WHAT IS SCIENTOLOGY?

*The Comprehensive Reference
on the World's Fastest Growing Religion*

Publications, Inc.

WHAT IS SCIENTOLOGY?

BASED ON THE WORKS OF
L. RON HUBBARD

Compiled by staff of the Church of Scientology International

Published by **Bridge Publications, Inc.**, 4751 Fountain Avenue, Los Angeles, California 90029

ISBN 1-57318-078-5

Published in other countries by **NEW ERA Publications International ApS**, Store Kongensgade 55, 1264 Copenhagen K, Denmark

ISBN 87-7816-636-5

Photography by Golden Era Productions except as listed (company and page number): Culver Pictures—65; © 1993 Sygma, Photographer: Bagglioni—77; The Bettman Archive—40, 75; © 1998 Ron Chapple/ FPG International Corp—154; © 1998 Ancil Nance/FPG International Corp—154; © 1998 Bob Gage/FPG International Corp—72; © 1992 Michael Krasowitz/FPG International Corp—465; © 1992 Dick Luria/FPG International Corp—469; © 1992 Peter Gridley/FPG International Corp—571, 573; © 1992 Arthur Tilley/FPG International Corp—577.

Printed in the United States of America

The full body of knowledge that comprises the Scientology religion is contained in more than forty million spoken and written words on the subject — all by L. Ron Hubbard, the source and founder of Scientology.

That public interest in Scientology is mounting rapidly is undeniable. This volume was first compiled in 1992 to fill the demand for a concise reference on Scientology. In the seven years since then, the explosive growth of Scientology churches, missions and groups around the world has necessitated the publication of this updated and expanded edition.

While continued expansion will inevitably change the numbers once again, much will remain constant, including, of course, the technology of Scientology and its effect upon all it touches. To provide an understanding of this phenomenon, contained herein is a complete description of Scientology: its religious philosophy, its practices, its organization, its activities and its growing influence on society.

Church of Scientology
International

TABLE OF CONTENTS

FOREWORD

Despite the twentieth century's torrent of technological advances, our civilization is in dire need of help. Since the advent of an atomic age which spawned the distinct possibility that all life on Earth could be extinguished at the push of a button, two generations have grown up under that specter. Partially in consequence, life in our society has taken many strange twists: Children are forcibly administered tranquilizing drugs in schools in the name of control; workers are taxed one hour's wages for every three on the job; and our youth emerge from their schools unable to read or write. Through media manipulation, whole populations are directed what to think, what to believe or what attitudes to hold. Such is the world that would be encountered by a time traveler from the start of this century, and surely he would find it strange.

It is not easy to live with purpose, dignity and happiness in a world so engrossed in materialism and so utterly blind to man's spiritual needs. Half an hour's walk through any urban landscape would convince virtually anyone that life could be a happier proposition.

Which brings up this relevant question: What is Scientology?

Scientology is an applied religious philosophy.

The fastest growing religious movement on Earth, Scientology has become a firmly established and active force for positive change in the world in less than half a century.

The Scientology religious philosophy contains a precise system of axioms, laws and techniques, exhaustively researched and documented as workable. As such, it provides the individual with the ability to dramatically improve conditions, not only in his own life but in the world around him.

In a word, Scientology works.

And this is why millions of people the world over use its principles in their daily lives, why a growing number of people find such relevance in Scientology for themselves, their families, their organizations, their nations and this entire civilization.

You will learn about Scientology in this book, about its basic principles, its history, its organizations, what it is doing to improve life in a troubled world and about the remarkable man who researched and developed Scientology — American philosopher and humanitarian L. Ron Hubbard.

Fundamentally, Scientology is about the individual man or woman. Its goal is to bring an individual to a sufficient understanding of himself and his life and free him to make improvements where he finds them necessary and in the ways he sees fit.

Scientology is a workable system. Evidence of this may be seen in the lives of millions of Scientologists and the positive effects they create. People improve their lives through Scientology. As Scientologists in all walks of life will attest, they have enjoyed greater success in their relationships, family life, jobs and professions. They take an active, vital role in life and leading roles in their communities. And participation in Scientology brings to many a broader social consciousness, manifested through meaningful contribution to charitable and social reform activities. Through hundreds of separate community outreach programs, Scientologists help the needy and disadvantaged on every continent.

Scientology contains effective answers to society's most crucial problems, among them drug abuse, crime, education and decay of moral values.

All Scientologists are drug-free, and spearhead effective actions in countries around the world to get others off drugs. Scientologists have helped millions of underprivileged children to dramatically improve their reading level, vocabulary and comprehension, and the record of Scientology's fight for human rights is unparalleled.

Scientology is not authoritarian. There is no enforced belief. Rather, a maxim in Scientology is that only those things which one finds true for himself are true. In Scientology one learns to think for himself — it is a voyage of self-discovery.

In the interests of making *What Is Scientology?* useful to as many as possible, it has been organized with the assumption that the reader has little or no familiarity with the subject. Consequently, the book is best read in sequence, since more advanced concepts build upon information in earlier chapters. The primary purpose was to produce a book that fully answers the question "What is Scientology?" Millions of words have been written on the subject of Scientology, and in this volume we present the fundamentals. Photographs, diagrams and graphs illustrate many points of importance.

Thus, as a broad overview of Scientology, this book will be a useful reference text, both to those with specific questions about the subject and, through the selected writings of L. Ron Hubbard, to those who wish to generally know more about his philosophy and principles.

The Scientology religion consists of a growing worldwide network of churches, missions and groups. And like any great movement that has advocated change for the better, it has not been a stranger to controversy, attracting media attention in many countries. *What Is Scientology?* both examines and explains this phenomenon, chronicling the history of its battles against vested interests and correcting much of the misinformation that has been manufactured in an attempt to hinder its forward progress.

Scientology is a dynamic, expanding religion. Since this book first went to press in 1992, the religion has expanded into more and more countries, cities, towns and hamlets of Earth, and continues to do so. The chapters

Scientology is about the individual man or woman. Its goal is to bring an individual to a sufficient understanding of himself and his life and free him to improve conditions in the ways that he sees fit.

describing Scientology's influence in society have already required augmentation and will again. But the basic ideas of Scientology, the benefits it offers, will not change and so, if this volume succeeds in answering the question posed by its title, the intention behind its publication will have been well served.

A civilization without insanity, without criminals and without war, where the able can prosper and honest beings can have rights, and where man is free to rise to greater heights, are the aims of Scientology.

In less than fifty years, Scientology has become an indelible part of this civilization's fabric. It is here to stay.

How has this happened in so short a time? The answers are contained within.

Scientology events, celebrations and briefings are held several times a year, attended by thousands of parishioners. Events held at a central location, such as this gathering, are telecast to churches around the globe. At such events, Church leaders have an opportunity to talk to other Scientologists and brief them on Church activities and expansion news from different parts of the world.

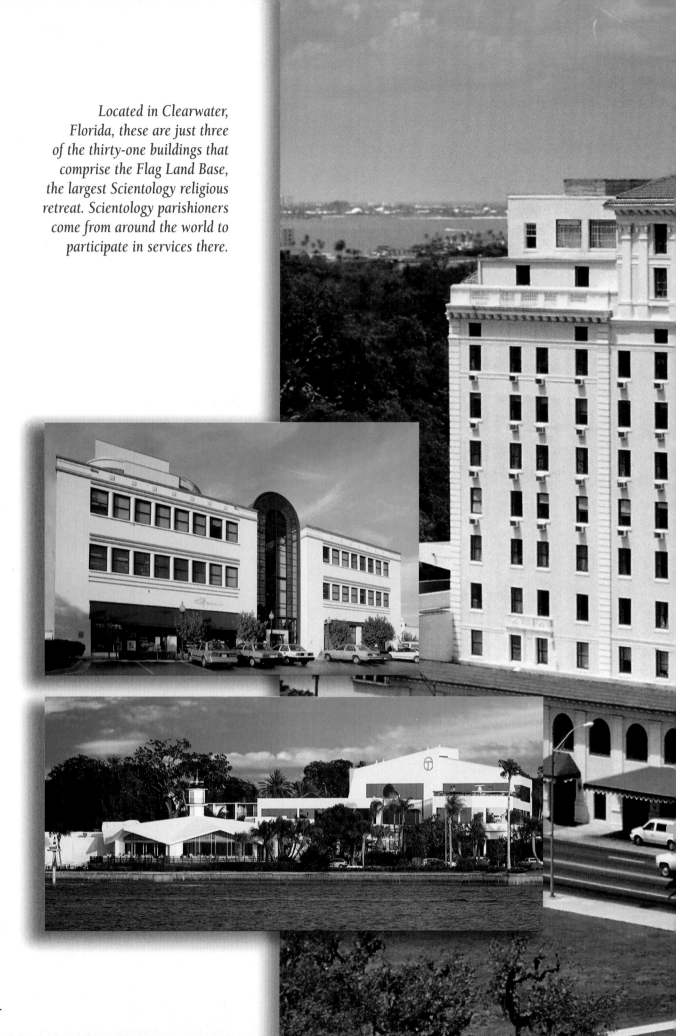

Located in Clearwater, Florida, these are just three of the thirty-one buildings that comprise the Flag Land Base, the largest Scientology religious retreat. Scientology parishioners come from around the world to participate in services there.

Advanced Organization Los Angeles

American Saint Hill Organization

L. Ron Hubbard Way, named by the
Los Angeles City Council in honor of the founder
of Scientology, is home to three churches serving
parishioners through increasing levels of
spiritual advancement.

Church of Scientology of Los Angeles

Celebrity Centre International, located in Hollywood, California, heads a worldwide network of organizations which help many Scientology artists, athletes and business professionals. Scientology Celebrity Centres can be found in major cities including Paris, Vienna, Düsseldorf, Munich, Florence, London, New York, Dallas, Portland, Las Vegas and Nashville.

*Scientology churches exist in most
major cities around the world.
Some of them are shown here.*

Tokyo, Japan

Zurich, Switzerland

Toronto, Canada

Washington, DC

Boston, USA

Miami, USA

Milano, Italy

Durban, South Africa

The Advanced Organization in Sydney, Australia, services parishioners from throughout the Southern Hemisphere, including the Far East.

Sydney, Australia

The Saint Hill College for Scientologists is situated on fifty-five acres of rolling countryside in East Grinstead, Sussex, England. Students from many countries come here to study the advanced graduate course it offers.

Copenhagen, Denmark

Located in Copenhagen, Denmark, the Advanced Organization Europe welcomes multinational Scientologists not only from across Europe but also from Africa and the Commonwealth of Independent States.

The Freewinds, operating out of her home port in the Caribbean, far from the turbulent crossroads of the world, offers Scientologists the highest levels of spiritual advancement.

PART ONE

SCIENTOLOGY: ITS BACKGROUND AND ORIGINS

Scientology follows a long tradition of religious practice. Its roots lie in the deepest beliefs and aspirations of all great religions, thus encompassing a religious heritage as old and as varied as man himself.

Though drawing upon the wisdom of some 50,000 years, Scientology is a new religion, one which has isolated fundamental laws of life and, for the first time, developed a workable technology that can be applied to help one achieve a happier and more spiritual existence. Scientology is therefore something one *does,* not merely something one believes in — an important point which will be greatly clarified as you read on.

That Scientology's development and rapid promulgation was made possible, in part, by advances in the physical sciences through the first half of the twentieth century is significant. Scientology constitutes man's first real application of scientific methodology to spiritual questions.

Part One of this volume provides a firm grounding on the subject of Scientology, covering three topics, with a chapter devoted to each. The first provides a brief introduction to the Scientology religion and a basic explanation of its principles. The second traces the history of religious thought in order to place Scientology into its proper context and clarify the path it follows. The third chapter introduces the reader to the founder of Scientology, L. Ron Hubbard.

CHAPTER 1

THE SCIENTOLOGY RELIGION

Thanks to scientific and technical advances over the last hundred years, most people are today materially wealthier than their forefathers. Yet, by their own accounts, the improvement in the quality of their lives has not matched their material gains. In fact, it may be argued that people once were happier and more fulfilled. For some, material affluence breeds anxiety, a gnawing fear that if someone doesn't take away their hard-earned acquisitions, the end of their days will prematurely arrive to finish the job. Others find death easier to face than a lifetime of assembly-line slavery, while most, in a less dramatic fashion, simply buckle down to lives of quiet desperation.

As the twenty-first century dawns, most individuals have no real grasp of the factors governing their existence. And yet, simply stated, if they had a greater understanding of themselves and their fellows they would be able to improve conditions and thus live happier lives. This, then, is the purpose of Scientology: to enable man to improve his lot through understanding.

Before Scientology, the tremendous scientific advances of this era were not matched by similar advances in the humanities. Man's knowledge of the physical universe had far outdistanced his knowledge of himself. The resulting pressures from such an imbalance account for much that has unsettled society and threatens our future. What Scientology represented to many when it appeared in the early 1950s was a restoration of the balance.

Despite its many successes, science has not provided answers to questions man has been asking himself since time immemorial: Who are we? What do we consist of? Where do we come from? Where are we going? What are we doing? These questions have always been the province of philosophy and religion, but traditional answers became inadequate in the face of the H-bomb. Scientology, drawing on the same advances in knowledge that led to the understanding of nuclear physics, provides modern answers to these questions. And it supplied workable methods of application which made it possible for man to reach the ancient goal he has been striving toward for thousands of years: to know himself and, in knowing himself, to know and understand other people and, ultimately, life itself.

Scientology is a religion. It holds in common many of the beliefs of other religions and philosophies. Scientology considers man to be a spiritual being, with more to him than flesh and blood. This, of course, is a very different view to that espoused by prevailing scientific thought which views man as only a material object, a complex combination of chemical compounds and stimulus-response mechanisms.

Scientology believes man to be basically good, not evil. It is man's experiences that have led him to commit evil deeds, not his nature. Often, he mistakenly seeks to solve his problems by considering only his own interests, which then causes trouble for both himself and others. Scientology believes that man advances to the degree he preserves his spiritual integrity and values, and remains honest and decent. Indeed, he deteriorates to the degree he abandons these qualities.

But because man is basically good he is capable of spiritual betterment, and it is the goal of Scientology to bring him to a point where he is capable of sorting out the factors in his own life and solving his own problems. Other efforts to help man have tried to solve his problems for him and in this respect Scientology is different. Scientology believes that an individual placed in a position where he can increase his abilities, where he can confront life better, where he can identify the factors in his life more easily, is also in a position to solve his own problems and so better his own life.

Life has tended to force the individual into certain values. The stresses of existence have tended to fixate his attention to a point where his awareness of himself and his environment has been greatly diminished. Attendant to this lowered spiritual awareness are problems, difficulties with others, illness and unhappiness. The goal of Scientology is to reverse this diminishing awareness and, in that sense, wake the individual up. As one becomes more and more alert, his abilities increase and he is capable of greater understanding and thus better able to handle his life.

Scientology, then, contains solutions to the problems of living. Its end result is increased awareness and spiritual freedom for the individual and rehabilitation of his basic decency, power and ability. It can and does accomplish these ends routinely, daily, all over the world.

The source and founder of the Scientology religion is L. Ron Hubbard, who devoted his life to finding answers to questions that have troubled mankind for millennia. Mr. Hubbard's intellectual rigor, his curiosity and boundless spirit of adventure inspired his search, even as a young man.

The first widely released results of Mr. Hubbard's researches did not lie in Scientology, however, but in another field of endeavor, "Dianetics." The word *Dianetics* comes from the Greek words *dia*, meaning "through" and *nous*, meaning "soul," and is defined as "what the soul is doing to the body."

Dianetics constituted L. Ron Hubbard's first breakthrough, and it was his initial discoveries in this area which led to further researches and the exact isolation of the source of life itself. Man does not *have* a spirit. He *is* a spirit. He *has* a mind and he *has* a body. Dianetics addresses and handles the effects of the spirit on the body. Dianetics thus helps provide relief from unwanted sensations and emotions, accidents and psychosomatic illnesses (ailments caused or aggravated by mental stress).

The word *Scientology* is taken from the Latin *scio*, which means "knowing in the fullest sense of the word," and the Greek word *logos,* meaning "study of." It literally means "knowing how to know." Scientology itself is defined as "The study and handling of the spirit in relationship to itself, universes and other life."

Scientology addresses the spiritual being. It directly raises his awareness and ability, and by so doing, he also becomes increasingly able to overcome the negative factors that impair him.

In over half a century of investigation, Mr. Hubbard isolated many, many fundamental truths about life, leading to his development of Scientology and the subsequent growth of the Scientology religion.

A testament to the truths contained in Scientology lies in the fact that in less than two generations, the Scientology religion now flourishes on every continent with thousands of churches, missions and groups touching millions of lives daily. Found in every facet of society, Scientologists are businessmen, housewives, students, artists, celebrities, laborers, scholars, soldiers, doctors, policemen and on and on.

Scientologists, ever involved in the world around them, naturally share with others what they have learned in Scientology.

Others, seeing the relevance Scientology can have in their lives too, also become interested in what Scientology can offer *them*. And so Scientology grows, in much the same way as every great religion in history has grown, from individual to individual, bringing knowledge, wisdom and hope for a better life.

With Scientology, millions know life can be a worthwhile proposition, that man can live a fulfilled life in harmony with others and that the world can be a happier place. Scientologists work to create such a world every day, joined by others who share this dream. The undeniable relevance of Scientology to the lives of these millions assures its permanence in our society. Millions upon millions more will follow in this quest to create a better world.

CHAPTER 2

THE RELIGIOUS HERITAGE OF SCIENTOLOGY

The dream of making the world a better place has been embraced by every religious movement in history. Indeed, throughout the ages religion has served as the primary civilizing influence on the planet.

The knowledge that man is a spirit is as old as man himself. Only recently, with the advent of Western psychology, have notions cropped up that man is nothing more than an animal, a stimulus-response mechanism. These pronouncements are at odds with every religious tradition, which speak of the "soul," the "spirit" or the "life force" — to encompass a belief held by all civilized men.

The Scientology religion follows just this tradition of man's search for his spiritual identity. In Scientology, the individual himself is considered to be the spiritual being — a thetan (pronounced "thay´-tn"). The term is taken from the Greek symbol or letter *theta* which has long served as a symbol for thought or spirit. Thus, although it is a new religious movement, Scientology is heir to the understanding of thinking men since the beginning of human history that man is a spiritual being who aspires to understand and improve life. The search has been long, but answers now exist in Scientology for anyone who wishes to reach for them.

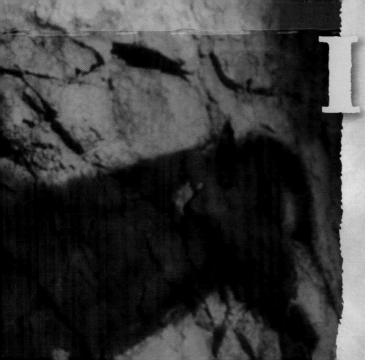

I n Lascaux, France, 15,000 years before Christ, early man painted bulls and other images deep inside the walls of caves. His underlying belief held that such representations would bring the living animal within their grasp, and so guarantee a successful hunt.

Like this ancient man with his primitive spear, in his attempt to conquer the raging bull, human beings have been trying to understand themselves and their relationship to other living things and the physical universe for countless eons. That which has been recorded in cave paintings, on stone tablets and in ancient myths stands as a testament to this search.

For all the mystery surrounding himself, one of the first things man has innately known was that he was more than merely another beast of the forest, more than mere muscle and bone, but that he was somehow endowed with a spark of the divine, a spiritual being.

Such wisdom formed the basis of the first great civilization—the Egyptian, whose culture endured for twenty-seven centuries. As the earliest people to conquer man's deep-rooted fear of ancestral spirits, they were also among the first to propose that each man must provide for his own happy afterlife.

Despite considerable advances in the physical sciences, their gift of organization and their monumental art and architecture, the Egyptians still lacked the means to reverse the internal decay of their society. Beset with immorality and decadence, they were soon too enfeebled to resist the onslaught of Rome.

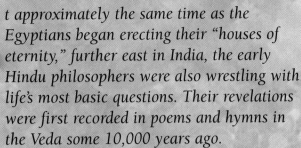

At approximately the same time as the Egyptians began erecting their "houses of eternity," further east in India, the early Hindu philosophers were also wrestling with life's most basic questions. Their revelations were first recorded in poems and hymns in the Veda some 10,000 years ago.

The doctrine of transmigration (the ancient concept of reincarnation)—that life is a continuous stream which flows ceaselessly, without beginning and without end—initially seemed to explain much of what plagued India. With the prospect of many lives, it was reasoned, a man had just as many opportunities to achieve self-knowledge.

But such a belief offered little succor to the multitudes of impoverished. And so, as that misery continued to spread, concerned religious leaders began to challenge traditional doctrine.

Siddhartha Gautama, son of a wealthy Hindu rajah, spent years in search of fundamental truths, and declared that man could live a "Middle Path" between the extremes of sensual indulgence and drastic asceticism. Man, he proclaimed, is a spiritual being who can achieve an entirely new state of awareness which he termed **bodhi.** For this reason, he is remembered today as the Buddha, revered for civilizing most of Asia. Unfortunately, however, he left no real means for others to actually attain those states of which he spoke.

In Persia and much of the ancient world, philosophers and religious men continued their quest to divine the true nature of man, even studying the movements of the sun and stars in hopes of unlocking the mysteries of life.

In the seventh century B.C., Zoroaster, born into a priestly family, came to believe himself a prophet. Forced to flee his native land for what he taught, he found asylum with King Vishtaspa in eastern Iran. There, the Persian religion of Zoroastrianism was born around the belief that only by defining "good" and "evil" could one hope to free himself of ignorance and achieve true happiness in the afterlife.

A century later, the Chinese philosopher Lao-tse believed the world moved according to a divine pattern, one reflected in the rhythmic and orderly movements of nature. Saddened by the corruption of politicians and general social decay, he saw man striving to be good, rather than let his inherent goodness come naturally from within. Eventually, so great was his disillusionment, he called for a return to a simpler golden age, and set out for the secluded countryside. Yet upon reaching the city's edge, Lao-tse was beseeched by the gatekeeper not to leave before recording his ideas for posterity.

is manuscript, the **Tao Te Ching**, became the basis of Taoism and held out yet another hope of higher states to which man could aspire.

Tao means simply "way" or "way to go." It is the way the universe moves—a universe to which man is inextricably linked. When men are most natural, they move according to the laws of interdependence and interaction of all universal laws, and so maintain a perfect harmony and balance. According to the **Tao**, it is the way—there is no other.

Unfortunately, Taoism too did not provide a **workable** means to reach that perfect harmony. Nor was any attempt made to provide such a means. For intrinsic in the Way, was the conviction that its basic truths were beyond words and could only be experienced. Hence the principles remained in the realm of esoteric knowledge.

When the Delphic Oracle proclaimed the Greek philosopher, Socrates (470–399 B.C.) to be the "wisest man in the world," Socrates countered that he was wise only in that he knew that he did not know. He believed man had a right to search for his own truth and that through increased understanding would become happier and more tolerant.

Socrates believed himself charged with a mission from God to make his fellow men aware not only of their own ignorance but also that knowledge could redeem them.

Socrates held that neither he nor anyone else had the right to force opinions on others. Rather, through systematic questioning, he sought to lead others to cast aside preconceptions and reach their own conclusions. He challenged falsehoods and pomposity, but his ironic criticisms and intellectual honesty were misunderstood by the authoritarians of his time.

Like many philosophers before him, Socrates' methods challenged established beliefs. As a result, in 399 B.C. he was convicted of both "denying the gods" and corrupting youth. Sentenced to drink a cup of hemlock, a bitter poison, he chose to die rather than compromise his stand against tyranny and suppression of the truth.

Prejudice and a general deviation from the road to philosophic truth about man sent even the highly learned Greek civilization to an inevitable and untimely end. First conquered by the Roman Empire, its cities were then mercilessly sacked by barbarians.

Like the philosophers of Greece, India and China, the Hebrews, too, sought to define the meaning of life. According to Jewish tradition, it was Abraham who first gained a special understanding of what lay at the heart of the universe and from that revelation came a belief in a personal god. He further believed that beneath the seemingly endless variety of life lay a single purpose, a single reality.

Judaism is the mother religion of both Christianity and Islam — the three dominant faiths in the Western world.

Two thousand years ago, Jesus of Nazareth brought new hope to man by preaching that this life was not all men might hope for, that man was more than only flesh and would continue to live, even after death. Implicit in his message was the promise of salvation from suffering and a promise of eternal peace.

At odds with the teachings of Jesus was traditional rabbinical belief that salvation would not come until the advent of a distant Messiah. Hence, the special appeal of Christ's message that the Kingdom of God was not only at hand, but lay within all those with faith.

L ong fearing popular revolt, the Romans equated Christ's words with political insurrection. Rome had decreed that nothing should be held above imperial order and thus viewed Christ's wholly spiritual message as dangerously revolutionary, particularly his talk of the coming Kingdom.

Though crucified, the hope that Christ brought to man did not die. Instead, his death became symbolic of the triumph of the spirit over the material body and so brought a new awareness of man's true nature.

The Romans, however, continued to insist that man was just a material object. The psyche (a word meaning "spirit" or "breath of life") was thought to be given up when the man "himself," his body, had perished.

For all their military strength, the Romans never acknowledged or found ways to develop man's true potential and so, as did so many empires before them, they too perished.

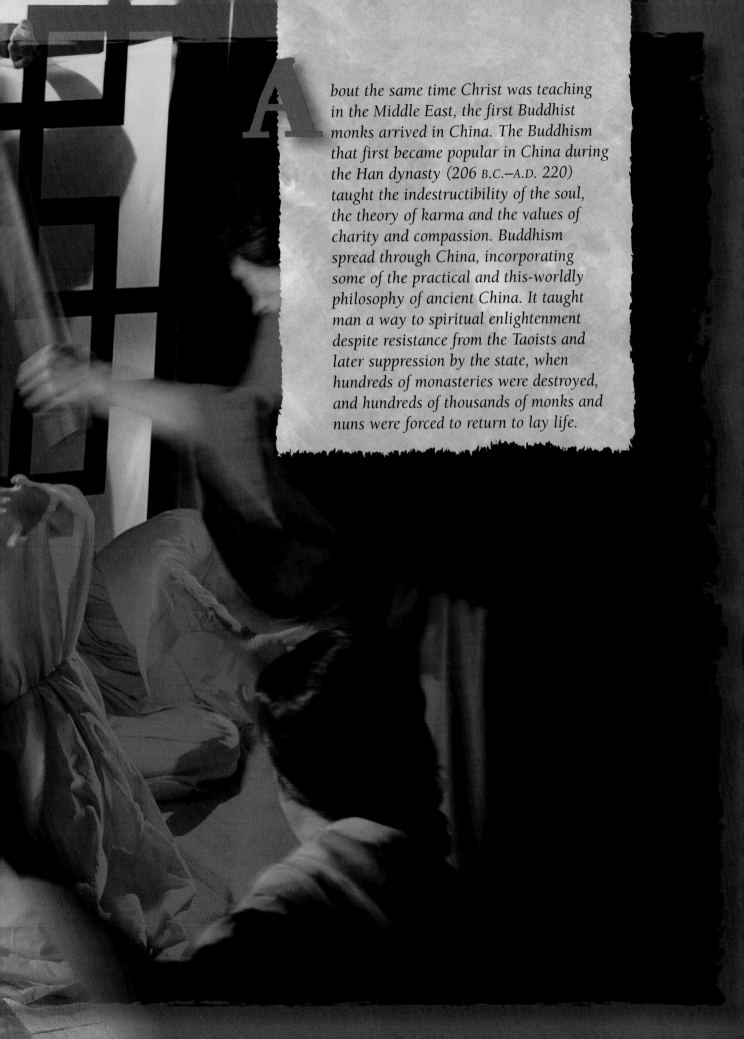

About the same time Christ was teaching in the Middle East, the first Buddhist monks arrived in China. The Buddhism that first became popular in China during the Han dynasty (206 B.C.–A.D. 220) taught the indestructibility of the soul, the theory of karma and the values of charity and compassion. Buddhism spread through China, incorporating some of the practical and this-worldly philosophy of ancient China. It taught man a way to spiritual enlightenment despite resistance from the Taoists and later suppression by the state, when hundreds of monasteries were destroyed, and hundreds of thousands of monks and nuns were forced to return to lay life.

Despite such suppression, belief in the spiritual nature of man received even more impetus in the sixth century when the prophet Mohammed preached that there was only one God and attempted to civilize an entire nation. He taught about the supremacy of the spiritual over the material, and beseeched man to seek his own salvation. His message was seen as a threat to the revenues of Mecca, and eventually led to his banishment.

Within eight years, however, he returned triumphant and began his "Holy War" against infidels. He built the great Islamic Empire, which eventually reached from Spain to the borders of China.

The Crusades, the subsequent wars "in the name of religion" which swept Europe for hundreds of years, involved tens of thousands of people in continuous bloodshed. Nonetheless, with the Crusades came a vital cultural exchange. Men who had never traveled beyond the immediate vicinity of their manor, village or fiefdom were suddenly exposed to an entirely new world across the Mediterranean.

Toward the end of this period, in 1215, English barons forced King John to sign the famous Magna Carta. This historic document, a formal recognition of the rights of others, was built on the belief that the basic nature of man was good, not evil, and that he was capable of determining his own destiny.

The provisions included the guaranteed freedom of the church, respect for the customs of towns, protection of the rights of subjects and communities, and what would later be interpreted as a guarantee of the right of trial by jury. These represented the triumph of law over king, and thus reason over force.

But the late fifteenth century ushered in the Inquisition, which again sought to quell man's sense of reason and his reach for spiritual enlightenment. Those subscribing to beliefs unacceptable to the Catholic church were tried and tortured until they renounced their "heretical views."

Anyone thought to have "strange" or "different" ideas could be labeled a blasphemer or even a witch, then burned at the stake if they refused to accept the established beliefs.

But man's desire to understand himself and the world around him could not be stopped and men like Leonardo da Vinci pursued their studies in the hope of finding the answers. A brilliant painter, engineer, astronomer and botanist, Leonardo helped launch the Renaissance and a new age of scientific discovery in the face of ridicule from the ignorant and bigoted. Even the most seemingly innocuous studies had to be undertaken with discretion, as the watchful eye of the Inquisition was ever present. In fact, many of his notes were written out so they could only be read in a mirror.

In the sixteenth century, Galileo dared to challenge long-held beliefs by publicly endorsing the Copernican theory that the Earth revolved around the sun and not the reverse. This was considered heresy by the still-active Inquisition.

Galileo was sentenced to an indefinite prison term by the Catholic church for his "crime." Only when he subsequently renounced Copernican theory was he allowed to return to his villa where he lived out the remainder of his life under house arrest by authority of the Inquisition, a broken man.

Fleeing suppression and intolerance in Europe, pilgrims of several faiths set sail for the New World where their aspirations of freedom were probably best summed up by Thomas Jefferson's Declaration of Independence. He wrote, ". . . that all men are created equal, that they are endowed by their Creator with certain inalienable Rights, that among these are Life, Liberty and the pursuit of Happiness." The light of spiritual freedom was once again burning bright.

There were some however, like Charles Darwin, who had a very different message: Man was but another rung on the evolutionary ladder, and could never hope to raise himself to greater levels of awareness. Darwin's man-from-mud theory, the idea that life was a chance happenstance resulting from a chain reaction in a sea of ammonia, soon took hold in the scientific community. Ironically, however, that very same theory may be traced to an ancient Egyptian myth wherein man was seen as emerging from a primordial ocean.

Professor Wilhelm Wundt, a German psychologist and Marxist at the University of Leipzig, proclaimed that man's soul—if indeed he had one—was irrelevant, as man could only be understood in terms of physically observable phenomena. A search for the spiritual nature of man, he reasoned, was a waste of time as there was no psyche. Thus psychology became the study of the spirit which denied the spirit. The subject of psychology thereafter became prevalent in universities.

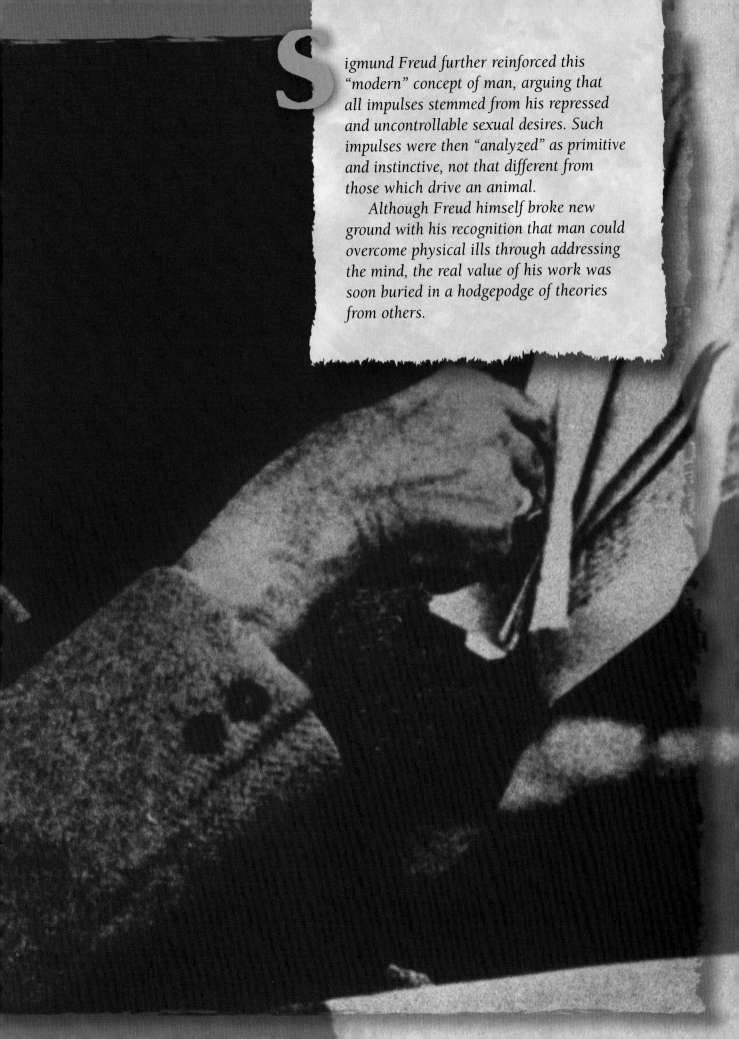

Sigmund Freud further reinforced this "modern" concept of man, arguing that all impulses stemmed from his repressed and uncontrollable sexual desires. Such impulses were then "analyzed" as primitive and instinctive, not that different from those which drive an animal.

Although Freud himself broke new ground with his recognition that man could overcome physical ills through addressing the mind, the real value of his work was soon buried in a hodgepodge of theories from others.

In Russia, former veterinarian Ivan Petrovich Pavlov served the dictator Stalin with experiments to discover how man could be controlled to better serve the state. He reasoned that if dogs could be made to slaver on command, so could human beings. Man had now been reduced to the level of a mindless animal — and thus psychiatry was born, as a tool for tyrannical governments.

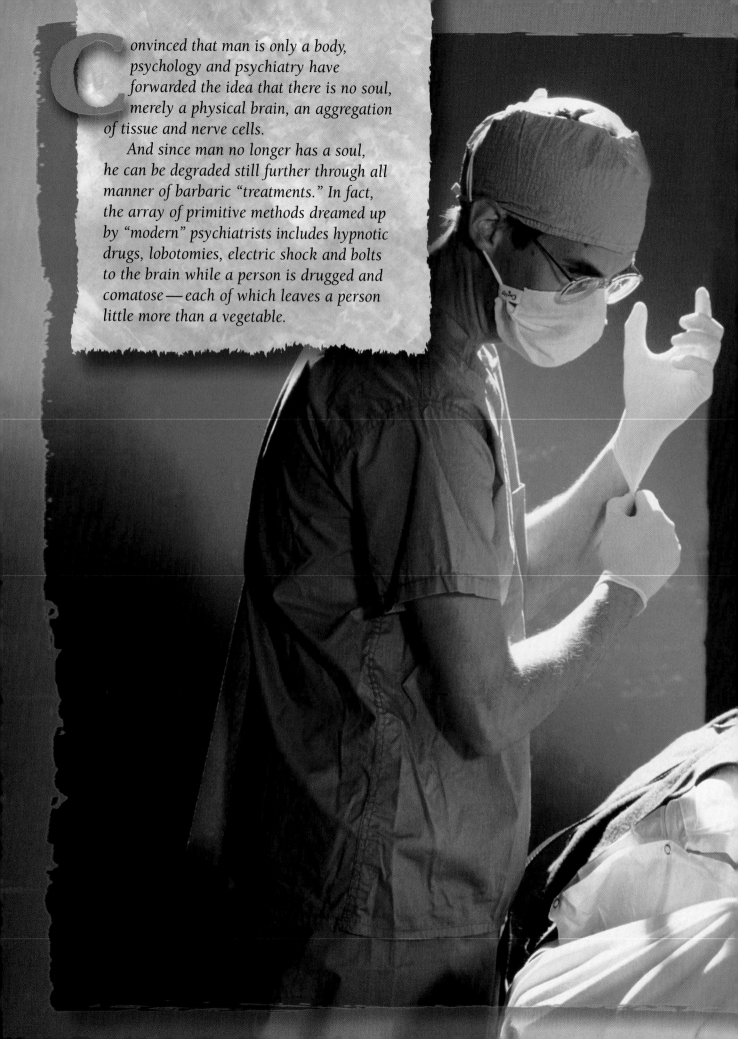

Convinced that man is only a body, psychology and psychiatry have forwarded the idea that there is no soul, merely a physical brain, an aggregation of tissue and nerve cells.

And since man no longer has a soul, he can be degraded still further through all manner of barbaric "treatments." In fact, the array of primitive methods dreamed up by "modern" psychiatrists includes hypnotic drugs, lobotomies, electric shock and bolts to the brain while a person is drugged and comatose—each of which leaves a person little more than a vegetable.

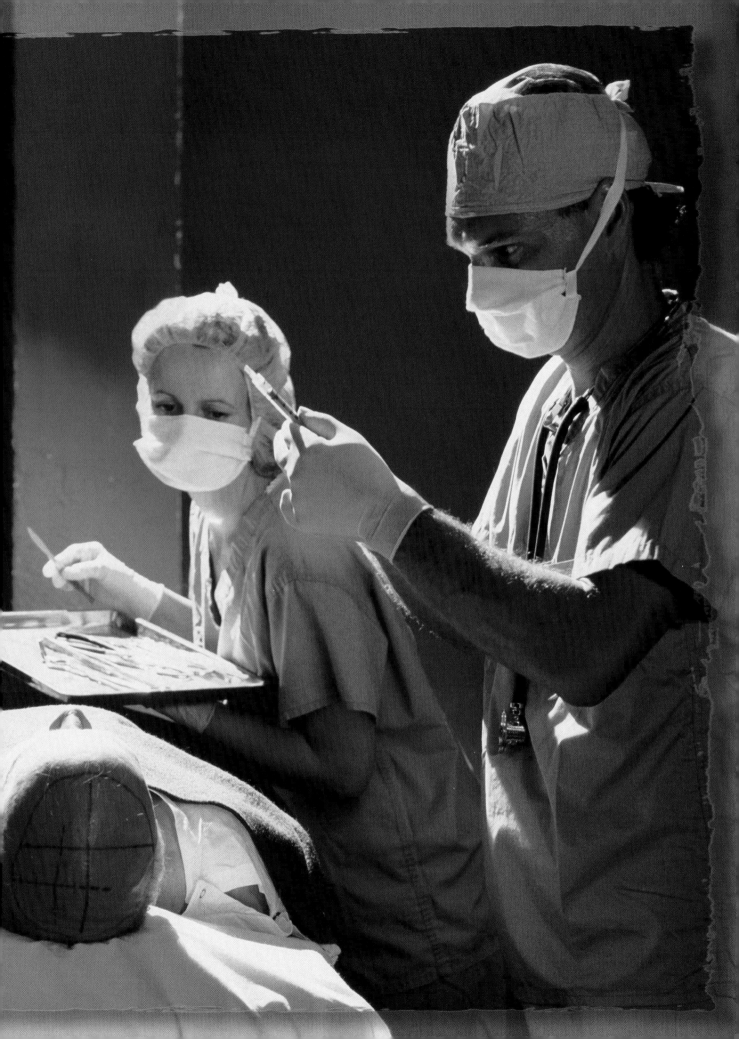

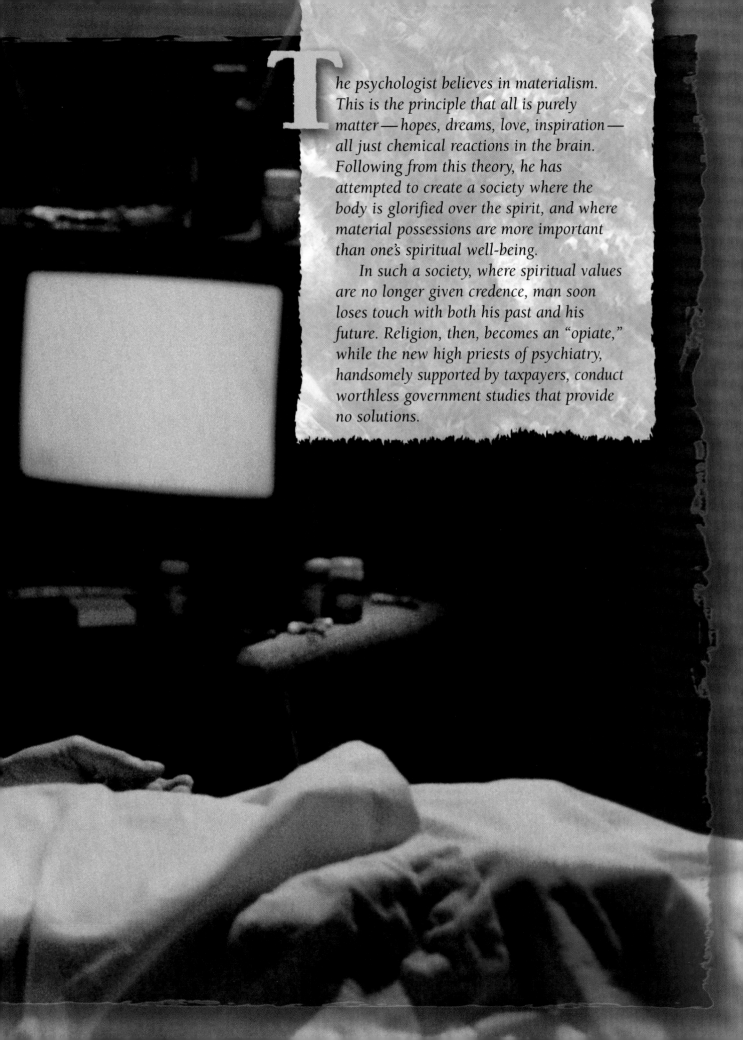

The psychologist believes in materialism. This is the principle that all is purely matter — hopes, dreams, love, inspiration — all just chemical reactions in the brain. Following from this theory, he has attempted to create a society where the body is glorified over the spirit, and where material possessions are more important than one's spiritual well-being.

In such a society, where spiritual values are no longer given credence, man soon loses touch with both his past and his future. Religion, then, becomes an "opiate," while the new high priests of psychiatry, handsomely supported by taxpayers, conduct worthless government studies that provide no solutions.

Even today, new ideas are fought by totalitarian states, and learning is restricted to the privileged few, in an attempt to keep the majority ignorant. Book burnings are another phenomenon of our own time, reminiscent of the Inquisition.

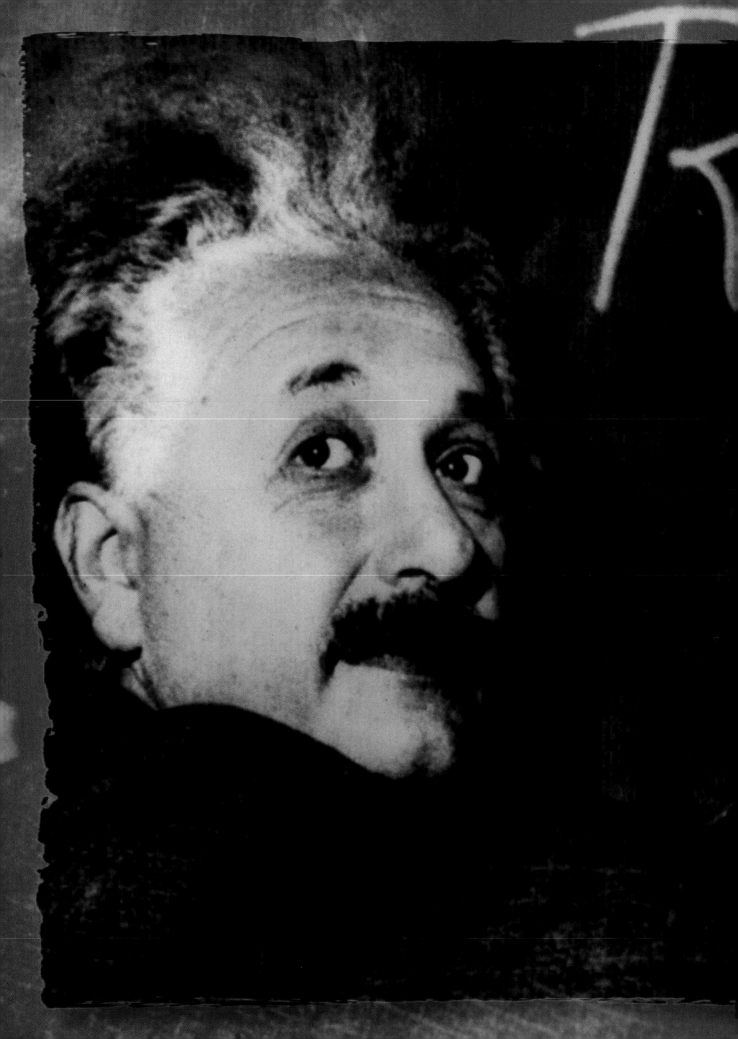

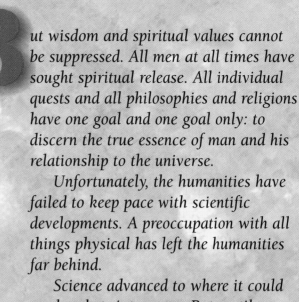

But wisdom and spiritual values cannot be suppressed. All men at all times have sought spiritual release. All individual quests and all philosophies and religions have one goal and one goal only: to discern the true essence of man and his relationship to the universe.

Unfortunately, the humanities have failed to keep pace with scientific developments. A preoccupation with all things physical has left the humanities far behind.

Science advanced to where it could send rockets into space. But, until now, the greatest challenge of all was ignored, the improvement of man himself.

At this point in the history of our civilization we have, frighteningly enough, developed the capabilities to destroy all life on the Earth.

One madman in a position of power could wreak the ultimate destruction for all living things. Lacking a real understanding of man or a workable technology to improve man, governments are unable to forge their own destinies and the potential for chaos is very real.

Perhaps it has taken the potential for ultimate destruction to bring about the ultimate in hope for mankind: a twentieth-century religion, utilizing a truly workable technology to bring man to an understanding of himself and his fellows. Both the atom bomb and this technology were born at the same time—in the crucible of the last world war. Fortunately, we can now end not only war, but crime and insanity on Earth, once and for all. We can reverse the dwindling spiral of life on this planet.

Man can find answers to his timeless questions and gain true spiritual freedom — with Scientology.

CHAPTER 3

L. RON HUBBARD: THE FOUNDER OF SCIENTOLOGY

L Ron Hubbard is the founder of Scientology. He has described his philosophy in more than 5,000 writings, including dozens of books, and in 3,000 tape-recorded lectures. Those who regularly employ his teachings to improve themselves and help their fellows come from all walks of life, while Scientology missions and churches have been established on six continents.

The universal acclaim for the man—including thousands of awards and recognitions from individuals and groups and the unprecedented popularity of his works among people from all walks of life—is but one indicator of the effectiveness of his technologies. More importantly, there are millions of people around the world who consider they have no greater friend.

Although long celebrated as a writer, novelist and explorer, it was the 1950 publication of *Dianetics: The Modern Science of Mental Health* that initially focused world attention on L. Ron Hubbard. That book, which marked a turning point in history, provided the first workable approach to solving the problems of the mind, the first hope that something could be done about the causes of irrational behavior—war, crime and insanity. Dianetics is something that anyone can use to help improve himself and his fellows. Hence, when the book was released, Amherst College Political Science Professor, Dr. Frederick L. Schuman's declaration in the *New York Times:* "History has become a race between Dianetics and catastrophe. Dianetics will win, if enough people are challenged in time to understand it."

Although most men might have been satisfied with such an accomplishment, L. Ron Hubbard did not stop at Dianetics. Yes, he had solved the riddle of the human mind, but there still remained unsolved questions regarding the nature of the human being himself, outstanding puzzles concerning that long-sought-after "something" we call *life*. And from his methodical and wholly scientific research into this problem came the applied religious philosophy of Scientology, offering not only greater happiness and ability but also solutions to such seemingly hopeless social problems as drug abuse, the decline of moral standards and illiteracy—always providing effective and workable solutions as he found them.

The story of Dianetics and Scientology began long before the publication of Mr. Hubbard's first book on the subject. Indeed, even in his early youth he exemplified a rare sense of purpose and dedication which, combined with his adventurous spirit, made him a living legend. His lifelong search for answers to the human condition was equally adventurous; for unlike other philosophers content to view events from an ivory tower, he knew that to really understand one's fellow man, one had to be part of life. One had to rub elbows with all kinds and types of people. And, one had to explore the nooks and crannies of all existence.

This chapter will cover the key incidents that shaped L. Ron Hubbard's life, and the important milestones on the road to his discoveries. By any measure, it was an immensely full and interesting life, but the true value of it lies in the legacy that he left mankind.

S on of naval commander Harry Ross Hubbard and Ledora May Hubbard, L. Ron Hubbard was born on March 13, 1911 in Tilden, Nebraska. At the age of two, he and his family took up residence on a ranch outside Kalispell, Montana, and from there moved to the state's capital, Helena.

As a young boy he learned much about survival in the rugged Far West—with what he called "its do-and-dare attitudes, its wry humor, cowboy pranks, and make-nothing of the worst and most dangerous." Not only could he ride horses at the age of three and a half, but was soon able to rope and break broncos with the best of them.

Ron Hubbard's mother was a rarity in her time. A thoroughly educated woman, who had attended teacher's college prior to her marriage to Ron's father, she was aptly suited to tutor her young son. Under her guidance, Ron was reading and writing at an early age, and soon satisfying his insatiable curiosity about life with the works of Shakespeare, the Greek philosophers, and other classics.

When his father's naval career necessitated that the family leave Montana for a series of cross-country journeys, Ron's mother was also on hand to help him make up what he missed in school.

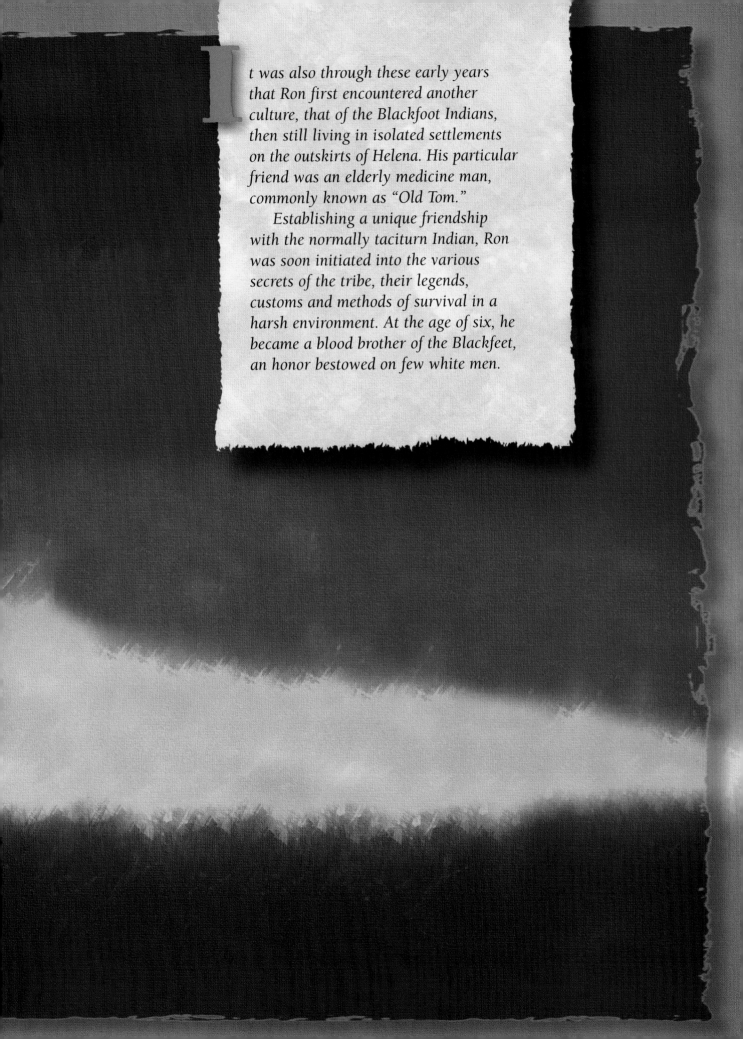

I t was also through these early years that Ron first encountered another culture, that of the Blackfoot Indians, then still living in isolated settlements on the outskirts of Helena. His particular friend was an elderly medicine man, commonly known as "Old Tom."

Establishing a unique friendship with the normally taciturn Indian, Ron was soon initiated into the various secrets of the tribe, their legends, customs and methods of survival in a harsh environment. At the age of six, he became a blood brother of the Blackfeet, an honor bestowed on few white men.

In early 1923, when Ron was twelve, he and his family moved to Seattle, Washington, where his father was stationed at the local naval base. He joined the Boy Scouts and that year proudly achieved the rank of Boy Scout First Class. The next year he became the youngest Eagle Scout ever, an early indication that he did not plan to live an ordinary life.

At the end of that year, young Ron traveled to the nation's capital via the Panama Canal, meeting Commander Joseph C. Thompson of the US Navy Medical Corps. Commander Thompson was the first officer sent by the US Navy to study under Sigmund Freud, and took it upon himself to pass on the essentials of Freudian theory to his young friend. Although keenly interested in the Commander's lessons, Ron was also left with many unanswered questions.

n 1927, at the age of sixteen, Ron took the first of his several voyages across the Pacific to Asia. There, both on his own and in the company of an officer attached to the British legation, he took advantage of this unique opportunity to study Far Eastern culture. Among others he befriended and learned from was a thoroughly insightful Beijing magician who represented the last of the line of Chinese magicians from the court of Kublai Khan.

Although primarily renowned as an entertainer, Old Mayo was also well versed in China's ancient wisdom that had been handed down from generation to generation. Ron passed many evenings in the company of such wise men, eagerly absorbing their words.

I t was also through the course of these travels that Ron gained access to the much talked-about but rarely seen Buddhist lamaseries in the Western Hills of China — temples usually off-limits to both local peasants and visiting foreigners.

Among other wonders, Ron told of watching monks meditate for weeks on end, contemplating higher truths. Once again then, he spent much of his time investigating and questioning, seeking answers to the human dilemma.

Beyond the lamasery walls, he closely examined the surrounding culture. In addition to the local Tartar tribes, he spent time with nomadic bandits originally from Mongolia. He further traveled up and down the Chinese coast exploring villages and cities, delving into the fabric of the nation. And everywhere he went, one question was uppermost in his mind: "Why?" Why so much human suffering and misery? Why was man, with all his ancient wisdom and knowledge accumulated in learned texts and temples, unable to solve such basic problems as war, insanity and unhappiness?

By the age of nineteen, long before the advent of commercial airplane or jet transportation, he had traveled more than a quarter of a million miles, including voyages not only to China but also Japan, Guam, the Philippines and other points in the Orient. In a very real sense, the world itself was his classroom, and he studied in it voraciously, recording what he saw and learned in his ever-present diaries, which he carefully preserved for future reference.

Everywhere he went, he also took the time to help and teach others. On a remote Pacific island, for example, he proved to the terrified natives that the groans of a ghost in a supposedly haunted cave were nothing more than the rushing of underground water.

In the South Pacific islands, Ron continued his search by venturing deep into the jungles of Guam where he located an ancient burial ground, a place steeped in the tradition of heroic warriors and kings. Though his native friends were fearful for him, he explored the sacred area—his initiative drawn from the ever-present desire to know more.

These sojourns in Asia and the Pacific islands had a profound effect, giving Ron a subjective understanding of an Eastern philosophy that had predated even the Greeks.

FRI
ENGLISH POET
5
iambic pentameter
he boy | out went | to meet | the b

Yet for all the wonders of these lands and all his respect for those whom he encountered, he still saw much that concerned him: Chinese beggars willing themselves to die above open graves in Beijing, children who were less than rags, widespread ignorance and despair. And in the end, he came to the inescapable conclusion that despite the wisdom of its ancient texts, the East did not have the answers to the miseries of the human condition. It remained evident in the degradation and sorrow of its people.

Returning to the United States in 1929, Ron resumed his formal education. After attending Swavely Prep School in Manassas, Virginia, he was graduated from the Woodward School for Boys in Washington, DC.

He enrolled at George Washington University. His university subject should probably have been ethnology, since he was already an expert in many different cultures — from the Philippine pygmies to the Kayan shamans of Borneo to the Chamorros of Guam. But fate and his father placed him, fortunately, in mathematics and engineering instead. With his knowledge of many cultures and his growing awareness of the human condition, his background in engineering and mathematics would serve him well in undertaking a scientific approach to solving the riddles of existence and man's spiritual potential.

Theorizing that the world of subatomic particles might possibly provide a clue to the human thought process, he enrolled in one of the first nuclear physics courses taught in the United States. Moreover, he was concerned for the safety of the world, recognizing that if man were to handle the atom sanely for the greatest benefit, he would first have to learn to handle himself. His aim, then, was to synthesize and test all knowledge for what was observable, workable and could truly help solve man's problems. And to that end, he set out to determine precisely how the mind functioned.

I n one of his first pioneering experiments on the subject, he employed a sound wave measuring device called a Koenig photometer. Two students read poetry from extremely different languages—Japanese and English—into the device. He found that the device identified the speech as poetry regardless of language. When haiku was read in the original Japanese, the wavelengths produced by the Koenig photometer were the same as those produced when English verse was read.

Here, then, he concluded, was scientific evidence that people were not so different as he had been led to believe, that there was indeed a meeting ground, and all minds did in fact respond identically to the same stimuli.

Reasoning that questions arising from his experiments would best be answered by those who were paid to know about the mind, Ron took these discoveries to the psychology department. Rather than answers, however, he found that the George Washington University psychologists had no comprehension or understanding of the results — but more importantly — they weren't even interested in such things.

Stunned, he soon came to the realization that no one knew how the mind worked. And furthermore, no one in the fields of psychology or psychiatry was about to find out.

Not only were there no answers in the East, there were none to be found in any Western center of culture.

To be very blunt," he put it, "it was very obvious that I was dealing with and living in a culture which knew less about the mind than the lowest primitive tribe I had ever come in contact with. Knowing also that people in the East were not able to reach as deeply and predictably into the riddles of the mind as I had been led to expect, I knew I would have to do a lot of research."

Deciding that formal study had nothing more to offer, L. Ron Hubbard left college in the depths of the Depression, again taking his quest to learn about life out into the world. He said of this period, ". . . my writing financed research and this included expeditions which were conducted in order to investigate primitive peoples to see if I could find a common denominator of existence which would be workable."

e directed two expeditions, the Caribbean Motion Picture Expedition, a two-and-a-half month, 5,000-mile voyage aboard the four-masted schooner, **Doris Hamlin,** and the West Indies Mineralogical Expedition, which completed the first mineralogical survey of the island of Puerto Rico under US rule. Upon his return to the United States, and with scientific grants few and far between, he began to write his way to fame and fortune, supporting his research by becoming one of the most popular writers of the 1930s.

As the editor of **Thrilling Adventures** magazine, one of the more than 30 magazines he headlined, wrote in October 1934, "L. Ron Hubbard needs no introduction. From the letters you send in, his yarns are among the most popular we have published. Several of you have wondered, too, how he gets the splendid color which always characterizes his stories of the faraway places. The answer is: He's been there, brothers. He's been and seen and done. And plenty of all three."

While continuing to write for his New York editors as well as screenplays for Hollywood such as **Secret of Treasure Island,** he never stopped his vital researches into man.

L Ron Hubbard was searching for a principle which would lead to the unification of knowledge and explain the meaning of existence—something other philosophers had set out to find in the past with varying degrees of success. In fact, many Western philosophers had given up on the idea that different peoples held anything in common and were no longer even asking questions about the life force or the essence of life. Man had become just another animal, mere flesh and bones.

Yet Mr. Hubbard saw man in a very different light. Although he had no name for it yet, he felt certain that life was more than a random series of chemical reactions, and that some sort of intelligent urge underlay our actions. Organizing the tremendous body of data he had acquired—from his travels, research and experiments—he embarked upon a new experimental path, this time to determine how cells functioned. And following an elaborate series of experiments in early 1938, he made a breakthrough of magnitude: he isolated the common denominator of existence. SURVIVE.

That man was surviving was not a new idea. That this was the single basic common denominator of existence was.

The predominant theory of the time held that life was simply a chance chain reaction in a sea of ammonia. Disproving this materialistic belief and forming the basis for all his later work, his findings were compiled into a philosophic manuscript, "Excalibur," written during the first weeks of 1938.

He wrote: "I suddenly realized that survival was the pin on which you could hang the rest of this with adequate and ample proof. It's a very simple problem. Idiotically simple! That's why it never got solved. Nobody has ever looked at anything being that simple to do that much. So what do we find as the simplicities of solution? The simplicities of solution lie in this: that life, all life, is trying to survive. And life is composed of two things: the material universe and an X-factor. And this X-factor is something that can evidently organize, and mobilize the material universe."

ecalling the writing of "Excalibur," the first of his many manuscripts on the subject of life, he noted, "I began to hammer out that secret and when I had written ten thousand words, then I knew even more clearly. I destroyed the ten thousand and began to write again."

The response of those who read this manuscript was dramatic, and more than a few publishers eagerly sought to publish it. He declined. " 'Excalibur' did not contain a therapy of any kind but was simply a discussion of the composition of life. I decided to go further," he added.

Ron continued to fund his research by his ever more popular fiction writing. His stories and novels spanned every genre from adventure and travel to mystery, western, romance, science fiction and fantasy. Writing not of machines and robots but of real men and real adventures, he pioneered a whole new era of science fiction writing as one of the creators of what came to be known as the "Golden Age of Science Fiction."

His expeditions continued as well. Elected a member of the prestigious Explorers Club in New York City, he was bestowed custody of their flag, a high honor in the field of exploration, for the Alaskan Radio Experimental Expedition in May 1940. This expedition greatly assisted in the codification of the coastal charts of British Columbia and Alaska, while augmenting his knowledge of more cultures—the Tlingit, the Haida and the Aleut Indians of Alaska.

In December 1940, L. Ron Hubbard earned his "License to Master of Steam and Motor Vessels" from the US Department of Commerce. Three months later, he obtained a second certificate attesting to his marine skill: "License to Master of Sail Vessels, Any Ocean."

Throughout all of this, however, Ron was continuing in his quest to answer the riddles of man. His writings and explorations had the purpose of financing his researches and expanding his knowledge of the world and life.

Then came the war.

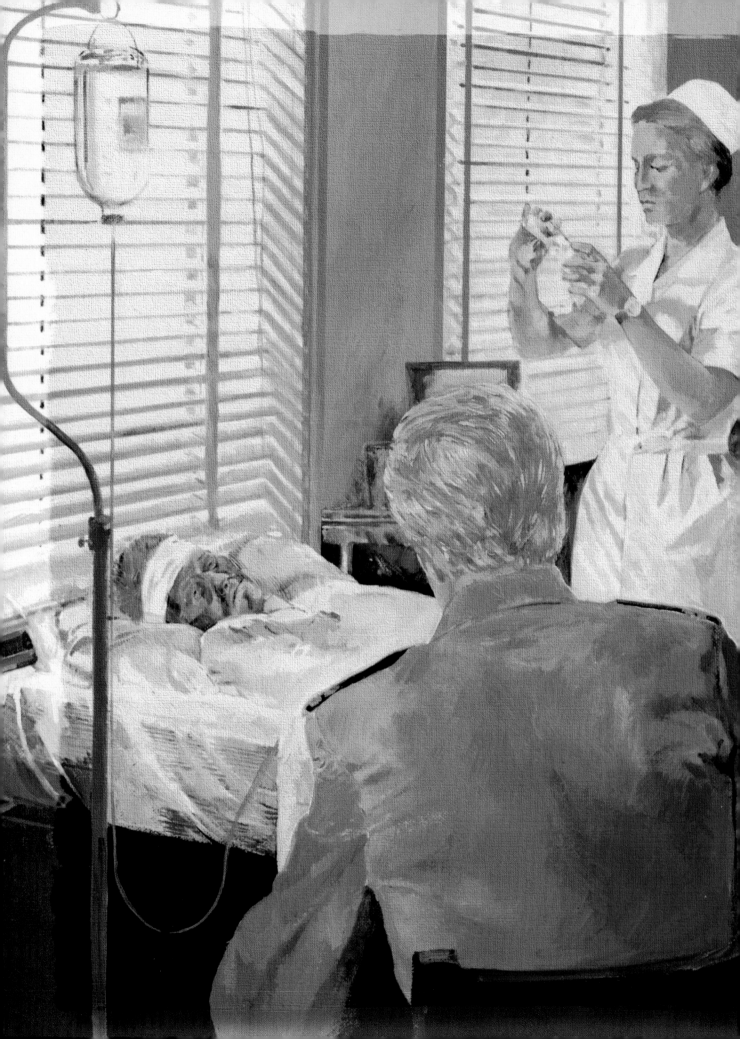

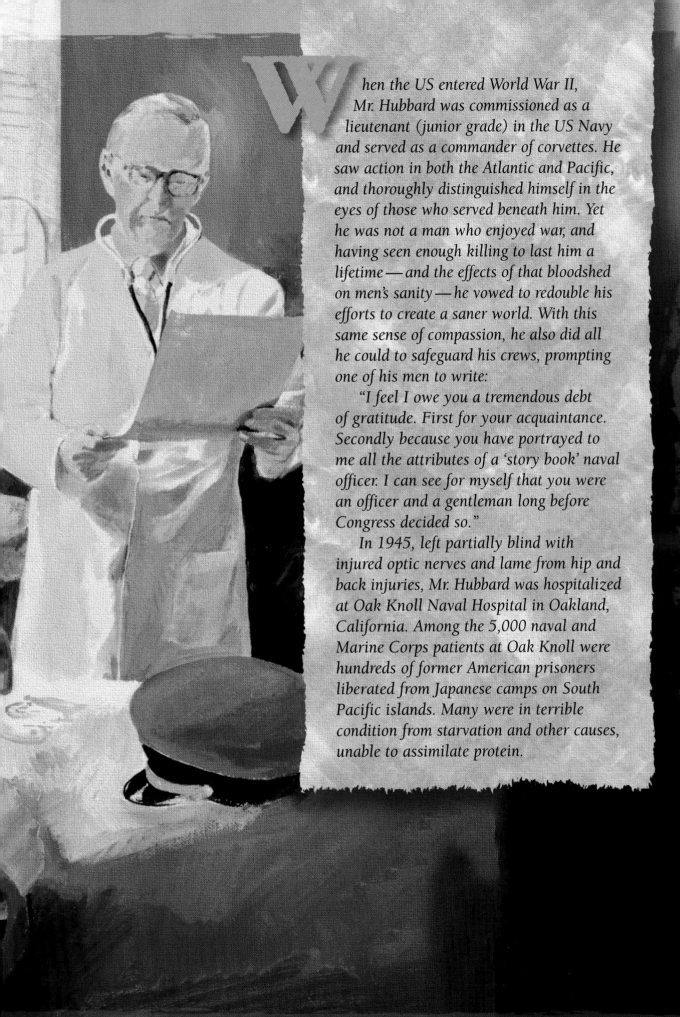

When the US entered World War II, Mr. Hubbard was commissioned as a lieutenant (junior grade) in the US Navy and served as a commander of corvettes. He saw action in both the Atlantic and Pacific, and thoroughly distinguished himself in the eyes of those who served beneath him. Yet he was not a man who enjoyed war, and having seen enough killing to last him a lifetime—and the effects of that bloodshed on men's sanity—he vowed to redouble his efforts to create a saner world. With this same sense of compassion, he also did all he could to safeguard his crews, prompting one of his men to write:

"I feel I owe you a tremendous debt of gratitude. First for your acquaintance. Secondly because you have portrayed to me all the attributes of a 'story book' naval officer. I can see for myself that you were an officer and a gentleman long before Congress decided so."

In 1945, left partially blind with injured optic nerves and lame from hip and back injuries, Mr. Hubbard was hospitalized at Oak Knoll Naval Hospital in Oakland, California. Among the 5,000 naval and Marine Corps patients at Oak Knoll were hundreds of former American prisoners liberated from Japanese camps on South Pacific islands. Many were in terrible condition from starvation and other causes, unable to assimilate protein.

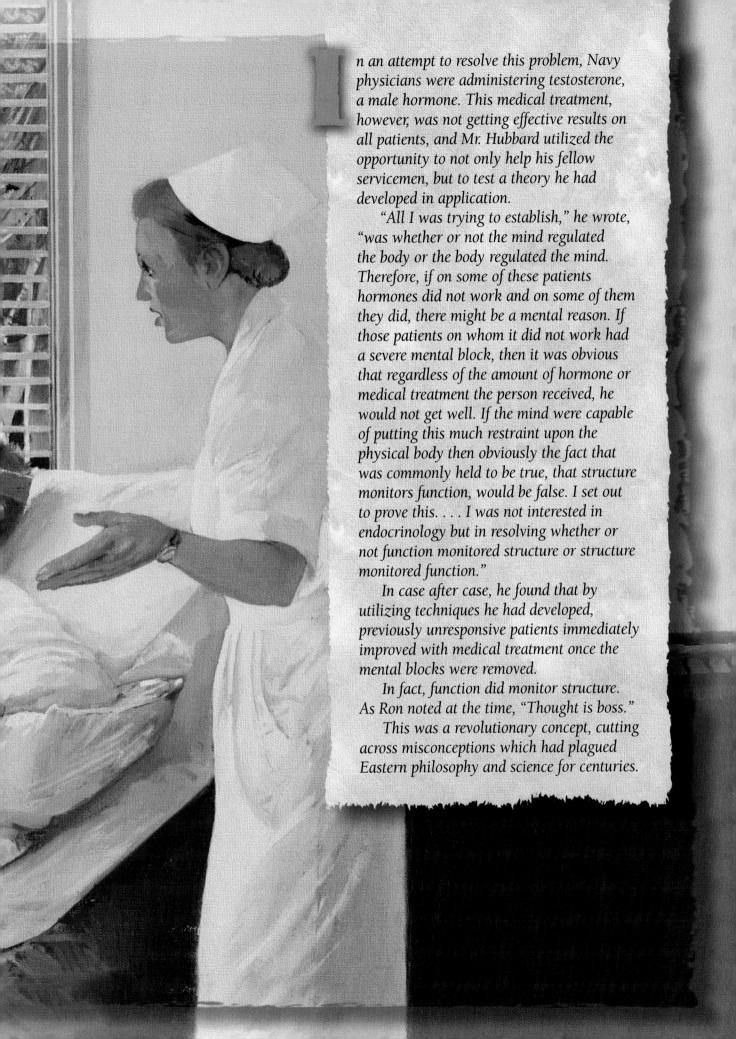

In an attempt to resolve this problem, Navy physicians were administering testosterone, a male hormone. This medical treatment, however, was not getting effective results on all patients, and Mr. Hubbard utilized the opportunity to not only help his fellow servicemen, but to test a theory he had developed in application.

"All I was trying to establish," he wrote, "was whether or not the mind regulated the body or the body regulated the mind. Therefore, if on some of these patients hormones did not work and on some of them they did, there might be a mental reason. If those patients on whom it did not work had a severe mental block, then it was obvious that regardless of the amount of hormone or medical treatment the person received, he would not get well. If the mind were capable of putting this much restraint upon the physical body then obviously the fact that was commonly held to be true, that structure monitors function, would be false. I set out to prove this. . . . I was not interested in endocrinology but in resolving whether or not function monitored structure or structure monitored function."

In case after case, he found that by utilizing techniques he had developed, previously unresponsive patients immediately improved with medical treatment once the mental blocks were removed.

In fact, function did monitor structure. As Ron noted at the time, "Thought is boss."

This was a revolutionary concept, cutting across misconceptions which had plagued Eastern philosophy and science for centuries.

ith peace restored at war's end, Mr. Hubbard immediately set out to further test the workability of his breakthroughs. This was intensive research. For subjects he selected people from all walks of life — in Hollywood, where he worked with actors and writers; in Savannah, Georgia, where he helped deeply disturbed inmates in a mental hospital; and in Washington, DC, New York City, New Jersey, Pasadena, Los Angeles and Seattle. In all, he personally helped over four hundred individuals before 1950, with spectacular results. And he used the same procedures to cure injuries and wounds he himself had received, fully recovering his health by 1949.

So complete was his recovery, that officers from the Naval Retiring Board reviewing Lt. Hubbard's case were actually upset. After all, they reasoned, how could a man physically shot to pieces at the end of the war pass his full physical examination? The only answer, they concluded, was that L. Ron Hubbard must be somebody else. And when they found that all was in order, they designated him fit for active duty.

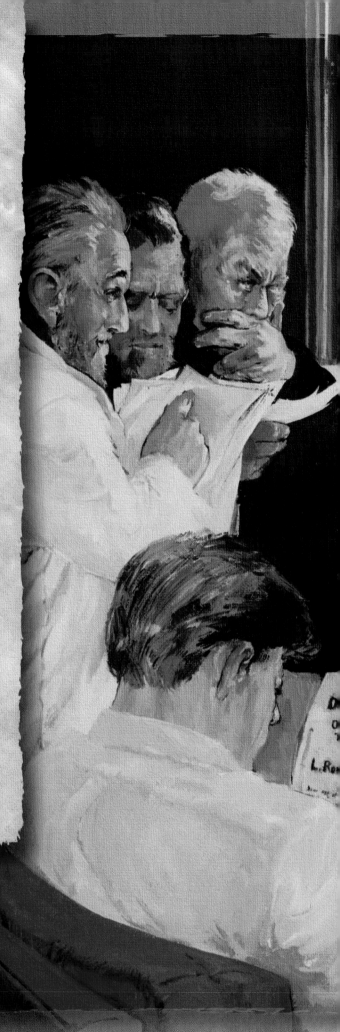

Returning to Washington, DC, Ron compiled his sixteen years of investigation into the human condition, writing the manuscript "The Original Thesis" (today published under the title **The Dynamics of Life**), a paper outlining the principles he was using. He did not offer it for publication. He gave a copy or two to some friends, and they promptly duplicated it and sent it to **their** friends who, in turn, made copies and sent it to others. In this way, passed hand to hand, Dianetics on its own became known the world over. Word spread that he had made a revolutionary breakthrough. L. Ron Hubbard had found the source of human aberration and had developed a technique of the mind that worked. Dianetics was born.

The first published article on Dianetics, entitled "Terra Incognita: The Mind," appeared in the Winter/Spring 1949–1950 issue of the **Explorers Club Journal**. Shortly thereafter, Ron found himself literally deluged with letters requesting more information on the application of his breakthroughs. Hoping to make his discoveries available to the broad public, and at the insistence of those working with him at the time, he offered his findings to the American Medical Association and the American Psychiatric Association. The response was most enlightening. Not only did the healthcare establishment claim no interest in his work, they declined to even examine his results.

Thereupon a new lesson was learned.

A workable technology of the mind, that anyone could use to help himself and others, was totally at odds with the entrenched medical and psychiatric establishment. They preached that the mind was so complex it could only be understood by "experts" (themselves). They depended upon government appropriations and research grants and perceived Dianetics as a threat to these vested interests (ignoring the fact that Mr. Hubbard had always funded his own research). A technology that anyone could use posed a threat to their monopoly and their billions of dollars. They not only refused to accept Dianetics, they tried to suppress its use. If helping others was their sole purpose, certainly they would have embraced a new, completely proven technological breakthrough and assisted its release for the benefit of society. But they did not, and thus one can only conclude that their true motives were more sordid—the control of others toward their own interests, or, in one word, greed.

L. Ron Hubbard's friends and associates were aghast at the responses from the bastions of healing. On the one hand were hundreds of case histories with rave testimonials from those who had studied and used Dianetics and thousands of letters from people wanting to know more. On the other hand were the few "experts," who had resorted to 220 volts of electricity to cure problems of the mind, who had never studied the subject of Dianetics but nonetheless, didn't want it.

And so the decision was made. L. Ron Hubbard would go directly to the public with a handbook, detailing his discoveries and the techniques he had developed. Never before had there been such a text on the mind, a work expressly written for the man on the street.

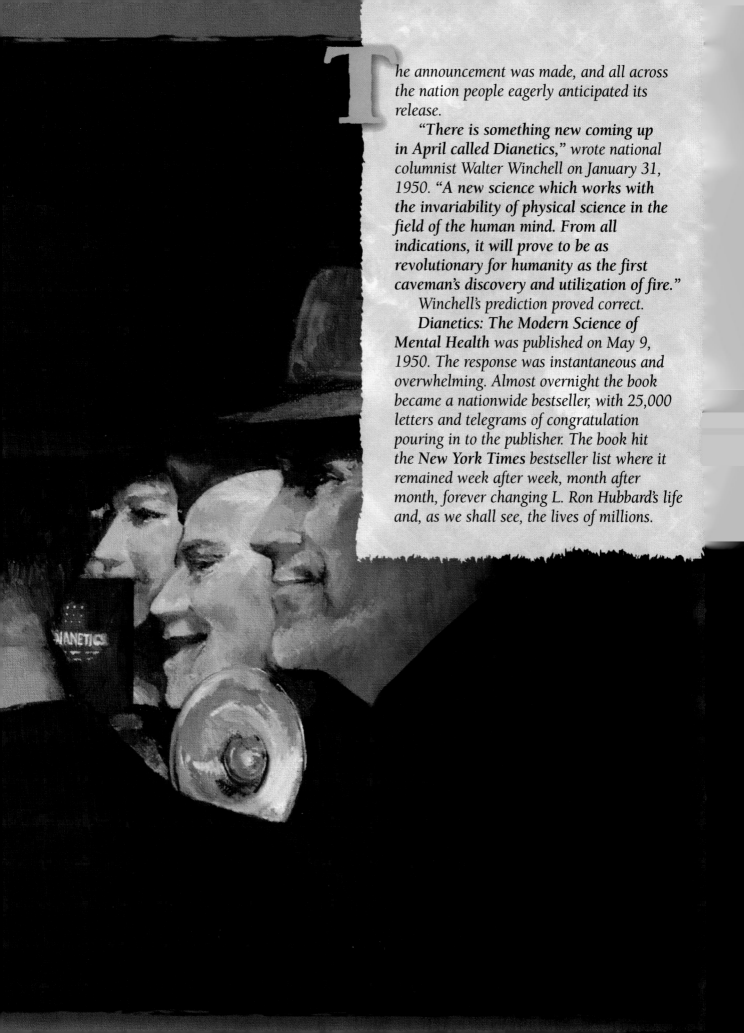

The announcement was made, and all across the nation people eagerly anticipated its release.

"There is something new coming up in April called Dianetics," wrote national columnist Walter Winchell on January 31, 1950. "A new science which works with the invariability of physical science in the field of the human mind. From all indications, it will prove to be as revolutionary for humanity as the first caveman's discovery and utilization of fire."

Winchell's prediction proved correct.

Dianetics: The Modern Science of Mental Health was published on May 9, 1950. The response was instantaneous and overwhelming. Almost overnight the book became a nationwide bestseller, with 25,000 letters and telegrams of congratulation pouring in to the publisher. The book hit the *New York Times* bestseller list where it remained week after week, month after month, forever changing L. Ron Hubbard's life and, as we shall see, the lives of millions.

A NEW ERA FOR MANKIND

The publication of *Dianetics: The Modern Science of Mental Health* ushered in a new era of hope for mankind, and with it a new phase of L. Ron Hubbard's life. Although from this point forward his life would prove just as adventurous as the previous 39 years, it is not the details that are most important, but the accomplishments which form the subject matter of this book.

The first indication that he was to be a public figure came immediately after the release of *Dianetics*. Although Mr. Hubbard had originally planned yet another expedition following the completion of his book, so great was the popular response to his work that he had to change those plans. Thus, instead of exploring islands off Greece, he soon found himself lecturing on Dianetics to packed halls across the nation. It was also at this time that the first Hubbard Dianetics Research Foundation was formed in Elizabeth, New Jersey, and people began arriving in droves to study the new techniques and find out more about the subject.

By late fall of 1950, there were 750 groups across the country applying Dianetics techniques, while newspaper headlines proclaimed, "Dianetics Taking US by Storm," and "Fastest Growing Movement in America."

Ron's research continued, and in March 1951 he completed his next book, *Science of Survival*. In this 500-page work, he further explored the nature of thought and life, offering readers an understanding of, and a new means to predict human behavior. The book is oriented around a chart, the Hubbard Chart of Human Evaluation, which exactly delineates the various emotional tones of individuals, and provides precise procedures to bring anyone to the highest level and thus ultimate survival.

In 1951 he wrote a total of six books, continuing to research and perfect the technologies of Dianetics with which he had resolved the problems of the human mind. But this still left many unanswered questions, questions which man had been pondering since the beginning of recorded history. "The further one investigated," he wrote, "the more one came to understand that here, in this creature *Homo sapiens,* were entirely too many unknowns."

And so, within a year and a half of the release of *Dianetics: The Modern Science of Mental Health,* L. Ron Hubbard had embarked upon another journey of discovery—entering the realm of the human spirit. This track of research, begun so many years earlier as a young man traveling the globe in search of answers to life, was to span the next three decades. And as breakthrough after breakthrough was codified, Scientology was born, giving man, for the first time, a route to higher levels of awareness, understanding and ability that anyone could travel.

Given the inherently religious nature of Mr. Hubbard's work through these years, it was only natural that those surrounding him would come to see themselves not only as students of a new philosophy but also as students of a new religion. And so, in 1954, Scientologists in Los Angeles established the first Church of Scientology. L. Ron Hubbard founded the subject—early Scientologists began the Church.

As more and more people discovered his breakthroughs, Scientology churches sprang up rapidly around the world. Meanwhile, through his writings and lectures, he continued to make his discoveries available to those who sought answers.

In 1959, Mr. Hubbard and his family moved to England, where he purchased the Saint Hill

Manor in East Grinstead, Sussex. This was to be his home for the next seven years, and the worldwide headquarters of the Church of Scientology. There, in addition to his constant writing and lecturing, he began intensively training Scientologists from around the world so that they, in turn, might return to their homelands and teach others. The mid-1960s saw him develop a step-by-step route for anyone to reach states of higher awareness. He also codified administrative principles for the operation of Scientology churches — work which brought about the expansion of Scientology into a global network.

On September 1, 1966, with Scientology established as a worldwide religion, Mr. Hubbard resigned his position as Executive Director of the Church and stepped down from the boards of all Church corporations in order to fully devote himself to researches into the highest levels of spiritual awareness and ability. On the threshold of breakthroughs that had never before been envisaged, he took to the sea, in part to continue his work in an undistracted environment.

On board ship for the next seven years, he again traveled extensively, while devoting his attention to ever-worsening problems facing society through the late 1960s and early 1970s. Of special note from this period is the drug rehabilitation program he developed, recognized today by government studies around the world as the most effective in existence. It was also during this period that he developed the highest levels of Scientology, refinements of application, new administrative principles, and advances in the field of logic — all of which are explained later in this book.

Returning to shore in 1975, Mr. Hubbard continued his travels — first from Florida to Washington, DC and Los Angeles before finally settling in the southern California desert community of La Quinta near Palm Springs, his home until 1979. There, searching for new ways to make Dianetics and Scientology more easily accessible, he wrote dozens of training films on the subjects to visually demonstrate proper application of technical principles. He directed many of these films himself.

Long concerned with accelerating social decay, in 1980 Mr. Hubbard wrote a nonreligious moral code based on common sense. Published in booklet form, it is entitled *The Way to Happiness*. In explanation of this work, L. Ron Hubbard said, "Reading the papers and wandering around in the society, it was pretty obvious that honesty and truth were not being held up to the standards they once had. People and even little kids in schools have gotten the idea that high moral standards are a thing of the past. Man has in his hands today a lot of violent weapons. He doesn't have the moral standards to go with them."

Loudly applauded by community and civic groups around the world, *The Way to Happiness* soon spread across the planet. An entire grass-roots movement formed to disseminate and use the booklet to uplift the decency and integrity of man. To date, more than 65 million copies have been distributed, with millions more being demanded each year.

In 1980, Mr. Hubbard also found time to resume his fiction career. Celebrating his 50th anniversary as a professional writer, he turned his prodigious energy to the authoring of *Battlefield Earth: A Saga of the Year 3000*. This epic science fiction novel was followed by the ten-volume *Mission Earth* opus, a satirical romp through the foibles of our civilization. All eleven books went on to become *New York Times* and international bestsellers, a consecutive bestseller record unmatched by any writer in history.

Returning to his more serious work with continued research into man's spiritual potentials, Mr. Hubbard traveled extensively through California in the early 1980s. In 1983, he took up residence in the town of Creston, near San Luis Obispo. Here he completed his research and finalized the Scientology technical materials he had spent most of his life developing.

The L. Ron Hubbard Life Exhibition, which opened in Hollywood in 1991, features multimedia displays on the works of L. Ron Hubbard, audiovisual presentations on the scope of his discoveries, and artifacts from his early years of exploration, writing and research. It is open daily to the public.

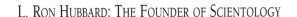

Today, those materials are recorded in the tens of millions of words on the subject of the human spirit which comprise Dianetics and Scientology philosophy. The over 25 million words of his lectures — just those that are on tape — are enough to fill over 100 volumes of text.

In fact, it may well be that L. Ron Hubbard's works include more literature, recorded research and materials than any other single subject of philosophy, the spirit or religion. All of these materials are available to anyone who desires an improvement in his life. Well over 120 million of his books are in circulation today.

Having fully completed his research and seen its broad application expand to six continents and over 60 countries, improving the lives of millions of people, L. Ron Hubbard departed this life on January 24, 1986. Instead

of an end, however, it marked the beginning of an unprecedented expansion of the religion of Scientology around the world, as more and more people continue to benefit from his technologies.

As just one indication of Mr. Hubbard's continued popularity, fully 38 years after its initial publication, *Dianetics: The Modern Science of Mental Health* achieved the unheard of, returning to the top of the *New York Times* bestseller list in 1988. It still rides on bestseller lists around the world to this day and has thus far sold more than 18 million copies.

No less dramatic was the popular acceptance of Mr. Hubbard's other discoveries. To date, for example, over a quarter of a million people have been freed from the effects of drugs, utilizing his rehabilitation methods in centers across the globe, including the world's largest drug rehabilitation and training facility in Oklahoma.

For many more throughout the world — two million in South Africa alone — the name L. Ron Hubbard means literacy and an ability to learn any subject, thanks to his developments in the field of study.

His breakthroughs in administration have enabled thousands of professionals in industry, business and community affairs to bring sanity and stability to their workplaces and their groups.

Every day, Mr. Hubbard's discoveries on the subject of ethics help bring new order into people's lives, into their families, their communities and their environment. A long-confused subject, it has been endowed with new clarity and workability.

Today, millions of people are using his principles and are finding they work. And through this application, L. Ron Hubbard's dream, a dream that perhaps summarizes the hopes of thinking men throughout the ages — "a civilization without insanity, without criminals and without war, where the able can prosper and honest beings can have rights, and where man is free to rise to greater heights" — is not only possible but attainable.

Although L. Ron Hubbard was first known as the popular author of more than 500 novels and short stories, the library of his works on Dianetics and Scientology consists of more than 3,000 lectures, 84 films, three encyclopedic series and over 40 million written words — an extraordinary attainment which reflects the genius of a man who paved the road to a new and better future for mankind.

Although best known as the founder of Dianetics and Scientology, L. Ron Hubbard cannot be so simply categorized. His life was too varied and his influence too broad. Bantu tribesmen in southern Africa know him as an educator; factory workers in Albania know him for his administrative discoveries; children in China know him as the author of their moral code; and readers in a dozen languages know him only for his novels. Had Mr. Hubbard stopped after only one of his many accomplishments he would still be celebrated today.

What follows in this book will provide a firm appreciation of L. Ron Hubbard's contributions to mankind, and everything contained in these pages derives from his work. Although one can enjoy the benefits of Scientology without fully knowing Mr. Hubbard, one cannot understand the man without understanding Scientology — for it is his work and his work alone.

Every few hundred or a thousand years, some genius rises and man takes a new step toward a better life, a better culture. Such a man is L. Ron Hubbard, the founder of Scientology.

MORE ABOUT
L. RON HUBBARD

One way to learn more about Mr. Hubbard's attainments is to visit the Internet site which bears his name (http://www.lronhubbard.org). The full text and photographs of the *RON* Series form a part of this large site, providing a close look at his achievements as writer, master mariner, explorer, poet/lyricist, music maker, educator and humanitarian.

The accolades for his work would fill a volume — awards recognizing his literary accomplishments, his humanitarian contributions, his discoveries. But the greatest reward, particularly in Mr. Hubbard's own estimation, were the lives he was able to help through Dianetics and Scientology.

PERSONAL INTEGRITY
BY L. RON HUBBARD

*HAT IS TRUE FOR YOU is what you have
observed yourself
And when you lose that
you have lost everything.*

*What is personal integrity?
Personal integrity is knowing what you know—
What you know is what you know—
And to have the courage to know
and say what you have observed.
And that is integrity
And there is no other integrity.*

*Of course we can talk about honor, truth, all these things,
These esoteric terms.
But I think they'd all be covered very well
If what we really observed was what we observed,
That we took care to observe what we were observing,
That we always observed to observe.*

*And not necessarily maintaining a skeptical attitude,
A critical attitude, or an open mind.
But certainly maintaining sufficient personal integrity
And sufficient personal belief and confidence in self
And courage that we can observe what we observe
And say what we have observed.*

*Nothing in Dianetics and Scientology is true for you
Unless you have observed it
And it is true according to your observation.
That is all.*

PART TWO

SCIENTOLOGY PRINCIPLES AND APPLICATION

The full story of the development and codification of Scientology can be found in scores of books, more than 15,000 pages of technical writing and more than 3,000 taped lectures. All told, these works represent a lifetime of research by L. Ron Hubbard to discover a workable means to set men spiritually free—to replace ignorance with knowledge, doubts with certainty and misery with happiness.

Today, the fruits of L. Ron Hubbard's work are available to anyone who wishes to reach for them. And no matter how different Scientologists may be—whether teachers and businessmen, housewives and athletes, artists and secretaries—they hold one vital factor in common: having significantly bettered their lives, they know that Scientology works.

Nothing in Scientology, however, need be taken on faith. Its truths are self-evident, its principles are easily demonstrable and its technology can be seen at work in any church of Scientology. One need only open the door and step through.

CHAPTER 4

A DESCRIPTION OF SCIENTOLOGY

Scientology: *Scio* **(Latin) know,** *logos* **(Greek)**
the word or outward form by which the inward
thought is expressed and made known.
Thus, Scientology means knowing about knowing.

Scientology is a twentieth-century religion. It comprises a vast body of knowledge extending from certain fundamental truths, and prime among those truths: Man is a spiritual being endowed with abilities well beyond those which he normally envisages. He is not only able to solve his own problems, accomplish his goals and gain lasting happiness, but also to achieve new states of awareness he may never have dreamed possible.

In one form or another, all great religions have held the hope of spiritual freedom—a condition free of material limitations and misery. The question has always been, however, how does one reach such a state, particularly while still living amidst a frantic and often overwhelming society?

Although modern life seems to pose an infinitely complex array of problems, Scientology maintains that the solutions to those problems are basically simple and within every man's reach. Difficulties with communication and interpersonal relationships, nagging insecurities, self-doubt and despair—each man innately possesses the potential to be free of these and many other concerns.

Scientology offers a pathway to greater freedom.

While the hope for such freedom is ancient, what Scientology is doing is new. The way it is organized is new. The technologies with which it can bring about a new state of being in man are likewise new.

Because Scientology addresses man as a spiritual being, it stands completely apart from other religions which see man as a product of his environment or his genes—fixed in the limitations under which he was born.

Rather, Scientology is the study and handling of the spirit in relationship to itself, universes and other life. Based upon the tradition of fifty thousand years of thinking men, it is built upon the fundamental truths of life. From these principles, exact methods by which one can improve conditions were derived; and unlike other efforts of improvement, which offered only rules by which men should live, Scientology offers real tools for use in everyday life. Thus, it does not depend upon a system of beliefs or faith. The emphasis is squarely on an exact application of its principles toward the improvement of one's life and the world in which we live.

To understand exactly how Scientology is utilized, something should be known of the track of research L. Ron Hubbard traveled and the antecedent of Scientology—Dianetics.

DIANETICS: UNDERSTANDING THE MIND

Dianetics: *Dia* **(Greek) through,** *nous* **(Greek) soul.**

*The Dianetics symbol uses the Greek letter **delta** as its basic form. The stripes are green for growth, and yellow for life. The four green stripes represent the four subdivisions of man's urge to survive which are delineated in Dianetics.*

Prior to 1950, prevailing scientific thought had concluded man's mind to be his brain, i.e., a collection of cells and neurons, and nothing more. Not only was it considered that man's ability cannot be improved, but it also was believed that with the formation of his cerebral cortex, his personality was likewise irrevocably established. These theories were, however, inaccurate, and as a consequence science has never evolved a workable theory of the mind nor a means to resolve problems of the mind.

L. Ron Hubbard changed all that with *Dianetics: The Modern Science of Mental Health.* Its publication in 1950 marks a watershed in the history of man's quest for a true understanding of himself.

Dianetics is a methodology which can help alleviate unwanted sensations and emotions, irrational fears and psychosomatic illnesses (illnesses caused or aggravated by mental stress). It is most accurately described as what the soul is doing to the body through the mind.

Like Scientology, Dianetics rests on basic principles, easily learned, clearly demonstrated as true, and every bit as valid today as when first released in 1950.

THE GOAL OF LIFE

The concise statement of the goal of life itself was one of the most fundamental breakthroughs of Dianetics. This, the dynamic principle of man's existence, was discovered by L. Ron Hubbard and from this many hitherto unanswered questions were resolved.

The goal of life can be considered to be infinite survival. That man seeks to survive has long been known, but that it is his primary motivation is new. Man, as a life form, can be demonstrated to obey in all his actions and purposes the one command: "SURVIVE!"

This is the common denominator of all life, and from it came the critical resolution of man's ills and aberrations.

Once "Survive!" was isolated as the primary urge which explained all of a life form's activities, it was necessary to study further the action of survival. And from that research it was discovered that when one considered pain and pleasure as part of the equation, he had at hand the necessary ingredients with which to understand all of life's actions.

Survival is not only the difference between

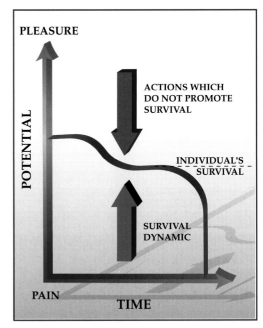

life and death. There are various levels of survival.

The better one is able to manage his life and increase his level of survival, the more he will have pleasure, abundance and satisfaction.

Pain, disappointment and failure are the result of actions which do not promote survival.

As a rough analogy, the time track could be likened to a motion-picture film, if that film were three-dimensional, had fifty-seven perceptions and could fully react upon the observer.

SURVIVAL AND THE MIND

Dianetics states that the purpose of the mind is to solve problems relating to survival.

The mind directs the individual in the effort of survival and bases its operations upon the information that it receives or records. The mind records data using what are called mental image pictures.

Such pictures are actually three-dimensional, containing color, sound and smell, as well as other perceptions. They also include the conclusions or speculations of the individual. Mental image pictures are continuously made by the mind, moment by moment. One can, for instance, examine the picture of what he had for breakfast this morning by recalling breakfast; and similarly recover a picture of an event which occurred last week by recalling it; or even recall something which happened a much longer time ago.

Mental image pictures are actually composed of energy. They have mass, they exist in space, and they follow some very, very definite routines of behavior, the most interesting of which is the fact that they appear when somebody thinks of something. If a person thinks of a certain dog, he gets a picture of that dog.

The consecutive record of mental image pictures which accumulates through an individual's life is called the time track. The time track is a very accurate record of a person's past. As a rough analogy, the time track could be likened to a motion-picture film — if that film were three-dimensional, had fifty-seven perceptions and could fully react upon the observer.

The mind uses these pictures to make decisions that promote survival. The mind's basic motivation, even though a person might fail in an undertaking or make a mistake, is always survival.

That being the case, why don't all of the actions dictated by the mind result in enhanced survival? Why do people sometimes experience irrational fears, doubt their own

Mental image pictures are recorded in the analytical mind.

But those mental image pictures containing physical pain and painful emotion are recorded in the reactive mind.

abilities or entertain negative emotions which seem uncalled for by circumstances?

THE PARTS OF THE MIND

L. Ron Hubbard discovered that the mind has two very distinct parts. One of these — that part which one consciously uses and is aware of — is called the analytical mind. This is the portion of the mind which thinks, observes data, remembers it and resolves problems. It has standard memory banks which

contain mental image pictures, and uses the data in these banks to make decisions that promote survival.

However, two things appear to be — but are not — recorded in the standard banks: painful emotion and physical pain. In moments of intense pain, the action of the analytical mind is suspended and the second part of the mind, the reactive mind, takes over.

When a person is fully conscious, his analytical mind is fully in command. When the individual is "unconscious" in full or in part, the reactive mind cuts in, in full or in part. "Unconsciousness" could be caused by the shock of an accident, anesthetic used for an operation, the pain of an injury or the deliriums of illness.

When a person is "unconscious," the reactive mind exactly records all the perceptions of that incident, including what happens or is said around the person. It also records all pain and stores this mental image picture in its own banks, unavailable to the individual's conscious recall and not under his direct control. Though it may appear that a person knocked out in an accident is unconscious and unaware of happenings around him, his reactive mind is actually industriously recording everything for future use.

The reactive mind does not store memories as we know them. It stores particular types of mental image pictures called engrams. These engrams are a complete recording, down to the last accurate detail, of every perception present in a moment of partial or full "unconsciousness."

This is an example of an engram: A woman is knocked down by a blow to the face. She is rendered "unconscious." She is kicked in the side and told she is a faker, that she is no good, that she is always changing her mind. A chair is overturned in the process. A faucet is running in the kitchen. A car is passing in the street outside.

The engram contains a running record of all these perceptions.

The problem with the reactive mind is that it "thinks" in identities, one thing identical to another. The equation is A=A=A=A=A. A reactive mind computation about this engram would be: the pain of the kick equals the pain of the blow equals the overturning chair equals the passing car equals the faucet equals the fact

that she is a faker equals the fact that she is no good equals the fact that she changes her mind equals the voice tones of the man who hit her equals the emotion equals a faker equals a faucet running equals the pain of the kick equals organic sensation in the area of the kick equals the overturning chair equals changing one's mind equals . . . But why continue? Every single perception in this engram equals every other perception in this engram.

In the future, when this woman's present environment contains enough similarities to the elements found in the engram, she will experience a reactivation of the engram. For example, if one evening the faucet were running and she heard the sound of a car passing outside and, at the same time her husband (the man in her engram) was scolding her about something in a similar tone of voice as used in the original engram, she could experience a pain in the side (where she was kicked earlier). And the words spoken in the engram could also become commands in the present: She might feel that she was no good, or get the idea that she was always changing her mind. The reactive mind is telling the woman that she is in dangerous quarters. If she stays, the pain in the areas where she was abused could become a predisposition to illness or a chronic illness in themselves. This phenomenon of "awakening" the old engram is called restimulation.

The reactive mind is not an aid to a person's survival for the excellent reason that though it is sturdy enough to hold up during pain and "unconsciousness," it is not very intelligent. Its attempts to "prevent a person from getting himself into danger," by enforcing its engram content, can cause unevaluated, unknowing and unwanted fears, emotions, pains and psychosomatic illnesses that one would be much better off without.

The reactive mind can cause unknowing and unwanted fears, emotions, pains and psychosomatic illnesses that one would be much better off without.

Dianetics can effectively "erase" the contents of the reactive mind and free a person from its adverse influence.

THE SOLUTION TO THE REACTIVE MIND

Having discovered the existence of the reactive mind and its engrams, L. Ron Hubbard developed very precise techniques to address it. These techniques can effectively "erase" the contents of the reactive mind and eliminate the ability of such recordings to affect the person without his conscious knowledge. Furthermore, it makes these formerly hidden memories available to the individual as memory in the analytical mind. The effectiveness of these techniques, astonishing in many cases, has been documented in a multitude of case histories over a half-century of application.

THE CLEAR

The goal of Dianetics is a new state for the individual, sought throughout history but never attainable before Dianetics. This state is called "Clear." A Clear is a person who no longer has his own reactive mind and therefore suffers none of the ill effects that the reactive mind can cause.

The Clear has no engrams which, when restimulated, throw out the correctness of his computations by entering hidden and false data.

Becoming Clear strengthens a person's native individuality and creativity and does not in any way diminish these attributes. A Clear is free with his emotions. He can think for himself. He can experience life

ANALYTICAL MIND

A person who no longer has his own reactive mind is called a Clear. What he is left with is all that is really <u>him</u>.

THE ATTRIBUTES OF CLEAR

Clear is a state that has never before been attainable in man's history. A Clear possesses attributes, fundamental and inherent but not always available in an uncleared state, which have not been suspected of man and are not included in past discussions of his abilities and behavior. The Clear is:

- *Freed from active or potential psychosomatic illness or aberration*
- *Self-determined*
- *Vigorous and persistent*
- *Unrepressed*
- *Able to perceive, recall, imagine, create and compute at a level high above the norm*
- *Stable mentally*
- *Free with his emotion*
- *Able to enjoy life*
- *Freer from accidents*
- *Healthier*
- *Able to reason swiftly*
- *Able to react quickly*

Happiness is important. The ability to arrange life and the environment so that living can be better enjoyed, the ability to tolerate the foibles of one's fellow humans, the ability to see the true factors in a situation and resolve problems of living with accuracy, the ability to accept and execute responsibility, these things are important. Life is not much worth living if it cannot be enjoyed. The Clear enjoys living to a very full extent. He can stand up to situations which, before he was cleared, would have reduced him to a shambles. The ability to live well and fully and enjoy that living is the gift of Clear.

unencumbered by inhibitions reactively dictated by past engrams. Artistry, personal force and individual character are all residual in the basic personality of the person, not the reactive mind.

Clears are self-confident, happy and generally successful in both careers and interpersonal relationships. It is a highly desirable state for any individual and is attainable by virtually anyone. In fact, thousands upon thousands of people have achieved the state of Clear, a living tribute to the workability of L. Ron Hubbard's discoveries and the technology he developed.

DIANETICS ON THE INTERNET

More information about Dianetics is available directly by visiting the award-winning Dianetics Internet site at **http://www.dianetics.org.**

This site features:
- *A multimedia tour of the human mind.*
- *A "Global Locator" which guides visitors to their nearest Dianetics Counseling Group, organization or mission.*
- *An On-line Dianetics Bookstore which provides information about every book and lecture on the subject of Dianetics by L. Ron Hubbard.*

This site can be viewed in English, German, French, Spanish and Italian.

(For a directory of all Dianetics and related sites, see Chapter 49, List of Churches of Scientology and Other Related Organizations.)

SCIENTOLOGY: A KNOWLEDGE OF LIFE

The Scientology symbol is an S imposed over two triangles. The S stands for Scientology. The two triangles represent important concepts in the Scientology religion. The lower triangle is made up of affinity, reality and communication, which together equate to understanding. The top triangle consists of another set of closely interrelated factors—knowledge, responsibility and control.

For all that Dianetics resolved in the field of human behavior and the mind, there still remained one outstanding question. When someone was looking at a mental image picture, who was looking at that picture?

The breakthrough came in the autumn of 1951, after Mr. Hubbard observed many, many people using Dianetics and found a commonality of experience and phenomena. After carefully reviewing all relevant research data, Mr. Hubbard isolated the answer: Man was neither his body nor his mind, but a spiritual being. This was the source of all that is good, decent and creative in the world: the individual being himself. With this discovery, L. Ron Hubbard founded the religion of Scientology, for he had moved firmly into the field traditionally belonging to religion—the realm of the human soul.

The term *soul*, however, had developed so many other meanings from use in other religions and practices that a new term was needed to connote precisely what had been discovered. The term Mr. Hubbard chose was *thetan*, from the Greek letter *theta, θ,* the traditional symbol for thought or life.

A thetan is the person himself, not his body or his name or the physical universe, his mind or anything else. It is that which is aware of being aware; the identity which IS the individual. One does not *have* a thetan,

something one keeps somewhere apart from oneself; he *is* a thetan.

Very pertinent to Mr. Hubbard's research at this juncture was his examination into the phenomena known as exteriorization. Although various religious texts make mention of it, no one had ever considered the matter with such careful scrutiny. From this research, Mr. Hubbard concluded that the thetan is able to leave the body and exist independent of the flesh. Exteriorized, the person can see without the body's eyes, hear without the body's ears and feel without the body's hands. Man previously had very little understanding of this detachment from his mind and body. With the act of exteriorization attainable in Scientology a person gains the certainty he is himself and not his body.

THE PARTS OF MAN

From this discovery, Mr. Hubbard went on to precisely delineate the parts of man.

First there is the body itself. The body is the organized physical composition or substance of man, whether living or dead. It is not the being himself.

Next, there is the mind, which consists essentially of pictures.

Finally, and most important, there is the thetan. The thetan is not a thing. It is the creator of things.

A man is composed of three parts: A body, a mind and the individual himself — the spiritual being or <u>thetan</u>.

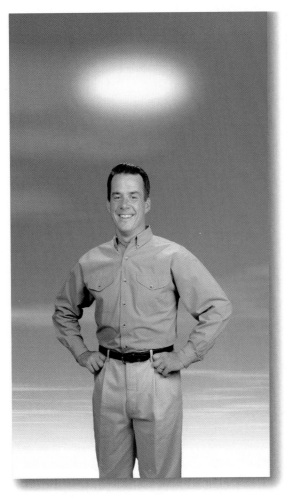

The thetan is the identity which IS the individual; it is not the body. In Scientology, it has been found that a thetan can leave the body and exist independent of the flesh. This phenomenon is called exteriorization. After exteriorization, a person gains certainty he is himself and not his body.

The seniormost of the three parts of man, obviously, is the thetan, for without the thetan there would be no mind or animation of the body, while without a body or a mind there is still animation and life in the thetan.

The thetan utilizes his mind as a control system between himself and the physical universe. The mind is not the brain. The brain is part of the body and does not determine intelligence. It can be likened to a switchboard. If one said that a telephone switchboard was the intelligence of the corporation it served, this would be like saying the brain was the intelligence of the person. It is just not true. The brain is simply a conduit that, like a telephone wire, carries messages. The mind accumulates recordings of thoughts, conclusions, decisions, observations and perceptions of a thetan throughout his existence. The thetan uses his mind in the handling of life and the physical universe. The body (including the brain) is the thetan's communication center. It is a physical object, not the being himself.

The thetan is the source of all creation and life itself. It becomes fully apparent for the first time in man's experience that the spirit is immortal and possessed of capabilities well in excess of those hitherto predicted. The exteriorization of the thetan from his body accomplishes the realization of goals envisioned — but questionably, if ever, obtained — in spiritualism, mysticism and such fields.

Recognition of the thetan makes possible gains in ability and awareness — improvements which are not attainable in any practice holding man to be only a body and thus entirely subject to physical universe limitations. Psychology, for instance, had worked itself into a dead end. Having no concept of the existence of an animating factor to life, it had degenerated into a practice devoted solely to the creation of an effect on living forms.

In Scientology, however, the thetan himself is directly addressed. Such an approach to improvement accomplishes increased spiritual freedom, intelligence and ability for the individual, and clarifies any part of life.

*The basic command "Survive!" obeyed by all of life can be compartmented into the eight dynamics (**dynamic** meaning urge, drive or impulse). A knowledge of the dynamics allows one to more easily inspect and understand any aspect of life.*

THE EIGHT DYNAMICS

Because the fundamentals upon which Scientology rests embrace all aspects of life, certain key principles can be broadly employed to better any condition. Scientologists use these principles in their daily lives, and their use alone can often make the difference between success and failure. Moreover, the principles greatly clarify what is so often confusing and bewildering.

Suppose, for example, life could be correctly compartmentalized so that its many activities, often confused and blurred, could suddenly assume a new clarity? Suppose, for instance, that all the activities in one's varied life could not only be understood for what they really are, but harmonized with all others?

This is possible in Scientology through delineation of the eight dynamics.

The basic command "Survive!" obeyed by all of life, is subdivided into eight compartments so that each aspect of life can be more easily inspected and understood. These compartments are called the eight *dynamics* (*dynamic* meaning urge, drive or impulse). L. Ron Hubbard had observed and delineated the first four of these dynamics in Dianetics. When his research led him into the realm of Scientology, he was able to amplify these first four and delineate the remaining four dynamics.

Through Scientology, a person realizes that his life and influence extend far beyond himself. He becomes aware also of the necessity to participate in a much broader spectrum. By understanding each of these dynamics and their relationship, one to the other, he is able to do so, and thus increase survival on all these dynamics.

The **first dynamic** is SELF. This is the effort to survive as an individual, to be an individual. It includes one's own body and one's own mind. It is the effort to attain the highest level of survival for the longest possible time for self. This dynamic includes the individual plus his immediate possessions. It does not include other people. It is the urge to survive as one's self. Here we have individuality expressed fully.

The **second dynamic** is CREATIVITY. Creativity is making things for the future and the second dynamic includes any creativity. The second dynamic contains the family unit and the rearing of children as well as anything that can be categorized as a family activity. It also incidentally includes sex as a mechanism to compel future survival.

The **third dynamic** is GROUP SURVIVAL. This is the urge to survive through a group of individuals or as a group. It is group survival, the group tending to take on a life and existence of its own. A group can be a community, friends, a company, a social lodge, a state, a nation, a race or in short, any group. It doesn't matter what size this group is, it is seeking to survive as a group.

The **fourth dynamic** is SPECIES. Man's fourth dynamic is the species of mankind. This is the urge toward survival through all mankind and as all mankind. Whereas the American nationality would be considered a third dynamic for Americans, all the nationalities of the world together would be considered the fourth dynamic. All men and women because they are men and women seek to survive as men and women and for men and women.

The **fifth dynamic** is LIFE FORMS. This is the urge to survive as life forms and with the help of life forms such as animals, birds, insects, fish and vegetation. This includes all living things whether animal or vegetable, anything directly and intimately motivated by life. It is the effort to survive for any and every form of life. It is the interest in life as such.

The **sixth dynamic** is the PHYSICAL UNIVERSE. The physical universe has four components. These are matter, energy, space and time. The sixth dynamic is the urge to survive of the physical universe, by the physical universe itself and with the help of the physical universe and each one of its component parts.

The **seventh dynamic** is the SPIRITUAL DYNAMIC, the urge to survive as spiritual beings or the urge for life itself to survive. Anything spiritual, with or without identity, would come under the heading of the seventh dynamic. It includes one's beingness, the ability to create, the ability to cause survival or to survive, the ability to destroy or pretend to be destroyed. A subheading of this dynamic is ideas and concepts and the desire to survive through these. The seventh dynamic is life source. This is separate from the physical universe and is the source of life itself. Thus there is an effort for the survival of life source.

The **eighth dynamic** is the urge toward existence as INFINITY. The eighth dynamic also is commonly called God, the Supreme Being or Creator, but it is correctly defined as infinity. It actually embraces the allness of all. That is why, according to L. Ron Hubbard, "when the seventh dynamic is reached in its entirety one will only then discover the true eighth dynamic."

Simply delineating these dynamics clarifies and brings order into existence. One can observe these dynamics in one's own life, note which one or ones need improvement and, through Scientology, bring these factors into greater harmony.

THE TONE SCALE

Another tool drawn from the body of Scientology and commonly used in everyday life is the emotional Tone Scale. Codified from many, many hours of exhaustive testing and observation, the Tone Scale plots emotions in an exact ascending or descending sequence. Until Mr. Hubbard's examination of this matter, emotions were something we all suffered or enjoyed, but never fully understood.

Have you ever attempted to raise the spirits of someone mourning a recent loss with a cheerful word? The response is usually a fresh outpouring of tears.

Or someone whose outlook and response to life is a chronic apathy, no matter what is happening around him? The person seems to be in good health, has a loving family and an enviable job, but nothing makes any difference. The person just is not interested.

The Tone Scale precisely illuminates what is occurring with individuals such as these, how best to communicate with them and how to help them.

One can find himself or any individual on this Tone Scale and thus know how, using Scientology, he may best be moved up to the higher tones where increased beingness, competence, self-esteem, honesty, well-being, happiness and other desirable attributes are manifested.

These emotional levels are thoroughly detailed in Scientology, but this simplified version will serve to show different emotions and their relative positions on the scale:

40.0	Serenity of Beingness
30.0	Postulates
22.0	Games
20.0	Action
8.0	Exhilaration
6.0	Aesthetic
4.0	Enthusiasm
3.5	Cheerfulness
3.3	Strong Interest
3.0	Conservatism
2.9	Mild Interest
2.8	Contented
2.6	Disinterested
2.5	Boredom
2.4	Monotony
2.0	Antagonism
1.9	Hostility
1.8	Pain
1.5	Anger
1.4	Hate
1.3	Resentment
1.2	No Sympathy
1.15	Unexpressed Resentment
1.1	Covert Hostility
1.02	Anxiety
1.0	Fear
0.98	Despair
0.96	Terror
0.94	Numb
0.9	Sympathy
0.8	Propitiation
0.5	Grief
0.375	Making Amends
0.3	Undeserving
0.2	Self-Abasement
0.1	Victim
0.07	Hopeless
0.05	Apathy
0.03	Useless
0.01	Dying
0.0	Body Death

4.0
ENTHUSIASM

3.0
CONSERVATISM

2.5
BOREDOM

2.0
ANTAGONISM

1.5
ANGER

1.1
COVERT HOSTILITY

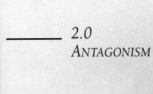

1.0
FEAR

0.5
GRIEF

0.05
APATHY

From knowledge of a man's level on the scale, much can be determined about his attitudes, behavior and survival potential.

When a man is nearly dead, he can be said to be in chronic apathy. And he behaves in certain specific ways. This is 0.05 on the Tone Scale chart.

When a man is chronically sad about his losses, he is in grief. And, once again, behaves in a predictable manner. This is 0.5 on the chart.

When a person is not yet so low as grief but realizes losses are impending, or is fixed chronically at this level by past losses, he is in fear, around 1.0 on the chart.

Just above fear, past or impending losses generate hatred in the person. However, he dare not express this as such, so the hatred comes forth covertly. This is 1.1, covert hostility.

An individual fighting against threatened losses is in anger and manifests predictable aspects of behavior. This is 1.5.

The person who is merely suspicious that loss may take place, or who has become fixed at this level, is resentful. He is in antagonism, which is 2.0 on the chart.

Above antagonism, the situation of a person is not good enough for him to be enthusiastic, not bad enough for him to be resentful. He has lost some goals and cannot immediately locate others. He is said to be in boredom, or at 2.5 on the Tone Scale chart.

At 3.0 on the chart, a person has a conservative, cautious aspect toward life, but is reaching his goals.

At 4.0 the individual is enthusiastic, happy and vital.

Very few people are naturally at 4.0 on the Tone Scale. A charitable average is probably around 2.8.

This scale has a chronic or an acute aspect. A person can be brought down the Tone Scale to a low level for ten minutes and then go back up, or he can be brought down for ten years and not go back up.

A man who has suffered too many losses, too much pain, tends to become fixed at some lower level of the scale and, with only slight fluctuations, stays there. Then his general and common behavior will be at that level of the Tone Scale.

The simplest thing to know about this scale is that people find it difficult to respond to communication which is too far above where they are stuck. If you try to help someone in apathy by talking to them in enthusiasm, you will probably not have much success. The gap between such extremes is not easily bridged unless you understand the Tone Scale.

Using knowledge of the Tone Scale, however, you would recognize the emotion one-half to one full tone above the person, communicate in that tone and thus bring him up to higher tones. By moving up the scale gradiently it is possible to help someone overcome fixed conditions and regain a more happy and vital outlook.

The Tone Scale is of enormous value in life and its relationships. Mr. Hubbard thoroughly researched human behavior and the full body of his work in this area furnishes an accurate description of the attitudes and behavior of others. By knowing where a person falls on the scale, one can precisely predict his actions. Knowledge of the Tone Scale gives one a greater understanding of his fellows than ever before available. It is a true technology of helping others to better their conditions.

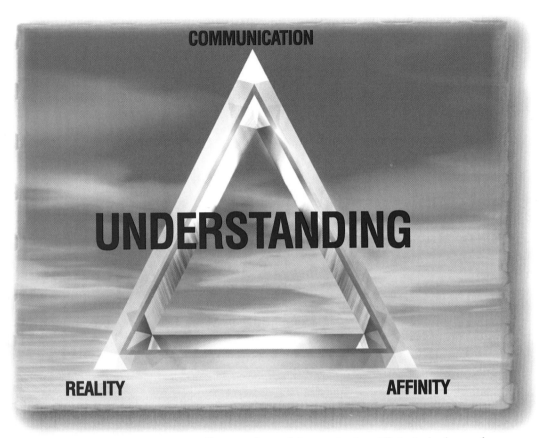

COMMUNICATION

UNDERSTANDING

REALITY   AFFINITY

The components of understanding are Affinity, Reality and Communication. Affinity is the degree of liking or affection. Reality is agreement, or that which appears to be, and communication is the interchange of ideas or objects. Together these form an interrelated triangle.

AFFINITY, REALITY AND COMMUNICATION

Another tool of considerable importance in Scientology, and one that greatly assists interpersonal relationships, is the principle of affinity, reality and communication. These three interdependent factors may be expressed in a triangle. The first corner of the triangle is affinity, which is the degree of liking or affection or lack of it. It is the feeling of love or liking for something or someone.

The second corner of the ARC triangle is called reality, which could be defined as "that which appears to be." Reality is fundamentally agreement. What we agree to be real is real.

The third corner of the triangle is communication, defined as the interchange of ideas or objects between two people. In human relationships this is more important than the other two corners of the triangle.

The interrelationship of the triangle becomes apparent at once when one asks, "Have you ever tried to talk to an angry man?"

Without a high degree of liking and without some basis of agreement there is no communication. Without communication and some basis of emotional response there can be no reality. Without some basis for agreement and communication there can be no affinity. Thus these three things form a triangle. Unless there are two corners of a triangle, there cannot be a third corner. Desiring any corner of the triangle, one must include the other two.

The ARC triangle is not equilateral. Affinity and reality are much less important than communication. It might be said that the triangle begins with communication, which brings into existence affinity and reality.

Great importance is placed in Scientology on the factor of communication, as Scientologists know that communication is the bridge to higher states of awareness and happiness.

These three terms — affinity, reality and communication — add up to understanding.

They are interdependent one upon the other, and when one drops the other two drop also. When one point of the ARC triangle rises, the other two rise also.

The ARC triangle has many uses in improving conditions in life. It answers the question of how to talk to someone — if one uses the triangle and chooses a subject on which the person being talked to can agree, affinity will rise and communication will be better. Using the principle that raising any corner of this triangle raises the other two, one can improve his relationship with anyone. This is the first step in helping others.

THE SCOPE OF SCIENTOLOGY

Although there are substantially many more ways in which these principles and others may be used to better conditions, one need not spend months studying Scientology before it can be used. People have been led to believe that life is complex and man unknowable, but Scientology holds the opposite view: It is possible for anyone not only to know himself in the fullest sense of the word, but also to gain control over life. Moreover, Scientology is organized so that one may easily employ just a single principle to work remarkable changes.

But quite apart from the immediate bettering of relationships, or sorting out the confusion in one's life, these principles are actually part of the practice of Scientology, and that practice is dedicated to—and has the technology to—consistently raise individuals on the Tone Scale, increase their ARC, and broadly improve their dynamics.

To fully appreciate the depth and scope of the religion, and the actual practice of these principles and others, it is necessary to gain some understanding of the most important practices of Scientology—auditing and training—the subject of the next chapter.

SCIENTOLOGY ON THE INTERNET

*Internet users can gain further understanding of Scientology and many of its churches by visiting the Scientology Global Information Center at **http://www.scientology.org.***

Among this site's many features are:

■ *"Virtual tours" inside many of the churches pictured at the beginning of this book, including the first Church of Scientology in Los Angeles, the Founding Church of Scientology in Washington, DC, the motor vessel **Freewinds,** the Flag Land Base, the Saint Hill College for Scientologists, Celebrity Centre International and the Advanced Organization Saint Hill for Europe.*

■ *A real-time audio presentation of L. Ron Hubbard's classic lecture, "The Story of Dianetics and Scientology."*

■ *A "Global Locator" through which visitors from anywhere in the world can find the exact location of their nearest Scientology church.*

■ *An ongoing series of scholarly studies by religious experts who have examined Scientology in depth and published their findings.*

*This site also includes the entirety of this book, **What Is Scientology?** and can be viewed in English, French, Spanish, German and Italian.*

(For a directory of all Scientology related sites, see Chapter 49, List of Churches of Scientology and Other Related Organizations.)

CHAPTER 5

THE PRACTICE OF SCIENTOLOGY

Within the vast amount of data which makes up Scientology's religious philosophy there are many principles which, when learned, give one a new and broader view of life. Knowing the Tone Scale, for instance, a person can see how best to deal with a grumpy child, mollify an upset friend or get an idea across to a staid employer. These principles amount to a huge area of observation in the humanities. The data exists for a person to think with, to work with, to wonder with, to accept or reject as he wishes. It is a body of knowledge there for the learning. There is nothing authoritarian in it. It is valuable purely as a body of knowledge.

From this body of wisdom the second division of Scientology—the application of the principles of Scientology's philosophy—is derived. The extraordinary achievement of Dianetics and Scientology has been the development of exact, precise methods to increase man's spiritual awareness and capabilities. Other efforts along this line provided only sporadic or temporary results—

if any. Using Scientology, life-enhancing improvements can be obtained when exactly applied.

The importance of *application* in Scientology comes from the fact that L. Ron Hubbard developed as part of the religion an actual technology that enables one to use his discoveries to better oneself and others. *Technology* means the methods of application of the principles of something, as opposed to mere knowledge of the thing itself. And, using L. Ron Hubbard's technology, applying the methods, one can heighten his perceptions and awareness, increase his abilities and lead a better, more fulfilling life. In short, one can be unhindered by others' ideas that man cannot change and that one can be no better than he was born to be.

Throughout the remainder of this book the term *technology* is used with regard to the application of Scientology principles. Many technologies are extant today, technologies to build bridges and technologies to fire rockets into space. But with the work of L. Ron Hubbard, for the first time there exists a proven, workable technology to improve the functions of the mind and rehabilitate the potential of the spirit. This is auditing.

A Description of Auditing

Although the purely philosophical aspects of L. Ron Hubbard's work are sufficient in themselves to elevate this civilization, only auditing provides a precise path by which any individual may walk an exact route to higher states of spiritual awareness.

The goal of auditing is to restore beingness and ability. This is accomplished by (1) helping the individual rid himself of any spiritual disabilities and (2) increasing individual abilities. Obviously, both are necessary for an individual to achieve his full spiritual potential.

Auditing, then, deletes those things which have been added to the reactive mind through life's painful experiences and addresses and improves one's ability to confront and handle the factors in his life.

Through auditing one is able to look at his own existence and improve his ability to confront what he is and where he is. There are vast differences between the technology of auditing, a religious practice, and other practices. There is no use of hypnosis, trance techniques or drugs during auditing. The person being audited is completely aware of everything that happens. Auditing is precise, thoroughly codified and has exact procedures.

A person trained and qualified to better individuals through auditing is called an auditor. *Auditor* is defined as one who listens, from the Latin *audire* meaning to hear or listen. An auditor is a minister or minister-in-training of the Church of Scientology.

A person receiving auditing is called a preclear—from pre-Clear, a person not yet Clear. A preclear is a person who, through auditing, is finding out more about himself and life.

The period of time during which an auditor audits a preclear is called an auditing session.

A session is conducted at an agreed-upon time established by the auditor and preclear.

Auditing uses processes—exact sets of questions asked or directions given by an auditor to help a person locate areas of spiritual distress, find out things about himself and improve his condition. There are many, many different auditing processes, and each one improves the individual's ability to confront and handle part of his existence. When the specific objective of any one process is attained, the process is ended and another can then be used to address a different part of the person's life.

An unlimited number of questions could, of course, be asked—which might or might not help a person. The accomplishment of Dianetics and Scientology is that L. Ron Hubbard isolated the exact questions and directions to bring about spiritual freedom.

The questions or directions of the process guide the person to inspect a certain part of his existence. What is found will naturally vary from person to person, since everyone's experiences are different. Regardless of experience or background, however, the individual is assisted in locating not only areas of spiritual upset or difficulty in his life, but in locating the source of the upset. By doing this, any person is able to free himself of unwanted barriers that inhibit, stop or blunt his natural abilities and increase these abilities so that he becomes brighter and more spiritually able.

There are no variables in the technology of auditing, no random results or haphazard applications. Auditing is not a period of vague free association. Each process is exact in its design and in its application, and attains a definite result when correctly ministered.

Scientology auditing can bring any person from a condition of spiritual blindness to the brilliant joy of spiritual existence.

THE IMPORTANCE OF COMMUNICATION

In point of fact, communication is one of Scientology's most fundamental doctrines and the basis for its core religious services, auditing and training. A substantial portion of the Scientology scripture is devoted to the understanding and application of communication, including books, tape-recorded lectures and training films. A Scientology auditor studies communication and practices communication techniques at many points in his training, continually working to achieve a perfect mastery of its formula.

Auditing becomes possible only through application of the communication formula. A person participating in auditing (a "preclear" in Scientology) must direct his attention inward to the deepest recesses of his reactive mind to confront occluded past incidents, including past lives, in order to find the answers to auditing questions, erase the harmful energy contained in the mental image picture recordings of these incidents, and thus experience relief from spiritual travail. The preclear is fully alert during an auditing session and becomes even more alert as auditing progresses. The auditor and preclear work together to help the preclear defeat the preclear's reactive mind. Auditing is not something done to the person, but involves his active participation to increase his self-determinism. Using communication alone, the auditor must direct the preclear's attention (with the preclear's agreement) to past moments of pain, unconsciousness or misemotion.

The preclear, knowing that the auditor is following the exact and predictable communication formula, feels sufficiently secure to allow the auditor to direct his attention and to tell the auditor about what he finds.

THE AUDITOR'S CODE

The auditor maintains and practices a code of conduct toward his preclear known as the "Auditor's Code." This is a doctrine of rules which must be strictly followed to ensure a preclear receives the greatest possible spiritual gain from auditing, and was evolved over many years of observation. It is the code of ethics which governs an auditor's actions.

For example, in keeping with the Auditor's Code, an auditor promises never to use the secrets divulged by a preclear in an auditing session. Traditionally, all communications between a minister and his parishioners have been privileged and confidential, and such is the case in auditing. The confidences given in trust during an auditing session are considered sacrosanct by the Church, and are never betrayed.

Auditing is only successful when the auditor conducts himself in accordance with the Code. An auditor never tells the preclear what he should think about himself, nor offers his opinion about what is being audited. A goal of auditing is to restore the preclear's certainty in his own viewpoint; evaluation for the preclear only inhibits attainment of this goal. Hence, such evaluation is prohibited by the Code.

The qualities instilled by the Auditor's Code are essentially those held to be the best in people. An auditor shows his preclear kindness, affinity, patience and other such virtues, to assist the preclear in confronting areas of spiritual upset or difficulty.

THE E-METER

Auditing is assisted by use of a religious artifact which helps the auditor and preclear locate areas of spiritual distress or travail. This religious artifact is called an Electropsychometer, or E-Meter. (*Electropsychometer* from *electrometer*, a calibrated device used for measuring extremely low voltages and *psyche*, the human soul, spirit or mind.) The E-Meter measures the spiritual state or change of state of a person and thus is of enormous benefit to the auditor in helping the preclear locate areas to be handled. The reactive mind's hidden nature requires utilization of a device capable of registering its effects—a function the E-Meter does accurately.

When the E-Meter is operating and a person holds the meter's electrodes, a very tiny flow of electrical energy (about 1.5 volts— less than a flashlight battery) passes down the wires of the E-Meter leads, through the person's body and back into the E-Meter. The electrical flow is so small, there is no physical sensation when holding the electrodes.

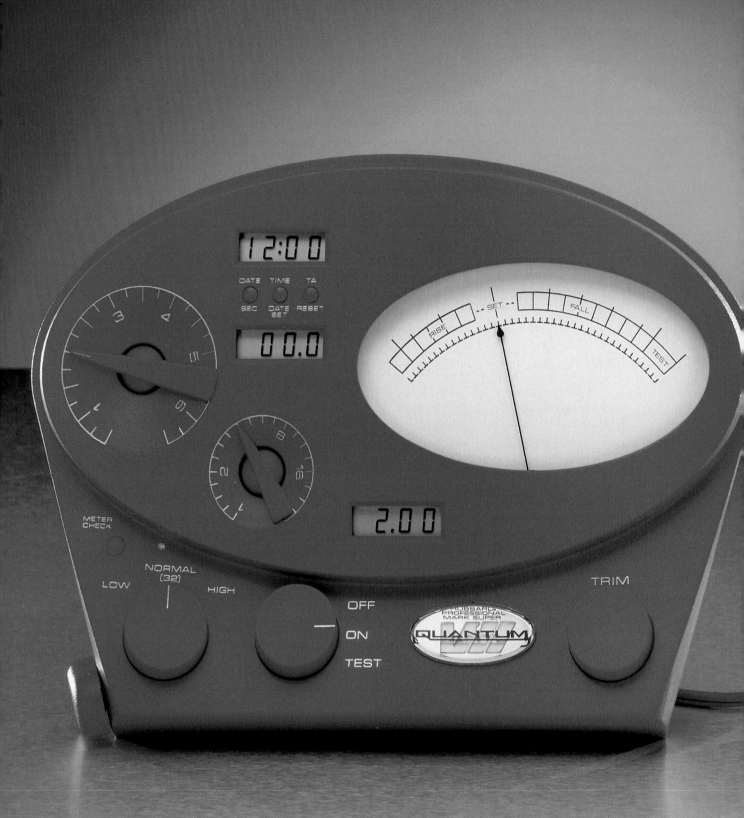

The pictures in the mind contain energy and mass. The energy and force in pictures of painful or upsetting experiences can have a harmful effect upon an individual. This harmful energy or force is called charge.

When the person holding the E-Meter electrodes thinks a thought, looks at a picture, reexperiences an incident or shifts some part of the reactive mind, he is moving and changing actual mental mass and energy. These changes in the mind influence the tiny flow of electrical energy generated by the E-Meter, causing the needle on its dial to move. The needle reactions on the E-Meter tell the auditor where the charge lies, and that it should be addressed through auditing.

Different needle movements have exact meanings and the skill of an auditor includes a complete understanding of all meter reactions. Using the meter, the auditor ensures the process covers the correct area in order to discharge the harmful energy connected with that portion of the preclear's reactive mind. When charge lessens, the person heightens his ability to think clearly in the area being addressed and his survival potential increases proportionately. As a result, the preclear discovers things about himself and his life — new realizations about existence, the milestones that mark his gains.

These realizations result in a higher degree of spiritual awareness and consequently a greater ability to succeed.

HOW AN AUDITING SESSION IS CONDUCTED

Auditing consists of certain elements: the preclear, the auditor, the auditing process, communication, the Auditor's Code and the E-Meter. In combination, they resolve the reactive mind.

An auditing session takes place in a quiet, comfortable place where it will not be

The Electropsychometer, or E-Meter, measures the mental state or change of state of a person, helping the auditor and preclear locate areas of spiritual distress or travail so they can be addressed and handled.

disturbed. Usually the auditor and preclear are seated across a table or desk from one another with an E-Meter set up for the auditor's use. Before a program of auditing begins, the preclear is familiarized with the elements of auditing during a period of orientation so he knows what to expect in a session. The auditor also ensures the preclear has no distractions or upsets to prevent him from devoting his full attention to the process used in the session.

Different types of auditing are used for each preclear, depending upon his concerns during the session and his earlier auditing. Although auditing addresses the individual, and each individual is different, a precisely delineated gradient of processing steps must be followed to achieve personal spiritual freedom for everyone.

By using exact questions and the E-Meter, the auditor first locates an area of charge in the preclear's reactive mind to address with the process. When the auditor finds something in the reactive mind, the meter needle surges, indicating that the subject of his questioning contains charge.

Once an area of charge or upset has been located, the auditor then asks the process question or gives the directions needed to assist the preclear in examining that upset. The preclear is now inspecting his reactive mind.

The auditor guides the preclear to look at this area more thoroughly. He continues the process and makes notes of the meter reactions and data recovered by the preclear to help chart progress. He abides by the Auditor's Code, never evaluating the data being recovered by the preclear. As the process continues, more and more data from that area of the reactive mind, heretofore hidden from the person's conscious awareness, becomes available in the analytical mind of the preclear. The questions and directions of the particular process help the preclear discharge the harmful energy or force connected with incidents or

This is an auditing session. The auditor is on the left; the preclear is on the right.

situations in his past. As the charge lessens, the preclear's awareness of the area increases.

The auditor continues to guide the preclear's attention to the area. Reactions on the E-Meter aid him to direct the preclear to pull more and more data, previously unknown to the preclear, out of the reactive mind and return it to his analytical awareness. Ultimately, the preclear becomes completely aware of the content and is able to view it as it is, without his awareness clouded by reactivity.

During auditing, a preclear has many realizations about life. Such discoveries are known in Scientology as cognitions. A cognition is something a person has come to realize. It is a "What do you know, I just realized why I always felt that way about . . ." kind of statement. Cognitions result in a higher degree of awareness and consequently greater abilities to succeed in life. When such a realization occurs, that portion of the reactive mind ceases to register on the E-Meter and the needle freely sweeps the dial rhythmically back and forth, a phenomenon plainly visible to the auditor.

The preclear has gained a higher degree of awareness and rid himself of, perhaps, an irrational fear, psychosomatic illness or psychosomatic disability. The source of what had been bothering him had been unknown, but, once discovered, its power is nullified. The process employed in the auditing session has served its purpose and can be ended. The auditor now proceeds on to additional processes in further auditing the preclear.

As more and more areas of the reactive mind are addressed and alleviated through auditing, its adverse effects continue to lessen and the individual becomes happier, more spiritually aware and more in control of his life.

WHY AUDITING WORKS

In a session, the analytical mind of the preclear is assisted by the analytical mind of the auditor in order to vanquish the preclear's reactive mind.

The preclear is victimized by his reactive mind. When the reactive mind is restimulated, a person is affected by the harmful energy it contains. Since the reactive mind is hidden, the preclear cannot handle it by himself. Witness the thousands of years man has philosophized, "soul searched" and tried to understand himself and his motives to no avail. In the absence of an auditor, the strength of the preclear's dynamic thrust is less than the force being exerted by the reactive mind.

One of the primary reasons auditing works is because the strength of the auditor's dynamic thrust is added to the preclear's dynamic thrust and these two combined are greater than the single force of the preclear's reactive mind. Working together and applying L. Ron Hubbard's precise technology, the preclear's reactive mind can be erased.

Each time an area of charge is released from the reactive mind, the preclear's awareness increases. This increase of awareness builds from auditing session to auditing session and the preclear gradually becomes more and more aware of who he actually is, what has happened to him and what his true spiritual potentials and abilities are.

VALIDATION OF RESULTS

Auditing gains which a person feels subjectively can also be shown objectively through testing during the course of an auditing program. Numerous tests are used by technical staff to help gauge a preclear's progress. These tests measure the preclear's ability prior to starting an auditing program and provide a prediction of how much auditing it may take to achieve a certain result with the preclear. When the preclear is retested afterwards, the improvements he is experiencing personally can be plotted on a graph which validates his gains. The results are used by the auditor to help determine further processes to audit.

Though testing is primarily meant to assist technical staff to ensure a preclear derives the greatest spiritual benefits in his auditing, the consistent results observed have changed man's viewpoint of himself in many regards. Prior to Dianetics, psychiatry and psychology were adamant in their assertion that a person's ability and intelligence could not be changed. Their pronouncements were disproven in the face of study after study wherein persons showed dramatic increases in both areas after auditing.

One routine test is the Oxford Capacity Analysis (OCA) which accurately measures ten different personality traits. These rise markedly in auditing, reflecting the preclear's gains. Preclears report being calmer, more stable, more energetic and more outgoing as a direct result of auditing, and scores on the OCA furnish corroborative data.

Aptitude tests are also a reliable indicator of auditing results. Improvements in aptitude test scores correlate with a decrease in propensity towards accidents. Many other tests are available which measure coordination and perceptions such as vision, hearing, colorblindness, balance and so on. These functions also improve as a result of auditing.

Naturally, individual progress is variable since it is largely influenced by the preclear's dedication and the frequency of sessions. Therefore, clearly defined rates of improvement are impossible to establish, and the Church makes no claims or guarantees of the gains someone will make in auditing. Church staff, however, have seen so many remarkable improvements in parishioners that they expect such results as a matter of course.

COMPARISON TO EARLIER PRACTICES

Auditing is quite different, both in terms of approach and result, from other efforts which purport to help man improve his lot in life.

In psychoanalysis, for instance, the analyst does not accept what the person says but interprets it, evaluates his condition for him, reads sexual significance into his statements and tells him why he is worried, all of which merely confuse a person further and have no helpful effect. In auditing, what the preclear says is never evaluated and his data is never refuted. To do so would totally violate the Auditor's Code. Nor in auditing is the preclear encouraged to ramble on without guidance, ransacking the millions of incidents in his reactive mind and restimulating many, in the hope he might stumble across the right one.

In the more brutal practice of psychiatry, force (physical, chemical or surgical) is used to overwhelm an individual's ideas and behavior and render the patient quiet. There is no thought of gain or help here but only of making patients more manageable. Auditing bears no resemblance to any part of this field.

Similarly, auditing bears no resemblance to psychology, which is primarily the study of observing responses to stimuli and provides no means of producing actual improvement. Other practices such as hypnotism consider that a person has to be put into a state of lessened awareness (i.e., a trance) before anything can be done. Auditing is quite the opposite and seeks to wake people up, not put them to sleep.

Past efforts to help man sought to do so by enforcing moral codes or standards of behavior and conduct but, having no knowledge of the reactive mind or means to relieve its irrational dictates, they achieved no lasting improvements.

Auditing is quite different from these past practices, many of which were impositive and some, like psychiatry, which are actually harmful. In auditing one follows a precisely mapped route which leads to specific improvements and it is only the individual being audited who says whether these have been achieved or not. The preclear determines when he has regained an ability or rid himself of a spiritual barrier to living, not anyone else. The auditor continues to minister to the preclear until the preclear knows of his own volition that he has succeeded. It is not the auditor or anyone else in Scientology who says the preclear has made a gain. The preclear himself knows. Given that the goal of auditing is rehabilitation of one's own potentials, the gains can really be determined in no other way.

Auditing is made up of common denominators which apply to all life. There are no variables in auditing; the same procedures apply to all cases. Only auditing restores to the individual his native potentials, enabling him to be the person he knows he really is. Only auditing frees a person from the traps of the reactive mind.

A DESCRIPTION OF TRAINING

A fundamental idea of Scientology is that increased spiritual awareness is the only factor which offers any road to increased survival and happiness.

Through auditing one becomes free. This freedom must be augmented by knowledge of how to stay free. Scientology contains the anatomy of the reactive mind in its axioms and the discipline and know-how necessary to handle and control the laws of life. The practice of Scientology, then, is composed in equal parts of auditing and training in Scientology principles which includes the technology of their application. Knowing the mechanisms by which spiritual freedom can be lost is itself a freedom and places one outside their influence.

Auditing lets one see how something happened, training teaches one why.

Therefore, because of the importance of training, one will find Scientologists studying the works of L. Ron Hubbard in any church of Scientology. If one were to look in on them, anywhere in the world, the scene would be the same:

Scientologists seated at tables read the written works of L. Ron Hubbard, dictionaries at hand. Some, wearing headphones, listen to his lectures, while others drill the principles of application—all in a precisely laid out sequence.

There are no teachers present. Instead, an ambulatory Course Supervisor moves from individual to individual, monitoring their progress, while a Course Administrator provides any needed materials. Here one sees enthusiastic people, not only assimilating data, but actually learning how to apply it.

This is Scientology training, and it is unique in the field of learning.

Training is the way to learn the technology of Scientology. Technology implies use. There is a gap between knowledge and the application of that knowledge. By becoming trained, a person becomes able to use the truths found in Scientology to actually improve conditions in life.

The practice of Scientology emphasizes application. What exactly does one do to reunite a father and a son, to ease the suffering of a widow or repair a failing marriage? Other religions and practices espouse how one must maintain faith, work out differences or endure with dignity. But does such advice, however well-meaning, actually make a difference?

When a Scientologist enrolls on a Scientology course aimed at providing him the means to better any relationship, he will actually acquire an understanding of the subject, and equally important, the skill to apply it.

By way of an example, let us suppose that a Scientologist is faced with the prospect of a friend's impending divorce. A trained Scientologist has learned why a marriage—any marriage—fails. He understands why good communication ceases between partners and how affinity becomes lowered. Knowing this, he can do something effective to salvage a marriage. He knows methods of reestablishing communication between estranged husbands and bitter wives, and how to rekindle love all but extinguished by marital transgressions. Training in Scientology gives him what nothing else can: a truly workable means of dealing with real-life situations. Someone who has only participated in auditing as a preclear might understand part of a problem in his own marriage but he will not have a complete understanding of it, much less the skills necessary to help others understand theirs.

The practice of Scientology therefore invariably includes gaining knowledge through training in Scientology principles. By learning the subject, one comes to own the philosophy of Scientology for himself and so is able to improve his own life and the lives of others.

How Do Scientologists Train?

During his research, L. Ron Hubbard made many advances in how best to educate people and these are applied in training services ministered by the Church. He isolated the fundamentals of learning and codified these into a technology of study. Study technology is a separate field in itself, with application to any subject of learning. It is used in all Scientology training but is equally useful in the study of any subject.

Among elements unique to Scientology course rooms is the Course Supervisor, an expert in the technology of study, adept at locating and handling any barriers or obstacles to understanding which one might encounter. The Supervisor does not lecture, nor in any way add his own rendition of the subject. This point is important because the results obtained in Scientology come only from closely following the technology exactly as written by Mr. Hubbard. The subject has already been researched, tested and well-proven as workable in application. Verbal renditions passed on from teacher to student would inevitably contain alterations from the original, however unintentional, until Scientology's efficacy would be lost. This is why considerable attention is paid to ensuring a student receives only the pure rendition as written or spoken by Mr. Hubbard himself.

Instead, the Supervisor helps the individual to grasp the materials, always stressing understanding and application. This method of education has been found to enable individuals to understand more and be far better able to use what they have learned than traditional methods of instruction.

Scientology training allows individuals to learn at their own pace. Each course is organized around what is called a checksheet, another innovation in the technology of study developed by Mr. Hubbard. A checksheet is a means of arranging and presenting the materials of a subject in a step-by-step manner to facilitate learning. Checksheets lay out the sequence of study and the practical application drills to be followed.

The materials of a Scientology training service consist of books, other publications, films and recorded lectures by L. Ron Hubbard. These are laid out in the checksheet and the student studies them in the order listed. The individual progresses from one step to the next only when he is ready. There is no "getting left behind," no expecting him to blindly accept the data, or other such humiliations all too prevalent in the society's educational system. A Scientology training service is solely for the benefit of the individual; his own advancement in knowledge is the determining factor of progress.

Since the emphasis is on doing, not study for the sake of study, the individual soon finds himself working with others on the practical aspects of his course, studying together to become proficient in what they have learned. An atmosphere of mutual assistance pervades every Scientology course room.

In addition to studying, each Scientology course requires direct application of the data learned. As one progresses through the checksheet, he is required to demonstrate concepts, apply the information to situations in his own life and practice the procedures or techniques being studied until proficient in their use. A balance is struck between study of Scientology principles and practical application of these principles. The product of a Scientology course is someone who not only understands what he has studied but who can demonstrate this understanding through application.

There are course rooms for reading assignments and listening to taped lectures, while other course rooms are reserved for people to drill the application of their materials.

Another feature of Scientology training is the use of films as a tool to teach correct technical application. These films cover specific aspects of Scientology, showing exactly how they are applied in auditing. The

In a Scientology course room, people study Dianetics and Scientology materials at their own pace with the help of trained Course Supervisors. Students practice the application of those materials to improve their own lives and help others.

films were written by L. Ron Hubbard and many of them were also produced, directed and narrated by him.

When someone completes a training service they are awarded a certificate of accomplishment to signify attainment of a particular level of knowledge or skill.

SCOPE OF TRAINING IN SCIENTOLOGY

The broad scope of Scientology is divided into numerous courses, ranging from introductory courses that teach basic principles, to more extensive ones that train auditors, to courses which contain knowledge about the ultimate capabilities of the thetan, to those that cover the full philosophic and technical materials of Dianetics and Scientology. There is much to know but all of it is knowable and as one learns more, his view of life becomes clearer and more understandable.

At the heart of all instruction in Scientology are the auditor training services offered in the Academy of Scientology in any church.

Scientology Academy training gives one an understanding of man, his potentials and the difficulties that confront him, far in excess of anything taught in the humanities or social sciences. Here, one becomes aware of how Scientology principles apply to situations anywhere in life. With this knowledge a person understands why some people are successful while others fail. He understands why one man is happy while another is not. He knows why some relationships are stable and why others fall apart. Life is not a mystery to someone who has studied Scientology. In this respect, training offers every bit as much personal insight as does auditing. All lives are occasionally beset with trouble. A child falls and gets a scrape, the drinking problem of a neighbor's wife is discovered, a friend's business is failing, a parent becomes ill. The trained Scientologist can bring to bear what he has learned in the Academy to any situation in life and he can do something about it.

The skills acquired in training are a discipline in living and a know-how of the parts of life. Training in Scientology is the bridge between one's own learning and experience and livingness, and the truths offered to him in Scientology. It is a bridge from every human being to an understanding of life.

The Academy training services teach different aspects of this understanding as well as methods of their application, a combination which brings about certainty that one does, in fact, know. Since life is an activity, the emphasis is on application. The student, then, learns the actions which constitute their most important application, auditing. This encompasses an understanding of the communication which takes place between auditor and preclear and how to foster good communication.

Once one has learned to do this within the discipline of auditing it becomes simple to do it in life. One thoroughly studies the theory and mechanics of the E-Meter and then drills with it until he is proficient in its handling and operation. He learns the basic rules of auditing and how to minister a session to a preclear. Each step is studied and then drilled to competence. He watches training films in the Academy film room in order to learn the correct way to perform a particular aspect of auditing. He learns the various codes, laws and axioms that pertain to auditing so that he has a thorough grasp of these basics.

Later steps of his training build upon earlier steps and he is gradually brought up to actual handling of specific laws by which life operates. He next learns exact auditing processes and drills them with other students to the point of proficiency.

After two weeks of intensive training the student can complete enough study and drilling to be ready to begin auditing another on elementary processes. His preclear can be a friend, a fellow student, church staff member or anyone. His sessions are carefully supervised by highly trained auditors in the church who help him correctly apply his materials. He audits his preclear daily and fulfills specific auditing requirements listed on his checksheet. Application, whether in life or in auditing, is the prime purpose of his training.

By bringing improvement to another person the student gains the certainty that he in fact does understand his materials. He confirms his competence in handling the elements of life and his certainty in his own abilities rises. This is a factor equally as important to one's spiritual advancement as the personal gains one receives from being audited.

L. Ron Hubbard stressed that half the gains in Scientology come from training in its principles. The truth of this becomes obvious when one considers how much a knowledge of Scientology clarifies a person's view of life. This naturally includes a greater understanding of what goes on in his own auditing sessions and so makes his own progress as a preclear more rapid and certain. Such understanding is gained by training.

In addition, there is considerable pride and personal satisfaction seeing another become more able and happier as a result of one's help. But regardless of whether one chooses to audit full time, one is alive and, trained in Scientology, he has new understandings he can use.

After completing the auditing requirements on the checksheet, he graduates from his course. An auditor does six major training services in sequence as part of his Academy training. The completion of each signifies a level of skill attained by the auditor and is denoted by a classification, Class 0 through Class V. More advanced classifications, numbering up through Class XII, can be obtained on higher-level training services available at specific churches around the world. Each level follows the efficient and thorough pattern of instruction described earlier, but adds more advanced theory and procedures. The result is an auditor who becomes more and more knowledgeable in the subject. In this way the different levels of training parallel the levels through which a preclear advances in auditing.

Upon completion of specific training services, the auditor gains further know-how in applying what he has learned under highly qualified supervision on an internship. Interning turns an auditor into an expert by doing. The auditor ministers auditing to many different preclears on actions in which he has been trained. Such experience imparts the unshakable certainty that comes only from the experience of doing something over and over.

Auditing techniques work 100 percent of the time if they are applied correctly. Though the basic principles of auditing are simple in themselves, skill in the application of auditing techniques must be gained by an auditor before he will be able to produce invariable results.

Precision is a requisite for accomplishing many things in life but when one is dealing with life itself, which is the preclear, slight variations in application of a procedure can considerably lessen the result obtained. It has long been established that greater gain accrues when the auditing procedure is ministered precisely in all its aspects. The miracles of auditing are the culmination of dozens, even hundreds, of precisely learned, drilled and applied points concerning the wording of procedures, operation of the E-Meter, communication with the preclear and so on. The many steps of an auditing session, correctly taken, result in giant strides of spiritual improvement for the preclear.

A highly trained auditor spends thousands of course-room hours learning his skills and perfecting them in practice. It is usual for an auditor-in-training to put in forty or more hours per week. He invests far more time in a study of the mind than does a practitioner in any similar field. At the highest levels of classification, an auditor will have studied a number of course hours comparable to twelve years of classes at a college or university.

Training in Scientology enables one to face and handle existence. The skills of effective communication, of how to really help another, and how to face whatever life may present — all of these attributes have as many applications as there are situations in life requiring a handling.

The need for auditors is great since it is plain that individuals can be salvaged only one at a time. Unlike many other religions, this salvation ultimately occurs in Scientology in the one-on-one relationship between auditor and preclear. Many Scientologists train to become auditors, and anyone who wishes to help his fellow man can do the same. But of no less importance, one can gain greater skill in handling life than he ever thought possible. There is no more worthwhile purpose than helping one's fellows and no better way to accomplish this purpose than by becoming an auditor. Auditors apply what they have learned to help others with auditing and to change conditions wherever they find that conditions need improving.

This is the mission of the trained Scientologist, and it is in his understanding, his compassion and his skill that the dreams of a better world reside.

THE VALUE OF SCIENTOLOGY

Through auditing and training, Scientologists have come to understand that much in our modern world is transitory and impermanent and based on things not surviving or on things that are in fact being destroyed. They know the practice of Scientology can rehabilitate the individual to his full potentials and that these gains last forever, bringing him to a realization of his own immortality.

Caught on an economic treadmill, hit at every side with the materialism of our age, it is hard for many to grasp that higher states could even exist.

But they do exist.

One sees this for himself when he reaches for them.

Once one starts moving up, there is no wish to stop. The scent of freedom is too strong.

The practice of Scientology is concerned with a better state for man and opens the way with a certain and sure bridge into a future. The way has been dreamed of in ages past. For man it never existed until now.

It exists in Scientology.

CHAPTER 6

THE BRIDGE TO A BETTER LIFE

That man could improve and better himself is a traditionally held belief. This idea tended to become obscured by the nineteenth-century theories of psychology which claimed otherwise—that we remain as we were born. More than that, psychology offered the novel but utterly false idea that man was only an animal and therefore could not improve his ability, could not improve his behavior and could not improve his intelligence.

Because of this, man in general now finds it rather hard to grasp the older and truer idea that man is a spirit and that he can reach for and attain higher states.

Yet betterment is a reality. Many higher states of existence are available to man, and these are attainable through Scientology. L. Ron Hubbard provided a precise delineation of these states, and then clarified how they could be attained by arranging them on a chart which graphically showed each step of the route upward.

Life is improved on a gradient. It is improved a little and then it is improved a little more and then a little more. It does not happen all at once. One cannot expect to be handed a totality of improvement in an instant, like being injected with a syringe that magically cures everything, unless of course one subscribes to the nonsensical idea that a living being has nothing to do with life. What is improved in Scientology is the individual and his awareness. It is not his body, his credit cards, his automobiles or other attendant and appendant machinery surrounding him. The individual himself is improved.

If one had a person with a very serious illness, his mind would be so thoroughly occupied with that condition that he could envision little more than recovery. If in this state someone were to propose the idea he might return to his job and play for the company football team within a week, it is doubtful he would even listen. When the pain subsided and he began to contemplate sitting up, this would be a substantial gain; after which he might even entertain the idea of going downstairs. But if at any point of improvement he were asked to consider the rigors of his job or the company team, it would constitute too big an improvement in too short a time.

Similarly, spiritual advance occurs a bit at a time and one cannot expect someone to immediately leap to the highest levels. The chart Mr. Hubbard devised indicates not only attainable improvements, but also the proper progression, thus avoiding the inevitable setback when attempting to attain too much too soon. An orderly progression, one improvement at a time, as Mr. Hubbard laid out, enables one to ascend at a satisfactory pace to a very high state indeed.

The chart which shows these gradations to betterment is called the Classification, Gradation and Awareness Chart of Levels and Certificates. It is divided into two sides — the left-hand side showing training steps one takes in Scientology, and the right-hand side showing the auditing steps.

Classification refers to training in Scientology and the fact that certain actions are required, or skills attained, before an individual is classified as an auditor at any particular level and allowed onto the next class.

Gradation refers to the gradual improvement that occurs in Scientology auditing. There are grades to a road and there are grades to steps. There can be shallow or steep steps, or even a vertical ascent, which is not a gradient. The desirable road is a gradual grade upward.

One's spiritual awareness improves as one progresses in Scientology. By receiving both training and auditing, each equally necessary, one's awareness increases. The levels of awareness are listed in the center of the chart and correspond precisely to one's progress in training and auditing.

Man, in his religious heritage, has long imagined a bridge across the chasm between where one is now and a higher plateau of existence. Unfortunately, many of those attempting to cross that chasm fell into the abyss.

Employing this metaphor, the Classification, Gradation and Awareness Chart represents, in fact, the bridge which spans the chasm and brings one to the higher plateau. This is the vision man has cherished for at least ten thousand years, and it is now attainable by following the steps as laid out on the chart. It is an exact route with precise procedures providing uniformly predictable spiritual gains when correctly applied. The bridge is complete and can be walked with certainty.

The series of awareness levels running up the center of the Classification, Gradation and Awareness Chart include, for example, unexistence, disconnection, need of change, demand for improvement, hope and ability, to name but a few. These levels represent what the individual person is aware of in his or her life. Everyone is somewhere on these levels of awareness. The goal of Scientology is to assist the individual to raise his awareness. Each rise in awareness is accompanied by increased ability, intelligence and survival potential.

The chart is a map of what one individual can become aware of. It is, however, important to note that the chart stresses one's personal awareness, not what others may have observed about his behavior. Thus, again, we find that what matters is the individual, for that is what is addressed and improved. Scientology is for the person who sincerely wants change, wants to become better and more able. Scientology thus helps the able to become more able.

As one moves up this bridge, he becomes a trained auditor and learns to help another as well as receive his own auditing. He achieves the state of Clear, advances to the highest levels of auditor training and the highest states of awareness as a spiritual being. The awareness levels are paralleled by the various techniques and activities which approximate them and bring about further improvements as one progresses.

To enjoy the full spiritual gains from Scientology, one must move up both sides, training and auditing, if one is to make it all the way. One must learn the axioms of existence by training in Scientology if one is to attain a higher awareness of life. One must experience how these axioms relate to himself through auditing if he is to fully understand himself and his relationship to life. Attempting to walk only one side of the Bridge is like trying to climb a hill by hopping on one leg. But an individual moving up both sides of this chart, one step after another, will arrive at the top.

The chart is a guide for the individual from his first awareness of Scientology to each higher state. Man has never before had such a map. It is the Bridge to Total Freedom. It is the route. It is exact and has a standard progression. One walks it and one becomes free.

THE GOAL OF SCIENTOLOGY

The goal of Scientology is making the individual capable of living a better life in his own estimation and with his fellows.

Although such a statement may seem simple and modest, the ramifications are immense and embody the dream of every religion: the attainment of complete and total rehabilitation of man's native but long-obscured abilities that place him at knowing cause over matter, energy, space, time, form, thought and life.

Yet even well before one reaches this state, the changes Scientology can bring are profound. Personal relationships can be repaired or revitalized. Personal goals can be realized and happiness restored. Where once there were doubts and inhibitions, there can be certainty and self-confidence. Where once there had been unhappiness and confusion, there can be joy and clarity.

Those who have seen Scientology at work today cannot easily close their eyes to the results or fail to acknowledge that it truly does work. For Scientology has taught that a man is his own immortal soul. In Scientology, the riddle has been solved and the answer found simple.

Note: The next several chapters cover the auditing and training services found on the chart, providing descriptions of the primary ones listed. One can turn to the appropriate chapter in Part Three for information about any particular service.

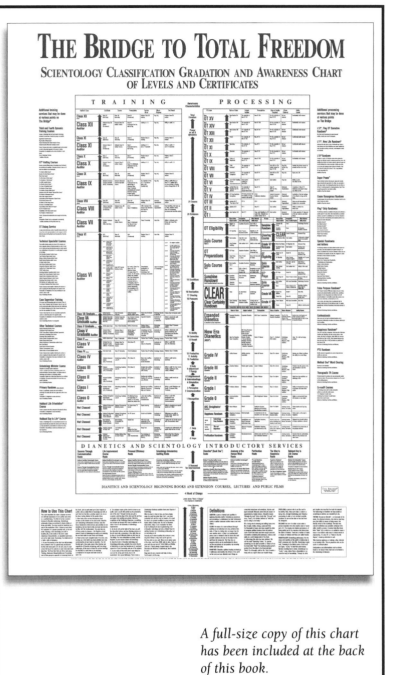

A full-size copy of this chart has been included at the back of this book.

PART THREE

THE SERVICES OF SCIENTOLOGY

People benefit from Scientology through specific services which translate its philosophy into religious practice—practical applications of Scientology principles. Auditing and training are the two central services of the Scientology religion. Each service has an end result, enabling a person to increase his spiritual awareness and ability. His problems resolve, his relationships improve and his outlook on life brightens. He understands himself better and becomes more able.

Scientology can be addressed to *any* area in one's life. An arrangement of clearly defined services makes it possible for anyone to learn and apply its different aspects. In this way people progress up the Bridge to spiritual freedom.

The chapters in this part describe the services of Scientology. These follow the pattern of the Classification, Gradation and Awareness Chart, starting with introductory books and services and progressing up to different auditing levels and courses of training. All of the categories of services offered at churches and missions are discussed, including the Scientology system of ethics which helps people apply Scientology for the greatest gains.

Each chapter describes a category of service and may be read independently of the rest. If the reader is especially interested in one category in particular, he can find it in the table of contents and read that chapter first. All chapters should be read in order to gain a full appreciation and understanding of the Scientology services that make up the Bridge to Freedom.

CHAPTER 7

BASIC DIANETICS AND SCIENTOLOGY BOOKS, FILMS, LECTURES & EXTENSION COURSES

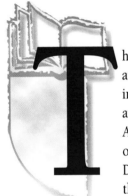

The fundamentals of Dianetics and Scientology are found in L. Ron Hubbard's books and lectures on these subjects. Any one of these books offers more insight into Dianetics and Scientology than can be gleaned from a thousand magazine articles or interpretations of his work. After all, the best way to find out about any subject is to go directly to its original materials. And in Dianetics and Scientology, these are Mr. Hubbard's books and lectures. There are also informative films specifically designed for those new to the subject. Many were written by Mr. Hubbard, and several are narrated by him.

Still, L. Ron Hubbard was first and foremost a writer, and his books have been read by millions, bringing him recognition as one of the most popular authors of all time. His first published book to explain the workings of the human mind, *Dianetics: The Modern Science of Mental Health*, remains a bestseller nearly fifty years after its initial publication, a feat unparalleled in publishing history. Today, it is still known to millions of Scientologists as "Book One."

There are many books one can read to find out about Dianetics and Scientology, to decide for oneself whether the observations and phenomena Mr. Hubbard describes are true. All of Mr. Hubbard's works on Dianetics and Scientology are straightforward, exact and written to be understood by anyone. Furthermore, they contain practical knowledge that lends itself to immediate application. The basic books for someone new to the subject contain explanations of the most fundamental principles underlying Mr. Hubbard's discoveries on the mind and the spirit and are described here. Additional information on the hundreds of other books, taped lectures and videos are described in Chapter 47, "The Books, Lectures and Videos of Scientology."

There are also many introductory services which provide more information and practical application in the fundamentals of Dianetics and Scientology. They are described in the next chapter, "Dianetics and Scientology Introductory Services."

Often, the first thing one who is interested in Dianetics and Scientology and their founder sees is the *Introduction to Scientology* video. This one-hour filmed interview, the only one ever granted by Mr. Hubbard, explains how he made his discoveries and breakthroughs during his explorations of the mind, spirit and life. He discusses his bestseller, *Dianetics: The Modern Science of Mental Health,* and how Scientology came about. And he answers the most commonly asked questions: What is Scientology? Why is it a religion? What is the difference between the mind and the spirit? What is man's true purpose? How do people benefit from Scientology? And what do people do in churches of Scientology?

DIANETICS

Dianetics: The Modern Science of Mental Health

Before Dianetics the world did not have a precise and workable means to resolve problems of the mind. Into this dark age, like a bolt from the blue, came the publication of *Dianetics: The Modern Science of Mental Health.*

Published on May 9, 1950, *Dianetics* was hailed as a breakthrough by Walter Winchell, noted columnist of the *New York Daily Mirror* "as revolutionary for humanity as the first caveman's discovery and utilization of fire." The book instantly became a *New York Times* bestseller, and has routinely outsold the average bestseller year after year for five decades. In fact, no other book in history has even appeared on the *New York Times* bestseller list nearly fifty years after its first publication and appearance. With 18 million copies sold, it is indisputably the most widely read and influential book on the human mind ever published. That its importance was immediately recognized can be seen in the fact that within the first year of its initial release, more than 750 Dianetics groups sprang up in the United States.

This book marks a turning point in man's knowledge and understanding of himself. It is *the* manual of Dianetics procedure. In *Dianetics,* L. Ron Hubbard details the dynamic principle of existence (*Survive!*) and provides the first accurate description of the human mind, what it consists of and how it operates. He describes in great detail the source of all human aberration: the reactive mind and its engrams. Having discovered the barrier to rationality and survival, L. Ron Hubbard then developed a technology to eradicate its harmful effects, resulting in a new state of existence for man, the state of Clear. The auditing techniques for erasing engrams and creating Clears are covered in vivid detail in *Dianetics* and continue to be widely used today.

This Dianetics package provides all the materials needed to start using Book One right away: a hardback edition of Dianetics: The Modern Science of Mental Health, *the* How to Use Dianetics *video and accompanying workbook,* Dianetics Lectures and Demonstrations, *and a Dianetics Pocket Guide listing each step of Dianetics procedure so one is ready to give a session at any time.*

The importance of this book was not underestimated when it was first published—and should not be today. Anyone who has not read *Dianetics* remains ignorant of the most important breakthroughs on the subject of the human mind.

Dianetics Lectures and Demonstrations

Following the release of *Dianetics: The Modern Science of Mental Health*, Mr. Hubbard gave a special course in Dianetics to an audience in Oakland, California, eager to find out more about this breakthrough technology. In a series of four lectures, he discusses engrams, the handling of grief in a preclear, how to get preclears who are having difficulty moving again, and other new developments in Dianetics. One of these lectures includes an actual session, demonstrating the techniques of Dianetics auditing—conducted by Mr. Hubbard himself. There is no better way for a beginner to understand how Dianetics is applied than to hear the Founder of the subject use it.

Video: *How to Use Dianetics: A Visual Guidebook to the Human Mind*

Especially for someone new to the subject of Dianetics, this 55-minute companion video to the book *Dianetics: The Modern Science of Mental Health* shows him how to *apply* the techniques in the book. The video visually describes the reactive mind, engrams, the dynamic principle of existence, the dynamics, exact Dianetics procedure and what is happening each step of the way. It contains all the information needed to start

The Dynamics of Life

The Story of Book One

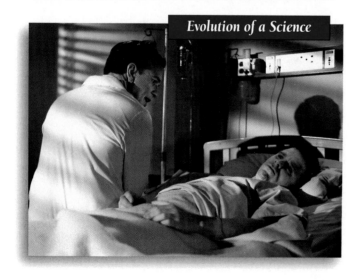

Evolution of a Science

Each of these films can be seen daily at local Scientology churches throughout the world.

auditing Dianetics immediately. For those who want to be able to effectively improve the lives of people they know, this video is invaluable.

Film: *The Story of Book One*

The Story of Book One is a chronicle of the adventure of Dianetics—its discovery and the widespread use of L. Ron Hubbard's breakthroughs which were first published in *Dianetics: The Modern Science of Mental Health. Dianetics* gave the world the truth about the mind and, as mentioned earlier, is known today as "Book One." This film tells the exciting story behind that story: how it came to be written, why it was written and published as a book, the obstacles Mr. Hubbard overcame to bring it to the common man, and the overwhelmingly popular response it received when it was released in public bookstores on May 9, 1950.

The Dynamics of Life

Written in 1947, this is the first formal record of L. Ron Hubbard's researches into the structure and functions of the human mind.

In his introduction, he writes: "Dianetics offers the first anatomy of the human mind and techniques for handling the hitherto unknown reactive mind, which causes irrational and psychosomatic behavior. It has successfully removed any compulsions, repressions, neuroses and psychoses to which it has been applied."

The Dynamics of Life was Mr. Hubbard's original thesis and includes the first description of auditing principles, including the code of conduct an auditor should follow, the nature of engrams and their effects upon individuals, and case histories showing the results of early Dianetics auditing. When it was first circulated, Mr. Hubbard was deluged with requests for more information. This led him to write his landmark manual of Dianetics procedure, *Dianetics: The Modern Science of Mental Health.*

Film: *Dianetics: The Dynamics of Life*

The true story of L. Ron Hubbard's historic exploration into the riddle of life itself, what led to his discovery of the dynamic principle of existence and the instant grass-roots demand for Dianetics technology the world over.

Dianetics: The Evolution of a Science

At a young age, L. Ron Hubbard became greatly intrigued by the mystery of man and his mind. *Dianetics: The Evolution of a Science* is the story of how he came to make the breakthroughs which solve this mystery.

Here, L. Ron Hubbard traces the exact sequence of events leading to his discoveries about the human mind and his detection of that hidden part of the mind responsible for all of man's nonsurvival behavior.

This book reveals how Mr. Hubbard was able to recognize and isolate an individual's true basic personality and details how painful or traumatic events in life can become fused with an individual's innermost self, causing fears, insecurities and psychosomatic ills. And it shows how, by first describing the full potential of the mind, he was able to discover these impediments. Because of his work, this potential is now attainable.

While *Dianetics: The Modern Science of Mental Health* details what Dianetics is and how to use it, this is the book that tells how Mr. Hubbard made those discoveries.

Film: *Evolution of a Science*

Evolution of a Science is a moving story that graphically illustrates the power of L. Ron Hubbard's discoveries in the field of the mind and spirit, and the dramatic results that can be achieved just by reading the book *Dianetics: The Evolution of a Science*.

Before Dianetics, many crippling conditions appeared inexplicable. When no physical cause could be identified, prevailing practices offered nothing but a future of "learning to live with it." This film dramatically presents the knowledge man was missing and the result when truth is realized.

Self Analysis

L. Ron Hubbard writes in this book: "Your potentialities are a great deal better than anyone ever permitted you to believe." *Self Analysis* is the first book to provide definite techniques to improve memory, speed reaction time, handle psychosomatic illness and reduce stress. It offers the means to spiritual self-discovery through a series of processes designed to give an individual the clearest look he has ever had into his past.

A series of tests at the beginning of the processing section enables the reader to assess his current emotional condition and spiritual state before starting, and provides a gauge of the improvements achieved as he progresses through the book. The reader then embarks on an analysis of his past, guided by simple and specific directions. Through the processing contained in *Self Analysis*, a person can discover that he is a much better friend to himself than he ever thought possible.

The Basic Dianetics Picture Book

The fundamental discoveries of Dianetics are all presented here with perfect clarity. Easy-to-understand text and illustrations *show* what the mind consists of, how it works and how the reactive mind impairs awareness and ability. The book describes the state of Clear — the goal of Dianetics — and how it is achieved. It pictorially demonstrates how an auditing session works and how it rids one of his reactive mind.

The Beginning Scientology Books Package provides the fundamental principles and technical data of Scientology and also includes a dictionary of basic Dianetics and Scientology terms.

SCIENTOLOGY

Scientology:
The Fundamentals of Thought

Mr. Hubbard regarded *The Fundamentals of Thought* as his first Scientology book. In this work, he introduces many of the powerful basic principles of the Scientology religion. It includes a broad summary of his research and contains a complete description of Scientology's most fundamental principles: the cycle of action, the conditions of existence, the ARC triangle and the parts of man — thetan, mind and body.

These are more than theories. They address *how* life works and *why,* thereby bringing the reader to a greater understanding of his real identity as a spiritual being, of his fellows and of the world around him. And one chapter consists of Scientology auditing techniques that can be immediately used to bring about changes for the better. *The Fundamentals of Thought* are, indeed, the fundamentals of life.

Scientology: A New Slant on Life

This collection of thirty essays by L. Ron Hubbard provides the reader with a new view of what life *can* be — what we all once dreamed it could be. Here, the reader will discover the two rules to follow for happy living, the exact anatomy of failure and how by knowing this one can win in life more often than he loses, how to live with children so that they grow up to be intelligent and happy, the key concept anyone can use to help someone change his destructive behavior patterns, how knowledge affects sanity and the first usable description of what constitutes true individual greatness.

Scientology: A New Slant on Life contains both a discussion of the profound principles and concepts on which Scientology is based and remarkable practical techniques anyone can use to improve his life.

Scientology 0-8: The Book of Basics

Here are the fundamental principles and technical data of Scientology. *The Book of Basics* is a distillation of the entire body of Scientology scripture. Indeed, the title of this book means, "Scientology, zero to infinity," the numeral 8 being the symbol for infinity standing upright.

Mr. Hubbard plotted many of his observations onto scales of attributes or characteristics of the spirit, mind and life. These invaluable discoveries are included in *The Book of Basics* and may be used to understand the extremes and intervening gradients of such things as responsibility, emotion, affinity, awareness and knowingness itself.

This book includes a thorough discussion of the Axioms of Dianetics and Scientology. These are the basic laws of life itself. With this knowledge one can understand and predict all human behavior. Included too are Mr. Hubbard's discoveries of the fundamentals underlying all forms of thought, known as the Logics.

Scientology 0-8 concisely provides the central, fundamental data of life.

The Problems of Work

Work is a large and important part of life for nearly everyone. It also can be a major source of upset, anxiety and frustration, and thus become a major barrier to spiritual progress. Those who do not like work usually do not enjoy life. This important book analyzes and explains the relationship between the individual and his work. It shows exactly what job-related factors can lead to exhaustion and discomfort and provides exact procedures the reader can use to overcome them. And it demonstrates how one can regain his enthusiasm for work.

In *The Problems of Work,* Mr. Hubbard isolates the problems encountered on the job—whether on the assembly line or in the CEO's office. He offers solutions to frayed tempers and the common feeling that one cannot possibly accomplish all there is to do. This book uncovers the way to handle the confusions that surround a job and opens the doors to efficiency. In fact, within these pages one will find the keys to success and personal satisfaction.

The Basic Scientology Picture Book

The basic principles of the Scientology religion are clearly illustrated in this book, including the parts of man—spirit, mind and body, and the relationship among the three. The concepts can be clearly understood by any reader of any age. The book describes how auditing is applied and leads to a better life and total spiritual freedom.

Comprehensive Reference: The Scientology Handbook

A companion volume to *What Is Scientology?* this handbook covers different practical applications of Dianetics and Scientology that anyone can use to improve life—both for himself and others. While it does not supplant the other books in this chapter, it does show how many of the fundamentals they contain can be put to immediate practical use in everyday life. See Chapter 28 for a more detailed description and why it is a book everyone should have. It is a book that shows one how to *use* Scientology to better every aspect of life.

TAPED LECTURES

To explain his discoveries firsthand, L. Ron Hubbard delivered thousands of lectures to eager audiences all over the world. He lectured extensively throughout the United States and in London, Melbourne and Johannesburg, among the many other cities that welcomed him. Mr. Hubbard lectured to both those newly acquainted with his works and to long-time Scientologists.

The selected lectures listed below are particularly good introductions to the Scientology religion. Each is roughly one hour in length and each provides some of the fundamental wisdom of Dianetics and Scientology, as well as insights into L. Ron Hubbard himself. Listening to Mr. Hubbard reveals his vitality, humor and enthusiasm as no written word can.

The lectures address a wide variety of topics, but each one communicates the essence of the Scientology religion and its positive view of man's spiritual potential. One gains a unique insight into Scientology from hearing L. Ron Hubbard discuss the subject. The titles in this series illustrate the point:

The Story of Dianetics and Scientology

This is the *first* taped lecture one should listen to for an insight into the subjects of Dianetics and Scientology. In this very personal and fascinating talk, L. Ron Hubbard introduces many of the people and experiences encountered during his search for the truth about the spirit, the mind and life itself.

From the friendship which sparked his interest in the mind at the age of twelve, through his travels in Asia as a teenager, and even his experiences at war, Mr. Hubbard describes a continuous journey of discovery culminating with the research and development of Dianetics and Scientology technology. He reveals exactly how he came to unlock the mystery of the human mind and spirit and how he finally uncovered the truth that meant freedom for all mankind.

Operation Manual for the Mind

Many people "wonder" how the mind works. Since we all have one—as people have had throughout history—why is the mind not understood? This lecture reveals a deep-seated belief which prevents man from finding out how his own mind operates. With this "secret" exposed, the door is opened for a true understanding of oneself.

The Road to Truth

What is truth? A question that has been asked since the beginning of time is now answered. In this lecture, Mr. Hubbard explains how to recognize the traps and half-truths that confound all who seek answers to life's most basic mysteries. And he explains what one must do to walk all the way on the "Road to Truth" and attain spiritual freedom.

The Hope of Man

L. Ron Hubbard praises the great spiritual figures of the ages, including Siddhartha Gautama, Lao-tse, Krishna and Christ and shows how they kept alive the flame of hope for spiritual freedom. He describes the role of the Scientology religion in this tradition and the practical path it provides so that man can at last attain this hope.

Man's Relentless Search

Man has been searching for answers to his own existence throughout recorded history. This lecture describes some of the answers provided by religions and philosophies down through the ages. And it reveals what they all missed that Scientology now provides.

Scientology and Effective Knowledge

The pursuit of knowledge has occupied the attention of philosophers, explorers, scholars and adventurers for thousands of years. Beyond technological advances, little of value has been learned about life itself. In this tape, L. Ron Hubbard reveals the one simple quality an individual must assume to better understand any aspect of life. With this key, anyone can obtain effective knowledge.

The Dynamics

The task of understanding life can seem daunting by virtue of its sheer enormity and complexity. By delineating and defining the eight "dynamics," or fundamental urges of all life, Mr. Hubbard not only makes life clear and suddenly easy to understand, but makes it possible for one to attain greater ability in handling life.

The Dynamic Principles of Existence

Why do some people succeed while others fail? Luck? Destiny? Can one change one's own "lot" in life? Yes, one can. There is a principle which directly monitors how alive an individual is. Mr. Hubbard explains this principle and outlines how to apply it in life.

The Machinery of the Mind

Whatever claims were made about the mind before Dianetics, virtually *nothing* was actually *known*. This fascinating lecture provides a clear understanding of the "machinery" of the mind, along with the processes of thought, decision-making and communication. In this lecture, Mr. Hubbard explains how a knowledge of these factors enables anyone to regain control of his life.

Power of Choice and Self-Determinism

Many factors influence the course of one's life. By far the most important is one's own power of choice. This lecture explains how to rehabilitate this ability and how then using it could affect an individual or society.

The Road to Perfection— The Goodness of Man

In contrast to some beliefs, Scientology views man as basically good. In this lecture one learns the truth about the basic nature of man and what it takes to restore an individual to a higher level of decency and ability.

Man: Good or Evil?

One question has been asked down through the ages: Is man evil or is he good? No answer has ever provided any certainty—until now. Mr. Hubbard describes what good and evil really are and illustrates the basic good nature of man.

Increasing Efficiency

Increased efficiency does not come from a change of diet, pills or anything else outside the mind. This lecture contains invaluable data that will restore anyone's efficiency, effectiveness and competence.

Health and Certainty

What is the connection between certainty and health? Certainty of what? In this remarkable analysis of the anatomy of certainty, Mr. Hubbard unlocks the door to more than mere physical health. Whether the health of a society or an individual, the secret is the same. The degree to which one can control one's own life depends on only one thing. That "one thing" is detailed in this lecture.

The Five Conditions of Existence and Formulas for Their Improvement

There is no such thing as an unchanging condition. Whether rapidly or slowly, everything is either growing or shrinking, expanding or contracting, improving or getting worse. This lecture defines the five basic conditions and the series of actions one can take to improve any aspect of life. A job, a relationship, one's state of mind—each can be improved by applying the formula of actions appropriate to the condition it is currently in.

The Affinity-Reality-Communication Triangle

Affinity, reality and communication are inextricably linked. When you increase your communication with someone, you will find your affinity for that person also rises. In fact, when any "corner" of this triangle is raised, the other two factors follow "automatically." This is the key to better relationships with others and a deeper understanding of all life.

Scientology and Ability

It is an old idea that teaching someone skills leading to self-sufficiency is better than charity for the recipient. This happens to be true in every aspect of life. The best solution to any difficulty would be to acquire the ability to solve it oneself. In this lecture, Mr. Hubbard reveals how Scientology restores one's full inherent ability.

Miracles

Everybody has some idea about what would constitute a miracle. But is there really such a thing? With no appeal to faith, this lecture defines exactly what miracles are and sheds light on how they can be experienced.

The Deterioration of Liberty

People and societies throughout history have pursued freedom. Despite strong foundations like the Declaration of Independence in the United States, for example, it is possible to see our freedoms eroding. This lecture covers how to preserve high ideals in a sometimes unfriendly world.

Differences Between Scientology and Other Philosophies

When told about Scientology, people often say, "Oh, so it's like . . ." In this lecture, Mr. Hubbard describes how Scientology may be compared to various religions—and also how it is not only different, but unique. Here, one gains an understanding of Scientology's true value to humanity today.

EXTENSION COURSES

To make the information found in Mr. Hubbard's books available for study at home, churches of Scientology provide extension courses on many Dianetics and Scientology books. Each extension course covers one of Mr. Hubbard's books in full and is designed to give the reader a complete understanding of the subject matter.

Lesson books are provided with the extension courses. The reader completes the corresponding lesson as he reads the book and then mails it to his local Scientology church or mission. There, a church staff member reviews the lesson, sends a reply and helps with any difficulties. Extension courses help to deepen one's understanding of Dianetics and Scientology books and are an excellent way to acquire such knowledge.

Extension courses on basic Dianetics and Scientology books described in this chapter include:

Hubbard Dianetics Extension Course

Dianetics: The Dynamics of Life Extension Course

Dianetics: The Evolution of a Science Extension Course

Hubbard Self Analysis Extension Course

Scientology: The Fundamentals of Thought Extension Course

Scientology: A New Slant on Life Extension Course

The Problems of Work Extension Course

These and other books and lectures by L. Ron Hubbard are available in bookstores and libraries, and through Scientology churches, missions and groups. They also may be ordered electronically from the Scientology Internet site at **http://www.scientology.org**, the Bridge Publications site at **http://www.bridgepub.com** or the New Era Publications site at **http://www.newera publications.com**.

CHAPTER 8

DIANETICS AND SCIENTOLOGY INTRODUCTORY SERVICES

It is easy for someone new to Scientology to take his first steps on the Bridge to Total Freedom. His introduction to the religion usually comes through reading one of L. Ron Hubbard's books and/or attending a lecture about Dianetics or Scientology given by a Scientologist at a church or mission. After realizing there are areas in his life and environment that he would like to change for the better, and that Scientology has a technology that will help him achieve this, he is usually eager to begin a service. And with this as the impetus, he finds Dianetics and Scientology introductory services which provide an accessible first step.

While the following services are described as "introductory," their power to bring about positive spiritual benefit should not be underestimated. Each service provides much insight into the basic precepts and practices of Dianetics and Scientology and furnishes valuable data one can immediately apply to improve life — one's own and that of others.

Dianetics and Scientology is a vast body of wisdom. It is presented in a series of gradient levels that enable one to rise in spiritual awareness and ability with certainty and stability. And like all services in Scientology, these initial ones are designed on an ideal gradient.

Introductory services are usually short in length and can be completed in a few evenings at any church or mission. Several, but by no means all, of these services are described below. While they are usually done in the order given below, this may vary according to an initial assessment which helps gauge a person's current spiritual state. This includes testing such as a personality profile which measures ten different traits, the person's knowledge of Scientology, what Scientology books he has read, and other factors. With the help of a Scientologist who knows exactly what part of Scientology best matches the individual's immediate needs, he can then progress in the sequence that is right for him.

His first action before beginning any service, however, will invariably be to see the *Orientation* film which, as described below, shows him what he will find in a church of Scientology. The next step is usually the Success Through Communication Course which provides invaluable tools which will help him progress more effectively in everything he does in Scientology. In addition, one finds a lineup of introductory services which address specific needs which may be appropriate depending upon the initial assessment that has been done. All exist, however, to move him through the introductory area and onto and up the Bridge to Total Freedom.

Orientation — the Film

Orientation answers the question, "What is Scientology?" and is the film everyone sees before beginning their first service. As its title suggests, the film thoroughly orients the viewer to what happens inside a Scientology church and, in fact, shows him exactly what to expect from the moment he enters. It also provides an understanding of the Scientology religion, its purpose and the vital role it plays in society. Scientologists from many walks of life describe what Scientology means to them and relate the profoundly positive effects they have experienced through its application in their lives. By the end of this film, the viewer will have a clear understanding of his role in Scientology and of what he is aiming for.

Life Improvement Courses

The Scientology Life Improvement Courses are designed to fit the different needs of individuals based on their knowledge of Dianetics and Scientology, what books they may have read and their situation in life. These contain the basics of Scientology technology which can bring immediate improvement to a *specific* aspect of an individual's existence.

The confusions of modern living require solutions. A difficulty in a relationship, a business or family situation can grow and consume far too much attention. In fact, it is these seemingly commonplace problems that often work to distract one from the more important things in life, particularly one's spiritual growth. Each Life Improvement Course contains Scientology breakthroughs one can use to rectify specific problem areas and improve conditions. There are services addressing interpersonal relations, overcoming the ups and downs in life, personal values and integrity, understanding others, working more efficiently, marriage, raising children, and many more.

In every sense of the word, then, these are practical courses. Each is illustrated to facilitate understanding, with an emphasis on practical application. One learns the theory of basic Scientology principles relating to each area, then applies these in course room exercises until they can be applied in life.

For example, in the Life Improvement Course which deals with improving relationships, one discovers ways, based on Scientology fundamentals, to improve relationships with others. He learns the true basis of interpersonal relations, the affinity, reality and communication (ARC) triangle, and then practices the precise steps set forth in the course for improving or repairing any relationship. He learns principles of communication and their application. He learns the Third Party Law, L. Ron Hubbard's discovery concerning the underlying cause of any conflict, and how to employ this discovery to resolve strife. Given these and other tools, he can change and improve his life. He learns things he can actually do, not only for his own benefit, but also for the benefit of others.

Life Improvement Courses are unique to Scientology. Unlike other religions, Scientology offers a practical technology about man that can be applied to actually improve conditions in life. As one applies this technology to day-to-day concerns to better himself and others, he finds he is now more able to continue his journey to higher levels of spiritual awareness and ability.

Life Improvement Courses:

- Overcoming Ups and Downs in Life Course
- Personal Values and Integrity Course
- How to Improve Conditions in Life Course
- How to Improve Relationships with Others Course
- Starting a Successful Marriage Course
- How to Maintain a Successful Marriage Course
- How to Improve Your Marriage Course
- How to Be a Successful Parent Course
- How to Make Work Easier Course
- Introduction to Scientology Ethics Course
- The Way to Happiness Course

The Success Through Communication Course

This course is a vital step for anyone new to Scientology. Many, many people experience difficulties in communicating. Some have trouble expressing themselves, while others feel uncomfortable in certain social situations. Still others find it difficult to initiate a conversation, while some do not know how to end one. Communication difficulties are among the biggest problems people have in everyday living. Yet in addition to creating problems in life, this inability is also a block to spiritual improvement. In fact,

A person can make rapid improvement in a specific area of his life with a Life Improvement Course. These provide Scientology fundamentals directly related to the area for which a person wants immediate help.

the key to such improvement is the ability to communicate.

One of the greatest discoveries of Scientology is the delineation of the components of communication. All the spiritual gains experienced in Scientology stem in one way or another from knowledge and application of communication. Effective communication is essential for a successful auditing session. And communication constitutes the primary corner of the ARC triangle, one of Scientology's fundamental principles. Effective communication is integral to every Scientology religious service and Scientologists have become known around the world as *the* experts on the subject of communication.

The exact technology of how to communicate effectively is taught on the Success Through Communication Course, which consists of eighteen separate communication drills for teaching the basic elements of good communication. Every student twins with another and the two work together, reading a drill and then doing it. Experienced Course Supervisors are always on hand to help with difficulties and ensure smooth progress.

An ability to communicate well is highly rewarded in life as evidenced by the esteem accorded artists, entertainers, television personalities and the like. But on a more personal scale, one who can truly communicate gets the more desirable job, has the better friends, the deeper relationships and a smoother life than one who cannot communicate. More importantly, once one gains the ability to communicate effectively, he has the key to worlds previously hidden, including one's true spiritual self.

SCIENTOLOGY SEMINAR COURSES:

The Anatomy of the Human Mind Course

After being introduced to either Dianetics or Scientology, people who want to know more about the mind and about the thetan's relationship to the mind take this service.

Here they learn that the human mind has an exact anatomy. Before Dianetics, this anatomy was essentially unknown because those seeking to understand the mind did so from a wholly material perspective.

The Anatomy of the Human Mind Course contains a precise description of the mind, its components, its workings and its relationship to man as a spiritual being. This extensive service includes twenty lectures, detailing every aspect of the mind. Each lecture is followed by demonstrations and practicals so one gains a comprehensive understanding of such basics as the reactive mind, mental image pictures, engrams, the analytical mind, the being, understanding, the body, its nervous system and aberration. The Anatomy of the Human Mind Course imparts a real understanding of these principles, one which brings about a vast new understanding of life.

Personal Efficiency Course

For many people, happiness is an elusive quality. Surveys show that "being happy" is what a majority of people want most in life. This fact begs the question: Why are some people happy and others not? And what can be done when happiness seems unattainable?

The first question is perhaps best answered by understanding exactly what happiness is. As to the second question, the answer requires understanding the obstacles to personal happiness and learning how to overcome them. This understanding may be found in a service offered at every Scientology church: The Personal Efficiency Course.

Taken either on a part-time schedule over a period of five days or more intensively over a weekend, this course provides answers to many of the problems and obstacles encountered in life and gives attendees the opportunity to test the principles for themselves. It is here, often for the first time, that the student experiences the gains available from auditing. This is done on a turnabout or "co-audit" basis where

On the Dianetics Seminar, students pair up and audit each other as much as they want, giving them the firsthand experience of the results of Dianetics and the mutual gain of helping another person.

students audit each other on basic Scientology processes. In short, this course offers both personal experience and an analysis of the "basics" of life, in very real and practical terms.

While there are numerous basic courses in Scientology that address specific problems or aspects of life, the Personal Efficiency Course is broader and more fundamental. It is for anyone who has ever wondered if there was more to life.

BOOK ONE SERVICES:

Hubbard Dianetics Seminar

Those familiar with Mr. Hubbard's *Dianetics: The Modern Science of Mental Health* can experience the workability of Dianetics technology for themselves by attending a Dianetics Seminar and participating in Dianetics auditing. One need not have read the book to participate.

In so doing, one can begin to rid himself of the barriers to his confidence, well-being and success.

A Dianetics Seminar begins with a video presentation that explains basic Dianetics principles and what occurs in an auditing session. Then one reads selected portions of *Dianetics: The Modern Science of Mental Health* and "pairs up" with another seminar participant to practice auditing procedures. After only a few hours he will be familiar enough with Dianetics technology to audit another person or to receive auditing himself, always under the guidance of experienced seminar supervisors who are highly trained in Dianetics auditing. During the seminar one may participate in as much Dianetics auditing as he wishes and thereby gain firsthand understanding and benefits of its power.

Hubbard Dianetics Auditor Course

A Hubbard Dianetics Seminar graduate is likely to want to continue co-auditing while learning more about Dianetics. If so, he will probably decide to take the Hubbard Dianetics Auditor Course, which provides the perfect way for him to sharpen his skills as a Dianetics auditor and gain more experience with, and benefit from, Dianetics auditing.

These are the course materials and books studied by students on the Hubbard Qualified Scientologist Course. They provide a firm grounding in many basic Scientology principles which can then be applied to life.

This is an extensive course containing tape-recorded auditing demonstrations by L. Ron Hubbard. Assisted by a trained and experienced Course Supervisor, individuals on the Hubbard Dianetics Auditor Course learn exactly how to deal with anything that could arise in an auditing session through hands-on application of the procedures in *Dianetics: The Modern Science of Mental Health.*

Introductory Dianetics Auditing

Anyone interested in experiencing Dianetics auditing, exactly as is learned on the Hubbard Dianetics Auditor Course, can receive auditing from an experienced Dianetics auditor. This is available in blocks of auditing to provide the greatest possible benefit. Just as it did in 1950, Dianetics auditing can bring about life-changing results by addressing the unwanted elements in life that hold one back. One can recognize and resolve the hidden sources of pain, nervousness, unwanted behavior patterns, psychosomatic illness, negative emotions and more. And it is available for everyone. There is no need even to have read a book or to have done a course to discover how Dianetics auditing can change one's life.

BEGINNING SCIENTOLOGIST GRADUATE COURSE:

Hubbard Qualified Scientologist Course

Everyone is involved in life whether he is happy about it or not. There are, however, basic laws on the way life operates, and a knowledge of these laws can make life easier to understand and provide tools to improve conditions. This is the subject of the Hubbard Qualified Scientologist Course, the last and most wide-ranging of the introductory courses, and is usually done following the Success Through Communication Course.

This service offers a broad and thorough grounding in key Scientology principles and introduces one to Scientology auditing. It consists of six of L. Ron Hubbard's basic books, a filmed interview with Mr. Hubbard in which he discusses how he developed Dianetics and Scientology and explains their principles, and many practical assignments that apply what has been studied to real life situations. From these practicals one can come to a certainty as to how to apply these principles rather than treating them as simply some kind of an intellectual pursuit. On this service one learns to audit basic Scientology processes and gains experience auditing others. He drills communication fundamentals and learns how to properly minister an auditing session. After drilling different auditing techniques, he then both audits another and receives auditing himself. These powerful techniques include methods to spiritually assist those suffering from illness or an accident, to make an intoxicated person sober, and processes which greatly raise one's awareness of his past.

The Hubbard Qualified Scientologist Course gives one an excellent general understanding of what Scientology is about, and how it is applied to help others as well as oneself. It could be said that after completing this course one has "graduated" from the introductory services and is now ready to move up the Bridge towards the state of Clear, and beyond.

INTRODUCTORY AUDITING:

The surest way to understand what Scientology auditing can accomplish towards bettering an individual's life is to go to a Scientology church or mission and actually experience an auditing session with a highly trained auditor. In fact, this is a vital step for new preclears.

In charting the route to higher spiritual states, L. Ron Hubbard developed processes for taking one to the next higher level of awareness. Many of these processes are designed specifically for the person just beginning auditing. There are hundreds of processes which can be used to introduce one to what auditing is and demonstrate the gains available from it. These are processes that deal, among other things, with increasing communication abilities, raising awareness, expanding affinity and willingness to assume responsibility, and even resolving the causes of unhappiness rooted in failures to adhere to a moral code or helping someone become able to learn. Introductory auditing can produce remarkable changes in conditions and increase spiritual awareness.

There are also many other kinds of introductory auditing, including:

Group Processing. Here, an auditor increases the ability of individuals being audited as part of a group. Group Processing improves a person's alertness and awareness of the environment, as well as his communication. Some individuals have reported spectacular wins including increased havingness and even exteriorization. For more than four decades Scientologists— newcomers and old-timers alike—have enjoyed the excitement, wins and gains of Group Processing sessions, and, in fact, the sheer fun of them.

Assists. These are actions that are taken to assist the spirit to deal with trauma, losses or upsets, or confront physical difficulties; while not intended to replace medical treatment, they do much to help alleviate physical pain and discomfort.

Marriage counseling. This addresses marital problems and, through the application of Scientology technology, helps couples create healthy marriages based on trust.

The fact that these services are introductory in no way diminishes their precision or their potential for providing insight into life. In fact, since these services provide an individual with his first spiritual gains from auditing, they often end up as among the most memorable services he will ever experience.

There are also other services an individual can do to begin his Scientology journey if, for example, he has difficulties with study or comprehension, or if he has a history of extensive drug use. These services all have the objective of assisting one to take his first steps onto the Bridge and continue on the path to total freedom. They are described fully in the chapters that immediately follow.

Life does not have to be an unhappy plight, but one would be hard pressed to find a person who has not had his share of knocks or who cannot name some aspect of life he would wish to improve. Millions have found the answers on introductory services at a Scientology church or mission. And, armed with these answers, they are ready to continue up the Bridge to Total Freedom.

CHAPTER 9

REVITALIZING THE INDIVIDUAL IN A POLLUTED AND DRUGGED WORLD

Research has demonstrated that the single most destructive element present in our current culture is drugs.

The use of street drugs—LSD, heroin, cocaine, angel dust, marijuana and others—has proliferated at all levels of society. College students atrophy their brains on marijuana; schoolchildren are shoved daily into pill popping by both peer and pharmaceutical pressures; and the seemingly everyday Smith down the street and Jones at the job harbor a habit they neither suspect nor deal with.

Widespread consumption of illegal drugs—many of which were originally prescription remedies—has created a $500-billion-a-year industry. By some estimates, marijuana is now the biggest cash crop in America. Cocaine and its derivatives, highly fashionable in the 1970s, are now widely abused, due in large part to claims by psychiatrists as recently as 1980 that cocaine usage was not addictive. They could not have been more deceptive.

In researching the barriers to spiritual gain caused by drugs, L. Ron Hubbard uncovered the existence of a *drug personality,* an artificial personality created by drugs.

"Drugs can apparently change the attitude of a person from his original personality to one secretly harboring hostilities and hatreds he does not permit to show on the surface," wrote Mr. Hubbard. "While this may not hold true in all cases, it does establish a link between drugs and increasing difficulties with crime, production and the modern breakdown of social and industrial culture."

The decline in mental alertness and ethical fiber in society is as glaring as the headlines trumpeting the devastating physiological effects of drugs. "The drug scene is planetwide," concluded Mr. Hubbard. "It is swimming in blood and human misery."

As vicious and damaging as street drugs have proven to be, medical and psychiatric drugs form an equally destructive vector in this biochemical trend. (See Chapter 29.) Statistics show that as early as the 1950s, daily dosages of sleeping pills or painkillers had become so commonplace that they were hardly considered drugs. Valium was the first drug to take its place amongst tranquilizers of choice. Today, however, we have the mind- and mood-altering drugs such as Thorazine, Stelazine, Zoloft, Prozac, Tofranil, Xanax and Ritalin, which are even more damaging than street drugs. The prevalence with which these are prescribed as a panacea is often shocking to the uninformed.

Mr. Hubbard's research, however, yielded this conclusion: "Unfortunately, it is not recognized that a person whose pain has been deadened by a sedative has himself been deadened by the same drug, and is much nearer the ultimate pain of death. It should be obvious that the quietest people in the world are the dead."

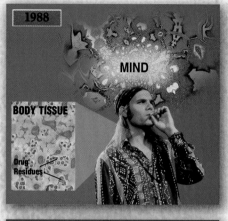

It is a proven fact that drug residues can be trapped in the body.

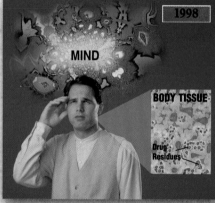

Years later, these residues can dislodge and begin to affect the person again.

Though a person is no longer taking drugs, he has mental image pictures of drugs and drug experiences . . .

. . . which can reactivate as long as toxic drug residues are locked in the body. A person's awareness, ability and attitudes can be adversely affected.

Drug taking is, in no small way, part of life in our modern world.

Additionally, the past century's technological advances have produced many an insidious byproduct, each of them threatening to an individual's well-being. Smog, for instance, was unknown before the rise of manufacturing centers in Britain. Every major city on Earth now advises its inhabitants daily about the quality of air they are breathing. A hundred years ago, the main food preservatives were salt or ice. Today, nearly any packaged food has a list of the artificial ingredients it contains that is longer than the list of natural ingredients. Environmental disasters such as the 1986 catastrophe at the Chernobyl nuclear power station in the former USSR—to say nothing of radiation exposure from widespread nuclear bomb testing—did not exist fifty years ago.

We live in a chemical-oriented society. The Environmental Protection Agency reports that the average American consumes four pounds of pesticides each year and has residues from over 400 toxic substances in his body. More than 3,000 chemical additives are found in the food we eat.

There is no escaping our contaminated civilization and, furthermore, it has been found that these substances can put an individual in a "wooden" sort of state: unfeeling, insensitive, unable, untrustworthy, a menace to his fellows trapped in the dramatizations of his reactive mind.

Neither toxic pollution nor drug abuse were of major concern in 1950 when L. Ron Hubbard released *Dianetics*. By the 1960s, however, the frightful specter of both had arrived and Mr. Hubbard's research showed that a person who had been heavily on drugs was not able to make spiritual gains from auditing. This condition had not been encountered earlier in his researches, as drugs had not yet encroached so deeply into society. But it became more and more prevalent and required a solution, as drugs now represented an increasingly serious block to auditing progress.

THE BIOCHEMICAL FACTOR

The way a being perceives much of existence is via the sensory channels of the body. The body is a communications center for the being, with the brain acting as a switchboard for translating thought into action. The biochemical actions of drugs alter the normal operations of this pattern, often with harmful or even disastrous consequences.

L. Ron Hubbard researched this barrier to spiritual freedom long before it was recognized by others as the huge social concern it is today. His work yielded a truly effective handling for the adverse biochemical effects of drugs and other toxins.

He made the discovery that residues from drugs and other toxins lodge in the fatty tissues of the body and stay there, even years after they have been ingested, and that these residues can continue to affect the individual adversely long after the effect of the drug has apparently worn off. Such deposits have been known to cause lessened perception, tiredness, confused thinking and a host of other symptoms—all of which are counter to what is being achieved through auditing. Documented cases show that an individual may reexperience the effects of LSD years after having taken the drug.

Realizing that this biochemical factor had to be handled before any lasting spiritual gain could be made through auditing, L. Ron Hubbard devised what independent researchers acknowledge as the safest, most effective—and only—detoxification program of its kind: the *Purification Rundown.*

In Scientology, a *rundown* designates a series of related actions which culminate in a specific end result. Developed solely to handle the biochemical barrier to spiritual gain, the Purification Rundown is a carefully designed combination of exercise, vitamins, nutrition and sauna use which dislodges drug residues and other toxins from the fatty tissues so that these substances can then be eliminated from the body. A person undergoing this program is closely monitored by specially trained personnel in liaison with medical doctors to ensure that each aspect of the program is administered correctly and the desired benefits are attained.

Once the person has been freed from the harmful effects of these drug residues and other toxins, he is in a far better position to improve as a spiritual being, to which many thousands of people have attested.

Validation by Independent Studies

After the release of the program in 1980, news of L. Ron Hubbard's breakthrough reached medical circles and the scientific community. Since then, numerous studies of his detoxification method have been undertaken, each validating the tremendous workability of the program.

Important studies over the past two decades provide repeated evidence of the program's efficacy in eliminating toxins from the body.

In Michigan, the accidental contamination of cattle with a toxic fire retardant resulted in 97 percent of the state's population with detectable amounts of the retardant in their fatty tissues a full five years later. A group of Michigan residents, who had been monitored since the initial contamination, was told by doctors that the toxins were there to stay. Then, in 1982, a group of these subjects was put through the Purification program. Biopsies of fatty tissue before and after showed a decrease of the fire retardant and other toxins of over 20 percent. A follow-up examination four months later proved even more significant: levels of toxins continued to decrease after the program had been completed and showed an average decrease of over 40 percent of the toxins.

Similarly, in 1983, independent researchers conducted tests on a woman who had done the Purification program after having been heavily exposed to industrial contaminants while on the job. A urine test done at the

207

On the Purification program, running is done to get the blood circulating deeper into the tissues where toxic residuals are lodged and thus act to loosen and release the accumulated harmful deposits and get them moving.

Very important, then, is that the running is immediately followed by sweating in the sauna to flush out the accumulations which have now been dislodged.

Regular nutrition and supplemental nutrition in the form of mega-vitamin and mineral dosages and extra quantities of oil are a vital factor in helping the body to flush out toxins and to repair and rebuild the areas that have been affected by drugs and other toxic residuals.

A proper schedule with enough rest is mandatory, as the body will be undergoing change and repair throughout the program.

beginning of the program showed high levels of mercury and lead in the woman's body. During the program, she secreted a black substance through the pores of her skin as chemicals were flushed out of her body. The study noted, "Removal of the toxic substances from her system was accompanied by remission of her subjective complaints as well. She no longer felt the extreme tiredness, malaise and lethargy she had been experiencing since her exposure."

Not surprisingly, such results generated interest from prominent medical and biochemical authorities. In study after study, Mr. Hubbard's research has been validated by official reports. For example, after conducting his own independent study, a US Environmental Protection Agency doctor concluded that dangerous environmental toxins, which had lodged in the body for two years, could be flushed out by doing the Purification program.

Among numerous recent correlative studies, one that bears significant mention was conducted in 1995 by Dr. Forest Tennant, executive director of the Research Center for Chronic Pain and Dependency Disorders, and Dr. Shelley Beckmann, a molecular biologist. Monitoring the rehabilitation of cocaine and Valium addicts using Mr. Hubbard's technology, they found that the detoxification procedure resulted in previously undetectable drugs appearing in both the urine and in the sweat of former drug users. In other words, these residual drugs were dislodged as a result of the program and eliminated once and for all, freeing the individual from their harmful effects.

The deadly chemical *dioxin*, Agent Orange, was used to defoliate trees during the Vietnam War. Exposure to the chemical resulted in dioxin poisoning of American servicemen. Years later no effective handling had been developed. Then a Florida cardiologist conducting tests on a person who had been exposed to the chemical but who had done the Purification program, found that his patient's level of the chemical had reduced

These books cover in detail the technology and exact procedures of the Purification program, including a full textbook, an illustrated booklet and a manual to guide one's progress step by step through the program.

by 29 percent immediately after the program and an astounding 97 percent eight months later—and that all symptoms of dioxin poisoning had disappeared.

At an early phase of his research into drug addiction and rehabilitation, Mr. Hubbard predicted that his program might also reduce body accumulations of radioactive particles— a prediction since supported by clinical trials in Russia among victims of the Chernobyl nuclear reactor disaster. The subjects in one trial of those who experienced radiation fallout included fourteen men from the Kaluga region and, according to three measures, body levels of radionuclides reduced as much as eightfold. Another trial, in which the subjects were fourteen children living in Bryansk, directly in the path of leakage from the reactor, gave equally remarkable results. This led a radiation safety expert to point out that after industrial or environmental accidents, when it is

crucial that treatment be simple, economic and quickly administered, the Hubbard detoxification procedure is one of the very few methods that meets these criteria.

These and other similarly impressive studies validate the workability of the Purification Rundown, a workability that people on every continent of Earth have experienced subjectively. They know on a deeply personal level that Mr. Hubbard's program is *the* solution to the blight of drugs. Many who have completed the program report that, along with eradicating any craving for drugs, they can see or hear better than before, they can study for the first time, they are able to learn new subjects much more easily, get along better with people, appreciate what is going on around them and generally feel healthier and happier.

The entire program is explained in detail in the book *Clear Body, Clear Mind: The Effective Purification Program,* including the discoveries which led to its development and an exact description of how and why it works. One can read this book and then, by following the procedures detailed in the text, administer the Purification program to himself to detoxify his own body, and join the more than 250,000 others who have freed themselves from the biochemical devastation caused by drugs and toxic substances.

THE *FULL* RESOLUTION

While the Purification Rundown rids one of the biochemical residues that reactivate past drug experiences, it is but the first step in a full resolution to the spiritual devastation caused by drug, medicine and alcohol abuse. Other mental and spiritual factors exist and to address these L. Ron Hubbard developed a series of auditing processes and actions that handle the harmful effects of drugs by getting to the very cause of one's decision to use them. These actions are ministered in churches and missions by highly skilled auditors.

Reorienting to the Present-Time Environment

A person who has been on drugs often becomes disassociated from the world around him or even his physical self, as evidenced by the neglect many drug takers show for their hygiene, dress, health, job, friends and family.

The reason is that, among other things, drugs dull a person's communication. This is most directly observed in the action of painkillers which shut off the person's feeling of pain, but it occurs with the use of other drugs as well. Emotions are suppressed with drug use, and perceptions become altered or shut off.

A person often becomes less aware of things and people around him and so becomes less considerate and responsible, less active, less capable and less bright. He

factually becomes less conscious of what is happening in the present. One does not have to have been a heavy narcotics addict to experience a lessening of alertness, fogginess or other effects as a result of drug use.

Drugs do something else too: They stick a person's attention at points in his past. Mental image pictures restimulated from the reactive mind appear in the visions of hallucinations a person sees while on certain drugs. Attention often becomes stuck in these pictures after the drug has worn off, with the cumulative effect of the person not feeling "with it" or cognizant of his present-time environment.

This can be dangerous to the person himself and to others, as seen in the number of drug-related automobile accidents that occur, to say nothing of less serious accidents or goofs that happen because a person is unaware of what is going on around him. Drug use makes a person less alert mentally, can harm memory and has a host of other effects on attitudes and behavior—all residual consequences of the drugs, which persist indefinitely unless audited.

The reason drugs are so harmful spiritually is that they can badly scramble the energy contained in the mind, disorienting and confusing the person. His awareness often diminishes and his capabilities of dealing with the energies and masses of reality are dramatically lessened. A person affected by drugs is thus less able to control the things in his environment and, despite whatever subjective feelings he may have to the contrary, he becomes less powerful and less able.

While on drugs, the pictures in one's reactive mind can violently turn on, overwhelming the being and making him afraid to confront anything in the reactive mind thereafter. As a result, the person is *stopped dead* from any mental or spiritual gain.

The attention of a person withdrawing from drug use can be very stuck on the body, and past incidents can be reactivated heavily.

Objective Processes can extrovert the person's attention and greatly ease any discomfort. Past incidents drop out of the present and no longer impinge on the person.

L. Ron Hubbard's breakthroughs in drug rehabilitation technology and his full drug handling program directly address each of the above-mentioned phenomena.

To assist those undergoing withdrawal symptoms, he developed a Therapeutic Training Routine (TR) Course. It consists of drills, called TRs, whose purpose is to increase and improve an individual's ability to confront (to face without flinching or avoiding) and *be there* in the present. If a person is experiencing withdrawal, this course is done concurrently with the Purification Rundown step to lessen the discomfort.

To further raise the ability to confront one's present-time environment, a person's next step is the TRs and Objectives Course. Here one participates in Objective Processing (auditing techniques which direct a person's attention to the real, observable, outward *objects* he encounters), which effectively unfix him from the significances of the mind that have him stuck in his past.

This is a very important factor in mental and spiritual ability. The more a person can exist in the present without his attention stuck in past incidents, the better able he is to deal with his life. He feels brighter, has increased perception, is better able to deal with his environment, and also becomes more able to deal with others.

THE DRUG RUNDOWN

Getting the person into present time is not the total answer, however. Drugs scramble the mind to such a degree that freeing the person from these effects requires a precise and thorough approach. Thus, the actual incidents from his reactive mind associated with drugs must also be addressed in a series of auditing processes that comprise the *Drug Rundown*.

Experiences the person had while taking drugs are the first to be addressed with these exact auditing steps, and the charge in the reactive mind which has accumulated around these incidents is in this way released. Attention that had been fixated by drugs, medicines and alcohol is freed, and the mental masses brought about by drugs are erased.

Drug taking also invariably has numerous unwanted physical sensations, emotions, attitudes and other feelings connected with it. Auditing on the Drug Rundown addresses unwanted feelings connected with specific drugs taken by the person. When these are fully handled, the person is freed from their psychosomatic effects.

L. Ron Hubbard found, though, that people begin taking drugs for a reason: To ease the agony of a physical condition, to numb themselves against certain situations in their lives, to relieve boredom, to feel better. The number of possible reasons is as great as the number of people taking drugs. By taking drugs the person was trying to handle or cure something. At the bottom, then, the drug problem is essentially spiritual. The being, in some way hurt, was led into the false solution that drugs could cure this. The solution, as many learned the hard way, turned out to be a trap from which there was no true escape until the drug-handling technology of L. Ron Hubbard.

A vital part of the Drug Rundown, then, includes finding the pains, emotions, sensations and other unwanted feelings the person was suffering from—and for which drugs became the cure. When these are found, each is addressed in auditing. Unless the reasons a person went onto drugs in the first place are resolved, the person is forever left with the original condition for which drugs were a "solution."

When the original problem is addressed, the person himself is at last free from any effects of drugs and free from the need to take them.

TOWARD A DRUG-FREE CIVILIZATION

On Earth today, drugs are very, very big business. We live in a society where human values are routinely shunted aside for the economic concerns connected with drugs, both legal and illegal. The cost in crime, the cost in trying to control the problem, the cost in inefficiency, the cost simply in lives lived under the numbing influence of drugs cannot be calculated. For to do that, one would have to put a price on life itself.

So, what price the headache remedies, the soporifics, the pain relievers, the antidepressants that fill our medicine cabinets?

What price the amphetamines given our schoolchildren, turning them into drug-dependent people? What price the narcotics that are used to negate a painful existence? What price the recreational drugs that provide escape from the boredom of affluence? What price these shackles that keep from us the sensations and joys of living itself?

A drug war rages on this planet. L. Ron Hubbard recognized the drug problem long before it became an international concern. And he developed a technology people can use to free themselves from this trap and remain free of it.

His technology is the weapon that can win this war.

For more information on how to get rid of the harmful effects of past drugs and toxic substances that dim one's life, visit **http://www.purification.org**.

CHAPTER 10

STUDY TECHNOLOGY: EFFECTIVE LEARNING AND EDUCATION

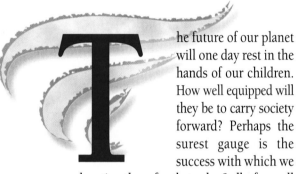

The future of our planet will one day rest in the hands of our children. How well equipped will they be to carry society forward? Perhaps the surest gauge is the success with which we are educating them for that role. Sadly, from all indications, this responsibility has not been met. At a time when quality education is more important than during any period in history, our schools are failing at an alarming rate.

Typical of the educational problems faced by most Western countries is the tragedy of the United States student. America once had one of the finest educational systems in the world, yet for nearly three decades that system continues to face a formidable crisis.

Over 25 percent of all students leaving or graduating high school lack the reading and writing skills required by the minimum demands of daily living.

The American high-school dropout rate hovers at around 30 percent to 50 percent in less privileged urban areas.

According to the president of one teachers' association, up to 50 percent of all new teachers quit the profession within the first five years. Another 1996 study put the figure at 30 percent. Regardless, it is a waste of a vital resource. Equally appalling was the report's finding that in the US more than 40 states hired teachers who were not fully qualified in their classroom subjects.

Little wonder, then, that SAT (Scholastic Aptitude Test) scores of American students have sunk to levels considerably lower than those achieved by students in the mid-1960s.

In fact, in the mid-1990s, the College Board (the body that sponsors the SAT) began to grade the SAT scores on a new curve, one that, according to a leading scholar, "has lowered the test's 'unchanging standard' and our country's educational aspirations." For years the average score was based on the performance of students in 1941, but the board decreed that the mathematical and verbal tests would be "recentered" and based on the results of students who took the tests in 1990. Considering that the student scores dropped steadily since the early to mid-1960s before leveling off in 1980, this was indeed a white flag on the part of US educators. Meanwhile, news media regularly report on the continuing decline of standardized test scores, on overcrowding in classrooms, on public disenchantment about pouring more tax dollars into what they perceive to be an increasingly poor investment, and growing teacher disillusionment.

Nor is it a coincidence that about three in five of America's prison inmates are illiterate. The link between illiteracy and crime has been well documented.

It is indeed a grim picture but is no better in most other parts of the world.

A British survey sponsored by the *Sunday Times* of London, for instance, found 42 percent of those surveyed were unable to add the menu prices of a hamburger, French fries, apple pie and coffee. One out of six British inhabitants could not correctly locate Great Britain on a world map.

From both official and media reports, the pattern of educational decline is evident in

READING LEVEL INCREASE AFTER APPLICATION OF L. RON HUBBARD'S STUDY TECHNOLOGY

In a project done in Brixton, England (a suburb of London), 8 to 13 year-old students were put through a specially prepared course in reading skills based on the study technology of L. Ron Hubbard. The course focused on finding misunderstood words in their current studies and each student spent 8 to 10 hours over 10 days doing the course. Based on standard reading tests, the students who went through this course gained an average of 1.3 years in reading age. A control group, students who weren't put through this course, actually dropped slightly in reading skills over the same period of time, losing an average of 0.03 years in reading age, attributable to misunderstood words.

-0.03 Years
Control Group

+1.3 Years
Students using L. Ron Hubbard's study technology

almost every Western country—places where excellence in public education was once taken for granted.

These dismal figures translate into an equally depressing economic scene. Internationally, the cost to business in lowered or wasted productivity, unemployment and crime is estimated at $300 billion annually. Businesses are forced to develop their own remedial programs to teach employees the basic reading, writing and computational skills necessary to function on the job.

There seems to be no shortage of ideas and theories on how to accomplish educational reforms. But these programs tend to create as many problems as they solve.

For example, after the crisis in education became headline news, America instituted "get tough" retention policies and added graduation requirements, on the assumption that a greater challenge for students would improve performance. The opposite occurred. The policies raised rather than lowered the dropout rate in some cities. The president of the American Federation of Teachers argued, "It's ridiculous to raise the hurdle for kids who are unable to jump in the first place."

A WORKABLE ANSWER: STUDY TECHNOLOGY

Failed attempts in recent decades to improve education raise one important question: With so much attention on improving the quality of education, with billions spent each year to remedy the situation, why has there been so little improvement?

There is an answer. Quite simply, these efforts have been directed at solving the wrong problems.

At the root of educational failures lies a fundamental situation that has been almost universally overlooked: Students have never been taught how to learn.

Students are thrown into their school years and basic subjects without ever first being taught how to go about learning those subjects. As they grow older they are confronted by more and more complex areas of study, still without ever having learned how to learn.

Learning how to learn has been the vital missing ingredient that has hampered all fields of study. It handicaps both children in school and people in life.

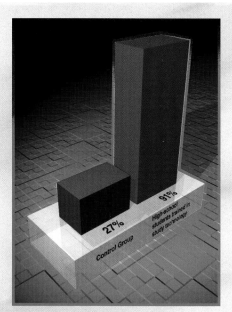

Comparison of passing scores on South Africa's Department of Education examinations between high-school students taught using L. Ron Hubbard's study technology and a control group.

Without knowing how to learn what they are studying, a majority of students find education a trying and difficult process. They never master the ability to rapidly learn something with certainty and ease. Others, who apparently have less difficulty studying, find they are unable to apply what they have read.

It is a reality of the modern world that anyone in the work force, whether on the factory floor or in the executive suite, must have an ability to assimilate important information, retain it and then be able to apply it. This process, whether formal or informal, is what is meant by "study."

L. Ron Hubbard recognized the failings of modern education and training in 1950, many years before educational horror stories began to make headlines.

His extensive investigation into the problems of teaching others led to a breakthrough — the first comprehensive understanding of the real barriers to effective learning. From this, Mr. Hubbard developed a precise technology on how to learn any subject — a technology that ensures a person will not only fully grasp what he is studying, but proficiently apply what he has studied in work or in life.

These breakthroughs came to be known as "study technology," and provide the first fully workable approach to teaching people exactly how to learn. Study technology helps anyone learn anything. Used throughout Scientology in all churches, missions and groups, it is also widely used outside the Church in schools and businesses. Study technology opens the door to effective training and makes it possible to raise the general quality of education to new heights.

Study technology is based on laws that underlie all learning. It delineates the barriers which block a person's ability to grasp information and provides precise methodologies to overcome those barriers.

Study technology has been extensively tested and proven to achieve uniform, consistent results wherever it has been applied. Because it is based on fundamentals common to everyone, it cuts across any economic, cultural or racial lines and can be used by all, regardless of age. It is as effective in the executive suites of multinational corporations as it is in elementary school classrooms.

Outstanding improvements have been made by students of all ages in reading level, comprehension, vocabulary and mathematics when they have been instructed in study technology. A Los Angeles study showed an average gain of 1.8 years in vocabulary and comprehension after only 10 hours of tutoring in study technology. One student gained an almost unbelievable 5 years and 9 months in his test scores after 20 hours of instruction. All teachers involved in this study also reported an overall improvement in their students' ability to learn, ability to read and, an unexpected gain, in the general behavior of students as a direct result of study technology.

An Arizona study tested students after the beginning of a school year and then six months later. Teachers ran the classroom using study technology throughout the duration of the study. Standard reading tests were administered and showed an average gain of two years in comprehension and vocabulary. This is four times the expected gain, a remarkable achievement considering individual tutoring was not part of the study.

In South Africa one class of underprivileged high-school students was trained in study technology, and at the end of the school year achieved a 91 percent pass rate on the country's Department of Education examination. A control group, not so trained, had a 27 percent pass rate on the same test.

The numbers collected from these and many similar studies translate, really, into effective education for young people and an assurance they will grow to a confident, self-reliant adulthood with learning skills they will use every day of their lives.

Many principles and procedures make up study technology, but it only takes a brief discussion of a few of the most basic to provide an insight into what it is and what it can accomplish.

THE BARRIERS TO STUDY

L. Ron Hubbard discovered three primary barriers which keep one from successfully studying a subject. Despite all that has been written on the subject, these three barriers, simple as they are, were never isolated as paramount to effective education. For want of this data, the toll in poorly educated students, unfulfilled potential and frustration is incalculable.

The First Barrier—Lack of Mass

Attempting to educate someone without the mass (or object) that he is going to be involved with can make study exceedingly difficult. This is the first barrier to study.

For example, if one is studying tractors, the printed page and the spoken word are no substitute for an actual tractor. Lacking a tractor to associate with the written word, or at least pictures of a tractor, can close off a person's understanding of the subject.

Definite physiological reactions occur when trying to educate a person in a subject without the thing actually present or available. A student who encounters this barrier will tend to feel squashed, bent, sort of spinny, sort of dead, bored and exasperated. He can wind up with his face feeling squashed, with headaches, and with his stomach feeling funny. He can feel dizzy from time to time and very often his eyes can hurt. These reactions are quite common but wrongly attributed to poor lighting or studying too late at night or any number of other incorrect reasons. The real cause is a lack of mass on the subject one is studying.

The remedy to this barrier is to supply the thing itself—in the example above, the tractor, or a reasonable substitute for one. Some educators have instinctively known this, but usually it was applied only to younger students and it certainly was never given the importance it warrants at any level of education.

The Second Barrier— Too Steep a Gradient

The next barrier is too steep a study gradient. That is, if a student is forced into undertaking a new action without having understood the previous action, confusion results.

There is a different set of physiological reactions which occur as a result of this barrier. When one hits too steep a gradient, a sort of confusion or reelingness is experienced.

Commonly, the difficulty is ascribed to the new action, when in fact it really stems from the previous action. The person did not fully understand some part earlier and then went into confusion on the new one. This barrier to study is very pronounced in subjects involved with activity.

Take the example of a person learning to drive. He cannot properly coordinate his feet and hands to manually shift the car into another gear while keeping to one lane. The difficulty will be found to lie in some earlier action about shifting gears. Possibly he was not yet comfortable shifting through the gears with the engine off and the car at rest. If this is recognized, the gradient can be cut back, and the person brought up to a point where he can easily shift the gears on a motionless car before performing the same action while in motion.

The Third Barrier— the Misunderstood Word

The third barrier to study is the most important of the three. It is the prime factor involved with stupidity and many other unwanted conditions.

This third barrier is the misunderstood word. A misunderstood definition or a not-comprehended definition or an undefined word can thoroughly block one's understanding of a subject and can even cause one to abandon the subject entirely.

This milestone in the field of education has great application, but it was overlooked by every educator in history.

Going past a word or symbol for which one does not have a proper definition gives one a distinctly blank or washed-out feeling. The person will get a "not-there" feeling and will begin to feel a nervous hysteria. These are manifestations distinct from either of the other two barriers.

The barrier of the misunderstood word is far more important than the other two, however. It has much to do with human relations, the mind and different subjects. It establishes aptitude or lack of aptitude and is the key to what psychologists were attempting to test for years without recognizing what it was.

A person might or might not have *brilliance* as a computer programer, but his ability to *do* the motions of computer programing is dependent exclusively and only upon definitions. There is some word in the field of computer programing that the person who is inept did not define or understand and that was followed by an inability to act in the field of computer programing.

This is extremely important because it tells one what happens to doingness and that the restoration of doingness depends only on the location and understanding of any word which has been misunderstood in a subject.

A reader coming to the bottom of a page only to realize he didn't remember what he had just read is the phenomenon of a misunderstood word, and one will always be

The materials comprising the Student Hat course contain all of L. Ron Hubbard's study technology, as contained in his written works and recorded lectures.

found just before the material became blank in his mind.

This sweeping discovery is applicable to any sphere of endeavor, and opens wide the gates to education.

STUDENT HAT

These barriers to study and their resolution are contained on a Scientology training course called the Student Hat. ("Hat" is a common English term for a particular duty or task assigned, taken from the fact that in many professions, the type of hat worn is a badge of specific authority. In Scientology too, the term refers to one's duties and responsibilities. It also describes the written materials one studies to learn how to perform a particular function, in this case study.) The Student Hat course covers the complete technology of how to study any subject effectively. These are the materials one needs to learn in order to study successfully. This is very important for Scientologists who wish to undertake Scientology training. It will provide them with the tool needed to comprehend everything they study. Much of the study technology is contained in nine lectures Mr. Hubbard gave on learning and education, and these are all included, along with many of his pertinent writings.

This course provides a full understanding of the barriers to study and how to recognize and fully handle them. It shows one how to clear up a misunderstood word so he fully understands it and can use it both orally and in writing.

As discussed in detail in Chapter 31, the study technology has been put to many uses: in schools, universities, businesses and other institutions. To make this technology available to all, the Church offers the following works in addition to the Student Hat materials:

Basic Study Manual

The major breakthroughs of study technology are described for any age or academic level from teenagers on up. All fundamentals are covered, giving a firm grounding to successful learning in any pursuit.

Learning How to Learn

Recommended as the first study book for children, this illustrated work teaches children how to study. Basic to all children's education, it teaches exact skills they need in order to begin learning.

Study Skills for Life

Written specifically for young teenagers, this book enables a person to learn the most basic aspects of study technology in an easy-to-understand format.

Two additional books exist to aid children in study:

How to Use a Dictionary Picture Book for Children

Many children have not been taught to use a dictionary. Thus, when a parent or teacher uses a word beyond their level of comprehension, they have no way to define it. *How to Use a Dictionary Picture Book for Children* teaches children how to find and understand words.

Grammar and Communication for Children

This simple English grammar book was written and illustrated to hold the interest of children. Its purpose is to show the young student the basics of grammar so he can understand and communicate well and does not develop a fear or distaste for the subject.

A Technology to Increase Comprehension

In the years following L. Ron Hubbard's breakthrough on the importance of the misunderstood word, he developed a considerable body of technology which enables one to deal with the misunderstood words or symbols he encounters.

The relay of ideas from one mind to another mind or minds depends upon words, symbols, sounds, pictures, emotions and past associations. Primary among these, in any developed culture, are words. These can be written or spoken. While whole subjects exist concerning the development and meaning of words, many of them very learned and worthwhile, practically no work was ever done on the effect of words or the consequences of their misuse or noncomprehension.

What was not studied or known before L. Ron Hubbard's development of study technology is that the flow of ideas in any message or field of learning can be blocked in such a way as to suppress further understanding or comprehension from that point forward. Further, the misunderstood word can even act in such a way as to bring about ignorance, apathy and revolt in the classroom and in the workplace depress productivity.

Not only did these factors remain undiscovered before Scientology, but also, of course, no technology existed to remedy the problem.

To enable a person to handle the effect of misunderstood words, L. Ron Hubbard developed the subject called Word Clearing. Word Clearing is part of the broader field of study technology, but in itself Word Clearing has many uses and applications. Word Clearing can be defined as "the subject and action of clearing away the ignorance, misunderstoods and false definitions of words and barriers to their use."

In his observations of society, Mr. Hubbard had noticed a deterioration in literacy during this century. This conclusion is inescapable if one compares the political speeches and literature of a hundred or even fifty years ago to those of today. He noticed that the public was more and more dependent upon radio, motion pictures and television, all of which contain the spoken word, and he considered the possibility that these messages were not being fully received or understood. His observations were confirmed when an advertising association undertook a survey which showed that television audiences misunderstood between one-quarter and one-third of all the material they watched—findings with alarming implications. Not only are there serious economic consequences, as the study pointed out, wherein up to one-third of advertising expenditures are wasted because the public does not understand the ads. More importantly, such a gross level of noncomprehension can generate antipathy and even aggression among viewers.

When one speaks or writes, one has the responsibility to others to do so in a way that he will be understood. Further, one has a responsibility to oneself to ensure that he understands what he sees and hears.

L. Ron Hubbard developed nine separate methods of Word Clearing and several related technologies for handling the effects of misunderstood words and false information. Each method provides a different way of locating noncomprehension, identifying the underlying misunderstood word and then helping the individual come to a full understanding of the word so he can use them in his own vocabulary. Thousands of hours of research and hundreds of thousands of case studies went into the development of these nine methods.

In the twelve or sixteen years or more that a student spends in school, the unknowing accumulation of undefined words and symbols can present a serious barrier to knowledge and productivity in life. Also, when a person comes across words or symbols in everyday activities outside of the classroom that he does not understand, these, too, will end up limiting his capabilities.

With the techniques of Word Clearing, whole subjects which were not understood at the time and therefore could never be applied in life can be "recovered" and actually understood and used. Such is the power of clearing misunderstood words. Wherever communication is being engaged in, given or received, the technology of Word Clearing will find beneficial use.

Mr. Hubbard once remarked, "The future is the only frontier without limit and the frontier that we will all enter and cross no matter what we do." Reading news headlines is enough to tell anyone that social problems are escalating in virtually every community and that these portend a bleak future. Drugs, crime, unemployment, poverty and violence are all indicators of how extensive educational failures have become. A great many of those enmeshed in such problems could have been happier, more productive individuals if they had simply learned how to learn. If used, study technology will salvage both our current and future generations.

To learn to study any subject more effectively, visit the Study Technology Web site at **http://www.studytechnology.org.**

CHAPTER 11

THE KEY TO LIFE: HANDLING A WORLD OUT OF COMMUNICATION

While L. Ron Hubbard has provided a troubled society with many of the benefits of his research into the mind and spirit through secular applications of the technology in a number of fields—drug and criminal rehabilitation, education, artistic revitalization, and administration, to name a few—he said that of all his many breakthroughs "none of them are as meaningful to the culture around us as the discovery and development of the materials that comprise the Hubbard Key to Life Course."

Which, of course, raises the question: What was so important about this course that led Mr. Hubbard to call it the "Key to Life"? And, for that matter, what *is* the Key to Life?

For the answer and, in fact, to be able to grasp the full significance of the answer, one must first appreciate one of the core problems facing our culture today—functional illiteracy.

"Functional illiteracy" describes the condition when an individual appears able to make his way in life, yet is actually so deficient in reading and writing that he is essentially illiterate. This is the product of school systems that have done little more than baby-sit many students for twelve years and then turn them loose with no chance of contributing to society and every chance that society will have to support them. The term *functional illiteracy* really means "illiteracy" and demonstrates the legacy of an educational system which, entrusted with educating our young people, fails them (and the rest of us) miserably.

More than 25 million Americans are illiterate, according to government figures. Another 45 million, at least, are only marginally capable of leading productive lives. These figures include nearly 49 percent of all adult Americans and underscore the general decline in literacy.

Tests by Mr. Hubbard conducted in the late 1970s revealed that college graduates, when examined on common materials they read for pleasure, did not understand much of what they read. While they could pronounce words, they could not define many of the words they pronounced and they did not really comprehend what they were reading. Their ability to learn had been stymied. These findings would not surprise educators in even the better private universities who routinely find students who cannot read with comprehension, regardless of how well they scored on standardized admission tests.

As shown in the previous chapter, Mr. Hubbard recognized the seeds of this problem in the 1950s, and by 1964 he had developed his breakthrough study technology. In the late 1970s, however, he saw that even this technology required a more fundamental handling because of the escalating cultural decline. By then we had produced generations of people who were being bombarded with large amounts of information they do not comprehend and who have taken on the role of spectators. They are out of communication with life, which essentially means that they cannot competently give or receive communications.

Furthermore, he clearly saw that if one could truly comprehend what he read and heard and could make himself understood by others, all of life would be open to him. Conversely, to the degree one could not express himself and make others understand him and could not understand what others communicated, life would be closed off to him. In solving the problem of a world out of communication, L. Ron Hubbard developed a method that not only can make an illiterate person literate but increase the ability of anyone to comprehend and to be understood.

And *this* is the Key to Life.

Key to Life is a major breakthrough in the field of communication. Step by step, it strips away the reasons why a person cannot comprehend what he reads, writes and hears and why others cannot understand him.

In his attempt to handle this problem of comprehension among Scientology students and staff, Mr. Hubbard embarked upon a process to which he was no stranger — addressing the problem with a series of undercuts. He had done this over and over again with other aspects of the spiritual technology of Scientology, on the premise that while virtually anything can be made too complicated to understand there is little liability in simplifying something down to its basics. And time and time again he had demonstrated a very special genius for finding the very basics of a subject, thus making it comprehensible to anyone.

In addressing this problem of illiteracy, however, he found himself facing a unique and problematic situation. Keep in mind that what he was attempting to do was no small task. It was to first discover the impediments to comprehension and then to provide the tools to overcome them and thus allow communication. In other words, first he had to discover *why* so many people were illiterate, and then he had to come up with a remedy. He had already discovered why Scientology students and, indeed, most people could not learn, the primary villain being the misunderstood word, accompanied by the other barriers to study mentioned in the previous chapter. But obviously this was not enough of a solution and needed to be further undercut.

And here we come to the conundrum he found facing him: How do you convey the meaning of a word to a student who does not even understand the meaning of the words you are using in attempting to convey the meaning?

His research had taken him to the heart of this problem—the dismaying reality that this phenomenon of misunderstood words extended to the very core of language— its simplest words. And by this we mean words such as *but, and, or, were, their, so, on, at,* and so on. The words we use most often. What he called "the small common words." The words that educators have assumed "everyone knows."

Not everyone suffers this liability, of course, but nearly everyone suffers from it in some degree. Offer the sentence "It's as good as gold" to a crowd of people and you will find that most will not be able to define the word "as." Yet this is a word that is used hundreds of times each day.

This deficiency does not automatically classify everyone as illiterate, but it does show that virtually everyone's comprehension can be increased. And when we throw into the equation the fact Mr. Hubbard had discovered early in the previous decade that when someone encounters a misunderstood word, he stops understanding and does not fully grasp or become aware of what follows, we see in this set of circumstances the source of a somewhat befuddled and out of communication world.

So, here again was the problem he faced: how can you teach the language, its use, its construction, and its words without addressing the problem of misunderstood words? It seemed impossible. There was no way to use words to define words with words when even the most basic words were not understood. Or was there?

What was needed, Mr. Hubbard decided, was a way to totally avoid the possibility of allowing the student to encounter words he might misunderstand. And the solution he developed reflected the simplicity of genius:

Pictures.

Illustrations, to be exact. Thousands of illustrations.

Words are most often used to communicate concepts between people. But people sometimes also use physical gestures and noises to get the job done. And, throughout history, he has also used pictures to illustrate objects and concepts.

Thus the Key to Life Course utilizes thousands of highly evocative and expressive illustrations drawn by world-renowned illustrators to define concepts along with words to ensure *full* comprehension.

By any standards this was a task of monumental proportions, one that resulted in central course materials that consisted of three singularly unique books.

The first of these takes up the problem of the small misunderstood words and is appropriately enough titled *Small Common Words Defined.* Here, one finds the sixty most commonly used English words, the ones that "everybody" assumes they understood and few do.

Each definition of each of these words is accompanied by an illustration which adds to an understanding of the word by providing a clear conceptual definition, a revolutionary procedure. True, most children's dictionaries are heavily illustrated to aid comprehension, but the illustrations are not integral to the written definitions as these are. This is an entirely original advancement in education.

The written definitions themselves are simplicity personified, and *every* word used in them, or in the book is also defined in a glossary in the back of the book. The opportunity to misunderstand words is virtually nil. As these are the words we learn to join or carry virtually everything we say, and as research has shown that they are the words that people most commonly misunderstand, this book alone is a giant step towards literacy.

The next step on the Key to Life Course, now that the student has been prepared, involves yet another crucial yet overlooked educational tool: the dictionary. Most students have never been taught exactly *how to use* a dictionary and when they attempt to do so, what they face is a potential minefield of misunderstood words and symbols. In view of the fact that a dictionary is supposed to be used to bring clarity and understanding, this was yet another problem Mr. Hubbard found himself confronting.

Consider this: given the potency of misunderstood words and symbols to block comprehension from the moment they are encountered, what does a student — young or old — make of this:

> *corvette:* \kor-´vet\ n. F, fr. MF, prob. fr. MD *corf,* a kind of ship, lit., basket — more at CORF (1636)

even before he reaches the definition of the word itself?

What he does *not* do, nine times out of ten, is go to the explanatory notes at the front of the dictionary, because he has already found that they are almost incomprehensible. So what he *does* do is struggle on through a fog of incomprehension, read the definition, not understand it and promptly forget it.

The Hubbard Key to Life Course breaks through the barriers to comprehension and assimilation of data, utilizing thousands of pictures to communicate the fundamental factors of language.

In fact, one can pick up a copy of *Merriam Webster's Collegiate Dictionary,* Tenth Edition, look at the explanatory notes concerning etymology and one will find a very learned and extremely complex discussion of the subject that does not even define MF and MD. Nor is it defined in the body of the dictionary itself.

Where all this leaves the student, of course, is nowhere.

Mr. Hubbard's answer was the *How to Use a Dictionary* book, which also utilizes illustrations to bring about understanding. *How to Use a Dictionary* defines not only every symbol and *abbr.* the student might encounter when attempting to clear up a word, but how to pronounce it and understand its derivation; how to identify parts of speech and identification marks; and even something as basic as exactly how words are alphabetized in a dictionary.

The result is a student who can use a dictionary without descending into a miasma of doubt, frustration and confusion, but instead gain the understanding he seeks.

Still, perhaps the most significant and far-reaching innovation Mr. Hubbard developed for this course is found in a book titled *The New Grammar.* Which is exactly what it is.

The mere mention of English grammar to virtually anyone who has ever been a student is enough to cause a pang of discomfort or even to send something approximating a chill of terror down their spines. Mention the words *gerund, split infinitive* or *past participle* to a friend and watch his eyes glaze over. Our experience with the stultifying complexity of grammar—like childhood diseases—is something most of us would rather forget.

At this point in the Key to Life Course, the student has an understanding of the most fundamental words of the language, knows how to clear up those he does not understand, and is ready to learn, through the proper use of grammar, how to communicate in a way that will be understood.

However, when Mr. Hubbard began to research the subject, he was appalled. As he put it in his introduction to the book, "Grammar is established by *common usage* and forwarded by *writers.* It got into a very dark eddy of a very dark river when it fell into the hands of the professors." (See page 230.)

Further, he pointed out that written and spoken communication was not invented by grammarians, who had turned the subject of grammar into "a *study* which belongs in the hands of the professors." No, he said, "It is obviously a *use* which belongs in the hands of the users."

And to place it back in the hands of users, Mr. Hubbard undertook a number of highly innovative measures, starting with that redefinition of grammar as something one uses, not something one studies. Among these measures was the stripping away of ambiguities and the elimination of the arbitrary distinction between various types of modifiers. As both adverbs and adjectives have the same function, which is to modify, they became simply "modifiers."

In short, in this extraordinary work, Mr. Hubbard clarifies the entire construction of the language and shows that grammar, when it is understood, is something one uses to facilitate and enhance meaningful communication. Other than that, he points out, it has no other useful purpose.

There is yet more to this remarkable course which has not been mentioned. For example, the very first step taken by the student on the Key to Life is a special auditing action that is unique to this course and found nowhere else on the Bridge. The results are spectacular. After this powerful auditing, one finds an individual with renewed certainty and unshakable stability.

Similarly noteworthy, after gaining an understanding of basic words, and with a firm grasp of grammar, the student examines in great depth "The Factors of Scientology," L. Ron Hubbard's concise and beautiful summation of thirty years of research into the human spirit and its relationship to the material universe. From these fundamental truths the student gains a profound understanding

The New Grammar focuses not on a study of stultified rules, but on the use of grammar to facilitate communication.

of Scientology and what it means to be a Scientologist.

The student who completes the Hubbard Key to Life Course is one who will be able to express himself easily and clearly, both verbally and in writing, and one who will fully understand the communication he receives from others. And his ability to now thoroughly understand Scientology will allow him to progress more rapidly on the Bridge.

Not only Scientologists can benefit from these breakthroughs, however, for each of these books was designed to stand alone in any educational field. And, a result of the demand from educators and educational institutions, the three component books of the Key to Life Course, *Small Common Words Defined*, *The New Grammar* and *How to Use a Dictionary*, are available to the growing numbers of those who see in Mr. Hubbard's work the tools for a desperately needed educational renaissance.

The Key to Life Web site on the Internet contains more information on this major breakthrough in the fields of communication and education. It can be found at **http://www. keytolife.org.**

THE IMPORTANCE OF *THE NEW GRAMMAR*

"English is now the language of international communication. It is the language used by heads of state. It is the language of international business negotiation. It is the language of the majority of the rapidly growing masses of computerized information.

"Unfortunately, most persons educated by the public education systems in the United States are not competent in understanding and using English. As a teacher in one of the better private universities in the United States I am well aware that many of our students, even though they are among those ranking very high on standardized tests, are unable to read with comprehension. Failing to master the full resources of the English language, students become functionally illiterate.

"This inability to fully understand and use language causes problems in schools and businesses, and these problems affect wider areas of society. In this time of widespread illiteracy L. Ron Hubbard introduces a book that makes grammar understandable and useful to all.

"This book takes grammar and makes it easy. It helps individuals to understand the basic building blocks of the English language and how to use those building blocks to better communicate, express their thoughts and understand what they read.

"L. Ron Hubbard first gained fame as a writer at a time when even the popular magazines of the day expected their readers to appreciate breadth of vocabulary and variety of style.

"Only a professional writer with a writer's sensitivity to language could have written such an innovative approach to grammar. Only such a writer would see grammar not as full of constricting rules, but full of possibilities for rich expressions of thought and action.

"Teaching writers how to write in the 1940s, L. Ron Hubbard has now come full circle with this grammar book and returned to the field of teaching language.

"This is a brilliant book by a brilliant mind. In fact, it is a revolution in thought."

David Rodier, PhD
Associate Professor of Philosophy
American University, Washington, DC

GRAMMAR
BY L. RON HUBBARD

L. Ron Hubbard offered the following explanation of grammar, its history and its function as an introduction to his highly acclaimed textbook *The New Grammar*, part of the Key to Life Course.

Grammar *is the way words are organized into speech and writings so as to convey exact thoughts, ideas and meanings amongst people. It is essentially a system of agreements as to the relationship of words to bring about meaningful communication.*

That is all that grammar is. If it is defined otherwise, students will think they are being taught classroom rules rather than how to talk and read.

*This definition will not be found in dictionaries because grammar fell into the hands of grammarians who themselves misunderstood the word **grammar**. It is that and that only which makes grammar tough. The objective of **The New Grammar** is to bypass the resulting complications.*

*Grammar is established by **common usage** and forwarded by **writers.** It got into a very dark eddy of a very dark river when it fell into the hands of the professors. This is basically what is wrong with it. It isn't even difficult to understand it. It is only difficult to understand the inability of the professors to write about it.*

*Grammar isn't the **study** of anything. It's the **use** of something. Now a "professor" believes that anything is a study. That's because he gets paid for telling people it is a study. Grammar is a part of **everyday existence** and if you don't know it and can't use it, nobody can understand you and you can't understand others and you will be in mystery about things and people a lot of the time.*

If grammar is defined as the way words are organized into speech and writings so as to convey exact thoughts, ideas and meanings amongst people, students will be eager to study it rather than thinking they are suffering under the yoke of "professors" who themselves couldn't talk or communicate. Grammar is something people need in order to understand and be understood and that is the end of it.

Grammarians of the past never understood what a word was and failed to properly define the most basic element of their subject.

They also failed to notice and stress the fact that the language is made up of words which, on the whole, have several meanings and can be used in several different ways. Without an understanding of this, the language and grammar can appear very confusing.

These and many other errors have made the subject difficult to learn and use.

The aim of this book is to make a person expert in the use and construction of words and language so that he can convey his concepts and thoughts clearly and lucidly and so that he can understand the thoughts and concepts of others.

That's all there is to grammar.

CHAPTER 12

THE LIFE ORIENTATION COURSE: ATTAINING COMPETENCE IN LIFE

It has been said that most people live lives of quiet desperation. While this may not be true of everyone, how many people can say that their lives are harmonious, rewarding and fulfilling? How many can say they are living the life they once dreamed of? While one is often defined, and remembered, by what he does in life — usually represented by his job — there is of course much more to life than this. True fulfillment and happiness comes when one is fulfilled on all eight dynamics — through family and friends, through the groups one belongs to, through what one contributes to and receives from the other dynamics. When any of these factors are missing from one's life or enturbulated or overbalanced we find the seeds of turmoil.

It is a fact, however, that one's job is usually one's main "hat" in life. It is what we primarily produce and how we support ourselves and it monopolizes a large amount of our attention. Consequently when this activity goes badly, it tends to affect all the other factors in our lives. Conversely, when our other hats, be it husband, wife, parent, become less than ideal, it tends to affect our jobs and all our other hats. Still our work is important. After all, it occupies more of our waking hours than any other single activity, and our success or failure affects our purposes and dreams on all dynamics. For example, the man who is unproductive and dissatisfied in his job brings his disgruntlement and anxiety home to upset his family life, suffers during his leisure time and often loses friends because of his negative attitude. He is certainly not as happy as he could be if he demonstrated a higher level of competency in his main activity. Competence is accompanied by many positive qualities, including pride, satisfaction and a sense of security.

Contrary to popular belief, however, competence is not necessarily something one is born with; it is a quality one develops. Most people depend upon "experience," but experience is a fickle teacher—not one we can always depend upon. It would be better if there were dependable tools, workable principles and procedures that have been verified in the crucible of life itself. Fortunately, the tools that can lead one to competence do exist. They can be found in L. Ron Hubbard's Life Orientation Course. In fact, as the course name implies, these are the tools one can use to get one's bearing in life and harmoniously align all the factors of this vast mosaic so that they are no longer confusing or overwhelming.

As mentioned, there are many parts to anyone's life: ambitions, friends and associates, a job and social involvements. There are obligations to fulfill, assets to protect, people to look after, a future to make, and more. The elements that make up a complete life, anyone's life, are myriad. And when one factor is missing or life is overbalanced in favor of another factor to the neglect of still others the consequences can be disheartening, if not disastrous.

The Life Orientation Course helps an individual become able to sort out every single area of his life, thus pointing all his activities towards the same end and aligning all his dynamics. The tools used to accomplish this remarkable achievement are varied and many. Some, used by themselves, have brought life-changing results. Yet when combined on the Life Orientation Course (together with other tools and procedures that are found nowhere else in Scientology) their power to help an individual bring about profound change in *every* aspect of his life is unprecedented.

For example, as noted in Chapter 4, life can be compartmentalized into eight urges or aspects and man's survival depends upon his participation in all eight of these dynamics and, thus, how his activities align with them. On this course, the individual undertakes a searching study of the eight dynamics. Yet, unlike previous attempts he

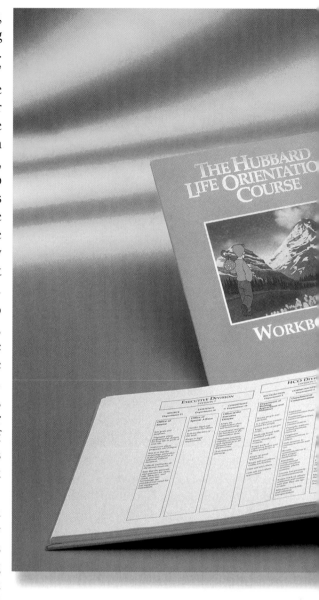

might have made in this direction, on this course a special auditing process provides an emphasis on his personal involvement on each dynamic, enabling him to even more closely inspect them and thus gain a view of all life with crystalline clarity.

Now, from a vantage point better than he has ever occupied, he can view his life, his dynamics, his influence over these dynamics, his decisions along these lines and how these have contributed to where he finds himself. Study alone could not bring about this awareness; the auditing is necessary.

With this sufficiently broad view, he can begin to distinguish those actions promoting

increased survival from those actions which are nonsurvival. This entails more auditing, developed by Mr. Hubbard especially for the Life Orientation Course, and results in a firm subjective understanding of what happens in life if the dynamics go out of alignment.

Then there are the conditions of existence, as described in Chapter 17, a vital tool that is fully utilized in the Life Orientation Course. Everything and everyone is in some condition at any given moment, be it low or high. Mr. Hubbard examined this fact and delineated twelve conditions which encompass every possible state a person, thing or activity can be in. These are not arbitrary opinions but

laws of life that can be verified by anyone through observation. These conditions range from utter confusion in which a person is useless and unable to produce anything, to one of power where he is functioning at a very high level indeed—with steps in between. Along with this, Mr. Hubbard also developed a series of steps or formulas for each condition. When these are diligently followed, the individual can move upwards, a step at a time, to new heights. Utilizing these conditions the Life Orientation student can improve his life on all dynamics treating *every* aspect of his existence more thoroughly than he has ever imagined possible.

Yet another tool, and one used in a way unique to this course, is the organizing board. Developed by Mr. Hubbard to aid and organize Church administration, the organizing board is more than it appears to be at first glance. With its seven divisions, twenty-one departments and their units, and the awareness levels which correspond to each department, what we have here is not just some kind of flow chart or method to signify the "posts" in an organization but what is actually a "philosophical machine."

To explain further: Philosophy, of course, in its original and widest sense is the love, study and pursuit of wisdom, or of knowledge of things and their causes, whether theoretical or practical. In actual usage, it is the science which investigates the most general facts and principles of reality and of human nature and conduct.

By "machine" is meant a system or organization for doing or making something. It is something which makes or does things and when given an impetus, it continues a sequence of action.

A philosophic machine, then, would be something you would draw up which gave some data which you could then combine with some other data and get some sort of answer.

The organizing board is a philosophic machine that can be used to analyze one's entire existence.

On the Life Orientation Course the student analyzes every aspect of his life against the twenty-one departments, discovers what is missing or incomplete and otherwise less than functional and optimum but also what they are doing successfully. In other words, the student divides every activity of his life into these twenty-one compartments, and then examines each activity to see what he is doing or not doing in that area.

By examining his life in this manner, nothing he does escapes his scrutiny. And because these departments contain *all* the actions that are vital for anyone to operate at a high level, he also sees what he is *not* doing

and *should* be doing in order to succeed. Essentially, then, on this course the student gains an entirely new view of the organizing board as a tool for life, one that he can apply long after he has graduated to better his existence.

Finally, to provide a view of the many remaining elements involved in this course, there is the matter of products. The fact is, to survive well the different activities of an individual's life must each result in something of real use and value. A person who has no valid purpose in life or in what he does or who produces nothing of value will be miserable. A specific product should result from activity in each part of his life.

His profession, for instance, results in a product which furthers his survival. A person produces something or provides some service for which he is given money on which to live. The establishment and maintenance of his living quarters results in a completely different product, but one which also helps promote a different aspect of his survival. A comfortable, clean home is a pleasant place in which to live, certainly a valuable product in itself. Likewise, each activity in a person's life has a product, and these either aid or inhibit his success and survival depending on how good they are.

Unfortunately, many people are not sure exactly what product they create in their everyday jobs, let alone in every activity of their lives. But on this course they gain an understanding of every product they have or *should* have to make each activity they are involved in rewarding and fulfilling.

Essentially, what this course does is it gets the person totally oriented to his *main* product in life, how this fits in with the rest of his dynamics, and brings him to clearly view what he needs to do to viably produce it. This is a major advance because it results in someone who is causative, competent and productive.

With this ability gained, the individual has truly straightened out his life. He sees clearly where he is headed, and is armed with the tools to make sure he arrives at the somewhere he always wanted to be. Rather than be blown here and there by the winds of chance, he gets his life in clear perspective and under control, with a certainty on the laws of life, knowing exactly, at every step of the way, what he is doing to forward his own true purposes.

On the Life Orientation Course, purpose, morale, spiritual fulfillment and happiness are in the offing.

A frank assessment of the lives of other people usually reveals that many are not leading the lives they would like, but rather the life they think it "has to be" for one reason or another. L. Ron Hubbard developed the Life Orientation Course to help people better understand where they are going in life and to help them make their lives more fulfilling. He has provided a route into the very activity of living itself. It is the gateway to a life of purpose, morality, spiritual freedom and happiness.

CHAPTER 13

THE GRADE CHART: AUDITING TO HIGHER STATES OF EXISTENCE

Through Dianetics and Scientology auditing, man's full spiritual potential, so often speculated about, can be realized. This potential is far, far higher than man ever thought possible.

The goal of auditing is greater cause and ability for the person, enabling him to better understand and handle his own life.

The degrees and stages of discovery as one comes to know oneself and attain total spiritual freedom are scaled upwards on the auditing steps of the Bridge. The person moves up step by step, graduating each time to a higher level.

HIGHER STATES

Man is so visibly MAN that he overlooked in most of his philosophies and *all* of his sciences that there is more than one state of existence attainable by man.

Indeed, until Scientology came along and changed their minds, all nineteenth-century psychologists *stated* that man could never change. And described only one state of existence—mortal man.

There are *many* states of existence besides that of man. This has been touched on by earlier philosophies. What is new about Scientology is that one being can attain several different states of existence in just one lifetime.

This is so novel an outlook man at large has never thought of it before. That he personally and in this lifetime could become something far higher and better than a man is brand-new to him. He has heard of dying and his soul going to heaven or hell, and he has variously regarded the prospect as good or boring or terrifying.

Some savants amongst the Himalayas have worked in this direction. Siddhartha Gautama (Buddha) spoke of it. Fifteen or twenty years of hard work were said to result in a nebulous conclusion.

With Scientology, there are no such uncertainties. These higher states can be attained through auditing.

These states are the whole of the horizon and attainment of Scientology. Rather than seeking to make the insane sane, Scientology is seeking to make a man into a higher being.

As one progresses through his first steps in auditing, he can be freed not only of the effects of drugs but of any "need" to take them. When he then does his Scientology Grades, he can become a being who can truly communicate—a higher being who can make new worlds. He frees himself from the hostilities and sufferings of life—and more. As he moves upward, he can become truly well and happy, free of maladies and disabilities rooted in his reactive mind. And, progressing yet further, he can then attain states never before described in man's literature, much less attained: Clear and beyond.

Scientology could be defined as a road to truth. The progressive auditing grades are, in reality, those *barriers,* in order, *which keep a person from going forward to an ultimate truth.* There are no other barriers to moving up to higher states than those addressed and resolved at each of the levels of the Grade Chart. And as he achieves higher levels, he moves closer to that transcendent truth.

L. Ron Hubbard developed many different auditing processes during his research. He arranged these in a sequence that enables an individual to achieve greater awareness and with this, higher states of existence leading to, finally, a recognition of his own immortal nature.

This road is known as *the Grade Chart.*

There are many auditing services available, and given that Scientology addresses all aspects of life, it is not surprising that there are many services which focus on one or more particular factors which may frustrate one's survival. Yet all of those factors are ultimately alleviated and resolved through following the Grade Chart. Mr. Hubbard described it as "the main program," senior to all other auditing concerns. In fact, *all* other auditing actions are designed to get a person back onto the Grade Chart or moving more swiftly along it.

The chart is the swiftest and surest path to higher states, and the *only* certain road to total freedom. What follows is a description, in sequence, of the auditing services which comprise that chart. It is the path everyone must take.

SERVICES OF THE GRADE CHART

Conditional Preparatory Steps

Every individual is unique, and thus there are different ways to begin one's progress up the Grade Chart, based on individual needs as determined by the Case Supervisor. One or all of these services may mark the first steps preparatory to the Scientology Grades on one's journey to total freedom. They are available at Scientology churches and missions.

Purification Rundown

The Purification Rundown can enable a person to advance spiritually through auditing. This rundown addresses the mental and spiritual factors that can come from the use of drugs or the effects of toxins and chemicals that remain in the body. The program detoxifies the body through a combination of exercise, vitamins, nutrition and sauna, closely supervised by trained Scientologists in liaison with medical practitioners. As drugs dull a person's ability to communicate and perceive, this is often one of the first steps on the Bridge. For more information, see Chapter 9.

TRs and Objective Processing

Objective Processes locate the person in his environment, establish direct communication with the auditor, and bring a person to present time. This latter result is an important factor in spiritual and mental sanity and ability, as a human being can be "stuck" in literally thousands of past moments. The result is an individual with increased perception who is more at cause over his body and his environment.

Further case gain comes through learning and drilling the TRs (training routines or drills) numbered 0 through 9, which help the individual better confront and handle his environment and life, and thus increase his ability to move up the Grade Chart.

Scientology Drug Rundown

Done after the Purification Rundown and TRs and Objectives, this auditing rundown unburdens the effects of a person's drug use, and allows him to attain all of the gains possible in his Grade Chart auditing. By addressing the mental and spiritual damage that results from drug use, one experiences considerable relief and expansion as a being. The result is a person released from the mental and spiritual effects of drugs, medicine and alcohol.

Scientology Expanded Grades

Expanded Grades can give any preclear enormous gains in life. These grades consist of a series of auditing processes which restore to the individual specific abilities and lay a strong foundation for more advanced auditing. (By "Expanded" is meant something that increases one's outlook. "Grades" is short for "gradation" and applies to the gradient steps of the ascending levels up the Bridge.)

The Expanded Grades consist of six separate grades, described below, and nearly 150 different processes on which a person may be audited. Each grade was designed by Mr. Hubbard to enable the individual to rehabilitate or strengthen specific spiritual abilities.

When a particular process has achieved its desired result, the person's awareness increases in that area and he becomes more able in that regard. Auditing more processes on a similar subject returns more ability. Further processes on a grade are then done until the person is rehabilitated on the whole subject of that grade, at which point the next grade, and another area of ability, can be addressed.

In this way, the Expanded Grades improve and restore a thetan's abilities — abilities so buried that he had come to believe his failings were simply a "natural" consequence of life. Yet such failings are not natural at all. Through Scientology Expanded Grades auditing an individual's native potentials and characteristics become evident, and flourish. They are available at Scientology churches and missions.

The six Expanded Grades are:

Expanded ARC Straightwire

The concept of ARC (affinity, reality and communication—the components of understanding) is one of the most important factors in all life. If a person can establish ARC for something, he can truly understand it. As noted, the subject of Scientology is the person himself, a spiritual being, and so it follows that the first grade would involve restoring a preclear's direct and immediate understanding of himself.

"Straightwire" refers to the action of putting one into better communication with his mind and the world.

The processes on this level free an individual from continued deterioration at a personal level. Here we have someone who will not get worse—and knows it. All of this can be accomplished through the processes of ARC Straightwire.

Expanded Grade 0

The ability to communicate is one of the most fundamental abilities of a being. A being who can communicate is in a state well above what we know as "man."

The processes of Expanded Grade 0 address a person's ability to communicate and free him, in his *own* estimation, from any blocks in the area. These processes restore the ability to communicate to anyone about any subject. And with the ability to communicate comes the joy of associating freely with others.

He who can truly communicate to others is a higher being who builds new worlds. Auditing can help an individual achieve this higher state of being—one who can communicate. It is achieved at the auditing level known as Expanded Grade 0.

Expanded Grade I

What distinguishes civilized man as MAN is that he is mired in PROBLEMS which just get worse the more he tries to "solve" them.

The being who can recognize the actual source of problems and so see them vanish is too rare to be easily comprehended. A being in a higher state looks at them and they "vanish"—meaning they cease to be problems.

The mechanisms and phenomena surrounding problems have never, before Scientology, been examined or understood. The breakthrough came when L. Ron Hubbard identified a precise mechanism common to *all* problems.

Through the auditing procedures of Expanded Grade I, the preclear gains the ability to recognize the actual source of problems, at which point they cease to be problems.

Expanded Grade II

Man has never known, except in some of the rare miracle workers he regarded as saints, how to bring relief to various sufferings.

The secret was that through misdeeds, harmful acts against one's fellows and other transgressions, one is connecting oneself to what he abhors.

When a person unthinkingly transgresses against the mores to which he has agreed or, with "good cause" knowingly offends them, his misery begins. Having transgressed, the person now feels he must hold back his deed from others, and he begins to withdraw or feel different from the person or group he has harmed. This is the mechanism by which people create misery, bitterness and hatred around themselves. This is the source of the guilty conscience, feelings of vengeance and, actually, all the sufferings and hostilities of life.

To be able to easily bring relief to oneself and others from the hostilities and sufferings of life is a skill man has seen only in healers.

Relief is obtained at Expanded Grade II.

Expanded Grade III

Man is chained to the upsets in his past. He has never understood why he felt so upset and misunderstood about his family or people or situations.

Most men dwell perpetually on troubles they have had. They lead sad lives.

On Grade III processes one locates specific incidents where upsetting change occurred in life and addresses these so that they no longer adversely affect one. Some of the processes also enhance the ability of the individual to create positive change in himself or his environment.

This grade gives the preclear the freedom to face the future with an enhanced ability to confront, experience and find advantage in the inevitable changes of life.

Freedom from the upsets of the past with the ability to face the future is almost an unknown condition to man. It is attained at Expanded Grade III.

Expanded Grade IV

Man's abilities tend to be individually specialized. One can be so intent upon one action that he is clumsy in performing others. Habit patterns can be nearly impossible to break, yet these fixed conditions hold a person down and inhibit his ideas and activities in ways that cloud his potential.

The processes of Grade IV enable the preclear to view himself in relation to all life and free himself from any patterns of thought and action which, while seeming to promote one's survival, in reality do everything but. When one moves out of fixed conditions, he can experience a huge resurgence in the ability to choose, partake in and enjoy new activities.

Moving out of fixed conditions and being able to do other things is attained at Expanded Grade IV.

———

A person who is able in a given area can produce, perform, function and control activity in that area. A being who has attained the abilities from the Scientology Expanded Grades is now able in *life* itself. As such he is more in control, more aware and enjoys more personal power. He is also now in a position to rid himself of his reactive mind and its content.

The Scientology Passport to Freedom, used by Scientologists to assist in tracking their orderly progress up the Bridge. As one finishes a grade, the passport is stamped to show completion.

NEW ERA DIANETICS AUDITING

The reactive mind plagues a person with the unthinking, irrational dictates of its contents and imposes anxieties, fears, unwanted sensations and feelings and a host of other undesirable effects. Freeing him from the command value such unwanted emotions exert over his volition provides new levels of self-determinism.

Initially, the reactive mind was addressed using only the techniques laid out in *Dianetics: The Modern Science of Mental Health*, also known as "Book One." But L. Ron Hubbard continued to refine the techniques. The culmination of more than a quarter of a century of research and improvement came in 1978 with New Era Dianetics and the widespread making of Clears.

The effectiveness of these New Era Dianetics techniques is nothing short of revolutionary. A 1950s Book One auditor would have been astonished to see the speed with which Dianetics results could be attained with the advent of NED. The ratio has been estimated at 100 to 1. What once could only be achieved in thousands of hours of auditing can now often be realized in only dozens of hours.

The question may arise: If one is directly addressing the reactive mind in Dianetics auditing, why then are the Scientology Grades necessary? Chronologically, Dianetics came before Scientology; and it would seem natural that one would give Dianetics to a preclear before he received Scientology auditing.

The answer lies in the fact that Scientology Grades were developed as an *undercut* to Dianetics. The preclear usually needs a lot of work on his life and his relationship to his environment before he can easily confront his reactive mind on NED. The Grades unburden a great deal of the reactive mind and environment, not to mention the fact that they provide enormous gains in his life. And by first giving him Scientology Expanded Grades, it is then far easier for him when he moves into New Era Dianetics and when he attains the state of Clear. Instead of increasing the number of hours to reach Clear, the Scientology Grades actually can shorten it up.

New Era Dianetics auditing consists of eighteen separate steps, specific rundowns and actions which address the engrams contained in the reactive mind. The different sensations, emotions, feelings and so forth are used to trace back engrams in the reactive mind. Utilizing Dianetics auditing procedure, the preclear erases those engrams, nullifying the reactive mind's ability to control the individual unwittingly.

The NED Drug Rundown, for example, resolves the factors in the reactive mind related to drug addiction, eradicating not only the unwanted aftereffects of drugs, but even those reactive forces that initially led one to turn to drugs. The harmful effects of drugs on the mind are erased and a person is freed from the compulsion to take drugs.

Another of the NED Rundowns, entirely tailor-made to the individual, handles anything a person considers to be a disability. There is no longer any need to adjust to one's limitations when he can eradicate the cause of them in the reactive mind.

Dianetics does not cure any physical condition, but does address those spiritual and mental factors that can predispose or precipitate illness or make medicine ineffective. As a result, by handling the psychosomatic causes, one can achieve a well and happy human being and often bring a person to that burst of glory and freedom known as the state of Clear.

NED is available at Scientology churches and missions.

STATE OF CLEAR

The state of Clear has often been described in Dianetics and Scientology. It has always been understated. Time has revealed that Clear is far above anything one had dreamed of previously.

Here is a being who has forever vanquished his own reactive mind, the source of man's misery. He has a very high degree of personal integrity and honesty, and is living proof that man is basically good. His own basic beingness returns and his own personality flourishes. When a person becomes Clear, he loses all the fears, anxieties and irrational thoughts that were held down by pain in the reactive mind and, in short, regains himself. Without a reactive mind, an individual is much, much more himself.

Until an individual is cleared, no matter how able he has become by virtue of earlier auditing, it is inevitable that he will sooner or later sink back into the reactive mind. That is why clearing is vital. Clear is total eradication of the individual's own reactive mind. Thus, Clear is a stable state, not subject to relapse.

Today, the state of Clear can routinely be attained in New Era Dianetics. And if a person does not achieve Clear on NED, he can attain it through the Alternate Clear Route and the Clearing Course (explained below and on page 246).

The full glory of the state of Clear has no comparable description in any writings existing in our culture. The state had been long sought but was impossible to achieve without the researches and breakthroughs of L. Ron Hubbard. No matter how able a being may have been, no matter what powers he possessed, no matter his strengths, the reactive mind was still there, hidden, and eventually dragged him down again. The state of Clear does exist today and is attainable by all men. Many thousands of Scientologists all over the world are Clear, joined by more each day.

Alternate Clear Route

The amount of auditing necessary to erase the reactive mind is unique to each person. If a person does not achieve Clear on NED, he

When a person attains the state of Clear he is entitled to wear a Clear bracelet.

continues with further levels on the Grade Chart and attains it on the Clearing Course. That the state of Clear can be attained is a certainty; the only question is whether a person will attain it through NED or this alternate route. Other grades or auditing services do not result in Clear.

The auditing steps comprising the Alternate Clear Route are available only at Scientology Advanced Organizations, Saint Hill Organizations and the Flag Service Organization.

Grades V and VA
Power and Power Plus

Grades V and VA are the next steps for a person who did not attain Clear on NED.

On Grade V (Power) one discovers and resolves those things that pin one to the reactive mind. And on Grade VA (Power Plus) a person tackles the beings, places and subjects he has long detested. These processes vastly increase one's abilities, potentials, intelligence and awareness, and free one from major and long-standing problems to restore previously hidden powers.

Man can seldom handle power. He retreats from it or abuses it. When he has it he often misdirects it. To have it and handle it is attained on Grades V and VA.

Available only at Scientology Advanced Organizations, Saint Hill Organizations and the Flag Service Organization.

Grade VI

This level delivers freedom from dramatizations. The theory includes four filmed lectures by Mr. Hubbard in which he reveals the fundamental anatomy of the reactive mind, and exactly why the human race reacts as it does.

Man's past is his "time track." There are three conditions concerning it. A being is first unaware he has one, then is fascinated by what he finds out about his own past and then finds what made him—and it— that way.

Some of this often shows up in lower auditing. But at this level, one comes to handle it.

At this grade, the state attained defies easy description. It is so far above common experience and totally missing in all of man's literature. It is a Grade VI Release.

Available only at Scientology Advanced Organizations and the Flag Service Organization.

Clearing Course

On this service the Grade VI Release studies the materials of the Clearing Course which include several technical films featuring lectures and Solo auditing demonstrations by Mr. Hubbard. Here, the student learns the anatomy and mechanics of the core of the reactive mind itself and then audits himself until his reactive mind—the basic cause of his decline—is vanquished and he is capable of regaining his full potential as a being at the newly attained state of Clear.

For those who do not go Clear on NED, this is the level on which they will achieve that state.

Available only at Scientology Advanced Organizations and the Flag Service Organization.

STEPS BEYOND CLEAR

Sunshine Rundown

This short action adds extra shine to the state of Clear. By doing it, the Clear is becoming self-determined in his new state. One does this rundown immediately after achieving the state of Clear, whether he has gone Clear on New Era Dianetics or the Clearing Course. This service is provided at Class V or higher level churches.

Solo Auditor Course and OT Preparations Auditing

Many of the OT levels, and certain steps of the Alternate Clear Route, require that the individual audit himself. This is called Solo auditing and requires that he learn all basic auditing skills and how to operate the E-Meter flawlessly.

The Solo Auditor Course is in two parts: On Part 1, the individual learns the fundamentals of Solo auditing and the required technical skills. This may be done at any Class V or higher church. On Part 2, one actually begins Solo auditing and becomes competent with his skills, ready to address the processes of the advanced levels. It is available only at Advanced and Saint Hill Organizations and Flag.

OT Preparations auditing varies from individual to individual according to their unique case needs. It is available from Advanced and Saint Hill Organizations and the Flag Service Org.

To acknowledge one's attainment of New OT VIII, a Scientologist may wear the OT bracelet.

OPERATING THETAN LEVELS

By "operating" is meant "able to act and handle things." And by "thetan" is meant the spiritual being that is the basic self. "Theta" is Greek for thought or life or the spirit.

An Operating Thetan then is one who can handle things without having to use a body or physical means.

Basically one is oneself, can handle things and exist without physical support and assistance. This state is Operating Thetan, or OT. It doesn't mean one becomes God. It means one becomes wholly oneself.

By eradicating the reactive mind one overcomes the barriers which made it so difficult to attain total spiritual independence and serenity. Thus, once a person achieves Clear he is now able to become refamiliarized with his native capabilities. As man is basically good, a being who is Clear becomes willing to trust himself with greater and greater abilities. This is done through the OT levels.

Like any other gain in Scientology, the state of OT is attained gradually. Just as it would not be as beneficial to give someone New Era Dianetics auditing before handling the negative effects of drugs and toxins with the Purification Rundown, so it is wrong to try to move someone onto the OT levels before he is ready for them. One might as well pull a baby out of its bassinet and demand that he run. He cannot run until he has first learned to crawl and then to walk. The reactive mind thoroughly blocks the thetan from regaining and exercising his native powers. But once this block is removed, an individual can learn to operate as himself, a spiritual being.

The OT levels contain the very advanced materials of L. Ron Hubbard's researches and it is here a person achieves the ultimate realization of his own nature and his relationship to life and all the dynamics. Abilities return as he advances up through the OT levels and he recovers the entirety of his beingness. Miracles of life have been exposed to full view for the first time ever on the OT levels. Not the least of these miracles is knowing immortality and freedom from the cycle of birth and death.

These levels are fifteen in number, each one a complete auditing service. OT Levels I through V are ministered at Advanced Organizations and the Flag

Service Organization. OT levels through VII are available at the Flag Service Organization in Clearwater. OT Level VIII, and higher OT levels when released, are available exclusively from the Flag Ship Service Organization, aboard the *Freewinds*.

ADDITIONAL SERVICES TO SPEED PROGRESS UP THE GRADE CHART

While the following steps are not done by everyone, each addresses and resolves certain difficulties a person may be encountering in his life. They can be done at various points on the Bridge.

Those who do one or more of them have found their progress up the Grade Chart greatly enhanced.

Happiness Rundown

Based on the precepts found in *The Way to Happiness,* L. Ron Hubbard's nonreligious, common-sense moral code, this powerful auditing rundown gives one the ability to create a happier, saner environment. While this code is nonreligious, its precepts are addressed spiritually in auditing. By clearing up any confusions an individual may have on the subject of morals, any transgressions against these morals and any other spiritual factors tying him to immorality, he is left with certainty that he can avoid tragedy and unhappiness and, indeed, live a happier life and achieve spiritual gain. Those who complete this rundown find they really are on the way to happiness.

The Happiness Rundown can be done at different points on the Grade Chart. One *should* get it at some point on the Bridge, ideally before the Grades. It is available at Scientology churches and missions.

False Purpose Rundown

A being who has accumulated hidden destructive purposes contrary to his own survival will operate far below his potential. This rundown slashes straight to the root of false purposes and makes them vanish. These false purposes are what hold a person back and prevent his ability to regain spiritual freedom and progress up the Bridge. Once these harmful effects are eradicated, the basic goodness of the individual is restored.

This rundown can be done at almost any point on the Grade Chart, and is especially beneficial for those who experience difficulty in moving up the chart. It is even beneficial for a Clear stalled in moving up to OT, as nonsurvival postulates and considerations can stand independently of mental mass. Resolving these factors through False Purpose Rundown auditing can improve his power as a being. This rundown is available at all Scientology churches.

Expanded Dianetics

This specialized branch of Dianetics addresses the basic reasons why a person restrains himself. Included in Expanded Dianetics are more than nine separate rundowns and other auditing steps which, following a program uniquely tailored to the individual, can help him remove these barriers and regain his innate power. At its conclusion, intentions and abilities which had been submerged for lifetimes can be restored, and one can regain a truer sense of self. It is available at missions and churches.

Method One

Method One auditing can clear up all misunderstandings in every subject one has studied. The result of properly completed Method One is the recovery of one's education.

It can be done on a "co-audit" basis, where two people audit together, each auditing one another in turn, once they have been trained in the procedure. The auditing directs one to misunderstood words or symbols from prior educational studies that are interfering with the ability to understand and clears these words up fully. By resolving past confusions, this can also smooth the way for more rapid auditing gains. It is available at all churches and missions.

PTS Rundown

It frequently occurs in life that one comes into contact with a suppressive person—someone who acts to invalidate and make less of him. At this point one can become "PTS," a potential trouble source, due to the fact that this suppressive person is making one's life difficult. L. Ron Hubbard found that the suppression that affects one the worst actually stems from connections one has had to hostile personalities before this lifetime. The PTS Rundown was developed by Mr. Hubbard to free one from the long-term spiritual effects of such suppression. It is available at Scientology churches and missions.

Suppressed Person Rundown

This is a miraculous rundown that can result in a formerly antagonistic person coming forward to the preclear with unprompted, friendly communication. It is available at Scientology churches and missions. (For other services available which address PTS conditions, see Chapter 46.)

Interiorization Rundown

One of L. Ron Hubbard's most remarkable achievements was to prove that man is not his body and that he can exteriorize from his body. Once a preclear exteriorizes during processing, he may run into difficulties if auditing continues. Prior to Mr. Hubbard's research on the Interiorization Rundown, auditors had to cease auditing preclears when they went exterior in auditing. In many cases, although the person would exteriorize once or twice it was not a stable state and the person would have difficulty exteriorizing again. As preclears often exteriorize in lower grade auditing, without solving this problem, they may have difficulty making further progress up through Clear and OT. This remarkable rundown solves this problem and permits preclears to continue up the Bridge after going exterior in auditing and makes further exteriorization possible. Available at Scientology churches and missions.

————

Of the higher states attainable by moving up the Grade Chart, L. Ron Hubbard wrote:

"...the way is true and plainly marked and all one needs to do is to place his feet upon the first rung of the ladder, ascend to Clear and then walk upward to and far beyond the stars.

"It is quite impossible to overstate the importance of such news. Two thousand five hundred years ago a statement similar to this and almost impossible to attain brought civilization to three-quarters of Asia.

"Yet day by day, Clears enrolled on the OT levels are walking that ladder and have already begun to reach the stars."

————

From "Dianetics, Scientology and Beyond," the full text of which can be found at page 274.

CHAPTER 14

THE CLASSIFICATION CHART: AUDITOR TRAINING SERVICES

Life for the individual quite commonly is looked upon as a descent into an abyss. Scientology's symbol of the Bridge to Total Freedom crosses this abyss and illustrates the idea of traveling from unknowingness to revelation. Remarkably, this Bridge is more than a mere symbol, however, for the Scientology Classification, Gradation and Awareness Chart shows how a person moves step by step to higher states. It contains the idea of the different states of existence and the entirely new idea that one can progress upward on it and improve his spiritual condition. To achieve maximum gain, one must travel up both sides of the Chart: the gradation or processing side on the right, and the classification or training side on the left.

Training is a vital necessity on the journey to true spiritual freedom. There are three reasons for training in Scientology: first, to be a professional auditor and to work at it in life; second, to be an auditor so that one can help one's friends and associates; and third, to help oneself achieve the greatest gains possible. There is no substitute for understanding, and an understanding of life comes from training.

Life can be a jungle. People get hurt, lives shatter. One may be continually surrounded with travail. To confront and resolve these factors requires not only attaining higher states of existence through auditing, but also achieving a complete understanding of what is happening around one and why. Without training, one can spend much of life in mystery about why things are the way they are. It has been said that a student spends less time getting trained than he would spend just wondering why life is the way it is.

Dianetics and Scientology offer the answers to life. Therefore to understand life—indeed, to be fully alive—one *must* get trained.

Even from the standpoint of a preclear receiving auditing, training has immense advantages. The untrained individual seldom knows why the auditor is asking what he asks. And even though he wins, he is in a position of still having much to learn about himself and others. These insights come through training. More than half of the spiritual gain to be had through Dianetics and Scientology can only be attained as a trained Scientologist.

As it is with auditing in Scientology, training follows a gradient series of steps up the Bridge. As one begins his ascent up the Classification Chart, he can achieve perfection in his ability to communicate and carry out his intended actions—skills far from commonplace in modern society. This prepares one for the study of the Academy Levels, where he learns how to handle virtually every aspect of life, the environment and the sufferings of those about him with the processes of the Scientology Grades. One then studies the procedures of New Era Dianetics, enabling him to bring his fellows to even higher states of existence—including the state of Clear. Moving on to advanced auditor training on the Saint Hill Special Briefing Course, he gains a mastery of the fundamentals of auditing, the philosophic basis of all aspects of Scientology and the secrets of life revealed therein. Then, as a Class VIII, he attains effortless competence as an auditor and learns how to apply the technology 100 percent standardly, 100 percent of the time. It is a level of proficiency without comparison in modern culture.

Scientology courses contain the books and other materials written by Mr. Hubbard, his tape-recorded lectures and Technical Training Films necessary to impart a complete understanding of theory and technique, accompanied by intensive drilling so that the student becomes fully competent in application.

There is no part of the mind, spirit and life Scientology training does *not* address. Every spiritual ability necessary to survive at an entirely new level is addressed and restored by following the Classification Chart, completing a training service and moving on to the next.

Thus the Classification Chart represents that route that every Scientologist should follow to learn this technology and thus advance on the road to total freedom.

SERVICES OF THE CLASSIFICATION CHART

STUDY TECHNOLOGY

The emphasis in Scientology training is on application. Correct application requires a full understanding of the materials. Thus, knowing how to study is crucial, and therefore the first studies one undertakes concern the subject of *study* itself.

Student Hat

The basic components of the subject of study, when fully understood, give one the exact means and tools to study any subject and apply what he has learned. While the technology of study taught on this course is useful for any subject, it is crucial to attaining the spiritual benefits of Scientology. Available in all Scientology churches and missions, the Student Hat is a prerequisite for all major training services in Scientology.

Hubbard Method One Co-audit Course

In Method One Word Clearing, a person clears up every misunderstanding in every subject he has ever studied. The end result of a fully completed Method One is the recovery of one's education.

In Method One co-auditing two people audit together, each auditing the other in turn. The course first teaches one how to deliver this auditing, and then one applies these procedures by co-auditing with another Scientologist similarly trained. The auditing directs one to misunderstood words or symbols from prior studies that are interfering with the ability to understand. It clears up these words fully. The course has no prerequisites and is open to anyone.

THE FUNDAMENTAL SKILLS OF AUDITING

Hubbard Professional TR Course

On the Hubbard Professional TR (Training Routine) Course, you gain professional communication skills which, when applied in an auditing environment, help people rid themselves of their aberrations forever, and help them regain their native spiritual abilities. In auditing, communication is more fundamental than the technique or process used. It is because of the critical importance of communication in auditing that the Hubbard Professional TR Course is an ironclad prerequisite to every Scientologist's auditor training.

Prior to L. Ron Hubbard's researches into the subject of communication, no one had isolated the exact working components of communication, nor its relationship to one's efforts to help his fellow man. Yet, as you soon discover on the Hubbard Professional TR Course, all human endeavor—particularly auditing—depends utterly on a full knowledge and understanding of the real basics of communication. Only the auditor who knows and uses the Scientology discoveries in the field of communication can hope to succeed.

This service teaches the theory of these discoveries, first by dissecting communication into each of its components, then by thoroughly and clearly showing the *use* of these basic elements in one's life. Technical Training Films written, directed and narrated by L. Ron Hubbard bring about an even more profound understanding.

Further, as part of this service, you participate in very special auditing processes that provide firsthand insight into these basic laws of Scientology and life-changing results.

Scientology auditor training begins with the Hubbard Professional TR Course, the Hubbard Professional Upper Indoc TR Course and the Hubbard Professional Metering Course.

Once you have completed your theory section and auditing, you begin practical drilling of the training routines. Each TR develops a specific skill in a basic part of communication. As one's ability to *confront* (in this sense, meaning *to face another person comfortably without flinching or avoiding*) underlies all communication, the first drill, called the "be there" TR, teaches one to just *be there,* comfortably, and confront. This is accomplished even with distractions, since one cannot hope to communicate well if he is shy, nervous or unwilling to simply be there to communicate.

On subsequent drills, you learn how to deliver a communication so it is received and understood by another; to acknowledge another's communication in such a manner that the other person knows he has been heard and understood; to deliver a communication with clarity and detect when any misunderstanding has occurred; to capably elicit and acknowledge answers to your questions (an important skill in living

and a vital one in auditing); to effectively address anything others say—and maintain ARC with them—no matter what they might bring up.

These drills are executed in an exact sequence, each one building on the ones done earlier, each mastered before going on to the next. By doing the drills in this manner, you not only become aware of poor communication habits or patterns you may have previously developed, but learn to communicate effectively. With these skills, an auditor can competently direct a preclear in auditing sessions so he achieves the full spiritual benefit of auditing.

And, with these higher-level abilities mastered, you become far more able to perceive and more confidently deal with the world around you. The end result is an individual who, with his communication skills alone, can handle *any* social situation no matter how rough and can expertly and flawlessly guide a preclear through any situations that arise in an auditing session.

Hubbard Professional
Upper Indoc TR Course

The next basic skill needed by an auditor or, for that matter, any successful person, is the ability to get that which one intends, his intention, across and carried out in life. Integral to this is one's control over the things he encounters in everyday living and his ability to competently direct people and situations.

One is successful in life to the degree that he can start, change or stop the things and people within his environment. And in auditing, there is no more important factor than the auditor's ability to guide a preclear through a session with positive, helpful control.

This skill is learned on the Hubbard Professional Upper Indoc TR Course. *Indoc* is short for *indoctrination* (meaning "to teach") and Upper Indoc TRs, as they are called, are the series of TRs that follow Professional TRs in auditor training.

If one looks squarely at the subject, one sees that it is not possible to accomplish anything in life if one cannot exert control. How, for example, can one drive a car one cannot start, change and stop? Control is vital to any endeavor, including auditing. Skillful control makes for more positive application of auditing techniques and greater, surer spiritual gain for the preclear.

When you complete this course you can adroitly start, change and stop communication and direct other people. Your abilities in this area are thoroughly drilled until this proficiency is attained.

Control is a subject all auditors must master and, factually, is something everyone needs to know. The Professional Upper Indoc TR Course is where such expertise is attained.

Hubbard Professional
Metering Course

Another factor crucial to the workability of Dianetics and Scientology technology is an *operational* understanding of the E-Meter: how to *use* it to accurately detect and systematically handle the barriers that keep people from being happy and spiritually free.

The E-Meter gives man his first keen look into the heads and hearts of his fellows. It detects things that otherwise would have been hidden from man forever. Simply stated, without precision use of the E-Meter, bringing others to the highest spiritual states is impossible.

The fact is, the E-Meter requires considerable knowledge and skill to use it to its full potential. However, as the art of using an E-Meter does not depend upon a knowledge of electronics, but of mental image pictures, a Scientologist can quickly acquire *professional* metering skills within a matter of weeks.

Gaining such a grasp of the E-Meter and its use first entails an understanding of the theory of both how the E-Meter works and its purpose in a session. Through this study, the auditor can correlate the meter's reactions to what is happening in the mind of the preclear in front of him in a session.

The course, therefore, has two parts.

The first part consists of basic E-Meter theory, followed by practical drills—each designed to give a grasp of how the meter is used in auditing.

Having gained a thorough familiarity with the meter, you then move to advanced metering theory and its full use in auditing.

No matter your unfamiliarity with the E-Meter at the outset, you can gain a complete understanding of what it is, how it works and the spiritual benefit one can accomplish through its use. Upon completion of the service you will fully understand and expertly operate the E-Meter and inspire confidence in the preclear.

As is the case in TR courses and at every level of auditor training, L. Ron Hubbard's Technical Training Films are an integral part of flawless metering. These films exist to clarify each component of the E-Meter and to set a performance standard by which you can learn exactly how to operate the E-Meter and master its precise use in auditing.

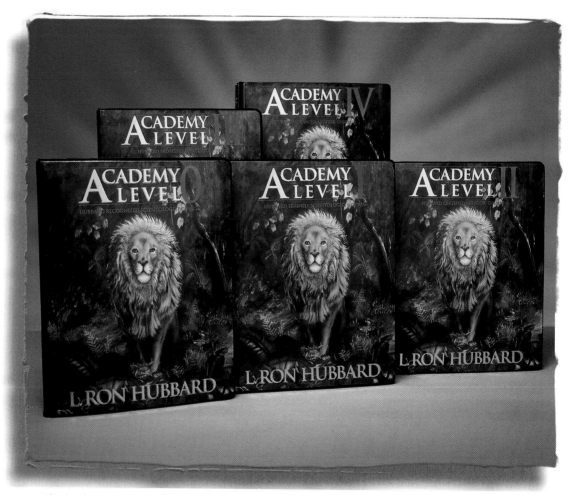

The Academy Levels—auditor training levels 0–IV.

ACADEMY AUDITOR TRAINING

What makes Scientology unique to earlier religions is that it contains a route to higher states of being that man can attain in just one lifetime.

That these higher states exist—and that one could be something far higher and better than that of "mortal man" in this lifetime—is perhaps difficult for some to grasp. Yet these states do exist, and through Scientology training and auditing one has the bridge to such levels—and to a future only dreamed of in the past. One's route to these states is made possible only by auditors skilled in the ministry of the Scientology Expanded Grades.

The Academy Levels are a series of five auditor classification services that parallel the Scientology Expanded Grades discussed in the preceding chapter. Each level contains the underlying principles and auditing processes of its corresponding grade. For those learning Scientology, the Academy is where the principles of Scientology—and what they achieve—become manifest. Each level consists of both theory study and practical application of a specific aspect of Scientology technology. A series of recorded lectures by Mr. Hubbard are an integral part of the theory study.

In short, each of these training levels contains answers to the spiritual barriers that hold people back from everything they set out to achieve in their lives. And because each level deals with a specific aspect of life and the way to improve that aspect, when you acquire the knowledge and skills of these levels you become much more causative in life overall.

Level 0—Class 0 Auditor
(Hubbard Recognized Scientologist)

The first state one achieves through Scientology Expanded Grades auditing is that of a being who is *in communication* in life. In developing the techniques of auditing to bring man to this state, L. Ron Hubbard wrote, "He who can truly communicate to others is a higher being who builds new worlds."

This Academy Level not only increases your ability to communicate, but teaches you the most basic actions of auditing, such as proper session form and how to use the E-Meter in specific auditing processes. Through your study of Mr. Hubbard's basic books and lectures you gain a full grasp of communication as a subject—what it is, what blocks it and how such barriers can ruin a person's life. In his practical training, the Level 0 Auditor learns each of the techniques of ARC Straightwire and Grade 0 (see Chapter 13). In so doing, you gain the skill to fully rehabilitate another's innate ability to communicate *freely* with anyone on any subject.

Level I—Class I Auditor
(Hubbard Trained Scientologist)

"The being who can recognize the actual source of problems and so see them vanish is too rare to be easily comprehended," L. Ron Hubbard wrote of the state of existence reached at Grade I. "Man *solves* problems. A being in a higher state looks at them and they vanish."

On this Academy Level, you discover the anatomy of problems: why people get them in the first place, what sticks an individual's attention to past troubles and worries, and what unfixes that attention so he can *be in present time* and, from there, create his own future. You discover how to handle confusions, increase efficiency and help others recover from illness and injury. And you develop a competence, certainty and ability to confront and handle life's problems—your own and others'.

Upon completion of this service you will be trained in the special auditing style, techniques and processes of Expanded Grade I and be fully capable of rehabilitating anyone's ability to recognize the *source* of their problems and make those problems vanish.

Level II—Class II Auditor
(Hubbard Certified Auditor)

It is an oft-proven fact that auditor training will help anyone become more himself and, in that respect, increase his personal well-being. This is profoundly the case on Academy Level II, which focuses on the full ramifications of harmful acts and how to undo the exact mechanism that drives an individual down to degraded states.

On this service, you become expert in processes that guide the preclear to *overt acts* (harmful acts or omissions) and *withholds* (those areas of his life he is restraining and withholding himself from), enabling him to be free of these restraints.

When man's level of awareness rises, he becomes more able to predict—and see the consequences to himself and others of evil actions. Academy Level II teaches how to raise another's awareness and rehabilitate his basic goodness.

The Level II-trained Auditor can expertly help anyone not only look at what is restraining him but act on it. You have the tools to end the hostilities and sufferings in anyone's life and to bring them to a state of existence marked by a return of their personal integrity, self-determinism, trustworthiness and honesty.

Level III—Class III Auditor
(Hubbard Professional Auditor)

Chained to the upsets of his past, man is unable to face the future. A Level III Auditor possesses the technology to free a preclear from deep-seated emotional turmoil that robs him of his ability to positively change conditions in life.

In Level III you discover the mechanisms behind personal upheavals and how to alleviate the harmful aftereffects. You learn to minister auditing services that achieve an *exact* result and become skilled in achieving that result in the smallest amount of time. Your practical training includes more advanced use of the E-Meter in session and more skilled auditing techniques that guide a preclear rapidly to areas that should be addressed, without a moment lost on wide excursions.

Upon completing this level you will have certainty of how to bring another freedom from the upsets of the past, a higher level of ARC in life and a greater ability to face the future and experience change without becoming upset.

Level IV—Class IV Auditor
(Hubbard Advanced Auditor)

This Academy Level gives you the skills needed to handle the *service facsimile:* that computation (a consideration that one must be consistently in a certain state in order to survive) generated by the preclear to make himself right and others wrong. It is this exact mechanism that traps a spiritual being and limits his ability.

By learning each of the Expanded Grade IV processes, you gain a full grasp of the technology of service facsimile handling and become fully capable of assisting another to face his life without the impulse to justify his actions, defend himself against others, make others wrong, or demand their sympathy. A Class IV Auditor is able to bring an individual to a level where his ability to accept and create new ideas is fully restored, and he can do new things and achieve his goals in life.

An Academy-trained Scientologist is someone with special knowledge in the handling of life. The better trained he is, the less mystery life holds for him. The emphasis of all Scientology training is on a flawless ability to *do* auditing, and a command of the theory and goals of Scientology. Thus, the Academy-trained Scientologist is able to *do* Scientology. You not only learn to help preclears by auditing them with excellent auditing results, but while helping others deal with their lives, you better handle your own.

NEW ERA DIANETICS AND GRADUATE AUDITOR TRAINING

Level V—Class V Auditor
(Hubbard New Era Dianetics Auditor)

Upon completing the Class IV Auditor level, your next step is the Hubbard New Era Dianetics Auditor Course, where you inherit the benefit of more than thirty years of Dianetics research to achieve in your preclears the dramatic results of well and happy human beings, many of whom will attain the state of Clear.

New Era Dianetics (NED) changes none of Mr. Hubbard's earlier theories or principles of Dianetics as he originally developed them. It is based on Mr. Hubbard's refinement of all previous Dianetics techniques dating back to 1948—and includes the milestone development of new and more precise procedure in 1978. NED consists of at least eighteen separate steps, including four rundowns, which address and resolve various areas of spiritual travail. The Relief Rundown, for example, relieves the losses an individual has suffered, such as the death of a loved one, after which the person's life may have changed for the worse. Others include the NED Drug Rundown, the Disability Rundown and the Identity Rundown. With these new techniques and the speed with which they bring results, New Era Dianetics as ministered by NED auditors makes widespread clearing possible for millions.

Level V Graduate— Class V Graduate Auditor
(Hubbard Class V Graduate Auditor)

This service puts the polish on all one's earlier auditing actions. It gives an auditor the advanced skills needed not only for

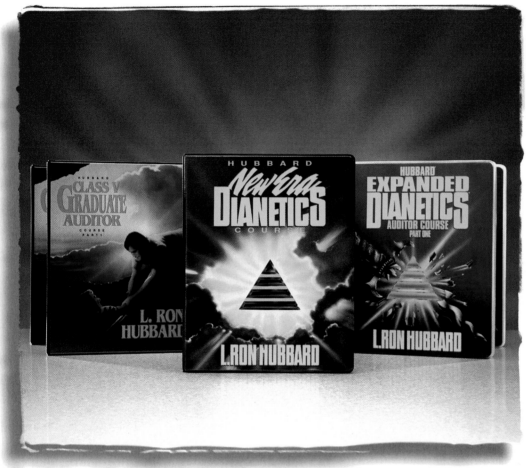

Above the level of Class IV, an auditor learns how to audit New Era Dianetics as a Class V Auditor. He can then develop advanced auditing skills on the Class V Graduate Auditor Course, followed by the specialized branch of Dianetics technology known as Expanded Dianetics, which enables him to become a Class VA Graduate Auditor.

perfect auditing, but the ability to repair any auditing difficulties that might arise. Here you become skilled in the technology needed to take any preclear to the doorway of Clear. This is the route for the individual who is not going on to the Saint Hill Special Briefing Course (Class VI) immediately after completing his NED (Class V) training.

Whether auditing in the field or in a mission or church, the Class V Graduate Auditor, once through this rigorously practical service, is equipped with all the tools necessary to keep his preclears progressing up the Bridge.

Familiarity with the full range of auditor tools and materials, dexterity with the E-Meter, positive direction of the preclear in session and the ability to perceive and instantly resolve any nonoptimum situation in an auditing session—these are the hallmarks of the Class V Graduate Auditor.

Level VA—Class VA Graduate Auditor
(Hubbard Expanded Dianetics Specialist)

At this level, the auditor learns the precise auditing skills needed to audit Expanded Dianetics, a specialized branch of Dianetics which addresses and handles those elements in a preclear's reactive mind that lie behind the aberrations that cause him to compulsively restrain himself. The Class VA Graduate Auditor Course is the highest level of training available in a Class V church. (See Chapter 13 for more on Expanded Dianetics.)

Those on the Saint Hill Special Briefing Course study all materials shown here, including 31 books, 29 Technical Training Films, 12,000 pages of technical volumes, more than 430 recorded lectures and 10 of L. Ron Hubbard's lectures on film.

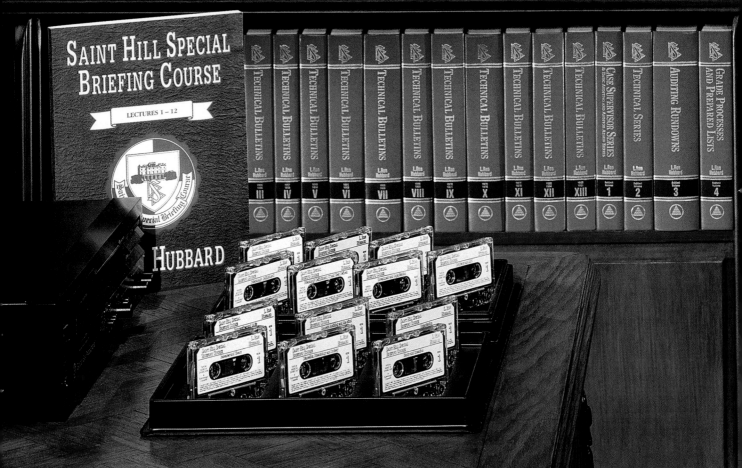

ADVANCED AUDITOR TRAINING

Level VI—Class VI Auditor
(Hubbard Senior Scientologist)

Those who have attained the state of Clear who are not Class V Auditors may enroll directly on the Briefing Course, the only prerequisite being that they have completed the Student Hat and Professional TRs and Metering Courses.

A full understanding of Scientology and, therefore, of life could only be arrived at in one way: by learning the consecutive, chronological series of Mr. Hubbard's breakthroughs, step by step, so you not only know *what* his discoveries are, but *why* they were arrived at and how they progressed. Once you see how these breakthroughs fit together, you can totally master the technology. Only on the Saint Hill Special Briefing Course can you achieve this.

With Scientology Academy training providing fundamental theory and techniques to handle the primary factors that complicate life and aberrate a being, the Saint Hill Special Briefing Course brings you to a superlative level of technical skill and competence.

The Saint Hill Special Briefing Course is the *most comprehensive* single auditor training service in Scientology. It contains the largest, broadest body of information on the subject of human behavior, the mind, life and spirituality that has ever been available. It exists to train superlative auditors. Its graduates are known as *The Dukes of the Auditor Elite.*

The course is named after Saint Hill Manor in England, Mr. Hubbard's residence during much of the 1960s, and where he personally ministered the services from March 1961 to December 1966. It covers an intense period of his research, leading to many important discoveries. Auditors came from all over the world to Saint Hill and were present when Mr. Hubbard developed the Bridge to Total Freedom and many of the procedures that today form a large part of any preclear's auditing.

The course was extremely popular and auditors who returned to their areas from Saint Hill were regarded with enormous respect. The desire by Scientologists to participate in the Briefing Course resulted in its establishment in other areas of the world in church organizations called "Saint Hills" as a tribute to the original home of the course. Due to the scope of the course and the facilities necessary to minister it, only these selected Scientology church organizations offer the Saint Hill Special Briefing Course.

Here, you study all of L. Ron Hubbard's books and technical bulletins and listen to recordings of his more than 430 Saint Hill lectures. The full service consists of sixteen individual checksheets, each a complete course of study in itself which may be done as a whole at one time or with intervals between the parts. Each requires an average of three to four weeks to complete.

Each checksheet covers a specific period of Dianetics and Scientology technology and gives you a full understanding of the theory and application of the materials of that period. In essence, you are gaining ever wider understandings of life and the handlings of man's aberrations.

On the final two parts of the course, you audit extensively and become expert in the application of Dianetics and Scientology technology. Special training aids helping you apply the materials are found only on the Saint Hill Special Briefing Course. And all of L. Ron Hubbard's Technical Training Films are seen on the course.

The vast panorama of understanding the human mind and the secrets of life are only attained by a sequential study of all the developments one by one as they occurred, a consecutive chain of breakthroughs, each one a milestone in man's understanding of man. These are the miracles available on the Saint Hill Special Briefing Course.

Several more levels of auditor training exist above the Saint Hill Special Briefing Course. Each of these auditor classifications teaches advanced auditing techniques and requires that the auditor be thoroughly trained on the lower classifications in order to apply them. As Mr. Hubbard's research reached into higher realms of awareness and ability, he codified auditing actions which would allow others to attain these levels.

Level VII—Class VII Auditor
(Hubbard Graduate Auditor)

The Class VII Auditor ministers Power Processes, which are everything the name implies. The procedures on this level are *extremely precise,* thus you are permitted to train on the Class VII Course at Saint Hills only after completing the Saint Hill Special Briefing Course and ministering flawless auditing on many, many preclears. Only when you attain this high level of professional skill, are you then authorized to study the Power Processes. One is then required to demonstrate a level of perfection in his skill with these processes before he may audit them on any preclear.

Level VII is not a prerequisite to further training levels. Rather, it is only for those staff auditors of Saint Hills, Advanced Orgs and the Flag Service Org who will be expected to audit Power Processes.

Level VIII—Class VIII Auditor
(Hubbard Specialist of Standard Tech)

The Class VIII Auditor Course is unique to all others in that it brings you to a standard of perfect understanding and application of the *basics* of auditing. Leading to Class VIII, in each training level the auditor learns different styles of auditing, processes, techniques and theory. On the Class VIII Course, an auditor (or case supervisor, as described under "Auditor Supervision" further in this chapter)

develops an *exact, unvarying* standard of application of every *fundamental* of auditing and the mind—all to achieve stellar results on *any* preclear.

At Class VIII, you must know and be able to apply all auditing skills instinctively and advance preclears to higher states of spiritual awareness and ability, no matter the level of auditing applied. And as there are no shortcuts to attaining this, the Class VIII service rigorously brings you to that level of flawless, invariable, precise skill.

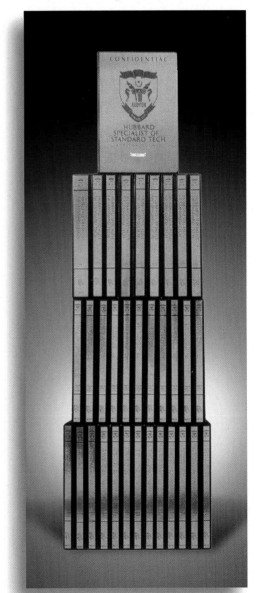

The Class VIII Course, one of the highest levels of auditor classification, stresses precision application of Scientology technology.

The highest standards of auditing are upheld until every auditing procedure is absolutely mastered. One must study the materials of the course three times, including nineteen original Class VIII Course lectures by Mr. Hubbard, in order to reach the understanding which underlies a Class VIII Auditor's effortless competence.

The basic fundamental learned on the Class VIII Course is this: That there are many ways to *incorrectly* do the processes of auditing. But there is only *one correct* way to do them, and that way is drilled in until it becomes *part* of one.

The power in the vast technical data of Scientology becomes concentrated into a relatively few essentials. In the hands of a Class VIII Auditor these essentials produce the high-velocity gains which result from perfect application.

Level IX–XII — Class IX–XII Auditor
(Hubbard Advanced Courses Specialist);
(Hubbard Class X–XII Auditor)

Class IX, X, XI and XII Auditor Courses are available to Sea Org members only. These are the most advanced and powerful levels of auditor skill. As such, these services are conducted only at the spiritual mecca of Scientology, the Flag Service Organization.

TECHNICAL SPECIALIST COURSES

Once you complete a major auditor training level at a Scientology church, special courses are available to broaden your technical skills and rapidly help you resolve particular problems a preclear may sometimes encounter. These special processes and rundowns are not contained in the normal course of auditing actions on the Bridge.

These courses comprise a body of studies which cover a panorama of specific rundowns and technical skills. (These techniques, in addition to the full philosophical theory underlying them, *are* included within the Saint Hill Special Briefing Course.)

Each Technical Specialist Course takes from two days to two weeks and requires no internship to enable you to rapidly acquire the skills you need. Each procedure learned will resolve an exact condition in the preclear, enabling him to continue his spiritual progress. These services are the most direct way for you to learn, for example, all the procedures necessary to repair victims of psychiatric invalidation and evaluation, to assist people to overcome specific fears and to help others rid themselves of false purposes.

These are all conditions that can slow a preclear's spiritual progress, but through Technical Specialist training, you become fully capable of helping any person resolve such barriers so that he may continue up the Bridge. See Chapter 46 for a complete listing of specialist courses.

The Technical Specialist Courses train an auditor on the specialized techniques to resolve a broad spectrum of mental and spiritual maladies. There are 19 separate courses, each covering a different subject.

PERFECTING SKILLS OF APPLICATION

Auditor Internships

"A course graduate becomes an auditor by auditing," L. Ron Hubbard once wrote. "That means LOTS of auditing."

After training on selected services, your auditor skills are developed and polished to top-caliber level through practical, on-the-job apprenticing under expert technical supervision. This is done through *internship* programs.

Newly trained auditors undergo a daily schedule of auditing a high number of hours on preclears, review of their sessions and correction of any errors, auditing, correcting, drilling, more auditing, correcting, auditing — each day gaining invaluable practical experience.

This intensive practical regimen brings to light any weakness in your ability to apply *all* materials studied in your training. Particular emphasis is given to these areas until the auditor becomes competent in them. Through this pattern of daily auditing, combined with inspection and any needed correction of errors, you will build up to an ability to flawlessly audit for many hours each day.

When an intern can routinely minister well-done auditing with a number of preclears, and polishes any rough edges so he can think with his materials without hesitation on what to do in an auditing session, he has completed his internship. Internships are rigorous and, through them, you will quickly become a top-flight, expert auditor — and invariably raise your competence in life.

AUDITOR SUPERVISION

Case Supervisor Training

Successful auditing is a team activity requiring the work of additional people besides the auditor and preclear. In order to ensure Scientology technology is ministered correctly in all cases, auditing is overseen by another technically trained person called the Case Supervisor (C/S). The Case Supervisor directs auditing actions for each individual preclear under his care. *Case* is a general term for a person being helped in auditing. The Case Supervisor's purpose is to see that the technology is ministered standardly for the greatest possible benefit of the preclear. Ultimately, it is the Case Supervisor who is responsible for the technical quality in his area. "A Case Supervisor," as L. Ron Hubbard succinctly described, "is specially trained to analyze cases and sessions."

The Case Supervisor is a highly trained and interned auditor who has completed additional training in the technology of supervising auditing. Not every auditor becomes a C/S, but every Case Supervisor is a highly skilled auditor.

The Case Supervisor reviews all auditing sessions ministered by auditors under his charge. A Case Supervisor goes over every session and tells the auditor what to do in the next one. Case Supervisors are the men and women who are behind the scenes of all good auditing that is done.

The C/S verifies that each auditor's sessions are standardly done and directs the auditor on what services to minister session by session, based on an overall program of auditing drawn up especially for each individual to ensure his maximum spiritual progress. He helps the auditor minister the technology correctly and, if some error in procedure is made, he sees that the auditor is corrected. The skill of an auditor is thus enormously improved by a good C/S.

The C/S, not being directly involved in the session, studies the technical report made by the auditor; this distance often furnishes a clear and valuable view of the preclear's overall progress. He is there *for the preclear* and is dedicated to getting the preclear through anything that may come up in his auditing. "Most pcs know the C/S is there," L. Ron Hubbard once wrote in an early bulletin to Case Supervisors. "This awareness is also a great trust and it is a trust that is earned by great results and is never betrayed."

Case Supervisor training consists of courses followed by internships of their own. In this way, you learn the technology of case supervision and then gain practical experience supervising the auditing of others. There are C/S courses following Class IV, Class V, Class V Graduate, Class VA Graduate, Class VI, Class VII, Class VIII, Class IX and Class XII.

The successful completion of a Scientology training course is validated with certification. When one has passed a thorough period of internship, he earns a gold seal signifying that his certificate is permanent.

AN AUDITOR'S VALUE

Auditor training services gradually make one more capable in life. Each course and internship builds on the preceding and makes an individual more and more confident and able.

Skills gained by training in the discipline of auditing are the superior skills of handling life. With them one can undo the pain, misery and failures of others and this has never been possible in history. The proficient auditor is valuable beyond compare to his fellows, to the world and to himself. An impulse to help resides in nearly everyone. Auditor training gives you the know-how to provide help of a higher order. An auditor is the only person in the world capable of actually undoing unhappiness in another. He is the only one who can help others restore their native spiritual powers. No better way to help exists, and no activity is more rewarding.

CHAPTER 15

RECOMMENDED COURSE OF PROGRESS

The amount of research L. Ron Hubbard conducted on man, the mind and life is astounding. He wrote millions of words and delivered many millions more in lectures. His own creed provides that wisdom is only worthwhile if it can be shared, and Mr. Hubbard spent years making his materials readily available for anyone with a desire to improve his life. Today, the Church of Scientology carries on that intention.

Why is there so much information? Dianetics and Scientology contain answers to the broadest field of all, the field of life. And the materials of Dianetics and Scientology are a precisely laid route to higher states of ability and awareness. Of greater importance than the sheer quantity and exactitude of material, however, is the fact that one can begin to apply the technology to one's own life and the lives of others as soon as he starts to learn it. One is not required to sequester himself away for twenty years on a mountaintop to see improvement. We are alive now. With L. Ron Hubbard's technology, we can improve now.

With the multitude of services available, the question naturally arises, "Which is the best way to travel up the Bridge?"

There are three general routes of progress up the Bridge. Each route has its advantages: (1) training as an auditor, (2) individual auditing as a preclear, and (3) a combination of individual auditing and auditor training, done concurrently. What follows is a discussion of each route with recommendations on how to make the most certain progress.

TRAINING AS AN AUDITOR

Decades of people moving up the Bridge to Total Freedom have recognized that training as an auditor is the most optimum way to progress in Scientology. The value of Scientology training cannot be overstated, since training provides the understanding of life necessary to live successfully. Before one will succeed in any game, he must learn its rules and develop the necessary skills. Without the rules, one upsets the other players. Without the skills, one can hardly play, much less win. Training in Scientology teaches one the rules and develops the needed skills, but here the game is life itself. With Scientology it is a game where everyone wins.

It is proven that a person who is technically trained in Scientology is much more able to handle work and personnel than an untrained individual. How can people handle life if they have no expert knowledge of how to go about it? Those who become trained as auditors in Scientology are not expected to only audit. That is a limited view of Scientology and its applications to life. While the skill of a trained auditor as applied to auditing someone is the most valuable skill of all, a trained Scientologist is also far more effective in the factories, the offices, the homes and the neighborhoods than someone who is not trained.

Training as a professional auditor has the further advantage of being the most economical route up the Bridge. As a trained auditor one can receive his own auditing by exchanging with another auditor, and in this fashion advance up the processing side of the Bridge. He is thus able to move up both sides of the Classification, Gradation and Awareness Chart at the same time and gain both an objective and subjective understanding of the technology.

As an auditor, one can do far more to improve people and conditions in life. Foremost amongst things an auditor can do is free another spiritually and there is nothing more valuable than that. Through auditing a person becomes spiritually free and only an auditor can make that happen.

The training side of the Classification, Gradation and Awareness Chart lays out the progression of courses necessary to become an auditor. This sequence usually begins with one or more introductory services, as described earlier, which lead up onto the training side of the Bridge. After completing one or more introductory services, the Student Hat course is a vital first major service.

Mr. Hubbard found that the single biggest pitfall in training was the inability to study properly. Mr. Hubbard remedied this with his discovery of the three barriers to learning and his subsequent development of a technology to overcome them. Since then, it has invariably been the case that the Scientologist who knows and applies Mr. Hubbard's study technology throughout his training speeds through his courses and becomes an accomplished auditor.

Another indispensable service is the Method One Word Clearing Co-audit Course. Method One is one of the nine methods of Word Clearing. A person can learn to audit this procedure and then co-audit it with another individual. Method

One Word Clearing is an auditing procedure in which the auditor and preclear search for and clear out of the way any basic word and meaning errors in the preclear's past. The value of this is appreciated when one realizes that with Method One Word Clearing, whole subjects and even entire educations that previously were not understood may be recovered. A person can fall permanently behind at points where he accumulated misunderstoods. Method One frees the person from these points and makes it possible for him to use his education.

Either the Student Hat or Method One Word Clearing may be done first, but both are necessary for successful and rapid study that will allow one to reap the full spiritual benefits of Scientology.

An individual with a history of drug use may find that the effects of drugs severely inhibit his studies. In some cases it is necessary that a student do the Purification program and the Drug Rundown before he can adequately progress up the Bridge. This requirement imposes no economic hardship, as the needed processes and actions may be co-audited at any church or mission.

The next subject to be learned if one is to progress on the Bridge are effective communication skills, which are taught on the Hubbard Professional TR Course and the Hubbard Professional Upper Indoc TR Course. Here, one masters the communication cycle, which is vitally important in auditing. He also masters the subject of control, which too is indispensable. Many difficulties in the application of auditing can be traced to a faulty understanding of TRs and how to use them.

Once a student has mastered study technology and the TRs, he is ready to learn how to use the E-Meter on the Hubbard Professional Metering Course. A fully trained Scientology auditor, at any given moment, knows precisely what is happening with regard to mental masses and charge in the preclear. On the Hubbard Professional Metering Course, the student auditor becomes deft at identifying the sources of trouble in another's life and monitoring the process that will eradicate the mental masses and charge that have accumulated in these areas. The difference between helping the preclear attain freedom from these hidden barriers in his reactive mind and not so helping falls squarely in the realm of meter training.

With mastery of E-Meter operation, the Scientologist then takes another major step in his training by learning the theory and techniques of Scientology Expanded Grades auditing. This material is covered in Academy Levels 0–IV, as described in previous chapters. The importance of applying the materials on any training course cannot be overstressed. One does drills to learn how to operate the E-Meter, drills to learn how to properly do each action associated with an auditing session, and drills on the techniques used in auditing. All this drilling leads up to an ability to apply the technology. It is essential then that one spends adequate time on drills and learns each one well.

After finishing the Academy Levels 0–IV, the auditor should now intern as a Class IV Auditor. An internship provides much needed experience as an auditor, polishes the skills learned in the Academy and develops certainty in oneself and one's abilities. Each higher classification attained should be followed by an internship for that class, so experience is gained at each level as one moves up.

Training in Scientology also should include the Saint Hill Special Briefing Course. This course contains all the materials of Dianetics and Scientology necessary for a full understanding of life. When studying the Saint Hill Special Briefing Course, one may also co-audit with another student on any process or action taught on the course, and the student is thus able to audit as he desires.

Complete mastery of auditing technology comes with training on the Class VIII Course. The Class VIII Course trains an auditor in the precise standard of application for any case.

By training as an auditor one moves up the entire Bridge in the most economical way possible, acquiring all the data and all the gains there are to be had. Many Scientologists have advanced far in Scientology by training as auditors. It is the most highly recommended way to progress.

INDIVIDUAL AUDITING

An alternate way to move up the Bridge is to receive individual auditing in the Hubbard Guidance Center of a church or mission. This is much faster than training as an auditor in terms of one's own personal progress up the auditing side of the Bridge. It is, however, not as economical because it requires special attention from several staff members to provide the individual service.

Auditing in the HGC enables one to receive service in intensive numbers of hours which makes for very rapid progress. There are minimal interruptions from the upsets of day-to-day life when auditing is done every day for several hours. A Scientologist soon rises above situations which would have dragged him down earlier. More gain is achieved per unit of time when auditing is done this way.

Before beginning auditing, it is wise to become fully familiar with a set of guidelines which, if followed, help ensure that the greatest gains are made in one's sessions. These are supplied by the person in the church who oversees the administration of all auditing, called the Director of Processing. (*Processing* is another word for auditing.) These guidelines cover such points as getting sufficient sleep the night before a session, eating properly and refraining from the use of drugs or alcohol for the duration of the auditing, except for medications administered under the care of a physician. The individual also should keep his personal life as ethical as possible, as problems in one's relationships with others may take up an inordinate amount of auditing time, time that could otherwise be spent on progress up the Bridge.

Any training a Scientologist receives before embarking on auditing will be to his advantage. Even a person who has read books on Dianetics and Scientology will be more conversant with what is taking place in his sessions. At some point, in order to make it all the way up the Bridge, auditor training will be required, so the more one knows about the technology early on, the better off he is.

It is important that enough auditing time be arranged at the outset to ensure that adequate progress can be attained. An estimate of how many hours will be required to reach a specified point on the Bridge can be ascertained by church technical staff before a preclear starts his auditing.

The specific auditing that a person does is determined by the Case Supervisor. Because everyone is different, it is impossible to state beforehand exactly how each preclear should progress. The basic route for all Scientologists, however, is laid out on the Classification, Gradation and Awareness Chart and includes, for any case, the Expanded Lower Grades; New Era Dianetics; clearing, either on New Era Dianetics or on the Clearing Course; and each OT level.

Many people who have experienced skilled auditing say it is the most valuable activity there is. Those who move up the Bridge through auditing will do so rapidly.

AUDITING AND TRAINING

A third route Scientologists use to progress up the Bridge is a combination of auditing in the Hubbard Guidance Center and auditor training in the Academy. When the Scientologist is not in session as a preclear, he is in a course room, studying to be an auditor. This combined route has the advantages of rapidity of progress up both sides of the Grade Chart. One's gains in auditing are augmented by the gains of training, making it an excellent way to progress for those who have the time to do both concurrently.

It should be noted that TRs are not undertaken simultaneously with auditing and so those who wish to study Academy Level training material while receiving auditing in the HGC should do their Professional TR Course and Professional Upper Indoc TR Course beforehand. Experience has taught that apart from teaching auditing skills, the TRs result in vast personal changes and gain as the individual's ability to confront and handle communication improves. For this reason, TR training should not be intermixed with auditing.

These are the three main ways Scientologists progress up the Bridge to Total Freedom. Regardless of the route one chooses, the adventure of Scientology is a journey of awakening and self-discovery unlike anything else in life.

RECOMMENDED COURSE OF PROGRESS

1

TRAINING AS AN AUDITOR

Most economical route up the Bridge

■ Teaches the most valuable skill of all — auditing

■ Provides the knowledge of life and increases the ability to handle it

■ Enables one to co-audit up the Bridge

2

INDIVIDUAL AUDITING

Fastest route up the Bridge

■ Intensive auditing makes further progress per hour of auditing

■ Full services of the Hubbard Guidance Center to ensure maximum gains

3

COMBINATION OF AUDITING & TRAINING

The route with the most gains

■ Enables progress up both sides of the Bridge

■ Person can study on course when not in session

■ Auditing gains are increased by gains in training

Dianetics, Scientology & Beyond
By L. Ron Hubbard

For thousands of years men have sought the state of complete spiritual freedom from the endless cycle of birth and death and have sought personal immortality containing full awareness, memory and ability as a spirit independent of the flesh.

The dream of this in Buddha's time was called "Bodhi," being the name of the tree under which he attained such a state.

But due to the unknown presence of the reactive mind and its effect upon the spirit as well as the body, such periods of freedom were difficult to attain and were, as we have found, temporary.

Further, few could attain even this temporary state and those who did acquired it at the cost of decades of self-denial and personal discipline.

In Scientology this state has been attained. It has been achieved not on a temporary basis, subject to relapse, but on a stable plane of full awareness and ability, unqualified by accident or deterioration. And not limited to a few.

By eradicating the reactive mind we not only achieve in the state of Clear an erasure of the seeming evil in man, who is basically good, we have overcome the barriers which made it so difficult to attain total spiritual independence and serenity.

We call this state "Operating Thetan." To **operate** something is to be able to handle it. **Thetan** is from the Greek letter "theta" the traditional philosopher's symbol (from the letter in the Greek alphabet "theta" θ) of thought, spirit or life. Thus it means a being who as a spirit alone can handle things.

The definition of the state of Operating Thetan is "Knowing and willing cause over Life, Thought, Matter, Energy, Space and Time."

As man is basically good, despite his evil reactions to his reactive mind, a being who is Clear becomes willing to trust himself with such abilities. And in any case none can have more power than they can control.

In Scientology a Clear can walk his way to Operating Thetan, not in the decades demanded even by a temporary state in past ages, but within months or at most a year or so. And when he attains the state he is no longer subject to sudden and inexplicable collapses as occurred 2,500 years ago. One is able to attain and retain the desirable condition.

Not the least of the qualities of OT is personal and knowing immortality and freedom from the cycle of birth and death.

The concept is rather vast for immediate grasp but chiefly because one has hoped and had his hope for this turned to despair and his despair turned to a total apathy concerning it too often down the ages to do more than extend a tremulous wonder.

But the way is true and plainly marked and all one needs to do is to place his feet upon the first rung of the ladder, ascend to Clear and then walk upward to and far beyond the stars.

It is quite impossible to overstate the importance of such news. 2,500 years ago a statement similar to this and almost impossible to attain brought civilization to three-quarters of Asia.

Yet day by day, Clears enrolled on the OT levels are walking that ladder and have already begun to reach the stars.

It is quite true. And quite attainable on the well marked road of modern Scientology.

PART FOUR

CHAPLAIN, MINISTERIAL, ETHICS AND JUSTICE SERVICES

While Scientology ministers perform many of the traditional ceremonies and services common to most religions, they also conduct services that are unique to Scientology. Scientology provides a clearly mapped pathway to full spiritual awareness, one which brings about an understanding of life. Yet on this planet life does contain distractions and problems that can divert one from this goal. One of the primary functions of a Scientology minister is to help one transcend these barriers. Armed with L. Ron Hubbard's technology, a Scientology minister is uniquely qualified to accomplish this purpose.

Even when progress in Scientology appears stalled or when difficulties arise, there are solutions which enable one to continue his spiritual advancement. Mr. Hubbard not only provided the technology which creates the path, but he also isolated reasons for any apparent failures in application and thoroughly codified methods to resolve these, making Scientology, as shown in Chapter 18, capable of correcting even itself. Scientology is a religion where, ultimately, everyone wins.

CHAPTER 16

CHAPLAIN AND MINISTERIAL SERVICES

Churches have always provided guidance and succor to their parishioners in times of need. In fact, beyond strictly spiritual concerns, churches traditionally have seen their mission as easing temporal suffering, helping where help is required and restoring dignity to men and women at pivotal points in their lives.

By longstanding tradition, Scientology ministers also have acted to ease suffering and provide counsel and succor to those in need, whether a member of their congregation or simply someone in the community who may need help. In fact, one cannot function as a Scientology minister without a genuine and overriding desire to help others, whether to ease current suffering or to help people advance up the Bridge. But unlike ministers and priests of other religions, Scientology ministers bring more than compassion and care to the needy—they bring a highly trained expertise in Scientology techniques that can resolve any problem at hand, no matter how insurmountable it may seem to the individual involved.

Ministerial services are important for any religion, but for individual Scientologists they take on special significance—it is by helping others that they help accomplish Scientology's goal of making this world a better place for everyone.

CHURCH CEREMONIES

Scientology ministers perform many of the same types of ceremonies and services that ministers and priests of other religions perform. Each Sunday, the church's Chaplain, or another minister, conducts a weekly service for members of the church, which is open to nonmembers as well. At this service, the minister will speak about some topic related to an important Scientology principle or practice and discuss how it can be applied in daily life. A typical Scientology sermon may address the idea that a person is a spiritual being, the eight dynamics, the Axioms of Scientology or perhaps the Creed of the Church. These weekly services do much to revitalize the religious commitment of Scientologists, but they also offer hope of a better life to the non-Scientologists who are always welcome to attend.

In addition, Scientology congregations celebrate weddings and christenings with their own formal ceremonies and mark the passing of their fellows with funeral rites. The Chaplain often conducts these ceremonies, although any ordained Scientology minister can also officiate. Scientologists find that Scientology services, which address the spirit in accordance with the religion's teachings, are uniquely suited to their needs and impart a special quality to these occasions.

A Scientology wedding ceremony

Scientology marriage counseling helps create an atmosphere of honesty and open communication between marital partners.

CHAPLAIN SERVICES

The Chaplain also ministers to Scientologists on a more personal level. Indeed, it is well known within the Scientology community that if there is some personal difficulty threatening one's progress up the Bridge and there seems nowhere to turn, the Chaplain is always available for counseling and guidance.

Such aid can take many forms.

For example, if a couple are experiencing marital discord and find that it is affecting their progress in auditing and training, they can turn to the Chaplain to help them work through their difficulties. Chaplains are trained in ministering Scientology marriage counseling, which is an exact technology for alleviating marital problems that addresses the root of all such difficulties: transgressions against the couple's previously agreed moral code which now inhibits their communication. Scientology marriage counseling not only restores communication, but also brings about a resurgence of the affinity and reality that go with it. Utilizing these techniques, Chaplains and other Scientology ministers have successfully salvaged thousands of marriages.

In addition to salvaging marriages, and as part of his larger effort to restore family unity, the Chaplain is often called upon to help the child. He can do so in many ways.

The young student suffering through his studies will find relief through the application of study technology. The child who cannot get along with his friends can quickly resolve the matter with communication skills learned on a course specifically designed for him.

The ill or injured child, and even infants, may be given assists — techniques developed by L. Ron Hubbard to alleviate the spiritual component of physical pain, shock and emotional trauma. Helpful to people of all ages, assists operate on the principle that one tends to withdraw mentally or spiritually from an injured area. Only by restoring communication with this area can one bring the spiritual element into healing, thereby greatly speeding the healing process. Assists are used to relieve stress and physical aches and pains, or to orient a confused or distraught individual to his present environment.

Possessing all these tools and more, the Chaplain is well equipped to counsel parents and help their children grow up happy, confident and able.

There are, of course, many problems in life capable of creating such difficulties that one's spiritual progress is hindered. These problems include, for example, a sudden dismissal from a job, an unexpected financial reversal, or the loss of a loved one. The Chaplain is there to help in all of these circumstances.

Regardless of whether the Scientologist is currently active on the Bridge or not, and regardless of his financial condition, the Chaplain is sure to help. By working closely with other local Scientologists or the Church's Free Scientology Center, or using his own auditing skills, the Chaplain will arrange for assists or other auditing to be ministered to one in need. Or the Chaplain may recommend a book by L. Ron Hubbard or a Life Improvement or extension course for more guidance. Sometimes merely the act of listening to, understanding and acknowledging someone who is troubled is sufficient to lift his spirits and start him on the road to recovery.

The Chaplain also acts as a "port of last call" for a Scientologist who may have encountered a problem while participating in religious services at his church. The Chaplain therefore is constantly alert for the rare occasion when an individual experiences some Scientology service that he is not happy with, invariably because it was not ministered correctly. In such instances the Chaplain either arranges for or himself provides auditing to the person. By applying the technology in strict accordance with the scripture, the Chaplain is able to save the individual and lead him back onto the path to spiritual freedom.

As discussed in more detail in Chapter 17 (Scientology Ethics and Judicial Matters), the Chaplain also helps Scientologists who are involved in a dispute, personal disagreement or misunderstanding by assisting them to resolve the problem through the application of Scientology religious principles in the Church's ecclesiastical justice procedures.

OTHER MINISTERIAL SERVICES

The Chaplain is just one of many other ministers on staff at local churches who also provide lifesaving services to Scientologists. For example, some ordained Scientology ministers are highly trained in the Scientology technology of confessionals. They hear confessionals from any parishioner who has committed some moral transgression and who wants to take responsibility for correcting his past conduct. They also are empowered to grant spiritual forgiveness to a Scientologist who honestly and fully partakes of the confessional. When forgiveness is granted, it always brings remarkable results—not only is the individual's desire for advancement on the Bridge renewed, but his life looks a whole lot brighter. True spiritual resurgence can thus be achieved.

Another minister on church staff who can play an important role in a Scientologist's spiritual life is the church's Ethics Officer. One of the main responsibilities of the Ethics Officer is to help parishioners resolve problems they encounter in their lives that are adversely affecting their progress up the Bridge. Trained Ethics Officers are able to help individuals sort out areas of their lives that may be spiritually distressing and preventing them from experiencing full gains in training or auditing. Ethics Officers also counsel Scientologists who are troubled by antisocial individuals whose intentions and actions are inimical to the parishioner's spiritual well-being. As described in the following chapter, L. Ron Hubbard discovered the basics of ethics and developed many tools that are used by Ethics Officers to help Scientologists lead happier, more ethical lives, and thus become more able to attain their spiritual goals.

A Scientology minister plays a role that is both traditional and uniquely nontraditional at the same time. That so much of his work is aimed at helping the infirm, the estranged and the saddened is traditional. What is not traditional, however, is that he can do more than offer them sympathy and compassion that is based upon common sense and faith. With the tools provided by L. Ron Hubbard, he can actually better their conditions.

CHAPTER 17

SCIENTOLOGY ETHICS AND JUDICIAL MATTERS

ecause it has long been acknowledged that spiritual progress and proper conduct are inextricably linked, all great religious philosophies contain some form of ethical, moral and/or judicial system. Most obviously, one finds the Ten Commandments aimed at outlawing those transgressions deemed most offensive to God and most injurious to the Jewish people. Similarly, the Buddhists developed the concept of Right Livelihood, while Christian notions of sin fill a thousand pages or more. But merely setting down rules has never appreciably led to improvement, and it was not until L. Ron Hubbard defined and codified the subject that there was any workable technology of ethics and justice for increased happiness, prosperity and survival.

When considering the ethics and justice of Scientology, there is another, equally relevant factor that must be taken into account: to a Scientologist, it is not enough to care only for one's own survival, to better his personal spiritual existence through Scientology, while leaving his fellows to their own devices. As Scientologists advance in their religion, they become increasingly aware of their environment and those around them, and their responsibility for the community and the world in general. The ethical and judicial systems of Scientology are therefore appropriately far more than a matter of personal concern; they are an integral part of the broader view of bettering conditions across all dynamics, of helping make a world free of the degradation, violence and suffering so common in modern culture.

ETHICS

The Scientology system of ethics is based wholly on reason. Whereas morals, Mr. Hubbard pointed out, are essentially laws of conduct laid down from accumulated experience out of ages past and thus may no longer be entirely relevant to survival, ethics consists wholly of rationality toward the highest level of survival for all dynamics. True, in the absence of anything else, a moral code can provide a general yardstick for optimum conduct, and ethical conduct always includes an adherence to society's moral codes. But over time, morals can become outmoded, burdensome, and so invite revolt. Thus, although moral codes are respected, it is the adherence to ethical standards that holds the channels of the Bridge firmly open, enabling Scientologists to progress smoothly and without distraction.

Ethics may be defined as the actions an individual takes on himself to ensure his continued survival across the dynamics. It is a personal thing. When one is ethical, it is something he does himself by his own choice.

The logic of Scientology ethics is inarguable and based upon two key concepts: *good* and *evil*. Like ethics and justice, *good* and *evil* have long been subject to opinion, confusion and obfuscation. But to appreciate what Scientology ethics is all about, it must be understood that *good* can be considered to be a constructive survival action. It is something that, to put it simply, is more beneficial than destructive across the dynamics. True, nothing is completely good, and to build anew often

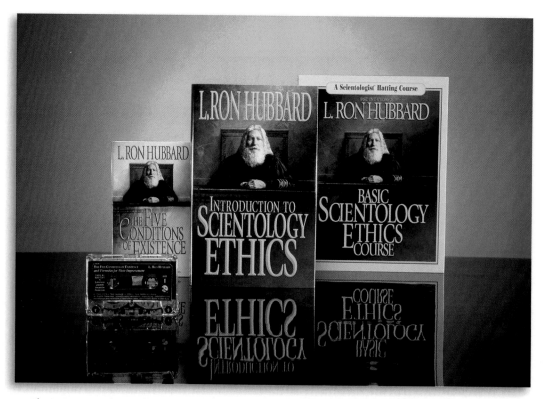

The Basic Scientology Ethics Course includes the **Introduction to Scientology Ethics** *book and the taped lecture by L. Ron Hubbard "The Five Conditions of Existence," to show one how to effectively apply Scientology ethics and justice technology.*

requires a degree of destruction. But if the *constructive* outweighs the *destructive*, i.e., if a greater number of dynamics are helped than harmed, then an action can be considered good. Thus, for example, a new cure which saves a hundred lives but kills only one is an acceptable cure.

Having thus defined what is good, evil then becomes the opposite of good, and constitutes anything which is destructive more than it is constructive along the dynamics. A thing which does more destruction than construction is evil from the viewpoint of the individual, the future race, group, species, life or physical universe matter that it destroys.

In summation, then, an act or conclusion is as *right* as it promotes survival across the dynamics and to be entirely right would be to survive to infinity. Conversely, an act or conclusion is *wrong* to the degree that it is nonsurvival across the dynamics, injuring more than it aids.

With a firm understanding of these definitions, the Scientologist is well equipped to rationally determine the course of his actions.

The logic behind maintaining high ethical standards is simple. Although modern conceptions of ethics have become hopelessly convoluted with common conflict of interest and gray areas of choice, it cannot be forgotten that greater survival for both individuals and groups comes through abiding by these agreements. Hence, the Scientologist is lawful with regards to his country, fair in his dealings with others and faithful in his relationships. He knows that because every individual is essentially good, he has an innately acute sense of what is ethical and what is not. Thus, when one violates one's personal sense of ethics, he soon loses self-respect and begins to deteriorate from that point forward.

CONDITIONS OF EXISTENCE

With the basic definitions of *ethics, good* and *evil* in place, and the basic *necessity* for ethical conduct established, Mr. Hubbard proceeded to develop a means of allowing one to gradually raise his ethics level and so increase survival in any area of his life. It is a system of betterment unlike any other, and contains nothing of the "Go-and-sin-no-more" approach that many find so difficult to follow. Rather, it is predicated on the idea that there are degrees of ethical conduct, that things may be surviving more or less well, but can still be greatly improved. Hence, Mr. Hubbard set out to delineate the various ethical states or *conditions* which constitute the degree of success or survival of something, and precisely how to better that condition of survival.

These conditions are not static states, but either improve or worsen, depending upon one's actions. Indeed, it is a fact that nothing remains exactly the same forever, for such a condition is foreign to life and the universe. Things grow or they lessen. They cannot apparently maintain the same equilibrium or stability. Everything in existence is in one condition or another. A person is in some condition personally, his job is in a condition, his marriage is in a condition and so on.

Mr. Hubbard isolated and described these states, then determined what it would actually take to move from any given condition to a higher one. In all, Mr. Hubbard delineates twelve separate conditions. They range from a state of complete confusion where an individual is in no position to produce any product to a condition of stable power wherein very little if anything can imperil his position. Along the way to power, he will pass through such other conditions as normal operation wherein he is gradually taking on more control, producing more and more, but has still not achieved permanent stability. As he continues to properly apply himself, he will eventually move into a condition of affluence—an abundance of those things which enhance his life. Or, failing to take proper steps, may sink into a state of emergency.

Like every fundamental truth in Scientology, the conditions encompass the whole of life. They represent descriptions of actual laws that apply to everything from the growth of trees to the running of an automobile to the raising of a child. Yet discovering these conditions of existence was not all Mr. Hubbard accomplished; he also discovered the exact actions or steps anyone under any circumstances can take to better any condition of existence.

Those steps to improving conditions are aptly called formulas. They are precisely laid out for each condition, and only by following the specific formula for the condition in which one finds oneself can an individual move on to the next higher condition.

To take a very common example, consider the subject of personal relationships between a man and a woman. Obviously, when a couple first begins dating, however strong the attraction, they are not in the same condition as a married couple. Likewise, the marriage beset with strife owing to adultery is not surviving well—and is thus in a lower condition than the entirely harmonious marriage. Yet regardless of how poorly a marriage may be surviving, how bitter the arguments, how seemingly unresolvable the strife, there are—always—steps one can do to better the condition of that marriage. And by continuing to apply those steps, ascending through successively better conditions, one can, with remarkable certainty, always improve that marriage.

The same conditions and their formulas can be used to better anything, from personal happiness to the performance of a high-school athletic team to the performance of a multinational corporation. If, to take another example, an employee suddenly finds himself demoted to a lower position in his company, there are precise ways and means by which he can climb back up the corporate ladder. Similarly, if the employee suddenly finds himself promoted to a higher position with a substantial pay increase, a precise application of the Scientology ethics conditions will keep him from falling into the trap of suddenly spending more than he makes or assuming that he is now forever blessed in the eyes of his boss.

The important point to recognize here is that the Scientology conditions formulas are not arbitrary. Yes, they serve to raise a Scientologist's ethics level and so speed his progress on the Bridge. But they also can raise the ethics level, and thus the survival, of anyone in any circumstance; for the conditions describe what governs all existence, and if followed, they *do* lead to improvement. Conversely, if these conditions are not followed, the individual, his career, his relationships or even his possessions will deteriorate to the next lower condition.

Scientologists use these conditions formulas to handle personal situations, family activities, successes and failures on the job and relationships with other people. The conditions formulas can be applied to *any* situation on *any* dynamic. They *are* the tools by which one makes changes in his life and the world around him.

Because the conditions formulas follow natural laws that embrace all life's endeavors, they naturally open the door to increased survival on any dynamic and in any course of action. Moreover, the conditions formulas are quickly learned, easily applied and can immediately set one on the road to happiness, success and well-being.

STATISTICS: THE MEASUREMENT OF SURVIVAL

As a further word on the Scientology ethics conditions, mention should be made of how Scientologists use statistical measurement to eliminate the guesswork of applying conditions formulas. Simply put, a statistic is a basic tool for the measurement of survival potential. A statistic is a number or amount compared to an earlier number or amount of the same thing. Statistics refer to the quantity of work done or the value of it and are the only sound measure of any production or any activity. Although one normally thinks of statistics in terms of, say, items sold or payment received, anything can be analyzed in terms of statistics— from gardening to golf. Moreover, only by monitoring statistics can one be certain that he is pinpointing the proper condition, whether bettering or worsening, and not relying on rumor or hearsay. Thus, with an understanding of how to compile, graph and compare statistics, the Scientologist is amply

equipped to determine exactly *what* condition an activity is in, and thus exactly what steps he must take in order to better that condition.

THE ANTISOCIAL PERSONALITY

Another key aspect of the Scientology ethics system is the recognition of the antisocial personality. Reflective in man's earliest ethical codes is an innate sense that there are those among us—about 2 1/2 percent of the population—who possess characteristics and mental attitudes that cause them to violently oppose any betterment activity or group. Within this category, one finds the Adolf Hitlers and the Genghis Khans, the unrepentant murderers and the drug lords. Although most blatantly antisocial types may be easy to spot, if only from the bodies they leave in their wake, others are less obviously seen. Enterprises may seem to crumble for no apparent reason, marriages may mysteriously disintegrate and a thousand more ills may affect those associated with the antisocial personality. In fact, all told, 20 percent of the entire population suffers, in one form or another, from a connection with the antisocial personality. For that reason Mr. Hubbard offers very specific guidelines for their detection.

To ensure that these guidelines never perpetuate a witch hunt or an unjust condemnation, he also provides a precise description of the social personality—the category that embraces the great majority of mankind. Moreover, Mr. Hubbard continually stresses that, regardless of apparent traits, all men are basically good—even the most seemingly unrepentant.

The importance of detecting the antisocial personality becomes eminently clear when one considers his effect on the lives of those around him. It has been found that a person connected to an antisocial personality will suffer greatly decreased survival, impeding not only his progress in Dianetics and Scientology but in all aspects of his life. Then, too, as his conditions worsen, his ensuing troubles tend to spill over into the lives of others. Hence such a person is designated a "potential trouble source." With the standard application of materials found in Mr. Hubbard's *Introduction to Scientology Ethics,* however, the potential trouble sources can be swiftly helped. Factually, Scientologists use these materials every day to repair marriages, bring parents and children closer together and trade misery for health and happiness.

THE THIRD PARTY LAW

Another key tool that Scientologists regularly use to better their lives, remove barriers that may slow their progress on the Bridge and generally improve conditions is the Third Party Law. This law, defined for the first time by Mr. Hubbard, illuminates the underlying cause of all human conflict—whether in the home, the community or the nation. Precisely stated, the law is this:

"A THIRD PARTY MUST BE PRESENT AND UNKNOWN IN EVERY QUARREL FOR A CONFLICT TO EXIST.

"or

"FOR A QUARREL TO OCCUR, AN UNKNOWN THIRD PARTY MUST BE ACTIVE IN PRODUCING IT BETWEEN TWO POTENTIAL OPPONENTS.

"or

"WHILE IT IS COMMONLY BELIEVED TO TAKE TWO TO MAKE A FIGHT, A THIRD PARTY MUST EXIST AND MUST DEVELOP IT FOR ACTUAL CONFLICT TO OCCUR."

The jealous business associate who continually slanders one to a boss, the spiteful neighbor who slyly belittles a wife to a husband, the disgruntled ex-employee who bad-mouths a company to customers—all may constitute the hidden third parties in a conflict that is severely injurious to survival. And unless those third parties are detected, that hidden but very real third party can wreak considerable havoc in terms of worsening conditions on any number of dynamics. Thus, it is not uncommon to find the Third Party Law used in conjunction with the conditions formula steps to, say, salvage a marriage or friendship. As with the detection of the antisocial personality, however, Mr. Hubbard was careful to precisely delineate the application of this tool so that it is not unjustly used.

SCIENTOLOGY JUSTICE

For all the tools that a Scientologist possesses to better his conditions and raise his ethics level, it is occasionally necessary, for the protection of the many, that the group step in and take proper action when the individual fails to take such action himself— hence the Scientology justice system. The basic idea behind Scientology justice is as simple and rational as the underlying theory of Scientology ethics. Justice exists to protect decent people. It is necessary in any successful society. Without it the brute attacks the weak, the good and the productive. The concept and practice of justice as it exists in society today, however, is increasingly ineffective.

The justice system of society is bogged down in a morass of Latinized grammatical complexities and has become, sadly, a matter of which attorney can present the better argument. Right and wrong, guilt and innocence are relegated to bit players in the show. A lawyer defending a criminal on trial for armed robbery, for instance, is not interested in establishing guilt or innocence; he is looking for a loophole or technicality on which the case can be dismissed and his client set free—whether guilty or not. Few have the wealth necessary to even try to pursue justice through the courts and even if one prevails, attorney costs often make it a Pyrrhic victory. The due process of the court system is in a virtual gridlock of court filings.

Scientology has another system, one unlike any other. Jurisprudence exists within Scientology which is both rapid and fair, and Scientologists utilize this to protect the decent and the productive.

Scientology justice is administered in accordance with a precise set of easily understandable ecclesiastical codes clearly delineated, broadly published and well known by Scientologists. Justice actions are conducted entirely in accordance with these codes, and whether they have been violated or not; suspicion, opinion or caprice play no part. The codes protect the rights of any Scientologist in good standing with the Church.

The sole purpose of justice in Scientology is to establish the truth of a matter and determine guilt or innocence. With this established, proper restitution of wrongs can be made. Scientologists with disputes can use Scientology justice to settle matters amicably. Any Scientologist can avail himself of the justice system to resolve civil disputes, be they with another Scientologist or even a non-Scientologist. And because Scientology justice is fair, economical and occurs without delay, Scientologists find it of great value.

Any justice action in Scientology is expected to be concluded within a week of being convened, saving the parties involved the unnecessary stress of lengthy delays. Situations are resolved rapidly, the outcome resulting in the greatest good for the greatest number.

Church justice codes delineate four general classes of crimes and offenses: errors, misdemeanors, crimes and high crimes. These range from minor unintentional errors or omissions in applying Church policy or Scientology technology, to felonies and serious ecclesiastical offenses.

Justice proceedings are effected by bodies formally convened by duly authorized members of the Church with the sole purpose of carrying out one particular justice action. These temporary bodies consist of Church staff members or other Scientologists who otherwise carry on with their normal duties and activities, but who are given the responsibility of acting on behalf of the group in the matter before them. No attorneys are used and the entire business of a justice action in Scientology is to determine with accuracy the truth of the situation and to see that any wrong is rectified accordingly. There are no legal maneuverings or technicalities which obscure establishing rightness or wrongness, innocence or guilt. One is expected to present the truth, and knowing that the procedures are fair, this is almost exclusively what then happens. An accused has access to any reports against him and has the right to face and question his accusers.

Four main types of bodies constitute the Scientology system of justice.

A *Court of Ethics* is convened when known evidence exists of an offense committed against the justice codes by a person. A staff member is appointed as hearing officer and adjudicates the facts of the matter and makes a recommendation based on these. The convening authority may direct amends based on the findings commensurate with the offense.

A *Board of Investigation* has the duty to discover the cause of conflicts amongst Scientologists or poor performance in an area in the Church. A three- to five-member board is appointed to conduct an investigation. The board reports on its findings but recommends no disciplinary actions. It may recommend a Committee of Evidence be convened should it uncover serious offenses.

A *Chaplain's Court* exists where grievances may be heard and disputes brought to speedy and equitable resolution. The Chaplain hears all matters, or when requested and allowed by the Chaplain, a body of three people is selected mutually agreeable to both parties. Scientologists use this means of civil justice because it is faster and fairer than what they would receive from any court system. If two Scientologists cannot resolve, say, a personal financial matter, they can bring this before the Chaplain's Court and get it handled rapidly and fairly. The alternative would be to bring costly and time-consuming suit in the legal system.

A *Committee of Evidence* is convened to try more serious matters. This is a fact-finding body composed of between four and seven members. Its duty is to conduct an inquiry into known offenses, hear evidence from witnesses it calls, arrive at a finding and make a full report and recommendation to its convening authority for his action.

Punishment is not a factor in Scientology justice, since it has long been proven in society that punishment more often than not simply hardens the punished person into patterns of destructive behavior. Instead, those guilty of ecclesiastical offenses are instructed to make amends for any damage done by their actions, perform what amounts to community service on behalf of those wronged, and other such actions. In this wise, Scientology justice helps an individual apply ethics to himself and his activities and move up the conditions.

Scientology justice protects the group from the destructive actions of individuals as well. A person who refuses to act ethically and who commits crimes against the group in general may be brought before a justice action in an effort to straighten him out. Depending on the severity of his offenses, a Committee of Evidence may recommend suitable restitution and penalties, taking into consideration any mitigating circumstances. The most extreme penalty that can be leveled at a person is expulsion from the Church. This can occur when blatant actions intended to destroy Scientology or Scientologists are committed, or when the person has clearly proven that he is no longer in agreement with and is actively opposing the Church's goals. Such a person has demonstrated that he opposes what Scientology stands for. By publicly announcing the person's expulsion, Scientologists in good standing are alerted and can avoid being harmed by him until such time as his actions are more in accord with the group.

No further action is taken by the Church or its members as justice has been done by expelling the individual from the group. The exclusion from Scientology is the harshest judgment faced by any Scientologist for it effectively bars any further progress on the Bridge. Once expelled, the person must go his own way and sort out his life without further communication, assistance or guidance from the Church, which is extremely busy giving its help to those who honestly desire it. The expelled individual is no longer a part of Scientology and its benefits are not his to enjoy, including access to Scientology justice procedures, no matter what difficulties he encounters.

With any justice action, even expulsion from the Church, if the individual concerned does not feel justice has been done, he has avenues of recourse to determine the facts and correct matters, if needed. Because Scientology justice is predicated solely on establishing truth, the honest individual is secure in the knowledge that he will receive fair treatment.

The Scientology justice codes align with the mores and legal codes of the society. Acts considered criminal by society are considered criminal by the Church and Scientologists. Scientologists do not tolerate illegal activities of any sort. Experience has taught that those who seriously violate the laws of the land are incapable of maintaining the ethical standards required to accomplish spiritual advancement.

In summary, Scientology justice is a new system, one which serves the individual and the group equally well. Its procedures are valuable to Scientologists as they offer a system where disputes can be resolved, truth is made known and increased survival occurs.

The book *Introduction to Scientology Ethics* contains the full scope of Scientology ethics technology and the Scientology justice system in clearly defined terms.

ETHICS, JUSTICE AND MANKIND

Scientology ethics, explained L. Ron Hubbard, are reason. They provide the means by which men conduct themselves toward their long-term survival, the survival of their families, their groups, their planet and more. Implicit within the subject is the recognition that all things are, to one degree or another, interdependent upon all else and that only by constantly considering the survival of the many can the individual ensure his own survival.

With this thinking firmly in mind the Scientologist obeys the law, remains faithful to his spouse, truthful in his business dealings and otherwise conducts himself in accordance with honesty, integrity and decency.

Scientologists understand that rules and laws form the agreements by which a group, society or nation survives, and that high ethical standards, far from inhibiting the enjoyment of life, foster it.

Yet what of the rest of the world?

For want of a workable system of ethics and justice, whole civilizations have gone to ruin, whole forests have been laid to waste and whole sections of our cities have been reduced to racial battlegrounds. Simultaneously, we have witnessed the steady disintegration of the family, a general decay of sexual values, escalating drug abuse, theft, assault and on and on until it seems there is no hope at all — except this: The Scientologist must also live in this society, and he truly does possess the tools to make a difference.

CHAPTER 18

ANY REASONS FOR DIFFICULTIES AND THEIR CORRECTION

ccording to the personal accounts of Scientologists in Chapter 19, the gains to be had in Scientology are considerable, even miraculous. By far the largest percentage of people who take part in Scientology training or auditing achieve gains comparable to those. Occasional failures have, however, been reported. But, when Scientology appears to go wrong, there is invariably a specific error that has been made in the application of technology which, when remedied, enables it to then work and achieve the expected results. The fact is: *Scientology works 100 percent of the time when it is properly applied to a person who sincerely desires to improve his life.*

Such a statement is all the more remarkable when one considers that the general attitude of man toward help or improvement has considerably worsened under the relatively recent influences of psychiatry and psychology. For concurrent with the rise of these two fields came soaring violent crime rates, the creation and rapid proliferation of drug abuse, plummeting educational standards, a weakening of moral standards and a legion of social, economic and other ills. Such a correlation is not coincidental.

These problems of modern living have a direct connection to the massive injection of false psychiatric and psychological solutions into the culture. The steady decay of social institutions over the past century followed the ill-considered adoption of psychiatric dogma in the management of our schools, family affairs, child rearing, interpersonal relationships, the arts, criminal justice, politics and other areas.

Furthermore, psychiatric propagandizing against traditional moral values has clouded the concepts of right and wrong and produced generations of people who are confused about themselves, their marriages, their families, their communities and where they are going in life.

Dianetics and Scientology entered a world battered by half a century of this false mental technology and two paramount facts became clear. The abilities of many people to actually perceive, think and reach rational conclusions had noticeably lessened; and many had grown chronically cynical, disabused of the notion that spiritual improvement or real help was possible. Dianetics and Scientology, however, *do* produce positive results, spectacular even, if one honestly studies, understands and applies the data. There are methods to produce results even among those who have been victims of this general societal malaise.

The technology of Dianetics and Scientology has proven to be invariably correct. It is therefore of some value to not only examine why there have been occasional failures, but see exactly how misapplication — and not flaws in the existing technology — is the major contributing factor.

Most importantly, this chapter affords one the opportunity to see how and why certainty of application *is* attainable through standard Scientology training. The fact is, any student can bring about the miracle results of Scientology expressed in the next chapter — and experienced by Scientologists around the world every day — through precise application of the technology.

As misapplication can occur in the course of one's training or auditing, which could prevent the technology from being ministered exactly, the following is a description of these errors and how they are easily remedied:

ERRORS IN TRAINING

Wrong Purpose for Studying

Before even starting to study a subject, a person can make a fundamental mistake — trying to study it for some other reason than to really learn, understand and apply it.

Some of the wrong reasons for study include: to earn a certificate or degree, to gain status, to pass an examination, to impress someone or to obey the wishes of a parent or family member.

These reasons might result in a degree, but are no guarantee that a person will be able to *apply* the material he has studied.

If a person studies Dianetics or Scientology for the wrong reason, he will only hinder his chances for real improvement.

This could result in a failure to really understand the course and get the full gains possible.

One should train with the purpose of application in mind. Scientology training services are arranged so that they are easy to get through, step by step. Upon completion of the service, one knows the materials he has studied and can apply the data to all of his life.

Lack of Confidence or Certainty

Scientologists new to training, while eager to discover the principles and procedures that will free any man from his aberrations, nonetheless may quaver at the considerable skills and processes they seek to master through auditor training.

The assuring factor lies in L. Ron Hubbard's researches, through which he developed the handling for *any* situation that might surface in auditor training and in auditing sessions themselves.

It is the heritage of Scientology training that Mr. Hubbard both made his milestone discoveries available to aspiring auditors and established all training programs. Initially supervising these courses, he routinely instilled flawless certainty in every auditor so that the benefits of his discoveries could be reached by every preclear. He also developed the technology of course supervision, turning this "hat" over to trusted technical specialists who shoulder the responsibility for the quality training of all auditors in Scientology churches worldwide.

Over decades of Scientology training, drills developed by Mr. Hubbard have proved to be the cornerstone of any auditor's unshakable certainty of application. "The key to professionalism is DRILL," he wrote. "When one is flawless in drill, he looks professional and inspires confidence in the preclear."

In 1996, a major advance in guaranteeing total auditor certainty—and perfect auditing sessions—was accomplished through the development of "Golden Age of Tech" (technology) auditor training programs. These programs today make it possible for any Scientologist in a matter of weeks, to learn and drill to flawless perfection every element of an auditing session.

Every "Golden Age of Tech" drill is based on the exact technical theory and auditing techniques developed by L. Ron Hubbard. They follow an exact *gradient* of difficulty which, when fully and honestly done, result in perfect application of auditing procedure and uniformly miraculous results—both in students and their eventual preclears.

And not in years, but in a matter of *weeks*.

The Barriers to Study

In his extensive study of education and learning, L. Ron Hubbard discovered the actual barriers to study which can prevent a person from understanding a subject or from even *wanting* to study. These barriers can interfere with one's training in Scientology or even in life.

The barriers to study have been fully researched and described by Mr. Hubbard; there are services at Scientology churches and missions where one can learn what these barriers are and how to easily overcome them.

Past Study Failures

After failures studying prior to Scientology, a person can become so convinced that he cannot study that he won't even try to study again, or when attempting to study, runs into past failures and doesn't progress. There are various remedies available in Scientology to help one overcome such problems and regain the ability to learn quickly and competently.

Past Bad Study Experiences

Past approaches to education have not known the precise causes of study difficulties and, due to this, the methods for handling have not always been effective.

Some of the past attempts to correct poor study included:

■ Dunce caps on the students while they sat in the corner. This activity has never made any student brighter, but only succeeded in humiliating students, leaving them with less desire to learn.

■ Trick methods of studying and memory systems whereby the student is taught to parrot off facts as a substitute for actual understanding. While a student employing such techniques might look like he has learned something, these methods impart no real knowledge a person can *use*.

■ The use of drugs to quiet a student and make him less active—purportedly to enable him to concentrate and to lengthen attention span. In actual fact, this method makes a student dull and less able to learn for he is less in communication with his physical surroundings. Such drugs also have extremely damaging side effects, which have included instances of suicide.

■ Pain and duress to force a person into obedient study. Examples of this are rapping knuckles with a ruler, spankings and other threats of punishment if a student did not learn as the teacher demanded. Students "taught" in this method often dislike study and have great difficulty with it in future attempts. Pain and duress also stand as a confession from the teacher that he has failed in his job.

It has never been successful to override a person's own determinism to "make" them do something. Consulting someone's understanding and encouraging their sincere willingness and desire to learn has always succeeded. Teaching someone with the idea they are stupid and must be forced to learn destroys the individual's initiative.

In Scientology the actual causes for study difficulties have been isolated. L. Ron Hubbard's study technology can handle reasons why anyone would have trouble in study and even more importantly, once a person is taught the technology of study, he can actually prevent difficulties from occurring again.

Problems with Earlier Similar Subjects

When a person has developed misconceptions or misunderstandings in subjects studied earlier, it can hinder him in current studies. The later subject can seem complicated or incomprehensible due to confusions stirred up by unwitting association with the earlier subject.

A housewife who has trouble baking may not realize that her botched recipes stem from earlier confusions in her study of arithmetic in school.

An advertising agency copywriter whose clients are unhappy with his ads does not see that his confusions on grammar from high school are ruining his professional life.

A photographer who cannot take a good picture might not connect his difficulties with earlier studies and misconceptions of color harmony in a painting class.

This inability to grasp a current subject is the result of confusions from earlier subjects. The housewife could make better cakes if she understood that half a pint was eight ounces, not four ounces. The ad copywriter could be more successful if he saw that behind his stilted prose lay confusions in grammar. The photographer might take award-winning photos if he knew how to use colors for more pleasing arrangements.

There is a specific handling for such examples as the above—to find the *earlier* subject and clear up the misconceptions and misunderstandings in *it*. The student will then be able to learn the current subject.

This procedure is followed in Scientology training and failures due to confusions in earlier studies are resolved or prevented.

False Ideas or Information

In day-to-day living people often accept ideas without question if they appear to make sense. False ideas and information can come from newspapers, radio, TV or textbooks. They can even come from parents or friends. If a person has been given a lot of false information or concepts in an area, it is difficult to study and apply the subject as it just doesn't make sense.

The subject of religion, for instance, has been seriously muddied up by the mechanistic philosophies of the last century with their false ideas that man is an animal.

Fortunately, there is a very simple procedure developed by L. Ron Hubbard for handling this problem. It helps the person locate the false data he has acquired on a subject, and helps him strip it away, thereby freeing up his ability to think in the area where he was formerly confused.

Studying While Tired, Hungry or on Drugs

Trying to study and learn without being well rested and well fed is an error. It is very hard to understand the information being studied when one's attention is fixed on one's body. It is also a mistake to drink alcohol or to take any kind of drugs while attempting to study.

Taking drugs while studying would defeat the purpose of training, which is to increase a person's awareness and ability. Drugs, whether medical or street drugs or even alcohol, have the opposite effect and impair the senses, the intelligence and the ability to view things clearly. Many medical drugs cause serious side effects, such as hallucinations or mental disturbances. For this reason, taking drugs while doing a Scientology service is forbidden.

Even if a person is no longer taking drugs, if he has taken many drugs in the past, he may have trouble studying until the effects of the drugs have been eradicated.

Persons who have used drugs do the Purification program and the Drug Rundown—auditing that addresses and handles the damage caused by drugs, enabling them to think clearly once again.

Receiving Training While Connected to Someone Who Is Against Spiritual Betterment

Someone connected to a person who does not want to see him become better and more self-determined will not be able to obtain and keep his gains from Scientology training. There is a great amount of information available in Scientology which fully describes this phenomenon and explains how to deal with it.

Suppose a wife is unhappy being a housewife and wants a career of her own where she can use her abilities yet she is too timid to resolve the matter with her husband, who is violently opposed to the idea and believes a wife's place is in the home.

She begins Scientology training and starts to become stronger and more self-confident. The husband, viewing her progress as a threat to his own plans and comfort, tells his wife that he will divorce her and leave her with no support if she does not stop attending Scientology services. Or perhaps she comes home after an evening at the church, tells her husband how much she is learning and how great she feels, and he sourly states that he does not see any difference in her. This situation will cause a phenomenon whereby the person feels much better at first and is steadily improving but then loses her gains.

Training must not be continued over such a situation, as training under this kind of duress will not produce the intended results.

Fortunately, the exact technology to resolve this exists in Scientology and it can be handled quite rapidly. The wife would sit down with a trained Scientologist who would assist her in communicating with her husband. The situation would be resolved in such a way that her own spiritual betterment was not slowed, but also so that her husband's wishes were also respected and accommodated.

In some cases, the cause of this "up-and-down" phenomenon in a person's life cannot be immediately located in the person's environment. If this is the case, there is also special auditing available to help a person discover the real causes and thus become stable in life.

The technology to help people communicate with and deal with others in their environment who are antagonistic to their plans or desires for personal and spiritual betterment is available at Scientology churches and missions.

Schedules

Scientology training services are provided to an agreed-upon schedule adhered to by all Scientology students. Services start and end at an exact time. Each student has the responsibility to arrive on time and to follow his schedule. Students shuffling in at odd hours can distract those already training and contribute to a failure to really understand the material. The remedy is simple: By sticking to the schedule, a minimum of time is wasted and everyone can get on with their training.

Anyone having difficulty following the schedule should see his Course Supervisor for assistance.

Illness

It is an error for a person to continue studying on a Scientology course if he is physically ill. If one is not feeling well while on a Scientology service or is unable to attend because of illness, he should let the Course Supervisor know right away and see a doctor if necessary.

Materials

All Scientology training services have specified materials that the student needs to have on hand. A lack of needed materials obviously would prevent progress. Fortunately, churches make these materials easily available, and many are available in different languages.

As part of an ongoing program, and as Scientology expands into new territories, the Church makes materials available in many languages so parishioners around the world can advance their study of Scientology.

Ask Only the Supervisor, Not a Student

Those engaged in Scientology training services agree to follow a guide for students which includes simple, common-sense rules that experience has shown make training much easier.

Included in these guidelines is the basic rule that if the student doesn't know something or is confused about course data, he should ask a Supervisor and clear up his confusion before continuing. He should not ask another student as this can create progressively worsening misconceptions, since they don't necessarily know the answers. If he asks the Supervisor he will be referred to the correct answer contained in his training materials.

Distractions While Studying

Significant personal problems can weigh heavily on a student during his time on training and distract his attention from what he is trying to learn. The Course Supervisor can often be of assistance in such matters and should be consulted, though sometimes auditing is necessary to resolve the situation.

In Scientology training it is the right of all students to learn undistracted by unethical interpersonal relationships. The basic rule is, "Do not engage in any sexual activities (or involvements) that could impede or interrupt the processing or training of another Scientologist." When this is violated, one's own spiritual progress is actually impeded. The correct action is not to engage in such activities.

Dishonesty

Occasionally an individual completes a training service dishonestly by falsely signing off items on his checksheet he hasn't done or by pretending to have completed the service with full understanding of the material when he *hasn't* fully understood it.

Such a person is only cheating himself. This is easily handled by applying the study technology and owning up to any prior failures to do so. The student will then be able to successfully complete his training.

Scientology training takes place on a gradient with more basic services coming before more advanced ones. If prerequisites to a course are falsified, the student will not grasp the materials or skills covered on the service. Any inclination not to honestly walk each step of the Bridge resolves with the application of auditing and other procedures. In this way the full gains can be attained.

Not Following the Auditor's Code

Even for auditors in training, the Auditor's Code, the code of conduct that must be followed by all auditors, still applies. Not following the Code can lead to not getting results on one's preclears. If one feels he can't apply the Code, he should get help from the Supervisor.

Supervisor's Permission

A Scientologist should not receive processing from or give processing to anyone under any circumstances without the direct permission of the Director of Training and the Case Supervisor. The exception is if an emergency assist is needed due to injury or illness.

Scientology was not designed to be mixed with other mental or spiritual practices; if a person is involved with any, he should simply inform the Director of Training who will either authorize him to go ahead with what he wishes to do or help him remedy the situation he is trying to handle.

It is also an error to audit anyone who:

1. Expects to be cured of any terminal illness.
2. Has an extensive institutional or psychiatric history which includes heavy drugs, shocks of various kinds and/or so-called psychiatric brain operations. By "institutional history" is meant having been knowingly or unknowingly given such treatment in a public or private institution for the insane, a psychiatric ward in a hospital, a psychiatrist's, psychologist's or other mental practitioner's clinic or office or a mental health center. It is not that such individuals cannot, in many instances, be helped. But they require many more hours of auditing than someone who has not been so harmed and often, too, due to the damage received in such "treatment" are so unstable as to require more attention and facilities than the church could possibly provide. Therefore, in order to do the greatest good for the greatest number, it is more survival to use Scientology to bring about improved conditions in the individuals in society who are already capable and who would progress fastest. These people, made even more capable, will increase their spheres of influence. The society will then support constructive reform measures such as eliminating the unworkable and even debilitating practices of psychiatry and psychology. Those who do have institutional or psychiatric history are, however, allowed to engage in Scientology training services, unless otherwise found to be unqualified.
3. Members of organizations who by their conduct show themselves to be hostile to the best interests of mankind. This category would include also those who have publicly attacked Scientology in the media.

It has been found that all such attacks on Scientology were instigated by those who either knew full well that their allegations were false or had no information on the subject in the first place. Such persons constitute a minor percentage of the population and work against any group or activity that strives to better others, for they perceive improvement as a threat to their power.

ERRORS IN AUDITING

Just as there are guidelines for training, there also are guidelines which the preclear should follow to get the most out of auditing. Some of the errors that a student can make in training also are applicable to preclears. The most common errors made by preclears and how these can be easily remedied are as follows:

Not Getting Sufficient Food or Sleep

Just as being well fed and well rested are requirements for training, so they are for auditing. Not getting enough sleep while auditing can slow one's progress and keep one's attention on the body. The preclear should get seven or eight hours of sleep a night (or more if he needs it) to ensure he is well rested.

Snacking on soft drinks and chips instead of nutritious meals with plenty of vegetables and protein is also a mistake. If the preclear feels run-down or has attention on his body, he will have less attention to give to the processes in session. To get the most gains, one's concentration has to be on the process.

Misunderstood Words

As mentioned in a previous chapter, one of the barriers to study is a phenomenon that occurs when words one reads or hears are not fully understood. This applies in processing as well. If a person who is being audited does not really understand what the auditor is saying or asking, he might well be trying to do something totally different from what the auditor and the process intend. He might experience a lack of gains, become puzzled, and possibly would not want to continue with any further auditing.

To prevent this situation from occurring, a person about to begin auditing is given a thorough understanding of the basic terms and concepts that will be used. The exact procedures to be followed are reviewed until the person feels confident that he understands them. If later during the auditing some question or uncertainty arises, the parishioner should tell his auditor immediately. The auditor will help him clear up any misunderstood words and answer any questions.

Having Attention on Something Else

Sometimes a person tries to receive auditing while his attention is on something else.

Perhaps he knows that the money he put in the parking meter will run out in half an hour, or he knows that if he has not completed his session at a certain time, no one is going to pick up his children from the baby sitter.

Situations like this must be handled *before* the auditing begins. The preclear simply works to find a solution, such as parking in another spot or asking someone else to pick up the children.

Not Following Instructions

An auditor knows what he is doing and in working with people his goal is to *free* the individual, not suppress him. No matter if it seems difficult at times to do as he says, it will be to the preclear's advantage to do so. Following instructions to the best of one's ability is the keystone of fast progress. The auditor will be the most understanding person the preclear knows; cooperation with him will save many hours.

Not Staying in Communication with the Auditor

The preclear should remain in communication with his auditor. If he feels an unusual or new sensation, he should inform the auditor; he can help to the degree that communication with him is maintained. If the auditor does something that the preclear doesn't like, the preclear should inform the auditor immediately. The communication should not be kept to oneself or saved for the neighbors. Failure to maintain good communication can stop auditing progress entirely. If the preclear feels something is wrong, he should say so. Auditors are usually perceptive but few are psychic.

To receive help as a preclear, a person has to be honest with his auditor. If he doesn't tell his auditor what is really going on — even things he's done that he is ashamed of or for which he thinks he'll be thought less of — he will simply block his own progress up the Bridge. A preclear should also take responsibility for his own case. As he consciously works toward his own improvement he will enhance his progress. He should follow instructions, but help the auditor by remaining in communication with him and by telling him whenever he feels there is something he would like to talk about or work on.

Not Understanding the Auditor's Code

The Auditor's Code (see Chapter 40) is the governing set of rules for the general activity of auditing. The preclear should understand that the auditor is guided in his conduct as an auditor by the Auditor's Code. One point of the Code states that he is not allowed to sympathize with the preclear, but instead must be effective in helping the preclear. He also is trained not to evaluate for a preclear or to tell him what to think about his case in session.

Confusions about the E-Meter

The E-Meter is a very accurate instrument and the full gains in auditing are impossible without its use. Confusions about what the E-Meter does or how it works can interfere with auditing. The meter does not diagnose or cure anything. Its value is in helping the auditor locate areas of spiritual travail and charge in the preclear's reactive mind, and in this capacity it is invaluable.

At the beginning of auditing the preclear is shown how to hold the meter electrodes, and has the meter's use in auditing explained to him. The meter electrodes and other conditions need to be adjusted to fit the preclear for comfort or else false readings can be obtained which can mislead the auditor in session. For instance, if the preclear's hands are excessively dry and calloused, a hand cream may need to be applied in order to ensure proper skin contact. Such things as an uncomfortably cool auditing room or wearing shoes that are too tight can also affect the operation of the meter. The auditor is trained to check for and handle this kind of thing before session.

Self-Auditing

Sometimes a person engages in what is called "self-auditing," which consists of applying processes on oneself. It is out-of-session wondering and chewing on one's reactive mind. This is an error, as the person himself does *not* know how to resolve the problem. Most people have been trying to figure out what is wrong with themselves all their lives without success, so the self-auditing approach does not work.

Auditing is a team activity, with the auditor and the preclear working together. The auditor gives the auditing command, the

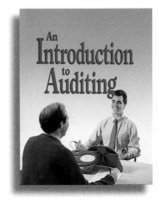

This booklet is provided to all persons newly beginning auditing. It lays out guidelines to follow in order to get maximum gain from one's auditing.

preclear looks to his reactive mind, gets the answer to the question, tells the auditor, and then the auditor acknowledges the answer. In this way the preclear and auditor work together to handle the preclear's reactive mind.

(Self-auditing is not to be confused with Self Analysis auditing. Self Analysis auditing uses the exact commands in the book *Self Analysis* by L. Ron Hubbard and actually amounts to being audited by the author. Neither is it the same thing as Solo auditing, which is a precise technology developed by Mr. Hubbard to enable one to attain various of the OT levels.)

Discussing One's Case

Case has an exact technical definition in Scientology. It means the entire accumulation of upsets, pain, failures, etc., residing in the preclear's reactive mind. This is what is handled with auditing.

Discussing one's case with anyone else besides an auditor in session is forbidden as this can cause problems in session. If a preclear has done this he should let his auditor or Case Supervisor know. The Case Supervisor is the staff member who directs the auditor and guides him in what auditing actions are needed for each individual preclear under his care.

Anyone who wishes to say something about his case before going into session or in between sessions should see his church's staff Examiner. The preclear can tell the Examiner anything he wishes the Case Supervisor to know, and the Examiner will ensure the Case Supervisor receives the communication.

Actions Unknown to Case Supervisor

Sometimes people get into situations where they are being audited by an auditor, and at the same time are given other Scientology services by someone else, such as another auditor or staff member or maybe even a friend or family member. This should be avoided, as such other actions, unknown to the Case Supervisor, could foul up the person's case. If this situation arises, it should be immediately communicated, so the auditor can act accordingly.

Fooling Around with Processes

Another error consists of fooling around with nonstandard processes outside of session, without a meter; it is sometimes done by students, stirring up cases. Such activity is forbidden. Standard auditing is ministered only by a trained auditor using proper procedures developed by L. Ron Hubbard.

Taking Drugs or Medicine

Taking drugs while receiving processing is an error just as it is while receiving training, and for the same reasons. Drugs, whether medical or street drugs or even alcohol, should not be consumed at these times.

Illness

It is important if a person becomes ill or has an injury while receiving auditing, even if it is just a cold, to let his auditor know. It is a mistake to not mention an illness or injury, as this will only slow progress. One's auditor must be informed right away of any such illness or injury so that medical attention can be suggested if needed.

If one needs to receive an assist on an emergency basis, this is fine, but make sure that the person who gives the assist writes down what occurred in the session and records it in the auditing folder (the folder which holds all the records of auditing sessions and other vital data on a preclear's case). In this way the Case Supervisor will be fully informed of all actions taken.

Auditing While Connected to Someone Who Is Opposed to Spiritual Betterment

Just as with training, it occasionally happens that a person receiving auditing is associated with someone who does not care for the fact the person is trying to improve himself. For reasons of their own, a friend or family member sometimes feels threatened if anyone in their vicinity seeks to grow spiritually or become more able and they will express their displeasure in any number of ways. One being audited while connected to such people may have trouble keeping their gains from auditing. The stress they are subjected to between sessions from the antagonistic person can pose too much of a distraction to the auditing. If the preclear feels this is occurring he should make the situation known. He can then receive assistance from staff in the organization to resolve the source of the antagonism and restore enough harmony so that auditing may progress as expected.

Breaking Auditing Appointments

An auditor's time is very valuable. If an auditing appointment is made, it is a mistake not to keep it. If the preclear doesn't show up for session one too many times, he shouldn't be surprised to find that his auditor has been assigned to audit others. If a session absolutely has to be missed or one has to go out of town, he should be sure to let his auditor know with plenty of advance warning.

Not Getting Enough Auditing

Auditing should be provided and received intensively and in sufficient quantity to ensure a stable improvement.

Life tends to knock a person about somewhat, and can prevent one from making steady gains if too much time passes between individual sessions. Additionally, it can be predicted based on a person's current case state that it will take a certain amount of hours of auditing to achieve a specific result. The preclear should secure enough services so as to attain the end result he desires.

Denying One's Integrity

One of the most basic truths of Scientology is that something is not true if it is not true for the individual himself. No one but the individual himself can determine whether he has been spiritually bettered from auditing. If one claims to have benefited for specious reasons such as to be better thought of by one's friends or to have the status of having attained a higher level on the Bridge, this inevitably causes problems sooner or later. Each level of auditing builds on the earlier levels below it and if one skips through lower levels in a desire to get to a higher level, this higher level will not be achieved. This is corrected by going back and honestly completing the missed levels.

Getting Discouraged Easily

Do *not* be discouraged easily. Give auditing a fair chance to work. A preclear will often experience different emotions or attitudes during auditing services, and discouragement can be one of them.

The only way out is the way through. Sometimes a preclear has to have the courage to persist through a difficult spot in auditing to emerge with the full gains that can be had.

But *do* persist. If the auditor and the preclear work together as a team, results will occur every time. Man has spent countless years sinking into his present state. Auditing will not handle every problem a person might have in a day or a week. But the technology is available to greatly increase a person's ability and to restore his health, self-confidence and happiness. Man *can* pull himself up.

Scientology does not claim to be a perfect system. It is a *workable* system, and does produce definite, predictable and positive results, far in excess of any other practice.

It is the responsibility of the individual to practice Scientology exactly as provided in Scientology scripture, just as it is the auditor's and Course Supervisor's. When applied exactly as written, Scientology services will give 100 percent success.

REMEDYING CASE DIFFICULTIES

Scientology's workability is enhanced by the unique aspect of being able to correct itself. Problems that arise or errors made can be rectified through a corrective technology L. Ron Hubbard developed.

Over the course of more than twenty years' research, Mr. Hubbard devised auditing techniques to remedy any error that can occur during the course of an auditing session. These techniques locate and resolve all errors. The result is a standard corrective technology that keeps the bumps on the road as incidental as can be expected when one is handling something as tumultuous as life.

Everybody is different. In moving up the Classification, Gradation and Awareness Chart, aspects of a person's life may need to be addressed that are not a part of the general auditing as shown on the Chart. Case conditions can exist which, while not requiring attention in the majority of people, nevertheless could stall the progress of some.

L. Ron Hubbard's intention was to provide a technology that brought freedom to *all*, not just to many or to most. To this end, he was constantly alert to phenomena arising in people's progress which indicated conditions that might require special auditing in order to completely resolve them.

As a result, Mr. Hubbard developed a number of auxiliary auditing actions to make one's progress up the Bridge smoother. Some of these help a person sort out a specific problem he may be having in his life, such as problems with his marriage. Others address past therapies the person had which created adverse effects. Difficulties one encountered in previous training might be the subject of another auditing action that concentrates on that area.

Life can present any number of situations that stall a person's spiritual progress. Sometimes these can knock the person off the Bridge entirely, but L. Ron Hubbard devised help even for that. People who have stumbled on the Bridge have been helped back on it, often at an improved rate of advance.

L. Ron Hubbard developed this corrective technology in order to minimize failures and errors. This is the reason why one finds so many successes in Scientology. Scientology truly is the only game where everyone can win.

Today, this is exactly what is being addressed by Golden Age of Tech programs in Scientology churches around the world. Any time a Scientologist does not achieve perfection with his application of Scientology technology in auditing or in life, the original intention to *help* — both himself and others — *appears* to have failed. But, applied in its purity, Scientology technology works 100 percent of the time. The answer to every Scientologist being able to achieve *perfect* application of Mr. Hubbard's technology can be experienced in any Scientology church today.

PART FIVE

THE EFFECTIVENESS OF SCIENTOLOGY

The experiences of millions over the course of several decades show Dianetics and Scientology to be the most effective and practical path to spiritual improvement of any religion this world has seen. The point cannot be stressed enough: Answers have been found to the problems of life. They exist in Scientology and people discover this fact for themselves every day.

At a time where many unworkable "solutions" are offered, disappointment can blind people to something which really does work. The effective results of Dianetics and Scientology, then, warrant some comment. The next chapter has been written by individual Scientologists for their statements are the best testament to its workability.

CHAPTER 19

SUCCESSES OF SCIENTOLOGY

I f one honestly avails himself of the technology and sincerely applies himself to gain the benefits offered, there are apparently no limits to what can be achieved.

This chapter is devoted to the stories of individual Scientologists and tells of the gains and results they have experienced. It is in these that the worth of Scientology finds its truest expression.

The opinions of experts or the pronouncements of authorities bear little importance. It is by each individual's reckoning whether or not he arrives at a better place.

People who have benefited come from all over the globe and from all walks of life. L. Ron Hubbard's technology knows no economic, ethnic, racial, political or religious barriers. Wisdom is for any man who chooses to reach for it.

Literally millions of stories are on file in churches and missions in all parts of the world. These are not the stories of the privileged or select. They are the successes of everyday people who were looking for answers and who were bright enough to know when the answers had been found.

The following should not be construed as claims made by the Church concerning personal benefits any individual will experience. The Church provides the services. The results speak for themselves.

In January of 1975 I was working on my first film in Durango, Mexico. There I met an actress who gave me the book **Dianetics**. During the five weeks we were filming she gave me some auditing sessions and applied some basic principles. That was when I became involved in Dianetics— because it worked.

When I returned to the United States I began Scientology training and auditing. My career immediately took off and I landed a leading role on the TV show "Welcome Back Kotter" and had a string of successful films. I have been a successful actor for more than twenty years and Scientology has played a major role in that success.

I have a wonderful child and a great marriage because I apply L. Ron Hubbard's technology to this area of my life.

As a Scientologist, I have the technology to handle life's problems and I have used this to help others in life as well.

I would say that Scientology put me into the big time.

John Travolta
Actor

The main thing that has really impressed me about Scientology is that there is the most brilliant tech for anything and everything in your life. I've become a more powerful individual with increased abilities. I never even conceived that I could experience these kinds of gains prior to Scientology.

There is a way to handle every part of life with Scientology, and a way to exist that is far beyond any dream that you could ever dream. All of my dreams keep becoming realities and that's very exciting!

Through Scientology, things happen a lot quicker. What used to take weeks or months sometimes happens in days or even minutes!

Life is at my fingertips and with Scientology I've found I can have or be whatever I want.

Kelly Preston
Actress

To tell you the honest-to-God truth: without Scientology, I would be dead. So, I can personally highly recommend it.

Kirstie Alley
Actress

Scientology is the gateway to eternity. It is the path to happiness and total spiritual freedom. Until one has experienced the technology of Scientology it's unlikely that one will ever experience these wonderful discoveries. I know because it has worked for me. The more time and effort I invest, the more I receive. I highly recommend it.

Isaac Hayes
Composer,
Musician & Actor

L Ron Hubbard researched Man and has carefully and precisely mapped a route out of the madness, misery and unwanted conditions one can encounter in life. When applied exactly, the technology produces incredible results. Those results are very definite and eternal.

Were it not for Scientology, I would either be completely insane or dead by now. I am forever grateful for the technology of Scientology and to Mr. Hubbard who dedicated his life to helping man and this planet, as well as to the people who have dedicated their lives to helping others through Scientology.

Lisa Marie Presley

I am no longer stuck in the bottomless pit of despair and apathy. Having achieved the state of Clear is the single most important thing that I've done for myself. It has allowed me to experience life in a way I only imagined.

Juliette Lewis
Actress

The single greatest thing that studying Scientology has done for me is that it's helped me become freer. Freer to create life as I want to, without being thrown off from my objectives. One of the first simple successes was that I learned to handle and remove my own self-imposed barriers and restraints. Through further study, my ability to handle life around me also increased. This freedom has been hard won, but the rewards are great.

My study of Scientology has also enabled me to write more music. I have become quicker and am able to use all of the musical abilities that I already have. I gained a new understanding of what the proper importances are in the process of creating music.

Scientology has helped me to live better. Using the basic principles of Scientology has become a natural way of life for me. From Scientology I've gotten a freedom to learn whatever I want to learn in life and I'm gaining new abilities all the time.

Chick Corea
Musician & Composer

I think the most essential thing for an artist, in order to develop and mature, is to get information that he or she can use in terms of communication skills and in terms of affinity and reality with people. The Tone Scale is invaluable wisdom for any artist. I think Scientology is essential. It's been the most practical tool for me to have. I love being a Scientologist. I'm proud to have parents and grandparents who are Scientologists. I love being an individual and expressing myself and Scientology has enabled me to do that.

Kate Ceberano
Singer, Songwriter
& Actress

In other philosophies, my questions would get answered to some degree, but then I would have a follow-up question and there would be no answer. The logic would dead-end. In Scientology you can find answers for anything you could ever think to ask. These are not pushed off on you as, "This is the answer, you have to believe in it." In Scientology you discover for yourself what is true for you.

No one is telling you. You gain your own knowledge of what is true for you. And so your ability to communicate, your ability to be certain about yourself and to know what your purposes, intentions and goals are, become much stronger. Scientology is about regaining total cause over your own life.

Jenna Elfman
Actress

I have always been a fairly happy person. From the time I was a boy I knew the difference between right and wrong. What I didn't understand was why others did not. I've seen so many people, some very close to me, do things so obviously contrary to life and happiness. When I began to study Scientology, these "unknowable" things suddenly became very simple to understand.

I now have a very broad understanding of people and of life. With that, I help people every day, help them answer questions for themselves.

People see that things are going well for me and usually want to know why I don't have the same problems others do. My answer is always the same, "Scientology."

Bodhi Elfman
Actor

Scientology makes people free, sane and able. It makes it possible to be more oneself, with the ability to create and change anything being a natural and expected phenomenon. It puts you at cause over your life and makes it easy for you to take responsibility not only for your own life, but for the world.

Scientology is sanity and if people who aren't in Scientology knew just how sane their lives could be, they would run to find out about it.

Anne Archer
Actress

I started in Scientology in 1977 and soon realized the data contained in Scientology would make a huge difference in my life. All the courses and auditing have been extraordinarily enlightening and valuable. My wife and I use Scientology to create a wonderful marriage. In fact, I'm sure there's not a day that I don't apply what I've learned in Scientology dozens (and probably hundreds) of times in a variety of ways.

Scientology is such a key part of my life today that it really constitutes an approach to living that is optimum for me as an individual, as a member of a family, as a member of the groups I belong to, and as a citizen of the world.

Scientology founder L. Ron Hubbard was a great man. We should all be thankful for the insights and knowledge he made available for all people.

Terry Jastrow
TV Producer & Director

Scientology has had a major impact upon both my personal life and my artistic life. It has contributed tremendously to the survival and expansion of both.

As an artist I have had difficulties that were very hard to confront—phenomena such as "stage fright" or "the blank page when writing that first line." The "solutions" to these and other problems, in the form of drugs and alcohol, had plagued me for a long time.

Scientology supplies a technology that assisted me in confronting and handling such situations very effectively. My ability to create impact as an artist has increased tremendously due to Scientology auditing and training.

Marital and familial relationships had long been an unstable area for me. Scientology handled this area of my life and has given me the ability to create a very sane and healthy family and the best possible environment in which to bring up my children.

Applying Scientology technology, for me, has been the smartest decision I could have possibly made toward the betterment of my life and the lives of those around me.

Mark Isham
Musician & Composer

Being involved in Dianetics and Scientology, I have become totally ethical about everything in my life. I think once you do that, things just fall in their own place.

My career has escalated tremendously. I seem to be doing one movie after the other. The quality of my life and the direction I am going to couldn't be more crystal clear.

Peter Medak
Director

I had been destroying myself for eight months with false information about the mind that a psychologist had given me, which had left me completely confused. There were many individuals in my life who told me that the mind could not really be understood. I saw others around me who were afraid of knowing anything about it. They acted as if it were a dark, dangerous cave that you didn't dare enter. This was completely false data. When I read the book **Dianetics** I realized the mind was comprehensible and it released tremendous pressure from my life.

This technology is a gift that has given me the ability to achieve what I have achieved. I owe much to L. Ron Hubbard and to this technology. It works. There are millions of people who need to know about it right now. They need answers.

Eduardo Palomo
Actor & Vocalist

For many years I was looking for a spiritual path and answers. After studying many other methods and philosophies I found Dianetics and Scientology. It was different than other things I had studied because it didn't make some other part of existence responsible for the state of one's life. In the works of L. Ron Hubbard, you find that you are responsible for and the total cause of your own life. In other words you are the one who has it in your hands to make the decisions that determine what direction your life will go. With Dianetics I have come to believe in myself and in the strength of my own decisions.

I would like people to know that this technology is simple. Anyone can apply it in life and see the changes. It works in any part of life where it is used.

Carina Ricco
Singer, Actress & Composer

There is a certain aspect of Scientology that helped me stay on my own path in creating life as a new game.

It is important to be able to handle the different considerations and viewpoints of those around you about your career and your life—about your dreams. These things become the subject of other people's opinions and intentions, both good and bad.

Scientology has given me certainty of myself. I have the ability to comfortably communicate with anyone in any situation and be certain of my own goals.

Giovanni Ribisi
Actor

Scientology has given me self-confidence. The first service I received in Scientology was introductory auditing. At the time, I was having problems with auditioning. I would get really nervous and blow it every time.

Through Scientology I got to the bottom of the spiritual difficulty which was holding that problem in place. I was cast as the star of what is now one of the prime-time series on television.

Catherine Bell
Actress

I sought out other solutions, I tried other philosophies and never found one that really indicated the truth to me. Scientology presented precepts to me that really made me feel like I had found, at last, the guidelines that I had been searching for.

Before Scientology I had one dream of making a living, doing voice-overs for animation. After I became a Scientologist my abilities expanded so far and above what I originally dreamed for myself that I've amazed even myself at my enormous increase of abilities.

I've won an Emmy, a platinum and a gold album. I've written and starred in a one-woman show and I have a bright future as a producer.

I've got two beautiful children, an incredibly supportive husband, a staff working with me for the same future dreams and goals, and all of this is because I became a Scientologist.

Nancy Cartwright
Actress, Writer & Producer

Scientology has enabled me to make my dreams come true, really. I know that it can do the same for anyone. It is a rocket ride to spiritual freedom. If life is a game, Scientology gives you the tools to play it with a stacked deck and win consistently.

Jason Beghe
Actor

I have been acting since age 4. I have always been working and I have always been in Scientology my entire life. (I was born into it.) Each service in Scientology is something I have added to my tool box of data for living.

The Purification Rundown lifted a cloud off my head and enabled me to think and see clearly.

Before I finished another level of Scientology auditing, I had a very hard time with being wrong and I always had to have my own way—and not in a good sense. After auditing, I was able to have my thoughts, communicate them and not have to be right all the time.

Then the Life Orientation Course defined even more clearly what I needed to do to stay on target with my goals and not waver into other things.

I have to say that one of the most important things Scientology has given me is the ability to keep my integrity together. I understand how people can get into unethical situations, and Scientology has always helped me keep my head clear and be in present time. I have been able to see situations for what they are.

Danny Masterson
Actor

Scientology has been my road out. There is nothing about my life that I feel apathetic or unhappy about. Scientology gives you hope and the certainty that you can improve any condition. This, to me, is priceless.

Leah Remini
Actress

S cientology auditing gives you the ability to be as great as you can be. And it takes the stops off the things that prevent you from succeeding.

Floyd Mutrux
Writer, Director
& Producer

T he wins that I've had with Scientology coincide directly with the rise in my career. It's hard to pick out any one specific piece of tech, suffice it to say that I as an artist was surrounded with nonsurvival considerations, actions and valences —all of my own making. Through my use of Scientology technology I have eradicated most of these things and continue to eradicate them, giving me more freedom and intention to create into the future. And, by the by, a great deal more altitude, a more inclusive point from which to view life—past, present and future.

I wish to acknowledge Ron's brilliant work, benevolence and stick-to-it-ness. He never gave up and I am thankful and happy to be a recipient of that knowledge.

Geoffrey Lewis
Actor

I live life and I have a great time. If something starts to get me down, I have the tools in Scientology to handle it. These are actual tools to handle life and make it better.

Michelle Stafford
Actress

I have been a working musician since I became a Scientologist and am fortunate to have played with many world-class songwriters. One minute I was buying their records or tickets to their shows and the next I was playing on their albums.

Many musicians are very technically skilled but they are missing a key ability—the ability to really communicate to an audience.

Communication is the basis of life and through Scientology I have learned how to communicate freely through my music.

K. Patrick Warren
Keyboardist

Scientology is simple. The better you know something the more capable you become. And when that something is yourself, things get better and the quality of life improves. Scientology has helped me realize the full range of my potential and ability as an artist and a person. I am more productive and better able to handle responsibility. At the same time I feel a greater sense of freedom and appreciation of life. I am a happier person in my marriage, my career and my associations with others.

Edgar Winter
Recording Artist

Scientology saved my life. I have always won at life, but never to my full potential. Since I've been in Scientology, I have a whole new career and I have a new life. And best of all, I have the knowledge to make it happen.

Before Scientology I succeeded a lot, but I also bombed out a lot. When I found Scientology I was not working much and I was personally very unhappy in life. I did not have the knowledge or the tech to get out of that condition or even that I was in a condition to get out of. Now I have the knowledge to create for myself the life I want.

Jennifer Aspen
Actress

Ever hear the advice "Just be yourself"? What if you don't know who that is? With the tools in Scientology, I finally answered that question for myself and I can promise you that I really do know exactly WHO I AM and what that means. Then there's the maxim "You're your own worst enemy." What if you don't want to be, but can't figure out how to accomplish that? Scientology showed me why that happens and how to replace the negative with ease. And what I love the most is that no one told me what to think or what to do, they just gave me the tools to answer the questions for myself.

Karen Nelson Bell
Producer, Director
& Musician

An aspect of Dianetics I really like is the auditing itself. It's amazing to feel light and feel the burden lifted. My hearing and my eyesight improved. I remember seeing a map on the wall in a room I was being audited in, and one day I looked at this map and saw every little letter clearly. I used to have to take a magnifying glass and look at those letters.

Michael Fairman
Actor

P rior to my knowledge of Scientology and the many tools and technology it makes available, I was extremely busy, going everywhere at a snail's pace. I was playing hide-and-seek with myself, a very frustrating game. But that game is over and the frustration that accompanied it is handled. Scientology allows me to have certainty about what I know. Personally and professionally, there's no more guessing about how to be. I calmly point and click. I know that I have hit the mark. Now I am free for the most important thing about me: creativity. What I want is a matter of choice—**my** choice. How I get it is a matter of "trust Scientology."

Haywood Nelson
Actor

I t would take more than a few words to tell how much Scientology has helped me during the past twenty-seven years. Life continues to improve to the extent that I continue using Scientology techniques. By now, I've achieved most of the life goals I've set at various points over the years and continue to reach for bigger ones. In recent years, after becoming a more highly trained counselor, I have been able to help others rid themselves of unwanted emotional burdens. This, in addition to being able to bring better art to people, is one of the greatest pleasures in life.

David Campbell
Composer & Arranger

My life is infinitely better since my first introduction to Scientology. Before Scientology, I was on an emotional "roller coaster." Anytime I'd win at something or gain a moment of happiness, if it was on a Tuesday, you could predict that by Wednesday I'd be down in the dumps again. This "up and down and up and down" was such a point of upset and hopelessness for me that I finally resigned myself to the fact that this was something I was going to have to live with for the rest of my life.

In 1988, as a result of Scientology auditing, this phenomenon ceased for all time. I was shocked. I couldn't believe it. I was no longer on the "helpless" receiving end of life. I am resilient, strong, more self-assured and most importantly, more able to handle what I encounter.

Physical aches and pains I'd associated with writing my songs have vanished. On stage, I feel much more creative and I am enjoying myself more up there.

My awareness of, interest in and love for other people has risen markedly and the more I study Scientology, the more I feel like I'm coming out of a long, deep sleep. What a relief!

David Pomeranz
Songwriter &
Recording Artist

Scientology has made it possible for me to change my life and the lives of others. It provided me with tools that I could apply to realize my potential. Not long after I became a Scientologist I got my role as Mary Ellen on the TV show "The Waltons." Through what I have learned in Scientology I am able to confront and handle difficult situations without relying on other people for solutions. I apply what I've learned to other people and have had a positive effect on their lives as well.

Scientology has made me much happier.

Judy Norton
Actress & Singer

I n my career Scientology is the thing that has made it possible to be in show biz for more than 25 years. I love the people, I love the work. Scientology has helped me to handle the everyday problems of life, handle confusions and keep my goals focused. It has made my life fulfilling as an actor, father and American citizen and has made it possible for me to fulfill my own American Dream. Being a Scientologist has clarified knowing what freedom really is.

Michael D. Roberts
Actor

B efore Scientology, I was quite introverted and lonesome at times. Scientology gave me the ability to communicate to people.

Through Scientology, I expanded personally and started to wonder what I should paint and what I should communicate. My first published artwork was done for the National Geographic Society in Washington. Since then I have painted many magazine covers and have become quite well-known throughout central Europe for my work.

In Scientology, I gained the technical knowledge behind life and, as a result, have grown in every aspect of life.

Carl-W. Röhrig
Artist

*W*ell, I didn't have an occupation. At the time, my idea toward life was to see how little I could do and basically how much and how many kinds of drugs I could take. I wasn't doing anything with my life. When I got into Scientology a lot changed right away. For the first time ever, I saw that there was hope and that was very encouraging. When I received Scientology counseling to handle my drug problem, my life started going up and up and up and hasn't stopped since.

Keith Code
Motorcycle Racing
Instructor

*S*cientology has saved my life, by enabling me to free myself from drugs. I regained many lost abilities, some of which I did not know I had or that I considered pure utopia. Through the study of Dianetics and Scientology I am now able to communicate better with others, to listen to them and to love them. I found again respect for myself. L. Ron Hubbard says: "What is true for you is what you yourself have observed."

This philosophy has an enormous value. In short, it has given me what I was looking for.

Xavier Deluc
Actor

The first thing that struck me about Scientology is that it made sense. I could think with the data. The second was that it actually WORKED and that is why I became a Scientologist. I've been a Scientologist for over twenty-five years and I'm still awed daily by the things I've learned through Scientology. Not only did my dreams come true but along the way the quality of my life became rich, filled with decency and integrity. My awareness and perception have increased a thousandfold and I have an unshakable certainty that, through Scientology, it is possible to achieve true spiritual freedom. Scientology is simply the finest thing I have encountered in my entire existence.

Today I have a magnificent wife, four incredible children and I wake up each morning knowing that I am contributing to the betterment of my family, society and the world around me.

Scientology has made it possible for me to lead a full and productive life.

Jeff Pomeranz
Actor

Since I did my very first course, a communications course, I've been able to apply Scientology to every part of my life. I'm co-founder and executive director of The School of the Natural Voice here in Los Angeles. I have hundreds of singers come to me for voice lessons. Most of my time is spent applying the simplest Scientology technology to their lives, just to help them gain confidence in themselves and their ability. My own singing career has flourished through the use of Scientology. I apply the administrative technology to my business and it's helped me build a business I never knew I had the potential to do. It's one thing for me to sit here and spout off about how great Scientology is and have someone else read what I'm saying and say, "Oh yeah, well you're just saying those things because someone asked you to." All I can say is take ONE PIECE OF DATA and apply it to a part of your life standardly and see what happens. I'm amazed at how it works exactly the way it's supposed to work every time.

Gloria Rusch-Novello
Singer, Writer & Actress

As a medical professional I am concerned with matters which deal with life. The knowledge about life which I have obtained from Scientology has been an incredible help to me. I have seen so many young doctors become hardened, disillusioned and lose compassion because of the suffering to which they are exposed.

Being a Scientologist and knowing Scientology has allowed me to grow in compassion and understanding and has made me more effective in helping my patients, my children and others.

Scientology has not only given me the tools I can use to help others, but a deep understanding of the spiritual aspects of life. Scientology is the road to true spiritual freedom. It is the most rewarding journey I have ever taken.

Megan Shields
Physician

With Scientology, I've gained an enormous understanding and love for life and my perceptions have increased. As an artist, that's priceless. My business has skyrocketed and the demand for my work keeps increasing. Scientology gave me the realization of my unlimited potential as a spiritual being and the ability to achieve any goal I set for myself. For this I am forever grateful.

James T. Sorensen
Photographer

A s a fire captain I regularly face incidents involving illness, injury, death, danger and disaster. I deal with life-threatening situations and strangers count on me to help them during some of the worst moments of their lives.

Not only must I be prepared to direct the actions necessary to handle these situations but I am ultimately responsible for the safety of my firefighters and the citizens that I serve while doing so. My job can be physically and emotionally overwhelming.

Scientology has given me the knowledge and skills to deal with all aspects of life. I am able to think clearly and calmly in any situation. This makes me very effective in assisting others and avoiding mistakes in dangerous environments.

Scientology has given me the ability to communicate, solve problems, organize and be productive. These are VITAL tools for living which I have used to improve my relationships with others. I have been able to achieve more than I ever hoped for and, more importantly, I have gained an increased awareness and a greater understanding of myself spiritually. And that is the most rewarding experience of all.

> Cory S. Trammell
> Fire Captain

B efore Scientology I was extremely shy. I had a big problem even beginning a conversation with someone. I had a lot of trouble making new friends and I was generally an introverted person.

Scientology completely handled this. I have lost my fear of communicating and can talk to people and make friends easily.

I am able to work out problems until all parties are happy. Scientology has made parenting really fun. My daughter grew up in Scientology, she is able to communicate, stays away from drugs and other teen insanities and she and I have a great relationship.

Scientology has given a sense of purpose to my life.

> Barbara Pease Stewart
> Businesswoman

*S*cientology is a clean and concise philosophy. It is truth. And you use it from your point of view, not someone else's. It helps you become more able.

Bob Salerno
Freestyle Skier

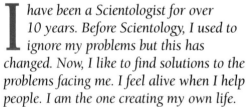

I have been a Scientologist for over 10 years. Before Scientology, I used to ignore my problems but this has changed. Now, I like to find solutions to the problems facing me. I feel alive when I help people. I am the one creating my own life.

Saila Domani
Consultant

*B*efore Scientology I had no real direction in life and was definitely the effect of it. I had a profession that I was pursuing (being a pilot) but I didn't have the data necessary to learn to do it.

Through studying Scientology I have learned how to communicate and to confront life head-on. I can honestly say that I am no longer the effect of my environment or my future and I'm doing exactly what I want to do in life.

Randy Hepner
Jet Pilot

W e really don't know how we would have kept our marriage together if it were not for Scientology.

There is so much stress that is placed upon a marriage that it's sometimes difficult to know that you are making the correct decisions. Through Scientology we look forward to each and every day as an adventure, instead of just "getting by." L. Ron Hubbard developed a great deal of technology that has enabled us to face the challenges brought on by day-to-day living. It's really helping our marriage work.

Scott and Susie Sutton
Writers, Illustrators
& Publishers

B efore Scientology I had my own company that was doing okay, but I didn't have the faintest idea how to get along with people on a professional level. I didn't know how to lead without building up animosity or how to be liked and still have control. It seemed that as a leader one had to continually assert oneself, much like a bull in the field running over a herd of cows. Very macho!

Needless to say, this approach didn't work very well.

Then I found Scientology.

I learned how to handle people effectively while still managing to keep my sense of humor. I learned how to understand people (including myself) and how to get the most out of people and also how to give. I learned how to help other people get along with others. All this has led me to a good, healthy, sane life.

Robert McFarlane
Businessman

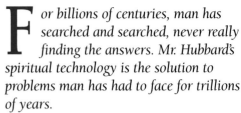

For billions of centuries, man has searched and searched, never really finding the answers. Mr. Hubbard's spiritual technology is the solution to problems man has had to face for trillions of years.

In my experience with Mr. Hubbard's processes and training, I have been able to confront and eliminate things that have caused ruin in my life. I have found that the barriers in life are the ones that I have created. As a result, I am more ethical, more creative and more successful. My goal of helping a billion human beings find answers to questions for themselves is unfolding right before my very eyes.

Rev. Alfreddie Johnson, Jr.
Founder of the World
Literacy Crusade

When I was first introduced to Scientology, I was doing well in life but I knew there was more. I wanted to know what made people tick and how one could improve his own condition. Now I have the answers to those questions and more. They are contained in the vast wealth of knowledge of Scientology.

Billy Evans
Publisher

Twelve years ago, I was successful in the business world but my life was really a mess. I was married to a banker hooked on drugs and had no strength to face the future. With Scientology, I now live a wonderful life and I truly enjoy what life has to offer. I am in control of my own life now and, best of all, I can help others live better and happier lives, thanks to Scientology.

Lily Guerrero
Sales Manager

S cientology counseling has expanded my reach for my family, my friends and mankind. I really want to help them survive. I find I have very little attention on myself personally as I have personal fulfillment, leaving time for involvement in my children's schooling and community activities. I now have a high personal esteem for my friends and family.

Barbara Levine
Housewife

A few years ago, I would never have thought that a wife and mother of two daughters could also become a successful television and radio announcer. Now I know that I create my own future. Whether a situation is a "good one" or a "bad one" depends totally on me. I found that I could not only progress in my career, but meet a man I trusted, build a family and raise two lovely daughters. Honesty, courage, trust, integrity and serenity are among the many things I have gotten from Scientology. My gratitude to L. Ron Hubbard continues to increase.

Franca Cerveni
Radio and Television
Announcer

One of the best things that I have gotten from Scientology is a future—a real future. I had what I considered was a good job, but I wasn't going anywhere that interested me.

I knew there was something missing in my life. Now I have no doubt about who I am or about the direction I am going. Without Scientology this just would not have happened. My activities are directed now and the goals I made much, much earlier in my life are now defined and real. I recommend Scientology to anyone who wants to put direction into their life and set their goals straight.

Gary Nordfors
Carpenter

I used to have a fear of crowded places. Every time I'd go to the grocery store or to a movie or almost any place where there were a lot of people, I'd go into a panic; my heart would race, my hands would sweat and I would feel as though I was about to pass out. This problem was completely handled in one hour of Scientology auditing and it has never recurred. If I had gone to a psychiatrist, I am sure it would have cost tens of thousands of dollars and years of therapy and still would not be handled.

Dianne Cook
Bookkeeper

Being a professional driver dealing with the public and their need to be across town NOW used to be stressful for me. Before Scientology I had no idea about being in control of my vehicle and therefore had my fair share of accidents. After each shift I would be wiped out. Now, I handle my car with certainty and do the impossible as far as my clients are concerned. I'm rarely stressed and when my shift is over I still have plenty of energy to play with my young son. Not bad for an old coot, eh?

Henry Baumgard
Taxi Driver

I found that embarking on a career in art had its drawbacks. Drugs seem to be everywhere in the art world. The myth that "artists need to be crazy to be creative" is rampant. It is no wonder that many artists have failed, given up their hopes and are no longer creating. When I discovered Scientology, I learned that you can overcome the critics and the drugs. And the myth? Well, that's all it is—a myth. A sane artist has a much better chance at succeeding and surviving as an artist. Scientology has given me the knowledge, ability and strength to maintain my sanity even when the world gets crazy.

Bobbie Kitchens
Artist

M an, I was a mess after getting out of college. Drugs, fear, alienation, stagnation; these were the makeup of my existence. By applying Scientology to myself and my environment I was able to pull myself up by the bootstraps. Today I'm married to a wonderful lady and have a daughter Molly who is the greatest. I have a new life and love it. I look forward to living it every day. Scientology is all about improving and living life with enthusiasm.

Bob Sullivan
Fisherman

S cientology has been a tremendous asset for my brothers and I as individuals, as a family and in our highly successful firm. The breadth of knowledge available from the subject is hard to conceive. Most notable is the ability to communicate on any subject. That, coupled with L. Ron Hubbard's enormous insights into the mind of man, and the study and administrative technology he has developed, gives one a huge leg up on any endeavor. Being happy with oneself, one's family, one's business activities and life generally is a fantastic accomplishment and the knowledge that one can improve from there still, is incredible; yet we have found it truly achievable with Scientology.

Matt Feshbach
Investment Manager

S cientology has helped me a lot. I'm a figure skater and have to confront doing difficult things on ice, sometimes even very early in the morning. Doing my TRs and Objectives especially helped me confront and get my jumps for competition. Now I'm not so afraid to just "go for it."

Alyssa Weller Campbell
Figure Skater

I have been involved in Scientology for nearly twenty years. Earlier as a student I had felt inadequate in my studies. In Scientology I found out that I had missed basic steps in my education and I was able to resolve my study problems and go on to fulfill my goals to work with children. Now I am a teacher and I use that same technology with my students. Once they have learned how to study and apply what they have learned, they have been able to come up two to three grades in eight months. The students are bright, confident and proud of their achievements. It has been a great joy and privilege to share L. Ron Hubbard's study technology with my students.

Carol Loweree
Teacher

Scientology has helped me bring up a teenage boy in a troubled world. We are the best of friends. With Scientology and the precepts of **The Way to Happiness** by L. Ron Hubbard, I have gotten through the rough years.

Bob Cook
Painter

As a kid growing up I was very shy, withdrawn, afraid of people and generally unhappy. All these uncomfortable feelings were still there during high school and later in college. The most I could hope for was to make each day as bearable as I could, yet I felt life should be happier.

These ill feelings weren't going to go away all by themselves. I was going to have to DO something about them and what I did was Scientology.

I enrolled on a Scientology communication course and to my surprise and delight my shyness started to disappear and my fear was less and one by one all these uncomfortable feelings started to go away. It was like shedding a skin. And what I found underneath all of this was ME! The more I used what I learned in Scientology the more ME I became. Scientology really works! I became more outgoing, more confident, honest and ethical. I found my integrity. I liked people a lot more, and life became FUN, just like I always thought it should be.

Michael Manoogian
Logo Designer

At thirty-five years old, I was not happy and wasn't getting what I wanted from life. I felt if I waited it out or tried harder, things would change. As each failure came my way, whether it be in relationships or career, my world just seemed to get a little smaller. I wondered why the fearlessness and enthusiasm I once had was gone. I did not have the ability to change things so passed time waiting for fleeting moments of happiness. I got interested in Scientology and found that something could be done. I found there is hope and made successes out of my failed purposes and goals. Due to Scientology I have a great marriage, my life is better and I'm able to win again.

Janice Sturgiss
Mother

W hen I got into Scientology, I found communication and friendships. And this, I think, is the true meaning of life. Communication. Friends.

Christina Kumi Kimball
Executive

A fter Vietnam I was floundering. The technology of Dianetics and Scientology revitalized my life. I was searching for answers to life and found them. The tools I got from Scientology ethics and administrative technology boosted me to the top of my profession. All of these tools have expanded my awareness and abilities to the point where I can make a difference.

Bill Moon
Research Analyst

Before I was introduced to Scientology, I was moving about in life uncertain of how to create stable success for myself as an artist, in my marriage and for others around me. I just left it to hard work and luck. I now have confidence that I can tackle any venture in life and be able to make it work for the benefit of myself and others around me. This confidence comes from the clarity and workability of a lifetime of research and hard work by L. Ron Hubbard. I am deeply indebted to him.

Scientology not only gives me the tools to enhance my life, but contains basic truths about my spiritual existence that lead to increased awareness and states of existence that are far higher than one can even imagine.

Pat Frey
Event & Floral Designer

Scientology has changed my whole life for the better. It has given me a better understanding of myself, of others and of life. This makes life much more livable. I would never have the terrific marriage I now have without Scientology. The gains I have had in Scientology enable me to experience events without getting overwhelmed by them, making me a better problem solver and more stable. My ethical and moral standards have risen incredibly, which is a real asset. With Scientology, life is easier, simpler and more fun.

Bill Greenwalt
Real Estate Broker

One of the principles of Scientology is "if one knows the technology of something he cannot be the adverse effect of it." In Scientology there is a wealth of know-how on life. I have achieved many goals using the technologies of L. Ron Hubbard. One of the things I have gained through Scientology is to set a target for goals that I want to achieve and then push them through to attainment.

Craig Hooks
Carpet Salesman

Scientology gave me and my family a new life. It enabled my kids to survive "teenage madness." It has enabled me to understand people so I can cooperate with others. I have increased my ability to help others just by talking and listening to them.

Joe Duncanson
Electrician

If anyone had told me years ago that I would be where I am today I would not have believed them, but here I am! I have an absolutely wonderful marriage. My husband and I have a growing and happy relationship. We can talk to our children about anything and they know they can talk to us. This fact alone is the most valuable thing about Scientology—it helps people get into real communication. Even my parents who are not Scientologists tell me the world would be a wonderful place if all children were as active, helpful and honest as ours are.

Dorda McDaniel
Store Owner

Before Scientology I knew that I wanted to have a good marriage, happy family and to be successful in life, but it seemed that I kept running into closed doors which I could not open. I got into Scientology in 1972 and knew that I had found a way to achieve my childhood goals and dreams.

Scientology gave me the tools I needed and the understanding which I so lacked, and what was even more important: a way to apply this knowledge to better my life. As I improved and became more capable, it had a definite effect on others as well.

Scientology literally saved my life. I look back on the course of destruction I was on, and had it not been for Mr. Hubbard's technology, I would not have been able to achieve what I have today, a happy family and success in what I do helping others make their lives more worthwhile.

Jane Allen
National Spokesperson
Citizens Commission
on Human Rights

I went with a friend to the Church of Scientology. I didn't believe them, I didn't trust them. I knew nobody could do what they had told me. But I made a deal with the person I saw. *"I will read your book* **Dianetics.** *If I like it, I will be back."* That was spring, 1975. Over the years Scientology and Dianetics has not failed to work when applied. I see it work every day!

Roy Brock
Roofer

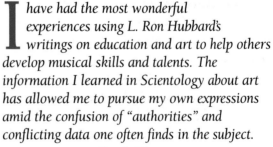

S cientology training has changed my life and made me able to function more at cause because I am now able to know that what I am doing is right.

Linda Tucker
Office Manager

I have had the most wonderful experiences using L. Ron Hubbard's writings on education and art to help others develop musical skills and talents. The information I learned in Scientology about art has allowed me to pursue my own expressions amid the confusion of "authorities" and conflicting data one often finds in the subject.

Carole Blum
Music Teacher

I have studied, for some twenty years now, the various technologies that exist in Scientology. I have firsthand knowledge and experience of the workability of this subject in assisting an individual to dramatically enhance the quality of his life. I can honestly say that I know who I am and that I am much more capable of controlling life (as opposed to life washing me downriver and into the ocean). I am happy. I am successful.

Bill Johonnesson
Management
Specialist

I began taking drugs when I was fourteen years old. By the time I was seventeen years old I had become an addict. I tried several programs to handle my addiction and none of them worked.

In 1973 I went to Narconon LA. There, using L. Ron Hubbard's drug rehabilitation technology I was able to successfully come off of drugs. After graduating the Narconon program, I read **Dianetics**, became a trained auditor and received auditing myself. My insecurities, fears and losses in life were handled with Scientology auditing. I can honestly say Scientology saved my life. Today I run a very successful Narconon drug rehabilitation center. I have three teenagers that I have raised successfully and most of all I have my life back. I would strongly suggest that anyone out there who is looking for a better life pick up a **Dianetics** book and read it. It will change your life forever!

Jeanne Trahant Stewart
Executive Director
Narconon Newport Beach

Before I was a Scientologist, I was unsure of myself and nervous and shy dealing with men. I got confused and annoyed easily if things did not go my way. Now, after nearly twenty-five years of being a Scientologist, I cannot believe that I am the same person. I feel so calm. I am self-assured. It's a great feeling.

Carmen Suarez
Manager

Before I found Scientology I was a stressed-out executive who was running on tranquilizers and martinis to get through the day. I had ulcers and back problems, and I felt I would burn out before I was forty. I was out of communication with my family and my business associates. Scientology helped me to discover who I really am, which enabled me to pursue my goals in life. I no longer require drugs or alcohol to remain stress-free and my body problems have ceased. As the result of Scientology training and counseling I now have a happy marriage, my own successful interior design firm and I have become an accomplished public speaker. Scientology works because it has the technology to change the conditions in life.

Lee Cambigue
Business Executive

About 5 1/2 years ago I was miserable. When things didn't go well I blamed someone else. I was always broke and relied heavily on my parents to bail me out. I was at a point where I knew I needed to change. I had read other self-help books, and I would get fired up for about a day, but that was it. Then I read **Dianetics.** Wow! Something clicked when I was reading it and I knew that this was it. It made sense and was something that I could do and see the results of, and they stayed with me. From that moment on, my life has been getting better.

Michael Klaumann
Photographer

I f religion has something to do with knowing oneself, then Scientology includes undoubtedly the new discoveries that make it unique in this context. For me, Scientology has been and is an extraordinary adventure in which one finds the most interesting thing in this world: oneself. Scientology has helped me discover dimensions that before I did not even think would exist.

Horst Mehler
Author

I owe my life to Scientology—both literally and figuratively. Prior to getting involved in Scientology I was heavily dependent on drugs. I was killing myself. One day a friend told me about Scientology. It contains so much simple data that is immediately applicable in life. I gained the ability to face life and learned the power of real communication. Scientology technology helped me free myself from drugs and create a new life.

Ron Penner
Caterer

Before Scientology I never felt confident in my abilities at work, I was introverted and my drive to succeed was getting weaker by the day. With Scientology I've been able to turn this all around. Scientology has increased my ability to handle all areas of my life. I now have a great husband who I love more and more each day and I also have a fantastic career. It is actually hard to think what life would be like without Scientology.

Stephanie Rose
Radio Broadcaster

As a child I had everything—wonderful parents, a beautiful home, a terrific life. Then my parents moved when I was a teenager and I snapped. We quit communicating and I spent years rebelling against them. We were so out of touch by 1969 it was unbelievable. I was on a quest to find out why I felt the way I did. In 1969 I read the book **Dianetics** by L. Ron Hubbard and that day my life changed. I started the Communications Course and immediately understood how to solve the problem with my parents.

I went from a rebellious individual trying to hurt my parents to a very happy person. I am now in terrific communication with my parents. I have handled the problems that held me down so I don't have to pass them on to my son. I am successful at **whatever** I do and I find life just gets better and better.

Tory Bezazian
Mother

SUCCESSES FROM SPECIFIC SERVICES

Millions of successes are on file in churches of Scientology around the world relating benefits received from Scientology training and auditing services. Here is a representative sampling of gains Scientologists report having experienced from individual services spanning the Bridge to Total Freedom.

INTRODUCTORY BOOKS AND SERVICES

Twenty years ago, although I had a good job and had recently gotten married, I was dissatisfied with life and was seldom really happy. My day-to-day existence seemed futile and had little direction or purpose. I suspected that there must be more to life than what I was experiencing, but it was all a mystery to me.

I picked up a book one day, entitled *A New Slant on Life*. In this book by L. Ron Hubbard I found answers to my problems. I went to the Church of Scientology and got onto a course on communication and suddenly had some tools to change unwanted conditions. My life started to turn around.

Today, I own my own successful business, the expansion of which I directly attribute to the use of L. Ron Hubbard's principles. I have been happily married for over twenty-three years and have a teenage daughter who is also happy and doing well in life. Not only am I happier and more successful than I thought possible, but I am now involved in the Church of Scientology's community affairs programs, helping other people to get off drugs and helping to make known the harmful effects of drugs. I am enjoying life and have never looked back!

R.T.

After reading some of L. Ron Hubbard's books in 1976 and taking a course, I found my teaching profession was more enjoyable and productive because now I could understand and therefore handle "problems" that came up.

My children in class were happier, too! My life changed dramatically. Old body aches and pains from an international track and field career vanished with the application of Mr. Hubbard's spiritual technology. With my new awareness and confidence, I stepped into the business world and started my own business. My life is a happy one, filled with new discoveries at every turn. I find it amazing that we are born into this life and are not given an instruction manual on how to live it! I now have one!

I highly recommend the use of L. Ron Hubbard's technology to anyone who wishes he had a "manual" that would better life. You will find, as millions have, that true joy and happiness can be achieved.

I.P.

I wish I had found Scientology twenty years ago when I was first looking for answers to my life. I went to a lot of meetings and read a lot of books and tried a lot of different things but then I just sort of got on with my life. I happened upon **Fundamentals of Thought** one day in a bookstore, stayed up all night reading it and my life has not been the same since. I immediately saw how I had a problem relating to others in many cases, and with the materials L. Ron Hubbard presented in the book I was able to improve the way I deal with other people which has made them and me a lot happier.

M.T.

Before the Success Through Communication Course I was having a rough time talking to people. I wouldn't be able to start a conversation or if I had to leave, I couldn't end one either. But then I did this course and I am now able to talk to people and get my communications across. I can also answer questions easily without being embarrassed and can make friends much more easily and just lead a happier life.

C.E.
*Success Through
Communication Course*

Sometimes in life achieving a goal large or small can seem very complex and possibly there are barriers to accomplishment. After having studied the entire book **Fundamentals of Thought** I found I was able to simply play the game of life, knowing with certainty that things would turn out right—and that's exactly what happened! I became more able to make a clear, precise decision about something I wanted to do. And this certainly made the greatest difference in getting it done. I was able to improve my relationship with my husband, my parents and my son through understanding them better. My work became not just easier, but more enjoyable. I was able to enjoy being with people so much more and better deal with even difficult circumstances. Best of all, I am in a much better position to help others. So many times I've had a friend or acquaintance who I could have helped. Before, I would have been sad for them because there was nothing I could have done. But now I have solutions that work.

T.L.

I was dancing ballet and teaching in a university. I had broken a bone in my left foot and was unable really to perform anymore. I'd opted to teach instead of dance. I had had an operation to remove the bone and in fact ended up standing up through my last four months of lectures at the university due to hip pain that started just after the foot operation.

One of my university colleagues told me I should get and read a book called **Dianetics: The Modern Science of Mental Health.** I read the book over three days practically night and day. It made so much sense to me I KNEW it must work.

I went with a friend to the Dianetics center and received some Dianetics auditing as mentioned in the book. After the second session I was entirely well. The pain in my hip disappeared and to this day has never returned. I resumed dancing and even started performing again.

D.A.
Introductory Auditing

My son died in an accident and in the weeks that followed I was constantly thinking about the moment when my father told me about his death. During all my daily activities I appeared to be functioning properly, but that moment was constantly replaying in my thoughts. I doubt I would have been able to continue to function much longer without it really driving me crazy. After one session of introductory Dianetics auditing, six weeks after his death, that "tape" stopped playing constantly and I was able to proceed with my daily routine and obligations much more easily.

I do not believe I would have been okay without this auditing. My life would probably have completely fallen apart.

S.R.
Introductory Auditing

My success ranks with biblical references to the blind seeing, the lame walking and people being raised from the dead! What the top medical authorities in the fields of internal medicine, orthopedics, radiology and neurology could not handle in three years, my auditor with LRH tech handled in one afternoon! I can move my previously debilitated left arm with ease and comfort now. This morning I could not raise it from my side without terrible pain!

The spiritual cause of the problem is resolved and the problem no longer exists.

P.W.
Introductory Auditing

The course has meant regained knowledge, regained awareness, abilities, freedom to speak my mind, listen better, hear more, speak more precisely and clearly and it goes on and on. A miracle has occurred to me!

M.A.
Success Through
Communication Course

I was withdrawn, extremely shy and afraid to communicate. Then I did the Success Through Communication Course. As a result, the world became brighter and people were less of a threat to me. I became happier and willing to hold a conversation with anyone. There was a feeling of control in my environment and the sensation of being very big as a spirit. It was the best feeling I had ever experienced.

N.D.
Success Through
Communication Course

ETHICS AND CHAPLAIN SERVICES

For many years, even though most things generally went well for me, one area of my life seemed constantly jinxed. Unexpectedly, the bottom would drop out and everything would suddenly start to go wrong. I would always pick myself up and start again, but continually lived in fear that the lightning would inexplicably strike again. One day, after my life had exploded yet one more time, a friend suggested I address the problem with Scientology ethics. What followed was a miracle. I discovered exactly why things around me remained in such a constant turmoil. Underlying all of my problems was a nonsurvival decision I had made many, many years earlier about myself. Life suddenly started going well. And it *kept* going well. Scientology increases your awareness and you realize that you are **fully responsible** for your own condition. As a spiritual being, you can create your life fully. And when you begin to live like that, all of your dreams start to come true.

R.W.

With the assistance of a church staff member trained in the ethics technology, I set out to resolve a situation that was troubling me in my professional life. When I looked into it closely, I discovered that the situation stemmed from a way of operating that I had adopted much earlier — to stay "low profile" and "invisible" — not just on the job but as an individual. Not a successful way to operate for a person or an executive! I worked this all out through applying the ethics conditions. I became more **myself,** and since doing this I have been willing to stick my neck out more in life and I take more responsibility for myself and others.

M.H.

My husband and I ran into a situation in our marriage that we just were not solving on our own, so we requested the assistance of the chaplain at our church. The chaplain listened carefully to both of us as we explained the situation. She then wrote out a series of simple steps, including studying Scientology materials, communicating with each other and addressing the **underlying** cause of the problem, which turned out to be quite different from what we thought. The problem that we had tried to "solve" for several months just **vanished** once we applied the ethics technology to it as directed by our chaplain. We were both utterly amazed at the results — and soon laughing together at ourselves and what we had thought of as a big problem. This was not "marriage counseling" in the traditional sense at all. This was the use of Scientology principles that recognize us as **spiritual beings,** enabling us to solve our **own** problem by understanding it, confronting it and communicating about it. That is Scientology in its essence and it creates what I call "miracles of the spirit" every day.

L.S.H.

PURIFICATION PROGRAM

I am an attorney specializing in tax law. I have been a newscaster with NBC and am a published author.

Prior to doing the Purification program developed by L. Ron Hubbard, I had experienced the effects of toxins in my body for years. As a young girl, I had rabies shots, as well as other medicinal drugs.

For years I have felt the effects of these poisons which I became acutely aware of while doing the program.

I never really knew how my perceptions were affected by these toxins until I got them out of my system. My ability to think clearly increased; I was sharper, brighter and generally more alert.

It is a medically recorded fact that my hearing was poor prior to doing the program, and as a result of doing the program my hearing improved. My IQ also went up ten points. This is on record, as I took a test prior to doing the regimen and took one after doing the program.

M.P.
Purification Program

I had used drugs ranging from marijuana to freebasing cocaine as well as others in between for three years straight. I was failing in school, disliked myself and had absolutely no inkling as to what I was doing or where I was going in life. The only time I had "fun" was when I was high on drugs.

I then started the Purification program and finished it in two weeks.

I have been a changed person ever since! My IQ rose fifteen points from the time I started to completion of the Purification program. I am alive, I no longer have a fog around me—I can see what is really going on in my life rather than living in a "fairyland." I have been off drugs for six years now and I am a productive person in the society.

The Purification program completely changed my life. Many thanks to L. Ron Hubbard for caring enough to invest his life in bettering mankind.

G.S.
Purification Program

I did the Purification program and the results were amazing. During the early part I felt for days like I was "stoned." I would get up in the morning in a mental fog. It was definitely reminiscent of the old times when it was miserable to go to work and the future seemed unimportant. My reaction to pressure situations was just to say, "To hell with it" and ignore it. After some time on this program this went away and by the time I was done I felt more bright and awake than I have ever felt. It has been a couple of years since I did the program, and this feeling has persisted. My life has changed.

S.G.
Purification Program

I did the Purification program shortly after getting started in Scientology. I was amazed at the changes it produced in me.

It enhanced my perceptions and as a fine artist this is invaluable. It also helped increase my speed in completing my artwork. I was far less moody and much more stable mentally than ever before. These factors allowed me to be more successful in my business relationships and with people in general. It was a great experience.

W.D.
Purification Program

As a Bachelor of Medicine, I found it very interesting to study the Purification program. I found it so interesting that I began the program at the Church of Scientology.

After completing the program, I noticed a tremendous upsurge in physical and mental well-being.

Mentally I feel relaxed, my memory has improved a great deal and I feel much less dispersed and freer emotionally. The changes are so vast that I must say that this program has changed my life and my only wish is that these discoveries by L. Ron Hubbard will be broadly implemented to handle our "drug society" which is in so much need of them.

J.M.B.
Purification Program

STUDY TECHNOLOGY

The technology of L. Ron Hubbard is really incredible—specifically his study technology. I studied for nineteen years. I was in a university and I noticed that I started to feel kind of "stupid." I couldn't grasp the information in my courses as fast as I could before. I started having trouble with my studies. With the study technology of L. Ron Hubbard, everything changed. All my troubles went away and my brightness came back. I was better than ever. Just to give an example: I'm French and I tried to learn English in French schools for eight years. At the end of that time, I knew only ten to twenty words. I started to learn English with L. Ron Hubbard's study technology. Three months

later I was able to have a conversation with any English-speaking person. Today, my ability to speak English is impressive. This technology is priceless.

P.M.
Student Hat

This is the most powerful course I have ever done. The wins, gains and changes have been phenomenal. I have changed so much as a student it is hard to believe. I can actually study comfortably now. This material hit into very basic inabilities and has totally changed them around. I have so much more power to operate and I have regained a marvelous sense of who I am and my own ability to communicate.

S.R.
Student Hat

I have been a teacher for nearly twenty years and a student for nearly fifty years. In that time I have seen and experienced much that has been described as "education." Some of it has been good, but an overwhelming amount of it had little or no lasting value.

As a student I found it very difficult to exercise anything other than my memorization skills. I just memorized things without really understanding why I was doing it. The purpose was really just "to get the grade."

My first course in the study technology developed by L. Ron Hubbard completely revitalized me as a student and provided me with the tools to approach study with a purpose and to really learn something for application. It was this technology that gave me my first real interest in teaching. I realized that with the basic tools provided by this exceptional technology, not only was I able to learn anything I set my mind to, but I could help someone else to learn successfully as well.

For nearly twenty years I have been working with students of all ages from around the world, and have found that they all suffer from the same study-related problems and that once in possession of Mr. Hubbard's breakthrough technology they have the tools necessary for successfully learning anything.

I can think of no greater gift than to give a child (or adult) these easily mastered study tools. They last for a lifetime; they open wide the doors of the future and they unlock potential that was always there.

B.W.
Student Hat

I just finished my Student Hat course and I feel great about it. My trouble in school was that I never knew how to study. I was always a kid with cheat sheets in the desk and instead of writing a report by myself, I'd copy the data verbatim from the source.

I now know how to study—and if someone can learn to study then they can learn anything they want to and do it. I never knew before how important proper study technology is, but now I love it. I apply the study technology constantly as it is invaluable. I'd never be without it.

E.B.M.
Student Hat

KEY TO LIFE COURSE

I have gained **myself** on this course; a certainty of my true beingness and an ability to duplicate others and to be duplicated by others. My confront of life and my willingness and ability to communicate has soared.

I feel like a new being who has shed tons of confusions and fears and who has tools that will enable me to live life.

T.P.
Key to Life Course

The Key to Life has been the most rewarding course I have done in my life.

"A man is as alive as he can communicate," L. Ron Hubbard wrote. I am ten times more alive than I was when I began this course and have the potential to become many times more so! So much of life's agony is just a failure to understand what was communicated.

R.F.
Key to Life Course

Thoroughly confused and stultified by the educational system, I somehow stumbled through life this far. How, I don't know.

It took this course to undo years of incorrect training and education and then put a foundation there that will stand for the rest of my life. I now feel that I have a *chance in life and that I have the ability to go forward and succeed.*

The course has indeed been aptly named—the Key to Life.

> F.A.
> Key to Life Course

I have just finished the Key to Life Course. It is indescribable in terms of personal wins and abilities regained or polished up.

If someone had told me that I would experience this much gain, this much revitalization and resurgence from doing the Key to Life, I don't think I would have believed them.

The wins are incomparable, that's just how basic and powerful this course is.

> S.S.
> Key to Life Course

AUDITOR TRAINING

The Academy Levels were the first courses I did where I learned how to audit and really help another person by handling any difficulties to do with communication. I finished studying the course and then took my first preclear into session. He was a very shy young man who talked with a slight stutter and walked through a room looking at the floor to avoid having to look at and talk to other people. I took him into session and audited him for a few hours. As we walked out of the room after session, he gave me a big grin and said, "Well, let's give this a test." He then walked right up to the first person we met and started chatting, laughing and really enjoying himself, and continued getting into communication in a

totally relaxed manner with the people in the room. There were no signs of his stutter. It was like watching a totally different person from the shy person of a few hours earlier, and it left me feeling very, very happy that I had been able to apply what I had learned to produce this incredible result.

> H.N.
> Academy Level Training

This was possibly the most demanding training I've ever done—and the most rewarding. In learning to audit, I've seen sick people jump out of bed and dance after a session. I've watched psychosis melt away before my eyes. I've seen preclears who felt they had no recall of the past suddenly remember. I've seen major life ruins vanish in one short session, after years of the preclear trying to handle them with other means.

> D.M.
> Academy Level Training

I just completed training on the Academy Levels and the knowledge contained in them has changed my life in numerous ways. I am now much more at cause and know how things are going to go in my life.

The most rewarding part of the Academy Levels is to sit down in the auditing room with another person and administer the processes and experience the elation when my preclear gets rid of some aberrated pattern he's had all his life.

One has to do it to experience it. The preclear's complexion gets bright, his eyes very bright and clear and a big smile comes across his face and he looks at you with a "what do you know, I thought I would have to live with that for the rest of my life!" expression that tells you what's occurred to him and you know you have made life and livingness a brighter activity for that person. I cannot thank L. Ron Hubbard enough for all the love and caring he put into this work, to ensure that each person who wants to help others change will understand and be able to apply his discoveries.

P.C.
Academy Level Training

I was educated for four years at one of the finest universities in the world but I honestly have to say that there were any number of lectures I heard while doing the Saint Hill Special Briefing Course which taught me more about myself, others and life than any ten courses I took in college. L. Ron Hubbard's depth of understanding of life and the mind was so far beyond anything my professors could teach me that doing the Briefing Course was like a university education several times over. By the time I did the course I was already a trained and experienced auditor but studying all the materials of Dianetics and Scientology in the order that L. Ron Hubbard discovered them gave me a total understanding of his technology and I was able to make it my own because I followed and understood exactly how he did it.

As an auditor I have all the technology under my belt now and I know I can help any person improve. Helping someone else discover more about himself is the most satisfying activity I know and the Briefing Course is the course that teaches you all the technology of how to do this. I have learned in Scientology that there is a technology to life and that once you've learned it, you know it forever. The Saint

Hill Special Briefing Course is the most thorough education in life that exists anywhere.

D.K.
Saint Hill
Special Briefing Course

My life changed radically from the knowledge gained on the Saint Hill Special Briefing Course, and I will continue to put every part of what I have learned into application.

Without doubt, the Saint Hill Special Briefing Course was the most spectacular adventure of my life. I gained a wealth of knowledge and understanding broad enough and technically perfected to the point where I know with absolute certainty how to set any individual free. I was put in awe many times over at the simplicities and truths presented on the course and I felt myself changing as I have never felt before.

While the course taught me the technology of auditing, what I really learned was the technology of LIFE. I stepped into a new realm of capability and stability and really assumed the beingness of an auditor the way L. Ron Hubbard intended.

I am forever grateful to L. Ron Hubbard for this legacy of technology, for it is a truly amazing body of truths expansive enough to fill the universe, yet maintaining a total simplicity. With it we can free and are freeing beings.

P.A.
Saint Hill Special Briefing Course

What I got out of the Saint Hill Special Briefing Course was an unshakable certainty and an understanding of a tremendous body of truths which left me with the true beingness of a Scientologist and an auditor.

I solved aspects of my own life just by mere knowledge of this data but above and beyond this I gained the know-how of clearing another being of the barriers to his freedom. That is the bottom line and is something that can never be taken away from me—the knowledge of how to free a being.

P.A.
Saint Hill Special
Briefing Course

Listening to the Saint Hill Special Briefing Course lectures was the most rewarding training I have ever done as an auditor. Every detail of research that L. Ron Hubbard did at Saint Hill during the 1960s is covered in these tapes and listening to them is really like sitting right next to him and learning how he developed the Bridge to Total Freedom, step by step.

These lectures not only cover all the basic underlying theory of the Bridge but also address just about every facet of life. Mr. Hubbard gives incredible facts about man's past, politics, religion, study, different cultures, music, art and a myriad of other subjects. Once you have heard all these lectures you have a comprehensive understanding of life. What I gained as an auditor from these tapes and this course was a complete certainty on auditing basics.

Auditing became the simplest thing in the world to do because any and all seeming complexities got swiftly eradicated and I just knew that I was able to get any preclear

through anything in auditing with ease and with 100 percent results every time.

G.M.
Saint Hill Special Briefing
Course

The Class VIII Course has resulted in a quantum leap in my auditing skills. Whereas earlier I felt that I had a mountain of information that I had to remember and use while auditing, now I am just there, relaxed and in communication with the preclear and naturally doing the next correct thing without having to think about it.

Auditing has been reduced to a simplicity where the tech is simply part of me—I own it and can use it with no effort, worry or thought. I can only liken it to an athletic skill. A great athlete is so highly trained that he doesn't think about his next action as that would be much too slow—he simply does it.

I feel honored and privileged to be among the elite of Scientology auditors and being able to help others so effectively in ways that have never before been possible.

Auditing is now easy and pure pleasure with every session ending in an excellent result. Thank you, Ron, for this priceless gift—you have made my life truly worthwhile.

L.D.S.
Advanced Auditor Training

DIANETICS AND SCIENTOLOGY AUDITING

I have had many personal successes with Scientology auditing. My ability to let others be, without the need to interfere and unnecessarily interrupt or control them, came way up. This was a big win, in the work environment particularly. Also, I found changes in life, often disconcerting in the past, became something I just took in stride. All in all, my ability to confront and handle the pressures and stresses of day-to-day interrelationships increased dramatically and I find myself calmer and enjoying life much, much more.

> K.R.
> *Scientology Auditing*

Scientology Expanded Grades have noticeably increased my ability to learn. In my business, I must do extensive reading and research, and I am now able to absorb and understand a much higher volume of material. This ability has been invaluable to me.

Due to Expanded Grades auditing I have become much happier and find my respect for others has increased. My energy level has risen to the point where I've started my own business and have become revitalized as a writer and financial lecturer.

Probably the most amazing thing which has happened to me was the fact of a 20 percent increase in my IQ.

> K.G.
> *Scientology Auditing*

After completing Grade II I feel terrific. I feel energetic, enthusiastic and yet at peace with myself. I also sense a new awareness. I can also look back at past hurts, anxieties and frustrations and feel that they will not have any impact on future decisions.

> P.N.
> *Scientology Auditing*

I was looking for a way to handle the emotional pain left over from being abused as a child. I went to a psychologist and she said, "I don't know how to help you." Another one said, "All we can do is 'reprogram' you." The third one told me maybe she could do something but that it would take thirty years. Then a friend told me Scientology could handle my problem, like that! It's true. Since I have had Scientology auditing I no longer have to live in the past—I can live in the present and create my future. And it all happened faster than I would have imagined possible!

> M.S.
> *Scientology Auditing*

The end result of my Drug Rundown restored me to my teenage years— when I was honest, didn't take drugs or alcohol; when I was so full of life and enthusiasm; when everything was new and wonderful and I could do anything. All I had to do was decide I wanted something or to do something and it happened. That state has been restored to me now.

I'm fifty-three.

> S.L.D.
> *Dianetics Auditing*

I have been a Scientologist for many years and I can say with no reservation whatever that the single most important thing for me is that through Scientology auditing I have gained total certainty that I am a spiritual being. To me that knowledge alone is more important than anything else in life.

> F.K.
> *Scientology Auditing*

Before I came into Scientology, I knew there was something more to understand about myself and about life. I would wonder "Who am I?" but never really found an answer, until Scientology. The most valuable thing I have gained from Scientology is a complete certainty of myself as a spirit. It may sound unbelievable to say that Scientology delivers the promise of personal immortality, but it's true. I know without doubt that I am a spiritual being and that I can create a future for myself that is bright, expansive and long-lasting. And to me, that knowledge is priceless.

L.G.
Scientology Auditing

Prior to coming into Scientology I had received a major operation on my nasal passages which were blocked, causing extreme sinusitis. The medical specialist told me that although he could help by removing the blockage, in his experience it would not fully resolve the problems I was having which he felt may be psychosomatic. He was right. Although I experienced relief, I was still crippled by blinding headaches and sinusitis and would literally have to go to bed as it hurt so much. Then came Scientology auditing. One day in my auditing I contacted something which had to do with the extreme pain I was suffering. Suddenly I felt a crunch— I could physically sense the bones in the left part of my face changing. Right afterwards my face felt as if it had woken up after being asleep. It began tingling. The huge pressure buildup from my sinuses had completely disappeared— gone.

I knew that it was over. I no longer felt any sinus pain—I could breathe— I felt alive again.

To this day, twenty years later, it's never returned. What happened to me during that auditing was a miracle.

C.M.
Scientology Auditing

Before I became involved in Scientology, I had an inkling that there was some kind of spiritual or transcendental aspect to existence. I saw this expressed by certain artists, for example, and had some concept that this was desirable, although it was not at all clear what this was all about.

By progressing through the levels of auditing and training, I have come to know myself as a spiritual being. This has not only been a route of increased analytical understanding, but also a very personal and subjective path.

This, of course, has also resulted in a much greater understanding of other people and why they act as they do. Scientology has therefore also helped me tremendously in the practical aspects of life as well.

N.L.
Scientology Auditing

I have been a Scientologist for more than 20 years. I always wanted to help others so I became an auditor. There is something very special about being able to use the technology of Scientology to help another person improve his own life. But even more important than that, Scientology addresses the individual as a being and resolves the spiritual blocks that ruin his existence. When these are gone, a person not only is more capable, happier and more confident, but has complete certainty of himself.

It is tremendously rewarding to me to see someone have that realization for the first time. Scientology opens the door to eternity.

L.W.
Scientology Auditing

My wife was seven months pregnant when she became very ill and had surgery performed in her abdomen. *After the operation the doctor told me she would need to remain in intensive care for several days. He explained that, being pregnant, the pain from the surgery would be very intense and would last for many days. He estimated it would take five days before she could walk.*

While she was in intensive care, I audited her and in less than twenty-four hours she was walking up and down the hall, and in forty-eight hours she was released from the hospital. The head doctor examined her and told me her recovery was miraculous!

E.E.
Scientology Auditing

I was wearing glasses when I went for my first Dianetics session. I had been wearing them for six years and my *vision was steadily deteriorating. During the session I discovered why I had started wearing glasses. All of a sudden I felt a tremendous surge of inner strength and certainty. I took my glasses off and I felt terrific. Things looked really clear. That was over twenty years ago and I haven't worn glasses since. Today my vision is almost perfect. Dianetics really works.*

R.B.
Dianetics Auditing

After getting Grade 0 I honestly feel like a new person. It's a wonderful feeling knowing that I can *communicate and that I want to communicate. Through this auditing I realized that I have an absolute love for being in communication with people and things. This was a life-changing experience.*

A.T.
Scientology Auditing

In the fall of 1990 I developed a physical condition which I had never encountered before. *Over three months I visited several doctors to try to determine what it was and to find out how to cure it. Finally after seeing a specialist it was diagnosed as a chronic vascular disease that there was no cure for. I was told by this specialist that I would probably have it for the rest of my life. This news was very upsetting to me. I was twenty-eight years old at the time. Then I got some auditing. After less than one hour I felt much better. Not only that, the physical condition stopped spreading.*

Within a week of daily auditing, all physical evidence of the condition was gone. It is 1 1/2 years later and the disease has not returned.

J.M.
Dianetics Auditing

New Era Dianetics auditing is absolutely incredible. I never realized really what an engram *could do and how solidly fixed they were in one's mind or how insidiously they aberrate you. Then I had a session of New Era Dianetics and I was utterly amazed* at what happened. This particular engram was quite severe and I was a little more than nervous to go through it, but with the help of my auditor, I made it through. We ran it several times, each time picking up more of the engram that was hidden beneath unconsciousness and pain. After we had run all the emotional pain out of this engram, I had an incredible realization about my life and why I had been unconsciously behaving in certain ways. That unwanted aspect of myself is gone now, never to return. I couldn't stop smiling for days after that! It was incredible, I felt as if I were floating when I walked. I had never felt so good, and this was just one engram.

J.J.
Dianetics Auditing

New Era Dianetics auditing has completely changed my life. Things that seemed unresolvable resolved in the first 4–5 hours. Until I experienced it for myself, the reactive mind was not really tangible to me; but let me tell you, when you get in session with an auditor trained on New Era Dianetics and an E-Meter you instantly find and resolve those things that have been haunting you for years. I would never have believed it if someone had told me what had been underlying all my fears and anxieties. Each session ended with me finding out something about myself that I didn't know before and with a new feeling of freedom. I can't say enough about New Era Dianetics auditing—there is no aberration that can hide from its incredible ability to dig out of the reactive mind that which keeps you pinned down in life.

L.D.
Dianetics Auditing

I used to have epilepsy. Through Dianetics auditing, I discovered that the convulsions which traumatized my life for more than sixteen years stemmed from a series of electric shocks that my mother underwent when she was pregnant with me.

During the sixteen years I suffered attacks of excruciating blinding and stabbing pains through my eyes and head. My body would go rigid and my throat, mouth and arms would go numb. Then I would throw up every twenty minutes for eight hours before the pain would subside.

These attacks occurred from the ages of eleven to twenty-seven years, until I had Dianetics auditing. These attacks vanished after Dianetics auditing at the age of twenty-seven. Today, ten years later, I have helped hundreds of people achieve similar results with Dianetics auditing.

J.B.
Dianetics Auditing

Years ago I was burglarized at home. Two guys entered and I was beaten severely and raped. I had twenty-seven fractures in my face and jaw. The doctors said I'd lose my eyes. I was an emotional wreck, unable to face my friends or any part of life. I was terrified by this experience and unable to confront it.

I turned to Scientology auditing. The improvement was so miraculous that one friend who had come with me dropped to her knees and cried. Within two days the emotional trauma was gone. I completely regained my self-confidence and self-respect. This made it possible for my body to heal much faster. Scientology auditing got me over a tragic experience and has enabled me to lead a better life than I ever thought possible.

V.F.
Scientology Auditing

Nearly one year ago my father was struck down by a massive heart attack which left him completely disabled. We were told by the doctor that he probably would not survive as he was seventy-eight years old and the damage was too great. He was discharged to a convalescent center renowned for its success in stroke rehabilitation.

Two days after he arrived we were told by the director that my father would not benefit from the program as he was too far gone, that it was hopeless and she would not be able to help him.

I gave my father Scientology auditing every day. Day by day he improved until finally six weeks later he walked out of that facility!!!

The same physical therapist who had told us that there was no hope confessed to my sister that in her twenty years' experience with stroke patients she had never seen anyone come back the way my father had.

A.A.
Scientology Auditing

I was very ill for months in the hospital. I was under intensive care for weeks with a bleeding ulcer infection and kidney failure. My heart stopped three times. I was unconscious for over a week, and I did not want to live. The doctors were going to give up on me and stop the treatment. The nurses did not expect me to survive. My wife had a very hard time with it and she couldn't even call to see how I was doing; she had to have someone else call for her. She then received some Dianetics auditing and came to grips with it, at which point she was able to come into my room in the hospital and give me some auditing. She came in every day.

I soon started becoming more aware of my environment and had a determinism to survive. It made life bright enough to live. I am now recovered and would not have lived if it weren't for the technology of L. Ron Hubbard that helped us get through it.

B.G.
Dianetics Auditing

In 1977 I had a serious problem with drugs. I was drinking morning, afternoon and night, as well as using cocaine five to six times a week. Life was gray. I felt hopeless, and there seemed to be no way out. Then I was introduced to the technology of L. Ron Hubbard and believe me, life has not been the same. My drug problem was history after three months. I began to take courses at the Church of Scientology on communication, auditing and life. Today, over ten years later, I still have no more urges or cravings for drugs and alcohol.

D.H.
Scientology Auditing

Before I got Expanded Dianetics auditing, I had problems and conflicts with those I worked with and was in trouble all the time. Expanded Dianetics is very powerful and thorough. I found the very source of my problems with other people and blew this away! It became a pleasure to work with others. I discovered why there were certain locations—cities and even whole countries—I hated or feared. This was fully resolved (prior to my auditing I disliked the city I was in so much that I stayed inside all the time and would only venture out when forced to).

Turmoil and strife disappeared and it was possible for other people to live happily with me for the first time!

A.A.
Dianetics Auditing

In this session, a series of incidents from my childhood that were causing me a tremendous amount of guilt and heartache was completely relieved. This was unconfrontable before. In fact, I'd never been able to talk about it, not in twenty-seven years. My auditor had me return to the moment it happened and go over the incident several times. I was wide awake and fully alert throughout.

As we began, I felt again the same fear and frustration I felt in the incident, but as we continued, the bad feeling was completely discharged and I began to feel much better. By the end of my Dianetics session I was totally free of any effects from this nightmare that had been ruining my life. It's a real miracle—I feel like a 200-pound weight is off my shoulders!

As a Doctor of Dentistry, I'd wholeheartedly recommend Dianetics auditing to anyone. I see now that when you get rid of the upsets, guilt, anger, etc., your whole life changes for the better.

S.C.
Dianetics Auditing

There is so much for me to say about this fantastic auditing. It handled areas of myself and my life that I've wanted handled for so long. I'm incredibly happy. I don't know when I've really ever attained this before.

One of the biggest things that occurred was that I gained self-respect—something I've been without for a very long time. I now have the ability to inspect situations with myself and others and handle accordingly without shame, blame, regret or worry about the future. It's a great life I have and will continue to have. I have a fresh start now!

K.S.
Scientology Auditing

Every two weeks I used to get a migraine headache which literally did not allow me to get up from bed. This was ruining everything I wanted to do in life.

Then I received New Era Dianetics auditing and in the three-hour session I eradicated the source of the migraines. Today, a year and a half later, I've not had another headache. I'm living a new life.

A.P.
Dianetics Auditing

Over two years ago I had a severe accident where I smashed both ankles. The bones were in fifteen pieces and the surgeon was not positive he could even put them all back together. He said I would never run and may not ever walk. It took all sorts of screws, pins, wire and steel plates just to hold all the pieces together while they healed. I got daily auditing starting the day after the accident, which not only greatly eased excruciating pain both mentally and physically but also produced miracles. My doctors were amazed as they could not believe my speedy recovery. I was walking within months and now I dance, run and play sports which my doctors doubted would ever be possible. There is absolutely no way this would have occurred without L. Ron Hubbard's technology.

G.C.
Dianetics Auditing

STATE OF CLEAR

Achieving the state of Clear is the most important thing that has happened in my life. Not only because I was relieved of my past unwanted emotions that were affecting my life and making it difficult to be happy, but also because I opened a new door of happiness. I'm now able to help others a great deal more as I can understand them in a way that was not possible before. Abilities that I did not know I had became evident and as a result I could experience and give greater happiness to others.

My dreams and goals are alive and I have certainty that they will happen. My strength and persistence as an individual have been unblocked.

T.L.
State of Clear

Do I feel wonderful! Having recently achieved the state of Clear, everything around me is so calm and my awareness of the environment and life itself has expanded tremendously. I am now able to view life's problems analytically and come up with sound, rational decisions for each and every one of them. My energy level has increased tenfold and I tackle life with an enthusiasm I never had before. Being Clear has enabled me to begin accomplishing all of those things I wanted in life.

J.L.
State of Clear

It's been many years since I went Clear but the feeling of vitality has never faded. Being Clear, I am able to see things as they are, rather than viewing them through my own reactivity. I notice that though other people might get very upset or frustrated about problems and troubles, I can just view the actual situation and decide on the best solution to handle it rather than automatically REACTING or losing my temper and saying something I would later regret. With my marriage, being Clear has had a tremendous effect. I feel that communication is the basis of a good marriage. Because I am Clear my ability to communicate is very good and I have a very happy marriage. I have been able to enter a newly chosen career full speed ahead, without veering off onto any side roads or worrying if it was all going to work. It's very easy to do things because I'm definite in my decisions. I know what I can achieve.

Achieving the state of Clear released me from the barriers of life and left me with a definite sense of freedom.

D.F.
State of Clear

I have just achieved the state of Clear! It is nothing short of miraculous to be rid of one's reactive mind and to have the accompanying freedom, happiness and newfound abilities that I know are lasting. When I first read the **Dianetics** book and learned for the first time the truth about the mechanics of the mind and how it all works, I wanted to go Clear.

It is an incredible relief to finally understand myself and to know with certainty the cause of man's aberrations, his downfalls, his sorrows and that these can be eradicated to make way for a new life of competence and happiness. The day-to-day problems and obstacles in life no longer pin me down in unwanted conditions. I am able to set and reach any goals that I create and positively affect my relationships with others and family.

Since achieving the state of Clear, I notice that my family and friends are doing far better as well, and I am much more capable of helping them. The doors to my future have blown wide open with potential and possibilities.

G.A.
State of Clear

It is nearly beyond my power of expression to describe the state of Clear—this crystal, shining, effortless state. It is the most basic and the most noble part of me. It is all that I knew I ever was, absolutely unadulterated by past failure, social machinery or false identity. I have the complete freedom of basic personality. Man has perhaps glimpsed this state when witnessing individual acts of mercy, kindness, creativity, courage, truth or any other attribute we commonly personify through art. It isn't a temporary condition or something that will pass, like the happiness we feel during some great moment in our lives. It is lasting and permanent. This is the beginning of something new and great for me and a brand-new vista for mankind as well.

N.K.N.
State of Clear

Before going Clear I was dissatisfied with life, I felt trapped in some way. I was on a treadmill, and there didn't seem to be any way to get off of it. Going Clear really opened the door to my life and my abilities.

I now see a strong, vibrant future and a way to achieve my goals. It's hard to imagine how I lived at all before I went Clear. My whole concept of what living means has changed and I wouldn't trade it for anything!

C.J.
State of Clear

OT LEVELS

It seems I've been searching for eons for what I know now. I feel at peace. I am calm and certain. Things that never made sense now make sense. It's so hard sometimes to say enough to really acknowledge the magnitude of what processing is and does. OT levels are the most precious thing in the universe.

R.M.
OT Levels

Moving through the OT levels is like nothing I've ever experienced before. Through them you find the answers to things you never imagined existed. These answers unlock the very truths of life for you. The OT levels are like removing shackles from yourself as a spiritual being—ones you weren't aware you carried with you. I found that I'd been so used to dealing with life in a certain way that I surprised myself when I no longer became upset or acted negatively on my job or in my relationships. My life became calm, it became sane and I became truly cause over each of my dynamics. The OT levels gave me the freedom and understanding of life that has enabled me to accomplish goals I never dreamed were possible.

S.M.
OT Levels

On the OT levels I learned the ultimate truths of man and myself. And the truth does make you free. And with that freedom has come a joy I have never known before. It is a happiness that spills over into the lives of everyone I touch. As if I am so rich in happiness I have plenty left over to give.

I have seen with clarity beyond the cycle of life and death, and risen to an immense vista of freedom where such things as friendships, affections and my personal identity can last beyond one life.

To say my future looks exceedingly bright is an understatement. I am a *free being!*

S.H.
OT Levels

This was truly the most amazing action I've ever done in Scientology. The power and simplicity of this OT level frequently left me at a loss of words for what had occurred in my universe—the changes were that fast and big. I am now looking forward to an eternal future of new abilities and a newfound insouciance to play the game of life.

M.H.
OT Levels

I can't describe how wonderful I actually feel. Calm, serene—that's it. Also a very deep knowingness. There are things now that I know about why we are like we are (or were, in my case!), about our true nature—and I can testify, MAN IS GOOD. There's no doubt about that. As for myself, I now know that I can be anything I want. It's that easy! I can choose my own path. Many, many additives are gone, leaving more and more and more of just myself. Life is truly beautiful and bright.

The amount of very deep-rooted basic stuff handled is almost unbelievable. The amount of gain is like nothing I've ever experienced in Scientology before. It's a quantum leap.

B.M.
OT Levels

The greatest change for me on this OT level is really finding myself more and more as I always wished to be. I have completely lost all self-invalidation. Things I previously thought as "too hard" or "impossible" or "too exhausting" are now reachable. This level goes deep into the salvation of man. I know I'll never make the same mistakes again.

M.B.
OT Levels

On this OT level I was able to resolve situations that had worried me for an eternity in a matter of minutes. I have become cause over any situation in my life. I can handle, resolve and accomplish what I decide to. Life can be handled totally and solely on a spiritual level. My ability to spot the exact *source of a situation and then handle it immediately is unstoppable.*

> B.R.
> OT Levels

The OT levels create such a feeling of freedom you become able to set your own future and go where you want to go. The OT levels take you to an incredible new realm of self-awareness — but the result is the ability to get more done in life!! I am more part of life and I have the ability to join in and make life happen the way I want it.

> C.M.
> OT Levels

I have regained the power of boundless and limitless persistence. I have regained myself and have no questions as to who I am or why I am. I have regained the spirit of play and the ability to permeate that I had lost and forgotten long ago. This was truly magnificent!

> N.B.
> OT Levels

My understanding of the human condition has vastly expanded. My care for other people has risen enormously. My life is much calmer now. I am much, much less likely to become upset. The gains I have achieved are greater than anything I have ever experienced. Peace of mind and spirit is priceless.

> P. J.B.
> OT Levels

On OT II I have gained competence, respect for myself and others, a deeper understanding of life, an amazement with the simplicity of things, and a sense of well-being.

> M.P.
> OT Levels

PART SIX

CHURCHES OF SCIENTOLOGY AND THEIR ACTIVITIES

The Scientology religion offers mankind the true path to spiritual freedom.

But for an individual to make that journey, there must be some form of organizational structure within which an individual church, or an entire international hierarchy, can function in order to help individuals move along this path.

This need has existed since the very earliest days of Dianetics and Scientology, when the first organization was formed in Mr. Hubbard's living room. As word of the miracles of his discoveries spread, more and more people arrived at his doorstep and it was soon very obvious some form of organization would be needed.

But what form would that organization take? As Mr. Hubbard soon discovered, a workable technology of groups was just as sadly lacking as a true understanding of the mind and spirit. After allowing the adoption of standard management practices of the day and seeing them fail miserably, Mr. Hubbard realized it would be necessary to develop an entirely new system of organizational administration.

And so he did. That pattern of operation became the administrative foundation upon which the entirety of Scientology was built.

Today, every church of Scientology in the world is organized into a standard pattern and organizational structure which makes it possible to minister to the needs of their ever-growing congregations. Individual churches are organized into a hierarchical structure which encompasses all churches and their supporting organizations. From the missions and groups at the entry point of Scientology to the advanced churches which minister the highest levels of Scientology religious services, individual churches of Scientology are the milestones which mark the road Scientologists walk as they cross the Bridge.

This section explains how individual churches of Scientology and the overall international ecclesiastical hierarchy are organized, and how they function to support Scientology's ministry.

CHAPTER 20

STRUCTURE OF SCIENTOLOGY CHURCHES

A church of Scientology is a special place, quite different from the popular conception of a church. It is, for example, not open only on Sundays. The Scientology community around a church comes and goes at different times during the week, and the church is an integral part of their lives. It is where they come to participate in Scientology religious services, engage in community activities, or simply meet friends. Through the church's doors, they walk a road that can be walked nowhere else, a road to personal discovery, awareness and truth.

The atmosphere in a Church of Scientology is also unique, reflecting a place where people are on a path of discovery, where they are attaining new heights of spiritual awareness, and where they are actively and successfully pursuing their goals. It is alive and cheerful, the hope of a better world seems to imbue every activity. Churches of Scientology are friendly, warm and welcoming.

Churches are staffed by dedicated Scientologists who leave their homes each morning knowing that when they return in the evening they will have spent the day helping their fellows become happier and freer. In a thoroughly materialistic and often cold world, there are not many who can claim such personal satisfaction.

The dedication of Church staff extends to serving the needs of parishioners by accommodating the busy schedules of active and involved individuals and families. Thus, churches of Scientology are open seven days a week, with services usually beginning at 9:00 A.M. and continuing throughout the day and evening. Many churches have two teams of staff, one for weekdays and another to serve parishioners on evenings and weekends. The Day staff work from 9:00 to 6:00. The second staff (called Foundation staff in honor of the original organization which was so called because it was considered to be a "FOUNDATION for a new world and a better life") take over from the Day staff at dinner time and keep the church open until 10:30 at night during the week and from 9:00 to 6:00 on weekends. When not working, both Day and Foundation staff tend to the rest of their lives, which includes their families, other personal obligations and, of course, their own progress in Scientology.

The church literally is always there, and Scientologists count on it as a stable reference point in their lives. They know that when they need something, their church always will be there to help them.

BUILDING THE BRIDGE

As an individual moves up the Bridge, making the journey from preclear to Clear to OT, he moves progressively up through increasingly higher stages of awareness, a gradient improvement, with each advance built upon the one before. It is here we find the key to the organizational structure of the religion of Scientology, for just as these stages of awareness comprise the backbone of the Bridge, so, too, are they fundamental to the pattern of organization used by individual churches—known as the organizing board.

In 1965, searching for the key to workable administration, Mr. Hubbard developed the organizing board, a pattern of operation based on seven internal "divisions" which express every function a Scientology church needs to attend to in order to minister to its congregation. The organizing board—or org board for short—also represents the cycle of expansion. As Mr. Hubbard discovered, for any activity to grow, it must move through a series of twenty-one states of awareness which are a part of this cycle.

The org board forms more than just an efficient pattern of operation, however. And while it is true that these administrative principles are applicable to any activity in any organization, Mr. Hubbard developed them specifically for churches of Scientology and, as a result, something very special occurs when one steps into a Scientology church and becomes a part of its administration. As a Scientologist enters the church and passes through these different divisions, he also moves through the twenty-one states of awareness.

These states are a direct reflection of his ascent up the Grade Chart, for it too is based on the twenty-one states of awareness that make up every cycle of expansion. Thus, it is easy to see how the administrative form that Scientology organizations take matches the spiritual steps of awareness one must pass through to reach the state of OT.

The org board, then, marks out a route of growth for the individual, and for the organization.

THE SEVEN-DIVISION ORG BOARD

Mr. Hubbard developed the seven-division organizing board administrative pattern in 1965. Since then, it has been used in all churches of Scientology, their supporting organizations and their related charitable and educational organizations as well. It is an arrangement of administrative functions specifically designed to support the spiritual purposes of a church.

As noted above, this pattern contains seven divisions which describe all the actions encompassed by the organization. Each division is subdivided into three departments. In these seven divisions and their twenty-one subdivisions one finds all the functions, duties, positions, sequences of action and channels of communication within the organization.

The first division is the Hubbard Communications Office—so named because its main functions were originally part of L. Ron Hubbard's office in the early days of Scientology. This division establishes, which means literally, keeps the church operating. Here, Department 1 provides new staff and ensures they get hatted for their church positions. A hatted staff member is one who is able to competently perform the specific functions of his position.

Division 2 is the Dissemination Division. *Dissemination* means to spread or scatter broadly. In a Scientology church, this division informs the public about Scientology services and scriptural materials. It produces mailings and publications, such as the church's magazines, which are sent to all parishioners, and operates the church bookstore. When parishioners write in to request information about or arrange for services, staff within this division respond to the requests.

Division 3 is Treasury. All corporations, even religious ones, are required to keep proper financial records. The church's fixed donation system of fund-raising provides the financial support necessary for it to disseminate Scientology, carry on its work in the community and continue its ministry to a growing congregation. Division 3 pays the bills and keeps financial records. It also provides for the upkeep of the church's premises and equipment.

Division 4 is the Technical Division, and its staff minister the church's core religious services of auditing and training. It is here where a parishioner participates in the services of the Grade Chart. Since auditing and training are the central activities of every church, this division often contains four to five times more personnel than other divisions. The other divisions of the organization support and facilitate these activities.

The next division, Division 5, is the Qualifications Division. This division sees to the enhancement, training and care of the staff. Any staff member who has any difficulty in performing his duties will receive immediate attention and help from Division 5. Division 5 also helps parishioners who have difficulty applying the principles they have learned in training, and conducts internships in auditor training. It also verifies that parishioners have realized the full spiritual gains and abilities in their auditing and training. The Qualifications Division is therefore the division that issues certificates, validating new states of spiritual ability and awareness.

Division 6 is called the Public Division. Here, individuals are introduced to Scientology through lectures and films, open houses, Sunday church services and tape plays and introductory religious services.

This division reaches out to the community to provide assistance when needed and contributes to local social programs. Through the Public Division, the church performs many goodwill activities which benefit the entire community. Division 6 personnel also help parishioners form "field groups" to minister basic Dianetics and Scientology services to the public so more people can benefit from Dianetics and Scientology.

The last division is the Executive Division, Division 7, which is responsible for ensuring through careful planning and supervision that the church as a whole remains viable and able to minister to its congregation. The Executive Director of the church also is Division 7's most senior staff member. Division 7 is also responsible for secular corporate functions, legal affairs and government relations.

Another important executive in each church who serves in Division 7 is the L. Ron Hubbard (LRH) Communicator—a position established when Mr. Hubbard served as Executive Director of the Church and maintained a local representative in each church to facilitate his communications. Today, the LRH Communicator is responsible for ensuring that the church adheres to Scientology scripture. This duty is especially critical for proper functioning of the church because it is only through the orthodox ministry of auditing and training, as precisely provided in the scripture, that the gains and accomplishments of Dianetics and Scientology are possible. The LRH Communicator also preserves the L. Ron Hubbard office maintained in every church as a mark of respect for the Founder of the religion.

By carrying out its specific functions, each division contributes to the overall ministry of the church. Each department within a division likewise has its own distinct duties which must be carried out for the division itself to function correctly.

ORGANIZING BOARD

(Simplified version, showing the organizational pattern used in all churches of Scientology)

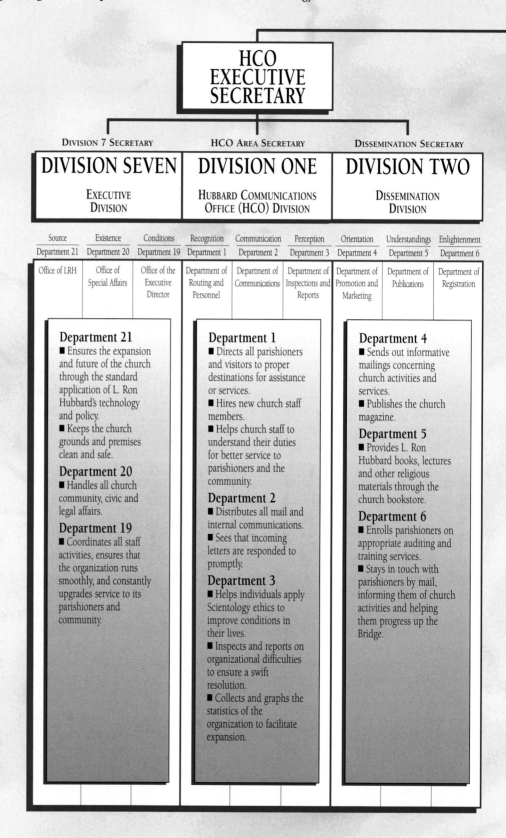

HCO EXECUTIVE SECRETARY

DIVISION 7 SECRETARY | HCO AREA SECRETARY | DISSEMINATION SECRETARY

DIVISION SEVEN
EXECUTIVE DIVISION

DIVISION ONE
HUBBARD COMMUNICATIONS OFFICE (HCO) DIVISION

DIVISION TWO
DISSEMINATION DIVISION

Source Department 21	Existence Department 20	Conditions Department 19	Recognition Department 1	Communication Department 2	Perception Department 3	Orientation Department 4	Understandings Department 5	Enlightenment Department 6
Office of LRH	Office of Special Affairs	Office of the Executive Director	Department of Routing and Personnel	Department of Communications	Department of Inspections and Reports	Department of Promotion and Marketing	Department of Publications	Department of Registration

Department 21
- Ensures the expansion and future of the church through the standard application of L. Ron Hubbard's technology and policy.
- Keeps the church grounds and premises clean and safe.

Department 20
- Handles all church community, civic and legal affairs.

Department 19
- Coordinates all staff activities, ensures that the organization runs smoothly, and constantly upgrades service to its parishioners and community.

Department 1
- Directs all parishioners and visitors to proper destinations for assistance or services.
- Hires new church staff members.
- Helps church staff to understand their duties for better service to parishioners and the community.

Department 2
- Distributes all mail and internal communications.
- Sees that incoming letters are responded to promptly.

Department 3
- Helps individuals apply Scientology ethics to improve conditions in their lives.
- Inspects and reports on organizational difficulties to ensure a swift resolution.
- Collects and graphs the statistics of the organization to facilitate expansion.

Department 4
- Sends out informative mailings concerning church activities and services.
- Publishes the church magazine.

Department 5
- Provides L. Ron Hubbard books, lectures and other religious materials through the church bookstore.

Department 6
- Enrolls parishioners on appropriate auditing and training services.
- Stays in touch with parishioners by mail, informing them of church activities and helping them progress up the Bridge.

EXECUTIVE DIRECTOR

ORGANIZATION EXECUTIVE SECRETARY

TREASURY SECRETARY	TECHNICAL SECRETARY	QUALIFICATIONS SECRETARY	PUBLIC SECRETARY
DIVISION THREE	**DIVISION FOUR**	**DIVISION FIVE**	**DIVISION SIX**
TREASURY DIVISION	TECHNICAL DIVISION	QUALIFICATIONS DIVISION	PUBLIC DIVISION

Energy	Adjustment	Body	Prediction	Activity	Production	Result	Correction	Ability	Purposes	Clearing	Realization
Department 7	Department 8	Department 9	Department 10	Department 11	Department 12	Department 13	Department 14	Department 15	Department 16	Department 17	Department 18
Department of Income	Department of Disbursements	Department of Records, Assets and Materiel	Department of Technical Services	Department of Activity	Department of Production	Department of Examinations	Department of Review	Department of Certifications and Awards	Department of Public Information	Department of Clearing	Department of Success

Department 7
■ Accepts donations and collects other income.

Department 8
■ Sees to the material needs of the church and its staff by purchasing all items required to keep the church functioning.
■ Pays any bills incurred by the church.

Department 9
■ Cares for all church furniture, equipment and the like, ensuring such property is well maintained and properly functioning.
■ Keeps records of church accounts.

Department 10
■ Helps preclears and students schedule their religious services.
■ Helps arrange housing for out-of-town parishioners.
■ Provides technical staff with supplies and materials to deliver auditing and training.

Department 11
■ Ministers Scientology training services to parishioners.
■ Trains auditors who can help others move up the Bridge.

Department 12
■ Ministers Scientology auditing services.

Department 13
■ Verifies that students and preclears have received the full spiritual benefit of their services.

Department 14
■ Corrects errors in the ministry of religious services.
■ Ministers religious services to staff.

Department 15
■ Issues certificates to those who complete church services.

Department 16
■ Makes Dianetics and Scientology more broadly known and delivers introductory lectures to inform people about the subjects.

Department 17
■ Provides introductory training, auditing and seminars.
■ Delivers chaplain services including marriage counseling.
■ Performs ministerial services including weddings, naming ceremonies and Sunday services.

Department 18
■ Appoints and assists volunteer ministers to perform their functions in the community.
■ Helps open new Dianetics and Scientology groups in the area.
■ Assists the local community church goodwill programs.

These volumes contain the codification of
the administrative technology used by all
Scientology churches and organizations.

ORGANIZATION EXECUTIVE COURSE

QUALIFICATIONS DIVISION
L. RON HUBBARD
5

PUBLIC DIVISION
L. RON HUBBARD
6

EXECUTIVE DIVISION
L. RON HUBBARD
7

MANAGEMENT SERIES
L. RON HUBBARD
VOLUME 1

MANAGEMENT SERIES
L. RON HUBBARD
VOLUME 2

MANAGEMENT SERIES
L. RON HUBBARD
VOLUME 3

OEC AND MANAGEMENT SERIES
POLICY INDEX
L. RON HUBBARD
INDEX

SCIENTOLOGY ADMINISTRATIVE POLICY

Having described the basic organizational form, one can now begin to understand the specific policies upon which that framework functions. These precise and workable administrative policies were developed by Mr. Hubbard through years of research and experience, and constitute a tremendous body of material relating to the survival of a group.

As with everything Mr. Hubbard accomplished, his discoveries came from hard-won experience. As Executive Director of Scientology churches internationally, he was familiar with virtually every position and function, ironing out difficulties and forming the policy for smooth and efficient operation. In fact, he isolated administrative fundamentals for every level of an organization from top to bottom. He wrote policies covering the theory and procedures of every facet of a Scientology organization. These policies define the basic laws of the third dynamic (group survival) and constitute a body of knowledge as important to administration of groups as his writings on Dianetics and Scientology are to rehabilitation of the spirit.

Mr. Hubbard arranged his administrative technology into a twelve-volume set of reference texts. Volume 0, the Basic Staff Hat, contains all policies pertinent to every Church staff member and provides a thorough orientation to organizational structure for new staff members. Seven of the remaining volumes, numbered one through seven, correspond to the same numbered divisions of the organizing board. Volume 1, for example, covers Division 1; Volume 2, Division 2; and so on. Each divisional volume contains all the policies pertaining to the purpose and functions of that division. Organized in this way, any Church staff member can easily find the policies which describe his own functions within the group or the functions of any other staff member. The remaining volumes encompass Mr. Hubbard's writings on the subject of management and executive know-how.

These books codify the administrative principles and techniques successfully operating Scientology churches, or any organization for that matter. When important functions are missing, the organization necessarily is, to that degree, unsuccessful. And to the extent each function is present and properly operating, the organization will be successful. Church executives train on courses which cover the totality of these volumes and learn to apply them in discharging their day-to-day responsibilities.

Mr. Hubbard discovered and delineated the basics on which any group operated and, as such, these breakthroughs are broadly applicable. Thus, although Mr. Hubbard developed this technology to help administer Dianetics and Scientology, Scientologists who worked outside the Church adapted these principles to other groups as well. Since then his administrative principles have been used by many other organizations around the world with extraordinary success.

THE CHURCH
AND ITS PARISHIONERS

Once a week, usually on Friday, parishioners gather for graduation, a time when they acknowledge their fellow parishioners who have completed a course or level of auditing. At this time they have the opportunity to share their successes during a spirited assembly which also serves to encourage others to progress up the Bridge.

While most people recognize the need for a stronger emphasis on religion in their lives, very few are as actively committed to the practice of their religion as Scientologists. Whereas members of many religions generally meet only on Sundays, Scientologists may spend several hours each day, five days a week for a period of several weeks at their church while auditing or training. Many are also highly committed to participating in church-sponsored community betterment programs.

CHAPTER 21

CHURCHES, MISSIONS AND GROUPS

Today, Scientology is practiced in more than 125 countries. Its churches comprise a hierarchy which ministers services from the most basic to the most spiritually advanced, raising man out of his day-to-day problems and carrying him to never-before envisioned spiritual vistas.

The millions of people who have been introduced to the miracles of L. Ron Hubbard's technology are a broad mixture of cultures, races and nationalities. Each day they are joined by thousands more to whom Scientology is brand-new.

A person discovering Scientology for the first time usually reads a book, learns about the subject from a friend, attends a lecture in someone's home or takes an introductory course at a local mission. As it was in the early 1950s, news about the miracles of Dianetics and Scientology is still most often spread by personal contact and word of mouth.

Those who carry forward this message of a bright and hopeful future are the field auditors, groups and missions of Scientology, which exist to minister the religion at the grass-roots level.

Above this level are the more established churches of Scientology which are the centers for Scientology in their cities and the focal points for many community outreach activities. Here, parishioners come to study Scientology scripture and learn to audit.

The more advanced Scientology churches minister the highest levels of auditing and training, including the OT levels. Here, parishioners are certain to rediscover their true potential as spiritual beings.

To serve the spiritual needs of congregations and to ensure all religious services are ministered in strict accordance with Scientology scripture, the worldwide churches of Scientology are organized in a hierarchical structure which includes churches that minister directly to Scientology parishioners, as well as church "management" organizations that oversee, support and guide their activities. This section provides an explanation of the former category of Scientology churches—those that directly minister to the needs of the growing number of Scientologists throughout the world.

FIELD AUDITORS, AND DIANETICS AND SCIENTOLOGY GROUPS

Auditing at the Grass Roots

When asked to describe a time when life seemed most fulfilling, a great many people will give the same answer: when they were able to help someone in a time of genuine need, whether a friend, family member, even a complete stranger.

Most would offer help more often — if they knew what to do, or felt confident that they could do it correctly. For many field auditors, this explains perfectly their dedication in pursuing their calling.

Each day, field auditors give new hope to the lives of those in their community. They audit, provide marriage counseling, help resolve drug habits, and in everything they do, help to make life less difficult for those they meet.

Field auditors exist all over the world — from the busiest cities to some of the most remote extremities of society. For many people, the field auditor is their first contact with the Scientology religion, and his ministry their first step on the Bridge to Total Freedom.

A couple in southern California who are field auditors gave just one of many examples of their success in helping others move onto the Bridge and discover that there is hope for a better life:

"We have had thousands of miracles in our lives and in our preclears' lives. . . . A recent one involved two professionals who came to us for auditing. With all the trappings of success, their lives had been devastated by drug abuse. Both had been using hard drugs for years. The wife was in particularly bad shape, and it took all the tools of ethics we knew to turn her life

around. Both she and her husband are now. . . receiving auditing from us. They are winning more than they ever thought possible."

A Scientologist in the northern suburbs of Chicago who has dedicated himself to serving his community as a field auditor says, "Every morning, come rain, shine, wind or snow, I get up, kiss my wife and the kids goodbye, and board the train for my office in Chicago. There I provide auditing and get people up the Bridge to Clear. . . . It's a powerful incentive to me to continue auditing others when I see the changes in their lives and their understanding of life itself."

Field auditors sometimes join together to form Auditors Associations or Dianetics Counseling Groups, expanding their outreach to the public by giving lectures and seminars and by ministering Dianetics and Scientology services. Field auditors everywhere are united and aided by a Church organization called International Hubbard Ecclesiastical League of Pastors (I HELP). (See Chapter 22 for more information.) Alone or with others, the field auditor serves the individual, the building block of the society, contributing to his ability to improve his own life and the world around him by setting him on the path to spiritual growth and understanding.

As L. Ron Hubbard wrote, "Let a man know he is himself, a spiritual being, that he is capable of the power of choice and has the right to aspire to greater wisdom and you have started him up a higher road."

And therein lies the true purpose of the field auditor.

Field auditors and Dianetics
Counseling Groups minister
the following services:

■ INTRODUCTORY LECTURES

■ TAPE PLAYS OF L. RON HUBBARD'S LECTURES

■ HUBBARD DIANETICS SEMINAR

■ SUCCESS THROUGH COMMUNICATION COURSE

■ OTHER INTRODUCTORY SERVICES FOR PEOPLE NEW TO SCIENTOLOGY

■ SCIENTOLOGY ASSISTS

■ PURIFICATION PROGRAM

■ DIANETICS AND SCIENTOLOGY AUDITING THROUGH NEW ERA DIANETICS

SCIENTOLOGY MISSIONS

Pioneering Dianetics and Scientology

Not unlike those early pioneers and missionaries who braved challenging environments in far-flung countries, opening up Scientology today in a new place— whether a small town in the USA or a mountain village in Nepal—is always an adventure. It usually starts with someone reading one or more of L. Ron Hubbard's books, which creates a thirst for more information about Dianetics and Scientology technology in the new area. A person calls in from a far-flung city in Siberia, or from the center of Indiana, says he has been co-auditing for a hundred or a thousand hours on Dianetics, and wants to know, "What do I do next?"

More often than not, a Scientology missionary arrives on his doorstep, and ignites the spark. He or she begins by inviting people in the community to a lecture on Scientology. The grass-roots interest grows and soon more people are co-auditing. A group forms and expands. It provides even broader services—basic courses, introductory lectures, and perhaps the Purification Rundown. More new people are introduced to Scientology and Dianetics and what was once a handful grows to a small community of Scientologists in the hundreds. Soon what was a group of twenty has become a mission.

Although missions start in a number of ways, the simple fact is that any Scientologist may qualify to open one and thereby contribute to the spiritual growth of his community. Often, missions are founded by individual Scientologists who, having experienced the benefits of Scientology, want to introduce their religion to others in new parts of the world. Starting a mission is truly a pioneering activity that fulfills the wishes of Scientologists who want to offer to others in sometimes remote corners of the world the spiritual gains they have themselves realized.

"Starting a new mission from scratch has been the most adventurous thing I have done this lifetime," said one Scientologist. "I can't tell you what a thrill it has been to help a brand-new person find the truth. Life just isn't the same for a person once he has come into contact with the technology."

Sometimes the reach for Dianetics and Scientology is dramatic, as was the case of a man in war-torn Croatia who decided the best way to start his country on the road to peace was to establish a mission in the capital city of Zagreb. "I was mobilized and had to spend two months serving in the Croatian army in command of twelve. I spent every moment of our free time telling them about Dianetics and Scientology." There on the battlefield he found many individuals drawn to Dianetics and Scientology, and from them came his first staff members and parishioners.

Through spirit such as this, Scientology has reached in recent years into India, Pakistan, Sri Lanka, the Philippines, Indonesia, Japan, Taiwan, Africa, Romania and across the vast face of the Commonwealth of Independent States. Hundreds pour into missions in Moscow and throughout Russia to get a seat in a crowded hall to hear about Dianetics, and to have the spark of spiritual freedom rekindled.

Missions minister all the introductory and beginning services of Dianetics and Scientology, including extension courses, the Personal Efficiency Course, Life Improvement Courses, Dianetics Seminars, the Success Through Communication Course, the Student Hat, the Hubbard Qualified Scientologist Course, the PTS/SP Course and certain co-auditing courses where Scientologists learn to audit each other on specific actions. Not surprisingly, it is during these co-audits that some of the most spectacular revelations occur, for here the individual not only experiences the power of the technology but sees its effects on another.

"I had my first experience auditing another person in a Dianetics co-audit," reported one parishioner. "It was the most thrilling moment of my life to see someone change for the better right before my eyes and to see a problem that had plagued him all his life vanish completely as he saw for himself where it had come from and why it had affected him."

Missions may also minister the Purification program and all auditing services up through New Era Dianetics, including introductory auditing and Expanded Lower Grades. Missions fulfill a vital need, for those who learn about Scientology at a mission are discovering basic skills and fundamental truths which they can immediately apply to improve their own lives and the lives of others. Missions in all countries are helped and guided by Scientology Missions International (SMI). (See Chapter 22 for more information.)

Standing at the entrance gates to the Bridge, missions reach out into their communities to inform people of the miracles of Dianetics and Scientology. Those who take their first steps on the Bridge in a mission are beginning what will become life-changing new voyages of self-discovery. They, too, are pioneers.

There are hundreds of missions located in scores of countries around the world. They minister the following services:

- INTRODUCTORY LECTURES, FILMS AND TAPES

- EXTENSION COURSES

- LIFE IMPROVEMENT COURSES

- PERSONAL EFFICIENCY COURSE

- HUBBARD DIANETICS SEMINAR

- SUCCESS THROUGH COMMUNICATION COURSE

- OTHER INTRODUCTORY SERVICES FOR PEOPLE NEW TO SCIENTOLOGY

- SCIENTOLOGISTS HATTING COURSES

- STUDENT HAT

- STUDY CERTAINTY COURSE

- PTS/SP COURSE

- PURIFICATION PROGRAM

- DIANETICS AND SCIENTOLOGY AUDITING THROUGH NEW ERA DIANETICS

CLASS V ORGANIZATIONS

A local Scientology church is both a spiritual *and* a social hub for its parishioners — a bustling center of activity and a focal point for the religion. The next level in the hierarchy above missions and groups, these churches express their own special ambience. It is partly the friendliness, partly the sense of dedication that permeates the place, and partly the dynamic mix of people, individuals of different ages, backgrounds and lifestyles all working so well together under one roof. All of these combine to result in what L. Ron Hubbard characterized simply as "the spirit of Scientology."

And that spirit is unique.

Like Scientology field groups and missions, a local church provides introductory lectures, workshops, seminars and other religious services to people new to Scientology. This is where those who are curious about Scientology can call or visit and immediately find out about — and participate in, if they wish — introductory services. And it is where they can also discover exactly how to chart their path to Clear and beyond.

What is most distinctive about these Scientology churches is that each is a *technical* hub as well. Here a young woman who wants to learn the exact technology that will help her resolve a difficult relationship sits next to a grandmother who is studying so she can help her grandchildren do better in life. And at the next table there may be a teenager who wants to learn auditing so he can help others. These parishioners are all intent on learning to apply L. Ron Hubbard's technology and achieving the spiritual results that technology delivers. Skillful Case Supervisors help them progress through the auditing levels of the Scientology Grades and New Era Dianetics (see Chapter 13) and guide them as they receive training through Class V Graduate Auditor level (see Chapter 14). For this reason, these churches are known to Scientologists as Class V organizations.

"My church is like no other place I have ever been," said a parishioner of a Scientology church in a large city. "I am *cared for* there, in the most valuable way possible — I learn about myself as a spiritual being, and then how to use that when I go out the doors of the church into my daily life. My auditing and training address the most important aspects of *my* life, and I love going into my church."

At a Class V church one finds parishioners of all walks of life actively moving up the Bridge. Here a Scientologist takes his first steps toward the states of Clear and Operating Thetan (OT). He usually takes courses, whether attending on a schedule at night and on weekends while he works, or arranges his life so he can study full time during the day.

Parishioners in these congregations have usually started their first steps on the Bridge at area Scientology missions or through field auditor services. And, in fact, Class V churches provide technical assistance to the executives and staff of area Scientology missions, as well as local field auditors and groups.

As Class V churches also work to make Dianetics and Scientology broadly known in their communities, many of these churches establish smaller offices in nearby areas and towns to provide introductory services. Similarly, these churches assist Scientologists to establish groups and missions, thus meeting the increasing grass-roots demand for L. Ron Hubbard's technology.

Scientologists gather at their local Scientology churches for marriages, funerals, naming ceremonies and ordinations of ministers to mark important points in the lives of the congregation. There are also weekly Sunday services at which a Scientology minister or other speaker addresses the congregation concerning some aspect of Scientology religious doctrine. At these services attendees also learn of upcoming events, recent news and specific Church of Scientology community actions.

Churches of Scientology hold congregational gatherings on Friday nights during which members of the church come together to share their recent accomplishments in the religion. Such gatherings are festive and lively affairs, often including a performance by a musical group of church members, or people telling of their latest community project. Parishioners also gather periodically at their church to listen to recorded lectures by L. Ron Hubbard.

But the highest points on the Scientology calendar are the Church celebrations of Scientology holidays, such as the annual L. Ron Hubbard birthday event or the Auditor's Day celebration. Broadcast live (or in some instances prerecorded) from the main centers of Scientology such as Clearwater, Florida; Los Angeles, California; or Saint Hill Manor in East Grinstead, England, these celebrations feature current news about the religion in general and specific accomplishments at churches throughout the world, presented by prominent ecclesiastical leaders. Even visitors often comment on the professional presentation of these gatherings—and their high emotional and artistic impact. More importantly, these events serve to strengthen the sense of community and the common spiritual purpose of Church members.

Class V churches not only provide a vital focal point for Scientology in their areas, but at this stage on the Bridge, a Scientologist stands on the threshold of new spiritual discoveries unlike any other. These churches provide a safe and stable place for all the Scientology activities in an area to help parishioners move up the Bridge to Total Freedom.

Scientology Class V Churches minister the following religious services:

■ ALL INTRODUCTORY SERVICES MINISTERED BY MISSIONS

■ ALL DIANETICS AND SCIENTOLOGY AUDITING THROUGH NEW ERA DIANETICS AND EXPANDED DIANETICS

■ AUDITOR TRAINING TO THE LEVEL OF CLASS V GRADUATE

■ THE MINISTER'S COURSE AND ORDAINING MINISTERS

■ TECHNICAL SPECIALIST COURSES

■ THE HUBBARD KEY TO LIFE COURSE

■ THE HUBBARD LIFE ORIENTATION COURSE

■ THE HUBBARD SOLO AUDITOR COURSE, PART ONE

■ CLEAR

■ SUNSHINE RUNDOWN

Celebrity Centres

L. Ron Hubbard once wrote, "A culture is only as great as its dreams, and its dreams are dreamed by artists." As an artist himself, Mr. Hubbard understood only too well just how important those dreams are to the creative person. He recognized, as well, that artists supply the spark of creativity and the vision of what could be leading us all into tomorrow.

It is an irrefutable fact that artists wield enormous influence over society, setting cultural trends and forwarding new ideas, both good and bad. For example, in the 1960s, musicians promoted drugs and helped lead an entire generation into the drug culture. On the other hand, many artists work to raise public awareness of environmental concerns, provide society with spiritual insights or urge reform of troubled areas.

In either case, by example and through their art, they communicate to millions. Thus, by improving the lives of artists, great progress can be achieved to better the condition of society—for any artist with an increased ability to communicate, who is drug-free and has high moral standards, imparts a positive influence on many others.

There is one type of Scientology church that is particularly reflective of how L. Ron Hubbard viewed the artist and his role in rebuilding what is plainly a troubled society: the Church of Scientology Celebrity Centres.

Founded in 1969 in accordance with explicit directions from L. Ron Hubbard, the Church of Scientology Celebrity Centre utilizes the full body of Dianetics and Scientology on behalf of the creative individual. And when Mr. Hubbard speaks of rehabilitating artistic creativity, he is actually speaking of rehabilitating the source of all creativity, the human spirit. Rekindling the artist spiritually enhances his creative potential, restores to him high ethical standards, and otherwise helps him to forward his work in the creative arts.

"I've been coming to Celebrity Centre for years now, and every time I'm there, I am revitalized," said one artist. "It's just such an aesthetic environment, it makes me feel free and ready to create again."

"Celebrity Centre is absolutely an oasis for me, and for any creative person," said a Scientologist. "My creativity and my spiritual life are intertwined, but in the harsh world of the entertainment industry, they sometimes seem to clash. At Celebrity Centre, I have a safe haven where I can enjoy my fellow artists and share our creative spirit as well as our spiritual lives. It is a *very* special church."

Such revitalization of the spirit of artists bodes well for society's future. And this occurs daily with thousands of such individuals around the world.

Celebrity Centre ministers the same services as other Class V organizations. The artist who comes to a Celebrity Centre takes the same spiritual journey across the Bridge as the millions of other parishioners who are not in the public spotlight. Art and music have been linked with man's religious quest throughout history. At the Church of Scientology Celebrity Centre, the religious services of the church elevate the individual artist to achieve his own spiritual goals and in turn, the artists routinely channel their inspiration in ways which contribute to the spiritual uplifting of society as a whole.

To date, Celebrity Centres exist in eleven major cities and cultural centers around the world, including Celebrity Centre's international headquarters appropriately located in Hollywood's historic Château Elysée, once an in-town getaway for some of that city's most memorable stars during its heyday.

Wherever Church of Scientology Celebrity Centres exist, the local community also benefits from the individual spiritual growth that comes with the rehabilitation of writers, musicians, actors and actresses. In each community, these artists — some of the brightest luminaries of stage and screen — regularly perform benefit concerts to support a wide range of local charities.

Through his creations, the artist creates a cultural renaissance. At Celebrity Centres that renaissance begins with the spiritual revitalization and rehabilitation of the artist.

Church of Scientology
Celebrity Centres minister
the following religious services:

■ ALL SERVICES MINISTERED BY CLASS V CHURCHES

SAINT HILL ORGANIZATIONS

The fountainhead of much of Scientology —technically and organizationally—is the heritage of the church of Scientology at Saint Hill in East Grinstead, Sussex, England. During the period L. Ron Hubbard resided there, from 1959 through 1966, some of the Scientology religion's most historically significant events took place.

"It was at Saint Hill that our growth began," Mr. Hubbard later wrote. "It was from here that the upper bastions of freedom and ability were issued."

This English manor was not only Mr. Hubbard's home, but the bustling site of some of his most important breakthroughs on the subject of the mind and spirit. The first Scientology Clears were made here, as were the first to reach the levels of OT— Operating Thetan.

"I arrived at Saint Hill in April 1965," recalls a Scientologist. "There were about fifty-six or fifty-seven staff. By August, there were two hundred staff. It was CROWDED. People audited elbow to elbow and nobody minded."

Another Scientologist said of the period: "My first impression of Saint Hill was it was *busy* and *friendly*. There were always new people arriving, but it was very orderly and stable.

"The atmosphere was enthusiastic. Clears were being announced all the time and there was a lot of very fast movement on the Grade Chart."

During these years, Scientologists came from all corners of the world to listen to Mr. Hubbard's daily lectures on his new discoveries. They applied these breakthroughs immediately, and from this came new techniques and procedures for training auditors to a level of skill not previously attainable on what was known as the original Saint Hill Special Briefing Course (SHSBC).

Today, *all* of the materials on which Mr. Hubbard briefed those first parishioners —in total, more than 430 recorded lectures— remain the very core of the Briefing Course.

When other churches were formed in Copenhagen, Los Angeles and Sydney to minister this advanced and special auditor training, they opened their doors as *Saint Hill Organizations* for they, too, specialize in conducting the SHSBC for all Scientology parishioners in their part of the world.

Saint Hill Organizations must maintain facilities for parishioners from both local areas and even other countries. Most parishioners who travel to a Saint Hill arrange their schedules so they can devote themselves to an intensive period of training— several months to a year—on the Briefing Course. Thus, Saint Hills have a high concentration of parishioners who devote their full time to religious services.

The intensity of discovery, of obtaining greater spiritual knowledge and practice is every bit as alive as in those earliest days of the Briefing Course.

Today, Scientologists still come to East Grinstead from around the world for the Briefing Course or simply to see an important place in Scientology's history. Visitors to the Manor see the course rooms where the first lectures of the original Briefing Course were given, and the research room where Mr. Hubbard made his historic breakthroughs into the states of Clear and OT, opening the Bridge to all mankind.

And today, when a Scientologist wishes to dedicate himself to the full understanding of his religion at the church which represents the very heart of Scientology, he does so at a Saint Hill.

Church of Scientology Saint Hill Organizations are found in four locations around the world: East Grinstead, Los Angeles, Sydney and Copenhagen.

They minister the following religious services:

■ ALL AUDITING AND TRAINING SERVICES MINISTERED BY SCIENTOLOGY CLASS V CHURCHES

■ POWER PROCESSING

■ THE SAINT HILL SPECIAL BRIEFING COURSE

■ CLASS VII AUDITOR TRAINING

■ AUDITING SERVICES ON THE GRADE CHART THROUGH ELIGIBILITY FOR OT LEVELS AUDITING

■ THE HUBBARD SOLO AUDITOR COURSE

ADVANCED ORGANIZATIONS

That man is a spiritual being is the most fundamental truth in Scientology and no matter where a parishioner receives Scientology services, his problems can be handled by addressing the underlying spiritual factors which hold those difficulties in place. At the advanced levels of Scientology, however, one begins to explore the true nature of the spiritual universe and to confront the long-hidden lies which have led him to drastically reduce his own potential as a spiritual being. Church of Scientology Advanced Organizations minister these OT (Operating Thetan) levels, as they are called, states of spiritual existence and ability heretofore unknown to man.

At an Advanced Organization, the individual recovers lost abilities and gains new insights into the nature of his own spirituality, his relationship to others, the material universe and the eighth dynamic. Thus it is not surprising to find that an atmosphere of spiritual discovery permeates these churches. Those who come to an Advanced Organization have studied long and hard to reach this point on the Bridge and moving up the OT levels is a significant step. It is here that individuals fully recover true certainty of their own spirituality and become confident of their ability to play and win the game of life, not only today but far into the future.

Advanced Organization churches minister to parishioners who move up the Bridge from missions and Class V churches in countries on every continent. Advanced Organization churches are located in Los Angeles, California; East Grinstead, England; Copenhagen, Denmark and Sydney, Australia. At these churches, one progresses through the OT levels to the completion of OT Section V. Advanced Organizations also minister the training services Class VIII Auditor and Case Supervisor Courses.

In the Advanced Organization of Los Angeles, Scientologists from throughout the United States, Canada, Mexico and South America participate in the OT levels or Class VIII Auditor training. Similarly, the Advanced Organization in Sydney, Australia, ministers to Scientologists from the Southern Hemisphere and the Orient. Parishioners from throughout Europe travel to the Advanced Organization in Denmark, where the OT levels are ministered in every major language of the continent. And Scientologists from the United Kingdom go to the Advanced Organization at Saint Hill in East Grinstead, Sussex, England.

Each OT level is a step on an exciting journey to spiritual discovery. As one parishioner described it, "Things which I never understood about myself and others were suddenly perfectly clear. My life was different every day."

Another parishioner described her experience: "As I walked through the door of the Advanced Organization, I knew I had come to an extraordinary place. The bustle and excitement and the familiar Scientology friendliness were my first impressions. I felt immediately at home even though this church was many times the size of the church in my community. I met Scientologists from all walks of life—a house painter, physician, architect, actor, fireman—and we became good friends during the weeks we were on the Advanced Courses together. There is no way to describe the exhilaration I felt as a result of experiencing these spiritual levels."

To a Scientologist, arrival at an Advanced Organization is a major landmark in his spiritual journey across the Bridge. At this juncture, he is fully prepared for his most important steps yet on the path which leads upward to true spiritual freedom.

Four Church of Scientology Advanced Organizations minister the following religious services:

■ ALL AUDITING AND TRAINING SERVICES MINISTERED BY CLASS V CHURCHES

■ ALL PROCESSING SERVICES FROM GRADE VI RELEASE THROUGH NEW OT V NEW ERA DIANETICS FOR OTs

■ DOCTORATE SERIES COURSE FOR OTs

■ CLASS VIII AUDITOR AND C/S TRAINING

FLAG SERVICE ORGANIZATION

The Flag Service Organization (FSO) is a religious retreat which serves as the spiritual headquarters for Scientologists from all over the world. It is the hub of the Scientology worldwide community, a dynamic, multilingual organization and is the largest single church of Scientology in the world. The FSO not only ministers the most advanced levels of training available anywhere, but all of the OT levels up to New OT VII, Solo New Era Dianetics for OTs (Solo NOTs).

From the late 1960s through the mid-1970s, the highest ecclesiastical organizations were located at sea aboard a flotilla of ships. The 350-foot vessel *Apollo* served as Mr. Hubbard's home. Because of this, it was then the most senior Scientology church, known as the "flagship" of the flotilla and called "Flag" for short. (See Chapter 33.)

At that time, special advanced auditing and training services were ministered only aboard Flag. However, as more and more Scientologists wanted to participate in these services, the lack of sufficient space required a move to land. And, in 1975, the Flag Service Organization established itself in Clearwater, Florida, where it occupied the eleven-story Fort Harrison Hotel. Since then, Flag has continued to expand. Today it also occupies the Sandcastle Hotel which ministers advanced auditing, the Coachman Building which at any given time serves as a training center for thousands of Scientologists and several other supporting facilities. Due to Flag's growing international congregation, new construction is always ongoing to provide still more facilities for its parishioners.

Today, nearly eight hundred staff minister to parishioners who travel from around the world to participate in auditing and training at the FSO. Because many stay for several weeks or even months at a time before returning home, the FSO also provides comfortable accommodations for its parishioners so they can progress up the Bridge free from the distractions and turbulence of the day-to-day world.

"Flag saved my life, really," said a Scientologist who is a television and film producer. "Flag is really the place to be. It's the best place in the world to get auditing. It's precise, and there's tremendous care in every action and service. It's simply the most theta place in the world."

Another Scientologist said, "I come to Flag for spiritual rejuvenation. Just being in the atmosphere is an incredible experience in itself. Being with other Scientologists from all over the world is very exciting, and Flag definitely lives up to its reputation as the friendliest place in the world."

The FSO ministers Dianetics and Scientology services from the bottom of the Bridge through to New OT VII, plus certain specialized auditing services only available there.

Here, also, Scientologists participate in training to the level of Class XII, which is the highest auditor classification in Scientology. Auditor training from Class IX and above is available only at the FSO and only to members of the Sea Organization. Only Flag staff may train on the highest levels of Class X to Class XII. Included among Flag staff are the most experienced and highly trained auditors, case supervisors, course supervisors and other training specialists anywhere in the world.

The excitement an auditor feels is often almost equal to that of the parishioner to whom he is ministering. "With each session, the person unfolds spiritually," said one auditor. "His perceptions reach a level never previously imagined. Aberration just falls away in moments—and it falls away forever, leaving him spiritually free of those restraints for eternity."

The FSO sets the technical standard in Scientology and enjoys a reputation for perfection. Flag thus serves an important role in the Scientology religion by training and interning ministerial staff from all lower churches and missions. Churches and missions from around the world send their technical staff to be trained to Flag standards.

Because it is the largest single church for Scientology in the world, Flag is also a worldwide focal point for the religion. Hundreds of parishioners gather each week in the church auditorium to acknowledge those who have completed OT levels. They also learn the latest news from other churches around the world and receive special briefings from the Church's international headquarters.

Several times a year Flag is host to globally telecast major Scientology religious gatherings, at which top Church executives present current news, briefings and plans for the future.

The FSO is also a hub of Scientology within its own community, sponsoring many different outreach activities to help those in need. Artists and musicians at Flag hold public exhibitions and concerts, and local public are always invited.

The Flag Service Organization is the mecca of the Scientology religion. Though it concentrates on ministering the most advanced spiritual levels of Scientology, its services span the entirety of the Bridge. Every Scientologist in the world aspires to come to Flag. And sooner or later, everyone does.

The Flag Service Organization ministers all religious services available at churches of Scientology up to its level. Additionally, it ministers:

■ **NEW OT VI AND NEW OT VII (SOLO NEW ERA DIANETICS FOR OTS)**

■ **AUDITOR TRAINING THROUGH CLASS XII**

■ **SPECIALIZED AUDITING MINISTERED ONLY AT THE FSO INCLUDING:**

- *L10 Rundown*
- *L11 Rundown*
- *L12 Rundown*
- *Case Cracker Rundown*
- *New Vitality Rundown*
- *Profession Intensive*
- *Knowledge Rundown*
- *Interiorization by Dynamics Rundown*
- *Dynamic Sort-out Assessment*
- *Fixated Person Rundown*

FLAG SHIP SERVICE ORGANIZATION

The Flag Ship Service Organization (FSSO) is a unique church of Scientology which is located aboard the Motor Vessel *Freewinds,* a 440-foot ship based in the Caribbean, with the home port of Curaçao. The ship was acquired in the mid-1980s shortly before the release of the highest advanced auditing level currently available, New OT VIII.

Needing a safe, aesthetic, distraction-free environment appropriate for ministration of this profoundly spiritual level of auditing, this church of Scientology returned to the sea, far from the crossroads of the workaday world. And while the Flag Service Organization ministers the highest levels of training and auditing from the bottom of the Bridge up to New OT VII, the most advanced OT level — OT VIII — is entrusted exclusively to the FSSO.

To a Scientologist, coming to the *Freewinds* for New OT VIII is the pinnacle of a deeply spiritual journey. Years of training and auditing have brought him to this ultimate point. It is the most significant spiritual accomplishment of his lifetime and brings with it the full realization of his immortality.

The *Freewinds* is a very special place. It is the one place on this planet that a Scientologist can go and be certain that he will be able to devote all of his attention to his religious practice and, at the same time, share the company of people who share his religious commitment and outlook on life in general. A voyage on the *Freewinds* is nowhere close to a vacation. Rather, it is the perfect religious retreat dedicated to enabling one to devote his full attention to spiritual growth.

One parishioner said, "Not only was I in a part of the world I had never seen, I was also there to embark on a spiritual journey of immense importance. The religious service I did there could only be accomplished at sea — literally off the crossroads of the world, where I and other Scientologists in a completely distraction-free environment could find out about ourselves and realms of spirituality that were quite beyond anything I had ever dreamed of."

"I've come to realize that my visit to the *Freewinds* was the launching point for my spiritual reawakening," wrote another parishioner after his first visit to the FSSO. "I've found where I was destined to be and know with certainty the group to which I truly belong."

Religious services ministered aboard the *Freewinds* are not limited to Scientologists who have reached OT VIII.

Rather, there are many specialized services ministered involving training in advanced spiritual concepts that would give a tremendous boost in awareness to any Scientologist, no matter where on the Grade Chart he may be. These services are based on several series of very popular lectures that L. Ron Hubbard gave in the 1950s on the state of OT, such as *The Route to Infinity, The Dawn of Immortality* and *The Creation of Human Ability.*

Other religious programs conducted aboard the *Freewinds* include religious conventions and seminars for staff and parishioners of churches of Scientology from around the world as well as specially arranged gatherings also for Scientologists from a particular country or community for a particular program of religious services.

Each year the annual Maiden Voyage event, commemorating the anniversary of New OT VIII, has come to be one of the most important gatherings of dedicated Scientologists and an opportunity for senior Church officials to meet and work directly with these parishioners to advance their religion. Scientologists who attend this annual spiritual cruise become "OT Ambassadors" and initiate programs to help Scientologists all over the world advance the aims of Scientology and to reach the top of the Bridge at New OT VIII.

The *Freewinds* is like no other place on Earth. It truly marks the beginning of a voyage to all eternity.

The Church of Scientology
Flag Ship Service Organization
ministers the highest levels of religious services,
as well as other select services to help one on his route to OT:

■ NEW OT VIII, THE HIGHEST AUDITING
   LEVEL IN SCIENTOLOGY

■ THE HUBBARD KEY TO LIFE COURSE

■ THE HUBBARD LIFE ORIENTATION COURSE

■ SPECIAL TRAINING SERVICES TO ENHANCE
   ABILITIES AS AN OT

CHAPTER 22

THE MANAGEMENT OF SCIENTOLOGY

As described in the previous chapters, Scientology churches are part of a hierarchical structure and arranged in a pattern which matches the Classification, Gradation and Awareness Chart of Scientology. In other words, at the lower level of this hierarchy individuals and Church organizations minister beginning-level auditing and training; and, at the upper level, Church organizations minister the highest levels of auditing and training. It is a logical sequence of organization, one that reflects the spiritual progress of Scientology parishioners up the Bridge.

This ecclesiastical hierarchy is paralleled by a corporate structure, as is the case in many religions. Each church corporation is organized on a nonprofit basis with its own board of directors and executives responsible for its activities. These churches together form the stable building blocks of an international network which spans the globe.

An integral part of this international structure are Church corporations that house the staff who form international management. These corporations are International Hubbard Ecclesiastical League of Pastors, the mother church for all Scientology volunteer ministers and field auditors; Scientology Missions International, the mother church for all Scientology missions; and above them all, Church of Scientology International, which serves as the mother church for the Scientology religion.

The church corporations at this level of the Scientology ecclesiastical hierarchy formulate broad planning which, when implemented, results in the stability and expansion of the religion worldwide. Below international management is a network of continental or zonal management organizations, each of which provides ecclesiastical support to individual churches within its sphere of influence.

It is these three churches that actually unite the rest of the churches in the Scientology ecclesiastical hierarchy to accomplish their common purpose.

INTERNATIONAL HUBBARD ECCLESIASTICAL LEAGUE OF PASTORS

The International Hubbard Ecclesiastical League of Pastors (I HELP) was created to provide auditors who minister religious services outside organized churches with the guidance they need to operate successfully.

Field auditors and volunteer ministers receive much needed assistance and guidance through I HELP, the support organization within the Scientology ecclesiastical hierarchy that was formed specifically for that purpose.

The international headquarters for I HELP, located in Los Angeles, California, provides planning, consultation and direction by creating and executing broad campaigns designed to increase the popularity of field auditing and I HELP membership. It keeps the membership informed by distributing newsletters and promotional materials to I HELP continental churches for their use. I HELP International also consults with these churches to assist them to become able to better service I HELP members in the field.

I HELP continental offices, in turn, hold local events, conventions and seminars where I HELP members attend special workshops that help them to improve their skills. I HELP offices also offer assistance with any administrative or technical difficulties members may encounter by providing training materials, publications and consultation services. Most importantly, I HELP ensures field auditors and groups maintain high standards of application and discipline as they are most often bringing Scientology to those who need to benefit immediately from standardly applied technology.

Local churches of Scientology also support these individuals in the field by establishing and supervising Auditors Associations and actively encouraging individual field auditors to become members of these groups. These local churches provide field auditors with support services to assist their ministry and, in turn, field auditors and groups direct new parishioners to their local churches for further religious services.

For anyone ministering Dianetics and Scientology services outside of organized churches and missions, I HELP provides guidance and assistance to enable them to be effective and successful in their communities.

SCIENTOLOGY MISSIONS INTERNATIONAL

Overseeing the Mission Network

As is the case with field auditors, those who operate the Scientology churches that are called missions are likewise supported by an ecclesiastical structure which provides guidance and assistance.

Scientology Missions International (SMI) is the mother church for all missions and comprises the level above field auditors in Scientology's ecclesiastical hierarchy. SMI's international offices provide guidance, help and direction for existing missions through a global network of continental offices.

SMI International provides overall planning and technical direction for the mission network. This includes not only direction which enables missions to continue to minister their growing congregations, but overall guidance on all legal, financial and corporate matters.

SMI continental offices help new missions in their area get off to a running start. They provide the new mission with the materials and training manuals it will need to function. SMI also arranges for the staff of the new mission to apprentice in a successful mission operated by veteran, proven mission staff. SMI monitors this training to ensure that when the doors of the new mission open, the staff will be confident in their ability to minister to the needs of their community.

Continental offices also distribute the magazines, newsletters and other materials which keep the vast mission network briefed on interesting activities and other current developments, and they inform the public whenever a new mission is established in the country. They also provide a variety of dissemination materials missions can use to introduce the Scientology religion to others, and encourage Scientologists to open missions of their own.

SMI continental offices also arrange regular conferences for mission holders, so that members of the missions in a particular region can meet, introduce themselves to one another and work together on coordinated plans for supporting their ministries.

As missions grow, they can eventually become large enough to reorganize as a Class V Scientology church. Many have done so.

Scientology missions are far more numerous than are Scientology Class V churches, and each mission reaches out into society and brings Dianetics and Scientology to mankind through basic services.

*The headquarters of the
Church of Scientology management
in Los Angeles, California*

THE CHURCH
OF SCIENTOLOGY INTERNATIONAL

At the top of the ecclesiastical structure is the Church of Scientology International (CSI), the mother church for all Scientology. Located in Los Angeles, CSI provides overall direction, planning and guidance for the network of churches, missions, field auditors and volunteer ministers which comprise the Scientology hierarchy it spans, and ensures these various organizations are all working effectively together.

Every church has one common and primary goal — to help its parishioners achieve spiritual freedom. Such a goal, however, is attained on a gradient, one step at a time, and this is reflected in the ecclesiastical hierarchy of Scientology.

CSI broadly plans and coordinates Scientology expansion. This planning is then carried out by the individual networks of organizations which comprise ecclesiastical management at the continental echelon.

Through CSI's ecclesiastical management activities, Scientology churches receive guidance in applying the scriptures both technically and administratively.

In addition to providing planning, direction and general support to the churches in the hierarchy, CSI also provides specialized programs for staff on Scientology administrative technology. This training is conducted at the International Training Organization at CSI's headquarters in Los Angeles, California.

CSI has a network of continental offices responsible for carrying out its activities on regional and local levels. These offices serve to support the actions of local churches in their respective areas and also serve as a coordinating and rallying point for all Scientology activities associated with those local churches. They also see to the well-being of these organizations and groups. In this way, the activities of missions,

churches, field auditors and other related groups integrate and ultimately result in spiritual advancement for all Scientologists in their continent or region.

In addition to guiding the growing Scientology hierarchy, CSI sees to the publication of Scientology scripture, both in written and audiovisual form, including some three thousand of Mr. Hubbard's tape-recorded lectures. A division within CSI, Golden Era Productions, is responsible for producing these recordings as well as E-Meters, religious training films, slide shows and videos of Scientology. It supports the religion worldwide by publishing informational brochures and posters, and parishioner magazines in many languages. Golden Era also compiles, designs and translates new books and other religious materials based on Mr. Hubbard's researches and writings into more than a dozen languages.

Two Church-affiliated publishing houses provide L. Ron Hubbard's works on Dianetics and Scientology to Scientology churches worldwide. They also provide Scientology books, tapes and videos to retail bookstores as part of the Church's effort to make Mr. Hubbard's works widely known.

Bridge Publications is located in Los Angeles, California, and publishes Mr. Hubbard's works for the Western Hemisphere. New Era Publications International, located in Copenhagen, Denmark, covers the rest of the world — including Europe, Africa, Australia, New Zealand and throughout Asia. More than 110 million of L. Ron Hubbard's books are in circulation today in over thirty languages.

Through its actions worldwide, CSI ultimately assures that Scientologists can progress to the highest levels of spiritual freedom through the thousands of churches, missions and groups which comprise the Scientology religion.

CHAPTER 23

THE GUARANTOR OF SCIENTOLOGY'S FUTURE

RELIGIOUS TECHNOLOGY CENTER

The powerful technologies of Dianetics and Scientology provide nothing less than the means to attain true spiritual freedom and immortality for everyone who begins the journey toward that goal. Technology like this never existed before, and millions around the world personally regard it as valuable beyond comparison. They know that when this technology is applied precisely as written by L. Ron Hubbard—and with their honest and ethical participation—they will achieve the spiritual benefit they seek through Scientology 100 percent of the time.

Religious Technology Center (RTC) exists to ensure that this can occur. Its purpose is to protect the public from misapplication of the technology and to see that the religious technologies of Dianetics and Scientology remain in proper hands and are properly ministered.

Monitoring and enforcing the purity of technical application, and guaranteeing standard administration, is no small task. Historically, every religion has experienced periods during which growth has met with alterations of religious doctrine and practice and even outright derailment from the initial mission. Spiritual movements and religious denominations throughout the ages have suffered the destructive influences of infighting and struggles for power.

Past religious teachings, traditionally passed down by word of mouth or recorded by scribes, were subject to both alteration and misinterpretation. In contrast, this century's technological advances have facilitated the permanent recording of Scientology scripture in books, tape-recorded lectures and films. Because the original writings and recordings by Mr. Hubbard can always be examined and verified, the technology, in truth, can never be lost. Yet despite the emergence of Scientology in an era of technological advances, the religion and its churches have nonetheless encountered the nemesis of alteration and reinterpretation that has plagued other religions.

Fortunately, coincident with advances in communication, bodies of copyright and trademark law have been developed and used to guard even religious scriptures and symbols from misuse and alteration. It is this fundamental function of protecting the Scientology religion's trademarks and advanced religious scripture that Religious Technology Center provides. It is a function that guarantees the purity and workability of Scientology far into the future.

GUARANTEEING THE PURITY OF THE RELIGION

Initially, Mr. Hubbard personally oversaw the orthodox practice of Scientology. As an integral part of that endeavor he also registered as legally protectable trademarks many of the religion's identifying words and symbols, such as "Dianetics" and "Scientology." These registered marks provided a legal mechanism for ensuring that the Scientology religious technologies are standardly ministered in exact accordance with the scriptures and not altered by misappropriation or improper use. They also provided a legal mechanism to prevent anyone from offering some altered or inauthentic version of Dianetics and Scientology and representing it as the real technology.

In 1982, Mr. Hubbard donated these religious marks to the newly formed Religious Technology Center and entrusted that church with the responsibility of protecting the religion of Scientology by enforcing the pure and ethical use and standard application of his technologies. RTC thus maintains the purity of the technology and guards against any misuse or misrepresentation by legally registering, and where necessary enforcing, certain words and symbols of the Scientology religion as trademarks and service marks in countries the world over.

It is RTC that grants Church of Scientology International (CSI), the mother church of the Scientology religion, the right to use the trademarks and to license their use to all other Scientology churches. Without CSI's written authority and RTC's ultimate approval, no entity can legally use the marks or call itself a Church of Scientology. With all Scientology churches bound to minister Dianetics and Scientology technologies in full compliance with their trademark licenses, the entire hierarchy up to the Church of Scientology International is self-correcting and ensures pure and orthodox Scientology.

In contrast, RTC investigates any departures from that standard administration and ensures that orthodoxy is restored. It also ensures that no individual or group misrepresents itself and offers an altered technology while calling it Dianetics or Scientology.

PROTECTING THE ADVANCED TECHNOLOGY

One of RTC's most crucial functions is its custodianship of the advanced religious scriptures of Scientology, called the *advanced technology*. The bulk of Scientology scriptures are broadly available to anyone seeking spiritual enlightenment. However, the advanced technology, which represents a very small portion of the scriptures, is maintained as strictly confidential. Before a parishioner is allowed to use these materials, he or she must meet the highest ethical standards and have completed earlier levels of spiritual release (see Chapter 13), which form the foundation for more advanced religious services. An individual who has not completed the prior levels of spiritual attainment will be unable to receive the full spiritual benefits of the more advanced technology.

Scientology churches that minister the advanced technology are monitored by RTC to ensure the materials of each level are kept secure, that each church's license requirements are strictly observed and that advanced services are ministered exactly as written by Mr. Hubbard.

THE INSPECTOR GENERAL NETWORK

To preserve its objective oversight function, RTC is not involved in any way in the management of churches or in the actual ministry of Dianetics and Scientology to parishioners. Therefore, those responsibilities fall squarely on the shoulders of CSI, which supervises the ecclesiastical management of all Scientology churches, along with the dissemination and propagation of the religion.

RTC stands apart as an external body which protects the Scientology religion and acts as the final arbiter of orthodoxy. At the apex of this pivotal function is RTC's Inspector General Network, which operates from seven offices on four different continents. The duties and authority of an RTC Inspector General are much like those traditionally associated with the inspector general title in other organizations. Namely, an Inspector General investigates and corrects instances in which departure from a standard, policy or ethic could betray an organization's service to its constituent public.

GUARANTEEING THE FUTURE OF DIANETICS AND SCIENTOLOGY

Religious Technology Center guarantees the continued purity of Dianetics and Scientology by ensuring that the trademarks and technology it protects are kept in proper hands and used properly throughout the world. Concurrently, by monitoring those responsible for Church administration and the ministry of services to parishioners, RTC ensures a strong and incorruptible Church management—one which can never be subject either to internal politics or external attempts to harm the religion. With this guarantee, the ecclesiastical hierarchy of the Scientology religion is protected against intrusion, and parishioners are able to attain the spiritual freedom they seek when they enter a Church of Scientology.

Through the exact application of the materials of Dianetics and Scientology, an individual will achieve not only a full understanding of himself as a spiritual being, but true spiritual freedom. Thus, Scientologists across the globe view the maintenance and incorruptibility of their religious technology—in precise accordance with the founder's source writings—to be essential to their very salvation.

Religious Technology Center works, then, to guarantee that L. Ron Hubbard's legacy of spiritual freedom continues to exist tomorrow, or ten thousand years from now. To millions of Scientologists around the world, there is nothing more important.

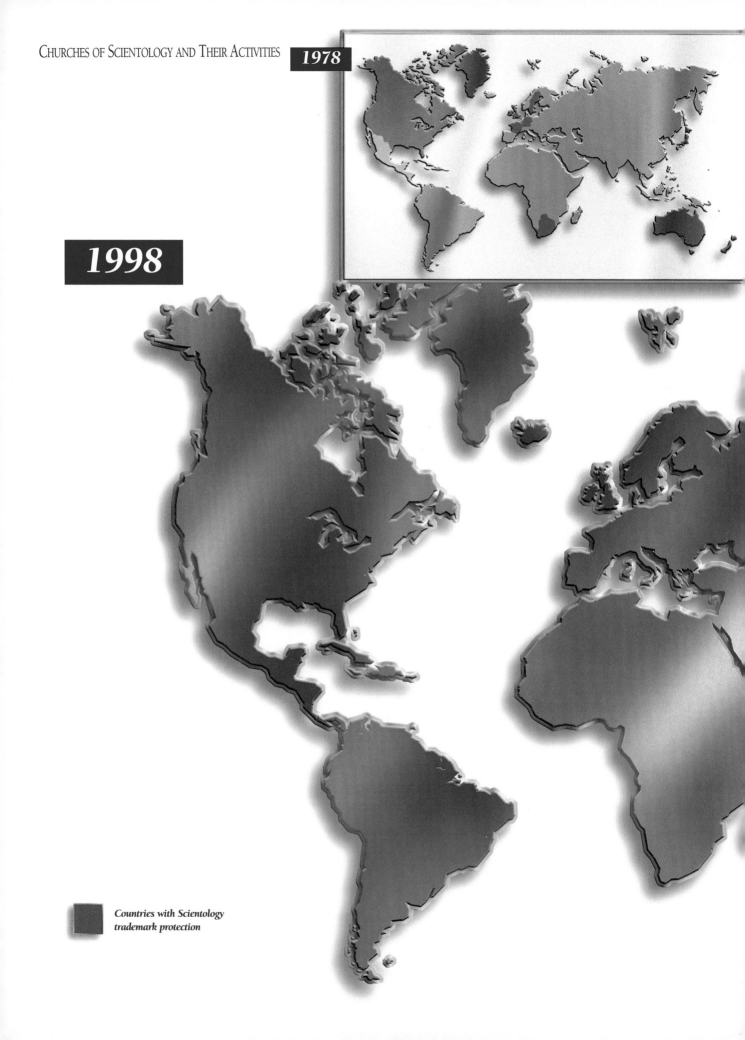

1978

1998

Countries with Scientology
trademark protection

RELIGIOUS TECHNOLOGY CENTER

Trademarks are legal assurances of the genuine origins of the materials they identify. Numerous words and symbols represent Scientology's many component parts. Indeed, the words "Scientology" and "Dianetics" are themselves trademarks, which along with the other marks prevent unauthorized use of the names, symbols and materials of Scientology, thus guaranteeing the purity of the religion and its practices. Below are but a few examples:

The Scientology Symbol is a trademark incorporating the letter "S" for Scientology, the ARC triangle, and the KRC triangle. It identifies materials and services of the Scientology religion throughout the world.

Introduced in 1950, the Symbol of Dianetics is a trademarked symbol whose stripes represent the four dynamics of Dianetics.

The state of Operating Thetan is represented by a specific trademark, the OT Symbol.

The Scientology Cross is a trademark, the eight points of which represent each of the eight dynamics.

CHAPTER 24

THE INTERNATIONAL ASSOCIATION OF SCIENTOLOGISTS

Without fireworks, without cheering crowds, but with pure unadulterated dedication, a small group of Scientologists who were determined not to let anyone stop man's chance for freedom, formed the International Association of Scientologists.

All new movements have at one time been faced with persecution and misunderstanding. And all great movements have succeeded because of the personal conviction and dedication of their members.

Regrettably, history has seen many attempts to suppress religious freedom and human rights. From the persecution of early Christians in Rome, to the slaughter of Jews in Nazi concentration camps and the recent discrimination against Jehovah's Witnesses in Greece, many faiths have suffered dearly.

Because of just such a lamentable history the International Association of Scientologists was formed to guarantee that the Scientology religion can be practiced for all time — through a strong group composed of those who believe in and are willing to fight for the rights of man and the freedom of all religions.

The IAS was established at Saint Hill Manor in East Grinstead, Sussex, England, in 1984 when delegates from around the world gathered in recognition of the need to unite all Scientologists as one international body.

Membership in the Association is open to any Scientologist. There are three categories of membership:

1. Introductory Membership:

All new Scientologists are invited to receive a free six-month introductory membership. Beginning members also receive magazines and informational mailings from the IAS about membership activities and recent news concerning the practice of Scientology around the world.

2. Annual Membership:

Annual membership is valid for one year. It entitles the holder to benefits granted by the Association including a membership card and copies of *IMPACT,* the Association's magazine.

Annual members also receive written briefings to keep them abreast of events and other important news in Scientology, invitations to events sponsored by the Association, and the right to participate in IAS award programs and projects.

3. Lifetime Membership:

Lifetime membership is valid for the lifetime of the holder and entitles him to all benefits and privileges granted by the Association.

Today the IAS is a membership organization open to all Scientologists from all nations. The strength of the individual members of the team, briefed and coordinated one with another, unifies and strengthens the group. For this reason, in addition to forming the IAS, adopting a constitution and electing a board, the first IAS delegates also formulated the Pledge to Mankind. To rededicate themselves to the aims of Scientology, they signed this pledge (a copy of which is included in the reference section of this book).

Catalyzed by this profound statement of purpose, Scientologists from around the world enthusiastically embraced the IAS and, through their financial support and membership activities, they rapidly made the IAS a major voice of religious freedom. IAS's purpose is to unite, advance, support and protect the Scientology religion in all parts of the world, so the aims of Scientology as originated by L. Ron Hubbard can be achieved. It also supports churches of Scientology and individual Scientologists in their social reform activities. It ensures that the religion is defended and protected, so Scientologists can carry forth and achieve their mission of spiritual salvation.

In 1993, the IAS established the United States IAS Members Trust (USIMT) to raise tax deductible contributions from IAS members in the United States. The USIMT supports the same worthwhile purpose as the IAS.

Each year, delegates representing Association members from all over the world gather at an annual convention of delegates to review the accomplishments of the previous year, establish goals for the next year and elect the board of the Association as necessary. The Association also holds an annual anniversary celebration, where significant recent accomplishments and progress toward the aims of Scientology are acknowledged. The celebration is broadcast to members around the world.

Membership in the Association

Members of the International Association are entitled to certain rights and privileges as granted by the Association. In addition, the Church of Scientology International has adopted membership in the International Association of Scientologists as its official Scientology membership system and provides special privileges and benefits to Association members so they may more quickly move up the Bridge.

In addition to different categories of membership, special honor statuses are awarded to acknowledge extraordinary contributions toward achieving the goals of the Association. These honor statuses are valid for the duration of the membership of the holder. Categories include: Sponsor of the Association, Crusader, Member on the Honor Roll, Patron of the Association, Patron with Honors, Patron Meritorious, Silver Meritorious, Gold Meritorious and Member on the Senior Honor Roll. Members attaining these statuses are acknowledged with publication of their names to all members and presentation of pins and plaques at special award dinners.

In addition, anyone in agreement with the Pledge to Mankind and the aims of Scientology, even if he does not attend a church of Scientology or participate in its religious services may, upon contribution to the Association, be accorded the status of Associate. Associate status does not entitle the holder to the benefits and privileges of membership.

IMPACT Magazine

All members receive IMPACT magazine which contains news and information of interest to every Scientologist, including official news of the Association, major activities undertaken by the Association and its members and other announcements.

IMPACT reports notable activities of Association members around the world who forward the aims of Scientology. IAS members contribute to the general good in many ways: They make Scientology more widely known, encourage others to practice its principles, and educate the public about the true practices and value of the Scientology religion.

Association Support

The Association provides support to projects its members undertake which either contribute to the well-being of mankind or help eradicate threats to religious freedom. It also supports projects initiated by the Church to protect the religion and to make Scientology more broadly known. The Association makes monetary grants to such worthy projects and calls upon its members to support them as well.

Requests for grants to fund such projects must be in full alignment with the goals of the IAS and should be directed to either the IAS or the USIMT.

In Frankfurt, Germany, members of the International Association of Scientologists joined religious leaders from around the world to take a stand for religious freedom. Such actions are helping produce a climate in countries throughout Europe where people of all religious denominations can freely practice their faiths.

The administration of grant funding is divided between United States proposals and proposals for all other countries. The IAS provides grants to projects conducted outside of the United States, while the US IAS Members Trust funds projects in the United States. Both support the same worthwhile purposes.

This extensive grant-making program has encouraged many Scientologists to volunteer their time and effort toward undertaking worthwhile projects to better their communities. For example, since its earliest years, IAS members have initiated and actively supported human rights, religious freedom, social betterment and community outreach activities. On every continent, one can find IAS members at the forefront of humanitarian anti-drug, criminal reform and literacy efforts. These outreach activities have

been widely recognized and include such programs as "Say No to Drugs" campaigns in Europe, as well as human rights activities aimed to stem the tide of psychiatric abuses in countries around the world. And IAS members have substantially contributed to actions which forward the Scientology religion and help produce a climate in countries throughout Europe that allows not only Scientologists, but people of all religious denominations, to freely practice their faiths.

An example of the impact of IAS support are the actions of an IAS member and educator in the United Kingdom. In 1994, with the help of IAS grants, she started bringing Mr. Hubbard's study technology to the country of Zimbabwe. By late 1996 an entire town had adopted this technology throughout its school system.

With additional IAS support over the following year, she began training teachers in one African school district. In coordination with officials of the Ministry of Education at both local and national levels, she brought L. Ron Hubbard's study technology to every school in that district. All one thousand teachers are now trained in it, use it every day and benefit more than thirty thousand students in seventy-eight schools.

The IAS has also provided support to the World Literacy Crusade, a program established in Compton, California in 1992 to bring L. Ron Hubbard's study technology to the inner cities. The program has since grown to thirty chapters worldwide, including to other cities in the United States, and Great Britain, Canada, Australia and New Zealand. The Association provided support to help establish the Compton Project as a model chapter, greatly assisting the expansion of the World Literacy Crusade by enabling it to train others and open new chapters elsewhere.

On a similar note, the IAS has sponsored the Hollywood Education and Literacy Project (HELP), a program which provides one-on-one mentoring and tutoring, delivering full reading and writing programs which utilize L. Ron Hubbard's study technology. Individuals unable to read when they arrived at the program are able to read and write with only a few weeks of tutoring.

Inside the most notorious state prison in Ensenada, Mexico, an IAS-sponsored drug and criminal rehabilitation program, based on L. Ron Hubbard's technology, has resulted in dramatic changes among the most hard-core of inmates. As a result, the program has come to the attention of government officials interested in establishing the program broadly in other penal institutions.

Association support has helped forward the eradication of psychiatric abuses through grants to the Citizens Commission on Human Rights. A series of IAS-funded publications exposing psychiatric abuses such as electroshock treatment, psychiatric drugging of the population and subversion of education and morality were distributed internationally. And with the help of the IAS, CCHR filed an official complaint with the South African Truth and Reconciliation Commission, established to promote national unity and reconciliation following the collapse of the apartheid government, detailing how psychiatric abuses had helped foment racism in that nation.

The crusade to bring religious liberty to people of all faiths in Europe has included the distribution of special editions of *FREEDOM* magazine for Austria, Italy, France, the United Kingdom, Denmark, Spain, Sweden, Switzerland and Greece. These publications present the truth about Scientology and expose those who are attempting to hinder implementation of real solutions to social problems.

Special publications have been produced which educate the public on how to protect their right to religious freedom and to suggest what protective actions to take should that right be abridged.

The IAS also helped forward campaigns to protect and expand the Scientology religion. IAS funded projects to educate the public about discrimination against Scientologists and members of other religions through publications and ad campaigns in major international newspapers, including the *New York Times* and the *International Herald Tribune*. When Scientologists from around the world gathered in Frankfurt, Germany, in a massive rally for religious freedom, the Association provided support. Similarly, the IAS has supported religious freedom efforts in France and Spain.

The Association has also provided support for a massive campaign to make Scientology well known throughout Europe. Forwarding the message, "Think for Yourself," the campaign has been carried on billboards, fliers and newspaper ads throughout the European continent.

Through activities such as these, the International Association of Scientologists has become a force for positive change in the world today. The IAS works ceaselessly to forward the aims of Scientology and welcomes the membership of all who would aid in bringing hope to mankind.

IAS FREEDOM MEDAL WINNERS

Each year since 1985, the IAS has recognized individuals who have defended the cause of religious freedom by awarding them the Freedom Medal at its anniversary celebration every October. This medal acknowledges exemplary courage and determination of these members for bringing greater freedom to mankind.

There is no higher honor accorded the contributions a Scientologist may make to society. No one better embodies this accolade than those who, by fighting for man's freedom, are daily advancing, uniting, supporting and protecting the Scientology religion.

Recipients have come from all walks of life —from educators to actors, racecar champions to champions of religious tolerance and individual liberty.

Lawrence Anthony (South Africa), for helping bring to justice apartheid-era psychiatrists for their human rights atrocities.

Jane Allen (USA), for exposing anti-humanitarian mental health practices and spearheading grass-roots action to end abuses.

Elena Roggero (Italy), for effectively leading and inspiring the national fight against drug abuse through the "Say No to Drugs" movement.

Chick Corea (USA), for exemplifying what it means to be a Scientologist and sharing this with millions of people around the world.

Isaac Hayes (USA), for bringing
L. Ron Hubbard's study technology to
less-privileged urban communities worldwide
as an international spokesman for the World
Literacy Crusade.

John Travolta (USA), for enlightening millions about the spectrum of
L. Ron Hubbard's technology including Dianetics, Scientology, study
technology and drug rehabilitation technology, and his unflagging support
of religious tolerance.

Martha Ballasteros
and Javier Ramirez
(Venezuela), for making
applications of
L. Ron Hubbard's
technology known to
millions throughout
South America.

Anne Archer (USA), for her support of anti-drug and educational causes
and her championing of religious freedom and human rights in the US
and abroad.

Ann Roberts (United Kingdom), for
implementing L. Ron Hubbard's study
technology for a quarter of a century, and
bringing literacy to tens of thousands in
Zimbabwe.

Keith Code (USA), motorcycle racing champion and trainer of
champions, for making L. Ron Hubbard's technology broadly known
in his field.

...ud Reichel (USA), for implementing L. Ron Hubbard's
...dministrative technology in the fields of education,
...overnment and industry throughout Russia.

CHAPTER 25

THE STAFF OF SCIENTOLOGY CHURCHES

L Ron Hubbard characterized churches of Scientology as islands of sanity in a difficult world, each established to succor man from the gathering darkness and decay of this earth's civilization. "Others talk about a better world," he wrote. "We are making one."

It is the dedicated objective of every Scientology church to begin making that better world by bettering each individual parishioner, bringing him to higher states of spiritual awareness and enabling him to create positive change in every activity of life he engages in. But no organization could possibly carry out such a mission without people, and thus it is the staff of missions and churches who form the backbone of the Scientology religion.

Holding a job in the workaday world is, for most people, a burdensome necessity. Few who work for a living are fortunate enough to be doing something they can enjoy, much less something they feel strongly enough about to dedicate their lives to the endeavor. In contrast, staff members of Scientology organizations recognize the importance of helping others achieve peace, sanity and true spiritual freedom. As L. Ron Hubbard described it, "A post in a Scientology organization isn't a job. It's a trust and a crusade."

STAFFS OF LOCAL SCIENTOLOGY CHURCHES

Local churches of Scientology are administered by Scientologists who have dedicated themselves to the religion for either a two-and-a-half or five-year period. Staff duties vary. Some require auditor or other specialized training; others hold administrative positions and help to keep the church functioning by providing the support necessary to minister auditing and training.

Though churches and missions have different functions and minister different religious services, staff duties are often similar. For example, every church has an executive structure responsible for the day-to-day operation of the church. The Executive Director and his staff are there to ensure each area of the church provides the best possible service to its parishioners and members of the community.

Another body of staff members is responsible for establishing the church, bringing aboard new staff, and ensuring that the communications of the church—phone calls, letters, and even internal messages from one staff member to another—are delivered.

There are staff who introduce new people to the church through lectures, workshops, films and other presentations about Scientology.

Of prime importance are the technical staff, those who supervise Dianetics and Scientology training and the auditors who minister spiritual counseling. Being an auditor is one of the most rewarding activities any staff member—indeed any Scientologist—can do. Only an auditor can assist a person up the path to Clear and ultimately to true spiritual freedom.

The staffs of churches and missions succeed because they are trained. Every function in a church or mission has a corresponding course of study which can be taken by any new staff member who assumes those duties. Staff engage in 2 1/2 hours of study or auditing each day. When they know how to do their jobs, they proceed on to other training, perhaps as an auditor, or use this time to move up the Bridge as a preclear.

Those staff who have dedicated themselves to five years of service may be sent for full-time training at a higher organization—either technical training at Saint Hill or the Flag Service Organization, or administrative training at the International Training Organization in Los Angeles, California, at the headquarters of the Church of Scientology International. This training can last up to a year, but in any event results in a highly trained church administrator, auditor or case supervisor.

Scientology staff members routinely face challenges involving the mastery of new abilities, for regardless of past training before joining staff, these individuals often must learn new skills in order to get the required tasks done. This may seem daunting to most people in the workaday world, but not to a Scientology staff member. Thus, in walking through a church of Scientology it would not be unusual to find the Rhodes scholar ministering auditing, the accountant supervising courses and the auto mechanic lecturing.

Regardless of the task at hand, staff members seize responsibility and learn how to do the job—and do it well. There are few people anywhere who have duties more challenging— or more fulfilling. For this reason, public Scientologists regard staff with more than a little respect and a great deal of admiration.

Staff members in a Scientology organization are known for their dedication to helping others achieve spiritual freedom, for their commitment to the aims of Scientology but perhaps above all, for their genuine friendliness.

CHAPTER 26

THE SEA ORGANIZATION
THE RELIGIOUS ORDER OF SCIENTOLOGY

The core of every great religion in history has been a group of individuals dedicated to achieving the goals of the religion. In Scientology, these individuals are part of a fraternal religious order known as the Sea Organization, or Sea Org. While relatively few in number, its members play a crucial role in virtually every aspect of the ministry and expansion of Scientology. And, like their counterparts in other faiths, Sea Organization members occupy the most essential and trusted positions in the senior churches in the Scientology ecclesiastical hierarchy.

The Sea Organization derives its name from its beginnings in 1967 when Mr. Hubbard, having retired from his position as Executive Director International, set to sea with a handful of veteran Scientologists to continue his research into the upper levels of spiritual awareness and ability.

The first Sea Org members, who were all Clears and OTs, formulated a one-billion-year pledge to symbolize their commitment to the religion as immortal spiritual beings. It is signed by all members today. They dedicate themselves to the goal of bringing spiritual freedom to all beings through the full application of Mr. Hubbard's technologies. The Sea Organization was born of a concern for the welfare of mankind—and it is with this viewpoint that members of the Sea Org continue to operate.

EXPANDED ROLE

Initially, Sea Org members lived and worked aboard a fleet of ships, headed by the flagship *Apollo*, which was also home to Mr. Hubbard, the Commodore of the Sea Organization. As Scientology continued to expand, the role of Sea Org members expanded, too. Today the majority of Sea Organization members are located on land, but in keeping with tradition, many still wear maritime uniforms, and all have honorary ranks and ratings.

Appropriate to their high level of dedication and commitment, Sea Org members bear a responsibility unique within Scientology. They are the only Scientologists entrusted to minister the advanced levels of training and auditing and the only individuals who may hold the senior ecclesiastic positions in the Scientology hierarchy. All advanced churches and management-level church organizations employ only members of the Sea Organization religious order. While Sea Org members enter into binding employment contracts and are responsible to the directors and officers of the church where they are employed, the eternal commitment to Scientology as a member of the Sea Organization is a fundamental requirement for employment.

The hallmark of any Sea Org member is competence and professional teamwork, no matter how diverse or challenging the duty assigned. New members undergo rigorous training to raise their ability to confront and deal with their environment.

Today, there are more than five thousand members of the Sea Org. They may be found in almost any area of endeavor in the religion. They are the cameramen, directors, artists, writers and designers who produce the dissemination materials for the religion internationally. They are the senior public relations personnel for the religion who constantly interact with media and governmental officials. They are the top technical staff in Scientology, the top auditors and case supervisors who not only minister the most advanced spiritual technology but, at the upper levels of the hierarchy, also oversee the purity of training and auditing worldwide.

No formalized structure exists for the Sea Org. Rather, its members are subject to the established lines of seniority and authority in the church organizations in which they work. Commitment to the Sea Organization is a sign of devotion to the religion and its objectives.

Having so dedicated their lives, Sea Org members work long hours and live communally with housing, meals, uniforms, medical and dental care provided by their Church employers. A portion of each day is dedicated to training and auditing but they otherwise devote themselves to whatever their assigned task may be in the furtherance of the objectives of Scientology. Their achievements over the more than three decades of the Sea Org's existence are phenomenal and members appropriately have a vibrant esprit de corps and sense of accomplishment. Because of this, they are held in high esteem by all Scientologists who recognize the important role they play in ensuring the religion continues to achieve its objectives around the world.

Members of the Sea Org are committed to achieving the goal of a cleared planet through the standard ministry of the religious technology of Scientology. It is a challenge met with unfailing determination and dedication.

All members of the Sea Organization are dedicated to the goal of bringing spiritual freedom to all beings through the full application of Mr. Hubbard's technologies. Although most members are now located on land, its maritime traditions are still observed.

PART SEVEN
COMMUNITY ACTIVITIES

That a church would involve itself in charitable works and community betterment is both natural and traditional. For if it can be said that all great religions sprang from what is decent and beneficent in man, then it follows that charity and social responsibility are logical extensions of spiritual values. Prior to government welfare programs, for example, only the church could be counted upon to provide for the needy and the destitute—and through much of the world it is still only the church that provides assistance.

The Church of Scientology has become a vital force in the community. Utilizing L. Ron Hubbard's breakthroughs and technology, Scientology churches have become not only catalysts for constructive change throughout the world, but also rallying points for those who seek to improve conditions in their communities.

CHAPTER 27

THE CHURCH OF SCIENTOLOGY ACTIVE IN THE COMMUNITY

The Church of Scientology and its members are committed to social betterment—in the local neighborhood, the nation or in the world as a whole. The tools employed are those acquired from study of L. Ron Hubbard's works, including his drug rehabilitation technology, his effective study methods, his essays on safeguarding the environment and, perhaps most important, the immense compassion for others that pervades everything he wrote.

ANTI-DRUG CAMPAIGNS

In support of its international grass-roots fight against drugs, the Church of Scientology unites concerned community groups and stages public awareness forums, anti-drug rallies and educational conferences.

In the United States, for instance, Church-sponsored anti-drug campaigns have helped millions of people by fighting further drug proliferation. It has done so through enlisting the aid of celebrities for concerts with anti-drug themes; by raising funds for youth groups such as the Police Activities League, which provides tutorial services for disadvantaged youth; and by hosting conferences of community leaders involved in anti-drug activities, such as that in Washington, DC, which led city commissioner Bob King to present the Church's local "Lead the Way to a Drug-

Free USA" program with a proclamation lauding its efforts in the war against drugs.

Nor was he by any means the only one to recognize the Church's efforts. Not long after establishment of "Lead the Way" in the District of Columbia, the director of the Office for Substance Abuse Prevention of the US Department of Health commended the Church for its drug-fighting initiative: "It is because of the participation of dedicated groups like yours that we are making progress in the reduction of alcohol and other drug problems."

Using programs developed and supervised by local churches, the Church has encouraged individual Scientologists to participate in Church-sponsored anti-drug campaigns.

Scientologists across the US rallied to join the "Lead the Way to a Drug-Free USA" program, and to encourage youth to be drug-free through the "Drug-Free Marshals" program. Spawned by the "Lead the Way" campaign in 1993, the program has become one of the most successful grass-roots endeavors of its kind and today is international in scope.

The program deputizes children as "Drug-Free Marshals" who pledge to keep themselves, their friends and family drug-free by:

"1. Living a drug-free life.

"2. Showing my friends that a drug-free life is more fun.

Young Drug-Free Marshals from around the United States represent tens of thousands of children and are supported by national and state legislators, mayors, judges and police chiefs. Here, on a visit to the US Capitol, they promote a drug-free lifestyle for youth to members of Congress.

"3. Helping my fellow Drug-Free Marshals.

"4. Learning more about how drugs really harm people.

"5. Telling people the truth about the harmful effects of drugs.

"6. Helping my family and friends be drug-free.

"7. Setting a good example to all children by leading the way to a Drug-Free USA."

The program began in April 1993 when two hundred children between the ages of six and thirteen were sworn in by the director of the Los Angeles FBI's Drug Demand Reduction Program. Since that time, tens of thousands of children and adults — including US senators and congressmen, state legislators, mayors, judges and police chiefs — have signed this pledge.

(For more information about the Drug-Free Marshals, visit **http://www.drugfreemarshals.org** on the Internet.)

Around the World

As drug abuse knows no international boundaries, Scientologists are active in anti-drug campaigns in many nations.

In Canada, for example, Scientologists founded the national "Say No to Drugs, Say Yes to Life" campaign, which serves as a key force in turning youth away from drugs before they start.

The campaign has gained the support and participation of entertainment and sports figures because of their appeal to youth — such as the Toronto Maple Leafs hockey team, the Toronto Blue Jays baseball team, the Toronto Argonauts and the Saskatchewan Roughriders football teams, all of whom have signed the "Say No to Drugs, Say Yes to Life" Honor Roll and serve as examples for Canada's young.

Canadian city officials have also lent their support to the campaign. In eleven cities in the province of Ontario, mayors have proclaimed March 13 — L. Ron Hubbard's birthday — "Say No to Drugs, Say Yes to Life" Day in their cities, commemorating the Church's campaign. The mayor of Brampton, Ontario specifically commended the Church for "helping educate communities toward an understanding that to achieve their goals, they must be drug-free."

Scientologists in Germany, France, Switzerland, Denmark, Belgium, Holland, Austria, Sweden, Norway, Italy and the United Kingdom also lead successful and popular "Say No to Drugs, Say Yes to Life" campaigns.

The Italians, who have a "Say No to Drugs" Honor Roll, enlisted the support of Philips, Italy's most famous volleyball team. And while touring Italy, members of the legendary Spanish football team, Real Madrid, each signed the honor roll. Further maintaining a high profile in the field of sports, the Church's anti-drug campaign sponsors major sporting events to heighten public awareness of the problem and its solution.

In Denmark, the "Say No to Drugs, Say Yes to Life" association has been educating members of Parliament, city officials, police chiefs and other community leaders on the dangers of drug use — particularly the liabilities of methadone. Danish Scientologists loudly decried this psychiatric "quick fix," with thousands of signatures on the "Say No to Drugs, Say Yes to Life" Honor Roll. Scientologists throughout Denmark also have spearheaded the creation of school environments entirely free from drugs, where students and teachers pledge to permit no tolerance toward drugs and to widely promote their school as drug-free.

In Germany, which also faces a methadone problem of frightening proportions, Scientologists in Hamburg published a brochure which described the destructiveness of methadone "therapy," distributing more than 50,000 copies of it throughout the city. This led to a long-overdue national exposé of abuses occurring in Hamburg's "Needle Park."

As elsewhere, concerts, rallies and broad-scale distribution of anti-drug literature effectively mobilized thousands of German citizens who pledged to lead drug-free lives.

In Switzerland, where anti-drug events have regularly been held in Lucerne, Basel, Bern, Lausanne and other cities, Scientologists, with other local organizations, have participated in the closing of an infamous park to drug addicts and pushers. Support for the Church's anti-drug activities has come from both federal and state members of Parliament.

French Scientologists have organized marches, concerts and street events to promote the Church's anti-drug message, and have reached hundreds of thousands of Parisians. Champion motorcyclist Marc Arrighi, who broke the world rear-wheel-stand speed record in 1996, is among those who have actively promoted the "Say No to Drugs" campaign.

In Spain, where drug trafficking has earned the nation the title "drug crossroads of Europe," local Scientologists formed a "Freedom Without Drugs" association and conducted a series of anti-drug events in Madrid.

Utilizing public events with just as much efficiency, Mexican Scientologists run a "Say No to Drugs" campaign, assisted by well-known entertainers in cities such as Torreón, Guadalajara and Mexico City. Similarly, South African Scientologists inaugurated a "Say No to Drugs, Say Yes to Life" Honor Roll, with events at schools, clubs and other organizations. To date, tens of thousands of South Africans have signed the honor roll, including the mayors from Port Elizabeth, Cape Town and Soweto.

In both Australia and New Zealand, Scientologists campaign against drug abuse with a "Say No to Drugs, Say Yes to Life" Honor Roll, receiving support from a wide range of sports celebrities, including the legendary New Zealand All Blacks rugby

To create a safer environment, Italian "Say No to Drugs" teams frequently lead city drives to clear local parks of used hypodermic syringes left by drug addicts.

team and many famous automobile and motorcycle racing stars.

Children in many countries have also adopted the "Drug-Free Marshals" campaign, adapting the name for their group according to their own choice.

Australia has a growing and active group of "Drug-Free Ambassadors" who have taken on projects such as painting murals with anti-drug messages in prominent city locations. The "Drug-Free Ambassadors" in Canada have enlisted city officials and celebrities in their efforts to keep their peers away from drugs. In South Africa, schoolteachers participate in the campaign, and thousands of "Drug-Free Marshals" participate in weekly activities including essays and lectures about the drug problem and its solutions. In Spain, the "Drugbusters" have formed a soccer team which promotes the benefit of keeping the world of sport drug-free.

Groups of church volunteers and celebrities in Italy lead regular citywide drives to round up and safely dispose of used hypodermic syringes, discarded in public parks by addicts—potentially lethal hazards. Rome, Verona, Padova, Torino, Brescia, Pordenone, Novara, Monza, Florence and Milan have all benefited from such cleanup drives. Officials in many of these cities support this important public service by providing equipment to collect and dispose of the discarded syringes.

Scientologists' industry in combating drug abuse has been widely recognized. Scores of cities throughout the world have issued commendations to the Church for its anti-drug work. From Perth to Adelaide in Australia, from Madrid to Stockholm to Milan in Europe, from Cape Town to Pretoria in South Africa, from more than forty cities in the United States and fifty in Canada, city governments have recognized the value of the efforts of Scientologists in this area. In fact, wherever one finds a Church of Scientology, one will find Scientologists making a concerted effort to turn youth and adults away from drugs.

REDUCING CRIME

Inexorably linked with both drug abuse and urban decay is crime. To the degree that a man perceives his environment as a threat, Mr. Hubbard wrote, he will not thrive. With that in mind, Scientologists have dedicated themselves to the reduction of criminality in an effort to further safeguard their environment. Of course, they believe the ultimate solution to crime is the genuine reform of individuals with criminal impulses—that reform made possible with L. Ron Hubbard's technology. Witness the case of a Melbourne, Australia, resident who, after receiving Scientology auditing, turned himself in to local authorities and confessed to having stolen eight hundred dollars, years earlier. His reason: He realized that he could not advance spiritually until he had taken full responsibility for past transgressions and repaid the money—which he did. The judge remarked that such action was unheard of and reduced the penalty to a suspended sentence, describing the man's behavior as exceptional and clearly displaying his rehabilitation.

At a community level, Scientologists have assisted the efforts of law enforcement in various cities. In San Francisco, for example, Scientologists spearheaded the creation of a Neighborhood Crime Watch program designed to protect those who live in the community near the church. Crime Watch programs have also been organized or actively contributed to by Scientologists in Los Angeles; Boston; Washington, DC; Florida and many other locations.

In Montreal, Canada, the Church of Scientology sponsors a contest inviting the public to write essays regarding crime reduction, as a means of raising public awareness of the problem, and appreciation for the daily task of law enforcement. In Mexico City, Scientologists conducted seminars to teach police officers better human relations techniques. And when riots shook Los Angeles in 1992, *The Times* of London reported, "Further east, at the fabled intersection of Hollywood and Vine, 300 members of the Church of Scientology ignored the citywide curfew and surrounded an entire block. . . . By midnight it was one of the very few blocks on Hollywood Boulevard where no business had been torched or looted."

ENVIRONMENTAL REVITALIZATION

Scientologists naturally tend to participate in environmental efforts because of their concern for the well-being of the communities in which they live and work.

Thus, in one city, Scientologists can be found heading recycling projects, public park cleanups and the removal of graffiti, while in another they can be found planting trees or protecting wildlife.

Ecologically minded South African Scientologists celebrate Earth Day each year with educational campaigns to stress the importance of safeguarding and improving their environment. A church-organized anti-litter campaign in Durban, South Africa, involving hundreds of volunteers from both the church and the community, received special recognition and a warm letter of thanks from the Durban City Council. In Australia, the "Clean Up Australia Day" organization recognized the Church of Scientology's community cleanup events with a proclamation acknowledging the Church's "outstanding contribution." Scientologists run an ongoing educational campaign in Melbourne and other Australian cities to reduce pollution in the environment.

In Spain, Scientologists have worked to reforest areas burned out by forest fires. In cities along the western US coast, Churches of Scientology have been involved in beach

Churches of Scientology, including the Founding Church in Washington, DC, shown above, support the US Marine Corps' "Toys for Tots" program.

cleanups and cooperative government and community-based programs in which sections of public beaches and highways are kept free of litter and graffiti.

Scientologists are constantly engaged in smaller, unreported projects— discouraging neighborhood youth from defiling property with spray cans, or encouraging those around them to keep streets and parks free of litter. These activities are all part of the Church's larger view that ultimately no dynamic can thrive unless all thrive, and that each man is not only vitally linked to all other men but also to the world in which he lives.

ETHNIC AND CULTURAL AFFAIRS

By the Creed of the Church, "All men of whatever race, color or creed were created with equal rights." In its efforts to secure freedom and human rights for all individuals, the Church of Scientology has provided effective assistance for members of minority groups who have suffered hardship owing to their race or beliefs.

In the United States, the Church of Scientology maintains an Office of Ethnic and Cultural Affairs to coordinate Church efforts on behalf of all minorities. One of the services of this office has been to publish a popular column, syndicated in newspapers around the country, providing positive guidelines on educational reform, self-esteem and other applications of L. Ron Hubbard's technology.

The Church provided the first national exposure of then-widespread racial discrimination against US Internal Revenue Service (IRS) employees by IRS officials. In the early 1990s, Scientologists investigated and exposed voluminous reports received on the IRS's discriminatory policies and practices in Chicago; New York; Los Angeles; Indianapolis; Kansas City; Jackson, Mississippi; and Norfolk, Virginia.

Scientologists have also investigated and challenged racially motivated police brutality on the streets of Los Angeles. The Church helped initiate reforms of the Los Angeles Police Department in the 1970s and 1980s, and today, through its efforts and those of other public-spirited groups and individuals, the department has been hailed for its progress.

In Washington, DC, Scientologists established an award-winning program which has assisted hundreds of African-American inner-city children to raise their scholastic competence and self-esteem. Many Scientologists volunteer their time every weekend to help these underprivileged children and, as a result, have received community awards for their hard work, dedication and results, including a proclamation by the City Council of Washington, DC, which declared October 21 "Church of Scientology Community Betterment Day."

Scientologists have also worked for years to better conditions, restore civil rights, and provide skills and hope to indigenous citizens of Canada, New Zealand, Australia and South Africa.

To increase understanding and tolerance between diverse groups, to ensure justice for all regardless of color or creed—these are not merely words to the Scientologist, but deeply felt convictions, seen as a true cornerstone for survival.

SUPPORTING GOODWILL AND COMMUNITY EFFORTS

In cities on every continent, members of the Church donate thousands of hours in community work and provide assistance to a wide range of other goodwill and community groups and activities.

Churches of Scientology support and contribute to a variety of other established community programs such as the Red Cross, the March of Dimes, the Cystic Fibrosis Foundation and local community groups in cities the world over. Church members' support of these programs ranges from broad participation in drug-free blood drives and "walk-a-thons," to citywide collection of holiday toys for needy children, and the donation of food and clothing for families in need.

For years, the Church of Scientology in Portland has provided assistance to the Northeast Emergency Food Program, sponsored by Ecumenical Ministries of Oregon. The Portland church displays the award certificate received for "outstanding contribution" to the program's fund-raising efforts. In 1997, Portland's Bureau of Buildings contacted the Church for help in caring for a low-income family it was evicting from a house that was no longer safe. Using building supplies donated by the community, a group of Scientologists, along with members of the Portland Police Department, freely gave their time and labor to the project. When they had finished, the house exceeded every local building standard and the residents were able to remain.

In Orange County, California, Scientologists helped form a local chapter of the "Food for All" program with Lutheran Social Services and Presbyterian and Catholic groups in the area which provides food for the homeless.

In Los Angeles, a murals project sponsored by the Church's Community Outreach Group and Visual Artists Association has created scores of large murals at Family Courts and related facilities, helping to uplift the spirits of abused and neglected children throughout Los Angeles County. The Community Outreach Group has received city, county and state recognition for its work and was named the community group of the year in Los Angeles. Church volunteers in Los Angeles have also worked for many years with the Red Cross on a variety of projects ranging from community blood drives to disaster relief.

The Church of Scientology of St. Louis raises funds for the United States Marine Corps' "Toys for Tots" program, while also carrying out a successful education program aimed at steering children clear of crime.

In Arizona, church volunteers participated in a telethon pledge drive to support public television, raising $25,000 in a few hours—more than double the target set by the local public television station for that time period.

Church volunteers in Sydney, Australia, conduct clothing drives for underprivileged families and provide musical entertainment for the elderly.

In Auckland, New Zealand, they run a literacy program to teach reading to young people who are unemployed or involved with drugs and crime. Many participants in the program have stopped taking drugs and expressed an interest in returning to school to complete their education, while others have found jobs and become productive members of the community.

In Germany, Church volunteers also provide musical entertainment for the elderly at old-age homes, and during the winter they give warm clothing, food and hot drinks to the homeless in Hanover, Stuttgart and Düsseldorf.

Volunteers in France also regularly distribute food and clothing to those in need, while in nearby Belgium, local Scientologists supported an annual 24-hour bicycle race, raising funds for cancer research.

In South Africa, Church volunteers visit prisons where they conduct seminars to show inmates how to live honest and more fulfilling lives.

At Saint Hill in Sussex, site of the Church of Scientology's headquarters in the United Kingdom, Scientologists hold annual fetes attended by some 2,000 people each year, to support charity organizations such as the Royal National Lifeboat Institute and the Youth Trust, a national organization working to keep children off drugs. British Scientologists also support the community activities of many other groups and organizations. One group participates every year in an annual fund-raising event which supports a national society's Teenage Cancer Trust. Another group took part in a 1997 cycling marathon to raise funds for the British Heart Foundation.

Honoring a long tradition of helping the needy, and particularly children, over the Christmas holidays, Scientologists help spread Christmas goodwill in cities all over the world. From California to New York, Scientologists in the United States collect food and gifts to cheer the holidays of those in need.

Such contributions have earned numerous recognitions. In 1996, the director of the Los Angeles Outreach Program was commended by President Bill Clinton for services rendered to foster children. The Program Director organized volunteer Scientologists who contributed more than 60,000 hours of work to the Los Angeles County Department of Children and Family Services. The commendation stated in part: "You have worked with energy and dedication to provide solutions to the many problems that government alone cannot fix. With your active involvement, you have brought hope and help to countless people in need. . . . Your work is going a long way toward healing and renewing your community, inspiring all who seek to improve our world."

The Church has also sponsored the popular "Winter Wonderland" in Hollywood, complete with the film capital's largest Christmas tree and snow by the ton. Santa lights the tree during the annual Christmas parade and the setting plays host to thousands of children and their parents. "Winter Wonderland" is also a yearly feature in Clearwater, Florida, where Scientologists construct a Swiss Alpine village, complete with Santa Claus, skating, train and pony rides, a petting zoo, snowmen

Church volunteers entertain the elderly, collect food and clothing for those in need and raise funds for charities, contributing to their communities in these and many different ways.

and a special Santa's Workshop. More than 30,000 children and their parents visit during the holiday season. Those who come to enjoy the festivities are encouraged to donate canned goods, clothing and toys which are then distributed to needy families in time for the holidays.

The Women's Auxiliary of the Church of Scientology in Clearwater provides hundreds of Christmas presents to underprivileged children in cooperation with the local Marine Corps Reserve. The Women's Auxiliary has also provided gifts for the children of Florida migrant workers.

Each year, Scientologists organize a toy drive and party for Clearwater's foster children. One such party in 1995 resulted in a unique project among the 250 foster children who attended, to bring attention to the plight of abused and neglected children everywhere. The children each traced their individual handprints onto one of a multitude of brilliantly colored and patterned fabrics, wrote their names on the cloth hand and placed it on a 121-square-foot black velvet tapestry. The "Hands of Hope" Quilt project culminated with a visit in 1996 to

Washington, DC, where the children and their parents received a warm welcome from First Lady Hillary Rodham Clinton in the East Room of the White House.

Scientologists in Ottawa and Montreal team up with local law enforcement officers and firefighters for annual toy drives and caroling for underprivileged youth and residents of care centers. Year-round, Canadian church members also greet and care for arriving immigrants and refugees and their families—around the clock as necessary. The Church of Scientology of British Columbia was acknowledged with a certificate of appreciation for "generous contribution" from the Immigrant Services Society of British Columbia for helping newly arrived refugee families.

In Montreal, the Church is an active fund-raiser, joining forces with the Canadian National Hockey Team for various charities. Scientologists in Montreal have supported the Cerebral Palsy Association, led by a Scientologist who has served as vice-president of the association's fund-raising committee.

SCIENTOLOGY IN THE COMMUNITY— THE LARGER PURPOSE

Although it may be reiterated that the Church has received thousands of awards and commendations for its work within communities, these are incidental to both the intention and the deed. Scientologists help because help is part of the fabric of their religion, and L. Ron Hubbard has always stressed the importance of taking responsibility for one's fellows.

It should also be pointed out that, in addition to these listed activities, a legion of unheralded Scientologists in countries all over the world engage in a host of unreported activities. Whether they are organized by the Church, or simply the actions of individual Scientologists who willingly accept responsibility for their fellows and their neighborhoods, it is part and parcel of the broader view that there is no finer satisfaction than that which comes from helping. Thus, wherever one finds a Church of Scientology, one also finds a steady, if unpublicized, effort to help wherever needed.

Reducing criminality and drug abuse, community cleanup and charitable contributions—when one considers the larger purpose of Scientology, it is no accident that members of the Church have chosen to focus their social betterment programs on these areas. For although the primary emphasis of Scientology remains on bettering the individual, on bringing him to greater heights of spiritual awareness, the long-range aim has always been the same—a civilization without insanity, without criminals and without war, where the able can prosper and honest beings can have rights, and where man is free to rise to greater heights. And so, as the numbers of Scientologists continue to grow, so, too, is their presence increasingly felt as a vital force in the community.

Some of the numerous recognitions the Church has received for its community activities.

CHAPTER 28

SCIENTOLOGY VOLUNTEER MINISTERS

GRASS-ROOTS MOVEMENT EXTENDS HELP WORLDWIDE

When asked to describe a time when life seemed most fulfilling, a great many people will give the same answer: when they were able to help someone in a time of genuine need, whether a friend, family member, even a complete stranger.

Most would volunteer help more often—if they knew what to do, or felt confident that they could do it correctly.

The solution is the Volunteer Minister Program—a worldwide grass-roots movement open to *anyone* interested in helping others. The program answers the question of *how* to help by providing a broad range of practical skills based on a true understanding of the spiritual nature of man and the factors which influence his survival. With these skills, the Volunteer Minister can relieve pain and sorrow, and remedy confusion, conflict, upset and even failure in virtually every aspect of life.

The program began in the mid-1970s after L. Ron Hubbard concluded that crime was rising in direct proportion to the decline of religious influence. He also saw that only religion was capable of exerting a positive influence over the social afflictions of man. When society depends solely on police agencies and duress to enforce morality and social change, it inevitably will fail. The real answer lies in restoring spiritual values and seeking solutions based on understanding, not force. With the Volunteer Minister Program,

Mr. Hubbard provided society the tools to achieve these aims and made them broadly available for use by Scientologists and non-Scientologists alike.

First announced in a 1976 essay, "Religious Influence in Society; Role of the Volunteer Minister," Mr. Hubbard defined the Volunteer Minister as "a person who helps his fellow man on a volunteer basis by restoring purpose, truth and spiritual values to the lives of others." (See page 448 for the complete text of this essay.) Thus was born a broad-based movement of individuals from all walks of life dedicated to providing practical assistance to others in communities throughout the world.

By applying fundamental Scientology techniques which anyone can use, Volunteer Ministers embody the truth that when Scientology is used, conditions improve.

The technology used by Volunteer Ministers is contained in the 950-page *Scientology Handbook*, a detailed compilation of fundamental and practical Scientology principles. Illustrations and clear guidelines on how to minister these techniques make them easily learned by anyone with a desire to help others overcome difficulties and better the conditions of their own lives. (For more information on *The Scientology Handbook*, see page 444.)

One chapter of *The Scientology Handbook* is devoted entirely to assists and their utilization of spiritual means in the healing process.

Volunteer Ministers have provided assists to people in need around the world in the aftermath of earthquakes, floods, fires and explosions.

United States

Africa

United States

Japan

In times of need and in the aftermath of disaster Volunteer Ministers play a vital role in helping to provide relief, not only in the form of food and clothing but also through the delivery of assists. These basic techniques alleviate the emotional and spiritual trauma of injuries and aid the healing process.

One successful team of Volunteer Ministers mobilized in January 1995, when Kobe, Japan, was hit by an earthquake—one of the most catastrophic of the twentieth century. Relief centers were set up throughout the city. Medical teams tended to the physical needs of the residents, followed by the Volunteer Ministers who gave more than four thousand assists. The assists were so popular that lectures were set up to teach others, including many Red Cross volunteers, how to administer them.

When a massive earthquake rocked Los Angeles in 1994, local Volunteer Ministers were among the first to provide assistance. Within twenty-four hours, they were distributing food, clothing, blankets and other supplies to those hit hardest by the disaster. Working together with Red Cross and volunteers from other churches, they set up relief shelters in the neighborhood which had been at the epicenter of the quake. Day and night, Volunteer Ministers delivered Scientology assists to those who had been injured or traumatized. In all, Scientologists contributed more than ten thousand hours of volunteer work, and were acknowledged by city, county and state leaders.

The effectiveness of Volunteer Ministers in disaster relief efforts has drawn the attention of government officials in many nations. When an earthquake struck Russia's Sakhalin Island in June 1995, the Ministry of Emergency arranged to fly a team of Volunteer Ministers to the disaster site. The Deputy Commanding Officer of the military for the region found their contributions so essential to his brigade's efforts that he later wrote that he considered it "absolutely necessary" to include trained Scientologists as part of any future disasters "to deliver help in emergency situations and also to increase the workability of the rescue teams."

Volunteer Ministers also trained Red Cross personnel in assist technology at the remote scene of the 1998 earthquake in Western China, so they could provide relief to earthquake victims. In Korea, another team ministered to children, after an industrial explosion. When floods hit St. Louis, Missouri, in 1997, Volunteer Ministers from around the country worked alongside the American Red Cross, which commended their support as "invaluable and vital to the success of the relief operation."

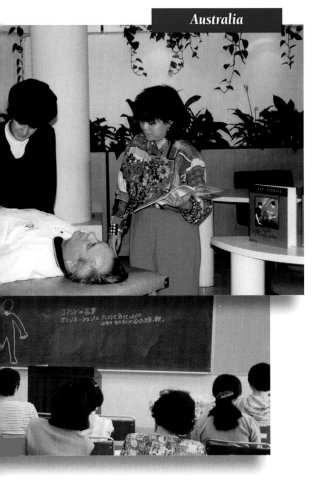

Australia

Volunteer Ministers were likewise active and on the scenes of the major 1989 San Francisco earthquake, the territories of Florida devastated by Hurricane Andrew, and the 1994 floods in northern Italy.

When the tragic news of the bombing of the federal building in Oklahoma broke on April 19, 1995, some 150 Volunteer Ministers from around the United States quickly mobilized, traveling to Oklahoma City to help those in need. Volunteer Ministers from Texas, New Mexico, Colorado, Kansas, Missouri, Nebraska, Oklahoma, Arkansas, Nevada, California and Minnesota delivered hundreds of assists to those injured or traumatized by the blast, with dramatic results. Their actions were so effective that they were given special access to the heavily secured blast site where they worked alongside rescue workers.

Just as the actions of Volunteer Ministers are not confined geographically, neither are they limited to serving others only in times of disaster. You can find them day in and day out, quietly working to make their communities a better place. In Australia, Volunteer Ministers

tutor aboriginal youth. In South Africa, they give lectures and classes on communication and how to study to the less privileged, and minister to prisoners.

In Nevada, a Volunteer Minister heard of a young girl who had been badly beaten by her father after he learned that she had stolen from a local store. When the Volunteer Minister contacted the Child Protective Services to offer help, the agency placed the girl in her care. Applying ethics and study technology from *The Scientology Handbook,* the Volunteer Minister helped the girl take an honest look at her life, work out how to take responsibility for her misdeeds and begin a more ethical life from that point on. This was neither an empty pep talk nor a stern "warning." The Volunteer Minister and the girl worked together to actually *do* a worked-out series of steps to improve the girl's attitude toward, and responsibility for, her own life. When the girl later returned to school, the dean was amazed at the change and began sending other children to the Volunteer Minister. The local juvenile hall and police department also began to refer troubled youth to the Volunteer Minister for help, after observing the effectiveness of her work.

To facilitate such vital activities, churches of Scientology take an active role to encourage Volunteer Ministers and to help them start their ministries. International Hubbard Ecclesiastical League of Pastors (I HELP), takes particular responsibility for ensuring the success of the Volunteer Minister Program and has established a 1-800 number (1-800-HELP-4-YU) to provide instantaneous referrals to Volunteer Ministers in emergencies.

While Scientology churches are an important source of support to many Volunteer Ministers, *anyone* who wishes to become a Volunteer Minister may do so regardless of religious affiliation. And there are no restrictions on the types of assistance they may provide. All it takes is a desire to help others and the initiative to read *The Scientology Handbook* or one of its chapters and begin applying its technology.

Volunteer Ministers also work closely with ministers of other denominations. In Sydney, Australia, Volunteer Ministers work hand in hand with the Salvation Army, running the local drive for food, clothes and toys. In Milwaukee, Wisconsin, Volunteer Ministers embarked on a tutoring program in conjunction with a local Baptist church that has greatly improved the literacy level of the children and adults it has served. The Volunteer Ministers also have given sermons at the Baptist church, providing others an insight into Scientology and its practical principles. In South Africa, working with other churches has enabled Volunteer Ministers to make the technology from *The Scientology Handbook* more broadly available.

As one newspaper reported, a South African pastor, sixty-nine-year-old Reverend William Mesilane of the Christ Assembly Church, is also a Volunteer Minister, and routinely utilizes Scientology technology to help people in his community. The story reported, "He eased someone's pain using the Touch Assist on the train from Maclear to Sterkstroom. He saw a woman crying, who jumped with terror if anyone spoke to her. He asked her what was wrong and she did not know. He offered to do a Touch Assist, which took twenty minutes. During that time, the train conductor came and watched him at work as well as curious passengers. At the end of the Touch Assist the woman was laughing and calm.

"William claims he took on a new lease in life when he began to study the *Handbook*. He eagerly plans to use all he learns to help his people further."

Whether it is one individual with a momentary upset, an entire community suffering the shock of natural disaster, or a widespread social ill like drug abuse or illiteracy, Volunteer Ministers help because they are able and because they care.

Our world can sometimes seem a cynical one. Newspapers tend to stress the bad news, and materialistic propaganda depriving life of purpose can have a depressing effect on anyone.

The flourishing growth of the Volunteer Minister Program is evidence that people do want to help, and do want to improve conditions, if only they knew how.

By freely offering assistance to those who need it, Volunteer Ministers are making the world a better place.

To find out more about the Volunteer Minister Program, or to order *The Scientology Handbook* or any of the booklets mentioned in this chapter, call 1-800-HELP-4-YU.

THE SCIENTOLOGY HANDBOOK

The technology used by Volunteer Ministers is found in a 950-page encyclopedic work, *The Scientology Handbook,* the companion volume to *What Is Scientology?* The *Handbook* sets out fundamental and practical Scientology techniques that anyone can learn to use to help others resolve difficulties and improve their lives.

The *Handbook* is so practical that anyone can pick it up, read it and apply its techniques to improve conditions in any aspect of life and on any scale. It is divided into chapters, each addressing a topic and providing solutions one can use to help others.

Each chapter of *The Scientology Handbook* teaches a body of basic Scientology technology about the subject addressed. And with each lesson learned, the Volunteer Minister becomes more able to deal with any situation he sees in life. After studying the appropriate chapters, the reader may find himself assisting one child with a difficulty at school or, as some Volunteer Ministers have done, assisting an entire nation to improve its education system, or he may volunteer to help resolve a neighbor's marital upset, or help bring an end to gang violence or ethnic conflict in his city, state or country.

Available in German, Italian, Spanish,

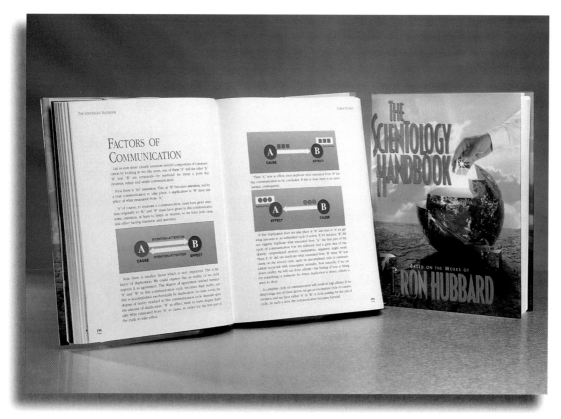

The Scientology Handbook provides fundamental Scientology technology that anyone can use to aid the injured and ill, handle troubled marriages, rescue drug addicts from their addiction and resolve many other difficulties.

French and English, *The Scientology Handbook* and its accompanying extension course are in constant use by a growing body of Volunteer Ministers around the world.

For ease of use and dissemination, each chapter of *The Scientology Handbook* has been published as a separate booklet, each of which may be used to immediately educate anyone on a particular subject. These booklets all have practical exercises, previous results of application and suggestions for further study. The booklets available include:

A Description of the Scientology Religion:

This introductory booklet describes the underlying causes of social ills in this century and describes the religion of Scientology. It shows exactly what the mind consists of and how it works, a description of auditing and provides a new understanding of the spirit and how you can help someone else to improve their life.

The Technology of Study:

Here is information that can help anyone understand the basics of learning and exact ways to overcome all the pitfalls one can encounter during study. It describes the three barriers to study and how to deal with each. This is the data needed to help anyone, child or adult, who wants to study effectively.

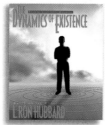

The Dynamics of Existence:

This covers the principle of the eight dynamics and explains how life is compartmented into these separate urges toward survival. By understanding how these interact one can use this information to help another achieve balance in his life, make rational decisions and clearly understand the difference between right and wrong.

The Components of Understanding:

Understanding is composed of Affinity, Reality and Communication. This booklet explains this fundamental principle and shows how these factors can be skillfully used to bring anyone to a higher level of understanding of anything, and how to improve relationships between people. An enormously useful tool to help others.

The Emotional Tone Scale:

Here are all the emotions people experience, plotted on a scale. Not only can one use this to accurately predict how people will behave, but it is also invaluable for bringing people up the scale to higher and happier levels.

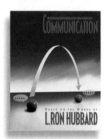

Communication:

Communication is one of the most valuable tools one has when attempting to assist others. Here, it is broken down into its component parts to give one a deep understanding of the subject. There are also detailed drills to make anyone a skilled communicator.

Assists for Illnesses and Injuries:

Physical difficulties have mental and spiritual aspects that can be addressed to alleviate them. The applications, developed by L. Ron Hubbard, are called assists and as described here, can be used by anyone to help the injured and ill, and even to sober up someone who is intoxicated. This booklet is a how-to guide on using these techniques to help others.

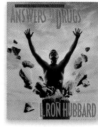

Answers to Drugs:

Using the principles in this booklet, one can help a person understand the effects of drugs and why he took drugs in the first place. There are even techniques one can use to help a person overcome the physical discomfort that accompanies drug withdrawal.

How to Resolve Conflicts:

This booklet shows how to effectively help others resolve their differences and restore peaceable relations, whether in the workplace or the home. There is a reason for conflicts between people and here one discovers what it is and how to use that knowledge.

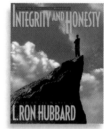

Integrity and Honesty:

There is an actual mechanism which makes people withdraw from relationships, families and groups. This booklet shows what it is and provides the remedies to help anyone regain pride and self-respect and restore broken relationships.

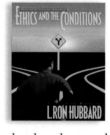

Ethics and the Conditions:

The fundamentals of ethics contained in this booklet provide the means for an individual to help a person raise his ethics level and move his entire life into a better condition. These basic laws can be used to help a person or a group improve their survival potential.

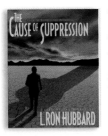

The Cause of Suppression:

There is a reason why some people become ill, have accidents and seem to attract failure. This booklet explains what it is and how one can help free others of this.

Solutions for a Dangerous Environment:

Applied on a broad scale, the principles in this booklet bring about an enormous calming influence; on an individual scale it gives one methods to help anyone overcome their fears and lead a calmer more orderly life.

Marriage:

Once the stable foundation upon which society was built, families are today threatened by a worsening marriage failure rate. This booklet shows how transgressions against a moral code can destroy a marriage and provides real methods for making a marriage work or for salvaging a failing marriage.

Children:

The application of these principles can help ensure children remain happy, loving and productive, and that they become valued members of the societies in which they live. Here are methods to handle a child's upsets, encourage his willing contributions and even how to help a baby be healthy.

Tools for the Workplace:

This booklet describes the actual relationship between the individual and his work. It describes the primary cause of job-related exhaustion and provides exact procedures to overcome it. Also included are ways to deal with confusion in the workplace. As one's life is largely comprised of work, one needs to understand what this subject is really about.

These *Handbook* booklets are so popular that they have been translated into Greek, Hungarian, Finnish, Russian, Swedish, Danish, Dutch and Portuguese, as well as the five languages of the *Handbook* itself. Every year over 80,000 copies of the booklets are distributed internationally.

The Scientology Handbook is the result of hundreds of thousands of hours of research and application. It teaches many of the most helpful Scientology practices and techniques in a series of simple and swiftly learned lessons. After studying these lessons, one can immediately go out on his own and begin ministering to the needs of the community in a volunteer capacity, or he can become even more effective by joining with other local Volunteer Ministers.

Religious Influence in Society
Role of the Volunteer Minister

By L. Ron Hubbard

An early twentieth century philosopher spoke of the impending decline of the West. What he failed to predict was that the West would export its culture to the rest of the world and thus grip the entire world in its death throes.

Today we are witnessing that decline and since we are involved in it, it is of utmost importance to us. At stake are whether the ideals we cherish will survive or some new abhorrent set of values win the day.

These are not idle statements. We are today at a watershed of history and our actions today will decide whether the world goes up from here or continues to slide into some new dark age.

It is important to understand bad conditions don't just happen. The cultural decay we see around us isn't haphazard. It was caused. Unless one understands this he won't be able to defend himself or reach out into the society with effectiveness.

A society is capable of surviving for thousands of years unless it is attacked from within or without by hostile forces. Where such an attack occurs, primary targets are its religious and national gods and heroes, its potential of leadership and the self-respect and integrity of its members.

Material points of attack are finance, communications, technology and a denial of resources.

Look around today and you will find countless examples of these points. They scream at us every day from the newspapers.

Probably the most critical point of attack on a culture is its religious experience. Where one can destroy or undermine religious institutions then the entire fabric of the society can be quickly subverted or brought to ruin.

As you read on in this book you will discover why this is such an important factor and what can be done about it.

Religion is the first sense of community. Your sense of community occurs by reason of mutual experience with others. Where the religious sense of community and with it real trust and integrity can be destroyed then that society is like a sandcastle unable to defend itself against the inexorable sea.

For the last hundred years or so religion has been beset with a relentless attack. You have been told it's the "opiate of the masses," that it's unscientific, that it is primitive; in short, that it is a delusion.

But beneath all these attacks on organized religion there was a more fundamental target: the spirituality of man, **your own basic spiritual nature, self-respect and peace of mind.** This black propaganda may have been so successful that maybe you no longer believe you have a spiritual nature but I assure you you do.

In fact, you don't have a soul, you **are** your own soul. In other words, you are not this book, your social security card, your body or your mind. You are you. This will become more apparent, if it isn't already clear, as you read this book.

Convince a man that he is an animal, that his own dignity and self-respect are delusions, that there is no "beyond" to aspire to, no higher potential self to achieve, and you have a slave. Let a man know he is himself, a spiritual being, that he is capable of the power of choice and has the right to aspire to greater wisdom and you have started him up a higher road.

Of course, such attacks on religion run counter to man's **traditional** aspirations to spiritual fulfillment and an ethical way of life.

For thousands of years on this planet thinking man has upheld his own spirituality and considered the ultimate wisdom to be spiritual enlightenment.

The new radical thought that man is an animal without a spiritual nature has a name: totalitarian materialism. Materialism is the doctrine that "only matter matters." The apostles of this new thought are trying to sell everybody on the idea that people really down deep are just a mass and what the person wants to do is cohese with this mass and then be protected by the mass.

This philosophical position was very handy to militaristic and totalitarian governments and their advocates of the last hundred years who wished to justify their atrocities and subjugation of populaces.

One of the tricks of the game has been to attack religion as unscientific. Yet science itself is merely a tool by which the physical universe can be better controlled. The joke is that science itself can become a religion.

Gerhard Lenski on page 331 of his **The Religious Factor, a Sociologist's Inquiry,** defines religion as "a system of beliefs about the nature of force(s), ultimately shaping man's destiny, and the practices associated therewith, shared by members of a group."

Scientific activities can be as fanatical as religious ones. Scientific groups can themselves be religious "orthodox science" monopolies. The Einsteinian concept of space and time can itself become a holy writ, just as Aristotle's writings were converted into dogmas by the orthodoxy to squash any new ideas in the Middle Ages. (Einstein himself until late in his life was looked upon as a maverick and denied admittance into learned societies.)

Science in itself can become a new faith, a brave new way of overcoming anxiety by explaining things so there is no fear of God or the hereafter.

Thus science and religion are not a dichotomy (pair of opposites). Science itself was borrowed from ancient religious studies in India and Egypt.

Religion has also been attacked as primitive. Too much study of primitive cultures may lead one to believe religion is primitive as it is so dominant in them and that "modern" cultures can dispense with it. The truth of the matter is that at no time is religion more necessary as a civilizing force than in the presence of huge forces in the hands of man, who may have become very lacking in social abilities emphasized in religion.

The great religious civilizing forces of the past, Buddhism, Judaism, Christianity, and others, have all emphasized differentiation of good from evil and higher ethical values.

The lowering of church attendance in the United States coincided with a rise in pornography and general immorality, and an increase in crime which then caused a rise in numbers of police without a subsequent decline in actual moral aberration.

When religion is not influential in a society or has ceased to be, the state inherits the entire burden of public morality, crime and intolerance. It then must use punishment and police. Yet this is unsuccessful as morality, integrity and self-respect not already inherent in the individual, cannot be enforced with any great success. Only by a spiritual awareness and inculcation of the spiritual value of these attributes can they come about. There must be more reason and more emotional motivation to be moral, etc., than threat of human discipline.

When a culture has fallen totally away from spiritual pursuits into materialism, one must begin by demonstrating they are each a soul, not a material animal. From this realization of their own religious nature individuals can again come to an awareness of God and become more themselves.

Medicine, psychiatry and psychology "solved" the whole problem of "human nature" simply by dumping it into the classification of material nature—body, brain, force. As they politically insist on monopoly and use social and political propaganda to enforce their monopoly, they debar actual search for real answers to human nature.

Their failures are attested by lack of result in the field of human nature. They cannot change man—they can only degrade. While asserting dominance in the field of human nature they cannot demonstrate results—and nowhere do they demonstrate that lack more than in their own persons. They have the highest suicide rate and prefer the use of force on others. Under their tutelage the crime rate and antisocial forces have risen. But they are most condemned by their attacks on anyone who seeks answers and upon the civilizing influences of religion.

Of course, if one is going to find fault with something, it implies that he wishes to do something about it and would if he could. If one does not like the crime, cruelty, injustice and violence of this society, he **can** do something about it. He can become a VOLUNTEER MINISTER and help civilize it, bring it conscience and kindness and love and freedom from travail by instilling into it trust, decency, honesty and tolerance.

Briefly, a Volunteer Minister fulfills the definition of religion in this increasingly cynical and hopeless world.

Let's look again at the definition of religion.

In a few words, religion can be defined as belief in spiritual beings. More broadly, religion can be defined as a system of beliefs and practices by means of which a group of people struggles with the ultimate problems of human life. The quality of being religious implies two things: first, a belief that evil, pain, bewilderment and injustice are fundamental facts of existence; second, a set of practices and related sanctified beliefs that express a conviction that man can ultimately be saved from those facts.*

Thus, a Volunteer Minister is a person who helps his fellow man on a volunteer basis by restoring purpose, truth and spiritual values to the lives of others.

A Volunteer Minister does not shut his eyes to the pain, evil and injustice of existence. Rather, he is trained to handle these things and help others achieve relief from them and new personal strength as well.

How does a Volunteer Minister accomplish these miracles? Basically, he uses the technology of Scientology to change conditions for the better—for himself, his family, his groups, friends, associates and for mankind.

A society to survive well, needs at least as many Volunteer Ministers as it has policemen. A society gets what it concentrates upon. By concentrating on spiritual values instead of criminality a new day may yet dawn for man.

L. RON HUBBARD Founder

* Reference: A Scientific Study of Religion by J. Milton Yunger, Oberlin College.

PART EIGHT

SOCIAL REFORM ACTIVITIES

While religious leaders have long recognized that man's spiritual well-being cannot be entirely divorced from temporal concerns, few churches have dedicated themselves so thoroughly to the cause of social reform as the Church of Scientology. Through its diligence and persistence, the Church is recognized by many as a leading champion of human rights, one that involves itself in arenas wherever injustice has been perceived.

It may seem unusual for a church to actively involve itself, as the Church of Scientology has done, in the exposure of psychiatric abuses around the world, governmental abuses of law and human rights, international law enforcement corruption and a host of other ills that plague society, but the fact is Scientologists care as much about the here and now as the hereafter. The Creed of the Church specifically addresses the inalienable rights of all men, regardless of race, color or creed, and the actions of Scientologists everywhere have given these words true substance.

CHAPTER 29

SPEARHEADING SOCIAL REFORM

Scientologists who care enough to investigate, to overcome the resistance of powerful vested interests, and even to place themselves at risk, have achieved remarkable results. Laws have been passed, lives saved, victims rescued, restitution paid, criminals arrested and life-threatening activities halted. In a word, they have resulted in justice, a sometimes rare commodity in today's world.

Scientologists have, in a very real sense, drawn the line. They have raised their voices in the collective cry: "Enough!" Enough butchery of innocents, enough enslavement of the weak, enough intolerance, enough abuse of power by those who hold it. Such statements may sound dramatic—but only to those too timid to see, those who huddle in the security of their homes and jobs, or those who, when they witness evil on the evening news or upon the streets of their cities say, "This has nothing to do with me."

That the presence of evil is as real as the shadows that dog our footsteps will be shown in this chapter. It is man's burden and will continue to be so for as long as it has nothing to do with us. No matter how technologically advanced our age, no matter how "enlightened" the opinions on talk shows or the advice so liberally handed out in magazines, it is not enough. As repugnant as the thought may be, there are those among us on a mission of destruction, and it will take more than talk to abort such missions.

Scientologists are acutely aware of this. And thus they have taken the task of man's freedom upon themselves. For as has been implied and discussed and stated in this book, the mission of Scientology involves spiritual freedom. But just as there can be no soaring flight while anchored to the ground, so there can be no true and lasting spiritual freedom while tyranny and injustice govern any man among us.

The Code of Honor of a Scientologist states quite plainly: "Your integrity to yourself is more important than your body." And while no ethical code can be enforced, it is a beacon that stands as an ideal. To many Scientologists it is even more—it is a reality to live by. Which is why they are willing to draw that line, to persist against unfriendly fire, and to show by deeds that enough is indeed enough.

To carry these battles forward, the Church and concerned Scientologists have founded a number of nonprofit organizations such as the Citizens Commission on Human Rights (CCHR) and the National Commission on Law Enforcement and Social Justice (NCLE) which seek social reform in the areas of psychiatric excess and government abuse, respectively. And, to quickly and broadly bring the results of its research in these areas and others into the light of day, the Church publishes an international journal.

FREEDOM MAGAZINE

Since it was founded in 1968, *Freedom* magazine has become widely recognized as one of the foremost voices for social reform and human rights. Originating in the United Kingdom as a newspaper broadsheet, *Freedom* magazine's flagship edition is now published in the United States by the Church of Scientology International in Los Angeles, California. By 1998, localized editions were published in fourteen countries and nine languages. *Freedom* is now available on the Internet at **http://www.freedommag.org**, offering past and current editions of the magazine in all major languages.

Today, leaders in government, business and the news media increasingly turn to *Freedom* for coverage of significant issues. Among the many notable contributors, US congressmen have published articles on important social concerns in *Freedom* and, just before the 1996 elections, the four major US presidential candidates, including the president of the United States, submitted articles presenting their views on solutions to the American drug problem.

A forum for hard-hitting investigative journalism, *Freedom* has taken on stories that other media have been reluctant to investigate or publish. And, as its readership has grown, so has public awareness of areas in need of social reform. *Freedom* has broken important stories on the forced drugging of schoolchildren, government chemical and biological warfare experimentation and psychiatric brutalities.

An award-winning publication, *Freedom* is a dependable source of information about a wide range of timely issues, from government corruption to workable solutions for the problems of drug abuse, illiteracy and violent crime, to protecting privacy, property rights and freedom of speech in the electronic age of the Internet.

In 1988, *Freedom*'s Human Rights Leadership Awards were created so that the positive contributions of individuals in government, the news media and other areas of society who have supported human rights were appropriately recognized.

These awards are presented to those at the forefront of efforts to advance the causes of freedom of expression, freedom of information, government reform, mental health reform, children's rights, religious freedom and social justice. Recipients have included Freedom of Information advocate US Senator Patrick Leahy, First Amendment expert Paul McMasters and former chairman of the US Commission on Civil Rights Arthur A. Fletcher.

Through awards to individuals who are improving conditions in society, positive contributions to our civilization and to the welfare of mankind are reinforced.

It is *Freedom*'s intention—and the evident trend—that the voices speaking out on behalf of human rights and individual freedoms will continue to become more and more powerful in the years ahead.

CITIZENS COMMISSION ON HUMAN RIGHTS

Among the codes and creeds Scientology parishioners unite under is the Code of a Scientologist, written by L. Ron Hubbard in 1954. The fourth point of the code is one in which the individual pledges: "to decry and do all I can to abolish any and all abuses against life and mankind," followed by agreements "to expose and help abolish any and all physically damaging practices in the field of mental health," "to help clean up and keep clean the field of mental health" and "to bring about an atmosphere of safety and security in the field of mental health by eradicating its abuses and brutality."

Since the Church of Scientology's inception, its parishioners have remained steadfastly opposed to the brutal treatments, criminal practices and human rights abuses which are the stock in trade of the mental health field.

Established in 1969 by the Church, the Citizens Commission on Human Rights (CCHR) has become an effective force for change in this area. A nonprofit and tax-exempt public benefit organization, it investigates and exposes psychiatric violations of human rights and actively works to eliminate harmful practices in the field of mental health. By 1998, CCHR had grown to 128 chapters in twenty-eight countries and become an internationally acknowledged authority on mental health reform.

A 1986 report presented by a Special Rapporteur to the United Nations Human Rights Commission refers to the reforms accomplished by CCHR in the field of mental health, stating, "CCHR has been responsible for many great reforms. At least thirty bills throughout the world, which would otherwise have inhibited the rights of patients, or would have given psychiatry the power to commit minority groups and individuals against their will, have been defeated by CCHR." By 1998, the number of such bills defeated, or bills that protected patient rights

passed because of CCHR's work, had risen to one hundred.

While the CCHR chapters that exist in many countries and cities manage their own immediate areas, they are extensively supported by the CCHR International office located in Los Angeles. Serving all these offices worldwide, CCHR International is responsible for ongoing research and analysis, the production of enlightenment and training publications, the creation of public relations and other campaigns, coordinating legislative watchdog and reform activities and many other actions concerned with cleaning up this once neglected field.

CCHR Commissioners

CCHR International appoints commissioners from all walks of life to provide professional advice and to help disseminate the truth about psychiatry's destructive agenda. Among other responsibilities, they hold public hearings into specific abuses which are uncovered during the course of CCHR's work, prepare reports for government officials and other authorities and conduct media interviews.

Currently CCHR International has forty-five commissioners representing the fields of arts and entertainment, religion, law, politics, science, medicine, health, education and business. With rapidly increasing public awareness of the dangers of psychiatry and psychology, these professional ambassadors provide a vital link with the community.

CCHR Human Rights Awards

CCHR has joined forces with many other courageous individuals throughout the world in its efforts to clean up the field of mental health. In 1994, as part of its 25th anniversary celebration, CCHR initiated its International Human Rights Award to recognize and honor individuals who have displayed extraordinary courage and commitment in the fight for the restoration of basic human rights.

In the first year, the recipients of the CCHR International Human Rights Awards were Patrick Griffin, a solicitor from Australia who worked tirelessly with CCHR to expose the atrocities of Chelmsford Hospital and the use of deep sleep treatment there; Senator Edo Ronchi from Italy, for his work with CCHR to expose to media and to government the horrendous conditions in Italian psychiatric facilities, effecting drastic change; Lorne Love from the United States, founder of the Committee to Stop the Federal Violence Initiative, a psychiatric initiative which targeted African-American children for their supposed genetic tendency to become violent later in life; Texas State Senators Mike Moncrief and Judith Zaffirini, for their persistence in holding hearings into psychiatric insurance fraud in their state, which led to one of the largest national healthcare fraud investigations ever; and Dr. Thomas Szasz, emeritus professor of psychiatry, for his articles, books and lectures, throughout a quarter of a century, exposing the truth about psychiatry.

Since then, CCHR has awarded its prestigious International Human Rights Awards to individuals from Greece, South Africa, Italy, Russia and the United States.

Psychiatry Unmasked

Interestingly enough, psychiatry has been a field which claims both humanitarian motive and leadership in the treatment of "mental health." It is a positioning that for many years has filled its trough with lucrative government appropriations and given it no small measure of societal power.

Based upon the realities discovered by the Church of Scientology, however, a more apt analogy might be that it has been looting the coffers for many years, for if, as is true for most of us in society, payment is received in return for a valuable service or product, psychiatry has been pulling the wool over government eyes for a very long time. Having taken the high ground much earlier this century simply due to the fact that nothing much had been done as far as

studies of the mind were concerned, psychiatry stepped into the void and declared its leadership position. There were no competitors to speak of, for medicine had its hands full with advances in physical treatment and had virtually no interest in the mind. And so, initially at least, in a society newly infatuated with the claims of science, there was little opposition to these new theories that claimed for themselves the same scientific status. Funded by governments interested in the control of populations, psychiatrists donned white cloaks in their laboratories, ran their tests on mice and monkeys and dogs and issued scholarly papers, written in a rapidly developed lexicon virtually incomprehensible to the layman—or the politician.

In truth, and as time finally proved, it was simply another case of an emperor with no clothes. The problem was not minor, however; it lay in the basic premise. Any researcher faces many choices in virtually limitless directions. And more than a century ago, psychiatry and its cousin, psychology, chose a certain path which has since, with minor exceptions, been slavishly followed. The premise was that man was an animal (thus the experiments on animals), that all mental activity originated in the brain (thus physical treatment of this physical organ was a primary solution), and that he responded to environmental stimuli (thus his behavior could be manipulated by such stimuli). Psychiatry has done little to diverge from this premise.

Unfortunately, the path has led only to a dead end. The fact of the matter is that these self-appointed experts do not, to this day, understand the mind or how it works. And although their name implies they are involved in the study of the psyche or soul—for that is what the word *psychiatry* originally meant—today's psychiatrist denies the existence of the spirit and sees man as only a pain-driven lump of matter and chemicals.

And as psychiatry still stumbles in circles around that cul-de-sac into which they were led, they have had to step over the bodies of the victims lying in their wake. Even a car mechanic learns about engines—what they are, what motivates them, how they work—before diving in with a wrench. Psychiatry has not only missed this basic premise, but its tools are dangerous. In lieu of understanding, their only instruments are a vast cornucopia of mind-altering pharmaceuticals, electroshock machines and surgeons' knives. And as the basic premise is inaccurate, and they actually have no idea *what* they are treating (other than easily observed symptoms) the results are naturally dismal, to say the least. In fact, psychiatrist Dr. Thomas Szasz has called psychiatry the single most destructive force to have affected the American scene in the last fifty years.

The obvious question that arises is what does one do in such circumstances? They have claimed a leadership position by virtue of the fact there were no other candidates, and now they are expected to deliver. Unfortunately, they have virtually no idea what they are doing. It is a difficult position to be in. And so we have the undeniably applicable maxim: Desperate men do desperate things.

L. Ron Hubbard was one of the first to notice the nakedness of this emperor—and the desperation of his acts. From his earliest contact with the field in the late 1940s, he saw that something was very wrong: an arrogance, a venality, a lack of concern for the individual and a serious incompetence. He noted with due outrage that for all the talk of enlightened psychiatric care, unmanageable patients were still routinely warehoused in dreadful conditions, drugged into vegetative states that left them permanently impaired, and punitively electroshocked. He also noted that, beyond food, clothing and a padded cell, psychiatry possessed no tools at all for dealing with the mentally ill.

To sum up, Mr. Hubbard wrote, psychiatry stood for ineffectiveness, lies and inhuman brutality. Its basic assumption revolved around the idea that with enough punishment, anyone could be restored to sanity; and if all else failed, one could always sever the patient's prefrontal lobes. With this and more in mind, Mr. Hubbard declared it to be the Scientologist's duty "to expose and help abolish any and all physically damaging practices in the field of mental health." Thus came about the formation of CCHR—the Citizens Commission on Human Rights.

Doctors of Death

Perhaps nowhere have the abuses of psychiatry been more widespread than in Europe. Yet diligent CCHR volunteers have made both the public and government increasingly aware of the atrocities perpetrated by those who practice this pseudoscience. It has been an effort requiring courage and, at times, strong stomachs.

In Germany CCHR has, for many years, actively investigated, documented and exposed the Nazi roots of modern psychiatry. While psychiatry has long tried to disassociate itself from the racial (and religious) acts of genocide in Nazi Germany, the facts are indisputable: Psychiatry spawned "racial purity" or "eugenics" almost three decades before the Nazis took power in 1933.

As early as 1895, psychiatrist Alfred Ploetz was eagerly promoting the murder of the "weakly and ill-bred child," although he, of course, misrepresented his intent by benignly calling for "a gentle death."

Within ten years, Ploetz founded the German Society for Racial Hygiene, joining with another psychiatrist, Ernst Rudin, who was grateful for the opportunity. "Only through the *Führer* did our dream of over thirty years, that of applying racial hygiene to society, become a reality," he said. Rudin was the director of the Kaiser Wilhelm Institute for Psychiatry, one of a number of institutes under the umbrella of the Kaiser Wilhelm

Society. The Society was the primary "think tank" behind the Nazi ideology and Rudin, as head of one of its major institutes, was bestowed with special awards by the Nazis and Hitler for his work. After the war the Society was renamed the Max Planck Society and Rudin's institute became the Max Planck Institute for Psychiatry.

It was against this background that the Church of Scientology in Germany established a CCHR chapter in 1972 which undertook a lengthy research project into the identity of the German psychiatrists behind the Nazi regime, the role they assumed in the "extermination camps" and how they escaped punishment during the Nuremberg Trials. What they discovered was that many returned to become "respectable" and influential members of society after the war. The result of more than twenty years of research finally culminated in the explosive and well-documented book, *Psychiatrists— the Men Behind Hitler,* released in Germany in 1994.

Psychiatry's legacy is no less bloody in other European countries.

In Italy, in 1979, CCHR investigated the Mombello Provincial Mental Health Center and discovered the mummified bodies of former mental patients. The grisly collection included twelve bodies without arms, several sawed-open heads, some fifty brains, kidneys, lungs, arms, legs and ears. These body parts were so well preserved that the embalming fluid used to mummify them had permeated nearly all the tissues—a result that could only have been accomplished by injecting the chemicals while the victims' hearts slowly pumped it into their bodies.

Mombello was by no means a singular example of psychiatry's activities in Italy. In April 1991, CCHR and several government officials raided the Lonigo Insane Asylum and found that conditions in psychiatric institutions were only slightly better than when mental patients were being embalmed

alive. Inmates were naked, locked into rooms where the floors and beds were covered with human feces and urine. Wallowing in filth and dying of disease proved to be the standard psychiatric treatment in Italy. Over the next seven years, CCHR Italy continued to raid mental hospitals throughout the country. Aided by Members of Parliament and covered by television news crews, CCHR not only documented and exposed similar abuses in dozens of other mental hospitals, but succeeded in closing down some of the worst of these psychiatric hellholes.

And these were by no means isolated abuses. Elsewhere in Europe, conditions have been much the same.

In France, which has the fourth largest per capita psychiatric presence in the world, there is likewise no lack of work for CCHR. There, hundreds of French citizens are subjected to psychiatric electroshock "treatments" every year. This barbaric practice passes up to 460 volts of searing current through a victim's head, causing bone-breaking convulsions and severe brain damage. As a result, CCHR has been inundated with tragic stories from people whose lives have been ruined by this so-called treatment.

CCHR has investigated numerous such cases and taken action to stop abuses by filing complaints with government agencies and acting as a civil party in suits to assist those in psychiatric institutions who had been force-fed, humiliated, beaten, drugged and even raped.

CCHR has also vigorously campaigned against involuntary commitment laws which allow individuals to be incarcerated without their consent. In 1989, it discovered that the Ministry of Justice had refused to release a report on the appalling conditions in France's psychiatric facilities and attempted to use various government channels to force the report into the open.

When the report was finally made public after intense political pressure by CCHR, it became clear why psychiatrists wanted it kept secret: Forty percent of the patients in the country's psychiatric hospitals, many of them elderly, did not need to be there; of these, half had no diagnosable "mental illness." The motivation for commitment was solely financial. As a result of CCHR's actions, France's involuntary commitment law was amended in 1990.

In Denmark, CCHR has a long history of exposing psychiatric abuses. In 1979, CCHR investigators discovered mind-control experiments using LSD were being conducted at Frederiksberg Hospital. As a result, the Justice Ombudsman initiated his own investigation. This resulted in a 75-page report strongly criticizing psychiatry and an order that all victims of mind-control experiments be compensated for the harm they suffered.

For years, Denmark's oppressive mental health laws empowered psychiatrists to force patients to undergo treatment. In 1995, widespread alarm at the growing and arbitrary use of coercive psychiatry led CCHR to bring together a number of humanitarian organizations to articulate their concerns in a public forum. The Parliamentary Assembly of the Council of Europe had already in 1994 recommended that proposals to strengthen the rights of psychiatric patients be implemented by the governments of all thirty-two Council of Europe member states—a significant recognition that human rights violations in psychiatry had reached extreme levels.

CCHR Denmark subsequently investigated, documented and exposed crimes in psychiatric institutions, including the use of forced drugging and other coercive treatments which even resulted in patient deaths. Submissions calling for the investigation of psychiatry in Denmark have been made to various judicial committees, health committees, the European Council and the prime minister of Denmark. By the mid-1990s, more than two hundred psychiatrists internationally had been convicted of exploitation, sexual abuse and fraud, while another five hundred were under investigation.

In Norway, members of CCHR exposed one of that country's greatest hidden scandals by revealing that between 3,000 and 4,000 people admitted to Gaustad psychiatric facility between 1945 and 1970 had been brutally lobotomized. Surgeons destroyed living brain tissue by sawing open the crown of the skull and slashing away at the prefrontal lobes with a knitting needle. In Sweden, CCHR has regularly produced a quarterly magazine entitled *Human Rights*. Sent to politicians, social workers, police and other officials, it regularly exposes such crimes as the sexual exploitation of patients by psychiatrists.

In Spain, CCHR documented psychiatric abuses and called for investigations into instances of psychiatric brutality and violations of human rights. Patients incarcerated in psychiatric hospitals and forced to receive brain-damaging electroshock treatments have been freed from psychiatric hands. Through an ongoing public information campaign, CCHR has warned government officials and legislators of psychiatry's role in creating violence, subverting education, preying on the elderly and sexually abusing patients.

Europe is, however, only the tip of the psychiatric iceberg. Exposing similar betrayals in the name of help in countries throughout the world has been the ongoing duty of other CCHR chapters.

Chelmsford—The Endless Sleep

Chelmsford is a name that Australian members of CCHR will probably never forget. For many, it was their first contact with unmitigated evil. And for all of them, it tested both their courage and their ability to persist in the face of derision, disbelief and an uncaring bureaucracy.

The Church's exposure of the atrocities at Chelmsford resulted in an international scandal and much needed psychiatric reform.

For Australians as a whole, the name of Chelmsford is today synonymous with madness, barbarism and horror; of psychiatry run amok, of bizarre experiments that, one magazine claimed, "rival those performed by Dr. Josef Mengele in Nazi Germany." New South Wales Health Minister, Peter Collins, called it "the darkest episode of the history of psychiatry in this country." And in mute witness, at least forty-nine crematoriums and cemeteries around Sydney hold Chelmsford's victims.

The Chelmsford Private Hospital in Sydney's northwest Pennant Hills was headed by Dr. Harry Bailey who by 1963 had started to administer what is called deep sedation therapy, or more commonly, deep sleep therapy. As a later story by the *Sydney Morning Herald* described it, the title was a misnomer.

"First of all it isn't a therapy," having shown no therapeutic benefits. "Nor is it sleep. It is a coma induced by large doses of barbiturates."

Bailey's technique for handling mentally disturbed Chelmsford patients who were sent to him for help and care was essentially simple, if heavy-handed. He would place them in a coma for up to two weeks, during which period he would administer daily doses of electroshock therapy and/or psychosurgery, often without the consent or knowledge of the "sleeping" patient.

From mid-1963 to 1979, during his autocratic reign at Chelmsford, the deaths from this "treatment" mounted. Then there were the suicides by patients who were able to make it out of the facility alive, although the number of these was difficult to verify.

In the mid-1970s, CCHR began to receive reports of what was happening at Chelmsford. And by 1978, after investigating, it had collected hard evidence of six deaths related to deep sedation therapy. At that point, CCHR went public. Exposure of these atrocities resulted in an international scandal and much-needed psychiatric reform.

What followed was a significant demonstration of the unwillingness of authorities to view emperors in their nakedness—and the failure of the psychiatric establishment to police itself. It was, in fact, a tedious merry-go-round of letter writing and lobbying. The Royal Australian and New Zealand College of Psychiatrists was given the evidence, and did nothing. The Minister of Health of the state of New South Wales was given the evidence, and did nothing. The Health Commission and the Medical Board were given the evidence, but they each referred CCHR to the other. Meanwhile, public relations attacks were mounted against CCHR.

It took CCHR ten years of persistent investigation and bulldog-like determination before the New South Wales government appointed a Royal Commission in 1988 to look into deep sleep therapy in Chelmsford and throughout the state. Finally, after the two-year inquiry was completed and the full litany of horrors was uncovered— which included the possibility of 183 patient deaths, either at Chelmsford or within a year of discharge—a thorough shake-up of mental health care in New South Wales was recommended, along with a mental health patient bill of rights.

And what of psychiatry's stance after CCHR first uncovered what was happening at Chelmsford? It was ignored for as long as possible. However, this comment by a leading international figure provides an apt summation of psychiatric concerns. On January 6, 1981, Sir Martin Roth, Professor of Psychiatry at Cambridge University, wrote to another psychiatrist, who was calling for an inquiry, that the "Scientologists and other organizations will have obtained ammunition for years or decades to come. There is, therefore, a pressing need for maintaining strict confidentiality at this stage until one can set these barbarities in the context of contemporary practice in psychiatry in a carefully prepared statement that comes from colleges and other bodies concerned."

Scientology's relentless work to uncover the truth was not without compensation. Deep sleep therapy was banned. Chelmsford was closed. And, of even more significance, many of the surviving victims who received electroshock therapy took their cases to the Victim's Compensation Tribunal. The Tribunal found that the deep sleep patients receiving electroshock had indeed suffered from "an act of violence," and in 1991 a victim of the now-outlawed deep sleep treatment was awarded the maximum $50,000.

Two of the psychiatrists who worked at Chelmsford finally faced criminal charges in 1992. And CCHR continued its work, exposing psychiatric abuses at Townsville Hospital in the northern state of Queensland. In practices frighteningly similar to Bailey's deep sleep treatments, sixty-five deaths were attributed to "unlawful and negligent treatment" after CCHR triggered a government investigation.

Finally, what of Bailey? In September 1985, having already confronted serious criminal charges in one legal case and due to appear in court the next day to answer in a civil damages suit, Harry Bailey avoided being brought to justice by ending his own life with an overdose of barbiturates. The wretched suicide note he left behind was tantamount to a confession of guilt. His enemies, he wrote, "have finally won."

Psychiatric Slave Camps

In the 1970s, a traveling windowpane salesman lost his way in the semirural countryside outside of Johannesburg, South Africa. Stopping to ask directions at what seemed to be a desolate mining compound, he happened upon a troubling sight: a naked and obviously terrified native woman was attempting to flee a uniformed guard.

The salesman was a Scientologist and reported what he had seen to the Church. As the South African edition of Freedom began to investigate, what emerged was a story that would long stand as a dark symbol of psychiatric greed and inhumanity.

That apparently abandoned mining compound was one of thirteen psychiatric facilities owned and operated by the Smith-Mitchell Holding Company, a group that by the mid-70s was absorbing about one-third of the South African mental health budget. Nine of these facilities were for black patients, four for whites.

What CCHR uncovered was shocking. In 1976, more than 70 percent of all black certified mental patients in South Africa were in the hands of this group. The Smith-Mitchell hospitals had a patient population of more than 10,000. And the blacks were treated little better than animals, providing twelve-hour-a-day forced labor to line the pockets of their keepers. Nutrition was minimal, patients slept on mats on bare concrete floors, and in some institutions there was only one nurse on duty for anywhere from 300 to 1,000 patients. Nor were there equipped medical facilities, and at least one patient died a day. Accurately

described by media as "hidden slave camps" and "human warehouses," most of these Draconian camps were hidden from view and surrounded by spiked fences.

Troublesome patients were made tractable with a trip to the nearest state hospital where electroshock therapy was administered — without anesthetic.

The exposure of these grim revelations in Church publications brought an understandable wave of public outrage, both in South Africa and overseas. The United Nations and the World Health Organization investigated and confirmed the atrocities uncovered by CCHR.

However, instead of investigating the horrifying reports and protests that flooded in, the then-apartheid South African government passed a law banning the publication of material or photographs about the psychiatric camps. By so gagging all opposition, the oppressive apartheid regime ensured that no further progress would be made while it was in power. The measure was so effective that when South Africa emerged from the tyranny of apartheid, CCHR found that the legally enforced silence surrounding the camps had made them "invisible" to the new government.

With the fall of apartheid in 1994, CCHR brought the psychiatric camps to the attention of officials in the new Government of National Unity with a submission calling for a public inquiry into psychiatry's apartheid crimes. In 1995, the Minister of Health ordered a government inquiry to "investigate and report on any malpractices or violation of human rights in psychiatric hospitals."

By February 1996, the Inquiry issued a damning report which laid the blame for this brutal racial discrimination on "the protective [mental health] legislation which prohibits publication of anything against the hospitals" and recommended that the offensive law be repealed. The news exploded across the country through extensive national media coverage.

Story after story detailed the committee's findings, which included the facts that:

Death certificates were falsified to cover up the real causes of patient deaths; there was extensive physical and sexual abuse, including the sodomy of male patients; and, many patients were drugged so heavily that they were reduced to zombie-like states.

The recommendations for reform loudly echoed those made in CCHR's submission:

That the practice of involuntary commitment was a gross abuse of human rights and required a further full inquiry; that a "Charter of Patients Rights" should be drawn up and adhered to; that regular inspections should be carried out by an independent panel, which should include "consumer representatives and leaders of local communities"; and that a similar panel should investigate every complaint of psychiatric abuse and recommend prosecution of any criminal abuse found.

Since the report's release, Members of Parliament who have been briefed on psychiatry's racist history have been speaking out in Parliament in support of CCHR's call for a further inquiry.

One Member of Parliament called for an independent inquiry into "psychiatry itself," saying, "Organized psychiatry and individual psychiatrists were at the heart of this entire disgraceful situation . . . How can they escape responsibility? An independent inquiry [is] needed into the nature and culture of psychiatric practice . . . otherwise, we will have psychiatrists investigating themselves."

CCHR and US Psychiatric Institutions

Since the late 1960s CCHR has investigated a virtually endless array of psychiatric abuses in the United States. In 1976, for instance, it provided California lawmakers with evidence and witnesses documenting the unexplained deaths of more than a hundred people at the Camarillo and Metropolitan state psychiatric institutions. These exposés led to an investigation by the California state legislature and resulted in substantial administrative changes in both institutions.

In 1990 a similar pattern of abuse was discovered at the Patton state psychiatric institution in San Bernardino, California. CCHR discovered that the death rate at Patton had increased five times since the head of the institution had assumed office. Again, the California legislature investigated and the executive director was forced to resign.

CCHR has been responsible for many legislative reforms over the years, including a 1976 law passed in California to restrict the use of electric shock and lobotomies on children, and to require full disclosure to adult patients of the damaging effects of the brutal procedures. In 1994, a similar law banning the use of ECT on children was passed in Texas due to the efforts of CCHR there. In Florida, where "for-profit" psychiatric hospitals indulged in schemes such as "patient brokering" and "referral fees," CCHR was instrumental in getting legislation passed to ban such fraudulent practices.

CCHR continues to work closely with local, state and federal authorities to uncover and expose fraud and patient abuses in psychiatric facilities. Its work has resulted in a heightened awareness by law enforcement of fraudulent practices and, consequently, more and more psychiatric facilities are being forced to close.

Psychiatrists and Sexual Abuse

Although the Chelmsford atrocities and the disgraceful South African mental health camps are broad and telling examples of psychiatric desperation, there is a less dramatic yet extremely pervasive form of abuse which, mainly through the efforts of CCHR, continues increasingly to make headlines around the world: psychiatric sexual abuse.

A growing problem among psychiatrists and psychologists, the sexual exploitation of patients — men, women and children — had long gone unreported owing to the unique and powerful control mental health professionals hold over their patients. Less than 5 percent of patients sexually assaulted by their therapists ever take action against them. And there are even cases on record wherein psychiatrists have actually used their instruments of trade — electroshock and heavy sedation — to silence patients they have sexually abused.

While there have been widespread reports of these abuses in institutions, CCHR investigations and the appearance of more and more newspaper accounts show the problem is not limited to those who have been committed to psychiatric care. It ranges from one-man practitioners in small towns and cities, to high officials. Early in 1992, for instance, John Hamilton, deputy medical director of the American Psychiatric Association, stepped down from office and had his license suspended for a year — after having sexual relations with a patient who was courageous enough to file a complaint. Ironically, Hamilton wrote and edited the APA peer review manual.

However, this type of rap on the knuckles is all too common — and, more unfortunately, all too rare. In the last ten years, the APA has suspended or expelled only 113 psychiatrists for exploiting patients. These are mild actions when one considers findings of the California task force that about 66 percent of those who are sexually exploited by mental health practitioners experience serious emotional repercussions, and 1 percent even commit suicide.

The intrinsic problem here, of course, is that like doctors and lawyers, psychiatrists righteously and loudly claim that a peer review system is firmly in place to handle member malfeasance. Outsiders, particularly those involved in enforcement of laws, are not needed, thank you. However, the reality demonstrated in all these professions shows serious flaws. Two factors come into play: A peer is after all an equal and a member of the same group and, unless one is motivated by deeply rooted ideals, it is, to say the least, uncomfortable to reprimand one's equals; and, perhaps of more pertinence, if judgments are too harsh they are invariably publicized, thus airing the profession's dirty linen. Bad publicity is anathema to a profession already standing on shaky ground. And faced with this disturbing threat, ranks tend to close rather quickly.

Therefore, knowing full well that the psychiatric community has consistently demonstrated an inability to police its own actions, CCHR has long felt it only just that the perpetrators of actions that break the law of the land should face criminal prosecution. And so, it has taken it upon itself to see that they do. Victims of psychiatric abuse have little other recourse. Virtually nobody else is willing to stand up for their rights, perhaps because of the societal stigma attached to mental difficulties. More and more, however, they turn to CCHR as the word goes out that Scientologists care.

Thus, over the years, CCHR investigations have led to the prosecution of scores of psychiatrists, psychologists, psychiatric workers and psychiatric facilities. Law enforcement has demonstrated an increasing willingness to prosecute psychiatrists who commit criminal acts, a major reversal of earlier decades when they could literally get away with murder.

While exploitation of women patients is common, CCHR's investigations have revealed that the majority of these cases involve even more distasteful acts against children.

■ One of the first cases CCHR investigated was that of Orange County psychiatrist, James Harrison White, who had sexually assaulted a 15-year-old boy. White was sentenced in 1990 to six years and eight months in prison. The Senior Deputy District Attorney, Dennis D. Bauer wrote to CCHR:

"I commend you and your staff for the tireless energy and unselfish commitment to solving one of society's neglected and secret problems . . . 'experimental psychiatry.' "

■ That same year, another case involved the Children's Farm Home, a residential center for children with behavioral and emotional problems, in Oregon. Three men, William Henry Dufort, the home's director, another counselor and a caseworker, were all charged with sexual abuse and/or sodomy of young boys under their care. Dufort was charged with forty-three counts and sentenced to forty-eight years in prison.

■ On July 27, 1992, Alan J. Horowitz of Schenectady, New York was sentenced to ten to twenty years in prison for sodomizing a nine-year-old psychiatric patient the previous year. Allegedly, he had assaulted a string of children from California to Israel to New York in the prior twenty years.

The problem is widespread. Each year, CCHR investigates scores of crimes such as these and ceaselessly lobbies for stronger laws against psychiatric rapists, in particular to make sexual relations with patients by psychotherapists and/or other mental health practitioners illegal. After many years of CCHR efforts, such a law was passed in California in 1989. By 1998 sixteen states had passed these laws and CCHR was actively working with other states to enact similar legislation.

Psychiatric Drugs

When LSD was accidentally discovered, it was not put on the shelf, but actively developed by its maker and subsequently heavily promoted by noted psychiatrists and psychologists from the 1950s on. By the mid-60s it started to become a campus fad.

Around the same time, however, as *Freedom* exposed, it was also being given to unknowing US soldiers by their government. The results of these experiments included death, birth defects in offspring and lifelong psychotic reactions for some of the victims.

Due to the work of the Church, which located a number of these unfortunate veterans, the Army conducted a program to locate and notify all who had been tricked

into participating in these covert psychiatric mind-control programs. Psychiatric drugs have long been a CCHR target. Mind-altering, with immensely powerful and dangerous side effects, they have been used extensively by psychiatrists who lack real answers to problems they don't understand.

A common tactic to gain acceptance for such drugs is to release each with massive public relations campaigns professing the drug's efficacy and safety. But often, cases discrediting the claims of safety and revealing instead harmful side effects soon begin to accumulate. In the mid-1800s, opium addiction begat morphine which was touted by the medical establishment as nonaddictive treatment for opium addiction. But by 1870, morphine was recognized as more addictive than opium. This led to the development of heroin, extolled as a nonaddictive substitute for morphine. Within fifteen years this claim had clearly been shown to be otherwise. Following World War II, psychiatrists began pushing a new drug, methadone, as a cure for heroin addiction, thus foisting a century-old con game on a growing number of victims—all while reaping huge appropriations of public funding for its implementation.

Other prescription drugs such as Valium, Librium, Xanax, Oraflex, Halcion and Prozac were all claimed to be safe, but each has been found to have harmful side effects. Psychiatrists have earned hundreds of millions of dollars prescribing these drugs—and then treating the problems created by their own prescriptions.

The pharmaceutical drug companies reap huge profits, literally tens of billions of dollars a year, from the widespread use of drugs to treat an ever-increasing list of symptoms for new illnesses "discovered" each year by the psychiatric profession. Hundreds of psychiatric drugs are consumed by millions to "solve" a multitude of modern problems such as sleeplessness, nervousness, stress or just plain boredom. These illnesses,

all of which are given credence with sophisticated names, become official during the American Psychiatric Association's annual convention. Psychiatrists proffer a newly discovered illness and a vote is taken, with a majority consensus creating an official new disease. Why "official"? Official diseases can be treated and paid for by insurance companies, and in that way the psychiatric/drug manufacturer coalition ensures an ever-increasing source of income. Without question this is one of the great frauds of the twentieth century. It is a fraud that remains suppressed through the billions of dollars vested interests have at their disposal for high-tech PR campaigns and expensive marketing strategies, which in turn create the advertising revenues for a largely compliant media which would have its revenues threatened if it exposed the scam.

Drugging and Labeling of Children

Psychiatric drugs have even become entrenched in the educational system. Ritalin, a powerful amphetamine-like drug prescribed by psychiatrists for so-called hyperactive children of all ages, has turned essentially normal, healthy children into depressed, listless and sometimes violent or suicidal addicts. In fact, Ritalin is bought on the street by heroin addicts. In the 1980s, a CCHR educational program warned parents of the dangers of Ritalin and cautioned them against claims that their children might be suffering from the stigma of "mental illness" simply because psychiatrists had chosen to label them so.

Indeed, the prescribing of Ritalin or any one of the hundreds of other psychiatric drugs to children is symptomatic of a much larger problem: the fraudulent diagnoses of "mental disorders" in children.

The lamentable truth is that every normal aspect of childhood behavior falls within

Some of the many issues of Freedom *magazine published and distributed by the Church to educate the public on important social issues.*

469

the broad spectrum of "symptoms" which comprise so-called "mental illness." By reading the "bible" of mental illness, psychiatry's *Diagnostic and Statistical Manual of Mental Disorders* (DSM) in the US, or its international counterpart, one could be led to believe that everyone is mentally ill. Psychiatry has literally covered every base with its invented criteria. Consider this: In 1880 there were seven categories of mental disturbance; in 1952, the first year the DSM was published, the number leaped to 112; in 1980 there were 224 mental disorders; and, by 1994 the number had climbed to 374.

Increased diagnostic capabilities? Hardly. This epidemic of mental disease is more likely to have its roots in the fact that once a new "illness" is listed in the DSM, insurance companies and governments are willing to pay for the "treatment" which today is usually a regimen of psychiatric drugs.

The chemical treatments which supposedly address psychiatry's multitude of mythical mental illnesses have spawned a worldwide, multibillion-dollar drug industry which has been growing steadily since the early 1960s. By the late 1970s, more than 82 million prescriptions for tranquilizers, 24 million prescriptions for sedatives/hypnotics and 16 million for antidepressants had been filled in the United States. Today one in every two adults in the United States has taken some form of psychotropic drug.

And today, psychiatrists are the pushers for the multibillion-dollar pharmaceutical industry.

Even the very young have become targets of this onslaught. More than four million children, whose only "problem" is that they are more active than their peers, are regularly being given powerful psychotropic drugs designed to dope them into submission. The natural energy and exuberance of childhood has been redefined as mental illness and millions are diagnosed as suffering from Attention Deficit Disorder (ADD).

Dr. Fred Baughman, a California pediatric neurologist for 35 years, bluntly summarized the situation in a letter to the *New York Times* on April 14, 1995: "The educational and medical establishments are engaged in a quid pro quo relationship to perpetuate illusions of diseases that reduce the schools' obligations to prepare children for adult life. Meanwhile, for-profit medicine and its business partners gain thousands of young patients.

"The invention of diseases satisfied medical-economic needs. Additional income for growing numbers of psychologists and psychiatrists is generated. . . . ADD was invented, in committee, at the American Psychiatric Association in 1980. . . . There is nothing a physician can see to confirm or refute it . . ."

Fraudulent diagnosis—which annually also involves millions of adults—is only one of the many psychiatric abuses CCHR has effectively exposed. While much has yet to be accomplished, the deadly social, financial and personal effects of this psychiatric creation of a "cash cow" will one day become a sordid chapter of the past.

Psychiatric Fraud

Greed is, of course, what motivates the fraudulent—a category of criminal that has been no stranger to the ranks of psychiatry. According to investigations by CCHR, the mental health system is riddled with them.

In 1992 a hearing before the US House of Representatives Select Committee on Children, Youth and Families heard numerous cases of such abuse provided to the committee by CCHR and others. These incidents ranged from adolescents and children subjected to psychiatric practices they never needed in the first place, to institutions that hired "bounty hunters" to kidnap patients they could hold against their will—all for the insurance money.

Insurance has, in fact, been a major area of psychiatric fraud, particularly among private, for-profit hospitals. CCHR's investigations which began in 1990 resulted in growing media exposure of fraud and patient abuse in these hospitals, and by 1991 the front pages of national newspapers were covering the stories of patients, mainly teenagers, being locked up against their will until their insurance benefits ran out. CCHR's persistent exposure of the abuses resulted in investigations not only by state lawmakers, but by insurance fraud investigators, state Attorneys General, the US Department of Justice, the FBI, the US Postal Inspection Service and other federal agencies. One US hospital chain had to pay nearly $1 billion in fines to the federal government and settlements to insurance companies. It subsequently left the psychiatric hospital business.

Other for-profit psychiatric hospital chains came under close scrutiny for their practices, such as paying "headhunter" fees for referrals of people for psychiatric treatment, whether needed or not. Nor is this only a US phenomenon. The Canadian government has also been subjected to the scam. Between 1987 and 1991, hundreds of psychiatric hospitals in the US billed the Ontario Health Insurance Plan (OHIP) for hundreds of millions of dollars for patients routinely sent there by "headhunters" who charged bounties to American psychiatric facilities for delivering patients. Thanks to the work of CCHR in Canada, the Ministry of Health filed suit against the psychiatric defrauders.

The widespread industry abuses discovered by CCHR and other investigators include sending patients back into the street as soon as insurance ran out after the thirty days most companies were willing to pay for inpatient care; paying social workers, school counselors, crisis hot-line workers and even ministers to refer patients; abusing children with violent therapy; diagnosing without sufficient detail; and multiple unnecessary treatments. Preying on the young and/or helpless is a common theme.

Fraud, however, wears as many faces as its participants can dream up schemes. In 1989 CCHR uncovered and exposed documents to show that two psychiatric facilities in Los Angeles that had been paid hundreds of thousands of dollars in government funding, did not even exist — except on paper.

Whether involving fraud, physical and mental abuse, unethical behavior or the destruction of our children with drugs, CCHR's tireless work against psychiatric wrongdoing has been lauded by law enforcement, politicians, human rights groups and those victims who had been unable to stand alone against these brutal practices.

Psychiatry too has recognized CCHR's work, although not necessarily with such admiration. In fact, with CCHR's revelations in South Africa, Australia, the United States, Germany, Canada, Italy, France, Switzerland and other countries, psychiatry had no choice but to realize that in Scientology it faced its worst enemy.

CCHR Publications

In more than twenty-five years of persistent and dedicated assault on the entrenched authority and abuses of psychiatry in the field of mental health, the major challenge confronting CCHR in its mission has not been psychiatry itself, but the lack of accurate information available to the public.

Consequently, in 1994, CCHR International embarked on its largest-ever public awareness campaign. Within three years, in addition to creating its own Web site on the Internet, it had researched, produced and released for international distribution two books and nine penetrating booklets which disclose the true story of psychiatry's influence upon our society. CCHR has since been inundated with positive responses from many countries and has expanded rapidly to meet the burgeoning needs of the world community for information by publishing even more of the booklets. The initial releases, which were published and distributed with help in the form of grants from the International Association of Scientologists, are described below.

Psychiatry:
The Ultimate Betrayal

This authoritative book uses psychiatry's own studies and opinions and utterances to show its destructive impact on society. Researched in fine detail, this comprehensive text provides readers with a profound understanding of how psychiatry's influence increased in spite of its lack of results, and how detrimental it has been for our homes, our schools, our courts and virtually every sector of our civilization.

Distributed to police chiefs, judges, attorneys, governors, ministers, educators, civil rights organizations, mayors, libraries, medical professionals and others, this popular work has significantly increased CCHR's role on the world stage of human rights leadership.

In the words of one grateful reader, a Chief of Police, "The book takes the reader inside the closed community of psychiatry, leaving it open to full inspection . . . This is not light reading. It will dismay, shock and anger all at once."

While many readers were indeed shocked and angered by the revelations, they turned the last page with a new understanding of psychiatry's negative influence on all our institutions and found themselves armed with the knowledge required to reverse the tide of irresponsibility that threatens our culture's survival.

Psychiatrists—the Men Behind Hitler

The culmination of more than twenty years of research by CCHR, this extensively documented book reveals the real scourge behind Hitler's Nazi regime—those responsible for both his indoctrination and inspiration—psychiatrists. It divulges what most historical texts have missed, that the plans for genocide were laid long before Hitler came to power. Psychiatry had planned the extermination of what it termed "life devoid of value" in the 1920s and, in fact, psychiatrists managed to engineer the murder of some 300,000 mental patients long before the war even began.

The book continues to meet critical acclaim. As one international religious leader said, "[It] is one of the most significant books and the most valuable reference tools in some of the very current issues posed by the continuation of the philosophy and physical patient abuses from this profession that constitutes a continuing threat to free men."

Booklets

By 1998, CCHR International had distributed more than 3.9 million copies worldwide of its now celebrated booklets exposing psychiatric human rights abuses committed in the guise of help—nine publications in numerous languages, distributed in sixteen countries.

Serving to both enlighten and warn the public, the booklets cover the ruinous effects of psychiatric intrusion into different areas of society. The nine publications listed here were the first of an ongoing series covering all facets of psychiatry's activities:

Creating Racism: Psychiatry's Betrayal
Destroying Lives:
    Psychiatry – Education's Ruin
Creating Crime:
    Psychiatry – Eradicating Justice
Denying Respect:
    Psychiatry – Victimizing the Elderly
Creating Chaos:
    Psychiatry – Destroying Morals
Betraying Women: Psychiatric Rape
Creating Evil:
    Psychiatry – Destroying Religion
Inflicting Pain:
    Psychiatry – Destroys Minds
Harming Artists:
    Psychiatry – Manipulating Creativity

While psychiatry claims humanitarian motives, its true harmful effects are exposed in a number of CCHR publications.

What started with a modest circulation of tens of thousands of the booklets rapidly expanded to millions in the early 1990s with translated editions in four major languages. As word spread at a grass-roots level, people from all over the world contacted CCHR in pursuit of additional copies— teachers, parents, lecturers, counselors, grandparents, lawyers, ministers, students, politicians and others.

That they were enlightened can be seen in the words of a school guidance counselor who said of the *Education's Ruin* booklet: "The sooner we get back to the proven methods of teaching and discard the nonsense, the better. There are so many truths in the booklet that it should be made compulsory reading for all politicians, lawmakers and educators. It will

take years to reverse the damage done, but we do have to start somewhere."

To women, to educators, to those laboring in the thankless arena of justice and to many others, the booklets explained what they had long suspected yet largely been unable to articulate, that the influence of psychiatry had contributed significantly to the collapse of mores and values that had long been the glue which held society together. Armed with the truth, they have been empowered to raise their voices and reverse the tide.

The Internet

As part of its commitment to better inform the broad public, CCHR released its massive international Web site in June 1996 — at **http://www.cchr.org**. The state-of-the-art site offers general information in five languages as well as complete copies of each of the booklets and abstracts from its books. Attracting thousands of visitors every week, the site has played a vital role in greatly expanding CCHR's help throughout the international community and speeding dissemination of the truth about psychiatric betrayal.

How to Start a CCHR

Forming a CCHR does not demand prior expertise or research. The primary prerequisite is a willingness and desire to do something to eliminate psychiatric abuse and restore human rights. Anyone wishing to start a CCHR chapter should merely contact their nearest CCHR office. (See Chapter 49 for a list of addresses.)

CCHR members have already compiled the successful actions needed to set up a local chapter, how to document abuses, what to look for when touring a psychiatric institution and numerous other helpful pointers. These are included in the information packets needed to start a CCHR chapter.

NATIONAL COMMISSION ON LAW ENFORCEMENT AND SOCIAL JUSTICE

In the words of L. Ron Hubbard, "Scientology exists to further and better the government of people and believes in the principles of democracy, the Magna Carta, the Constitution of the United States and also the Bill of Rights."

To promote and advance the cause of civil rights, the Church of Scientology in 1974 created the National Commission on Law Enforcement and Social Justice (NCLE), a nonprofit and tax-exempt organization. Although its original mandate was to focus on issues in the United States, it has since taken on international responsibilities as a civil rights watchdog.

The problem of false reports in government agency files has, for many years, been of primary concern to NCLE. It found that the basic rights and freedoms of citizens in any

country could be seriously jeopardized by uncorrected information in government files. And the potential for harm and abuse was compounded by the fact that agencies from many nations shared data bases.

Documents obtained by NCLE proved conclusively that false reports were being fed from law enforcement groups to government agencies in countries around the world. Numerous cases were documented by NCLE of individuals who had been jailed, harassed and even physically abused by police officials because of these reports in countries such as Germany, France and the United States. In some cases, corrupt officials were paid for personal information about private individuals.

In the United States, NCLE has contributed to several investigations by the US General Accounting Office, an arm of the US Congress, on such subjects as the security of sensitive law enforcement files maintained on computerized data bases.

Through the years, NCLE has worked with many individuals and grass-roots groups to broadly educate people on the importance of preserving and advancing individual rights and freedoms within the framework of constitutional government.

NCLE has also conducted extensive research into problems with justice systems internationally. Based on these findings, a task force was launched to educate and propose reforms to lighten court loads and expedite justice.

In the United States, NCLE investigated instances of constitutional violations by officials of the Food and Drug Administration (FDA) and found evidence that vested interests were using the agency for personal gain. It became evident that armed raids and arbitrary actions by certain FDA officials had violated constitutional protections and civil rights of many individuals in the health food industry. NCLE found that the FDA had approved drugs and other consumer items despite clear indications that they were harmful to adults and children, and took action accordingly to expose the abuses which had come to light.

In 1996, confronted with growing evidence that civil unrest has injustice at its core, and in the interest of making equal justice a reality for all minorities, NCLE initiated a grass-roots campaign for judicial reform. Carried forward by the commission's Judicial Reform Coalition in Los Angeles, and led by civil rights activists and attorneys, this campaign has brought together numerous religious, racial and ethnic minorities who have been denied equal treatment by the US judiciary. Their goal is the exposure of abuses and the attainment of lasting reforms.

Throughout the world, NCLE is alerting government and law enforcement officials to the dangers of civil rights abuses and the need to institute and maintain constitutional protections. And the reform measures enacted continue to spread, little by little, ensuring individual rights for all.

How to Start an NCLE Chapter

If you care about civil rights, privacy and freedom, you can start an NCLE chapter by contacting NCLE's main office in Los Angeles, California. (See Chapter 49 for address.)

Exposing Government Abuses

A key area of concern to the Church of Scientology has been the subject of government testing on unwitting human subjects, including experiments with harmful chemicals and other substances. Such investigations have exposed not only how the civil rights of test victims were violated, but how illegal activities by individuals in the responsible agencies were never prosecuted.

Scientologists have campaigned to discover and expose harmful tests with LSD and other substances carried out by government agencies. As a result of this campaign the United States Army announced a program to locate and notify those who had been unknowing participants in these covert

mind-control operations. A press wire at the time stated that the "Army's action followed a concerted campaign by the Church of Scientology, which located a number of veterans who underwent experiments with LSD and hallucinogenic drugs."

Church investigations of government chemical and biological warfare tests included the 1980 exposure of "Operation Big City," five consecutive days of covert biological warfare experiments conducted in 1956 by the CIA with the cooperation of US Army personnel.

In 1979, the Church released an analysis of CIA records which revealed that the agency had sponsored biological warfare tests in Florida in 1955. These tests were linked to an outbreak of whooping cough in that state which claimed the lives of twelve people, half of them children under the age of one. Also that year, *Freedom* magazine was first to break the story of how the CIA had spent more than $150,000 to continue biological warfare work in apparent defiance of a 1969 presidential order. The documents showed that the CIA continued to spend money through 1972 on a project intended for the development and testing of biological warfare "harassment systems" and for the "large-scale production of microorganisms," despite the 1969 order, which banned the production and stockpiling of biological weapons. Another *Freedom* article in 1984 revealed that the US Army had conducted secret biological warfare experiments on American citizens.

Church revelations have exposed the participation of government officials from various nations in drug smuggling, collusion between the US Food and Drug Administration and pharmaceutical companies, and other abuses.

More recently, *Freedom* investigated and exposed the real cause behind Gulf War illness, a malady which has afflicted veterans of Operation Desert Storm with a variety of long-lasting ailments ranging from constant searing headaches to fatigue, rashes, and joint and muscle pains. In the face of continued government insistence that Gulf War illness is only a "psychological problem," *Freedom* revealed that these maladies resulted from exposure to deadly chemical and biological warfare agents used during the Persian Gulf conflict. The US Defense Department finally admitted that some veterans had come into contact with such agents and a subsequent Presidential Commission found that the government had consistently misrepresented the facts.

Governments are entrusted to protect their peoples. When this trust is betrayed, the Church of Scientology feels it should be made known so that steps can be taken to prevent future abuses.

FREEDOM OF INFORMATION

In 1822 James Madison, fourth president of the United States and a primary creator of the democratic principles which form the American system of government, wrote a letter putting forward a basic proposition concerning democracy:

"A popular government, without popular information, or the means of acquiring it, is but a prologue to a farce or a tragedy; or, perhaps, both. Knowledge will forever govern ignorance; and a people who mean to be their own governors must arm themselves with the power which knowledge gives."

Passed into law in 1966 and greatly strengthened in 1974, the US Freedom of Information Act is a worthy effort by Congress to breathe life into Madison's words.

Under this act, a citizen can request access to any records of the executive branch of the federal government. The act provides that those records must be released to the requester unless they are shielded from disclosure by some provision of the Freedom of Information Act itself, or by some other federal law.

As Madison implied, a knowledgeable and informed citizenry is able to make intelligent decisions regarding its own future. And

the Freedom of Information Act is one of the most valuable tools allowing people to learn exactly what their government is doing—and if government agencies have files about them. When one considers that Martin Luther King, Jr., was the subject of tens of thousands of government documents peppered throughout FBI and IRS files, one can see why this is sometimes worth knowing. However, King had no access to a workable Freedom of Information Act at that time.

The concept of freedom of information has not been without opposition. More than a few government agencies have waged pitched court battles to preserve their secrecy.

To help counter these and other attempts to circumvent the law, the Church of Scientology submitted an open letter to Congress on July 4, 1981, signed by 146 organizations opposing an effort at that time to limit the effectiveness of the act.

Widely recognized among public interest groups as a leading expert on freedom of information legislation, the Church of Scientology has also earned a substantial reputation for its role in informing US citizens of their rights under the Freedom of Information Act. Nor have Scientologists limited their energies in these matters to the United States. When freedom of information legislation was passed in France (1978), Canada (1982), Australia (1982), New Zealand (1983), Italy (1991) and Belgium (1991), members of the Church played a decisive role to bring these laws about.

In 1991 Scientologists also assisted passage of a new law in France providing individuals greater access to the files of *Renseignements Généraux* (General Information), the French intelligence police, known as the "RG."

In 1992 an international conference on freedom of information, organized by a Scientologist, was held in Hungary with speakers from the United States, Canada, Sweden, Portugal, Scotland and Germany, and delegates from Czechoslovakia, Yugoslavia,

Romania, Albania, Bulgaria, the Ukraine, Latvia and Poland. This three-day international meeting, attended by 120 people and cosponsored by the Hungarian Ministry of the Interior and Ministry of Justice, under the auspices of the Council of Europe, brought a vital message on the subject for all those emerging from former political repression.

Broad public education concerning freedom of information is essential if people are to understand their rights. In the mid-1970s the Church of Scientology published the first of its informative booklets on freedom of information—a layman's guide for filing requests and overcoming arbitrary refusals to provide valid information.

A revised and updated edition has since been published. It has been distributed as a public service to more than 60,000 individuals and groups. Entitled *How to Use the Freedom of Information Act: Holding the Government Accountable for Its Actions*, the revised handbook received countless accolades by letter and in the media, and the Church still receives numerous requests for copies years after its publication.

This handbook printed and distributed by the Church to hundreds of thousands of citizens, has made individual rights known and has provided individuals with simple directions for using the Freedom of Information Act and informed them of their rights under this law.

Fighting for Freedom of Information

Ever willing to fight unwarranted government secrecy in the courts, the Church of Scientology's litigation with various US government agencies has established legal precedents further empowering the citizen with his right to monitor his government.

In May 1991, for example, a federal court in the United States credited the Church, in a case it brought against the Internal Revenue Service, for helping bring about significant reform. "Furthermore," the court stated, "communications between the IRS and the Church indicate that this litigation contributed to the IRS' decision to review its procedures and that resulting improvements in these procedures will enable better handling of over 1,000 cases involving identical legal issues."

In another precedent-setting case of broad value, the US Court of Appeals for the District of Columbia ruled that the National Security Agency could not simply assert that it was unable to locate records in response to a Church FOIA request. The court ordered the agency to conduct new searches, stating, in part, "If the agency can lightly avoid its responsibilities by laxity in identification or retrieval of desired materials, the majestic goals of the act will soon pass beyond reach."

In yet another case, a federal judge in Los Angeles granted *Freedom* magazine's motion to require the IRS to produce a detailed and specific index of records being withheld by the agency, rather than merely listing them out by general category.

And with each success through and for the Freedom of Information Act comes not just another victory for Scientology, but a victory for all those who might one day suffer from government secrecy.

It was in acknowledgment of such unprecedented efforts that noted author and expert on US intelligence matters, Victor Marchetti, declared:

"I would like to commend the Church of Scientology for its faith in itself and its determination to work within the constitutional democratic system of our nation. It has fought the good fight against great odds openly and legally . . . and it has survived . . . which is more of a tribute to its membership than it is to our own government. By its tenacity and determination, the Church of Scientology has forced that government to adhere to the Constitution . . . something that will benefit all Americans in the long run."

Protecting Freedom of Information in the Electronic Age

With the advent of modern computer networks, "freedom of information" has taken on new meaning. Today's worldwide information superhighway, the Internet, offers a wealth of readily accessible knowledge.

As do all historic champions of free expression, the Church of Scientology applauds and embraces the Internet as a promising new frontier, where knowledge can conquer prejudice, truth can overcome fear, and the free exchange of public debate can liberate mankind from lies and oppression. L. Ron Hubbard succinctly captured the essence of the Internet's potential when he wrote that "Ideas and not battles mark the forward progress of mankind."

But as is true of any new frontier, the acts of a lawless few can jeopardize the promise of progress and compromise the rights and freedoms of the responsible, law-abiding majority. Thus the news media — print, broadcast and electronic — all report the sad and shocking truth on a daily basis: the Internet can be abused as easily as it can be employed for good. Finding "free speech" a convenient cloak to disguise their aberrational

conduct, denizens of the darker corners of cyberspace espouse perversion, exploit children through molestation and pornography, commit fraud and other forms of commercial crime, invade zones of personal privacy, and infringe the intellectual property rights of artists, musicians and thinkers. In the corrupt corridors of cyberspace, unscrupulous people literally threaten the rights and the well-being of people everywhere.

As always, the Church of Scientology has stepped into the breach in the defense of the free exchange of ideas and in the name of respect for the rights of everyone. While legislatures debate ultimately arbitrary or even destructive means of regulation, the Church of Scientology has emerged in the forefront of efforts to guarantee free speech on the Internet through protecting intellectual property rights. Just as the US Constitution guarantees freedom of speech, it also states that "The Congress shall have power to promote the progress of science and useful arts, by securing for limited times to authors and inventors the exclusive right to their respective writings and discoveries . . ." Those parallel rights have coexisted for more than two hundred years, and the advent of the Internet can neither diminish nor revoke either of them.

The Church has emerged as an experienced, recognized voice in the debate surrounding the survival of both free speech and intellectual property rights in cyberspace. For example, as a result of a watershed case involving the potential liability of Internet access providers — who provide the facilities that enable all participants to access the Internet, whether for socially beneficial or ultimately destructive purposes — the Church pioneered a protocol to enable access providers to respond quickly to Internet abuses without interfering with the privacy or free speech interests of the vast and lawful majority of Internet users. Likewise, in court decisions both in the United States and abroad, procedures were developed by the

Church to reveal the identities of individuals responsible for transmitting unlawful material such as child pornography and counterfeit copies of intellectual property, without unnecessarily intruding into the privacy of others. The Church's experiences and accomplishments in this regard have been guideposts for legislators here and abroad who are attempting to fashion laws and regulations affecting the Internet.

Through *Freedom* magazine, the Church has investigated and exposed a number of now-notorious Internet outlaws who threatened those freedoms by their lawlessness in the on-line world. The Church has also pioneered innovative protocols with Internet access providers that facilitate the free exchange of ideas, information and public debate on the Internet while securing the intellectual property rights guaranteed by law to the creators of works of public interest. When reason and the law have gone unheeded, the Church has taken legal action to protect Scientology intellectual properties from unauthorized copying and distribution resulting in landmark legal precedents which secure and preserve the freedoms and legal rights of all who travel the information superhighway.

The result of the Church's dedication has been to the benefit of both freedom and the Internet itself. As leading Internet columnist and attorney Jonathan Rosenoer noted, "the Internet will never expand if people don't have the ability to protect their creative works under a strong copyright framework. The Church of Scientology's cases are helping to develop it."

Church members also work alongside top cyberspace experts such as "father of the Internet" Vinton Cerf and pioneers on legal aspects of information access to find new ways to protect the Internet from abuse. Observing that technology generally possesses—or can create—the solutions to the problems of cyberspace, the Church supported initiatives which ultimately led to software which enables users to "screen" or block undesired content, without the need for government intervention or censorship.

Solving problems of speech should not—indeed, must not—involve abridgment of freedom of speech. Thus the efforts of Church members contribute significantly to the strength of the Internet and help to keep it free of burdensome regulation, while protecting the rights of those creative individuals who generate new ideas and works of art and scholarship.

RELIGIOUS FREEDOM

According to the Creed of the Church of Scientology, Scientologists believe that all men have inalienable rights to their own religious practices and their performance, and that no agency less than God has the power to suspend or set aside these rights.

However, like all of man's treasured freedoms, freedom of religion is maintained only through vigilance and refusal to succumb to those who seek to enslave and suppress.

Over the years, the Church of Scientology has been a leader in championing the cause of religious freedom for all. It strongly believes that as the United States was founded on this principle, separation of church and state forms an essential base for all other freedoms. And that continuous attempts by government to encroach upon this right must be strenuously fought, for this is the sign of an oppressive government.

During the 1970s one of the methods used by vested interests to undermine religious freedom in the United States was a broad-scale propaganda and lobbying campaign directed at both state and federal legislatures. Efforts were made to introduce bills which would have legalized the activities of antireligious hate groups, restricted the legitimate dissemination activities of churches and given state agencies the green light to take control of day-to-day church operations.

Through the dedicated work of Scientologists and friends in other religious groups,

Strong advocates for religious freedom, Scientologists here march through a European city.

antireligious legislation of this type met defeat in Alabama, California, Connecticut, Delaware, Florida, Illinois, Kansas, Massachusetts, Michigan, Minnesota, New Jersey, New York, Nevada, North Carolina, Ohio, Oregon, Pennsylvania and Texas.

Milestone Victories

A landmark California case, which began in 1979 as an attempt to subjugate religion under a psychiatric yoke, ended with passage of a law that protects churches from punitive damages claims by antireligious interests.

The case, involving a frivolous lawsuit filed against a Christian church over the suicide of a parishioner, progressed through a series of rulings and appeals in California state courts over a period of ten years. The Church of Scientology worked with more than 1,500 religious organizations in opposing the suit and making its ramifications known to other religions and the public.

In the eventual 1989 decision, the US Supreme Court endorsed a California Supreme Court decision which held that the state's laws forbid the filing of such cases against churches. The right to free practice of religion was upheld, and this attempt to position psychiatrists as overseers of religion was dismissed.

In another milestone victory, the Church of Scientology mustered interfaith support for a bill prohibiting claims for punitive or exemplary damages against religions, with strictly defined exceptions.

Many religious groups joined the Church in support of the bill, including the California Catholic Conference, the California Council of Churches, the Church of Jesus Christ of Latter-day Saints and the National Congress for Religious Liberty.

Two years of concerted efforts culminated on September 26, 1988, when California Senate Bill No. 1 was signed into law by the California governor.

Establishing an Important Precedent

Churches have traditionally been guardians of freedom, protecting citizens against government attempts to dilute or eradicate their rights, and therefore they have often come under attack. To help protect churches from unwarranted government intrusion the 1984 Church Audits Procedures Act was passed by Congress "to give churches a special audit procedure to require the IRS to take greater care in the examination of churches."

This law is a step intended to help close the door on IRS intimidation and attempts to silence religions and subvert their role in society.

The Church of Scientology blocked efforts by the Internal Revenue Service (IRS) to undermine this act, and in the course of doing so has preserved the rights of all religions in the United States.

The Church of Scientology has long been a vocal critic of government abuses, and some IRS officials saw the law as an obstacle to their habitual circumvention of constitutional safeguards. The IRS commissioner from 1981 to 1986 called the law's regulations "little more than a series of mechanistic tests and hoops for the Service to jump through."

The Church of Scientology established the first major court precedent strengthening the Church Audit Procedures Act in 1990 when the US District Court in Boston ruled against the IRS' request to rummage through 200,000 pages of church documents.

This Church of Scientology case was observed widely by many religious leaders as the first major test of the law—with an outcome that would be significant for all churches in the United States.

After the Church's courtroom triumph, the *Legal Times* reported, "Other church groups are hailing the decision as a victory for religious freedom, and warn that the IRS had better think twice before sticking its nose in religious organizations' business again."

The Church of Scientology has been at the forefront of efforts to preserve religious freedom and human rights.

Establishing Religious Freedom Week

With the groundswell of public support for religious freedom generated by Church of Scientology initiatives, leaders of other mainstream religions joined in petitioning the US Congress to enact an annual national Religious Freedom Week.

The original Religious Freedom Week resolution was enacted by the president of the United States on September 20, 1988, and has now become an annual national tradition.

The Religious Freedom Week celebrations, in which churches of nearly every faith participate, have brought about a renewed awareness throughout the country of the importance of defending the right for all citizens to practice their faith according to their own conscience.

In 1995, the same coalition which made Religious Freedom Week a reality tackled a new yet related issue: resolving the contentious debate over the role of religion in public schools. The Church's interest was more than incidental. The suppression of religion in all aspects of society, including education, has clearly contributed to a catastrophic decline in morality; yet it was equally important to keep schoolchildren from having religious views imposed upon them in an educational context.

The coalition found the answers within the fabric of the Constitution itself and seminal Supreme Court cases. Expanding their ranks to include more than three dozen religious and civil liberties organizations, the coalition prepared "Religion in The Public Schools: A Joint Statement of Current Law," which clearly and concisely set forth the true state of US law pertaining to religion and religious expression in public schools—and, for many, led to amicable resolution of the issue. President Bill Clinton praised the joint statement as "wise and thoughtful."

Preserving Religious Freedom

Throughout Europe, Religious Freedom Crusades organized by the Church of Scientology have been conducted in response to threats from antireligious influences.

In France, 2,500 Scientologists assembled in Strasbourg to proclaim a "Declaration of Religious Freedom" which was subsequently accepted by the Council of Europe.

In Denmark, the Danish Interfaith Forum, with the Church of Scientology among its active members, has become a notable voice for religious freedom throughout that country.

In Brussels, Belgium, the Church of Scientology united with a number of other religions, academics and human rights advocates to establish the "Council for Human Rights and Religious Freedom." Its multidenominational members from countries throughout Europe represent their respective churches and organizations on important religious freedom and human rights issues.

In its battles against attempts to violate or negate religious freedom, the Church of Scientology and its members have maintained a firm stance that religious freedom must be preserved for all faiths.

Nowhere has this been more true than in today's Germany, where synagogues are destroyed by fire, Muslims are attacked in the streets and other religious minorities are savaged in the press through hate campaigns supported by the government itself. Here, churches of Scientology and individual Scientologists have also had to battle severe discrimination.

As the German government has denied these ongoing human rights abuses, Scientologists have made the truth about the religious discrimination in Germany broadly known through international public information campaigns in major world newspapers.

Scientologists have also brought the matter of discrimination in Germany to the attention of international bodies and the results have been far-reaching for churches and groups that are the targets of such discrimination. In annual reports of the Special Rapporteur of the United Nations Commission on Human Rights, he has warned the international community about those countries in which individual freedoms were most severely threatened. Following his eleven-day visit to Germany, with senior officials at federal and state levels, leaders and members of minority religions, the Rapporteur issued his findings in March 1998, which exposed a wide range of religious minorities which were being subjected to intolerance, suspicion and discrimination.

The Rapporteur's reports expanded upon a series of five successive US State Department human rights reports. These State Department reports, which strongly criticized government-instigated discrimination against religious and ethnic groups, also warned of growing antisemitism in Germany.

Other international human rights bodies have issued similar reports. These organizations include Amnesty International, the Organization on Security and Cooperation in Europe (the "Helsinki Commission"), a British ad hoc human rights committee of lords and scholars and the Human Rights Centre of Essex University in England—in all, seventeen separate reports critical of Germany's treatment of religious and racial minorities.

International protests have been held in Germany to decry these human rights abuses. In October 1997, more than 10,000 Scientologists and members of other religious denominations held a massive march in Berlin in support of religious freedom for people of all faiths. Gathering at the Brandenburg Gate, the marchers called world attention to human rights violations by the German government and demanded religious freedom in Germany.

While individuals in the German government continue to wage war on religious minorities, German courts have stood fast, upholding the constitutional guarantee to freedom of religion.

In a one-year period between August 1995 and August 1996, the Church of Scientology and individual Scientologists prevailed in 107 cases involving the right to practice one's religion.

When the German judiciary upholds the constitutional rights of one religion, of course, they uphold the constitutional rights of every other religion. Such rulings have thus significantly contributed to freedom of religion for all faiths in Germany.

Carrying forward its commitment to religious freedom, the Church of Scientology has contributed towards bringing about peace in the war-torn former nation of Yugoslavia. Scientologists with the Citizens Commission on Human Rights investigated and broadly exposed the fact that leading psychiatrists had stirred up religious and ethnic hatreds in the area and fomented the "ethnic cleansing" which had victimized religious minorities and bathed the Balkans in blood. They also publicized that these psychiatrists who orchestrated the violence were operating off an agenda similar to the "racial hygiene" of Nazi psychiatrists during World War II. One of the psychiatrists exposed was Serb leader Radovan Karadzic who was subsequently indicted for crimes against humanity by the International Criminal Tribunal in The Hague. CCHR provided the Tribunal with extensive documentation to support the charges against Karadzic.

The Church has also been effective in exposing the criminal activities of antireligious hate groups such as the Cult Awareness Network (CAN) in the United States and similar movements in Europe. It exposed not only CAN's brutal tactics during its "deprograming" activities but its coercive recruiting and referral techniques and its financial motivations. CAN had been involved in violent "deprogramings" of members of many religions, including Roman Catholics, Episcopalians, Baptists, Buddhists and others.

In 1996, CAN declared bankruptcy and went into liquidation after losing a multimillion-dollar lawsuit to a man affiliated with a Christian religion who had been assaulted by a CAN deprogramer. In 1997, CAN was revived by a new, multifaith board of directors, headed by a Baptist minister and Bible college professor. Restored to its original stated purpose—"To educate the public on religious rights, freedoms and responsibilities"—CAN now works with religious groups of all faiths to foster understanding and tolerance.

The work of Scientologists on behalf of religious freedom is nondenominational; it is carried out with the view that liberty of religious belief and practice is the cornerstone of freedom itself, and that when one religion is infringed upon, the rights of all men are endangered.

Ongoing Crusade Against Injustice

These are just some of the highlights of the Church of Scientology's ongoing work to eradicate injustice, abuse of the weak and betrayals of public trust. It is no easy task; social reform requires constant vigilance and a willingness to confront those ugly facts most would like to ignore.

A just and enlightened civilization does not tolerate brutalities toward the helpless among its citizens. Nor does a true civilization allow monolithic governments to subvert the rights of its most honest and productive people. It is often said that power corrupts. And so it has been in many civilizations that have come and gone in ages past. When citizens feel they can no longer do something about injustice, they have taken a giant step toward abdicating their rights to freedom.

Scientologists have the courage and determination to do something about it. They have, indeed, drawn the line, not just for themselves, but for all men of goodwill. While some of the dreadful things that happen in this world may seem far distant from the life you live, you should know this: that what Scientologists are doing, they are doing for you. And in doing so, they are bringing all mankind closer to a higher and better civilization.

For more information about topics in this chapter, visit the following sites on the Internet:

http://www.freedommag.org, and
http://www.cchr.org.

Scientologists care enough to speak out against the injustice, brutality and abuse found in our society.

PART NINE

WORLD INSTITUTE OF SCIENTOLOGY ENTERPRISES (WISE)

If Scientologists are to survive this world, L. Ron Hubbard explained, they must see to the survival of all men. They must dedicate themselves to the eradication of injustice, constantly work to raise levels of ethics and restore sanity in all sectors of society.

Although members of the World Institute of Scientology Enterprises ("WISE") represent a diverse group — from presidents of advertising companies to owners of auto repair shops — each has discovered a vital fact: the principles and techniques of organizational administration that L. Ron Hubbard developed for churches of Scientology could be adopted to run their own organizations — whether a Boy Scout troop, governmental agency or industrial giant — with phenomenal results. And because this philosophy and technology of administration reflects Mr. Hubbard's strict standards of ethical conduct, they found out that, along with unparalleled successes, their workplaces had become havens of stability, sanity and ethics.

WISE plays a pivotal role in bringing this about. Originally formed as a fellowship of Scientologist businessmen and women, WISE now also is the entity responsible for making Mr. Hubbard's administrative technology available to the business community. By functioning as an autonomous corporation separate and apart from churches of Scientology, WISE insulates them from activities that do not belong in a church and would distract staff from their real purpose — the ministry of Scientology.

WISE accomplishes its goal through a variety of activities. It authorizes use of symbols and copyrighted works relating to Mr. Hubbard's administrative technology by individuals who want to use them in teaching business administration to others or in consulting with other businesses. It helps its members resolve business disputes they may be involved in by providing them the mechanism for applying the principles and techniques of Scientology's system of ethics and justice. And WISE stands ready at any time to answer questions businessmen and women may have as to the many ways in which they can benefit from Mr. Hubbard's discoveries.

CHAPTER 30

WISE: ENABLING GROUPS TO FLOURISH AND PROSPER

Until Dianetics and Scientology, no one knew the principles of a successful group any more than they knew the principles of the human mind.

Recognizing that what all too often passes for life in the modern workplace is endless drudgery, inefficiency, insecurity and bureaucratic entanglements, individuals began to utilize the same administrative principles L. Ron Hubbard developed for use in Scientology churches to improve their own businesses, organizations, groups and even their personal lives.

Their reasoning was simple: As Mr. Hubbard's administrative policies are based on natural laws of life and living, they certainly could be applied to bring sanity, stability and expansion to any organization outside of the Church. Why, for example, must any individual suffer sleepless nights worrying about the future of their business or favorite club or other organization when Mr. Hubbard has so plainly outlined practical means of survival in *any* group endeavor?

Why, too, must anyone — employee, executive or volunteer — suffer from continual infighting, backbiting and day-to-day duress when Mr. Hubbard so precisely lays out rules for group harmony? Moreover, many had long been utilizing principles from such Scientology books as *The Problems of Work* to help resolve problems in group and work situations. Some even compiled their own manuals using some of Mr. Hubbard's material for use in training their employees, while others used what they knew to assist colleagues.

MAKING THE TECHNOLOGY AVAILABLE

WISE was formed in 1979 as a religious fellowship organization of businesspersons and professionals in numerous fields who share a common certainty of the value of Mr. Hubbard's administrative technology.

Their tools, available in many bookstores and public libraries, are the twelve encyclopedia-sized volumes comprising the *Organization Executive Course* (OEC) and *Management Series* volumes. This body of work addresses the subject of life in a group with the same thoroughness and attention to fundamental truths as Mr. Hubbard's writings on Scientology address the life of an individual. Thus, just as Dianetics and Scientology opened the way to an understanding of the mind and the spirit, the volumes of the OEC lead to an understanding of just what comprises a successful group. Be it a local civic group or the largest government agency, with the principles contained in the OEC, one can turn any group into a productive, smooth-running and expanding concern.

These volumes contain practical knowledge in all areas of organizational administration, structure and management. With their principles, one can solve problems ranging from the hiring of a secretary to the implementation of multinational corporate plans. Similarly, by employing the principles contained in the organizing board (see Chapter 20) Mr. Hubbard developed, one can remarkably streamline all aspects of operation and make it productive. The fundamentals of the

The offices of WISE International, located in Los Angeles.

organizing board apply equally well to a business of either ten or ten thousand; in fact, with the application of the data in even a single volume, any group or personal activity can be immediately bettered.

Simply put, this technology encompasses the basic laws needed to succeed in any endeavor in any zone of application. No wonder then that individuals regularly use this technology not only in their careers but also their personal lives. With such knowledge so readily available, it was only natural that businessmen and professionals would begin implementing these discoveries to better relationships within their fields of practice and with their friends and families. Today, this technology is utilized with excellent results by tens of thousands of individuals, groups and organizations. Its use results in increased survival and well-being, allowing any group to flourish and prosper.

THE BENEFITS OF MEMBERSHIP

WISE members share a keen interest in L. Ron Hubbard's administrative technology, and through WISE they are able to reach others who share that interest and discuss projects and matters of mutual concern. WISE holds regular conventions and seminars during which members can get together and learn new methods of applying in their own businesses or professions the principles and techniques of organizational administration that Mr. Hubbard discovered. WISE also distributes newsletters and other publications to its members to keep them informed about current news and upcoming events involving subjects as diverse as management by conditions, personnel and ethics in business.

But WISE provides its members with other benefits as well, including several that have had a beneficial impact on the business community in general. For example, while many WISE members employ the administrative principles solely within their own business or profession, some study Mr. Hubbard's administrative breakthroughs and want to show others how they too can benefit from this technology. To do so, they must be licensed by WISE so they can use Mr. Hubbard's name and the other words and symbols associated with his administrative technology.

WISE's licensing function is critically important for ensuring the integrity of these trade and service marks. By licensing only qualified individuals and organizations, WISE helps safeguard against offbeat activities or the publication of altered versions held out to be Mr. Hubbard's true technology. Because of WISE's oversight, the business community can be more assured of both the competence and high ethical standing of anyone offering business services under these marks. They know, for example, that any WISE-licensed consultant has completed a course of study in administrative technology and is skilled in helping others apply it.

WISE itself does no consulting. But individual WISE members who are professional consultants can produce spectacular results when called to help. They have rightly earned a reputation for their ability to resolve situations that others, lacking their know-how, have been unable to crack. For the technology they have at their fingertips can correct even the most difficult organizational problems.

Another benefit WISE provides its members arises through its issue authority function. This authorizes educators, consultants, businesses and other organizations to publish (or "issue") training material containing Mr. Hubbard's copyrighted works. Many WISE members want to publish passages from Mr. Hubbard's writings and recorded lectures on organizational administration in materials

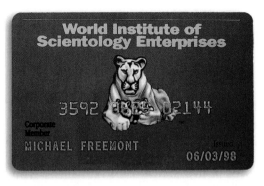

A membership card for WISE International.

they use in training their own personnel or personnel of other companies, or in providing business management consulting services. These members will incorporate Mr. Hubbard's quotations in textbooks and other materials that they specially adapt to businesses or specific industries. WISE serves as the central authority which permits such use and — of equal importance — ensures that the material as published is consistent with Mr. Hubbard's writings.

THE WISE CHARTER COMMITTEE

WISE helps its members maintain high ethical standards by sponsoring local Charter Committees, composed of the most ethical WISE members, known as Charter members. These committees help create a more ethical business environment by applying Mr. Hubbard's ethics technology.

Charter Committees are responsible for assisting WISE members in their communities to resolve business disputes that may have arisen between them and other WISE members, or even businesses that are not members of WISE. By applying Mr. Hubbard's ethics technology to mediate and resolve these disputes, Charter Committees rapidly and fairly dispose of conflicts that otherwise would languish for years — at great cost — in the "normal" legal system. And unlike the parties in a "normal" legal proceeding, *both* sides in a Charter Committee dispute-resolution proceeding are satisfied with the outcome of their case.

As one WISE member reported: "The thought of a mediation used to cause me to sweat cold bullets . . . Then I got a dispute handling from WISE. The results were amazing. And yes, I felt much better afterwards. But the real bonus was the end result—fairness. Both parties had to confront their own responsibility in the matter and the ethics of the situation was taken into account, not just the technicalities of some obscure law."

The owners of two large European companies engaged for nearly a decade in a corporate dispute, then met with a WISE Charter Committee mediator, specialist-trained in the application of the ethics technology. He brought the two parties, step by step, to a level of agreement and communication from which they could, with finality, work out their own resolution.

One of the former disputants reported, "To anyone who may be convinced that he has the most flagrant dispute ever—and that it cannot be solved—believe me, there *is* a way out. And the way out is: standard application of Mr. Hubbard's technology through standard WISE mediation."

The other told of his experience: "Over the past couple of days, I have been involved in the resolution of a nine-year-old conflict that has caused tremendous upset. This is now fully handled and, by the use of L. Ron Hubbard administrative and ethics policy, I have gained a better understanding of how a conflict can occur, and how I—being responsible no matter what—can end it."

THE HUBBARD COLLEGE OF ADMINISTRATION

Because so many public and private sector administrators now use Mr. Hubbard's technology, WISE has established the Hubbard College of Administration, a degree-granting institution with a two-year curriculum, to provide the public with the knowledge and techniques they need to tackle every possible challenge that can be encountered in administering and running any group, company or organization.

Whether one is learning specific tools to apply to his or her own organization or studying to become a consultant to help others, the Hubbard College provides the highest caliber of training in L. Ron Hubbard's administrative technology.

The curriculum at the Hubbard College is arranged so that even the novice can rapidly grasp the basics and move on to more advanced training within a very short period of time. Hubbard College courses may be taken on either a full-time or part-time basis.

Every new student at the Hubbard College initially spends time with an adviser to clarify the purpose of his or her study. Then an individualized program is developed with the focus on taking courses that present the administrative technology that will be most helpful to him. Graduates routinely experience increased production, reduced stress, streamlined organization, bettered management/staff relations and heightened ethical levels amongst employees.

For example, one of the most popular courses at the Hubbard College, the Elementary Data Series Evaluator Course, provides a comprehensive approach to undesirable group situations and teaches the student to apply Mr. Hubbard's discoveries in the field of logic to resolve these. Through this course, the business professional or consultant can expertly see beyond the "apparent" reasons for a problem and zero in on the true underlying source of the decline or difficulty.

Hubbard Colleges of Administration worldwide offer the highest caliber training in the management technology of L. Ron Hubbard.

The Hubbard College also offers specialist courses covering such subjects as:

- use of the organizing board in groups
- use of the organizing board to analyze one's life
- sales and marketing
- executive essentials and leadership
- management by statistics
- conditions of existence and formulas for their improvement
- financial management
- public relations
- the use of surveys
- how to increase personnel and company efficiency
- effective communication skills
- how to put planning into implementation
- hiring and the use of personnel testing
- developing effective company policy
- the application of ethics to business
- debug technology
- troubleshooting
- computers

On the Net

More information about the Hubbard College of Administration—including case studies of companies, photographs and maps of College locations, and an on-line study materials catalog—is available on the Internet at **http://www.hubbardcollege.org**.

Through courses in L. Ron Hubbard's administrative technology, one can learn the organizational know-how to completely reverse any downtrend in life and successfully manage <u>any</u> group endeavor.

DELIVERING LIFE-CHANGING RESULTS

Some 40,000 of these specialist courses had been given by the late 1990s. And successes reached far beyond business and professional applications. Many of the College's course graduates report that, as a result of the organizational know-how they have gained, other areas of their life improve as well—they have a more positive overall outlook, salvaged marriages, happier family life, and have achieved many of the personal goals they have been striving for.

As stated by one executive, "I can honestly say that L. Ron Hubbard's organizational material has made a profound difference in the employees and my company—not only adding great value to our business, but also to our personal lives."

Worldwide availability of this extraordinary technology became a reality in the 1990s when the Hubbard College expanded behind the former iron curtain. As reported by one recent graduate, the general director of a Fortune 500 company's subsidiary in Russia:

"I would like to express my respect and compliments, and say it is an honor to write this in appreciation of your personal efforts, and those of your colleagues of Hubbard College of Administration, who shared their knowledge and experience so generously with us. Your supervisors led us by the example of their professionalism to new heights of experience in business ... The introduction of the elements of Hubbard technology yielded positive results, no question about it."

WHY IS WISE IMPORTANT?

For all the talk of fortunes made on Wall Street, of how we are better off now than four years ago and other such statements which paint a generally rosy economic picture, the realities faced by millions give less cause for optimism. The grim realities include (depending upon where you live) inflation, recession, lowered productivity, imbalance of trade, bankruptcy, national debts, strikes, unemployment, poverty and want. And these well-known symptoms of economic instability are actually indicators of a much deeper problem: a crippling lack of administrative know-how. If today's businesses and governments could grasp and competently apply the basic principles of organization and administration, they would enact workable solutions to end social and economic chaos rather than perpetuate it. Increased survival on the third and fourth dynamics would inevitably result.

Instilling the workable technology of administration into a society which is suffering from a severe lack of workable management tools is a mammoth task. And viewed against the background of boom-and-bust economics and unstable societal and governmental structures, the urgency of the situation is even more apparent.

WISE offers the hope of improvement. Its members bring sanity and order into the business community. In fact, every WISE member is a point of stability that reduces confusion in this uncertain world. Businesses can prosper, governments can rule wisely and populations can live without economic duress. With L. Ron Hubbard's administrative technology, the goals that have evaded society for so long are within reach.

WISE on the Internet

For more information about WISE and the administrative technology of L. Ron Hubbard, visit the WISE Web site at http://www.wise.org.

Features include:

■ tools for the workplace that can help anyone on any job
■ the benefits of WISE membership
■ essays and articles on administration by Mr. Hubbard and successful applications of his technology in the business world

THE WORKABILITY OF L. RON HUBBARD'S ADMINISTRATIVE TECHNOLOGY

Robert Goldscheider, a management consultant for thirty-three years, has been special counsel to multinational corporations, the UN Industrial Development Organization and the World Intellectual Property Organization. He observed the application of Mr. Hubbard's administrative technology in the business world.

"Having had a firsthand opportunity to delve rather deeply into the administrative writings of L. Ron Hubbard, I am impressed. The technology is infused with common sense and practicality.

"Particular aspects, proven to be successful at all levels of the corporations I visited and analyzed, include:

"AVAILABILITY—The entire body of his administrative technology is carefully recorded in bound volumes, indexed and cross-referenced by title, subject and date. This affords a stability at all levels where corporate executive and staff alike can become acquainted with policy and cooperate as a group.

"THE ORG BOARD—The organizing board pattern is an innovative discovery which can be adapted to accommodate a large multipurpose corporation or customized to the needs, purposes and strategies of a particular organization.

"MANAGEMENT BY STATISTICS—A carefully organized reporting system, broken down to quantify and qualify virtually every aspect of operations relevant for sensitive management control. The ability to react very promptly to developments is one of the attributes of LRH administrative technologies, and is perhaps the key reason they have been successfully applied so consistently.

"INDIVIDUALITY—The techniques and systems developed to choose the correct personnel for a job, and how to train and stabilize them to perform their functions, has never before been so well described or completely delineated.

"In my opinion, the management technologies of L. Ron Hubbard superbly take into account long-run policies and daily needs of modern business and administrative operations. If the MBA products of our most eminent business schools had measured up to these standards in the past decade, I doubt that the American and world economics would be in their current disarray.

"I know of no other body of administrative laws and methods which is as complete, as workable and as broadly applicable as Mr. Hubbard's. His philosophy of organizational know-how and his lucid explanations for its application deserve wide use in industry, commercial enterprises and government."

Robert Goldscheider, Chairman
The International Licensing Network, Ltd.,
Technology Management Consultants

SUCCESSFUL APPLICATION

Tens of thousands of WISE members—from every strata of organization—not only benefit from the solutions found in L. Ron Hubbard's administrative technology, but affect the productivity of countless more around them. Here are some of the testimonials received daily by WISE offices throughout the world.

My practice had a lot of disorder and inefficiencies before you came in. Thanks to the Hubbard data and your help, I am now achieving the success I have worked so hard for.

Seven weeks ago I was unsure as to whether or not I would continue practicing chiropractic. I had lost my sense of purpose and felt overwhelmed with confusion and sadness at the condition of the world, where I found myself, and in life. Not a pretty picture. As a last resort I attended [a WISE] introductory seminar.

On December 30, I took myself to the introductory seminar. On December 31st I decided to sign up for a complete management package. I immediately noticed a dramatic change in one of my chiropractic assistants, and for myself the decision to begin the management program signified a clear commitment to my belief in myself. All was not lost after all.

Now only seven weeks later, my original failing practice has almost doubled and . . . I know my purpose and willingly accept the responsibility that goes along with it. I am filled with energy and find true happiness in my work. I feel like this is my first year in practice instead of my seventh.

Chiropractor

I have operated a company for the last twenty years which is a large complex of property and businesses in southern California. The major business is a 500-seat restaurant which has been operating for twenty-five years. In addition, there are 47 apartment units, a 40-room hotel and a private club on the property.

Although the restaurant has always done well, the efficiency with which it was operated resulted in slow growth and little profit. I, with my staff of 120 managers and employees, began working with and using the organizational technology of L. Ron Hubbard and this has done more in the last eleven months than the twenty years before to make the restaurant an efficient, effective and profitable organization. In my opinion, no other investment could have come close to that performance. Sales for the eleven months I have worked with LRH technology were up 14 percent. Profits for the same period are up 67 percent and the effect of many of the efficiency measures are just beginning to be felt. In fact in the last month, the sales were up 19.8 percent . . .

Most significant, formerly stagnating, uninspired managers are now excited, motivated and effective beyond what I ever thought them capable. This has indeed been a miracle.

Vice President of
Operations,
Restaurant/
Business Complex

I have enjoyed incredible successes since beginning the executive director apprenticeship [at the Hubbard College of

Administration]. A few simple personnel changes, bright ideas and basics put in have acted in a very earthshaking way to put my companies into affluence and get them under controlled expansion.

I have implemented policies on statistics and not even "almost immediately" but IMMEDIATELY, our income and other statistics doubled.

I know that when I get a key basic point in, it WILL cause immediate expansion. I have seen this direct cause-and-effect relationship so often while doing this apprenticeship that I know with certainty it is not just "chance," "an amazing coincidence," or "luck." It is the POWER of Hubbard Management Technology in ACTION—ACTION being the key word.

Owner,
Property Title Transfer Service

My two businesses were losing money for five straight months. Our financial situation was grim and I knew that if we didn't turn the situation around soon, we would lose our restaurants.

I started studying L. Ron Hubbard's administrative and managerial technology. There wasn't a whole lot I could do to turn things around. I was depending on other people, and they were failing me.

I'll let the results speak for themselves: For the first five months of the year we lost a lot of money. In the following three months (after studying LRH administrative tools) our sales volume increased by a total of 15.7 percent and our total net profit, year to date, was considerable. (More than the last three years' profits combined.) Not only did we make up the loss, but exceeded it and became profitable right away (we even made this profit after we took out money for extensive renovations)!

Owner,
Franchised Restaurant Chain

My business was at an all-time low, not to mention my life, my marriage and my health. I had employees who had little respect for me, and a marriage which had many doubts for the future. I had been in business for approximately seven years and had lost all interest and enthusiasm for my work.

Over a few months I would be changed into a new person using Mr. Hubbard's administrative material. I continually worked at stripping away all the false data I had about organizations and life.

I now have a business that is gearing up to three times its size of a year ago, expansion is existing everywhere, my marriage is reaching new heights of enthusiasm, companionship and love that I never realized were possible. I have a staff that is totally trained and who work together now as team players. This has allowed me to prosper again in ways that I never believed were possible. I have enthusiasm in my business and life.

Healthcare Professional

L Ron Hubbard's management technology is world-class. It is an innovative and remarkably workable method of improving conditions. Being a WISE member and using this technology has allowed me to improve my business and to face head-on the challenges of work and life with a smile and with enthusiasm.

This is priceless data. It's also simple and basic. Results are immediate. If you are having any business difficulties this stuff can turn your entire career or business around in a matter of days. It's that powerful.

Investment Counselor

With the help of Mr. Hubbard's management technology we have been able to introduce the organizational structure of the organizing board, the use of statistics, Mr. Hubbard's communications system and the development of "hats" for our staff. As a result the responsibility of our personnel has increased and the use of LRH management technology has allowed us to avoid redundancy and breaks in production and survive in the difficult economical situation here in Russia.

Deputy General Director,
Electrical Component
Production Company

Our industry was really undergoing a big shake-out. Businesses similar to mine were going under at a very fast rate. Those that weren't going under were struggling.

LRH management tools helped me to predict the future trends of my industry and to find out what was really needed and wanted by my customers and my vendors. We were able to then restructure and implement plans to respond effectively to the changes coming down. As a result of really knowing where things were going, I was able to get out in front and lay the track to create my own future.

In the first year of using LRH tools our total revenues doubled; in the second year we doubled again, and then again in the third year; and in our fourth we more than tripled . . .

Owner,
Truck and Freight Company

I just wanted to say how much I appreciate the administration tools of L. Ron Hubbard. So far this year has been nothing short of phenomenal . . . Even what we now think of as the slow weeks are easily above my minimum profit quota. We have routinely had sales that I would have thought impossible a year ago.

Though I can't single out any single tool, there is one which I deem more significant than others—LRH's executive system. It gave me the courage to finally quit working on cars and start running my business. That, coupled with better knowledge on my finances through the use of statistics, a successful marketing plan and a well-designed work-order routing and tracking system, have made me successful beyond my wildest dreams . . .

Though I did fairly well before using LRH technology, the days of wondering how I am going to make the payroll during those "slow times" are gone forever.

Owner,
Automobile Repair Shop

Our staff is more supportive and dedicated to developing our company to its highest level. I simply can't explain how much weight that takes off the shoulders of top management, when so many employees take the responsibility to make their company succeed.

Owner,
Formal Wear Rental Business

I highly recommend that any serious student in the business world observe for himself the practical methods that Mr. Hubbard has developed.

*Technology Consultant
and Staff Scientist,
Massachusetts Institute
of Technology*

This was the first real training I encountered in my life . . . Next to me at their tables were others sitting and sweating over booklets, like college freshmen—solid businessmen from the largest aircraft building companies, the oil kings. They, just like me, were going through all those checkouts, through the same stages . . .

There was nothing surprising about it, because Ron Hubbard himself, exactly in the same manner, walked from idea to more and broader ideas. His researches became a foundation of the management technology which includes the principles of building an organization, personnel management, production ethics, as well as the formulas of how to salvage a company from any difficult situation and bring it to success . . .

Behind the seeming simplicity of the course there was something really invaluable: we were taught to think, compare, make conclusions, look for the solutions using our own enterprises and firms as examples.

*Journalist,
Russian Press Association*

L Ron Hubbard administrative technology has been the management technology that I have followed since I started our insurance adjusting company in 1979. This technology has taken my company from a one-man operation out of a rented house to the fastest growing insurance adjusting company in southern California, with over 140 employees.

Prior to studying and applying this technology, I studied business administration throughout my more than six years in college. I had been attempting to get answers in the areas of personnel, client relationships, finance, production, quality of work product and marketing. Somehow the answers I got were vague and not data that could be readily applied.

I came upon Hubbard Management Technology in the early 1970s and decided it was worth looking into. And that it was. I have taken courses in this technology and apply it to my company on a daily basis. Almost all of our employees have graduated from the more advanced programs.

Through WISE membership this technology has been made available. I urge all businessmen to become WISE members and take advantage of its services and benefits.

*Senior Executive,
Insurance Adjustment
Company*

PART TEN

SOCIAL BETTERMENT ACTIVITIES

It is impossible to ignore the signs of decay in modern society—drug abuse, criminality, failing education and moral decline. Each of these devastating social ills, if left unremedied, will ultimately destroy the very foundations upon which any civilized society is structured.

Scientologists always have been concerned about this decline in society at large, well knowing that L. Ron Hubbard's technology has wide secular applications that are of inestimable benefit beyond the religious arena. The word "technology" is used to describe "the *methods of application* of the principles of something, as opposed to mere knowledge of the thing itself." Mr. Hubbard was no ivory tower theorist. The principles he discovered are meant to be *used*. Thus, *technology* refers to the methods he developed through which these principles can be applied.

It is the workability of this secular technology in its broad application that has united both Scientologists and non-Scientologists since the 1960s to effectively arrest the decline of our society and rid the world of its devastating social ills.

CHAPTER 31

SOLUTIONS TO A TROUBLED SOCIETY

While the severity of society's ills is such that to some their resolution might seem impossible, and indeed may well have been impossible just a few short decades ago, they can be—and in fact are being—resolved by social betterment organizations that apply Mr. Hubbard's technologies and principles:

Drug and alcohol abuse. Narconon International, which oversees a global network of drug rehabilitation and drug education centers, is dedicated to restoring drug-free lives to drug-dependent people through the use of Mr. Hubbard's drug rehabilitation methods. Narconon also provides educational programs to help school-age children and others avoid the trap of drugs.

Crime. Criminon International helps incarcerated criminals learn to be productive members of society and brings about reform so that prisons actually rehabilitate.

Education. Applied Scholastics International assists students, parents, tutors, teachers and educational organizations around the world to eradicate illiteracy with Mr. Hubbard's study technology.

Morals. Utilizing Mr. Hubbard's non-religious moral code, *The Way to Happiness,* The Way to Happiness Foundation is creating a groundswell of international support for moral reform amongst both children and adults.

Each of these international organizations are separate, secular organizations in their own right, and each has its own history of vital contributions to society. Through the application of Mr. Hubbard's secular technology, they have successfully improved the lives of millions in this troubled world.

These social betterment groups exist to bring about genuine improvement of conditions on a planetwide scale—a goal shared by all Scientologists. Their activities, while secular in nature, are supported by churches of Scientology and individual Scientologists around the world who volunteer their time and talents.

Every society is composed of individuals. When a large number of them reach a point where they lack self-worth and competence, are unable and/or unwilling to contribute productively, lack respect for the rights of others and themselves, and see no solution to their predicament, we then have a society in serious trouble. However, when the majority is salvaged and placed upon a path to greater survival for themselves and others, we have a society willing to resolve the problems of the present and able to create a future in which a civilization can thrive.

It is such a future that these social betterment groups work to achieve. The following chapters describe their activities and the work they are doing to make this future a reality.

NARCONON:
A NEW LIFE FOR DRUG ADDICTS

Narconon (meaning no drugs) began in 1966 through the efforts of Arizona State Prison inmate William Benitez. A hard-core addict from the age of thirteen, then serving his fourth prison term, Benitez had unsuccessfully tried numerous ways to kick his drug habit.

In Mr. Benitez's words:

"My failure to come off drugs wasn't due to not wanting to. Believe me, I really tried. I read and read ... Freud, Jung, Menninger—and studied one philosophy after another, everything I could get my hands on to find out about myself. I underwent psychiatric aid and participated in all sorts of programs and as time went on, I knew less about myself instead of more. The only thing that kept me from putting a gun to my head was that I knew someday I would make it. I felt so sorry for my friends who were constantly trying to get off drugs. I wanted to help them and yet I couldn't even help myself.... I was so tired of the life of addiction, thieving, prostitution and all that goes with it. On my fourth and last trip to Arizona State Penitentiary, I was tried as a habitual criminal, which sentence carried a mandatory fifteen years to life, of which I received fifteen to sixteen years. It was at this point that I began to go into agreement with the idea that once you were an addict, you remained an addict."

His search for solutions led him to L. Ron Hubbard's *Scientology: The Fundamentals of Thought,* and with the principles in this book, he was at last able to kick his addiction.

As Mr. Benitez continued his studies, he soon realized that Mr. Hubbard's mental and spiritual discoveries offered the first real hope for addicts, and began applying that material to help other inmates.

"When first applied to a pilot group at Arizona State Penitentiary in 1966," Mr. Benitez reported, "it consisted only of the basic communication exercises. Yet, seven out of ten of the first group in their own words, 'made it.' Their success spread at grass-roots level to other prisons, and drawing on further research by L. Ron Hubbard, the program was expanded."

An initial group of ten grew to one hundred inmates within the first year, and, although originally organized to help heroin addicts, Narconon's usefulness and workability led to enormous interest from the general prison population. In 1967 prison officials granted permission for any inmate to join the group, and thereafter Narconon was opened to all who wished to improve their lives.

Mr. Benitez wrote to L. Ron Hubbard, who encouraged him to expand the program. The Church of Scientology in Phoenix also assisted by donating materials, and the most effective drug rehabilitation program in the world was born.

By 1970, Mr. Benitez had been released from prison and traveled to Los Angeles to assist in opening the national office of Narconon. This became known as Narconon US, and commenced a program of drug rehabilitation that was soon to spread throughout the United States.

Initial Narconon programs in institutions such as California's Rehabilitation Center in Norco, the California Men's Colony in San Luis Obispo and the Youth Training

School in Ontario, California, were well received and highly successful.

An official evaluation of the ten-month program at the Youth Training School showed that disciplinary offenses among the control group increased 10 percent during the second five-month period, while those of the Narconon group decreased by 81 percent. The grade average of the control group increased from C to C+, while that of the Narconon group increased from C– to B–.

Narconon successes continued to mount. In May 1972, a program was started at the Ventura School for Boys and Girls in Ventura, California. After considerable expansion it later received funding from the California Youth Authority.

That same year, Narconon opened its first residential programs, making it possible to take an addict through the Narconon withdrawal program and other Narconon courses. This expansion was an important step for Narconon as it brought all stages of rehabilitation into the safety of a residential environment.

The Narconon Program:
Producing New Lives Without Drugs

The need for effective drug rehabilitation technology is today greater than ever before, for the scope of the problem is vast. Internationally, the illegal narcotics industry generates estimated annual revenues of $500 billion to $1 trillion.

This astonishing statistic is only one indicator of the many social repercussions of drug abuse. Criminals on drugs, for example, are responsible for the vast majority of all crimes committed. According to US Justice Department studies, three out of four suspects arrested for crimes of violence test positive for illegal drugs.

To meet this crucial need for effective drug rehabilitation, Narconon has expanded greatly in the years since its founding. As the program moved into other countries, Narconon International was formed to direct the drug education and rehabilitation activities and provide assistance and support to Narconon centers and their staffs throughout the world. Narconon International has a goal to achieve a drug-free Earth. It provides effective and complete drug rehabilitation for those enslaved by drugs and works to prevent our future generations from ever becoming addicted. Located in Los Angeles, Narconon International today supervises worldwide drug education and drug rehabilitation programs.

Today, commensurate with the more than a quarter-million drug-free lives achieved through L. Ron Hubbard's technology has been the expansion of Narconon centers internationally. Narconon centers providing rehabilitation and/or education services are currently administered in 50 centers located in 21 countries: Argentina, Australia, Brazil, Canada, Colombia, Denmark, France, Germany, Ireland, Italy, Kazakhstan, Mexico, the Netherlands, New Zealand, Russia, Spain, Sweden, Switzerland, Ukraine, the United Kingdom and the United States. In addition, an estimated one million people worldwide have availed themselves of Narconon's drug education services, including more than 115,000 schoolchildren in 1997 alone.

Narconon also operates one of the largest training and rehabilitation facilities of its kind in the world, the Narconon International New Life Center. This facility brings a new life to many in need of rehabilitation, with the highest quality and most effective drug rehabilitation program available in the world. It is also here that Narconon personnel come from many countries for training to administer this Narconon program to others. Narconon

The Narconon program consists of a series of exercises, drills and study steps done in a precise sequence. The study materials and workbook shown here guide the individual through the program.

New Life Center is the international training center, turning out highly qualified and competent staff fully trained in L. Ron Hubbard's technology. These dedicated Narconon staff return to their cities and countries to bring a new life to drug and alcohol abusers throughout the world.

Narconon's efficacy comes entirely from the technology developed by L. Ron Hubbard who, years before the drug crisis became headline news internationally, had extensively researched the antisocial side effects of drugs.

He discovered the insidious effects not only of illegal or "street" drugs but also of alcohol and psychiatric drugs—the latter often far more devastating and injurious than the original condition they were intended to "cure."

Narconon utilizes a completely *drug-free* rehabilitation program to restore life to drug and alcohol abusers and give them back control of their lives.

In a field loaded with drug programs that substitute addictions with yet more drugs, L. Ron Hubbard developed exact techniques to deal with the physical and mental damage brought about by substance abuse. None of these techniques involve the use of methadone or any other substitute drug.

The Narconon program today consists of a series of exercises, drills and study steps done in a precise sequence. The techniques and learning programs help the individual withdraw from current drug use, get into communication with others and the environment, remove the residual drugs from his body, gain control of himself and his environment and reach the point where he can take responsibility not only for himself, but also for others. The Narconon program consists of the following:

Among the thousands who have been salvaged by Narconon are once hard-core heroin addicts at this Mexican prison.

1. Drug-Free Withdrawal — The first step of the Narconon program helps the individual cease current drug use rapidly and with minimal discomfort through proper nutrition, vitamins and care from experienced Narconon staff. Various assists help the person come off the drugs with minimal discomfort.

2. The Narconon Therapeutic TR Course — Once withdrawal is complete, a series of communication drills (called training routines, or "TRs") are used to extrovert the person and raise his ability to confront his life — that is, to comfortably face others and situations in his environment. Each TR increases the person's ability to face life and communicate with others.

3. The Narconon New Life Detoxification Procedure — Next, the person cleanses his body of drug residues and other toxic substances through a regimen of exercise, sauna and nutritional supplements as described in the book *Clear Body, Clear Mind: The Effective Purification Program* by L. Ron Hubbard. Drug residues remain locked in the fatty tissues of the body and can be released into the bloodstream years after the person has stopped taking drugs, thus rekindling old cravings for drugs. This step purges the body of these residues and other toxins.

4. Narconon's Learning Improvement Course — Here, the individual gains the ability to study and retain knowledge, along with the ability to recognize and

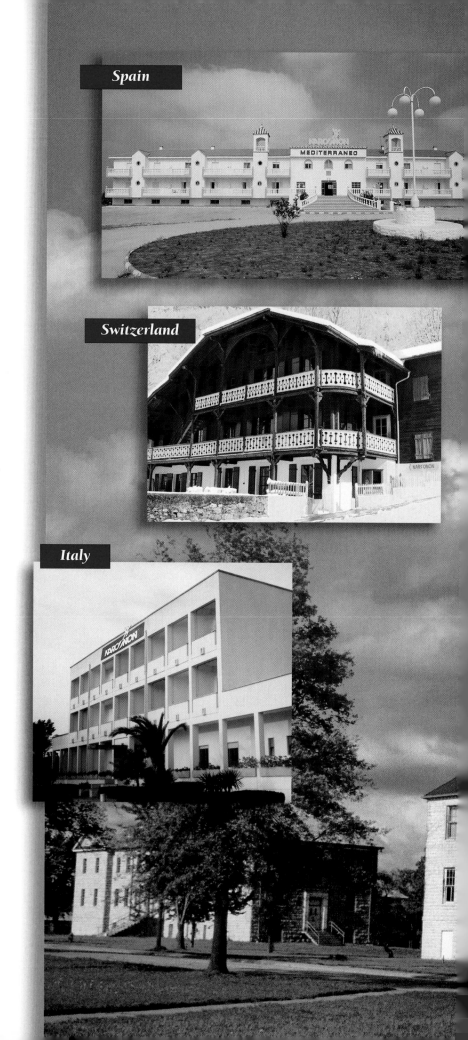

Spain

Switzerland

Italy

Narconon centers provide rehabilitation and/or educational services at 50 centers located in 21 countries, from Argentina to the Ukraine.

overcome the barriers to study. He can now proceed with further educational steps to prepare him to lead a productive and ethical life.

5. Narconon Communication and Perception Course—On this step, the individual repeats the TRs, plus additional exercises which get him into full communication with others and his environment. The exercises pull the person's attention off himself, where it has been fixed by drugs, and out to the world around him. He also helps another person on the course do the exercises, which not only gives him increased responsibility, but a tremendous sense of pride and satisfaction because of this newly gained ability to help others.

6. Narconon's Ups and Downs in Life Course—Now the individual gains the knowledge to spot and handle those influences in his environment that would cause him to lose any gains he has made. He learns the characteristics of the antisocial personality and the social personality so he can recognize the two, spot the differences between them and better choose his friends and associates. Completing this course makes a person less susceptible to those who would influence a reversion to drugs.

United States

Germany

Sweden

United States

7. Narconon's Personal Values and Integrity Course—Here the individual gains the data he needs to improve his survival potential. The course teaches him about the eight dynamics, ethics, honesty and integrity, showing him how to correct antisocial behavior by ridding himself of the effects of past harmful deeds.

8. The Narconon Changing Conditions in Life Course—This course covers the ethics technology of L. Ron Hubbard and shows the individual exactly how to apply it to improve conditions in his life, something he needs if he is to reassert his self-determinism.

9. Narconon's "The Way to Happiness" Course—Based on a nonsectarian moral code called *The Way to Happiness,* this course gives the individual a guide to living a life where real happiness is attainable.

This comprehensive program addresses and handles the reason why the individual started using drugs in the first place and arms him with the knowledge and certainty he needs to lead a happy, drug-free life. Vocational training programs are also available to develop needed job skills so graduates can better support themselves.

The Narconon program's exceptional success rate speaks for itself. A study in Spain, for example, found 78.37 percent still drug-free a year after the program.

In the United States, the average cost for incarcerating offenders is $25,000 to $40,000 per year per inmate. Yet prisons and county jails are a "revolving door," with 80 percent or more offenders returning to jail after release. A very large percentage of those arrested commit their crimes either while drugged or intoxicated or as a result of trying to support their addictions.

Thus, of great significance is Narconon's effectiveness in dramatically reducing criminal recidivism. Every single study done of the Narconon program's effect on criminal offenders with drug and alcohol histories has shown a stunning reduction in their rate of return to the justice system. As early as 1975, a study at Delaware Correctional Center revealed that 84 percent of the Narconon graduates who had done more than just one Narconon course had *no further arrest.* In Connecticut, there were zero arrests within a year, compared to 66 percent in the control group. An ongoing formal outcome study of program results from two US Narconon centers treating addicts with heavy drug and criminal histories has shown an eighteen-month to two-year 83 percent reduction in criminal activity and 95 percent reduction in arrests.

Another evaluation of the Narconon program at this same time was conducted in what was then West Berlin. It showed a 92 percent reduction in the arrest rate in the year following program completion. This compared to a 50 percent rearrest rate in the control group.

Narconon International has also worked in close coordination with prestigious scientific researchers and research institutes to study the healthfulness and specific application of L. Ron Hubbard's body detoxification procedure, a vital component of Narconon delivery. A sufficient number of fully realized studies accumulated from areas as far spread as California, Yugoslavia, Russia and Kazakhstan leading to two International Conferences on Human Detoxification that were hosted by Narconon International and other organizations in Los Angeles in 1995 and in Stockholm, Sweden, in 1997. In Los Angeles a study was presented by Megan

Shields, MD, and Shelley Beckmann, PhD, that clinically demonstrated cocaine and Valium metabolites being excreted in the sweat and urine as a result of this detoxification procedure. At the Stockholm conference, a group of sixteen doctors and scientists from Russia's esteemed Academy of Medical Science and Kazakhstan presented a coordinated battery of two-year studies they had performed on participants in the detox program, demonstrating uniformly significant improvements in physical health and overall well-being. In consequence, several new Narconon programs opened in Russia, Ukraine and Kazakhstan.

Narconon programs are administered by dedicated individuals who choose to work with Narconon because it has proven itself in the drug rehabilitation field. In some cases these staff are Scientologists. In many other cases, they are those who have progressed themselves from addict to ex-addict to contributing Narconon staff member.

Effective Drug Education Lectures

Prevention is also an important part of the Narconon program. The international spokesperson for Narconon is actress Kirstie Alley. She tirelessly promotes the benefits of a drug-free life attainable through Narconon, with numerous radio and television interviews and public appearances at fund-raising events. Other Narconon spokespersons gave nearly ten thousand lectures on drug abuse to approximately one million students in the 1980s and 1990s. These "Truth About Drugs" lectures result in a dramatic change in attitude toward drugs. As early as 1989, a study by the Foundation for Advancements in Science and Education measured the attitude change of students from the second grade to twelfth grade in high school and concluded:

Film and television actress, Kirstie Alley, is Narconon's international spokesperson.

"Narconon's drug education program is effective in teaching students about the adverse consequences of drug abuse and has a very positive influence on the attitudes of students toward drugs. The most dramatic effect on attitude [was] observed in the borderline group of students — those indicating that they might use drugs in the future."

Of the students in this category, 86 percent indicated that they were less likely to use drugs following the presentation.

Narconon Boston has also delivered many years of "peer leadership" training to high-school youth in the New England area, training them not only on drugs, but also on public speaking and conflict resolution.

Narconon lecturers have worked in close association with police or police agencies in many areas of the world including Canada, the United States, Sweden, Norway and Italy. Narconon Sweden and local, regional and national police officers have cooperated for well over a decade, including, for example, delivering a full briefing on the Narconon drug education method to all police officers who themselves work on drug prevention in the Stockholm area.

Narconon staff regularly deliver professional lectures on issues of drugs and the workplace to corporate and business executives throughout the world. One such executive wrote in response, "The second part of the meeting on the subject of the consequences of a world on drugs was presented by [a Narconon staff person]. It was very interesting for [our] Vilnius staff. Despite the fact that the drug problem is not a new issue for Lithuania, most of us were not familiar with the problem and its dramatic consequences: the crime, the deaths, the costs, the victims. We got acquainted with Narconon's highly effective program to rehabilitate drug abusers. The presentation was interesting and informative."

In Italy, Narconon centers have distributed tens of thousands of Narconon drug education booklets on how to talk to youth about drugs, how drugs affect the mind, and methadone (as a very poor solution to the heroin problem). Schools and municipalities throughout Italy continue to request thousands more copies of these booklets that share a vital, new perspective on drugs, addiction and treatment methods.

Scientologists Support Narconon

While talk of drug and alcohol abuse is endless, solutions do not come as easily. Nearly 80 percent of the American public, for instance, believe that drug abuse is a concern that the US government must deal with immediately, yet 70 percent feel their government's "war on drugs" is ineffective.

Scientologists strongly believe that both drug education and real rehabilitation are vital. Based on results, Mr. Hubbard's technology provides the most effective solutions to drug and alcohol abuse.

In more than 30 years of service in the war against drugs, Narconon has shown itself to be the most effective rehabilitation program there is. It is something that the peoples of Earth urgently need. Thus, Scientologists support Narconon. Many contribute time and energy to help Narconon staff, serving as part-time volunteers in Narconon's community and prison programs.

Administrative staff in Narconon's worldwide network help acquire donations for new premises or materials, and help to recruit staff for these programs. Individual Scientologists and churches of Scientology have enthusiastically supported the Narconon program by providing millions of dollars' worth of funding and material support.

This combination of dedicated staff and L. Ron Hubbard's technology has served Narconon for more than three decades as the acknowledged pacesetter in the field of drug and alcohol prevention, education and rehabilitation.

Expansion Because of One Reason: Results

From the simple beginnings of a single L. Ron Hubbard book, to the full lineup of today's Narconon program, the fact of workability lies at the core of Narconon's success. Professionals in the field of drug rehabilitation from many countries have attested to Narconon's results.

A nationally respected American drug abuse consultant whose career in drug prevention began with then-President Richard Nixon's "war on drugs," said this about Narconon:

"I have been to some of the high-powered programs in the nation and I can say, unequivocally, that what you are doing here is better than anything I have seen anywhere else. Even to the point that if [my sons] . . . had a drug problem, I would bring them here. And that's over the other programs I talked about."

A leading drug rehabilitation expert who has studied a number of different rehabilitation programs has remarked that "The drug-free procedure used by Narconon during drug withdrawal is in my opinion sound."

He also pointed out that "an important aspect is the systematic application of techniques to improve communication and interpersonal skills in persons dependent on alcohol and/or drugs. The techniques include training in personal values, integrity and in general cover ethical principles. This aspect of the program is implemented using a methodology developed by L. Ron Hubbard . . .

"This area is in my opinion critical in the treatment of persons afflicted with addictive disorders. Although experts often note that addictive disorders should not be viewed from a moralistic perspective, a view which is often misunderstood, there is no question that one of the central problems in addictive behavior is the restructuring of the normative system of patients affected by the disorder. Addicts characteristically subordinate values such as work, family relationships and community responsibilities to the ingestion and unwise use of alcohol and/or drugs. Social neglect and criminal behavior are frequent companions of drug abuse and alcoholism. Efforts to develop a functional normative system as is done by Narconon should result in favorable outcomes. Narconon has demonstrated that this redefinition of the normative system of addicts is possible to implement with empathy, compassion and respect for the addict."

Narconon is accredited by the prestigious Commission for Accreditation of Rehabilitation Facilities (CARF), widely recognized as the foremost authority on drug rehabilitation programs in the United States. CARF's standards are the highest in the nation and have been adopted by many states and federal agencies as the benchmark for all rehabilitation programs to measure up to.

Narconon is also recognized by numerous governments as a safe and highly effective program. In Sweden, Denmark, Italy, the Netherlands and Switzerland, governments provide funding for Narconon's drug education efforts and support delivery of the drug rehabilitation program.

The Parliamentary Assembly of the Council of Europe recognized the success of L. Ron Hubbard's drug rehabilitation technology and Narconon in a resolution passed in January 1988.

More and more, judges and government agencies today refer drug addicts to Narconon for rehabilitation, rather than to jail or prison. Such an option is given by courts in Denmark, Germany, Italy, the Netherlands, Spain, Sweden and the United States.

Three decades of success prove that the Narconon program gets *real* results, far better than any other drug rehabilitation program in the world. Narconon has documented many, many cases of successful release from drugs and resultant drug-free lives.

A parole agent from the California Department of Youth Authority commented on the effectiveness of Narconon:

"I am very impressed by some of the gains I have seen in wards placed in Narconon. One of the most dramatic changes I ever noted was produced in a ward who had failed to show improvement in other local drug treatment programs. At Narconon he made rapid and outstanding improvement. The improvement was due to the Narconon program alone since all other factors remained constant."

Another California Youth Authority representative had this to say about Narconon's approach to drug abuse prevention and rehabilitation:

"As one of our more congenial community resources, Narconon has produced results with some of our wards, where other programs have failed. It is reassuring to have an organization such as Narconon that meets the needs of our parolees and goes a little beyond—they care."

Like many others, a New London, Connecticut, attorney who studied the results of Narconon's residential program responded to the Narconon program with great admiration:

"Without equivocation, of all the social agencies with which I have had contact over the past two years, Narconon is the one to which I turn when all other possibilities have vanished. It is staffed with youthful, outgoing, knowledgeable and dedicated men and women who can communicate properly with their 'clients.' Let me offer my highest possible commendation: that this is the number one social agency serving the community in the reduction of crime and drug abuse."

An official with the Canadian Penitentiary Service wrote:

"The Narconon program is the only program I have observed to produce quick and stable results in assisting addicts to give up their dependency on drugs. I have been employed in Corrections since 1964 and have had the opportunity to participate in and observe varied treatment programs for addicts, but this is the first program that I have observed to achieve what it claims to achieve."

A former Los Angeles public health official who witnessed results in the early years of Narconon's residential program said this:

"It is one of the few programs which has enabled drug/alcohol abusers to evolve a rational, humanistic approach to social and personal tensions. Narconon has proven its success inside institutions and on the streets. It is well staffed and well organized; people associated with its programs are dedicated and cooperative. I therefore highly recommend Narconon."

The most extraordinary example of Narconon methodology becoming a major force for rehabilitation inside institutions is the program at Ensenada State Prison in Baja, Mexico. (This began as a pilot project with volunteers administering the full Criminon criminal reform program, incorporating the Narconon drug rehabilitation method, to a number of inmates.) The crisis of daily heroin use inside the prison had been estimated by prison officials at 80 percent. But with the introduction of these programs, literally hundreds of inmates have been brought through drug-free physical withdrawal and gone on to cleanse their bodies of drug residuals and to study the Narconon course, many of them learning to read in the process. The staff of the program are now almost entirely inmates who have themselves recovered from drug addiction and then trained on the Narconon method inside the prison. One prison official estimated that heroin use has dropped 80 percent from its former use level since the Narconon program was introduced. And justice officials outside the prison in Ensenada reported that the crime rate in the whole city has significantly dropped. Thus, Narconon has returned to the social environment in which it was founded three decades ago to continue to rescue prisoners from drug-induced oblivion.

The head of a Russian delegation from the Ministry of the Interior, which seeks solutions to the drug problem in Russia, concluded after his study of several Narconon facilities:

"The only place in the world where I have seen with my own eyes drug addicts fully cured from heroin and cocaine is Narconon. This technology is not only taking the person off the addiction, it also . . . keeps them cured and ethical and in a high moral state.

" . . . I see these methods as the future hope for all those unfortunate addicts in Russia and the other republics."

How a Narconon Program Is Started

Individuals interested in pioneering a Narconon program based on Mr. Hubbard's technology first contact the nearest Narconon center or Narconon International representative for the assistance they need. Narconon International will then provide them all the advice, guidance and materials they will need to commence activities. (Centers and offices are listed in the back of this book.)

The first step to opening a Narconon is recruiting others interested in working in the field of drug rehabilitation. A willing and able staff is the nucleus of any successful Narconon. These individuals are then trained to deliver the program. Staff training facilities exist to make this as easy as possible.

Narconon International helps obtain suitable premises and ensures that all local regulations and requirements are met. Manuals and other materials are available from Narconon offices to set up and operate one's own Narconon center and to contact and help those in need of Narconon's services. Representatives from Narconon International and Narconon's regional offices assist in all aspects of getting the new center set up and running successfully. They place one in contact with referral agencies that lead to people in need of the program, help locate local sources of funding and provide organizational advice and direction. Donations may be needed for beginning expenses and course materials. In many cases the local community has assisted in donating furnishings, bedding, food and sometimes money to new Narconon programs. Narconon International will give guidance on how to go about obtaining donations for these important prerequisites.

SUCCESSES OF NARCONON GRADUATES

The drug problem ranks high among the vital concerns of society. Untold numbers of lives have been ruined. But there is a viable solution, one that restores self-respect and a willingness to be a part of life once more. L. Ron Hubbard's technology, applied throughout the world by Narconon, is the road back. Each time a person is rehabilitated through Narconon, the scourge of drugs disappears a little more from the world. Narconon offers hope that drug abuse will one day be a thing of the past.

I came here already destroyed. I had lost about twenty kilos in the streets. I was gaunt, pale and could not physically move as a result of daily drug abuse. This was occurring physically, but it was not all [of it], as morally I arrived with no hope of anything and full of doubts as to whether or not I would ever want to make it in life. Nothing mattered in life.

I had been in two [other rehabilitation] centers, but I got nothing from being in these centers. I started the [Narconon] program and bit by bit I became freer of drugs. I started to regain my lost hopes and desire to live again. But not only that, I am now happy without having to live with drugs—to wake up in the morning with a desire to smile and with the thought that I start a new beautiful day and that the road for better days will continue.

M.B.

I was a drug addict for four years. During this time I used every drug there is. For two years I was very, very heavily addicted to heroin. I almost died from this. Since joining Narconon my whole life has changed. I am now able to communicate much easier with anybody. I have learned to control myself and my environment much better. I now have responsibility (which I couldn't face up to before). I don't need drugs anymore because I am now higher than I have ever been on drugs. I thank you L. Ron Hubbard and everyone helping people with Narconon.

D.K.

The first time I walked in the Narconon office I was desperate. My son had not spent more than a few months out of jail at any given time period for over five years and all of his incarcerations had been directly related to drug and alcohol offenses. Counseling, and even hospitalization, had not helped. You were my last hope.

As I read the letters on the wall in the waiting room I remember my eyes stinging with tears. I wondered if I would ever be able to write a letter thanking Narconon for the successful treatment of my son.

There were a lot of rocky moments for all of us during the instruction stage—phone calls, home visits, even a few disappointments. When he finished the program I don't think any of us knew for sure what the final outcome would be.

That was almost two years ago and with a happy, grateful heart I am writing you and your dedicated, wonderful, committed staff to let you know that the program proved successful. The nightmare of drug and alcohol abuse is finally in the past. My son has become a happy and confident individual, with your assistance. The program established itself to be the best investment we could have ever made. Would I recommend Narconon to anyone? In a heartbeat!

May God bless each and every one of you. Keep up the great work.

N.N.

For a while, I thought drugs were fun. But then they almost killed me the way they have so many other musicians. I did the Narconon program and it literally saved my life. I have lived drug free for a number of years now and continue to reach new levels of creativity and satisfaction with life. Now it's life that's fun. I would have hated to have missed it!

N.H.

From this day on I will be all I can be in this world thanks to Narconon. The staff are very brave people here at Narconon. They are good people and without them and their kindness I would never have made it. I feel great today, and I will feel great tomorrow too, because I am a drug-free person.

S.B.

I came here beaten up by the use of drugs. I was at the point where I wanted to die, my attitude and perception of life was all screwed up. I am now a new person. This program has saved my life. I have had so many wins and realizations. I do know that I have the ability, the technology and the courage to lead a drug-free life. I would really encourage others to do this program and get the gains I have got.

D.K.

Narconon saved my life. For years, seventeen to be exact, I battled with drugs and alcohol. This program was the only one that showed me how to stay off drugs and how to live my life honestly, and work toward happiness.

L.V.

Having now completed this program I can say without any reservation whatsoever, I feel I am living proof that there is certainly more to life than three bottles of wine or the equivalent consumption each evening.

Without the Narconon program and the compassion of the staff who deliver it, I would not be as alive as I am today and I would certainly not be looking forward to life as I am. So a big, big thank you and my eternal affinity and love for saving my life.

M.B.

I am a fully recovered drug addict. My life was in total ruin before I entered the Narconon program in 1989.

Today I have a happy and productive life. After I completed my program at Narconon, I wanted to give others what was given me. Narconon gave me my life back and I have seen and helped countless others to achieve what I have.

Drugs only bring about insanity and health problems that put us all at risk. L. Ron Hubbard has given us the technology so that we all can be free. I am more than happy to help make this happen.

K.D.

I am a staff member here at Narconon Los Angeles. Working here is the best thing I have ever done. I am a former drug user who was addicted to drugs for twenty years.

It wasn't until I came to Narconon that I came to a total understanding of why I did drugs. I not only learned why I did drugs, but I also learned how to confront difficult situations, how to communicate with people and how to control my life. I now can handle situations logically and analytically rather than running for a syringe or a pill.

Working at Narconon I have seen people walk in the door messed up on drugs and alcohol. They're in bad shape mentally and physically.

To see these people turn their lives around and become happy, confident and productive is the most rewarding feeling a person can ever feel. To really help people and see the results of the Narconon program is nothing short of a miracle.

P.J.

Narconon on the Internet

Further information about Narconon can be found on its Internet site located at: **http://www.narconon.org.**

CRIMINON:
TRUE REHABILITATION FOR CRIMINALS

Each day in the United States, more than 31,000 petty and hard-core criminals are released back into their communities. Within one year, up to 80 percent of these men and women will have committed ten or twenty more crimes before being arrested again and sent back to prison.

The figures speak for themselves. The 80 percent recidivism rate makes a mockery of current psychiatric-oriented rehabilitation methods, demonstrating that, for all intents and purposes, there is in fact no such thing as criminal rehabilitation. A report published by the National Council on Crime and Delinquency in America concurred, stating that there was "little evidence that either institutional programs or noninstitutional efforts to rehabilitate offenders make any appreciable difference."

And so go the revolving doors of the US penal system.

L. Ron Hubbard once quite accurately pointed out that although the percentage of criminals is relatively small, the amount of grief and turmoil they create in the world is out of all proportion to their numbers. "Thus," he concluded, "the criminal mind is a subject one cannot avoid in research as it is a major factor in the distortion of a culture."

From the need to remedy this glaringly destructive societal flaw—and through the fruits of Mr. Hubbard's research—Criminon (which means "without crime") was born in New Zealand in 1970. A branch of Narconon, it is an organization that operates within the penal system to rehabilitate criminals and restore their sense of worth so that they can become productive members of society.

Criminon actually grew out of the very successful Narconon prison programs. By the 1980s, with increased drug usage in all sectors of society, the Narconon program shifted its emphasis to community-based activities. At that point, Criminon expanded into the correctional facilities to fill a need.

Rehabilitating a Sense of Responsibility

Headquartered in Los Angeles, Criminon operates programs across the United States. By the start of 1998, 4,000 inmates in 750 prisons were being helped weekly, up from 200 prisons just four years earlier. Such expansion has not been limited to prisons. In Los Angeles, Criminon initiated a remarkably successful program in Central Juvenile Hall among youngsters who were gang members charged with serious crimes. The supervising detention officer wrote, "The results of the program well exceeded our expectations in my unit, and I would therefore recommend Criminon to any corrections facility."

Small wonder then that the program is spreading. A southern California municipal court judge has sentenced more than five hundred misdemeanor offenders to Criminon instead of to jail. In his words, "The efficacy of Criminon has far surpassed even our most optimistic expectations. We have seen a significant increase in compliance with all terms and conditions of probation, restitution, fine payments and community service for those who have completed the program.

"Compliance approximates 90 percent. Additionally of great significance is the reduction of recidivism. Less than 1 percent of those who have completed the program have reoffended." Because of its success, this court's referral approach is gaining more and more popularity. Additionally, Criminon has become active in other locations around the world, ranging from Australia to England and Hungary to Mexico.

The success of the Criminon program is best told in the words of those whose lives are changed by it. A remarkable letter was received by the judge from a man he had sentenced to the Criminon program for driving without a license:

". . . I have been in and out of the justice system since I was 12 years old — I'm now 42 and I spent from age 13 to 23 behind bars. I don't have a high-school degree and until recently I barely knew how to read. I have lived a very hard life. I have seen the worst that the street could give me. It has caused me great suffering.

". . . When I walked into the Criminon center my goal was to just get through it, satisfy your sentence and walk away. What I didn't realize was that I was going to grow mentally, morally and to become a much better person. This program taught me first how to read, study and comprehend information I'm trying to learn. This simple key unlocked in me the ability to understand and comprehend what the teachers could not make me comprehend in school. I now have the key to study and read and understand what I read . . .

". . . This program gives more back to the society than I think anyone really knows. Punishment or jail time is a complete waste. It does no one any good. Let me tell you as someone who has spent years creating 'hell' for society, I have done the punishments the justice system has given me. I got a trade out of it, but it didn't give me my self-respect back. This sentence you gave me was very different. Criminon has given me my self-respect back. It has changed me. It has shown me that I can have everything I want in life — without breaking any laws. I used to get respect in the streets from what I did

there, but today I receive respect from society for what I'm doing now. This program will open more minds than the jail system ever will.

". . . I am going to take a learning course that Criminon offers so I can become an instructor at this center and do all I can to help others who want to become a more productive member of society like I did. If there is ever anything I can do for you, please don't hesitate to ask. I hope with all the influence you have, that you can make people understand how valuable the Criminon course is and how it can help society and in the end, make your job easier." — G.S.

Such success naturally raises basic questions: What makes Criminon different? What does it do? Perhaps the best place to start is with what Criminon does *not* do:

Criminon does not drug inmates. It does not use punitive restraints. It does not use aimless conversation for lack of a better tool. It is not psychiatry or psychology.

From psychiatry's ineptitude within the penal system — in spite of the immense funding and power bestowed upon it — the uncharitable conclusion could be drawn that rehabilitation is not necessarily what it intends to accomplish. However, the more obvious and arguable point is that it is unable to rehabilitate criminals because it has no knowledge of what makes a criminal. Unproven theories are easy to come by, and psychiatry/psychology has no lack of them. Criminality is blamed on everything from poor environmental conditions, inherited drives, biological imbalances in the brain, to "sluggish nervous systems."

Criminon's success, on the other hand, directly stems from workable rehabilitation methods. Mr. Hubbard extensively researched criminality until he found the actual source of what makes a criminal, and from this point of truth, he was able to develop effective solutions.

Criminon programs work with offenders to help them regain their self-respect and moral values.

"Do you know that there is not a criminal anywhere in any prison who is not a criminal because he was degraded and lost his personal pride?" Mr. Hubbard asked in one of his lectures. "I have done a very thorough cross-check of this—what they call 'bad women,' 'criminal men.' Their badness and criminality is immediately traceable to a loss of their powers and personal pride, and after that they were 'bad'; they were 'dangerous.'

"If you want to rehabilitate a criminal, just go back and find out when he did lose his personal pride. Rehabilitate that one point and you don't have a criminal anymore."

By addressing this point of rehabilitation, people of all faiths and walks of life, through their support of Criminon, are taking effective action to end this repeating cycle of criminality and reform the prison system.

The Program

L. Ron Hubbard made an important discovery more than three decades ago—he conclusively proved that man was basically good. This is in fact nowhere more evident than in our prison population—men who commit wrongful deeds against their fellows want to be caught, which explains why criminals invariably leave clues and make the job of the police that much easier.

What they do not necessarily want, however, is punishment. As all men are basically good, those who err actually seek to be rendered less harmful to society, and they can be rehabilitated.

The key element of the Criminon program is The Way to Happiness Extension Course, based on a booklet of the same name. As the first step toward rehabilitation, this correspondence course is designed to give inmates knowledge of right and wrong conduct. A nonreligious moral code, *The Way to Happiness* is practical and incisive, and provides fundamental guides to behavior—a vital step, often overlooked in the family life and education of the criminal. Critical values ranging from love and kindness to basics such as hygiene and common courtesy are covered.

Inmates complete practical exercises on this course and mail them in to Criminon staff and volunteer groups of Scientologists around the country who grade the exercises. These staff maintain communication with the inmate and encourage him, and when he finishes the course he receives a certificate from Criminon.

Other parts of the Criminon course are similar to those used in the Narconon drug rehabilitation programs and are actually administered to the inmates in prison, either by Criminon staff or volunteers. These elements include:

1. Criminon's Learning Improvement Course—As many inmates suffer literacy problems, this course in study skills is invaluable as a tool both during incarceration and upon release. As it provides the ability to learn any subject, it is a fundamental that will help in vocational and other training.

2. Criminon's Communication Course— These communication exercises increase the inmate's ability to face life and not withdraw from it—the very act that exacerbated the criminal condition.

3. Criminon's Handling Suppression Course—As recidivism is often due to the return of an inmate to his previous environment, this invaluable course helps him learn the social and antisocial characteristics of his friends and associates. The person is thus less susceptible to bad influences.

4. Criminon's Personal Integrity Course— This study of the eight dynamics, ethics and integrity, helps the inmate take responsibility for, and rid himself of, his past misdeeds. And as with the Narconon program, other courses address subjects such as how to change conditions in life, how to contribute effectively and other basics vital to successful living.

All in all, the Criminon program totally replaces the unworkable rehabilitation methods that only exacerbate crime. It directly and effectively rehabilitates individuals so that criminal behavior becomes a thing of the past and remains that way. Because of its workability, word of Criminon is spreading rapidly from prison to prison. And of the thousands of prisoners released every day, more and more will be truly rehabilitated. In time, the revolving door will be closed.

PRISONERS SPEAK OF RESULTS

Thousands of letters and testimonials from prisoners describe how Criminon helped them cope with prison life, increased their self-worth and happiness, and began to change their outlook and behavior for the better.

I believe that if The Way to Happiness can help someone such as myself—who is a three-time convicted felon and ex-drug abuser of any substance, a thief, liar, manipulator, etc.—then this course can help even those who feel that all hope has been lost.

A.B.

This course has taught me the many changes that life can take and it has polished my ability to deal with those changes. It has taught me the importance of trust and the importance of fulfilling my obligations. I have to be an industrious individual in society. I have a four-year-old son and I am a single parent and it is very important to remember that setting good examples enhances your child's chances of becoming a more successful and industrious member in this society. It has also taught me a little of what my religion teaches me and that is knowledge of self and discipline, which are the main ingredients that 75 percent of this nation lacks.

Q.W.B. Detroit

This class has helped me find the true happiness within myself. I've made a lot of new positive changes in my life and just by using all of the precepts in my everyday life things just keep getting better. More opportunities are opening up for me. I have control of my life now and have set some new goals to achieve. As long as I stay true to myself I will succeed.

T.B. California

This course should be mandatory. It has turned my life around in a very important manner. The most important change is that it has allowed me to stop using heroin for the very first time in sixteen years. I really can't pinpoint what it was, but for sure it is a combination of the instructors and what's in the course itself. But you should continue this as long as possible. Thank you for this once-in-a-lifetime opportunity.

R.D.P. California

I am so thankful to you for The Way to Happiness Course. I had lost all my self-respect and personal pride. I didn't care for myself or anyone else. However, through this course I have gotten all my pride back and my self-respect as well. I didn't think I could ever face my family or the world again. But thanks to The Way to Happiness Course I can hold my head up again. I also know for sure that I will never again commit another crime or come back to prison.

*C.P. Western
United States*

The Way to Happiness Course has been a large part of my getting back my self-respect. The time I spent working the lessons, and then putting the lessons to work, were a big part of my feeling human again. I believe so strongly in this program that I have told many others about the course and will continue to do so in the future. Thank you Criminon for making these programs available to me and others in my position.

J.C. Oklahoma

Before entering this program [Criminon] I didn't know what success was. I didn't even know the tremendous feeling of self-assurance you adopt from this program. I can now honestly say that the works of L. Ron Hubbard are very inspiring. They have taught me the value of hard work and self-awareness.

Others around me have noticed the change in my whole being. My attitude, my patience, my ability to deal with hostile situations with calm assurances, this is something I never had or was able to do. But with what I have learned on this program I have attained those characteristics and more.

I feel in control of my life, and although I am presently a guest of the state (prisoner) in a correction facility, I never felt more free in my life!!

I know when I am released I can truly be happy and prosper in society because I no longer have a destructive nature. Rather I have come to learn of a productive and positive way to go about life thus making my survival and those around me safe with room to grow.

T.W. Delaware

We are very grateful and appreciative of the books and tapes that you donated. Your books were very beautiful and from the moment we received them they became very much in demand because they relate to us as people in a way we never have seen before. There is great truth in this philosophy you gave us, and we are very much in your debt.

The tape lectures of Mr. Hubbard's have changed the lives of a lot of people here. We started a night class and over fifty inmates have attended. Some of the men said that if they heard this tape before they got in trouble with the law, they would have never wound up in jail.

How can we make it available to more people? This stuff really can prevent crime.

S.P. Florida

For many years I seemed to be living in a very dark room. When I completed the [Criminon] course it was like someone had switched the light on in this dark room and I beheld some pretty good things in there. I saw kindness, love, respect, self-control, honesty and many, many more beautiful things. What's amazing in all of this, it was myself that I saw. I realized for the first time in my life I had sincerely and truly found myself. The other amazing thing is, I didn't hate myself anymore because I understood.

R.P. Ontario,
Canada

Since I've been doing this course, I have gone seven months major ticket free [without major disciplinary action], which I have never done and I'm involved in a trade called food tech and I'm steadily bettering myself. I would like everyone to know that this course has done a great deal for me and I'm very thankful for it. 'Cause now I feel ready for the real world and ready for the people around me. Thank you!

J.W. Michigan

While taking The Way to Happiness Course I felt a renewed sense of pride in who I really am and my capabilities to do good. I have regained certainty that I am not a bad person. I made a mistake and I have paid my debt to society. Now this course has relighted in me to be good and do good, because only that will ensure my happiness and the happiness of others.

T.A.C. Indiana

Criminon on the Internet

Further information about Criminon can be found on its Internet site located at: **http://www.criminon.org.**

APPLIED SCHOLASTICS:
A REVOLUTION IN EDUCATION

As early as 1950, L. Ron Hubbard expressed his deep concern over the poor quality of so-called "modern" education.

"Today's children will become tomorrow's civilization," he wrote. "The end and goal of any society as it addresses the problem of education is to raise the ability, the initiative and the cultural level, and with all these the survival level of that society. And when a society forgets any one of these things it is destroying itself by its own educational mediums."

Decades later, Mr. Hubbard's observation has proven accurate. And, unless the deterioration of society's educational systems is arrested, continued societal disintegration can be predicted. There is hope, however, for Mr. Hubbard developed breakthrough educational technology capable of turning schools into institutions of unprecedented learning excellence, and of transforming today's alarmingly widespread illiteracy into new vistas of opportunity.

Improving Education with
L. Ron Hubbard's Study Technology

The ability to understand and retain data, to actually be able to *learn,* is vital for almost anyone in today's world, adult or child. New technologies, the constant avalanche of information, even something as simple as reading the directions of household electronic equipment requires comprehension.

L. Ron Hubbard's study technology is thus an advance of gigantic significance in a world of steady educational decline, a world in which the field of education has abdicated its role to the extent that today students are not even taught *how* to learn. Study technology is a vast body of knowledge that not only consistently teaches people to learn how to learn, but delineates the previously unknown three major barriers to effective study. Armed with this knowledge, anyone can now successfully study. And altogether this represents nothing less than a revolution in the field of education.

It is the job of Applied Scholastics to place this technology in the hands of the world's students and educators. Applied Scholastics International is a nonprofit public benefit corporation whose purpose is to provide educators, governments, vocational trainers, community groups, parents and students with the learning tools they need to achieve a world free from illiteracy, where individuals know how to learn and can achieve their chosen goals.

Located in Los Angeles, it has affiliated offices in Australia, Austria, Belgium, Canada, Commonwealth of Independent States, Czech Republic, Denmark, France, Germany, Holland, Hungary, Japan, Mexico, South Africa, Sweden, Taiwan, the United Kingdom and New Zealand.

Although founded in the early 1970s, the organization had its beginnings in the previous decade, when government schoolteachers who knew of L. Ron Hubbard's study technology began using it in their classes and reported great improvement in learning abilities among their students. In 1971, the first educational organization specializing in the use of study technology was started in California by a Scientologist teacher.

Applied Scholastics was founded the following year as the operating entity with the mission of advancing public education by

L. Ron Hubbard's study technology is delivered throughout the world by more than 250 groups in 29 countries on 6 continents. Shown here are just some of the fully illustrated educational study materials which can be applied to a wide range of academic levels.

ensuring that those outside churches of Scientology could avail themselves of Mr. Hubbard's study technology. Formed by a team of educators and teachers from a number of American schools and universities, Applied Scholastics today is international in scope, coordinating the many programs throughout the world which utilize study technology. Many Scientology churches and their members support and sponsor Applied Scholastics in recognition not only of its proven results but of its potential to improve life for the students of today and tomorrow.

To date, more than 3 million people have participated in Applied Scholastics programs throughout the world. And Mr. Hubbard's study technology is used in programs conducted by more than 250 educational organizations in 29 countries on 6 continents.

Multilevel Approach

Working at the grass-roots level and with educational authorities, Applied Scholastics addresses seven main areas of education: teacher training, schools, community education programs, English as a second language, individual tutoring and training human resource professionals so that they, in turn, can train their staff.

Among the Applied Scholastics International affiliates throughout most of Europe, there is the Association for Effective Basic Education in Denmark; Centers of Individual and Effective Learning in Switzerland; Studema in Sweden; the Effective Education Association and Basic Education and Supplementary Teaching Association in the United Kingdom. New organizations and affiliates open each year.

In the growing number of schools and colleges affiliated with Applied Scholastics, students who are taught study technology from an early age are routinely eager, bright and interested in life around them, as numerous studies show.

One of the many schools which use study technology is Oregon's Delphian School,

Since 1975, Education Alive has introduced more than 2 million African students such as these from Zimbabwe to L. Ron Hubbard's study technology.

which occupies an 800-acre campus near Portland, enrolling students from around the world in a full-time academic program. It also operates training and apprenticeship programs for teachers, educators, school administrators and parents.

Ability Plus School in southern California, which teaches students ranging from toddlers through high school, also uses study technology at all levels of teaching. And the Clearwater Academy International in Florida, which caters to students from many parts of the world, similarly uses study technology in all of its classes.

In Europe, the Amager International School in Copenhagen has a student body made up of children from more than thirty nations. It provides a standard education in Danish and other key European languages with a curriculum using all aspects of study technology.

In fact, all Applied Scholastics affiliated schools utilize study technology and provide their students with the tools to be self-learners and successes in their chosen careers. The above-average results speak for themselves.

Teacher Training Programs

An additional and highly important aspect of Applied Scholastics is its programs which train teachers to apply study technology. These activities, conducted throughout the world, supply teaching skills based on Mr. Hubbard's methods and rekindle the enthusiasm for learning which good teachers so frequently bring to their classrooms.

In consequence, today teachers throughout the world are giving new meaning to their endeavors. Education Alive, the Applied Scholastics affiliate which utilizes L. Ron Hubbard's study technology in educational programs in South Africa and other parts of the African continent, was established in 1975, and since then more than two million students have been introduced to study tech through seminars and workshops. Greatly aiding in improving the then deplorable educational standards for blacks in that nation, Education Alive has also trained literally tens of thousands of teachers since its inception. In one teachers' college, the dropout rate for teacher trainees fell dramatically to only 2 percent after Education Alive implemented a program there.

Such results bring to life what Mr. Hubbard hoped for some three decades ago. Following his visit to South Africa in the early 1960s, he predicted massive social upheavals and a severe rift between black and white communities. To avert potential disaster, he advised measures and provided the technology that would enable the country's large black population to become literate.

The appreciation and increased hope and human dignity resulting from Education Alive's programs is clear from this teacher's remarks:

"I stand like a warrior to conquer all difficulties I have come across with much ease. The entire world has become a phenomenon that needs restudy and to be observed with a different perspective . . ."

Encouraged by Education Alive's results, major corporations have provided financial support for its vital work.

"Education Alive has rescued me, and saved the lives of many pupils, students and teachers, as well as employees," said one grateful teacher. "I honor L. Ron Hubbard and his successors for the work they have done for the African child. Everybody who has heard these lectures is thirsty for further lessons and, at the same time, in a hurry to go out and experiment with these wonderful methods of teaching."

In nearby Zimbabwe, where L. Ron Hubbard once lived and worked, Applied Scholastics, with the permission of the Ministry of Education and Culture, instituted a study technology teacher training program which has proven so successful, it has been expanded to the entire district of Shurugwi. There, more than 1,000 teachers have been trained in Mr. Hubbard's study technology, and they are currently using it to raise the literacy levels and study skills of 31,000 students throughout the district.

Such numbers are impressive, but represent a much larger tale. In the People's Republic of China, a country with many millions of illiterate citizens, Applied Scholastics International has trained more than 5,000 teachers since 1984. In the Yunnan provincial capital city of Kunming, the City Education Bureau now requires that junior high school English teachers use the Chinese translation of Mr. Hubbard's study materials for their teacher training. The Shandong Education Commission cosponsored a correspondence course for teachers to allow the study technology to reach the population more quickly. And the major textbook publisher in China, in preparation for more extensive use of study technology throughout the country, trained its editorial staff in Applied Scholastics courses.

Extensive teacher training on study technology in Costa Rica has resulted in a more rapid and thorough application of English as a second language for teachers. In recognition of the role Mr. Hubbard's study technology has played in raising the standard of education there, a representative of the Costa Rican Ministry of Education presented a special award to Applied Scholastics at its twentieth anniversary celebration in Los Angeles in 1992.

In Mexico, study technology has been in use since 1976, benefiting thousands of students. In 1995 alone, more than 1,200 teachers in one state were trained in the use of the *Basic Study Manual*.

And offering a broader perspective of the value of study technology in teaching are these words from a long-term professor of English and award-winning teacher:

"I have never felt so good about my work nor achieved such consistent academic successes as I have since I incorporated the study technology of L. Ron Hubbard into my classes. No teacher should enter a classroom without this knowledge. No student should exit a school without this knowledge. This is what we all should have known long ago and didn't. Thank you, L. Ron Hubbard, for your gift to humanity."

Each week hundreds of students avail themselves of the services of the Hollywood Education and Literacy Project (HELP), dubbed a "model facility" by the California Youth Mentoring Initiative of the governor's office.

Grass-roots Programs Bring Hope — and Success

Recognizing that illiteracy has been identified as a cause for many other social ills including poverty and juvenile crime, many have put study technology to work broadly in nonscholastic settings, working directly in communities untouched by meaningful education.

In the Los Angeles area city of Compton, California, the World Literacy Crusade, a nonprofit educational organization founded by a Baptist minister, works in association with Applied Scholastics International to establish community-based literacy and learning programs which utilize study technology (including in Compton itself). These programs have been described by youth counselors as "heaven sent." Not only have younger children markedly increased their reading and communication skills with the application of Mr. Hubbard's study materials, but even gang members, normally disdainful of any remedial education programs, are willingly attending study classes. "These study materials,"commented a community minister who works with the program, "will set people free."

In Lynwood, California, World Literacy Crusade tutors were invited to assist low-achieving public school students to improve reading and math skills. The average reading grade level increased by eight months in just seven weeks of part-time tutoring. Math tests improved 10 percentage points in the same time period. Working with African-American churches, Applied Scholastics initiated a program to train parents as tutors so they could pass study skills to their families and other members of the community. Since then, the program has expanded to other US cities. In fact, inspired by the Crusade, by 1998 more than thirty similar community education programs were underway in the US, Canada, Australia, Malaysia and New Zealand, all working with ethnic groups and indigenous races.

World Literacy Crusade International spokesperson Isaac Hayes, an Academy award-winning musician, entertainer and actor, placed this program in perspective, saying that it "hits at the heart of violence among our youth. It's about more than getting an education. It is about getting hope and finding a way out."

Similarly working at the grass-roots level is the Hollywood Education and Literacy Project (HELP), a tutoring/mentoring facility. Part of the California Youth Mentoring Initiative of the California governor's office—and dubbed a "model facility" by that office—HELP uses Mr. Hubbard's study technology to enable youth and adults to read and write and become successful and productive in life. The project, which works in collaboration with the Police Activities League and Jeopardy programs of the Los Angeles Police Department and other public and private endeavors, has attracted attention from state, local and government officials throughout the United States and now has more than half-a-dozen sister projects. At this writing, hundreds have availed themselves of HELP's services, and in any given week close to two hundred people receive tutoring and mentoring from trained tutors at HELP's Hollywood facility.

The program also trains teachers and mentors to deliver study technology in their classrooms. Those who complete the program report the birth of a newfound excitement for education.

Results

The documented results of Applied Scholastics programs speak volumes of their value. A representative sample:

1. At one school in Los Angeles where study technology is used throughout the curriculum, students taking the Scholastic Aptitude Test regularly score 30 percent above the national average. And, in the nationally recognized California Achievement Test, fourth grade students score two or more grade levels above the norm in reading, math and language.

2. From a literacy program in South Africa, the average gain in reading age was two years and three months. Further, students trained in study technology in government schools have demonstrated an outstanding increase in pass rates for all subjects. From June and December 1995, as an example, the average pass rate in 19 schools increased from 43 percent before the use of study technology to 78 percent after it was implemented.

3. Another study conducted in England showed that students shot ahead 1.3 years in their reading levels after just ten hours of study using Mr. Hubbard's study technology. Comparatively, no gain in reading levels was found in a control group of students not instructed in study technology.

4. In Mexico City, study technology was introduced into a private school. High-school students in one class had failed 95 percent of their materials. After application of study technology, the class passed 90 percent of the materials the following year.

Applied Scholastics International and its associated groups are bringing L. Ron Hubbard's study technology to people from all walks of life and at every level of society—methods which are not only successful beyond any other approach to education, but fully capable of generating a renaissance in learning.

England

Oregon, USA

New Jersey, USA

Among the hundreds of schools from around the world which exclusively use L. Ron Hubbard's study technology

Canada

Massachusetts, USA

Denmark

Virginia, USA

531

SUCCESSES IN APPLICATION

Every day, in schools, learning centers and training programs all over the world, more and more individuals are having the door of opportunity opened to them through the study technology of L. Ron Hubbard.

As a teacher of English as a second language in a large inner-city high school in Manhattan, I have successfully used study technology to help my students become more able people and acquire a greater understanding of the lessons they were taught.

Other teachers and administrators in my school have noticed the change and improvements in my students' test scores and speaking ability, as well as the atmosphere in my classroom.

Their praise has validated my application of Mr. Hubbard's study technology and its goals: that being a good teacher produces students who can apply what they have learned.

L.K.

Over the past six years I have worked as a special education teacher in public schools.

My students could be described as kids who have given up on learning, or the belief that they can learn. After using Mr. Hubbard's study technology with my students it is wonderful to see their self-esteem return, their purpose as a student rekindled and most important—their skills improve. When I see reading and math scores improving with children who have not

moved in their skill levels for two to five years, I know this technology works.

V.G.

At the time I was first introduced to Mr. Hubbard's theories and methods, I was very discouraged about what was happening to student literacy and motivation. I was even considering tendering my resignation. However, after learning about the basic barriers to study and what could be done about them, I began using more and more of the data with students. Eventually, I created an entire study skills course and also taught my grammar and writing course fully utilizing study technology. The result has been one rehabilitated English teacher and hundreds of enthusiastic, rejuvenated students.

B.E.P.

I had to send my daughter to a state school in Holland. After one year at school she had to wear glasses, started to stutter and had a lot of trouble with her math. Even though I was helping her at home, the problems became worse and she became very unhappy.

My son also went to the same school and he became very withdrawn and quiet. His teacher told me he was deaf (reason for being quiet) and he had an underlying psychological problem. Well, he had been a very lively child up until then and not deaf—I can assure you of that!

We decided to move and bring our children to Greenfields School which uses L. Ron Hubbard's study technology in all its classes. Even though there was a language barrier they both felt much happier at their new school.

Within no time my son was a happy, very lively boy again and all the signs of his "problems" were gone, and he could still hear very well.

My daughter's problem with math came down to not knowing the three barriers to study and how to handle them. She actually loves math now and her stuttering completely disappeared.

The use of study technology has saved my children's school life without a doubt!

I.M.H.

I have been in a school without study technology and I know that L. Ron Hubbard's study technology that I use is much better. When I study I learn much faster and I love what I learn about. When I use this, I stay at a nice steady pace. I also know now what I am learning, I can use it, because I really understand what I am learning.

C.B.

I am a teacher at the Ohio Institute of Technology. This is an electronics technical school and we have students from all social backgrounds and educational levels. I used the methodology as laid out in the Basic Study Manual for two quarters at the Institute and met with tremendous success. The school administration was so impressed with my results that they have given me three months' leave of absence to get more training in the technology developed by Mr. Hubbard.

C.K.

Resources are needed that provide teachers with materials to teach students reading. I believe that L. Ron Hubbard's materials, such as the Basic Study Manual, provide a resource that is not currently covered in the K–12 curriculum. I see these texts as an important resource that fill a definite need for reading instruction. I would like to suggest their use as supplementary texts to be used at the discretion of California teachers.

S.C.

Using L. Ron Hubbard's basic study techniques, we found profound jumps in productivity among staff. Employees stopped making costly mistakes.

R.H.

I've finally gotten the data that's been denied to me for so long! I've wanted to know how to study so earnestly throughout my so-called education. It is safe to say that I've learned more on this course than the entirety of my previous schooling.

J.D.

I can think of no more valuable and necessary element of any course of study, practical or theoretic, than study technology courses.

R.V.D.

Some people try to say common things with uncommon words instead of saying uncommon things with common words. But this course taught me to understand simple words which turn out to be the ones we often don't understand. I have changed a great deal in just two days of this course. Yesterday I spent my day practicing what I learned and it became great fun. I no longer worry about how I am going to study. L. Ron Hubbard's study technology is amazing.

P.R.N.

Applied Scholastics on the Internet

Further information about Applied Scholastics can be found on its Internet site located at: **http://www.appliedscholastics.org.**

THE WAY TO HAPPINESS FOUNDATION:
IMPROVING MORALS IN TODAY'S WORLD

Every culture in every age has relied upon a moral code to promote positive, constructive conduct and discourage destructive, harmful acts. Although much in these past moral codes may not seem particularly applicable at the close of the twentieth century or the beginning of a new millennium, when those codes were written they were entirely relevant. They helped perpetuate the family, the group and nation. They provided means by which individuals upheld basic tenets of honesty and mutual trust. In short, moral codes supplied the overriding principles by which men could live peaceably, prosperously and in harmony with one another.

Today's declining morality has long been a point of grave concern. If art and entertainment are any reflection of our culture, then we live in genuinely frightening times. It is an era of gratuitous violence wherein we have the potential for immense destruction, but no corresponding moral standards to check that destruction. It is an age of senseless killing, unrestrained greed and such profoundly deep cynicism that even the concept of morals often brings a sneer. From textbooks which teach that man is an animal to the banning of school prayer, materialists and so-called "authorities" in mental science have helped create a social and academic climate hostile to morality, where human life is viewed as something temporal and accidental.

But just as all ancient cultures required a moral code for their survival, so too does our own culture desperately need such a code by which we may live. Judging by modern crime rates, divorce rates, substance abuse and falling confidence in government, one could predict the seeds have been sown for serious social upheaval unless countered by a commensurate effort to restore traditional values.

L. Ron Hubbard was keenly aware of this situation in 1980 when he observed that our modern world lacked a code of morals befitting our fast-paced, high-tech, pragmatic society. Old values had been broken but not replaced, and many people were left to flounder on rapidly shifting sands of societal change. Moreover, the moral codes of ages past were religiously based and demanded faith that few could muster in this era of waning church attendance.

Even as he continued with his religious researches, Mr. Hubbard always endeavored to bring solutions to the world from a purely humanitarian perspective. And in this instance, quite separate from his religious works — the Scientology religion already had a moral and ethics code — he saw the need for a nonreligious moral code.

That moral code he wrote is *The Way to Happiness*. It is the first moral code based wholly on common sense, and the only one entirely nonreligious in nature. It carries no other appeal than to the good sense of the individual man or woman, boy or girl who reads it.

Beneath the many differences of national, political, racial, religious or other hue, each of us as individuals must make our way through life. Such a way, *The Way to Happiness* teaches, can be made better if the precepts it presents are known and followed, and if one gets others to know and follow them as well.

Life in an immoral society can be much worse than simply difficult. One's own survival is constantly under threat as even the most basic human values are held up to ridicule. To counter such declining moral trends, *The Way to Happiness* contains twenty-one separate precepts — each constituting a rule for living — and has relevance for anyone. "Safeguard and Improve Your Environment" it advises. "Be Worthy of Trust." "Fulfill Your

Obligations." These and the other precepts are fully explained with examples of how each should be applied in one's life and how one can make it known by others. Regardless of the course of any person's life, the precepts can be likened to the edges of the road: Violating them, one is like the motorist who suddenly swerves off the highway—the result can be wreckage of the moment, the relationship, the life. Abiding by the precepts gives one a chance to attain true and lasting happiness.

Loudly applauded by community and civic groups around the world, *The Way to Happiness* rapidly spread across the planet. Soon, *The Way to Happiness* booklets were being passed out by hand on city streets, offered by local businesses and banks and even in classrooms and hotel rooms. To date, copies of the booklet have been passed out to more than 50 million people in more than sixty countries and translated into twenty-two languages.

A Better Life for Millions

The Way to Happiness Foundation, based in Los Angeles, was organized to meet the grass-roots demand for *The Way to Happiness* and to provide copies to the many millions interested in improving moral standards. By promoting the booklet's distribution and use, The Way to Happiness Foundation is changing the lives of the many people reached by it—and thereby improving conditions in communities around the world.

The booklet enjoys widespread popularity because it effectively reestablishes moral values wherever its message is heard and used. It has received more than a dozen US Congressional recognitions and has been enthusiastically endorsed by police, civic leaders, businessmen, educators and other groups who have distributed it broadly. Hundreds of groups and officials have used the booklet to bring about greater harmony in their communities. In recent years the booklet has enjoyed even greater exposure through a series of public service announcements that have aired on more than two hundred television stations in the United States and internationally through the Entertainment and Sports Programing Network.

The Way to Happiness Public Service campaign is popular, not only with the general public—over 23,000 of whom have called The Way to Happiness Foundation for more information on its programs—but also with the PSA directors of the TV stations themselves. One such programing executive, after having seen the ads, said that this material on morals was mandatory to air, as people had to pay attention to it. Another PSA director at a TV station after seeing the ads ordered booklets to distribute to family and colleagues.

The book is distributed through sponsorships: any individual, business or group may donate copies to youth groups, schools, clubs, social service agencies, military organizations or a multitude of other groups. These groups then distribute the booklets to their members or others with whom they are in contact.

Thousands of schools and millions of students participate in the broad promotion of *The Way to Happiness* precepts. With the help of sponsoring groups, local schools and youth organizations initiate projects that range from cleaning up the environment to setting good examples for peers and helping rid schools of drugs. As a case in point, a sheriff in Alabama integrated *The Way to Happiness* into his presentations to local schools as part of the D.A.R.E. national anti-drug program and requested dozens of copies of the book for his officers.

One of the many sponsoring groups is the Concerned Businessmen's Association of America (CBAA), a nonprofit, charitable educational organization founded in 1981. Through its efforts, many young people are no longer involved in drug abuse, crime and gang violence. Since CBAA began, millions of copies of *The Way to Happiness* booklet have been distributed throughout the national school systems, with more than seven million students participating in its programs involving over ten thousand elementary, junior high and high schools.

CBAA has conducted two very successful nationwide campaigns based on *The Way to Happiness:* "Set a Good Example" and "Get Drugs off School Grounds." These consist of two contests, one for individual students who demonstrate how they use the precept "Set a Good Example" in their lives, and one for schools, promoting their efforts to keep drugs off their campuses. More than thirty state governors, along with directors of state alcohol and drug-abuse programs and departments of education in hundreds of communities, have endorsed the "Set a Good Example" contest using *The Way to Happiness.*

One Ohio school, prior to becoming involved with one of these contests, suffered routine violence, crime and drug abuse among its students and tested well below the average national reading level. After participating in the program for two years, the school was declared drug-free and reading levels had risen well above the national level.

Similar results were found in a middle school in Nashville, Tennessee. Before using *The Way to Happiness* book in the contest program the school averaged nineteen referrals for fighting and misbehavior to the principal's office per week. After the Way to Happiness contest was implemented, the principal reported that "We decreased the violence by 70 percent to 80 percent over the school year."

An independent study of the results of the "Set a Good Example" contest found that 90 percent of teachers whose students participated in the contest reported positive attitude changes in their children. Students were described as more positive and proud of their accomplishments, working together and being more friendly and helpful. The study also found 80.5 percent of the students felt they had learned much from the program, and that 77 percent were using what they learned from *The Way to Happiness* booklet in their everyday lives.

The Way to Happiness is also reaching into the hearts of cities, where gang violence and street warfare have been a way of life. The simple reading of this booklet has actually brought reform to hundreds of gang members.

As a dramatic case in point, in Los Angeles, after hard-core gang members read (or, in some cases, were read to from) *The Way to Happiness,* they voluntarily removed graffiti from 130 buildings in their neighborhood, while passing out hundreds of copies of the booklet to neighbors.

Many concerned citizens use *The Way to Happiness* to bring their communities together. Such was the case during and after the 1992 civil unrest in Los Angeles. *The Way to Happiness* Foundation volunteers passed out hundreds of thousands of copies throughout the city while assisting on food drives and cleanup actions.

A director of a community improvement association in south central Los Angeles said, "The statistics for major crime in this area have been considerably down for each of the first four months of the year. I know that the distribution of 16,000 *The Way to Happiness* booklets has had a lot to do with this. With the tool of this booklet, we are winning and will have a final victory over the degradation that surrounds us."

Many other campaigns have been sponsored around the world. In the South African township of Soweto, a campaign based on the precept "Safeguard and Improve Your Environment" was supported by the largest food chain in the country and two major labor unions. Still another campaign in the South African city of Pietermaritzburg in the province of Natal was highly successful in easing racial tensions. And in 1992, the South African police requested 114,000 copies of *The Way to Happiness*—one for every policeman in the country.

The booklet has been in such demand throughout South Africa that it was translated into Zulu and more than 130,000 copies were printed and distributed in the Zulu newspaper *Ilanga.*

The president of the National Traditional Healers Association of Southern Africa, Dr. Patience Koloko, after being introduced to *The Way to Happiness* booklet, immediately started using it and has been conducting a campaign amongst her people for the past several years.

Dr. Koloko stated that she has "found this booklet to be of such fundamental grass-roots value in everything that I do that I just have to tell how wonderful it is . . ." She also said, "Personally, I find myself reading and rereading this booklet. It is so small, yet it is so big, its bigness is difficult to describe—somehow when times are dark, and the road is rough, *The Way to Happiness* somehow opens the door to a way forward." She uses the booklet with her association's members, and "the members repeatedly ask for more and more copies of this wonderful booklet."

And readers of the booklet are in no way limited to those who receive it through schools or hand-distribution. Throughout the United States, tens of thousands of businessmen, executives and other travelers read copies of *The Way to Happiness* compliments of hotels that provide the booklet in their guest rooms. Upon ordering a stock of books for his guests, one Hilton Hotel manager remarked, "It is obvious that the morals and integrity of a large portion of our population are lacking today. Your book says it simply, as it should be, and hopefully will play on the conscience of many people to realize the need to adjust their lifestyles for a more healthy and vital environment, not only for themselves but for everyone around them."

For an even more impressive index of the influence of *The Way to Happiness* booklet, consider Russia, where, just five years after the first printing of its Russian translation, more than 13,000,000 copies had been distributed nationwide, its text also reprinted in *Arguments and Facts*, one of the most popular Russian newspapers.

"I read lots of literature about the harmful effects of alcohol and various indulgences," said one reader who wrote to *The Way to Happiness* Foundation's Moscow offices, "and now I have *The Way to Happiness* booklet by L. Ron Hubbard. I have been reading it just about every day and as a result I no longer smoke or drink, my relationships with my wife and four kids totally changed. This book will save our long-suffering people from trouble that is hanging about us."

MORAL PRECEPTS FROM THE WAY TO HAPPINESS

1   *Take Care of Yourself*
2   *Be Temperate*
3   *Don't Be Promiscuous*
4   *Love and Help Children*
5   *Honor and Help Your Parents*
6   *Set a Good Example*
7   *Seek to Live with the Truth*
8   *Do Not Murder*
9   *Don't Do Anything Illegal*
10   *Support a Government Designed and Run for All the People*
11   *Do Not Harm a Person of Good Will*
12   *Safeguard and Improve Your Environment*
13   *Do Not Steal*
14   *Be Worthy of Trust*
15   *Fulfill Your Obligations*
16   *Be Industrious*
17   *Be Competent*
18   *Respect the Religious Beliefs of Others*
19   *Try Not to Do Things to Others That You Would Not Like Them to Do to You*
20   *Try to Treat Others As You Would Want Them to Treat You*
21   *Flourish and Prosper*

Worldwide Recognition

In one year alone, 324 major recognitions were received by the Foundation, 131 of them from government officials worldwide acknowledging *The Way to Happiness* for its role in fostering greater social responsibility and tolerance.

One former Toledo, Ohio, police officer remarked, "After having read *The Way to Happiness*, I've never felt so uplifted. In a world so wrought with destruction these days, it's a blessing to have such a publication available to help instill strong moral values in our youth today."

In Moscow, the chief of the city's police force — one of the largest in the world — ordered 5,000 copies of the Russian edition of the book for his officers noting: "This book is recommended to you by the Moscow City Police Department in hopes that it will help you lead a better and happier life."

A major of the Ural army stationed in Chechnya decided to help make peace in that region by handing out copies of *The Way to Happiness* to Chechnyan soldiers. He wrote in a letter: "When I read this booklet I understood that it really is the way that leads to a happy life, to love and respect between people . . . therefore I decided that soldiers need to know this book. When I gave this booklet to a person and explained why I gave it to him, he became good-willed towards me and some even became friends."

The troubled nations of Croatia, Serbia and Bosnia have also benefited, with tens of thousands of copies of the booklet distributed and printed in newspapers and magazines. Wrote one Bosnian official after reading Mr. Hubbard's common-sense precepts in *The Way to Happiness*: "This booklet is the most important thing for the people of my country. It is even more important than food."

Even the drug-torn nation of Colombia has felt the impact. The country's largest and most influential newspaper, *El Tiempo,* distributed copies of the booklet to all subscribers and printed a series of quotes from the booklet in its editions. Referring to the violence that had shaken the nation, the newspaper president stated, "The root of this illness is not in politics but in the soul of our people. When I read

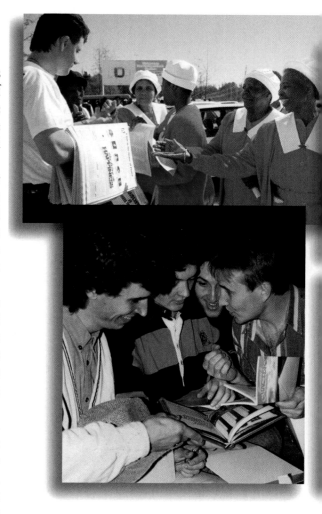

The Way to Happiness, I realized that this is our solution for social and personal illness."

One Colombian army general was so taken with the work that he had 30,000 copies distributed to soldiers fighting the drug war. Yet another general urged judges in Colombia's demoralized justice system to follow *The Way to Happiness* to restore justice in the country.

Colombia's Minister of Education endorsed the booklet, announced a "Set a Good Example" contest, and suggested all teachers, alumni, directors of education and parents organize classrooms where *The Way to Happiness* would be available to help people discuss and handle their problems.

In Mexico, gangs in the cities of Ensenada and Tijuana are using *The Way to Happiness* to get other gang members to reform. A gang leader in Tijuana got gang members educated in the precepts of *The Way to Happiness* and created a mural competition in which gang members depicted these precepts from the booklet. And in

The Way to Happiness *has received more than a dozen US congressional recognitions and has been enthusiastically endorsed and broadly distributed by police, civic leaders, business, educational and other groups.*

another contest in Ensenada, twenty-three murals were painted. Through *The Way to Happiness*, gang members in the area are being transformed into contributing members of society.

The president of Olympian International (and a world-renowned trainer and sports physician) helped get copies of *The Way to Happiness* to many Olympic athletes, explaining: "It's a wonderful way to educate the people on the harmful effects of drugs and to build their self-esteem for better understanding right and wrong by using their common sense."

After reading his special edition copy of the book, the United Nations ambassador from Slovakia stated: "While reading it I found it one of the most moving and touching ways to speak about life and the horrible senselessness of the war. My suggestion would be to print as many copies of the book as possible in all languages and distribute it to the widest groups of people all over the world."

And, in Austria, a government minister said: "After reading about your international campaign based on tolerance, trust and understanding I must say that the values expressed in your activities should be the basis of human life on this Earth."

The Way to Happiness Foundation's humanitarian activities stretch far afield across the world. Following civil unrest in Algeria, a branch of The Way to Happiness Foundation in France rallied volunteers to provide thousands of *The Way to Happiness* booklets to help resolve the conflict.

In *The Way to Happiness*, L. Ron Hubbard has given everyone a guide by which they can chart a course to a world where violence is not a solution to the bumps in the road and where mutual respect and trust make the way smoother for all. Like gentle oil spread upon a raging sea, the calm generated by *The Way to Happiness* will flow outward and outward. The Way to Happiness Foundation helps the revitalization of moral values in our world by assisting in every way possible the spreading of this common-sense guide to better living.

WINNING WITH THE WAY TO HAPPINESS

Moral values have been heavily assaulted in this century. Many people have recognized the decline within their own lifetimes and avidly support the concepts expressed in The Way to Happiness. It has been used by tens of millions around the world, helping spread a common-sense approach to living in our turbulent world.

I am writing this letter in reference to one of the greatest self-esteem/self-help books I have come across in quite a while, The Way to Happiness.

As a police officer, many situations that I see along with other officers are often sad ones. So many people seem to be unable to pull within themselves to find good. The Way to Happiness book encourages people to search for the goodness within themselves and spread that goodness to others.

Officer F.P.
Hartford Police Department

We think that the publication of the book in Lithuanian would be useful and beneficial. Our community, having experienced a long and severe period of communist oppression, is in great demand of spiritual values such as honesty, conscientiousness, sincerity and tolerance. These qualities will help us to overcome the severe inheritance and to advance on the road of freedom and independence to the European community of nations.

Professor L.A.
Ministry of Energy
Lithuania

We like The Way to Happiness booklet because the way we work with children around here is to recognize that they seem to be in the dark about how to handle life. They need real direction, so we try to provide the lantern that lights up the road for them.

The Way to Happiness booklet has the true ingredients for this. It provides moral support, common sense, the real basic things these children need to know to avoid trouble and it is not so lengthy that they can't get through it.

The mother I gave the booklet to told me it helped her to phrase what she had always wanted to tell her children but couldn't find the words for. She said, "This booklet refreshes the things I have always known. Things I felt I myself or someone ought to write a book on so our children could know them. That won't be necessary now that we have The Way to Happiness booklets."

Everyone we give booklets to expresses their appreciation. Teachers, parents, clergy and the citizens here have all wanted extra copies for their friends so they have joined us in efforts to get the booklet into the hands of every parent in the area. We already have requests for over 25,000 copies.

A.H.
Director, Parents of Watts

Participating with The Way to Happiness has been most rewarding to me. I have thoroughly enjoyed hearing my patients' favorable responses. Many have personally thanked me for The Way to Happiness booklet and were pleased to get another to pass it on to friends.

I encourage anyone considering participating in The Way to Happiness program to do so. The more people who have access to this booklet, the better our society will be.

M.S. D.D.S.

Thank you so much for the beautiful book, The Way to Happiness. It is beautifully bound and has a beautiful message. It is a wonderful and insightful guide to living a more peaceful life on a personal and worldwide basis.

T.L.
United States Senate
Washington, DC

Reading the book was very interesting and helpful. I have no doubt that reading and using this guide can help people think and behave in a more positive way. Allow me to express to you my sincere appreciation of the blessed activity of The Way to Happiness Foundation and my best wishes to your success in disseminating the message of peace and harmony.

R.A.
Knesset Member
Jerusalem, Israel

We love your Way to Happiness booklet. The values, moral and ethical, are exactly what we believe schools should emphasize. Maybe, if we start them young, they will have the foundation for happiness. Our students find it easy to understand, and direct and to the point.

L.H.
Principal, Board of Education
City of New York

After having read The Way to Happiness, I've never felt so uplifted. We here at ADD LOVE Productions, have provided our children's performing group, The Positive Force Performers, each with their own copy to study. To date, we've distributed over 1,500 copies throughout Toledo, Ohio and Detroit, Michigan during our special presentations. Everyone who has received a copy only had the highest praise for its positive message.

In a world so wrought with destruction these days, it's a blessing to have such a publication available to help instill strong moral values in our youth today.

D.A.
Executive Producer
ADD LOVE Productions

Thanks for sending copies of The Way to Happiness! We love the whole concept, and it goes hand in hand with our mission which is to inspire girls in the highest ideals of character, conduct and patriotism in order to help them reach their full potential. The book will be invaluable for use in troop meetings, service unit gatherings, and as inspiration to many of our volunteers.

M.C.
West Texas Girl Scout Council, Inc.

Please accept my thanks for the wonderful book, The Way to Happiness. It is filled with gems, and it certainly gives some interesting pointers on happiness.

G.P.
US Congressman
Washington, DC

The Way to Happiness Foundation on the Internet

Further information about The Way to Happiness Foundation can be found on its Internet site located at:
http://www.thewaytohappiness.org.

THE ASSOCIATION FOR BETTER LIVING AND EDUCATION

The powerful social betterment technologies developed by L. Ron Hubbard have given humanity the tools to reverse the deteriorating condition of our society, a fact first recognized by those who themselves experienced his life-saving methods. These individuals have since played a leading role in bringing improvement to society's most troubled areas. Inspired by Mr. Hubbard's words, "We have the answers to human suffering, and they are available to everyone," teachers in the US and England found that their students who used his study technology realized exceptional gains in reading, learning and understanding. Likewise, there was the individual in prison who found that after reading one of Mr. Hubbard's books, he had in his hands tools that enabled him to overcome drug addiction. Others utilized methods that allowed criminals to truly rehabilitate themselves. So it spread. And small miracles began to happen.

These miracles were recognized and application of Mr. Hubbard's social betterment methods quickly expanded into areas across the globe where they were desperately needed. Yet despite the spectacular demand and support for these methods in recent decades, society's decline has rapidly accelerated, fueled by provenly unworkable and even harmful psychiatric-based attempts at education and rehabilitation.

It became clear that only through broad and standard application of Mr. Hubbard's study technology, his drug and criminal reform methods and his common-sense moral code could continued beneficial results be assured, both for individuals served by these breakthroughs and for society as a whole. Thus the need was recognized for an organization to provide these technologies in a form that would always be available for use by secular groups wishing to improve conditions in society—and one which would champion their accomplishments in reforming the abuses so rampant today.

That organization is the Association for Better Living and Education (ABLE), an international nonprofit public benefit corporation dedicated to social betterment. Formed in 1988, ABLE is empowered to authorize qualified social betterment groups to use L. Ron Hubbard's technologies in purely secular charitable and educational activities. ABLE also is charged with the important responsibility of ensuring that this technology is made known and available to anyone who needs it and that the organizations authorized to utilize the technology under the social betterment trademarks are doing so correctly.

ABLE's Commitment to Life-Saving Results

Based in Los Angeles, ABLE International carries out its programs both directly and through a network of continental and national offices located throughout the world. ABLE and its affiliated offices closely monitor the activities and accomplishments of the four international social betterment organizations discussed in the previous chapters covering Narconon International, Criminon International, Applied Scholastics International and The Way to Happiness Foundation.

These international organizations each shoulder the primary responsibilities for their respective areas of concern—whether drug rehabilitation, criminal rehabilitation, education or raising public morals. Through their own network of continental offices, each provides direct guidance, assistance and support to the social betterment groups working on the front lines—all the local Narconon, Criminon,

Applied Scholastics and Way to Happiness groups.

ABLE's function is to ensure that the entire social betterment network is applying Mr. Hubbard's life-saving technology properly so the programs conducted under the names and symbols associated with this technology—such as "Narconon" and "Applied Scholastics" and their logos—are as effective as they can be. ABLE also informs the public of the incredible successes that are accomplished through these social betterment programs. Thus, ABLE not only helps those who directly receive or use this technology to achieve previously unheard of results, it also makes those results known to every sector of society seeking to eradicate drug abuse, illiteracy and crime, and improve declining morality.

ABLE carries out its responsibility by:

1. Researching and chronicling the accomplishments of organizations that administer Mr. Hubbard's social betterment technology in each of its secular applications;

2. Increasing public awareness of all the programs that utilize Mr. Hubbard's social betterment technology through the production of publications and other educational materials;

3. Providing secular groups that use Mr. Hubbard's technology with material they can use to inform interested members of the public about their accomplishments;

4. Overseeing the compilation and publication of texts that contain Mr. Hubbard's social betterment technology, including courses and course materials that guide people in the use of this technology;

5. Permitting only organizations that agree to apply Mr. Hubbard's social betterment technology properly—and only for charitable and educational purposes—to use the names and symbols associated with this technology.

In short, ABLE works to ensure that Mr. Hubbard's technology is applied exactly as written and that the remarkable results of his discoveries are made available to all.

ABLE's Commitment to a New Civilization

ABLE's support and promotion of these invaluable social betterment programs offers new hope for individuals across the world. From the addicted who find new meaning in drug-free lives, to the illiterate who learn to read and suddenly find a future, the criminals who once again find pride in who they are and their potentials, and the children who discover the value of morals, ABLE is helping and changing lives.

While ABLE's mission is to reverse the decline of our civilization—to once again make learning a joy, our streets safe, our people able to face life sanely and rationally—the satisfaction gained by the staff of ABLE and its supporters and volunteers comes from helping individuals, those basic building blocks of our society so often ignored and overlooked. There is no greater fulfillment in any act than there is in restoring hope and pride and competence to such individuals.

The aims of Scientology seek a civilization without insanity, without criminals and without war, where the able can prosper and honest beings can have rights, and where man is free to rise to greater heights. Since the activities of ABLE and the social betterment groups it supports contribute vitally to this goal, churches of Scientology and individual Scientologists alike will continue to do all they can to support their programs.

Man is desperately seeking solutions that *work*. ABLE ensures that such solutions are readily available. As a result of ABLE's work, those who so desire also are able to create a new civilization here on Earth, one in which crime, illiteracy, drugs and immorality are things of the past.

ABLE on the Internet

Further information about the Association for Better Living and Education can be found on its Internet site located at: **http://www.able.org** .

CITY OF MONTGOMERY
PROCLAMATION
BY THE MAYOR

City of Austin
Proclamation
Be it known by these presents that
I, Bruce Todd, Mayor of the City of Austin, Texas,
do hereby proclaim

August 28, 1993
as
Applied Scholastics Day
in Austin, and call on all citizens to join me in recognizing that

Office of the Mayor
Proclamation
Whereas:

WHEREAS: The future of our planet will be in the hands of the youth of today; and

WHEREAS: society lives and works more productively in an environment free of litter and pollution; and

WHEREAS: it is up to the present generation to "Set a Good Example" for the youth of today by demonstrating the need to safeguard and improve the environment; and

WHEREAS: The Way to Happiness Campaign for three years now supported the ideals of the City's litter programs and

CITY OF CARSON
PROCLAMATION
RECOGNIZING THE 25TH ANNIVERSARY OF
APPLIED SCHOLASTICS

State of Louisiana
Buddy Roemer
Governor
Proclamation

City and County of Denver
Proclamation

Office of the Mayor
Proclamation
OAKLAND CALIFORNIA

CITY OF TUCSON OFFICE OF THE MAYOR
PROCLAMATION

The City of Inglewood
Proclamation

STATE OF INDIANA
EXECUTIVE DEPARTMENT
INDIANAPOLIS
PROCLAMATION
To All To Whom These Presents May Come, Greeting:

WHEREAS, the youth of Indiana and America are the hope of the future; and

WHEREAS, drug abuse, crime and violence are a threat to the happiness and well-being of our future society; and

City of Los Angeles
Congratulations
Applied Scholastics International

Lexington-Fayette

City of Flagstaff
Office of the Mayor
Proclamation

The City of San Diego
Proclamation
MAKING AMERICA SAFE MONTH

WHEREAS, the youth of San Diego and the nation are the hope of the future for our society; and

State of Rhode Island and Providence Plantations
OFFICE of the GOVERNOR
GUBERNATORIAL PROCLAMATION

PROCLAMATION

City of Memphis
PROCLAMATION BY THE MAYOR

WHEREAS, Applied Scholastics has been providing quality education around the world for 21 years; and

Proclamation
CITY OF ATLANTA
APPLIED SCHOLASTICS
25th Anniversary

Whereas, The year, 1997, marks the 25th Anniversary of Applied Scholastics, a non-profit educational organization that promotes the improvement of the quality of education for Americans' youth; and

WHEREAS, Narconon an organization founded to rehabilitate drug users is celebrating its 25th Anniversary; and

WHEREAS, Narconon's worldwide efforts to prevent drug addiction and rehabilitate those that have become addicted is headquartered in Hollywood, California; and

WHEREAS, there are now 24 Narconon Centers located in the United States, Canada, Australia, Denmark, Germany, France, Holland, Italy, Spain, Sweden, Switzerland and the United Kingdom treating thousands of individuals addicted to drugs each year; and

WHEREAS, Narconon is fighting the war on drugs on the

WHEREAS, Applied Scholastics provides the tools of literacy and learning known as Study Technology developed by humanitarian and educator, L. Ron Hubbard; and

The State of Wisconsin

OFFICE OF THE GOVERNOR

CITY OF PALO ALTO
PROCLAMATION
"SET A GOOD EXAMPLE MONTH"

WHEREAS, today's youth are tomorrow's civilization and the youth of California and America are the hope of the future; and

WHEREAS, drug abuse reduce the desire to learn, the skills and comprehension of students which directly undercuts the objectives of our schools, whose purpose is to prepare youth for life in our society; and

STATE OF IN
EXECUTIVE DEPARTM
INDIANAPOLIS
PROCLAMA

City of Los Angeles
State of California
PROCLAMATION
Set A Good Example
MONTH

County of Chatham
Georgia

Proclamation

County of Los Angeles
NARCONON
25TH ANNIVERSARY

Whereas, FOR A QUARTER OF A CENTURY, NARCONON HAS PROVED ITSELF TO BE A UNIQUELY EFFECTIVE DRUG REHABILITATION PROGRAM WORLD-WIDE; AND

Whereas, BECAUSE OF UNPARALLELED RESULTS OF THE DRUG REHABILITATION METHODS DEVELOPED BY HUMANITARIAN L. RON HUBBARD, NARCONON HAS EXPANDED FROM ONE SMALL PROGRAM IN AN ARIZONA STATE PRISON TO AN INTERNATIONAL NETWORK OF 24 NON-PROFIT CENTERS IN 12 COUNTRIES; AND

Proclamation

CITY OF ALBANY, NEW YORK
Office of the Mayor

WHEREAS: The Concerned Businessmen's Association of America out of a concern for our youth and their future, created the American SET A GOOD EXAMPLE Contest and campaign TO GET DRUGS OFF SCHOOL GROUNDS and out of our community; and

WHEREAS: This nationwide campaign encourages young people across the United States to set a good example, to educate themselves and their peers in common sense standards of right and wrong conduct as contained in the book THE WAY TO HAPPINESS; and

WHEREAS: The City of Albany proudly recognizes the accomplishments of a special group of students who are the members of Wildwood School, Unit 12 of Shaker Senior High School for the honor of

TOWN of LOS GATOS
Proclamation

STATE OF OKLAHOMA
EXECUTIVE DEPARTMENT
Proclamation

City of Elsa, Texas
proclamation

WHEREAS, The children of Elsa, Texas and America are the hope of the future and drug abuse, violence, and illiteracy are a serious threat to their happiness and well being and that of our future society; and

WHEREAS, 1997 is the 25th Anniversary of Applied Scholastics, a non-profit educational organization; and

WHEREAS, The Concerned Businessmen's Association of America out of a concern for our youth and their future have created the American "SET A GOOD EXAMPLE CONTEST" to help youth get active in their own campaign to prevent drug abuse, violence and illiteracy.

WHEREAS, This contest encourages youth to educate themselves and use the common sense guidelines for living contained in the book THE WAY TO HAPPINESS book by noted author, L. Ron Hubbard to set good examples for their peers of honesty, trust and competence; and

WHEREAS, Schools enrolled in this annual competition have been commended every year in the United States Congressional Record, by Governors of 41 states, by Mayors across the country and leaders of business and industry across; and

WHEREAS, Lyndon B. Johnson Elementary School

Borough of McKees Rocks
Office of the Mayor
ALLEGHENY COUNTY, PENNSYLVANIA
PROCLAMATION

WHEREAS, 1997 is the 25th Anniversary of Applied Scholastics, a non-profit educational organization; and

WHEREAS, literacy is the basic tool of learning, and the people of McKees Rocks, their success, and the success of forthcoming generations depend upon advancing learning skills to meet the technological challenges of the information age; and

WHEREAS, Applied Scholastics provides the tools of literacy and learning known as Study Technology developed by humanitarian and educator, L. Ron Hubbard; and

County of Los Angeles
With sincere congratulations and best wishes, the Board of Supervisors of the County of Los Angeles does hereby join in the celebration of the
Benefit Event
Narconon Chilocco
New Life Cente

CITY OF INDIANAPOLIS
WILLIAM H. HUDNUT, III
MAYOR
PROCLAMATION
"SET A GOOD EXAMPLE MONTH"
June 1991

The youth of Indiana and America are the hope of the future, and drug abuse, crime and violence are a threat to the happiness and well-being of our future society; and

CITY OF SANTA MONICA
Proclamation

WHEREAS, Twenty-five years ago, inside the walls of Arizona State Prison, inmate William Benitez founded the Narconon Program and began the 1st and 2nd phase rehabilitation of himself and other inmates addicted to heroin and other drugs, including alcohol; and

WHEREAS, there are now twenty-four Narconon Centers located in the United States, Canada, Australia, and Europe, treating thousands of individuals addicted to drugs each year; and

WHEREAS, NARCONON is fighting the war on drugs on two fronts: 1) through drug education/prevention programs delivered in schools, juvenile facilities, community organizations, and 2) through rehabilitating those who have become addicted to alcohol and other drugs; and

WHEREAS, NARCONON volunteers are dedicated to fighting the war on drugs to prevent our future generations from becoming addicted.

City of Los Angeles
PROCLAMATION
Safeguard - Improve Your Environment
WEEK
WHEREAS, YOUNG PEOPLE FROM ALL OVER THE LOS ANGELES AREA WILL BE PARTIC

Office of the Mayor
City of Washington
Proclamation

WHEREAS, 1997 is the 25th Anniversary of Applied Scholastics, a non-profit educational organization; and

WHEREAS, literacy is the basic tool of learning, and the people of this city, their success, and the success of forthcoming generations depend upon advancing learning skills to meet the technological challenges of the information age; and

WHEREAS, Applied Scholastics provides the tools of literacy and learning known as Study Technology developed by humanitarian and educator, L. Ron Hubbard; and

WHEREAS, Applied Scholastics is successfully spreading these effective learning tools across the world as well as providing hope for the future to thousands of educators, millions of students and hundreds of educational institutions on every continent of earth; and

WHEREAS, the results achieved through the application of Study Technology over the last twenty-five years continues to raise the learning rate of employees to become 100% proficient in the workplace, better the lives of children and students in schools, learning centers, vocational schools and colleges, as well as save the lives of youth in violent and poverty-ridden areas;

NOW, THEREFORE, I, ____, Mayor of the City of Washington,

PROCLAMATION
From the Office of the Mayor
City of Toledo, Ohio

WHEREAS, 1997 is the 25th Anniversary of Applied Scholastics, a non-profit educational organization; and

WHEREAS, literacy is the basic tool of learning, and the people of this city, their success, and the success of forthcoming generations depend upon advancing learning skills to meet the technological challenges of the information age; and

WHEREAS, Applied Scholastics provides the tools of literacy and learning known as Study Technology developed by humanitarian and educator, L. Ron Hubbard; and

WHEREAS, Applied Scholastics is successfully spreading these effective learning tools across the world as well as providing hope for the future to thousands of educators, millions of students and hundreds of educational institutions on every continent of earth; and

WHEREAS, the results achieved through the application of Study Technology over the last 25 years continues to raise the learning rate of employees to become 100% proficient in the workplace, better the lives of children and students in schools, learning centers, vocational schools and colleges, as well as save the lives of youth in violent and poverty-ridden areas;

NOW, THEREFORE, I, Carleton S. Finkbeiner, Mayor of the City of Toledo, by the powers vested in me, do hereby proclaim 1997 as

THE YEAR OF LITERACY AND LEARNING

Proclamation
OFFICE OF THE MAYOR
City of Orange

WHEREAS   1997 is the 25th Anniversary of Applied Scholastics, a non-profit educational organization; and

WHEREAS   Literacy is the basic tool of learning, and the people of this city, their success, and the success of forthcoming generations depend upon advancing learning skills to meet the technological challenges of the information age; and

WHEREAS   Applied Scholastics provides the tools of literacy and learning known as Study Technology developed by humanitarian and educator, L. Ron Hubbard; and

WHEREAS   Applied Scholastics is successfully spreading these effective learning tools across the world as well as providing hope for the future to thousands of educators, millions of students and hundreds of educational institutions on every continent of earth; and

WHEREAS   The results achieved through the application of Study Technology over the last 25 years continues to raise the learning rate of employees to become 100% proficient in the workplace, better the lives of children and students in schools, learning centers, vocational schools and colleges, as well as save the lives of youth in violent and poverty-ridden areas;

NOW THEREFORE   I, James D. Gilliam, Mayor of the City of Orange, Texas, do hereby proclaim 1997 as

THE YEAR OF LITERACY AND LEARNING

CITY OF SAN PABLO
PROCLAMATION
Applied Scholastics Day
August 28, 1993

WHEREAS, Applied Scholastics has been providing quality education around the world for 21 years; and

PROCLAMATION
APPLIED SCHOLASTICS - 25TH ANNIVERSARY

WHEREAS, 1997 is the 25th Anniversary of Applied Scholastics, a non-profit educational organization; and

WHEREAS, literacy is the basic tool of learning, and the people of this city, their success, and the success of forthcoming generations depend upon advancing learning skills to meet the technological challenges of the information age; and

WHEREAS, Applied Scholastics provides the tools of literacy and learning known as Study Technology developed by humanitarian and educator, L. Ron Hubbard; and

WHEREAS, Applied Scholastics is successfully spreading these effective learning tools across the world as well as providing hope for the future to thousands of educators, millions of students and hundreds of educational institutions on every continent of earth; and

WHEREAS, the results achieved through the application of Study Technology over the last 25 years continues to raise the learning rate of employees to become 100% proficient in the workplace, better the lives of children and students in schools, learning centers, vocational schools and colleges, as well as save the lives of youth in violent and poverty-ridden areas;

NOW, THEREFORE, I, Harold Gray, do hereby proclaim 1997 as

City Of Raleigh
North Carolina
PROCLAMATION

WHEREAS, Applied Scholastics has been providing quality

NOW, THEREFORE, I, ROXANNE QUALLS,
as Mayor of the City of Cincinnati, do hereby proclaim the year 1997 as

"THE YEAR OF LITERACY OF LEARNING"

PART EIGHT

THE STATISTICS AND GROWTH OF SCIENTOLOGY

While religious leaders have long recognized that man's spiritual well-being cannot be entirely divorced from temporal concerns, few churches have dedicated themselves so thoroughly to the cause of social reform as the Church of Scientology. Through its diligence and persistence, the Church is recognized by many as a leading champion of human rights, one that involves itself in arenas wherever injustice has been perceived.

It may seem unusual for a church to actively involve itself, as the Church of Scientology has done, in the exposure of psychiatric abuses around the world, governmental abuses of law and human rights, international law enforcement corruption and a host of other ills that plague society, but the fact is Scientologists care as much about the here and now as the hereafter. The Creed of the Church specifically addresses the inalienable rights of all men, regardless of race, color or creed, and the actions of Scientologists everywhere have given these words true substance.

DEMOGRAPHIC AND STATISTICAL FACTS ABOUT SCIENTOLOGY

This chapter presents facts and figures about Scientology which detail its rapid dissemination and growth around the world. These include results of an extensive demographic survey of Scientologists from every continent which provide a picture of who they are, what they are like, their attitudes, lifestyles and more.

Scientologists represent a tremendously varied cross section of society and include Kenyan farmers, Norwegian fishermen, Brazilian soccer players, Japanese businessmen, Italian educators and on and on. To typify a Scientologist, one must disregard age, race, occupation, nationality or political allegiance, for Scientologists cover the entire spectrum.

Scientologists are healthy (over half do not miss a single day of work in any given year), active (a majority are involved in some form of church, human rights, environmental or charitable activity) and successful in their work (3/4 in the US earn more than the national average wage). Scientologists are also drug-free (none at all use illegal street drugs).

Such figures run counter to many current trends in society and underscore the fact that Scientology helps people lead better lives. More people are discovering and embracing Scientology every day. Its expansion increases because it continues to offer meaningful solutions to universal problems.

WORLD EXPANSION OF DIANETICS AND SCIENTOLOGY

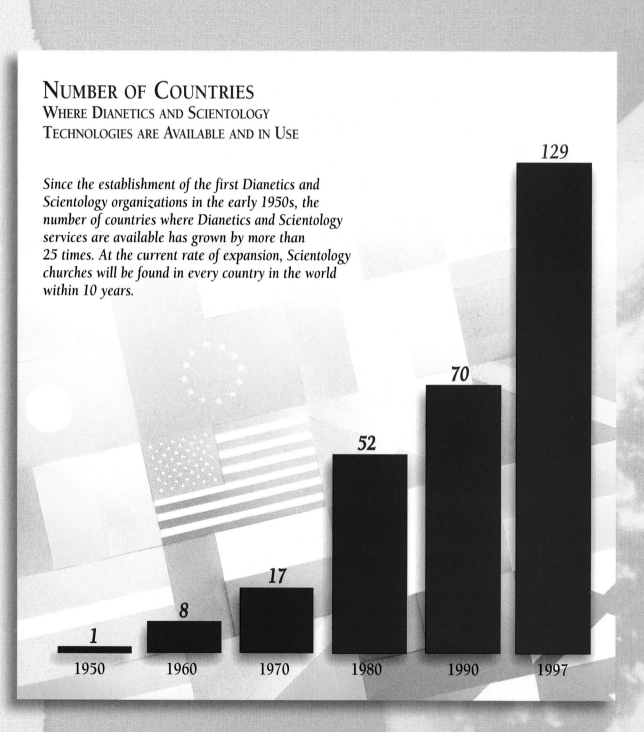

NUMBER OF COUNTRIES
WHERE DIANETICS AND SCIENTOLOGY
TECHNOLOGIES ARE AVAILABLE AND IN USE

Since the establishment of the first Dianetics and Scientology organizations in the early 1950s, the number of countries where Dianetics and Scientology services are available has grown by more than 25 times. At the current rate of expansion, Scientology churches will be found in every country in the world within 10 years.

129

70

52

17

8

1

1950   1960   1970   1980   1990   1997

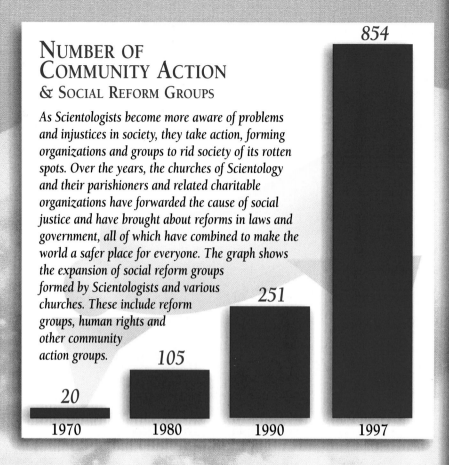

NUMBER OF COMMUNITY ACTION
& SOCIAL REFORM GROUPS

As Scientologists become more aware of problems and injustices in society, they take action, forming organizations and groups to rid society of its rotten spots. Over the years, the churches of Scientology and their parishioners and related charitable organizations have forwarded the cause of social justice and have brought about reforms in laws and government, all of which have combined to make the world a safer place for everyone. The graph shows the expansion of social reform groups formed by Scientologists and various churches. These include reform groups, human rights and other community action groups.

854
251
105
20
1970   1980   1990   1997

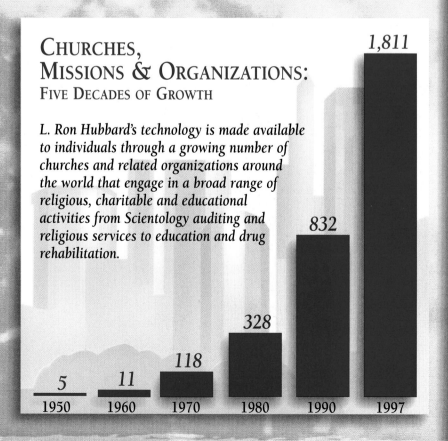

CHURCHES, MISSIONS & ORGANIZATIONS:
FIVE DECADES OF GROWTH

L. Ron Hubbard's technology is made available to individuals through a growing number of churches and related organizations around the world that engage in a broad range of religious, charitable and educational activities from Scientology auditing and religious services to education and drug rehabilitation.

1,811
832
328
118
5   11
1950   1960   1970   1980   1990   1997

COUNTRIES
IN WHICH DIANETICS AND SCIENTOLOGY SERVICES ARE MINISTERED

Albania
Algeria
Argentina
Armenia
Aruba
Australia
Austria
Azerbaijan
Bangladesh
Belarus
Belgium
Benin
Bolivia
Botswana
Brazil
Bulgaria
Burkina Faso
Cameroon
Canada
Chile
China (including Hong Kong)
Colombia
Costa Rica
Croatia
Cuba
Cyprus
Czech Republic
Denmark (including Greenland)
Djibouti
Dominican Republic
Ecuador
Egypt
El Salvador
Estonia
Ethiopia
Fiji
Finland
France (including Martinique)
Gabon
Gambia
Georgia
Germany

Ghana
Greece
Grenada
Guatemala
Guinea
Haiti
Honduras
Hungary
Iceland
India
Indonesia
Iran
Ireland
Israel
Italy
Ivory Coast
Jamaica
Japan
Kazakhstan
Kenya
Kyrgyzstan
Latvia
Lebanon
Liechtenstein
Lithuania
Luxembourg
Macedonia
Madagascar
Malawi
Malaysia
Malta
Mauritius
Mexico
Moldova
Mongolia
Morocco
Mozambique
Namibia
Nepal
Netherlands
Netherlands Antilles
New Zealand
Nicaragua
Nigeria
Norway
Pakistan
Peru

Philippines
Poland
Portugal
Romania
Russia
Rwanda
St. Kitts-Nevis
St. Lucia
Saudi Arabia
Senegal
Serbia
Sierra Leone
Singapore
Slovakia
Slovenia
South Africa (including Bophuthatswana)
South Korea
Spain
Sri Lanka
Suriname
Sweden
Switzerland
Taiwan
Tajikistan
Tanzania
Thailand
Trinidad and Tobago
Turkey
Turkmenistan
Uganda
Ukraine
United Arab Emirates
United Kingdom
United States (including Puerto Rico)
Uruguay
Uzbekistan
Venezuela
Zaire
Zambia
Zimbabwe

CHURCH OF SCIENTOLOGY STAFF

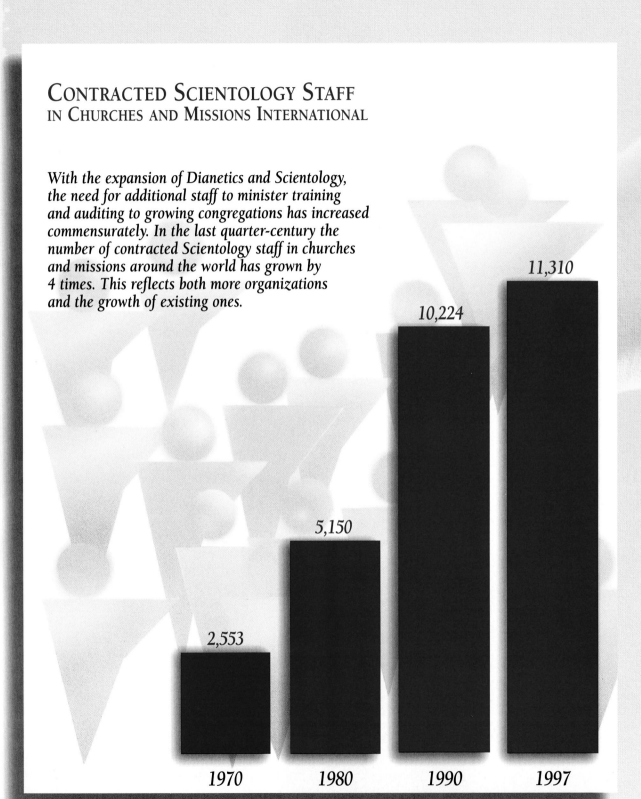

CONTRACTED SCIENTOLOGY STAFF
IN CHURCHES AND MISSIONS INTERNATIONAL

With the expansion of Dianetics and Scientology, the need for additional staff to minister training and auditing to growing congregations has increased commensurately. In the last quarter-century the number of contracted Scientology staff in churches and missions around the world has grown by 4 times. This reflects both more organizations and the growth of existing ones.

11,310

10,224

5,150

2,553

1970   1980   1990   1997

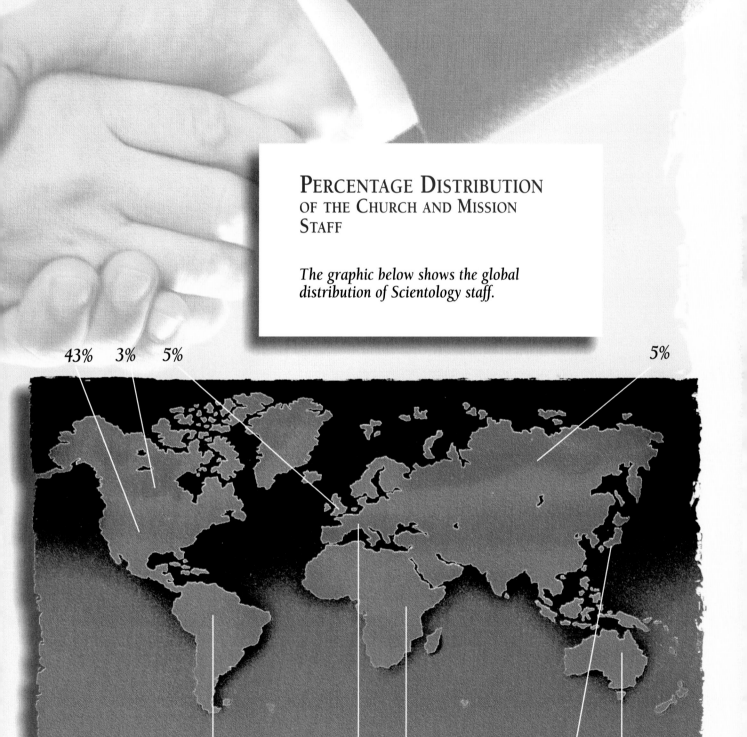

PERCENTAGE DISTRIBUTION
OF THE CHURCH AND MISSION
STAFF

*The graphic below shows the global
distribution of Scientology staff.*

43%   3%   5%

5%

7%

27%   3%

2%   5%

Services of the Church of Scientology

Number of People
Participating in Scientology for the First Time (per Year)

A fair gauge of just how many people are interested in Scientology is the following graph, which reflects the annual number of individuals entering a church or mission for the first time, participating in a service, obtaining a book or hearing a lecture. The number each year increased by nearly 8 times from 1970 to well over a half-million new people by the end of 1997.

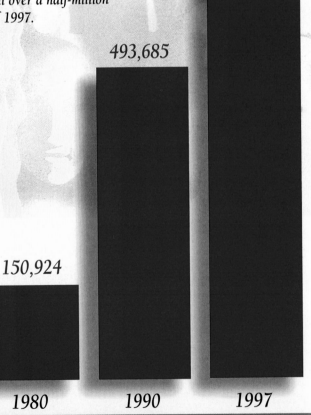

642,596

493,685

150,924

87,045

1970   1980   1990   1997

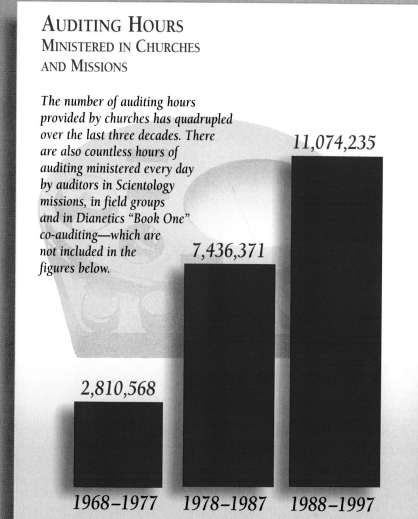

AUDITING HOURS
MINISTERED IN CHURCHES AND MISSIONS

The number of auditing hours provided by churches has quadrupled over the last three decades. There are also countless hours of auditing ministered every day by auditors in Scientology missions, in field groups and in Dianetics "Book One" co-auditing—which are not included in the figures below.

11,074,235

7,436,371

2,810,568

1968–1977   1978–1987   1988–1997

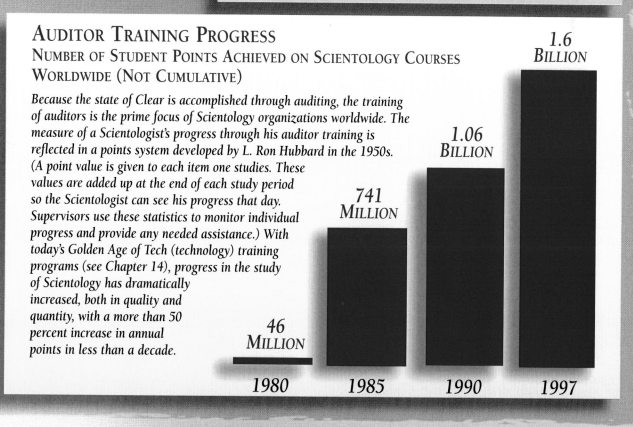

AUDITOR TRAINING PROGRESS
NUMBER OF STUDENT POINTS ACHIEVED ON SCIENTOLOGY COURSES WORLDWIDE (NOT CUMULATIVE)

Because the state of Clear is accomplished through auditing, the training of auditors is the prime focus of Scientology organizations worldwide. The measure of a Scientologist's progress through his auditor training is reflected in a points system developed by L. Ron Hubbard in the 1950s. (A point value is given to each item one studies. These values are added up at the end of each study period so the Scientologist can see his progress that day. Supervisors use these statistics to monitor individual progress and provide any needed assistance.) With today's Golden Age of Tech (technology) training programs (see Chapter 14), progress in the study of Scientology has dramatically increased, both in quality and quantity, with a more than 50 percent increase in annual points in less than a decade.

1.6 BILLION

1.06 BILLION

741 MILLION

46 MILLION

1980   1985   1990   1997

DISSEMINATION OF SCIENTOLOGY INFORMATION

MAGAZINES GROWING IN CIRCULATION

Three of the more important publications for members are **The Auditor**, *the magazine of all Saint Hill Organizations,* **Source** *magazine, the publication of the Flag Service Organization, and* **Advance**! *which is the magazine of the Advanced Organizations. Their increasing circulation reflects the continuous growth of these organizations.*

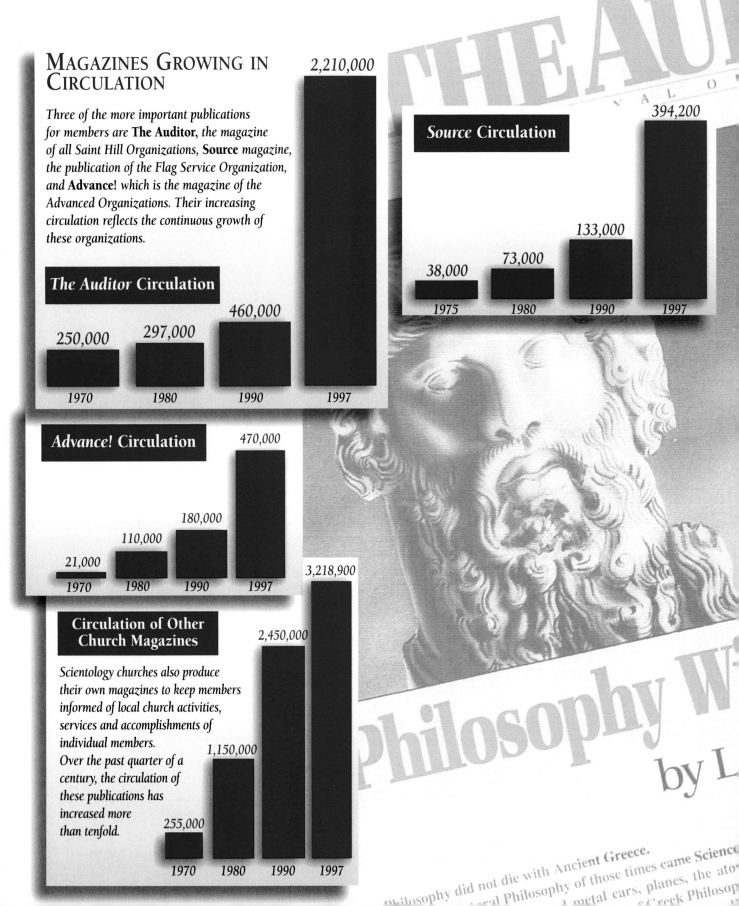

The Auditor Circulation

1970	1980	1990	1997
250,000	297,000	460,000	2,210,000

Source Circulation

1975	1980	1990	1997
38,000	73,000	133,000	394,200

Advance! Circulation

1970	1980	1990	1997
21,000	110,000	180,000	470,000

Circulation of Other Church Magazines

Scientology churches also produce their own magazines to keep members informed of local church activities, services and accomplishments of individual members.

Over the past quarter of a century, the circulation of these publications has increased more than tenfold.

1970	1980	1990	1997
255,000	1,150,000	2,450,000	3,218,900

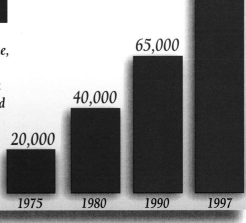

Celebrity Circulation

The Celebrity Centres' magazine, **Celebrity,** *was started in the early 1970s, and by 1975 had a circulation of 20,000. By the end of 1997, circulation had risen nearly 500 percent to 97,000.*

97,000

65,000

40,000

20,000

| 1975 | 1980 | 1990 | 1997 |

International Scientology Magazine Circulation

Throughout the 1980s and 1990s, church publications grew with the expansion of local and international Scientology organizations. With the additions of **International Scientology News,** **Freewinds** *(the magazine of the Church of Scientology Flag Ship Service Organization) and* **Cause** *(the magazine of the International Hubbard Ecclesiastical League of Pastors) in this period, Scientologists in every corner of the world are kept abreast of Scientology news and expansion. At the end of 1997, the circulation of local and international Scientology publications was 400 percent greater than two decades earlier.*

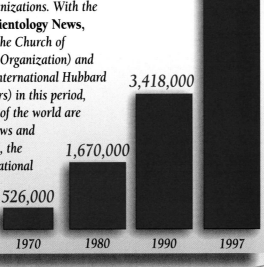

6,630,000

3,418,000

1,670,000

526,000

| 1970 | 1980 | 1990 | 1997 |

Web Page Requests (Hits) to Scientology-Related Internet Sites

42,000,000

10,000,000

250,000

| 1995 | 1996 | 1997 |

SCIENTOLOGY ON THE INTERNET

The dissemination of information about Dianetics and Scientology via the Internet began in late 1995. With the emergence of the L. Ron Hubbard, Scientology and Dianetics sites on the World Wide Web in March 1996, there were as many as 1,000 visitors a day. In two years, traffic to these sites increased 40 times.

Visitors to Scientology-Related Internet Sites

2,000,000

500,000

40,000

| 1995 | 1996 | 1997 |

POSITIVE RESPONSE TO DIANETICS AND SCIENTOLOGY

An independent national research company conducted two public opinion surveys for the Church of Scientology International: one survey of those who had purchased copies of **Dianetics: The Modern Science of Mental Health** and a second survey of members of the Church.

An extraordinarily high consensus was revealed. In fact, the research company concluded it had never seen responses so uniformly favorable.

DIANETICS IMPROVES LIVES

When **Dianetics** bookbuyers were asked, "Would you say that applying the techniques in **Dianetics** has changed your life?" 79 percent responded affirmatively. Ninety percent felt that **Dianetics** was successful in "helping man to improve his potential," while 84 percent felt that the book "helped people become more successful" and "taught people how to be happier."

79%
YES
"Dianetics Changed my Life"

90%
"Helps Man Improve His Potential"

84%
"Helps People Become Successful"

84%
"Teaches People How to Be Happier"

SCIENTOLOGY MAKES A DIFFERENCE

In a survey among Church of Scientology members, 97 percent responded that Scientology has made "a great deal" of difference in their lives, with the remaining 3 percent responding that it had made some difference. Ninety-one percent stated that Scientology had "exceeded" or "met" their expectations.

97%

"Scientology Made a Great Deal of Difference"

91%

"Scientology Exceeded/Met My Expectations"

Ninety-six percent of Church members reported that they had participated in auditing with 97 percent of those who had been audited saying it was helpful and 95 percent saying they desire to continue to participate in auditing services.

97%

"Auditing Was Helpful"

95%

"Desire to Continue Auditing"

One hundred percent of those surveyed agreed that Scientology successfully "teaches people to think more clearly."

These responses are testimony to the workability of Dianetics and Scientology.

100%

"Scientology Teaches People to Think More Clearly"

L. RON HUBBARD'S BOOKS

PUBLIC POPULARITY

The popularity of Scientology can be measured by the number of Dianetics and Scientology books in public hands. The total number of L. Ron Hubbard's nonfiction titles sold since 1950 is more than 62,000,000. The rate of increase in public demand is possibly best seen in the number of Dianetics: The Modern Science of Mental Health *books sold since its release in 1950. The graph below shows the cumulative Dianetics sales since 1950.*

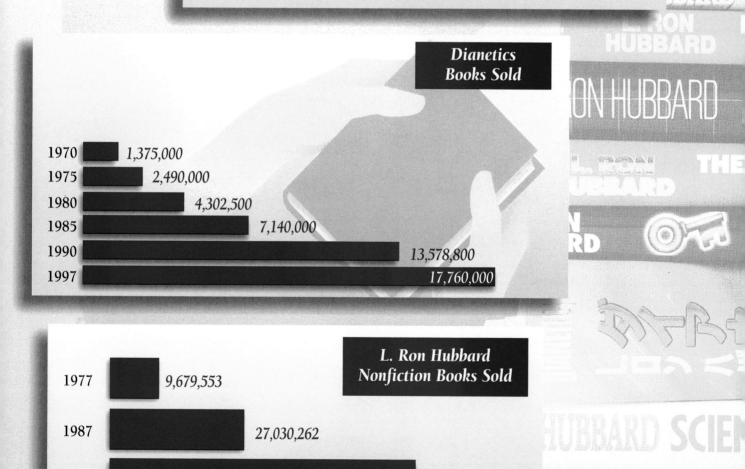

Dianetics Books Sold

Year	Books Sold
1970	1,375,000
1975	2,490,000
1980	4,302,500
1985	7,140,000
1990	13,578,800
1997	17,760,000

L. Ron Hubbard Nonfiction Books Sold

Year	Books Sold
1977	9,679,553
1987	27,030,262
1997	62,152,965

L. Ron Hubbard's works are in huge demand around the world and distributed in the 138 countries listed below.

1. Albania
2. Algeria
3. Argentina
4. Armenia
5. Aruba
6. Australia
7. Austria
8. Azerbaijan
9. Bahamas
10. Bangladesh
11. Belarus
12. Belgium
13. Benin
14. Bolivia
15. Botswana
16. Brazil
17. Bulgaria
18. Burkina Faso
19. Cameroon
20. Canada
21. Chile
22. China
(including Hong Kong)
23. Colombia
24. Congo
25. Costa Rica
26. Croatia
27. Cuba
28. Cyprus
29. Czech Republic
30. Denmark
(including Greenland)
31. Djibouti
32. Dominican Republic
33. Ecuador
34. Egypt
35. El Salvador
36. Estonia
37. Ethiopia
38. Fiji
39. Finland
40. France
(including French Guiana, Guadeloupe, Martinique, Réunion Island, Polynesian Islands—Tahiti, St. Pierre and Miquelon)
41. Gabon
42. Gambia
43. Georgia
44. Germany
45. Ghana
46. Greece
47. Grenada
48. Guatemala
49. Guinea
50. Guyana
51. Haiti
52. Honduras
53. Hungary
54. Iceland
55. India
56. Indonesia
57. Iran
58. Ireland
59. Israel
60. Italy
61. Ivory Coast
62. Jamaica
63. Japan
64. Jordan
65. Kazakhstan
66. Kenya
67. Kuwait
68. Kyrgyzstan
69. Latvia
70. Lebanon
71. Liechtenstein
72. Lithuania
73. Luxembourg
74. Macedonia
75. Madagascar
76. Malawi
77. Malaysia
78. Mali
79. Malta
80. Mauritius
81. Mexico
82. Moldova
83. Monaco
84. Mongolia
85. Morocco
86. Mozambique
87. Namibia
88. Nepal
89. Netherlands
90. Netherlands Antilles
91. New Zealand
92. Nicaragua
93. Nigeria
94. Norway
95. Pakistan
96. Peru
97. Philippines
98. Poland
99. Portugal
100. Romania
101. Russia
102. Rwanda
103. St. Kitts and Nevis
104. St. Lucia
105. Saudi Arabia
106. Senegal
107. Serbia
108. Sierra Leone
109. Singapore
110. Slovakia
111. Slovenia
112. South Africa
(including Bophuthatswana)
113. South Korea
114. Spain
115. Sri Lanka
116. Sudan
117. Suriname
118. Sweden
119. Switzerland
120. Taiwan
121. Tajikistan
122. Tanzania
123. Thailand
124. Trinidad and Tobago
125. Tunisia
126. Turkey
127. Turkmenistan
128. Uganda
129. Ukraine
130. United Arab Emirates
131. United Kingdom
(including Bermuda, Gibraltar and Montserrat)
132. United States
(including Puerto Rico)
133. Uruguay
134. Uzbekistan
135. Venezuela
136. Zaire
137. Zambia
138. Zimbabwe

To meet the worldwide demand for L. Ron Hubbard's works, his books have been published in the 33 languages listed below.

1. Afrikaans
2. Arabic
3. Bahasa Indonesia
4. Bosnian
5. Chinese
6. Czech
7. Croatian
8. Danish
9. Dutch
10. English
11. Finnish
12. French
13. German
14. Greek
15. Hebrew
16. Hungarian
17. Italian
18. Japanese
19. Korean
20. Norwegian
21. Polish
22. Portuguese
23. Punjabi
24. Russian
25. Serbian
26. Sotho
27. Spanish
28. Swahili
29. Swedish
30. Taiwanese
31. Urdu
32. Xhosa
33. Zulu

SOCIAL BETTERMENT AND REFORM ACTIVITIES

NUMBER OF
SOCIAL BETTERMENT GROUPS

One way the Church of Scientology and its members actively participate in bettering society is by establishing non-church groups and organizations around the world. Using L. Ron Hubbard's technology, Scientologists help children with school and study problems, work to rehabilitate drug addicts and criminals, and bring about a safer environment through programs to increase moral values. The graph above shows the number of officially established and recognized groups using L. Ron Hubbard's technology to better social problems. There are many thousands of others less formally organized and not reflected in these figures, but no less dedicated or effective.

457

164

38

6

1970   1980   1990   1997

NARCONON
DRUG EDUCATION

The Narconon drug rehabilitation program that uses L. Ron Hubbard's technology gets people off drugs and also delivers drug education lectures and seminars to schools and community groups.

Launching its educational program in the early 1980s in response to the onslaught of cocaine and crack addiction among Western youth, Narconon has delivered thousands of lectures and helped nearly 1 million students and adults avoid the horrors of drug use.

The figures below are cumulative for each area.

NARCONON CENTER	NUMBER OF LECTURES	NUMBER OF ATTENDEES
Greater Los Angeles	5,665	215,990
Boston	3,544	380,559
Italy	1,651	302,102
Chilocco	540	24,796
Spain	35	2,580
Sweden	1,125	36,487
Switzerland	73	2,793
Denmark	400	13,326
Canada	160	10,999
Cumulative Total:	13,193	989,632

Effectiveness of Narconon
Demonstrated by Government Study

A study completed and released by an independent sociological research group in Spain on the success of Narconon confirmed the remarkable results of Narconon.

Of the students surveyed, 78.4 percent were still off drugs two years later and had completely ceased all criminal activity. Over two-thirds of those who had received other types of rehabilitation treatment stated the effects from these treatments had been negative and unsuccessful, while 86.5 percent rated Narconon as very positive and 89.2 percent stated that the Narconon staff were very qualified.

78.4%

**Still off Drugs
after 2 Years**

86.5%

**Positive Results
from Narconon**

89.2%

**Narconon Staff Are
Very Qualified**

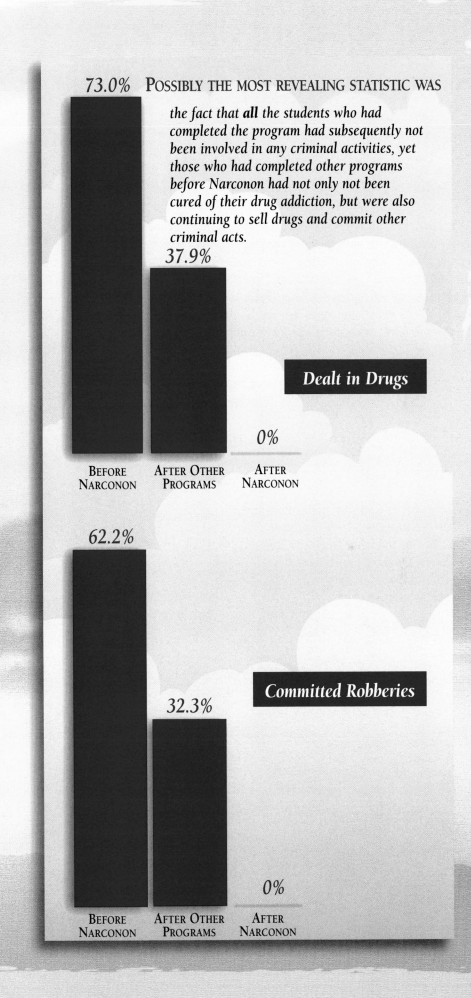

73.0% POSSIBLY THE MOST REVEALING STATISTIC WAS

the fact that **all** the students who had completed the program had subsequently not been involved in any criminal activities, yet those who had completed other programs before Narconon had not only not been cured of their drug addiction, but were also continuing to sell drugs and commit other criminal acts.

37.9%

Dealt in Drugs

0%

BEFORE
NARCONON

AFTER OTHER
PROGRAMS

AFTER
NARCONON

62.2%

Committed Robberies

32.3%

0%

BEFORE
NARCONON

AFTER OTHER
PROGRAMS

AFTER
NARCONON

VITAL STATISTICS OF SCIENTOLOGISTS ACROSS THE WORLD

WHAT ARE SCIENTOLOGISTS LIKE?

What are their backgrounds and how do they live? What is important to them and what are their habits and interests? To answer these questions, surveys were mailed to Scientologists around the world. The statistics and graphs on the following pages reflect the results—showing attitudes, lifestyles and backgrounds of Scientologists. (A margin of ±3 percent is allowed to cover both statistical and sampling errors.)

HOW WERE YOU INTRODUCED TO SCIENTOLOGY?

Scientologists want their friends to know about what they find helpful. It is no surprise then that well over half of today's Church members were first introduced to Scientology through a friend or relative.

AGE WHEN FIRST INTRODUCED TO SCIENTOLOGY

Lecture
3.1%

Through an advertisement
4.8%

Other
0.9%

Through reading a Dianetics or Scientology book
20.6%

Through a personality test
18.0%

Through a friend or relative
52.6%

26–30 years
19.5%

31–40 years
12.4%

21–25 years
36.6%

Over 40 years
4.3%

Under 20 years
27.1%

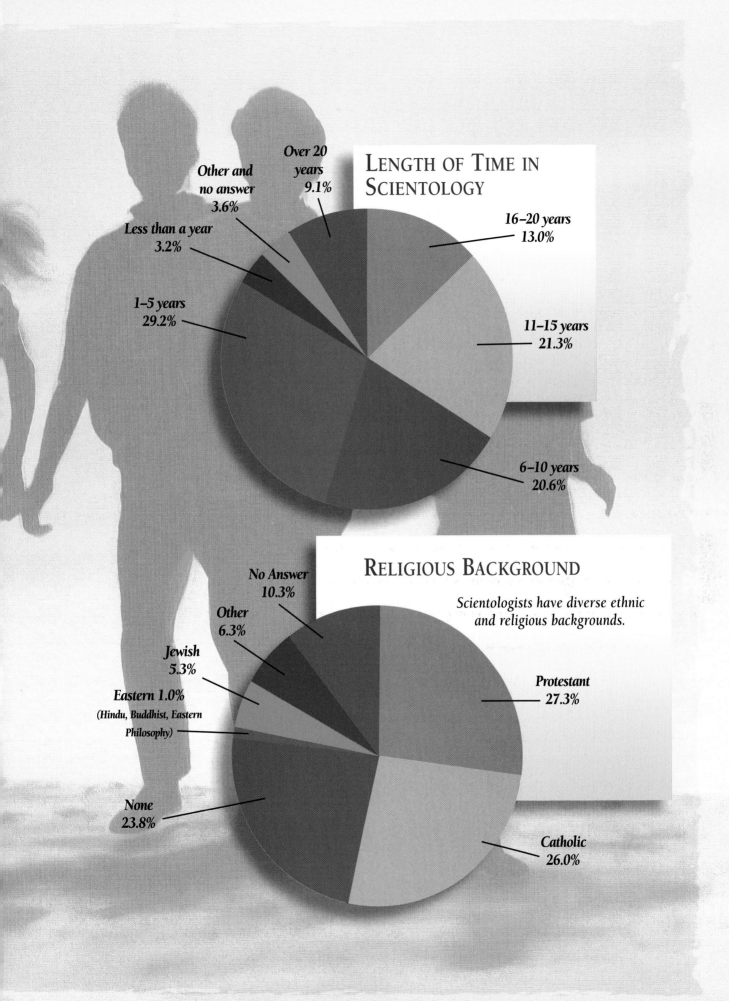

LENGTH OF TIME IN SCIENTOLOGY

Over 20 years
9.1%

Other and
no answer
3.6%

Less than a year
3.2%

1–5 years
29.2%

16–20 years
13.0%

11–15 years
21.3%

6–10 years
20.6%

RELIGIOUS BACKGROUND

*Scientologists have diverse ethnic
and religious backgrounds.*

No Answer
10.3%

Other
6.3%

Jewish
5.3%

Eastern 1.0%
(Hindu, Buddhist, Eastern
Philosophy)

None
23.8%

Protestant
27.3%

Catholic
26.0%

MARITAL STATUS

Statistics show that the marriage rate more than doubles after involvement in Scientology. Marriage is seen as vital to almost three times as many after Scientology as before. More than just recognizing the value of creating and maintaining successful relationships, Scientologists have the technology to bring these about which results in close, happy families and long-lasting marriages.

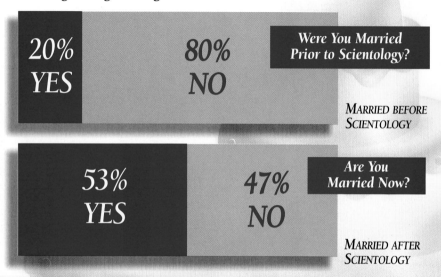

20%
YES

80%
NO

Were You Married Prior to Scientology?

MARRIED BEFORE SCIENTOLOGY

53%
YES

47%
NO

Are You Married Now?

MARRIED AFTER SCIENTOLOGY

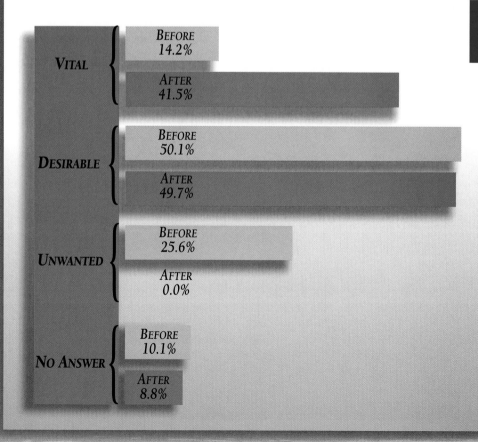

What Was Your Attitude Toward Marriage Prior to and after Becoming a Scientologist?

VITAL
BEFORE 14.2%
AFTER 41.5%

DESIRABLE
BEFORE 50.1%
AFTER 49.7%

UNWANTED
BEFORE 25.6%
AFTER 0.0%

NO ANSWER
BEFORE 10.1%
AFTER 8.8%

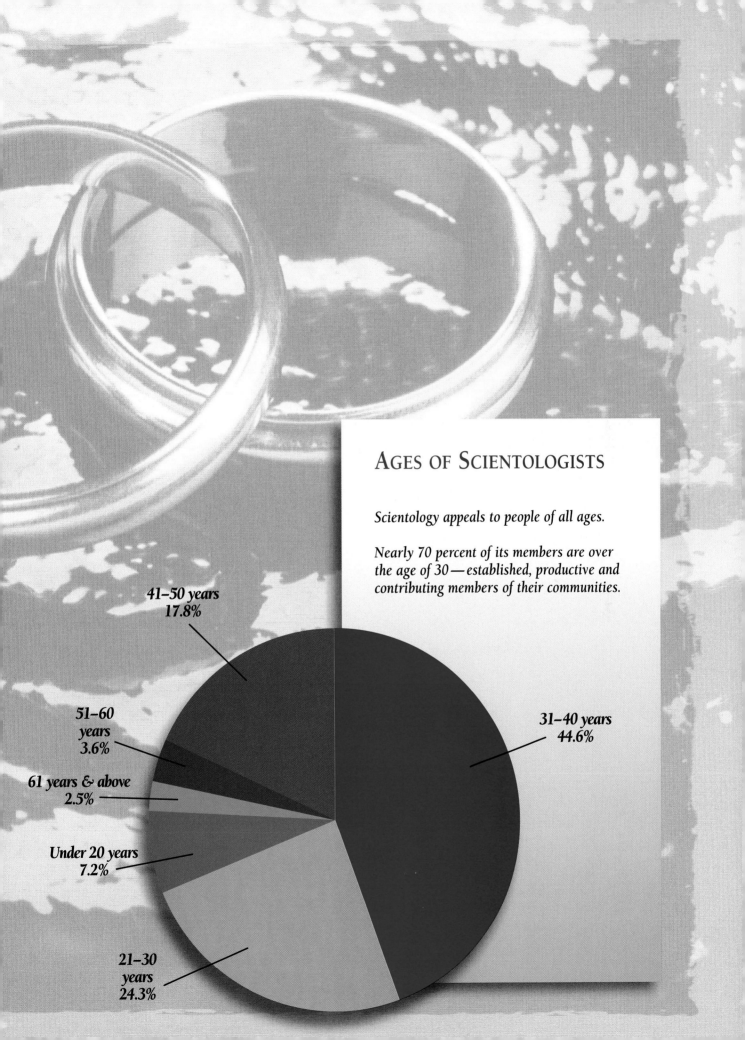

AGES OF SCIENTOLOGISTS

Scientology appeals to people of all ages.

Nearly 70 percent of its members are over the age of 30 — established, productive and contributing members of their communities.

**41–50 years
17.8%**

**51–60
years
3.6%**

**61 years & above
2.5%**

**Under 20 years
7.2%**

**31–40 years
44.6%**

**21–30
years
24.3%**

SCIENTOLOGISTS
AND THEIR FAMILIES

Over 97 percent of married couples who are Scientologists have children. They enjoy raising children and ensure that their children are involved in community and school projects, sports and other activities to give them a well-rounded upbringing. (As a comparative, US census statistics show that 51 percent of America's married couples do not have children.)

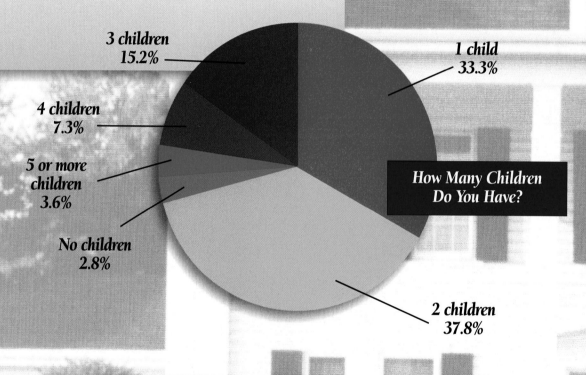

3 children 15.2%

4 children 7.3%

5 or more children 3.6%

No children 2.8%

1 child 33.3%

How Many Children Do You Have?

2 children 37.8%

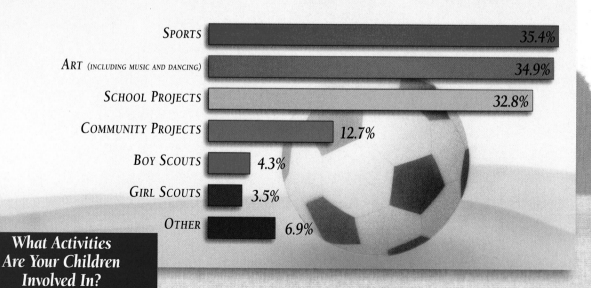

SPORTS	35.4%
ART (INCLUDING MUSIC AND DANCING)	34.9%
SCHOOL PROJECTS	32.8%
COMMUNITY PROJECTS	12.7%
BOY SCOUTS	4.3%
GIRL SCOUTS	3.5%
OTHER	6.9%

What Activities Are Your Children Involved In?

SCIENTOLOGISTS'
RESIDENCES

With over 50 percent of Scientologists married with children, corresponding numbers own or rent homes.

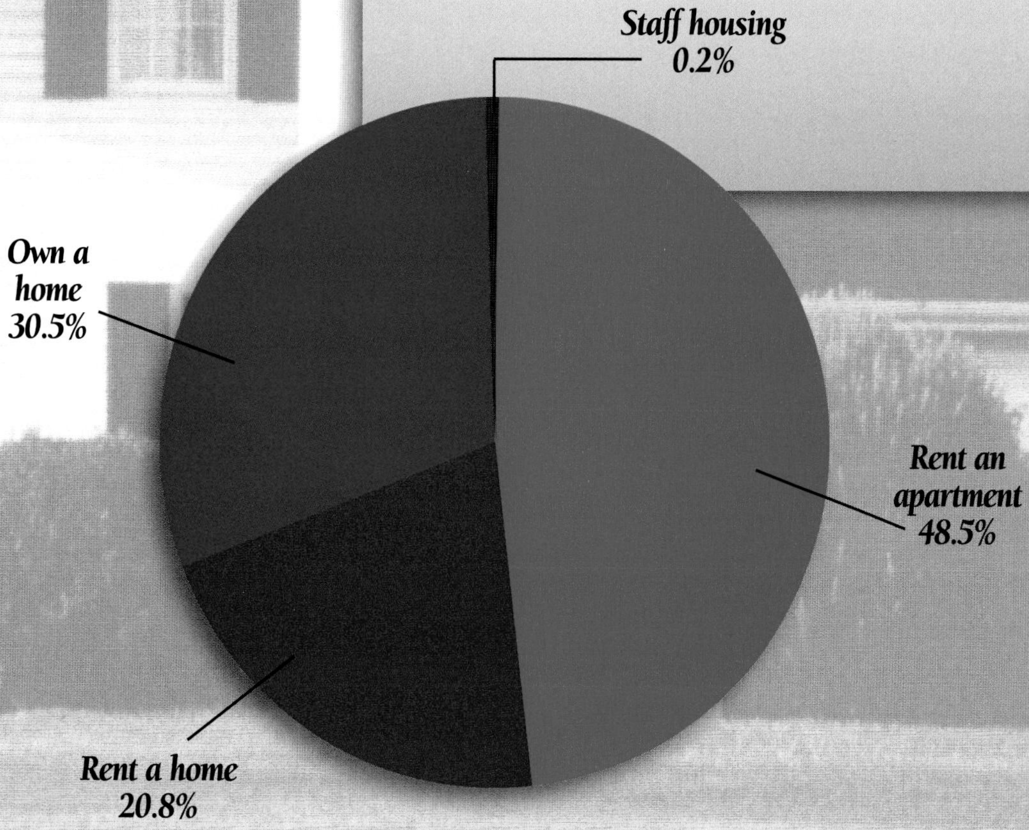

**Staff housing
0.2%**

**Own a
home
30.5%**

**Rent an
apartment
48.5%**

**Rent a home
20.8%**

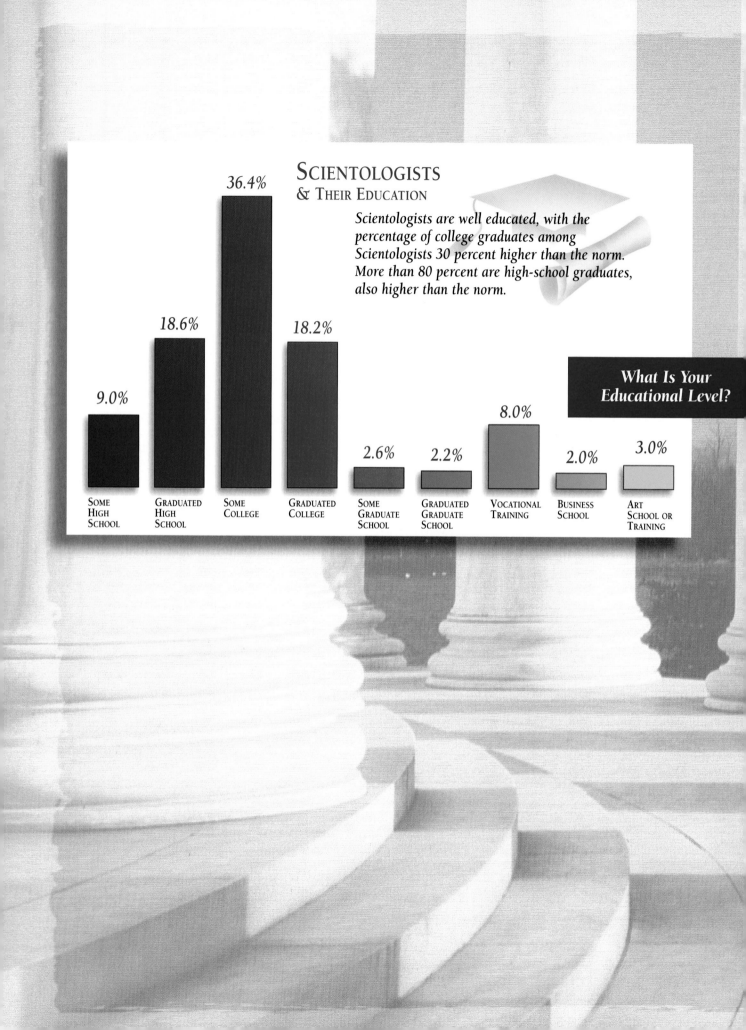

SCIENTOLOGISTS
& THEIR EDUCATION

Scientologists are well educated, with the percentage of college graduates among Scientologists 30 percent higher than the norm. More than 80 percent are high-school graduates, also higher than the norm.

What Is Your Educational Level?

36.4%

18.6%

18.2%

9.0%

8.0%

2.6%

2.2%

2.0%

3.0%

SOME HIGH SCHOOL

GRADUATED HIGH SCHOOL

SOME COLLEGE

GRADUATED COLLEGE

SOME GRADUATE SCHOOL

GRADUATED GRADUATE SCHOOL

VOCATIONAL TRAINING

BUSINESS SCHOOL

ART SCHOOL OR TRAINING

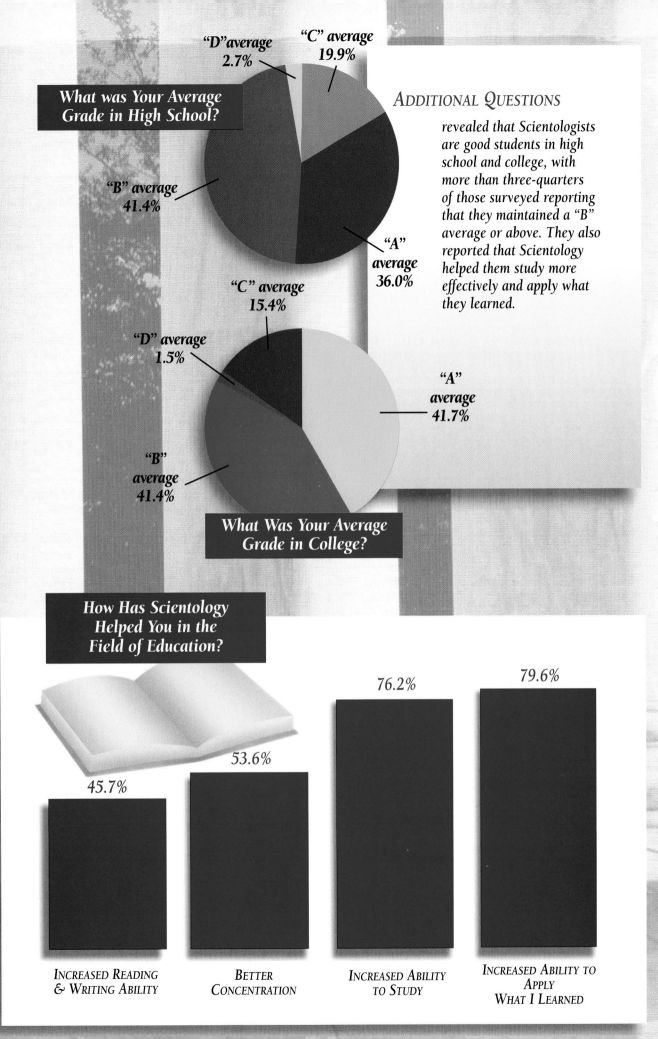

What was Your Average Grade in High School?

"D"average 2.7%

"C" average 19.9%

"B" average 41.4%

"A" average 36.0%

ADDITIONAL QUESTIONS

revealed that Scientologists are good students in high school and college, with more than three-quarters of those surveyed reporting that they maintained a "B" average or above. They also reported that Scientology helped them study more effectively and apply what they learned.

"C" average 15.4%

"D" average 1.5%

"B" average 41.4%

"A" average 41.7%

What Was Your Average Grade in College?

How Has Scientology Helped You in the Field of Education?

45.7%

53.6%

76.2%

79.6%

INCREASED READING & WRITING ABILITY

BETTER CONCENTRATION

INCREASED ABILITY TO STUDY

INCREASED ABILITY TO APPLY WHAT I LEARNED

75.1% *Improved Competence*

50.5% *More Able to Deal with Stress at Work*

48.3% *Improved Relationships with Other Employees*

3.0% **Other**

What Have Your Occupational Gains Been As a Result of Scientology?

SCIENTOLOGISTS & WORK

Scientologists find that no matter what their occupation, Scientology helps them improve their competence. As a result they are more productive and valuable to their profession.

What Is Your Current Occupation?

Managerial Position	16.5%
Arts, Technical & Engineering	15.6%
Owner or Part-owner of Company	14.0%
Sales	10.2%
Computers	8.1%
Teaching	6.2%
Medical (including Nursing, Dental, etc.)	5.8%
Construction	5.5%
Student	4.8%
Marketing & Advertising	4.6%
Clerical	4.5%
Secretarial	4.0%
Communications	2.7%
Law	1.3%
Sports	0.9%
Civil Service	0.8%
Armed Forces	0.5%

INCOME INFORMATION

Per an independent national research group study of individuals who have purchased and read the book **Dianetics: The Modern Science of Mental Health**, *84 percent of* **Dianetics** *book readers felt that Dianetics helped people become more successful. One measurement of success is the amount of income one makes.*

An average annual wage in the United States in the 1990s was $22,563: Of Scientologists surveyed, nearly 80 percent earn in excess of the national average.

Scientologists do not look toward others to help them survive. They work hard to support themselves and their families. The percentage of Scientologists on welfare (which includes Scientologists in such countries as Sweden, Denmark and the United Kingdom where public assistance is even more prevalent than in the United States) is less than half of the average in the United States, which today is estimated at 4 percent.

What is your average yearly income bracket since Scientology?

Above US National Average

80.0%

Do you receive welfare?

NO

98.1%

SCIENTOLOGISTS' HEALTH

Scientologists make productive employees. Almost 75 percent report they are ill less often than they were before Scientology. More than half report that, in the last year, they did not miss any days of work due to illness, and over 85 percent miss less than the United States absenteeism average of almost 5 days missed a year due to illness.

A health-and-employee-benefits insurance expert reviewed the medical expenses for the 1,200 staff of the Church of Scientology International. He stated that its per capita medical costs ran between 10 percent and 20 percent of the national average.

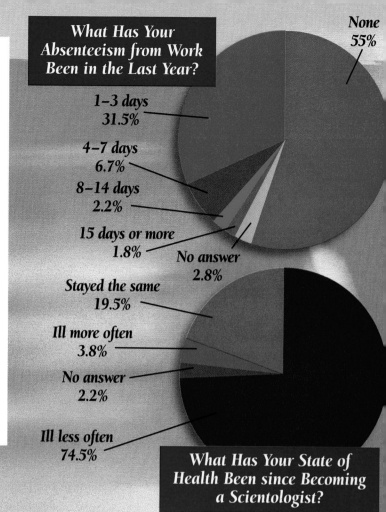

What Has Your Absenteeism from Work Been in the Last Year?

None 55%

1–3 days 31.5%

4–7 days 6.7%

8–14 days 2.2%

15 days or more 1.8%

No answer 2.8%

Stayed the same 19.5%

Ill more often 3.8%

No answer 2.2%

Ill less often 74.5%

What Has Your State of Health Been since Becoming a Scientologist?

SCIENTOLOGISTS ARE LESS ACCIDENT-PRONE

Scientologists find that auditing and training greatly improve awareness of surroundings. In being more aware of the environment, Scientologists tend to be less accident-prone than others. The following statistics show that after Scientology the number of individuals involved in accidents is dramatically decreased.

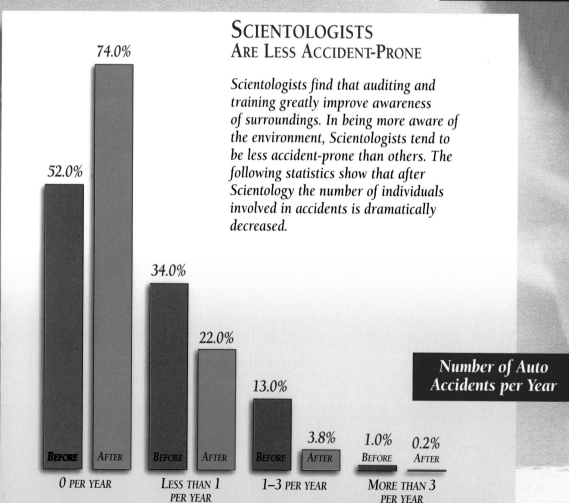

Number of Auto Accidents per Year

74.0%

52.0%

34.0%

22.0%

13.0%

3.8%

1.0%

0.2%

| BEFORE | AFTER | BEFORE | AFTER | BEFORE | AFTER | BEFORE | AFTER |

| 0 PER YEAR | LESS THAN 1 PER YEAR | 1–3 PER YEAR | MORE THAN 3 PER YEAR |

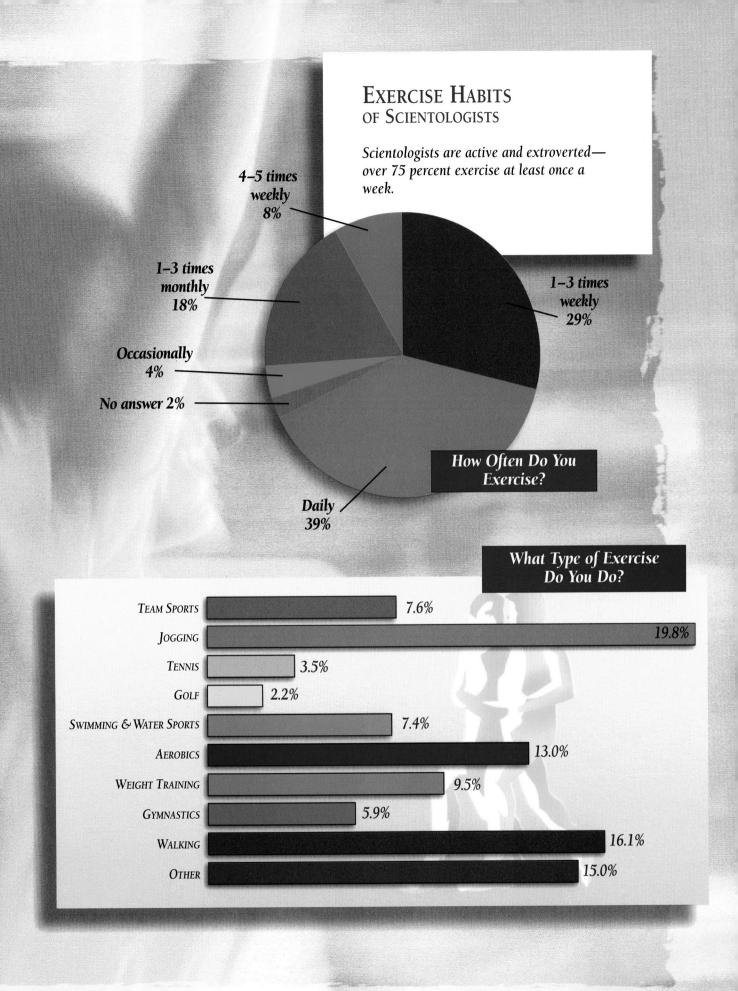

EXERCISE HABITS
OF SCIENTOLOGISTS

Scientologists are active and extroverted—over 75 percent exercise at least once a week.

4–5 times weekly
8%

1–3 times monthly
18%

Occasionally
4%

No answer 2%

1–3 times weekly
29%

Daily
39%

How Often Do You Exercise?

What Type of Exercise Do You Do?

TEAM SPORTS	7.6%
JOGGING	19.8%
TENNIS	3.5%
GOLF	2.2%
SWIMMING & WATER SPORTS	7.4%
AEROBICS	13.0%
WEIGHT TRAINING	9.5%
GYMNASTICS	5.9%
WALKING	16.1%
OTHER	15.0%

DRUG INTAKE OF SCIENTOLOGISTS

In a drug-ridden culture, it is a fact that all Scientologists are drug-free. 100 percent say they take no street drugs at all. This statistic is even more dramatic when compared to the 1990 US government figures showing that over 50 percent of the general population between the ages of 18 to 25 use drugs.

Had You Taken Street Drugs Prior to Being in Scientology?

No 38.5%

Yes 61.5%

No 100%

Do You Currently Take Street Drugs?

One time 11.1%

Currently taking medical drugs as prescribed 2.3%

More than one time 5.0%

Have You Used Medical Drugs During the Last Year?

No 81.6%

ALCOHOL USE BY SCIENTOLOGISTS

Alcohol-use surveys done in the United States revealed that 7 percent drank alcohol daily, 56 percent sometimes and 37 percent never. In comparison, Scientologists' use of alcohol is lower than averages for the US and no Scientologist surveyed drinks on a daily basis.

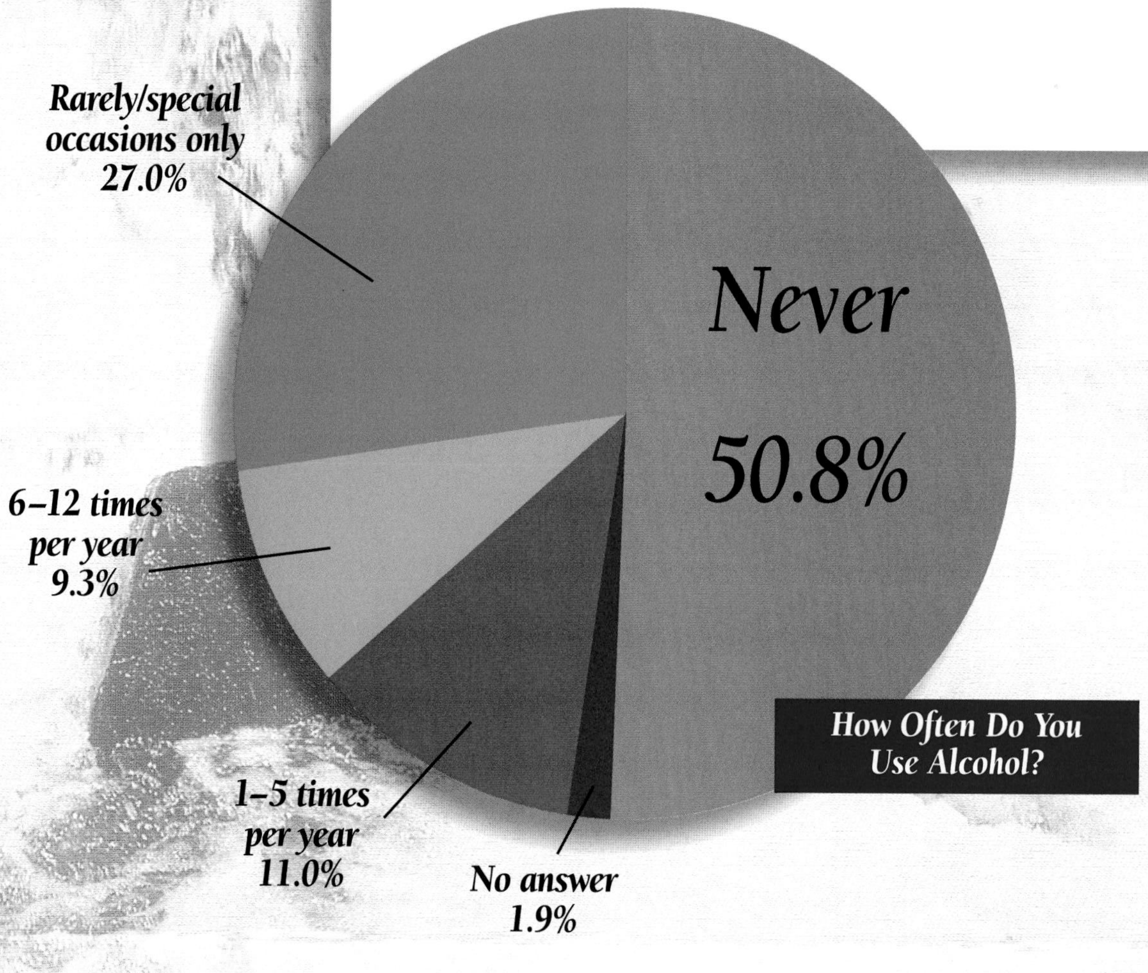

Rarely/special occasions only 27.0%

6–12 times per year 9.3%

1–5 times per year 11.0%

No answer 1.9%

Never 50.8%

How Often Do You Use Alcohol?

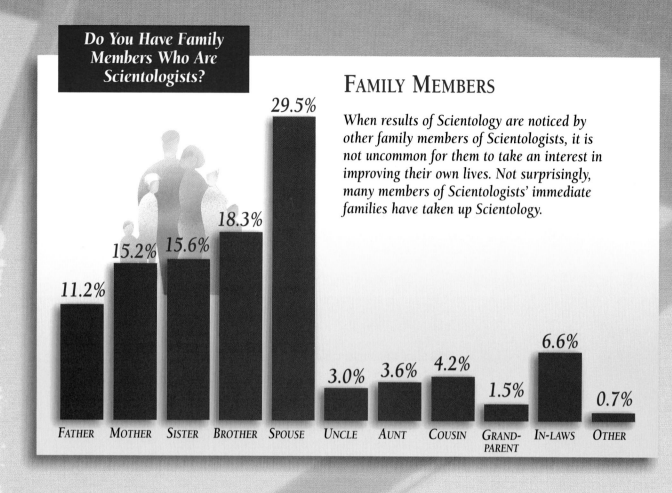

Do You Have Family Members Who Are Scientologists?

FAMILY MEMBERS

When results of Scientology are noticed by other family members of Scientologists, it is not uncommon for them to take an interest in improving their own lives. Not surprisingly, many members of Scientologists' immediate families have taken up Scientology.

29.5%

18.3%

15.2% 15.6%

11.2%

3.0% 3.6% 4.2% 1.5% 6.6% 0.7%

FATHER MOTHER SISTER BROTHER SPOUSE UNCLE AUNT COUSIN GRAND-PARENT IN-LAWS OTHER

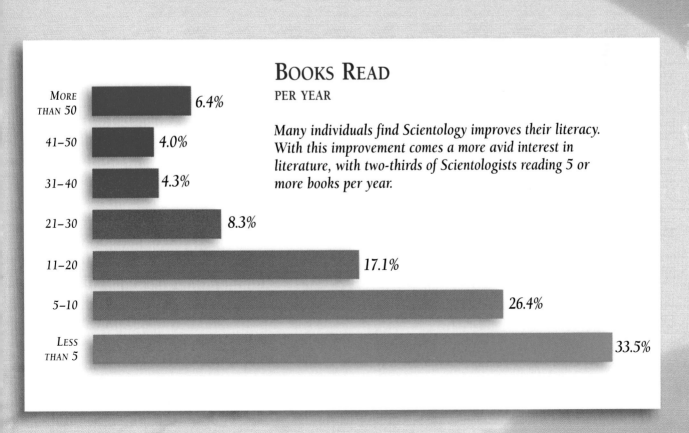

BOOKS READ
PER YEAR

Many individuals find Scientology improves their literacy. With this improvement comes a more avid interest in literature, with two-thirds of Scientologists reading 5 or more books per year.

MORE THAN 50	6.4%
41–50	4.0%
31–40	4.3%
21–30	8.3%
11–20	17.1%
5–10	26.4%
LESS THAN 5	33.5%

SCIENTOLOGISTS' ATTITUDES TOWARD LIFE

Scientologists live honest and ethical lives. They are interested in the well-being of others while achieving their own potentials. They have a positive outlook on life.

96.3%	LIVING A LIFE OF HONESTY AND MORAL INTEGRITY
95.8%	DEVELOPING FULLY AS AN INDIVIDUAL
95.3%	HAVING SOMETHING MEANINGFUL TO WORK TOWARD
94.0%	USING MY FULL POTENTIALS
91.7%	ENJOYING GOOD HEALTH
91.6%	REALLY HELPING OTHERS
89.3%	HAVING LOVING RELATIONSHIPS
88.9%	HAVING A STABLE FAMILY LIFE
84.9%	PROVIDING FOR MY FAMILY
82.9%	CREATING A FUTURE FOR MY CHILDREN
76.1%	HAVING GOOD, CLOSE FRIENDS
71.8%	HAVING ENOUGH MONEY TO LIVE WELL
69.2%	HAVING NEW EXPERIENCES AND EXCITEMENT
61.6%	HAVING A STEADY JOB
53.9%	HAVING THE BEST THINGS IN LIFE

What Is Important to You in Life?

SCIENTOLOGISTS' INVOLVEMENT
IN COMMUNITY ACTIVITIES

As seen in the preceding pages, Scientology helps improve and better one's own life. But for Scientologists it is just as important to become involved in activities to better the quality of life around them. As seen in this graph, Scientologists are involved in diverse activities to better the community and society.

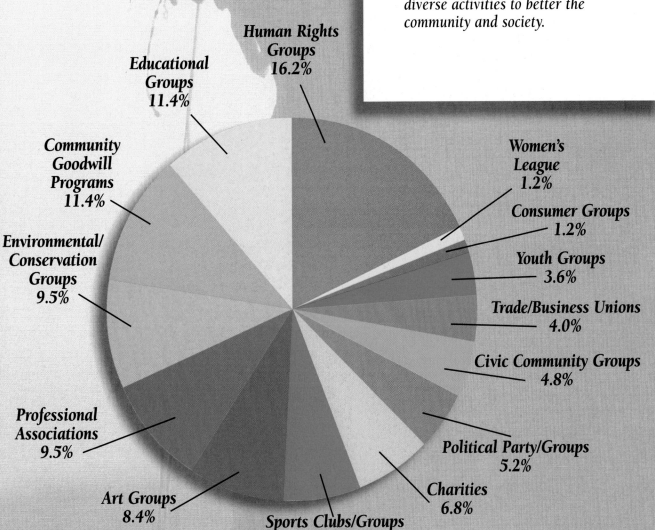

Human Rights Groups
16.2%

Educational Groups
11.4%

Community Goodwill Programs
11.4%

Environmental/ Conservation Groups
9.5%

Professional Associations
9.5%

Art Groups
8.4%

Sports Clubs/Groups
6.8%

Charities
6.8%

Political Party/Groups
5.2%

Civic Community Groups
4.8%

Trade/Business Unions
4.0%

Youth Groups
3.6%

Consumer Groups
1.2%

Women's League
1.2%

SCIENTOLOGY WORKS

As you read these words, the statistics of Scientology will have changed. A week, a month, a year from now they will have changed again as this vital religion reaches further into a troubled world. Its presence will be felt in more countries; its materials will be translated into more languages; it will continue to be the fastest growing religion in the world.

The only possible reason for this phenomenon is that Scientology works. And once people read a book, hear a lecture or take a course they find for themselves that it works and pass the news on to others. Scientology offers man his greatest hope for a new world, free of the misery, pain and conflict that has plagued us for so long.

THE HISTORY OF SCIENTOLOGY'S EXPANSION

The story of Dianetics and Scientology expansion is a simple one. Having developed the world's first workable technology of the mind and an applied religious philosophy that struck a vital chord in so many people, L. Ron Hubbard found that word of his discoveries began to spread. As he continued researching, his further milestone discoveries created greater and greater interest.

To make these discoveries available, training centers, missions and churches were founded; and as more and more people discovered that Dianetics and Scientology worked, the cycle perpetuated itself.

This is the broad view. For a real sense of the story, however, one must return to early January 1950, when word of the forthcoming *Dianetics: The Modern Science of Mental Health* generated so many advance orders, the publisher literally had to force his way past a mound of envelopes that had been dropped through the mail slot of his office door.

Dianetics Bursts on the Scene

Published on May 9, 1950, *Dianetics* quickly led to a national movement. Bookstores, unable to keep copies on the shelves, slipped them beneath the counters for favored customers. Campus discussion groups and Dianetics clubs sprang up from coast to coast. Having grasped the essentials of Dianetics from their reading, thousands were either auditing or receiving auditing, while a number of hospitals adopted Mr. Hubbard's technology as the *only* effective means of helping those suffering from psychosomatic ills. As for the author, by summer 1950, readers were actually camping on his lawn in the hopes that he might consent to offer personal instruction.

To meet this demand, the Hubbard Dianetics Research Foundation opened in Elizabeth, New Jersey, in June 1950. There, Mr. Hubbard delivered the first Professional Auditor Course to students arriving from across the nation. With sales of the book approaching the 100,000 mark, five more branch offices soon opened—in Chicago; New York; Washington, DC; Los Angeles and Hawaii.

Concurrent with the establishment of the Dianetics offices, those first hectic months after publication saw Mr. Hubbard on the lecture circuit—first to Los Angeles where, with little promotion, more than 6,000 people welcomed him to the Shrine Auditorium; then on to the San Francisco Bay area for a series of lectures in Oakland.

Returning to Los Angeles, Mr. Hubbard continued lecturing and instructing students. When these students returned to their hometowns to audit friends, family members and associates, the word continued to spread.

Having spent the spring of 1951 in pre-communist Havana, Cuba, where relative anonymity afforded him the opportunity to complete his second major work on Dianetics, *Science of Survival,* Mr. Hubbard accepted an offer to pursue his research and instruction at a newly opened Dianetics Foundation in Wichita, Kansas.

Here Mr. Hubbard formed the first organization that he himself actually administered, the Hubbard College. This organization trained auditors under his personal supervision, and only when those auditors could competently demonstrate auditing skills and results were they certified.

As news of Mr. Hubbard's return to the United States circulated, scores of students appeared, so that by June 1951 the First Annual Conference of Hubbard Dianetics Auditors brought leading auditors from around the nation to Wichita. Thereafter, Mr. Hubbard continued to lecture and oversee auditor training, while delivering a series of evening talks to the Wichita Chamber of Commerce on how his discoveries might be employed to expand their community.

Scientology Is Announced

With the continuation of his research through the autumn and early winter of 1951, Dianetics auditors were invited to study a new subject, one which would place them squarely in the spiritual realm — Scientology. By early spring 1952, some 15,000 persons were utilizing Scientology principles toward the betterment of their lives.

To train and audit these founding Scientologists, a Scientology center was established at 1407 North Central Avenue, Phoenix, Arizona. There, the recently formed Hubbard Association of Scientologists International (HASI) offered two classes of membership, one technical and one general. To keep HASI members informed of technical breakthroughs and Association news, the first *Journal of Scientology* was published in August 1952 — a typewritten mimeograph, partially funded with paid notices from HASI members offering instruction and auditing in such cities as Boston, Detroit, Philadelphia, Chicago, Honolulu, and Little Rock, Arkansas.

As news of Scientology moved east across the Atlantic and interest took root in England, Mr. Hubbard was asked to lecture in London. Arriving in September 1952, he found a surprisingly substantial Scientology community. Under his supervision, England soon had a growing number of certified Scientology auditors and many more students in training at the London center.

Back in the United States, Scientologists were equally enthusiastic, touring the length and breadth of California to offer auditing demonstrations and Group Processing — all, as the *Journal* reported, "in a very spirited fashion."

The Philadelphia Doctorate Course

After delivering a series of lectures to the newly formed Hubbard Association of Scientologists in London and completing his landmark work, *Scientology 8-8008,* Mr. Hubbard returned to the United States for a celebrated series of December 1952 lectures in Philadelphia. Known as the *Philadelphia Doctorate Course,* these lectures described the full range of man's spiritual potential as well as a wide analysis of human behavior. As recordings of these lectures began to circulate throughout the Scientology field, and a third printing of his book *Scientology 8-8008* rolled off the press, the ranks of Scientology kept increasing on both sides of the Atlantic.

By early 1953, Mr. Hubbard resumed his instruction of auditors at the Hubbard Association of Scientologists International center in Marlborough Place, London. The organization now boasted many more auditors in training and a burgeoning field of preclears. Concurrently, American Scientologists opened new centers in Houston, Texas, and in Hollywood and El Cerrito, California. To apprise them of the latest technical breakthroughs, the Hubbard Communications Office in London opened and the first *Professional Auditor's Bulletins* were published.

The Church Is Born

"After a very careful examination of a poll," declared Scientologists in a 1954 *Journal of Scientology,* "one would say very bluntly: Scientology fills the need for a religion." Consequently, and independently of Mr. Hubbard, the first Church of Scientology was founded by parishioners in Los Angeles.

At about the same time, in Phoenix, a major Scientology and Dianetics congress was underway. Featuring L. Ron Hubbard's lectures, seminars and auditing demonstrations, the congress attracted 450 Scientologists from across the United States.

Also indicative of expansion through this period: news that Scientology had taken root in Australia; word from South Africa where 35 Scientologists had enrolled on a course taught in Durban; a notice from New Zealand (which now had a church in Auckland) that a Phoenix-trained auditor opened a course for some two dozen new Scientologists; and letters from Tel Aviv and Cairo where Scientologists were desperately hungry for more books. All told, by the summer of 1955 there were eight buildings in Mr. Hubbard's Phoenix center and 22 full-time staff members.

Although still lagging in comparison, Great Britain now boasted nearly 500 auditors in such towns as Farnham, West Croydon and Liverpool. As the worldwide Scientology network grew, Mr. Hubbard moved to more centrally located Washington, DC, where, in July 1955, the Founding Church of Scientology and the first Academy of Scientology were formed. Here also, the first Scientology distribution center was established to oversee the printing and dissemination of material around the world. To ease the administration of this now sizable organization, Mr. Hubbard drafted the first of what would ultimately be volumes of administrative policies laying out the functions, actions and duties of the organization.

Books Create Worldwide Growth

Dissemination, L. Ron Hubbard advised in January of 1957, was a matter of getting Scientology books to the public. The prolific Mr. Hubbard had by now written *Scientology: The Fundamentals of Thought, The Problems of Work, Scientology: A History of Man, Self Analysis in Scientology* and *How to Live Though an Executive*. Inspired by his words, Scientologists distributed books at an unprecedented rate. As a result of the growth

that followed, the Hubbard Association of Scientologists International gathered in Washington, DC, to appoint a new secretary for Great Britain to help oversee the broadening activities throughout the British Isles. Also resolved at that Washington conference: the establishment of offices in the Union of South Africa, where the Church of Scientology of Johannesburg had also been founded. Nor was South Africa the only far-flung land where Scientology was taking root, for as of June 1958 *Scientology: The Fundamentals of Thought* had been translated into Greek.

Returning to London in the fall of 1958, after lectures in Washington, Mr. Hubbard found plans in place for a new London educational center. The center was to utilize Scientology study techniques to help British schoolchildren learn more effectively. The project sparked so much interest among Londoners that a number of those who turned up for the first public lecture had to be turned away for want of available seating.

The hall was also crowded in New Delhi when a sister project initiated a course to train ranking members of the Indian government (including the Minister of Labor) on how Scientology principles might be utilized in the educational realm.

A few thousand miles to the southeast, excitement continued to build in Auckland, New Zealand, where the book campaign was in full swing and demand was so high that the local Scientology bookstore regularly sold out its stock. Keeping books in stock also proved a problem in Australia, South Africa, France and outlying areas of England and the United States — continents now dotted with Scientology churches and missions. The largest concentration, however, still remained in the United States, where some 500 turned up at the Washington, DC, Shoreham Hotel in July 1959 for nine hours of lectures by L. Ron Hubbard on new clearing procedures. Eight weeks later another 400 met at London's Royal Empire Society Hall in Trafalgar Square, while dozens of advanced students attended the First Melbourne Advanced Clinical Course.

The Move to Saint Hill

To establish a central training, management and dissemination point, Mr. Hubbard and his family moved to Saint Hill Manor in East Grinstead, Sussex, England. Here, in July 1959, the Hubbard Communications Office Worldwide was established. In keeping with his advice from two years earlier, one of the first departments to be established was a shipping office for books — and orders poured in so quickly that they could not be filled fast enough. To help staff members cope with the demand for books and services, 1959 saw such administrative policy letters as "How to Handle Work" and "How to Get Approval of Actions and Projects."

"Hubbard Communications Office is now safely and securely established at Saint Hill Manor, East Grinstead, Sussex," Mr. Hubbard wrote in the autumn of 1959, and by early 1960 the half-hundred acres at Saint Hill were the scene of much activity. Cables and telegrams arrived at all hours of the day and night with requests for more books, advice and reports of expansion in 11 different countries.

To ensure orderly growth, Mr. Hubbard continued his study of administrative procedure, codifying the basic principles and drafting appropriate policy letters. Meanwhile, the call went out for staff to help with everything from delivering messages and typing, to training and auditing, to executive functions.

With the firm establishment of these worldwide organizational basics at Saint Hill the previous summer, Scientology entered into an accelerated period of expansion through 1960. After yet more lectures at his home, Mr. Hubbard set off to South Africa in September. There, he standardized the administration of a steadily building organization before moving on to Washington for another series of lectures. Returning to Saint Hill in early January 1961, he found letters from such frontiers as Cuba, where a resident doctor was attempting to organize a correspondence course; Thailand, where pioneer Scientologists offered an introductory Scientology course to the monks of a Bangkok monastery; and Israel, where a number of teachers were reading *Dianetics*. There were also letters from Bombay where educators were utilizing Scientology principles, and more orders for books from Peoria, Illinois, to Auckland, New Zealand.

The Saint Hill Special Briefing Course

Following another trip to South Africa in late January of 1961, when another church was founded in Cape Town, Mr. Hubbard returned to Saint Hill and initiated the famed Saint Hill Special Briefing Course. In a matter of months, study space was at such a premium that students were regularly found auditing on the tennis court and lawns — prompting Mr. Hubbard to initiate plans for the conversion of buildings. And as those Briefing Course graduates returned to their hometowns telling of their successes, new pioneer groups were soon established.

Armed with the fruits of new technical breakthroughs, Scientologists continued to reach into society — into Mexico where a Spanish translation of *Scientology: The Fundamentals of Thought* had sparked a small movement in Mexico City; and into France where a pair of Scientologists had recently founded a Parisian church of Scientology and now needed French translations of Scientology materials.

Once again, to guarantee a steady but orderly rate of expansion, Mr. Hubbard drafted further administrative policy letters in 1963 to outline such organizational fundamentals as the delineation of duties for a staff member and the importance of administration. Through the implementation of these and other policy letters, as well as steady dissemination in the field, the mid-60s saw four newly founded Scientology churches around the world, including Port Elizabeth and Durban, South Africa; Detroit, Michigan; and Honolulu, Hawaii. With these churches in place, the total number of Scientology churches had reached 13 by the end of 1964.

Meanwhile, as Scientologists had continued to arrive at Saint Hill for training and auditing, the organizational staff likewise increased. Mr. Hubbard, continuing his technical research and breakthroughs, presented seven lectures on the field of education in 1964, which formed the basis of study technology.

By 1965, more than 200 staff provided services to Scientologists and, all told, some 1,000 hours of auditing were given every week. To impress upon them just how vital it was to maintain standard application of Dianetics and Scientology through each and every one of those hours, and, in fact, for all time, Mr. Hubbard issued two more administrative policy letters: the very critical issues "Keeping Scientology Working" and "Safeguarding Technology."

Additionally, the first Foundation (at Saint Hill) was founded in June to meet the increasing demand of the local population for services during evenings and weekends.

The Bridge to Freedom

With the release of the Classification and Gradation Chart in September 1965, delineating the exact steps of auditing and training on the Bridge to Total Freedom, Scientologists now had an exact route to follow to achieve the state of Clear. This included the release of the Scientology Grades 0 – IV to establish a firm foundation at the beginning of the Bridge.

Concurrent with his technical research, Mr. Hubbard had been examining the very basics of organization as part of his continuing efforts to make his technology readily available and standardly delivered. As a result, in November Mr. Hubbard announced the seven-division organizing board — immediately implemented at Saint Hill, sent out to organizations around the world, and becoming the standard pattern of operation still in use today.

In consequence, Scientology continued to reach new areas in Australia where more Scientology lectures and demonstrations were organized; in South Africa where a Cape Town Scientologist launched a course for businessmen; and in New Zealand where Scientologists wrote in their thanks for the new international The Auditor magazine which told of technical advances and success.

And with every issue of The Auditor came news from other corners of the world, instilling a sense of unity among Scientologists, whether in Alberta, Canada; Port Elizabeth, South Africa; Puerto Rico; or Glenrock, Illinois.

The State of Clear and Beyond

Continuing his technical research through the early months of 1966, L. Ron Hubbard announced a breakthrough of supreme importance: The state of Clear was now attained with certainty by any well-trained auditor. A few months later, Mr. Hubbard released the first two OT levels beyond the state of Clear, and with these new levels now available Scientologists flocked to Saint Hill from around the world.

By mid-May 1966, the first Clears were attesting at Saint Hill, and the routine attainment of this long-dreamed-of state was particularly meaningful to Scientologists. Clears were often featured on the cover of The Auditor, and returning to their homelands, were regularly called upon to speak. Their success, in turn, inspired others to move out into the world — auditing, setting up introductory courses and generally spreading the word. To that end, two enterprising Scientologists began translating Scientology materials into Danish, while others were either opening or expanding Scientology centers in Austin, Texas; Buffalo, New York; Manchester, England; Guadalajara, Mexico; and The Hague, Netherlands.

With the pattern of organizations now in place and the field continuing to expand at a healthy rate, Mr. Hubbard took another critical step for the future. He resigned his Scientology directorship to devote himself fully to further research. In September 1966, all his administrative duties were turned over to Executive Council Worldwide and 100 staff charged with the responsibility of administering the existing Scientology network and ensuring its further expansion.

The Sea Organization Begins

To support L. Ron Hubbard's ensuing research and the delivery of soon-to-be-released

OT Levels III, IV, V and VI, the Sea Organization was formed on August 12, 1967. Its first operational vessels were the *Enchanter* (later rechristened the *Diana*) and the *Avon River* (rechristened the *Athena*). Within a few months the *Royal Scotman* (rechristened the *Apollo*) became the third vessel. With these research vessels operating and a dedicated team for support, Mr. Hubbard continued to provide Scientology with technical breakthrough after technical breakthrough.

OT III Released

On September 20, 1967, in a particularly important recorded message, Mr. Hubbard announced that he had discovered the means to eradicate those spiritual factors which stand in the way of peace and tolerance for mankind.

Further growth followed, with 104 organizations, missions and field groups in twelve countries around the world. All told, Scientologists were now ministering some 50,000 auditing hours per year. By the end of 1967 there were also over 500 Clears.

To provide Scientologists with the fruits of Mr. Hubbard's upper-level research, 1968 saw Sea Organization teams establish Advanced Organizations in Edinburgh, Scotland and Los Angeles, as well as an American Saint Hill Organization in Los Angeles.

The year 1968 additionally signaled a significant boom in churches around the world. For instance, hundreds of students could be found in the Academy during any given course period. Likewise, San Francisco's newly formed church of Scientology, with 23 staff members, reported large numbers of students on course, as did Detroit, Toronto and London. More than 400 Scientologists convened at a Saint Hill graduation to hear those who had recently completed the OT levels and the one-thousandth Clear attested in March. A broader look at statistics revealed 15,000 professional auditors, and by this time some 3,000,000 people had purchased Scientology books or services from 37 official Scientology churches worldwide.

As Scientologists continued to reach deeper and deeper into society, however, they increasingly came face to face with society's problems — in particular, drug abuse which had risen to epidemic proportions by 1968. To help reverse the trend, Mr. Hubbard began a comprehensive research program to search out a means to alleviate not only the effects of drug abuse but also the causes. This work led to the first Drug Rundown in 1968, allowing still more individuals to ascend the Bridge.

The First Class VIII Auditors

To ensure that each and every organization offered orthodox auditing services, Mr. Hubbard launched a new advanced training course in September 1968 to emphasize standard technical application. This was the Class VIII Auditor Course conducted aboard the *Apollo* and attended by top auditors from churches around the world.

With the release in 1969 of the Hubbard Standard Dianetics Course to simplify and standardize Dianetics procedures, and the earlier arrival of the first Class VIII graduates to ensure the standard application of all auditing, Scientology course rooms were soon packed, from New York to New South Wales. As more and more students continued up the Bridge, a third Advanced Organization and Saint Hill was opened in Denmark.

"By rehabilitating the artist," Mr. Hubbard had said, "one does much for rehabilitating the culture." With this incentive, the first Scientology Celebrity Centre was established in 1969. Aimed at assisting the now numerous artists and celebrities who had found Scientology technology indispensable to their creative well-being, the course rooms of the Los Angeles Celebrity Centre were soon also filled with students. In addition to regular Scientology services, Celebrity Centre provided a forum for poets, playwrights, actors, painters and musicians — all part of the effort to help revitalize the arts.

Meanwhile, by August 1970, as demand for advanced levels continued to increase, the Edinburgh Advanced Organization was forced to move to larger quarters at Saint Hill.

Flag Management Is Formed

In the interest of further expansion, L. Ron Hubbard developed a completely new system of management and established the Flag Bureaux aboard the *Apollo* in 1970 to carry out this function for all of Scientology. To relay and implement the Flag Bureaux's orders, liaison offices were opened in Los Angeles for the United States, Saint Hill for the United Kingdom and in Copenhagen for Europe.

In April 1970, Mr. Hubbard invited executives from all churches to attend his Flag Executive Briefing Course on the flagship *Apollo*. The end result placed true administrative experts in all local churches. And with the later publication of the *Organization Executive Course* and *Management Series* volumes, all policy was now readily available to the 2,553 staff of the 118 churches and missions in 20 nations.

As of early 1971, 250 professional auditors had joined the Los Angeles Auditors Association to deliver the newly expanded Scientology lower grades. Later this same year, Mr. Hubbard released three new auditing rundowns: L10, L11 (the New Life Rundown) and L12 (the Flag OT Executive Rundown). These rundowns were delivered only by the first, specially trained Class XII Auditors aboard the *Apollo*. At the same time, fellow auditors were busy at newly formed churches in Las Vegas, Nevada; Pretoria, South Africa; Göteborg and Stockholm, Sweden; Copenhagen, Denmark; Munich, Germany; Plymouth, England; Buffalo, New York; and Boston, Massachusetts.

Employing new technical releases containing refinements of study techniques to greatly speed students through their courses, 1972 saw Scientology increase in size under Sea Organization guidance. All told, these breakthroughs helped push the number of Clears to the 4,000 mark by early 1974, while future Clears stepped onto the Bridge at newly opened Scientology churches in Sacramento, California; Ottawa, Ontario; Manchester, England; Mälmo, Sweden; Vancouver, British Columbia; Portland, Oregon; and Vienna, Austria.

After months of research and compilation, the *Dianetics and Scientology Technical Dictionary* was completed in early 1975. This long-awaited work defined all Dianetics and Scientology words and abbreviations used in connection with auditing and training, and thus greatly aided study.

The Flag Land Base Established

Another milestone for 1975 was the landing of the Sea Organization and establishment of the Flag Land Base in Clearwater, Florida. Located in the eleven-story Fort Harrison Hotel and the nearby Clearwater Bank Building, the Flag Land Base constituted the largest single Scientology organization in history. As the spiritual headquarters of the Church and the only place where preclears could receive the special L Rundowns, it was soon drawing Scientologists from all over the world.

Nineteen seventy-five also saw the opening of Chicago's Church of Scientology, another church in Philadelphia and the first Canadian paperback edition of *Dianetics*.

A new Spanish translation of *Dianetics* was released in Mexico in 1976, and some 12 million television viewers watched as Hispanic celebrities told of its benefits.

In August, 10,000 Scientologists convened for a convention in Anaheim, California. And all the while, Scientology and Dianetics continued to repair lives around the world: in the Philippines where business leaders discovered L. Ron Hubbard's technology, and in the slums of London where his study technology was put to good use helping impoverished children.

Approximately one hundred miles east of Los Angeles, at the desert community of La Quinta, Mr. Hubbard established a Scientology training film studio (Source Productions) in 1977. Under his personal direction, in an eight-month period, Source Productions produced a public Scientology information film and seven technical instruction films to preserve the standard training and application of Scientology long into the future.

The same year, to accommodate the flood of Scientologists arriving for services, the 520,000-square-foot Cedars of Lebanon complex in Hollywood was purchased — soon to be the new home of the Church of Scientology Los Angeles, the American Saint Hill Organization, the Advanced Organization and various administrative offices. This was also a big year for the Flag Land Base with the release of two L. Ron Hubbard written and directed public information films, *The Secret of Flag Results* and *The Case He Couldn't Crack*. And to help keep all running smoothly, L. Ron Hubbard's dictionary of Scientology management terms was released.

The Year of Technical Breakthroughs

Christened "The Year of Technical Breakthroughs," 1978 was another landmark with the release of New Era Dianetics, providing lightning-fast gains for those who were not yet Clear. In cities across the world — now including Oslo, Norway; Bern, Switzerland; and Milano, Italy — students entered course rooms to learn the techniques of NED.

Later that year, New Era Dianetics for OTs (New OT V) was introduced. As word of the truly extraordinary gains this level offered circulated, more and more Scientologists began congregating at the Flag Land Base.

Still more technical releases were celebrated in 1979, most notably the Purification program to rid the body of harmful residuals of drugs and environmental pollutants.

To accommodate the vast number of Scientologists arriving at Flag, the 100-room Sandcastle Hotel, half a mile from the Fort Harrison Hotel, was purchased and renovated.

By the end of June 1980, more than twenty new churches had been founded in locations as diverse as Brussels, Belgium, and Bogotá, Colombia.

New OT VI and VII Released

The most significant achievement of 1980 was the release in September of another two OT levels, New OT VI and VII. Expanding the scope of gains available for the individual beyond any commonly envisioned state, these levels were soon bringing still more Scientologists to the Flag Land Base.

Mr. Hubbard issued several new bulletins on how best to make Scientology known in the early 1980s. Cities where demand was so great that new Scientology churches were opened included Phoenix, Arizona; Cincinnati, Ohio; Albuquerque, New Mexico; Berlin, Germany; Geneva, Switzerland; Tel Aviv, Israel; Canberra, Australia; Edmonton and Quebec, Canada; and four in Mexico City.

The first L. Ron Hubbard lecture series on cassette was released in 1980 by Golden Era Productions — then known as Source Productions at La Quinta and now relocated to a nearby 500-acre property to facilitate not only film production, but also audio and technical compilations for speeding Scientologists up the Bridge. And for an indication of just how big Scientology had grown by 1980: Dianetics and Scientology were now available in 52 countries at 328 organizations, missions and auditor groups, serviced by 5,150 staff who helped provide 794,990 auditing hours that year.

With liaison offices now established for Canada and Latin America, a total of eight such offices were ensuring steady expansion under Sea Organization direction. As of 1981, twelve of Mr. Hubbard's Technical Training Films were completed and released to help standardize Scientology training. Mr. Hubbard also released the Sunshine Rundown to heighten one's awareness of new abilities as a Clear.

The Foundation of a New Era

Nineteen eighty-one was also the year of important administrative changes initiated in response to a problem many organizations suffer in periods of rapid expansion. These changes were ultimately designed to safeguard the purity of the technology, the integrity of the Church and the future of the Scientology religion. That year, inspections conducted by dedicated, long-term Scientologists revealed that the Guardian's Office or "GO" had lost sight of its charter and so grossly exceeded its authority that the Church's stability was being jeopardized.

The GO was a small unit of the Church, established in 1966, to protect Scientology organizations from external threats. Over time, it had evolved into a separate, insular, entirely autonomous unit, answering to no one and operating without regard to Mr. Hubbard's policies.

Thus, in July of 1981, a new era dawned in the Church. The group of dedicated Scientologists that uncovered the GO's misdeeds and out-ethics put an end not only to that but to the GO as well. The GO's leadership was removed. Those who had instigated wrongdoing were expelled. The Guardian's Office itself was disbanded entirely, and a major reorganization of the Church's corporate structure was implemented to prevent any possibility of a future recurrence of anything resembling the autonomy of the GO.

It was a new era and saw the birth of new organizations and new directions. Church of Scientology International (CSI) was created as the new mother church of the Scientology religion, established to provide ethical, effective ecclesiastical management for Scientology churches throughout the world. It was also at this time that the senior ecclesiastical body over Scientology missions, Scientology Missions International (SMI), was formed. (See Chapter 22.)

In 1982, Religious Technology Center (RTC) was formed as an entirely new Church with an entirely new, distinct and unique function.

That year, L. Ron Hubbard donated all the trademarks of Dianetics and Scientology to RTC, which was chartered expressly to guarantee the purity of the Scientology religion and the integrity of the use of the powerful technologies of Dianetics and Scientology by ensuring the proper use of these marks. While RTC did not inherit any corporate, ecclesiastical or management function, it was created to meet the need to ensure the standard application of the technology and to eliminate any possibility of Scientology falling into the wrong hands. (See Chapter 23.)

To cope with the new administrative load, July of 1982 saw the establishment of the International Network of Computer Organized Management (INCOMM). Utilizing computer systems based upon Mr. Hubbard's developments in the field, INCOMM fully computerized international church management to facilitate efficiency of operations and the huge rate of Scientology expansion.

As a result of these changes, the religion began a period of growth unlike any before it. The Scientologists who had purged the GO proved their leadership qualities, and in combination with the newly streamlined and cohesive church structure, preclears began moving far more speedily and confidently to Clear and beyond. The total number of Clears and OTs produced at the Flag Land Base and Advanced Organizations surged.

And as just one more indication of how quickly Scientology was now expanding through the early 1980s, a new Advanced Organization opened in Sydney, Australia.

Dianetics: Perennial Bestseller

To spread word of technical breakthroughs and generally inform the world of just what Scientology has to offer, the Planetary Dissemination Organization was founded in 1983. One of the organization's first tasks: to make *Dianetics* even more widely available. And the result a few months later: *Dianetics* once again reached the bestseller lists with the seven-millionth copy sold.

Concurrently, new churches were founded in Hamburg, Bern, Zurich and Verona, soon followed in the US with churches in Long Island, New York, and Orange County, California. And to serve the artistic community in New York, a Celebrity Centre organization was opened there.

Two more German churches opened in 1984 and by then, scores of Scientology churches and missions spanned the globe. It seemed only appropriate, then, that on

October 7, 1984, the International Association of Scientologists was formed at Saint Hill in England, to unite Scientologists from all nations.

Man has long suffered from inability to consistently pursue his true purposes, and in 1984 Mr. Hubbard released the solution to such problems: the False Purpose Rundown. As with all earlier technical releases, Scientology course rooms from Sydney to St. Louis were soon filled with auditors learning how to remove those factors which obscure a being's real purposes. So great were the numbers of students and preclears at the Flag Land Base that the Flag Bureaux, previously located in Clearwater, was moved to Los Angeles in order to make more room for more delivery to parishioners and consolidate management. As an added bonus, Scientologists were soon to be listening to the first of Mr. Hubbard's lectures in Clearsound — a revolutionary development in tape restoration making possible the release of all of Mr. Hubbard's lectures from 1950 forward.

Nineteen eighty-five saw the 150th church open in Monza, Italy. To meet the demand around the world for taped lectures (over 90,000 students and preclears completed services in 1985) a full production and recording studio was established at Golden Era Productions. And, looking to the future for a glimpse of what was to come, Sea Organization teams began scouting for a new motor vessel where Scientology's most advanced auditing level could be offered in a distraction-free environment.

While the Sea Organization was ensuring the availability of the OT levels, other Scientologists were making L. Ron Hubbard's work better known to those who had not yet stepped onto the Bridge. As a result of these efforts: copies of Dianetics appeared in Gdańsk, Poland, for the first time; a Peruvian mission was established in Lima; a team of Scientologists distributed Scientology materials in Hong Kong; and a Celebrity Centre in Nashville, Tennessee, opened its doors in 1987. New Scientology missions also opened in Puerto Rico, North Carolina, Palm Springs and Zaire and — fulfilling the long-laid seeds — in Ambala, India.

And lest one had any doubts as to just how many were now reaching for L. Ron Hubbard's works, Dianetics reached the number one position on the New York Times bestseller list. Concurrently, Dianetics was released, and became instantly popular, in a new quarter — mainland China — with the first printing selling out in less than two weeks.

Painstakingly researched, the new fully updated Scientology Academy Levels were released in the first days of 1988. Also in 1988, the greatly improved Mark Super VII E-Meter was released. Further plans to make L. Ron Hubbard technology available in more secular settings led to the formation of the Association for Better Living and Education (ABLE). Among other projects ABLE would soon help initiate was to bring L. Ron Hubbard's study technology to classrooms in China where 190,000 copies of Dianetics had been distributed by this point. In order to handle equally impressive North American sales of L. Ron Hubbard's books, Bridge Publications (formerly the Publications Organization, United States) moved into new and larger quarters in Los Angeles.

New OT VIII — Truth Revealed

After four years of intensive work locating, purchasing and refitting, the Sea Organization motor vessel was christened the Freewinds. Setting sail on June 6, 1988, she was not only the first Sea Organization vessel to see service in thirteen years, but she is the only place where Scientologists can take the highest available step on the Bridge: New OT VIII, Truth Revealed.

The unveiling of two new facilities was further cause for celebration among Scientologists in 1989. The first was the twelve-story, 110,000 square-foot Hollywood Guaranty Building, which was to serve as the home of international Church management. The second was the Saint Hill Castle, a building modeled after a medieval English castle, that Mr. Hubbard originally conceived and designed in 1965. It now offered advanced Scientology services and the Saint Hill Special Briefing Course. Three more new churches opened in 1989: one in Atlanta, Georgia; another in Hanover, Germany; and the third in Stuttgart.

These three churches brought the total number of Scientology organizations, missions and field groups up to 830, with some 10,000 staff members ministering to more than 200,000 students and preclears for a grand total of 1.4 million auditing hours per year. That same year also saw the technology moving into society with 251 social reform groups and 164 social betterment groups supported by Scientologists.

While the demand for Dianetics and Scientology in China was growing, another Asian nation was responding in a significant way to Mr. Hubbard's technology: Japan. In a matter of months, the first Scientology church in Tokyo was offering courses and auditing to scores of Japanese citizens.

Into the Nineties

The 1990s heralded a new era of unprecedented expansion which resulted in so many milestones that it may be remembered as one of the most significant decades in Scientology history.

It began as thousands of Scientologists poured into their churches to enroll on the Hubbard Key to Life Course, first made available on May 9, 1990; the March 13, 1991 release of the complete *Organization Executive Course* and *Management Series* volumes containing all of L. Ron Hubbard's organizational policies; soon followed by the eighteen-volume collection of Mr. Hubbard's technical writings.

More than 700 invited guests — including leaders of the business community, the arts and political dignitaries — were on hand for the 1991 opening of the L. Ron Hubbard Life Exhibition in Hollywood.

Auditor's Day 1991 celebrated the completion of a five-year program to compile, verify as totally accurate, and make available all of L. Ron Hubbard's auditing and training

technology on the Bridge to Total Freedom. And with this, the final Classification, Gradation and Awareness Chart was released at an event at Saint Hill in England.

And with the iron curtain down, such formerly inaccessible nations as Russia, Hungary and what had been East Germany were soon reaching for L. Ron Hubbard's technology. To meet their needs, a Sea Org liaison office opened in Russia, while teams flew in to deliver Mr. Hubbard's educational and administrative technologies.

By the end of 1991, with those formerly Eastern-bloc nations now enjoying Mr. Hubbard's materials, there were 74 countries offering Scientology. New translations followed and the number of translated titles rose to 422, available in 31 languages.

There were 1,039 Scientology organizations, missions and groups around the world — the yearly number of Scientology book sales of 1967 were being exceeded every day. There were also 1.5 million auditing hours provided that year, and more auditing took place in just 12 days than occurred in the whole of 1967. A 1991 survey revealed that Dianetics and Scientology had become so widely known they were household words.

Impressive as those numbers were, they were but the beginning of a boom.

Nowhere was Scientology's expansion more rapid than in Russia, where in 1992, hundreds attended Dianetics seminars, as groups formed across the face of the Commonwealth of Independent States. *Dianetics* was translated into Russian and released the following year and the thousands and thousands who had already learned about it soon became millions as stories on Dianetics flooded radio, television and the printed media.

In July 1992, the newly restored Celebrity Centre International was officially opened to service the many artists in Scientology.

May 1993 brought the opening of the Moscow mission, the first Church of Scientology in Russia. As the news about Dianetics and Scientology continued to spread, groups formed from the Black Sea to Siberia, from the Mongolian border to the edge of the Arctic.

While Scientology spread across Russia, other countries were also introduced to L. Ron Hubbard's technology: Cyprus, Iceland, Malta, Paraguay, Peru, San Marino, Ukraine, Zambia, Uruguay, Suriname and a score more.

More than 20,000 top government officials learned about Scientology and Dianetics for the first time through distribution of this book, *What Is Scientology?*, to United Nations representatives, judges, business leaders and representatives of major religions in the United States, Canada, Africa, Australia, Europe and South America.

In September, the L. Ron Hubbard Images of a Lifetime photo exhibition opened at the Flag Land Base in Clearwater, Florida. Hundreds of never-before-seen photographs provided tens of thousands of Scientologists and non-Scientologists with new insights into Mr. Hubbard's life.

The most significant legal recognition of the Scientology religion came in October 1993 when the United States Internal Revenue Service issued ruling letters which recognized the tax-exempt status of more than 150 Scientology churches, missions, social reform organizations and other entities because they operate exclusively for religious and charitable purposes.

IRS religious recognition was universal and unconditional, and it was the result of the most detailed and exhaustive examination of a religious organization in the agency's history. The IRS was given unfettered access to every echelon of the Church's ecclesiastical hierarchy. Thus, the IRS examination was not limited to United States entities, but specifically included the financial and other affairs of church organizations from Australia to Canada and from Europe to South Africa.

As a result, Church of Scientology International (CSI), the mother church of the Scientology religion, received not only exempt recognition, but also received a group exemption letter embracing all Scientology churches within its ecclesiastical oversight.

The Church's spiritual meccas were also individually recognized as tax exempt, as were the Church's publishing entities.

Scientology Missions International received its own exemption. It also received a separate group exemption letter for all Scientology missions within its ecclesiastical oversight.

RTC was individually recognized as tax exempt and received its own separate ruling letter.

The IRS also recognized the International Association of Scientologists as a tax-exempt organization.

In addition to ruling favorably on tax exemption, the IRS rulings made all donations to all United States churches of Scientology deductible against personal income taxes to the full extent permitted by law.

The decision had international repercussions. Though hundreds and hundreds of courts around the world had already recognized Scientology as a bona fide religion, there could no longer be even a trace of doubt as to that religiosity. The flag of victory planted on American soil served as a guidon to the many other nations where Scientology had been established.

Almost immediately the International Criminal Police Organization, Interpol, a long-time adversary in Europe, also fully recognized Scientology as a religion and agreed to purge all false information about the Church contained in its files internationally.

With Scientology now moved firmly into the mainstream, Church management was able to devote its attention fully to creating further growth and expansion for the religion in 1994. And it was thus appropriate that the early months of that year saw the full renovation and expansion of the Church's Advanced Organization in Sydney, Australia.

In March, *The Scientology Handbook,* the most comprehensive manual on the basics of Scientology ever published, was released in five languages. Provided in its 984 pages and more than 700 photographs and illustrations are easy-to-apply solutions for a myriad of day-to-day problems.

With release of the *Handbook* also came the launch of the "Crusade for a Better World," a program designed to activate Volunteer Ministers who, by applying the fundamentals from *The Scientology Handbook,* could help people in all walks of life with difficulties ranging from handling relationships and stress in the workplace to resolving the problems of drugs and education and a myriad of spiritual challenges.

Volunteer Ministers became a vital force in communities the world over, introducing thousands to L. Ron Hubbard's technology.

As an index of how rapidly Scientology was growing, May brought the release of the *How to Use Dianetics* video in ten new languages — German, Italian, French, Spanish, Swedish, Danish, Japanese, Greek, Russian and Hungarian — making Dianetics available to more than 1 billion people.

Two new churches of Scientology opened — the Celebrity Centre Nashville and the Church of Scientology of Buenos Aires. Ten new missions opened in the Commonwealth of Independent States.

Nineteen ninety-four also marked the fortieth anniversary of the Church of Scientology. As part of the year-long celebration, the What Is Scientology? exhibition opened in December at the National Press Club in Washington, DC. Heightened interest in Scientology brought hundreds of government officials and members of the media to tour the exhibit to learn more about the Church and its membership.

In 1995, Scientology books and materials were made available in more languages than ever before, to millions of new people. Released in March in fourteen different languages was *L. Ron Hubbard: A Profile,* a comprehensive look at his life and work which chronicled Mr. Hubbard's contributions to a broad number of fields including philosophy, education, drug rehabilitation, photography, music and literature, among others. This publication launched a whole new *RON* Series offering unique insights into Mr. Hubbard's many endeavors and his dedication to helping others.

In 1995, sales of *Dianetics* reached 17 million in May. In the Commonwealth of Independent States, L. Ron Hubbard technology became available in Georgia, Armenia, Azerbaijan and Turkmenistan.

In the spring of 1995, a new Scientology mission was opened in Wichita, Kansas. This city was where Mr. Hubbard discovered the source of life — the thetan — and established the first national Dianetics Foundation headquarters in the 1950s. Once again Mr. Hubbard's route to spiritual freedom was welcomed by the city that stood at the historic crossroads of Scientology's development. And, seven months later, the new premises of the Founding Church of Scientology in Washington, DC, were opened at the fully restored Fraser Mansion on Dupont Circle. It was in this city that forty years earlier Mr. Hubbard had established the first auditor training Academy.

To meet an increasing demand for Scientology in Europe, the Advanced Organization and Saint Hill in Copenhagen, Denmark, was fully renovated to provide new facilities for the flood of European Scientologists coming for advanced spiritual studies. Concurrently, the Advanced Courses of Scientology and Mr. Hubbard's accompanying filmed lectures on the subject were translated and released in French, German, Spanish and Italian, making the OT levels available in these languages for the first time.

By the beginning of 1996, Scientology reached every corner of the world, including for the first time Latvia, Sri Lanka, Botswana, Hong Kong, Romania and Nepal.

In February, leaders of the Shinto religion, one of the world's oldest faiths, traveled from Japan to Clearwater, Florida, and Los Angeles, California, to learn more about L. Ron Hubbard and Scientology.

In March, fulfilling the ever-increasing demand for information about Scientology and Dianetics, the Church released *Orientation,* the most important film about Scientology ever produced. *Orientation* takes the viewer on a guided tour of a model church of

Scientology and provides a firsthand look at the religion, its beliefs and practices, its purposes, results and how Scientology relates to one's future as a spiritual being.

Also in March, Scientology and Dianetics entered cyberspace, the vast computer network of the Internet which provides information to an estimated 50 million people around the world. The Scientology and Dianetics site is among the largest on the Internet. It comprises 32,000 pages and 7,000 photos and high-tech features such as virtual-reality tours of churches of Scientology. During its first six months, the site was visited by more than 2 million people.

The dramatic upsurge of interest in Dianetics and Scientology brought with it the necessity to streamline Church management. A corps of 100 highly trained and experienced executives assumed key positions of responsibility in all major continental zones, preparing the Church to meet the demands of expansion as Scientology moves into the future.

In May came the announcement of a watershed in Scientology history—the dawn of a Golden Age of Technology. What was meant was simply this: New technical programs and breakthroughs designed to not only bring about perfect auditors, but to make that level of perfection available to millions. For millions auditing millions was the goal that Mr. Hubbard envisioned.

The announcement was preceded by an extensive investigation to standardize all auditor training in any org regardless of country, no small undertaking considering differences in language and the far-flung orgs around the world. The result was a massive series of precise auditor training drills taken from Mr. Hubbard's writings for use by auditors-in-training. And the result of application of these drills was not only to greatly speed up training but also to raise auditing skill to previously unattained levels.

The drills were made available in twelve languages, including English, French, Italian, Spanish, German, Dutch, Danish, Norwegian, Swedish, Portuguese, Hebrew and Japanese.

At the same time came another history-making announcement — the release of the Hubbard Professional Mark Super VII Quantum E-Meter. Made possible by space-age advances in computer technology, the Quantum is the most advanced E-Meter ever developed, produced exactly according to Mr. Hubbard's specifications.

And finally came the release of the Hubbard E-Meter Drills Simulator, a revolutionary tool which enabled students for the first time to simulate every aspect of a live auditing session, including E-Meter reads.

The breakthroughs of the Golden Age of Tech formed nothing less than a complete revolution in the application of Scientology technology. The immediate result was Scientology Academies filled with students around the world. In June 1996, a new series of training drills for the Advanced Courses were released.

As training at both ends of the Bridge became faster and more flawless than ever, new materials continued to be released in all major languages. In September, L. Ron Hubbard's lectures for all Scientology courses up to Level 0 were released in Spanish, German, French and Italian; by December all of his lectures to Level IV were completed. At the same time, *The Problems of Work* was released in Norwegian, Portuguese, Danish and Hebrew, and *Scientology: The Fundamentals of Thought* was published in Portuguese and Hebrew.

As the worldwide implementation of these new training programs gained even greater impetus, further expansion and even broader acceptance of L. Ron Hubbard and his works appeared in 1997.

In Los Angeles in early April 1997, in recognition of Mr. Hubbard's humanitarian contributions, the street where the Church of Scientology of Los Angeles, American Saint Hill Organization and the Advanced Organization of Los Angeles are located was renamed "L. Ron Hubbard Way." Following several months of reconstruction to make it one of the most beautiful city streets in the world, L. Ron Hubbard Way was opened with a daylong celebration attended by state and city officials, local dignitaries and more than 7,000 Scientologists from around the world. Both the Governor of California and the Mayor of Los Angeles sent personal representatives to deliver messages of support and congratulations. The speakers praised L. Ron Hubbard for his humanitarian works and his contributions toward helping to eradicate illiteracy, drug abuse and criminality not only in Los Angeles but in many other cities around the world.

In this respect, L. Ron Hubbard's technology has taken an even greater prominence in areas long plagued by ethnic discord. Nineteen ninety-seven brought the opening of a new Scientology mission in Memphis, Tennessee, through which its sponsors resolved to bridge racial differences in that city. From newly liberated southern African nations to feuding Balkan States to the teething democracies of former Soviet republics to Latin American communities in the firing line of violent drug lords, the expansion of Dianetics and Scientology represents a constant, growing voice for tolerance and sanity among people, no matter their seemingly unresolvable conflicts.

Nineteen ninety-seven represented a major leap in worldwide recognition of this and other truths about Scientology. In June, the Church of Scientology launched an historic international crusade to expose and dismantle the long-ingrained false premises upon which the walls of conflict are built. Some of the most destructive thinking of the late twentieth century — commonly accepted and seldom inspected lies perpetrated throughout society, such as "You're just a piece of meat," "Man is a stimulus-response animal," "IQ can't be improved" and "People can't change" — were exposed on television, in newspapers and magazines, on billboards and bus-shelter posters and on an expanded Scientology Web site on the Internet. Through this crusade, L. Ron Hubbard's workable solutions to life's problems were brought to the homes of millions of people each day — first in North America, then expanding to Europe — in the form of the broad release of his basic books and a new introductory Personal Efficiency Course.

By 1997, Scientology was available in more than 120 countries. And at the Flag Land Base alone, more than 1 million auditing sessions were provided. And every five minutes of every day, a new person started his first service in a Scientology mission.

But however great the numbers become — the new preclears and auditors sitting down for their first session, the new readers picking up their first copies of *Dianetics* — the story of Scientology expansion is still a simple one: Having discovered that L. Ron Hubbard's technology works, people make it known to others.

CHAPTER 34

FUTURE PREDICTION OF SCIENTOLOGY:

THOUGHTS AND STATEMENTS ABOUT THE SCIENTOLOGY RELIGION FROM PROMINENT SOCIAL AND RELIGIOUS LEADERS

If a founding Scientologist had been asked in the 1950s to predict the impact of Scientology on the world a half-century later, would he have been able to imagine the extent to which it has grown today? Would he have been able to envision from a stucco building in Phoenix, Arizona, the more than one thousand churches, missions and groups that exist today? Would he have been able to envision the hundreds of thousands who have been helped to rid themselves of the curse of drugs, or the millions who have been placed on the road to literacy through the use of L. Ron Hubbard's technologies?

Surely, these pioneer Scientologists had some idea of what potential L. Ron Hubbard's discoveries held for mankind, just as today's Scientologists envision even greater expansion in the future.

Today, Scientology is the fastest growing religion on the planet—and so long as Mr. Hubbard's technologies are available to all who wish to reach for them, and so long as they are applied standardly, Scientology will continue to grow.

To understand what this growth might mean to a troubled world, religious leaders, professionals, educators and others have offered the following predictions on the future impact of the Scientology religion.

The movement founded by L. Ron Hubbard will engage itself increasingly in the design of a new world following the collapse of the Soviet Union and communism. A new awakening of spiritual powers is taking place and his vision will help shape events.

Hans Janitschek
President
Society of Writers
United Nations

The Church of Scientology has taken an active role in the fight for social justice and equal rights for minorities.

Community programs which utilize the study methods of L. Ron Hubbard have helped thousands of inner-city children as well as adults. And Mr. Hubbard's moral code, The Way to Happiness, *has been used to rehabilitate gang members and given them a chance to become honest and productive citizens. Scientologists have been instrumental in providing minorities tools which enable them to accomplish their goals.*

As a new religion, the Scientologists have had their share of discrimination but work tirelessly to preserve not just their religious freedom but the religious freedom for all people around the world.

I believe the Church will continue to be a strong force to protect the rights of all men, women and children far, far into the future.

Jeanetta Williams
National Board Member
NAACP (National Association for the Advancement of Colored People)

Scientology has come a long way, and has grown in numbers.

There are so many people of different types—and into different activities—art, human rights, rehabilitation and more.

Obviously, it will last. It can be geared to individual interests, and even if the interests change, people can use the basic technology to adapt to new ones.

Loretta Needle
BA, University of Toronto

Scientology is a practical religious theology which embodies the technology of helping people discover themselves and at the same time to become aware of the evils that plague our society, such as the prevalent use of dangerous psychiatric drugs.

The pastoral counseling program of Scientology puts man in touch with reality and enhances and strengthens his relationship with God and his fellow man.

The beauty of Scientology is you don't have to give up your religious upbringing to become a Scientologist. You can still remain in your original church.

Scientology has a great future because it helps those who are in frustration and despair to shift their position to a helpful and useful one.

The late Rev. Dr. Leo Champion
Pastor
Fellowship Missionary Baptist Church
Milwaukee, Wisconsin

Having won legal recognition as a religion, I believe the Church of Scientology will gain acceptance in the community of the world's religions as a distinctive combination of Eastern spirituality and Western pragmatism.

Dr. Lonnie D. Kliever
Professor and Chair
Department of Religious Studies
Southern Methodist University

Like so many relatively new religions, the Church of Scientology has been forced to spend much of its time and resources fighting religious prejudice and prosecution. Despite those pressures, the Church has been a real force for good in the lives of many of its adherents and a champion of religious freedom.

Robin Johansen
Attorney and Religious
Freedom Fighter

I have observed the Church of Scientology over the past few decades. Its critics have come and gone. It has emerged victorious from struggles with powerful governmental institutions and with organized bigotry. In the wake of every controversy, the Church has grown and prospered.

I have also had the opportunity to interact with ordinary Scientologists in everyday settings. I never fail to be impressed by the solidness, clarity and high ethical standards of Church members. Thus, at both an institutional and an individual level, Scientology has a strength of character that bodes well for its future.

I would finally like to mention that the Church of Scientology has taken responsibility for the surrounding society. Critics never seem to find the room to mention the Church's work in educational reform, in the fight against drugs, in the publicizing of medical abuse and in other areas of social reform. Thus Scientology continues to work toward a brighter future for all of us, and I, for one, wish the Church every success in its endeavors.

Prof. James R. Lewis
Chairman, Department of
Religious Studies
World University of America

Scientology, as a movement, has firmly dedicated itself to advancing the cause of human rights for all people, regardless of race, color, creed or nationality. Scientologists not only speak out against social injustices they encounter, but take effective action to remedy them.

I have fought for and marched for civil rights for nearly two decades. I know how much courage it takes to look into the face of oppression and take a stand against it. Members of the Church of Scientology are leading and winning the battle for religious rights.

I am proud to stand together with Scientologists in this fight. I am sure Scientology will continue to come out on top and continue to be instrumental in creating a better world for all.

Ernest Johnson, Esq.
President, NAACP
Louisiana State Conference

Your Church's noble principles of high ideals and ethical living along with the beliefs of accepting so many aspects of knowledge meets very close to the ideals of the American Institute of Islamic Studies. I find it a pleasure and privilege to reach out for common thoughts. The future looks so optimistic that we shall convey our common principles to the world side by side.

Amir Gillani
President
American Institute of Islamic Studies
Toronto, Canada

I've always been impressed with the founder of Scientology, L. Ron Hubbard, because he was a man of multiple and comprehensive talents. As I understand Scientology, it incorporates a philosophy which is a way of living and tools for the betterment of the society. With those tools the coming millennium has tremendous promise and I think Scientology will be there as a guiding light.

Senator Diane Watson
California State Senate

It's a new religion, and it will meet many difficulties. But Scientology stands on fine ground, and all resistance will be broken down.

Harry Widemyr
Social Inspector
Sweden

The mission of the Church of Scientology has a special importance for post-totalitarian countries.

The experience of the Church of Scientology in building a community, and its technologies of spiritual training, can and already do play a significant role in creating a new spiritual foundation in places with nontotalitarian governments.

Dr. Michael A. Sivertsev
Chairman for New Religions
Board of Cooperation with Religious Organizations
Office of the Russian President

Through its religious and educational initiatives, the Church of Scientology has established its place among the religions of South Africa.

It is a therapeutic religion that diagnoses the problem of the human condition and provides specific techniques of spiritual healing and an applied religious philosophy designed to cure that problem.

Although Scientology is often described as a "new religious movement" it actually is not new. In South Africa, as we have seen, Scientology has been present for forty years.

As a religion that is both old and new, the Church of Scientology has continued to advance religious aspirations that have gained adherents all over the world. At the very least, the Church of Scientology merits continued recognition and attention as a religion in South Africa.

David Chidester
Professor of Comparative Religion
University of Cape Town,
South Africa

The Church of Scientology is an important force in our society seeking to enhance the people's ability to know what our government is doing, is not doing and why, and otherwise striving to enable citizens to make the government more accountable for its actions. I believe that in the future, when the need for such efforts will be more necessary, the Church's role will be even stronger and more effective.

Quinlan J. Shea
Former Senior Justice
Department Official
Director, Center for Citizen Access
to Government Information

It is notable that while the major denominations in Canada are careless about religious rights (and, therefore, careless about the ultimate welfare of our people), Scientologists have courageously and at great cost struggled against state abuses of these and other rights. If they hold out and succeed, all of us will one day have to bring our proper thanks that through their endurance we enjoy our freedom.

Juris Calitis, DD
The Right Reverend
Evangelical Lutheran Church
of Canada

Drugs are the scourge of mankind, and they are the problem we must solve as we exit the twentieth century. The twenty-first century promises hope because Scientology is here and has the solutions to drugs.

Bob King
Former Advisory
Neighborhood Commissioner
Washington, DC

There are many Bible-believing Evangelicals and others in the established Christian community who have not yet accepted the Church of Scientology. Nevertheless, they should thank the Lord for them, because the Scientologists have fought a lot of battles that have helped protect and safeguard freedom for us all.

Because of these efforts, Scientology is continuing to gain more and more acceptability among leaders in the religious community, and the Church has won most of its battles. However, while they are enjoying a breathing period, be assured there are a lot more battles to be fought, and won, down the road.

Rev. Jim Nicholls
Producer of Voice of Freedom
Radio and TV Show

I have seen firsthand the work the Church has done to forward social betterment through its support of ABLE International and the Narconon drug and alcohol rehabilitation programs.

In my eight years as Medical Director for Narconon's treatment center in Oklahoma, I have witnessed the strong dedication and commitment from ABLE and Narconon in addressing substance abuse, one of society's most damaging and widespread problems.

This in itself will make its mark as more and more people overcome addiction through the application of L. Ron Hubbard's discoveries in the treatment of chemical dependency.

Dr. Ray E. Stowers, DO
Board Certified
in Addiction Medicine

Scientology has a background of benefiting its members as well as the general public through a number of social betterment programs in areas like drug rehabilitation, education and government reform. This broad spectrum of beneficial activities is a tribute to the Church as well as its members and is something I believe guarantees the Church of Scientology a bright future.

Dr. Isaac N. Brooks, Jr. PhD
Executive Director
National Task Force on Religious Freedom
Legislation and Litigation
Washington, DC

Based on the time I've been in Hollywood and seen what the Church of Scientology has accomplished, all indications appear that the Church in the next five years will continue to make progress in the community, specifically as it relates to handling gang violence, graffiti, etc.

The outreach achieved is significant and I think it is very positive. The Church continues to have faith and continues to help those in need of direction, upgrade their properties, and contribute to community development.

Frank L. Buckley
Board Member
Hollywood Chamber of Commerce

With one of the most ambitious religious Internet sites ever created—the result of an international team of workers and thousands of hours of labor—the Church of Scientology has clearly established itself as a pioneer in the dissemination of its beliefs via the premiere communications medium of the twenty-first century. There is no doubt in my mind that on-line spiritual seekers will be challenged and informed by this vital work.

At the same time, I believe Scientology's trailblazing efforts in protecting the on-line rights of intellectual property owners will be of tremendous benefit to every writer as the years progress and as more and more information is published on-line.

Mark A. Kellner
Author, God on the Internet

My experience working with the Church of Scientology on the L. Ron Hubbard Way streetscape project showed me that the Church and its members are genuinely committed to improving the quality of life for all people in our community. Through this experience I also learned about the Church's efforts to combat drug abuse and illiteracy. The Church has more than proven that they practice what they preach. I believe that the Church of Scientology is providing much needed solutions to many of our society's plaguing problems and the Church may very well be not only a model for all of us to follow today, but for generations to come.

Tod A. Burnett
Commissioner
Los Angeles Board of Public Works

I think the Church's involvement in such issues as religious freedom and ending psychiatric abuses within the field of mental health demonstrate the Church is interested in more than just spirituality, but in enabling all people to enjoy their human rights. The support for these efforts can only grow.

Cedric Hendricks
Congressional Aide
Washington, DC

There is and will be a more positive view of Scientology through the actions of community work and the various community outreach programs that the Church presents.

It has been a fulfilling experience working with Community Outreach staff for over ten years.

I look forward to a long relationship utilizing the talent, the time, and dedication to helping young people which has been our source of contact over the years.

Carole J. Simpson
County of Los Angeles
Department of Children Services

It is inevitable that Scientology will expand because from my experience, the types of people I have met are walking advertisements for it. I think more and more people are looking for a practical philosophy.

The Hon. Herbert Graham
Former Deputy Premier
Western Australia

I have traveled far and wide throughout my professional life and see the peoples of Earth as incredibly diverse in character as well as needs. Oftentimes our efforts to understand and help them have been too narrow. In the many years I have worked with the Church of Scientology the one thing which has impressed me the most and which will characterize the Church far into future centuries is its ability to deal with humankind as a whole.

At the heart of Scientology's activities is the betterment of all people no matter what creed, what race, what socioeconomic status to develop themselves spiritually and mentally so that each individual can improve his own life. Scientology's far-reaching goals are designed to tend to each individual uniquely with compassionate concern and commitment. These rare attributes are essential in these times of trouble and uncertainty and most assuredly provide the Church with a platform for growth and strength in the years to come.

L. Fletcher Prouty
Col. US Air Force (Ret.)

On the threshold of the twenty-first century Scientology will continue to grow and be very strong and effective in its impact around the world. They will continue to be admired for putting hands and feet to their beliefs. Their example in fighting for religious freedom will continue to inspire all other faith groups in the ongoing struggles for religious freedom. Keep on keeping on.

Rev. William Solomon
Executive Minister
Metro Toronto Black Clergy
Association

It's far better known than it was a few years ago. People are more aware now. As society becomes more complex, people will want to associate with something to get a handle on life. I see this as a religious movement with all churches.

Michael Franchetti
Former Deputy Attorney General
California

I feel [Scientology's] future is good, given the conditions in society today and the need for people to find themselves. It's a good future, but a rough one, as long as organizations with strong religious prejudices exist and want to create problems for others. It's unfortunate, but inevitable.

Professor J. Stillson Judah
The Graduate Theological Union
San Francisco

As the Church of Scientology is a well-arranged organization, I see very good survival chances for its future. This is because the survival of a religion depends very much on its organization.

Dr. Rainer Flasche
Philipps University
Marburg, Germany

Observers of the Church [of Scientology] seem to be predominantly of the opinion that as a phenomenon it will develop and become larger due to the symptoms shown by unsolved problems and conflicts in our technical-scientific world.

Rudolf Grimm
Journalist

I expect the Church of Scientology increasingly to contribute positively to interfaith understanding in a true spirit of dialogue. This will be a valuable and welcome development. Such cooperation and dialogue will, in itself, help to break down barriers and increase trust, and will produce a broad stream of people of faith and ethics seeking and working for world peace.

Rev. Brian Cooper
*Chairman, Christian Peace
Conference England*

I am confident that the Church of Scientology will continue to be on the cutting edge of government reform simply because the Church has been doing it for years and doing it well. Scientology does this type of work better than any other organization in the country.

Wayne C. Bentson
*Freedom of Information Act
Specialist
Western Information Network*

The clearest indication of a religion is its practitioners. I see Scientologists engaged in the philosophy of L. Ron Hubbard by their promoting the development of human rights for all persons.

As to the future, I see the Scientology religion increasing the ability of humanity to achieve its best potential for good.

Ted Eagans
*Co-Founder and Director
Lift Every Voice, Inc.*

I have personally seen the verve and vitality of Scientologists across Europe, revitalizing the cause of religious freedom as we approach the year 2000. I have observed their actualization of the Universal Declaration of Human Rights in its 50th Anniversary in 1998. Scientologists are bringing together human rights and religious groups in a concerted push to restore those rights that are a part of every nation that has signed the Universal Declaration.

L. Ron Hubbard's philosophy of human and spiritual freedom is helping to create a future where individuals and humanity will flourish in a world of freedom. Scientologists have already staked a claim for liberty, not only for themselves but for others as well. In bringing people together, the Scientologists are ensuring that the Universal Declaration of Human Rights forged in this century will only become stronger in the coming centuries.

Irving Sarnoff
*Founder
Friends of the United Nations*

I feel that the Church has been a great help to many people. It has brought enlightenment— I hope you continue in your strides.

Lilyann Mitchell
*Argus Newspaper
England*

It is obvious that the Church of Scientology feels a moral responsibility to attack serious social problems and improve conditions. I see the Church building on this background and expanding its activities into the practical, hard-nosed field of education where it can play a major role in resolving some of the bitter conflicts which are preventing the proper education of our children. We need our children to be literate to have real-world skills. I see the Church of Scientology playing a major role in making this happen.

> Patrick Groff, EdD
> Professor Emeritus
> San Diego State University

Because the Church of Scientology has a legitimate philosophy on the human situation, it will endure. I see it outliving and speeding the demise of its main antagonist, the state-sponsored religion of psychiatry. Despite the current financial power of psychiatry and its ability to spread its dark message that man is but an animal, I believe the day will come when the Church of Scientology will be joined by other churches dancing on psychiatry's coffin.

> Seth Farber, PhD
> Executive Director
> Network Against Coercive
> Psychiatry

We should honor the Citizens Commission on Human Rights, established by the Church of Scientology in 1969, because it is really the organization that for the first time in human history has organized a politically, socially, internationally significant voice to combat psychiatry. This has never happened in human history before.

> Dr. Thomas Szasz, MD
> Professor Emeritus
> State University of New York

We, at the Bible Holiness Movement, have—over the years—been gratefully aware that the Church of Scientology has actively endeavored to express its committal to the God-given rights and liberties, including religious freedom, that are essential to society, and this with them has not been an abstract ideal but an essential practical effort along

with other religious and concerned bodies of people.

It is also good to have known personally of many instances when these Scientologists have acted on behalf of others who would differ with them, simply on the basis of principle and human compassion. Two instances come to mind, one where an Evangelical youth was under illegal effort to force a denial of faith in Christ, and the other of compassionate and effective effort in improving the lot of South African Black mental patients who were suffering vicious abuse in a form of virtual slavery.

What of the future? It would be our hope and expectation that the Scientologists will continue in their social conscience and concern for human liberty.

> Wesley H. Wakefield
> Bishop General of the
> International Bible Holiness
> Movement

As we enter a new century, global awareness of our environment—and the human consequences that accompany our dependence on chemicals—is greater than ever. L. Ron Hubbard may be the only person in the twentieth century to offer individuals a practical solution to the devastating aftermath of chemical exposure and drug abuse. The importance of the detoxification program that he developed, and that Scientology churches throughout the world have delivered to hundreds of thousands of individuals, cannot be overestimated. Mr. Hubbard's program may well be looked back upon as the breakthrough that enabled man to maintain a high quality of life in an increasingly toxic environment.

> Dr. David Root, MD, MPH
> (Master of Public Health)
> Occupational Medicine Specialist

*I bring to your attention two of the works of writer and philosopher L. Ron Hubbard—*Dianetics *and* The Way to Happiness—*to emphasize the wisdom of his philosophy regarding the creation of harmony amongst mankind. His scientific truisms and passionate talks about the rights of mankind inspire hope for an optimistic future.*

I know that implementation of new projects will be a real investment in bringing about the realization of L. Ron Hubbard's wishes to strengthen the moral health of a growing generation.

Stanislav S. Pylov
*Russian Academy of
Humanitarian Sciences*

The Declaration of Human Rights as released to the world by the United Nations in 1948 was a huge stride forward for humanity. The tenets of the Scientology religion not only support the hopes and aspirations for humanity as contained in the Declaration, but give us all an understanding of why it is so important people are brought together when they have this understanding. The principles contained in Scientology will be a major element in bringing the peoples of the world together.

Cecile Vowles
*National Vice President
United Nations Association of
Australia*

The trend today is for people to go back to conservatism.

As long as the Church of Scientology provides a visible alternative it's going to grow and expand.

We are through the permissive age and people are questioning values. You will get larger if you continue to provide an active social side to the Church.

If you continue to reassure people that it isn't all hopeless and the world isn't coming to an end you'll continue to do well.

Robert Carr
*Journalist
Ontario Parliament*

Each church has its unique role. Basically I see the role of the Church of Scientology as cleaning man's thinking, redirecting man's thinking, because obviously the old thought process has gotten us in the mess that we have. We must look at old values, old ways of doing things and not be afraid to question. And if we find that these values are incorrect in view of new enlightenment, then be willing to change—not feel threatened by new ideas, but embrace them and give them a chance to be proved or disproved.

Rev. E. L. Woods
*Pastor of Ebony Missionary Baptist
Church
Los Angeles, California*

Although these views greatly vary, all have common denominators. Among them are: Scientology is a practical religion; it has improved the spiritual lives of millions; it is a growing authority in the humanities; and, it is a vital source of wisdom about the spiritual nature of man.

The future, L. Ron Hubbard said some thirty years ago, would tell more than he ever could about the value of his work.

Thus far it has told an extraordinary story—a story of millions who have found a way to better themselves and their fellows through the use of this technology, of new rights for the mentally ill, of new lives for drug abusers and of new hope for the illiterate.

But what does the future hold from this point forward? Many of those who have attempted to halt Scientology in the past are still with us, and it is not unreasonable to assume that there may be future battles to fight. But in the final analysis, authority belongs to those who can DO the task in any given field. Authority sustained by pompousness, the laws passed and "we who know" cannot endure.

Scientology has the answers. Authority belongs to those who can do the job. And Scientology will inherit tomorrow as surely as the sun will rise.

CHAPTER 35

THOSE WHO OPPOSE SCIENTOLOGY

Dianetics did not come quietly into the world. Even before publication of L. Ron Hubbard's *Dianetics: The Modern Science of Mental Health,* excitement had been created on a relatively small scale—small, in hindsight of what was to come later. It had begun with a mimeographed copy of his earlier work *Dianetics: The Original Thesis,* which was passed hand to hand around the country, and continued with an article in the *Explorers Club Journal.*

Then, on May 9, 1950, *Dianetics: The Modern Science of Mental Health* reached the bookstores. Almost immediately, a groundswell of public enthusiasm vaulted the book onto national bestseller lists. Stores simply could not keep copies in stock as hundreds of thousands across the nation formed themselves into auditing groups, and Mr. Hubbard's discoveries even began to take root on distant shores. To meet the astonishing response from all sectors of society—the fashionable, the academic and, most importantly, the man on the street— the publisher instantly ordered further printings. Yet still supply could barely keep pace with demand. By the end of six weeks, Dianetics was not merely a phenomenon; it was the beginning of the global movement that continues to grow today.

There were, however, a scant few among society's ranks who were not quite so enthusiastic, i.e., certain key members of the American medical/psychiatric establishment. That their numbers were pitifully small— literally measured in the dozens—did not necessarily concern them. They were well-entrenched and well-connected; and when they decided that Dianetics must be stopped to preserve their kingdom, they were fully prepared to make use of every one of those connections.

Thus it was that two diametrically opposed forces were unleashed on May 9, 1950. On the one hand stood the hundred thousand and more everyday men and women who eagerly read and applied *Dianetics* with extraordinary success. On the other stood a small clique of medical and psychiatric practitioners, who knew nothing of the human mind and had not even read *Dianetics.* Nonetheless, they were certain that a handbook which made self-improvement possible to anyone would constitute a severe financial loss to the healthcare establishment. After all, they reasoned, how could psychiatrists expect to command large salaries if the man on the street knew more about the mind than they did? Seen within this context then, May 9, 1950, not only saw the birth of Dianetics, but also psychiatry's first shot that began a war.

THE REAL ISSUES

To understand the forces ranged against L. Ron Hubbard, in this war he never started, it is necessary to gain a cursory glimpse of the old and venerable science of psychiatry —which was actually none of the aforementioned. As an institution, it dates back to shortly before the turn of the century; it is certainly not worthy of respect by reason of age or dignity; and it does not meet any known definition of a science, what with its hodgepodge of unproven theories that have never produced any result—except an ability to make the unmanageable and mutinous more docile and quiet, and turn the troubled into apathetic souls beyond the point of caring.

That it promotes itself as a healing profession is a misrepresentation, to say the least. Its mission is to control.

Psychiatry as we know it today is more priesthood than science. Its conglomeration of half-baked theories is handed down by an arbitrary elite—authorities who have attained such status through who they know and who can sweet-talk the government into parting with yet more grant money. While as for what they actually do, there are only three primary methods of "treatment"—electroshock, psychosurgery and psychotropic drugs.

To illustrate the unscientific basis of this "science," in fascist Italy in the 1930s, Professor Ugo Cerletti noted that back in A.D. 43 or so, Roman citizens would sometimes try to rid themselves of headaches by putting a torpedo fish on their heads. A torpedo fish generates about twenty-five volts of electricity. Perhaps it was just coincidence that the Empire fell soon after that, but be that as it may, Cerletti was undeterred by this observation and set off on a new path. He began his experiments by killing dogs with huge jolts of electricity. However, before he could significantly reduce Rome's canine population, inspiration came in the form of a visit to a pig slaughterhouse. There, much to his delight, he found that pigs were not killed by the electricity administered, but only sent into epileptic convulsions, whereupon their throats could conveniently be cut by the butchers. After experimenting further—and losing a great many pigs—to discover how much electricity it would take to kill one of the porcine creatures, he was ready for man.

The unfortunate vagrant he chose (generously supplied by the police) received 70 volts to the head, fell, then shouted, "Not a second [one]. It will kill!" Later, it was discovered that human beings could withstand between 140 and 150 volts to the brain. Thus electroconvulsive shock therapy (ECT) was born.

Psychosurgery had equally shabby beginnings, according to the medical historians. In 1848, Phineas Gage of Vermont was peering into a blasting hole when a charge detonated and blew a metal tamping rod through his brain—an unfortunate accident that he managed to survive.

But, his astute physician noted with amazement, Gage had changed! A most noticeable change—from efficient and capable to self-indulgent and profane. Thus Gage may take his place in history as the first person to survive a lobotomy. The man who actually established himself as the father of the lobotomy (a procedure conducted on intractable patients to make them more manageable) was Dr. Egas Moniz. He operated on about one hundred patients. However, in at least one case, the operation might have been a success but the doctor died: he was shot by one of his lobotomized patients. That in 1949 he was given the Nobel prize for this questionable advancement is one of the saddest ironies of medical history. Nonetheless, it assured that many followed his path.

As for drugs, witch doctors have used the natural variety for centuries. Today's pharmaceutical psychotropic drugs began their development with attempts to brainwash recalcitrant citizens and political prisoners. Virtually all of the original research—in Russia, Germany and the United States—was funded by intelligence agencies. Once again, the aim was to make individuals more tractable and malleable. And in the United States, at least most of it was illegal, conducted on unknowing servicemen and citizens. Except, of course, in the oft-cited instance of CIA psychiatrist, Dr. Louis Jolyon West, who was the only man known to have killed an elephant with LSD.

That all of this experimentation—drugs, psychosurgery, ECT—has never cured anyone of anything but, on the contrary, has either made people more manageable or damaged them beyond recognition, has never stopped the psychiatric community from continuing these practices. After all, these are the only tools they have. Without them, they would have nothing to sell.

Which brings up a crucial point: to whom do they sell their services? Not to the broad public (and only sometimes even to their own patients), for the majority have no faith in this parody of science and would never even entertain the idea of actually visiting a psychiatrist. Then, of course, there is also the shame and embarrassment associated with going to a psychiatrist—which is largely due to the way psychiatrists themselves have characterized mental illness in a sales campaign that backfired. The only customers they have, the only ones willing to pay for their services (and very generously) are governments, particularly the clandestine arms of the government, or those that desire to control people, be they prisoners, children or society's unwanted.

These, then, constitute the force that tried to stop Dianetics and Scientology.

And this is the world Dianetics entered. A world where psychiatry was entrenched among the US intelligence services, living off the fat of government grants, and experimenting—with the help of ex-Nazi scientists—on an oblivious public. A world where their critics were simply labeled insane and "in need of psychiatric help."

Thus the battle lines were drawn. Dianetics offered a means to happiness, stability and success. It provided a solution to psychosomatic illnesses. It created an interest in the workings of the mind among people of all classes and ages. And it gave the man in the street a method that, for the first time, he himself could utilize to improve his own condition. Additionally, it should be kept in mind that L. Ron Hubbard achieved something that psychiatrists have long been attempting to achieve: to write a book about the mind that was genuinely popular, that people actually wanted to read, that was both understandable and applicable.

But *Dianetics* did more. It labeled the latest and greatest psychiatric drugs as dangerous. And it directly exposed the inhuman crimes of psychiatrists and the harm they caused with ECT and lobotomies, clearly substantiating the irreparable damage these treatments caused to healthy brain tissue.

That mental health professionals were incensed by Mr. Hubbard's not-so-gentle upbraiding is understandable, particularly as he was not a member of their elitist clique.

But when all was said and done, the issue was clearly financial: How long could one continue to convince the American taxpayer to foot the bill for multimillion-dollar psychiatric appropriations in the face of what Dianetics could accomplish for the price of a book?

THE MARSHALING OF FORCES

Among the many, many positive reviews and articles on *Dianetics* were a few strategically placed "hits" specifically designed to dampen public enthusiasm.

These first negative "reviews" on *Dianetics* came through the American Medical Association—a group instinctively opposed to any unregulated or nonmember means to better health and living. But it was not as it appeared; it was more the result of a ventriloquism act. The actual link to the AMA was made by the American Psychiatric Association (APA) medical director, Dr. Daniel Blain, who well knew that psychiatry enjoyed nothing close to the credibility of its medical colleagues, and none of the clout. The voice of the AMA was essentially that of him and his colleagues.

But using the AMA to take potshots was only the first round. The full APA plan was far more elaborate. First, false propaganda was to be published in "authoritative" journals. Then, once the "experts" had passed judgment, these opinions would be given to mainstream media sources. Dossiers would be created to contain all this unflattering "information" and passed still further afield including, of course, to appropriate government agencies.

Although simple in both design and execution, the consequences would be far-reaching. Indeed, to one degree or another, the subsequent attacks on Dianetics and Scientology were but a result of this original scheme to fabricate dossiers and then spread them far and wide.

MIND CONTROL EXPOSED

During the continual process of Dianetics research, both as an auditor and as an observer of other auditors, Mr. Hubbard naturally came into contact with a wide variety of cases. And it was inevitable that these would include those who had been in the hands of psychiatrists closely allied to the intelligence community.

Thus it came about, fully twenty-five years before the facts were made public by Congress, that Mr. Hubbard was the first to announce and decry government mind manipulation programs. Eventually, of course, these and other revelations about Central Intelligence Agency

(CIA) misconduct would entirely reshape public perception of this agency.

The vehicle for his revelation was his 1951 book *Science of Survival,* and in it Mr. Hubbard described in no uncertain terms the combined use of pain, drugs and hypnosis as a behavioral modification technique of the worst kind. It was, he said, so extensively used in espionage work, it was long past the time people should have become alarmed about it. It had taken Dianetic auditing to discover the widespread existence of these brainwashing techniques, and, he added, the only saving grace was that Dianetics could undo their effects.

With such covert government activity so openly addressed by Mr. Hubbard and Dianeticists, he had compounded his "crime": In his first book, he offended psychiatrists; in his second, the intelligence community. That the two, already closely connected, should now draw even closer in the common effort to stop him was not surprising. What was surprising was the velocity and frequency of subsequent attacks. By the mid-1950s, at least half a dozen federal agencies, including the Federal Bureau of Investigation (FBI), the Internal Revenue Service (IRS) and the Food and Drug Administration (FDA), were brought into the effort to suppress Dianetics and its assault on the mental health field.

"You would have thought that at the very least I was inciting whole populations to revolt and governments to fall," a slightly bemused Mr. Hubbard later wrote of these events. "All I really was doing was trying to tell man he could be happy, that there was a road out of suffering and that he could attain his goals."

THE BATTLE MOUNTS

Yet even while Mr. Hubbard successfully told man he could be happy and the numbers of Scientologists mounted, psychiatry was attempting to strengthen its grasp on society.

The plan involved what came to be known as the Siberia Bill, actually named the Alaska Mental Health Bill. The more popular title came from the fact that the proposed outcome of this cherished psychiatric plan was likened to a Siberia-type camp for mental health patients in the frozen wastelands of Alaska. Presumably, this was far enough away from the well-traveled roads of the world to allow psychiatrists to conduct their mind control and other experiments on a captive population, unhindered by the glare of publicity. To ensure a captive population, the measure incorporated a "simplified commitment procedure," so simple, in fact, that it eradicated such wasteful and costly activities as jury trials and legal defenses and allowed any peace officer, friend, medical doctor and, of course, psychiatrist, to institute commitment proceedings.

But just after January 1956 and the bill's unanimous, yet barely noticeable, passage through Congress, a coalition of members of the Church of Scientology and civil rights groups launched a campaign to inform the American public just what this bill held in store for them. Under the rallying cry, "Siberia, USA!" a massive letter-writing campaign inspired political opposition.

When it was over, the commitment section of the bill was deservedly dead, leaving merely an act to authorize mental health funding to the territory of Alaska.

A wounded psychiatry struck back, this time utilizing the FDA as its main battering ram. Thanks to the Freedom of Information Act, Scientologists later uncovered a mountain of documents which well demonstrated the activities of the participants—egged on by members of both the AMA and APA. A veritable beehive of activity took place, with letters and meetings between interested psychiatric parties; the Department of Justice; the Washington, DC, police department;

the United States Post Office; the IRS; the AMA of course; and even the US Army's Criminal Investigation Command—all continuously linked and regularly prodded by a now extremely nervous psychiatry.

The upshot of all these schemes? The first action was a ludicrous failure, the second a waste of time, the third an embarrassment.

The first, based on a psychiatrist's "tip" that the Church was using illegal drugs, led to a "raid" on the Washington, DC, church by a US deputy marshal who seized a few bottles of said drug. When it turned out to be a compound of the commonly available vitamin B_1, vitamin C, niacinamide and calcium, that case obviously went nowhere.

Drug dealing proving an unworkable premise, the FDA and other interested agencies decided that Scientology practicing medicine without a license would prove fertile ground for exploration. On March 19, 1959, FDA agent Taylor Quinn infiltrated the church, taped a religious service, and passed the information on to the US Attorney's Office.

Unfortunately, as he reported to the FDA, the church had required him to sign a contract that he was not to learn to cure anyone. Nor was there any evidence of fraud.

With both drugs and illegal healing dead-ended, the only avenue remaining to the FDA was the E-Meter. Perhaps, they theorized inaccurately, it was used to "diagnose" or "cure illness." So, on January 4, 1963, US marshals, deputized longshoremen and armed police barged their way into the Founding Church of Scientology in Washington, DC, threatened the staff, and left with two vans of not only E-Meters, but books, scriptures and other materials.

Still, as outrageous as it was, it did not match the sheer audacity of what happened in Seattle where the FDA's fingerprints were figuratively all over the handgun that was used to murder the head of the church there.

A local resident, Russell Johnson, who had heard about the FDA's actions in Washington, DC, thought they would provide a sympathetic ear to his current problem. He called them to complain about "the practices of a Dr. William Fisk who operates as the Church of Scientology" and claimed Fisk was attempting to seduce his wife.

The enterprising FDA official he spoke to immediately suggested that Johnson join forces with the FDA as an "undercover agent" and infiltrate the church. Johnson dutifully did this, reported in, and was instructed to return and get further information.

Johnson carried his duties as an intelligence agent into tragic and bloody extremes. On September 10, 1963, he walked into the Seattle church and shot and killed the Executive Director before a roomful of horrified congregation members.

The FDA then carried the concept of expediency to new and distasteful heights. Instead of confessing that one of its "agents" had just committed murder, it contacted the Seattle police department and arranged to send its own people illegally into church premises with the homicide team, to further gather information for its "investigation." As usual, however, the FDA discovered nothing illegal in the church.

For more than a decade the FDA would remain obsessed with the E-Meter. With other government agencies, it would repeatedly infiltrate the Church with agents and informants, employ bugging devices, place a "cover" on Church mail, and obtain confidential Church bank account information.

It went nowhere. In 1969, the Washington, DC, Federal Appeals Court ruled the Church a bona fide religion protected by the US Constitution, and that the E-Meter had not been improperly labeled or used.

Still, it was not until 1973 that a reluctant FDA finally returned those stolen Church materials: 5,000 books, 2,900 booklets, and the E-Meters.

MEDIA-GOVERNMENT COLLUSION

There remains one illuminating point to the FDA fiasco. It involves the enlistment by the FDA of *The Saturday Evening Post* and their star feature writer, James Phelan.

After being approached by the AMA to do a story on Scientology, the *Post* assigned the piece to Phelan, who traveled to England to interview Mr. Hubbard. He was warmly welcomed and assisted in every manner possible, as befits a seemingly interested and unbiased journalist, which is how he represented himself.

That Phelan was anything but that was borne out by two facts: Immediately upon his return to Washington and before the story was published, he gave his story to the FDA for coordination purposes; and the resulting story was a hatchet job of the first order—an unrestrained attempt to smear both Mr. Hubbard and Scientology, obviously a flanking action to the FDA's attempted case against use of the E-Meter.

Phelan was followed by many others—a long string of stories through the years, concocted to create a climate conducive to governmental harassment. It was a similar pattern to that which occurred in Germany in the 1930s—the very successful media actions to create public "indignation" that would legitimize not only the most blatant violations of civil rights, but, indeed, the Holocaust.

THE IRS CAMPAIGN

The FDA had conclusively proven its incompetence, not only by botching its mandate to destroy Scientology, but by taking so long to do it—and allowing Scientology to grow meteorically, both in the United States and around the world. Thus, the FDA was dismissed to do what it does best: harass vitamin salesmen, and give carte blanche to powerful drug companies well before completion of the product safety tests.

The weight of the mission soon fell on IRS shoulders—more specifically, on the shoulders of an attorney in the office of the IRS' Chief Counsel, one Charlotte Murphy. A noteworthy fact is her attendance at meetings in the mid-1950s of the DC Medical Society's Committee on Mental Health—along with the main sponsors of the Siberia Bill, along with the psychiatrist who had falsely "tipped" the FDA that the Church was involved in illegal drugs, and along with a number of leading psychiatrists who had been at the forefront of the attacks on Dianetics from day one. It is therefore not surprising that Murphy herself requested that she deal exclusively with any IRS matters regarding Scientology. Nor were her intentions surprising. She made them quite clear in a memo to the Director of the Washington Branch of the IRS in which she asked whether there were "any local statutes or ordinances available as tools to curtail or close down the operation."

What followed was an all-out effort to harass the Church by denying tax-exempt status to various Scientology churches, and issuing federal tax liens against others. Information was provided to the post office to "support a charge of misrepresentation," and later a host of other government agencies were forwarded blatantly ludicrous falsehoods on the order of: "LSD and perhaps other drugs are widely used by the members while assembled" and that the Church used "electric shock" on its parishioners in an "initiation ceremony"— fabrications that would have been laughable if not for the consequences.

The harassment of the Church and its leaders for purposes totally removed from proper enforcement of the tax laws was definitively exposed during a series of Congressional investigations and hearings in the 1970s. These hearings focused on,

among other things, the infamous 1969 Nixon White House "enemies list," and revealed previously secret and illegal IRS programs against individuals and organizations, including the Church of Scientology.

History shows us that of the 213 names on the Nixon list, 211 were left bankrupt, collapsed, disbanded or dead. Indeed, of the individuals and organizations on that infamous "enemies list," only two survived intact: L. Ron Hubbard and the Church of Scientology. That these attacks continued for as many years as they did serves as a study in how bureaucratic momentum can carry raw animus forward long after the initial "reason" has been forgotten.

The whole tiresome history of IRS attacks would fill a book. Faced with the choice of defending itself or perishing, the Church used the Freedom of Information Act (FOIA) to obtain and ultimately expose government documents which demonstrated a broad range of discriminatory conduct and illegal acts against the Church and its parishioners by certain elements within the IRS. When the agency balked at releasing the information, the Church was forced to litigate hundreds of cases which ultimately resulted in precedent-setting legislation—and exposure and confirmation of the very matters alleged by the Church, and more. One federal judge credited the Church with reforming IRS procedures which directly benefited "over 1,000 cases involving identical legal issues." An official of the US Department of Justice remarked that the Church's actions "significantly contributed to the preservation of democracy for everyone." Indeed, it is virtually impossible to read a page in a legal textbook about the FOIA today without finding a precedent set by the Church of Scientology.

The documents obtained under the FOIA filled scores of filing cabinets and revealed a genuinely shocking parade of dirty tricks authored by those in the IRS who hoped for the Church's destruction. They tell of IRS attempts to redefine the term "church," expressly to disqualify Scientology from tax-exempt status. When that did not work, an even more incredible story unfolded: In an attempt to circumvent the absence of any wrongdoing on the Church's part, rogue IRS employees engaged for years in a corrupt scheme of vast dimensions.

Directing this effort was the infamous Los Angeles branch of the IRS Criminal Investigations Division (CID), a unit whose abuses of the Church and countless other taxpayers eventually became the focus of extensive congressional hearings in 1989 and 1990, and ultimately led to substantial IRS reforms. Before that, however, the Los Angeles IRS CID, with the offices of the mother church of the Scientology religion nearby, held sway over certain key IRS matters relative to Scientology.

The CID plan called for nothing short of complete destruction of the Church. Yet even as attempts were made to infiltrate church premises and plots were hatched to forge and plant documents to later be "discovered" and used as evidence, Church attorneys and staff exposed all. Thus, in addition to concerns over growing public outrage resulting from this exposure, the CID now had to contend with another problem: It had spent several years investigating the Church at enormous cost to taxpayers, only to find no crimes committed.

Still, in a last-ditch effort to save face, the Los Angeles CID sought to persuade the Department of Justice to bring some kind — any kind — of prosecution to justify what it had done. Justice may be blind but it is rarely stupid, and Justice Department attorneys rebuked the unit and refused to support any prosecution or even further investigation.

Throughout this assault, the Church persisted in efforts to gain fair treatment from the IRS. Finally, in 1991, senior executives of church organizations met with IRS officials in Washington, DC. Once dialogue began, outside the purview and without the poisonous influence of the Los Angeles CID, the result was inevitable. Still, it was neither fast nor easy, for the IRS conducted a two-year examination of an intensity and depth without parallel in the history of exempt organizations.

IRS officials subjected Scientology churches to the most intensive scrutiny any organization ever faced — including a meticulous review of its operations and financial records, as well as a comprehensive review of every aspect of Church policy and practices at all levels, including the most senior echelons of its management.

The IRS review resulted in hundreds of detailed questions, requiring thousands of pages of narrative and many more thousands of pages of financial records. Six teams of between four and eight agents conducted a full-time review for periods of up to ten continuous weeks. And by the end of its examination, the IRS had reviewed more than one million pages of information concerning the Scientology religion.

The IRS also reviewed and fully investigated sensationalized media stories about Scientology based on the allegations of a few disgruntled former members. The agency found these apostates unreliable and dismissed their media stories as utterly baseless.

By the time the churches of Scientology received the IRS final decision, the largest administrative record ever for any exempt organization — twelve linear feet — had been compiled. These churches and their representatives had been subjected to hundreds of hours of exhaustive meetings and examined by the most senior officials over exempt organizations at the IRS National Office, spanning the administrations of three IRS Commissioners.

In the end, the IRS came to the only conclusion possible after such a thorough examination: Scientology churches and their related entities were organized and operated exclusively for charitable and religious purposes.

So, on October 1, 1993 the United States Internal Revenue Service issued ruling letters which recognized the tax-exempt status of more than 150 Scientology churches, missions, social reform organizations and other entities because they operate exclusively for religious and charitable purposes.

IRS religious recognition was universal and unconditional, and it was the result of the most detailed and exhaustive examination of a religious organization in the agency's history. The IRS was given unfettered access to every echelon of the Church's ecclesiastical hierarchy. Thus, the IRS examination was not limited to United States entities, but specifically included the financial and other affairs of church organizations from Australia to Canada and from Europe to South Africa.

As a result, Church of Scientology International (CSI), the mother church of the Scientology religion, received not only exempt recognition, but also received a group exemption letter embracing all Scientology churches within its ecclesiastical oversight. The Church's spiritual meccas were also individually recognized as tax-exempt, as were the Church's publishing entities.

Scientology Missions International (SMI) received its own exemption. It also received a separate group exemption letter for all Scientology missions within its ecclesiastical oversight.

Religious Technology Center (RTC) was individually recognized as tax-exempt and received its own separate ruling letter.

The IRS also recognized the International Association of Scientologists as a tax-exempt organization.

In addition to ruling favorably on tax exemption, the IRS rulings made all donations to all United States churches of Scientology deductible against personal income taxes to the full extent permitted by law.

The IRS recognition brought not only an end to decades of conflict between churches and the tax agency, but a formal acknowledgment of Scientology's religious nature and its benefit to society as a whole.

In the wake of that victory, and the Church's efforts to expose IRS wrongdoing, came many reforms benefiting all US citizens. The Taxpayer Bill of Rights, now a legislative reality, exists today in no small part due to the perseverance of the Church and its parishioners who exposed widespread IRS abuses and demanded a curb of future abuses. Through their use of the FOIA, the Church ultimately brought into public view agency misconduct and computer errors which could have resulted in $1 billion in incorrect assessments. The movement now gaining momentum in Congress to make sweeping tax reform reality rather than rhetoric is, to no small degree, traceable to the groundbreaking work of Scientologists.

In short, when the war with the IRS ended, the ground gained on the road to that resolution yielded victories enjoyed today by all Americans.

AN END TO THE WORLDWIDE CAMPAIGN

Although the more than forty-year assault against Scientology assumed large proportions, the source must be remembered —that small but influential circle of psychiatrists. Nor did the means change over the years: false allegations selectively planted in the media, then seeded into federal files as background "fact."

It is a method, with small adjustments, that also served to cause trouble overseas. The international pipeline left the US, primarily through IRS and FBI links, traveled through the channels of the International Criminal Police Organization (Interpol), located in France, and was

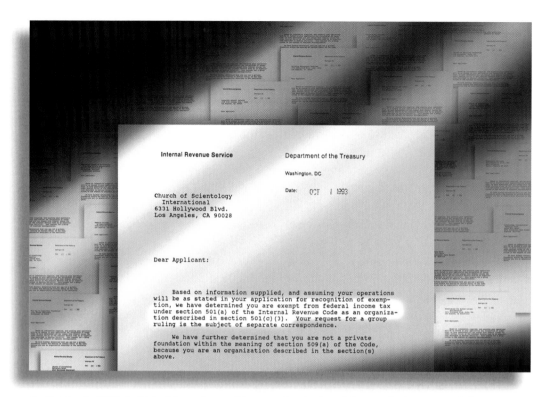

On October 1, 1993 the United States Internal Revenue Service issued letters which recognized the tax exempt status of more than 150 Scientology churches, missions and social reform organizations.

discharged among the law enforcement and intelligence bodies of various nations.

What happened was fairly predictable: attacks against Scientology by government agencies in England, France, Germany, Italy, Spain and Australia—all with fervent media support involving the most outrageous allegations. Still, as usual, Scientology prevailed.

And, just as there had been some within the IRS who were willing to examine the facts and dismiss the lies about Scientology, so it was with Interpol. Following the IRS recognition, Church officials were able to meet with top Interpol officials to present the truth.

Interpol, too, recognized the religiosity of Scientology. The Church and the police agency peacefully resolved all issues between them. Following its own charter not to involve itself in religious matters, Interpol today keeps no files on the Church of Scientology.

SKIRMISHES

The IRS recognition of Scientology was a stunning blow to those who had kept the attacks on the Church going for so many decades. Yet despite this, and despite the end to the international campaign of disinformation which had also been waged for so many years, the psychiatrists who had fueled this campaign from behind the scenes continued sniping on other fronts.

One vector of attack was through so-called "anti-cult" groups. For many years, psychiatry had used a variety of antireligious front groups to assault Scientology and other churches, both in the United States and Europe. One of the most notorious of these was the "Cult Awareness Network," known as CAN.

CAN had been a clearinghouse in the US for false and biased information which was used to incite prejudice, hatred and fear about Scientology and many other religions, both old and new. It was an organization that preyed on the gullible and violated the civil rights of the innocent for financial reward. Its members were continually linked to kidnappings, assaults and rapes.

The Church responded with a national public information campaign which provided the truth about this organization to police departments, judges, district attorneys and religious and charitable organizations across the country. And the resulting groundswell of public indignation and condemnation created a backlash against CAN.

In 1996, CAN was forced into liquidation after unsuccessfully seeking to escape a $1.1 million damages verdict handed down by a US District Court in Seattle by filing for bankruptcy. The case involved a young Christian man who had been kidnapped and assaulted by a CAN "deprogramer."

Yet another attack on the Church was mounted from a different direction—the technological frontier of the Internet. Here, a handful of apostates, with the support of psychiatric and media apologists who had figured prominently over the years in assaults on Scientology, began to broadly distribute copyrighted and confidential religious scriptures which had been stolen from a Church of Scientology in Denmark.

When the Church brought legal action against these copyright pirates, those involved claimed the protection of "free speech" for their criminal acts.

The courts disagreed. Judges in three different cases ruled unequivocally against those distributing the stolen materials, and upheld the right of the Church of Scientology to protect its sacred scriptures from illegal distribution on the Internet.

So it goes. Key psychiatric figures, their US government allies and psychiatric colleagues overseas, together have spent untold millions of dollars around the world to stop Scientology.

And they never have.

THE END OF THE FIGHT

While psychiatry had US government agencies infiltrating, raiding and investigating the Church in the early and mid-1960s and inquiries in Australia and Great Britain underway during the same decade, the technologies of Scientology and Dianetics were widely available in five countries. Despite unabated attacks, these technologies became available in five more countries by the mid-1970s, in fifty-six countries in the late 1980s, and in seventy-four countries by the turn of the 1990s. By 1998, there were more than 1,400 churches, missions and groups located in over 130 countries. All of which demonstrates that psychiatry has been about as effective in stopping Scientology as it has been in treating mental illness.

It has, in fact, become increasingly evident that psychiatry offers no valuable contribution to society whatsoever. Electric shock, brain operations and indiscriminate drugging of patients in nineteenth-century-like horror chambers passed off as mental hospitals have killed and maimed people on a daily basis. And during the period psychiatry has held its position of authority, the most dramatic era of social unrest, civil disobedience, drug proliferation and criminality in the history of the Western world has gained momentum.

Today, there are 500 Dianeticists and Scientologists to every psychiatrist, and while Scientology expands, enrollment in psychiatric university curriculums has slid to a drastic low since a peak in the 1960s. Without government appropriations, even these few psychiatrists would not be able to economically survive, for they have nothing to offer worth a cent of the public's money.

Hence, while Scientology is more visible than ever, with churches dotting every continent on Earth and millions of parishioners around the world, one is hard-pressed to find even a single psychiatrist with a shingle on his door. True, one can still find them in scuffed-linoleum offices of state and county hospitals, and lodged in the federal bureaucracy. But when was the last time anyone saw a sign advertising lobotomies, electric shock and seriously incapacitating drugs?

In short, then, while psychiatry, which lives off government handouts, is shrinking, Scientology, which receives only public donations from people who know it works, is growing faster than any religion in the world. And if Scientology had anything to hide, it would not have survived the relentless attacks detailed in this chapter.

Thus the story of the attacks against Scientology is basically very simple. Dianetics and Scientology cut across vested interests which then ruthlessly attempted to destroy it. The issue was never any wrongdoing by the Church, merely encroachment on turf claimed by a mental health industry that would stop at nothing to preserve its stake.

Still, while psychiatry's offensive against Scientology has been all but defeated, the battle is not over and the skirmishes continue.

In spite of the IRS recognition in the United States of the religiosity of the Church of Scientology, there are less enlightened countries that do not have a tradition of religious freedom, that are dominated by state religions which consider others to be competition, and that have a long and painful tradition of intolerance. In these countries, the strategy is the same as it once was in the United States. The same false reports are seeded into government files, the same type of psychiatrists make authoritative announcements, and the same kind of media blindly repeats wild accusations.

But just as in the United States truth once again demonstrated its power by prevailing against odds that would have overwhelmed any lesser cause, so too will it in these countries. It is clear now that when any government agency demonstrates enough integrity to actually investigate the Church of Scientology, to examine the false reports,

libel, rumor and innuendo, to see for themselves what the Church actually is and actually does, it has no choice but to recognize the religiosity of Scientology and the benefit it brings. While some still cling to the musty old files with yellowing clippings dating back to those early days in 1950, they too will sooner or later have to enter the present and step into the tide of the future.

It would thus be well to remember, then, that when alarming reports are heard about Dianetics and Scientology, they stem from those who would prefer to manhandle problems with mind-altering drugs or enough electricity to throw a pig into convulsions—and as any fool knows, sticking one's finger in a light socket or clamping electrodes to one's skull cures nothing. (Even psychiatrists are not that stupid. When widely offered $10,000 to undergo their own "treatment," not one has ever agreed to subject himself to electroconvulsive therapy.)

The lessons of history provide the best context within which to consider such attacks. Every great movement which has opened new vistas and shaken the strongholds of archaic thought has been attacked by those who profit from the persistence of outmoded ideas. Thus, as Scientologists continue their work toward a new civilization without insanity, criminality or war, those with billion-dollar vested interests in just those ills will continue to lash out.

Yet it is ironic to view these attacks in the context of time. Scientology did not choose to fight this battle with psychiatry and, indeed, was not the one to fire the opening salvos. Mr. Hubbard was simply the one to come up with real answers to problems of the mind. Perhaps sensing that implicit in a solution to the mind lay their own demise, psychiatrists decided to destroy him and his technology. And just as they feared, Scientology has become their nemesis, exposing their brutality and their crimes.

What remains of the old guard stands increasingly alone and the shrill voices of their heirs grow fainter and fainter. For try as they might to maintain their privileged positions and spread their falsehoods, the ears and eyes of the world have changed. Truth, after all, sheds light. The dark shadows in which they have hidden have grown ever more insubstantial.

But even as their tirades drone on, there is another point they should consider: The world which they helped create, a world where the wasted insane wander aimlessly through our inner cities, where senseless criminality claims a new life every few minutes, and entire generations sag under the double onslaught of drug dependency and illiteracy, this is a world in which they too must live.

And so, in the end, even those who attempted to stop Scientology will ultimately benefit from its victory.

THE TRUE STORY OF SCIENTOLOGY
BY L. RON HUBBARD

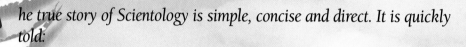

The true story of Scientology is simple, concise and direct. It is quickly told:

1. A philosopher develops a philosophy about life and death.

2. People find it interesting.

3. People find it works.

4. People pass it along to others.

5. It grows.

When we examine this extremely accurate and very brief account we see that there must be in our civilization some very disturbing elements for anything else to be believed about Scientology.

These disturbing elements are the Merchants of Chaos. They deal in confusion and upset. Their daily bread is made by creating chaos. If chaos were to lessen, so would their incomes.

The politician, the reporter, the medico, the drug manufacturer, the militarist and arms manufacturer, the police and the undertaker, to name the leaders of the list, fatten only upon "the dangerous environment." Even individuals and family members can be Merchants of Chaos.

It is to their interest to make the environment seem as threatening as possible, for only then can they profit. Their incomes, force and power rise in direct ratio to the amount of threat they can inject into the surroundings of the people. With that threat they can extort revenue, appropriations, heightened circulations and recompense without question.

These are the Merchants of Chaos. If they did not generate it and buy and sell it, they would, they suppose, be poor.

For instance, we speak loosely of "good press." Is there any such thing today? Look over a newspaper. Is there anything **good** on the front page? Rather there is murder and sudden death, disagreement and catastrophe. And even that, bad as it is, is sensationalized to make it seem worse.

This is the coldblooded manufacture of "a dangerous environment." People do not need this news; and if they did, they need the facts, not the upset. But if you hit a person hard enough he can be made to give up money. That's the basic formula of extortion. That's the way papers are sold. The impact makes them stick.

A paper has to have chaos and confusion. A "news story" has to have "conflict," they say. So there is no good press. There is only **bad** press about everything. To yearn for "good press" is foolhardy in a society where the Merchants of Chaos reign.

Look what has to be done to the true story of Scientology in order to "make it a news story" by modern press standards. Conflict must be injected where there is none. Therefore the press has to dream up upset and conflict.

Let us take the first line. How does one make conflict out of it? No. 1, **A philosopher develops a philosophy about life and death.**

The Chaos Merchant **has** to inject one of several possible conflicts here: He is not a doctor of philosophy, they have to assert. They are never quite bold enough to say it is not a philosophy. But they can and do go on endlessly, as their purpose compels them, in an effort to invalidate the identity of the person developing it.

In actual fact, the developer of the philosophy was very well grounded in academic subjects and the humanities, probably better grounded in formal philosophy alone than teachers of philosophy in universities.

The one-man effort is incredible in terms of study and research hours and is a record never approached in living memory, but this would not be considered newsworthy. To write the simple fact that a philosopher had developed a philosophy is not newspaper-type news and it would not disturb the environment. Hence the elaborate news fictions about No. 1 above.

Then take the second part of the true story: **People find it interesting**. It would be very odd if they didn't, as everyone asks these questions of himself and looks for the answers to his own beingness, and the basic truth of the answers is observable in the conclusions of Scientology.

However, to make this "news" it has to be made disturbing. People are painted as kidnapped or hypnotized and dragged as unwilling victims up to read the books or listen.

The Chaos Merchant leaves No. 3 very thoroughly alone. It is dangerous ground for him. **People find it works.** No hint of workability would ever be attached to Scientology by the press, although there is no doubt in the press mind that it **does** work. That's why it's dangerous. It calms the environment. So any time spent trying to convince press Scientology works is time spent upsetting a reporter.

On No. 4, **People pass it along to others,** the press feels betrayed. "Nobody should believe anything they don't read in the papers. How dare word of mouth exist!" So, to try to stop people from listening, the Chaos Merchant has to use words like **cult.** That's "a closed group," whereas Scientology is the most open group on Earth to anyone. And they have to attack organizations and their people to try to keep people out of Scientology.

Now, as for No. 5, **It grows**, we have the true objection.

As truth goes forward, lies die. The slaughter of lies is an act that takes bread from the mouth of a Chaos Merchant. Unless he can lie with wild abandon about how bad it all is, he thinks he will starve.

The world simply must **not** be a better place according to the Chaos Merchant. If people were less disturbed, less beaten down by their environments, there would be no new appropriations for police and armies and big rockets and there'd be not even pennies for a screaming sensational press.

So long as politicians move upward on scandal, police get more pay for more crime, medicos get fatter on more sickness, there will be Merchants of Chaos. They're paid for it.

And their threat is the simple story of Scientology. For that is the true story. And behind its progress there is a calmer environment in which a man can live and feel better. If you don't believe it, just stop reading newspapers for two weeks and see if you feel better. Suppose you had all such disturbances handled?

The pity of it is, of course, that even the Merchant of Chaos needs us, not to get fatter, but just to live himself as a being.

So the true story of Scientology is a simple story.

And too true to be turned aside.

PART TWELVE

A SCIENTOLOGY CATECHISM

Throughout history, religions have traditionally published summaries of their basic principles in catechism form. The following chapter will answer some of the most commonly asked questions people have about the fundamentals of Dianetics and Scientology.

When individuals first hear about the subject, their questions are usually quite diverse. They range from "Why is Scientology called a religion?" and "What is the difference between Dianetics and Scientology?" to "Who was L. Ron Hubbard?" to "What is the E-Meter and how does it work?"

These questions, and many others, are answered in the following pages.

CHAPTER 36

ANSWERS TO COMMON QUESTIONS

hat does the word Scientology mean?

The word *Scientology,* conceived by L. Ron Hubbard, comes from the Latin *scio* which means "know" or "distinguish," and from the Greek word *logos* which means "reason itself" or "inward thought." Thus it means the study of wisdom or knowledge. It means knowing how to know. Scientology, however, is defined as the study and handling of the spirit in relationship to itself, universes and other life.

What is Scientology about?

Developed by L. Ron Hubbard, Scientology is a religion that offers a precise path leading to a complete and certain understanding of one's true spiritual nature and of one's relationship with self, family, groups, mankind, all life forms, the material universe, the spiritual universe and the Supreme Being, or infinity.

Scientology addresses the spirit—not simply the body or mind—and believes that man is far more than a product of his environment, or his genes.

Scientology comprises a body of knowledge which extends from certain fundamental truths. Prime among these are:

Man is an immortal spiritual being.

His experience extends well beyond a single lifetime.

His capabilities are unlimited, even if not presently realized.

Scientology further holds man to be basically good, and that his spiritual salvation depends upon himself and his fellows and his attainment of brotherhood with the universe.

Scientology is not a dogmatic religion in which one is asked to believe anything on faith. An individual discovers for himself that Scientology works by applying its principles and observing or experiencing the results.

The ultimate goal of Scientology is true spiritual enlightenment and freedom for the individual.

How did Scientology start?

L. Ron Hubbard began his studies of the mind and spirit in 1923, resulting in a manuscript entitled "Excalibur" in 1938. It was in this unpublished work that the word "Scientology" first appeared to describe what Mr. Hubbard termed "the study of knowing how to know." He decided against publishing the book, saying, "Excalibur did not contain any therapy of any kind but was simply a discussion of the composition of life." And he added, "I decided to go further."

The "going further" resulted in Dianetics, a subject which was, in fact, introduced into the much broader field of Scientology to provide some kind of "therapy" that could be easily utilized by the man in the street. Thus, in 1947, he wrote a manuscript detailing some of these discoveries.

It was not published at that time, but circulated among friends, who copied it and passed it on to others. (This manuscript was ultimately formally published in 1951 as

Dianetics: The Original Thesis and later republished as The Dynamics of Life.)

As copies of the manuscript circulated, Mr. Hubbard began to receive a flood of letters requesting further information and more applications of his new subject. He soon found himself spending all his time answering letters and decided to write a comprehensive text on the subject.

He first published an article on the subject. "Terra Incognita: The Mind," appeared in the Winter-Spring 1950 issue of the Explorers Club Journal. This was followed by the book Dianetics: The Modern Science of Mental Health, published in May 1950. It became a nationwide bestseller almost overnight. By late summer, people across the country were not only reading the book, but were also organizing their own groups for the purpose of applying Dianetics techniques. The book has remained a bestseller ever since, becoming number one on the New York Times bestseller list almost four decades after its initial publication. It continues to appear on bestseller lists around the world.

In the course of thousands of hours of Dianetics counseling on tens of thousands of individuals all over the country, it soon became apparent that many people audited on these procedures were coming into contact with incidents that seemed to occur in previous lives. Although certain officials in the Dianetics organizations attempted to suppress research into this phenomenon, L. Ron Hubbard refused to allow this. In his subsequent investigation, during which he asked himself the question of "Who was looking at these mental image pictures?" (a question raised in 1950 in Dianetics: The Modern Science of Mental Health as a vital matter to resolve), Mr. Hubbard believed that it had to be something other than the mind itself. He came to the conclusion that it was man's spiritual self that was doing so. Eventually, Mr. Hubbard confirmed that he was dealing with an individual who was a spirit inhabiting a body and using a mind, and that man had a fundamentally spiritual nature.

It was this discovery, in the fall of 1951, that completed the circle for Mr. Hubbard and brought him back to the broader subject of Scientology and what Dianetics had been addressing all along—the spirit. It was then that he publicly announced Scientology. As he put it, "I found out what was looking at the pictures. And described it. And found out that you could do things with it from a very practical standpoint that nobody had ever done before and found myself suddenly in the field of religion . . ."

In 1954 the first Church of Scientology was formed in Los Angeles by a group of Scientologists, and within a few years churches were formed across the country and around the world.

In the years that followed, L. Ron Hubbard completed his research into the spiritual nature of man. Today, all his writings on the subject are available to anyone who wishes to study Scientology. Although Mr. Hubbard departed his body in 1986, he is still with us in spirit and the legacy of his work continues to help people around the world realize their true spiritual nature.

Is it all based on one man's work?

Although Dianetics and Scientology were discovered by L. Ron Hubbard, he wrote: "Acknowledgment is made to fifty thousand years of thinking men without whose speculations and observations the creation and construction of Dianetics would not have been possible. Credit in particular is due to:

"Anaxagoras, Thomas Paine, Aristotle, Thomas Jefferson, Socrates, René Descartes, Plato, James Clerk Maxwell, Euclid, Charcot, Lucretius, Herbert Spencer, Roger Bacon, William James, Francis Bacon, Sigmund Freud, Isaac Newton, van Leeuwenhoek, Cmdr. Joseph Thompson (MC) USN, William A. White, Voltaire, Will Durant, Count Alfred Korzybski, and my instructors in atomic and molecular phenomena, mathematics and the humanities at George Washington University and at Princeton."

Why is Scientology called a religion?

Scientology certainly meets all three criteria generally used by religious scholars around the world to determine religiosity: (1) a belief in some Ultimate Reality, such as the Supreme or eternal truth that transcends the here and now of the secular world; (2) religious practices directed toward understanding, attaining or communing with this Ultimate Reality; and (3) a community of believers who join together in pursuing this Ultimate Reality.

Scientology's beliefs in an Ultimate Reality that transcends the material world include its concepts of the thetan, the spiritual world (the seventh dynamic) and the Supreme Being (the eighth dynamic). The second element can be found in Scientology's life-rite ceremonies such as naming, marriage and funeral services, but predominantly in the religious services of auditing and training, through which Scientologists increase their spiritual awareness of themselves and attain an understanding of the spiritual world and, ultimately, their relationship with the Supreme Being. As to the third element, a very vital community of believers can be found at any church of Scientology at almost any time of the day.

Scientology is thus a religion in the most traditional sense of the term. Scientology helps man become more aware of God, more aware of his own spiritual nature and that of those around him. Scientology scripture recognizes that there is an entire dynamic (urge or motivation in life) devoted to the Supreme Being (the eighth dynamic), and another dynamic that deals solely with one's urge toward existence as a spirit (the seventh dynamic). Acknowledgment of these aspects of life is a traditional characteristic of religions.

Scientology holds in common with all great religions the dream of peace on Earth and salvation for man. What is new about Scientology is that it offers a precise path for bringing about spiritual improvement in the here and now and a way to accomplish it with absolute certainty.

Why is Scientology a church?

The word *church* comes from the Greek word *kyrios* meaning "lord" and the Indo-European

base *kewe,* "to be strong." Current meanings of the word include "a congregation," "ecclesiastical power as distinguished from the secular" and "the clerical profession; clergy."

The word *church* is not only used by Christian organizations. There were churches ten thousand years before there were Christians, and Christianity itself was a revolt against the established church. In modern usage, people speak of the Buddhist or Muslim church, referring in general to the whole body of believers in a particular religious teaching.

A church is simply a congregation of people who participate in common religious activities. Church is also used to refer to the building where members of a religious group gather to practice their religion and attain greater spiritual awareness and well-being.

In the 1950s, Scientologists recognized that L. Ron Hubbard's technology and its results dealt directly with the freeing of the human spirit, and that greater spiritual awareness was routinely being achieved. There was no question in their minds that what they were dealing with was a religious practice; thus, in the early 1950s, they voted that a church be formed to better serve the spiritual needs of themselves and others who shared their belief. The first Church of Scientology was then incorporated in 1954.

Thus, Scientology is a religion and the use of the word *church* when referring to Scientology is correct.

Does Scientology have a scripture?

Yes. The writings and recorded spoken words of L. Ron Hubbard on the subject of Scientology collectively constitute the scripture of the religion. He set forth the Scientology theology and technologies in more than 500,000 pages of writings, including dozens of books and over 2,000 tape-recorded public lectures.

What is the Scientology cross?

It is an eight-pointed cross representing the eight parts or dynamics of life through which each individual is striving to survive. These parts are: the urge toward existence as self, as an individual; the urge to survive through creativity, including the family unit and the rearing of children; the urge to survive through a group of individuals or as a group; the urge toward survival through all mankind and as all mankind; the urge to survive as life forms and with the help of life forms such as animals, birds, insects, fish and vegetation; the urge to survive of the physical universe, by the physical universe itself and with the help of the physical universe and each one of its component parts; the urge to survive as spiritual beings or the urge for life itself to survive; the urge toward existence as infinity. To be able to live happily with respect to each of these spheres of existence is symbolized by the Scientology cross.

As a matter of interest, the cross as a symbol predates Christianity.

What does the Scientology symbol, the S and double triangle, represent?

The "S" stands for Scientology.

The lower triangle is called the ARC triangle (pronounced by the letters A, R, C); A for affinity, R for reality and C for communication. These three interdependent factors combined add up to understanding and are expressed as a triangle. ARC is a fundamental principle of the Scientology religion.

The first corner of the triangle is affinity, which is the degree of liking or affection for someone or something. Reality is the second corner and is, fundamentally, agreement. The third corner is communication, defined as the interchange of ideas between two people.

All three of these are interrelated. Without a degree of liking and some basis of agreement, there is no communication. Without communication and some basis for affinity, or emotional response, there can be no reality. Without some basis for agreement and communication, there can be no affinity. And

when one corner of this triangle is improved, the other two corners are likewise improved.

The upper triangle is the KRC triangle. The points are K for knowledge, R for responsibility and C for control. Like the points of the ARC triangle, these three elements are interrelated. When one corner of the KRC triangle is raised, the other two also rise.

This symbol first appeared in 1952.

What religious holidays do Scientologists celebrate?

Scientologists celebrate several major holidays annually. These include the birthday of L. Ron Hubbard (March 13); the date marking the initial publication of *Dianetics* (May 9); Auditor's Day, in honor of all auditors (second Sunday in September); and the anniversary of the founding of the International Association of Scientologists, which unites, supports and protects the Scientology religion and Scientologists throughout the world (October 7).

Additionally, Scientologists in particular geographic areas may observe their own significant dates, such as the founding of the church in their area. Members of the Church also observe traditional religious holidays such as Christmas.

Why does Scientology have ministers? How does one become a Scientology minister?

Like many other religions the Church of Scientology has ministers who minister Scientology religious services to its church parishioners. Only those who specifically enroll in and graduate from the Scientology Minister's Course and its prerequisites and fulfill the requirements for ordination may become Scientology ministers. All Scientology auditors are required to become ordained ministers.

WHAT SCIENTOLOGY DOES FOR THE INDIVIDUAL

How does Scientology work?

The Scientology religion provides answers to many questions about life and death. It encompasses an exact, precisely mapped-out path. Through application of Scientology technology principles in an auditing session, a person is able to remove barriers and unwanted conditions and so become more himself. As a person progresses, he often reaches out to help others in the ways he has been helped.

In developing Scientology, L. Ron Hubbard found the means to develop a technology to free the human spirit and thereby allow man to really know himself. He thoroughly tested all of his procedures and recorded for future use those that proved most workable in bringing about uniformly predictable results. These comprise standard Scientology technology.

That which is real to the person himself is all one is asked to accept of Scientology. No beliefs are forced upon him. By training and processing, he finds out for himself the answers he is looking for in life.

What does Scientology accomplish?

Scientology stresses the application and workability of its principles and techniques. When properly practiced, Scientology enables one to develop in all aspects of life, both spiritual and temporal. It addresses the individual and brings about greater happiness, self-confidence and ability by increasing a person's awareness and effectiveness in life. It differs from other religious philosophies in that it supplies the means through which a person can increase his ability to effectively resolve the problems and situations he and others face in life.

A fundamental premise of Scientology is that man is basically good and can improve conditions in his life. However, Scientology cannot promise to do anything by itself. Only the individual can bring about his own improvement by applying the teachings of Scientology to himself and those around him.

How do people get into Scientology?

Usually by word of mouth, often by reading a book or seeing promotional materials or visiting a church of Scientology. Sometimes a person becomes interested by meeting a Scientologist and seeing that he has "something"—a positive attitude toward life, certainty, self-confidence and happiness—which they too would like to have. Fundamentally, people get into Scientology because they want to improve something in their lives or because they want to help others improve themselves and thus create a better civilization.

How does Scientology view marriage and the family?

Scientology regards the family as the building block of any society and marriage as an essential component of a stable family life.

People often find that after they begin practicing Scientology, their relationships with their spouses and other family members strengthen dramatically. That is because Scientology teaches an individual to communicate more freely with others, raises his capacity to love other people and puts him in better communication with family and friends.

Surveys have found that after participating in Scientology services, individuals are more likely to marry or stay married and to have children than before they became Scientologists.

How does the Church view relationships between a Scientologist and family members who are not Scientologists?

The Church encourages and helps its members to have excellent family relationships, whether or not their relatives are Scientologists. In fact, relationships between a Scientologist and the rest of his family routinely improve after he begins practicing Scientology because he has acquired the means to increase communication and address and resolve any problems that might have existed.

The Church goes to great lengths to reconcile family differences should a problem arise. For example, Scientology Chaplains will assist family members to come together and work to discover the real cause of their disagreements. Friends and family of Scientologists are always welcome to visit the Church, to meet other Scientologists and to have any questions they may have about Scientology answered. Regardless of whether the other family members choose to become Scientologists or not, Scientologists take deep pride in their record of resolving family problems and conflicts.

Is Scientology open to anyone?

Scientology is open to anyone who seeks spiritual betterment.

The materials that make up Scientology scripture are readily available at churches of Scientology and public libraries throughout the world. Churches and missions are always open to the public and anyone can come in for a tour and personally see what the Church is all about.

Scientologists come from all walks of life, and range from teachers to businessmen and women, doctors, housewives, attorneys, engineers, nurses, construction workers, celebrities, marketing and administrative personnel, secretaries, athletes, civil servants and others.

Is Scientology a secret society?

Not at all. One may go into a Scientology church at any time. Scientology scripture and other literature are readily available to anyone. There is no demand for one to withdraw from society when he begins Scientology; on the contrary, Scientologists are widely known for becoming very involved in life around them as they are eager to take responsibility for improving conditions.

Scientology
and Other Practices

Is Scientology like hypnotism, meditation, psychotherapy or other mental therapies?

There is no resemblance. In fact, it was as a result of L. Ron Hubbard's investigation of hypnotism and many other mental practices that he saw the need for practical answers to man's problems. In his book, *Dianetics: The Modern Science of Mental Health,* he wrote that he had found hypnotism and psychotherapy to be dangerous and impractical. Nearly all other methods of alleged mental science are based on principles that are quite the opposite of those used in Scientology. They treat man as a "thing" to be conditioned, not as a spiritual being who can find answers to life's problems and who can improve enormously.

In what way does Scientology differ from other religions?

Nearly all religions share a belief in helping man live a better life. In Scientology, this concept is expressed as one of the aims of the Church, which is to achieve a world without insanity, war and crime.

While Scientology has much in common with other religions in this regard, particularly in terms of its basic religious concepts and its outreach into the community with social reform programs, the most valuable asset that Scientology has to offer is a wealth of technology which brings about greater spiritual awareness.

Unlike some religions which believe that man is intrinsically evil, Scientology believes man is basically good. The Scientology religion offers practical tools one can use to better oneself and others. Some religions offer salvation in the hereafter, while Scientology offers certainty of eternal salvation now.

Scientology makes it possible for *any* religion to attain its goals and is therefore a religion of religions.

Is Scientology a cult?

No. It is a religion in the fullest sense of the word.

"Cult" is usually meant in a disparaging sense to imply a secret or closed group with limited membership and mysterious beliefs. Religious scholars point out that the term has become almost meaningless, since its modern use reflects a growing prejudice against all religions. For example, a government report in Belgium labeled the Hasidic Jews and even the YWCA as "cults." The French Parliament included Baptists on their list.

Religions that grow and endure do so to the degree that they assist people in their spiritual lives. To fulfill this role, the scripture of Scientology is fully codified, broadly published and available to anyone, and its churches and missions are always open to the public.

Scientology is unique in that it does not require or tell anyone to "believe" anything. Rather, Scientology believes every individual should think for himself. In Scientology, what is true for the individual is only what he has observed personally and knows is true for him. Scientology is not authoritarian, but offers a technology one can use and then decide whether it works for him.

SCIENTOLOGY BELIEFS

Is man a spirit?

Yes. A short exercise can quickly answer this for anyone: If you have someone close their eyes and get a picture of a cat, they will get a mental image picture of a cat. But who exactly is looking at that picture in the mind? The answer, of course, is the human spirit itself. In Scientology we call the spirit a thetan, from the Greek letter *theta,* meaning thought or life or the spirit.

How does one know that he is a spirit?

It is a matter that each individual must examine for himself. Scientologists believe man is more than a mind and body and that it is he, himself, the spirit, who can control the mind and the body.

Do you think your body would do anything by itself if it were not guided by you, the being?

Does Scientology have a concept of God?

Most definitely. In Scientology, the concept of God is expressed as the eighth dynamic—the urge toward existence as infinity, as God or the Supreme Being or Author of the Universe. As the eighth dynamic, Scientology's concept of God rests at the very apex of universal survival.

As L. Ron Hubbard wrote in *Science of Survival:* "No culture in the history of the world, save the thoroughly depraved and expiring ones, has failed to affirm the existence of a Supreme Being. It is an empirical observation that men without a strong and lasting faith in a Supreme Being are less capable, less ethical and less valuable to themselves and society. . . . A man without an abiding faith is, by observation alone, more of a thing than a man."

Unlike religions with Judeo-Christian origins, the Church of Scientology has no set dogma concerning God that it imposes on its members. As with all its beliefs, Scientology does not ask individuals to believe anything on faith. Rather, as one's level of spiritual awareness increases through participation in Scientology auditing and training, he attains his own certainty of every dynamic and, as he moves from the seventh (spiritual) dynamic to the eighth, will come to his own understanding of infinity and God and his relationship to it.

Scientology seeks to bring one to a new level of spiritual awareness where he can reach his own conclusions concerning the nature of God (or the Supreme Being or infinity) and what lies in store for him after his present lifetime. Thus, like many Eastern religions, salvation in Scientology is attained through personal spiritual growth and enlightenment.

Can't God be the only one to help man?

Scientologists take the maxim quite to heart that God helps those who help themselves. They believe that each person has the answers to the mysteries of life; all he requires is awareness of these answers, and this is what Scientology helps him achieve. Man is accustomed to asking for pat answers. Scientology requires that the person think for himself and thus help himself become more understanding, able, happy and healthy.

Does Scientology believe in brotherly love?

Yes, and perhaps goes a step further. L. Ron Hubbard wrote that "To love is the road to strength. To love in spite of all is the secret of greatness. And may very well be the greatest secret in this universe."

Why do Scientologists want to help people?

For several reasons. First, because Scientologists themselves have been helped enormously—and they want others to share the same successes. Second, Scientologists understand that life is not lived alone. An individual has more than just one dynamic (the urge to survive as self). He wants to help his family, his groups, mankind itself and living things survive better.

Does Scientology recognize good and evil?

Yes, in Scientology, a very clear distinction is made between good and evil. Those actions which enhance survival on the majority of the eight aspects or dynamics of life are good, and those which destroy or deny these aspects of life are evil. Scientologists strive to make decisions that will enhance the majority of these dynamics of life.

Good may be defined as constructive. Evil may be defined as destructive.

Does Scientology believe man is sinful?

A fundamental tenet of Scientology is that man is basically good but has become "aberrated" (capable of erring or departing from rational thought or behavior) through spending many lifetimes in the physical universe and therefore commits harmful acts or sins. These acts further reduce his awareness and potential power as a spiritual being.

Through Scientology he can confront his actions, erase the ignorance and aberration which surrounds them, and come to know and experience truth again.

All religions seek truth. Freedom of the spirit is only to be found on the road to truth.

Sin is composed, according to Scientology, of lies and hidden actions and is therefore untruth.

Will Scientology put one in control of his mind?

Yes. As man is a spiritual being, quite separate from his mind and his body, Scientology will help him achieve a far better command over his mind, just as it helps him to control in an intelligent way all aspects of his life.

Is Scientology about the mind?

No. Scientology is about the individual himself as a spiritual being separate and distinct from the mind.

Does Scientology believe in mind over matter?

In practicing Scientology you address yourself—not your mind, not your body, but you.

Scientologists have found that the spirit is potentially superior to material things, and that the spirit, i.e., you, if cleansed of past traumas, transgressions and aberrations, can make miraculous changes in the physical universe that would not otherwise be possible.

Does Scientology believe one can exist outside of the body?

Before entering Scientology many people experience the feeling of looking down on one's body, but they do not understand what is happening. Once they have achieved greater spiritual awareness through Scientology auditing and training they find that this experience becomes nothing out of the ordinary. Scientology believes that man is not his body, his mind or his brain. He, a spiritual force, energizes the physical body.

Scientology proved, for the first time, that man was a spiritual being, not an animal.

Does Scientology believe in reincarnation or past lives?

Reincarnation is a definite system and is not part of Scientology. It is a fact that unless one begins to handle aberrations built up in past lives, he doesn't progress.

The common definition of reincarnation has been altered from its original meaning. The word has come to mean "to be born again in different life forms" whereas its actual definition is "to be born again into the flesh or into another body." Scientology ascribes to this latter, original definition of reincarnation.

Today in Scientology, many people have certainty that they have lived lives prior to their current one. These are referred to as past lives, not as reincarnation.

Past lives is not a dogma in Scientology, but generally Scientologists, during their auditing, experience a past life and then know for themselves that they have lived before.

To believe one had a physical or other existence prior to the identity of the current body is not a new concept—but it is an exciting one.

In Scientology, you are given the tools to handle upsets and aberrations from past lives that adversely affect you in present time, thus freeing you to live a much happier life.

Does Scientology believe in charity and welfare?

It does. However, Scientologists also believe in the principle that some form of exchange is necessary in any relationship. If a person only receives and never gives, he will lose his own self-respect and become an unhappy person. Therefore, Scientology-sponsored charity programs often encourage those receiving the charity to make their own contribution in exchange by personally helping others who are in need. Such contributions enable one to receive help and yet maintain his self-respect.

Does Scientology hold any political views?

Scientology is nonpolitical and does not engage in any political activity whatsoever. By its creed, "All men have inalienable rights to conceive, choose, assist or support their own organizations, churches and governments." Scientologists are free to hold their own political views, vote for the candidates of their choice, etc., and are not given direction from the Church as to what position to take on political issues or candidates. The Church believes there should be a complete separation of church and state.

Can children participate in Scientology? How?

Yes, many children do and there are no age restrictions as to who can participate in Scientology auditing or training. Some Scientology churches conduct courses and study programs specifically designed for young people. Children below the age of majority must first obtain written consent from their parents or guardian to participate in Scientology services. Like adherents of other religions, Scientologists are very proud when their children join them in the practice of their religion.

What does Scientology say about the raising of children?

L. Ron Hubbard has written a great deal about raising children. In Scientology, children are recognized as people who should be given all the respect and love granted adults.

Scientologists believe children should be encouraged to contribute to family life and not just be "seen and not heard" as the old saying goes. Children are spiritual beings, and as such they need to exchange with those around them in order to thrive and live productive, happy lives. For more information on raising children, the book *Child Dianetics* and the course "How to be a Successful Parent" are recommended reading.

Most children raised in good Scientology homes are above average in ability and quickly begin to understand how and why people act as they do. Life thus becomes a lot happier and safer for them.

Can one make up his own mind about Scientology?

One can and indeed one should. Scientology enables a person to think for himself. There is no purpose served in practicing or studying Scientology because someone else wants him to. But if a person has taken a good look at his life and has decided that he wants to make it better, the best thing is to start and find out for himself what Scientology can do for him. One should read one of the basic books by L. Ron Hubbard, such as *Dianetics: The Modern Science of Mental Health*, or *Scientology: The Fundamentals of Thought*.

What is real in Scientology for you is what you find in it that is real for you.

SCIENTOLOGY'S FOUNDER

Who was L. Ron Hubbard?

L. Ron Hubbard is the founder of Dianetics and Scientology and the author of the Scientology scripture. His research on the spirit, the mind and life is recorded in the tens of millions of words which comprise Dianetics and Scientology. His works cover subjects as diverse as drug rehabilitation, education, marriage and family, success at work, administration, art and many other aspects of life.

His best-selling book *Dianetics: The Modern Science of Mental Health* alone has sold millions of copies and continues to appear on the *New York Times* and other bestseller lists around the world, nearly five decades after its original publication.

L. Ron Hubbard dedicated his life to helping others. He saw that this world had to change drastically, and he created a workable technology so that needed changes could occur.

Testimony to the effectiveness of his discoveries are the millions of happy and successful people and the hundreds of Dianetics and Scientology churches, missions and groups internationally.

Is L. Ron Hubbard still alive?

No. L. Ron Hubbard passed away on January 24, 1986, but he remains with us in spirit and through the legacy of his technology and its continual application around the globe.

What was L. Ron Hubbard's role in the Church?

L. Ron Hubbard founded the Scientology religion. The first Church of Scientology was formed by a group of Scientologists in Los Angeles in 1954.

Mr. Hubbard directly managed the early Scientology organizations until 1966, when he resigned as Executive Director and turned this function over to Scientology Church executives. Although he continued to take an interest in the Church's activities and provided his advice on administrative matters when asked, he devoted almost all his time to researching the upper levels of Scientology and codifying the technology he had discovered.

Has L. Ron Hubbard's death affected the Church?

L. Ron Hubbard recorded the results of all his research in writing, on film or in taped lectures so that the technology could be preserved. As a result, Scientology has continued to expand and its future survival is assured.

All great religious leaders of the past have died. Their work flourishes. Men die. Wisdom and ideas do not. As long as men and women communicate and read and use the knowledge L. Ron Hubbard has organized, Scientology will grow and serve mankind.

How did L. Ron Hubbard rise above the reactive mind when others did not?

He applied to himself the principles he had found.

Did L. Ron Hubbard make a lot of money out of Scientology?

Like other authors, he made his money from the royalties on his books. As noted, one book alone, *Dianetics*, has sold millions of copies, and his total book sales of both fiction and nonfiction are in excess of one hundred million copies around the world, including more than twenty national bestsellers in the 1980s.

On his death, Mr. Hubbard willed the vast bulk of his estate, including the royalties from the sale of these books, to the religion to help ensure its future practice to the betterment of mankind.

Was L. Ron Hubbard a millionaire?

L. Ron Hubbard was one of those fortunate people who never made problems over money. He inherited some wealth at an early age, but in the early 1930s became one of the highest paid writers in America, long before

Dianetics. He was a millionaire several times over from his book royalties. His public book sales continue to be astronomical.

How is it that one man could discover so much information?

He simply cared enough to want it and had the intelligence and persistence to research and find it.

Few men have been trained in all the Eastern philosophies and in the highest levels of Western science as well.

Knowing that his research was only as valuable as it provided workable solutions to man's problems, he tested all of his discoveries and found the most effective methods for applying the results of his research. His workable methods enabled him to continue research into higher and higher realms of spiritual awareness.

Do Scientologists believe that L. Ron Hubbard was like Jesus Christ?

No. L. Ron Hubbard personally stated he was a man as others are men. He was a much-loved friend and teacher and continues to be respected and loved.

Did L. Ron Hubbard go Clear?

Yes. In order to map the route for others he had to make it himself.

SCIENTOLOGY ATTITUDES AND PRACTICES

How do Scientologists view life?

As a game — a game in which everyone can win. Scientologists are optimistic about life and believe there is hope for a saner world and better civilization and are actively doing all they can to achieve this.

What moral codes do Scientologists live by?

There are four main codes that Scientologists apply in life. One is the Auditor's Code, which gives the basic rules an auditor must abide by to ensure excellent auditing results. Another is the Code of a Scientologist, guidelines which Scientologists agree to follow in order to achieve the aims of Scientology. There is an ethical code, called the Code of Honor, that Scientologists follow in their day-to-day activities with their fellow men. L. Ron Hubbard also has written a nonreligious moral code called *The Way to Happiness* which gives basic precepts for a happy life. This moral code is used by Scientologists and non-Scientologists alike, and tens of millions of copies have been distributed in communities all around the world.

What is Scientology's view on drugs?

Scientologists consider that drugs cause extremely damaging effects on a person — physically, mentally and spiritually. They decrease awareness and hinder abilities. They are a "solution" to some other problem, but then they become an even bigger problem.

Scientologists do not take street drugs or mind-altering psychiatric drugs. Scientologists do use prescribed drugs as part of medical programs from competent physicians.

For more information about drugs and what can be done about them, the book *Clear Body, Clear Mind: The Effective Purification Program* is recommended.

Are there many young people on staff in Scientology?

We find that young Scientologists enjoy the lifestyle of working in the Church, and many staff members are between the ages of 22 and 35. It may be that due to the expansion of Scientology they find that there are opportunities to achieve responsible positions quite rapidly. Many families have three generations in Scientology. But bear in mind that there are also a great many older people in Scientology, so it is not uncommon to meet staff who are 50, 60, 70 or even 80 years old.

Are there any special dietary laws or rules against smoking or drinking in Scientology?

No. There are no dietary laws whatsoever and no general prohibitions against smoking or drinking. However, Scientology does have a mandatory rule banning the consumption of any alcohol within twenty-four hours of or during an auditing session or training. The effects of the alcohol would make it impossible to benefit from these religious services.

Smoking is forbidden in course rooms or during auditing sessions since it would distract oneself and others. Rules for student behavior are laid out in a Church policy called the "Student's Guide to Acceptable Behavior."

Do Scientologists use medical doctors?

Yes. The Church of Scientology has always encouraged its staff and parishioners to see medical doctors to handle the physical aspect of any illness or injury. Once a Scientologist with a physical condition receives the needed medical treatment he can resume his auditing and so handle any spiritual trauma connected with the physical condition. Many medical doctors also are Scientologists.

In *Scientology does one have to sacrifice one's individuality?*

No. People are unique, despite all the problems and aberrations they have in common. As they become disentangled from the stimulus-response part of their mind, they become more themselves, more unique, more individual and learn to believe in themselves. In fact, becoming more aware of and able to express one's own unique beingness is encouraged in Scientology. Scientology teaches one to maintain his personal integrity and develop fully as an individual.

What benefits can one get from Scientology?

Scientology resolves the problems of man by addressing the spiritual travails which hold those difficulties in place. As these barriers begin to fall away, one gains the ability to communicate in relationships, whether with family members and spouses, friends or even mere acquaintances. He becomes free of stress and finds new enjoyment in life. Yet more importantly, a Scientologist gains an understanding of himself spiritually, discovers his true potentials and recovers the certainty of his own immortality as a spiritual being.

What is Scientology's system of ethics?

The Scientology system of ethics is based wholly on reason.

L. Ron Hubbard has defined ethics as "reason and the contemplation of optimum survival." He has also pointed out: "Dishonest conduct is nonsurvival. Anything is unreasonable or evil which brings about the destruction of individuals, groups, or inhibits the future of the race."

Ethics may be defined as the actions an individual takes on himself to ensure his continued survival across the dynamics. It is a personal thing. When one is ethical, it is something he does himself by his own choice.

The Scientology ethics system includes a body of technology called conditions formulas. L. Ron Hubbard discovered that there are various states of existence and that there are exact formulas connected with these states. A person can determine what condition any area of his life is in and apply a formula to immediately improve this condition. While very simple, such actions are quite powerful and have enabled millions of individuals to improve their lives in ways never thought possible.

Another part of Scientology's ethics system is what is known as Confessionals. Man has long postulated a means by which he could put himself on the right path. As long ago as 500 B.C., religions recognized that confession frees a person spiritually from the burden of sin. In Scientology, it has been found that a Confessional (a type of auditing) assists the person who has transgressed against his own and his group's moral code to unburden himself and again feel good about himself and be a contributing member of the group.

As L. Ron Hubbard has written: "No man who is not himself honest can be free — he is his own trap. When his own deeds cannot be disclosed, then he is a prisoner; he must withhold himself from his fellows and is a slave to his own conscience."

These are just two of the tools from the wealth of ethics technology that exists in Scientology. Complete information on this subject is contained in *Introduction to Scientology Ethics* by L. Ron Hubbard.

What does "clear the planet" mean?

It means that Scientologists want to rid the planet of insanity, war and crime, and in its place create a civilization in which sanity and peace exist. In order to do this, they must help individuals become free of their own individual insanities and regain awareness that they are basically good.

What does "suppressive person" mean?

According to L. Ron Hubbard, a suppressive person is "a person who seeks to suppress, or squash, any betterment activity or group. A suppressive person suppresses other people in his vicinity. This is the person whose behavior is calculated to be disastrous." Well-known examples of such a personality are Napoleon and Hitler. Mr. Hubbard found that a suppressive person, also called an antisocial personality, has definite antisocial attributes.

The basic reason the antisocial personality behaves as he or she does lies in a hidden terror of others. To such a person every other being is an enemy, an enemy to be covertly or overtly destroyed. The fixation is that survival itself depends on "keeping others down" or "keeping people ignorant." If anyone were to promise to make others stronger or brighter, the antisocial personality would suffer the utmost agony.

Because of this, the suppressive person seeks to upset, continuously undermine, spread bad news about and denigrate betterment activities and groups. Thus the antisocial personality is against what Scientology is about—helping people become more able and improving conditions in society. For the good of the Church and the individuals in it, such a person is officially labeled a suppressive person so that others will know not to associate with him.

For more understanding of suppressive persons and how to handle them, the book *Introduction to Scientology Ethics* is recommended.

What is disconnection?

A Scientologist can have trouble making spiritual progress in his auditing or training if he is connected to someone who is suppressive or who is antagonistic to Scientology or its tenets. All spiritual advancements gained from Scientology may well be lost because he is being invalidated by an antagonistic person. In order to resolve this, he either "handles" the other person's antagonism with true data about the Church, or as a last resort when all attempts to handle have failed, he "disconnects" from or stops communicating with the person.

The terms "disconnect" and "handle," as defined by L. Ron Hubbard, mean:

"The term *handle* most commonly means to smooth out a situation with another person by applying the technology of communication.

"The term *disconnection* is defined as a self-determined decision made by an individual that he is not going to be connected to another. It is a severing of a communication line.

"The basic principle of handle or disconnect exists in any group and ours is no different.

"It is much like trying to deal with a criminal. If he will not handle, the society resorts to the only other solution: It 'disconnects' the criminal from the society. In other words, they remove the guy from society and put him in a prison because he won't *handle* his problem or otherwise cease to commit criminal acts against others."

A person who disconnects is simply exercising his right to communicate or not to communicate with a particular person. This is one of the most fundamental rights of man. "Communication, however, is a two-way flow," Mr. Hubbard pointed out. "If one has the right to communicate, then one must also have the right to not receive communication from another. It is this latter corollary of the right to communicate that gives us our right to privacy."

With the technology of handle or disconnect, Scientologists are, in actual fact, doing nothing different than any society or group has done down through thousands of years.

Does Scientology engage in brainwashing or mind control?

No. In fact, what we do is exactly the opposite. We free people and enable them to think for themselves.

Millions of Church members from literally all walks of life have attested to the positive benefits received from Scientology. A common theme to their personal success stories is that they are now more in control of their lives than they ever have been.

Factually, Mr. Hubbard was one of the first to discover and expose actual mind control and brainwashing experimentation conducted by United States military and intelligence agencies during and after World War II. Not only did he uncover blatantly destructive experimentation, he also discovered that the technology he developed, Dianetics, could undo the effects of an insidious form of hypnotism called pain-drug-hypnosis and free a person from its grip.

Years after Mr. Hubbard learned about these government-sponsored psychiatric mind control experiments, documents released under the Freedom of Information Act detailed the extent to which these techniques were being used. Over the years, the Church of Scientology has exposed numerous instances of brainwashing or mind control practices, such as those involved in so-called "deprograming." Such practices are diametrically opposed to the aims of Scientology, which are to free man and return to him his ability to control his own life.

Does Scientology actively proselytize for new members?

Yes. Scientologists make Scientology technology broadly available to others because they want others to receive the same gains they have experienced. The Church wants more people to know and apply the works of L. Ron Hubbard and actively and vigorously promotes this.

Does one really need Scientology to do well in life?

That is a question one must answer for oneself. A Scientologist's viewpoint is that while some people might be surviving quite well without Scientology, they can always do better and expand their potentials even further. In fact, Mr. Hubbard founded Scientology for the precise purpose of helping the able become more able, and one usually finds that the people doing best in life are those who first embrace Scientology.

Does one have to believe in Scientology?

No. One is not expected to "believe" in Scientology. One is only expected to study

and apply Scientology religious principles and practices and see for himself if Scientology works for him.

To quote L. Ron Hubbard, "Anything that isn't true for you when you study it carefully isn't true."

Why do Scientologists sometimes seem so intent on what they are doing?

If you had a chance to change yourself and civilization so greatly, you would be interested as well.

What do the terms preclear and auditor mean?

A preclear is someone who is receiving Scientology or Dianetics auditing on his way to becoming Clear. Through auditing he is finding out more about himself and life.

An auditor is a Dianetics or Scientology practitioner trained in the technology of auditing. Auditor means "one who listens" (from the Latin word *audire*). An auditor listens and computes, applying standard technology to preclears to help them achieve the abilities stated on the Classification, Gradation and Awareness Chart. An auditor's job is to ask the preclear to look, and get him to do so.

Are auditors governed by a code of conduct?

Yes.

Auditors maintain and practice a code of conduct known as the Auditor's Code, exactly followed rules that ensure the person being audited gets the greatest possible gain. The Auditor's Code evolved over many years of observation, and it is the code of ethics which governs an auditor's conduct.

Auditing is most successful when the auditor acts according to the Code. For example, one goal of auditing is to restore the individual's certainty in his own viewpoint; evaluation for him only inhibits attainment of this goal. Hence, the Code flatly prohibits the auditor from telling the person he is auditing what he should think about himself, or offering any opinion about what is being audited.

Auditing must be conducted within a framework of complete trust; thus, as with ministers of other religions, the Auditor's Code requires auditors to treat communications from parishioners with total confidentiality.

The qualities instilled by the Auditor's Code are essentially those held to be the best in people. An auditor shows kindness, affinity, patience and other such virtues while assisting the person being audited to confront areas of upset or difficulty.

Is information divulged during auditing sessions always kept confidential?

Absolutely and without exception.

Traditionally, all communications between a minister and his parishioners have been privileged and confidential. That is certainly the case in the Scientology religion, and this trust is never violated. In fact, the Church would invoke all legal protections under its clergy-penitent privilege to safeguard this confidentiality.

What is the E-Meter and how does it work?

E-Meter is a shortened term for electropsychometer. It is a religious artifact used as a spiritual guide in auditing. It is for use only by a Scientology minister or a Scientology minister-in-training to help the preclear locate and confront areas of spiritual upset.

In itself, the E-Meter does nothing. It is an electronic instrument that measures mental state and change of state in individuals and assists the precision and speed of auditing. The E-Meter is not intended or effective for the diagnosis, treatment or prevention of any disease.

The book *Understanding the E-Meter* offers a simple explanation of how the E-Meter works and what it actually measures. In order to understand what the E-Meter does, it is necessary to understand some basic Scientology concepts.

There are three basic parts of man — mind, body and thetan. The thetan is an immortal spiritual being — the individual himself. He (the thetan) inhabits a body, which is a carbon-oxygen machine. He has a mind, which is a collection of mental image pictures he has created. These pictures have weight and

mass and can impinge on the person when he is emotionally upset.

This is what makes the E-Meter read — the impingement of such pictures against the body. The E-Meter puts a very small electrical current (approximately one-and-a-half volts) through the body. This is about the same amount of current as in the average battery-powered wristwatch. When a person thinks a thought, looks at a picture, reexperiences an incident or when he shifts some part of the pictures in his mind, he is moving and changing actual mental mass and energy. These changes in the person's mind affect the tiny flow of electrical energy generated by the E-Meter, which causes the needle on its dial to move.

The E-Meter thus measures changes that are caused by the spiritual being in his own mind (i.e., the movement of mental masses around him) and in this capacity, it is a religious artifact.

The E-Meter is used to help the individual who is being audited uncover truth. By locating areas of mental or spiritual trauma, the E-Meter helps both the auditor and the preclear locate exactly what to address in auditing.

What is training?

Training is the way to learn the spiritual technology of Scientology. It is the word used to describe the study of Scientology principles by a parishioner so they can be applied to accomplish the purpose of improving conditions in life, both his own and the lives of others.

Study programs range from the introductory where an individual learns the basics of Scientology, to the advanced where individuals study the higher levels of scripture on their path to advanced spiritual levels. Programs also exist for those who seek to become ministers and apply the auditing technology to others as an auditor.

In every church of Scientology are special rooms where parishioners study the written works and listen to taped lectures of L. Ron Hubbard in the precise order set forth on a checksheet. A Course Supervisor is present in each course room to assist Scientologists to attain full understanding of the material they are learning. A Course Supervisor does not teach, lecture or interpret in any way, but instead refers the individual to the correct material if the student is experiencing difficulty. Because of the checksheets and Supervisor's role, parishioners studying Scientology materials are able to proceed at their own individual pace.

Auditor training includes an intensive series of drills on each and every aspect of delivering an auditing session and use of a special computerized E-Meter simulator for teaching a student to flawlessly handle an E-Meter. Films on important aspects of auditing also are used to facilitate learning the practical applications of auditing. A student learns his techniques cold and in every church of Scientology around the world there is but one passing standard: A student who graduates is expected to minister a 100 percent perfect auditing session every time.

Through Scientology training, that standard is reached daily.

The end result of training is that an individual is able to minister auditing to another person. Because Scientology offers an understanding of human behavior, training as an auditor also provides individuals with a means of dealing with real-life situations by understanding their causes. Training gives Scientologists the know-how to resolve difficulties in life that might otherwise appear unsolvable.

What is study technology?

Study technology is the term given to the methods L. Ron Hubbard developed to enable individuals to study effectively. Learning the methods to grasp the materials of the Scientology scriptures is the first step in an individual's spiritual journey and renders the student better able to use and apply what he or she has learned. The "study tech," as it is sometimes referred to colloquially, can be applied by anyone to the study of any subject and in addition to its use in churches of Scientology is broadly used in the secular world as well.

L. Ron Hubbard recognized the failings of modern education and training in 1950, many years before educational horror stories began to make headlines. He observed that students were simply unable to learn with comprehension. Sometimes they could repeat, parrot-fashion, what they had been taught, but were unable to apply the subject supposedly "learned" with any facility or understanding.

Mr. Hubbard then researched the subject and isolated the actual barriers to effective learning. He found that the problem was not overwork, crammed study schedules or incompetent teachers. Rather, he discovered that the main impediment to students' ability to retain and effectively use data was the absence of a technology of *how* to study.

Study technology is not a gimmicky "quick-study method," but an exact technology that anyone can use to learn a subject or to acquire a new skill.

THE ORGANIZATIONS OF SCIENTOLOGY

How are churches of Scientology administered?

Each individual church of Scientology is separately incorporated and governed by its own board of directors. The officers and directors also form the ecclesiastical management of the church and are fully responsible for ministering services to their parishioners.

Church of Scientology International (CSI), the mother church of the Scientology religion, is headquartered in Los Angeles. CSI oversees the ecclesiastical activities of all Scientology churches, organizations and groups throughout the world, and sees that individual churches receive guidance in their ministries. CSI also provides the broad planning and direction needed to support the Church's international growth.

(For more information about the structure of the Church, see Part Six.)

How many people work in a Scientology church?

The number of staff varies from church to church. Small churches may have twenty and large ones more than five hundred.

Where are Scientology churches located?

Scientology churches and missions exist all over the world. There are a great many churches and far more missions in every continent. A complete listing of Scientology churches and missions and their locations is provided in Chapter 49, and on the Scientology Internet site at http://www.scientology.org.

What does a Scientology church or mission actually do?

The main activities of Scientology churches and missions are ministering to their parishioners and providing them the religious services of their faith — Scientology auditing and training, Sunday services, weddings, funerals and christenings as well as other such chaplain services.

What is the Office of Special Affairs?

The Office of Special Affairs (OSA) is responsible for directing and coordinating all legal matters affecting the Church. It also publishes public information material about the social betterment works of Scientology, for the general public, governments, the media, and other religious and community groups with interests similar to those of the Church. OSA also oversees the social reform programs of the Church, among which are those that expose and rectify violations of human rights.

What is the Flag Service Organization?

The Flag Service Organization (FSO), often referred to as "Flag," is one of the Church's international religious retreats. Located in Clearwater, Florida, it offers advanced spiritual training and auditing. It retains its name from the days when it used to operate from the flagship *Apollo*. ("Flag" in nautical terms means "the flagship," which is the vessel from which orders are given to others. Flag, today is a *service* organization and no longer functions in a managerial capacity.)

What is the Flag Ship Service Organization?

The Flag Ship Service Organization is located aboard the 450-foot ship *Freewinds*, another of the Church's advanced religious retreats. It ministers the level of auditing called New OT VIII as well as specialized training.

What is the purpose of advanced Scientology religious retreats?

In Scientology, some upper levels of spiritual counseling require the parishioner's full-time participation for a period of several weeks in order for the person to achieve the full spiritual benefits of the religious service. Thus, the Church maintains religious retreats, away from the distractions of the world, which provide the ideal environment for advanced religious studies and spiritual counseling. While freedom from distraction is important during all counseling, it is vital at the most advanced levels.

What is the Sea Organization?

The Sea Organization (commonly referred to as the Sea Org) is the religious order for the Scientology religion and is composed of the most dedicated Scientologists in the world — individuals who have dedicated their lives to the service of their religion.

The Sea Organization is a fraternal religious order and is not incorporated or otherwise organized as a legal entity. Members of the Sea Org therefore are wholly responsible to the church of Scientology for which they work and are subject, as are all other employees of that church, to the orders and directions of its board of directors.

The Sea Org was established in 1967 and once operated from a number of ships. It was set up to help L. Ron Hubbard with research of earlier civilizations and supervise Church organizations around the world. It is also entrusted to minister the advanced services of Scientology.

The Sea Organization retains its name in celebration of the fact that Mr. Hubbard's life was frequently connected with the sea. It exists to help keep Scientology working.

Is it true that people in the Sea Org sign a billion-year contract?

Yes, they do. It is a symbolic document which, similar to vows of dedication in other faiths and orders, serves to signify an individual's eternal commitment to the goals, purposes and principles of the Scientology religion. Sea Org members have dedicated their lives to working toward these ends and toward a world without war, drugs, crime and illiteracy.

What are field staff members?

Field staff members are individual Scientologists who disseminate Scientology and help raise funds for the Church by providing basic Scientology books to interested friends, family members and acquaintances, and introducing other interested individuals to the Church. Field staff members are appointed by their nearest Scientology church. Because they have had immense spiritual gains from Dianetics and Scientology, field staff members naturally want to share the technology with others.

Why is everything copyrighted and trademarked in Scientology?

Scientology and Dianetics are technologies that work if applied exactly. If they are altered, the results will not be uniform.

For this reason, the writings of the Church are protected by copyright and the words and symbols which represent the technology are protected by trademarks. This way, nobody can misrepresent something as Scientology or Dianetics when it really is not.

In fact, some unscrupulous persons have tried, through dishonest conduct, to profit from the technologies of Dianetics and Scientology. The subjects were developed for spiritual salvation, not for anyone's personal enrichment. By owning the trademarks and copyrights of the religion and enforcing their proper use, the Church can ensure such ill-intentioned actions will never occur.

Why does the Church have confidential scriptures?

The vast majority of Scientology scriptures are widely available to the general public and can be read and studied by anyone. However, a very small portion of the scriptures that deal with the most advanced levels of spiritual counseling is restricted to those parishioners who have attained the prior levels of spiritual awareness.

Scientologists believe that one must be properly prepared — spiritually and ethically — to receive these materials and that premature exposure could impede spiritual development. For this reason, the information in these advanced scriptures is kept confidential.

It is not unusual for a religion to have confidential scriptures and practices. Similar religious practices exist in Judaism and Mormonism, for example.

CHURCH FUNDING

How are churches of Scientology supported financially?

By their members, just like every other church.

Some churches have a system of tithes, others require their members to pay for pew rentals, religious ceremonies and services. In the Church of Scientology, parishioners make donations for auditing or training they wish to receive. These contributions by Scientologists are the primary source of financial support for the Church and fund all the religious and social betterment activities the Church engages in. Scientologists are not required to tithe or make other donations.

Scientology does not have hundreds of years of accumulated wealth and property like other religions—it must make its way in the world according to the economics of today's society. When one considers the cost of ministering even one hour of auditing, requiring extensively trained specialists, and the overhead costs of maintaining church premises, the necessity of donations becomes clear.

The Church selected the donation system as its primary method of funding because it is the most equitable method. Those who use the facilities of the church should be the ones who contribute most to its maintenance. Of course, no donation is expected from members who are at the church to participate in services other than auditing and training—listening to tape plays of L. Ron Hubbard's lectures, reading scriptural works in the church library, meeting with fellow parishioners, receiving counseling from the Chaplain or attending Sunday services, sermons, weddings, christenings and funerals.

Scientologists' donations keep the Church alive and functioning, fund its widespread social reform programs, make Scientology known to people who may otherwise never have the opportunity to avail themselves of it, and help create a safe and pleasant environment for everyone.

What about those who cannot afford to make donations for services?

There is a Free Scientology Center in churches of Scientology where those who cannot afford to donate may receive auditing without donation. As described above, many Scientology services do not require donation, and Scientology scripture is available at local churches of Scientology and libraries.

There are also books, books, books and free public lectures, Sunday services and other religious services for which there is no donation. Books can be obtained in the local area by going to a church of Scientology, a public bookstore or local library.

Is the Church profit-making?

No. Scientology churches are nonprofit organizations, and all donations they receive are used exclusively in their ministries.

How much does it cost to go Clear?

The cost varies depending on which path one takes.

One way is to donate for auditing and participate in auditing services all the way up to Clear. The preferred route, however, is to become trained as an auditor and co-audit with another Scientologist. The co-auditing route to Clear requires far less in donations than to only have auditing ministered to oneself, plus one helps another to progress spiritually. As auditing costs much more for the church to supply (requiring several staff for each parishioner) donations necessarily must be higher. Training is much more economical and an incentive for persons to receive training and then co-audit, without cost, to the state of Clear.

No matter which path one chooses, all who have attained the state of Clear express the pricelessness of the increased spiritual freedom they have achieved.

SCIENTOLOGY AND DIANETICS BOOKS

What is the best book for a beginning Scientologist to read?

Dianetics: The Modern Science of Mental Health, which has been repeatedly on bestseller lists, is the book recommended for beginners who are interested in the mind and how it works. This book has been a bestseller for nearly fifty years.

In 1977, *Publishers Weekly* called *Dianetics: The Modern Science of Mental Health* "perhaps the best-selling non-Christian book of all time in the West." In 1988, *Publishers Weekly* awarded *Dianetics* its prestigious "Century Award" for appearing for more than 100 weeks on its bestseller list.

For those more interested in starting with a broad summary of L. Ron Hubbard's research and findings about man as a spiritual being and basic principles of life, the first recommended book is *Scientology: The Fundamentals of Thought.* (Chapter 47 gives a more detailed explanation of the books available and suggested course of reading.)

Are the books difficult to understand?

Not at all. The books are quite easy to understand. Depending on what aspect of Scientology and Dianetics a person is interested in, any church Bookstore Officer can recommend the best sequence in which the books should be read.

Where can L. Ron Hubbard's books be purchased?

All of his books are available at missions and churches of Scientology. Many of his books are also available in bookstores and in libraries in cities all over the world.

What books should one read to get information about:

1. Basic Scientology principles:

The Basic Scientology Picture Book

Scientology: The Fundamentals of Thought

Scientology: A New Slant on Life

Scientology 0-8: The Book of Basics

2. Procedures to increase one's spiritual awareness and abilities:

The Creation of Human Ability

Advanced Procedure and Axioms

Scientology 8-8008

Scientology 8-80

3. Past lives and how they relate to this life:

Have You Lived Before This Life?

Scientology: A History of Man

4. The application of basic Scientology technology to help others improve their lives:

The Scientology Handbook

5. Dianetics:

The Basic Dianetics Picture Book

Dianetics: The Modern Science of Mental Health

The Dynamics of Life

Dianetics: The Evolution of a Science

Child Dianetics

6. Handling the residual effects of drugs and toxins:

> *Purification: An Illustrated Answer to Drugs*
>
> *Clear Body, Clear Mind: The Effective Purification Program*

7. Basic principles of communication:

> *Dianetics 55!*

8. The principles of ethics and how to use them to live a more productive life:

> *Introduction to Scientology Ethics*

9. Study methods:

> *Basic Study Manual*
>
> *Learning How to Learn*
>
> *Study Skills for Life*
>
> *How to Use a Dictionary Picture Book for Children*

These books were all written by L. Ron Hubbard or compiled from his works, and are just a few of the dozens and dozens of Scientology and Dianetics books available at churches of Scientology.

How can one get happiness out of a book?

The key to happiness is knowledge. Scientology and Dianetics books contain knowledge that can actually be applied to improve all aspects of one's life — from day-to-day routines to the most fundamental questions about life and eternity.

Being able to accomplish these improvements definitely makes people happier.

Dianetics

What is Dianetics?

L. Ron Hubbard discovered the single source of stress, worry, self-doubt and psychosomatic illness—the reactive mind. In his book *Dianetics: The Modern Science of Mental Health* he described the reactive mind in detail and laid out a simple, practical, easily taught technology to overcome it and reach the state of Clear. Dianetics (which means "through soul") is that technology.

What is the mind?

The mind is basically a communication and control system between the thetan—the spiritual being that is the person himself—and his environment. It is composed of mental image pictures which are recordings of past experiences.

The individual uses his mind to pose and solve problems related to survival and to direct his efforts according to these solutions.

What is the reactive mind?

The reactive mind is the portion of a person's mind which works on a totally stimulus-response basis, which is not under his volitional control, and which exerts force and the power of command over his awareness, purposes, thoughts, body and actions.

What is the difference between Scientology and Dianetics?

Dianetics comes from the Greek *dia* meaning "through" and *nous*, "soul." It is further defined as "what the soul is doing to the body."

Dianetics uncovers the source of unwanted sensations and emotions, accidents, injuries and psychosomatic illnesses, and sets forth effective handlings for these conditions. Further research into the spiritual aspects of Dianetics led to the discovery of Scientology.

Scientology, on the other hand, is the study and handling of the spirit in relationship to itself, to universes and to other life. Through the practice of Scientology one can increase his spiritual awareness and ability and realize his own immortality.

Dianetics and Scientology both utilize the E-Meter and basic rules of auditing.

SCIENTOLOGY AND DIANETICS TRAINING SERVICES

What training should a person take first?

The first action a person should take in his Scientology training is to read a book, such as *Dianetics: The Modern Science of Mental Health* or *Scientology: The Fundamentals of Thought* in order to learn the basic principles of Scientology. These books can be studied at home through what is called an "Extension Course," where lessons are completed and mailed in to the church. A staff member informs the student by return mail of any parts of the book he may have misunderstood.

One can also obtain the video *How to Use Dianetics,* which gives the basics of Dianetics auditing in visual form, enabling one to start auditing at home immediately. This video is a companion to the book *Dianetics* and gives the basics of Book One auditing in visual form so one can start auditing immediately. It places within one's reach the miracle results of Dianetics and gets one moving forward on the way to Clear.

The individual should next visit a church and meet with staff there for assistance and guidance in deciding which service he should participate in next, based on his own personal spiritual needs. There are many services available including the Personal Efficiency Course which teaches how to improve any condition in life through the fundamentals of Scientology, including the conditions of existence, the eight dynamics and the ARC triangle, as well as Scientology auditing which individuals learn and then apply.

There are also Life Improvement Courses on such subjects as marriage, children, work, relationships with others and personal integrity. As one progresses spiritually as a result of studying these Scientology materials, he becomes more effective and in control of his own life. There is also the Hubbard Dianetics Seminar which utilizes Dianetics auditing techniques based on *Dianetics: The Modern Science of Mental Health,* providing as much Dianetics auditing to a person as he wants and giving him the experience of applying Dianetics to another. There is also the Success Through Communication Course which teaches the basic communication skills one needs to improve his life.

What does one get out of Scientology and Dianetics training?

Training not only familiarizes one with the theology and tenets of the Scientology religion, but also gives a person the knowledge and tools to handle life. A basic datum in Scientology is that what one learns is only as valuable as it can be applied to help one do better in life. The principles and techniques do not just increase one's understanding (although it will definitely do that as well), but are for USE.

Although many Scientologists become practicing Scientology ministers, many others simply use this valuable technology in their everyday lives, on the job and with their friends and family members. They report that life becomes more confrontable, their abilities increase and they are happier because they are winning in the game of life.

Should I participate in auditing services before training?

L. Ron Hubbard has written many times about the fact that 50 percent of one's gains from Scientology are from training and 50 percent are from auditing. It is actually impossible to successfully advance through the upper processing levels of Scientology without having received certain training. Therefore, to get the most from Scientology, one should progress in training at the same rate as in auditing.

When can I participate in Scientology training?

Most churches of Scientology are open from 9:00 in the morning until 10:30 at night weekdays and 9:00 A.M. to 6:00 P.M. on weekends. Several different training sessions are scheduled within these hours.

What form does Scientology training take?

Scientology training is unique. Services are organized around a "checksheet," which is a list of materials, divided into sections, that lay out the theory and practical techniques and drills that form the subject matter to be mastered. These are found in the books, tape-recorded lectures and other written materials referred to in the checksheet. Each student moves through his checksheet at his own speed, so no one is ever held back or pressured to go too fast. A trained Course Supervisor is always available to help the parishioner, to refer him to the exact materials, to answer his questions and to ensure he is applying standard study technology to gain the full benefits from his studies.

When do I actually gain experience in auditing others?

Every major training service in Scientology is followed by an internship. This is a period of auditing others under the supervision of technical experts. In this way, an auditor's skills are honed and polished to a very high level of proficiency.

When can I take the Minister's Course?

This can be studied by any Scientologist who is training in Scientology or Dianetics. The program provides an appreciation of the world's great religions, the religious background and philosophy of Scientology, the ethical codes of Scientology and the ceremonies of the Church. It also shows how to conduct religious services and carry out basic ministerial duties.

How long do training services take?

Each service takes as long as it takes for the individual to go through the checksheet at his own pace. The length of each service will also depend on how many hours he studies per week. On the average, Scientology training takes anywhere from a few days (for most introductory services) to several months (for more advanced training).

Introductory services are designed to take one week at two hours a day. Academy training to become an auditor is generally two weeks, at forty hours a week, for each individual level.

The required time to complete the more advanced levels is quite extensive. The Saint Hill Special Briefing Course, which is a chronological study of Scientology and Dianetics from 1948 to the present, takes approximately one year, at forty hours a week. This study gives the Scientologist the entire philosophic and technical development of the subject, and is the most extensive training course in Scientology.

Are Scientology Course Supervisors university trained?

A university degree is not a prerequisite for becoming a Scientology Course Supervisor.

In Scientology, there is a very precise technology of how to supervise and successfully help individuals through their programs. All Scientology Course Supervisors are thoroughly trained in this technology to ensure that parishioners get the most from their training.

SCIENTOLOGY AND DIANETICS AUDITING

What is the difference between the two Scientology paths of auditing and training?

The reference that best explains the difference between these two routes is the Classification, Gradation and Awareness Chart (also known as the Grade Chart).

On the right side of the chart there are various steps of "grades" a person moves through as he participates in auditing. Each grade listed has a column for "Ability Gained" that describes the increasing levels of spiritual awareness and ability rehabilitated at each stage. This is done on a gradient (a gradual approach to something, taken step by step), so those states of being which are seemingly "too high above one" can be achieved with relative ease.

The left-hand side of the chart describes the gradient steps of training on which one gains the knowledge and abilities necessary to minister each level to others. Each training service listed includes a description of the specific subject matter for that level. In training, one is learning about the various facets of life with a view to helping others.

These two different paths parallel each other. Optimally, a person follows both paths.

The chart is a guide for the individual from the point he first enters Scientology, and shows him the basic sequence in which to proceed with his auditing and training services.

Do all Church staff participate in auditing and training?

Yes, of course.

Why does one have to wait six weeks to participate in auditing if one has been habitually using drugs?

Research has shown that it takes at least that long for the effect of drugs to wear off. Quite simply, auditing is not as effective while drugs are in the system because a person on drugs is less alert and may even be rendered stupid, blank, forgetful, delusive or irresponsible.

Will taking antibiotics prevent me from participating in auditing?

No. Antibiotics work differently than drugs. A preclear taking antibiotics pursuant to a doctor's prescription should be sure to let his Director of Processing know, but this will not prevent him from receiving auditing. Many people claim that antibiotics work more rapidly and effectively when they receive auditing at the same time.

Is it okay to take any sort of drugs when you are in Scientology?

Except for antibiotics or other prescribed medical drugs by a medical doctor, no. Any other drug use, such as the use of street drugs or psychiatric mind-altering drugs, is forbidden.

If one has a medical or dental condition requiring treatment and wishes to take some medical drug other than antibiotics, he should inform the appropriate staff member and consult his doctor or dentist.

Drugs are usually taken to escape from unwanted emotions, pains or sensations. In Scientology, the real reasons for these unwanted conditions get handled and people have no need or desire for drugs. Drugs dull people and make them less aware. Scientology's aim is to make people brighter and more aware.

Drugs are essentially poisons. Small amounts may act as a stimulant or as a sedative, but larger amounts act as poisons. Drugs also dull one's senses and affect the reactive mind so that the person becomes less in control and more the effect of his reactive mind, a very undesirable state.

Despite the claims of psychiatrists that drugs are a "cure-all," at best they cover up what is really wrong, and at worst, actually cause harm. The real answer is to handle the source of one's troubles—and that is done through Scientology.

How many hours of auditing a day can one participate in?

This depends upon one's particular auditing program. Some participate in auditing for a longer time than others. An average probably is around 2 1/2 hours a day for the five weekdays. Auditing is best done intensively, at least 12 1/2 hours a week (2 1/2 hours a day for the five-day week). The more intensively one is audited, the more rapid progress he makes as he is not distracted by day-to-day routines or upsets. Of course, one is not always receiving auditing so when one is, his best chance of making rapid progress is intensively.

Has the technology of auditing changed since the early days of Scientology?

The basics of auditing have not changed, but there have been considerable advances and refinements in auditing processes over the years. L. Ron Hubbard continued his research and development of Scientology auditing technology throughout his life, and completed it before he passed away. All of his technology is now available and presented in an exact sequence of gradient steps in which it should be used.

What will I get out of auditing?

Scientology auditing is ministered in a specific sequence which handles the major barriers people encounter when trying to achieve their goals. After receiving auditing, you will start to recognize for yourself that you are changing, that your outlook on life is improving and that you are becoming more able. In Scientology, you will not be told when you have completed an auditing level — you will know for yourself, as only you can know exactly what you are experiencing. This gives you the certainty that you have attained the spiritual advances that you want to attain from each level.

There will also no doubt be some outwardly demonstrable or visible changes that occur: Your IQ may increase, you might look healthier and happier, and may well have people comment on how calm or cheerful you look or, for instance, how you are doing better on your job.

We are not making any claims for Dianetics or Scientology. When you have experienced what can be, it is *you* who will make the claims.

Does auditing really work in all cases?

Dianetics and Scientology technologies are very exact and well-tested procedures that work in 100 percent of the cases in which they are applied in 100 percent accordance with L. Ron Hubbard's direction as preserved in the Scientology scripture.

The only proviso is that the preclear must be there on his own determinism and must abide by the rules for preclears during his auditing to ensure optimum results. The Church makes no guarantee of results as auditing is something which requires the active participation of the individual. Auditing is not something done to an individual — it is something done in which the individual is *the* active participant.

What auditing handles physical pains or discomfort?

Dianetics auditing is used to help handle physical pains or discomfort stemming from the reactive mind.

What can auditing cure?

Scientology is not in the business of curing things in the traditional sense of the word. Auditing is not done to fix the body or to heal anything physical, and the E-Meter cures nothing. However, in the process of becoming happier, more able and more aware as a spiritual being through auditing, illnesses that are psychosomatic in origin (meaning the mind making the body ill) often disappear.

Can one go exterior (be separate from the body) in auditing?

Exteriorization is the state of the thetan, the individual himself, being outside his body with or without full perception, but still able to control and handle the body.

Exteriorization is a personal matter for each individual. Many Scientologists have been known to go exterior, so it would not be at all surprising if you do too at some point during your auditing.

This can happen at any time in auditing. When a person goes exterior, he achieves a certainty that he is himself and not his body.

THE STATE OF CLEAR

What is Clear?

Clear is the name of a specific state achieved through auditing, or a person who has achieved this state. A Clear is a being who no longer has his own reactive mind, and therefore suffers none of the ill effects the reactive mind can cause.

How does one go Clear?

Simply by taking one's first step in Scientology, or by taking the next step as shown on the Classification, Gradation and Awareness Chart and then continuing up the levels set forth on this chart.

How long does it take to go Clear?

It varies from person to person, but it takes an average of anywhere from one year to two years to go from the bottom of the Grade Chart through Clear, depending on how much time one spends each week on his auditing. Those who participate in intensive auditing services and do not stop along the way progress the fastest.

If one goes Clear, will he lose his emotions?

No, on the contrary, a Clear is able to use and experience any emotion. Only the painful, reactive, uncontrolled emotions are gone from his life. Clears are very responsive beings. When one is Clear, he is more himself. The only loss is a negative—the reactive mind—which was preventing the individual from being himself.

What can you do when you are Clear?

A Clear is able to deal causatively with life rather than react to it. A Clear is rational in that he forms the best possible solutions he can with the data he has and from his own viewpoint. A Clear gets things done and accomplishes more than he could before he became Clear.

Whatever your level of ability before you go Clear, it will be greatly increased after you go Clear.

Are Clears perfect?

No, they are not perfect.

Being a Clear does not mean a person who has had no education, for example, suddenly becomes educated. It does mean that all the abilities of the individual can be brought to bear on the problems he encounters and that all the data in his analytical memory banks is available for solution to those problems.

A Clear has become the *basic individual* (himself) through auditing. The basic individual is not a buried, unknown or a different person, but an *intensity* of all that is best and most able in the person.

Do Clears get colds and get sick?

A Clear can still get sick, but this occurs much less often than before he became Clear. In other words, a Clear still has a body, and bodies are susceptible at times to various illnesses. However, no longer having his reactive mind, he is much more at cause and is not adversely affected by many of the things that would have caused psychosomatic illnesses before he went Clear.

To measure a Clear only by his health, however, would be a mistake because this state has to do with the individual as a spirit not as a body.

If Clears no longer have a reactive mind, why do they still need to participate in auditing?

There are many more states of awareness and ability that can be achieved above the state of Clear, as one is only Clear on the first dynamic. Once Clear, an individual wants to continue his auditing to achieve these higher spiritual states and expand his understanding and responsibility on the remaining dynamics.

The State of Operating Thetan

What is meant by Operating Thetan (OT)?

Operating Thetan is a spiritual state of beingness above Clear. *Thetan* refers to the spiritual being, and *operating* means here "able to operate without dependency on things." An Operating Thetan (OT) is able to control matter, energy, space and time rather than being controlled by these things. As a result, an OT is able to be at cause over life.

There are numerous auditing steps on the Bridge called OT levels. People on these levels are progressing to the spiritual state of full OT and becoming more and more OT along the way.

How would you describe the state of Operating Thetan?

The goal of Operating Thetan is to overcome the travails of existence and regain the certainty and abilities of one's native spiritual beingness. At this level one knows that he is separate and apart from such material things as physical form or the physical universe.

OT (Operating Thetan) is a state of spiritual awareness in which an individual is able to control himself and his environment. An OT is someone who knows that he knows and can create positive and prosurvival effects on all of his dynamics. He has been fully refamiliarized with his capabilities as a thetan and can willingly and knowingly be at cause over life, thought, matter, energy, space and time.

As a being becomes more and more OT, he becomes more powerful, stable and responsible as a spiritual being.

A Scientology Career

Can one audit as a career?

Yes. There are many Scientology ministers who audit full time as their life's work. Auditing provides a rewarding career as it is one in which you are always helping people and constantly seeing miraculous results on your preclears. It is very satisfying to know that you are making people's lives happier and saner.

Auditors are very valuable and in great demand.

L. Ron Hubbard's opinion of auditors is well known: "I think of an auditor as a person with enough guts to *do something about it*. This quality is rare and this quality is courageous in the extreme. It is my opinion and knowledge that auditors are amongst the upper tenth of the upper twentieth of intelligent human beings. Their will to do, their motives, their ability to grasp and to use are superior to that of any other profession."

Of what value would it be to have my child trained as an auditor?

First of all, it would provide a young person with certainty and knowledge in dealing with every possible type of human problem, be it interpersonal, familial, organizational, ethical, moral, religious or spiritual. Secondly, it would provide a career of fulfillment in aiding people from all walks of life to gain greater awareness and respect for themselves and other spiritual beings.

Auditors are in demand in every church of Scientology and mission throughout the world. Therefore, any young person would be fulfilling a great demand and contributing greatly to making this world a saner place by becoming trained to minister auditing.

Can one make Scientology a career in some other way than by being a minister?

Yes, there are thousands of Scientologists who work full time in churches and missions throughout the world as executives or administrative staff. There are also those who further the dissemination of Scientology on a one-to-one basis or through the dissemination of Scientology materials and books, those who hold jobs in the Church's social reform groups and those who work in the Office of Special Affairs involved in community betterment or legal work. All of these provide rewarding careers as each forwards the expansion of Scientology and thereby makes it possible for more and more people to benefit from its technology.

SCIENTOLOGY IN SOCIETY

I've heard that Scientologists are doing good things for society. What are some specific examples?

These activities would fill a book in themselves, and are covered in more detail in Part Seven of this book, but here are just a few examples that are typical of the things that Scientologists are doing around the world.

Scientologists regularly hold blood drives to get donations of blood for hospitals, the Red Cross and other similar organizations. As Scientologists do not use harmful drugs, these donations of drug-free blood are welcomed by those in charge of healthcare. Scientologists also regularly hold drives for donations of toys, food and clothing to make life happier for those in need.

During the annual holiday season, Scientologists are particularly active in this sphere. In downtown Hollywood, California, and Clearwater, Florida, for example, Scientologists build a "Winter Wonderland" scene each Christmas, complete with a large Christmas tree, Santa Claus and even "snow," creating a traditional Christmas setting for children who otherwise might never see one.

In Canada, a group of Scientologists spends many weeks each year raising funds to sponsor visits to summer camps by underprivileged children. Church members utilize their artistic talents to bring new experiences and joy to children by performing puppet shows in orphanages, schools and shopping malls, and magic shows for children in foster homes.

Scientologists can also be found in many communities contributing to the care of the elderly. They visit old-age homes and provide entertainment, draw sketches or just drop by and talk with senior citizens. You will find Scientologists helping with "community cleanup" campaigns and assistance to the injured at Veterans Administration hospitals.

Scientologists have taken a leading role fighting drug abuse, actively educating community officials and groups on the dangers of drugs and solutions to the problems. There are many groups utilizing L. Ron Hubbard's technology and freeing people from the devastating effects of drugs.

Mr. Hubbard's technology on how to study has been used by Scientologists and like-minded non-Scientologists around the world to help students and teachers alike. One place where this technology has made major inroads in combating illiteracy is in South Africa, where it has helped more than two million native Africans improve their ability to study.

Another important area of activity for Scientologists is raising moral standards in society. With the support and cooperation of Scientologists, local community service, business and governmental organizations have distributed tens of millions of copies of the nonreligious moral code, *The Way to Happiness,* now available in more than twenty different languages. Its use has led to a revitalization of purpose for people of all ages who apply its simple truths to their lives and to the environment around them.

Another prevalent activity for Scientologists is to expose and eradicate the violations of human rights perpetrated by psychiatry. Many Scientologists do this as members of the Citizens Commission on Human Rights (CCHR), a reform group which was established by the Church in 1969.

They actively investigate psychiatric abuses and bring these to the attention of the media, legislators and groups concerned with protecting people from brutal psychiatric techniques. Such practices as psychosurgery, electroshock and the administration of dangerous psychiatric drugs have destroyed the minds and lives of millions of individuals. Through the efforts of Scientologists working with CCHR, public awareness of the disastrous results of psychiatric methods has been raised and major steps taken to outlaw such practices.

Is Scientology active in black communities and countries?

Definitely. By the Creed of the Church, "All men of whatever race, color or creed were created with equal rights." Thus, there are no limitations placed on who may participate in Scientology services.

There are Scientologists of all races and colors.

For example, there are Scientology churches or Dianetics organizations in Ghana, Zaire, Zimbabwe, Ethiopia and Sierra Leone, among other countries, and black Scientologists are applying Scientology technology in their communities wherever possible.

Mr. Hubbard's study technology is used in many countries to help students and teachers alike. As earlier mentioned, in South Africa, these programs helped over two million underprivileged black Africans improve their ability to study, well before their fate became a popular cause and the walls of apartheid came down.

The Church maintains a Department of Ethnic Affairs specifically to interact and work with minorities. One example of this is a literacy project in Compton, California, which with the Church's effort, successfully turned drug abusers and gang members into responsible members of the community. The program has won endorsements from both community leaders and educators.

Does the Church engage in interfaith affairs?

Absolutely. The Church is a strong advocate of the interfaith approach on issues important to all religions. Scientologists work with representatives of many religions to support and encourage interreligious dialogue, religious freedom and respect for religion in society.

The Church has been involved for many years in actions to protect religious liberty and is active in the American Conference on Religious Movements (ACRM). This multidenominational association of religious organizations is dedicated to the advancement of religious liberty and dialogue.

Scientologists worked with leaders of other religions to petition the US Congress to enact a Religious Freedom Week. The result was just such a designation in 1988. It has now become an annual national tradition.

The Church mustered interfaith support for a bill which severely limits punitive damages claims against religions. Many religious groups, including the National Council of Churches, joined the Church of Scientology in support of California Senate Bill No. 1, which was signed into law by the governor in September 1988.

The bill had arisen following a frivolous lawsuit filed against a Christian church. The Church of Scientology worked with more than 1,500 religious organizations to oppose the suit and make its ramifications known to other religions and the public. In 1989, the US Supreme Court endorsed a California Supreme Court decision which held that the state's laws forbid the filing of such cases against churches.

The Church of Scientology International is an active member of the Coalition for the Free Exercise of Religion, a broad-based religious and civil liberties group that, in 1995, resolved the long and contentious debate over the role of religion in public schools. Through the united efforts of more than three dozen religious and civil liberties organizations, the coalition prepared "Religion in The Public Schools: A Joint Statement of Current Law," which established a model for public policy that led to a final and amicable resolution of the issue. President Bill Clinton praised the joint statement as "wise and thoughtful."

For more than a decade, the Church has exposed and defused assaults on religious freedom from organizations which support "deprograming," the violent practice of kidnappers who, for pay, try to break an individual's faith through such tactics as forcible restraint, food or sleep deprivation, beatings and even rape.

Over the years, deprogramers have attacked members of many different religions, including Baptists, Catholics, Episcopalians,

Methodists, Mormons and Muslims. As a result of coordinated interfaith actions, deprogramers have been arrested, convicted and jailed for their role in such illegal activities.

What does Scientology do to protect the environment?

Individual churches and their parishioners are very active in local environmental campaigns, including recycling projects, public park cleanups, removal of graffiti, murals projects that beautify inner-city streets and highways, Earth Day educational campaigns and community clean-up campaigns, and projects in various cities in Europe to round up and safely dispose of hypodermic syringes discarded by drug addicts in parks.

Do doctors, schools, social workers, businessmen and other professional people use L. Ron Hubbard's technology?

Yes, they do. Members of all these professions use Mr. Hubbard's technology to improve their lives and the lives of those they are helping or working with.

Schools and universities in many countries apply his study methods to improve literacy and teaching success, drug rehabilitation groups use his drug rehabilitation technology to successfully get people off drugs, doctors observe basic Dianetics principles to speed up the recovery of their patients, and businessmen apply L. Ron Hubbard's administrative procedures to create thriving businesses.

Mr. Hubbard's technologies apply to all spheres of life and uniformly get results when standardly used. Therefore, in virtually every area of social or community concern will be people using some aspect of these technologies.

Why do some people oppose Scientology?

There are certain characteristics and mental attitudes that cause a percentage of the population to oppose violently any betterment activity or group. This small percentage of society (roughly 2 percent) cannot tolerate that Scientology is successful

at improving conditions around the world. This same 2 percent is opposed to *any* effective self-betterment activity. The reason they so rabidly oppose Scientology is because it is doing more to help society than any other group. Those who are upset by seeing man get better are small in number compared to the millions who have embraced Scientology and its efforts to create a sane civilization and more freedom for the individual.

Why has Scientology sometimes been considered controversial?

Like all new ideas, Scientology has come under attack by the uninformed and those who feel their vested interests are threatened. As Scientologists have openly and effectively advocated social reform causes, they have become the target of attacks. For those vested interests who cling to a status quo that is detrimental to society, Scientology's technology of making the able more able and teaching people to think for themselves poses a serious threat.

As the falsehoods are proven lies, the controversy quickly fades, and the truth about Scientology, what the Church really is and what its members do, replaces it. The source of these attacks and the controversy that have generated are detailed in Chapter 35 of this book.

Why has Scientology been to court a lot of times?

The Church has gone to court in many countries to uphold the right to freedom of religion. In Australia, as one example, legal actions by the Church brought about a landmark victory which greatly expanded religious freedom throughout that country.

In the United States, the Church's use of the Freedom of Information Act, taking government agencies to court and holding them accountable to release vital documents to the public on a variety of subjects, has been heralded as a vital action to ensure honesty in government.

In certain cases, the Church has used the courts to protect its copyrighted materials, or to ensure its rights and the rights of its members are safeguarded.

During the history of the Church, a few unscrupulous individuals, lusting for money, have observed how Scientology is prospering and rapidly expanding, and unsuccessfully have abused the legal system, in an attempt to line their own pockets.

Are there any laws against the practice of Scientology? Has it been banned?

Of course not.

In fact, the Church has received numerous recognitions, citations and validations from various governments for contributions to society in the fields of education, drug and alcohol rehabilitation, crime reduction, human rights, raising moral values and a host of other fields.

How does Scientology view deprogramers and groups that attempt to force people to denounce their chosen religion?

These so-called "deprogramers," better described as psychiatric depersonalizers, are money-motivated individuals who kidnap others for profit. Their methods include brainwashing, imprisonment, food and sleep deprivation and various forms of torture. Such activities are clearly against the principles held by Scientologists—and have been proven to be against the law as well.

Why is Scientology opposed to psychiatric abuses?

As the stepchildren of the German dictator Bismarck and later Hitler and the Nazis, psychiatry and psychology formed the philosophical basis for the wholesale slaughter of human beings in World Wars I and II. Psychiatry uses electric shock, brain-mutilating psychosurgery and mind-damaging drugs to destroy a person and make him "docile and quiet" in the name of "treatment."

Psychiatric methods involving the butchering of human beings and their sanity are condemned by the Church. Scientologists are trying to create a world without war, insanity and criminality. Psychiatry is seeking to create a world where man is reduced to a robotized or drugged, vegetable-like state so that he can be controlled.

Scientologists do not believe that psychiatrists should tell their patients what they think is wrong with them. This interjects lies or ideas which are not true for the individual himself, thereby violating his basic integrity. Scientologists believe that one should find out for himself the source of his troubles since this gives him the ability to improve conditions in his own life and environment.

Scientology and psychiatry will always be working at cross-purposes. Scientology is a religion and recognizes that man is a spiritual being. Psychiatrists view man as an animal. Psychiatry is strongly opposed to all religions as it does not even recognize that man is a spiritual being.

Scientologists disagree with the enforced and harmful psychiatric methods of involuntary commitment, forced and heavy drugging, electroconvulsive shock treatment, lobotomy and other psychosurgical operations.

By the Creed of the Church of Scientology, the healing of mentally caused ills should not be condoned in nonreligious fields. The reason for this is that violent psychiatric therapies cause spiritual trauma. At best, psychiatry suppresses life's problems; at worst, it causes severe damage, irreversible setbacks in a person's life and even death.

Is Scientology trying to rule the world?

No. Scientology's aim, as expressed by L. Ron Hubbard, is that of creating "a civilization without insanity, without criminals and without war, where the able can prosper and honest beings can have rights, and where man is free to rise to greater heights . . ."

"We seek no revolution. We seek only evolution to higher states of being for the individual and for society."

Scientology does want to improve and reform societal ills, and Scientologists believe there can be a better world by doing so. It is not Scientology's mission to save the world. It is Scientology's mission to free you.

Can Scientology do anything to improve the world situation?

Yes, and it does so every single day. By making the able individual in society more able and more certain of his spirituality and abilities, and by helping more and more people through its religious and social reform programs throughout the world, the Church is helping the world become a better place.

It is possible to bring people to higher levels of communication with the environment and those around them. And as one raises the level of communication, one raises also the ability to observe and change conditions and thereby create a better world and a better civilization.

For more information about Scientology, visit the Internet Web page "The President of the Church of Scientology Answers Your Questions," where the most commonly asked questions about the Scientology religion are answered (**http://faq.scientology.org**).

CHAPTER 37

THE BONA FIDES OF THE SCIENTOLOGY RELIGION

T he only major new religion to emerge in this undeniably turbulent twentieth century, Scientology offers mankind the hope of resolving our most pressing societal problems and of creating a true renaissance of the spirit in the coming century.

As a new religion—which *all* religions once were, unfamiliarity with this vital movement has led some people to ask whether Scientology really is a religion. To its members and experts who have studied it, the answer is unequivocally affirmative.

Comparing specific Scientology doctrines and practices with those of other religions, similarities and differences emerge which make it clear that although Scientology is entirely new, its origins are as ancient as religious thought itself.

Different from older religions, Scientology's approach to the mysteries and problems of life is based on fundamental axioms that isolate and describe the very factors of life. And because the principles of Scientology encompass the entire scope of life, the answers it provides apply to all existence and have broad-ranging applicability.

Although several of the most central doctrines of Scientology are not unlike those of Judeo-Christian religions, many who are familiar with Scientology prefer the comparison to Eastern religions, particularly Buddhism. Yet, Scientology is truly unlike any religion that has preceded it. In fact and in substance it is its own religion with its own unique system of beliefs and practices. And, notably,

it is the only great religion to emerge in the twentieth century.

Nonetheless, because Scientology is a relatively new religion, founded in the early 1950s by L. Ron Hubbard, to gain a clearer understanding of its religious teachings it is of benefit to compare them to the doctrines of several other well-known religions that are older and therefore more familiar to more people.

Perhaps the best place to start is with what may well be the most fundamental doctrine of the Scientology religion, the doctrine of the "thetan." The cornerstone of Scientology theology is the belief that man is himself an immortal spiritual being who has lived through a great many lifetimes and has the potential of infinite survival. Scientologists call this spiritual being the "thetan." The word comes from the Greek letter *theta*, θ, the traditional symbol for thought or life.

While the Scientology concept of the thetan may appear identical to the Judeo-Christian concept of the soul, it is not; there are at least three critical differences between the concepts.

One difference is that Scientologists believe that man also has two other separate and independent parts: the mind and body. And that these are secondary to the thetan, which is considered to be the actual person himself. In sum, the mind and body are vehicles through which the thetan interacts with the material world. Judeo-Christian religions do not hold this view. Although there is no consistent description of man in the New Testament, it essentially retains the Hebrew teaching of unity of body and soul and that one is not complete without the other: Just as one has a body, so one has a soul. In

Scientology, on the other hand, the individual himself *is* his soul, or more accurately, thetan.

A second difference is that Scientologists believe that the thetan will live through a great many lifetimes. Jews and Christians believe the soul lives only once. This explains why Scientologists are eager to make this world a better place — they know they will be back to live in it again.

A third critical difference between the Scientology concept of thetan and the Judeo-Christian concept of soul is that Scientologists believe the thetan, and therefore man, is basically good. Jews and Christians follow the Old Testament teaching that man has two intrinsic impulses — one good and the other evil and man's plight is to overcome this evil impulse. Jewish and Christian theology holds that salvation from this plight occurs after death.

Salvation in the Scientology religion is different, and much more immediate. Although Scientologists hold that the immortal thetan is intrinsically good, they believe that he has lost his true spiritual identity and operates at a small fraction of his natural ability. It is this loss of spiritual identity and the thetan's own experiences, whether in current or prior lives, that causes man to be unhappy or to act irrationally and with evil intent, even though inherently he is good and highly ethical. And, as these experiences accumulate over time, they cause the thetan to become enmeshed with the material universe, from which these very experiences originated.

According to Scientology scripture, the experiences of the thetan are recorded on what is called a "time track," which consists of the mental image picture recordings of all perceptions of the past, much like a movie film. Thus, the time track records experiences of the thetan's current life as well as his experiences in all prior lives.

In addition to moments of pleasure, the time track also records moments of pain and other trauma which thereafter remain hidden from conscious view. It is these recorded, painful experiences that entrap the thetan. When the thetan is reminded of such traumatic past incidents, the relevant portions of the time track can reactivate and exert an involuntary influence on the thetan and the body. These may cause the thetan to experience pain or negative emotions or even to act irrationally.

This plight need not be permanent, however. Scientology offers humanity freedom from this needless suffering, both now and for all future time. By following the path outlined in the scripture of the Scientology religion, the thetan can progress through higher and higher levels of spiritual awareness and return to his native state and thereby achieve complete spiritual freedom. Now, in this lifetime complete spiritual freedom can be achieved.

The primary path to this spiritual freedom is through "auditing," one of the two central religious practices of the Scientology theology. With this freedom comes release from the eternal cycle of birth and death and full awareness, memory and ability independent of the flesh. And with it comes a spiritual being who is "knowing and willing cause over life, thought, matter, energy, space and time."

It should not be hard to see why Scientology so often is compared to Eastern religions. Many point to Scientology's ascending levels of spiritual awareness and self-searching path to enlightened understanding as similar to Buddhism's path to knowledge and strict practices of meditation and right living, and to the step-like levels of spiritual understanding of the Vedic "revealed knowledge" or the "way of knowledge" expounded by many of the schools of Hinduism. Others believe the Buddhist and Hindu goals of complete liberation from *samsara,* their view of the endless cycle of rebirth, may not be unlike reaching Scientology's highest levels of spiritual awareness. However, this is not the case.

Scientology is its own religion, and an absolute comparison between it and any other religion is impossible. There are significant differences between Scientology and other religions, including those of the East.

One very important distinction between Scientology and the religions of the East concerns their notion of the Supreme Being. Hinduism is a polytheistic religion. Buddhists do not believe in a Supreme Being in any form.

As many religious scholars note, Scientology in this respect is more like Western religions and shares their view that places the Supreme Being at the pinnacle of the cosmos. And it is the clarity with which Scientologists view this entire cosmos that enables them to create a vital and vibrant spiritual life on this earth.

Scientologists further identify another common unifying factor that runs throughout their view of the cosmos. This factor is that the primary goal of all life forms—from the thetan to the Supreme Being—is the urge towards infinite survival. Scientologists call this urge the "dynamic principle of existence."

This dynamic principle of existence is itself divided into eight distinct parts, which are called the eight dynamics. The specific dynamics include survival of self as the first dynamic, of the family as the second, of or as one's groups as the third, through man as a species as the fourth, for all life forms as the fifth, of the physical universe as the sixth, as a spiritual being as the seventh and the Supreme Being or infinity as the eighth.

While the eighth dynamic may be identified as the Supreme Being, as infinity or even as the God dynamic, it actually is the allness of all. Yet Scientology differs from religions of the West as to how it presents the Supreme Being to its members.

Many religions are quick to characterize their Supreme Being (whether called Yahweh, God or Allah) in such terms as omnipotent, omniscient, beneficent, judgmental, or demanding, and in most instances even describe it in anthropomorphic terms.

In Scientology, each individual is expected to reach his own personal conclusions regarding the eight dynamics, including the Supreme Being, through the religious practices of auditing and study of Scientology scripture. Thus, an individual's understanding as to his relationship with the Supreme Being is developed over time as he comes to understand and participate more fully in each of the preceding seven dynamics.

This is a necessary approach for, in Scientology, no one is asked to accept anything on faith. Instead, everyone is expected to test knowledge for themselves, on a purely personal level. Knowledge will be true for someone only when that person actually observes it and determines that it is true according to his own observation.

Thus by following the Scientology religious path, each person's relationship with the Supreme Being is on a truly personal, individual level.

That is why, according to L. Ron Hubbard, "when the seventh dynamic is reached in its entirety one will only then discover the true eighth dynamic."

Still, Mr. Hubbard also cautions: "No culture in the history of the world, save the thoroughly depraved and expiring ones, has failed to affirm the existence of a Supreme Being. It is an empirical observation that men without a strong and lasting faith in a Supreme Being are less capable, less ethical and less valuable to themselves and society. . . . A man without an abiding faith is, by observation alone, more of a thing than a man."

As may be apparent, Scientology also differs from Judeo-Christian religions in its form of worship. This difference arises from the relationship the specific religion expects its members to form with the Supreme Being. In the case of Judeo-Christian religions, which mandate a particular relationship with an anthropomorphic God, prayer is a logical mode of expression and communion. But this is not appropriate for Scientologists, since Scientology does not impose such a specific relationship with the Supreme Being.

Auditing and training are the two central religious services of the Scientology faith.

Through them, Scientologists are able to transcend this secular world, progress through ever-increasing levels of spiritual awareness, and develop a relationship with the Supreme Being that is meaningful and true for them.

But, it is important to bear in mind that Scientology is not at all just a set of spiritual beliefs divorced from the world in which we live. Scientology provides a guide for individuals to cast their spiritual values into action. Thus, as Scientologists become fully responsible for all eight of their dynamics, they actively work to improve the quality of all life and to make this a better world for everyone.

As shown within the pages of this book, they work to free drug addicts of their vices, to rehabilitate criminals, to bring literacy to the disadvantaged, to introduce a moral code to all sectors of society, to protect the weak, to fight injustice and prejudice, to promote human rights, and to participate in many charitable activities.

Scientology unquestionably is thus a holistic religion embracing all aspects of a person's life. Scientologists live their religion and apply its principles and ethical precepts in their relationships with family, friends, co-workers, community and environment, up through all eight dynamics to, and including, the Supreme Being. And in doing so, they follow a code of ethical conduct that is without rival in this day and age.

Thus, while auditing is a purely religious service, the benefits obtained from it pervade all planes of existence. These benefits include tangible benefits such as improved family life and relationships, good health and prosperity, as well as the primary benefits that are wholly spiritual—increased spiritual awareness and abilities, knowledge of the Supreme Being and the ultimate attainment of spiritual freedom.

It is for all these reasons—along with the belief of millions of adherents—that Scientology is indeed a religion. And although its doctrines and rites are not identical to any other religion, it would be well to remember that unlike these religions, Scientology was born in the twentieth century and is a religion of its times.

RELIGIOUS SCHOLARS VALIDATE SCIENTOLOGY

In view of its importance to our modern culture, it is not surprising that Scientology has drawn the attention of the world's leading religious scholars and sociologists from institutions as diverse and prestigious as Oxford University and universities in Rome, Paris, Cape Town, Stockholm, Buenos Aires, Helsinki, Tokyo and throughout the world.

Because of their interest in emerging religions, these scholars have tested Scientology against the norm by which they judge all religions. Many have even published written reports of their findings, which provide a unique view of Scientology.

Although each of these experts proceeded from his or her own unique cultural background and method of analysis, it is interesting to note that they all approached the classification of religion with similar criteria. Basically, they looked for three general characteristics:

1. A belief in some Ultimate Reality, such as a supreme or eternal truth that transcends the here and now of the secular world;
2. Religious practices directed towards understanding, attaining or communing with this Ultimate Reality; and
3. A community of believers who join together in pursuing this Ultimate Reality.

Based on these criteria, every scholar to examine Scientology has concluded that it has the requisite elements for a religion.

Each has found that Scientology meets the first element because it posits an Ultimate Reality that transcends the material world.

The scholars found the second element through both Scientology's life-rite ceremonies common to all religions (birth, marriage and funeral services, etc.), but predominantly through Scientology practices of auditing and training, since it is through these practices that Scientologists increase their spiritual awareness and, ultimately, attain an understanding of their relationship with the Ultimate Reality.

As to the third element, the religious experts found the religious community through which Scientologists pursue their quest for the Ultimate Reality is manifest through both the specific churches that have been established through the common belief and goals that cause adherents to join together to form and support their respective church.

Dr. Bryan Ronald Wilson, Reader Emeritus in Sociology at Oxford University and internationally respected as one of the most distinguished authorities on religious issues, has written extensively about the Scientology religion.

Scientology, he wrote, "embraces features which correspond in certain respects to some of the trends evident in the mainstream of Western religion. It employs language which is contemporary, colloquial and unmystical; and it presents its dogmas as matters of objective fact. Its conception of salvation has both proximate and an ultimate dimension."

Describing the basic tenets of the religion, Dr. Wilson noted that Scientology "offers adherents a graduated path of spiritual enlightenment. It claims to disencumber adherents of the untoward effects of past traumas, whether experienced in the present or in past lives. It is free from dogmas, and whilst, in abstract terms, as the 'eighth dynamic,' Scientology acknowledges a Supreme Being, it draws short of attempting to describe his attributes." In simple summation, he wrote, "Scientology is a genuine system of religious belief and practice which evokes from its votaries deep and earnest commitment."

Similar sentiments have been expressed by Regis Dericquebourg, Professor of Sociology of Religion of the University of Lille III in Lille, France. After an exhaustive study of Scientology, which included interviews with 285 French Scientologists, Professor

Dericquebourg concluded it was a bona fide religion.

"It enables the follower to give sense to cosmic, historical and personal events," he wrote, further pointing out that, "it offers the believer the conviction that he holds the solution to personal and group salvation; it enables the individual to be at cause in his life and not the effect of external causes."

He further concluded that Scientology rested on a personal experience which enables each parishioner to contact his or her own spiritual nature.

Another who has reached like conclusions is Professor Lonnie D. Kliever. A distinguished American expert on religion who has published several books and taught and lectured extensively on the subject over the past thirty-three years, he stated that "Scientology clearly meets the scholarly definition of any religious tradition, clearly pursues the goals of any religious quest and clearly exhibits the dimensions of any religious community."

Dr. Kliever pointed out that, to Scientologists, the "problems besetting the human race are ultimately spiritual rather than physical or mental." Scientology addresses those problems by freeing the individual from the spiritual debilities which have weighed down his existence.

Dr. J. Gordon Melton is the founder and director of the Institute for the Study of American Religion in Santa Barbara, California and has been engaged in the study of new religions for more than three decades. The author of over twenty books, including the *Encyclopedia of American Religions,* he has written that the "Church of Scientology is very much a religion in the fullest sense of the word."

According to Dr. Melton, the "Church of Scientology does espouse a belief in and devotion to and worship of a 'Supreme Being' as well as a belief in the immortality of the spirit and that man is a spiritual being."

Dr. Frank K. Flinn, adjunct professor in religious studies at Washington University, St. Louis, Missouri, has been studying emerging religions since 1962. A graduate of Harvard Divinity School, Dr. Flinn has conducted advanced religious studies and was a Professor in the Department of Religious Studies at the University of Windsor of Ontario, Canada.

After conducting research into the Church of Scientology, Dr. Flinn wrote, "I can state without hesitation that the Church of Scientology constitutes a bona fide religion. It possesses all the essential marks of religions known around the world: (1) a well-defined belief system, (2) which issues into religious practice (positive and negative norms for behavior, religious rites and ceremonies, acts and observances), and (3) which sustain a body of believers in an identifiable religious community, distinguishable from other religious communities."

COUNTRY BY COUNTRY EXPERTS AGREE

Dr. M. Darroll Bryant, Professor of Religion and Culture at Renison College, University of Waterloo, in Ontario, Canada, has also conducted a lengthy review of the Church of Scientology, after first becoming aware of the Church in the mid-1970s.

He stated, "According to Scientology, our humanity is composed of different parts: the body, the mind and the 'thetan.' The thetan in Scientology is analogous to the soul in Christianity and the spirit in Hinduism. Part of the problem of life is that human beings have lost an awareness of their true nature. In Scientology, this means an awareness of themselves as thetans."

Dr. Bryant also wrote that it was "apparent that Scientology is a religion. It has its own distinctive beliefs in and account

Expressed in these academic studies are the authoritative opinions of the world's leading social and religious scholars. Further commentary by these and other prominent leaders about the impact of the Scientology religion are presented in Chapter 34.

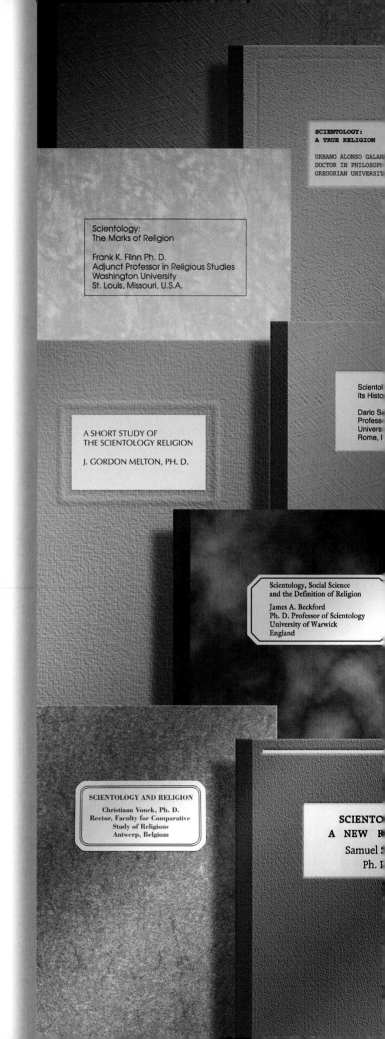

The Religious Status
of Scientology

Irving Hexham, Ph. D.

SCIENTOLOGY AND ISLAM

An Analogous
Study

Haji Muhammad al-Qaaim Safa Sav
President, Ahlul-Bait Center
Japan

The Church of Scientology

Juha Pentikäinen, Ph. D.
Marja Pentikäinen, MSC
Helsinki, Finland

SCIENTOLOGY:
A Comparison with
Religions of the East and West

Per-Arne Berglie
Professor, History of Religion
University of Stockholm
Stockholm, Sweden

RELIGIOUS PHILOSOPHY, RELIGION AND CHURCH

G. C. OOSTHUIZEN, TH. D.

PROFESSOR [RETIRED], DEPT. OF SCIENCE
OF RELIGION
UNIVERSITY OF DURBAN-WESTVILLE
NATAL, SOUTH AFRICA

SCIENTOLOGY
A Worshipping Community

Lonnie D. Kliever, Ph. D.
Professor of Religious Studies
Southern Methodist University
Dallas, Texas, U.S.A.

SCIENTOLOGY

RÉGIS DERICQUEBOURG
PROFESSOR, SOCIOLOGY OF RELIGION
UNIVERSITY OF LILLE III
LILLE, FRANCE

Is Scientology a Religion

Alan W. Black
Associate Professor of Sociology
University of New England
Armidale, New South Wales
Australia

SCIENTOLOGY
A Way of Spiritual
Self-identification

Michael A. Sivertsev, PH. D.
Chairman for New Religions
Board of cooperation
with religious organisations
Office of the Russian President

SCIENTOLOGY
An Analysis and Comparison
of its Religious Systems and Doctrines

Bryan R Wilson, PH. D.
Emeritus Fellow
Oxford University
England

SCIENTOLOGY
A RELIGION IN SOUTH

DAVID CHISHESTE
PROFESSOR OF COMPARATI
UNIVERSITY OF CAPE
SOUTH AFRICA

of an unseen spiritual order, its own distinctive religious practice and ritual life, it has its own authoritative texts and community-building activity."

James A. Beckford, Professor of Sociology at the University of Warwick, England, pointed out that developing modern religions normally "lack the benefits of inherited property-wealth, endowments, patronage and a 'birthright' membership," yet these are not characteristics of religion itself. And while there are various scholarly opinions on exactly how one does define "religion," it does not matter which approach one chooses in viewing Scientology, he wrote, for it meets "all the criteria conventionally applied by social scientists," no matter the definition employed.

Many scholars observed and commented upon the altruistic work performed by Scientologists. In one typical example, Dr. Alan W. Black, Associate Professor of Sociology at the University of New England in New South Wales, Australia, wrote that, "agencies established by the Church of Scientology have been active in anti-drug campaigns, in rehabilitating drug addicts and criminals, in eradicating illiteracy and remedying educational disadvantaged, in improving the environment, in providing disaster relief and in defending human rights."

A treatise by Michael A. Sivertsev, Chairman for New Religions of the Board of Cooperation with Religious Organizations in the office of the Russian president, provided an important cultural perspective.

"The religious message and the religious practice of the Church of Scientology," he wrote, "come and are taught to mankind in a time [of] mass secularization of public consciousness [and when] traditional religious systems, doctrines and practices leave the majority of contemporaries uninspired."

In his analysis he sought to examine, "what are the reasons . . . which make the image of Scientology attractive for independently thinking, active and distrustful persons in

the post-totalitarian era?" And in part, he concluded that "Scientology is an open religious system [and] that at the center of spirituality of Scientology lies, first and foremost, one's own personal experience of the realization of a spiritual identity, a new spiritual infinite self."

Another equally fascinating perspective — of religion in general and Scientology in particular — was provided by Mr. Fumio Sawada, the Eighth Holder of the Secrets of Yui-itsu Shinto, the oldest religion in Japan. His predecessors include Emperor Tenmu of A.D. 673, who also ordered the first written historical record of Japan. Mr. Sawada is one of Japan's foremost authorities on religion and a former director at the distinguished Sophia University.

"The term *religion* in Japan means to teach the origin, teach the source of the origin," he wrote. Quoting a poem which "predates Christianity's arrival in Japan," he expressed the Japanese view that "there are many paths at the foot of the mountain, but the view of the moon is the same at the peak." The point, he stated, is that "when there are so many similarities among religions, why concentrate on the differences?"

He added, "The concept of a person having lived before is old and fully accepted by Eastern religions. Scientology theory and practice is based around this concept, that one is a spiritual being which Mr. Hubbard has called a 'thetan,' and that one can recall his past lives, and that as a spiritual being his actions of the past determine his situation in the present.

"Japan is a country where religions place an accent on the raising of one's spiritual ability. From a Japanese point of view, Scientology is indeed a similar religion to others already here.

"It has more similarities to Japanese religions than Western religions, and for this reason it may be misunderstood in the West for not being similar to other mainstream religions."

Nonetheless, he concluded, "one cannot reach any other decision than that Scientology is a religion."

THE RELIGION FOR THE TWENTY-FIRST CENTURY

There can be no doubt that Scientology is a religion. Religious scholars from throughout the world unequivocally and unambiguously say so based on objective criticism developed in the halls of academia.

But Scientology is more than just any religion. It is the only religion that offers mankind a proven and practical path to freedom from the travails of the past and attainment of spiritual freedom beyond imagination. It is the only religion that offers personal immortality—now, in this lifetime. Because Scientology is the only religion that can answer such questions as who we are, why we are here, and what happens when we die, more people than ever are embracing it as their religion.

Born in the twentieth century, Scientology has become a great religion in terms of the number of its adherents, and in its beneficial effects upon society.

RECOGNITION BY THE COURTS

The religiosity of Scientology has not only been recognized by internationally known scholars but by courts and government agencies of major nations throughout the world.

The most significant legal recognition of the Scientology religion came in October 1993 when the United States Internal Revenue Service (IRS) issued ruling letters which recognized the tax-exempt status of more than 150 Scientology churches, missions, social reform organizations and other entities because they operate exclusively for religious and charitable purposes.

The IRS's religious recognition was universal and unconditional, and the result of one of the most detailed and exhaustive examinations in the agency's history. The IRS was given unfettered access to every echelon of the Church's ecclesiastical hierarchy. Thus, the IRS examination was not limited to United States entities, but specifically included the financial and other affairs of church organizations from Australia to Canada and from Europe to South Africa.

As a result, Church of Scientology International (CSI), the mother church of the Scientology religion, received not only exempt recognition, but also received a group exemption letter embracing all Scientology churches under its ecclesiastical oversight. The Church's spiritual meccas were also individually recognized as tax-exempt, as were the Church's publishing entities.

Scientology Missions International received its own exemption. It also received a separate group-exemption letter for all the Scientology missions under its ecclesiastical oversight.

RTC, the church that holds the trademarks of Dianetics and Scientology, was individually recognized as tax-exempt and received its own separate ruling letter.

The IRS also recognized the International Association of Scientologists as a tax-exempt organization.

In addition to ruling favorably on tax exemption, the IRS rulings make all donations to all United States churches of Scientology deductible against personal United States income taxes to the full extent permitted by law.

Although the IRS decision was the most significant recognition of the Scientology religion, it was by no means the first or last government confirmation of the Church's status. That conclusion has been echoed again and again by courts and government agencies everywhere.

Earlier, on January 19, 1983, in *Founding Church of Scientology of Washington, DC v. Director, Federal Bureau of Investigation*, the United States District Court, District of Columbia, ruled:

"The Church of Scientology must be treated the same as any established religion or denominational sect within the United States, Catholic, Protestant or other."

On February 27, 1984, the United States District Court, *Central District of California in Peterson v. Church of Scientology of California,* ruled:

"This court finds that the Church of Scientology is a religion within the meaning of the First Amendment. The beliefs and ideas of Scientology address ultimate concerns — the nature of the person and the individual's relationship to the universe. The theories of Scientology involve a comprehensive belief system. Additional indicia of the religious status of Scientology include the following: (a) Scientology has ordained ministers and ceremonial functions; (b) it is incorporated as a tax-exempt religious organization; and (c) it characterizes itself as a church."

After reviewing the judicial precedents concerning the religious nature of Scientology, the United States 11th Circuit Court of Appeals in *Church of Scientology Flag Service Organization v. City of Clearwater,* succinctly summed up US legal history on September 30, 1993:

"The history, organization, doctrine and practice of Scientology has been thoroughly recounted in numerous judicial decisions. We need not reiterate this background because the district court found that no genuine factual issues existed to dispute Scientology's claim of being a bona fide religion."

In a British Commonwealth country, on October 27, 1983, the full bench of the High Court of Australia — the highest court in the land — unanimously ruled that "The conclusion that it [the Church of Scientology] is a religious institution entitled to the tax exemption is irresistible." As a result of this case, the Church established the legal definition of religion for the Australian Constitution for the first time in history.

Scientology is treated as a religion with respect to all facets of its activities by courts and agencies at all levels of government.

The Assessment Appeal Board, province of British Columbia ruled in 1990:

"The Church of Scientology is a religious organization."

On December 21, 1993, the Inspector General of Financial Institutions for the government of Quebec recognized the Church of Scientology of Montreal and the Church of Scientology of Quebec City as religious corporations.

And on August 16, 1994, the province of Ontario determined that Scientology is a true religion and issued certificates to Scientology ministers authorizing them to perform marriages. As a result, the religious status of Scientology is now recognized in every Canadian province where churches exist.

More recently, in 1996, the British Ministry of Defense said that Scientology was "an officially recognized religion" in the Royal Navy.

Courts in Europe have also recognized the religiosity of Scientology.

In Germany, on January 30, 1985, in In Re Karl-Friedrich Munz, the Stuttgart District Court ruled:

"[The Church of Scientology's] purpose in this world is considered to help man in his striving for spiritual freedom and to completely free him from problems and burdens to reach total freedom in order to recognize himself as a spiritual being and experience the existence of a Supreme Being . . ."

On February 23, 1989, the Regional Court in Frankfurt found that the Church of Scientology constituted a religious community within the full meaning of German law.

In Stuttgart, on December 9, 1992, the District Court ruled that auditing is a religious activity. A few months later, regional courts in Munich and Frankfurt issued similar rulings.

In Baden-Württemberg on August 2, 1995, the court again held the Church of Scientology to be a religious entity.

The County Court of Freiburg im Breisgau, on February 6, 1996, ruled:

"Under no circumstances can it be accepted that the Church of Scientology is denied the protection of Article 4, paragraph 2 of the Constitution," the provision which guarantees freedom of religion.

In Italy, in the case of *State v. Eight Defendants,* the Trento Court of Appeals made the following finding:

"Scientology . . . has the objective to achieve an inner and outer freedom, one that transcends the human, one that belongs to the field of spiritual things, and that moves up to infinity; indeed, the progress toward realization of the eighth dynamic force — concerning Infinity and God — actually is the characteristic that describes Scientology as a religion and as a church."

And on December 12, 1991, the court of Lecco, in Italy, ruled that the Church and its followers were actively engaged in what could only be described as religious activities.

In Switzerland, the Statthalteramt of the District of Zurich on September 6, 1994, determined that Scientology was a religion and that the Church and its members were entitled to the protection guaranteed by freedom of religion.

In Austria, the Independent Administrative Senate in Vienna, on August 1, 1995, concluded that Scientology is a religion and that auditing is a religious activity conducted solely for a religious purpose.

On August 13, 1996, the Supreme Court of Austria ruled that Scientologists are protected by the nondiscrimination clause of the European Convention and cannot be discriminated against because of their religious beliefs.

In France, the Court of Appeal in Lyon ruled on July 28, 1997, that "the Church of Scientology is entitled to call itself a religion and is entirely free to develop its activities, under the existing law, including its missionary activities or even its activities of proselytism."

On the heels of this decision, on October 8, 1997, the Supreme Court of Italy issued a landmark decision for the Church of Scientology overruling a lower court decision which had very narrowly defined the concept of a bona fide religion by applying only Judeo-Christian principles. The Supreme Court noted that this view of religion was "based on philosophical and historical/social assumptions that are incorrect; and it is vitiated by manifest illogic in the reasoning supporting it."

In a precedent-setting decision in Germany on November 6, 1997, the Federal Administrative Court recognized that "auditing, per the statutes, is a form of 'spiritual counseling' and seminars and courses 'for the attainment of a higher level of being' are based on the commonly held convictions of members."

In many countries in which the Church of Scientology has been more recently established, governments have come to the same conclusion. For example, in 1991 the court of the capital city of Budapest officially recognized the Church of Scientology of Hungary. Then recognition came in Albania, and in December 1996, Kazakhstan acknowledged the religiosity of the Church there.

A RELIGION IN THE TRUEST SENSE

Governments, courts and religious scholars from every major country in the world unequivocally agree that Scientology is a religion. And while such recognitions are welcome and appreciated, Scientology would still be a religion even without them.

Scientology is a religion because it recognizes man as a spiritual being and provides a proven and workable path which, when walked, frees man from the travails of the past and enables him to achieve spiritual freedom and personal immortality. And it is a religion because millions of people from all walks of life in well over 100 countries consider it to be *their* religion.

THE AIMS OF SCIENTOLOGY
BY L. RON HUBBARD

A civilization without insanity, without criminals and without war, where the able can prosper and honest beings can have rights, and where man is free to rise to greater heights, are the aims of Scientology.

First announced to an enturbulated world in 1950, these aims are well within the grasp of our technology.

Nonpolitical in nature, Scientology welcomes any individual of any creed, race or nation.

We seek no revolution. We seek only evolution to higher states of being for the individual and for society.

We are achieving our aims.

After endless millennia of ignorance about himself, his mind and the universe, a breakthrough has been made for man.

Other efforts man has made have been surpassed.

The combined truths of fifty thousand years of thinking men, distilled and amplified by new discoveries about man, have made for this success.

We welcome you to Scientology. We only expect of you your help in achieving our aims and helping others. We expect you to be helped.

Scientology is the most vital movement on Earth today.

In a turbulent world, the job is not easy. But then, if it were, we wouldn't have to be doing it.

We respect man and believe he is worthy of help. We respect you and believe you, too, can help.

Scientology does not owe its help. We have done nothing to cause us to propitiate. Had we done so, we would not now be bright enough to do what we are doing.

Man suspects all offers of help. He has often been betrayed, his confidence shattered. Too frequently he has given his trust and been betrayed. We may err, for we build a world with broken straws. But we will never betray your faith in us so long as you are one of us.

The sun never sets on Scientology.

And may a new day dawn for you, for those you love and for man.

Our aims are simple, if great.

And we will succeed, and are succeeding at each new revolution of the Earth.

Your help is acceptable to us.

Our help is yours.

PART THIRTEEN

L. RON HUBBARD

To say that L. Ron Hubbard was a remarkable man seems somehow incomplete. As any reader can see by now, Mr. Hubbard left an extraordinary legacy: an immense body of wisdom that leads man to spiritual freedom; the fastest-growing religion in the world today; and an extraordinary organizational structure which allows the religion to expand without limit.

Furthermore, his works have touched the lives of millions, and not only the lives of those who are Scientologists. His study technology, his Purification Rundown, his administrative technology, his drug rehabilitation program, his nonreligious moral code and more, all have broad secular application.

In the following chapters, the reader can discover more about L. Ron Hubbard by reading a chronology of his life and a discussion of how thoroughly his discoveries have permeated our culture. Additionally, there is a list of publications, each dedicated to an aspect of his many accomplishments.

CHAPTER 38

L. RON HUBBARD
A CHRONICLE

To appreciate the scope of L. Ron Hubbard's life, his varied experiences and the many lands he visited in pursuit of answers to the human dilemma, the following chronicle has been provided. It is designed to give readers some feel for his progress and the sequence of steps leading to the discoveries for which he is so respected today.

13 MARCH 1911:

L. Ron Hubbard is born in Tilden, Nebraska. In September the Hubbard family—Ron, his father, Harry Ross Hubbard, an officer in the US Navy, and mother, Ledora May—move to Durant, Oklahoma.

1913–1917:

In 1913, settling in the city of Kalispell, Montana, Ron first encounters the Blackfoot Indians at a tribal dance on the outskirts of town. The Indians are much taken with young Ron's inquisitiveness and the beginnings of a bond are established.

From Kalispell, Ron moves to Montana's capital at Helena, where during the summer months he usually resides at the family ranch, affectionately known as the "Old Homestead." During the harsh winter months, a three-story red brick house near the corner of Helena's Fifth and Beatty Streets serves as Ron's home.

Among other colorful figures in this still pioneer setting, Ron meets Old Tom, a Blackfoot Indian medicine man. A unique and rare relationship is established as the elderly shaman passes on much of the tribal lore to his young friend.

Many a Saturday finds Ron and his friends panning for gold in the gullies for pocket money, while afternoons are spent riding broncos on the surrounding plains.

At the age of six, Ron is honored with the status of blood brother of the Blackfeet in a ceremony that is still recalled by tribal elders.

1918–1921:

In the spring of 1918 Ron and his grandfather embark on an "automotive adventure"—from Helena to Portland, Oregon, in a Model T Ford.

After returning to Helena, Ron takes his first adventure by himself, traveling to Tacoma, Washington to meet up with his father. He then moves with his parents first to San Diego and then a year later to Oakland, California.

1922–1923:

Ron moves north to Puget Sound in Washington State. He joins the Boy Scouts of America in April 1923. As a member of Tacoma Troop 31, he becomes a Second Class Scout on 8 May and two months later, on 5 July, advances to First Class Scout.

In October, Harry Ross Hubbard receives orders to report to the nation's capital. Ron and his parents board the USS *Ulysses S. Grant* on 1 November 1923 and sail to New York from San Francisco through the recently opened Panama Canal. They then journey to Washington, DC. During this voyage, Ron meets Commander Joseph "Snake" Thompson, who has recently returned from Vienna and studies with Sigmund Freud. Through the course of their friendship, the commander spends many an afternoon in the Library of Congress teaching Ron what he knows of the human mind.

By 11 December 1923, Ron, now part of Washington's Boy Scout Troop 10, earns his Carpentry, First Aid and Fireman merit badges.

1924–1925:

In the month of January 1924 Ron earns his Electricity, Personal Health, Photography and Public Health merit badges.

In February, after earning his Safety First, Craftsmanship, Swimming, Physical Development and Pioneering merit badges, Ron obtains his Life Scout and Star Scout medals.

In March, Ron obtains his Handicraft, Automobiling and Pathfinding merit badges. On 20 March Ron represents Troop 10 while visiting President Calvin Coolidge and five days afterwards, on 25 March, becomes the nation's youngest Eagle Scout. The next day, Ron leaves Washington and returns to Montana by cross-country train.

While in Montana, Ron continues his scouting activities, organizes scouting events and acts as an Assistant Scoutmaster. In 1925 Ron moves to Seattle where he attends Queen Anne High School.

1926–1929:

After completing the school year in early June 1927, Ron travels to San Francisco, boarding a steamer to meet his father in Guam. By way of Hawaii, Japan, China, the Philippines and Hong Kong, Ron arrives at the island of Guam during the first week of July 1927. There, he befriends the local Chamorros and teaches in the native schools. Throughout these travels, Ron's observations and adventures are carefully recorded in diaries. A few years later, Ron will draw upon these experiences for his adventure and action fiction.

By late September 1927, Ron returns to Helena where he joins the Montana National Guard's 163rd Infantry. While at Helena High School he becomes an editor of the school's newspaper.

For the annual Vigilante Day Parade on 4 May, Ron organizes and enters a group of classmates dressed as pirates of the Spanish Main and wins the prize for "Most Original" cast.

Finding classrooms and schools too confining, Ron ventures out alone again and travels aboard the USS *Henderson,* returning to the Orient.

Through the next fourteen months Ron journeys inland to the Western Hills of China, out again to Japan, then down to the Philippines and further south to Java. He plies the waters of the China coast as a helmsman and supercargo aboard the *Marianna Maru,* a twin-masted coastal schooner.

In China, he becomes close friends with British intelligence officers, Buddhist priests, US Marines and the last remaining magician from the line of Kublai Khan's court.

By late September 1929, he returns to the United States, completing his high-school education in Washington, DC. Writing and delivering a speech on the United States Constitution and the guarantees of individual liberty, he wins a scholastic oratory contest.

1930–1933:

Graduating from Woodward School for Boys in 1930, Ron enrolls at George Washington University. Here he studies engineering and atomic and molecular physics and embarks upon a personal search for answers to the human dilemma. His first experiment concerning the structure and function of the mind is carried out while at the university.

Ron joins the 20th Regiment, Company G of the US Marines, becoming a drill sergeant and turning out a prize-winning company. He performs as the balladeer for the local radio station WOL and writes serial drama shows. He also becomes a surveyor as part of a team sent to verify the Canadian/US border in Maine.

Taking his thirst for adventure to the skies, he is introduced to glider flying and quickly becomes recognized as one of the country's most outstanding pilots. With virtually no training time, he takes up powered flight and barnstorms throughout the Midwest. Due to reports he files on airport conditions, twelve unsafe airports are closed.

A national aviation magazine reports that Ron set a national soaring record for sustained flight over the same field.

Writing for the nationwide *Sportsman Pilot* magazine, Ron details the latest aviation developments and advises fellow pilots on flight procedures in adverse conditions.

He helps run the university flying club and is secretary of the George Washington University chapter of the American Society of Civil Engineers. As an editor and writer with the college newspaper, *The University Hatchet,* he writes his first published fiction story, *Tah.* He also wins the Literary Award for the best one-act play, *The God Smiles.*

In the spring of 1932, Ron organizes and heads the Caribbean Motion Picture Expedition. The two-and-a-half-month, 5,000-mile voyage aboard the 200-foot, four-masted schooner, *Doris Hamlin,* proves a unique and rewarding experience for over fifty college students. The voyage collects numerous floral and reptile specimens for the University of Michigan, and photographs are sold to the *New York Times.*

Shortly after Ron's return to the US he embarks on another adventure, the West Indies Mineralogical Expedition. Through April of 1933, Ron not only completes the first mineralogical survey of Puerto Rico, but writes articles for *Sportsman Pilot* magazine on flying through the Caribbean islands. He additionally investigates and explores some of the area's diverse cultures and beliefs, including that curious blend of Catholicism and voodoo known as Espiritismo.

Returning to the mainland in the spring of 1933, Ron begins his professional fiction-writing career. Ron writes a story a day and after a few short weeks of work nets his first sale to New York publishers. February 1934 sees the publication of Ron's first adventure fiction story, *The Green God.*

1934–1936:

Throughout this period, L. Ron Hubbard writes. Seated at his Remington manual typewriter, he easily produces 100,000 words of fiction a month.

Ron writes western, detective, adventure, action, and even romance stories. In 1935 he is elected president of the New York chapter of the American Fiction Guild, offering leadership to such stellar names as Raymond Chandler, Dashiell Hammett and Edgar Rice Burroughs. In his capacity as president, he also pens articles for writer magazines. He appears on radio shows advising both novice and professional colleagues on how to improve the quality and salability of their stories.

Illustrating his prolific output as a writer, he completes 138 novels, novelettes and short stories in six years in just the genres of adventure, action, western, mystery and detective. This is an average of over one published story every two weeks, three times the output of most other writers.

So great is his production in so many varied styles and genres that he employs numerous pseudonyms so as not to dominate too many magazine covers. Among them: Winchester Remington Colt, Lt. Jonathan Daly, Capt. Charles Gordon, Bernard Hubbel, Michael Keith, Legionnaire 148, Rene Lafayette, Ken Martin, B.A. Northrup, Scott Morgan, Kurt von Rachen, Barry Randolph, Lt. Scott Morgan, Legionnaire 14830, Capt. Humbert Reynolds.

So intense is the demand for Ron's stories, that one complete issue of *Top-Notch* magazine is entirely written by him. In 1936 Ron writes his first book, *Buckskin Brigades.*

1937–1940:

Ron's popularity is now such that Hollywood seeks film rights to his stories

and then enlists his services as a writer. After purchasing film rights to his novel, *Murder at Pirate Castle,* Columbia Pictures requests that he adapt this work for the screen under the title *Secret of Treasure Island.* Arriving in Hollywood in May 1937, Ron begins work on *Secret of Treasure Island* and goes to work on three other big screen serials for Columbia: *The Mysterious Pilot, The Great Adventures of Wild Bill Hickok* and *The Spider Returns.* Ron thus works on four of Columbia's big screen super serials. In his ten weeks in Hollywood, he not only writes over a quarter of a million words of scripts, but also continues producing for his New York editors.

Upon returning to New York, executives from Street & Smith, one of the world's largest publishing concerns, enlist Ron's expertise for their newly acquired magazine, *Astounding Science Fiction.* Ron is asked to help boost sagging sales with stories about real people—not robots, planets and spaceships. He accepts their proposal and the face of science fiction is changed forever.

His first science fiction work, *The Dangerous Dimension,* appears in the July

1938 issue of *Astounding Science Fiction*. Among other L. Ron Hubbard stories appearing in the pages of *Astounding* is the much acclaimed *Final Blackout* which is later released as a best-selling book.

In 1939 Street & Smith launch a second new magazine, *Unknown*, and it is soon filled with Ron's fantasy writings which could not be accommodated in *Astounding*. His first story in this genre is *The Ultimate Adventure*, appearing in the April 1939 issue. Many more L. Ron Hubbard fiction works appear for the first time in *Unknown* including such legendary stories as *Fear, Death's Deputy, Typewriter in the Sky* and *Slaves of Sleep*. These stories are subsequently released as books in their own right.

On 19 February 1940 Ron is elected a member of the prestigious Explorers Club. Concurrently he plans an Alaskan expedition, and on 27 July 1940 his Alaskan Radio Experimental Expedition embarks from Seattle. His vessel is the 32-foot ketch *Magician*, and she sails under Explorers Club flag number 105. Ron completes a voyage of some seven hundred miles, charting previously unrecorded hazards and coastlines for the US Navy Hydrographic Office. He also conducts experiments on radio directional finding, and examines local native cultures, including the Tlingit,

the Haidas and the Aleutian Island natives. On 17 December 1940 the US Bureau of Marine Inspection and Navigation awards Ron his Master of Steam and Motor Vessels license.

In December he returns to Seattle, resuming his writing while presenting the US Navy with the hundreds of photographs and notations they had requested.

1941–1945:

On 29 March 1941 Ron receives his Master of Sail Vessel license for "Any Ocean."

On 2 July 1941 he is commissioned as Lieutenant (jg) of the United States Navy Reserve. With the outbreak of war in December 1941, Ron is ordered to Australia where he coordinates intelligence activities.

Returning to the United States in March, Ron takes command of a convoy escort vessel in the Atlantic, then a subchaser in the Pacific. He also serves as an instructor and chief navigation officer, and is selected to Princeton University's Military Government School.

In early 1945, while recovering from war injuries at Oak Knoll Naval Hospital, Ron conducts a series of tests and experiments dealing with the endocrine system. He

discovers that, contrary to long-standing beliefs, function monitors structure. With this revolutionary advance, he begins to apply his theories to the field of the mind and thereby to improve the conditions of others.

1946:

After discharge from the US Navy in February 1946, Ron returns to writing, although his primary thrust continues to be the development of a means to better the condition of men. To help support this research, he writes thirty-one science fiction, fantasy, western, mystery and detective stories over the next three years. A few of the titles included in his work at this time are: *Blood on His Spurs, Ole Doc Methuselah, Killer's Law, Hoss Tamer* and *The Obsolete Weapon.*

1947:

Ron opens an office near the corner of La Brea Avenue and Sunset Boulevard in Los Angeles, where he tests the application of Dianetics among actors, directors, writers and others of the Hollywood community. These are the people who first receive the benefits of Ron's revolutionary breakthroughs in the field of the mind.

With test cases and research material in hand, Ron travels to Washington, DC where he compiles into manuscript form his sixteen-year investigation to determine the dynamic principle of existence. (The result of this work is published today as the book *The Dynamics of Life.*)

1948:

Ron accepts an appointment as a Special Police Officer with the Los Angeles Police Department and uses the position to study society's criminal elements.

Moving on to Savannah, Georgia, he volunteers his time in hospitals and mental wards, saving the lives of patients with his counseling techniques.

1949:

His as yet unpublished manuscript on Dianetics, which had been passed to a few friends for review, is copied and copied again until it circulates around the world. As a result of this enthusiastic response, Ron is urged by associates to write a popular book on the subject of Dianetics.

Late in the year, L. Ron Hubbard's "Terra Incognita: The Mind," the first published article on Dianetics, appears in the Winter - Spring 1950 issue of the *Explorers Club Journal.*

1950:

Ron is contracted by Hermitage House Publishing to write *Dianetics.*

In the first week of March he completes *Dianetics: The Modern Science of Mental Health.*

Ron writes *Dianetics: The Evolution of a Science* for magazine publication to promote and accompany the release of *Dianetics.*

On 9 May 1950, *Dianetics* is released and appears on the *New York Times* bestseller list,

18 June 1950. It remains on the bestseller list for twenty-eight consecutive weeks and launches a national movement which will soon become the fastest growing such movement in America.

On 7 June Ron delivers his first recorded lectures on Dianetics in Elizabeth, New Jersey, where the Hubbard Dianetics Research Foundation is formed.

On 10 August, after moving to a new residence in Los Angeles, California, Ron

delivers a lecture on Dianetics to a sell-out crowd of over 6,000 people at the Shrine Auditorium.

Through the remainder of the year, Ron continues to tour and speak in major cities and by the end of December he has delivered over one hundred lectures and crisscrossed the country.

1951:

Ron writes six books which outline his discoveries in the field of the human mind and give practical technology to better human existence.

In addition to the printed word, he delivers more than 100 lectures on the subject of Dianetics.

After returning from Havana, Cuba, where he completes the book *Science of Survival,* he opens the first Hubbard College in Wichita, Kansas, delivering lectures and conducting courses.

In the fall of 1951, having discovered that man is most fundamentally a spiritual being, he begins a new line of research to determine what can be done to help an individual regain natural abilities. These discoveries form the basis of Scientology.

1952:

Ron moves to Phoenix, Arizona where he opens his office and establishes the Hubbard Association of Scientologists International.

In September, traveling to England, he establishes the Hubbard Association of Scientologists International in London.

In late November Ron returns to the United States, where in Philadelphia he delivers a Doctorate Course in Scientology with 62 lectures in 18 days providing a wide analysis of human behavior. The lectures are known as the Philadelphia Doctorate Course Lectures. He then travels back to England where he begins plans for a research trip across Europe.

In addition to delivering 190 lectures on subjects such as emotional tones, communication and creativity, Ron writes of his further research on man's spiritual potential in four new books.

1953:

Motoring across Europe to Barcelona, he follows World War II invasion routes to study the effects of devastation on populations; he also researches European university systems.

Ron returns to Phoenix, where he releases new breakthroughs which enable the individual to explore his past and improve his reactions toward life. During this period, Ron also researches the basics of organization, developing principles that any group can use to survive and prosper. He delivers 232 lectures and writes two more books.

1954:

In recognition of the spiritual nature of Ron's philosophy, a number of Scientologists in Los Angeles, California form the first Church of Scientology in February.

Ron further researches and develops the religious philosophy of Scientology in Phoenix, delivering more than 460 lectures and continuing to write extensively.

1955:

In March, Ron moves from Phoenix to Washington, DC, where the Founding Church of Washington, DC is formed with Ron as Executive Director. He drafts organizational policies and intensifies his work in developing an administrative technology to allow Scientology churches to run smoothly and expand.

During October Ron returns to England to deliver lectures in London, while further establishing the London organization. Ron delivers over 200 lectures in this year, on subjects from counseling techniques to education and alcoholism. In December he travels to Ireland to initiate the formation of an Irish organization in Dublin and then returns to England.

1956:

Returning to Dublin, Ron researches and develops the exact steps and actions a person follows to establish a successful Scientology mission anywhere in the world.

He also writes a book containing simple but powerful precepts that allow anyone to immediately improve their life.

In Barcelona, Spain he conducts additional research, then returns to Washington, DC where he delivers a series of lectures which cover spiritual and material requirements of man. He then sails back to England aboard the *Queen Elizabeth,* during which time he writes a book providing solutions to day-to-day

job stress. After delivering 12 lectures on human problems in London, he again returns to Washington, DC.

While delivering more than 130 lectures, detailing solutions to such problems as environmental radiation and the failings of groups, Ron also runs both the Washington and London organizations during this year and finds the time to write two more books.

1957:

In February Ron travels to Puerto Rico where he continues researching and writing. In April he flies to London to deliver a series of lectures on auditing techniques and then travels to Washington. While still concentrating on further organizational and administrative developments and delivering over 145 public lectures, Ron also writes two books to better speed an individual's spiritual progress.

1958:

Ron delivers 133 lectures in 1958, including the Clearing Congress Lectures in Washington, DC, the first six of which are filmed. In October Ron sails to London aboard the RMS *Statedam.* In England, he delivers 45 lectures, while reorganizing local offices. With this accomplished, he sets sail back to Washington in early December aboard the *Saxonia*.

1959:

Ron defines the duties in various Scientology churches and delivers 16 lectures on auditing refinements in Washington, DC.

In March he begins negotiations to purchase Saint Hill Manor in Sussex, England which will be his home for the following seven years. By May, negotiations are completed and Ron moves his residence to the 55-acre estate. The worldwide headquarters of Scientology is moved to Saint Hill.

In yet another line of research, this one involving different orders of life, Ron conducts horticultural experiments in greenhouses at Saint Hill which bring about major increases in plant growth. His discoveries are written up in horticultural magazines internationally and receive wide coverage in daily newspapers.

The first E-Meter designed and built to Ron's exact specifications is produced.

On 16 October Ron begins an around-the-world trip, traveling to Greece, India, Melbourne, Hawaii, San Francisco and New York, arriving back at Saint Hill the first week of December.

In Melbourne alone, he delivers 38 lectures, and while in the United States he writes and issues an organizing board for American Scientology churches (a board which shows what functions are done, the order they are done in, and who is responsible for getting them done).

Upon his return to England, Ron appears on BBC television discussing his horticultural experiments. Shortly afterwards Ron travels to Washington, DC.

In all he gives 102 lectures this year and writes one book.

1960:

While in Washington, Ron delivers 18 lectures in one week outlining his discoveries on such subjects as the importance of honesty and individual responsibility. He then returns home to Saint Hill.

In March, after extensive research and investigation, Ron writes the book, *Have You Lived Before This Life?*

After delivering over 30 more lectures at Saint Hill and London, he travels to South Africa in September where he standardizes the operation and administration of South African organizations. At the end of the year, he once more returns to Washington, DC and finishes out the year by delivering three lectures.

1961:

After extending his stay in Washington for an additional 13 lectures he returns to Saint Hill for a week, then travels back to South Africa in late January. Here he not only delivers more than 20 lectures which further detail the means of realizing man's spiritual goals, but also develops a refined pattern of organization for Scientology churches.

Ron is awarded his second Explorers Club flag for his "Ocean Archaeological Expedition to study underwater sites of historical interest such as submerged cities."

In late March Ron returns to Saint Hill and in May he begins to give lectures to Scientologists on the Saint Hill Special Briefing Course — a comprehensive training program for Scientology auditors in which the entire history of technical development is covered.

For the following five years, Ron dedicates his time to continuing his research into states of existence and releasing his breakthroughs and new technology to students of the Saint Hill Special Briefing Course. His discoveries and developments from this period become an important part of the route to Clear and advanced spiritual states. This time is also devoted to developing and standardizing administrative policy for the churches.

1962–1963:

In the first week of September, Ron takes a short break from Saint Hill and travels to Washington, DC to deliver an eight-lecture congress in three days.

In addition to running the Saint Hill organization and the Briefing Course, during 1963, Ron films a movie entitled *An Afternoon at Saint Hill*. The film provides a tour of Saint Hill and a view of activities there.

1964:

While continuing his work at Saint Hill, Ron conducts photographic shoots in the surrounding area and carries out a study of promotional actions at the request of a well-known local promoter of events.

In June Ron begins a series of lectures in which he unravels the complexities of study and education, giving a technology which anyone can use to improve the study of any subject. This becomes study technology, which is used around the world today in both Scientology churches and in private and public education systems.

1965:

In January Ron travels to the Canary Islands to begin intensive research on the spiritual nature of man and his origins. He returns to Saint Hill later that month.

His activities during the remainder of the year bring major organizational and technical breakthroughs as a result of his years of work at Saint Hill.

The Classification and Gradation Chart is released, laying out the exact steps to follow in Scientology counseling and training to achieve higher states of awareness and ability.

In November Ron announces and implements the seven-division organizing board. This is a major breakthrough in the successful pattern of operation of any group. It has universal application and is in use today in all churches of Scientology and an increasing number of other organizations.

1966:

In February Ron returns to the Canary Islands to continue his advanced research of the spiritual nature of man. On 18

March he flies to Rhodesia where he investigates the ability of a single individual to single-handedly assist a small country to overcome its problems.

In July he returns to England and delivers the final lectures of the Saint Hill Special Briefing Course.

He releases the first advanced levels of Scientology auditing which take one beyond the state of Clear originally postulated in Dianetics. On 1 September 1966, L. Ron Hubbard resigns from all directorships and management of Scientology churches.

He subsequently accepts his third Explorers Club flag for the Hubbard Geological Survey Expedition, which will find and examine ancient Mediterranean civilizations, amplifying man's knowledge of his history.

In December Ron purchases the sailing vessel, *Enchanter* (later renamed *Diana*).

1967:

On January 2, Ron arrives in Tangier, Morocco, to continue his research into higher states of spiritual being. He travels to Las Palmas, Canary Islands, where he meets the *Enchanter* which arrives on 25 February.

With a group of dedicated Scientologists, most of whom had never been to sea, Ron forms the Sea Organization. He trains this inexperienced crew into a team of competent and professional mariners in a matter of months.

Joined by yet another vessel, the *Avon River* (later renamed the *Athena*), Ron and his crews conduct the Hubbard Geological Survey Expedition in the Mediterranean.

Ron's search for the truth results in one of his most significant breakthroughs in removing the barriers to man's ability to achieve full spiritual freedom. This research is fully codified and made available to advanced Scientologists.

In November Ron travels to England and accepts delivery of the 3,200-ton vessel *Royal Scotman* as a further expansion of the Sea Organization.

1968–1969:

Ron continues training the ships' crews while living aboard the *Royal Scotman* (which is renamed *Apollo*). Ron issues more than three hundred instructional letters, covering all nautical duties from engine room maintenance to fire drills and from navigation to small boat handling.

In the fall of 1968, aboard the *Apollo,* he delivers 19 lectures and develops a new advanced course, the Class VIII Course, to train auditors to a point of complete, invariable certainty on all the fundamentals of auditing, and flubless application of those principles.

During 1969 he researches the effects and causes of drug addiction and drug use, developing procedures which address and solve the causes of, and remove the harmful mental effects brought about by such abuse. He issues these findings for broad use.

1970–1973:

Having developed a successful and standardized pattern of organizational form and function, Ron turns to resolving the problems of how to manage an international network of organizations.

Ron streamlines organizational management technology—laying out highly workable principles of personnel, organization and financial management and handling which are found today in the *Management Series* volumes.

His breakthroughs at this time include the first significant advances on the subject of logic since ancient Greece. Ron conducts a comprehensive study of all existing public relations theories and practices and also releases his discoveries in the field of public relations, providing an entirely analytical and ethical approach to the subject.

In 1972 Ron carries out a sociological study in and around New York City. Through the remainder of the year and into 1973, he researches vitamins and nutrition which will later become significant in his

breakthroughs in the handling of the residual effects of drugs.

1974–1975:

In February 1974, while aboard the *Apollo,* Ron forms a music and dance troupe to provide entertainment and goodwill at Spanish and Portuguese ports of call. He personally instructs the musicians and dancers in artistic presentation, music, composition, sound, arranging and recording.

During October 1974 the *Apollo* sails across the Atlantic to Bermuda and then on to the Caribbean.

From February through June 1975, while in Curaçao, Ron takes a series of photographs for the island's tourist bureau and completes six photography projects for release in Scientology books and publications.

By mid-1975 the activities on the *Apollo* outgrow the vessel's capacity. Ron returns to the United States.

Ron settles in Dunedin, Florida, where he continues his research into music, examining choir music at local churches. He writes the scripts for the first Scientology educational films.

1976–1979:

Ron moves to a southern California desert ranch in La Quinta and establishes, trains and supervises a film production unit. Over the following three years he writes not only a feature-length screenplay, *Revolt in the Stars,* but also the scripts for thirty-three Scientology instructional films.

During this same three-year period he also shoots, directs and produces seven films which are used in training Scientology counselors.

Ron discovers that drugs remain in the body even years after usage has ceased.

Consequently, he develops the Purification Rundown to rid the body of harmful residual substances. Coupled with his 1969 discoveries, Ron's development of the drug rehabilitation program is complete. These techniques used by churches of Scientology and drug rehabilitation organizations around the world, allow anyone to free himself from the debilitating effects of drugs.

It is also in 1979 that Ron isolates and solves the problem of increasing illiteracy. His discoveries and solutions later become the published Key to Life Course widely acclaimed for its miraculous results.

1980–1981:

During this period Ron devotes the majority of his time to writing.

He composes a nonreligious moral code, *The Way to Happiness,* as a solution to the eroding morals in society. The broad distribution and widespread acceptance of this code contributes to a grass-roots movement for improved moral values.

Ron also writes two feature-length screenplays and fifty film treatments for public films on Dianetics and Scientology.

To mark his fiftieth anniversary as a professional writer, Ron writes the international blockbuster, *Battlefield Earth: A Saga of the Year 3000,* the largest science fiction novel written to date.

As part of his two-million-word output during this period, he also writes his science fiction satire, ten-volume magnum opus, *Mission Earth.*

1982–
24 January 1986:

Ron establishes a California home on a ranch outside of San Luis Obispo. He researches and releases new Scientology technical materials which further expand the route to total freedom, all the way to the highest levels of Operating Thetan.

Battlefield Earth is released in 1982 and becomes an international bestseller. Ron composes music and lyrics for an accompanying album—the first-ever soundtrack for a book.

While the acclaim for *Battlefield Earth* continues to grow with its publication in new languages, the first volume of Ron's *Mission Earth* is published in 1985. As each volume of the dekalogy is released it becomes an immediate bestseller. The

successive appearance of these volumes on the *New York Times* bestseller list constitutes a first in publishing history. Ron accompanies *Mission Earth* with another new music album.

In 1986 the music album *The Road to Freedom* is released. With music and lyrics written by LRH, it is Ron's statement of many basic principles of Scientology.

On 24 January 1986, having accomplished all he set out to do, Ron departs his body. With millions using his technology daily and crediting him with providing the sole means for their happiness and spiritual fulfillment, he has become one of the most beloved men in history. His many friends continue to express their thanks in acknowledgment of the fact that although his physical presence is gone, he is still very much with us in spirit and the legacy of his work lives on.

CHAPTER 39

L. RON HUBBARD HOW HIS WORK HAS INFLUENCED THE WORLD

Throughout history, the most important advances in our culture and civilization have not come about because man invented a stronger sword for the foot soldier, a better longbow for the archer, more powerful tanks for the cavalry or atomic bombs. Rather, progress has come from the new ideas of thinking men.

As L. Ron Hubbard wrote in *Science of Survival,* "Ideas and not battles mark the forward progress of mankind." When an idea represents fundamental and workable truths, it is adopted by many and achieves a lasting endurance. Plato's *Republic,* written more than three hundred years before the birth of Christ, catalyzed political thinkers for centuries and many of its fundamental concepts are woven into the fabric of modern governments. Descartes' seventeenth-century laws of mathematics are taught today in modern universities and continue to be used as tools to aid scientific inquiry.

Today, at the dawn of a new millennium, the last hundred years have seen some of the most rapid advances in technology ever.

These advances, unfortunately, have been accompanied by a commensurate decline in the beneficial influence of religion and the systematic removal of the humanities from our educational systems. The results have been mixed. While we have seen a rise in material living standards, we have also lived through the horrors of two world wars, political, racial and religious genocide on an unprecedented scale and social turmoil, reflected by plummeting moral standards, the breakdown of the family unit, violent crime, widespread drug abuse in all economic sectors and failing educational systems.

Amid this turmoil, L. Ron Hubbard researched the spiritual breakthroughs which led to his development of Scientology and ultimately the founding of the Scientology religion — the only major new religion established in the twentieth century. But the birth of Scientology has meant more than just the growth of a worldwide religion of eight million adherents. As has happened throughout history, the ideas of one man have been taken up and carried forward by many — Scientologists and non-Scientologists alike — and have become part of the fabric of modern culture.

THE QUESTION OF MAN'S INTELLECTUAL ABILITIES

Prior to 1950, popular thinking held that man's intelligence was *fixed*. The growing influence of materialistic science and its "man from mud" theories had stripped man of his soul and redefined man as an animal, no more than the sum of his genes. Stimulated by Darwinian theory of inherited attributes, variation in intelligence became the subject of intense study throughout the end of the nineteenth century. Prevailing thought, as most famously forwarded by Darwin's younger cousin, Sir Francis Galton, held that intelligence was hereditary and largely monopolized by Britain's first families. "Social Darwinism" proved that the most financially and socially successful owed their positions to genetic superiority. And shackled by genetic inferiority, the destitute deserved their lot. In the extreme, such thinking eventually led to a Third Reich eugenics program, complete with wholesale sterilization and plans for selective breeding. But even in less totalitarian terms, the thinking permeated society: One's intelligence was unalterably defined by genetic code.

A fairly representative statement on the matter, published in 1951, espoused the prevailing party line: "We believe that you can help your child make the most of his intelligence if you have a good idea of what it is. You don't have to know his IQ—we'll talk about that later—but you should at least be sure as to whether or not your child is superior."

General thinking on the subject was firm: Intelligence, as measured by the standard IQ tests, was determined by birth, and with it was determined the general course of one's life—whether rich or poor, white collar or blue.

DIANETICS AND A NEW VIEW

This, then, was the world which confronted L. Ron Hubbard in May 1950, when he published *Dianetics: The Modern Science of Mental Health* with its bold proclamation that not only was intelligence fluid, but one could improve it with the easily learned techniques of Dianetics. Then, too—and this was particularly startling—one could improve his intelligence beyond normally imagined limits.

The key which unblocked man's ability to reason was the discovery of the engram, the reactive mind and Dianetics proper. In the summer of 1950 the Hubbard Foundation verified and measured intelligence gains relative to auditing. The results were surprising to say the least. Thousands of testimonials attested to these gains and the consequent word of mouth laid waste the cornerstone of the man-from-mud school. Thinking on the subject reversed so rapidly and dramatically that even the mental health community, firmly rooted in genetic theory, came to embrace the idea that intelligence *could* be improved. By the late 1950s, even noted behaviorist B. F. Skinner had remarked that human intelligence could be changed. Meanwhile, Dianetics continued to be used widely by the man in the street and the idea that his abilities could improve soon spread far beyond the ivory walls of learning to become a popularly accepted fact.

Just how thoroughly this seminal discovery by Mr. Hubbard has permeated society, however, was seen in the controversy which surrounded publication of *The Bell Curve: Intelligence and Class Structure in American Life* in 1994. That book's authors vainly attempted to present evidence to support the theory that intelligence was hereditary, fixed and impossible to change. Almost instantly, the authors were burned at the intellectual stake as educators decried the book, pointing to a mountain of accumulated evidence which proved conclusively that IQ *could* be raised, a fact considered common knowledge by then. The backlash experienced by the authors of *The Bell Curve* is a testament to how a single discovery by one man can completely reverse the status quo in a span of less than fifty years.

A "QUIET" REVOLUTION IN HEALING

Mr. Hubbard's discoveries concerning the reactive mind—and specifically the crucial finding that an unconscious person continues to record all of the sounds, smells, pains and conversation and other events which are taking place around him—proved very influential in the realm of traditional familial and surgical medicine. Unheard of when first described in *Dianetics: The Modern Science of Mental Health*—and even met with disdain from some—decades later, this fundamental Dianetics principle has led to silence in operating rooms in many countries. A half-century ago, surgeons believed that an unconscious patient was incapable of perceiving or recording anything and operating rooms were often filled with needless chatter. But as the principles of Dianetics circulated through society, surgical procedures evolved . . . and surgeons were urged to speak only when absolutely necessary.

These observations also left an indelible mark on the field of emergency medicine. Today many emergency medical technicians take it for granted that silence and calm should be maintained around an accident victim. Indeed, they will tell you this is how they were taught—not only by their instructors but through instructional videos on first aid and emergency care which urge maintaining a silent environment.

Also now broadly accepted and in invaluable use are Mr. Hubbard's emergency assists, first announced in the 1950s. He provided the first delineation of how an injury affects the communication channels of the body—how a knowledge of nerve and energy flows can lead to truly lifesaving results through a restoration of communication to injured body parts. What followed from Mr. Hubbard's assists technology was a revelation in healing, much of it fueling the later spiritual wellness movement in Western culture. Today, doctors, nurses, chiropractors and entire Red Cross disaster relief teams are aided daily by the widespread knowledge and use of assist technology in their ranks.

Mr. Hubbard's influence in the healing arts can also be found in other, very different corners of medicine. His finding that much of what was characterized in psychiatric circles as "mental illness" had physical ailment at its root led, in many quarters, to a genuine metamorphosis in treatment models for unstable patients. When he voiced that finding in the early 1950s, it was utterly contrary to the conventional wisdom of his day, where inhumane "treatments" reminiscent of those found in medieval torture chambers were the rule; yet say it he did, and more than four decades later, the truth of his words is now gaining ground. As a very telling case in point, when dozens of Italian psychiatric asylums were closed by government order, scores of patients were taken to medical practitioners (whose services were priorly secured for that purpose) who found and treated bodily injuries and maladies which had contributed significantly to their anguish.

AWARENESS OF THE UNBORN

Mr. Hubbard's discoveries on the mind and life have also touched those who care for the unborn. Prior to 1950, prevailing theory held that the human child was incapable of recording memory until the formation of myelin sheathing at the age of about four years. The only exception being speculative ideas about "birth trauma" heard on the psychoanalytic fringe.

Then came this from L. Ron Hubbard: "The only test is whether or not a fact works. If it does work and can be used, it is a scientific fact. And the prenatal engram is a scientific fact. Tested and checked for objective reality, it still stands firm. And as for subjective reality, the acceptance of the prenatal engram as a working fact alone makes possible the Clear."

The ensuing years represented a silent revolution in popular thought: from "everybody knows" the unborn child sees, hears and feels nothing, to the virtually universal notion that mothers should take care to avoid harmful stimuli.

Once again, the ramifications of a bold new idea were considerable, heartening and flew squarely in the face of the broadly accepted fallacy that a man was only sentient in proportion to his physical development and that his emotions were wholly the result of biological chemistry. Carried along by the acceptance which continued to be generated by *Dianetics,* it was not long before Mr. Hubbard's revolutionary finding began to seep into the fabric of mainstream society.

There was *Pic* magazine, which began bold-typing such stories as, "Can Dianetics Decide Paternity? The Amazing New Science of the Mind . . . May Hold Answers to Prenatal Questions." That story, incidentally, went on to tell of a highly skeptical physician, "who volunteered to undergo a [Dianetics] run especially to prove to his own satisfaction that nothing would happen . . ." Whereupon, he was soon heard groaning from the pain of a restimulated backache. Likewise, the equally disbelieving *Pic* journalist reported how a close friend "curled up like an unborn child" when recounting his own birth. He then reported the startling point: "Dianetics maintains that those of us with brains which have not been damaged physically can go back into the past to conception itself, and can recount who was there, what was said, what went on."

By 1969, Dr. L. W. Sontag was able to inform the American Association for the Advancement of Science that experiments with sound had proved that "the fetus is not in a world by itself." A *Newsweek* article on a New Zealand fetologist's derivative work proclaimed "both physicians and mothers are coming to regard the fetus not as a vegetable, but as a vital, living individual. . . . The fetus hears sound, ranging from its mother's heartbeat to an automobile backfire, and will react to the noise by moving." In the 1980s came Dr. Thomas Verny's *The Secret Life of the Unborn Child* wherein he declared a child's personality to be quite significantly shaped by prenatal and birthing experiences—all of which became the standard of the natural childbirth movement through the late 1970s and early 1980s.

And today, thousands upon thousands of expectant mothers have insisted on silent childbirth, while hundreds of medical practitioners offer nothing but to their maternity patients. Thus, while it has taken five decades for the scientific and medical communities to begin to catch up with the discoveries of L. Ron Hubbard in recognizing the awareness of the unborn child, they are now virtually part of the medical mainstream.

PAST LIVES

There can be no argument that the discoveries that intelligence can improve, that memory can be traced as far back as conception, and that physical healing can be profoundly affected by mental and spiritual factors influenced popular thinking. Yet Mr. Hubbard's quest to find the root cause of human aberration led him far beyond human development. In July 1950, after an initially skeptical review of mounting data, L. Ron Hubbard was suddenly heard addressing auditors on "the procedures of running former lives." It was not a phenomenon he had been searching for, and he regarded it a bit tentatively at the outset. But in the end, and notwithstanding the objections from others, past lives became altogether routine. It soon became abundantly clear that man was indeed not a summation of flesh, bone and chemicals. Rather, he was a spiritual being with infinite memory and, as of then, unknown capabilities.

For the next three decades, Mr. Hubbard devoted himself to researching the fundamental nature of the human spirit and constructing an exact and workable path to total spiritual freedom which any man could walk.

Millions have.

By the mid-1950s, the subject of past lives had become almost passé for the thousands of Scientologists who, in daily auditing sessions, routinely recalled the details of earlier lives, memories that reached back not just a few hundred or a few thousand years, but to tens of millions of years and even earlier.

This growing acceptance of past lives had a subtle but noticeable influence in the culture at large. First came the mid-1950s book, *The Search for Bridey Murphy*. Remarking on it later, Mr. Hubbard explained, "When Bridey Murphy came up, some London researchers came to me and asked me to prove the existence of past lives, using Dianetics. Naturally I refused, because I'd already done that anyhow."

By the mid-1960s, more popular books were being written on the subject. Press accounts of those who had recalled past lives appeared in newspapers and magazines in the United States, England and as far away as New Zealand. Underscored by both the quantity of material and the popularity of such works as *Out On a Limb* and *Lives Unlimited*, past lives became a popular craze that included such activities as "come as you were" parties.

Eventually, even those in ever-skeptical scientific circles began to acknowledge the validity of past lives. One clinical psychologist told of hypnotically regressing patients through former incarnations to relieve suffering in this life. Another told of using various past-life techniques in therapy for a decade.

By the early 1980s, past lives were very much in the national consciousness. In fact, surveys now report that 27 percent of all Americans—an extraordinary number when one recalls how alien was the concept only forty years before—have finally come to accept that they live not once, but over and over again.

Books and newspaper articles told the story of popular acceptance with such headlines as "She Remembers Well That Winter of 1200," "Children Who Have Lived Before" and popular titles like *Life After Life*. It should be noted, of course, that by this point in our recent history, thousands and thousands of Scientology auditors had been routinely helping to free others from the layers of past-life trauma for nearly three decades.

OUT-OF-BODY EXPERIENCES

Of course, if man is a not a body but a spiritual being, it follows that he could experience things independent of his body. And, starting in the late 1950s and early 1960s, the first references to what eventually became known as "out-of-body experiences" began to appear in the para-psychological community. Titles such as "Near Death Experience" reported case studies of men and women, having died on operating tables or in car accidents, only to return with complete memory and perceptions of a brief existence completely separate from mortal flesh.

It was not long after that a then nascent New Age movement grabbed the concept, and promptly pushed it into the mainstream. By the beginning of the 1990s, public interest in out-of-body experiences was strong enough to boost books on the subject to the top of the *New York Times* bestseller list. Yet in all the New Age discussions of out-of-body experiences, one important fact has been routinely overlooked. A decade before those first instances of out-of-body experiences were reported by the popular authorities of the day, L. Ron Hubbard had already succeeded in getting individuals to exteriorize from their bodies using procedures he described in *The Creation of Human Ability*. And as Scientologists across the world utilized his same techniques—with the accomplishment of identical results—exteriorization, like past lives, became a broadly accepted consensus which gradually permeated the rest of society.

SOLUTIONS FOR A TOXIC WORLD

While greater spiritual freedom for man has always been the focus of Mr. Hubbard's work, he also examined both the body's effect upon the spirit and the spirit's effect on the body.

One example is Mr. Hubbard's discovery that residual deposits of drugs and other chemicals lodged in body fat and continued to affect one mentally and spiritually for many years. Because drug residue poses a major barrier to an individual's spiritual progress, a solution was needed. Mr. Hubbard's answer was the Purification program, a regimen of vitamins, exercise and sauna which flushes toxic substances out of the body and frees one from their harmful effects.

That discovery soon found broad use in other fields. Almost immediately it was seized upon as an effective contribution to drug rehabilitation. Mr. Hubbard had earlier developed methods to ease an individual's withdrawal from drugs and to put him back in communication with his environment. These methods were being used routinely in the Narconon program for nearly ten years to free addicts from the grip of chemical dependency.

Release of the Purification program prompted Narconon programs around the world to adopt this regimen to further increase their effectiveness. By the mid-1980s, its efficacy was recognized by scientific studies and by the early 1990s, experts in the field of drug rehabilitation were recommending Narconon as the most effective drug rehabilitation program in existence.

The Purification program provided more than just a solution to society's growing problem of drug abuse. It could also be used to combat the threat posed by our polluted environment made increasingly toxic through widespread use of pesticides, chemical contamination and the gradual erosion of the ozone layer.

In 1984, a Rand Corporation study estimated that by the year 2020, more than 75,000 American workers would die as a result of workplace exposure to toxic materials. A solution was obviously needed. A number of scientific studies were subsequently conducted to determine how effective Mr. Hubbard's methods were in addressing the problem of environmental contamination. In 1984, the *Journal of California Law Enforcement* reported that Purification had significantly aided police officers exposed to toxic chemicals to rid their bodies of such substances. Two years later, a report published by the Royal Swedish Academy of Science told of similar

results with poisoned chemical workers. Soon, the news of these innovative studies began to appear in more widely distributed occupational safety newsletters.

Mr. Hubbard's methods were also acknowledged in popular books on the subject of environmental pollution. In 1991, the author of *Diet for a Poisoned Planet* was found to be advocating what he called the Hubbard Method as the *only* solution to ridding the body of dangerous chemicals and environmental toxins.

If there were still any doubt as to how much this discovery permeated society, one need only witness how the Purification program helped Vietnam veterans recover from the effects of exposure to Agent Orange or how it provided a solution to those who had been exposed to deadly levels of radiation following the Chernobyl nuclear disaster. Even more recently, the Purification program had been successful in relieving symptoms of Gulf War Syndrome in veterans exposed to powerful chemical and biological agents during that conflict.

In 1995, discussions at the first International Conference on Human Detoxification unveiled the Purification program as the only effective method of handling drug detox, chemical poisoning and radiation contamination. A second summit two years later found authorities from fifteen nations gathered to discuss how Mr. Hubbard's Purification program could be implemented broadly as *the* solution to the problem of human detoxification.

The Breakthrough in Education

In the mid-1960s, Mr. Hubbard's researches into the field of education resulted in the release of a series of breakthrough techniques of study. Used routinely by parishioners in churches of Scientology throughout the world, these methodologies spread rapidly to tutoring programs and educational projects in many countries. The impact of these discoveries has had far-reaching consequences in providing an answer to the crisis in education.

The failure of our educational systems began with the introduction of experimental psychology into classrooms during the 1950s and continued with the gradual transformation of schools from institutions of learning to centers for therapy.

The fact that Johnny could no longer read and write became less important than how Johnny felt about being illiterate. The 3 R's were soon being replaced by "Values Education," "Self-Esteem Training," and "Outcome-Based Education," and our educational statistics crashed.

The statistics are frightening; they represent a picture not just of students discouraged by the system, but also turning into criminals. By the early 1990s, as many as 100,000 students were bringing guns to class every day. Juveniles accounted for 17 percent of all violent crime arrests. The number of children arrested for murder increased by 85 percent between 1987 and 1991. Justice Department estimates found that nearly one million young people between twelve and nineteen were being robbed, raped or assaulted by their peers. And of the juvenile offenders arrested, 85 percent were illiterate. In other words, those perpetrating the dangerous conditions in schools were the very same ones the educational system had failed.

What Mr. Hubbard's technology introduced to that dismal picture was nothing less than revolutionary. It isolated not only the true cause of illiteracy but provided a workable solution. Within three decades of being introduced, study technology brought the gift of literacy to millions around the world, through teachers in Africa, educators in China, and tutors in the inner cities of the United States.

Mr. Hubbard's contributions to education have not been limited to these benefits. As early as 1938, in a letter to a university dean, Mr. Hubbard criticized mass education which was resulting in "frozen, fact-laden minds." Students, he pointed out, "were not being taught to think or study, they were being taught to gorge facts, however disrelated, obtuse or useless." At the core of that problem was an educational establishment which, "through no particular fault of its own and despite every effort it has made to free itself, yet, through lack of tools, is forced to follow scholastic methods." The solution to resolving problems in education was not to try and fix something wrong in the student. Rather, the answer lay in correcting the educational system itself. It was a solution he would expand upon again and again, particularly after 1950.

Throughout the ensuing decades that sentiment permeated society. Headlines began to pose the question, "What's wrong with our schools?" And by 1997, the widespread demand to improve educational methods had become front cover feature material for weekly newsmagazines.

Once again, Mr. Hubbard's innovative view had become the accepted norm in society and was being forwarded by those who had no clue Mr. Hubbard's ideas had catalyzed the change. And just as those ideas seeped into society, so too did Mr. Hubbard's study techniques. By the end of the 1990s, even our public school systems began to seek ways to implement his study methods in their classrooms, and soon educators around the world were recognizing his techniques as common practice.

Restoring Society's Moral Anchor

Educational failures, rampant drug abuse and rising rates of crime and violence, though catastrophic, in and of themselves are symptoms of a deeper malaise affecting the social fabric of our culture — the loss of moral values.

The collapse of ethical standards walked hand in hand with the pronouncement that man had no soul. That is, if man's destiny was predetermined by a few strands of DNA, he was thus absolved of any responsibility for his own actions. "If it feels good, do it," became a rallying cry for a generation which was soon taking issue with any and all forms of morality. *Time* magazine announced that God was dead and religion passé. The result was a society cut free from any moral anchor. Even those who wished to stem this tide found themselves balked. As one popular magazine bemoaned, "Suppose for a moment that we wish to obey the rules: What do they mean and where are they written?"

Throughout history religion has been the driving force behind the establishment of a moral and ethical society. However, at the same time that morals were declining in mid-twentieth-century Western "civilization," that traditional religious role was being systematically weakened. As L. Ron Hubbard observed, courts in the United States had banned the display of the Ten Commandments in public schools—and that code, designed for a people of several millennia past, was already largely in disuse.

In 1980, having witnessed society's quagmire and recognizing this urgent need for timely moral direction, L. Ron Hubbard wrote *The Way to Happiness,* the world's first nonreligious moral code. Through its twenty-one precepts, this code provided man with the rules of behavior he so urgently needed.

No matter where the booklet was used (and by the mid-1990s well over fifty million had been circulated) the results were telling, as more fully described in Chapter 31. And it is far from coincidence that since the introduction and broad distribution of this powerful little booklet, morality has taken its rightful place in public debate. And what this shows is the simple fact that though society appeared to have lost its moral compass, L. Ron Hubbard's *The Way to Happiness* gave the world a new sense of moral direction for the first time in decades.

REHABILITATION OF THE CRIMINAL

If *The Way to Happiness* proved to be a boon to society at large, it came to represent something even more than that to thousands and thousands of men and women locked behind prison bars.

Long before the authorities in charge of modern prison systems had written off criminals as unsalvageable and came to accept an 80 percent recidivism rate as "normal,"

L. Ron Hubbard had traced the cause of crime to the loss of self-respect. The consequences of this loss are disastrous for it amounts to an individual who has broken *the contract with himself.* With this simple yet powerful datum in mind, a modest reform program was first established in London in the early 1950s aimed at the rehabilitation of juvenile delinquents. Four years later, a similar effort was launched in California's Folsom Prison, and the stage was effectively set for the founding of Criminon (without crime) and the introduction of Mr. Hubbard's methods of criminal reform directly into the prison system.

In 1970, the first Criminon program officially opened in New Zealand and by the end of the decade, as described in Chapter 31, L. Ron Hubbard's technology had become an international movement.

Letters from inmates in the United States, Great Britain, Mexico, Hungary and Poland all reported a return of self-respect. And with their self-respect came the knowledge that they could—perhaps for the first time in their lives—learn to function as honest citizens in society.

One index of just how far Mr. Hubbard's methods have permeated the field of criminal reform came in mid-1997 at a New York State convention of judges, district attorneys and prison administrators. Many visited the Criminon display during that convention and remarked that they were not only aware of Mr. Hubbard's programs, but believed that it was the only program which produced results.

Workable criminal rehabilitation has finally become reality. What that means for the rest of society was perhaps best summed up by a Los Angeles municipal court judge who began a pilot Criminon program in August 1996.

"What we are looking at with *The Way to Happiness* and Criminon programs are technologies which are much more than just shunting someone into custody for a long period of time," he said. "These programs present the only real hope for the future of this country in terms of a safe environment and neighborhood."

Global Movement in Administration

Mr. Hubbard's landmark breakthroughs in education, drug rehabilitation and criminal reform helped to make the name L. Ron Hubbard well known throughout many sectors of society. Yet these are still only a few of the discoveries which have impacted positively upon our civilization. A complete listing of Mr. Hubbard's discoveries would take volumes to describe.

There are, for example, his extremely significant strides in the field of administration—today codified as an administrative technology comprising 12 volumes and 62 recorded lectures, altogether containing more than 3.2 million words. Although originally designed for the growth and permanence of Scientology churches and never expressly intended for secular use, these works represent the world's most broadly utilized system of administration. Indeed, with some 75,000 concerns having adopted Mr. Hubbard's administrative solutions at the time of this writing, the scope of application is impressive—and all the more so when considering the diversity of those concerns. One finds industrial plants, retail outlets, service centers, agricultural combines, healthcare facilities, educational institutions, government agencies and more—all independently utilizing Mr. Hubbard's administrative tools in what has been legitimately described as a global movement.

Seminal among those administrative tools is a revolutionary organizational design known as the organizing board or "org board," which delineates every necessary function for perfectly coordinated effort. The whole is described in seven "divisions," corresponding to a sequence known as the Cycle of Production. That is, any activity will uniformly and universally follow the seven steps within the Cycle of Production. Thus the organizing board represents not the design of an assembly line or an assemblage of human cogs and wheels, but the genuinely ideal form for all concerted endeavors. Moreover, the organizing board is entirely elastic, and as applicable to the conglomerate as the single craftsman.

This is a tool adopted today by literally thousands upon thousands of businesses, groups and other organized activities around the world, including governmental offices in the states of Texas and Vermont and in the corridors of political parties in South Africa. By the end of the 1990s, the use of Mr. Hubbard's administrative technology had become such a familiar part of society that a representative of the Ministry of Interior of the governor's office in Russia's Ryazan Region gained approval to train fifty area mayors in Mr. Hubbard's administrative technology.

An Influence Profound and Lasting

His discoveries in many other areas, now similarly widespread in their influence, were equally ahead of their time. Yet among people of all walks of life, his ideas—such as the awareness of the unborn child—have achieved widespread popularity, whether or not he is recognized as their originator.

To Mr. Hubbard, who once said he was "the lesser part of my project," this would not have been disturbing in the least. Rather, that many millions have been helped—and continue to be helped—directly or indirectly by his far-reaching researches and writings, would certainly have been seen as possibly the best reward imaginable.

BIOGRAPHICAL PUBLICATIONS ABOUT L. RON HUBBARD

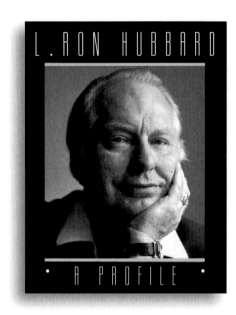

L. RON HUBBARD: A PROFILE

The most comprehensive work to date on Mr. Hubbard's achievements, *L. Ron Hubbard: A Profile* provides a broad perspective on all his works as humanitarian, educator, administrator, philosopher and artist. The publication also provides a chronological overview of his life and accomplishments, and how that life has touched millions, from industrial workers in Albania to young schoolchildren in Zimbabwe.

IMAGES OF A LIFETIME

Images of a Lifetime is a photographic biography drawn from some fifty thousand archival prints and representing nearly two decades of work. It chronicles L. Ron Hubbard's life from his childhood years in the rough and tumble American West to his youth in the elegant and mysterious Far East; as an author in Manhattan; a leader of expeditions across three seas and a researcher and lecturer in cities across four continents. This large-format, elegant book contains more than four hundred images of Mr. Hubbard, nearly half of which had never been published before. Woven throughout the book is the photographic trail of Mr. Hubbard's greatest work, the founding of Dianetics and Scientology.

THE *RON* SERIES

To present a life as rich and varied as L. Ron Hubbard's is a sizable task—and all the more so when one considers the sheer quantity of Ron's material, including his journals, diaries, letters and unpublished manuscripts (not to mention his more than sixty million words of published works). Drawing upon the entirety of those materials the *RON* Series presents both the many facets of Ron's life and his profound and lasting influence on the world in which we live. Contained within this collection are two categories: *RON* Series issues each focusing upon a specific avenue of his many and varied accomplishments; and *RON Letters and Journals,* drawn from the extensive collection of L. Ron Hubbard correspondence and personal journals.

RON
Letters and Journals:
The Dianetics Letters

From the greater body of materials assembled for the *RON* Series, and particularly pertaining to *The Rediscovery of the Human Soul* and *Auditor/Case Supervisor,* comes *RON Letters and Journals: The Dianetics Letters.* When originally published in 1950, Dianetics unleashed an unparalleled storm of enthusiasm. Return to those epic days and behold the birth of Dianetics from the eye of that storm, with Ron's letters and correspondence. Travel through time to the first days of Dianetics and see what he saw, what he felt and how he expressed himself in this issue of the *RON* Series.

RON
The Philosopher:
The Rediscovery
of the Human Soul

Since time immemorial, man has been asking the same eternal questions. But unlike all before him, L. Ron Hubbard did not stop until discovering the eternal answers. Here is both the story of how Ron forged the philosophy of Scientology, and what that philosophy means to this world.

RON
The Auditor/Case
Supervisor

If Scientology is an applied religious philosophy, then the central means of application is auditing. How Ron himself conducted an auditing session, how he came to develop the various techniques of auditing and to codify the role of the Case Supervisor—this is *RON The Auditor/Case Supervisor.*

RON
The Philosophy of Administration

Drawn from the laws of life for enhancement of life, this is the administrative philosophy of L. Ron Hubbard. Here is both the story of how he came to shape that philosophy, and how it fuels a worldwide Bridge to Total Freedom.

RON
The Horticulturist

In the summer of 1959, L. Ron Hubbard conducted a series of horticultural experiments that forever changed the way in which we view organic life. Here is a most remarkable, and previously untold, story of how Ron explored and came to revolutionize the world of horticulture and greater view of all living things.

HUMANITARIAN SERIES

RON
The Humanitarian: The Road To Self-Respect

"We have the answers to human suffering," L. Ron Hubbard wrote, "and they are available to everyone." In evidence of the statement stands all Ron provided for the rehabilitation of society's offenders. Here is a comprehensive look at L. Ron Hubbard's criminal reform techniques and his greater path of discovery—from the worst Los Angeles mean streets and the bowels of a federal penitentiary to a New York City so devastated by degradation he found it all but unrecognizable. Here, too, are Ron's answers to one of the most pressing problems facing this civilization.

RON
The Humanitarian: Rehabilitating a Drugged Society

There is no sector of today's society unaffected by drug abuse. Revealing the dark psychiatric root of the problem, here is the story behind the famed L. Ron Hubbard drug rehabilitation methods employed in hundreds of facilities worldwide.

ADVENTURER SERIES

RON
The Humanitarian:
Education

Here is the story of L. Ron Hubbard's lifelong devotion to learning and the trail he blazed to the only technology capable of salvaging today's education crisis. From Ron's experience as a sixteen-year-old English teacher to his training of officers and crews in World War II, this issue provides the definitive view of Ron the educator and development of his study technology.

RON
Adventurer/Explorer:
Daring Deeds and
Unknown Realms

Prepare for the white-knuckle adventures of a man who lived larger than life. Whether it's dueling with death in a blacked-out mine shaft; surviving a 400-foot free-fall glider crash; dodging flaming boulders on the rim of a live volcano; barnstorming across America or dining on iguana's tail—share in these adventures and more in this issue of the *RON* Series.

RON
The Humanitarian:
Freedom Fighter:
Articles and Essays

Through forty-six essays and articles presented we come to Ron's long, hard look at precisely what plagues twentieth-century Earth. Here are the "whys" and "wherefores" of planetary suppression, and what one can do about it. Here, too, is the never previously published "Strong Voices in the Land" in which Ron defines what it means when our collective voices are raised in opposition to the worst of oppression.

RON
Letters and Journals:
Early Years
of Adventure

Experience the real texture of living in Ron's letters and journals from beyond the social veneer. This issue of the *RON* Series takes you straight to the exotic locales he explored, from prerevolutionary China to the deepest jungles of Central America.

ARTIST SERIES

RON
The Master Mariner:
Sea Captain

Pace the decks of a dozen ships with the adventurous master of the world's waterways and sail the seas of China, Alaska, the Northwestern Pacific Ocean and the Mediterranean. There is indeed something magical about L. Ron Hubbard, sea captain.

RON
The Master Mariner:
Yachtsman

Share in Ron's adventures and challenges with Old Man Sea. Read his ships' logs from his Alaskan Expedition, the newspaper accounts of his yachting experiences in the Caribbean and his unpublished essays chronicling his expertise as master mariner.

RON
The Artist:
Art and the Philosophy
of Art

Author, photographer, music maker, filmmaker—L. Ron Hubbard truly embodied the word *creativity*. Presenting not only a broad view of Ron's artistic achievements, but all else he provided as our most relevant philosopher of art, here is the creative life of L. Ron Hubbard.

RON The Photographer

Photography, as L. Ron Hubbard was fond of pointing out, means light writing, and given the ways in which his photographs communicate, the statement is apt. Presented are photographs, essays and articles from some sixty years of writing with light by one of this century's most accomplished photographers.

RON The Filmmaker

From first-draft script to final print, there is no step of the art of filmmaking L. Ron Hubbard did not master. Here is a look at Ron's revolutionary statements on acting, scripting, cinematography and more.

RON
The Writer:
The Shaping of Popular Fiction

What if one, right now, could study the art of writing with such a master as L. Ron Hubbard? Presented in this issue of the *RON* Series is the mind behind the ideas, the technique behind the style and the genius behind the words of L. Ron Hubbard. In articles such as "The Manuscript Factory," "Arts vs. Eats," "How to Drive a Writer Crazy" and "The Pulp Paper Puzzle," Ron approaches the profession of writing with all the vibrancy and brilliance for which he is famous, and all of it drawn from his own colorful experiences.

RON Letters and Journals: Literary Correspondence

Drawn from the extensive collection of L. Ron Hubbard literary correspondence and journals, this is the definitive view of an author's world with all its passion, brilliance and intensity. Every letter takes one into the whirlwind life of a high-adventure writer in the heyday of the great American pulps. From his first furious days in Manhattan's pulp fiction jungle to his final letters from the 1980s — one is right there with Ron.

RON The Music Maker

Composer, performer, arranger and director — the story of Ron's musical legacy is a vast one. In the photographs, articles and never-before-released essays, *RON The Music Maker* details his lifelong love of the art of music, how he used the Scientology Emotional Tone Scale in teaching musicians and how he composed the melodies and songs for his *Battlefield Earth*, *Mission Earth* and *Road to Freedom* albums.

RON The Poet/Lyricist

If poetry is "the language of life," then L. Ron Hubbard spoke it fluently. *RON The Poet/Lyricist* presents a collection of sixty-five poems, lyrics and ballads — fifty-three never before published — and all to provide a wholly unique view of Ron.

MY PHILOSOPHY
BY L. RON HUBBARD

If philosophy can be defined as an investigation of the truths and principles of being, or the love, study or pursuit of wisdom, then L. Ron Hubbard deserved the title of "philosopher." He never claimed to be more than that. When his investigations led into the field of religion — the truths and principles of the *spirit* — he was the first to announce that he was no prophet or messiah. Still, he *was* the founder of the Scientology religion, and for this he is respected by millions around the world. The following essay tells us more about the man, his motives and why he has earned the admiration of so many, than any editorial comment can possibly do.

T*he subject of philosophy is very ancient. The word means: "The love, study or pursuit of wisdom, or of knowledge of things and their causes, whether theoretical or practical."*

All we know of science or of religion comes from philosophy. It lies behind and above all other knowledge we have or use.

For long regarded as a subject reserved for halls of learning and the intellectual, the subject, to a remarkable degree, has been denied the man in the street.

Surrounded by protective coatings of impenetrable scholarliness, philosophy has been reserved to the privileged few.

The first principle of my own philosophy is that wisdom is meant for anyone who wishes to reach for it. It is the servant of the commoner and king alike and should never be regarded with awe.

*Selfish scholars seldom forgive anyone who seeks to break down the walls of mystery and let the people in. Will Durant, the modern American philosopher, was relegated to the scrapheap by his fellow scholars when he wrote a popular book on the subject, **The Story of Philosophy**. Thus brickbats come the way of any who seek to bring wisdom to the people over the objections of the "inner circle."*

The second principle of my own philosophy is that it must be capable of being applied.

Learning locked in mildewed books is of little use to anyone and therefore of no value unless it can be used.

The third principle is that any philosophic knowledge is only valuable if it is true or if it works.

These three principles are so strange to the field of philosophy, that I have given my philosophy a name: SCIENTOLOGY. This means only "knowing how to know."

A philosophy can only be a **route** to knowledge. It cannot be crammed down one's throat. If one has a route, he can then find what is true for him. And that is Scientology.

Know thyself . . . and the truth shall set you free.

Therefore, in Scientology, we are not concerned with individual actions and differences. We are only concerned with how to show man how he can set himself free.

This, of course, is not very popular with those who depend upon the slavery of others for their living or power. But it happens to be the only way I have found that really improves an individual's life.

Suppression and oppression are the basic causes of depression. If you relieve those a person can lift his head, become well, become happy with life.

And though it may be unpopular with the slave master, it is very popular with the people.

Common man likes to be happy and well. He likes to be able to understand things, and he knows his route to freedom lies through knowledge.

Therefore, since 1950 I have had mankind knocking on my door. It has not mattered where I have lived or how remote, since I first published a book on the subject my life has no longer been my own.

I like to help others and count it as my greatest pleasure in life to see a person free himself of the shadows which darken his days.

These shadows look so thick to him and weigh him down so that when he finds they **are** shadows and that he can see through them, walk through them and be again in the sun, he is enormously delighted. And I am afraid I am just as delighted as he is.

I have seen much human misery. As a very young man I wandered through Asia and saw the agony and misery of overpopulated and underdeveloped lands. I have seen people uncaring and stepping over dying men in the streets. I have seen children less than rags and bones. And amongst this poverty and degradation I found holy places where wisdom was great, but where it was carefully hidden and given out only as superstition. Later, in Western universities, I saw man obsessed with materiality and with all his cunning; I saw him hide what little wisdom he really had in forbidding halls and make it inaccessible to the common and less favored man. I have been through a terrible war and saw its terror and pain uneased by a single word of decency or humanity.

I have lived no cloistered life and hold in contempt the wise man who has not **lived** and the scholar who will not share.

There have been many wiser men than I, but few have traveled as much road.

I have seen life from the top down and the bottom up. I know how it looks both ways. And I know there **is** wisdom and that there is hope.

Blinded with injured optic nerves, and lame with physical injuries to hip and back, at the end of World War II, I faced an almost nonexistent future. My service record states: "This officer has no neurotic or psychotic tendencies of any kind whatsoever," but it also states "permanently disabled physically."

And so there came a further blow . . . I was abandoned by family and friends as a supposedly hopeless cripple and a probable burden upon them for the rest of my days. I yet worked my way back to fitness and strength in less than two years, using only what I know and could determine about man and his relationship to the universe. I had no one to help me; what I had to know I had to find out. And it's quite a trick studying when you cannot see.

I became used to being told it was all impossible, that there was no way, no hope. Yet I came to see again and walk again, and I built an entirely new life. It is a happy life, a busy one and I hope a useful one. My only moments of sadness are those which come when bigoted men tell others all is bad and there is no route anywhere, no hope anywhere, nothing but sadness and sameness and desolation, and that every effort to help others is false. I know it is not true.

So my own philosophy is that one should share what wisdom he has, one should help others to help themselves, and one should keep going despite heavy weather for there is always a calm ahead. One should also ignore catcalls from the selfish intellectual who cries: "Don't expose the mystery. Keep it all for ourselves. The people cannot understand."

But as I have never seen wisdom do any good kept to oneself, and as I like to see others happy, and as I find the vast majority of the people can and *do* understand, I will keep on writing and working and teaching so long as I exist.

For I know no man who has any monopoly upon the wisdom of this universe. It belongs to those who *can* use it to help themselves and others.

If things were a little better known and understood, we would all lead happier lives.

And there is a way to know them and there is a way to freedom.

The old must give way to the new, falsehood must become exposed by truth, and truth, though fought, always in the end prevails.

PART FOURTEEN

REFERENCES

CHAPTER 40

THE CREEDS AND CODES OF SCIENTOLOGY

The adherents of every religion are bound together by creeds and codes.

These creeds state their aspirations, their duties, their mores and their beliefs. They align the religion's purposes and reinforce the basic tenets of the religion.

The codes and creeds of Scientology were written by L. Ron Hubbard in the 1950s during the formative years of the religion.

They set the guidelines for the practice and expansion of Scientology and still serve those ends today.

Included in these creeds are codes for the auditor, the supervisor, the manager and additional codes by which all Scientologists strive to live. Like Scientology, the usefulness of these principles determines their worth. Scientologists follow these precepts in applying Scientology technology, in dealings with others, and in the administration of their groups and the practice of their religion.

The Creed of the Church of Scientology

The Creed of the Church of Scientology was written by L. Ron Hubbard shortly after the Church was formed in Los Angeles on February 18, 1954. After Mr. Hubbard issued this creed from his office in Phoenix, Arizona, the Church of Scientology adopted it as its creed because it succinctly states what Scientologists believe.

We of the Church believe:

That all men of whatever race, color or creed were created with equal rights;

That all men have inalienable rights to their own religious practices and their performance;

That all men have inalienable rights to their own lives;

That all men have inalienable rights to their sanity;

That all men have inalienable rights to their own defense;

That all men have inalienable rights to conceive, choose, assist or support their own organizations, churches and governments;

That all men have inalienable rights to think freely, to talk freely, to write freely their own opinions and to counter or utter or write upon the opinions of others;

That all men have inalienable rights to the creation of their own kind;

That the souls of men have the rights of men;

That the study of the mind and the healing of mentally caused ills should not be alienated from religion or condoned in nonreligious fields;

And that no agency less than God has the power to suspend or set aside these rights, overtly or covertly.

And we of the Church believe:

That man is basically good;

That he is seeking to survive;

That his survival depends upon himself and upon his fellows and his attainment of brotherhood with the universe.

And we of the Church believe that the laws of God forbid man:

To destroy his own kind;

To destroy the sanity of another;

To destroy or enslave another's soul;

To destroy or reduce the survival of one's companions or one's group.

And we of the Church believe that the spirit can be saved and that the spirit alone may save or heal the body.

The Auditor's Code

This code first appeared as a chapter in the book *Dianetics: The Original Thesis* (later retitled *The Dynamics of Life*) written by L. Ron Hubbard in 1947 and published in 1951.

Subsequently, many hours of auditing ministered by auditors other than Mr. Hubbard provided him with information he was able to apply to refine the code and thus improve the discipline of auditing.

The Auditor's Code was revised in 1954, appearing in Professional Auditor's Bulletins 38 and 39.

Over the next four years, several additions were made to the 1954 Code, one of which appeared in the book *Dianetics 55!* Another was released in Hubbard Communications Office Bulletin of 1 July 1957, ADDITION TO THE AUDITOR'S CODE, and two more items were added when the Auditor's Code of 1958 was published.

The Auditor's Code 1968, released in October of that year, was issued as a Hubbard Communications Office Policy Letter. It was released in celebration of the 100 percent gains attainable by standard tech.

Hubbard Communications Office Policy Letter 2 November 1968, AUDITOR'S CODE, added three more clauses to the Code.

The final version of the Code was published by Mr. Hubbard on 19 June 1980.

The Auditor's Code is a fundamental tool of auditing and of life. As L. Ron Hubbard wrote in *Dianetics*, "The Auditor's Code outlines . . . the *survival conduct pattern* of man. The Clear operates more or less automatically on this code." Because the basic axioms of Dianetics and Scientology comprise the fundamentals of thought itself, what works in auditing also works in life.

I hereby promise as an auditor to follow the Auditor's Code.

1 I promise not to evaluate for the preclear or tell him what he should think about his case in session.

2 I promise not to invalidate the preclear's case or gains in or out of session.

3 I promise to administer only standard tech to a preclear in the standard way.

4 I promise to keep all auditing appointments once made.

5 I promise not to process a preclear who has not had sufficient rest and who is physically tired.

6 I promise not to process a preclear who is improperly fed or hungry.

7 I promise not to permit a frequent change of auditors.

8 I promise not to sympathize with a preclear but to be effective.

9 I promise not to let the preclear end session on his own determinism but to finish off those cycles I have begun.

10 I promise never to walk off from a preclear in session.

11 I promise never to get angry with a preclear in session.

12 I promise to run every major case action to a floating needle.

13 I promise never to run any one action beyond its floating needle.

14 I promise to grant beingness to the preclear in session.

15 I promise not to mix the processes of Scientology with other practices except when the preclear is physically ill and only medical means will serve.

16 I promise to maintain communication with the preclear and not to cut his communication or permit him to overrun in session.

17 I promise not to enter comments, expressions or enturbulence into a session that distract a preclear from his case.

18 I promise to continue to give the preclear the process or auditing command when needed in the session.

19 I promise not to let a preclear run a wrongly understood command.

20 I promise not to explain, justify or make excuses in session for any auditor mistakes whether real or imagined.

21 I promise to estimate the current case state of a preclear only by standard case supervision data and not to diverge because of some imagined difference in the case.

22 I promise never to use the secrets of a preclear divulged in session for punishment or personal gain.

23 I promise to never falsify worksheets of sessions.

24 I promise to see that any donation received for processing is refunded, following the policies of the Claims Verification Board, if the preclear is dissatisfied and demands it within three months after the processing, the only condition being that he may not again be processed or trained.

25 I promise not to advocate Dianetics or Scientology only to cure illness or only to treat the insane, knowing well they were intended for spiritual gain.

26 I promise to cooperate fully with the authorized organizations of Dianetics and Scientology in safeguarding the ethical use and practice of those subjects.

27 I promise to refuse to permit any being to be physically injured, violently damaged, operated on or killed in the name of "mental treatment."

28 I promise not to permit sexual liberties or violations of patients.

29 I promise to refuse to admit to the ranks of practitioners any being who is insane.

The Code of Honor

The Code of Honor first appeared in Professional Auditor's Bulletin 40 on 26 November 1954. As Mr. Hubbard explained:

"No one expects the Code of Honor to be closely and tightly followed.

"An ethical code cannot be enforced. Any effort to enforce the Code of Honor would bring it into the level of a moral code. It cannot be enforced simply because it is a way of life which can exist as a way of life only as long as it is not enforced. Any other use but self-determined use of the Code of Honor would, as any Scientologist could quickly see, produce a considerable deterioration in a person. Therefore its use is a luxury use, and which is done solely on self-determined action, providing one sees eye to eye with the Code of Honor.

"If you believed man was worthy enough to be granted by you sufficient stature so as to permit you to exercise gladly the Code of Honor, I can guarantee that you would be a happy person. And if you found an occasional miscreant falling away from the best standards you have developed, you yet did not turn away from the rest of man, and if you discovered yourself betrayed by those you were seeking to defend and yet did not then experience a complete reversal of opinion about all your fellow men, there would be no dwindling spiral for you.

"The only difference between paradise on Earth and hell on Earth is whether or not you believe your fellow man worthy of receiving from you the friendship and devotion called for in this Code of Honor."

1   Never desert a comrade in need, in danger or in trouble.

2   Never withdraw allegiance once granted.

3   Never desert a group to which you owe your support.

4   Never disparage yourself or minimize your strength or power.

5   Never need praise, approval or sympathy.

6   Never compromise with your own reality.

7   Never permit your affinity to be alloyed.

8   Do not give or receive communication unless you yourself desire it.

9   Your self-determinism and your honor are more important than your immediate life.

10   Your integrity to yourself is more important than your body.

11   Never regret yesterday. Life is in you today, and you make your tomorrow.

12   Never fear to hurt another in a just cause.

13   Don't desire to be liked or admired.

14   Be your own adviser, keep your own counsel and select your own decisions.

15   Be true to your own goals.

Code of a Scientologist

The Code of a Scientologist was first issued as Professional Auditor's Bulletin 41 in 1954. In this code, L. Ron Hubbard provides a Scientologist with guidelines for fighting for human rights and justice through social reform. It is a vital code for any Scientologist active in the community. The code was reissued in 1956 in the book, *The Creation of Human Ability.* Revised in 1969 and again in 1973, the code is given here in its final version.

As a Scientologist, I pledge myself to the Code of Scientology for the good of all.

1 To keep Scientologists, the public and the press accurately informed concerning Scientology, the world of mental health and society.

2 To use the best I know of Scientology to the best of my ability to help my family, friends, groups and the world.

3 To refuse to accept for processing and to refuse to accept money from any preclear or group I feel I cannot honestly help.

4 To decry and do all I can to abolish any and all abuses against life and mankind.

5 To expose and help abolish any and all physically damaging practices in the field of mental health.

6 To help clean up and keep clean the field of mental health.

7 To bring about an atmosphere of safety and security in the field of mental health by eradicating its abuses and brutality.

8 To support true humanitarian endeavors in the fields of human rights.

9 To embrace the policy of equal justice for all.

10 To work for freedom of speech in the world.

11 To actively decry the suppression of knowledge, wisdom, philosophy or data which would help mankind.

12 To support the freedom of religion.

13 To help Scientology orgs and groups ally themselves with public groups.

14 To teach Scientology at a level it can be understood and used by the recipients.

15 To stress the freedom to use Scientology as a philosophy in all its applications and variations in the humanities.

16 To insist upon standard and unvaried Scientology as an applied activity in ethics, processing and administration in Scientology organizations.

17 To take my share of responsibility for the impact of Scientology upon the world.

18 To increase the numbers and strength of Scientology over the world.

19 To set an example of the effectiveness and wisdom of Scientology.

20 To make this world a saner, better place.

The Supervisor's Code

Just as auditors must follow a code of conduct, so too does the supervisor in a Scientology course room. Unlike teachers in many traditional classrooms, Course Supervisors do not set themselves up as "authorities" who tell their students what to think, nor do they espouse their opinions on the subject. Instead, students are guided to find the answers for themselves in Dianetics and Scientology materials.

In the following code, Mr. Hubbard sets forth the key guidelines that ensure the course room is standard and professional, with maximum benefit to the students. This code is followed by supervisors in churches of Scientology throughout the world, guaranteeing a high level of training in the technology. It was first published in 1957.

1 The Supervisor must never neglect an opportunity to direct a student to the actual source of Scientology data.

2 The Supervisor should invalidate a student's mistake ruthlessly and use good ARC while doing it.

3 The Supervisor should remain in good ARC with his students at all times while they are performing training activities.

4 The Supervisor at all times must have a high tolerance of stupidity in his students and must be willing to repeat any datum not understood as many times as necessary for the student to understand and acquire reality on the datum.

5 The Supervisor does not have a "case" in his relationship with his students, nor discuss or talk about his personal problems to the students.

6 The Supervisor will, at all times, be a source-point of good control and direction to his students.

7 The Supervisor will be able to correlate any part of Scientology to any other part and to livingness over the eight dynamics.

8 The Supervisor should be able to answer any questions concerning Scientology by directing the student to the actual source of the data. If a Supervisor cannot answer a particular question, he should always say so, and the Supervisor should always find the answer to the question from the source and tell the student where the answer is to be found.

9 The Supervisor should never lie to, deceive or misdirect a student concerning Scientology. He shall be honest at all times about it with a student.

10 The Supervisor must be an accomplished auditor.

11 The Supervisor should always set a good example to his students: such as giving good demonstrations, being on time and dressing neatly.

12 The Supervisor should at all times be perfectly willing and able to do anything he tells his students to do.

13 The Supervisor must not become emotionally involved with students of either sex while they are under his or her training.

14 When a Supervisor makes any mistake, he is to inform the student that he has made one and rectify it immediately. This datum embraces all phases in training, demonstrations, lectures and processing, etc. He is never to hide the fact that he made the mistake.

15 The Supervisor should never neglect to give praise to his students when due.

16 The Supervisor to some degree should be pan-determined about the Supervisor–student relationship.

17 When a Supervisor lets a student control, give orders to or handle the Supervisor in any way, for the purpose of demonstration or other training purposes, the Supervisor should always put the student back under his control.

18 The Supervisor will at all times observe the Auditor's Code during sessions and the Code of a Scientologist at all times.

19 The Supervisor will never give a student opinions about Scientology without labeling them thoroughly as such; otherwise, he is to direct only to tested and proven data concerning Scientology.

20 The Supervisor shall never use a student for his own personal gain.

21 The Supervisor will be a stable terminal, point the way to stable data, be certain, but not dogmatic or dictatorial, toward his students.

22 The Supervisor will keep himself at all times informed of the most recent Scientology data and procedures and communicate this information to his students.

The Credo of a True Group Member

In our bureaucratic age, members of a group are often left feeling hopeless and ineffective in the face of seemingly insurmountable difficulties. Some may even come to feel they would be better off without allegiance to any group. But inevitably, no one can survive alone, and denying oneself membership in a group is denying oneself the pride and satisfaction which can only come through teamwork.

In his research into the technology of groups, L. Ron Hubbard codified the key principles which members of any group should follow to attain its goals. These are offered in the following code, written in January 1951. Using this code, a person can greatly increase his contribution to a group, while at the same time maintaining his own self-determinism.

1 The successful participant of a group is that participant who closely approximates in his own activities the ideal, ethic and rationale of the overall group.

2 The responsibility of the individual for the group as a whole should not be less than the responsibility of the group for the individual.

3 The group member has, as part of his responsibility, the smooth operation of the entire group.

4 A group member must exert and insist upon his rights and prerogatives as a group member and insist upon the rights and prerogatives of the group as a group and let not these rights be diminished in any way or degree for any excuse or claimed expeditiousness.

5 The member of a true group must exert and practice his right to contribute to the group. And he must insist upon the right of the group to contribute to him. He should recognize that a myriad of group failures will result when either of these contributions is denied as a right. (A welfare state being that state in which the member is not permitted to contribute to the state but must take contribution from the state.)

6 Enturbulence of the affairs of the group by sudden shifts of plans unjustified by circumstances, breakdown of recognized channels or cessation of useful operations in a group must be refused and blocked by the member of a group. He should take care not to enturbulate a manager and thus lower ARC.

7 Failure in planning or failure to recognize goals must be corrected by the group member for the group by calling the matter to conference or acting upon his own initiative.

8 A group member must coordinate his initiative with the goals and rationale of the entire group and with other individual members, well publishing his activities and intentions so that all conflicts may be brought forth in advance.

9 A group member must insist upon his right to have initiative.

10 A group member must study and understand and work with the goals, rationale and executions of the group.

11 A group member must work toward becoming as expert as possible in his specialized technology and skill in the group and must assist other individuals of the group to an understanding of that technology and skill and its place in the organizational necessities of the group.

12 A group member should have a working knowledge of all technologies and skills in the group in order to understand them and their place in the organizational necessities of the group.

13 On the group member depends the height of the ARC of the group. He must insist upon high-level communication lines and clarity in affinity and reality and know the consequence of not having such conditions. *And he must work continually and actively to maintain high ARC in the organization.*

14 A group member has the right of pride in his tasks and a right of judgment and handling in those tasks.

15 A group member must recognize that he is himself a manager of some section of the group and/or its tasks and that he himself must have both the knowledge and right of management in that sphere for which he is responsible.

16 The group member should not permit laws to be passed which limit or proscribe the activities of all the members of the group because of the failure of some of the members of the group.

17 The group member should insist on flexible planning and unerring execution of plans.

18 The performance of duty at optimum by every member of the group should be understood by the group member to be the best safeguard of his own and the group survival. It is the pertinent business of any member of the group that optimum performance be achieved by any other member of the group whether chain of command or similarity of activity sphere warrants such supervision or not.

The Credo of a Good and Skilled Manager

Leadership is a rare commodity, a gift possessed by a few uncommon individuals. As part of his management technology, L. Ron Hubbard developed a large body of guidelines to enable executives and managers not only to apply their powers with intelligence but also to exercise sane leadership that will enable their groups to flourish and prosper. Following this code will increase one's success as a manager in churches of Scientology but also any other group, from a business to a commonwealth of nations. This code was also written by Mr. Hubbard in 1951.

To be effective and successful a manager must:

1 Understand as fully as possible the goals and aims of the group he manages. He must be able to see and embrace the *ideal* attainment of the goal as envisioned by a goal maker. He must be able to tolerate and better the *practical* attainments and advances of which his group and its members may be capable. He must strive to narrow, always, the ever-existing gulf between the *ideal* and the *practical*.

2 He must realize that a primary mission is the full and honest interpretation by himself of the ideal and ethic and their goals and aims to his subordinates and the group itself. He must lead creatively and persuasively toward these goals his subordinates, the group itself and the individuals of the group.

3 He must embrace the organization and act solely for the entire organization and never form or favor cliques. His judgment of individuals of the group should be solely in the light of their worth to the entire group.

4 He must never falter in sacrificing individuals to the good of the group both in planning and execution and in his justice.

5 He must protect all established communication lines and complement them where necessary.

6 He must protect all affinity in his charge and have himself an affinity for the group itself.

7 He must attain always to the highest creative reality.

8 His planning must accomplish, in the light of goals and aims, the activity of the entire group. He must never let organizations grow and sprawl but, learning by pilots, must keep organizational planning fresh and flexible.

9 He must recognize in himself the rationale of the group and receive and evaluate the data out of which he makes his solutions with the highest attention to the truth of that data.

10 He must constitute himself on the orders of service to the group.

11 He must permit himself to be served well as to his individual requirements, practicing an economy of his own efforts and enjoying certain comforts to the wealth of keeping high his rationale.

12 He should require of his subordinates that they relay into their own spheres of management the whole and entire of his true feelings and the reasons for his decisions as clearly as they can be relayed and expanded and interpreted only for the greater understanding of the individuals governed by those subordinates.

13 He must never permit himself to pervert or mask any portion of the ideal and ethic on which the group operates nor must he permit the ideal and ethic to grow old and outmoded and unworkable. He must never permit his planning to be perverted or censored by subordinates.
He must never permit the ideal and ethic of the group's individual members to deteriorate, using always reason to interrupt such a deterioration.

14 He must have faith in the goals, faith in himself and faith in the group.

15 He must lead by demonstrating always creative and constructive subgoals. He must not drive by threat and fear.

16 He must realize that every individual in the group is engaged in some degree in the managing of other men, life and MEST and that a liberty of management within this code should be allowed to every such submanager.

Thus conducting himself, a manager can win empire for his group, whatever that empire may be.

CHAPTER 41

THE AXIOMS OF DIANETICS AND SCIENTOLOGY

epresenting the basic truths of life, the Logics and Axioms form the foundation upon which Dianetics and Scientology were built. Mr. Hubbard spent more than fifty years distilling the accumulated sum of man's wisdom, probing ever deeper into life's mysteries in order to discover these Axioms.

These are the central considerations and natural laws which contain the answers to life and its interaction with the physical universe. Dianetics and Scientology in their entirety flow from these basic truths. All later discoveries fall within the bounds of truth described in these Logics and Axioms.

The chapter ends with The Factors, which embody the general considerations by which the game of life is played.

The Logics

The Logics were written by L. Ron Hubbard from a summary of information which began in November of 1938 and were published in 1951. They have never varied since that time.

The Logics form a gradient scale of association of facts necessary to understand and resolve any problem. They are used to predict behavior and clarify the entire field of thought. The Logics are a method of thinking and could be called "how to think." The basic common denominators of all education may be found in the Logics.

Logic 1 Knowledge is a whole group or subdivision of a group of data or speculations or conclusions on data or methods of gaining data.

Logic 2 A body of knowledge is a body of data, aligned or unaligned, or methods of gaining data.

Logic 3 Any knowledge which can be sensed, measured or experienced by any entity is capable of influencing that entity.

COROLLARY: That knowledge which cannot be sensed, measured or experienced by any entity or type of entity cannot influence that entity or type of entity.

Logic 4 A datum is a symbol of matter, energy, space or time, or any combination thereof, in any universe, or the matter, energy, space or time itself, or any combination thereof, in any universe.

Logic 5 A definition of terms is necessary to the alignment, statement and resolution of suppositions, observations, problems and solutions and their communication.

DEFINITION: Descriptive definition: one which classifies by characteristics, by describing existing states of being.
DEFINITION: Differentiative definition: one which compares unlikeness to existing states of being or not-being.

DEFINITION: Associative definition: one which declares likeness to existing states of being or not-being.
DEFINITION: Action definition: one which delineates cause and potential change of state of being by cause of existence, inexistence, action, inaction, purpose or lack of purpose.

Logic 6 Absolutes are unobtainable.

Logic 7 Gradient scales are necessary to the evaluation of problems and their data.

This is the tool of infinity-valued logic: Absolutes are unobtainable. Terms such as good and bad, alive and dead, right and wrong are used only in conjunction with gradient scales. On the scale of right and wrong, everything above zero or center would be more and more right, approaching an infinite rightness, and everything below center would be more and more wrong, approaching infinite wrongness. All things assisting the survival of the survivor are considered to be right for the survivor. All things inhibiting survival from the viewpoint of the survivor can be considered wrong for the survivor. The more a thing assists survival, the more it can be considered right for the survivor; the more a thing or action inhibits survival, the more it is wrong from the viewpoint of the intended survivor.

COROLLARY: Any datum has only relative truth.

COROLLARY: Truth is relative to environments, experience and truth.

Logic **8** A datum can be evaluated only by a datum of comparable magnitude.

Logic **9** A datum is as valuable as it has been evaluated.

Logic **10** The value of a datum is established by the amount of alignment (relationship) it imparts to other data.

Logic **11** The value of a datum or field of data can be established by its degree of assistance in survival or its inhibition to survival.

Logic **12** The value of a datum or a field of data is modified by the viewpoint of the observer.

Logic **13** Problems are resolved by compartmenting them into areas of similar magnitude and data, comparing them to data already known or partially known, and resolving each area. Data which cannot be known immediately may be resolved by addressing what is known and using its solution to resolve the remainder.

Logic **14** Factors introduced into a problem or solution which do not derive from natural law but only from authoritarian command aberrate that problem or solution.

Logic **15** The introduction of an arbitrary into a problem or solution invites the further introduction of arbitraries into problems and solutions.

Logic **16** An abstract postulate must be compared to the universe to which it applies and brought into the category of things which can be sensed, measured or experienced in that universe before such postulate can be considered workable.

Logic **17** Those fields which most depend upon authoritative opinion for their data least contain known natural law.

Logic **18** A postulate is as valuable as it is workable.

Logic **19** The workability of a postulate is established by the degree to which it explains existing phenomena already known, by the degree that it predicts new phenomena which when looked for will be found to exist, and by the degree that it does not require that phenomena which do not exist in fact be called into existence for its explanation.

Logic **20** A science may be considered to be a large body of aligned data which has similarity in application and which has been deduced or induced from basic postulates.

Logic **21** Mathematics are methods of postulating or resolving real or abstract data in any universe and integrating by symbolization of data, postulates and resolutions.

Logic **22** The human mind* is an observer, postulator, creator and storage place of knowledge.

The human mind by definition includes the awareness unit of the living organism, the observer, the computer of data, the spirit, the memory storage, the life force and the individual motivator of the living organism. It is used as distinct from the brain which can be considered to be motivated by the mind.

Logic **23** The human mind is a servo-mechanism to any mathematics evolved or employed by the human mind.

POSTULATE: The human mind and inventions of the human mind are capable of resolving any and all problems which can be sensed, measured or experienced directly or indirectly.
COROLLARY: The human mind is capable of resolving the problem of the human mind. The borderline of solution of this science lies between why *life is surviving and* how *life is*
surviving. It is possible to resolve how *life is surviving without resolving* why *life is surviving.*

Logic **24** The resolution of the philosophical, scientific and human studies (such as economics, politics, sociology, medicine, criminology, etc.) depends primarily upon the resolution of the problems of the human mind.

Note: The primary step in resolving the broad activities of man could be considered to be the resolving of the activities of the mind itself. Hence, the Logics carry to this point and then proceed as axioms concerning the human mind, such axioms being substantiated as relative truths by much newly discovered phenomena. The ensuing axioms, from Logic 24, apply no less to the various "ologies" than they do to de-aberrating or improving the operation of the mind. It should not be thought that the following axioms are devoted to the construction of anything as limited as a therapy, which is only incidental to the resolution of human aberration and such things as psychosomatic illnesses. These axioms are capable of such solution, as has been demonstrated, but such a narrow application would indicate a very narrow scope of view.

The Dianetic Axioms

L. Ron Hubbard discovered that man obeys very definite laws and rules which can be set forward in axioms. The very first and most fundamental of these axioms and the basic axiom of Dianetics is: The dynamic principle of existence is survive.

The Dianetic Axioms were put together in the fall of 1951 after careful examination over a long period of time. These 194 Dianetic Axioms contain a codification of the factors underlying all mental aberration.

Axiom **1** The source of life is a static of peculiar and particular properties.

Axiom **2** At least a portion of the static called life is impinged upon the physical universe.

Axiom **3** That portion of the static of life which is impinged upon the physical universe has for its dynamic goal, survival and only survival.

Axiom **4** The physical universe is reducible to motion of energy operating in space through time.

Axiom **5** That portion of the static of life concerned with the life organisms of the physical universe is concerned wholly with motion.

Axiom **6** The life static has as one of its properties the ability to mobilize and animate matter into living organisms.

Axiom **7** The life static is engaged in a conquest of the physical universe.

Axiom **8** The life static conquers the material universe by learning and applying the physical laws of the physical universe.

SYMBOL: The symbol for the LIFE STATIC in use hereafter is the Greek letter THETA.

Axiom **9** A fundamental operation of THETA in surviving is bringing order into the chaos of the physical universe.

Axiom **10** THETA brings order into chaos by conquering whatever in MEST may be prosurvival and destroying whatever in MEST may be contrasurvival, at least through the medium of life organisms.

SYMBOL: The symbol for the PHYSICAL UNIVERSE in use hereafter is MEST, from the first letters of the words MATTER, ENERGY, SPACE and TIME, or the Greek letter PHI.

Axiom **11** A life organism is composed of matter and energy in space and time, animated by THETA.

SYMBOL: Living organism or organisms will hereafter be represented by the Greek letter LAMBDA.

Axiom **12** The MEST part of the organism follows the laws of the physical sciences. All LAMBDA is concerned with motion.

Axiom **13** THETA operating through LAMBDA converts the forces of the physical universe into forces to conquer the physical universe.

Axiom **14** THETA working upon physical universe motion must maintain a harmonious rate of motion.

The limits of LAMBDA are narrow, both as to thermal and mechanical motion.

Axiom **15** LAMBDA is the intermediate step in the conquest of the physical universe.

Axiom **16** The basic food of any organism consists of light and chemicals.

Organisms can exist only as higher levels of complexities because lower levels of converters exist.
THETA evolves organisms from lower to higher forms and supports them by the existence of lower converter forms.

Axiom **17** THETA, via LAMBDA, effects an evolution of MEST.

In this we have the waste products of organisms on the one hand as those very complex chemicals which bacteria make and, on the other hand, we have the physical face of the Earth being changed by animals and men, such changes as grass holding mountains from eroding or roots causing boulders to break, buildings being built and rivers being dammed. There is obviously an evolution in MEST in progress under the incursion of THETA.

Axiom **18** LAMBDA, even within a species, varies in its endowment of THETA.

Axiom **19** The effort of LAMBDA is toward survival. The goal of LAMBDA is survival. The penalty of failure to advance toward that goal is to succumb.

DEFINITION: Persistence is the ability to exert continuance of effort toward survival goals.

Axiom **20** LAMBDA creates, conserves, maintains, requires, destroys, changes, occupies, groups and disperses MEST.

LAMBDA survives by animating and mobilizing or destroying matter and energy in space and time.

Axiom **21** LAMBDA is dependent upon optimum motion. Motion which is too swift and motion which is too slow are equally contrasurvival.

Axiom **22** THETA and thought are similar orders of static.

Axiom **23** All thought is concerned with motion.

Axiom **24** The establishment of an optimum motion is a basic goal of reason.

DEFINITION: LAMBDA is a chemical heat engine existing in space and time motivated by the life static and directed by thought.

Axiom **25** The basic purpose of reason is the calculation or estimation of effort.

Axiom **26** Thought is accomplished by THETA FACSIMILES of physical universe, entities or actions.

Axiom **27** THETA is satisfied only with harmonious action or optimum motion and rejects or destroys action or motion above or below its tolerance band.

Axiom **28** The mind is concerned wholly with the estimation of effort.

DEFINITION: Mind is the THETA *command post of any organism or organisms.*

Axiom **29** The basic errors of reason are failure to differentiate amongst matter, energy, space and time.

Axiom **30** Rightness is proper calculation of effort.

Axiom **31** Wrongness is always miscalculation of effort.

Axiom **32** THETA can exert itself directly or extensionally.

THETA *can direct physical application of the organism to the environment or, through the mind, can first calculate the action or extend, as in language, ideas.*

Axiom **33** Conclusions are directed toward the inhibition, maintenance or accelerations of efforts.

Axiom **34** The common denominator of all life organisms is motion.

Axiom **35** Effort of an organism to survive or succumb is physical motion of a life organism at a given moment in time through space.

DEFINITION: Motion is any change in orientation in space.
DEFINITION: Force is random effort.
DEFINITION: Effort is directed force.

Axiom **36** An organism's effort can be to remain at rest or persist in a given motion.

Static state has position in time, but an organism which is remaining positionally in a static state, if alive, is still continuing a highly complex pattern of motion, such as the heartbeat, digestion, etc.
The efforts of organisms to survive or succumb are assisted, compelled or opposed by the efforts of other organisms, matter, energy, space and time.
DEFINITION: Attention is a motion which must remain at an optimum effort. Attention is aberrated by becoming unfixed and sweeping at random or becoming too fixed without sweeping.
Unknown threats to survival when sensed cause attention to sweep without fixing. Known threats to survival when sensed cause attention to fix.

Axiom **37** The ultimate goal of LAMBDA is infinite survival.

Axiom **38** Death is abandonment by THETA of a life organism or race or species where these can no longer serve THETA in its goals of infinite survival.

Axiom **39** The reward of an organism engaging upon survival activity is pleasure.

Axiom **40** The penalty of an organism failing to engage upon survival activity, or engaging in nonsurvival activity, is pain.

Axiom **41** The cell and virus are the primary building blocks of life organisms.

Axiom **42** The virus and cell are matter and energy animated and motivated in space and time by THETA.

Axiom **43** THETA mobilizes the virus and cell in colonial aggregations to increase potential motion and accomplish effort.

Axiom **44** The goal of viruses and cells is survival in space through time.

Axiom **45** The total mission of higher organisms, viruses and cells is the same as that of the virus and cell.

Axiom **46** Colonial aggregations of viruses and cells can be imbued with more THETA than they inherently contained.

Life energy joins any group, whether a group of organisms or group of cells composing an organism. Here we have personal entity, individuation, etc.

Axiom **47** Effort can be accomplished by LAMBDA only through the coordination of its parts toward goals.

Axiom **48** An organism is equipped to be governed and controlled by a mind.

Axiom **49** The purpose of the mind is to pose and resolve problems relating to survival and to direct the effort of the organism according to these solutions.

Axiom **50** All problems are posed and resolved through estimations of effort.

Axiom **51** The mind can confuse position in space with position in time. (Counter-efforts producing action phrases.)

Axiom **52** An organism proceeding toward survival is directed by the mind of that organism in the accomplishment of survival effort.

Axiom **53** An organism proceeding toward succumb is directed by the mind of that organism in the accomplishment of death.

Axiom **54** Survival of an organism is accomplished by the overcoming of efforts opposing its survival. (Note: Corollary for other dynamics.)

DEFINITION: Dynamic is the ability to translate solutions into action.

Axiom **55** Survival effort for an organism includes the dynamic thrust by that organism for the survival of itself, its procreation, its group, its subspecies, its species, all life organisms, material universe, the life static and, possibly, a Supreme Being. (Note: List of dynamics.)

Axiom **56** The cycle of an organism, a group of organisms or a species is inception, growth, re-creation, decay and death.

Axiom **57** The effort of an organism is directed toward the control of the environment for all the dynamics.

Axiom **58** Control of an environment is accomplished by the support of prosurvival factors along any dynamic.

Axiom **59** Any type of higher organism is accomplished by the evolution of viruses and cells into forms capable of better efforts to control or live in an environment.

Axiom **60** The usefulness of an organism is determined by its ability to control the environment or to support organisms which control the environment.

Axiom **61** An organism is rejected by THETA to the degree that it fails in its goals.

Axiom **62** Higher organisms can exist only in the degree that they are supported by the lower organisms.

Axiom **63** The usefulness of an organism is determined by the alignment of its efforts toward survival.

Axiom **64** The mind perceives and stores all data of the environment and aligns or fails to align these according to the time they were perceived.

DEFINITION: *A conclusion is the* THETA FACSIMILES *of a group of combined data.*
DEFINITION: *A datum is a* THETA FACSIMILE *of physical action.*

Axiom **65** The process of thought is the perception of the present and the comparison of it to the perceptions and conclusions of the past in order to direct action in the immediate or distant future.

COROLLARY: *The attempt of thought is to perceive realities of the past and present in order to predict or postulate realities of the future.*

Axiom **66** The process by which life effects its conquest of the material universe consists in the conversion of the potential effort of matter and energy in space and through time to effect with it the conversion of further matter and energy in space and through time.

Axiom **67** THETA contains its own THETA UNIVERSE effort which translates into MEST effort.

Axiom **68** The single arbitrary in any organism is time.

Axiom **69** Physical universe perceptions and efforts are received by an organism as force waves, convert by facsimile into THETA and are thus stored.

DEFINITION: Randomity is the misalignment through the internal or external efforts by other forms of life or the material universe of the efforts of an organism, and is imposed on the physical organism by counter-efforts in the environment.

Axiom **70** Any cycle of any life organism is from static to motion to static.

Axiom **71** The cycle of randomity is from static, through optimum, through randomity sufficiently repetitious or similar to constitute another static.

Axiom **72** There are two subdivisions to randomity: data randomity and force randomity.

Axiom **73** The three degrees of randomity consist of minus randomity, optimum randomity and plus randomity.

DEFINITION: Randomity is a component factor and necessary part of motion, if motion is to continue.

Axiom **74** Optimum randomity is necessary to learning.

Axiom **75** The important factors in any area of randomity are effort and counter-effort. (Note: As distinguished from near perceptions of effort.)

Axiom **76** Randomity amongst organisms is vital to continuous survival of all organisms.

Axiom **77** THETA affects the organism, other organisms and the physical universe by translating THETA FACSIMILES into physical efforts or randomity of efforts.

DEFINITION: The degree of randomity is measured by the randomness of effort vectors within the organism, amongst organisms, amongst races or species of organisms or between organisms and the physical universe.

Axiom **78** Randomity becomes intense in indirect ratio to the time in which it takes place, modified by the total effort in the area.

Axiom **79** Initial randomity can be reinforced by randomities of greater or lesser magnitude.

Axiom **80** Areas of randomity exist in chains of similarity plotted against time. This can be true of words and actions contained in randomities. Each may have its own chain plotted against time.

Axiom **81** Sanity consists of optimum randomity.

Axiom **82** Aberration exists to the degree that plus or minus randomity exists in the environment or past data of an organism, group or species, modified by the endowed self-determinism of that organism, group or species.

Axiom **83** The self-determinism of an organism is determined by its THETA endowment, modified by minus or plus randomity in its environment or its existence.

Axiom **84** The self-determinism of an organism is increased by optimum randomity of counter-efforts.

Axiom **85** The self-determinism of an organism is reduced by plus or minus randomity of counter-efforts in the environment.

Axiom **86** Randomity contains both the randomness of efforts and the volume of efforts. (Note: An area of randomity can have a great deal of confusion, but without volume of energy, the confusion itself is negligible.)

Axiom **87** That counter-effort is most acceptable to an organism which most closely appears to assist its accomplishment of its goal.

Axiom **88** An area of severe plus or minus randomity can occlude data on any of the subjects of that plus or minus randomity which took place in a prior time. (Note: Shut-off mechanisms of earlier lives, perceptics, specific incidents, etc.)

Axiom **89** Restimulation of plus, minus or optimum randomity can produce increased plus, minus or optimum randomity respectively in the organism.

Axiom **90** An area of randomity can assume sufficient magnitude so as to appear to the organism as pain, according to its goals.

Axiom **91** Past randomity can impose itself upon the present organism as THETA FACSIMILES.

Axiom **92** The engram is a severe area of plus or minus randomity of sufficient volume to cause unconsciousness.

Axiom **93** Unconsciousness is an excess of randomity imposed by a counter-effort of sufficient force to cloud the awareness and direct function of the organism through the mind's control center.

Axiom **94** Any counter-effort which misaligns the organism's command of itself or its environment establishes plus or minus randomity or, if of sufficient magnitude, is an engram.

Axiom **95** Past engrams are restimulated by the control center's perception of circumstances similar to that engram in the present environment.

Axiom **96** An engram is a THETA FACSIMILE of atoms and molecules in misalignment.

Axiom **97** Engrams fix emotional response as that emotional response of the organism during the receipt of the counter-effort.

Axiom **98** Free emotional response depends on optimum randomity. It depends upon absence of or nonrestimulation of engrams.

Axiom **99** THETA FACSIMILES can recombine into new symbols.

Axiom **100** Language is the symbolization of effort.

Axiom **101** Language depends for its force upon the force which accompanied its definition. (Note: Counter-effort, not language, is aberrative.)

Axiom **102** The environment can occlude the central control of any organism and assume control of the motor controls of that organism. (Engram, restimulation, locks, hypnotism.)

Axiom **103** Intelligence depends on the ability to select aligned or misaligned data from an area of randomity and so discover a solution to reduce all randomity in that area.

Axiom **104** Persistence obtains in the ability of the mind to put solutions into physical action toward the realization of goals.

Axiom **105** An unknown datum can produce data of plus or minus randomity.

Axiom **106** The introduction of an arbitrary factor or force without recourse to natural laws of the body or the area into which the arbitrary is introduced brings about plus or minus randomity.

Axiom **107** Data of plus or minus randomity depends for its confusion on former plus or minus randomity or absent data.

Axiom **108** Efforts which are inhibited or compelled by exterior efforts effect a plus or minus randomity of efforts.

Axiom **109** Behavior is modified by counter-efforts which have impinged on the organism.

Axiom **110** The component parts of THETA are affinity, reality and communication.

Axiom 111 Self-determinism consists of maximal affinity, reality and communication.

Axiom 112 Affinity is the cohesion of THETA.

Affinity manifests itself as the recognition of similarity of efforts and goals amongst organisms by those organisms.

Axiom 113 Reality is the agreement upon perceptions and data in the physical universe.

All that we can be sure is real is that on which we have agreed is real. Agreement is the essence of reality.

Axiom 114 Communication is the interchange of perception through the material universe between organisms or the perception of the material universe by sense channels.

Axiom 115 Self-determinism is the THETA control of the organism.

Axiom 116 A self-determined effort is that counter-effort which has been received into the organism in the past and integrated into the organism for its conscious use.

Axiom 117 The components of self-determinism are affinity, communication and reality.

Self-determinism is manifested along each dynamic.

Axiom 118 An organism cannot become aberrated unless it has agreed upon that aberration, has been in communication with a source of aberration and has had affinity for the aberrator.

Axiom 119 Agreement with any source, contra- or prosurvival, postulates a new reality for the organism.

Axiom 120 Nonsurvival courses, thoughts and actions require non-optimum effort.

Axiom 121 Every thought has been preceded by physical action.

Axiom 122 The mind does with thought as it has done with entities in the physical universe.

Axiom 123 All effort concerned with pain is concerned with loss.

Organisms hold pain and engrams to them as a latent effort to prevent loss of some portion of the organism.
All loss is a loss of motion.

Axiom 124 The amount of counter-effort the organism can overcome is proportional to the THETA endowment of the organism, modified by the physique of that organism.

Axiom 125 Excessive counter-effort to the effort of a life organism produces unconsciousness.

COROLLARY: Unconsciousness gives the suppression of an organism's control center by counter-effort.

DEFINITION: The control center of the organism can be defined as the contact point between THETA *and the physical universe and is that center which is aware of being aware and which has charge of and responsibility for the organism along all its dynamics.*

Axiom 126 Perceptions are always received in the control center of an organism whether the control center is in control of the organism at the time or not.

This is an explanation for the assumption of valences.

Axiom 127 All perceptions reaching the organism's sense channels are recorded and stored by THETA FACSIMILE.

DEFINITION: Perception is the process of recording data from the physical universe and storing it as a THETA FACSIMILE.
DEFINITION: Recall is the process of regaining perceptions.

Axiom 128 Any organism can recall everything which it has perceived.

Axiom 129 An organism displaced by plus or minus randomity is thereafter remote from the perception recording center.

Increased remoteness brings about occlusions of perceptions. One can

perceive things in present time and then, because they are being recorded after they passed THETA *perception of the awareness unit, they are recorded but cannot be recalled.*

Axiom 130 THETA FACSIMILES of counter-effort are all that interpose between the control center and its recalls.

Axiom 131 Any counter-effort received into a control center is always accompanied by all perceptics.

Axiom 132 The random counter-efforts to an organism and the inter-mingled perceptions in the randomity can reexert that force upon an organism when restimulated.

DEFINITION: Restimulation is the reactivation of a past counter-effort by appearance in the organism's environment of a similarity toward the content of the past randomity area.

Axiom 133 Self-determinism alone brings about the mechanism of restimulation.

Axiom 134 A reactivated area of the past randomity impinges the effort and the perceptions upon the organism.

Axiom 135 Activation of a randomity area is accomplished first by the perceptions, then by the pain, finally by the effort.

Axiom **136** The mind is plastically capable of recording all efforts and counter-efforts.

Axiom **137** A counter-effort accompanied by sufficient (enrandomed) force impresses the facsimile of the counter-effort personality into the mind of an organism.

Axiom **138** Aberration is the degree of residual plus or minus randomity accumulated by compelling, inhibiting or unwarranted assisting of efforts on the part of other organisms or the physical (material) universe.

Aberration is caused by what is done to the individual, not what the individual does, plus his self-determinism about what has been done to him.

Axiom **139** Aberrated behavior consists of destructive effort toward prosurvival data or entities on any dynamic, or effort toward the survival of contrasurvival data or entities for any dynamic.

Axiom **140** A valence is a facsimile personality made capable of force by the counter-effort of the moment of receipt into the plus or minus randomity of unconsciousness.

Valences are assistive, compulsive or inhibitive to the organism.
A control center is not a valence.

Axiom **141** A control center effort is aligned toward a goal through definite space as a recognized incident in time.

Axiom **142** An organism is as healthy and sane as it is self-determined.

The environmental control of the organism motor controls inhibits the organism's ability to change with the changing environment, since the organism will attempt to carry forward with one set of responses when it needs by self-determinism to create another to survive in another environment.

Axiom **143** All learning is accomplished by random effort.

Axiom **144** A counter-effort producing sufficient plus or minus randomity to record is recorded with an index of space and time as hidden as the remainder of its content.

Axiom **145** A counter-effort producing sufficient plus or minus randomity when activated by restimulation exerts itself against the environment or the organism without regard to space and time, except reactivated perceptions.

Axiom **146** Counter-efforts are directed out from the organism until they are further enrandomed by the environ at which time they again activate against the control center.

Axiom **147** An organism's mind employs counter-efforts effectively only so long as insufficient plus or minus randomity exists to hide differentiation of the facsimiles created.

Axiom **148** Physical laws are learned by life energy only by impingement of the physical universe producing randomity, and a withdrawal from that impingement.

Axiom **149** Life depends upon an alignment of force vectors in the direction of survival and the nullification of force vectors in the direction of succumb in order to survive.

COROLLARY: Life depends upon an alignment of force vectors in the direction of succumb and the nullification of force vectors in the direction of survive in order to succumb.

Axiom **150** Any area of randomity gathers to it situations similar to it which do not contain actual efforts but only perceptions.

Axiom **151** Whether an organism has the goal of surviving or succumbing depends upon the amount of plus or minus randomity it has reactivated. (Not residual.)

Axiom **152** Survival is accomplished only by motion.

Axiom **153** In the physical universe the absence of motion is vanishment.

Axiom **154** Death is the equivalent to life of total lack of life-motivated motion.

Axiom **155** Acquisition of prosurvival matter and energy or organisms in space and time means increased motion.

Axiom **156** Loss of prosurvival matter and energy or organisms in space and time means decreased motion.

Axiom **157** Acquisition or proximity of matter, energy or organisms which assist the survival of an organism increase the survival potentials of an organism.

Axiom **158** Acquisition or proximity of matter, energy or organisms which inhibit the survival of an organism decrease its survival potential.

Axiom **159** Gain of survival energy, matter or organisms increases the freedom of an organism.

Axiom **160** Receipt or proximity of nonsurvival energy, matter or time decreases the freedom of motion of an organism.

Axiom **161** The control center attempts the halting or lengthening of time, the expansion or contraction of space and the decrease or increase of energy and matter.

This is a primary source of invalidation, and it is also a primary source of aberration.

Axiom **162** Pain is the balk of effort by counter-effort in great intensity, whether that effort is to remain at rest or in motion.

Axiom **163** Perception, including pain, can be exhausted from an area of plus or minus randomity, still leaving the effort and counter-effort of that plus or minus randomity.

Axiom **164** The rationality of the mind depends upon an optimum reaction toward time.

DEFINITION: Sanity, the computation of futures.
DEFINITION: Neurotic, the computation of present time only.
DEFINITION: Psychotic, computation only of past situations.

Axiom **165** Survival pertains only to the future.

COROLLARY: Succumb pertains only to the present and past.

Axiom **166** An individual is as happy as he can perceive survival potentials in the future.

Axiom **167** As the needs of any organism are met it rises higher and higher in its efforts along the dynamics.

An organism which achieves ARC with itself can better achieve ARC with sex in the future; having achieved this it can achieve ARC with groups; having achieved this, it can achieve ARC with mankind, etc.

Axiom **168** Affinity, reality and communication coexist in an inextricable relationship.

The coexistent relationship between affinity, reality and communication is such that none can be increased without increasing the other two and none can be decreased without decreasing the other two.

Axiom **169** Any aesthetic product is a symbolic facsimile or combination of facsimiles of theta or physical universes in varied randomities and volumes of randomities with the interplay of tones.

Axiom **170** An aesthetic product is an interpretation of the universes by an individual or group mind.

Axiom **171** Delusion is the postulation by the imagination of occurrences in areas of plus or minus randomity.

Axiom **172** Dreams are the imaginative reconstruction of areas of randomity or the resymbolization of the efforts of theta.

Axiom **173** A motion is created by the degree of optimum randomity introduced by the counter-effort to an organism's effort.

Axiom **174** MEST which has been mobilized by life forms is in more affinity with life organisms than nonmobilized MEST.

Axiom **175** All past perception, conclusion and existence moments, including those of plus or minus randomity, are recoverable to the control center of the organism.

Axiom **176** The ability to produce survival effort on the part of an organism is affected by the degrees of randomity existing in its past. (This includes learning.)

Axiom **177** Areas of past plus or minus randomity can be readdressed by the control center of an organism and the plus or minus randomity exhausted.

Axiom **178** The exhaustion of past plus or minus randomities permits the control center of an organism to effect its own efforts toward survival goals.

Axiom **179** The exhaustion of self-determined effort from a past area of plus or minus randomity nullifies the effectiveness of that area.

Axiom **180** Pain is the randomity produced by sudden or strong counter-efforts.

Axiom **181** Pain is stored as plus or minus randomity.

Axiom **182** Pain, as an area of plus or minus randomity, can reinflict itself upon the organism.

Axiom **183** Past pain becomes ineffective upon the organism when the randomity of its area is addressed and aligned.

Axiom **184** The earlier the area of plus or minus randomity, the greater self-produced effort existed to repel it.

Axiom **185** Later areas of plus or minus randomity cannot be realigned easily until earlier areas are realigned.

Axiom **186** Areas of plus or minus randomity become increased in activity when perceptions of similarity are introduced into them.

Axiom **187** Past areas of plus or minus randomity can be reduced and aligned by address to them in present time.

Axiom **188** Absolute good and absolute evil do not exist in the MEST universe.

Axiom **189** That which is good for an organism may be defined as that which promotes the survival of that organism.

COROLLARY: Evil may be defined as that which inhibits or brings plus or minus randomity into the organism, which is contrary to the survival motives of the organism.

Axiom **190** Happiness consists in the act of bringing alignment into hitherto resisting plus or minus randomity. Neither the act or action of attaining survival, nor the accomplishment of this act itself, brings about happiness.

Axiom **191** Construction is an alignment of data.

COROLLARY: Destruction is a plus or minus randomity of data.
The effort of constructing is the alignment toward the survival of the aligning organism.
Destruction is the effort of bringing randomity into an area.

Axiom **192** Optimum survival behavior consists of effort in the maximum survival interest in everything concerned in the dynamics.

Axiom **193** The optimum survival solution of any problem would consist of the highest attainable survival for every dynamic concerned.

Axiom **194** The worth of any organism consists of its value to the survival of its own THETA along any dynamic.

The Scientology Axioms

In the Scientology Axioms, written by L. Ron Hubbard in 1954, we find a recapitulation of all the earlier Axioms and Logics, boiled down to a more practical, more fundamental and more forthright list. These axioms are best compared to the axioms of geometry. But the axioms of geometry are really much cruder than the Scientology Axioms, since geometry proves itself by itself and the Axioms of Scientology prove themselves throughout all of life.

Axiom **1** Life is basically a static.

DEFINITION: *A life static has no mass, no motion, no wavelength, no location in space or in time. It has the ability to postulate and to perceive.*

Axiom **2** The static is capable of considerations, postulates and opinions.

Axiom **3** Space, energy, objects, form and time are the result of considerations made and/or agreed upon by the static and are perceived solely because the static considers that it can perceive them.

Axiom **4** Space is a viewpoint of dimension.

Axiom **5** Energy consists of postulated particles in space.

Axiom **6** Objects consist of grouped particles.

Axiom **7** Time is basically a postulate that space and particles will persist.

Axiom **8** The apparency of time is the change of position of particles in space.

Axiom **9** Change is the primary manifestation of time.

Axiom **10** The highest purpose in the universe is the creation of an effect.

Axiom **11** The considerations resulting in conditions of existence are fourfold:

a. AS-ISNESS is the condition of immediate creation without persistence, and is the condition of existence which exists at the moment of creation and the moment of destruction, and is different from other considerations in that it does not contain survival.

b. ALTER-ISNESS is the consideration which introduces change, and therefore time and persistence, into an AS-ISNESS to obtain persistency.

c. ISNESS is an apparency of existence brought about by the continuous alteration of an AS-ISNESS. This is called, when agreed upon, reality.

d. NOT-ISNESS is the effort to handle ISNESS by reducing its condition through the use of force. It is an apparency and cannot entirely vanquish an ISNESS.

Axiom **12** The primary condition of any universe is that two spaces, energies or objects must not occupy the same space. When this condition is violated (a perfect duplicate) the apparency of any universe or any part thereof is nulled.

Axiom **13** The cycle of action of the physical universe is create, survive (which is persist), destroy.

Axiom **14** Survival is accomplished by alter-isness and not-isness, by which is gained the persistency known as time.

Axiom **15** Creation is accomplished by the postulation of an as-isness.

Axiom **16** Complete destruction is accomplished by the postulation of the as-isness of any existence and the parts thereof.

Axiom **17** The static, having postulated as-isness, then practices alter-isness, and so achieves the apparency of isness and so obtains reality.

Axiom **18** The static, in practicing not-isness, brings about the persistence of unwanted existences, and so brings about unreality, which includes forgetfulness, unconsciousness and other undesirable states.

Axiom **19** Bringing the static to view as-is any condition devaluates that condition.

Axiom **20** Bringing the static to create a perfect duplicate causes the vanishment of any existence or part thereof.

A perfect duplicate is an additional creation of the object, its energy and space, in its own space, in its own time using its own energy. This violates the condition that two objects must not occupy the same space, and causes the vanishment of the object.

Axiom **21** Understanding is composed of affinity, reality and communication.

Axiom **22** The practice of not-isness reduces understanding.

Axiom **23** The static has the capability of total knowingness. Total knowingness would consist of total ARC.

Axiom **24** Total ARC would bring about the vanishment of all mechanical conditions of existence.

Axiom **25** Affinity is a scale of attitudes which falls away from the coexistence of static, through the interpositions of distance and energy, to create identity, down to close proximity but mystery.

By the practice of isness (beingness) and not-isness (refusal to be) individuation progresses from the knowingness of complete identification down through the introduction of more and more distance and less and less duplication, through lookingness, emotingness, effortingness, thinkingness, symbolizingness, eatingness, sexingness, and so through to not-knowingness (mystery). Until the point of mystery is reached, some communication is possible, but even at mystery an attempt to communicate continues. Here we have, in the case of an individual, a gradual falling away from the belief that one can assume a complete affinity down to the conviction that all is a complete mystery. Any individual is somewhere on this Know to Mystery Scale. The original Chart of Human Evaluation was the emotion section of this scale.

Axiom **26** Reality is the agreed-upon apparency of existence.

Axiom **27** An actuality can exist for one individually, but when it is agreed with by others it can be said to be a reality.

The anatomy of reality is contained in isness, which is composed of as-isness and alter-isness. An isness is an apparency, not an actuality. The actuality is as-isness altered so as to obtain a persistency.

Unreality is the consequence and apparency of the practice of not-isness.

Axiom 28 Communication is the consideration and action of impelling an impulse or particle from source-point across a distance to receipt-point, with the intention of bringing into being at the receipt-point a duplication and understanding of that which emanated from the source-point.

The formula of communication is: cause, distance, effect, with intention, attention and duplication with understanding.
The component parts of communication are consideration, intention, attention, cause, source-point, distance, effect, receipt-point, duplication, understanding, the velocity of the impulse or particle, nothingness or somethingness.
A noncommunication consists of barriers. Barriers consist of space, interpositions (such as walls and screens of fast-moving particles) and time. A communication, by definition, does not need to be two-way. When a communication is returned, the formula is repeated, with the receipt-point now becoming a source-point and the former source-point now becoming a receipt-point.

Axiom 29 In order to cause an as-isness to persist, one must assign other authorship to the creation than his own. Otherwise, his view of it would cause its vanishment.

Any space, energy, form, object, individual or physical universe condition can exist only when an alteration has occurred of the original as-isness so as to prevent a casual view from vanishing it. In other words, anything which is

persisting must contain a "lie" so that the original consideration is not completely duplicated.

Axiom 30 The general rule of auditing is that anything which is unwanted and yet persists must be thoroughly viewed, at which time it will vanish.

If only partially viewed, its intensity, at least, will decrease.

Axiom 31 Goodness and badness, beautifulness and ugliness are alike considerations and have no other basis than opinion.

Axiom 32 Anything which is not directly observed tends to persist.

Axiom 33 Any as-isness which is altered by not-isness (by force) tends to persist.

Axiom 34 Any isness, when altered by force, tends to persist.

Axiom 35 The ultimate truth is a static.

A static has no mass, meaning, mobility, no wavelength, no time, no location in space, no space. This has the technical name of "basic truth."

Axiom 36 A lie is a second postulate, statement or condition designed to mask a primary postulate which is permitted to remain.

EXAMPLES:
Neither truth nor a lie is a motion or alteration of a particle from one position to another.

A lie is a statement that a particle having moved did not move, or a statement that a particle, not having moved, did move.

The basic lie is that a consideration which was made was not made or that it was different.

Axiom **37** When a primary consideration is altered but still exists, persistence is achieved for the altering consideration.

All persistence depends on the basic truth, but the persistence is of the altering consideration, for the basic truth has neither persistence nor impersistence.

Axiom **38** 1. Stupidity is the unknownness of consideration.
2. Mechanical definition: Stupidity is the unknownness of time, place, form and event.
1. Truth is the exact consideration.
2. Truth is the exact time, place, form and event.

Thus we see that failure to discover truth brings about stupidity.

Thus we see that the discovery of truth would bring about an as-isness by actual experiment.

Thus we see that an ultimate truth would have no time, place, form or event.

Thus, then, we perceive that we can achieve a persistence only when we mask a truth.

Lying is an alteration of time, place, event or form.

Lying becomes alter-isness, becomes stupidity.

(The blackness of cases is an accumulation of the case's own or another's lies.)

Anything which persists must avoid as-isness. Thus, anything, to persist, must contain a lie.

Axiom **39** Life poses problems for its own solution.

Axiom **40** Any problem, to be a problem, must contain a lie. If it were truth, it would unmock.

An "unsolvable problem" would have the greatest persistence. It would also contain the greatest number of altered facts. To make a problem, one must introduce alter-isness.

Axiom **41** That into which alter-isness is introduced becomes a problem.

Axiom **42** Matter, energy, space and time persists because it is a problem.

It is a problem because it contains alter-isness.

Axiom **43** Time is the primary source of untruth.

Time states the untruth of consecutive considerations.

Axiom **44** Theta, the static, has no location in matter, energy, space or time, but is capable of consideration.

Axiom **45** Theta can consider itself to be placed, at which moment it becomes placed, and to that degree a problem.

Axiom **46** Theta can become a problem by its considerations, but then becomes MEST.

MEST is that form of theta which is a problem.

Axiom **47** Theta can resolve problems.

Axiom **48** Life is a game wherein theta as the static solves the problems of theta as MEST.

Axiom **49** To solve any problem it is only necessary to become theta, the solver, rather than theta, the problem.

Axiom **50** Theta as MEST must contain considerations which are lies.

Axiom **51** Postulates and live communication not being MEST and being senior to MEST can accomplish change in MEST without bringing about a persistence of MEST. Thus auditing can occur.

Axiom **52** MEST persists and solidifies to the degree that it is not granted life.

Axiom **53** A stable datum is necessary to the alignment of data.

Axiom **54** A tolerance of confusion and an agreed-upon stable datum on which to align the data in a confusion are at once necessary for a sane reaction on the eight dynamics. (This defines sanity.)

Axiom **55** The cycle of action is a consideration. Create, survive, destroy, the cycle of action accepted by the genetic entity, is only a consideration which can be changed by the thetan making a new consideration or different action cycles.

Axiom **56** Theta brings order to chaos.

COROLLARY: Chaos brings disorder to theta.

Axiom **57** Order manifests when communication, control and havingness are available to theta.

DEFINITIONS:
Communication: the interchange of ideas across space.
Control: positive postulating, which is intention, and the execution thereof.
Havingness: that which permits the experience of mass and pressure.

Axiom **58** Intelligence and judgment are measured by the ability to evaluate relative importances.

COROLLARY: The ability to evaluate importances and unimportances is the highest faculty of logic.
COROLLARY: Identification is a monotone assignment of importance.
COROLLARY: Identification is the inability to evaluate differences in time, location, form, composition or importance.

The above is a summary of states of being which can be used to create, cause to persist, or destroy.

Having agreed to the mechanics and retaining the agreements, the thetan can yet make innumerable postulates which by their contradiction and complexity, create, cause to persist, and destroy human behavior.

The Prelogics

L. Ron Hubbard analyzed life in its relationship to matter, energy, space and time and as a result discovered the Prelogics. These were published in late 1951 following many years of research into the nature of life and the spirituality of man. All manifestations of thought and all difficulties of thought find their basis in the Prelogics.

Knowledge is a pyramid, and knowledge as a pyramid has a common denominator which evaluates all other data below it. At the top point of this pyramid, we have what could be called a Q or a common denominator. It is in common to every other datum in this pyramid full of data.

The Qs are the highest echelon from which all other things are derived. "Q" comes from *quod* in Q.E.D. (*quod erat demonstrandum*, meaning "which was to be shown or demonstrated," used especially in mathematical proofs). Q may be further defined this way: It is the level from which we are now viewing the common denominator to all experience which we can now view.

Q simply means the most common datum that sums all other data.

Q1 The common denominator of all life impulses is self-determinism.

Q2 Self-determinism may be defined as the location of matter and energy in space and time, as well as a creation of time and space in which to locate matter and energy.

Q3 The identification of the source of that which places matter and energy and originates space and time is not necessary to the resolution of this problem at this time.

Q4 Universes are created by the application of self-determinism on eight dynamics.

Q5 Self-determinism, applied, will create, conserve, alter and possibly destroy universes.

The Factors

(Summation of the considerations and examinations of the human spirit and the material universe completed between A.D. 1923 and 1953.)

1 Before the beginning was a Cause and the entire purpose of the Cause was the creation of effect.

2 In the beginning and forever is the decision and the decision is TO BE.

3 The first action of beingness is to assume a viewpoint.

4 The second action of beingness is to extend from the viewpoint, points to view, which are dimension points.

5 Thus there is space created, for the definition of space is: viewpoint of dimension. And the purpose of a dimension point is space and a point of view.

6 The action of a dimension point is reaching and withdrawing.

7 And from the viewpoint to the dimension points there are connection and interchange. Thus new dimension points are made. Thus there is communication.

8 And thus there is light.

9 And thus there is energy.

10 And thus there is life.

11 But there are other viewpoints and these viewpoints outthrust points to view. And there comes about an interchange amongst viewpoints; but the interchange is never otherwise than in terms of exchanging dimension points.

12 The dimension point can be moved by the viewpoint, for the viewpoint, in addition to creative ability and consideration, possesses volition and potential independence of action; and the viewpoint, viewing dimension points, can change in relation to its own or other dimension points or viewpoints. Thus comes about all the fundamentals there are to motion.

13 The dimension points are each and every one, whether large or small, *solid*. And they are solid solely because the viewpoints say they are solid.

14 Many dimension points combine into larger gases, fluids or solids. Thus there is matter. But the most valued point is admiration, and admiration is so strong its absence alone permits persistence.

15 The dimension point can be different from other dimension points and thus can possess an individual quality. And many dimension points can possess a similar quality, and others can possess a similar quality unto themselves. Thus comes about the quality of classes of matter.

16 The viewpoint can combine dimension points into forms and the forms can be simple or complex and can be at different distances from the viewpoints and so there can be combinations of form. And the forms are capable of motion and the viewpoints are capable of motion and so there can be motion of forms.

17 And the opinion of the viewpoint regulates the consideration of the forms, their stillness or their motion, and these considerations consist of assignment of beauty or ugliness to the forms and these considerations alone are art.

18 It is the opinions of the viewpoints that some of these forms should endure. Thus there is survival.

19 And the viewpoint can never perish; but the form can perish.

20 And the many viewpoints, interacting, become dependent upon one another's forms and do not choose to distinguish completely the ownership of dimension points and so comes about a dependency upon the dimension points and upon the other viewpoints.

21 From this comes a consistency of viewpoint of the interaction of dimension points and this, regulated, is TIME.

22 And there are universes.

23 The universes, then, are three in number: the universe created by one viewpoint, the universe created by every other viewpoint, the universe created by the mutual action of viewpoints which is agreed to be upheld — the physical universe.

24 And the viewpoints are never seen. And the viewpoints consider more and more that the dimension points are valuable. And the viewpoints try to become the anchor points and forget that they can create more points and space and forms. Thus comes about scarcity. And the dimension points can perish and so the viewpoints assume that they, too, can perish.

25 Thus comes about death.

26 The manifestations of pleasure and pain, of thought, emotion and effort, of thinking, of sensation, of affinity, reality, communication, of behavior and being are thus derived and the riddles of our universe are apparently contained and answered herein.

27 There *is* beingness, but man believes there is only becomingness.

28 The resolution of any problem posed hereby is the establishment of viewpoints and dimension points, the betterment of condition and concourse amongst dimension points, and, thereby, viewpoints, and the remedy of abundance or scarcity in all things, pleasant or ugly, by the rehabilitation of the ability of the viewpoint to assume points of view and create and uncreate, neglect, start, change and stop dimension points of any kind at the determinism of the viewpoint. Certainty in all three universes must be regained, for certainty, not data, is knowledge.

29 In the opinion of the viewpoint, any beingness, any thing, is better than no thing, any effect is better than no effect, any universe better than no universe, any particle better than no particle, but the particle of admiration is best of all.

30 And above these things there might be speculation only. And below these things there is the playing of the game. But these things which are written here man can experience and know. And some may care to teach these things and some may care to use them to assist those in distress and some may desire to employ them to make individuals and organizations more able and so give to Earth a culture of which we can be proud.

Humbly tendered as a gift to man by L. Ron Hubbard, 23 April 1953

CHAPTER 42

IMPORTANT DATES IN SCIENTOLOGY

Considering the scope and influence of Scientology worldwide, it may be hard to believe the religion is only a few decades old. Yet despite its comparatively recent founding, Scientology has enjoyed a history that is remarkably rich in accomplishments. The most significant dates and events in this history as chronicled in the following pages provide great insight into Scientology's extraordinary vitality and growth.

1948

Dianetics: The Original Thesis distributed in manuscript form.

Winter–Spring 1950

Terra Incognita: The Mind published in the *Explorers Club Journal*.

April 1950

Dianetics: Evolution of a Science published.

9 May 1950

Dianetics: The Modern Science of Mental Health published. The book became an immediate bestseller, appearing on the *New York Times* bestseller list on 18 June, and remaining there for 28 consecutive weeks.

7 June 1950

Hubbard Dianetics Research Foundation established. This was the first organization of Dianetics and headquartered, until 1951, in Elizabeth, New Jersey. Branch offices were located in New York; Chicago; Washington, DC; Los Angeles and Hawaii.

July 1950

The first Dianetic Auditor's Bulletin published.

November 1950

Notes on the Lectures of L. Ron Hubbard compiled for early auditor training, then subsequently published (in January 1951) in book form.

1951

First Dianetics group formed in Australia.

28 June 1951

Science of Survival released at the first Annual Conference of Hubbard Dianetics Auditors in Wichita, Kansas, as a limited edition manuscript.

August 1951

Hardcover edition of *Science of Survival* first published.

Self Analysis book published.

October 1951

Child Dianetics book published.

November 1951

Advanced Procedure and Axioms book published in Wichita, Kansas.

December 1951

Dianetics: The Original Thesis book published.

Handbook for Preclears book published.

1952

First Dianetics groups formed in Israel and New Zealand.

12 February 1952

The Hubbard College, the first organization established and directed by L. Ron Hubbard, founded in Wichita, Kansas, to train Dianetics auditors.

May 1952

The Wichita training center moved to Phoenix, Arizona. There L. Ron Hubbard publicly announced the formal establishment of Scientology and the formation of the Hubbard Association of Scientologists International (HASI).

June 1952

Technique 88 lectures given in Phoenix, Arizona on the subjects of effort and energy.

July 1952

Scientology: A History of Man book published.

21 September 1952

L. Ron Hubbard began offering the first training course for auditors in England. He also established the first British Scientology organization, and a London branch of the Hubbard Association of Scientologists International.

November 1952

Scientology 8-80 book published.

December 1952

Scientology 8-8008 book published.

1 December 1952

The first lecture of the Philadelphia Doctorate Course was presented by L. Ron Hubbard in Philadelphia, Pennsylvania, and he presented the first copies of the *Scientology 8-8008* book.

April 1953

How to Live Though an Executive book published.

May 1953

The first Professional Auditor's Bulletin published.

30 September 1953

L. Ron Hubbard lectured at the First International Congress of Dianeticists and Scientologists in Philadelphia.

18 February 1954

The first Church of Scientology founded in Los Angeles, California.

19 July 1954

The first of the Phoenix Lectures delivered in Phoenix, Arizona.

December 1954

Dianetics 55! book published.

28 January 1955

The Church of Scientology of Auckland, New Zealand, founded.

April 1955

The Creation of Human Ability published.

Mid-1955

The Distribution Center in Silver Spring, Maryland, founded to publish and make Scientology materials easily available around the world.

21 July 1955

Founding Church of Scientology of Washington, DC, founded along with the first Academy of Scientology.

15 November 1955

Church of Scientology of New York founded.

Early 1956

Ron traveled to Dublin, Ireland, to establish Dianetics and Scientology in that country.

22 July 1956

The first Hubbard Communications Office Bulletin (HCOB) published.

28 July 1956

Following protests by Scientologists, unconstitutional provisions of the Alaska Mental Health Bill defeated in the United States Senate.

3 August 1956

The first Hubbard Communications Office Policy Letter (HCO PL) published.

September 1956

Scientology: The Fundamentals of Thought published.

30 November 1956

Church of Scientology of Seattle, Washington, founded.

December 1956

The Problems of Work published.

11 March 1957

Church of Scientology of Miami, Florida, founded.

12–15 April 1957

London Congress on Nuclear Radiation and Health Lectures delivered. They formed the basis for the book *All About Radiation*.

May 1957

All About Radiation published.

11 November 1957

Church of Scientology of Johannesburg, South Africa, founded.

July 1958

Clearing Congress Lectures, Washington, DC. The first six lectures of this congress were filmed in color and are available today in video cassette format.

1959

Release of the Hubbard Mark I E-Meter.

Spring 1959

Saint Hill Manor purchased by L. Ron Hubbard. Located in East Grinstead, Sussex, England, the Manor served as Mr. Hubbard's residence and as the communications center of Scientology.

26 June 1959

Hubbard Communications Office Worldwide established at Saint Hill Manor.

26 October 1959

Church of Scientology of Paris, France, founded.

7 and 8 November 1959

Melbourne Congress Lectures given in Melbourne, Australia.

23 November 1959

International Council for Dianetics and Scientology appointed.

1960

Release of the Hubbard Mark II E-Meter, soon followed by the Hubbard Mark III E-Meter.

1 January 1960

State of Man Congress Lectures given at the Shoreham Hotel in Washington, DC, between 1 and 3 January 1960.

March 1960

Have You Lived Before This Life? book published.

20 June 1960

Hubbard Association of Scientologists International established in Cape Town, South Africa.

30 December 1960

Hubbard Communications Office, Ltd., incorporated in the United States.

31 December 1960

Anatomy of the Human Mind Congress Lectures in Washington, DC, on 31 December and 1 January 1961.

3 January 1961

Release of the Hubbard Mark IV E-Meter.

28 January 1961

Church of Scientology of Cape Town, South Africa, founded.

24 March 1961

The Saint Hill Special Briefing Course began, drawing students from around the world. Mr. Hubbard personally conducted this course until 13 December 1966.

April 1962

Church of Scientology of Port Elizabeth, South Africa, founded.

Summer 1962

Release of the Hubbard Mark V E-Meter.

4 January 1963

FDA E-Meter raid: Agents of the United States Food and Drug Administration (FDA), assisted by longshoremen, raided the Founding Church of Scientology in Washington, DC, and seized Scientology books and E-Meters. Years of litigation resulted in a landmark religious recognition for the Church on 30 July 1971 and eventually won a full victory against the FDA on 1 March 1973. [See corresponding entries.]

4 November 1963

Church of Scientology of Detroit, Michigan, founded.

1 December 1963

Church of Scientology of Durban, South Africa, founded.

24 January 1964

Scientology Library and Research, Ltd., established to safeguard and preserve all Scientology materials.

May 1964

L. Ron Hubbard released the exact auditor training regimen, now known as the Academy Levels. These levels set exact standards and training requirements for certification.

June–September 1964

A series of lectures delivered to the Saint Hill Special Briefing Course by L. Ron Hubbard detail his breakthroughs in the field of education. These are later released as the Study Tapes.

November 1964

The Book of Case Remedies published.

8 December 1964

R6EW and Solo auditing released at Saint Hill Manor.

Church of Scientology of Hawaii founded.

7 February 1965

HCO Policy Letter *Keeping Scientology Working* issued to provide for the continued and exacting application of Scientology throughout the world.

May 1965

Power Processing, Grades V and VA on the Grade Chart released at Saint Hill. L. Ron Hubbard personally trained the first auditors.

5 May 1965

The Classification, Gradation and Awareness Chart, listing the levels of training and grades of processing, and laying out the Bridge to Total Freedom, was released at Saint Hill. With the release of the "Grade Chart," Grades 0 through IV were also released.

25 May 1965

The seven-division organizing board developed and released by L. Ron Hubbard to provide the basic pattern for all Scientology churches worldwide and facilitate their survival and expansion.

11 June 1965

Hubbard College of Scientology Saint Hill Foundation founded. Subsequently, Church Foundations, which operate in the evenings and on weekends, were established in all Scientology organizations so members who worked during the day could still participate in training and auditing.

5 September 1965

L. Ron Hubbard inaugurated the Clearing Course at Saint Hill Manor; the course is now available at the Advanced Organizations in Australia, United States, United Kingdom and Denmark, as well as the Flag Land Base.

28 September 1965

Victoria, Australia inquiry report on Scientology by Kevin V. Anderson released, which resulted in legislation against Scientology practices. This was overturned when the Church was granted religious recognition in February 1973. On 27 October 1983, after further legal victories, the Australian High Court granted the Church full religious tax exemption. [See entries at 15 February 1973 and 27 October 1983.]

December 1965

Scientology: A New Slant on Life published.

30 December 1965

Church of Scientology of Twin Cities (Minneapolis and St. Paul, Minnesota) founded.

19 February 1966

Narconon drug rehabilitation program founded.

April 1966

An Introduction to Scientology, one-hour interview with L. Ron Hubbard, filmed.

August 1966

OT I released.

September 1966

OT II released.

1 September 1966

L. Ron Hubbard resigned from the Board of Directors and post of Executive Director of Scientology organizations to continue his writing and research. He was given the title of Founder and his administrative duties were taken over by Executive Council Worldwide.

January 1967

Mr. Hubbard traveled from Saint Hill to Tangier, Morocco.

27 June 1967

Church of Scientology of Austin, Texas, founded.

12 August 1967

The Sea Organization (or Sea Org) officially established.

8 September 1967

Church of Scientology of Toronto, Canada, founded.

18 September 1967

Church of Scientology of Bulawayo, Zimbabwe, founded.

20 September 1967

In *Ron's Journal 67* (a recorded message to Scientologists) the major breakthrough level, OT III, the "Wall of Fire," announced and released.

27 November 1967

The first Scientology publications organization (Pubs Worldwide) established at Saint Hill Manor, England.

27 December 1967

The first Advanced Organization to offer the OT levels to Scientologists established aboard the *Royal Scotman*. (This ship became the flagship of the Sea Organization and was renamed the *Apollo*.)

January 1968

OT IV, V and VI released.

23 May 1968

Advanced Organization, Edinburgh, Scotland, established.

June 1968

Scientology publications organization moved from Saint Hill Manor to Edinburgh, Scotland.

5 June 1968

Church of Scientology of Denmark founded in Copenhagen.

12 June 1968

Hubbard Academy of Personal Independence of Edinburgh, Scotland, founded.

17 June 1968

Church of Scientology of San Francisco, California, founded.

July 1968

The first book to introduce Scientology ethics principles and formulas, *Introduction to Scientology Ethics*, released.

August 1968

American Saint Hill Organization (ASHO) and Advanced Organization Los Angeles (AOLA) opened in Los Angeles, California. During this month L. Ron Hubbard released and personally supervised the Class VIII Course aboard the flagship *Apollo*. He also released the Drug Rundown — his breakthrough in handling the effects of drugs.

The Phoenix Lectures published.

Freedom magazine established in the United Kingdom. With its main editorial offices in Los Angeles, this award-winning publication is now distributed worldwide.

24 September 1968

The first of the Class VIII Auditor Course Lectures given.

31 October 1968

Church of Scientology of Las Vegas, Nevada, founded.

12 December 1968

Church of Scientology of Pretoria, South Africa, founded.

1969

First Dianetics groups in Germany, Greece and Mexico established.

1969

The Citizens Commission on Human Rights (CCHR) founded in England. Now headquartered in Los Angeles, California.

31 January 1969

The Church of the New Faith founded in South Australia. This corporation included Scientology churches in Adelaide, Melbourne, Perth and Sydney.

14 February 1969

Publications organization moved from Edinburgh, Scotland, to Copenhagen, Denmark.

April 1969

Standard Dianetics released.

16 April 1969

Church of Scientology of Göteborg, Sweden, founded.

7 July 1969

Advanced Organization Denmark founded in Copenhagen to serve European and African Scientologists.

Church of Scientology of Saint Hill Europe founded.

22 July 1969

Church of Scientology of Copenhagen (a second church in Copenhagen, Denmark) founded.

9 October 1969

Church of Scientology of Stockholm, Sweden, founded.

1970

Criminon, the criminal rehabilitation program utilizing the discoveries of L. Ron Hubbard, founded.

22 February 1970

Church of Scientology Celebrity Centre Los Angeles founded.

25 June 1970

Expanded lower auditing grades (Grades 0 through IV) released.

17 August 1970

Advanced Organization United Kingdom moved from Edinburgh, Scotland, to Saint Hill, Sussex, England.

9 September 1970

OT VII released.

November 1970

Scientology 0-8: The Book of Basics published.

The Flag Executive Briefing Course initiated by L. Ron Hubbard, who personally supervised and lectured students aboard the *Apollo*.

13 November 1970

The Flag Bureaux established by the Sea Organization aboard the *Apollo* to supervise Scientology expansion around the world.

19 November 1970

Continental Liaison Offices (CLOs) established to supervise Church affairs in their respective continental areas: United States; United Kingdom; Europe; Australia, New Zealand and Oceania (ANZO); and Africa.

1971

Three new rundowns released: L10, L11 (the New Life Rundown) and L12 (the Flag OT Executive Rundown).

20 January 1971

Hubbard Scientology Organization of Plymouth, England, founded.

11 February 1971

Church of Scientology Publications Organization United States established.

9 March 1971

Church of Scientology of Buffalo, New York, founded.

13 March 1971

Church of Scientology of Boston, Massachusetts, founded.

31 March 1971

Church of Scientology of Vienna, Austria, founded.

13 April 1971

Church of Scientology of San Diego, California, founded.

26 April 1971

Church of Scientology of Portland, Oregon, founded.

June 1971

Word Clearing Methods 1, 2 and 3 released.

30 July 1971

After eight years of litigation against the United States Food and Drug Administration (FDA), the Founding Church of Scientology of Washington, DC, won full religious recognition for the E-Meter as a religious artifact which can only be used by Scientology ministers and ministers-in-training. [See 1 March 1973 entry.]

21 December 1971

Release of inquiry report by British Member of Parliament John Foster calling for an end to a then three-year ban on foreign Scientologists entering the United Kingdom to study Scientology. On 16 July 1980 the UK Home Office formally lifted the ban, although it had not been enforced. [See 16 July 1980 entry.]

1972

First Dianetics groups in Belgium and the Netherlands formed.

27 January 1972

Church of Scientology of St. Louis, Missouri, founded.

22 February 1972

Word Clearing Method 4 released.

13 March 1972

Church of Scientology of Amsterdam, Holland, founded.

4 April 1972

Primary Rundown released.

15 April 1972

Expanded Dianetics released.

22 May 1972

Church of Scientology of Melbourne, Australia, reincorporated (formerly the Church of the New Faith).

6 June 1972

Church of Scientology of Vancouver, Canada, founded.

21 June 1972

Word Clearing Methods 5, 6, 7 and 8 released.

21 July 1972

Church of Scientology of Sydney, Australia, reincorporated (formerly the Church of the New Faith).

28 July 1972

Applied Scholastics founded.

18 August 1972

Church of Scientology of Malmö, Sweden, founded.

17 October 1972

Church of Scientology of Perth, Australia, reincorporated (formerly the Church of the New Faith).

8 November 1972

Continental Liaison Offices established in Eastern United States (New York City) and in Western United States (Los Angeles).

30 January 1973

Word Clearing Method 9 released.

15 February 1973

The Church of Scientology in Australia recognized to perform marriages.

1 March 1973

After ten years of litigation against the United States Food and Drug Administration (FDA), the Founding Church of Scientology of Washington, DC, won final victory, and the E-Meters and books taken in the 1963 FDA raid were ordered returned to the Church.

23 January 1974

Introspection Rundown released.

12 March 1974

Church of Scientology of Manchester, England, founded.

13 March 1974

Church of Scientology of Montreal, Canada, founded.

Church of Scientology of Ottawa, Canada, founded.

22 March 1974

Church of Scientology of Sacramento, California, founded.

18 April 1974

Ministers of the Church of Scientology in New Zealand licensed to perform marriages.

15 June 1974

Church of Scientology of Denver, Colorado, founded.

July 1974

The first *Organization Executive Course* volumes published making Mr. Hubbard's administrative policies broadly available around the world.

6 October 1974

Vital Information Rundown released.

Setting sail from Madeira on 6 October, the *Apollo* crossed the Atlantic Ocean to Bermuda, arriving on 16 October.

24 December 1974

Church of Scientology of Arizona founded in Phoenix.

13 March 1975

Church of Scientology of Chicago, Illinois, founded.

16 March 1975

Church of Scientology of Philadelphia, Pennsylvania, founded.

June 1975

Dianetics and Scientology Technical Dictionary published.

October 1975

The Flag Service Organization moved ashore to temporary quarters in Daytona Beach, Florida, and retired the flagship *Apollo*.

24 November 1975

Education Alive founded in South Africa.

6 December 1975

The Flag Land Base established when the Flag Bureaux and the Flag Service Organization moved to the Fort Harrison Hotel and Clearwater Building in Clearwater, Florida.

Spring 1976

Universal Media Productions established in Clearwater, Florida, to produce Scientology films.

24 August 1976

The technical bulletins of Dianetics and Scientology released in published books for the first time.

International Prayer Day, the Church's International Conference for World Peace and Social Reform, held in Anaheim, California, and attended by 10,000 Scientologists from around the world.

December 1976

Modern Management Technology Defined—Hubbard Dictionary of Administration and Management published.

8 December 1976

The Church of Scientology in Stuttgart, Germany, won a decision recognizing it as a religious community.

1 January 1977

The former Cedars of Lebanon Medical Center in Hollywood acquired as a major center for Scientology in the Los Angeles area.

27 September 1977

The Church of Scientology of Los Angeles, moved into the former Cedars of Lebanon Medical Center building complex.

Fall 1977

Universal Media Productions reorganized as Source Productions in La Quinta, California, to produce Scientology technical instructional films.

9 December 1977

The Secret of Flag Results, a film written by L. Ron Hubbard, released.

9 March 1978

Church of Scientology of Milano, Italy, founded.

21 June 1978

The first Hubbard Communications Office Bulletin on New Era Dianetics (NED) written, introducing an effective refinement of Dianetics by L. Ron Hubbard based on thirty years of experience in the application of the subject.

20 July 1978

Church of Scientology of Bern, Switzerland, founded.

September 1978

Audited New Era Dianetics for OTs (New OT V) released.

24 September 1978

"Dianetic Clear" Hubbard Communications Office Bulletin released.

1979

The first Dianetics group in Ecuador formed.

1 February 1979

The World Institute of Scientology Enterprises (WISE) founded as a religious fellowship for Scientologists in the business community and to assist them in improving the ethical standards of their own businesses as well as of the business community at large.

13 March 1979

The Hubbard Mark VI E-Meter released.

30 April 1979

Watchdog Committee established.

1 July 1979

The Sandcastle Hotel in Clearwater, Florida, purchased as part of the Flag Land Base, an advanced religious retreat for Scientologists.

20 September 1979

Instituto de Filosofía Aplicada A.C. (Asociación Civil), Durango (IFAD), Mexico City, founded.

December 1979

The Purification Rundown released.

3 January 1980

Church of Scientology of Brescia, Italy, founded.

29 January 1980

OT Drug Rundown (New OT IV) released.

31 January 1980

Church of Scientology of Cincinnati, Ohio, founded.

February 1980

Senior Executive Strata established, comprised of International Executives covering each of the twelve points of expansion. These specialists serve on the staff of the Executive Director International.

7 February 1980

Asociación Cultural Dianética A.C., founded in Mexico City.

14 February 1980

Church of Scientology of Edmonton, Canada, formed.

13 March 1980

Church of Scientology of Brussels, Belgium, founded.

Church of Scientology of Novara, Italy, founded.

1 May 1980

Instituto Tecnológico de Dianética A.C., along with the Organización Desarrollo y Dianética A.C., founded in Mexico City.

8 May 1980

Church of Scientology of Birmingham, England, founded.

Instituto de Filosofía Aplicada A.C., Roma in Mexico City, founded.

Church of Scientology of Sunderland, England, founded.

15 May 1980

Church of Scientology of Albuquerque, New Mexico, founded.

Church of Scientology of Columbus, Ohio, founded.

Centro Cultural de Dianética of Bogotá, Colombia, founded.

22 May 1980

Church of Scientology of Basel, Switzerland, founded.

Church of Scientology of Angers, France, founded.

29 May 1980

Church of Scientology of Canberra, Australian Capital Territory, founded.

June 1980

An extensive project to transcribe and publish all of L. Ron Hubbard's lectures on Dianetics and Scientology resulted in the release of the original *Research and Discovery Series Volume 1.* This series represents the complete running record of L. Ron Hubbard's research into the subject of the mind, life and spirit.

5 June 1980

Church of Scientology of Berlin, Germany, formed.

Church of Scientology of Rome, Italy, founded.

Church of Scientology of Pasadena, California, founded.

12 June 1980

Church of Scientology of Santa Barbara, California, founded.

Church of Scientology of Kitchener, Canada, founded.

Church of Scientology of San Fernando Valley, California, founded.

19 June 1980

Church of Scientology of Padova, Italy, founded.

26 June 1980

Church of Scientology of Oslo, Norway, founded.

10 July 1980

Centro de Dianética Polanco, Mexico City, founded.

Church of Scientology of Geneva, Switzerland, founded.

Church of Scientology of Pordenone, Italy, founded.

16 July 1980

The United Kingdom Home Office officially lifted the ban on foreign Scientologists entering the United Kingdom to study Scientology.

17 July 1980

Church of Scientology of Madrid, Spain, founded.

August 1980

Golden Era Productions, established as the international dissemination center for Scientology to produce religious films, recordings and other material.

The Success Through Communication Course released.

7 August 1980

Church of Scientology of Saint-Étienne, France, founded.

September 1980

New OT VI and VII released. The Hubbard Solo New Era Dianetics for OTs (Solo NOTs) Course (New OT VI), utilizes techniques Mr. Hubbard developed to help one be both auditor and preclear and audit oneself on the level of OT VII, Solo New Era Dianetics for OTs, which has as its end result Cause over Life.

25 September 1980

Scientology and Dianetics College in Tel Aviv, Israel, founded.

2 October 1980

Church of Scientology of Harare, Zimbabwe, founded.

Church of Scientology of Quebec, Canada, formed.

1981

CLO Canada established in Toronto and CLO Latin America (LATAM) established in Mexico City.

19 February 1981

The Way to Happiness published.

Spring 1981

Celebrity Centre moved into the famous Château Elysée, a French Normandie-style hotel in Hollywood, the home of many prominent actors, actresses and other celebrities in the 1930s and 1940s. In 1987, this building was registered as an historic landmark in the state of California.

19 March 1981

Church of Scientology of Johannesburg North, Johannesburg, South Africa, founded.

Asociación Cultural Dianética de Venezuela A.C., formed.

19 May 1981

Church of Scientology Flag Service Organization established as an independent corporation.

26 May 1981

Church of Scientology of Los Angeles, originally founded in 1954 as part of Church of Scientology of California, incorporated as a separate corporation.

September 1981

The Case He Couldn't Crack, a film written by L. Ron Hubbard, released.

1 October 1981

Church of Scientology Celebrity Centre Las Vegas founded.

19 November 1981

Church of Scientology International (CSI) founded as the mother church of Scientology. CSI's staff manages Scientology's international ecclesiastical hierarchy of churches.

3 December 1981

Church of Scientology of Winnipeg, Canada, founded.

9 December 1981

Operation and Transport Liaison Office Iberia established in Madrid, Spain.

22 December 1981

Scientology Missions International (SMI) founded.

31 December 1981

Church of Scientology of Aarhus, Denmark, founded.

Church of Scientology of Barcelona, Spain, founded.

7 January 1982

Church of Scientology Celebrity Centre Paris founded.

11 February 1982

Church of Scientology of Torino, Italy, founded.

4 March 1982

Church of Scientology of Clermont-Ferrand, France, founded.

11 March 1982

Church of Scientology of Tampa, Florida, founded.

Church of Scientology of Lyon, France, founded.

1 April 1982

Church of Scientology of Verona, Italy, formed.

Church of Scientology of Orlando, Florida, founded.

16 May 1982

Religious Technology Center (RTC) incorporated. L. Ron Hubbard donated all trademarks of Dianetics and Scientology to RTC.

28 May 1982

Church of Spiritual Technology founded.

17 June 1982

Church of Scientology of Lisbon, Portugal, founded.

Church of Scientology of Kansas City, Missouri, founded.

15 July 1982

Church of Scientology of Long Island, New York, formed.

19 July 1982

The International Network of Computer Organized Management (INCOMM) formed within the Church of Scientology International. INCOMM developed and today operates a major management computer system which fully supports the international ecclesiastical operations of the Church of Scientology.

29 July 1982

Church of Scientology of New Haven, Connecticut, founded.

5 August 1982

Church of Scientology of Brisbane, Australia, founded.

12 August 1982

Church of Scientology of Ann Arbor, Michigan, founded.

1983

The Planetary Dissemination Organization formed to provide dissemination campaigns to make Dianetics and Scientology even more widely available.

6 January 1983

Organización Cultural Dianética de Guadalajara A.C., founded in Guadalajara, Jalisco, Mexico.

3 March 1983

Agents of the Ontario Provincial Police raided the Church of Scientology in Toronto, Ontario, seizing millions of pages of documents. On 2 December 1991, the court declared that the raid violated the Canadian Charter of Rights and Freedoms. [See 2 December 1991 entry.]

5 May 1983

Church of Scientology of Hamburg, Germany, formed.

16 June 1983

Church of Scientology of Zurich, Switzerland, formed.

7 July 1983

Led by a team of Sea Organization members, the Advanced Organization Saint Hill Australia, New Zealand, Oceania (AOSH ANZO) opened its doors in Sydney, Australia to minister Advanced Courses.

8 September 1983

Church of Scientology of Orange County, California, formed.

27 October 1983

The Australian High Court granted the Church full religious recognition. The case also set the criteria for defining religion in Australia. [See entries at 15 February 1973 and 28 September 1965.]

10 November 1983

Church of Scientology Celebrity Centre New York founded.

December 1983

Formation of the Office of Special Affairs International, a network within the Church of Scientology International which plans and supervises the legal affairs of the Church under the board of directors.

1 March 1984

Church of Scientology of Celebrity Centre Hamburg founded. Later became Church of Scientology of Eppendorf.

Church of Scientology of Düsseldorf, Germany, founded.

1 June 1984

First cassette lectures by L. Ron Hubbard on the subjects of Dianetics and Scientology released in Clearsound, a new sound-reproduction technology developed by Mr. Hubbard.

5 June 1984

False Purpose Rundown released.

31 July 1984

The Way to Happiness Foundation incorporated in the state of California.

September 1984

Purification: An Illustrated Answer to Drugs released.

Purification Rundown Delivery Manual published.

7 October 1984

The International Association of Scientologists (IAS) formed by a group of dedicated Scientologists and the Pledge to Mankind signed at Saint Hill in England, further uniting Scientologists everywhere.

8 November 1984

Celebrity Centre International formed to give guidance to the network of Celebrity Centres throughout the world.

29 November 1984

Church of Scientology of Stevens Creek in San Jose, California, founded.

December 1984

The Flag Bureaux moved to Los Angeles to allow expansion of service delivery at the Flag Service Organization in Clearwater.

1985

New OT I released.

May–July 1985

Religious Freedom Crusade in Portland, Oregon drew tens of thousands of Scientologists from around the world to protest an outrageous verdict in a court case involving religious bigotry and intolerance. The case was declared a mistrial in July.

4 July 1985

Church of Scientology of Monza, Italy, founded.

5 October 1985

International Association of Scientologists (IAS) Freedom Medal instituted at first annual IAS convention in Copenhagen to acknowledge outstanding contributions toward the betterment of life and preservation of freedom on Earth.

IAS Medals are presented to:

Jeff Pomerantz, actor, for tireless devotion to protecting religious freedom and as a spokesman for and leader of Religious Freedom Crusades in Portland and Los Angeles.

Michel Raoust, for his outspoken defense of religious freedom in France, and for spearheading two major Religious Freedom Crusades throughout that country.

Barbara Ayash, for bringing the precepts of the nonreligious moral code *The Way to Happiness* to gang members in the inner city of Los Angeles, thus helping to put an end to violence and criminality.

17 November 1985

Clear Certainty Rundown released.

1986

First groups in Chile and Nigeria formed.

24 January 1986

L. Ron Hubbard departed this life at his ranch near San Luis Obispo, California, leaving the legacy of his life's work to the religion he founded.

16 March 1986

The Road to Freedom music album, which set to music many basic principles of life, released internationally. All music and lyrics were written earlier by Mr. Hubbard.

19 June 1986

Church of Scientology Celebrity Centre of Portland, Oregon, founded.

July–September 1986

Religious Freedom Crusade in Los Angeles, California.

16 September 1986

The Sea Organization Motor Vessel *Freewinds* purchased.

11 October 1986

IAS Freedom Medals are presented to:

Dennis Dubin, for his work to make Scientology well-known and well thought of among community and national leaders and for establishing major international cultural events at the Flag Land Base.

Paul Rood, for leading religious freedom campaigns in Europe. He was instrumental in establishing the Church of Scientology European Human Rights office and introducing many government officials to Scientology.

Don Moore, for conducting community affairs activities for the Church of Scientology and promoting the Canadian Charter of Rights and Freedoms.

16 October 1986

Church of Scientology of Nuoro, Italy, founded.

4 December 1986

On 4 December 1986, all orgs, missions and Narconon centers in Italy raided and closed down in a suppressive effort to stop Scientology in Italy. Churches and Narconons reopened the next day. Scientologists from around the world responded with a massive crusade for religious freedom. [See entry of 8 October 1997.]

1987

First groups in Ghana and Dominican Republic formed.

12 March 1987

Church of Scientology Celebrity Centre of Dallas, Texas, founded.

11 October 1987

IAS Freedom Medals are presented to:

Peter Schless, for leading internationally known musicians and celebrities who joined thousands of Scientologists in Religious Freedom Crusades in Portland and Los Angeles.

Andrik Schapers, for his dedication to religious freedom, leading Crusades in the United States and Europe.

Philippe de Henning, who as a champion driver on the international racing circuit, brought word of Dianetics and Scientology to millions with his "Dianetics" race car.

Dennis Clarke, for exposing ongoing abuses in the field of psychiatry. Through his efforts, millions of people across the country were warned of the dangers of psychiatric drugging and practices such as electric shock treatment and lobotomy.

24 December 1987

Church of Scientology of Brighton, England, founded.

1988

First groups in Hungary and Kenya formed.

7 January 1988

Church of Scientology of Lausanne, Switzerland, founded.

Evolution of a Science, a public Scientology motion picture, released.

789

March 1988

History of the E-Meter, a Technical Training Film, released.

13 March 1988

Advanced Organization Los Angeles and the Church of Scientology Orange County (California) acknowledged for achieving the size of old Saint Hill. (The original Saint Hill Organization, located at Saint Hill Manor, East Grinstead, Sussex, England, was very large when L. Ron Hubbard was its Executive Director. One of the first goals of all Scientology churches and organizations is to achieve the size of Saint Hill when it was under Mr. Hubbard's direction in the mid-1960s. As each church or organization achieves this goal, they are acknowledged at the annual celebration of Mr. Hubbard's birthday.)

Hubbard Professional Mark Super VII E-Meter released, developed according to L. Ron Hubbard's specifications and directions.

20 March 1988

Thirty-eight years after its initial publication, *Dianetics* returned as number one on the *New York Times* bestseller list, and remained on the list for a total of seventy weeks.

12 April 1988

The Church of Scientology in Portugal received religious recognition.

May 1988

What Happened to These Civilizations? a public Scientology motion picture, released.

9 May 1988

Hubbard Dianetics Seminar released.

Hubbard Dianetics Auditor Course released.

6 June 1988

Christening of the Sea Organization Motor Vessel *Freewinds* in Curaçao. Maiden voyage of the *Freewinds*.

The Flag Ship Service Organization and the *Freewinds* Ship Organization began operation aboard the Sea Organization Motor Vessel *Freewinds*.

7 June 1988

At sea: The New OT VIII course room opened aboard the *Freewinds,* and with it began the ministry of New OT VIII, Truth Revealed.

15 September 1988

Church of Scientology Celebrity Centre Düsseldorf, Germany, founded.

October 1988

The Technical Training Film *The Classification, Gradation and Awareness Chart*, written by L. Ron Hubbard, released.

8 October 1988

IAS Freedom Medals are presented to:

Jan Eastgate, for spearheading Citizens Commission on Human Rights social reform actions in Australia, where she initiated a major government investigation into "deep sleep therapy" (drug-induced coma, accompanied by electroshock), which was given to scores of patients, many of whom later died. This brutal practice was subsequently banned.

Rena Weinberg, for establishing Education Alive and bringing L. Ron Hubbard's study technology to black South African teachers and students. Tens of thousands of teachers and millions of students benefited.

Chick Corea, internationally popular jazz musician, for setting an example to millions of the benefits of Dianetics and Scientology and tirelessly crusading for religious freedom around the world.

30 October 1988

Dianetics released in Chinese to the people of mainland China and became a number one bestseller overnight.

14 November 1988

Association for Better Living and Education incorporated.

17 November 1988

Church of Scientology of Frankfurt, Germany, founded.

December 1988

The Married Couple, a public Scientology motion picture, released.

31 December 1988

Ten new Life Improvement Courses released, including: Overcoming Ups and Downs in Life; Starting a Successful Marriage; How to Maintain a Successful Marriage; How to Be a Successful Parent; How to Improve Relationships with Others; Personal Values and Integrity Course; and How to Make Work Easier.

Church of Scientology of Tokyo, Japan, founded.

1989

First groups formed in East Germany, Panama and South Korea.

13 March 1989

Advanced Organization Saint Hill United Kingdom and the Church of Scientology Hamburg (Germany) formally acknowledged at the annual celebration of L. Ron Hubbard's birthday for achieving the size of old Saint Hill.

May 1989

Release of *Assists*, a Technical Training Film, written by L. Ron Hubbard.

13 May 1989

The Flag Command Bureaux moved to the newly renovated Hollywood Guaranty Building, a twelve-story office building for international Scientology management and training of church executives from around the world.

August 1989

Between August of 1989 and the fall of 1990, the Church conducted an extensive dissemination campaign in the United States consisting of publishing advertisements in major US news and consumer magazines, each one featuring a basic Scientology precept.

5 October 1989

Church of Scientology of Hanover, Germany, opened.

6 October 1989

Completion and official opening of the Saint Hill Castle, a college for Scientology on the grounds of Saint Hill, first envisioned and designed by L. Ron Hubbard in 1965. The first castle to be built in England for fifty-nine years, it was inspired by other historic castles, particularly an eleventh-century Norman castle at Tonbridge, Kent. It provides greatly expanded facilities for the Advanced Organization and Saint Hill UK and Saint Hill Foundation.

7 October 1989

IAS Freedom Medals are awarded to:

Judy Norton, actress, for reaching millions via newspaper and magazine articles and more than 1,000 interviews, each carrying the message that Dianetics is the answer to improving lives.

Nicky Hopkins, renowned rock keyboardist and recording artist, for making Dianetics and Scientology broadly known in country after country throughout the world, bringing the news of LRH technology to millions.

Boris Levitsky, for his role in opening China to Dianetics and Scientology and introducing the people of China to L. Ron Hubbard's study technology.

12 October 1989

Church of Scientology of Atlanta, Georgia, opened.

December 1989

The Narconon Chilocco New Life Center, located on 167 acres on the Great Plains of Oklahoma, began conducting the Narconon program. It is the largest drug rehabilitation center in the world.

Release of *The Professional TR Course*, a Technical Training Film, written and narrated by L. Ron Hubbard.

28 December 1989

Church of Scientology of Stuttgart, Germany, founded.

31 December 1989

The Professional TR Course released with Clay Table Processing on communication.

1990

First groups formed in Taiwan, China, Romania, Algeria and Argentina; and, as a result of earlier missionary activity, groups are also formed in the former Eastern European countries of Czechoslovakia, Yugoslavia and Russia.

17 March 1990

The Churches of Scientology Stevens Creek (California), Munich (Germany) and Zurich (Switzerland) formally acknowledged at the annual celebration of L. Ron Hubbard's birthday for achieving the size of old Saint Hill.

May 1990

The Dynamics of Life, a public Scientology motion picture, released.

12 May 1990

The Hubbard Key to Life Course, the solution to a world out of communication, released to the public.

TRs and Objectives Co-audit Course released.

Clear Body, Clear Mind: The Effective Purification Program released.

Purification: An Illustrated Answer to Drugs released.

The Churches of Scientology Milano (Italy) and Stuttgart (Germany) formally acknowledged for achieving the size of old Saint Hill.

17 May 1990

Church of Scientology of Catania, Italy, founded.

June 1990

False Tone Arm, a Technical Training Film written by L. Ron Hubbard, released.

6 June 1990

The Hubbard Life Orientation Course released.

30 June 1990

The official opening of the Narconon Chilocco New Life Center at Chilocco, Oklahoma.

October 1990

Upper Indoc TRs, a Technical Training Film written by L. Ron Hubbard, released.

6 October 1990

IAS Freedom Medals are awarded to:

Jane Allen, for exposing psychiatric abuses in Colorado and establishing the Church of Scientology as a major force for social reform in the United States.

Julia Migenes, internationally acclaimed opera star, for supporting religious freedom and spearheading Dianetics and Scientology information campaigns in both Europe and the United States.

December 1990

Release of *Start, Change, Stop*, a Technical Training Film written by L. Ron Hubbard, released.

28 December 1990

Church of Scientology of Salt Lake City, Utah, founded.

31 December 1990

Basic Study Manual published.

Elementary and Executive Data Series Evaluator's Courses released.

1991

First groups formed in Poland, Bulgaria and Malaysia.

19 February 1991

Twenty-fifth anniversary of Narconon, grown from one program started by a prison inmate to a network of centers in twelve countries.

March 1991

The Solo Auditor, a Technical Training Film written by L. Ron Hubbard, released.

The Church of Scientology of Mountain View, California, founded.

15 March 1991

The new *Organization Executive Course (OEC)* and *Management Series* volumes released, containing over 10,000 pages of L. Ron Hubbard's administrative technology, twice as many as in the OEC volumes issued in the 1970s. Along with the 43 tapes on the OEC, the Flag Executive Briefing Course tapes and the Establishment Officer tapes, also released, these materials comprise the complete technology of organization.

20 April 1991

Grand opening celebration of the L. Ron Hubbard Life Exhibition at the Hollywood Guaranty Building. The president pro tem of the California Senate and the president of the Hollywood Chamber of Commerce cut the ribbon at the opening ceremony.

6 May 1991

Newly built 25,000-square-foot Sandcastle Technical Delivery Building in Clearwater, Florida, opened, especially for providing advanced level religious services.

10 May 1991

The *Technical Bulletins* volumes released in a new edition of 18 volumes and over 11,000 pages. These contain all of L. Ron Hubbard's technical articles and bulletins on Dianetics and Scientology.

7 June 1991

Christening of the historic Sea Org vessel, *Diana*, a 62-foot ketch which played an important role in the early history of the Sea Org as the first Sea Org vessel. Completely restored, she returns to service to provide sea training for Sea Org members.

17 July 1991

The Church of Scientology of Hungary registered as a religious body.

28 May–2 August 1991

Largest public information campaign in the history of Scientology in national newspaper *USA Today*. The two-month campaign featured full-page advertisements four times per week and two publication inserts.

August 1991

The Story of Book One, a public Scientology motion picture, released.

7 September 1991

The new Saint Hill Special Briefing Course released, including 437 taped lectures in Clearsound with written transcripts.

Updated, finalized and totally complete Grade Chart released, including all new technical releases since its original issuance in 1965.

26 October 1991

IAS Freedom Medals are awarded to:

Keith Code, motorcycle racing champion and trainer, for helping to make L. Ron Hubbard's technology of Dianetics broadly known.

Kirstie Alley, award-winning television and screen actress and international Narconon spokesperson, for enlightening millions throughout the world on L. Ron Hubbard's drug rehabilitation technology.

Gabriele Segalla, who founded the Citizens Commission on Human Rights in Italy, for investigating and exposing the horrors and brutalities taking place in psychiatric hospitals throughout the country and later helping bring about a major religious recognition for Scientology in Italy.

December 1991

Church of Scientology Puerto Rico founded.

2 December 1991

On 3 March 1983, agents of the Ontario Provincial Police raided the Church of Scientology in Toronto, Ontario. On 2 December 1991, the trial court declared the raid violated the Canadian Charter of Rights and Freedoms.

1992

First groups formed in the Philippines, Honduras, Brazil and Ivory Coast.

10 March 1992

L. Ron Hubbard Study Hall, housing a full library of L. Ron Hubbard's works, opens at Moscow State University in Russia. Additionally, an entire section of the Professors' Study Hall in the principal library of the university is dedicated to L. Ron Hubbard's books and he is awarded an Honorary Doctorate of Literature degree by the university.

8 May 1992

Children's Communication Course released.

Twenty-three Technical Specialist Courses released for more intensive technical training of auditors.

7 June 1992

How to Use Dianetics Video—A Visual Guidebook to the Human Mind released.

25 July 1992

Celebrity Centre International and the Manor Hotel (formerly the Château Elysée, a French Normandie-style hotel in Hollywood) restored and officially opened, now ministering to celebrities and professionals from around the world.

August 1992

To support growing missionary activity throughout Russia and the new independent states, an OTL is formed by Sea Org members in Moscow.

September 1992

First group formed in Albania.

12 September 1992

Auditor's Day—Hubbard British Mark V E-Meter back in production and made available for the first time since the late 1970s. Manufactured by Golden Era Productions for all auditing through the state of Clear.

17 October 1992

IAS Freedom Medals are presented to:

John Travolta, who throughout his career, has enlightened millions worldwide about Dianetics and Scientology. While actively and vocally supporting drug rehabilitation efforts at a grass-roots level, he also became an international spokesman for L. Ron Hubbard's study technology.

Debbi Mace, for conducting popular Dianetics Seminars in Moscow and establishing programs in the United States and Russia which utilize L. Ron Hubbard's study technology.

Jerry Boswell, president of the Citizens Commission on Human Rights Texas, for his significant role in exposing psychiatric fraud, assault and false imprisonment in the United States. His work resulted in new legislation that effectively curtailed the use of electric shock treatment in the State of Texas.

The all new *What Is Scientology?* is released at the annual IAS convention aboard the *Freewinds*.

May 1993

The Technical Training Film, *Estimating Case Conditions by Tests and the E-Meter*, written by L. Ron Hubbard, released.

August 1993

The *L. Ron Hubbard Images of a Lifetime Exhibition*, a photo exhibit of hundreds of never-before-seen photos of L. Ron Hubbard and his life, premiered at the Flag Land Base in Clearwater, Florida.

7 August 1993

Freedom magazine 25th anniversary as the social reform voice of the Church of Scientology celebrated with international event in Los Angeles.

September 1993

The Technical Training Film *How the E-Meter Works*, written by L. Ron Hubbard, released.

The Tone Scale film, written and narrated by L. Ron Hubbard, released.

30 September 1993

In the early 1980s, the city of Clearwater, Florida, passed an ordinance that was aimed at excluding Scientology from the city. Many other religious groups joined with the Church of Scientology to challenge the ordinance in court on grounds that it was unconstitutional. In September 1993 the Church won a resounding victory in the US Eleventh Circuit Court of Appeals, fully recognizing that Scientology is a religion.

1 October 1993

The United States Internal Revenue Service determined that Scientology churches and their related entities were organized and operated exclusively for religious and charitable purposes and issued letters recognizing their tax-exempt status.

These churches included the Church of Scientology International, the mother church of the Scientology religion; all US Scientology churches and several major Church organizations located abroad; Scientology Missions International; and the Hubbard Ecclesiastical League of Pastors (I HELP). In addition to the tax-exemption rulings, in separate rulings the IRS issued group exemption letters to Church of Scientology International and Scientology Missions International authorizing them to confer tax-exempt status on the churches and missions subject to their ecclesiastical guidance.

The IRS recognition included the Church's related charitable and educational institutions—it issued separate exemption letters to the Association for Better Living and Education (ABLE) and all the affiliated social betterment groups that were not already tax-exempt.

The IRS also issued individual letters of exemption to the Church's publishing organizations, Bridge Publications in Los Angeles and New Era Publications in Denmark, recognizing the publishing of L. Ron Hubbard's books on Scientology as a religious activity.

In a separate ruling letter the IRS individually recognized the tax-exempt status of Religious Technology Center, the Scientology church which ensures the purity of the religion and the integrity of the use of the technologies of Dianetics and Scientology.

December 1993

Release of *The Tone Scale Drill Film,* written and narrated by L. Ron Hubbard.

21 December 1993

Church of Scientology of Quebec recognized as a religion by the Inspector General of Financial Institutions in Montreal, Quebec, Canada.

14 January 1994

Following its premiere at the Flag Land Base, the L. Ron Hubbard Images of a Lifetime Exhibition opened at Saint Hill in England.

25 January 1994

With missionary activity and desire for Dianetics and Scientology rapidly growing throughout Russia in the 1980s and 90s, the Church of Scientology in Moscow is formed.

February 1994

How to Set up a Session and an E-Meter, a Technical Training Film written by L. Ron Hubbard, released.

10 March 1994

Introduction of Dianetics to the republic of Serbia.

11 March 1994

Two new churches of Scientology opened—the Church of Scientology of Buenos Aires and the Celebrity Centre Nashville.

The Scientology Handbook released at L. Ron Hubbard's birthday event. With 984 pages and more than 700 photographs and illustrations, published in five languages, it is the most comprehensive manual on the basics of Scientology.

7 April 1994

The Church of Scientology in Albania recognized as a religious organization.

6 May 1994

The *How to Use Dianetics* video released in 10 new languages—German, Italian, French, Spanish, Swedish, Danish, Japanese, Greek, Russian and Hungarian—making Dianetics available to more than one billion people around the world.

New sound technology developed by Golden Era Productions, enables archivists to hear and transcribe previously unintelligible LRH lecture recordings. As a result, the first of a new series of verified and compiled transcripts called the *Research and Discovery Series* is released.

19 May 1994

First auditing ministered in Croatia.

9 June 1994

First auditing ministered in Saudi Arabia.

23 June 1994

The Hamburg Senior State Prosecutor concluded a three-year politically motivated investigation into the Church of Scientology and declared *no* wrongdoing.

August 1994

Tone 40 Assessment, a Technical Training Film, written by L. Ron Hubbard, released.

16 August 1994

Church of Scientology ministers in Ontario, Canada, granted the right to perform marriages. This marked the attainment of religious recognition for Scientology in all Canadian provinces where Scientology churches are located.

September 1994

A series of full-page advertisements placed in the *Washington Post* and *New York Times* by Church of Scientology International exposing the religious bigotry and harassment of Scientologists by the German government.

8 October 1994

The International Association of Scientologists celebrated its 10th Anniversary at Saint Hill in England.

IAS Freedom Medals are awarded to:

Roberto Cestari, president of the Citizens Commission on Human Rights Italy, for leading the battle against psychiatric brutality in his country, conducting more than 18 raids on abusive institutions and helping to initiate more than 25 parliamentary interrogations into psychiatry.

Joan Lonstein, president of Criminon Los Angeles, for initiating highly successful criminal reform programs that use L. Ron Hubbard's technology to salvage the lives of thousands of men, women and juvenile offenders.

Bud Reichel, for implementing LRH administrative technology in Russian organizations of all kinds.

Jeanne Trahant Stewart, for her 20 years of service with Narconon Los Angeles, including 14 as executive director. She greatly expanded Narconon and has brought the miracles of LRH drug rehabilitation technology to thousands of drug addicts.

13 October 1994

The Secretary General of Interpol, the International Criminal Police Organization, recognized that there were no further disputes between Interpol and the Churches of Scientology.

December 1994

Release of *Use of a Doll in Auditing and TRs*, a Technical Training Film written by L. Ron Hubbard.

5 December 1994

As part of the year-long celebration of the 40th Anniversary of the Church of Scientology, the What Is Scientology? Exhibition opened at the National Press Club in Washington, DC.

16 February 1995

Dianetics technology introduced in Lebanon.

18 February 1995

On the 41st anniversary of the founding of the Church of Scientology in Los Angeles, it held a grand reopening in fully renovated quarters.

11 March 1995

L. Ron Hubbard: A Profile released, a comprehensive look at Mr. Hubbard's life and work, launching a series of *RON* publications focusing on the 29 professions in which L. Ron Hubbard excelled. Published in 14 languages.

25 March 1995

A model Scientology mission opened in Wichita, Kansas, the city where L. Ron Hubbard made major technical breakthroughs in the early 1950s and established the headquarters of the national Dianetics Foundation.

April 1995

Release of *The Art of Communication*, a Technical Training Film written by L. Ron Hubbard.

19 April 1995

Scientology ministers and Volunteer Ministers from throughout the United States gave assists and counseling to the survivors of the bombing of the federal building in Oklahoma City, Oklahoma.

22 April 1995

The Advanced Courses of Scientology and accompanying filmed lectures by L. Ron Hubbard on the subject of OT released in French, German, Spanish and Italian, making the advanced spiritual technology of Scientology available for the first time in these languages.

23 April 1995

Fully redesigned and remodeled, the Advanced Organization and Saint Hill Europe held its grand opening.

May 1995

Release of *Confessional TRs*, a Technical Training Film written by L. Ron Hubbard.

6 June 1995

The Road to Freedom compact disc, featuring Scientology music and lyrics written by L. Ron Hubbard, released in eight languages.

8 June 1995

L. Ron Hubbard's technology of Dianetics and Scientology introduced in the country of Kyrgyzstan in the Commonwealth of Independent States.

July 1995

Release of five Technical Training Films, featuring lectures and demonstrations by L. Ron Hubbard, which are now part of the Clearing Course.

4 July 1995

L. Ron Hubbard's technology of Dianetics and Scientology introduced in the country of Madagascar, an island nation east of South Africa.

August 1995

L. Ron Hubbard's Dianetics technology introduced in Georgia, Armenia, Azerbaijan and Turkmenistan in the Commonwealth of Independent States.

6 October 1995

IAS Freedom Medals awarded to:

Isaac Hayes, legendary recording artist, entertainer and screen actor, for bringing L. Ron Hubbard's study technology to cities across America as an international spokesman for the World Literacy Crusade.

Gurris de Nieto, for introducing thousands of educators and students to L. Ron Hubbard's study technology and making Dianetics and Scientology known to millions in Latin America.

Elena Roggero, one of Italy's most popular female vocalists and an award-winning songwriter, for effectively leading and inspiring the fight against drug abuse through a "Say No to Drugs" campaign that became a national movement.

21 October 1995

The Founding Church of Scientology of Washington, DC, moved to its new home in the historic Fraser Mansion. A centerpiece for Scientology in the United States capital, the new quarters provide an appropriate setting to receive top government officials in Washington and dignitaries from around the world.

4 November 1995

Grand opening of the fully renovated Clearwater Building to house administrative offices for the Flag Land Base.

21 February 1996

Central Bureaux Order 1015 was issued, establishing the Flag Liaison Office and new Continental Liaison Offices in: Africa; Australia, New Zealand and Oceania (ANZO); Canada; Europe; Eastern United States; Latin America; United Kingdom; and Western United States; and ushering in the New Era of Management.

29 February 1996

LRH's birthday declared a legal holiday in Ontario, Canada, for provincial workers.

March 1996

Release of *The Cycle of Communication*, a Technical Training Film written and narrated by L. Ron Hubbard.

15 March 1996

Scientology enters cyberspace with the largest multimedia presence on the Internet, tens of thousands of pages in five languages, featuring Scientology, Dianetics and L. Ron Hubbard.

Images of a Lifetime: A Photographic Biography released. Written by the official L. Ron Hubbard biographer, the 298-page edition contains more than 400 photographs, many published for the first time.

The film *Orientation* released worldwide. This film introduces Scientology by taking the viewer on a guided tour of a typical church and providing a complete description of Scientology belief and practices.

Scientology management streamlined to conform exactly to L. Ron Hubbard's administrative patterns. As part of this "New Era of Management," 100 top Church executives assume key positions of responsibility in all major continental zones.

22 March 1996

The Church of Scientology in Caracas, Venezuela, received full tax exemption.

29 March 1996

Sixteen Italian Scientologists acquitted of all false tax charges brought against them in Torino, Italy, with full religious recognition given to Scientology in the decision.

13 April 1996

The American Saint Hill Organization, in Los Angeles, with the capacity to train more than 500 auditors at a time, celebrated its grand opening with thousands of Scientologists in attendance.

23 April 1996

Independent Television Commission (UK) lifted its ban on advertising by the Church of Scientology, opening the door for the first time to broad dissemination campaigns in the United Kingdom.

May 1996

The Problem of Life, written by L. Ron Hubbard, released.

10 May 1996

The Golden Age of Technology launched, making it possible to train perfect auditors in every Scientology organization. Following one of the most extensive reviews of auditor training in the history of the Scientology religion, new auditor training drills were released in 12 languages, covering every technical procedure.

As part of the Golden Age of Technology, the Hubbard Professional Mark Super VII Quantum E-Meter, the most accurate and sensitive ever developed, is released.

Additionally, release of the Hubbard E-Meter Drills Simulator enables students for the first time to drill with precision any situation that might arise in an auditing session.

6 June 1996

New Golden Age of Technology drills for the Solo and Advanced Courses released during the *Freewinds* anniversary cruise.

5 July 1996

The Norwegian government formally recognized the Church of Scientology as a religious movement in its "Central Coordination Register of Legal and Entities."

14 September 1996

All Academy Level 0 lectures released in Spanish, German, French and Italian.

9 October 1996

Scientology acknowledged as an officially recognized religion in the British Royal Navy.

19 October 1996

IAS Freedom Medals awarded to:

Eduardo Palomo and Carina Ricco, international TV, film and recording superstars, for bringing word of Dianetics and Scientology to more than a billion people internationally.

Vladimir Kuropiatnik, for his instrumental role in expanding Scientology missionary activity across the Commonwealth of Independent States and getting *Dianetics* into the hands of millions of his countrymen.

Lawrence Anthony, South African freedom fighter, for helping to bring apartheid-era psychiatrists to justice for their egregious human rights violations, while also helping thousands of all races with L. Ron Hubbard's technology.

During the celebration at Saint Hill Manor in England, the new course "How to Confront and Shatter Suppression" was released.

October–November 1996

A seven-week series of full-page advertisements placed in the *New York Times* by Church of Scientology International exposing the religious bigotry and harassment of Scientologists by the German government.

October–December 1996

A public information campaign on Scientology for Europe and the UK was launched with a series of full-page advertisements in the *New York Times*, *The Economist* magazine and the *International Herald Tribune* by Church of Scientology International.

25 December 1996

The Church of Scientology of Alma-Ata registered as a religious association in Kazakhstan.

31 December 1996

All remaining L. Ron Hubbard lectures for Academy Levels up to Level IV released in Spanish, German, French and Italian.

28 January 1997

A penal tax case against a board member of the Church in Rome was dismissed with the Court of Appeals concluding that the religiosity of Dianetics and Scientology is fully confirmed.

5 April 1997

In recognition of L. Ron Hubbard's humanitarian contributions to mankind, the street where the Church of Scientology of Los Angeles, the American Saint Hill Organization and the Advanced Organization of Los Angeles are located, was renamed as L. Ron Hubbard Way. Prior to its official opening, the street underwent a complete reconstruction to make it one of the most beautiful avenues in the world. The grand opening ceremony was attended by state and city officials, local dignitaries and thousands of Scientologists.

26 April 1997

The National Association for the Advancement of Colored People (NAACP) issued its prestigious Dr. W.E.B. Du Bois Outstanding Leadership Award to L. Ron Hubbard for his humanitarian achievements in literacy, education and civilization.

10 May 1997

The new L. Ron Hubbard film, *Man the Unfathomable*, released internationally.

Also released are the new Hubbard Dianetics Auditor Course, the new Hubbard Dianetics Seminar Course and all L. Ron Hubbard lectures for New Era Dianetics in nine languages: German, Spanish, French, Italian, Danish, Swedish, Russian, Japanese and Hungarian.

27 June 1997

Major Scientology dissemination campaigns launched, first in the United States on 27 June 1997, and later in the UK (12 November 1997) and Europe (22 November 1997).

July 1997

Release of two Technical Training Films written by L. Ron Hubbard: *E-Meter Reads* and *E-Meter Reads Drill Film*.

21 July 1997

A march, rally and celebrity concert took place in Frankfurt attended by 2,000 people from Europe who came to protest against discrimination in Germany.

7 August 1997

First Dianetics and Scientology missionaries into Fiji.

September 1997

The Auditor's Code, a Technical Training Film written by L. Ron Hubbard, is released.

18 September 1997

The Commission for Security and Cooperation in Europe held a day of public hearings into religious intolerance in Europe, chaired by Senator Alfonse D'Amato. Along with members of different minority religious faiths, Scientologists John Travolta, Isaac Hayes and Chick Corea testified about religious discrimination against American and German citizens by the German government. German Scientologists, including a family who had left Germany to settle in the United States to escape the discrimination, testified.

4 October 1997

The first Scientology mission in Memphis, Tennessee, opened.

8 October 1997

On 4 December of 1986, all orgs, missions and Narconon centers in Italy were raided and closed down in a suppressive effort to stop Scientology in Italy. Scientologists from around the world responded with a massive crusade for religious freedom. On 2 July 1991 the First Instance Court in Milano acquitted all the defendants of the charges of criminal association, illegal medical practice and tax evasion. The government appealed. On 8 October 1997, the Italian Supreme Court affirmed the dismissal of these charges and held that Scientology is a religion.

24 October 1997

International Association of Scientologists 13th anniversary celebration and annual convention at Saint Hill in England.

IAS Freedom Medals are presented to:

Anne Archer, world-renowned screen actress and humanitarian, for establishing and promoting L. Ron Hubbard study technology programs and playing a crucial role in the crusade for religious freedom in Europe.

Ann Roberts, educator, for disseminating and implementing L. Ron Hubbard's study technology internationally for a quarter of a century, and instituting teacher training programs in Zimbabwe, which since 1994 have brought literacy to tens of thousands of students.

Javier Ramirez and Martha Ballesteros, for enlightening millions throughout South America on all applications of L. Ron Hubbard's technology and opening major humanitarian programs in his name.

27 October 1997

A march, rally, celebrity concert and candlelight vigil in Berlin. More than ten thousand Scientologists and representatives of many other religions attended, calling upon the German government to "Break down the wall of Intolerance."

November 1997

A major Scientology dissemination campaign launched in the UK.

6 November 1997

Germany's Federal Supreme Administrative Court ruled that a Scientology mission was not a business enterprise, as alleged by the government. The Court held that auditing is understood as "spiritual counseling" and that the mission's seminars and courses are based upon the sincerely held convictions of Scientologists. The Federal Supreme Administrative Court ignored an earlier adverse ruling by the Federal Labor Court, which had violated the due process rights of the Church.

22 November 1997

A major Scientology dissemination campaign launched in Europe.

December 1997

Release of *Body Motion Reads*, a Technical Training Film written by L. Ron Hubbard.

14 February 1998

Celebrating 30 years of religious service to Scientologists in the Western Hemisphere, the Advanced Organization of Los Angeles opened the doors to its fully redesigned and newly renovated 48,000-square foot building on L. Ron Hubbard Way.

March 1998

The Technical Training Films, *PC Indicators* and *PC Indicators Drill Film*, released.

16 May 1998

The L. Ron Hubbard Technical Training Film, *TRs in Life*, released internationally.

Release of the Technical Training Film, *The Different TR Courses and Their Criticism*.

concerning the Church and ordered the documents released. The court ruled the Church of Scientology was to be treated like all other mainstream denominations.

18 JUNE 1983

A bogus probate case alleging that L. Ron Hubbard had passed away was dismissed. The judge found that L. Ron Hubbard was doing very well, that his personal affairs were in good order and that he was entitled to his privacy.

28 JUNE 1983

A Massachusetts Superior Court judge ruled that the Church of Scientology "satisfies the criteria of a religion" as "the teachings involve a theory of the spiritual nature of man." The ruling also stated that the practice of auditing is central to the practice of Scientology, and that the organization of the Church has many resemblances to recognized hierarchical religious institutions.

27 OCTOBER 1983

The Church of Scientology won a case against the high commissioner for payroll tax in Australia. In a 5–0 decision issued by the High Court of Australia, the judges stated: "The conclusion that it is a religious institution entitled to the tax exemption is irresistible." During this case, the Church established the legal definition of religion for the Australian Constitution for the first time in history.

23 JANUARY 1984

The Church of Scientology in Sydney, Australia, was granted exemption from the payment of land tax, based on the fact that Scientology is a religion.

27 FEBRUARY 1984

In four consolidated cases in Los Angeles, California, the US District Court of the Central District of California, ruled: "This court finds that the Church of Scientology is a religion within the meaning of the First Amendment. The beliefs and ideas of Scientology address ultimate concerns — the nature of the person and the individual's relationship to the universe."

27 MARCH 1984

An appeals court upheld a November 1982 decision that found the Vancouver Church of Scientology exempt from property tax as a religious organization.

11 MAY 1984

A judge in Boston, Massachusetts, ruled: "As far as I am concerned, Scientology is a religion. I don't think there should be any serious doubt about that. I will take judicial notice that it is a religion, period."

30 JANUARY 1985

The Stuttgart District Court reversed an earlier negative lower court ruling concerning church proselytizing because: "The conduct of the concerned served a direct religious purpose."

30 APRIL 1985

The US Department of Justice was ordered to pay $17,097.72 to the Church of Scientology for improperly withholding documents which the Church had a right to receive, and for noncompliance with court orders.

15 MAY 1985

The Social Security Agency of Angers, France, ruled that a staff member of the Church of Scientology of Angers was not required to make social security payments because his commitment to the Church was of a purely spiritual nature and his work could not be compared to that of a normal wage earner.

20 MAY 1985

A case was won in the District Court of Stuttgart acknowledging the Church's dissemination activities as part of the pursuit of its religion.

5 JUNE 1985

In the case of the Church v. the City of Munich, the appeals court announced that the court accepts (a) that auditing is an essential part of the teachings of Scientology according to the self-understanding of the Church; (b) that based on this, the term "commercial enterprise" cannot be applied to the Church.

11 JUNE 1985

The Social Security Agency in Pau, France, issued a decision granting exemption from making social security payments due to the religious nature of the Scientologists' work.

16 JULY 1985

A judge in Multnomah County, Oregon, declared a mistrial in a second case involving a former parishioner of the Church who had been kidnapped by deprogramers and then forced to renounce her religion. The judge's decision threw out a $39-million-dollar verdict against the Church and declared that the court had not properly protected the rights of the Church as a religion during the trial. This reversal came about after tens of thousands of Scientologists from around the world traveled to Portland for the first Religious Freedom Crusade and stood shoulder to shoulder for sixty days until justice prevailed. [See 3 May 1982 entry.]

28 OCTOBER 1985

The Church of Scientology of Melbourne, Australia, was exempted from paying city taxes on the basis of being a religion.

20 NOVEMBER 1985

A proceeding in the Padova Court in Italy for alleged labor law violations was dismissed because no violations were found; the Church pursued religious aims, and Church staff did not fall within the purview of the labor law.

1986

Education Alive South Africa was granted official tax-exempt status from the Commission of Inland Tax Revenue.

26 MARCH 1986

In the United Kingdom, a permanent injunction was obtained against a group of individuals using copyrighted Church scriptures without permission. The group was also ordered to pay the costs of the case and £5,000 in damages.

5 MAY 1986

The Bologna Court in Italy dismissed a baseless prosecution against Scientology staff on the basis that no crime was committed, also finding the Church to be a religion.

5 JUNE 1986

A case involving the incorporation of the Scientology Mission of Ulm, Germany, was decided in the Church's favor, validating the mission as a religious organization.

23 JUNE 1986

In a court case involving an individual using copyrighted Church scriptures without permission, the United States Court of Appeals for the Second Circuit upheld the Religious Technology Center's ownership of the trademarks of Dianetics and Scientology and the right of the Church of Scientology International to enforce the proper use of the marks.

16 JULY 1986

Five Seattle "deprogramers" pleaded guilty to charges that they had attempted to force a Scientologist to give up her chosen religious beliefs. The deprogramers were sentenced to one year's probation and fined $5,000.

11 AUGUST 1986

A court in Denmark ordered three individuals to pay $175,000 in damages for theft of confidential Scientology scriptures from the Church of Scientology.

4 SEPTEMBER 1986

All Scientology churches and missions in California were exempted from California state unemployment insurance taxes, retroactive to January 1, 1984.

8 DECEMBER 1986

The Immigration and Naturalization Service (INS) National Office issued an official ruling to regional and local INS offices, stating that the Church of Scientology is a bona fide religion and is to be treated as any other religion.

1987–1988

All Canadian churches of Scientology received official recognition from the Revenue Department of the federal government, validating staff members of those churches as religious workers and exempting the churches from unemployment insurance and pension plan payments for their staff.

29 JUNE 1987

An injunction was granted by the Court of Appeal in Bern, Switzerland, against the illegal duplication of copyrighted taped lectures on Scientology by L. Ron Hubbard.

19 NOVEMBER 1987

Deprogramer Ted Patrick was ordered by a US District Court judge in Los Angeles to pay $184,900 in attorney fees and sanctions to a member of the Church of Scientology who had been kidnapped by Patrick in 1981 and held against her will for thirty-eight days.

29 DECEMBER 1987

Two deprogramers from England were convicted in Germany on charges of kidnapping a 32-year-old Scientologist. They spent six weeks in jail, were tried, sentenced and deported to England.

31 DECEMBER 1987

The Tax Office in Pau, France, issued a decision concerning the Pau mission, stating that donations for Scientology courses and auditing were tax-exempt.

17 FEBRUARY 1988

The Regional Court in Hamburg, Germany, recognized Scientology as a bona fide religion and granted incorporation as a religious organization to the Church of Scientology's Hamburg Celebrity Centre.

17 MARCH 1988

A German court cancelled proceedings against the Frankfurt mission, reaffirming the mission's incorporation as a charitable organization.

7 APRIL 1988

The Church of Scientology in Portugal was recognized and registered as a religious organization.

10 JUNE 1988

The inspector of corporate taxes in Amsterdam, Holland, granted exemption from value-added tax (VAT) and corporate tax to the Church of Scientology Amsterdam and cancelled assessments for corporate taxes for prior years.

16 JUNE 1988

The Utah State Tax Commission found the Church of Scientology Mission of Salt Lake City to be a religious institution and granted exemption from state sales and use tax.

11 JULY 1988

Narconon in Germany was recognized as a nonprofit organization.

20 JULY 1988

A Los Angeles Superior Court judge dismissed a billion-dollar lawsuit filed "on behalf of all disaffected Scientologists in the world." This was a total of six people out of eight million adherents around the world. Although the plaintiffs' allegations were carried widely in the media, the judge dismissed the suit as entirely unsubstantiated. The judge ordered the plaintiffs on seven separate occasions to provide evidence in support of their claims. They were unable to do so—he dismissed the suit as groundless. The dismissal was upheld on appeal in 1990 and costs of conducting this litigation were awarded to the Church.

20 SEPTEMBER 1988

The week of September 25 was proclaimed by Congress and President Ronald Reagan as National Religious Freedom Week, due in large part to the work of members of the Church of Scientology.

28 SEPTEMBER 1988

The California governor signed into law a bill that protects churches and religious organizations from unfounded punitive damages claims. The law, first conceived by Scientologists, requires stringent proof of actual damages before such a claim is accepted for trial.

12 OCTOBER 1988

In a Berlin, Germany, decision, the court recognized the church as a religion.

30 DECEMBER 1988

The Tax Commission of the city of New York granted full property tax exemption to the church as a religious organization.

23 JANUARY 1989

In Bolzano, Italy, the court threw out charges against eleven Scientologists involved in administering the Bolzano church's Purification Rundown. The charges, all based on false information supplied by a psychiatrist, were ruled as "unfounded" and the Scientologists were acquitted.

23 FEBRUARY 1989

The Department of Public Prosecution at the Regional Court Frankfurt am Main affirmed that the church was an established religious community and, as such, its dissemination, books and teachings are afforded constitutional protection.

MARCH 1989

The District of Schöneberg in Berlin recognized the church as a religious organization.

7 JUNE 1989

The Frankfurt, Germany, court ruled that auditing was the central religious practice of the Church and was covered under freedom of religion guarantees. The court further ruled that the religious services of the Church cannot be measured in monetary terms, and that they serve to forward the overall activity of the Church.

21 JUNE 1989

The Church of Scientology was victorious in a United States Supreme Court ruling that upheld the right of federal courts to place legal restraints on the IRS when there is reason to suspect that the tax agency is likely to violate the law and abuse its powers.

19 JULY 1989

The city of Munich, Germany, dropped a case against the church and affirmed its religious status.

10 OCTOBER 1989

A Munich court ruled that the church should have no restrictions placed on its dissemination activities on city streets.

FEBRUARY 1990

The Federal Finance Office in Germany exempted Scientology Missions International, the mother church for Scientology missions, from paying tax on the tithes from German missions, and made the decision retroactive to 1982.

15 FEBRUARY 1990

The Church of Scientology Mission of Anchorage in Alaska was granted property tax exemption based on religious status.

Following thirteen years of rejections of Church applications for trademark registration, the German Patent Court ruled that the term "Scientology" could be registered as a trademark.

27 MARCH 1990

The Monza Tax Commission in Italy ruled that the Church of Scientology was a tax-exempt organization and should not be subject to taxation because it is a religion.

23 MAY 1990

The Citizens Commission on Human Rights was granted tax-exempt status by the IRS.

18 JUNE 1990

A judge ruled in favor of the Church of Scientology of Boston and denied the IRS access to church records in the IRS' attempt to repeal the tax-exempt status of the Boston church, which had been granted in 1975. The judge also reprimanded the IRS for intrusive and abusive practices. The IRS appealed the decision but lost again in the higher court. The church set a nationwide precedent that protects all religions from IRS meddling in church affairs.

4 SEPTEMBER 1990

A Frankfurt, Germany, court affirmed the religiosity of Scientology and its right to set up information stands and distribute information about Scientology throughout the city.

18 SEPTEMBER 1990

A Valencia court ruled that Narconon is noncommercial and exempt from the payment of social security tax.

19 SEPTEMBER 1990

The Hanover District Court in Germany ruled that the exercise of religion includes expressions of religious and ideological life, especially missionary activities which promote one's own faith. The Land Treasury, defeated in its attempt to restrict free exercise of the Scientology religion, was made to pay court expenses.

20 SEPTEMBER 1990

A tax assessment against the Church of Scientology in Torino, Italy, was withdrawn because Scientology is a religion.

31 OCTOBER 1990

In Hanover, Germany, a court upheld the Church's constitutional right to disseminate its religion. The decision recognized the religiosity of the Church of Scientology.

16 JANUARY 1991

In a lawsuit filed against two trademark infringers in Brisbane, Australia, a decision was obtained in favor of New Era Publications against all unauthorized use of the copyrighted materials of L. Ron Hubbard.

21 FEBRUARY 1991

The local tax commission confirmed that the Scientology mission in Lecco, Italy, did not have to pay value-added tax because it is a church delivering religious services.

18 MARCH 1991

The United States Supreme Court issued a ruling that vacated an earlier $2.5 million judgment against the Church in a case involving a former member and sent the case to the California Court of Appeals with instructions to review its procedures in light of the requirements of the US Constitution.

15 APRIL 1991

A Milano tax court found the Church of Scientology of Italy to be exempt from value-added tax assessments as it is a religious organization.

24 MAY 1991

A US District Court judge in Los Angeles ruled that a Freedom of Information case brought by the Church against the Internal Revenue Service clearly served public benefit and caused the IRS to review its procedures, which led to the resolution of nearly 1,000 similarly situated cases brought by other US citizens against the agency. The judge awarded monetary compensation to the Church of Scientology for the expenses it incurred in this suit against the IRS.

21 JUNE 1991

A US District Court judge ordered monetary penalties against the IRS, which had filed a motion solely to "harass, cause unnecessary delay, or needlessly increase the cost of litigation" in two Freedom of Information Act suits filed by the Church.

2 JULY 1991

The Milano court in Italy, after a two-year-long trial, acquitted all Scientologists; fully affirmed the religious nature of the Church; acknowledged the goal of Scientology as spiritual freedom; recognized the E-Meter as a religious artifact; and cited the technology of Scientology as effective in drug rehabilitation.

17 JULY 1991

The capital city court of Budapest, Hungary, officially recognized the religiosity of the Church of Scientology of Hungary and acknowledged its members' right to freely practice their religion.

SEPTEMBER 1991

The Dresden mission in Germany became the first officially registered Scientology association in the former East Germany, handing a defeat to the local antireligious movement opposing the registration.

18 OCTOBER 1991

The Federal Constitutional Court of Germany, the highest court in the land, overturned a decree by the city of Hamburg which had forbidden the Citizens Commission on Human Rights, a Church-supported group, to distribute fliers in the streets.

4 NOVEMBER 1991

After three years of investigation by Spanish authorities, the national court in

Spain dropped all charges that were an attempted direct attack against the religion of Scientology and had earlier resulted in the unwarranted arrest of several members of the Church based on false information.

2 DECEMBER 1991

In Toronto, the court ruled that the Ontario Provincial Police 1983 raid of the church, the largest raid in Canadian history, was illegal and that all two million documents seized in the raid had to be returned.

12 DECEMBER 1991

The tax court in Lecco, Italy, determined that the activities of the Church were of a wholly religious nature and thereby dismissed a tax assessment claim against the Dianetics and Scientology Institute of Oggiono.

23 JANUARY 1992

The Hamburg Administrative Court recognized the local church's right to freely disseminate its religion and lifted all bans on promotion that had been placed by the city of Hamburg.

14 MAY 1992

The tax court in Verona, Italy, found that Scientology books and courses presented a religious and philosophical system which formed the foundation of the Church internationally. The court further ruled that this underlying religious view could not be questioned by the legal system.

17 JUNE 1992

The Superior Court in Germany accepted the religious and philosophical nature of the Church and concluded that the insinuations of a newspaper in Stuttgart were false and a violation of personal rights.

4 AUGUST 1992

Having expanded missionary activity through the 1980s and early 90s, Russian Scientologists in St. Petersburg incorporated the Scientology Center of St. Petersburg.

14 AUGUST 1992

The Oklahoma Board of Mental Health and Substance Abuse Services granted Narconon Chilocco an exemption from their certification process on the basis of Narconon's certification by the Commission on Accreditation of Rehabilitation Facilities.

17 AUGUST 1992

In the first ruling of its kind, the US Ninth Circuit Court of Appeals ruled that the public have the right to sue the IRS to remove false information from their files. The case was brought to court by two Scientologists who had discovered a false and damaging report in their IRS files.

19 AUGUST 1992

In cases involving the Church of Scientology International and the Church of Scientology Western United States, the US Court of Appeals for the Ninth Circuit held that the IRS must be held to a higher standard of proof when seeking records from churches.

26 OCTOBER 1992

The Oklahoma State Department of Health granted Narconon Chilocco its license — the final administrative step that officially sanctioned Narconon Chilocco to operate as a drug rehabilitation facility.

16 NOVEMBER 1992

In a case brought against the IRS, the Church of Scientology of California won a unanimous decision by the US Supreme Court which protects the constitutional rights to privacy of all US citizens. The precedent-setting ruling by all nine justices ruled that "A person's interest in maintaining the privacy of his 'papers and effects' is of sufficient importance to merit constitutional protection."

8 JANUARY 1993

The US District Court in Los Angeles issued a permanent injunction against a hypnotherapist who was infringing on a Church trademark, forbidding him further use of the mark. Religious Technology Center was awarded damages and all legal fees totaling more than a quarter of a million dollars.

24 FEBRUARY 1993

A Frankfurt, Germany, court ruled that the services of Scientology are of a religious and ideological character and are based on the principle of free religious practice.

5 APRIL 1993

A judge in Atlanta, Georgia, dismissed a suit brought against the Atlanta church on the basis that the suit violated the Church's religious freedoms under the United States Constitution.

28 APRIL 1993

In a tax case involving the Church of Scientology of Monza, Italy, the court stated that the religious nature of Scientology was self-evident and found that donations made for auditing and training constituted contributions given by members in conformity with the religious purposes of the Church.

4 MAY 1993

A United States District Court judge in California issued a permanent injunction against a copyright infringer and protected Church scriptures, both written material and tape-recorded lectures, from illegal usage. This landmark decision set a precedent for protecting intellectual property rights and guaranteeing freedom of speech for all those who use the Internet.

28 SEPTEMBER 1993

A federal judge in San Diego, California, awarded the Church of Scientology International a permanent injunction against a trademark infringer. The ruling upholds the Church's rights to use US copyright and trade secret laws to protect Scientology scriptures from unlawful copying and use. The same judge later ordered the infringer to pay $52,000 in damages to the Church.

30 SEPTEMBER 1993

The United States Court of Appeals for the Eleventh Circuit ruled overwhelmingly in favor of the Flag Service Organization, overturning a Clearwater, Florida, ordinance designed to harass the Church by entangling the city in the internal affairs of the religion. The court described the objective of the city in passing the ordinance as "patently offensive to the First Amendment [of the United States Constitution]."

1 OCTOBER 1993

The IRS issued a series of letter rulings, expressly recognizing Scientology churches, missions and other entities as tax-exempt organizations operated exclusively for religious and charitable purposes. Church of Scientology International was individually recognized as tax-exempt, and also received a separate group exemption ruling letter for all Scientology churches under its ecclesiastical guidance.

Scientology Missions International (SMI) received its own exemption letter, and it also received a group exemption letter for all the Scientology missions under its ecclesiastical guidance.

The Association for Better Living and Education received a separate letter ruling recognizing its exemption, as did the affiliated charitable, educational organizations that did not already have tax-exempt status.

Separate letters of exemption were also issued for the International Hubbard Ecclesiastical League of Pastors (I HELP); for the International Association of Scientologists (IAS) and for IAS' United States fund-raising entity, the US IAS Members' Trust; for the Church's publishing organizations, Bridge Publications in Los Angeles and New Era Publications in Denmark.

In a separate ruling letter, the IRS individually recognized the tax-exempt status of Religious Technology Center, the Scientology church which ensures the purity of the Scientology religion.

Those rulings signified that the IRS — and the US government — had formally recognized that Churches of Scientology operated exclusively for religious purposes and that Scientology, as a bona fide religion, was beneficial to society as a whole. Another consequence of these individual and group rulings was that donations to the Church in the US, including those for auditing and training, qualified as charitable contributions and for deduction for determining state and federal income tax.

31 JANUARY 1994

The Supreme Court of the State of New York determined auditing to be a spiritual precept of the Scientology religion and fully protected under the First Amendment.

26 OCTOBER 1994

The California Franchise Tax Board determined the Church of Scientology International to be exempt from corporate income tax.

17 NOVEMBER 1994

The California Franchise Tax Board determined Religious Technology Center to be exempt from corporate income tax.

29 DECEMBER 1994

The Church of Scientology of Los Angeles was determined by the California Franchise Tax Board to be tax-exempt from corporate income tax.

The International Hubbard Ecclesiastical League of Pastors was determined by the California Franchise Tax Board to be exempt from corporate income tax.

31 DECEMBER 1994

The Illinois Department of Revenue exempted the Church of Scientology of Illinois from sales and use tax.

8 FEBRUARY 1995

Scientology Missions International was determined by the California Franchise Tax Board to be exempt from corporate income tax.

16 JUNE 1995

The Stuttgart Court of Appeals upheld the right of the Church of Scientology to publicly distribute religious material.

AUGUST 1995

In the case of Stuttgart Mission Neue Bruecke v. Baden-Württemberg, in Germany, the court upheld that the Church was a religious entity.

1 AUGUST 1995

The Independent Administrative Senate in Vienna, Austria, concluded that Scientology is a religion and that auditing is a religious activity conducted solely for a religious purpose.

21 NOVEMBER 1995

In a significant ruling for all owners of copyrighted materials, a federal judge in California ruled that Internet access providers may be liable for copyright infringement by their subscribers. In a case involving Scientology religious materials, the court ruled that access providers who are aware of infringement but take no action to prevent its continuance, can also be charged with copyright infringement as they are "contributory infringers."

28 DECEMBER 1995

In Germany in a case involving the Karlsruhe Mission of Scientology, the Stuttgart Court of Appeals upheld the Church's right to freely distribute religious material to the public.

1 MARCH 1996

The Tax Appeals Court in Bergamo, Italy, ruled that the religious purpose of the Church qualified it for tax exemption.

4 MARCH 1996

In Lanciano, Italy, in a tax case involving the Narconon Revitalization Center in Palombaro, Italy, the court found Narconon exempt from all taxes at issue.

15 MARCH 1996

The Department of Finance and Revenue of the District of Columbia ruled the Founding Church of Scientology of Washington, DC, to be exempt from property taxes.

29 MARCH 1996

In Torino, Italy, the court found Scientology to be a bona fide religious denomination and, as Scientology services are religious in nature, the Church is exempt from taxation.

23 APRIL 1996

Scientology organizations in the United Kingdom won the right for fair treatment of religious advertising on British television, opening the doors for broad dissemination of Dianetics and Scientology on radio and television throughout the country.

13 AUGUST 1996

The Supreme Court of Austria ruled that Scientologists are protected by the nondiscrimination clause of the European Convention and cannot be discriminated against because of their religious beliefs.

29 OCTOBER 1996

The Church of Scientology of Ravenna, Italy, was found to be a religious association and exempt from laws which govern nonreligious organizations.

23 FEBRUARY 1997

Sea Org members established an Operation and Transport Liaison Office (OTL) in Budapest, Hungary, to support the Hungarian and east-central European boom of Scientology.

16 MARCH 1997

In a decision overturning a lower court ruling, the Court of Appeals of Rome, Italy, fully recognized the religious nature of Scientology and stated that the sale of L. Ron Hubbard books is an activity which supports the religious aims of the Church.

28 APRIL 1997

In a significant ruling affecting all Internet users, a federal judge in Washington, DC, granted a permanent injunction, damages and costs against a copyright infringer who had posted Church of Scientology religious scriptures on the Internet. The court ruled that copyright protections applied equally to copyrighted works posted on the Internet as to intellectual properties in any other medium.

16 JUNE 1997

A federal judge in California granted a permanent injunction against an infringer who had posted a copyrighted work on the Internet, overruling all of his defenses and finding that he knew the material was copyrighted when he posted it.

28 JULY 1997

The 4th Chamber of the Appeals Court of Lyon recognized the religiosity of Scientology, stating its free practice has full protection under the French constitution and European human rights covenants.

8 OCTOBER 1997

In a landmark decision, the Supreme Court of Italy cancelled a lower court ruling which had narrowly defined religion as Judeo-Christian. The Supreme Court stated this limited view was illogical and would exclude many of the great religions of the world, including Taoism and Buddhism. The Court further stated that, as the Church of Scientology was recognized in the United States, it should also be recognized in Italy and cited in support mutual human rights treaties between Italy and the United States which have existed since 1948.

6 NOVEMBER 1997

Setting a precedent throughout Germany, the Federal Administrative Court clarified that Church member donations for services are fully acceptable, noting "auditing, per the statutes, is a form of 'spiritual counseling,' and seminars and courses 'for the attainment of a higher level of being' are based on the commonly held convictions of members."

12 MAY 1998

A US District Court jury in San Jose, California, found unanimously that a northern California computer user willfully infringed a copyright in an unpublished Scientology religious work and ordered that he pay $75,000 in damages, plus fees and costs, to Religious Technology Center. The verdict, which may be the largest ever handed down for an infringement of a single work, sends a clear signal that federal law and property rights are not "suspended" in cyberspace.

CHAPTER 44

PLEDGE TO MANKIND

In 1984, the International Association of Scientologists adopted a pledge to mankind as a statement of its position and aims. The pledge was signed by representatives of Scientologists from around the world at Saint Hill Manor, in Sussex, England. It underscores the dedication and commitment of Scientologists everywhere to work for religious freedom and to better mankind.

"Time and again, throughout the troubled history of civilization on this planet, new ideas, new religions and constructive thought have met with violent opposition. Such attacks come from those who would preserve the status quo and particularly from those who seek to preserve and enhance their position through the domination, subjugation and even destruction of others. For this reason new religions have been born in blood at the cost of great sacrifice and suffering by adherents. It is only through a unity of purpose and unswerving commitment by a dedicated group that new ideas and new religions survive and expand.

"Scientology has been in existence now for some thirty-four years. During that time it has suffered all manner of attacks from the forces of oppression in various countries. Yet Scientology has survived and expanded because of the dedication of its members and because it is a force for goodness and freedom which is easily recognized by men of goodwill; despite the vicious lies which are spawned by those who would enslave mankind and which are carried by the media.

"Scientology is experiencing the greatest expansion and prosperity in its history. International in scope, Scientology each week frees more people from the debilitating effects of drugs, ignorance and other sources of aberration and moves them on the path to greater awareness, self-respect and dignity than all other groups combined.

"Yet as we have learned in our thirty-four years, whenever we expand, we are attacked, commensurate with that expansion. And today is no exception.

"In the United States, which was once thought to be a haven of religious liberty, we are the targets of unprincipled attacks in the court system by those who would line their pockets from our hard won coffers. Bigots in all branches of government, fearing the success of Scientology, are bent on our destruction through taxation and repressive legislation.

"We have been subjected to illegal heresy trials in two countries before prejudiced and malinformed judges who are not qualified or inclined to perceive the truth.

"In Canada and Germany, our Churches have been subjected to vicious raids reminiscent of the historical genocide attacks on religions that took place in 'less informed' times and societies.

"The news media chooses to ignore the good works and miraculous successes of Scientology and instead seeks to poison public opinion through vilification of the religion and its Founder.

"The detractors of Scientology know full well that it is a proven, effective and workable system for freeing mankind from spiritual bondage. That is why they attack. They fear that they will somehow be threatened by a society which is more ethical, productive and humane through the influence of Scientology and Scientologists. Thus when we expand, to that degree we are attacked.

"Up to this day, the responsibility for defending Scientology has been on the shoulders of a desperate few. And so it will continue in large measure.

"Yet, in order to continue the quest for a new civilization where honest men have rights and freedoms abound, the assistance and dedication of each and every Scientologist and other men of goodwill is essential. The road may be difficult and may get worse due to the rapid decline of civilization and erosion of personal liberties at this time. But united in purpose and dedication, we shall prevail for the benefit of all mankind.

"We, the undersigned, pledge ourselves, without reservation or any thought of personal comfort or safety, to achieving the aims of Scientology: 'A civilization without insanity, without criminals and without war, where the able can prosper and honest beings can have rights, and where Man is free to rise to greater heights.'

"We invite Scientologists and other well-intentioned people everywhere to join us in this pledge.

"Witness our hand this Seventh Day of October, AD 34, Saint Hill Manor, East Grinstead, Sussex, England."

CHAPTER 45

THE HOLIDAYS OF SCIENTOLOGY

To commemorate important dates in its history, the Church of Scientology observes holidays in all parts of the world through the course of the year. The most significant are celebrated with internationally telecast events to link all Scientology churches and missions around the world. In those cities where the local church cannot accommodate the thousands of parishioners attending the event, suitable auditoriums are rented. Major events are important to every Scientologist, whether in Africa, America, Asia, Australia or Europe, as they provide a special spirit of unity.

The major Scientology events feature briefings by senior ecclesiastical leaders on such subjects as the introduction of L. Ron Hubbard's works into new nations or sectors of society, the outstanding accomplishments of individual Scientologists and reviews of worldwide expansion. Events also feature releases of new Scientology books, materials, courses and news regarding the activities of social betterment programs—all cause for celebration. Although highly dignified affairs, Scientology events are also joyous.

Other notable events, such as the founding or anniversary of the founding of the church in a particular country or a city, may be locally observed. Traditional holidays, such as the United States Independence Day and French Bastille Day are not singled out, although Scientologists celebrate these occasions in their own countries according to custom. The following calendar lists notable days in Scientology history.

JANUARY

16 Recognition Day Africa, to celebrate recognition in 1975 of the Church of Scientology in South Africa.

25 Recognition Day Russia, to celebrate the registration of the first Russian Church of Scientology in Moscow in 1994.

Criminon Day, to celebrate the 1970 founding of Criminon, the criminal rehabilitation program.

28 National Founding Day New Zealand, to celebrate the founding of the first church in New Zealand, the Church of Scientology Auckland, in 1955.

FEBRUARY

15 Recognition Day Australia, to celebrate the recognition in 1973 of the Church of Scientology in Australia, by Federal Attorney General, Senator Lionel Murphy. Scientology was recognized under Section 26 of the Commonwealth Marriage Act, 1961–1966.

18 National Founding Day United States, to celebrate the founding of the first church in the US, the Church of Scientology Los Angeles, in 1954.

19 Narconon Day. On this day in 1966, an Arizona State Prison inmate initiated the Narconon drug rehabilitation program, which utilizes the technology of L. Ron Hubbard. Narconon has expanded to a network of more than thirty programs in countries throughout the world.

22 Celebrity Day, to celebrate the opening of the Celebrity Centre International in Los Angeles in 1970, dedicated to the rehabilitation of the culture through art.

MARCH

5 CCHR Day, to mark the formation in 1969 of the Citizens Commission on Human Rights. First formed in England, the commission is now a worldwide organization which has achieved major reforms internationally against psychiatric abuses.

9 National Founding Day Italy, to celebrate the founding of the first church in Italy, the Church of Scientology Milano, in 1978.

13 MARCH

L. Ron Hubbard's Birthday

The birthday of the Founder of Dianetics and Scientology, March 13, 1911, is commemorated each year with a major celebration honoring L. Ron Hubbard's achievements and his continuing contributions to mankind. Outstanding churches and missions are recognized for service to their parishioners and communities during the previous year.

13 National Founding Day Belgium, to celebrate the founding of the first church in Belgium, the Church of Scientology Brussels, in 1980.

National Founding Day Holland, to celebrate the founding of the first church in Holland, the Church of Scientology Amsterdam, in 1972.

19 National Founding Day Venezuela, to celebrate the founding of the first Dianetics center in Venezuela, the Asociación Cultural Dianética de Venezuela, A.C., in 1981.

24 Student Day, to celebrate the commencement of the Saint Hill Special Briefing Course in 1961. The course was begun at Saint Hill Manor, East Grinstead, Sussex and in 1968 was expanded to the American Saint Hill Organization in Los Angeles. Today, the Saint Hill

Special Briefing Course is also available in Copenhagen, Denmark; Sydney, Australia and at the Flag Land Base in Clearwater, Florida. This course, the largest in Scientology, covers the chronological development of Dianetics and Scientology.

31 National Founding Day Austria, to celebrate the 1971 founding of the first Scientology church in Austria, the Church of Scientology of Vienna.

APRIL

7 Recognition Day Albania, to celebrate the official recognition in 1994 of the Church of Scientology in Albania as a religious organization.

Recognition Day Portugal, to celebrate the recognition of the Portuguese Church of Scientology in 1988.

16 National Founding Day Sweden, to celebrate the founding of the first church in Sweden, the Church of Scientology Göteborg in 1969.

18 Recognition Day New Zealand, to celebrate recognition of the Church in 1974, with Scientology ministers licensed to perform marriages.

20 L. Ron Hubbard Exhibition Day, to celebrate the 1991 opening in Hollywood, California, of the L. Ron Hubbard Life Exhibition, a multimedia presentation of the life and accomplishments of L. Ron Hubbard.

MAY
9 MAY

Anniversary of Dianetics

The annual international celebration on this day salutes the publication of *Dianetics: The Modern Science of Mental Health* on May 9, 1950. It is the occasion when Scientologists

and community leaders from around the world acknowledge the contributions Dianetics has made to the betterment of individuals and society at large and the daily miracles that occur through its widespread application.

15 National Founding Day Colombia, to celebrate the founding in 1980 of the first Dianetics center in Colombia, the Centro Cultural de Dianética in Bogotá.

22 National Founding Day Switzerland, to celebrate the expansion of Scientology activities in this country with groups opening up in Bern, Basel and Zurich in 1974.

25 Integrity Day, to mark the 1965 release by L. Ron Hubbard of his studies on ethics—reason and the contemplation of optimum survival.

JUNE

5 National Founding Day Denmark, to celebrate the founding of the first church in Denmark, the Church of Scientology Denmark, in 1968.

6 JUNE

Maiden Voyage Anniversary

On this date in 1988, the Sea Org Motor Vessel *Freewinds* began her maiden voyage, during which New OT VIII was released. To celebrate the monumental advance to the highest levels of OT, OT VIIIs convene aboard the *Freewinds* each year for a week of special briefings and acknowledgments of their work in bringing a greater understanding of Scientology to others and helping improve conditions through Scientology.

12 National Founding Day Scotland, to celebrate the founding of the Hubbard Academy of Personal Independence in Edinburgh, Scotland, in 1968.

18 Academy Day, in celebration of the 1964 release of L. Ron Hubbard's study technology.

26 National Founding Day Norway, to celebrate the founding of the first church in Norway, the Church of Scientology Oslo, in 1980.

JULY

7 Advanced Organization Founding Day Europe, to celebrate the opening of the Advanced Organization Denmark in 1969.

Advanced Organization Founding Day Australia-New Zealand-Oceania, to celebrate the opening in 1983 of the Advanced Organization and Saint Hill in Sydney.

17 Recognition Day Hungary, to celebrate the registration in 1991 of the Church of Scientology of Hungary as a religious body.

21 Founding Day Washington, DC, to celebrate the incorporation in 1955 of the Founding Church of Scientology and the opening of the first Academy of Scientology.

28 Applied Scholastics Founding Day, to celebrate the 1972 inception of Applied Scholastics in Los Angeles.

AUGUST

12 Sea Org Day, commemorating the establishment of the Sea Organization in 1967, celebrated by all Sea Organization members throughout the world.

13 Advanced Organization Founding Day Los Angeles, to celebrate the opening of the American Saint Hill Organization and the Advanced Organization Los Angeles in 1968.

16 Recognition Day Canada, to celebrate the 1994 granting of licenses to Church of Scientology ministers to perform marriages in the province of Ontario. This marked the attainment of religious recognition for Scientology in all Canadian provinces where Scientology churches are located.

17 Advanced Organization Founding Day United Kingdom, to celebrate the opening of Advanced Organization United Kingdom at Saint Hill in Sussex, England, in 1970.

SEPTEMBER

5 Clear Day, to mark the inauguration of the Clearing Course in 1965. First released at Saint Hill Manor, the course is now available to Scientologists at Advanced Organizations in the United Kingdom, the United States, Denmark, Australia and at the Flag Service Organization in Florida.

8 National Founding Day Canada, to celebrate the founding of the first church in Canada, the Church of Scientology Toronto, in 1967.

Second Sunday in September
Auditor's Day

On this day auditors are acknowledged for their skill and dedication in bringing man up the Bridge to Total Freedom. Top auditors from around the world are recognized.

18 National Founding Day Zimbabwe, to celebrate the founding of the first church in Zimbabwe, the Church of Scientology Bulawayo, in 1967.

20 National Founding Day Mexico, to celebrate the forming of the first Dianetics institute in Mexico, the Instituto de Filosofía Aplicada, A.C., in 1979.

21 National Founding Day England, to celebrate the beginning in 1952 of Scientology in England, marking the opening of the London branch of the Hubbard Association of Scientologists International.

25 National Founding Day Israel, to celebrate the opening of the first Scientology and Dianetics college in Tel Aviv, Israel, in 1980.

OCTOBER
7 OCTOBER

International Association of Scientologists (IAS) Anniversary

Members of the IAS gather each year at Saint Hill in England to commemorate the founding of the IAS in 1984 and to rededicate themselves to its aims. The annual IAS freedom awards are presented and the annual convention of IAS delegates is held.

15 National Founding Day Germany, to celebrate the founding of the first church in Germany, the Church of Scientology Munich, in 1970.

26 National Founding Day France, to celebrate the founding of the first church in France, the Church of Scientology Paris, in 1959.

NOVEMBER

11 National Founding Day South Africa, to celebrate the founding of the first church in South Africa, the Church of Scientology Johannesburg, in 1957.

27 Publications Day, to celebrate the opening of the first publications organization, Publications Worldwide, at Saint Hill Manor in 1967.

DECEMBER

6 Flag Land Base Day, to celebrate the opening of the Flag Land Base in Clearwater, Florida, in 1975.

24 National Founding Day Spain, to celebrate the founding of the first church in Spain, the Church of Scientology Barcelona, in 1981.

25 Recognition Day Kazakhstan, to celebrate the recognition in 1996 of the Church of Scientology of Alma-Ata as a registered religious association in this nation, formerly part of the Soviet Union.

30 Freedom Day US, to celebrate the official recognition in 1974 of the Church of Scientology in the United States.

31 National Founding Day Japan, to celebrate the beginning of Scientology in Japan, which marks the opening of the Scientology Organization Tokyo in 1988.

31 DECEMBER
New Year's Eve

This event welcomes in the new year with a review of accomplishments of the previous twelve months and a look forward to plans for further reach into new areas of society with L. Ron Hubbard's technology. Stellar accomplishments of Scientology parishioners helping new people to move up the Bridge to Total Freedom are acknowledged.

CHAPTER 46

The Complete Auditing and Training Services of Scientology

Scientology services cover the full range of its religious philosophy and practice. There are auditing and training services which address every aspect of existence, for no matter what a person's condition in life, Scientology can help improve it.

The listings in this chapter categorize and provide information about Dianetics and Scientology auditing and training in the recommended sequence.

The vast majority of Scientology services are ministered by thousands of field auditors, field groups, missions and churches located throughout the world. Thus, no matter what city one may be in, one should be able to participate in Scientology services very easily. The approximate length of time a particular service takes is noted, in addition to which churches normally provide that service, from the most basic to the most advanced levels of training and auditing. One may become a classed auditor at a Class V or higher church only, not at a field group or mission.

Although advanced training and auditing services are available only at higher-level churches, due to the degree of skill and experience they require, even these services are very accessible since there are a number of higher-level churches located throughout the world—the Saint Hills, the Advanced Organizations, the Flag Service Organization. These all minister lower-level auditing and training, although they do not specialize in these. The highest church, the Flag Ship Service Organization, specializes in the highest OT level, OT VIII, and courses which deal with OT abilities.

For more information about any Dianetics or Scientology service, contact the Scientology church nearest you. A list of Scientology churches is included at the back of this book.

INTRODUCTORY SERVICES

There is an introductory service available for everyone, depending on personal interest or immediate concerns. These services provide information to people who have had little or no prior contact with Scientology, and will answer their questions and even help them begin to understand themselves better.

Introductory services are most frequently ministered by field auditors, field groups, missions and Class V churches. Many introductory services are described in greater detail in Chapter 8.

The following services contain basic data and technology to use to improve one's spiritual awareness. Course lengths are figured on a part-time schedule of three hours per day, five days per week.

■ Introductory Lectures

These lectures by experienced Scientologists introduce one to the fundamentals of Scientology, including basic truths about life and living such as understanding how to use the basic principles of communication to improve life.
Approximately 1 hour

■ Introductory Tape Plays of Mr. Hubbard's Lectures

The informative and lively lectures of L. Ron Hubbard provide a person with practical information he can immediately use to create beneficial changes in his life. Churches often play individual selections from the more than 2,000 public lectures delivered by Mr. Hubbard, or a complete series of lectures as originally given during one of the many congresses Mr. Hubbard delivered. These are commonly played, a lecture each day, on consecutive days.
Approximately 1 hour

■ Introductory Films

Many films provide information about Dianetics and Scientology or show how a person can improve his life. For titles and synopses of some of these films, see Chapter 7.
Length varies from 30 minutes to 1 hour each.

■ Books and Extension Courses

L. Ron Hubbard's books open the route to spiritual freedom and a better life. Extension courses, done at home, are designed to accompany many of these books. For additional data, see Chapter 7.

INTRODUCTORY COURSES

■ *Life Improvement Courses*

On these courses, one gains the knowledge of basic Scientology truths and tools he can use to apply to life. Relationships with others, successful parenting, personal integrity and honesty, making work easier, overcoming ups and downs in life, improving one's marriage and many other common problem areas that distract one from attaining spiritual freedom can be fully resolved through the use of the principles discovered on these courses. See Chapter 8 for more data on these courses.

Most can be completed in approximately 1 week.

Overcoming Ups and Downs in Life Course

Personal Values and Integrity Course

How to Improve Conditions in Life Course

How to Improve Relationships with Others Course

Starting a Successful Marriage Course

How to Maintain a Successful Marriage Course

How to Improve Your Marriage Course

How to Be a Successful Parent Course

How to Make Work Easier Course

Introduction to Scientology Ethics Course

The Way to Happiness Course

■ *Success Through Communication Course*

For the first time ever, Scientology fully defines the subject of communication to give one a complete understanding. Through a series of precise training drills, one gradiently improves his ability to communicate by learning exact and precise skills for guiding and controlling communication. See Chapter 8.

Approximately 1 week

■ *Hubbard Qualified Scientologist Course*

A person's ability and spiritual freedom increases as he progresses through the levels of Scientology and it is essential that his knowledge of life increases at a comparable rate. This course provides data and procedures to help increase one's awareness and ability to communicate with the world around one. It also provides simple techniques which can be used to assist people in physical pain or discomfort and ease their difficulty. On this course, one audits another on basic Scientology processes and receives auditing himself.

Approximately 4 weeks

■ *Hubbard Dianetics Seminar*

One who has read "Book One" and wishes to experience Dianetics for himself can participate in a Dianetics Seminar and gain firsthand and practical knowledge of Dianetics by applying basic techniques from *Dianetics: The Modern Science of Mental Health* to another and having them applied to oneself.

Seminars can be completed in two days full time (over a weekend) or during a week of evening classes, meeting each night for three hours. Naturally, this may take longer depending on how much auditing one would like to participate in. See Chapter 8.

■ *Hubbard Dianetics Auditor Course*

This theory and practice course contains further auditing techniques in addition to those learned during the Hubbard Dianetics Seminar and a series of L. Ron Hubbard's lectures on Dianetics. Students co-audit as much as they want in their progress toward Clear.

Approximately 3 weeks

■ *Anatomy of the Human Mind Course*

The exact anatomy of the human mind is one of the basic discoveries of Dianetics and Scientology. This course takes one step by step through an analysis of the parts of man, the mind and man's relationship to the physical universe; it includes theory, demonstrations and practical application. See Chapter 8.

Approximately 4 weeks (one lesson per evening for 20 evenings)

■ *Personal Efficiency Course*

On this course one discovers the secrets of efficiency, and is given the opportunity to test out each datum so he can decide for himself if it works. See Chapter 8.

Approximately 1 week

■ *Introductory Auditing*

The goal of auditing is to give the individual greater cause and ability and free him as a spiritual being. Auditing also enables one to better handle his own life. Basic auditing services introduce a person to Scientology and the personal awareness that Scientology works. In addition to a vast array of available processes, they can also include Group Auditing and Assist Auditing. You can experience for yourself the workability of Scientology — through receiving auditing by a thoroughly trained auditor. Individual sessions vary in length depending on the process being audited, but may last an hour or more. See Chapter 8.

AUDITING SERVICES

Auditing services to Clear are ministered in missions and Class V churches. Auditor training for New Era Dianetics (NED) and the Scientology Grades, however, takes place in Class V or higher churches. On this part of the Bridge one can progress through the life-changing Scientology Grades 0–IV and then attain the glorious state of Clear on NED auditing.

Note: Lengths of time for completing a given series of actions or grades are approximations only and should be used as guidelines. Each preclear varies in how long he will take to attain the designated spiritual result. An auditing process can take as little as minutes or as long as many, many hours over a number of sessions before the desired result is achieved.

CONDITIONAL PREPARATORY STEPS

The services below are often the first steps up the Grade Chart for many. For further information see Chapter 8.

■ Purification Rundown

The purpose of this rundown is to clean out and purify one's body of all accumulated impurities such as drugs, insecticides, pesticides, food preservatives and other toxins which could delay one's spiritual progress in Scientology. It is taken under the skilled supervision of a Purification Rundown Case Supervisor and only with approval from a licensed medical doctor. See Chapter 9 for more information.

Approximately 2 to 4 weeks at 5 hours per day

■ TRs and Objectives Co-audit Course

On the TRs and Objectives Co-audit Course one works with another student on the TRs (training routines) drills and then co-audits on Objective Processes which extrovert a being by directing his attention outward to the environment and increasing his ability to control himself and things around him. The benefits are multiple. One becomes spiritually aware and oriented to his present environment, while helping another achieve increased awareness and ability.

Co-audit course study is 4 days; length of auditing is approximately 25 hours

■ Therapeutic TR Course

Those who do not do the TRs and Objectives Co-audit Course may receive Objective Auditing in a church Hubbard Guidance Center. Therapeutic TRs provide direct personal benefits and also aid in further auditing. Offered as part of a person's case handling. Required before New Era Dianetics auditing if no other TRs course has been done. Available at all churches and missions.

Approximately 1 week

■ *Scientology Drug Rundown*

A preclear with a history of drug use has difficulty making and holding on to gains in auditing. This rundown releases a person from the harmful effects of drugs, medicines or alcohol, making it possible to receive the full and lasting spiritual benefits of Dianetics and Scientology auditing. Length of auditing is usually one 12 1/2 hour intensive which is available from field auditors, and at missions and churches.

One may, if he wishes, co-audit this rundown by doing the Scientology Drug Rundown Co-audit Course. Co-audit course study is approximately 3 days and is only available at Class V churches and above.

■ *Scientology Expanded Grades*

Step by step, the six levels of the Expanded Grades increase one's spiritual abilities and unburden much of the charge associated with his environment and his reactive mind so that he is better able to confront it on New Era Dianetics. The gains from these levels far exceed anything man previously has had available. The amount of time it takes one to move up through the Grades may vary, but the more intensively audited, the faster the progress. For greatest benefit and speed, it is recommended one make time for 25 hours a week but, at a minimum, at least 12 1/2 hours. It is quite common for students training in the Academy to co-audit each other through all the Grades. For further information see Chapter 13.

■ *ARC Straightwire Expanded*
Recall Release

This auditing is an exploration into the capabilities of one's mind. Aside from improving one's memory, an important ability in later auditing, on this level one realizes he is not going to get any worse.

■ *Grade 0 Expanded*
Communications Release

The processes of this grade gradually restore ability to communicate freely with anyone on any subject.

■ *Grade I Expanded*
Problems Release

The processes of Expanded Grade I give the preclear the ability to recognize the actual source of problems and make them vanish.

■ *Grade II Expanded*
Relief Release

Grade II addresses the mechanism by which bitterness and hatred come into existence. The processes of Grade II enable a person to eradicate these hostilities and sufferings from his life.

■ *Grade III Expanded*
Freedom Release

On Grade III processes one locates specific incidents during which upsetting change occurred in life and addresses these. The end result is the freedom to face the future with an enhanced ability to confront, experience and find advantage in the inevitable changes of life.

■ *Grade IV Expanded*
Ability Release

Old habits die hard, sometimes nearly impossible to break. The processes of Grade IV enable the preclear to move out of fixed conditions and gain the ability to do new things.

■ New Era Dianetics Auditing (NED)

Millions of people have experienced tremendous gains over the past 50 years auditing Dianetics exactly as Mr. Hubbard described it in 1950 in *Dianetics: The Modern Science of Mental Health.* But he did not stop there. His continued research, and his distillation of the results of a quarter of a century of application of Dianetics, resulted in the release of New Era Dianetics, a precise application of the basic Dianetics principles 100 times as powerful as the original techniques. It consists of numerous separate steps and distinct rundowns which go to the very root of unwanted and intolerable conditions.

On completion of NED one often has attained the state of Clear.

Length of time to audit varies, but it can result in the state of Clear. It is recommended one make time for 25 hours a week but, at a minimum, at least 12 1/2 hours.

■ Expanded Dianetics

This specialized branch of Dianetics addresses the basic reasons why a person restrains himself. It helps him remove these barriers and regain his innate power. At its conclusion, intentions and abilities which had been submerged for lifetimes can be restored. This is available at Class V churches.

Length of time varies but can result in Clear for those who did not go Clear on New Era Dianetics.

■ Clear

The state of Clear is far above anything one has previously dreamed of. Here, the being is forever free of his own reactive mind. Though long sought throughout the ages, the state was impossible to achieve before the research and breakthroughs of L. Ron Hubbard.

Initially, the state of Clear was attained through the techniques described in *Dianetics: The Modern Science of Mental Health.* Mr. Hubbard continued to research, however, seeking technology that offered faster and easier-to-attain results.

The state of Clear may now be attained on New Era Dianetics. If a person does not achieve Clear on NED, he will attain it on the Clearing Course, as described in the Alternate Clear Route below.

■ Clear Certainty Rundown

When someone has gone Clear on NED auditing, his next step is the Clear Certainty Rundown. This results in a being fully experiencing the glory of Clear, and ready to achieve Operating Thetan.
Approximately 5 hours

■ Sunshine Rundown

This short action adds extra shine to the state of Clear. By doing it, the Clear is becoming self-determined in his new state. One does this rundown immediately after achieving the state of Clear, whether he has gone Clear on New Era Dianetics or the Clearing Course (which is covered later in this chapter). This service is provided at Class V or higher-level churches.
1 day

■ Alternate Clear Route

The state of Clear is attainable by everyone. For those who do not attain Clear in New Era Dianetics, it is available through the Alternate Clear Route at Scientology Advanced Organizations, Saint Hill Organizations and the Flag Service Organization. This requires special auditing and then Solo auditing where the preclear audits himself.

■ Grades V and VA: Power and Power Plus

Power and Power Plus, both Saint Hill specialties, are the next steps for the NED Case Completion who did not go Clear on NED.

On Grade V (Power) one handles those things that pin one to the reactive mind. And on Grade VA (Power Plus) a person tackles the beings, places and subjects he has long detested. See Chapter 13.

Approximately 12 1/2 to 25 hours

■ Grade VI

This confidential level delivers freedom from dramatizations and the return of power to act on one's own determinism. The theory includes four confidential filmed lectures by Mr. Hubbard. This service is delivered to Power Plus Releases who have passed their Eligibility for OT levels. It is a Solo auditing action. See Chapter 13.

■ Clearing Course

Here one studies the materials of the Clearing Course, which includes technical films featuring lectures and Solo auditing demonstrations by Mr. Hubbard. On this course, one learns the anatomy and mechanics of the core of the reactive mind itself and then audits himself until his reactive mind — the basic cause of his decline — is vanquished and he attains the state of Clear. See Chapter 13.

SOLO AUDITOR COURSES

■ *Hubbard Solo Auditor Course*
Part One

Due to the nature of the highest spiritual states, many advanced services require the individual to audit himself. This is called Solo auditing.

Here one learns Solo auditing skills so that he can audit himself to achieve the state of Operating Thetan (and Clear, if not yet attained on NED).

The first part of the Solo Auditor Course teaches one all of the basic auditing skills—both theory and practical—plus the E-Meter skills needed to be a successful Solo auditor. This part of the course may be taken at a Class V church, so the Scientologist can attain these skills near his home and be ready to commence Solo auditing as soon as possible when he travels to an Advanced Org for the OT levels.

Approximately 6 weeks on a full-time schedule of 40 hours per week (8 hours per day, 5 days a week)

■ *Hubbard Solo Auditor Course*
Part Two

Here one audits oneself with exact directions provided by the Solo Case Supervisor until he has total certainty that he can handle anything that may come up in his Solo sessions. One does practical auditing which covers basic auditing procedures before engaging in an OT level.

Approximately 3 days

THE OT LEVELS

By eradicating the reactive mind one overcomes those factors which make total spiritual independence and serenity unattainable. A Clear is thus able to be reoriented to his native capabilities and becomes willing to trust himself with greater and greater abilities. This is done through the OT levels.

On the first 7 OT levels, which are designated pre-OT levels, the thetan is resolving factors which inhibit his ability to regain his native abilities as an OT. OT VIII, the first actual OT level, and those thereafter, directly address the spiritual being himself to accomplish the full attainment of his true potentials. Length of time required to complete these levels which are solo audited can vary greatly from person to person.

■ *OT Preparations Auditing*

This tailor-made program is designed to use L. Ron Hubbard's exact guidelines to handle any case areas that could cause one difficulty on the OT levels. It is personally addressed to one's own case. It is required in order to do the Solo auditing practice sessions on Solo Part Two and is ministered after the Sunshine Rundown for pcs who go Clear on NED or after Power Plus Release.

■ OT Eligibility

The OT levels are by invitation only to those whose ethics and responsibility level meet the standards necessary to receive and benefit from these powerful levels. Eligibility is determined by passing an FPRD Confessional for which one is awarded an "Eligibility for OT Levels" slip. If one is not immediately eligible for upper-level services, he receives a program to help him obtain his eligibility.

■ New OT I

This Solo-audited level is the first step a Clear takes toward full OT abilities, and that first step is a fresh, causative OT viewpoint of the MEST universe and other beings.

■ OT II

By confronting hidden areas of one's existence on the whole track, vast amounts of energy and attention are released. Those on this Solo-audited level experience a resurgence of self-determinism and native ability. OT II unlocks the aberrative factors on the whole track that have allowed the thetan to lose his innate freedom and ability and one achieves the ability to confront the whole track.

■ OT III—"The Wall of Fire"

This Solo-audited level takes one through what is called the "Wall of Fire" that surrounds a previously impenetrable whole track mystery. What prevents a being from being himself? This level answers that question. Once complete, a being is free of the whole track overwhelm that has trapped him. Here he confronts and eradicates the fourth dynamic engram that has plagued this universe for millennia.

These first three OT levels are available at an Advanced Organization or Flag. The part of the Bridge between Clear and OT III is called the Non-Interference Zone and includes the most crucial steps in one's progress to OT.

These levels can together require several months of daily Solo auditing to complete and should be done in succession at one time.

■ New OT IV—OT Drug Rundown

This level handles the hidden problems and stops in a being's universe caused by the effects of drugs and poisons on the whole track. This is the final polish that rids one of any last vestige of the effects of drugs on the spirit. Ministered at Advanced Organizations or Flag.

Approximately 12 1/2 to 25 hours

■ New OT V
New Era Dianetics for OTs

The Second Wall of Fire consists of 26 separate rundowns and has been described as dealing with "living lightning, the very stuff of life itself." This level addresses the last aspects of one's case that can prevent him from achieving total freedom on all dynamics. An audited level ministered at Advanced Organizations or Flag.

Approximately 50 hours

■ New OT VI
Hubbard Solo New Era Dianetics for OTs (Solo NOTs) Auditing Course

The training one receives before starting to solo audit on New OT VII is so powerful that it actually constitutes an entire OT level. On Solo NOTs one is dealing with complexities intended to crush one's true power and abilities as a thetan. Solo NOTs auditors acquire a wide range of auditing skills to handle the vast phenomena that can occur on OT VII.

Approximately 3–4 weeks with the new Solo Auditor Course done

■ New OT VII
Hubbard Solo New Era Dianetics for OTs Auditing

On New OT VII one Solo audits at home daily. This is a lengthy level, requiring a considerable amount of time to complete. It is the final pre-OT level, and culminates in attainment of the state of CAUSE OVER LIFE.

■ New OT VIII Truth Revealed

This Solo-audited level addresses the primary cause of amnesia on the whole track and lets one see the truth of his own existence. This is the first actual OT level and brings about a resurgence of power and native abilities for the being himself.

This may be done at the Flag Ship Service Organization only.

■ OT Levels Not Yet Released

Further OT levels to New OT XV to be released include levels which address Orders of Magnitude, Character, Operating and Future. An abundance of OTs must attain the previous states of OT before these levels are released.

RUNDOWNS AND ACTIONS THAT CAN BE DELIVERED AT DIFFERENT POINTS ON THE BRIDGE

(May be ministered by field auditors, missions and Class V churches or higher.) The length of time for these rundowns may vary, but as with any auditing, it is recommended they be done intensively.

■ *Happiness Rundown*

While the 21 precepts laid out in *The Way to Happiness* are nonreligious, by spiritually addressing them in auditing, one gains the certainty that he can be a more moral and therefore happier person. This rundown removes any spiritual factors tying one to immorality and he is left with certainty that he can lead a happy and spiritually fulfilling life.

■ *Confessional*

Auditing dealing with overts gives the highest gain in raising cause level because they are the main reason a person restrains himself and withholds self from action. Cases who have withholds will not progress in their auditing. Confessional auditing helps the individual straighten out his interpersonal relationships and achieve the maximum spiritual gain from his auditing.

■ *False Purpose Rundown*

A being who has accumulated hidden destructive purposes contrary to his own survival will operate far below his potential. This rundown slashes straight to the root of false purposes and makes them vanish. These false purposes are what hold a person back and prevent his ability to regain spiritual freedom and progress up the Bridge. Once these harmful effects are eradicated, the basic goodness of the individual is restored. This rundown is especially beneficial for those who experience difficulty moving up the Bridge. It is even beneficial for a Clear, stalled in his progress up to OT, as nonsurvival postulates and considerations can stand independently of mental mass.

■ *Method One*

Method One auditing can clear up all misunderstandings in every subject one has studied. The result of properly doing Method One is the recovery of one's education. The auditing directs one to misunderstood words or symbols from prior educational studies that are interfering with the ability to understand and clears these words up fully.

■ *PTS Rundown*

It frequently occurs in life that one comes into contact with a suppressive person—someone who acts to invalidate and make less of him. At this point one can become "PTS," a potential trouble source, due to the fact that this suppressive person is making one's life difficult. L. Ron Hubbard found that the suppression that affects one the worst actually stems from connections one has had to hostile personalities before this lifetime. The PTS Rundown was developed by Mr. Hubbard to free one from the long-term spiritual effects of such suppression.

■ *Suppressed Person Rundown*

This is a miraculous rundown that can result in a formerly antagonistic person coming forward to the preclear with unprompted, friendly communication.

■ *Interiorization Rundown*

One of L. Ron Hubbard's most remarkable achievements was to prove that man is not his body and that he can exteriorize from his body. Once a preclear exteriorizes during processing, he may run into difficulties if auditing continues. In many cases, although the person would exteriorize once or twice it was not a stable state and the person would have difficulty exteriorizing again. This rundown solves this problem and permits preclears to continue up the Bridge after going exterior in auditing and makes further exteriorization possible. Available at Scientology churches and missions.

■ *Introspection Rundown*

This service helps a preclear locate and correct those things which cause him to have his attention inwardly fixated. He then becomes capable of looking outward so he can see his environment, handle and control it.

■ *South African Rundown*

While living in South Africa, Mr. Hubbard discovered a spiritual case phenomenon peculiar to those indigenous to that country. He developed a series of processes which were especially designed to help the people of that country on their road to spiritual freedom. One learns to expertly audit this rundown and produce the result of a preclear who is willing to help and be helped without *any* qualms.

■ *Student Booster Rundown*

This rundown produces dramatic improvement by handling specific case manifestations that may be blocking one's ability to study and learn in Scientology.

FLAG ONLY RUNDOWNS

■ Vital Information Rundown

Sometimes hidden blocks can prevent a person from relaying knowledge or information, and this can wreak havoc on any group he is part of. On this rundown one finds and rids himself of those case factors that cause this to occur, allowing him to participate much more effectively in any group.

■ Allergy or Asthma Rundown

This special rundown can relieve mental and spiritual troubles underlying suffering by allergies or asthma sufferers.

■ Fear of People List

People often are unwilling to reach out in certain areas of life, making them ineffective. The Fear of People List handles the aberrating spiritual factors that cause this previously inexplicable spiritual disability, making it possible to face other people no matter who they are.

■ Est Repair Rundown

Some people formerly involved in the practices of a group called est (Erhard Seminars Training), have been found to need case repair. This rundown corrects any damage caused by est's practices, so that it does not hinder spiritual progress in Dianetics and Scientology auditing.

■ Repair List for Treatment from Psychiatrists, Psychologists and Psychoanalysts

This action frees one from damage caused by false data, invalidation and evaluation from psychiatrists, psychologists and psychoanalysts, so that preclears can make permanent spiritual gains in Dianetics and Scientology.

■ L Rundowns

These three powerful OT rundowns, designated by the letter "L"—L10, L11 and L12, contain the only direct processes used to accomplish exteriorization. Audited by the most highly trained Scientology auditor, the Class XII, they result from research Mr. Hubbard conducted to discover why people who exteriorized on other processes did not stably maintain this state. Once this was established and resolved, he then examined why some people did not exteriorize at all. The result was the Ls. The Ls also bring other remarkable gains, allowing the being to fully realize his own innate power, putting him in a state in which he is unlikely ever again to suffer the effects of suppression, and, in truth, giving the individual a new life.

■ Case Cracker Rundown

This rundown locates any and all factors preventing advancement as a spiritual being and literally "cracks" these previously unrelenting case barriers, solving any case. Once resolved, one can achieve the benefit of all Grade Chart levels, no longer hindered by hidden spiritual disabilities unique to his case. This service requires advanced precision auditor skill and is only available at Flag.

■ New Vitality Rundown

For those who have not progressed well due to suppression and other factors. Some beings inexplicably dramatize the effects of PTSness, even after PTS handling. This rundown reveals why. It searches out the blocks to one's spiritual advancement, and revitalizes a preclear who has not progressed well due to suppression and other factors. It is only offered at Flag due to the technical skill required.

FLAG RUNDOWNS NOT YET RELEASED

■ *Interiorization by Dynamics Rundown*

This rundown handles case factors interiorizing a pc or pre-OT into any dynamic, resulting in reversal of the barriers to exteriorization on any dynamic.

■ *Profession Intensive*

There are a multitude of case factors that can prevent one from obtaining the spiritual gains of each step of the Grade Chart, and the achievement of freedom as a spiritual being. One's work occupies at least 33 percent of anyone's life. This rundown addresses the aberrative spiritual effects on one's case that can be caused by this present life activity.

■ *Knowledge Rundown*

This rundown helps an individual overcome case barriers he may have to gaining knowledge about life.

■ *Dynamic Sort-Out Assessment*

This rundown locates the preclear's charged dynamics, which in turn bleeds charge off his entire case that is preventing his spiritual expansion across all dynamics.

■ *Fixated Person Rundown*

Sometimes a preclear has his attention fixated on another person to the point where it prevents him from putting his attention on other aspects of his auditing, his job or his life. Instead, he is looking through the viewpoint of another and in auditing is unable to as-is his own case because he is not addressing it through his own viewpoint. The Fixated Person Rundown handles this case condition.

■ *Havingness Rundown*

"Havingness" is the concept of being able to reach and not being prevented from reaching. The Havingness Rundown helps a person to increase his ability to reach and to achieve greater responsibility, and the ability to have.

■ *Super Power*

Consisting of 12 separate rundowns which address such areas as a thetan's 57 perceptics (and full rehabilitation of them), ethics, power of choice and the reasons why an individual becomes disassociated, Super Power unleashes the individual's full power as a spiritual being and raises him into a new realm of ability.

■ *Cause Resurgence Rundown*

This special rundown addresses the thetan himself and greatly boosts his levels of cause and control. The rundown assists in returning to a being more and more control of his own thetan energy flows and enhances his ability to handle life and his relations with others.

TRAINING SERVICES

Training in Scientology principles enables one to unveil the reactive mind, understand its machinations and render them powerless. By understanding the factors of life and developing skills to handle them, happiness can be achieved.

There is factually no higher ability than the ability to restore life to its native potentials. And that is what an auditor does. This section describes the training services offered in Scientology by which people learn this technology.

Length of courses may vary, as each person progresses at his own speed. The approximate times listed here are based on 40 hours of study per week (5 days at 8 hours per day).

PRELIMINARY AUDITOR TRAINING

STUDY:

■ *Student Hat*

The basic components of the subject of study, when fully understood, give one the exact means and tools to study any subject and apply what he has learned. While the technology of study taught on this course is useful for any subject, it is crucial to attaining the spiritual benefits of Scientology. Available in all Scientology churches and missions, the Student Hat is a prerequisite for all major training services in Scientology.

For more information about the study technology see Chapter 10.
Approximately 3 weeks

■ *Hubbard Method One Co-audit Course*

Method One co-auditing will clear up all misunderstandings in every subject one has studied. The result of properly completed Method One is the recovery of one's education.

In Method One co-auditing two people audit together, each auditing one another in turn. The course first teaches one how to deliver this auditing, then one applies these procedures by co-auditing with another Scientologist similarly trained. The auditing directs one to misunderstood words or symbols from prior educational studies that are interfering with the ability to understand and clears these words up fully. The course has no prerequisites and is open to anyone.
Approximately 3 weeks

■ *Primary Rundown*

This rundown includes Method One Word Clearing which is used to clear any subject one has studied in the past. Additionally one thoroughly clears the more than 2,000 words found in the Study Tapes and Student Hat course. One then is able to fully duplicate the study tech and gains an unsurpassed ability to apply the knowledge of *how* to study any subject. Individuals who complete this service are "superliterate" and have a full conceptual understanding of any material they read or seek to learn.
Approximately 4 weeks

TRs:

■ *Hubbard Professional TR Course*

One must fully understand the subject of communication and be able to communicate to others with flawless skill in order to audit effectively. The Professional TR Course results in an individual who can handle anyone with communication alone and whose communication skills can stand up faultlessly to *any* situation in auditing or life itself. See Chapter 14.
Approximately 2 1/2 weeks

■ *Hubbard Professional Upper Indoc TR Course*

After one completes the Professional TR Course, there is an even higher level of skill that may be attained through the drills on the Upper Indoc TR Course. These TRs which one does with another increase one's ability and willingness to deal with people and show one how to effortlessly communicate his intentions. See Chapter 14.
Approximately 1 week

METERING:

■ *Hubbard Professional Metering Course*

The E-Meter provides the only possible way for man to find his freedom, to rise to heights never before dreamed of. The meter enables the auditor to see the spiritual blocks which trap the individual. On the Hubbard Professional Metering Course, one learns how to operate an E-Meter and how to recognize E-Meter reads and know what they mean instantly. Even if he has never operated a meter before, by the time he completes this course, he will have mastered it and will be able to use it perfectly. See Chapter 14.
Approximately 3 weeks

■ *Scientology Minister's Course*

On this course one trains to become a minister of the Scientology religion, learns about the fundamental beliefs of the great religions of the world and enhances his own understanding of the religious nature of Scientology and the duties of a minister of the Church. Includes all Church ceremonies. It is a prerequisite for permanent certification as an auditor, and upon completion the Scientologist is officially ordained a minister of Scientology.
Approximately 4 weeks

AUDITOR CLASSIFICATION COURSES

Auditor training gives a person a thorough understanding of life and the skills to handle it. As one progresses through each level he learns fundamental Scientology principles and the skills to apply them in session and in life. Upon completing each level, one receives a certificate authorizing him to audit the processes of that level which correspond to the processing side of the Bridge (i.e., Academy Level 0 teaches one to audit Grade 0 processes). One can also advance up the processing side of the Bridge, through the Expanded Grades, by co-auditing with another similarly classed auditor.

The Academy Levels contain some of the most fundamental breakthroughs ever discovered regarding the mind, spirit and life. See Chapter 14 for further information.

Auditor training on the following Academy Levels teaches one to audit the processes to attain the full results of each Grade.

Course times listed require 40 hours study per week, at 8 hours a day for 5 days

■ *Academy Level 0*
(Hubbard Recognized Scientologist)

This course trains one to audit the processes of ARC Straightwire (recall of past incidents) and the processes of Grade 0, which enable one to bring any person to the point where he can communicate freely to anyone on any subject.
Approximately 2 weeks

■ *Academy Level I*
(Hubbard Trained Scientologist)

This course trains one to audit Level I processes so preclears attain the ability to recognize the source of problems and resolve them.
Approximately 2 weeks

■ *Academy Level II*
(Hubbard Certified Auditor)

In this service one learns how to audit Level II processes with the result that his preclear can gain the full end result of Grade II—relief from the hostilities and sufferings of life.
Approximately 2 weeks

■ *Academy Level III*
(Hubbard Professional Auditor)

This course trains one how to make a Grade III Release, one who has attained freedom from the upsets of the past with the ability to face the future.
Approximately 2 weeks

■ *Academy Level IV*
(Hubbard Advanced Auditor)

At this level one learns to audit the processes that free people from fixed conditions and handle their considerations that one must be consistently in a certain state in order to survive. Free of these fixated ideas, a person gains the ability to do new things.
Approximately 2 weeks

On an auditor internship one gains practical experience as an auditor, auditing preclears in the church's Hubbard Guidance Center (HGC). One works under the supervision of trained Case Supervisors, so that he can perfect his auditing skill and achieve all the results offered on the Bridge to Total Freedom. See Chapter 14 for more information.

■ *Class IV Internship*

At this level one works under experienced case supervision and learns to audit all levels up to and including Class IV processes flawlessly.
Approximately 3 weeks

■ *Class V*
(Hubbard New Era
Dianetics Auditor Course)

"New Era Dianetics" is the result of a quarter of a century of application of Dianetics, streamlined and refined by L. Ron Hubbard to the powerful technology it is today. This course trains a person to audit the many auditing rundowns of New Era Dianetics. Here, one inherits the benefit of *all* Mr. Hubbard's research and learns to apply it to eradicate the harmful reactive mind of his preclears and attain the state of Clear.
Approximately 3 weeks

■ *Class V Internship*

One gains valuable experience by auditing many sessions of New Era Dianetics until, through hours of application, he achieves the skill to flublessly use the techniques of NED, with consistently excellent results.
Approximately 3 weeks

■ *Class V Graduate*
(Hubbard Class V Graduate
Auditor Course)

At this level one trains on advanced auditing skills that will ensure his preclears will make rapid progress on their auditing programs on their way to spiritual freedom.
Approximately 3 weeks

■ *Class V Graduate Internship*

Here one audits intensively under specialist case supervision on the exact advanced actions needed on cases so that one can audit these actions flawlessly.
Approximately 3 weeks

■ *Class VA Graduate*
(Hubbard Expanded Dianetics Auditor
Course)

On this course one learns the precise auditing skills needed to audit Expanded Dianetics to handle those elements in a case that lie behind the aberrations that cause a person to compulsively restrain himself.
Approximately 1 week

■ *Class VA Graduate Internship*

On this internship, one audits the precise actions of Expanded Dianetics under skillful case supervision to the point where he can audit these processes perfectly.
Approximately 3 weeks

■ *Class VI*
Saint Hill Special Briefing Course
(Hubbard Senior Scientologist)

This course takes one through the comprehensive, chronological study of all the breakthroughs and discoveries of Dianetics and Scientology, step by step, to bring about a total mastery of the technology. Here, one is provided all the technology that has ever been issued, covering all steps of the Grade Chart up to Clear. This provides a complete understanding of the mind and spirit and all factors that can affect a spiritual being. Auditing sessions are supervised and polished, and students receive auditing on their grades. One becomes a superlative auditor who can audit to perfection all grades of auditing up to Class VI, including technical specialist processes. Graduates are known as the Dukes of the Auditor Elite. See Chapter 13 for more information.

Available only at Saint Hill Organizations and the Flag Service Organization.

Level A: The Fundamentals of Dianetics

Approximately 3 weeks

Level B: The Fundamentals of Scientology

Approximately 3 1/2 weeks

Level C: The Fundamentals of Havingness and Objectives Processing

Approximately 3 1/2 weeks

Level D: The Basics of the E-Meter

Approximately 3 weeks

Level E: The Principles of Auditing

Approximately 3 weeks

Level F: The Handling of Problems

Approximately 2 weeks

Level G: The Fundamentals of Confessionals

Approximately 4 weeks

Level H: The Basics of Listing

Approximately 3 weeks

Level I: The Basics of Listing and Nulling

Approximately 3 1/2 weeks

Level J: The Handling of ARC Breaks and Service Facsimiles

Approximately 3 1/2 weeks

Level K: The Recognition of Pc Indicators

Approximately 3 weeks

Level L: The Fundamentals of the Grade Chart

Approximately 3 weeks

Level M: The Basics of Case Repair and Resistive Cases

Approximately 3 weeks

Level N: The Developments and Techniques of Modern Auditing

Approximately 3 1/2 weeks

Level O: Auditing the Expanded Lower Grades, New Era Dianetics and Repair Actions

Approximately 4 weeks

Level P: Auditing Expanded Dianetics and the Specialist Rundowns

Approximately 4 weeks

Each level can be done as a course, the next to be studied at a later time, or one after the other. The course is available in this manner so that all Scientologists can avail themselves of it while attending to the needs of daily life that may prevent one from studying 40 hours per week for the year or so this course requires.

■ *Class VI Internship*

Approximately 4 weeks

■ *Class VII Auditor Course (Hubbard Graduate Auditor)*

Here one learns highly advanced auditing skills requiring complete mastery of all auditing fundamentals to produce spectacular results on any preclear. The Power Processes are aptly named and require an extremely skilled auditor who has a full grasp of the reactive mind to audit them. Auditing these processes is the ability one acquires on the Class VII Course. Staff only.

Approximately 1 week

ADVANCED AUDITOR CLASSIFICATION COURSES

With the exception of Class VIII, advanced auditor training is only available to contracted staff members of Advanced Organizations and Flag. These courses are available at Saint Hills (Class VII), Advanced Organizations (Class VIII) and the Flag Service Organization (Class VII to XII).

■ *Hubbard Class VIII Auditor Course (Hubbard Specialist of Standard Tech)*

A trained Class VIII Auditor aligns the full spectrum of knowledge below this level to audit to even higher standards, to give flawless, 100 percent standard auditing sessions that produce faster and greater spiritual gains for one's preclears. A Class VIII is a flubless, smooth-as-silk specialist in standard technology. He can audit any case with ease. He is a dedicated advocate for standard technology in his area and sets an example by his own performance.

Approximately 6 weeks

■ *Class VIII Internship*

On this service one interns as a Class VIII, hones his auditing skills to perfection and becomes an uncompromising champion of standard technology.

Approximately 3 weeks

■ *Hubbard Class IX Auditor Course (Hubbard Advanced Courses Specialist)*

This course trains the auditor to become a New Era Dianetics for OTs Auditor, capable of auditing New OT V, New Era Dianetics for OTs. This is the Second Wall of Fire and only when one has successfully walked through it is it possible to regain his true nature and abilities. Only available to staff of Advanced Organizations and above and only given at Flag.

■ *Class IX Internship*

On this service one interns as a Class IX and perfects his skill at this level.

■ *Hubbard Class X–XII Auditor Courses*

These, the highest levels of auditor classification, train an auditor in unique auditing skills, with confidential specialized TRs and metering skills necessary to audit the special L Rundowns, incredible case boosters that are only offered at Flag. The Class XII is the highest classed auditor in Scientology and the few who achieve this level have attained the mastery of all technology used to return one to his native state as a spiritual being. Available only to staff of the Flag Service Organization.

■ *Class X–XII Internships*

On these services one audits intensively under a highly skilled Class XII Case Supervisor to achieve nothing short of perfection in the skills required to audit the L Rundowns.

C/S COURSES

Once a fully interned auditor for any level, one can train as a case supervisor (C/S) for that level. This is a skilled activity which involves responsibility for the training of other auditors and for the results they achieve on their preclears.

There is a case supervisor training course and a case supervisor internship for each training classification level and each technical specialist course.

See Chapter 14 for more information.

C/S training and internships are offered by the same organizations where one can participate in the corresponding auditor classification levels.

Offered at Class V churches and above:

Class IV C/S Course

Class IV C/S Internship

Class V C/S Course

Class V C/S Internship

Class V Graduate C/S Course

Class V Graduate C/S Internship

Purification Rundown C/S Course

Purification Rundown C/S Internship

False Purpose Rundown C/S Course

False Purpose Rundown
  C/S Internship

Class VA Graduate C/S Course

Class VA Graduate C/S Internship

Offered at Saint Hills:

Class VI C/S Course

Class VI C/S Internship

Class VII C/S Course
  (Church staff only)

Offered at Advanced Organizations:

Class VIII C/S Course

Class VIII C/S Internship

Offered at Flag:

  (Church staff only)

Class IX C/S Course

Class IX C/S Internship

Class XII C/S Course

Class XII C/S Internship

COURSES WHICH CAN BE DONE AT DIFFERENT POINTS ON THE BRIDGE

The courses listed below can be done almost anywhere on the Bridge. Many have no or minimal prerequisites.

KEY TO LIFE AND LIFE ORIENTATION COURSES

■ *Hubbard Key to Life Course*

This service boosts the potential abilities of any person.

The most fundamental method of raising one's overall level of ARC is to increase communication. Because the components of theta itself are affinity, reality, communication, this is a remarkably effective action. The course begins with a special and powerful auditing action found nowhere else on the Bridge which brings the individual certainty and newfound stability. Then, through a series of breakthroughs which take apart the fundamentals of language and communication itself, the Key to Life strips away the reasons one is unable to communicate with others. Finally, there is an in-depth study of "The Factors of Scientology," L. Ron Hubbard's summation that unlocks the very riddles of life. For additional data, see Chapter 11. Available at all Class V churches and above.

Approximately 5 weeks

■ *Hubbard Life Orientation Course*

The Hubbard Life Orientation Course shows one how to improve every aspect of his life. Based on Mr. Hubbard's observation that the totality of one's survival can be analyzed against the eight dynamics, and all of life's *activities* can be analyzed against the seven divisions and 21 separate departments of the organizing board, this course provides a clear picture of one's entire existence and then provides the tools needed to rectify any missingnesses. This results not only in the alignment of one's purposes and activities in life, but allows one to more readily obtain the spiritual gains from the rest of Scientology. For additional data, see Chapter 12. Available at all Class V churches and above.

Approximately 4 weeks

HOW TO CONFRONT AND SHATTER SUPPRESSION

■ *PTS/SP Course*

This service trains one to detect and handle suppressive persons—those people who specialize in acting covertly to keep people around them invalidated, ineffective, introverted and small as spiritual beings. As suppression can block spiritual progress in Scientology, the ability to locate and deal with suppressive people and the effects they create is vital. This course is offered at Scientology missions and churches.

Approximately 3 weeks

KEEPING SCIENTOLOGY WORKING

■ *Keeping Scientology Working Course*

Here one learns the vital necessity of standardly applying the technologies of Dianetics and Scientology to know how to keep Scientology working, and to do so.

Approximately 1 week

ETHICS

■ *Scientology Ethics Specialist Course*

It has been said that the ultimate in ethics is the ultimate in survival. The Scientology Ethics Specialist Course enables one to approach that ultimate in all aspects of life. On this course, one studies the dynamics, statistics, the conditions of existence and their formulas, human evaluation and predicting behavior, the anatomy of suppression, the philosophy of ethics and justice and the use of those principles to assist any individual to lead a happier, more honest life. The result of this course is a person who fully understands and applies standard ethics and justice technology to the benefit of all dynamics.

Approximately 4 weeks

PRODUCT DEBUG COURSE

■ *Professional Product Debug Course*

This course teaches one how to find the exact block that is stopping the cycle of production or *any* cycle of action and the steps necessary to get desirable products or cycles of action done. While developed to debug progress in churches, one can use this simple but very effective technology in any area of life. Most recommended after Life Orientation Course.

Approximately 4 days

INTRODUCTORY AUDITOR COURSES

■ *Hubbard Introductory and Demonstration Auditor Course*

This course trains the auditor to competently audit any of the more than 200 introductory processes in Scientology. Each of these processes can bring about life-changing results, and the full body of the Introductory and Demonstration processes provides an auditor the entire battery of technology to help anyone making their first entrance to the Bridge. The course manual is the *Introductory and Demonstration Processes Handbook*.
Approximately 3 days

■ *Hubbard Assists Processing Auditor Course*

This course teaches a Scientologist more than 130 different assist processes, and provides the exact tool to alleviate the spiritual trauma associated with injury and preventing its healing. Includes assist auditing and processes to help people with injuries, burns, bruises, aches, pains, upsets in life, losses and more. Application of assist processes greatly speeds recovery. The manual for this course is the *Assists Processing Handbook*.
Approximately 3 days

■ *Hubbard Group Auditor Course*

Group Processing is formal auditing ministered to a group of people by a trained auditor. In this service one learns all the basic theory and procedures of Group Processing to effectively provide processing to groups of any size and produce spectacular results.
Approximately 3 days

TECHNICAL SPECIALIST COURSES

A classed auditor is qualified to study technical specialist courses, which give the skills to handle a wide variety of specialized auditing rundowns. These are short, fast courses that can be done at an Academy or Saint Hill Organization, giving an auditor the precise auditing skills he needs to help his preclears and handle any spiritual case condition requiring address to advance up the Grade Chart. These services are ministered in Class V churches.

Hubbard Senior
Confessional Auditor Course
Approximately 2 weeks

Hubbard False Purpose Rundown
Auditor Course
Approximately 2 weeks

PTS/SP Auditor Course
Approximately 10 days

Hubbard Happiness Rundown
Auditor Course
Approximately 5 days

Scientology Drug Rundown
Auditor Course
Approximately 2 days

Student Booster Rundown
Auditor Course
Approximately 2 days

Allergy or Asthma Rundown
Auditor Course
Approximately 2 days

Vital Information Rundown
Auditor Course
Approximately 2 days

South African Rundown Auditor Course
Approximately 10 days

Introspection Rundown Auditor Course
Approximately 2 days

Scientology Marriage Counseling
Auditor Course
Approximately 3 days

Handling Fear of People Auditor Course
Approximately 2 days

Est Repair Auditor Course
Approximately 2 days

Psych Treatment Repair Auditor Course
Approximately 2 days

PDH Detection and Handling
Auditor Course
Approximately 5 days

SUPERVISOR AND SERVICE DELIVERY COURSES

The following courses are available in Class V churches or higher and are intended to train church of Scientology staff to minister Dianetics and Scientology courses and services.

■ *Hubbard Mini Course Supervisor Course*

A Course Supervisor is responsible for seeing that his students are able to *apply* their materials. The Hubbard Mini Course Supervisor Course provides all the fundamentals of study technology and teaches the supervisor how, through two-way communication, to isolate any problem a student may be having and resolve it.

Approximately 5 days

■ *Hubbard Professional Word Clearer Course*

Among the many revolutionary discoveries made by L. Ron Hubbard was his discovery of the effects of the misunderstood word. A student who studies past misunderstood words will feel blank and be unable to understand what he has just read. He will also experience a variety of other nonoptimum mental and physiological effects.

The Professional Word Clearer Course teaches one how to find and clear misunderstood words in another. With this technology, one can handle a stalled student and restore his entire education to an individual. Misunderstood words are *the* reason behind the failure to learn and understand any material. A professional Word Clearer not only has the skills necessary to salvage the individual, he has in his hands tools which can be used to revert the decline of civilization itself. Available at Class V churches and above.

Approximately 2 weeks

■ *Hubbard Professional Course Supervisor Course*

The duty of the Course Supervisor is to ensure that students duplicate and can fully apply the materials of their courses. The Course Supervisor is responsible for training standard auditors—a large responsibility as only a 100 percent standard auditor will produce gains in his preclears.

This course teaches the tools of a Course Supervisor, including all forms of Word Clearing, full use and understanding of the study technology, use of clay table training, correct theory checkouts and how to obtain a completely F/Ning course room.

The result of this training is a professional Course Supervisor who has full knowledge of the technology of course supervision and is able to produce graduates who can and do apply the materials they study.

Approximately 3 weeks

■ *Hubbard Co-audit Supervisor Course*

To run a successful co-audit (a course room where students minister auditing to one another on a turnabout basis) one must have good administrative skills as well as an understanding of the processes ministered. On this service one learns the functions necessary for a successful, efficient co-audit. Available at Class V churches and above.

Approximately 4 weeks

■ TR Clay Table Processing Delivery Course

Life is composed of affinity, reality and communication. One of Mr. Hubbard's most fundamental breakthroughs was his analysis of the cycle of communication. By breaking communication down into its component parts it can be understood and one becomes able to remedy any lapse in his own ability to communicate. While vital to all aspects of living successfully, a flawless communication cycle is essential when auditing another being.

The Clay Table Processing Delivery Course, which is only available to staff members, trains a Supervisor to administer Clay Table Processing to students in the course room. This processing results in remarkable increases in the ability to communicate, and is done as part of the Professional TR Course, making it possible for one to perfect his communication skills.

Approximately 2 days

■ Purification Rundown In-Charge Course

This course trains a person to administer the Purification Rundown so that he has the knowledge and skill to see that everyone participating in the program achieves the full gains available.

Approximately 1 week

■ Cramming Officer Course

In examining the structure of organizations, L. Ron Hubbard discovered a missing function which he called the Qualifications Division or Qual — which is responsible for correcting an organization and its people. That duty belongs to the Cramming Officer, who functions to locate the exact reason behind technical or administrative flubs and gets these immediately corrected. Cramming is vital for making a flubless auditor, for every auditor is expected to be 100 percent standard. Any time an auditor goofs, he is immediately crammed and corrected to ensure he can apply the technology flawlessly. And exactly the same thing holds true for administrative personnel. The Cramming Officer guarantees the quality of the delivery of Scientology technology by locating and eliminating anything which cuts across its exact application.

Approximately 5 days

OT DEBUG AND HATTING COURSES

These special courses are comprised of L. Ron Hubbard's lecture series on the subject of Operating Thetan. Offered at the Flag Ship Service Organization, aboard the Motor Vessel *Freewinds,* each course covers a different body of knowledge about the thetan's potentials and capabilities. Though particularly relevant to Scientologists on the OT levels, the courses are recommended for any Scientologist, for by learning about what comprises and what blunts OT ability, one also becomes more capable in life. Available only at the FSSO, except where noted.

OT DEBUG SERVICE

The OT Debug Service is a special service delivered only aboard the *Freewinds* that helps a person isolate and resolve any blocks and barriers which are preventing him from progressing in Scientology. This service is for any Scientologist who needs assistance moving up the Bridge, or for those who simply wish to make faster progress. It consists of a series of specific actions done in an exact sequence by a trained specialist, and includes at least one of the OT Hatting Courses.

OT HATTING COURSES

■ *Time Track of Theta Course*

This service provides insight into man's true capabilities, how these can be recovered and how to use this data to improve conditions in his life and the lives of others.
Approximately 3 days

■ *The Route to Infinity Course*

Here one discovers how a being's decisions and postulates create change in the physical universe, and how to restore the ability to make his postulates become reality. He also learns more about the true nature of the thetan.
Approximately 3 days

■ *Secrets of the MEST Universe Course*

On this service one learns the capabilities of a thetan and how it is possible for one to locate, invent, change, convert and conserve time and space itself and then locate matter and energy in it. One discovers that he is not limited by this universe.
Approximately 5 days

■ *Universes and the War Between Theta and MEST Course*

In Scientology, a universe is defined as "a whole system of created things." The effort of the physical universe is to destroy all life within it, while the universe of theta seeks to master and use the physical universe. This service teaches the individual the weapons needed to win this war. One gains command of the cycle of action of create-survive-destroy; a knowledge of the fundamentals of communication; the laws of affinity and the true nature of reality and agreement. A student learns how to free himself from the traps of the physical universe.
Approximately 16 days

■ *The Perception of Truth Course*

To suddenly be confronted with the raw, naked truth about himself and his relationship to the physical universe can leave a being in a very unstable condition. This leads not to freedom, but further entrapment. This service describes how one resolves this dilemma and remains free. Here is a description of the "Qs," the highest common denominators of all experience.
Approximately 3 days

■ *The Phoenix Lectures Course*

In 1954, L. Ron Hubbard delivered a series of lectures which traced the religious and philosophical roots of Scientology back more than 10,000 years to the Vedic hymns. By taking the collective wisdom of the ages and adding to it the "impatience and urgency" of Western science, he arrived at the fundamental truths of Scientology. This service teaches the student the Axioms of Scientology, those self-evident truths which form the very fabric of existence and give him the ability to be at cause over any reality.
Approximately 5 days

■ *The Creation of Human Ability Course*

"Pan-determinism means 'the willingness of an individual to monitor two or more identities, whether or not opposing,'" L. Ron Hubbard stated. This course covers the subject of pan-determinism and other basic fundamentals of Scientology—fundamentals which makes it possible for one to not only increase his own spiritual abilities but also those of others around him.
Approximately 12 days

■ *The Power of Simplicity Course*

Though life is a game of complexities, winning that game lies not in the direction of greater complexity or more force, but greater and greater simplicity. This service teaches one the basics of simplicity, what it is, why it is valuable, what it means to confront life and thus operate better as an OT.
Approximately 12 days

■ *The Anatomy of Cause Course*

To set about to increase one's ability is a lie for the ability already exists. An auditor is simply increasing the individual's willingness to be, do, have, confront and create. This course explains how understanding these factors makes it possible to bring about spiritual improvement in oneself and others.
Approximately 9 days

■ *Whole Track Course*

On this course, one gains a profound understanding of the whole track (the moment-to-moment record of one's existence in this universe in picture and impression form), how it affects a being and how one can use this information to better the conditions of his life and the lives of those around him.
Approximately 3 days

■ *The Solution to Entrapment Course*

This universe punishes a being for communicating, yet only communication can undo the traps and free a being. Here, the student learns the mechanics and formulas of communication, the basics to life itself. One experiences life to the degree he is able to communicate and this course gives one a firm grasp on the principles of communication.
Approximately 10 days

■ *The Ability Congress Course*

The mission of Scientology is to increase the ability of people to live well. On this service one learns OT principles that will enable him to create, participate in and be responsible for the groups to which he belongs and thus enhance his survival on the third dynamic.

Approximately 5 days

■ *The State of Man Congress Course*

How has man arrived in his current state? What caused him to be in the condition he is in? On this course, the student discovers the simple reasons behind why an individual ceases to create along any of his dynamics. Here one learns how to salvage a marriage, rehabilitate the artist and make a government more ethical.

Approximately 4 days

■ *The Doctorate Series Course for OTs*

"The universe doesn't have any existence except the capability of a thetan . . . to perceive, to do, to create space and to handle energy and objects in that space," L. Ron Hubbard wrote. This course, consisting of 76 different lectures on the state of Operating Thetan, teaches one how to disagree with the illusion of the physical universe. The result is a being who understands the anatomy of universes and how to create them. Available at Advanced Organizations.

Approximately 4 weeks

■ *The Dawn of Immortality Course*

On this course, one finds out what happened to him and to his powers as a spiritual being—and how to recover them. He also learns the fascinating story of the very beginnings of Scientology.

Approximately 7 days

■ *The Skills of a Theta Being Course*

How does a being plummet from a total knowingness down to complete ignorance of his own creations and postulates? Here one not only discovers the answer to that question, but the route back from ignorance to total cause.

Approximately 5 days

■ *Exteriorization and the Phenomena of Space Course*

In Camden, New Jersey on October 6, 1953, a group of ten auditors chosen by L. Ron Hubbard were lectured on the latest breakthroughs and advanced techniques in exteriorization. This course, made up of the 84 lectures in that series, imparts techniques of rehabilitating a spiritual being using processes which address certainty, beingness, viewpoints and space. Available at Advanced Organizations.

Approximately 4 weeks

■ *Responsibility and the State of OT Course*

A being is responsible for his own condition. Only he can limit himself to blindness, ignorance and inability. The student learns the exact mechanics of how one becomes a victim of life and how to remedy this to bring a person to a high level of responsibility so that he can reach the state of Operating Thetan.

Approximately 2 weeks

■ *The First Postulate Course*

What existed before the beginning? On this course one learns the answer to that age-old question. He also learns how a being postulates his own case into existence and how he obsessively continues to create his own difficulties. If one wishes to address the core of irrationality and insanity, one must address the original intentions which cause the being to aberrate himself in the first place.

Approximately 2 weeks

CELEBRITY CENTRE COURSE

■ *The Principles of Creation Course*

This series covers the most basic principle of creation, which is restoring the individual's self-determinism and his ability to create anything. What is evil to a person are those things which are other-determined, over which he believes he has no control. The destructive power of valences—another person's identity unknowingly assumed by the individual—is revealed. When the individual becomes himself, fully self-determined and "captain of his own destiny" he regains his own native goodness and ability to create. Available at Advanced Organization Saint Hill ANZO.

Approximately 4 days

■ *The Rehabilitation of the Human Spirit Course*

The restoration of one's true beingness and the ability to grant beingness to others is the focal point of this service. Here one learns the techniques used to rehabilitate the power to postulate and create his own future. On this course, made up of 67 lectures, one discovers previously hidden knowledge of the human spirit, exteriorization and the creation of space, time and matter.

Approximately 2 weeks

■ *Hubbard Basic Art Course*

The restoration of a thetan's creative impulses and faculties is an integral part of true spiritual freedom. Indeed, Mr. Hubbard noted that aesthetic impulses are those closest to the inherent nature of the being himself. By studying fundamentals of art, aesthetics and creativity on this course and mastering their use, one can dramatically rehabilitate native creative abilities, and thus similarly restore the ability to confront the universe with a strong and ethical face. Offered only by Celebrity Centre churches and higher-level churches.

Approximately 4 days

CHILDREN'S COURSES

Designed for children ages 8 through 11, each course provides important skills for succeeding in school and with people. Fully illustrated, they cover a range of Scientology fundamentals but are presented at a level for young readers. Subjects include communication, the parts of man, the Tone Scale, how to use a dictionary, grammar and others. There are also children's courses which teach L. Ron Hubbard's study technology.

Children's Communication Course

Learning How to Learn Course

Study Skills for Life Course

How to Use a Dictionary Course

Grammar and Communication for Children Course

Basic Study Manual Course

Also offered by field auditors, groups and missions, they generally require 1 to 3 weeks of part-time study to complete.

ADMINISTRATIVE TRAINING

■ *Staff Status 0*

This is the first step taken by a new staff member to get familiar with the church organization and his fellow staff. This short checklist of actions takes the new staff member into each department of the organization where he learns of their duties and gets answers to any questions he may have.

Approximately 5 hours

■ *Staff Status I*

As a new church staff member a person studies the materials for Staff Status I which give him a basic knowledge of church organization and orient him to his duties and responsibilities as church staff. He achieves provisional status in the church organization through completing this course. This is the first step on the way to becoming a contributing church staff member. Available at missions and churches.

Approximately 2 days

■ *Staff Status II*

Trains one on the materials necessary for full church staff member status and gives the staff member a firm grasp of organizational fundamentals. It also qualifies one for future promotion to an executive position. Although dealing in the technology of administration, the material one studies on this course springs from L. Ron Hubbard's philosophical discoveries. Where auditing technology deals primarily with the application of these principles to the first dynamic, their application on the third dynamic is no less remarkable in their workability. Available at missions and churches.

Approximately 5 days

■ *Organization Executive Course (OEC)*

The materials for this course are contained in the *Organization Executive Course* Volumes 0–7 and the courses for each volume may be done individually. These volumes contain the basic laws of organization. While developed by Mr. Hubbard for Church organizations, the OEC covers *any* organization and contains fundamentals vital to any successful activity. Before *Dianetics* was published, man did not really know the principles of organization any more than he knew what made his mind work.

The OEC includes a complete study of the revolutionary organizational design known as the organizing board or "org board," which delineates every necessary function for perfectly coordinated effort. If anyone fully knew the OEC and could use it, he could completely reverse any downtrending group or organization. This is available at Class V churches and above. For more information about the organizing board, see Chapter 20.

Approximately 16 weeks

Basic Staff Hat
(Organization Executive Course, Volume 0)
Approximately 2 weeks

Organization Executive Course, Volume 1
Approximately 3 weeks

Organization Executive Course, Volume 2
Approximately 2 weeks

Organization Executive Course, Volume 3
Approximately 1 week

Organization Executive Course, Volume 4
Approximately 3 weeks

Organization Executive Course, Volume 5
Approximately 2 weeks

Organization Executive Course, Volume 6
Approximately 3 weeks

Organization Executive Course, Volume 7
Approximately 3 1/2 weeks

■ *Hubbard Consultant Course*

This course may be done after completing all volumes of the Organization Executive Course and preliminary auditor training. It is a prerequisite to advanced administrative training on the Flag Executive Briefing Course. It gives administrators enough technical training so they can be auditors on the *third dynamic,* without having to do full Academy training. A graduate of this course is skilled in two-way communication and can use an E-Meter to aid staff in administrative situations.

Approximately 1 1/2 weeks

■ *Flag Executive Briefing Course (FEBC)*

This course is built around Mr. Hubbard's *Management Series* volumes and related tape-recorded lectures and is based on an understanding of the principles and know-how imparted in the Organization Executive Course. Being himself a leader of men, he wrote up the philosophical and practical truths he applied in dealing with groups, to ensure the survival of the third and fourth dynamics. This service is available for public and mission staff only at the Flag Service Org, and for Class V staff and above at the International Training Organization in Los Angeles.

Approximately 6 weeks

■ *Hubbard Elementary Data Series Evaluator's Course*

Any thetan's survival potential depends on his ability to think. The technology of this course—the Data Series—is the greatest breakthrough in logic and rational thought in man's history. Through the exact application of this technology, one can find the underlying reason that causes any situation, good or bad, to exist. This gives one the magic key that opens the road to success in any endeavor. Delivered at Class V churches and above.

Approximately 2 weeks

■ *Hubbard Executive Data Series Evaluator's Course*

Building on an in-depth familiarity of organizations and their different parts and products, one becomes an expert in using the Data Series to rapidly and accurately locate the exact reasons for any situation. Mastering this course results in effective programs that will enhance any organization. Only available at Flag.

Approximately 4 weeks

FIELD MINISTRY COURSES

■ *Hubbard Dissemination Course*

On this service one drills not only how to apply basic Scientology principles to others to show them that these techniques work, but how to interest them in Scientology, and to apply its principles and techniques to their own lives.

Approximately 1 1/2 weeks

■ *Field Staff Member Specialist Course*

This course teaches the basics of how to effectively disseminate the knowledge of Scientology to other people and enlighten them on what Scientology is about. It includes FSM TRs, through which one gains the confidence to disseminate to anyone, at any time.

Approximately 2–3 days

■ *Special Course in Human Evaluation*

Here one finds out how to tell if someone he meets can be trusted, whether in business, friendship and even a marriage. Once one knows some of the basic fundamentals of human thought, he can accurately predict behavior and guarantee his own survival in relationships with others.

Approximately 1 week

OTHER CHURCH SERVICES

The traditional functions of churches are covered here, as well as services that do not involve auditing to help parishioners with specific needs. These services are ministered by Scientology ministers. See Chapter 16 for more information.

Sunday Church Services

Weddings

Funerals

Naming Ceremonies

Chaplain's Assistance

Ethics Consultation

Word Clearing

Qual Consultation

Qual Corrective Actions (Cramming)

Preclear Case Check

Preclear and Pre-OT Case Folder Review

CHAPTER 47

THE BOOKS, LECTURES AND VIDEOS OF SCIENTOLOGY

The best source of information on Dianetics and Scientology is the books and recorded lectures of L. Ron Hubbard. To guide the reader interested in learning more about Dianetics and Scientology, this chapter contains a selection of suggested books, lectures and videos. A complete chronological list of all Dianetics and Scientology materials including all administrative and technical issues and articles, insignia and more follow in Chapter 48.

One may wonder where to begin and in what sequence to study these materials. In general, the categories below begin with basic materials and progress to the more advanced or specialized. In addition to the individual books described in these pages, selected volumes are available in special packages. These selections were compiled to present the books in the ideal sequence, so your reading parallels your progress in Scientology and your advancement in auditing and training services.

The wisdom of L. Ron Hubbard can be found in these materials. They are available to anyone who wants them, whether near or far from a Scientology church. Many of these books are available in public bookstores and libraries; the rest can be obtained at any of the Scientology organizations listed in Chapter 49. Many have been translated into a number of different languages.

DIANETICS BOOKS

Dianetics: The Modern Science of Mental Health

Before Dianetics, the world did not have a precise and workable means to resolve problems of the mind. Into this dark age, like a bolt from the blue, came the publication of *Dianetics: The Modern Science of Mental Health*.

Published on May 9, 1950, *Dianetics* was hailed as a breakthrough by Walter Winchell, noted columnist of the *New York Daily Mirror* "as revolutionary for humanity as the first caveman's discovery and utilization of fire." The book instantly became a *New York Times* bestseller, and has routinely outsold the average bestseller year after year for five decades. In fact, no other book in history has even appeared on the *New York Times* bestseller list nearly fifty years after its first publication and appearance. With 18 million copies sold, it is indisputably the most widely read and influential book on the human mind ever published. That its importance was immediately recognized can be seen in the fact that within the first year of its initial release, more than 750 Dianetics groups sprang up in the United States.

This book marks a turning point in man's knowledge and understanding of himself. It is *the* manual of Dianetics procedure. In *Dianetics*, L. Ron Hubbard details the dynamic principle of existence (*Survive!*) and provides the first accurate description of the human mind, what it consists of and how it operates. He describes in great detail the source of all human aberration: the reactive mind and its engrams. Having discovered the barrier to rationality and survival, L. Ron Hubbard then developed a technology to eradicate its harmful effects, resulting in a new state of existence for man, the state of Clear. The auditing techniques for erasing engrams and creating Clears are covered in vivid detail in *Dianetics* and continue to be widely used today.

The importance of this book was not underestimated when it was first published —

and should not be today. Anyone who has not read *Dianetics* remains ignorant of the most important breakthroughs on the subject of the human mind.

The Dynamics of Life

Written in 1947, this is the first formal record of L. Ron Hubbard's researches into the structure and functions of the human mind. Although written before "Book One" (*Dianetics: The Modern Science of Mental Health*), it was published after it.

In his introduction, he wrote: "Dianetics offers the first anatomy of the human mind and techniques for handling the hitherto unknown reactive mind, which causes irrational and psychosomatic behavior. It has successfully removed any compulsions, repressions, neuroses and psychoses to which it has been applied."

The Dynamics of Life was Mr. Hubbard's original thesis and includes the first description of auditing principles, including the code of conduct an auditor should follow, and the nature of engrams and their effects upon individuals. There are also case histories showing the unprecedented results of early Dianetics auditing. Not surprisingly, when it was first circulated, Mr. Hubbard was deluged with requests for more information. This led him to write his landmark manual of Dianetics procedure, *Dianetics: The Modern Science of Mental Health* — the "textbook" of Dianetics. *The Dynamics of Life* offers a more concise view of how the mind works and how Dianetics can be used to alleviate man's suffering.

Dianetics: The Evolution of a Science

At a young age, L. Ron Hubbard became greatly intrigued by the mystery of man and his mind. *Dianetics: The Evolution of a Science* is the story of how he came to make the breakthroughs which solve this mystery.

Here, L. Ron Hubbard traces the exact sequence of events leading to his discoveries about the human mind and his detection of that hidden part of the mind responsible for all of man's nonsurvival behavior.

This book reveals how Mr. Hubbard was able to recognize and isolate an individual's true basic personality and details how painful or traumatic events in life can become fused with an individual's innermost self, causing fears, insecurities and psychosomatic ills. And it shows how, by first describing the full potential of the mind, he was able to discover these impediments. Because of his work, this potential is now attainable.

While *Dianetics: The Modern Science of Mental Health* details what Dianetics is and how to use it, this is the book that tells how Mr. Hubbard made those discoveries.

Self Analysis

Self Analysis is an indispensable volume of tests and techniques based on the discoveries of Dianetics. This book takes the reader on the most interesting adventure of all, the adventure of self, and the realization of one's potentials, which are "a great deal better than anyone ever permitted you to believe."

Central to the book is a self-evaluation chart, where one can plot one's improvement in tone level through the use of Self Analysis processes. Specifically, processes one can do on himself are included. Indeed, as one progresses through these procedures, he is in fact being audited by Mr. Hubbard himself. Readers report that using this handbook for just half an hour a day can dramatically improve memory, reaction time, alertness, and just the plain ordinary ability to be happy in life and enjoy things. By reevaluating oneself, an individual can see his own progress and advancement. This is the adventure of Dianetics one can employ right at home.

Science of Survival

This is the book that changed forever the way we look at life and the universe. Prior to the publication of this book, life was looked on by science as a sort of heat-energy machine operating on stimulus-response. L. Ron Hubbard's breakthrough, first described in this book, was the isolation of "life energy" as a type of energy existing separate from the physical universe. He used the Greek letter *theta* (θ) to describe this energy. It is the impact of this energy on the physical universe of matter, energy, space and time (MEST) that gives us the entire range of human experience. This breakthrough became known as the "theta–MEST theory."

It was this breakthrough that led to the development of the Chart of Human Evaluation, which is central to this book. This amazing chart is the most profound and insightful look at human character and behavior ever developed. This chart and its use in the accurate assessment of people and the prediction of their future behavior are described in detail.

Dianetics is pervasive. Human behavior and human thought are the foundation of human endeavor. Once one has the answer to these basic riddles there is almost nothing which will not eventually resolve.

Dianetics 55!

Called "the second book of Dianetics," this book contains a summary of the developments and breakthroughs in the five years following the publication of "Book One" (*Dianetics: The Modern Science of Mental Health*) in 1950. It further explores what was called in *Dianetics* the "awareness of awareness unit"—the person himself—and defines the components of freedom (affinity, reality and communication) and of entrapment (matter, energy, space and time).

Dianetics 55! also provides the fundamentals of communication—a subject so vital to spiritual freedom that one can state that a person is as alive as he can communicate. This text is used today in Scientology courses as the definitive manual of effective communication.

Child Dianetics

Published to meet the demand from parents for a book on how to better understand and bring up children using the principles of Dianetics, *Child Dianetics* reveals the true cause and remedy of childhood upsets, irrationality and fears. This book shows parents how to truly understand a child and establish an honest and loving relationship based on trust and mutual respect. It is a guide no parent should be without.

Notes on the Lectures of L. Ron Hubbard

In late 1950, Mr. Hubbard gave a series of pivotal lectures on Dianetics, the affinity-reality-communication triangle and the Tone Scale. At his request, the staff of the Hubbard Dianetics Research Foundation took detailed notes—including copies of his chalkboard diagrams—and compiled them into this comprehensive textbook.

Here is some of the earliest and best material on the ARC triangle and the Tone Scale—a detailed look at how one's attitude towards life, ability to communicate with others, behavior and even physical well-being shift as one goes up and down the scale.

Handbook for Preclears

This Dianetics workbook can be used both as a processing handbook by an auditor, or as a self-processing handbook that the individual uses by himself. It is designed to raise the individual on the Tone Scale, lessening the effect of the reactive mind and restoring self-determinism, intelligence and abilities. If one wants to experience the miraculous results of Dianetics auditing, one only needs this book and one's own desire to improve.

Handbook for Preclears contains the famous Chart of Attitudes. Using this chart, one can gain a profound understanding of people just by observing their attitudes towards life.

Advanced Procedure and Axioms

Dianetics is the first subject to codify life into axioms. In this book one finds the fundamental principles that govern life and the mind. When one knows and uses these basic laws, one can achieve spiritual freedom. There are three points of address in any case—thought, emotion and effort. Here is their anatomy and description with exact processing for each.

This book reveals for the first time the power of an individual's own thoughts and decisions in shaping life.

SCIENTOLOGY BOOKS

Scientology: The Fundamentals of Thought

Mr. Hubbard regarded *The Fundamentals of Thought* as his first Scientology book. In this work, he introduces many of the powerful basic principles of the Scientology religion. It includes a broad summary of his research and contains a complete description of Scientology's most fundamental principles: the cycle of action, the conditions of existence, the ARC triangle and the parts of man — thetan, mind and body.

These are more than theories. They address *how* life works and *why*, thereby bringing the reader to a greater understanding of his real identity as a spiritual being, of his fellows and of the world around him. And one chapter consists of Scientology auditing techniques that can be immediately used to bring about changes for the better. *The Fundamentals of Thought* are, indeed, the fundamentals of life.

Scientology: A New Slant on Life

This collection of thirty essays by L. Ron Hubbard provides the reader with a new view of what life *can* be — what we all once dreamed it could be. Here, the reader will discover the two rules to follow for happy living, the exact anatomy of failure and how by knowing this one can win in life more often than he loses, how to live with children so that they grow up to be intelligent and happy, the key concept anyone can use to help someone change his destructive behavior patterns, how knowledge affects sanity and the first usable description of what constitutes true individual greatness.

Scientology: A New Slant on Life contains both a discussion of the profound principles and concepts on which Scientology is based and remarkable practical techniques anyone can use to improve his life.

Scientology 0-8: The Book of Basics

Here are the fundamental principles and technical data of Scientology. *The Book of Basics* is a distillation of the entire body of Scientology scripture. Indeed, the title of this book means "Scientology, zero to infinity," the numeral 8 being the symbol for infinity standing upright.

Mr. Hubbard plotted many of his observations onto scales of attributes or characteristics of the spirit, mind and life. These invaluable discoveries are included in *The Book of Basics* and may be used to understand the extremes and intervening gradients of such things as responsibility, emotion, affinity, awareness and knowingness itself.

This book includes a thorough discussion of the Axioms of Dianetics and Scientology. These are the basic laws of life itself. With this knowledge one can understand and predict all human behavior. Included too are Mr. Hubbard's discoveries of the fundamentals underlying all forms of thought, known as the Logics.

Scientology 0-8 concisely provides the central, fundamental data of life.

The Problems of Work

Work is a large and important part of life for nearly everyone. It also can be a major source of upset, anxiety and frustration, and thus become a major barrier to spiritual progress. Those who do not like work usually do not enjoy life. This important book analyzes and explains the relationship between the individual and his work. It shows exactly what job-related factors can lead to exhaustion and discomfort and provides exact procedures the reader can use to overcome them. And it demonstrates how one can regain his enthusiasm for work.

In *The Problems of Work,* Mr. Hubbard isolates the problems encountered on the job — whether on the assembly line or in the CEO's office. He offers solutions to frayed tempers and the common feeling that one cannot possibly accomplish all there is to do. This book uncovers the way to handle the confusions that surround a job and opens the doors to efficiency. In fact, within these pages one will find the keys to success and personal satisfaction.

Have You Lived Before This Life?

With more than forty individual accounts of past lives revealed during auditing sessions, this book started a huge international upsurge of interest in the subject. Per survey today, 27 percent of the population believe they have lived before. *Have You Lived Before This Life?* started it all. It describes the life-changing benefits from recalling past lives and how this knowledge can increase spiritual awareness. It answers such questions as "What happens when a person dies?" and "Are there such things as ghosts?"

All About Radiation

Written by Mr. Hubbard and two well-known medical doctors, this book provides one the facts surrounding the effect of radiation on the body and spirit and offers solutions to those harmful effects. An immediate sellout in bookstores when originally released, *All About Radiation* tells the truth about the little known and talked about subject of radiation, and introduces the Purification Rundown as the technology to handle the cumulative effects of radiation.

Scientology 8-80

The discovery and increase of life energy is a goal as old as man himself. That goal has been realized in Scientology, and this book reveals how. Technique 8-80 is a specialized form of Scientology. It is, specifically, the electronics of human thought and beingness. It is basic in answering the riddles of life and its goals in the physical universe.

The goal is *survival*. The means to survival for life is the handling and use of energy.

The "8-8" stands for "infinity-infinity" upright, the "0" represents the static, theta.

Here Mr. Hubbard describes how the thetan acts as a mirror. Here is the truth of man's nature as a spiritual being that *creates* and *uses* the energies of aesthetics, thought, emotion and effort to operate in the physical universe.

Scientology 8-8008

The meaning of "8-8008" is that one attains infinity (the symbol 8 laid on its side)

through the reduction of the apparent infinity of the physical universe to zero and the increase of one's own creative ability from an apparent zero to infinity. In other words, it is the study of how to free the human spirit from the effects of the physical universe.

This is where the Factors (summations of the considerations and examinations of the human spirit and physical universe) are presented. Originally presented to attendees of Mr. Hubbard's Philadelphia Doctorate Course lectures, they describe the native beingness of man and the interaction of theta and MEST.

Scientology: A History of Man

This book is, as Mr. Hubbard stated in the introduction, "a coldblooded and factual account of your last sixty trillion years."

"The test of any knowledge is its usefulness. Does it make one happier or more able? By it and with it, can he better achieve his goals?"

"Like all useful knowledge it was hardly won. I began search into the backtrack of mankind some years ago. There was no actual knowledge of it in existence. There were numberless superstitions, countless guesses, as many theories in favor of one thing as in favor of another. People believed, some of them, that man had lived before. They had no proof. Others believed that man was born innocent and died and went to a place called Hell. Most believed that when you had lived once, that was all, fellow.

"Such a number of conflicting theories must have truth in them. It became my business to discover, against considerable odds, that truth."

History of Man gives those discoveries, containing a description of the principal incidents on the whole track.

The Creation of Human Ability

This book charts the route to the ultimate human ability—operating as a spiritual being exterior to one's body. With more than 80 powerful processes, this book forms a comprehensive handbook for the rehabilitation of man's true abilities.

REFERENCE HANDBOOKS

The Scientology Handbook

A companion volume to *What Is Scientology?*, this handbook covers the basic principles anyone needs to survive.

You've read *What Is Scientology?* Here is the book that shows you how to *use* Scientology.

Many people want to help others and would if only they knew what to do. This book fills that need. It is the key book used by Scientology Volunteer Ministers in their crusade to do something effective about conditions on this planet.

The Scientology Handbook provides miracle-working Scientology technology on how to preserve marriages, get delinquent children back in the fold, handle dissident elements in the society, get families out of the red, solve human conflict, handle illiteracy, resolve drug, alcohol and many other problems.

With more than 950 pages of practical solutions to the real problems of life, this book is a vital survival manual to living in today's world. (See Chapter 28.)

Introductory and Demonstration Processes Handbook

The more than 200 processes in this handbook are designed specifically for the person just beginning auditing. They address one's immediate life concerns and give him a reality of what Scientology auditing is and what it can accomplish—immediate spectacular results!

These processes are simple to learn and easy to apply. They may be put to use with no more preparation than studying one simple chapter. L. Ron Hubbard introduced this handbook by saying, "I refuse to take responsibility for any miracles you pull off. But for sure you are going to make some eyes pop. Have fun."

Assists Processing Handbook

Assists are processes that help a person to recover more rapidly from bruises, burns, illnesses, upsets or other mishaps. They alleviate the spiritual aspects of physical pain, shock and emotional trauma. Assists are used routinely to help anyone regardless of where he is on the Bridge.

This handbook contains more than 130 individual processes which are very easy to learn. Noticeable improvement can occur from performing an assist, which makes it an ideal way to introduce someone to Scientology.

Group Auditor's Handbook

Group Processing is a form of auditing which can produce startling results. These processes are ministered by a single auditor to a group of individuals gathered in one room and provide gains to many individuals at once. Anyone can partake regardless of how little or how much auditing they have had in Scientology. This book contains 33 simple to perform Group Auditing processes.

The Book of Case Remedies

A text for the full-time auditor, *The Book of Case Remedies* locates and handles the source of any obstacles to successful auditing. Here is a formidable array of remedies that the auditor can use to help people overcome any spiritual barriers that are preventing them from winning in life.

THE E-METER

Understanding the E-Meter

The E-Meter is a religious artifact which aids in auditing by measuring mental state and change of state in individuals. Without the E-Meter, one could not achieve the miracles occurring daily in Scientology.

With over seventy illustrations, the book *Understanding the E-Meter* provides insight into why and how the E-Meter reacts to thought and explains the mind and its relation to the physical universe. With this book one understands the basics behind auditing and how individuals are helped to locate and then handle their reactive mind and aberrations through the use of the E-Meter. The E-Meter makes possible spiritual freedom. This book describes how.

Introducing the E-Meter

This book contains very clear large-format photographs of what each E-Meter needle reaction looks like and means. Included here is information on how a change in the preclear's mental or spiritual state registers on the E-Meter, the parts of the E-Meter and how one sets up an E-Meter for use in an auditing session.

E-Meter Essentials

Skill in meter use depends upon fully familiarizing oneself with an actual meter. *E-Meter Essentials* provides a thorough coverage of the E-Meter, its use in various situations that may arise in an auditing session and a detailed description of the meter and needle reactions and what each one means.

The Book of E-Meter Drills

Use of the E-Meter is a very precise activity and requires familiarity and expertise. This book is key to gaining that expertise. It contains the entire gradient scale of E-Meter Drills used in training in Dianetics and Scientology.

For a further description of the E-Meter, see pages 165-167.

PURIFICATION

Clear Body, Clear Mind: The Effective Purification Program

Through extensive research, L. Ron Hubbard discovered that certain drugs can lodge in the fatty tissues of the body, and cause "flashbacks," tiredness, mental dullness and other adverse reactions, for years after their use ceases. He then developed the exact technology to rid an individual of the adverse effects of drugs, chemicals, radiation and toxins which can inhibit spiritual progress. This book explains that technology and provides the procedures of the Purification Rundown, the most effective program known to handle toxic residues in the body. Thousands of people from around the world have completed this lifesaving program and freed themselves from the harmful effects of drugs and toxins.

For a further description of the Purification Rundown, see Chapter 9.

Purification: An Illustrated Answer to Drugs

This fully illustrated book describes the Purification Rundown and exactly how it addresses the restimulative effects of drugs and toxins in the body. Included here in text and illustrations are the steps of the Purification Rundown. The book explains how the rundown removes drugs and toxins that have been stored in the body, and how this purification restores the ability to think more clearly.

ETHICS

Introduction to Scientology Ethics

In *Introduction to Scientology Ethics* Mr. Hubbard presents the first basic and workable ethics technology ever developed. Terms like *ethics, justice* and *morals* are defined, formulas to improve the survival of individuals and groups alike are provided, and codes to honest and happy living are revealed. By using these powerful principles of Scientology ethics every day a person can live a life of integrity and ever-increasing survival.

EXECUTIVE

How to Live Though an Executive

Recognizing that the role of the executive in an organization is planning and supervision, L. Ron Hubbard, after a broad study of communications theory and systems and a survey of many organizations, originated and composed the organizational communications system presented in *How to Live Though an Executive*. This is a communication manual for any organization. It details the exact factors an executive needs to successfully run an organization—from handling mail to raising morale to setting group goals.

ART

Art

In this book L. Ron Hubbard answers a question that has puzzled people for centuries: "What is art?" Mr. Hubbard not only provides the first clear definition of art, but also discusses the components necessary to create a truly artistic communication. This is knowledge that any artist, any viewer of art or anyone who intends to communicate successfully will recognize as infinitely valuable.

QUOTATIONS

Understanding: The Universal Solvent

L. Ron Hubbard said of wisdom, "It belongs to those who can use it to help themselves and others." This book was created to meet the demand of those who wanted to do just that. This inspiring collection of more than four hundred of Mr. Hubbard's favorite quotations spans such subjects as Understanding, Communication, Survival, Goals, Happiness and Freedom.

Knowingness

The popularity of *Understanding* prompted a second volume of LRH quotations. This collection from L. Ron Hubbard's writings covers more advanced concepts of life and spirituality including Imagination, Thought, Universes, Aesthetics, Force, Lies and Truth, Work, Play, Power, Responsibility and more.

REFERENCES SERIES

The Technical Bulletins of Dianetics and Scientology

The eighteen volumes of *The Technical Bulletins of Dianetics and Scientology* contain all of L. Ron Hubbard's technical bulletins, articles and essays on Dianetics and Scientology. In chronological order and fully referenced for easy use by anyone, these volumes are the broadest, most complete written record available on the spirit, the mind and life.

These books are vital to a full understanding of the technology of Dianetics and Scientology and are used extensively in the Academies of churches of Scientology. They are also invaluable as a key reference archive to have at home or at work to provide the exact technology needed to handle any situation in life.

Research and Discovery Series

Compiled from more than 25,000,000 words on archived tapes, this series contains a complete record of all of L. Ron Hubbard's recorded technical lectures and demonstrations. These volumes comprise all the advances which made possible the handling of the human mind and spirit, and contain more data than ever released in written bulletins by many times. There is no similar record.

Each volume also chronicles Mr. Hubbard's travels, providing reproduced photographs of L. Ron Hubbard as well as the letters, telegrams, charts and articles he wrote during those times.

The Organization Executive Course (OEC) and Management Series Volumes

If one knows the basic truths of life and the universe as contained in Dianetics and Scientology he can then effectively resolve and handle any area of human endeavor.

These twelve encyclopedia-sized volumes address the human dynamics of the workplace with the same thoroughness and insight with which Scientology addresses the life of the individual.

The OEC volumes correspond to the seven divisions of a Scientology organization, with an additional volume containing the fundamentals of organizational technology. This seven-division organization form, itself a breakthrough of magnitude, contains all of the actions and activities needed to secure the continued success and expansion of any organization.

The *Management Series* volumes contain revolutionary breakthroughs in how to organize, establish and operate any activity or group. A major advance contained in these volumes is on the subject of logic. Modern man has no real system of logic or rational thinking and thus reaches wrong conclusions and takes incorrect actions. The logic system contained in this series enables anyone to find the exact reason for any problem or situation, no matter how large, and open the door to handling it.

This technology applies to endeavors ranging from one person to thousands of people and when put into use expands either with predictable and phenomenal results.

RECORDED LECTURE SERIES

L. Ron Hubbard's discovery of the true nature of man as an immortal spiritual being of near infinite capacity, senior to the mechanics of matter, energy, space and time, opened new and unexplored horizons. He coined a new word, *thetan,* to describe this spiritual being. A thetan is defined as the person himself—not his body or his name, the physical universe, his mind or anything else; that which is aware of being aware; the identity which *is* the individual.

Mr. Hubbard spent much of his life exploring the spiritual potentials of man—what blocks those potentials, why is man trapped, and how can man become all that he is capable of becoming? In short, how high can man go?

During his more than half-century of research, Mr. Hubbard delivered thousands of lectures traveling throughout the United States, to England, Australia and South Africa, speaking to large Scientology congresses, groups of students and packed public auditoriums. All told, he gave more than three thousand lectures, sometimes delivering as many as four a day. Enthralled audiences not only gained priceless data but a personal insight into a man of broad intellect, with a keen sense of humor and boundless compassion. Whether interested new public, a select group of top auditors or staff of the earliest Scientology churches, their lives were changed in myriad ways by these lectures. There is still no way to get closer to L. Ron Hubbard than through listening to these recordings, as people around the world discover every day.

Below are the lecture series that have been released to date. They form the only complete record of this history-making research in existence. Those who have listened to them report dramatic changes in their viewpoint, ability and cause level in life just by gaining the knowledge they contain.

The lectures in each series are listed in the order in which they were given, beginning with the earliest lectures in 1952.

L. RON HUBBARD ON VIDEO

An Introduction to Scientology

This one-hour filmed interview, the only one ever granted by Mr. Hubbard, explains how he made his discoveries and breakthroughs during his explorations of the mind, spirit and life. He discusses his bestseller, *Dianetics: The Modern Science of Mental Health,* and how Scientology came about. And he answers the most commonly asked questions: What is Scientology? Why is it a religion? What is the difference between the mind and the spirit? What is man's true purpose? How do people benefit from Scientology? And what do people do in churches of Scientology?

The Clearing Congress
(6 lectures)

This is the only series of lectures given by Mr. Hubbard that was filmed in color, and provides a rare look at the warmth, vitality and humor of the man who unlocked the mysteries of the mind and life.

This series of lectures comprises one of the most extensive descriptions of the state of Clear ever given. The state of Clear is the achievement of a goal man has had for at least 2,500 years, and this series announces the fact of clearing, fully describes the factors involved in clearing others, and describes the four freedoms of Clear—freedom from illness, pain, ignorance and death. A key breakthrough, announced at this congress, was the fact that someone other than Mr. Hubbard himself had audited a person to the state of Clear. This opened the door to the achievement of the tens of thousands of Clears that exist today.

CLASSIC LECTURE SERIES

The selected lectures listed below are particularly good introductions to the Scientology religion. Each is roughly one hour in length and each provides some of the fundamental wisdom of Dianetics and Scientology, as well as insights into L. Ron Hubbard himself. Listening to Mr. Hubbard reveals his vitality, humor and enthusiasm as no written word can.

The lectures address a wide variety of topics, but each one communicates the essence of the Scientology religion and its positive view of man's spiritual potential. One gains a unique insight into Scientology from hearing L. Ron Hubbard discuss the subject. The titles in this series illustrate the point:

The Story of Dianetics and Scientology

This is the *first* taped lecture one should listen to for an insight into the subjects of Dianetics and Scientology. In this very personal and fascinating talk, L. Ron Hubbard introduces many of the people and experiences encountered during his search for the truth about the spirit, the mind and life itself.

From the friendship which sparked his interest in the mind at the age of twelve, through his travels in Asia as a teenager and even his experiences at war, Mr. Hubbard describes a continuous journey of discovery culminating in the research and development of Dianetics and Scientology technology. He reveals exactly how he came to unlock the mystery of the human mind and spirit and how he finally uncovered the truth that meant freedom for all mankind.

Operation Manual for the Mind

Many people "wonder" how the mind works. Since we all have one—as people have had throughout history—why is the mind not understood? This lecture reveals a deep-seated belief which prevents man from finding out how his own mind operates. With this "secret" exposed, the door is opened for a true understanding of oneself.

The Road to Truth

What is truth? A question that has been asked since the beginning of time is now answered. In this lecture, Mr. Hubbard explains how to recognize the traps and half-truths that confound all who seek answers to life's most basic mysteries. And he explains what one must do to walk all the way on the "Road to Truth" and attain spiritual freedom.

The Hope of Man

L. Ron Hubbard praises the great spiritual figures of the ages, including Siddhartha Gautama, Lao-tse, Krishna and Christ and shows how they kept alive the flame of hope for spiritual freedom. He describes the role of the Scientology religion in this tradition and the practical path it provides so that man can at last attain this hope.

Man's Relentless Search

Man has been searching for answers to his own existence throughout recorded history. This lecture describes some of the answers provided by religions and philosophies down through the ages. And it reveals what they all missed that Scientology now provides.

Scientology and Effective Knowledge

The pursuit of knowledge has occupied the attention of philosophers, explorers, scholars and adventurers for thousands of years. Beyond technological advances, little of value has been learned about life itself. In this tape, L. Ron Hubbard reveals the one simple quality an individual must assume to better understand any aspect of life. With this key, anyone can obtain effective knowledge.

The Dynamics

The task of understanding life can seem daunting by virtue of its sheer enormity and complexity. By delineating and defining the eight "dynamics," or fundamental urges of all life, Mr. Hubbard not only makes life clear and suddenly easy to understand, but makes it possible for one to attain greater ability in handling life.

The Dynamic Principles of Existence

Why do some people succeed while others fail? Luck? Destiny? Can one change one's own "lot" in life? Yes, one can. There is a principle which directly monitors how alive an individual is. Mr. Hubbard explains this principle and outlines how to apply it in life.

The Machinery of the Mind

Whatever claims were made about the mind before Dianetics, virtually *nothing* was actually *known*. This fascinating lecture provides a clear understanding of the "machinery" of the mind, along with the processes of thought, decision-making and communication. In this lecture, Mr. Hubbard explains how a knowledge of these factors enables anyone to regain control of his life.

Power of Choice and Self-Determinism

Many factors influence the course of one's life. By far the most important is one's own power of choice. This lecture explains how to rehabilitate this ability and how then using it could affect an individual or society.

The Road to Perfection— The Goodness of Man

In contrast to some beliefs, Scientology views man as basically good. In this lecture one learns the truth about the basic nature of man and what it takes to restore an individual to a higher level of decency and ability.

Man: Good or Evil?

One question has been asked down through the ages: Is man evil or is he good? No answer has ever provided any certainty—until now. Mr. Hubbard describes what good and evil really are and illustrates the basic good nature of man.

Increasing Efficiency

Increased efficiency does not come from a change of diet, pills or anything else outside the mind. This lecture contains invaluable data that will restore anyone's efficiency, effectiveness and competence.

Health and Certainty

What is the connection between certainty and health? Certainty of what? In this remarkable analysis of the anatomy of certainty, Mr. Hubbard unlocks the door to more than mere physical health. Whether the health of a society or an individual, the secret is the same. The degree to which one can control one's own life depends on only one thing. That "one thing" is detailed in this lecture.

The Five Conditions of Existence and Formulas for Their Improvement

There is no such thing as an unchanging condition. Whether rapidly or slowly, everything is either growing or shrinking, expanding or contracting, improving or getting worse. This lecture defines the five basic conditions and the series of actions one can take to improve any aspect of life. A job, a relationship, one's state of mind—each can be improved by applying the formula of actions appropriate to the condition it is currently in.

The Affinity-Reality-Communication Triangle

Affinity, reality and communication are inextricably linked. When you increase your communication with someone, you will find your affinity for that person also rises. In fact, when any "corner" of this triangle is raised, the other two factors follow "automatically." This is the key to better relationships with others and a deeper understanding of all life.

Scientology and Ability

It is an old idea that teaching someone skills leading to self-sufficiency is better than charity for the recipient. This happens to be true in every aspect of life. The best solution to any difficulty would be to acquire the ability to solve it oneself. In this lecture, Mr. Hubbard reveals how Scientology restores one's full inherent ability.

Miracles

Everybody has some idea about what would constitute a miracle. But is there really such a thing? With no appeal to faith, this lecture defines exactly what miracles are and sheds light on how they can be experienced.

The Deterioration of Liberty

People and societies throughout history have pursued freedom. Despite strong foundations like the Declaration of Independence in the United States, for example, it is possible to see our freedoms eroding. This lecture covers how to preserve high ideals in a sometimes unfriendly world.

Differences Between Scientology and Other Philosophies

When told about Scientology, people often say, "Oh, so it's like . . ." In this lecture, Mr. Hubbard describes how Scientology may be compared to various religions—and also how it is not only different, but unique. Here, one gains an understanding of Scientology's true value to humanity today.

AUDITOR COURSE LECTURE SERIES

For many years, L. Ron Hubbard personally trained Scientology auditors, giving hundreds of lectures and auditing demonstrations. Those lectures were recorded and today form a vital part of the Scientology religion. In addition to their value in training auditors, these lectures contain the first real understanding of the mind, the human spirit and life itself.

The Study Tapes
(9 lectures)

Study technology is *the* breakthrough that undercuts the reasons for illiteracy. The basic blocks to learning—the three barriers to study—were found by Mr. Hubbard, and in these lectures he shows exactly how one unblocks his ability to study and learn. Mr. Hubbard's discoveries have revolutionized the field of study and made it possible for anyone to read, fully understand any subject and *apply* what they have learned—which is crucial to reaping the spiritual benefits of Scientology.

The New Hubbard Professional TR Course Lectures
(7 lectures)

The essentials for any auditor seeking to bring spiritual gains to others—and for anyone determined to resolve *any* life situations—are taught and demonstrated by L. Ron Hubbard in these tapes. Presented in these lectures and auditing demonstrations are the fundamentals of communication: how an individual can better observe, look and confront, exchange communication with others and be communicated to. One learns exactly *how* the simplicity of observation and communication will take man from the bottom to the top.

Freedom Congress Lectures
(16 lectures)

The key to accomplishing anything in life is one's intention. These lectures cover how to increase one's own intention and ability to control life. They also describe the Upper Indoctrination TRs and their use in auditing.

The Academy Level Lectures

The Academy Levels contain some of the most fundamental discoveries regarding life and the human mind. The recorded lectures studied on the Academy Levels are available to anyone. They provide a grasp of the fundamentals of life.

Academy Level 0 Lectures— Communication
(7 lectures)

The person who can truly communicate to others is a higher being who builds new worlds. Here are the fundamentals of communication found nowhere else.

Academy Level I Lectures— Problems
(11 lectures)

Man "solves" problems. These lectures establish that a higher being recognizes the true source of problems and sees them vanish.

Academy Level II Lectures— Relief
(15 lectures)

These lectures illustrate how to easily bring relief to oneself and others from the hostilities and sufferings of life—a skill man previously has seen only in healers.

Academy Level III Lectures— Freedom
(7 lectures)

Here Mr. Hubbard discusses how to gain freedom from the upsets of the past, with a renewed ability to face the future.

Academy Level IV Lectures— Ability
(7 lectures)

These lectures address how to move oneself and others out of fixed conditions and become more able.

New Era Dianetics Lectures
(5 lectures)

These lectures to student auditors detail the theory and practical fundamentals of Dianetics, the time track, and the refinement of Dianetics based on years of application and results. The information learned in these tapes is an important part of mastering the streamlined and powerful techniques of New Era Dianetics, to give "miracles as usual" results at a speed a hundred times faster than the original techniques described in Book One.

The Saint Hill Special Briefing Course Lectures
(437 lectures)

In 1961, L. Ron Hubbard called the top Scientology auditors of the day to his home, Saint Hill Manor in the south of England, for a special training course. Over the next five years, he personally supervised the Saint Hill Special Briefing Course, releasing his discoveries and breakthroughs as they occurred, in a series of 437 lectures.

This is the most comprehensive series of lectures ever delivered on the philosophy and practice of Dianetics and Scientology. Mr. Hubbard continued his research into the mind and life during this period, including his upper-level research into the capabilities of man as a spiritual being, culminating in the development of the Classification and Gradation Chart, mapping the route to Clear. These lectures form a running record of that research. Listening to them is an unparalleled adventure of discovery into the true nature of man and his ultimate potentials. Contained herein are the answers, how he came to discover them and why they *are* the answers.

It was from this vast record of research and discovery that *all* of the lectures from the individual Academy Levels were compiled. Still, a far greater number of these lectures are available only in the Saint Hill Special Briefing Course series.

OT Lectures

The Dawn of Immortality:
Secrets of the Track Before Earth
(23 lectures)

These 23 lectures, recorded in 1952, were the first course in Scientology ever delivered. They in fact form a crash course in who we are, where we came from, why we are here on this planet and what our spiritual abilities really are. Mr. Hubbard describes the origin of the thetan and the entrance of the thetan into the physical universe, the collision of thought with matter, energy, space and time (MEST), and how this collision brings the individual down scale into greater and greater mystery, effort, anguish and pain. He also describes, in chilling detail, some of the ancient incidents common to all thetans on Earth, in particular the age-old "iron cover" which has blocked every effort towards spiritual freedom for eons: "Facsimile One." This is the story we were never meant to know—the story of how to regain our full abilities.

The Route to Infinity
(7 lectures)

"To be or not to be" is the most basic question faced by the thetan, and one's fate and future hangs on the answer. These lectures explore the full implications of that sweeping decision "to be" and show how this continuing decision affects every facet of one's life, every day. Here are the mechanics of how thoughts and dreams become a reality in the physical universe. And how to revitalize the ability to postulate, to decide, to create one's own future—and to be whatever one chooses to be.

The Perception of Truth
(4 lectures)

An individual suddenly confronted with the raw naked truth about himself, who realizes that what he thought were barriers are only shadows, can go "up the pole"—that is, achieve ecstasy without knowledge. This is a highly unstable condition in a universe

devoted to stopping thetans! This lecture series describes how one resolves this by gaining the knowledge to get out of and stay out of the traps of this universe, and how one can clearly differentiate truth from lies. Included is a description of the "Qs"—the highest common denominators of all experience.

Secrets of the MEST Universe
(5 lectures)

The universe of matter, energy, space and time, "MEST," seems terrifically solid, impenetrable and formidable to an individual. How can one match his own force against the tremendous force of great flaming suns and exploding supernovas? Yet that was a thetan's first mistake—trying to fight force with force. In these lectures, Mr. Hubbard describes the secret of the MEST universe—and the secret to rehabilitating the highest potentiality of theta.

The Philadelphia Doctorate
Course Lectures
(76 lectures)

Easily the most comprehensive body of data ever assembled on the potentials and capabilities of the spirit in relation to the universe, these lectures are the ultimate statement of what each one of us is capable of achieving.

We are taught the "natural laws" of the physical universe in school, such as physics or chemistry—but in the Philadelphia Doctorate Course, Mr. Hubbard explores the nature of reality itself. Are the laws of the physical universe "natural laws" or just agreements? Is the physical universe a reality or an illusion? What is the anatomy of universes—their construction, maintenance and destruction?

The purpose of this series, as stated in the first lecture, is to undo a person's agreement with the "natural laws" which became the MEST universe, thus enabling him to step out of the MEST universe and operate exterior to its flows and traps. It is a very thorough education as a spiritual being—priceless stable data that enable a person to operate at cause in the universe.

The text that accompanies these lectures is *Scientology 8-8008*.

Admiration and the Renaissance of Beingness
(18 lectures)

Why do the things that you most dislike—the ugly and unwanted things in life—persist? This lecture series describes how an individual fights hardest those things that he is not willing to BE. The "universal solvent" is revealed—a postulated factor which dissolves any unwanted thing. Here is the secret to remedying the individual's ability to BE and to create on a much higher plane of existence.

Exteriorization and the Phenomena of Space
(84 lectures)

Delivered in late 1953 to a hand-picked group of top auditors, this series of lectures reveals some of the most powerful knowledge ever released about the rehabilitation of a spiritual being.

In this series, Mr. Hubbard shows how a thetan, under constant bombardment from the physical universe, becomes at last unable to emanate energy and so collapses in on himself, like a dark star, interiorized into a body and at the effect of matter, energy, space and time. More importantly, he demonstrates how to reverse this process, rehabilitating the thetan's ability to emanate, create space and BE. The exteriorized thetan has the power to create and to be CAUSE in the universe without effort.

The Rehabilitation of the Human Spirit
(67 lectures)

Mr. Hubbard began this series of lectures with the admonishment, "Be surprised at nothing." What he then revealed was new technology that returned knowledge, skill and knowingness to the being, while enhancing perception, reaction time and serenity.

Delivered in Camden, New Jersey in late 1953, this lecture series reveals previously hidden knowledge on the human spirit and the creation of space, time and matter. The path to restoration of one's true beingness is detailed here, along with techniques to rehabilitate the power to postulate, predict and cause the future.

The Creation of Human Ability
(32 lectures)

This training course, based on the text *The Creation of Human Ability*, describes in detail the miracle-making auditing procedures from the book, which are designed "to bring an individual into such thorough communication with the physical universe that he can regain the power and ability of his own postulates." Here are the methods used to rehabilitate the full abilities of a thetan.

The Phoenix Lectures
(28 lectures)

In this series of lectures given in 1954, Mr. Hubbard traces the religious and philosophical roots of Scientology, going back more than ten thousand years to the Vedic hymns, and tracing the history of man's knowledge forward to present time. He shows how Scientology has taken the collective wisdom of the ages and added to it the "impatience and urgency" of Western science to arrive and thus bring to fruition the ambitions of thousands of years of thinking men. He covers the basics of Scientology, including the four basic attitudes towards existence or reality. A knowledge of these enables an individual to handle any unwanted reality and create any desired reality. He also describes how an individual can control time, and gives a detailed explanation of the Axioms of Scientology, those self-evident considerations that form the very fabric of existence.

Universes and the War Between Theta and MEST
(32 lectures)

This series describes a war "between an effort on the part of the physical universe to destroy all life within it, and an effort on the part of life to master and use the physical universe." Here is a full description of the "weapons" we have in Scientology to win that war—a knowledge of the physical universe; a knowledge of the spiritual being, or thetan, and his true capabilities; a command of the cycle of action of create-survive-destroy; a knowledge of the fundamentals of communication; the laws of affinity; and the true nature of reality and agreement. Here are the answers to riddles that have kept life enslaved by the physical universe.

The Solution to Entrapment
(35 lectures)

Given in early 1955, just prior to the publication of *Dianetics 55!* these lectures cover the fundamental principles of communication, including how communication relates to beingness, space, terminals, scarcities and games. Mr. Hubbard shows how this universe punishes beings for communicating and convinces people they should not communicate. Yet it is only through communication that one can undo the traps and free a being. He reveals the mechanics and formulas of communication, which are the keys to life itself. As he says in one lecture, "The amount of communication that an individual does determines directly the amount of life he experiences."

Conquest of Chaos
(6 lectures)

People will commonly seize on a stable datum as the solution to chaos and confusion. Yet choosing the wrong stable datum can lead to entrapment and insanity for an individual or for an entire society. One learns the "idiotic secret" that holds the material universe together, and it is demonstrated how

an understanding of the four postulates—not know, know, forget and remember—revitalize a person's awareness and power of choice.

Anatomy of the Spirit of Man Congress Lectures
(15 lectures)

Delivered in 1955 in Washington, DC, this lecture series heralded the development of a practical technology that would bring about a new state of being in man. In this series Mr. Hubbard explains and actually demonstrates the address of a spiritual being and its anatomy—postulates, communication, affinity, reality, understanding, the Tone Scale, ownership, immortality and exteriorization. These lectures contain the practical doingnesses involved in surviving as a spiritual being in the material world. One could look at it as a spiritual survival kit—square zero where a spirit is concerned.

Games and the Spirit of Play
(13 lectures)

This intriguing and often humorous lecture series reveals all aspects of games, problems and postulates. One learns about the various types that exist and have existed for eternity and how one may be involved in games without even knowing it. These types of games are by no means fun; discovering them and being free from them is one way to continue on a road to spiritual advancement. Also covered here is the basic anatomy of human problems, the common denominator of illness and the mechanics behind the human emotion known as jealousy.

The Power of Simplicity
(26 lectures)

Life is a game which consists of tremendous complexities, yet the power of an individual does not lie in the direction of greater complexity and more force, but in greater and greater simplicity. Exactly how you bring a person back to that simplicity is the subject of these lectures.

The Anatomy of Cause
(29 lectures)

Here, Mr. Hubbard discusses how to bring a person to cause in this universe, and why it is a lie that you are going to increase anyone's ability: the ability is already there. All you are doing in auditing is increasing the person's willingness to be, do, have, confront and create. These lectures cover the subjects of communication, control and havingness, and the anatomy of a game—freedom, barriers and purposes.

Illusion or Truth
(22 lectures)

"There is a condition worse than blindness," Mr. Hubbard states in the opening lecture, "and that is thinking you see something that isn't there." The stress in Scientology is the simplicity of observing what is there, not accepting the illusions of earlier studies. These lectures set forth the answers to age-old enigmas such as the true nature of death, the anatomy of sleep, what laughter is, and more. Here is how to dissolve the lies of the past and discover the truth about life.

The Ability Congress
(9 lectures)

This 1957 congress centered on the most basic of abilities—the ability to live. This includes improving the individual's ability to understand, to communicate, to have, to achieve goals and to tolerate a vast range of experience. The mission of Scientology is to increase the livability of people.

The First Postulate
(35 lectures)

In this series Mr. Hubbard reveals a discovery of magnitude—how a being postulates his own case into existence, that is, how he obsessively creates his own difficulties. While one could go on handling an individual's problems and difficulties in life, a more direct approach is to address the being's original intention that got him aberrated in the first place. This is the core of irrationality, insanity, and the limitation of a being's abilities. This series also answers the age-old question of what existed before the beginning.

The Origin of Aberration
(6 lectures)

Delivered in London in 1958, these lectures cover the breakthrough discoveries concerning the reactive mind, what makes it more solid and a detailed explanation of what "basic-basic" is. Also revealed in this lecture series is the "true" story of the creation of the universe, the actual source of successful beingness, the mechanics of confusion and how to handle one, no matter how large it is.

Cause and Spheres of Influence
(6 lectures)

These lectures were delivered in Washington, DC, in January of 1959 and give insight into the dramatic breakthroughs that made it possible to start clearing people on a large scale—making the goal of a cleared planet a reality. Covered in this series is invaluable information on the subject of leadership, the techniques of engram running, the overt–motivator sequence and how to estimate the state of case in a preclear.

Skills of a Theta Being
(26 lectures)

What are the skills that a spiritual being needs in order to be cause in life and win in this universe? This is a very thorough coverage of the fundamentals of Scientology, which is to say, the basics of life and knowingness. Subjects covered include an in-depth look at the anatomy of universes, the eight dynamics, what a mind is and the electronic phenomena of the mind. Here is the story of how a thetan goes from total knowingness down to "forgetting" and "remembering," and the route back from ignorance to cause over one's creations and postulates.

The Principles of Creation
(6 lectures)

This series covers the most basic principle of creation, which is restoring the individual's self-determinism and his ability to create anything. What is evil to a person are those things which are other-determined, over which he believes he has no control. The destructive power of valences is revealed—another person's identity unknowingly assumed by the individual. When the individual becomes himself, fully self-determined and "captain of his own destiny" he regains his own native goodness and ability to create.

Responsibility and the State of OT
(32 lectures)

A thorough and in-depth rundown on the self-created factors that limit a thetan's ability, causativeness and creativeness. Here are the mechanics of how a spiritual being limits himself and condemns himself to blindness, ignorance and inability. These lectures show how an individual begins to identify creation and communication with destruction, and so ceases to create or communicate. Here are the mechanics of exactly how a person becomes a victim of life, and how to remedy this, bringing the person to a high level of responsibility so he can reach the state of Operating Thetan (OT).

State of Man Congress
(9 lectures)

What is the current state of man? And how did he get in the condition he is in? In this lecture series Mr. Hubbard explores the sweeping ramifications of the statement that "True recovery of one's beingness goes along with one's realization that he has been the cause of any difficulty he has ever had." These lectures cover the subject of marriage and how one goes about creating one, the rehabilitation of artists, how to make governments more ethical, and an eye-opening lecture entitled "Why People Don't Like You."

The Anatomy of the Human Mind Congress
(5 lectures)

Given in late December 1960 in Washington, DC, these lectures provide a complete, concise description of the mind, its makeup and function and the basic principles of Dianetics and Scientology and their utilization in dissemination and expansion. In this series one learns what the brain is actually used for, the different types of minds that exist, how Dianetics and Scientology evolved and the different approach each of them takes in resolving the problems of the human mind.

Expansion of Havingness
(9 lectures)

Here is Mr. Hubbard's discovery of the hidden core of the reactive mind, black masses of mental energy, burned down to the last notch, that no one has ever been able to get rid of. This is the "raw meat" of human aberration and difficulty, and why an individual can carry his problems from lifetime to lifetime. He reveals how these masses are handled, and how to dramatically increase a person's reach and havingness.

A Series of Lectures on the Whole Track
(6 lectures)

The whole track is defined as the moment-to-moment record of a person's existence in this universe in picture and impression form. This compilation of lectures, taken from different periods, explores the back track on man, extending millions of years into the past. What is the true history of man, and how did he end up on this planet?

SPECIAL INTEREST SERIES

Special Course in Human Evaluation
(9 lectures)

This series details the subject of human evaluation and how people can be expected to react under certain circumstances. Key to this series was the Tone Scale, the gradient scale of Scientology which shows the emotional tones of a person ranging from the highest level—serenity of beingness—down to levels such as boredom, grief and apathy. Here are details and demonstrations of how people react at the various tone levels and how one uses the Tone Scale to improve communication skills. Attended by businessmen, this lecture series focuses on the application of the Tone Scale in business, politics and domestic activity.

How to Present Scientology to the World
(18 lectures)

This planet is in dire need of the knowledge and practical technology of Scientology. In this series of lectures, Mr. Hubbard tells Scientologists how to make Scientology better known and accomplish the goal of "a superior civilization in which peace can exist on Earth." This series includes data on how to deliver beginning courses in Scientology, methods of effective education, the importance of providing books to new people, and even how to overcome stage fright when addressing small and large groups.

Radiation and Your Survival
(10 lectures)

Delivered in 1957 at the London Congress on Nuclear Radiation and Health, these lectures give an in-depth study on the subject of radiation, covering several of the most important discoveries in this field including the development of nuclear fission and the adverse effect of gamma rays and radiation on the body. These lectures reveal how this one subject—radiation—though very little known, is the one thing that poses an end to one's future survival as a spiritual being. The series concludes with the direction man must take in the future and what barrier we have to surmount in order to survive.

Creating the Second Dynamic
(4 lectures)

This series deals primarily with the subject of the second dynamic (the urge toward existence as a sexual activity—including the sexual act itself, the family unit and the rearing of children). Covered in the series is a lecture on children with exact technology on handling them and processes one can deliver to them. From these lectures one learns how to achieve excellent communication with, and gain greater understanding of, the second dynamic—which enables anyone to create a sane, successful second dynamic.

CHAPTER 48

COMPLETE LIST OF ALL MATERIALS

T he following pages contain a complete listing of Dianetics and Scientology books, technical and administrative issues, articles, films, recorded lectures, cassettes, E-Meters, insignia and special publications from 1948 to the present.

For ease of reference the categories of books, films and recorded lectures are noted in the listings by symbols.

BOOKS

L. Ron Hubbard is one of the most acclaimed and widely read authors of all time, with more than 100 million copies of his works published throughout the world. The books listed here include only his nonfiction works on Dianetics and Scientology. Also included in this listing are the *RON Series*—a series of special publications chronicling his life and accomplishments. They contain a great deal of vital information about Dianetics and Scientology and their founder.

Each entry lists title, publication date, original publisher and where first published, and a notation if the book is a compilation of L. Ron Hubbard's works.

FILMS

Films are also included among Scientology materials. After extensive research on photography and film, Mr. Hubbard began producing films to make it easier for Scientologists, particularly auditors, to learn the theory and procedures of Scientology auditing technology. While valuable tools for learning the technology, these films also help to preserve the scripture of Scientology.

Many of the films were made between 1958 and 1970. In 1978, Golden Era Productions began producing a large number of new films, both technical training films for use in Scientology training and films dealing with specific problems and concerns of society, intended for a general audience. Because this film production project is continuing, the following listing includes only films that have been released at the time of publication.

Each film is listed by title and date of release.

RECORDED LECTURES

Starting in 1948, L. Ron Hubbard delivered more than 3,000 public lectures on every aspect of the mind, life and spirit. Some 25 million words exist on tape recordings that are stored in archives providing consecutive history of the discovery of the Scientology religion. These lectures cover vitually every aspect of Scientology religious belief and practice, including the technologies of auditing, training and administration of the religion.

Since 1977, many of Mr. Hubbard's recorded lectures have been released to the public singly or as part of a series, together with transcripts and glossaries. In order to ensure the highest quality sound, most have been produced using Clearsound state-of-the-art sound-reproduction technology. The project of reproducing these lectures is still in progress, and new lectures are released regularly so the extensive technology of Dianetics and Scientology that has been recorded on tape can be easily accessible to all.

ISSUES AND ARTICLES

In addition to his books, Mr. Hubbard continuously wrote bulletins detailing technical breakthroughs as they occurred. Beginning with Dianetic Auditor's Bulletins (DABs) in 1950, and later in Professional Auditor's Bulletins (PABs), Hubbard Communications Office Bulletins (HCOBs) and other technical issues, he recorded and issued valuable advice and data on his new discoveries.

Administrative breakthroughs were likewise issued immediately as policy letters for staff and public use. Various types of issues cover the administrative technology of Scientology churches, the earliest of these being policy letters written for specific organizations such as the Hubbard Association of Scientologists International (HASI PLs) and the Founding Church of Washington, DC (FC PLs). Mr. Hubbard also recorded policy in several other forms, including LRH Executive Directives (LRH EDs), Secretarial Executive Directives (Sec EDs) and, most often, Hubbard Communications Office Policy Letters (HCO PLs).

Magazine articles provided another medium for the communication of Dianetics and Scientology technology. Magazines for Scientologists, such as the *Journal of Scientology* (JOS), *Certainty, Ability,* and *The Auditor,* often carried articles by Mr. Hubbard, as did the *Freedom* magazine put out by the Church.

Each of these individual writings has been included in the following list, along with the type of issue, the date of its original publication and date of any revision.

INSIGNIA

Each of the insignia of Dianetics and Scientology is shown and described for the year it was adopted. Only official insignia are listed.

E-METERS

The progression of models of the E-Meter throughout the years of its development is shown. Each meter is listed with its year of release.

ADDITIONAL MATERIALS

Several special categories of materials are listed, including charts and tools for auditors. Mr. Hubbard also composed music for several films, and their sound tracks are available.

There are hundreds of course packs that accompany Dianetics and Scientology courses. While these packs are not listed, there is one pack for every course.

TRANSLATIONS

Translations of books, tapes, films and course packs have been completed in many languages. The translations listed are those available as of publication date of this book. Many more translated materials and new languages are added regularly.

1948

**DIANETICS:
THE ORIGINAL
THESIS**
by L. Ron Hubbard

L. Ron Hubbard's original thesis on Dianetics. This manuscript, released in 1948, was the result of his independent research in the field of the mind. It was formally published in 1951 as Dianetics: The Original Thesis *and later republished as* The Dynamics of Life. *Today published by Bridge Publications and New Era Publications.*
TRANSLATIONS: *Danish, Dutch, French, German, Italian, Norwegian, Portuguese, Spanish and Swedish.*

1950

In early 1950, Mr. Hubbard published an article on Dianetics in the prestigious *Explorers Club Journal,* then went on to release *Dianetics: The Modern Science of Mental Health* in May of 1950.

News of Dianetics soon spread nationwide, and he was deluged with demands for more information.

In August he lectured to an audience of 6,000 at the Shrine Auditorium in Los Angeles, and within a few short months more than 750 groups in the US alone were practicing Dianetics, led by the Hubbard Dianetics Research Foundation in Elizabeth, New Jersey, and its offices in New York; Washington, DC; Chicago; Los Angeles and Hawaii.

Mr. Hubbard spent much of his time traveling across the US to lecture to the public but still found the time to write articles and technical bulletins describing new techniques and to begin work on upcoming books covering his further advances in Dianetics.

ARTICLE   Terra Incognita: The Mind

**DIANETICS:
THE EVOLUTION OF
A SCIENCE**
by L. Ron Hubbard

Written in early 1950, this manuscript was published first as a magazine article in April 1950 and then as a book in September 1955, by the Hubbard Dianetics Research Foundation, Phoenix, Arizona. Today published by Bridge Publications and New Era Publications. TRANSLATIONS: *Danish, Dutch, French, German, Greek, Hebrew, Italian, Japanese, Spanish and Swedish.*

**DIANETICS:
THE MODERN SCIENCE
OF MENTAL HEALTH**
by L. Ron Hubbard

Written in early 1950 in Bay Head, New Jersey, and published by Hermitage House, New York, New York, 9 May 1950. Today published by Bridge Publications and New Era Publications.
TRANSLATIONS: *Chinese, Danish, Dutch, Finnish, French, German, Greek, Hebrew, Hungarian, Italian, Japanese, Norwegian, Portuguese, Russian, Spanish, Swedish, Swahili and Taiwanese.*

ARTICLE   The Aims of the Hubbard Dianetic Research Foundation

**SESSIONS AND
DEMONSTRATIONS**
ELIZABETH, NEW JERSEY

Following the publication of *Dianetics: The Modern Science of Mental Health,* the first Hubbard Dianetics Research Foundation was formed by a group of Dianeticists in Elizabeth, New Jersey. LRH lectured to staff and students at the Foundation, and recorded many of the auditing sessions he gave.

7 Jun	Bringing Preclear to Present Time
7 Jun	Auditing Toward Clear
7 Jun	Repairing Past Auditing
8 Jun	LRH Auditing Demonstration
8 Jun	Auditing a Chronic Somatic
8 Jun	LRH Auditing Demonstration
9 Jun	LRH Auditing Demonstration
9 Jun	LRH Auditing Demonstration
9 Jun	LRH Auditing Demonstration
10 Jun	Dianetics: First Lecture of Saturday Course
10 Jun	LRH Auditing Demonstration
10 Jun	LRH Auditing Demonstration
10 Jun	LRH Auditing Demonstration
12 Jun	LRH Auditing Demonstration
12 Jun	The Conduct of an Auditor—Part I
12 Jun	The Conduct of an Auditor—Part II
14 Jun	Diagnostic Procedure
15 Jun	Sound and Aberration
15 Jun	Clears in This Society
15 Jun	Case Factors
16 Jun	LRH Auditing Demonstration
16 Jun	Memory and Diagnosis—Part I
16 Jun	Memory and Diagnosis—Part II
17 Jun	Recognizing Contact of Engram
17 Jun	The Somatic Strip
19 Jun	Handling of Cases
19 Jun	Auditing an Illness Chain
19 Jun	The Fifteen-Minute Assist
20 Jun	Valences
20 Jun	Analytical Mind
21 Jun	Engrams
21 Jun	To Auditors About Diagnosis
23 Jun	Institutional Dianetics
24 Jun	Running Out Birth
26 Jun	Hypnosis
26 Jun	Demon Circuits
26 Jun	Testing for the Right Engram
27 Jun	Birth
27 Jun	Sense of Reality
28 Jun	Conception
28 Jun	Reduction of Engrams
29 Jun	Research and Discovery—Part I
29 Jun	Research and Discovery—Part II
1 Jul	Address of Auditor to Pc
3 Jul	Entering a Case
3 Jul	Demonstration of Handling a Case
4 Jul	Handling Somatics
5 Jul	Application of Procedure
5 Jul	Types of Cases
5 Jul	The File Clerk and Valence Shifters
6 Jul	Vicissitudes of the Preclear
7 Jul	Review of Material
7 Jul	Operation of Valences and Demon Circuits
8 Jul	How to Become an Auditor in One Easy Lesson
8 Jul	About Psychotics
10 Jul	Getting a Case Rolling
10 Jul	A Summary of Standard Procedure
11 Jul	Standard Procedure and Accessibility
12 Jul	Review of Standard Procedure
13 Jul	Auditor's Skill—Part I
13 Jul	Auditor's Skill—Part II
14 Jul	Conception—The Sperm Sequence
14 Jul	Circuitry
14 Jul	Things an Auditor Must Not Do
14 Jul	The Tone Scale in Action
15 Jul	Erasures
15 Jul	Processing Children
17 Jul	Derivation of Laws—Part I
17 Jul	Derivation of Laws—Part II
19 Jul	The Part Played by the Analytical Mind
21 Jul	Manifestations Which Assist the Auditor
22 Jul	Running Former Lives
22 Jul	The Anatomy of the Demon Circuit
24 Jul	Diagnosis Data
2 Aug	The Importance of Getting Engrams
4 Aug	Relation of Affinity, Communication and Reality

In addition to delivering lectures, Mr. Hubbard began writing bulletins which were distributed to auditors practicing Dianetics, to warn them of common errors and to impart new developments in the technology.

ISSUES

PRECAUTIONARY BULLETIN NO. 1
1 Jul   Auditor's Code—Breaking Of

PRECAUTIONARY BULLETIN NO. 2
1 Jul   Insanity "Caused by" Dianetics

RESEARCH BULLETIN NO. 2
1 Jul   Stuck on the Time Track

RESEARCH BULLETIN NO. 3
1 Jul   Sperm Sequence as Basic-Basic

DAB   Jul-Aug   Standard Procedure
VOL. 1, NOS. 1–2

**PUBLIC AND
PROFESSIONAL COURSE
LECTURES**
LOS ANGELES, CALIFORNIA

Following the introductory lecture to 6,000 at the Los Angeles Shrine Auditorium, Mr. Hubbard delivered a series of lectures and demonstrations at the Los Angeles Hubbard Dianetics Research Foundation.

10 Aug	Introducing Dianetics—Shrine Auditorium
15 Aug	The Anatomy of the Engram
16 Aug	Affinity, Reality, Communication
17 Aug	Straightwire
18 Aug	Denyers, Bouncers, Holders
18 Aug	The Guk Formula
21 Aug	Taking Inventory, SOP Step One
22 Aug	Opening the Case, SOP Step Two
22 Aug	Demonstration of Getting a Case Moving
23 Aug	The Tools of the Trade
24 Aug	Running Engrams, SOP Step Two
24 Aug	Checking Perceptics
25 Aug	Removing Demon Circuits and Valence Commands, SOP Step Three
25 Aug	Paralleling the Mind
28 Aug	Spectrum from Psychosis to Clear
28 Aug	Analytical Mind
29 Aug	Educational Dianetics
30 Aug	Preventive Dianetics
30 Aug	The Professional Auditor
31 Aug	General Discussion of Auditing
31 Aug	Medical Dianetics
31 Aug	Demonstration of Running Down a Chain
1 Sep	Child Dianetics
1 Sep	Guk vs. Drugs: Effects in Auditing
1 Sep	Auditing a Blind Preclear
4 Sep	Advertising—Propaganda Push Buttons
5 Sep	Political Dianetics
7 Sep	Language Adjustment
7 Sep	Valences and Valence Shifters

ISSUE

DAB   Sep   How to Release a
VOL. 1, NO. 3   Chronic Somatic

**OAKLAND PUBLIC
LECTURE SERIES**
OAKLAND, CALIFORNIA

Traveling from Los Angeles to
Oakland, Mr. Hubbard delivered
the following series of lectures and
demonstrations at the Oakland
Municipal Auditorium. (Four of
these lectures are available from
Golden Era Productions in a series
entitled, "Dianetics Lectures and
Demonstrations." TRANSLATIONS:
French, German, Italian, Spanish,
Hungarian and Russian.)

23 Sep   Introduction to Dianetics
23 Sep   What Dianetics Can Do
26 Sep   Auditor's Code
26 Sep   Standard Procedure Chart
26 Sep   Demonstration of Procedure
27 Sep   Different Types of Cases
27 Sep   Demonstration
28 Sep   How to Resolve Stalled Cases
28 Sep   Running an Engram
29 Sep   Guk and Freewheeling
29 Sep   Running a Secondary

ARTICLE   Oct The Analytical Mind

ISSUE

DAB   Oct   Dianetics and
VOL. 1, NO. 4   Religion

KANSAS CITY LECTURES
KANSAS CITY, MISSOURI

From Oakland, Mr. Hubbard traveled
to Kansas City, where he gave these
public lectures.

25 Oct   A Summary of Standard
          Procedure — Clarification
          of Operation
25 Oct   Demonstration
26 Oct   Types of Cases and Methods
          of Resolving Them
26 Oct   Demonstration
27 Oct   Demonstration
27 Oct   Restarting or Reopening
          Stalled Cases
28 Oct   Improved and Unpublished
          Techniques
28 Oct   Demonstration

ISSUES

DESPATCH 1 Nov The Intensive
                Processing Procedure
DAB   Nov The Processing of
VOL. 1, NO. 5 Children

**PROFESSIONAL COURSE
LECTURES**
ELIZABETH, NEW JERSEY

Returning from Kansas City to his
home in New Jersey, Mr. Hubbard
brought the students and staff of the
Foundation up to date on his latest
discoveries and advancements in
Dianetics techniques.

2 Nov   Starting Off a New Preclear
4 Nov   ARC and the Tone Scale
4 Nov   Use of ARC in Auditing
7 Nov   Practical Auditing
7 Nov   The Art of Processing
8 Nov   Child Dianetics — Part I
8 Nov   Child Dianetics — Part II
9 Nov   Group Dianetics — Part I
9 Nov   Group Dianetics — Part II
10 Nov   Handling Psychotics
11 Nov   Education and Dianetics
11 Nov   Axioms and Fundamentals
         About Data

ISSUES

ORGANIZATIONAL MEMORANDUM

16 Nov   An Addition to Standard
         Procedure

**PROFESSIONAL COURSE
LECTURES**
LOS ANGELES, CALIFORNIA

After delivering the Professional
Course in New Jersey at the
beginning of November, Mr. Hubbard
traversed the continent again to bring
his newest developments to Los
Angeles area Dianeticists.

20 Nov   Thought, Life and the
         Material Universe
21 Nov   Spectrums of Logic and
         Emotion
21 Nov   Tone Scales of Affinity,
         Reality and Communication
22 Nov   The Auditor's Code
22 Nov   Accessibility
24 Nov   The Accessibility Chart
24 Nov   Opening the Case
25 Nov   ARC and the Dynamics
25 Nov   Running Standard Procedure
25 Nov   The Anatomy of Circuitry
27 Nov   Handling Chronic Somatics,
         Stuck Cases
27 Nov   Straight Memory, Tone Scales
28 Nov   Valences and Demon
         Circuits — Part I
29 Nov   Valences and Demon
         Circuits — Part II
29 Nov   A New Straightwire
         Technique
30 Nov   Questions and Answers
1 Dec   Rudimentary Data
         on Groups
1 Dec   Groups

ISSUES

HCO PL 24 Nov Instruction Protocol,
                Official
DAB   Dec Handling the
VOL. 1, NO. 6   Psychotic
DESPATCH 12 Dec Certification Board
                Duties and
                Responsibilities

LOS ANGELES LECTURE
LOS ANGELES, CALIFORNIA

After delivering the Professional
Course, Mr. Hubbard remained in

Los Angeles to do further research,
where he delivered a lecture on Chain
Scanning — a new technique which
was still under development at the
time.

19 Dec   Chain Scanning

1951

Early in 1951 Mr. Hubbard was in
Palm Springs, California, compiling
the Hubbard Chart of Human
Evaluation. In the late spring, he
traveled to pre-Communist Cuba,
where he dictated the book *Science
of Survival.*

By this time a Dianetics Foundation
had formed in Wichita, Kansas, and
in June Mr. Hubbard lectured there
to over 100 auditors attending the
First Annual Conference of Dianetic
Auditors.

He spent much of the rest of the
year giving lectures, doing research
and writing up what he had found
into books, issues and articles.

**NOTES ON THE
LECTURES OF
L. RON HUBBARD**

*Detailed notes and diagrams of
Mr. Hubbard's November 1950 lectures
in Los Angeles, made by staff of the
Hubbard Dianetics Research
Foundation; assembled and published
at Mr. Hubbard's request so they would
be available for training purposes. First
published by the Hubbard Dianetics
Foundation, Inc., Wichita, Kansas,
1951, and today by Bridge Publications
and New Era Publications.*

ARTICLE   Jan Dianometry, Your
                   Ability and State of
                   Mind

ISSUE

DAB   Jan   Group Dianetics
VOL. 1, NO. 7

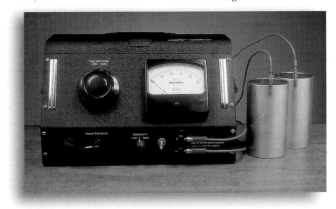

THE DIANETICS SYMBOL

*The Greek letter delta is the basic
form. The dark stripes are green,
which stands for growth. The light
stripes are yellow, for life. The four
green stripes represent the four
dynamics described in Dianetics:
the urge to survive as self, family,
group and mankind. This symbol
was designed in 1950 and has been
in use ever since.*

**MATHISON MODEL B
ELECTROPSYCHOMETER**

*Volney Mathison presented
L. Ron Hubbard with the first
electropsychometer (or E-Meter) in
1951, the Model B. It was used for
research throughout 1951.*

ELIZABETH LECTURES
ELIZABETH, NEW JERSEY

Taking a short break from his intensive work on the Hubbard Chart of Human Evaluation, LRH traveled from Palm Springs, California, to Elizabeth, New Jersey to brief auditors there on new techniques.

17 Jan The Third Dynamic

18 Jan Gradients of Accessibility

18 Jan Hurdy-Gurdy Straightwire and Haywire

ARTICLE Jan Diagnosis and Repair of Groups

ISSUES

CODE Jan The Credo of a True Group Member

CODE Jan The Credo of a Good and Skilled Manager

DAB Feb The Theory of
VOL. 1, NO. 8 Affinity, Reality and Communication

 RADIO BROADCAST LECTURES

MATHISON PROJECTION METER MODEL A

Also in 1951 the first projection meter was developed, the Model A. This E-Meter was useful in the instruction of auditors because it was designed to project an image of the meter, allowing students to see needle reactions while LRH demonstrated auditing techniques.

The following series of fifteen-minute talks was recorded and broadcast over a network of 126 radio stations across the US.

7 Feb How to Straighten Out a Group

8 Feb Dianetics

9 Feb Valences and Straight Memory

12 Feb Grief and Valences

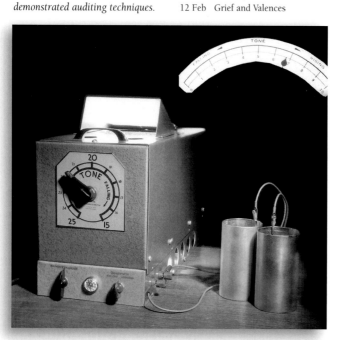

13 Feb Husbands and Wives Auditing Each Other

14 Feb Communication Breaks

15 Feb The Tone Scale of Groups and Nations

ISSUES

DAB Mar The Problem of
VOL. 1, NO. 9 Sedation

DAB Apr-May Lock Scanning
VOL. 1, NOS. 10–11

 RECORDED MESSAGE

This recorded address was sent by Mr. Hubbard from Wichita, Kansas, to be played for those attending the New York Dianetics Association's first anniversary of Dianetics celebration.

15 May Ron's May 15 Message

 PROFESSIONAL COURSE LECTURES
WICHITA, KANSAS

After completing his latest book, *Science of Survival,* Mr. Hubbard lectured to Professional Course students at the Hubbard Dianetics Foundation in Wichita, Kansas, on the theory and procedures detailed in the book.

21 May Theta–MEST Theory

4 Jun All Possible Aberrations

12 Jun Theory Behind Theta and MEST

12 Jun Demonstration: Validating Theta

ISSUE

DAB Jun Preventive Dianetics
VOL. 1, NO. 12

 SCIENCE OF SURVIVAL: SIMPLIFIED, FASTER DIANETIC TECHNIQUES
by L. Ron Hubbard

This book was released as a limited manuscript edition in June 1951, at the First Annual Conference of Hubbard Dianetic Auditors in Wichita, Kansas. The hardcover edition was published in August 1951 by the Hubbard Dianetics Foundation. The title was later changed to Science of Survival: Prediction of Human Behavior. *Included in each edition of* Science of Survival *is the Hubbard Chart of Human Evaluation. Today published by Bridge Publications and New Era Publications.*
TRANSLATIONS: *German and Italian.*

 FIRST ANNUAL CONFERENCE OF HUBBARD DIANETIC AUDITORS
WICHITA, KANSAS

L. Ron Hubbard gave attendees at the First Annual Conference of Hubbard Dianetic Auditors lectures centered on the latest advances in Dianetics, as covered in his book *Science of Survival.*

25 Jun New Techniques

25 Jun Review of the Theta–MEST Theory

25 Jun Goals of Theta and MEST

26 Jun Chart of Human Evaluation — Part I

26 Jun Chart of Human Evaluation — Part II

27 Jun Validation Processing

27 Jun Uses of Validation Processing

27 Jun Demonstration of Validation Processing

28 Jun The Complete Auditor — Part I

28 Jun The Complete Auditor — Part II

30 Jun MEST Straightwire

ISSUES

DAB Jul Education and the
VOL. 2, NO. 1 Auditor

DAB Jul Aberrations and
VOL. 2, NO. 1 Genius

ARTICLE Teaching

 PROFESSIONAL COURSE LECTURES
WICHITA, KANSAS

For a period of five weeks Mr. Hubbard gave lectures each Monday afternoon to students at the Hubbard Dianetics Foundation in Wichita, covering auditing basics as well as his latest discoveries and refinements of procedure.

9 Jul Review of Validation Processing

9 Jul MEST Processing

16 Jul Some Educational Data

16 Jul More on MEST Processing

23 Jul Basic Processing — Part I

23 Jul Basic Processing — Part II

30 Jul Basic Reason — Part I

30 Jul Basic Reason — Part II

6 Aug Survival and the Human Mind

6 Aug Survival Processing

 SELF ANALYSIS
by L. Ron Hubbard

First published by the International Library of Arts and Sciences, Wichita, Kansas, August 1951. Today published by Bridge Publications and New Era Publications. Contains a simplified version of the Hubbard Chart of Human Evaluation. TRANSLATIONS: *Bulgarian, Danish, Dutch, French, German, Greek, Hungarian, Italian, Norwegian, Portuguese, Spanish and Swedish.*

SPECIAL COURSE IN HUMAN EVALUATION
WICHITA, KANSAS

This series of lectures on human evaluation and its application in business, politics and domestic activities was given to a group of Wichita businessmen. (Available from Golden Era Productions.)

13 Aug	The Purpose of Human Evaluation
13 Aug	The Dynamics of Existence
14 Aug	Conquest of the Physical Universe
14 Aug	Personality
15 Aug	Self Analysis
15 Aug	The Tone Scale
16 Aug	Motion and Emotion
16 Aug	Motion and Emotion (cont.)
17 Aug	Motion and the Tone Scale
17 Aug	The ARC Triangle

ISSUES

LETTER	15 Aug	"Dear H.D.A.;..."
DAB VOL. 2, NO. 2	Aug	An Essay on Management
DAB VOL. 2, NO. 2	Aug	How to Pick Up Occluded Data
DAB VOL. 2, NO. 2	Aug	The "26" Percepties
DAB VOL. 2, NO. 3	Sep	Basic Reason — Basic Principles
SUPPLEMENT NO. 1 TO SCIENCE OF SURVIVAL	Sep	All Possible Aberrations
SUPPLEMENT NO. 2 TO SCIENCE OF SURVIVAL	Sep	Validation Processing

PROFESSIONAL COURSE LECTURES
WICHITA, KANSAS

In lectures to students attending the Professional Course at Wichita, Mr. Hubbard discussed a variety of subjects, including a new auditing technique known as Effort Processing. This powerful procedure addressed the effects of time, motion and directed effort on an individual.

20 Aug	Motion and Effort, Part I
20 Aug	Motion and Effort, Part II
27 Aug	Motion and Emotion in Processing
27 Aug	Line Charge
4 Sep	Time and Motion
4 Sep	Illusion
10 Sep	Mimicry
10 Sep	Theta Facsimiles
17 Sep	Some Notes on Black Dianetics
17 Sep	The Cellular Postulate
20 Sep	Self-determined Effort Processing
20 Sep	Randomity and Effort
24 Sep	Effort Processing Fundamentals, Part I
24 Sep	Effort Processing Fundamentals, Part II
1 Oct	Self-determinism and Effort Processing

1 Oct	Progress, Procedure and Demonstration

THE OCTOBER CONFERENCE
WICHITA, KANSAS

This series of lectures was given to more than fifty auditors from all over the country gathered for a conference in Wichita.

8 Oct	Axioms and Effort Processing
8 Oct	The Logics
9 Oct	Statics and Motions and Axioms 1–14
9 Oct	Effort Processing Summary
10 Oct	Axioms 14–32
10 Oct	Theory of Epicenters
11 Oct	Axioms 33–49
11 Oct	Epicenters and Self-Determinism
12 Oct	Randomity and Emotion
12 Oct	Effort in Engrams

THE DIANETICS AXIOMS
by L. Ron Hubbard

First published by Hubbard Dianetics Foundation, Wichita, Kansas, October 1951. This book was issued during the October Conference and was the first release of the Axioms of Dianetics. The Dianetics Axioms are now available in the books Advanced Procedure and Axioms, Handbook for Preclears, *and* Scientology 0-8 *by L. Ron Hubbard, published by Bridge Publications and New Era Publications.* TRANSLATIONS: Scientology 0-8: *Dutch, French, German, Italian and Spanish.*

PROFESSIONAL COURSE LECTURES
WICHITA, KANSAS

While continuing his research and auditing through 1951, Mr. Hubbard also took time to lecture to students attending the Professional Auditor Course, staff auditors at the Wichita Foundation and conference attendees.

15 Oct	ARC and Effort Processing
15 Oct	Postulate Processing
22 Oct	How to Handle the Human Mind as You Would an Electronic Computer
22 Oct	How to Handle the Human Mind as You Would an Electronic Computer (cont.)

CHILD DIANETICS, DIANETIC PROCESSING FOR CHILDREN
by L. Ron Hubbard

Compiled from the research and lecture materials of L. Ron Hubbard by the staff of the Hubbard Dianetics Foundation of Los Angeles, and first published in Wichita, Kansas, by the International Library of Arts and Sciences, October 1951. Mr. Hubbard wrote the introduction in August 1951, about the same time the book was actually typeset. Today published by Bridge Publications and New Era Publications. TRANSLATIONS: *German, Italian and Spanish.*

ISSUE

DAB VOL. 2, NO. 4	Oct	Self-Determined Effort Processing

THE FOUNDATION AUDITOR'S COURSE
WICHITA, KANSAS

23 Oct	Methods of Processing
23 Oct	Self-determinism on the Dynamics
24 Oct	Being Right
24 Oct	Introduction to the Service Facsimile
25 Oct	The Service Facsimile, Part I
25 Oct	The Service Facsimile, Part II
26 Oct	The Evolution of Man
26 Oct	How to Talk About Dianetics
29 Oct	The Theta Facsimile, Part I
29 Oct	The Theta Facsimile, Part II

PROFESSIONAL COURSE LECTURES
WICHITA, KANSAS

5 Nov	Postulates and Emotion
12 Nov	Love
12 Nov	Basic Postulates
12 Nov	Prime Thought
19 Nov	Cause and Effect, Part I
19 Nov	Cause and Effect, Part II
26 Nov	An Analysis of Memory and Human Aberration and Psychosomatic Illness, Part I
26 Nov	An Analysis of Memory and Human Aberration and Psychosomatic Illness, Part II
3 Dec	Advanced Procedure
3 Dec	Cause and Effect: Full Responsibility
10 Dec	Dead Men's Goals, Part I
10 Dec	Dead Men's Goals, Part II
17 Dec	Seriousness and Approval
17 Dec	Counter-Effort, Counter-Emotion and Counter-Thought

ADVANCED PROCEDURE AND AXIOMS
by L. Ron Hubbard

First published by the Hubbard Dianetics Foundation in Wichita, Kansas, in November 1951, and today by Bridge Publications and New Era Publications. It was written as a companion book to Handbook for Preclears, *which was published in December 1951.*

ISSUES

DAB VOL. 2, NO. 5	Nov	An Essay on Authoritarianism
DAB VOL. 2, NO. 5	Nov	A Brief History of Psychotherapy
SUPPLEMENT NO. 3 TO SCIENCE OF SURVIVAL		MEST Processing
DAB VOL. 2, NO. 6	Dec	Postulate Processing

HANDBOOK FOR PRECLEARS
by L. Ron Hubbard

This was the main theme of the Second Annual Conference of Hubbard Dianetic Auditors at which it was introduced. First published in December 1951 at Wichita, Kansas. It was later republished by Scientific Press in Phoenix, Arizona, under the title of Scientology Handbook for Preclears *and is today published by Bridge Publications and New Era Publications. It contains the Hubbard Chart of Attitudes.*

ARTICLE	Dec	Suggested Method of Handling Handbook

SECOND ANNUAL CONFERENCE OF HUBBARD DIANETIC AUDITORS
WICHITA, KANSAS

The theme of this conference was the new book *Handbook for Preclears*, which had recently been written and released, containing the Hubbard Chart of Attitudes.

27 Dec	Miracles in Dianetics
27 Dec	Counter-Emotion
28 Dec	The Chart of Attitudes
28 Dec	The Life Continuum Theory
29 Dec	The Emotional Curve
29 Dec	The Goal of Processing: The Ideal State of Man
29 Dec	Cause on All Dynamics
29 Dec	Handbook for Preclears
30 Dec	Effort Processing and the Life Continuum
30 Dec	Yes, No and Maybe
31 Dec	Informal Discussion with Ron

1952

In 1952 LRH made spectacular new discoveries concerning man, his mind and his true spiritual nature. He had earlier discovered mental image pictures, and had been studying their characteristics and behavior: the reactive, stimulus-response mechanisms that psychology had observed, but never analyzed or understood.

Now he found out what was looking at the pictures. And described it. And found out that you could do things with it from a very practical standpoint that nobody had ever done before.

Exteriorization and exteriorization processes, formation of the Hubbard College and the Hubbard Association of Scientologists were only a few of Mr. Hubbard's activities in 1952.

 **THE AUDITOR'S MANUAL**

Staff written and edited. Published by the Hubbard Dianetics Foundation, Inc., Wichita, Kansas, 1952.

In addition to research, writing and administrative work, Mr. Hubbard responded to continuing demands with a full schedule of lectures and demonstrations to Professional Course students, Foundation staff and the general public.

 PROFESSIONAL COURSE LECTURES
WICHITA, KANSAS

7 Jan — Survival

7 Jan — Questions and Answers

11 Jan — Service Facsimiles

11 Jan — Past Life Auditing: Effort Processing

11 Jan — Running Regret and Emotional Curve

14 Jan — The Impact of Dianetics on Society

14 Jan — The Emotional Curve

16 Jan — Running the Service Facsimile Chain

17 Jan — Effort Processing: Intentions and Overt Acts

21 Jan — The Anatomy of the Overt Act, Part I

21 Jan — The Anatomy of the Overt Act, Part II

28 Jan — The Anatomy of a Service Facsimile

28 Jan — The Anatomy of a Service Facsimile (cont.)

2 Feb — The Psychogalvanometer

2 Feb — Mysticism

 PUBLIC LECTURE
WICHITA, KANSAS

6 Feb — Dianetics: The Modern Miracle

 PROFESSIONAL COURSE LECTURES
WICHITA, KANSAS

8 Feb — Summary of the Service Facsimile Chain

18 Feb — The Code of Behavior

18 Feb — Care of the Body

 HUBBARD COLLEGE LECTURES
WICHITA, KANSAS

25 Feb — Review of Progress of Dianetics and Dianetics Business

25 Feb — Summary of Aberrative Incidents

 SUMMARY COURSE LECTURES
WICHITA, KANSAS

(Available from Golden Era Productions as a series entitled "The Dawn of Immortality.")

3 Mar — Scientology: Milestone One

3 Mar — Outline of Therapy

3 Mar — Demonstration of E-Meter

4 Mar — The Axioms and How They Apply to Auditing

4 Mar — Thought, Emotion and Effort

4 Mar — Discovery of Facsimile One

5 Mar — Auditing Facsimile One

5 Mar — Thought and Preclears

5 Mar — Emotion

5 Mar — Whole Track Facsimiles

6 Mar — Effort and Counter-Effort

6 Mar — Attack on the Preclear

7 Mar — Facsimiles: How to Handle Recordings

7 Mar — Indoctrination of the Preclear

8 Mar — Effort and Counter-Effort: Overt Acts

8 Mar — Indoctrination in the Use of the E-Meter

9 Mar — Thought, Emotion, Effort and the Overt Act

9 Mar — Demonstration: Metered Straightwire and Overt Act

9 Mar — Training Auditors

10 Mar — Running Effort and Counter-Effort

10 Mar — Organization of Data

10 Mar — Theta Lines

10 Mar — History of the Theta Line

10 Mar — Principal Incidents on the Theta Line

ISSUES

DESPATCH 24 Jan "To the Students:..."

DAB Feb Cause and Effect
VOL. 2, NO. 8

SUPPLEMENT NO. 4 Feb Effort
TO *SCIENCE OF SURVIVAL* Processing

ARTICLE Feb Processing of Auditors

 SCIENTOLOGY AND DIANETICS ADVANCED PROCEDURES

Notes and transcripts on lectures by L. Ron Hubbard and others; Wichita, Kansas; January through March 1952. Compiled and published by the Central Pennsylvania Dianetics Group, Middletown, Pennsylvania.

ARTICLE Apr A Story

After moving his office from Wichita to Phoenix, Arizona, Mr. Hubbard resumed lecturing, covering his startling new discoveries and their application to improve people's awareness and abilities.

 LECTURES
PHOENIX, ARIZONA

15 Apr — The Success of Dianetics

15 Apr — Theta Bodies

16 Apr — Anatomy of the Theta Body

16 Apr — How to Audit a Theta Line, Part I

16 Apr — How to Audit a Theta Line, Part II

16 Apr — How to Search for Incidents on the Track, Part I

16 Apr — How to Search for Incidents on the Track, Part II

16 Apr — Theta Body Demonstration

 TECHNIQUE 80 LECTURES
PHOENIX, ARIZONA

(Available from Golden Era Productions as a series entitled "The Route to Infinity". TRANSLATIONS: French, German, Italian and Spanish.)

19 May — Beingness

19 May — Outline of Technique 80

19 May — Wavelengths of ARC

20 May — Decision

20 May — Decision: Cause and Effect

21 May — Therapy Section of Technique 80, Part I

21 May — Therapy Section of Technique 80, Part II

ARTICLE 21 May Dianetics Jingles

 SUMMER SESSION TECHNIQUE 88 LECTURES
PHOENIX, ARIZONA

23 Jun — Introduction

23 Jun — Time

23 Jun — Obsession

24 Jun — Attention Unit Flows

24 Jun — Attention Unit Running

24 Jun — Concept Running

25 Jun — Invalidation

25 Jun — Overt Acts, Motivators and DEDs

26 Jun — The Actions of Energy

26 Jun — Technique 88 and the Whole Track, Part I

26 Jun — Technique 88 and the Whole Track, Part II

27 Jun — Confusions

27 Jun — Acquisition of Bodies

27 Jun — Theta and Genetic Lines

28 Jun — Technique 88: Questions and Answers

MANUAL Jun Electropsychometric Auditing Operator's Manual

 **INDIVIDUAL TRACK MAP**
by L. Ron Hubbard

Published by the Office of L. Ron Hubbard, Phoenix, Arizona, June 1952. (The text of this book is printed in full in the Technical Bulletins volumes.) New updated edition for use on New Era Dianetics was published in 1988. Today published by Bridge Publications and New Era Publications.

 A KEY TO THE UNCONSCIOUS, SYMBOLOGICAL PROCESSING
by L. Ron Hubbard

Published by the Scientific Press, Phoenix, Arizona, June 1952. (The text of this book is printed in full in the Technical Bulletins volumes.)

 TECHNIQUE 88 SUPPLEMENTARY LECTURES
PHOENIX, ARIZONA

24 Jul — Behavior of Energy as It Applies to Thought Flows

24 Jul — E-Meter Behavior versus Flow Lines and Patterns

7 Aug — Straightwire — Technique 88

7 Aug — Standard Process of 88, Lecture I

Aug — Standard Process of 88, Lecture II

28 Aug — Talk for Associates

28 Aug — Individualism

28 Aug — Ridge Running

4 Sep — Where We Are At

 **WHAT TO AUDIT**
by L. Ron Hubbard

Published in Phoenix, Arizona, by the Scientific Press, July 1952. The same text was issued as History of Man in London in July 1952.

HISTORY OF MAN
by L. Ron Hubbard

Published by the Hubbard Association of Scientologists, London, July 1952. It contained the same text as in What to Audit. *A later edition was entitled* Scientology: A History of Man, *which is its current title, as published today by Bridge Publications and New Era Publications.* TRANSLATIONS: *French, German and Italian.*

ARTICLE   Jul   A Step-by-Step Breakdown of 88

ISSUES

JOS Aug ISSUE 1-G	What Is Scientology?
JOS Aug ISSUE 1-G	Electronics Gives Life to Freud's Theory
JOS Aug ISSUE 1-G	The Handling of Arthritis
JOS Sep ISSUE 2-G	The Running of Concepts

THE PROFESSIONAL COURSE LECTURE SUMMARY
(also known as Professional Course Booklets)

Compiled and rewritten from transcripts of lectures given by L. Ron Hubbard during the spring and summer of 1952. This set comprised a list of 50 booklets. The first 27 booklets were originally entitled the Summary Course Booklets, *published by the Scientific Press, Phoenix, Arizona, March 1952. In May of 1952, Professional Course Booklets 28–31 were published by the Scientific Press. The balance of the* Professional Course Booklets *were issued throughout June, July and August 1952, published by the Hubbard Association of Scientologists, Inc., Phoenix, Arizona.*

SCIENTOLOGY: 88
by L. Ron Hubbard

A unique limited edition, handwritten by L. Ron Hubbard and printed on special lithographic plates. Distributed by the Hubbard Association of Scientologists, Phoenix, Arizona, September 1952. The technology from Scientology: 88 *can be found in* Scientology 8-80.

In September Mr. Hubbard flew to London, England, where he immediately began training auditors, writing a new book, establishing a new organization and launching several research projects. His agenda included several series of lectures to staff and students.

TECHNIQUE 88 SUPPLEMENTARY LECTURES
LONDON, ENGLAND

21 Sep	Basics of Scientology and Dianetics, Part I
21 Sep	Basics of Scientology and Dianetics, Part II
22 Sep	Tone Scale Characteristics— Flows, Part I
22 Sep	Tone Scale Characteristics— Flows, Part II
23 Sep	Blanketing—Exteriorization
24 Sep	The Three Types of Energy Flows
Oct	Theory of Flows—Counter-Elasticity
Oct	Flows
Oct	Present Time Use of Energy Manifestations
Oct	Basic Summary on SOP of Technique 8-80
Oct	Phenomena of the Thetan
Oct	Service Facsimile Chain
Oct	The Resolution of the Second Dynamic
Oct	Summary of Technique 8-80
Oct	Activity of the Auditor in Theta Clearing

ARTICLES

JOS Sep ISSUE 3-G	Danger: Black Dianetics!
JOS Oct ISSUE 4-G	The Loophole in Guarded Rights
JOS Oct ISSUE 4-G	"Being Cause" Is Society's Major Aberration
JOS Oct ISSUE 5-G	Records of Mind Are Permanent

SELF ANALYSIS IN DIANETICS— A HANDBOOK OF DIANETIC THERAPY
by L. Ron Hubbard

Published in London, England by Derricke Ridgway Ltd., October 1952. This was a revised edition of the original Self Analysis and is now out of print—the original version was reinstated and is the book which is used today.

ARTICLES

| JOS Nov ISSUE 6-G | Procedures for Theta Clearing |
| JOS Nov ISSUE 6-G | E-Meter Is Precision Instrument When Used Skillfully by Auditor |

SCIENTOLOGY 8-80
by L. Ron Hubbard

Originally published by the Hubbard Association of Scientologists, Phoenix, Arizona, November 1952, and today by Bridge Publications and New Era Publications. TRANSLATION: *French.*

LONDON LECTURES
LONDON, ENGLAND

Nov	Illusion Processing
Nov	The Role of Earth
Nov	Illusion Processing and Therapy
17 Nov	ARC, Motion, Emotion, Tone Scale, Flows, Ridges
17 Nov	Ridges, Self-determinism— Tone Scales
19 Nov	Attention, Part I
19 Nov	Attention, Part II
20 Nov	Creative Processing— Validation of MEST
20 Nov	Creative Processing— Breaking Pc's Agreement with Natural Laws

(Available from Golden Era Productions as a series entitled "Secrets of the MEST Universe")

6 Nov	Methods of Research— The Thetan as an Energy Unit
7 Nov	Force as *Homo Sapiens* and as Thetan—Responsibility
14 Nov	Be, Have and Do, Part I
14 Nov	Be, Have and Do, Part II

(Available from Golden Era Productions as a series entitled "The Perception of Truth." TRANSLATIONS: *French, German, Italian and Spanish.)*

10 Nov	Introduction: The Q List and Beginning of Logics
10 Nov	Logics 1–7
12 Nov	Precision Knowledge: Necessity to Know Terminology and Law
12 Nov	Logics 7–9 and 10–23

THE SCIENTOLOGY SYMBOL

There are two triangles, over which is imposed the S, which stands for Scientology. The lower triangle is the ARC triangle, whose points are Affinity, Reality and Communication. These are the three elements which combined give Understanding. The upper triangle is the KRC triangle. The points are K for Knowledge, R for Responsibility and C for Control.

The KRC triangle acts like the ARC triangle. When one corner is increased the other two also rise.

The Scientology Symbol first appeared in 1952.

It appears on auditors' blazer badges, Release pins and Clear bracelets. In addition it has been worn as lapel pins, tie tacks, rings of various designs, earrings, key rings, money clips, neckties, cigarette lighters, brooches and necklaces, and otherwise displayed in car badges, decals, flags, etc.

MATHISON MODEL H-52-1R

The model H-52-1R E-Meter became available in 1952 and was in use through 1954.

LONDON PROFESSIONAL COURSE LECTURES
LONDON, ENGLAND

10 Nov   Definitions of Dianetics and Scientology, Other Philosophies

12 Nov   8-8008 Continued, Time and Space

12 Nov   Time, Create, Destroy, Have

14 Nov   Standard Operating Procedure Issue 2, Part I

14 Nov   Standard Operating Procedure Issue 2, Part II

17 Nov   Self-determinism and Creation of Universes

17 Nov   Creative Processing

19 Nov   The Control of the Individual by an Unknown — Sound

19 Nov   Responsibility

20 Nov   Creative Processing — Handling Illusions

20 Nov   Assessment of Pc — The Dynamics: Be, Do, Have

ARTICLES

JOS Nov ISSUE 7-G   Sanity Needs Creation – Destruction Balance

JOS Nov ISSUE 7-G   The Components of Experience

ARTICLE Nov   My Going Away Present

SCIENTOLOGY 8-8008
by L. Ron Hubbard

Written by L. Ron Hubbard in England in October and November 1952. He had the first copy with him when he flew to the United States and presented it at the opening of the Philadelphia Doctorate Course on December 1st in Philadelphia, Pennsylvania. First published by the Hubbard Association of Scientologists, London, England, December 1952, and today by Bridge Publications and New Era Publications.

PHILADELPHIA DOCTORATE LECTURES
PHILADELPHIA, PENNSYLVANIA

This series of lectures was delivered to a class of thirty-eight auditors. Covering a wide analysis of human behavior, they gave a complete coverage of the latest auditing techniques and an expansion of the new professional course textbook, *Scientology 8-8008.* (Available from Golden Era Productions.)

1 Dec   Opening: What Is to Be Done in Course

1 Dec   E-Meter: Demo

1 Dec   Creative Processing: Demo of E-Meter Auditing

2 Dec   Locks, Secondaries, Engrams — How to Handle Them

2 Dec   The Gradient Scale of Handling Space, Energy and Objects

2 Dec   The "Q": Highest Level of Knowledge

2 Dec   A Thetan Creates by Postulates — Q2

3 Dec   The Track of the Thetan/GE — Space/Time

3 Dec   Anatomy of Processing — Energy, Phenomena/Sensation

3 Dec   Specific Parts of Self-determinism, Spacation

4 Dec   Spacation: Energy Particles and Time

4 Dec   Spacation: Locating, Space, Time

4 Dec   Spacation: Anchor Points, Origin

4 Dec   The Logics: Methods of Thinking

4 Dec   The Logics: Infinity-Valued Logic

5 Dec   Cycles of Action

5 Dec   The Tone Scale: Moving the Pc Up the Scale

5 Dec   Conditions of Space/Time/Energy

6 Dec   Axioms and Logics: Further Data

6 Dec   Formative State of Scientology, Definition of Logic

8 Dec   ARC/Cycles: Theory and Automaticity

8 Dec   More on Automaticity

8 Dec   ARC, Force, Be/Do/Have

9 Dec   What's Wrong With This Universe: A Working Package for the Auditor

9 Dec   Flows: Reverse Vector of Physical Universe

9 Dec   Flows: Characteristics Of

9 Dec   Flows: The Part Force Bears in Clearing

9 Dec   Flows: The Part Space Bears in Clearing

10 Dec   Flows: Patterns of Interaction

10 Dec   Flows: Rate of Change, Relative Size, Anchor Points

10 Dec   Flows: Basic Agreement and Prove It!

10 Dec   Flows, Dispersals and Ridges

10 Dec   Anatomy of the Genetic Entity

11 Dec   8-8008: Understanding the Phenomena

11 Dec   The DEI Scale

11 Dec   Structure/Function: Selective Variation Of

11 Dec   Chart of Attitudes: Rising Scale Processing

11 Dec   Rising Scale Processing

12 Dec   Game Processing

12 Dec   Games/Goals

12 Dec   SOP Issue 3: Postulate, Creative Processing

13 Dec   Standard Operating Procedure (SOP)

13 Dec   On Auditing: How to Succeed/Fail, Assess

13 Dec   SOP: Assessment (cont.)

13 Dec   Development of Scientology: Characteristics of a Living Science

13 Dec   Goal: Rehabilitation of Thetan, Case Step 1

15 Dec   SOP: Issue 5

15 Dec   SOP: Spacation

15 Dec   SOP: Spacation (cont.)

16 Dec   SOP: Spacation Step III, Flow Processing

16 Dec   SOP: Issue 5

16 Dec   Memory (Not Human Memory)

16 Dec   Memory and Automaticity

17 Dec   Summary to Date: Handling Step I and Demo

17 Dec   Demonstration on Step I (cont.)

17 Dec   Discussion of Demo: Above Agreement with Flows

17 Dec   Continued Demonstration Step 4

18 Dec   About the "Press" Tone Level: Psychometry

18 Dec   Chart of Havingness

18 Dec   How To Talk About Scientology

18 Dec   How To Talk to Friends About Scientology

18 Dec   Your Own Case: To You, the Student

ISSUE

MIMEOED Dec   "The aberration (above time)..."

ARTICLES

JOS Dec ISSUE 8-G   New Data Doesn't Invalidate Early, Proven Techniques

JOS Dec ISSUE 9-G   Thetan, to Be "Sane," Must Learn How He's Been Caring for Body

1953

At the beginning of 1953, L. Ron Hubbard was operating from his office in London and delivering lectures. New lines for the issue of technical releases and updates were established with the Associate Newsletter and Professional Auditor's Bulletin.

In April, he released a book covering his breakthroughs on the technology of communication in management, entitled *How to Live Though an Executive.*

The Factors were also released in April. A masterpiece of simplicity and wisdom, these thirty statements comprise, as Mr. Hubbard put it, a "Summation of the considerations and examinations of the human spirit and the material universe completed between 1923 and 1953 A.D."

During the summer months, he traveled across Europe continuing his research. Before the year was over he was again back in the US, delivering the first and second American Advanced Clinical Courses.

ARTICLE

JOS Jan ISSUE 10-G   Preclears Must Be Audited According to Their Condition

Traveling between England and the United States, Mr. Hubbard lectured on such developments as the application of auditing to groups, and expanded on the material covered in his latest books.

LONDON GROUP AUDITOR'S COURSE LECTURES
LONDON, ENGLAND

10 Jan   Educational System, How to Group Process

10 Jan   Educational System, How to Group Process (cont.)

10 Jan   What We Are Doing in Processing

10 Jan   Mechanics of the Mind

10 Jan   The Missing Particle

10 Jan   The Missing Particle (cont.)

10 Jan   The Processing of Groups by Creative Processing

10 Jan   Creative Admiration Processing

PHILADELPHIA DOCTORATE COURSE SUPPLEMENTARY LECTURES
LONDON, ENGLAND

(Available from Golden Era Productions as part of the Philadelphia Doctorate Course Lectures.)

12 Jan   Agree and Disagree: Have, Not Have

12 Jan   Agree and Disagree: Have, Not Have (cont.)

12 Jan   Anchor Points: Driving Them In and Out

14 Jan   Group and Individual Processing

14 Jan   SOP 5 Long Form Step I

16 Jan   SOP 5 Long Form Step II

16 Jan   SOP 5 Long Form Step II: Demonstration

19 Jan   SOP 5 Long Form Step III: Differentiation on Theta Clearing

19 Jan   SOP 5 Long Form Step III: Spacation

21 Jan   SOP 5 Long Form Step IV: GITA

21 Jan   SOP 5 Long Form Step IV: GITA (cont.)

23 Jan   SOP 5 Long Form Step V: Additional Techniques

23 Jan   SOP 5 Long Form Step VI

24 Jan   Concluding Long Form of Step V: Admiration Processing

ISSUES

DESPATCH 30 Jan   Processing Notes

BULLETIN late Jan   Bulletin to Auditors

DESPATCH   Scientology 8-8008, Standard Operating Procedure 8

ARTICLES

JOS Feb ISSUE 11-G   Preclears Should Be Processed; Education Isn't Auditor's Task

JOS 15 Mar ISSUE 12-G   Auditor First Should Know Tools Before He Goes in for Artistic

LONDON SPRING LECTURES
LONDON, ENGLAND

Continuing his education of Scientologists in England, Mr. Hubbard gave these twenty hours of lectures covering his latest procedures and theory. (Available from Golden Era Productions as a series entitled "Admiration and the Renaissance of Beingness.")

23 Mar Review of Dianetics, Scientology and Para-Dianetics/Scientology
23 Mar What's Wrong with the Pc and How You Can Do Something About It
24 Mar SOP Issue 5: Steps I to VII
24 Mar SOP Issue 5: Steps I to VII (cont.)
25 Mar The Elements with Stress on How to Run Matched Terminals
25 Mar The Elements with Stress on How to Run Matched Terminals (cont.)
26 Mar How and When To Audit
26 Mar Present Time
27 Mar SOP Utility
27 Mar SOP Utility (cont.)
27 Mar Types of Processes
27 Mar Beingness, Agreement, Hidden Influence, Processes
7 Apr Data on Case Level 5, Step for Case 5
7 Apr Data on Case Level 5 (cont.)
7 Apr Demonstration
7 Apr Exteriorization—Demonstration and Explanation
8 Apr Case Level VI and VII, Psychotic
8 Apr Case Level VI and VII (cont.)
24 Apr The Factors
24 Apr SOP 8

ISSUES
LRH RESEARCH NOTES Spring "Anything to which the pc agreed..."
DESPATCH Apr Advance Copy on Case Level V

HOW TO LIVE THOUGH AN EXECUTIVE: COMMUNICATION MANUAL
by L. Ron Hubbard

First published by the Hubbard Association of Scientologists, Phoenix, Arizona, April 1953 and today by Bridge Publications and New Era Publications. TRANSLATIONS: Italian and Spanish.

SELF ANALYSIS IN SCIENTOLOGY
by L. Ron Hubbard

Published by the Hubbard Association of Scientologists, Philadelphia, Pennsylvania, April 1953. This was a modified version of the original Self Analysis and is now out of print (although its text is contained in the Technical Bulletins volumes). The original 1951 edition of Self Analysis is in use.

ARTICLES
JOS ISSUE 13-G Apr Marital Scientology
15 Apr 3 Admiration Processing

ISSUES
ASSOCIATE NEWSLETTER 23 Apr "Several items of interest..."
ASSOCIATE NEWSLETTER 28 Apr "It probably has not occurred to the field..."

ARTICLES
JOS ISSUE 14-G Apr Child Scientology
JOS ISSUE 15-G May "The Old Man's Casebook"
ARTICLE 1 May Scientology 8-8008, Unlimited Techniques

ISSUE
ASSOCIATE NEWSLETTER NO. 2 early May "Associate, please send me..."

BIRMINGHAM LECTURES
BIRMINGHAM, ENGLAND

21 May Three Universes
21 May Tone Scale—ARC, Present Time

ISSUES
DESPATCH May The Theta–MEST Theory Extended
ASSOCIATE NEWSLETTER NO. 3 mid-May "Enclosed herewith, prior to release..."
PAB 1 10 May General Comments, Group Processing and a Summary of New Work: Certainties
PAB 2 end May General Comments, SOP 8 and a Summary of SOP 8-A, General Comment
ASSOCIATE NEWSLETTER NO. 4 end May "This newsletter concerns itself..."
DESPATCH Give and Take Processing

THIS IS SCIENTOLOGY, THE SCIENCE OF CERTAINTY
by L. Ron Hubbard

Published by the Hubbard Association of Scientologists, Philadelphia, Pennsylvania, June 1953. This book was later combined with Scientology: Auditor's Handbook and other material to make the book The Creation of Human Ability. Its text is contained in the Technical Bulletins volumes, as Journal of Scientology Issue 16-G.

ARTICLE
JOS ISSUE 17-G Jun The Limitations of Homo Novis

ISSUES
PAB 3 mid-Jun Certainty Processing
ASSOCIATE NEWSLETTER NO. 5 18 Jun "After a fast and violent passage..."

PAB 4 end Jun Beingness and Certainty Processing
ASSOCIATE NEWSLETTER NO. 6 Jul "This is a brief one about organization..."
PAB 5 mid-Jul About PABs
ASSOCIATE NEWSLETTER NO. 7 late Jul "Strategy and Tactics..."

ARTICLE
JOS ISSUE 18-G Jul Off the Time Track

ISSUES
PAB 6 end Jul Case Opening
PAB 7 mid-Aug "Come on and bear a hand..."
ASSOCIATE NEWSLETTER NO. 8 late Aug "The big news is the international congress..."
PAB 8 late Aug Viewpoint Processing
PAB 9 early Sep Formula H
ASSOCIATE NEWSLETTER NO. 9 4 Sep "Requested Report..."
PAB 10 late Sep Change Processing
ASSOCIATE NEWSLETTER NO. 10 late Sep Technique Bulletin

INTRODUCTION TO SCIENTOLOGY

Taken from the works of L. Ron Hubbard, published by the Hubbard Foundation, Philadelphia, Pennsylvania, late 1953. This notebook was awarded to all the students who successfully completed the course of the Foundation during the span of its existence: March 1952 through October 1953.

ON AUDITING

Taken from the works of L. Ron Hubbard, published in Ann Arbor, Michigan, late 1953.

MATHISON H-53-DS

Since the range of earlier meters was insufficient to register all preclears, the Model H-53-DS (Double Scale) was designed with an expanded range. It was released in late 1952.

FIRST INTERNATIONAL CONGRESS OF DIANETICISTS AND SCIENTOLOGISTS LECTURES

PHILADELPHIA, PENNSYLVANIA

This series of lectures was delivered to the nearly 300 delegates attending the First International Congress of Dianeticists and Scientologists.

LOOK DON'T THINK

Transcripts of lectures delivered by L. Ron Hubbard at the Philadelphia Congress, 30 September through 4 October 1953. Published by Scientology Northern California, 1953.

FIRST AMERICAN ADVANCED INDOCTRINATION COURSE LECTURES

CAMDEN, NEW JERSEY

The lectures listed below, covering his latest and most advanced discoveries, were given by Mr. Hubbard to a handpicked group of ten of the best auditors in the world. (Available from Golden Era Productions as a series entitled "Exteriorization and the Phenomena of Space.")

MATHISON HM-4

The Model HM-4 E-Meter was also introduced in 1953. HM-4 stands for Hubbard Meter 4—the first meter was the Model B in 1951, the second was the H-52-1R of 1952 and the third was the H-53-DS.

ARTICLE

ISSUES

PAB 11 early Oct What the Thetan Is Trying to Do

DESPATCH This Is a List to Be Run by Change of Space Processing

PAB 12 late Oct The Cycle of Action of an Explosion

DESPATCH 28 Oct Step III Auditing Commands

PAB 13 mid-Nov On Human Behavior

SECOND AMERICAN ADVANCED CLINICAL COURSE LECTURES

CAMDEN, NEW JERSEY

Due to the success of the First American Advanced Indoctrination Course and to meet demand for advanced training, a second, similar course followed almost immediately. (Available from Golden Era Productions as a series entitled "The Rehabilitation of the Human Spirit.")

17 Nov Opening Lecture: Emotional Tone Scale
17 Nov SOP 8-C: First Lecture
17 Nov Getting Up Speed, Part I
17 Nov Getting Up Speed, Part II
18 Nov Step I of 8-C: Orientation
18 Nov Black Mock-ups, Persistence, MEST
18 Nov Step II: Automaticities
18 Nov Waste a Machine
19 Nov Effects, Reaching End of Cycle
19 Nov Footnote to Effects, Reaching End of Cycle
19 Nov More on Machines
20 Nov Resistance to Effect
20 Nov Plan of Auditing
23 Nov Formula Phi, Creation of MEST
23 Nov Summary of Steps I, II, III of SOP 8-C
24 Nov Anchor Points, Knowingness of Location
24 Nov Steps V, VI, VII; Duplication, Unconsciousness
24 Nov Additional Remarks: End of Cycle Processing
25 Nov Steps V, VI, VII—Time
25 Nov SOP 8-C, Summary Of
26 Nov Electronic Theory, Anchor Points
26 Nov Additional Remarks: Electronic Theory, Anchor Points
26 Nov Exteriorization
27 Nov Anchor Points, Justice
27 Nov Symbols
28 Nov Demonstration: Group Processing
28 Nov Special Session: Experimental Group Process
30 Nov Space, Perception, Knowingness, Part I
30 Nov Additional Remarks: Space, Perception, Knowingness
30 Nov Space, Perception, Knowingness, Part II
1 Dec Lack of Space
2 Dec Blackness
3 Dec Time: Cause and Effect, Part I
3 Dec Time: Cause and Effect, Part II
4 Dec Plan of SOP 8-C
4 Dec LRH Questions the Class on Exteriorization

7 Dec Barriers, Occlusion
7 Dec Outline of SOP 8-C
8 Dec Essence of SOP 8-C
8 Dec Problems of Auditing
9 Dec Summary: Failures on Exteriorization
9 Dec Examples of SOP 8-C Patter
10 Dec Knowingness
10 Dec SOP 8-C: General Discussion
11 Dec SOP 8-C Patter
13 Dec Force, Part I
13 Dec Force, Part II
14 Dec SOP 8-C Step VIII, Definitions
14 Dec Cause and Effect—Assignment of Cause, GE
15 Dec SOP 8-C: Step V
15 Dec Energy Problems
15 Dec Additional Remarks: Energy Problems
16 Dec Techniques Which Do or Do Not Assign Cause
16 Dec Comm Line: Overt Act
17 Dec SOP 8-C: Formulas
17 Dec Space Opera
18 Dec The "Only One"
18 Dec Beingness
19 Dec SOP 8-C: General
19 Dec Mass
20 Dec Communication
20 Dec Auditing by SOP 8-C, Formula H
20 Dec Reach/Withdraw
21 Dec Ability to Accept Direction
21 Dec Knowingness and Certainty
22 Dec Remedy of Havingness
22 Dec Postulates

ISSUES

ASSOCIATE 19 Nov "Dear Associates:
NEWSLETTER Since coming back..."
PAB 14 Nov On Human Character

ARTICLE

JOS Dec What an Auditor
ISSUE 22-G Should Know

ISSUES

PAB 15 mid-Dec Acceptance Level Processing
LRH RESEARCH NOTES
Dec "Motto of the MEST Universe"

INTERNATIONAL CONGRESS OF DIANETICISTS AND SCIENTOLOGISTS LECTURES

PHOENIX, ARIZONA

The latest Scientology techniques, which had been developed and perfected at the Advanced Clinical Courses, were presented to Scientologists from around the world at this congress.

28 Dec Goals of Scientology
28 Dec Mock-ups, Energy
28 Dec Basic Theory of Definitions
28 Dec Basic Theory of Definitions (cont.), Group Processing
28 Dec Group Processing, Part I
28 Dec Group Processing, Part II
28 Dec How to Be a Group Auditor
28 Dec Group Processing
29 Dec Create, Survive, Destroy Curve

29 Dec Use of SOP 8-C
29 Dec Role of the Auditor
29 Dec Group Processing—Short Lecture
29 Dec Design of SOP 8-C: Process for Groups, Percentages of Successes and Failures
29 Dec Group Process
30 Dec Talk on E-Meter
30 Dec Automaticity
30 Dec Group Processing
30 Dec Group Processing
31 Dec Step V, SOP 8-C (Group Processing)
31 Dec Group Processing, Short Lecture
31 Dec Group Processing, Step I, SOP 8-C
31 Dec Group Process for HAS Associate Groups
Dec Group Processing—Reach and Withdraw Across the Dynamics

ISSUE

PAB 16 late Dec Acceptance Level Processing

1954

Mr. Hubbard spent 1954 in Phoenix, Arizona, at the Hubbard College, where he lectured and delivered Group Processing on a nearly continuous basis. He delivered eight Advanced Clinical Courses (ACCs), each course six weeks in length. During this time period he gave more than 490 recorded lectures and Group Processing sessions to meet the demand for the technology.

He also originated two new publications to get the tech further disseminated: Operational Bulletins and *Ability* magazine.

ISSUE

PAB 17 mid-Jan Future Processing

ARTICLE Jan An Invitation to Freedom, Man *Can* Save His Soul

MATHISON E-54

The Mathison E-54 meter was presented at the First International Congress of Dianeticists and Scientologists, September 1953, in Philadelphia, Pennsylvania, but it was overly complex and was never used much in auditing.

THIRD AMERICAN ADVANCED CLINICAL COURSE
PHOENIX, ARIZONA

(To be released by Golden Era Productions.)

4 Jan	Introduction to the Third ACC
4 Jan	Perception and Ownership
5 Jan	Communication Lag and State of Case
5 Jan	Boredom, Pace of Living, Truth
5 Jan	Symbols and a Group Processing Demo
6 Jan	Symbols and a Group Processing Demo (cont.)
6 Jan	Randomity Plus Automaticity
7 Jan	Communication
7 Jan	Anchor Points, Flows
8 Jan	Exteriorization from Masses
8 Jan	How to Know What the Pc Is Doing
11 Jan	Basic Theory and Application
11 Jan	Exteriorization and Demonstration
11 Jan	Agreement, Motion and Perception
12 Jan	Exteriorization, Acceptance and Rejection of Ideas
12 Jan	Exteriorization, Lecture and Demo
12 Jan	Exteriorization and Stuck Cases
13 Jan	Competence of Prediction, Demo
13 Jan	Competence of Prediction, Demo (cont.)
13 Jan	Exteriorization: Step I Procedure
14 Jan	Labels: In Society and Preclears
14 Jan	Labels and Beingness
14 Jan	Beingness, Justice, Identity
15 Jan	Present Time, Self Analysis
15 Jan	Present Time and Demonstration
18 Jan	Time: Barrier

BEEP METER

Though more a curiosity than an auditing tool, the "beep" meter was first available in 1954. It would give off a beep sound when a painful area of the body was located with a probe. LRH demonstrated and discussed this meter in his 20 January 1954 lecture entitled "Audio (Beep) Meter Demonstration."

18 Jan	Time: Basic Process On
18 Jan	Time: Sense, Particles, Survival Pace
18 Jan	Processing Time on a Group
19 Jan	Summary of Course to Date
19 Jan	Exteriorization: Demonstration
19 Jan	Communication by Emotion: Flows, Ridges
19 Jan	Group Processing
20 Jan	E-Meter, Use Of
20 Jan	Audio (Beep) Meter Demonstration
20 Jan	Exteriorization, Communication in Theta and MEST
21 Jan	Livingness Processing
21 Jan	Livingness Processing: Dyingness
22 Jan	Livingness Processing: Machinery
22 Jan	Livingness Processing: Demonstration
25 Jan	Goals of 8-O (OT) Abilities
25 Jan	Basic Data on 8-O (OT)
26 Jan	Exteriorization, Knowingness, Reality
26 Jan	Instruction Simplicities
27 Jan	OT, Inversion: Courage and Nobility
28 Jan	Exteriorization: Courage and Serenity
28 Jan	Courage Processing
29 Jan	Parked Personality: Exteriorization, Stuck Flows
29 Jan	Simple Basis of Evaluating Cases
1 Feb	Exteriorization, Taking Direction
1 Feb	Processing Havingness
2 Feb	Acceptance and Rejection of Havingness
2 Feb	Havingness: Comm Lines
3 Feb	Havingness: Ownership
3 Feb	Repairing a Case and Demo
4 Feb	Review on Havingness and Demo
4 Feb	Certainty: Maybes, Problems, Case Entrance
5 Feb	Endowment of Livingness: Extroverting Attention
5 Feb	Group Processing on Certainty
8 Feb	Summary of Course Data and Machinery
8 Feb	Group Processing: Automaticities
8 Feb	Group Processing: Assignment of Cause
9 Feb	Auditing Groups
9 Feb	Group Processing: Barriers
9 Feb	Short Discussion and Group Processing Demo
10 Feb	Group Processing: Being the MEST Universe
10 Feb	Group Processing: Being the MEST Universe (cont.)
10 Feb	Group Processing: Being the MEST Universe, Specific Manifestations
11 Feb	Group Processing: Things You Can Be
11 Feb	Group Processing: Resisting Effect
11 Feb	Group Processing: Exterior
12 Feb	Group Processing: Sound
12 Feb	Group Processing: Balance

RECORDED ADDRESSES

While delivering the Third Advanced Clinical Course in Phoenix, Arizona, Mr. Hubbard made recordings especially for delegates to congresses being held in London and New York.

12 Jan	Special LRH Message to London Congress of Dianeticists and Scientologists
22 Jan	LRH Message to New York Congress of Dianeticists and Scientologists

ARTICLES

JOS ISSUE 23-G	15 Jan	Man's Search for His Soul
JOS ISSUE 24-G	Jan	SOP 8-C: The Rehabilitation of the Human Spirit

ISSUES

PAB 18	late Jan	Overt Acts
PAB 19	early Feb	The Circuit Case
PAB 20	mid-Feb	Two Answers to Correspondents: The Nonpersistence Case and Ridge Running

FOURTH AMERICAN ADVANCED CLINICAL COURSE LECTURES
PHOENIX, ARIZONA

(To be released by Golden Era Productions.)

15 Feb	Introduction to Fourth American ACC
16 Feb	Group Processing: Ownership
17 Feb	Group Processing: Things Not Suppressing Time
17 Feb	Exteriorization Demonstration Process
17 Feb	Demonstration Processing: Exteriorization and Certainty of Perception
18 Feb	Group Processing: Spotting Things Which Don't Have to Be Suppressed
18 Feb	Demonstration Process: Exteriorization
18 Feb	Group Processing: Things Telling Where Things Are
19 Feb	Demonstration: Exteriorization
19 Feb	Group Processing: Second Dynamic
19 Feb	Group Processing: Imagination
22 Feb	Group Processing: Handling Energy and Thought
22 Feb	Group Processing: Consideration
23 Feb	Group Processing: Certainty
23 Feb	Group Processing: Omens, Consequences, Ownership
24 Feb	Group Processing: Time
24 Feb	Group Processing: Stabilization Process
25 Feb	Group Processing: Goals, Duplicating

PUBLIC LECTURE
PHOENIX, ARIZONA

ISSUES

ARTICLE

FIFTH AMERICAN ADVANCED CLINICAL COURSE LECTURES
PHOENIX, ARIZONA

(Available from Golden Era Productions as a series entitled "Universes and the War Between Theta and MEST.")

ISSUES

ARTICLE

ISSUES

ISSUES

SIXTH AMERICAN ADVANCED CLINICAL COURSE LECTURES
PHOENIX, ARIZONA

(To be released by Golden Era Productions.)

MATHISON E-SERIES METER
More fancy and complex meters were also made available during 1954, called the E-Series meters; few were ever used in auditing as they were too complicated to be workable.

PUBLIC LECTURE
PHOENIX, ARIZONA

UNIVERSE PROCESSES CONGRESS LECTURES
PHOENIX, ARIZONA

At the Universe Processes Congress (also called the Fourth International Congress of Dianeticists and Scientologists), delegates received fourteen hours of lectures and Group Processing from Mr. Hubbard. (To be released by Golden Era Productions.)

GROUP AUDITOR'S HANDBOOK, VOLUME ONE
by L. Ron Hubbard

First published by Hubbard Association of Scientologists International, Phoenix, Arizona, June 1954, and today by Bridge Publications and New Era Publications. The Group Auditor's Handbook, Volume One, was released at the Universe Processes Congress given in Phoenix, where it was made available to delegates and used by seminar leaders.

SCIENTOLOGY WORKBOOK

Taken from the works of L. Ron Hubbard, published by the Hubbard Association of Scientologists International, Phoenix, Arizona, June 1954.

THE MINISTER'S MEDALLION AND PIN

The minister's ceremonial medallion and ribbon was first introduced in 1954.

It is a gold cross on a white field, 2 1/2 inches in diameter, 3/8 inch thick. The ribbon is black.

The minister's lapel pin is the same design as the minister's medallion but smaller.

These insignia are worn by ordained ministers of the Church of Scientology.

ISSUE

PAB 28 11 Jun "My Dear Mr. Clouston:..."

SEVENTH AMERICAN ADVANCED CLINICAL COURSE LECTURES
PHOENIX, ARIZONA

(To be released by Golden Era Productions.)

23 Jun Opening Procedure 8-C
23 Jun Further Uses of Opening Procedure 8-C
24 Jun Summary of Plan of Course
25 Jun Review of Procedure: PTP, ARC Straightwire, Two-way Comm
25 Jun Review of Procedure: Starting a Session, Two-way Comm
25 Jun Opening Procedure of 8-D: Demonstration
25 Jun Opening Procedure of 8-D: Demonstration (cont.)
28 Jun Exteriorization
28 Jun Exteriorization (cont.)
29 Jun General Lecture: Straightwire, Communication
30 Jun Rundown of Essentials
30 Jun Group Processing
30 Jun Group Processing and Lecture, Something, Nothing
30 Jun Lecture: Being Made Nothing and Having to Be Something
1 Jul Group Processing: Communication, Duplication, Spotting Spots
1 Jul Communication, Duplication and the Step V
1 Jul Exteriorization by Distance, Cause
1 Jul Exteriorization, Distance and Time
4 Jul Scientology and Living
5 Jul Things in Time and Space
5 Jul A Bright Resistive Case
5 Jul The Role of Laughter in Processing—Dangerousness
5 Jul Rundown of Cases
6 Jul Remedy of Havingness and Spotting Spots in Space
6 Jul ARC, Time, Life and Universe
7 Jul Intensive Procedure— Lecture 1
7 Jul Intensive Procedure— Lecture 2
7 Jul Intensive Procedure— Lecture 3
7 Jul Intensive Procedure— Lecture 4, Basic Processes, Patter
8 Jul Basic Individual Processes
9 Jul The Nature and Effect of Communication in Games
9 Jul Communication and Barriers in Society and the Pc
12 Jul Two Types of Cases
12 Jul Time: Havingness
12 Jul Intensive Procedure: Nothing–Something
13 Jul Auditor's Code in Practice
14 Jul Power of Life and Death

14 Jul Application of Theory to Cases, Life and Death, Only One
15 Jul The Difference Between a Good and a Bad Auditor
15 Jul SOP 8-D: Its Application
15 Jul SOP 8-D: Orientation Points
15 Jul Training of Auditors
16 Jul Teaching Formula: Duplication
19 Jul Duplication, Part I
19 Jul Duplication, Part II
19 Jul Scientology, Its General Background—Part I
19 Jul Scientology, Its General Background—Part II
19 Jul Scientology, Its General Background—Part III
20 Jul Bridge Between Scientology and Civilization
20 Jul Consideration, Mechanics and the Theory Behind Instruction
20 Jul Consideration and Isness
23 Jul Isness
23 Jul The Four Conditions of Existence—Part I
23 Jul The Four Conditions of Existence—Part II
23 Jul The Four Conditions of Existence—Part III
23 Jul The Four Conditions of Existence—Part IV
23 Jul The Four Conditions of Existence—Part V
26 Jul Two-way Communication and Present Time Problem
26 Jul Opening Procedure of 8-C
27 Jul Question and Answer Period
27 Jul Handling of Theta Bodies
27 Jul Things an Auditor Should Know
27 Jul Afternoon Lecture Remarks Especially on Telepathy and ESP
28 Jul Description Processing
28 Jul Group Processing
Jul Time
Jul Types of Processes
30 Jul Control
30 Jul Certificates of Dianetics and Scientology

ISSUES

DESPATCH 15 Jul Training
DESPATCH 23 Jul Group Auditing Sessions

SCIENTOLOGY: AUDITOR'S HANDBOOK— INCLUDING INTENSIVE PROCEDURE
by L. Ron Hubbard

Published by the Hubbard Association of Scientologists International, Phoenix, Arizona, August 1954. (This book, combined with other material, was published as The Creation of Human Ability, *1955.)*

ISSUE

PAB 32 7 Aug Why Doctor of Divinity?

AXIOMS LECTURES
PHOENIX, ARIZONA

These four half-hour talks were recorded by Mr. Hubbard in his Phoenix office with no audience present, for use on the Professional Course. (Available from Golden Era Productions as part of the series entitled "The Phoenix Lectures.")

20 Aug Axioms, Part I
20 Aug Axioms, Part II
20 Aug Axioms, Part III
20 Aug Axioms, Part IV

GROUP AUDITOR'S HANDBOOK, VOLUME TWO
by L. Ron Hubbard

First published by the Hubbard Association of Scientologists International, Phoenix, Arizona, September 1954, and today by Bridge Publications and New Era Publications.

ISSUES

PAB 34 4 Sep Opening Procedure, SOP 8-C
DESPATCH 13 Sep Communication
CREED The Creed of the Church of Scientology

GROUP PROCESSING SESSION
PHOENIX, ARIZONA

14 Sep Dianetic Group Processing

ISSUE

PAB 35 18 Sep "What I Learned in Training"

LECTURE
PHOENIX, ARIZONA

28 Sep Church of Scientology Training Program and Lecture on Group Processing

ISSUES

Bulletin Sep Fighting Process
PAB 36 1 Oct The Use of Scientology Materials

EIGHTH AMERICAN ADVANCED CLINICAL COURSE LECTURES
PHOENIX, ARIZONA

(Available from Golden Era Productions as a series entitled "The Creation of Human Ability.") See also the book entitled *The Creation of Human Ability,* originally published in 1955, today published by Bridge Publications and New Era Publications.

4 Oct Introduction to the Eighth Unit
5 Oct Basic Elements of Processing

6 Oct Two-way Communication
7 Oct Elementary Straightwire
8 Oct Opening Procedure of 8-C
11 Oct Opening Procedure by Duplication
12 Oct Remedy of Havingness
13 Oct Spotting Spots
19 Oct Axioms of Dianetics
20 Oct The Parts of Man: Overt Acts and Motivators
21 Oct R2-61: Good and Evil; R2-62: Overt Act–Motivator Sequence
22 Oct Second Lecture on Two-way Communication
25 Oct Communication and Straightwire
26 Oct Survive
27 Oct Hypnotism
28 Oct What Would You Do If... ?
29 Oct The Factors
1 Nov Third Lecture on Two-way Communication
2 Nov *Homo Sapiens*
3 Nov Shame, Blame and Regret
5 Nov Factors Present in Good and Bad Auditing
8 Nov Nonverbal Communication
9 Nov Application of Axioms to Auditing
10 Nov Definitions: Axioms
11 Nov The Scope of Dianetics and Scientology
12 Nov Question and Answer Period: Dissemination

ROUTE ONE LECTURES
PHOENIX, ARIZONA

These twelve fifteen-minute lectures give additional data on specific processing steps laid out in the *Scientology Auditor's Handbook* which was released in August 1954 (the original edition of the book now known as *The Creation of Human Ability*). (Available from Golden Era Productions as part of the series entitled "The Creation of Human Ability.")

8 Oct Route 1, Step 4
8 Oct Route 1, Step 5
10 Oct Route 1, Step 6
10 Oct Route 1, Step 7
10 Oct Route 1, Step 8
10 Oct Route 1, Step 9
10 Oct Route 1, Step 10
10 Oct Route 1, Step 11
18 Oct Route 1, Step 12
18 Oct Route 1, Step 13
18 Oct Route 1, Step 14
18 Oct Route 1, Step 15

ISSUES

PAB 37 15 Oct The Communication Lines of Scientology
DESPATCH Oct Dianetics and Scientology, A Crusade

PUBLIC LECTURE AND GROUP PROCESSING SERIES
PHOENIX, ARIZONA

Throughout October, November and December of 1954, Mr. Hubbard gave Wednesday night public lectures and Group Processing sessions geared toward newer public interested in finding out more about Scientology. From mid-November through the beginning of December, he also lectured each morning to auditors on the Phoenix Certification Course.

20 Oct On Comprehending the Incomprehensible

20 Oct "Rising Scale" on the Tone Scale and "Find Something Incomprehensible"

20 Oct Group Processing

27 Oct Principal Difference Between Scientology and Dianetics

27 Oct "Electing Cause"— Something You Can't Control

27 Oct Life of Dynamics

3 Nov Organization of Scientology

17 Nov "Accept" and "Reject" (Group Processing)

17 Nov The Wrong Thing to Do Is Nothing

24 Nov Creation of Human Ability

24 Nov Group Process—"Find Shortest Communication Line"—"Create a Memory"

1 Dec Awareness of Awareness

1 Dec "Decide to Be Silent"—"Find Some Secrets"

8 Dec "Waiting," Something You Can Associate With

8 Dec Group Processing

15 Dec Acceptance Level

ISSUES

PAB 38 29 Oct The Auditor's Code 1954

PAB 39 12 Nov The Auditor's Code 1954 (Concluded)

PHOENIX CERTIFICATION COURSE LECTURES
PHOENIX, ARIZONA

16 Nov Elementary Straightwire

17 Nov Background of Six Basic Steps

19 Nov Remedy of Havingness

22 Nov Levels of Case Ability

23 Nov Addressing Groups and Starting Sessions

24 Nov Following Orders

24 Nov Two-way Communication

30 Nov Solving Cases

1 Dec Opening Procedure of 8-C

3 Dec The Importance of Two-way Comm During Opening Procedure by Duplication

4 Dec Last Lecture

ARTICLE

JOS Nov Validation of
ISSUE 40-G Scientology

ISSUES

PAB 40 26 Nov The Code of Honor

FOUNDATION Dec Accent on Ability,
BULLETIN VOL. 1, NO. 3 New Trend Takes Form

ARTICLE

JOS Dec Is It Possible to Be
ISSUE 41-G Happy?

NINTH ADVANCED CLINICAL COURSE LECTURES
PHOENIX, ARIZONA

(Available from Golden Era Productions as a series entitled "The Solution to Entrapment.")

6 Dec Introduction to 9th ACC— Havingness

7 Dec Essence of Auditing, Know to Mystery Scale

8 Dec Rundown on Six Basics

9 Dec Communication Formula

10 Dec The Practice of Dianetics and Scientology

13 Dec Conduct of the Auditor

14 Dec Mechanics of Communication

15 Dec Havingness

16 Dec Pan-determinism and One-way Flows

17 Dec History and Development of Processes—Games and the Limitations in Games

17 Dec History and Development of Processes—Question and Answer Period

20 Dec Games (Fighting)

21 Dec Anatomy of Games, Part I

21 Dec Anatomy of Games, Part II

22 Dec One-way Flows in Processing

22 Dec One-way Flows in Processing: Question and Answer Period

23 Dec Havingness and Communication Formulas

24 Dec Pan-determinism

24 Dec Pan-determinism: Question and Answer Period

27 Dec Training New People

27 Dec Curiosa from *Dianetics 55!*

(The Ninth Advanced Clinical Course went through the end of 1954 and into 1955. See continued listing of Ninth Advanced Clinical Course Lectures at the beginning of 1955.)

ISSUES

PAB 41 10 Dec The Code of a Scientologist

PAB 42 24 Dec Six Basic Processes

UNIFICATION CONGRESS OF DIANETICISTS AND SCIENTOLOGISTS LECTURES
PHOENIX, ARIZONA

This congress was marked by the release of a limited manuscript edition of Mr. Hubbard's newest book,

Dianetics 55! The material in the book was expanded upon in the lectures to delegates. So successful was this congress that it was repeated in four additional places: New York City, London, Australia and New Zealand. (To be released by Golden Era Productions.)

28 Dec Introduction

28 Dec Group Processing

28 Dec History of Dianetics

28 Dec Dianetics 1955

28 Dec Communication and ARC

29 Dec Games

29 Dec Group Processing, Part I

29 Dec Group Processing, Part II

29 Dec Terminals and Communication

29 Dec The Aims and Goals of Dianetics and Scientology

30 Dec Communication and Problems

30 Dec Group Processing, Part I

30 Dec Group Processing, Part II

30 Dec Problems and Games

30 Dec Group Processing

30 Dec Pan-determinism

DIANETICS 55!
by L. Ron Hubbard

A limited manuscript edition was available at the Unification Congress in Phoenix, Arizona, December 1954. *Dianetics 55!* was published in April 1955 by the Hubbard Dianetics Research Foundation, Phoenix, Arizona. Today published by Bridge Publications and New Era Publications.
TRANSLATIONS: Danish, French, German, Hebrew, Italian and Spanish.

1955

Continuing his busy lecture schedule, Mr. Hubbard gave many talks at the Hubbard Professional College in Phoenix, Arizona, through the end of May.

In June he traveled to Washington, DC, where he delivered two series of lectures and formed the Founding Church of Washington, DC. By October he had returned to London and begun delivery of the Fourth London Advanced Clinical Course (the first ACC that Mr. Hubbard himself conducted in England). He continued to research, write and lecture in England through the rest of the year.

NOTES ON LECTURES GIVEN BY L. RON HUBBARD AT PHOENIX, 1954

Taken from the lectures of L. Ron Hubbard, published by the Hubbard Association of Scientologists International, Johannesburg, South Africa, early 1955.

THE ELEMENTARY SCIENTOLOGY SERIES

Taken from the works of L. Ron Hubbard. Published by the Scientology Council, Los Angeles, California, early 1955.

L. RON HUBBARD'S PROFESSIONAL AUDITOR'S BULLETINS BOOK 1
(Professional Auditor's Bulletins 1–15)

Published by the Hubbard Communications Office, Washington, DC, 1955. (Note: The Professional Auditor's Bulletins written by L. Ron Hubbard also appear in the Technical Bulletins volumes.)

ARTICLE

JOS Jan Phoenix Clinic
ISSUE 43-G

NINTH ADVANCED CLINICAL COURSE LECTURES
PHOENIX, ARIZONA

1955 opened with the completion of the Ninth Advanced Clinical Course, which had begun in December 1954. (Available from Golden Era Productions as part of the series "The Solution to Entrapment.")

3 Jan Auditing Requirements, Differences

4 Jan Time

4 Jan Question and Answer Period

5 Jan Exteriorization by Gradient Scale

5 Jan Auditing at Optimum

6 Jan Exteriorization

7 Jan Elementary Material: Know to Mystery Scale

10 Jan Education: Goals in Society—Adult Education

11 Jan Fundamentals of Auditing

11 Jan Auditors' Conference

12 Jan Definitions: Glossary of Terms—Part I

13 Jan Definitions: Glossary of Terms—Part II

14 Jan Definitions: Glossary of Terms—Part III

17 Jan Auditing Demo: Six Basics in Action

17 Jan Auditors' Conference

18 Jan Auditing Demo: Spotting Spots

18 Jan Auditors' Conference

19 Jan Auditing Demo: Exteriorization

20 Jan Background Music to Living

21 Jan Axioms: Laws of Consideration—What an Axiom Is

ISSUE

PAB 43 7 Jan Plotting the Preclear on the Tone Scale

PUBLIC LECTURES AND GROUP PROCESSING SERIES
PHOENIX, ARIZONA

Despite a heavy schedule of Advanced Clinical Courses, Mr. Hubbard made time for a series of Wednesday evening lectures and Group Processing sessions for the general public.

5 Jan	The Society at Large
5 Jan	Group Processing
12 Jan	Group Processing
12 Jan	Games
19 Jan	The Affinity-Reality-Communication Triangle (released as one of the Personal Achievement Series)
19 Jan	Group Processing
26 Jan	Goals of Dianetics and Scientology
26 Jan	Group Processing
2 Feb	Alcoholism
2 Feb	Group Processing
2 Feb	Variation on Six Basic Processes
9 Feb	Miracles (released as one of the Personal Achievement Series)
9 Feb	Session: Control of Body, Think a Thought
23 Feb	Scientology and Ability (released as one of the Personal Achievement Series)
23 Feb	Group Processing
23 Feb	Session: Find a Mystery
2 Mar	Increasing Efficiency (released as one of the Personal Achievement Series)
9 Mar	Health and Certainty (released as one of the Personal Achievement Series)
9 Mar	Session: Only One, Things Real and Unreal
9 Mar	Group Processing
16 Mar	Knowingness
23 Mar	Scientology: A Technical Subject—Communication Lag, Principal Kinds Found in a Pc
30 Mar	Conquered Territory
30 Mar	Group Processing
6 Apr	On the Second Dynamic
6 Apr	Session: "What Could You Say To... ?"
13 Apr	The Dynamic Principles of Existence—The Eight Dynamics (released as one of the Personal Achievement Series)
13 Apr	Session: Find Present Time
20 Apr	Para-Scientology—or Things That Go Boomp in the Night
20 Apr	Session: Change and No-Change
27 Apr	The Direction of Modern Scientology
27 Apr	Gray Dianetics
27 Apr	Session: "Something You Could Say to People" and Ownership
4 May	Cause and Effect and Its Use in Processing
4 May	Session: Cause and Effect
11 May	Operation Manual for the Mind (released as one of the Personal Achievement Series)
11 May	Session: "Enchantment" Processing

STAFF AUDITORS' CONFERENCES
PHOENIX, ARIZONA

During January and February 1955, several conferences were held with staff auditors in Phoenix, briefing them on advances and refinements and discussing the results they were achieving.

10 Jan	Staff Auditors' Conference Lecture: Exteriorization
11 Feb	Staff Auditors' Conference
28 Feb	Staff Auditors' Conference

RECORDED ADDRESS

While delivering Advanced Clinical Courses in Phoenix, Arizona, Mr. Hubbard made a recording especially for delegates to the Third International Congress of Scientologists which was being held in London, England.

16 Jan	Address to Congress Delegates

ISSUES

PAB 44	21 Jan	Two-way Communication in Action
PAB 45	4 Feb	Mimicry
PAB 46	18 Feb	Straightwire
PAB 47	4 Mar	Opening Procedure 8-C

AUDITING DEMONSTRATIONS
PHOENIX, ARIZONA

Presented on closed-circuit television to Advanced Clinical Course students, these sessions were also recorded on audio tape for future study and use.

8 Mar	LRH Auditing Demonstration
14 Mar	LRH Auditing Demonstration
14 Mar	LRH Auditing Demonstration
15 Mar	LRH Auditing Demonstration, Parts I and II
16 Mar	LRH Auditing Demonstration, Parts I and II
17 Mar	LRH Auditing Demonstration, Parts I and II
18 Mar	LRH Auditing Demonstration, Parts I and II
21 Mar	LRH Auditing Demonstration, Parts I and II
22 Mar	LRH Auditing Demonstration, Parts I and II
23 Mar	LRH Auditing Demonstration, Parts I and II
24 Mar	LRH Auditing Demonstration, Parts I and II
25 Mar	LRH Auditing Demonstration, Parts I and II
28 Mar	LRH Auditing Demonstration, Parts I and II
29 Mar	LRH Auditing Demonstration, Parts I and II
1 Apr	LRH Auditing Demonstration

1 Apr	LRH Auditing Demonstration
4 Apr	LRH Auditing Demonstration
7 Apr	LRH Auditing Demonstration
19 Apr	LRH Auditing Demonstration
20 Apr	LRH Auditing Demonstration
21 Apr	LRH Auditing Session—Demonstration Rud Session
25 Apr	LRH Auditing Demonstration
26 Apr	Discussion and Education of the Pc
26 Apr	LRH Auditing Demonstration
27 Apr	LRH Auditing Demonstration
27 Apr	LRH Auditing and Discussion
28 Apr	Demonstration Auditing—More Education on Ownership Process
29 Apr	LRH Discussion and Auditing of Ownership and Control
7 May	LRH Auditing Demonstration
8 May	LRH Auditing Demonstration
9 May	LRH Auditing Demonstration
10 May	LRH Auditing Demonstration
13 May	LRH Auditing Demonstration, Parts I and II

HUBBARD PROFESSIONAL COLLEGE LECTURES
PHOENIX, ARIZONA

14 Mar	"Death Wish" The Only One (The Mechanics and Solution of the Occluded Case)
26 Mar	Axiom 51
2 Apr	Axiom 51 in Action
9 Apr	A New Understanding of the Six Basic Processes
16 Apr	The Service Facsimile
23 Apr	Thinkingness
30 Apr	Ownership Processing
7 May	Meaningness, Parts I and II
14 May	The Tone Scale

AUDITORS' CONFERENCES
PHOENIX, ARIZONA

14 Mar	Auditors' Conference
14 Mar	How to Audit Paying Pcs
1 Apr	First Hour Staff Auditors' Conference
4 Apr	Scale of Awareness
8 Apr	Staff Auditors' Conference
18 Apr	Auditors' Conference
19 Apr	Staff Auditors' Conference
21 Apr	Auditors' Conference
29 Apr	Sixth Hour of Staff Auditors' Conference
2 May	Talk on "Think a Thought" in Connection with Ownership

THE SCIENTOLOGY CROSS

The Scientology sunburst cross, the basic design of which was found by L. Ron Hubbard in an ancient Spanish mission in Arizona, is the official insignia for Scientology ministers.

The cross is three inches high and two inches wide, made of sterling silver and hangs on a fine silver chain. It is worn by both men and women. Each of the eight points of the cross represents one of the eight dynamics.

Large Scientology crosses of wood and other materials are displayed in Scientology churches.

Very small versions are also worn as pins.

THE HUBBARD COMMUNICATIONS OFFICE INSIGNIA

This is a shield with the S and double triangle and the initials "HCO" placed vertically, to the right.

Below the shield on a banner is the motto of HCO, the Hubbard Communications Office, "Bring Order."

THE SCIENTOLOGIST, A MANUAL ON THE DISSEMINATION OF MATERIAL
by L. Ron Hubbard

Published by the Hubbard Association of Scientologists International, Phoenix, Arizona, March 1955. The text of this manual has been reprinted in full in the Technical Bulletins and Organization Executive Course volumes. Today published by Bridge Publications and New Era Publications.

ISSUE

PAB 48 18 Mar Opening Procedure by Duplication

THE CREATION OF HUMAN ABILITY
by L. Ron Hubbard

Published by Scientology Publications in London, England, in April 1955 and in the United States a few weeks later. Today published by Bridge Publications and New Era Publications.

ISSUES

PAB 49 1 Apr The Remedy of Havingness

PAB 50 15 Apr Remedy of Havingness— The Process

LECTURE
PHOENIX, ARIZONA

18 Apr Dianetics and Scientology

ISSUE

PAB 51 29 Apr Spotting Spots

KEY TO TOMORROW
(also entitled *Scientology: Its Contribution to Knowledge*)

Taken from the works of L. Ron Hubbard, published by the Hubbard Communications Office, Phoenix, Arizona, in May.

ARTICLE

ABILITY early May The Scale of Issue
MINOR 4 Awareness

ISSUES

PAB 52 13 May Auditing the "Whole Track"

PAB 53 27 May Ownership, Special PAB

ANATOMY OF THE SPIRIT OF MAN CONGRESS LECTURES
WASHINGTON, DC

One of the highlights of this congress was LRH's announcement of the new, expanded Tone Scale, showing how it complemented the Tone Scale already familiar to Dianeticists and Scientologists. (Available from Golden Era Productions.)

3 Jun The Hope of Man

3 Jun Practicalities of a Practical Religion

3 Jun History of Research and Investigation

4 Jun Direction of Truth in Processing

4 Jun The Tone Scale—Three Primary Buttons of Exteriorization

4 Jun Group Processing: Meaningness

4 Jun Component Parts of Beingness

4 Jun Group Processing: Time and Location

5 Jun The Descent of Man

5 Jun How to Chart the Preclear— Knowingness and Unknowingness

6 Jun Six Basic Steps—Some Fundamentals of Auditing

6 Jun The Mechanisms of Ownership in Living

6 Jun Group Processing: Additional Processing on Meaningness

6 Jun The Game Called Man

6 Jun What Scientology Is Doing

ISSUES

CHART 4 Jun The Tone Plotting Scale

PAB 54 10 Jun Reality Level of Preclear

ARTICLE

ABILITY mid-Jun The Hope of
MINOR 5 Man

STRAIGHTWIRE: A MANUAL OF OPERATION
by L. Ron Hubbard

Published by Hubbard Communications Office, Washington, DC, July. The text of this manual has been reprinted in its entirety in the Technical Bulletins volumes.

ISSUE

PAB 56 8 Jul Axiom 51 and Communication Processing

LECTURE
PHOENIX, ARIZONA

11 Jul Seven Basic Steps (Codification of the Hubbard Certified Auditor Course)

ARTICLES

ABILITY mid-Jul The Adventure of
MINOR 6 Scientology

ABILITY early Aug With ARC
MAJOR 5

CERTAINTY Aug An Idea Versus
VOL. 2, NO. 8 War

ISSUE

DESPATCH 5 Aug "The secret is..."

ACADEMY LECTURE SERIES
WASHINGTON, DC

Delivered at the Academy of Religious Arts and Sciences in Washington, DC, these lectures covered the latest techniques being taught on Scientology auditor training courses. (Available from Golden Era Productions as a series entitled "Conquest of Chaos.")

23 Aug The Auditor's Public

23 Aug Axiom 53: The Axiom of the Stable Datum

30 Aug Rugged Individualism

30 Aug Union Station—R2-46

14 Sep The Unknown Datum— A MEST Shaking Lecture

14 Sep Postulates 1, 2, 3, 4 in Processing—New Understanding of Axiom 36

ARTICLE

ABILITY early Sep Basic Processes
MAJOR 6

ISSUE

PAB 60 2 Sep "Anything— Everything—Nothing"

ARTICLE

ABILITY 14 mid-Sep Start That Practice!

ISSUES

PAB 61 16 Sep Selling

PAB 62 30 Sep Psychiatrists

FOURTH LONDON ADVANCED CLINICAL COURSE LECTURES
LONDON, ENGLAND

Traveling to London in the autumn of 1955, Mr. Hubbard delivered an Advanced Clinical Course and a series of lectures to the general public. (To be released by Golden Era Productions.)

3 Oct Fundamentals of Scientology and Rudiments of Auditing, Parts I and II

4 Oct 1st and 2nd Postulates in Living

4 Oct 1st to 4th Postulates in Living

5 Oct Smoothness of Auditing, Parts I and II

6 Oct Communication and "I Don't Know" (Confusion)

6 Oct Stable Datum and Confusion

7 Oct Relations to Time Continuum

7 Oct Base Time and Time Continuum

10 Oct Establishing of the Auditor

10 Oct The Subject of Communication

11 Oct Data of Comparable Magnitude

11 Oct Communication Bridge, Confusion, Time Factor

12 Oct Communication and Intentions, Deterioration Of

13 Oct The Antiquity of Auditing

13 Oct Affinity, Reality and Communication

14 Oct Exteriorization and Interiorization

14 Oct Further Aspects of Exteriorization

17 Oct Tolerance of Havingness

17 Oct Establishing a Session

18 Oct Beginning and Continuing a Session

18 Oct Processing: Level One

19 Oct The Senior Desire of a Thetan

19 Oct Third Level of a Process

20 Oct The Pc's Present Time Problem—The Body

20 Oct An Understanding of Creative Processing

21 Oct Native State and Postulates 1, 2, 3, 4

21 Oct Native State and Communication

24 Oct Résumé of Creative Processes

24 Oct Lack of Terminals

25 Oct Engrams—Dissemination of Material

25 Oct The Handling of Confusion in the Preclear or on Any Dynamic

26 Oct Stable Datum and the Study of Science

26 Oct Solving Engrams with Stable Datum, Communication Terminals

27 Oct The Role of a Scientologist

28 Oct The Anatomy of Terminals

28 Oct Six Basic Levels of Processes

28 Oct Intolerance

31 Oct How to Audit

31 Oct Training of an Auditor

1 Nov The Preclear's Reality

1 Nov Improvement in Technology

2 Nov Trying and Communication

2 Nov Randomity and Automaticities

3 Nov A Review of the Fourth London ACC

3 Nov Attitude and Conduct of Scientology

16 Nov New Understanding of Universes

17 Nov End of Course Lecture

LONDON PUBLIC LECTURE SERIES

LONDON, ENGLAND

8 Oct Goals of Dianetics and Scientology

8 Oct Processing the Third Dynamic

15 Oct How Good Can You Get

15 Oct The Dynamics

22 Oct The Road to Perfection—The Goodness of Man

22 Oct Man: Good or Evil?

29 Oct The Machinery of the Mind

29 Oct Power of Choice and Self-Determinism

(The last five lectures of this series are available from Golden Era Productions as part of the Personal Achievement Series.)

ISSUES

PAB 63 14 Oct Playing the Game

OPERATIONAL 20 Oct "The following
BULLETIN 1 auditing commands..."

PAB 64 28 Oct First Postulate

ARTICLE

CERTAINTY Nov The Six Levels of
VOL. 2, NO. 11 Processing

HUBBARD PROFESSIONAL COURSE LECTURES

LONDON, ENGLAND

8 Nov Six Levels of Processing, Issue 5, Level One

8 Nov Six Levels of Processing, Issue 5, Level Two

9 Nov Six Levels of Processing, Issue 5, Level Three

9 Nov Six Levels of Processing, Issue 5, Level Four

10 Nov Six Levels of Processing, Issue 5, Level Five

10 Nov Six Levels of Processing, Issue 5, Level Six

ISSUES

OPERATIONAL 11 Nov Six Levels of
BULLETIN 4 Processing—Issue 5

PAB 65 11 Nov From a Lecture by L. Ron Hubbard on MEST Processing, 7 July 1951

OPERATIONAL mid-Nov "Limited
BULLETIN 5 company proceeding..."

ARTICLES

ABILITY mid-Nov What Are You
MAJOR 16 Going to Do About It?

ABILITY late Nov Letter to Ability
MAJOR 18 Editor

ISSUES

PAB 66 25 Nov First, Second, Third and Fourth Postulates

OPERATIONAL late Nov Processing
BULLETIN 6 Futures

LONDON AUDITORS' MEETING LECTURES

LONDON, ENGLAND

At these meetings with auditors in London, Mr. Hubbard delivered lectures on his latest developments. (To be released by Golden Era Productions.)

1 Dec The Lowest Level Case

1 Dec Fundamentals of Auditing Style

15 Dec Exteriorization by Separateness from Weakest Universe

22 Dec Matching Auditing to Tone

ISSUES

OPERATIONAL 6 Dec Intensive in
BULLETIN 7 Progress

OPERATIONAL 13 Dec Handling
BULLETIN 8 Press

OPERATIONAL 19 Dec The Turn of
BULLETIN 9 the Tide

PAB 68 23 Dec First and Second Postulate

OPERATIONAL 28 Dec "I am giving
BULLETIN 10 here in outline form..."

1956

Early in 1956, Mr. Hubbard traveled from London, England, to Dublin, Ireland, where he opened a new Dianetics and Scientology organization.

Researching, writing and lecturing all the while, LRH then traveled from Dublin back to London, then to Barcelona, Spain, back to London, to Washington, DC, back once more to London (sailing on the famous ocean liner *Queen Elizabeth* and writing *The Problems of Work* during the voyage), then again to Washington, DC, where he ended this very active and productive year with the Anti-Radiation Congress lectures.

LONDON AUDITORS' MEETING LECTURES

LONDON, ENGLAND

Continuing a series of technical lectures that he had started in December 1955, LRH gave the following talks at the London Auditors' Meetings in early 1956. (To be released by Golden Era Productions.)

3 Jan Solution to Body Behavior, Part I

3 Jan Solution to Body Behavior, Part II

10 Jan Auditor Insight

12 Jan Anglo-Saxon Thought

16 Jan Repair and Remedy of Havingness

19 Jan Exteriorization

24 Jan The Role of Creation in Aberration

31 Jan Basic Lecture on Havingness

31 Jan GE Scientology

7 Feb The Game of Life (Exteriorization and Havingness)

9 Feb Sixth Dynamic Decisional Processing

14 Feb Aims and Goals of Scientology 1956

14 Feb Games Processing Applied to Auditing

ISSUES

OPERATIONAL 3 Jan "Now that the
BULLETIN 11 happy holidays are over..."

PAB 69 6 Jan Six Levels of Processing, Issue 7 (Revised)

OPERATIONAL 10 Jan An Experimental
BULLETIN 12 Arrangement of Level One

OPERATIONAL 17 Jan Operational
BULLETIN 13 Bulletins Growing Up

OPERATIONAL 17 Jan Scientology
BULLETIN 13, Schools Curriculum
APPENDIX 1

OPERATIONAL 24 Jan After the
BULLETIN 14 Flood

DESPATCH 25 Jan "The recent reports on preclears show..."

OPERATIONAL 31 Jan Long
BULLETIN 15 Continued Run

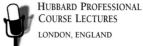

CREATIVE LEARNING— A SCIENTOLOGICAL EXPERIMENT IN SCHOOLS

Based on the works of L. Ron Hubbard. Published by the Hubbard Communications Office, London, England, in early 1956.

HUBBARD PROFESSIONAL COURSE LECTURES

LONDON, ENGLAND

6 Feb SLP 8, Level One, Theory

7 Feb SLP 8, Level One, Summation of Basic Theory

8 Feb Practical Application of Games to Processing

8 Feb SLP 8, Motives Of

10 Feb Application of Games to Processing (cont.)

10 Feb Use of Games Theory in Processing

14 Feb Application of Games to Processing—Comms and Vias

14 Feb The Various Ways of Processing a Preclear

14 Feb Games Applied to Processing Techniques

ISSUES

OPERATIONAL 7 Feb "Scientology
BULLETIN 16 US"

CEREMONY 7 Feb Founding Church of Scientology Funeral Service

OPERATIONAL 14 Feb Processing
BULLETIN 17 Results

PAB 72 21 Feb Changes for the PABs

PAB 74 6 Mar Office in Ireland

PAB 78 3 Apr Administration

PAB 79 10 Apr The Open Channel

PAB 80 17 Apr Scientology's Most Workable Process
PAB 81 24 Apr Purpose
PAB 82 1 May Scientology, The Fundamentals of Thought

LONDON PUBLIC LECTURE SERIES
LONDON, ENGLAND

5 May Latest Processes Today
31 Jul Games Processing

ISSUES

PAB 83 8 May The Conditions of Existence
DESPATCH 8 May Test Results
PAB 84 15 May The Reason Why
CEREMONY 15 May Scientology Wedding Ceremony
PAB 85 22 May The Parts of Man
PAB 86 29 May Causation and Knowledge
PAB 87 5 Jun Scientology Processing
PAB 88 12 Jun The Conditions of Auditing (concluded)
PAB 89 19 Jun Scientology, Revision of Translator's Edition
DESPATCH 26 Jun Current Processes
PAB 90 26 Jun The Organizations of Dianetics and Scientology
PAB 91 3 Jul The Anatomy of Failure
PAB 92 10 Jul A Critique of Psychoanalysis
DESPATCH 14 Jul Five Types of Valences
DESPATCH 20 Jul How to Really Split a Valence
DESPATCH 22 Jul Technical Bulletin
PAB 93 24 Jul A Critique of Psychoanalysis (cont.)

HUBBARD PROFESSIONAL COURSE LECTURES
LONDON, ENGLAND

Aug The Auditor's Code
Aug The Code of a Scientologist
Aug Auditing Positions
3 Aug Axioms 1–5
Aug Axioms 6–10
Aug Facsimiles (Solids)
Aug Opening Procedure of 8-C
Aug Start, Change and Stop
Aug Games Theory
Aug Problems and Consequences
Aug Valences
Aug Knowingness
Aug Creative Processing, Motion Stops, Perception
Aug Exteriorization Procedures
Aug Scales, Motion
Aug Scales, Curiosity, Not-Know
17 Aug Confusion and Stable Datum

Aug Chronic Somatics
Aug The Auditing of Solids
Aug Not-Knowing
20 Aug Auditing as a Profession
27 Aug Auditors' Conference

ISSUES

HCO PL 3 Aug I Mail Line
HCOB/PL 3 Aug Organizational Health Chart
BULLETIN 13 Aug Scientology Process Chart
PAB 94 15 Aug The Anatomy of Traps
HCOB 20 Aug HGC Procedure of Aug. 20
DESPATCH Aug The Goal of Auditors
DESPATCH 21 Aug Summary of Intensives since June
BRIEFING BULLETIN Games Congress, Shoreham Hotel

ARTICLE

ABILITY 34 late Aug Havingness

GAMES CONGRESS LECTURES
WASHINGTON, DC

This congress included thirteen hours of Group Processing and lectures covering the subject of games and their importance in understanding man and improving his happiness and abilities. (Available from Golden Era Productions as a series entitled "Games and the Spirit of Play.")

31 Aug Spiritual and Material Requirements of Man
31 Aug Group Processing: Crave to Know
31 Aug The Anatomy of Human Problems
1 Sep Games Conditions vs. No-Games Conditions
1 Sep Third Dynamic Application of Games Principles
1 Sep Group Processing: "Keep It from Going Away"
1 Sep Auditing Procedure 1956
1 Sep Universe
2 Sep Havingness
2 Sep Group Processing: Hold It Still, Mama and Papa
2 Sep Group Processing: Hold It Still, Mama and Papa (cont.)
2 Sep Effectiveness of Brainwashing
2 Sep Demonstration of SCS

SCIENTOLOGY: THE FUNDAMENTALS OF THOUGHT
by L. Ron Hubbard

First published as a series of Professional Auditor's Bulletins starting in 1956. Scientology: The Fundamentals of Thought was published in book form by the Hubbard Association of Scientologists International, Washington, DC, in September 1956. Today published by Bridge Publications and New Era Publications. TRANSLATIONS: Danish, Dutch, Finnish, French, German, Greek, Hebrew, Italian, Japanese, Norwegian, Portuguese, Spanish and Swedish.

ISSUES

PAB 95 1 Sep Valences
HCO TECH BULL 12 Sep The Summary of a Bulletin from the Academy in Washington, DC, Concerning Training
PAB 96 15 Sep Justice

CONFERENCE AND LECTURE
LONDON, ENGLAND

20 Sep London Auditors' Conference
25 Sep Review of SLP 8

ISSUES

HCO PROCESSING SHEET 20 Sep "The following are useful..."
HCOB 24 Sep Organizational Indoctrination
HCOB 26 Sep Registrar
ORG BULLETIN 26 Sep Procedure for Putting Auditors on Staff
HCO PL 26 Sep II Flow Line for Personnel
PAB 97 1 Oct Start-Change-Stop
HCOB 4 Oct High School Indoctrination

LONDON CONGRESS ON HUMAN PROBLEMS
LONDON, ENGLAND

This congress was held to discuss the major problems afflicting man at the time. *Certainty* magazine reported that in Mr. Hubbard's lectures to the more than 200 delegates, "He showed how salvation in our time lay in the application of the basic principles of modern knowledge as discovered, correlated and aligned in Scientology." (To be released by Golden Era Productions.)

5 Oct Man's Relentless Search (released as one of the Personal Achievement Series)
5 Oct Portions of You
5 Oct Group Processing: Putting the MEST Universe There
6 Oct Youth—Today's Displaced Person
6 Oct Group Processing: "Keep It from Going Away" and "Granting Life"
6 Oct Uses of Scientology
7 Oct Salvation 1956
7 Oct Personnel Efficiency
7 Oct Group Processing: Keeping Objects From Going Away
8 Oct Group Processing: Keep Him/Her From Going Away
8 Oct March of the Atom
8 Oct Today's Battle of Britain

ISSUES

LETTER 10 Oct "Dear Jean..."
PAB 98 15 Oct Creative Processes, Motions, Stops and Perceptions
HCOB 15 Oct Summary Research Project

ABILITY 36 mid-Oct Randomness and Automaticity

FIFTEENTH AMERICAN ADVANCED CLINICAL COURSE LECTURES
WASHINGTON, DC

In addition to recent developments in auditing technology, this course included several important lectures on learning and education. (Available from Golden Era Productions as a series entitled "The Power of Simplicity.")

15 Oct Opening Lecture
16 Oct Mimicry
17 Oct Complexity
18 Oct More on Mimicry
19 Oct Mechanics
22 Oct Scale of Reality
23 Oct "CRA" Triangle
24 Oct Cut Comm Lines (In and Out)
25 Oct Games Versus No-Games
26 Oct Learning Rates
29 Oct The Mind
30 Oct Education: Point of Agreement
31 Oct Rest Points and Confusion
1 Nov Coordination of Classes of Processes
2 Nov Wind-up on Stable Datum and Rest Points
5 Nov Radiation
6 Nov Time Track
7 Nov Creation
8 Nov Simplicity
9 Nov Skull Gazing
12 Nov Simplicity Versus Alter-Isness
13 Nov Aberration and the Sixth Dynamic
14 Nov Training Methods
15 Nov Diagnosis: How To
16 Nov Summary Lecture
23 Nov Farewell Lecture

ORGANIZATION SERIES LECTURES
WASHINGTON, DC

These lectures, given to church staff and students, cover how to succeed and make progress in an auditing practice, in supervising a Personnel Efficiency Course, and in group activities of any sort. (Available from Golden Era Productions as a series entitled "How to Present Scientology to the World.")

18 Oct How to Create and Instruct a PE Course, Part I
18 Oct How to Create and Instruct a PE Course, Part II
25 Oct Education
25 Oct Methods of Education
1 Nov Tone Scale (Autumn 1956)
1 Nov How to Handle Audiences
8 Nov Research Report: Radiation and Its Relationship to Processing
8 Nov Definition of Organization, Part I
15 Nov Definition of Organization, Part II
15 Nov Testing
22 Nov The Consequences of Organization

22 Nov The Deterioration of Liberty (released as one of the Personal Achievement Series)

29 Nov Hope

29 Nov The Scale of Havingness

6 Dec Money

6 Dec A Postulate Out of a Golden Age

13 Dec Confusion and the Stable Datum

13 Dec Randomity

ISSUES

HCOPL 26 Oct Gradient Scale of Personnel Procurement

HCOB 26 Oct HPA/HCA Training Processes

DESPATCH Oct/Nov Policy on Payment for Training and Processing

PAB 99 1 Nov Facsimiles and Solids

HCOB 9 Nov I Accounting Department, Washington

HCOB 9 Nov II Activities of Legal Department

HCOB 15 Nov HGC Preclear Complaints

PAB 100 15 Nov The Auditing of Solids

DESPATCH 19 Nov Staff Policy on Training and Indoctrination Courses

HCO 30 Nov SLP 8
TRNG BULLETIN

PAB 101 1 Dec Games Conditions Theory

HCOB 3 Dec BScn—HAA Techniques

HCO PL 11 Dec Tape Color Code

PAB 102 15 Dec A Case Report

THE PROBLEMS OF WORK
by L. Ron Hubbard

First published by Scientology Consultants, Inc., Washington, DC, December 1956, and today by Bridge Publications and New Era Publications. TRANSLATIONS: *Danish, Dutch, French, German, Hebrew, Italian, Japanese, Norwegian, Portuguese, Russian, Spanish and Swedish.*

L. RON HUBBARD'S PROFESSIONAL AUDITOR'S BULLETINS BOOK 2
(Professional Auditor's Bulletins 16–30)

Published by Hubbard Communications Office, Washington, DC, 1956.

L. RON HUBBARD'S PROFESSIONAL AUDITOR'S BULLETINS BOOK 3
(Professional Auditor's Bulletins 31–46)

Published by Hubbard Communications Office, Washington, DC, 1956.

L. RON HUBBARD'S PROFESSIONAL AUDITOR'S BULLETINS BOOK 4
(Professional Auditor's Bulletins 47–69)

Published by Hubbard Communications Office, Washington, DC, 1956.
(Note: The Professional Auditor's Bulletins written by L. Ron Hubbard also appear in the Technical Bulletins Volumes.*)*

ANTI-RADIATION CONGRESS LECTURES
WASHINGTON, DC

The fourteen hours of lectures to this congress include discussion of the problem of nuclear radiation, its effects on society and on the individual, and how these can be dealt with. (To be released by Golden Era Productions.)

29 Dec Opening Lecture

29 Dec Scientology View on Radiation

29 Dec Proofing Up a Body

29 Dec Group Processing: "Put It There"

29 Dec Group Processing: Confrontingness

30 Dec Solution to Psychosis

30 Dec Project Third Dynamic

30 Dec Insanity—Scarcity and Importances

30 Dec Group Processing: Mocking Up Bodies

30 Dec Group Processing: Making Problems and Confusions

31 Dec Background on Scale of Havingness

31 Dec Subzero Scales—Relation to Scale of Awareness

31 Dec Confrontingness

1957

Mr. Hubbard taught three Advanced Clinical Courses in Washington, DC, during 1957 and lectured at three congresses—one in London and two in Washington.

The lectures given to one of these congresses, the London Congress on Nuclear Radiation and Health, form the basis of the book *All About Radiation,* also first published during this year.

LRH's research into the field of education in 1957 resulted in vital technical issues on education in general and on the training of auditors—the foundations of modern Scientology study and training technology.

ISSUES

PAB 103 1 Jan The Code of a Scientologist

HCO PL 1 Jan FC Policy Letter

SCIENTOLOGY TRAINING COURSE MANUAL: FIELD VALIDATION AND HUBBARD APPRENTICE SCIENTOLOGISTS
(also known as HAS Training Manual)

Taken from the works of L. Ron Hubbard, published by the Hubbard Association of Scientologists International, Washington, DC, 1957.

SIXTEENTH AMERICAN ADVANCED CLINICAL COURSE LECTURES
WASHINGTON, DC

Mr. Hubbard's lectures to students on this course included talks on the anatomy of traps, evil and how it affects man's abilities, and individual identity. (Available from Golden Era Productions as a series entitled "The Anatomy of Cause.")

2 Jan Course Outline

3 Jan Reality Scale in Action

4 Jan Havingness in General and Bodies in Particular

7 Jan Learning Processes: No-Game Condition

8 Jan Agreements and Postulates of the Eight Dynamics

9 Jan Obnosis

10 Jan The Postulate of Game

11 Jan Postulates of Action–Reaction

4 Jan Control

15 Jan Evil

16 Jan Havingness

17 Jan The Randomities of Communication

18 Jan Auditing Techniques: Self-Denial, Responsibility

18 Jan Question and Answer Period

22 Jan Auditing Techniques: Order of Processes

22 Jan Order of Processes: Question and Answer Period

23 Jan Auditing Techniques: Scale of Processes

24 Jan Auditing Techniques: Altering Cases

24 Jan Altering Cases: Question and Answer Period

25 Jan Auditing Techniques: Specifics

25 Jan Specifics: Question and Answer Period

28 Jan Auditing Techniques: Stimulus-Response

28 Jan Stimulus-Response: Question and Answer Period

29 Jan Auditing Techniques: Action and Reaction

29 Jan Action and Reaction: Question and Answer Period

30 Jan Auditing Techniques: Workable and Unworkable

30 Jan Workable and Unworkable: Question and Answer Period

31 Jan Auditing Techniques: Solids

31 Jan Solids: Question and Answer Period

1 Feb Auditing Techniques: Games Conditions

4 Feb Auditing Techniques: Procedure CCH

---

5 Feb Auditing Techniques: How Far South?

5 Feb How Far South?: Question and Answer Period

6 Feb Auditing Session on Processes of Intensive CCH

7 Feb Summation

7 Feb Summation: Question and Answer Period

8 Feb General Use of Procedure

8 Feb General Use of Procedure: Question and Answer Period

11 Feb Question and Answer Period

12 Feb Final Lecture: Question and Answer

ISSUES

PAB 104 15 Jan Dissemination

HCO PL 25 Jan I Referrals to Field

HCO PL 25 Jan II Concerning the Separateness of Dianetics and Scientology

PAB 105 1 Feb The Story of a Static

HCO 6 Feb Procedure CCH
TRAINING BULLETIN

HCO PL 12 Feb "HCO is entitled..."

HCO PL 13 Feb "We will no longer..."

PAB 106 15 Feb Good Processes

SEVENTEENTH AMERICAN ADVANCED CLINICAL COURSE LECTURES
WASHINGTON, DC

(To be released by Golden Era Productions.)

25 Feb Opening Lecture, CCHs, The Future of Scientology

25 Feb Opening Lecture: Question and Answer Period

26 Feb ARC Triangle and Associated Scales

27 Feb Communication and Isness

27 Feb Communication and Isness: Question and Answer Period

28 Feb The Parts of Man

28 Feb The Parts of Man: Question and Answer Period

1 Mar Problems: Their Handling and Running

1 Mar Question and Answer Period About Problems and Responsibility

4 Mar Control

5 Mar The Scale of Techniques

6 Mar The Scale of Techniques: Question and Answer Period

6 Mar Control—The Lowest Possible Process

6 Mar Control—The Lowest Possible Process: Question and Answer Period

7 Mar Ought to Be

7 Mar Ought to Be: Question and Answer Period

10 Mar Valences—Basic Personality

10 Mar Valences—Basic Personality: Question and Answer Period

11 Mar Summary of Techniques

11 Mar Summary of Techniques: Question and Answer Period

12 Mar Survival

LONDON CONGRESS ON NUCLEAR RADIATION AND HEALTH LECTURES
LONDON, ENGLAND

These lectures include data on nuclear radiation, its effect on health, and the latest advances in Scientology. (Available from Golden Era Productions as a series entitled "Radiation and Your Survival.") See also the book *All About Radiation*. First published in May 1957. Today published by Bridge Publications and New Era Publications.

LECTURE
LONDON, ENGLAND

HUBBARD CERTIFIED AUDITOR COURSE LECTURES
WASHINGTON, DC

ALL ABOUT RADIATION
by L. Ron Hubbard

First published by the Hubbard Communications Office, London, England, May 1957. Today published by Bridge Publications and New Era Publications. TRANSLATIONS: Danish, Dutch, French, German, Italian, Spanish and Swedish.

STAFF AUDITOR CONFERENCE
WASHINGTON, DC

ADVANCED CLINICAL COURSE (ACC) PREPARATORY MANUAL FOR ADVANCED STUDENTS IN SCIENTOLOGY

Taken from the works of L. Ron Hubbard. Published by Hubbard Communications Office, London, England, Summer of 1957.

FREEDOM CONGRESS LECTURES
WASHINGTON, DC

The Freedom Congress was so named because its subject was freedom from human confusion. In addition to lectures, Mr. Hubbard gave demonstrations of specific processes and training drills and delivered Group Processing to the congress delegates. (Available from Golden Era Productions. TRANSLATIONS: French, German, Italian and Spanish.)

4 Jul	How We Have Addressed the Problem of the Mind
4 Jul	Man's Search and Scientology's Answer
4 Jul	Definition of Control
5 Jul	Basic Theory of CCHs
5 Jul	Group Processing: Acceptable Pressures
5 Jul	Group Processing: Hold It on Earth
5 Jul	Purpose and Need of Training Drills
5 Jul	Training Drills Demonstrated
6 Jul	Third Dynamic and Communication—High School Indoctrination Demonstration
6 Jul	Demonstration of High School Indoctrination
6 Jul	Tone 40 on an Object
6 Jul	Levels of Skill
6 Jul	Tone 40 on a Person
7 Jul	Child Scientology
7 Jul	CCH: Steps 1–4 Demo
7 Jul	CCH: Steps 5–7

ISSUES

HCO PL	5 Jul	Lonesome?
FC PL	10 Jul	Hiring of Staff Auditors
PAB 116	15 Jul	Solids and Chronic Somatics
HCO TRNG BULLETIN	15 Jul	"Our first lesson in training…"

EIGHTEENTH AMERICAN ADVANCED CLINICAL COURSE LECTURES
WASHINGTON, DC

Twenty-two lectures in which Ron shed light on subjects intimate to everyday living—such as sleep, laughter, time and the past. (Available from Golden Era Productions as a series entitled "Illusion or Truth.")

15 Jul	Scientology and Effective Knowledge
15 Jul	Question and Answer Period
16 Jul	CCH Related to ARC
17 Jul	Theory and Definition of Auditing
18 Jul	What Scientology Is Addressed To
19 Jul	The Five Categories
22 Jul	Control
23 Jul	The Stability of Scientology
24 Jul	Auditing Styles
25 Jul	Scales (Effect Scale)
26 Jul	The Mind: Its Structure in Relation to Thetan and MEST
29 Jul	The Optimum 25-Hour Intensive, Anatomy of Problems, Training Athletes
30 Jul	Death
31 Jul	Surprise—The Anatomy of Sleep
1 Aug	Thinnies
2 Aug	Ability—Laughter
5 Aug	Factors Behind the Handling of IQ
6 Aug	The Scale of Withhold
7 Aug	CCH
8 Aug	Confronting
9 Aug	Instructing a Course
16 Aug	The Future of Scientology

ISSUES

HCO TRNG BULL	17 Jul	Changes in Training Drills
HASI PL	26 Jul	Funds or Favors Received

ARTICLE

ABILITY 51	late Jul	The Adventure of Communication

ISSUES

HCOB	29 Jul	Withholds and Communication
HCOB	31 Jul	"More workable commands for testing…"
PAB 117	1 Aug	Confronting Present Time
FC PL	8 Aug	Power of Veto
ACC BULL	10 Aug	CCH 18

ARTICLE

ABILITY 52	early Aug	Confronting

ISSUES

HCO PL 15 Aug R Rev. 12 Jun 58		Ministerial Qualifications
PAB 118	15 Aug	Validation Committee
HCO PL	19 Aug	Certificates Release and Validation

ARTICLE

ABILITY 53	late Aug	Communication

LECTURE
WASHINGTON, DC

23 Aug	Axiom 53

ISSUES

HCOB	29 Aug	Government Project Stable Data
PAB 119	1 Sep	The Big Auditing Problem
HCO PL	2 Sep	Field Certificates
HCOB	2 Sep	"When a verbal direction is given…"
HASI PL	2 Sep	Executives
HCO PROC LETTER	3 Sep	Method of Opening and Invoicing Mail
HCO TRNG BULL	3 Sep	HPA/HCA Course Processes
HCO BULL	4 Sep	Stable Data for TRNG Instructors
HASI PL	5 Sep I	Validation of Staff
HASI PL	5 Sep II	"All preclears are expected to…"
HCO PL	5 Sep	Testing

ARTICLE

ABILITY 54	early Sep	More Confronting

ISSUES

HCOB	9 Sep	Processes to Be Run on HGC Preclears from This Date
PAB 120	15 Sep	Control Trio
HASI PL	16 Sep	HGC Policy, Results or Else
HCO TRNG BULL	24 Sep	Curriculum of CCH Class
HASI PL	26 Sep	Filling Posts

HASI PL	27 Sep	"It has come to my attention…"

ARTICLES

ABILITY 55	late Sep	The Saga of the 18th ACC
ABILITY 56	early Oct	The Eighteenth ACC

ISSUES

PAB 121	1 Oct	Rudiments and Goals
PAB 122	15 Oct	The Five Levels of Indoctrination and Procedure CCH
HASI PL	24 Oct	"Any staff member…"
HCO PL	29 Oct	HCO Files
CHART	29 Oct	A Basic Chart of Process Types

ARTICLES

ABILITY 57	late Oct	Escape
ABILITY 58	early Nov	We Are the Free People

ISSUES

PAB 123	1 Nov	The Reality Scale
HCOB 2 Nov RA Rev. 22 Feb 75		An Objective Rundown
ORG INFO SHEET	6 Nov	Duties of the Executive Director of the HASI (FC)
HCOB	13 Nov	Project Clear Check Sheet
PAB 124	15 Nov	Communication and Isness

ARTICLE

ABILITY 59	late Nov	Why You Should Come to a Congress

HUBBARD CERTIFIED AUDITOR STUDENT MANUAL

Taken from the works of L. Ron Hubbard. Published by Hubbard Communications Office, London, England, November 1957.

ARTICLE

ABILITY 60	early Dec	Scientology: The Philosophy of a New Age

SCIENTOLOGY: CLEAR PROCEDURE, ISSUE ONE
by L. Ron Hubbard

Published by Hubbard Communications Office, London, England, December 1957. Also printed in the Technical Bulletins Volumes. TRANSLATIONS: Dutch, French, German, Spanish and Swedish.

ARTICLE

ABILITY 62	Dec	We Begin a Campaign

ISSUES

PAB 125	1 Dec	The Parts of Man
HCOB	3 Dec	Clear Procedure, Rewritten and Expanded from 30 Nov. 57, Definitions, Goals
HCOB	4 Dec	Clear Procedure Continued, Step One: Participation in Session by the Pc

HCOB	7 Dec	HGC Procedure
PAB 126	15 Dec	Problems: Handling and Running
HCOB	16 Dec	Present Time Problem
HCOB	18 Dec	Psychosis, Neurosis and Psychiatrists
HCO PL	19 Dec	Phone Bill
HCO PL	20 Dec	Clarification of Public Relations Post
RESEARCH NOTE	Dec	Ability Book

ABILITY CONGRESS LECTURES
WASHINGTON, DC

The lectures of this congress centered on the return of ability to live—to understand oneself and others, to communicate, to have and achieve goals. (Available from Golden Era Productions.)

29 Dec	Experience—Randomity and Change of Pace
29 Dec	The Clear Defined
29 Dec	Clear Procedure
30 Dec	Cause and Effect
30 Dec	Creating a Third Dynamic
30 Dec	Upper Route to Operating Thetan
31 Dec	Responsibility—How to Create a Third Dynamic
31 Dec	The National Academy of American Psychology
31 Dec	Creative Processing Steps

CONTROL AND THE MECHANICS OF SCS

Taken from the works of L. Ron Hubbard. First published by Hubbard Association of Scientologists International, Washington, DC, in December 1957, and today by Bridge Publications and New Era Publications.

1958

Mr. Hubbard spent much of his time in 1958 working and lecturing in London and in Washington, DC. He was involved in organizations on both sides of the Atlantic simultaneously, while keeping up a heavy schedule of research, writing and lecturing.

Among his major technical breakthroughs in 1958 were refinements of clearing technology, as detailed in the Nineteenth American ACC lectures and Clearing Congress lectures, both given in Washington. Six of the Clearing Congress lectures were captured on color film and can still be heard and watched today.

Mr. Hubbard also made major developments in the technologies of auditing and auditor training, recorded in lectures, issues and articles.

ACADEMY OF SCIENTOLOGY— INSTRUCTIONS AND INFORMATION FOR STUDENTS IN HCA, VALIDATION OR SPECIAL COMMUNICATION COURSES

Based on the works of L. Ron Hubbard. Published by the Hubbard Association of Scientologists International, Washington, DC, 1958.

ISSUES

PAB 127   1 Jan   The Threat to Havingness

HCO PL   4 Jan R Field Offices
Rev. 30 Dec 58

ORG PL   10 Jan   Inspection of Hat Folders

DESPATCH 11 Jan HGC Procedure

HCOB   13 Jan   HGC Running of Pcs

PAB 128 15 Jan   The Factors Behind the Handling of IQ

HCOB   15 Jan   Field Office Communication

HCOB   18 Jan   "The reason the auditor is having trouble..."

NINETEENTH AMERICAN ADVANCED CLINICAL COURSE LECTURES
WASHINGTON, DC

(To be released by Golden Era Productions.)

20 Jan   The Four Universes
20 Jan   The E-Meter
21 Jan   Intensive Procedures
21 Jan   Intensive Procedure: Question and Answer Period
22 Jan   The Bank Out of Control and Its Stabilization
22 Jan   The Bank Out of Control and Its Stabilization: Question and Answer Period
23 Jan   Clearing Fields
23 Jan   Clearing Fields: Question and Answer Period
24 Jan   E-Meter, Identification and Association
24 Jan   E-Meter, Identification and Association: Question and Answer Period

HUBBARD AMERICAN BLUE E-METER

The new "American Blue" transistorized E-Meter was ready in time for the Nineteenth American Advanced Clinical Course in January 1958. A meter was also developed around this time that projected and displayed the meter dial and the tone arm. It was used in auditing demonstrations for training purposes.

27 Jan   What It Is You Clear, Something and Nothing
27 Jan   What It Is You Clear, Something and Nothing: Question and Answer Period
28 Jan   Man the Animal and Man the God
28 Jan   Man the Animal and Man the God: Question and Answer Period
29 Jan   History of Clearing
29 Jan   History of Clearing: Question and Answer Period
30 Jan   Test for Clears
30 Jan   Test for Clears: Question and Answer Period
31 Jan   Importance of Theory Behind Clearing Procedure
31 Jan   Importance of Theory Behind Clearing Procedure: Question and Answer Period
3 Feb   The Phenomena of Entrapment in the Physical Universe
3 Feb   The Phenomena of Entrapment in the Physical Universe: Question and Answer Period
4 Feb   How to Find a Preclear, Responsibility and Help
4 Feb   How to Find a Preclear, Responsibility and Help: Question and Answer Period
5 Feb   The Basic Approach to Clearing, Finding the Auditor
5 Feb   The Basic Approach to Clearing, Finding the Auditor: Question and Answer Period
6 Feb   CCH 0, SCS, Connectedness
6 Feb   CCH 0, SCS, Connectedness: Question and Answer Period
7 Feb   Help—How to Get Started
7 Feb   Help—How to Get Started: Question and Answer Period
10 Feb   Conduct of Clear
10 Feb   Conduct of Clear: Question and Answer Period
10 Feb   The Key Processes of Clearing
11 Feb   The Key Processes of Clearing: Question and Answer Period
12 Feb   Havingness, Anaten, Flows, in Relation to Clearing
12 Feb   Havingness, Anaten, Flows, in Relation to Clearing: Question and Answer Period
13 Feb   Other Processes, the Help Button
13 Feb   Other Processes, the Help Button: Question and Answer Period
14 Feb   Responsibility for Mock-ups
14 Feb   Responsibility for Mock-ups: Question and Answer Period

ISSUES

HCOB   21 Jan I   MEST Clear Procedure
HCOB   21 Jan II "An ACC is a special activity..."
HCOB   24 Jan   Outline of Activities
ORG PL 25 Jan   Inept Students
HCOB   25 Jan II Reviewing Week's Profiles
HCOB   26 Jan   Future Plans
HCO PL 27 Jan   Duties of Personnel Post
HCOB   1 Feb   Clearing of Fields
PAB 129 1 Feb   Confronting
HCOB   3 Feb   Free Clearing Project

ARTICLE

ABILITY 66   early Feb   The Attainment of Clears

ISSUES

HCO PL   5 Feb   "No new charters or contracts..."
HCOB   6 Feb   CCH 0b—Help in Full, Starting Session
FC PL   8 Feb   "Since people will begin to expect..."
HCOB   13 Feb   Rules Governing the Running of CCH 0b "Help"

ARTICLE

ABILITY 67   mid-Feb   Man's Contest with the Machine Age

ISSUES

PAB 130 15 Feb   Death
HCOPL   25 Feb   Routing of Communication

ARTICLE

ABILITY 68   late Feb   We Did It!

ISSUES

HCOB   1 Mar   Processes
PAB 131 1 Mar   The Scale of Withhold
PAB 132 15 Mar   Report on Two Cases that Have Received Psychiatric and Euro-Russian Therapy from the Government
HCO PL 17 Mar   Body Routing in Central Organizations
FC PL   19 Mar   Transportation, Dir Admin Responsibility
HCOB   22 Mar   Clearing Reality
FC PL   26 Mar   Salary and Unit Pay

STAFF AUDITORS' CONFERENCES
WASHINGTON, DC

27 Mar   Comments on Auditing
27 Jun   Processing on Clearing

ARTICLE

ABILITY 70   late Mar   Does Clearing Cancel the Need for Training?

ISSUES

HCOB   28 Mar   Only Organization Offices Can Certify Clears
PAB 133 1 Apr   Procedure CCH
HCOB   2 Apr   ARC in Comm Course
HCO PL   7 Apr   Routing of Org Board Changes
HCOB   8 Apr   Auditing the Pc on Clear Procedure
HCOB   8 Apr II A Pair of Processes
HCOB   11 Apr   CCH 88—Enforced Nothingness
PAB 134 15 Apr   Procedure CCH Continued
HCOB   23 Apr   Four Vital Training Data for Training Hats and Registrar

ARTICLE

ABILITY 72   late Apr   How We Work on the Third Dynamic

ISSUES

HCOB   1 May   Signs of Success
HCO PL   1 May I Employment Qualifications

HCO PL 1 May II Financial Management

PAB 135 1 May Procedure CCH Continued

HCOB 2 May Beingness Again

ARTICLE

ABILITY 73 early May Assists in Scientology

ISSUES

HCOB 9 May Who Should Take Which Class

PAB 136 15 May Procedure CCH Continued

HCOB 22 May "List the enemies of pc..."

ARTICLE

ABILITY 74 mid-May Scientology and the Reactive Mind

ISSUES

HCOB 24 May A Comment on Beingness Processing

FC PL 27 May Outside Auditing

HCO PL 28 May Incoming Calls for LRH

HCOB 29 May Standard Clear Procedure and an Experimental Road: Clearing by Valences

HCOB 29 May An Example of Clearing by Valences

PAB 137 1 Jun Some More CCH Processes

HCO PL 1 Jun Purchase Orders

ARTICLE

ABILITY 76 early Jun Offbeat Processing

ISSUES

HCOB 4 Jun Running Valences

FC PL 19 Jun Freeloaders

ARTICLE

ABILITY 77 late Jun Learning How to "Clear"

ISSUES

HASI PL 30 Jun Clear Bracelet Procedure

HCOB 30 Jun Procedure for Certifying Clears

CLEARING CONGRESS LECTURES
WASHINGTON, DC

The first six lectures of this congress were filmed in color and are available today from Golden Era Productions on video. They contain a complete and simple presentation of the subject of clearing for the general public as well as for Scientologists—a spanning of interests and a presentation of unusual accomplishment in itself.

4 Jul The Fact of Clearing

4 Jul The Factors of Clearing

4 Jul The Freedoms of Clear

5 Jul Prerequisites to Auditing

5 Jul Clear Procedure, CCH 0, Help

5 Jul Clear Procedure, Creativeness

6 Jul The Magic Button

6 Jul The Goal of Auditing

6 Jul Violence

ISSUES

HCOB 7 Jul Contents and Coverage of HCA/HPA Course

HCOB 9 Jul Staff Clearing

HCOB 12 Jul Standardization of Clear Processes for Guidance and Use of the HGCs

TWENTIETH AMERICAN ADVANCED CLINICAL COURSE LECTURES
WASHINGTON, DC

In this Advanced Clinical Course, Ron taught auditors how to find the basic incident on any preclear's case and the processes and skill necessary to handle it and clear individuals. (Available from Golden Era Productions as a series entitled "The First Postulate.")

14 Jul Opening Lecture

14 Jul Opening Lecture: Question and Answer Period

15 Jul ACC Procedure Outlined— E-Meter TRs

15 Jul ACC Procedure Outlined— E-Meter TRs: Question and Answer Period

16 Jul Course Procedure Outlined

16 Jul Course Procedure Outlined: Question and Answer Period

17 Jul Beginning and Ending Session—Gaining Pc's Contribution to the Session

17 Jul Beginning and Ending Session: Question and Answer Period

18 Jul ACC Training Procedure

18 Jul ACC Training Procedure: Question and Answer Period

21 Jul The Key Words (Buttons) of Scientology Clearing

21 Jul The Key Words (Buttons) of Scientology Clearing: Question and Answer Period

22 Jul The Rock

22 Jul The Rock: Question and Answer Period

23 Jul Special Effect Cases, Anatomy Of

23 Jul Special Effect Cases, Anatomy Of: Question and Answer Period

24 Jul Anatomy of Needles— Diagnostic Procedure

24 Jul Anatomy of Needles— Diagnostic Procedure: Question and Answer Period

25 Jul The Rock: Putting Pc at Cause

25 Jul Question and Answer Period: Clearing the Command

28 Jul ACC Command Sheet— Goals of Auditing

29 Jul ACC Command Sheet (cont.)

30 Jul ACC Command Sheet (cont.)

31 Jul Running the Case and the Rock

1 Aug Case Analysis—Rock Hunting

1 Aug Case Analysis—Rock Hunting (cont.)

4 Aug Case Analysis—Rock Hunting (cont.)

4 Aug Case Analysis—Rock Hunting: Question and Answer Period

5 Aug ARC

6 Aug The Rock, Its Anatomy

7 Aug The Most Basic Rock of All

7 Aug The Most Basic Rock of All: Question and Answer Period

8 Aug Auditor Interest

8 Aug Requisites and Fundamentals of a Session

15 Aug Summary of 20th ACC

ISSUES

HCOB 14 Jul 20th ACC Training Procedure

HCOB 15 Jul Carrying On

HCOB 28 Jul Clear Procedure

HCOB 29 Jul The Rock

HCOB 30 Jul The Handling of Hubbard Communications Offices

HCOB 5 Aug "The basic locating question of the Rock..."

HCOB 10 Aug ACC Auxiliary Procedure

HCOB 20 Aug I Present Time Problem—Running Of

HCOB 20 Aug II Out of Sessionness

AXIOMS AND LOGICS
by L. Ron Hubbard

First published by Hubbard Communications Office, London, England, August 1958; this book was a compilation of materials originally published between the years 1951 and 1955. Its contents are now found in Scientology 0-8: The Book of Basics, published by Bridge Publications and New Era Publications.

ISSUES

HCOB 25 Aug Administrative Stable Data

HCO PL 27 Aug I "The Washington, DC Central Organization..."

HCO PL 27 Aug II Executives of Scientology Organizations

HCOB 28 Aug Change Auditor's Code

HUBBARD "GREEN AND GOLD" UK METER

In Great Britain the "Green and Gold" meter was built. This E-Meter was used at the Fifth London Advanced Clinical Course.

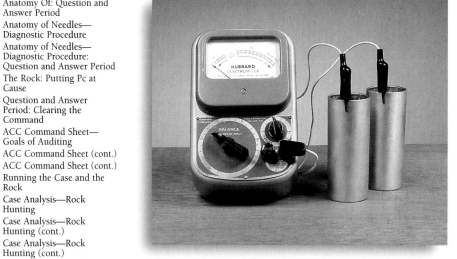

STAFF AUDITORS' CONFERENCES
WASHINGTON, DC

1 Sep   How to Run Present Time Problems

27 Sep   HGC Auditor Conference on Clear Procedure and Clearing People

ISSUES

HCOB   3 Sep   "The cost for an individual..."

HCOB   12 Sep I   Post Case Analysis Routine

HCOB   12 Sep II   Havingness—New Commands

HCO PL   12 Sep   Color Flash System Rewritten

HCOB   15 Sep   More on Training Drill Two

HCO PL   17 Sep   Who Can Order Printing

HCO PL   19 Sep   A Model Hat for an Executive

HCOB   29 Sep   Vital Training Data

HCO PL   1 Oct   HCO Board of Review

HCO PL   2 Oct   Sale and Conduct of Academy Courses

HCO PL   5 Oct   How to Fill Jobs

FC PL   6 Oct   Who Can Be Processed, Who Can Be Trained

FC PL   9 Oct   Departments of FCDC

HCOB   15 Oct   ACC Clear Procedure

ACC CLEAR PROCEDURE (TWENTIETH AMERICAN ACC)
by L. Ron Hubbard

Published by Hubbard Communications Office, Washington, DC, October 1958. The text of this book appears in full in the Technical Bulletins volumes.

ISSUE

PAB 146   15 Oct   Procedure CCH

ARTICLE

ABILITY 83   mid-Oct   New HCA Course You Can Begin at Home

LECTURE
LONDON, ENGLAND

Mr. Hubbard arrived in London on 17 October 1958 to give the London Clearing Congress, scheduled to start the following day. On arrival he gave a talk to the London staff on past ACCs, a new organization chart and organizational basics.

17 Oct   Talk to Staff on Arrival in England

LONDON CLEARING CONGRESS LECTURES
LONDON, ENGLAND

In this congress Mr. Hubbard covered a broad range of subjects—from his experiences developing the technologies of Dianetics and Scientology, to the characteristics of Clears and the skills necessary to produce them, to the effects of Scientology's activities on the future of this civilization. (Available from Golden Era Productions as a series entitled "The Origin of Aberration.")

18 Oct   The Story of Dianetics and Scientology

18 Oct   The Skills of Clearing

18 Oct   Confronting

20 Oct   The Rock

20 Oct   Confusion and Order

20 Oct   The Future of Scientology and the Western Civilization

ISSUES

HCO PL   24 Oct I   *Ability* Magazine

HCOB   25 Oct   Abbreviations

DESPATCH   Oct   ACC Preclear Check Sheet, Fifth London ACC

HCOB   27 Oct   How to Read Profiles on OCA: Comparing Current Week Profile with Week Before

FIFTH LONDON ADVANCED CLINICAL COURSE LECTURES
LONDON, ENGLAND

Auditing case histories from this month-long course, the most heavily attended ACC yet held, appear in the book *Have You Lived Before This Life?* (To be released by Golden Era Productions.)

27 Oct   Clearing and What It Generally Means to Man

28 Oct   Compartmentation of Four Universes

28 Oct   Compartmentation of Four Universes: Question and Answer Period

29 Oct   Types of Pictures

29 Oct   Types of Pictures: Question and Answer Period

30 Oct   Mental Image Pictures, Engrams

30 Oct   Mental Image Pictures: Question and Answer Period

31 Oct   Engrams

31 Oct   Engrams: Question and Answer Period

3 Nov   The Detection of Engrams

3 Nov   The Detection of Engrams: Question and Answer Period

4 Nov   The Detection of Engrams with an E-Meter

4 Nov   The Detection of Engrams with an E-Meter: Question and Answer Period

5 Nov   The Detection of Engrams, Part III

5 Nov   The Detection of Engrams, Part III: Question and Answer Period

6 Nov   The Moral, Ethical and Social Aspect of the Detection of Engrams

6 Nov   E-Meter Needle Manifestations

7 Nov   Detection of Circuits and Machinery

7 Nov   Detection of Circuits and Machinery: Question and Answer Period

10 Nov   Auditing—Its Skills

10 Nov   Auditing—Its Skills: Question and Answer Period

11 Nov   The Skill of an Auditor, Part I

11 Nov   The Skill of an Auditor, Part I: Question and Answer Period

12 Nov   The Skill of an Auditor, Part II

12 Nov   The Skill of an Auditor, Part II: Question and Answer Period

13 Nov   The Attitude of an Auditor

13 Nov   The Attitude of an Auditor: Question and Answer Period

14 Nov   What an Auditor Is Supposed to Do with an Engram

14 Nov   What an Auditor Is Supposed to Do with an Engram: Question and Answer Period

17 Nov   The Effect of the Environment on an Engram

17 Nov   The Effect of the Environment on an Engram: Question and Answer Period

17 Nov   How to Audit an Engram, Use of an E-Meter

17 Nov   How to Audit an Engram, Use of an E-Meter: Question and Answer Period

19 Nov   How to Start and Run a Session

19 Nov   How to Start and Run a Session: Question and Answer Period

19 Nov   Attitude and Approach to Auditing

28 Nov   The Plan of Clearing

28 Nov   Final Lecture

ISSUES

HASI PL   30 Oct   Personnel Efficiency Foundation

HASI PL   31 Oct   "Only 75 copies..."

PAB 147   1 Nov   Communication Course

HCOB   3 Nov   American College of Personnel Efficiency, Dublin

HASI PL   6 Nov   The Three-Basket System

HASI PL   7 Nov   Registrar

HASI PL NO.2   7 Nov   "The output of special letters..."

HCOB   7 Nov   HPA Courses for Staff

HCOB   11 Nov   ACC Schedule

HCOB   13 Nov   TR 9(b) and TR 9(c)

HASI PL   15 Nov I   Informing Public of Test Results

HASI PL   15 Nov II   How to Procure People

HCO PL   15 Nov I   The Substance and First Duty of HCO

HCO PL   15 Nov II   Legal Aid—HCO

HCO PL   15 Nov III   Outstanding Copyrights and Marks

HASI PL   17 Nov   Free Clear Estimates, Free Clear Tests

HCO PL   17 Nov I   Project Engineering

HCO PL   17 Nov II   Project Engineers, Three Types

HCO PL   17 Nov IV   HCO Project Engineer: "Have You Lived Before?"

HCOB   17 Nov   Clear Bracelets

OFFICE OF THE ED HASI   18 Nov   Letter Policy

HCO PL   19 Nov   Organization

HCO PL   22 Nov   Owner of Materials, the Legal View

SEC ED   23 Nov   Scientometric Testing

HCO PL   24 Nov RI   Magazine Policy
Rev. 11 Feb 80

HCO PL   24 Nov II   HASI Group Secretary

HCO PL   25 Nov   HCO Board of Review, Function and Practice

HCOB   25 Nov   Step 6

HCO TECH PL   25 Nov   Techniques to Be Used on HGC Preclears

HCOB   26 Nov   ACCs

HCO PL   27 Nov III   Basic Financial Policy, HCO

MEMO   29 Nov   Future Programs

ARTICLES

CERTAINTY VOL. 5, NO. 22   late Nov   Violence

ABILITY 85   late Nov   The Theory of Training in Scientology

ISSUES

PAB 149   1 Dec   Dummy Auditing, Step Two: Acknowledgment

HCOB   1 Dec I   "The enrollees of the 5th London ACC..."

HCOB   1 Dec II   Actions to Start an HCO

SEC ED   1 Dec   Materiel Administrator Hat

HCOB   6 Dec   How to Run an Engram, Brief Summary for HGC Use

ARTICLES

L. RON HUBBARD'S PROFESSIONAL AUDITOR'S BULLETINS BOOK 5

(Professional Auditor's Bulletins 70–80)

Published by Hubbard Communications Office, Washington, DC, December 1958.

(Note: The Professional Auditor's Bulletins written by L. Ron Hubbard also appear in the Technical Bulletins *volumes.)*

1959

In 1959, Mr. Hubbard purchased Saint Hill Manor in Sussex, England, and moved his offices there.

Once established at Saint Hill he began a number of projects, including a series of experiments with plants and the nature of their life energy. His experiments and findings were widely publicized in the media. Many administrative policies were also formed here, because at that time LRH was Executive Director International, directing the Scientology churches and developing organizational technology to increase efficiency.

In addition to his projects at Saint Hill, LRH continued researching and writing; he also made time to travel, giving lectures and congresses in Washington, DC; London, England; and Melbourne, Australia.

ISSUES

SUCCESS CONGRESS
WASHINGTON, DC

Delegates to this congress were given lectures on new breakthroughs in the handling of engrams and the skills needed to apply them in making Clears. (Available as a series entitled "Cause and Spheres of Influence.")

LECTURE
WASHINGTON, DC

TWENTY-FIRST AMERICAN ADVANCED CLINICAL COURSE
WASHINGTON, DC

(To be released by Golden Era Productions.)

ARTICLES

ISSUES

HUBBARD MARK I E-METER

By 1959, Mathison's E-Meter had become unworkable. Mr. Hubbard retained a new company, Fowler and Allen Electrical, and following his instructions, it produced the Hubbard Mark I E-Meter. The Mark I was the first of a series of dependable and truly workable meters.

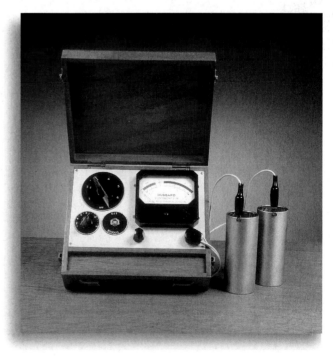

ARTICLE

ABILITY 88M late Jan A Campaign for Ethical Auditing

ISSUES

HCO PL 23 Jan Ethics

HCOB 24 Jan Scientology Axiom 58

HCO PL 26 Jan Scientology Magazines

SEC ED 29 Jan Secretarial to the Executive Director Hat

HCO PL 29 Jan HCO Communicator Hat

SEC ED 30 Jan Department of Promotion and Registration

SEC ED 31 Jan Promotional Letters

PAB 153 1 Feb CCH

HCOB 3 Feb I HGC Current Procedure

HCOB 3 Feb II Flattening a Process

HCOB 4 Feb Op Pro by Dup

SEC ED 4 Feb Policy—Certifying Clears

HCO PL 6 Feb HCO Accounts Worldwide

HASI PL 10 Feb Group Secretary

SEC ED 10 Feb The Advisory Council

SEC ED 10 Feb Central Files and the Addressograph (Use Of)

SEC ED 11 Feb The Dept of Promotion and Registration and CF Promotion Liaison

HCO PL 12 Feb Book Administrator

SEC ED 13 Feb Staff Processing and Training Policy

PAB 154 15 Feb CCH (Concluded)

HCOB 16 Feb HGC Processes for Those Trained in Engram Running or Trained in These Processes

STAFF AUDITORS' CONFERENCE
WASHINGTON, DC

16 Feb Staff Auditors' Conference

ISSUES

TRANSCRIPT 16 Feb Staff Auditors' Conference of February 16, 1959 Regarding HCOB 16 Feb. 59

SEC ED 17 Feb Extension Course Students, Letters

SEC ED 18 Feb Director of Materiel

SEC ED 18 Feb HGC Auditing Policies

SEC ED 18 Feb Thermostats in Buildings

SEC ED 19 Feb Use of Addresses in Letter Writing

HCOB 19 Feb Auditor's Code #19

SEC ED 23 Feb How to Interview People

SEC ED 24 Feb FC Communicator Basic Hat

SEC ED 24 Feb Secretary to Training Department Hat (Temporary Hat)

SEC ED 24 Feb Despatches to Advisory Council

SEC ED 24 Feb Shipping Department Invoices

HCOB 24 Feb Selected Persons Overt–Withhold Straightwire

HCOB 26 Feb I Identification

HCOB 26 Feb II Engram Running on Old Dianetic Cases or Restarted Cases

SEC ED 26 Feb HCO Executive Secretary Continental

SEC ED 26 Feb Responsibilities of Assistant Org Sec

HCO PL 27 Feb Duty of Area Sec Re Personnel

HCOB 27 Feb How to Select Selected Persons

HCO PL 28 Feb HCO Board of Review Duties

ARTICLE

ABILITY 90M late Feb How to Study Scientology

ISSUES

HCOB 28 Feb I Analysis of Cases

HCOB 28 Feb II ARC Breaks with Auditors

HCOB 28 Feb III Clearing Commands

HCOB 1 Mar II Two Rules for Happy Living

PAB 155 1 Mar Processes Used in 21st ACC

HCO PL 1 Mar HCO Forbidden Activities

SEC ED 2 Mar Accounting System

HCO PL 2 Mar I HCO Cable and Despatch, Designation System

HCO PL 2 Mar II HCO Theory of Communication

SEC ED 3 Mar Book Section: Credits and Debits

SEC ED 3 Mar Staff Auditors

SEC ED 5 Mar Addressing Department—Hats

HCOB 6 Mar I Training Drills

HCOB 6 Mar II How to Do a Diagnosis on Dynamic Straightwire

SEC ED 7 Mar Materiel Administrator—Hat

SEC ED 7 Mar Processing Administrator—Hat

SEC ED 9 Mar The Purpose of the Lead Auditor

HASI PL 10 Mar "Permanent staff members..."

HCOB 10 Mar Supplemental Data Sheet to HCO Bulletin of 16 February 1959 and Staff Auditors' Conference of 16 February 1959

HCOB 13 Mar Muzzled Auditing

PAB 156 15 Mar Processes Used in 21st ACC

SEC ED 16 Mar HGC Psychotic Applicants

HCOB 17 Mar I An Insanity Questionnaire

HCOB 17 Mar II Do-It-Yourself Therapy

HCO PL 18 Mar "The following are..."

HCO PL 20 Mar Certificates Handling

ARTICLE

ABILITY 92M late Mar The Subject of Clearing

ISSUES

HCOB 24 Mar I HAS Co-audit

HCOB 24 Mar II Minimum Standards

HCOB 25 Mar HAS Co-audit and Comm Course

HCO PL 25 Mar Book Policy

PAB 157 1 Apr Processes Used in 21st ACC (Concluded)

HCOB 3 Apr HAS Co-audit and Comm Course

SPECIAL HUBBARD PROFESSIONAL AUDITOR'S COURSE LECTURES
LONDON, ENGLAND

The lectures given on this course were recorded and subsequently used in the training of Hubbard Professional Auditors the world over. (Available from Golden Era Productions as a series entitled "The Skills of a Theta Being.")

6 Apr Beingness and Communication

7 Apr Universes

7 Apr The Dynamics

8 Apr Scales

8 Apr States of Being

9 Apr Anatomy

9 Apr What Can be Done With a Mind (Reality Scale)

14 Apr Mechanisms of the Mind

14 Apr Overt Act–Motivator Sequence

15 Apr Codes

15 Apr The Code of a Scientologist

16 Apr The Logics and Axioms of Dianetics and Scientology

16 Apr Axioms—Second Lecture

21 Apr Types of Auditing

21 Apr Modern Auditing Types

22 Apr Types of Cases

22 Apr Assessment

23 Apr Present Time

23 Apr Use of the E-Meter in Locating Engrams

28 Apr Theory of Processes

28 Apr Processes

29 Apr Specialized Auditing

29 Apr Processing of Children

30 Apr HAS Co-audit

30 Apr Electronic Phenomena of the Mind

1 May End of Course Lecture

ISSUES

HCO PL 6 Apr Clear Ads

SEC ED 6 Apr "The organization is as apparent..."

SEC ED 8 Apr A Promotion Plan

SEC ED 8 Apr The Hats of the Department of Promotion and Registration

SEC ED 9 Apr Voluntary Help

SEC ED 9 Apr Addressograph Tabbing—Libraries

HCO PL 14 Apr New Book

HCOB 14 Apr Letter from Australia

HCOB 15 Apr Emotional Tone Scale Expanded

HCO PL 16 Apr Books, Cost Of

SEC ED 18 Apr "Bookbuyers should be sold..."

SEC ED 18 Apr Addresses

HCOB 22 Apr Old and New Reality Scale

HCO PL 23 Apr I HCO Communicator Writes from South Africa

HCO PL 23 Apr II HAS Co-audit Courses

HCO PL 24 Apr I Final HPA Exam, HCO Board of Review

HCO PL 24 Apr III Organization Posts—Two Types

SEC ED 24 Apr Registrars— Materials Available To

HCO PL 29 Apr Defacing Books and Proper Addresses in Them

SEC ED 29 Apr Registrar—Dir of Processing, The Most Frequently Lost Line

HCO PL 30 Apr I Additional Staff Auditors

HCO PL 30 Apr II Long-Distance Program

HCO PL 1 May HAS Certificates

HCOB 3 May Solution to Solutions

HCOB 4 May I An Affinity Process

HCOB 4 May II How to Write a Curriculum

HCO PL 5 May Policy on SEC EDs and Hats

HCOB 7 May New Process

HCOB 8 May An Undoable Command

SIXTH LONDON ADVANCED CLINICAL COURSE LECTURES
LONDON, ENGLAND

(To be released by Golden Era Productions.)

12 May Clearing

13 May Second Lecture on Clearing Methodology

14 May Clearing Technology

19 May The Theory of Clearing

20 May Clearing, Practice of

21 May Clearing Processes—Special Cases

26 May Clearing: Theta Clear Procedure, Continued

27 May Clearing: General Processes, Lecture Two

28 May Clearing: General Cases— Communication Processes

2 Jun Clearing: Fixed Ideas

3 Jun Clearing: Communication Processes—Specific

THETA CLEAR CONGRESS LECTURES
WASHINGTON, DC

Mr. Hubbard's lectures to congress delegates included the importance of co-auditing in accomplishing widespread clearing. (To be released by Golden Era Productions.)

MELBOURNE CONGRESS LECTURES
MELBOURNE, AUSTRALIA

This congress, given during one stop on a round-the-world tour, covered a wide range of subjects including current political systems, how to improve one's chances of surviving an atomic attack and the relation between complexity and unworkability. (Available from Golden Era Productions as a series entitled "The Principles of Creation.")

FIRST MELBOURNE ADVANCED CLINICAL COURSE LECTURES
MELBOURNE, AUSTRALIA

New discoveries on responsibility and its relation to attainment of higher states of being and ability are covered in the thirty-two lectures of this course. (Available from Golden Era Productions as a series entitled "Responsibility and the State of OT.")

9 Nov	The Know-How of Auditing
9 Nov	Demo of an Assist
10 Nov	Valence Splitting—Entering a Mind Process
10 Nov	Demo of Knocking Down a Tone Arm
11 Nov	Cycle of Action; Create, Destroy, Relative Importances
11 Nov	Demo: Force Process—Discreditable Creation
12 Nov	The Rule of the Weak Valence
12 Nov	Demo: Dynamic Straightwire Assessment
12 Nov	The Rehabilitation of Judgment
13 Nov	How to Have a Game Instead of a Case
16 Nov	The Collapsed Cycle of Action
16 Nov	Getting the Pc into Session
17 Nov	Case Assessment, Part I
17 Nov	Case Assessment, Part II
18 Nov	Alter-isness—Keynote of All Destruction
18 Nov	Demo: Minus Randomity Areas
19 Nov	Minus Randomity, Clue to Case Assessment
19 Nov	Intricacies of Create—Create Series
20 Nov	Rationale of Create Series
20 Nov	Responsibility of Creation
23 Nov	Responsibility for Zones of Creation

HUBBARD MARK II E-METER

The Hubbard Mark II E-Meter was released in 1960.

23 Nov	Demo: Responsibility for Destruction
24 Nov	The Universe of a Thetan
24 Nov	Demo: Turning on Pictures
25 Nov	Counter-Creation
25 Nov	Individuation
26 Nov	The Constancy of Fundamentals of Dianetics and Scientology
26 Nov	The Handling of Cases—Greatest Overt
27 Nov	A Brand-New Type of Auditing
27 Nov	Principal Incidents on the Track
30 Nov	The Anatomy of Havingness
30 Nov	Processes

ISSUES
HCOB	12 Nov	Acknowledgments in Auditing
HCOB	18 Nov	1st Melbourne ACC Material
HCO PL	20 Nov	Validation of Certificates
HCO PL	23 Nov	Employment of Criminals Forbidden
HCO PL	27 Nov	Key to the Organizational Chart of the Founding Church of Scientology of Washington, DC
HCOB	30 Nov	Allowed Processes 1st Melbourne ACC
HCO PL	7 Dec I	Former Saint Hill Staff
HCO PL	7 Dec II	Scientology Cleanup
HCOB	11 Dec	New Horizons in Scientology
HCOB	15 Dec	Urgent Change in All Co-audit Courses
HCOB	16 Dec	Responsibility for O/Ws

ARTICLE
ABILITY 110 late Dec Techniques of Child Processing

ISSUES
HCOB	23 Dec	Responsibility
HCO PL	28 Dec	Personnel Departure Requirement
HCOB	31 Dec R	Blow-Offs

Rev. 9 Feb 89

ARTICLE
CERTAINTY Is It Possible to Be Clear?
SPECIAL ISSUE 3

CEREMONIES OF THE FOUNDING CHURCH OF SCIENTOLOGY
by L. Ron Hubbard

Published by Hubbard Communications Office, Washington, DC, 1959.

1960

Mr. Hubbard's schedule of lectures, congresses and Advanced Clinical Courses for 1960 took him to Washington, DC; London, England; Johannesburg, South Africa and to Saint Hill in England for the First Saint Hill Advanced Clinical Course.

His research led to major advances in auditing addressed to the subjects of help, responsibility and harmful acts. He also devoted time to finding new ways to apply Scientology broadly, to the betterment of large sectors of society.

ISSUE
| HCO PL | 1 Jan | Administrative Procedure for Reducing Overts |

STATE OF MAN CONGRESS LECTURES
WASHINGTON, DC

In this congress, given at the Shoreham Hotel in Washington, DC, Mr. Hubbard covered the eight dynamics in detail, with particular attention to how the dynamics interrelate and how to improve conditions across the dynamics. (Available from Golden Era Productions. TRANSLATIONS: French, German, Italian and Spanish.)

1 Jan	Opening Lecture
1 Jan	Responsibility
1 Jan	Overts and Withholds
2 Jan	Why People Don't Like You
2 Jan	Marriage
2 Jan	Group Auditing Session
3 Jan	Zones of Control and Responsibility of Governments
3 Jan	Create and Confront
3 Jan	Your Case

ISSUES
| HCOB | 2 Jan | HAS Certifications |
| HCOB | 3 Jan | A Third Dynamic for Scientology |

HUBBARD CLEARING SCIENTOLOGIST COURSE LECTURES
WASHINGTON, DC

Personally addressing the students of this course, Mr. Hubbard reiterated and expanded on auditing basics such as handling blocks to free communication and precise use of the E-Meter. (To be released by Golden Era Productions.)

4 Jan	E-Meter Phenomena
4 Jan	E-Meter and Time Track Structure
5 Jan	Processing Against an E-Meter
5 Jan	Operating an E-Meter in Processing
6 Jan	Auditing
6 Jan	Identity
7 Jan	Inability to Withhold
7 Jan	Case Level and Needle State
8 Jan	Sessioning and Withholds—Final Lecture

ISSUES
HCOB	7 Jan	The Unmoving Case
HCOB	8 Jan	OT Procedure for HCS/BScn Courses
HCOB	14 Jan	The Black Case
HCOB	18 Jan	Zones of Authority and Regulations of Saint Hill

ARTICLE

ISSUES

SPEECH
LONDON, ENGLAND

HAVE YOU LIVED BEFORE THIS LIFE?
by L. Ron Hubbard

Published by Hubbard Communications Office, Saint Hill Manor, East Grinstead, Sussex, England, March 1960. Revised and expanded in 1977. Today published by Bridge Publications and New Era Publications.
TRANSLATIONS: Danish, Dutch, French, German, Italian and Spanish.

ISSUES

ARTICLE

ISSUES

ARTICLE

ISSUES

LONDON OPEN EVENING LECTURES
LONDON, ENGLAND

In addition to his schedule of research, writing and lectures and conferences with staff, Mr. Hubbard made time in June and July to give several lectures to newer public. (To be released by Golden Era Productions.)

ISSUES

HUBBARD MARK III E-METER

The Mark II was soon followed by the Hubbard Mark III E-Meter, also released in 1960.

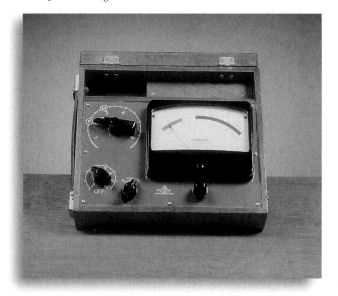

LONDON CONGRESS ON DISSEMINATION AND HELP
LONDON, ENGLAND

These lectures were given at a two-day congress with the theme of "dissemination and help," sponsored by the London Scientology organizations. (To be released by Golden Era Productions.)

FIRST SAINT HILL ADVANCED CLINICAL COURSE LECTURES
SUSSEX, ENGLAND

The lectures given at the first ACC delivered at Saint Hill Manor included discussion of the sixth and seventh dynamics and the use of the E-Meter in clearing. (To be released by Golden Era Productions.)

AUDIBLE E-METER

This meter, on which reads were heard rather than seen, was developed for use by the blind. Several prototypes of this meter were made, the first in the early 1960s.

ISSUES

ANATOMY OF THE HUMAN MIND CONGRESS LECTURES
WASHINGTON, DC

At the end of 1960, Mr. Hubbard traveled from South Africa to Washington, DC, to deliver this congress on 31 December and 1 January 1961. (Available from Golden Era Productions.)

31 Dec   The Genus of Dianetics and Scientology

31 Dec   The Things of Scientology

1 Jan   The Whole Answer to the Problems of the Mind

1 Jan   The Field of Scientology

1 Jan   Scientology Organizations

1961

1961 began with Mr. Hubbard in Washington, DC, delivering the Anatomy of the Human Mind Course and the Twenty-second American Advanced Clinical Course. Before the end of March he had traveled first to Saint Hill and from there to Johannesburg, South Africa, where he delivered more than twenty lectures and released a new organizational chart for use in Scientology organizations.

Certainly one of the most major events of 1961, though, was the opening of the most comprehensive, exhaustive auditor training course ever—the Saint Hill Special Briefing Course. Inaugurated on the 24th of March at Saint Hill Manor, this course rapidly became known the world over as the course where truly expert auditors were made.

TWENTY-SECOND AMERICAN ADVANCED CLINICAL COURSE LECTURES

WASHINGTON, DC

(To be released by Golden Era Productions.)

2 Jan   Why Cases Don't Move, Part I

2 Jan   Why Cases Don't Move, Part II

3 Jan   E-Meter

3 Jan   Withholds

4 Jan   The Mechanics of the Reactive Bank

4 Jan   Clearing Procedure

5 Jan   Dianetics and Present Time Problems

5 Jan   Methods of Clearing Technology—Finding of Havingness and Confront Processes

6 Jan   Dianetic Assist and Presession 38

6 Jan   Clearing Routine

ISSUES

HCO PL   4 Jan I   Urgent Mimeo Change

HCO PL   9 Jan   Duties of HCO

HCO PL 10 Jan   A Brief Outline of an HGC as Currently Done

HCOB   12 Jan   New Help Data

HCO PL 16 Jan I   Help Me Put in the New Lines

HCO PL 16 Jan II   New Road

HCOB   19 Jan   Additional HAS Processes

ANATOMY CONGRESS LECTURES

JOHANNESBURG, SOUTH AFRICA

The content and method of delivery of the Anatomy of the Human Mind Course was the key topic of the lectures at this congress. (To be released by Golden Era Productions.)

21 Jan   Opening Lecture

21 Jan   The Parts of the Mind

21 Jan   Aberration and the Handling Of

22 Jan   Evolution of Early Research—Prehav Scale

22 Jan   Things of Scientology: Cycle of Action, Time Track, Stable Datum

22 Jan   Clearing Certs for Clears

THIRD SOUTH AFRICAN ADVANCED CLINICAL COURSE LECTURES

JOHANNESBURG, SOUTH AFRICA

(Reproduced by Golden Era Productions for auditors learning to audit the South African Rundown.)

23 Jan   HAS Co-audit Processes and E-Meter

24 Jan   Presession 38

25 Jan   Model Session Revised

26 Jan   Difference Between Dianetics and Scientology—Presession 38

27 Jan   Creative Ability

2 Feb   Auditor Failures

3 Feb   Regimen and Prehavingness—Advances

6 Feb   Making Formulas Out of the Prehav Scale

7 Feb   What Are You Auditing?

8 Feb   Case Behavior Under Processing

9 Feb   Mental Healing: Sanity and Insanity

10 Feb   Organization Lines

13 Feb   The Three Therapies of Earth

14 Feb   Fundamentals of Auditing

15 Feb   Havingness and Confront Scales

16 Feb   Machines and Havingness

17 Feb   Case Conditions

ISSUES

HCO PL 23 Jan   PE Course Abolished

HCO PL 24 Jan   A Test Policy on MD Referrals

HCOB   25 Jan   Handling of Rudiments

HCOB   26 Jan   The "Ultimate" Processes

HCOB   28 Jan   New Assessment Scale

HCO PL 30 Jan II   Case Files

HCO PL 31 Jan I   Spheres of Influence

HCO PL 31 Jan II   Message Placement

HCO PL 31 Jan III   Academy Meters

ARTICLE

ABILITY 125   Feb   Personal Integrity

ISSUES

HCOB   2 Feb I   Command Sheet, Prehavingness Scale

HCOB   2 Feb II   UK Cases Different

HCO PL   4 Feb   Types of Letters Established

HCO PL   7 Feb   Proper Public Routing

HCOB   9 Feb   New Presession Data and Script Change

HCO PL 10 Feb   Professional Charges

HCO PL 12 Feb   Certificates and Awards Revised List

HCO PL 13 Feb   Permanent Staff Requirement Changes

HCO PL 14 Feb I   Personnel Procurement

HCO PL 14 Feb II   The Pattern of a Central Organization

HCOB   16 Feb   Formula 19

HCO PL 17 Feb I   HCO Continental

HCO PL 17 Feb II   State of Emergency

HCO INFO LETTER   18 Feb   Magazines

HCOB   18 Feb   SOP Goals, Marvelous New Breakthrough— Be-Do-Have Coordinated

HCO PL 19 Feb II   Accounts: How to Do a Payroll

HCOB   20 Feb   Important Data on Goals SOP

HCO PL 21 Feb I   Pattern for City Offices

HCO PL 21 Feb II   Choosing PE and Registration Personnel

HCO PL 22 Feb I   My Program to Raise Your Unit

HCO PL 22 Feb II   Permanent Staff Exam

HUBBARD BRITISH MARK IV E-METER

The British Mark IV E-Meter was introduced in early 1961 and by June 1961 was the only meter allowed in Academies of Scientology.

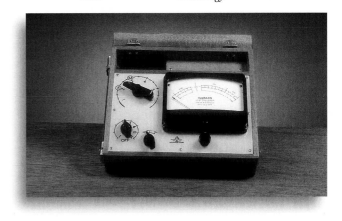

E-METER ESSENTIALS
by L. Ron Hubbard

First published by Hubbard Communications Office, Saint Hill Manor, East Grinstead, Sussex, England, May 1961. A new edition was published in 1988.

MAN FREE FROM MAN

Based on the works of L. Ron Hubbard. Published by Hubbard Communications Office, Saint Hill Manor, East Grinstead, Sussex, England, May 1961.

The following lectures, marking the beginning of the famous Saint Hill Special Briefing Course, were delivered personally by L. Ron Hubbard at Saint Hill from 1961 through 1966. During the next five and a half years, Mr. Hubbard lectured regularly to the students and personally oversaw their training so as to make them true experts who could be counted on to carry the latest technology and the highest standards of competence back to their communities. (The full set of 437 Saint Hill Special Briefing Course Lectures, from 1961 through 1966, is available from Golden Era Productions.)

SAINT HILL SPECIAL BRIEFING COURSE LECTURES
SUSSEX, ENGLAND

9 Nov Effective Auditing
14 Nov Routine 3D
15 Nov Routine 3D (cont.)
16 Nov Points in Assessing
21 Nov Running 3D
22 Nov Reading the E-Meter
23 Nov Auxiliary Prehav 3D Scale
28 Nov Havingness
29 Nov E-Meter Tips
30 Nov Parts of 3D
5 Dec Aspects of 3D
6 Dec Sec Checks Necessary
7 Dec Expectancy of 3D
12 Dec Sec Checks in Processing
13 Dec Assessing 3D
14 Dec Anatomy of Problems
19 Dec 3D Packages
20 Dec Upgrading Auditing
21 Dec Probabilities of 3D

ISSUES

HCO PL 10 May Staff Auditors
HCO PL 11 May I Student Training, Auditing Has Priority
HCOB 11 May I E-Meter Horror
HCOB 11 May II Assessment by Elimination, SOP Goals
HCOB 13 May Assessing for SOP Goals Improved
HCO PL 16 May HPA/HCA Requirement
HCOB 19 May Assessment Data
HCO PL 22 May The Only Valid Security Check
HCOB 23 May Prehav Scale Revised
SCALE May Prehavingness Scale
HCO INFO LETTER 23 May Telex From Ron to D of P London
HCO PL 24 May SOP Goals Assessments
SEC ED 24 May Responsibility for Results
HCOB 25 May Releasing and Preparing a Case for SOP Goals
HCO PL 26 May I Modification of HPA/HCA, BScn/HCS Schedule
HCO PL 26 May II Quality Counts
KSW Series 2
HCO PL 26 May III Basic Staff Auditor's Hat
HCOB 29 May Clarification of "Change Processing"
HCO PL 29 May I Quality and Admin in Central Orgs
KSW Series 3
HCO PL 29 May II Security of House
HCO PL 30 May I Current Office Work
HCO PL 30 May II How to Confess in HCO
HCOB 1 Jun Assessing
HCOB 5 Jun Processes Allowed
HCOB 7 Jun Academy Schedule, Clarification Of
HCO PL 7 Jun Orders
HCOB 8 Jun R E-Meter Watching, Are You Waiting for the Meter to Play Dixie?
Rev. 22 Feb 79

ARTICLE

ABILITY 129 Jun The Sad Tail of PDH

ISSUES

HCO PL 9 Jun Technical Hat Checking
LRH Comm N/W Series 22
HCOB 16 Jun CCHs and Routine 1
HCOB 17 Jun Primary Scale Amended
HCOB 19 Jun Sec Check Whole Track
HCOB 23 Jun Running CCHs
HCOB 27 Jun Routine One
HCO PL 29 Jun R Student Confessional List
Rev. 8 Nov 80
Confessional Form 5R

ARTICLE

ABILITY 130 Jul News News News

ISSUES

HCOB 6 Jul Routine 1A
HCO PL 7 Jul R II Auditor Confessional List
Rev. 5 Nov 80
Confessional Form 3R
HCOB 10 Jul Metering Rudiments
HCO PL 22 Jul Executives' Pay

ARTICLE

ABILITY 131 Aug Scientology's Future

ISSUES

HCO PL 4 Aug Private Mail and Telephone Calls
HCOB 10 Aug Information on Clears
HCO PL 14 Aug I City Offices
HCO PL 23 Aug HPA/HCA Policy
HCOB 23 Aug New Clearing Breakthrough!
HCOB 24 Aug Valences Key to Clearing
HCO PL 24 Aug HCO Organization, Future Plans
HCOB 31 Aug Advances in Technology
HCO PL 3 Sep HCO Vol Sec Policy Revised
HCOB 7 Sep New Facts of Life
HCO PL 12 Sep Curriculum for Clearing Courses
HCO PL 13 Sep I General Office Orders
HCO PL 13 Sep II HCO WW Security Form 7A
HCOB 14 Sep New Rudiments Commands
HCO PL 18 Sep R HCO WW Security Form 7B
Rev. 16 Mar 89
HCO PL 19 Sep Reality Test for Students
HCO PL 20 Sep Training Policy
HCO PL 21 Sep I Despatch Lines
HCO PL 21 Sep II Laundry
HCOB 21 Sep Security Check Children
HCO PL 28 Sep HCO WW Security Forms 7A and 7B
HCO PL 29 Sep HGC Allowed Processes
HCO PL 2 Oct II Mission Policies
HCO PL 5 Oct Repairs and Cleaning of My Office
HCOB 5 Oct Clean Hands Make a Happy Life

HCO PL 6 Oct Staff Clearing
HCOB 6 Oct Training of Staff Auditors
HCO PL 7 Oct Friday Cables
HCO PL 9 Oct I Academy Training
HCO PL 9 Oct Rudiments, Change In
HCO PL 9 Oct II HPA/HCA Rundown Change
HCO PL 10 Oct Problems Intensive for Staff Clearing
HCOB 12 Oct Student Practice Check
HCO PL 16 Oct Income Records
HCOB 17 Oct Problems Intensives
HCO PL 18 Oct Examinations
HCOB 19 Oct Security Questions Must Be Nulled
HCO PL 20 Oct RB Non-Scientology Staff
Rev. 11 Jan 85
HCO PL 23 Oct I E-Meters to Be Approved
HCO PL 23 Oct II HGC Preprocessing Security Check
HCO PL 23 Oct III Pay of Executives
HCO PL 25 Oct New Students Sec Check
HCOB 26 Oct Safe Auditing Table
HCO PL 27 Oct Professional Rates Restored
HCO PL 1 Nov HCO WW Security Form 5A
HCOB 2 Nov I The Prior Confusion
HCOB/PL 2 Nov II Training Quality
KSW Series 16
HCOB 7 Nov Routine 3A
HCOB 9 Nov The Problems Intensive, Use of the Prior Confusion
HCO INFO LETTER 14 Nov Routine 3D
HCO PL 14 Nov Stabilization of Clears
HCO INFO LETTER 15 Nov Add Routine 3D
HCOB 16 Nov Sec Checking
HCOB 20 Nov Routine 3D Commands
HCO PL 21 Nov I Letter Writer's Code
HCO PL 21 Nov II HGC Processing Liability
HCO PL 23 Nov I Accounts
HCOB 23 Nov I Meter Reading
HCOB 23 Nov II Auxiliary Prehav 3D Scale
COMMAND SHEET 27 Nov Routine 3D Command Sheet
COMMAND SHEET 27 Nov Routine 3D Improved Commands of 28 November 1961
HCO PL 29 Nov Classes of Auditors
COMMAND SHEET 30 Nov Routine 3D Improved Commands of 30 November 1961
HCOB 30 Nov ARC Process 1961
HCOB 3 Dec Running 3D Levels
HCO PL 6 Dec Saint Hill Training Candidates from Organizations
HCOB 7 Dec Sec Checks Vital
COMMAND SHEET 7 Dec Command Sheet for Routine 3D

HCO PL 11 Dec RB Organization Rudiments
Rev. 16 Mar 89
HCO PL 12 Dec Training Activities
HCO PL 13 Dec Extension Course Completion
HCOB 13 Dec Varying Sec Check Questions
HCOB 14 Dec Rudiments, Modernized
HCO PL 15 Dec R Rudiment Checklist for Orgs
Rev. 16 Mar 89
HCO PL 19 Dec II Saint Hill Retreads
HCO PL 20 Dec Student E-Metering
COMMAND SHEET 26 Dec Command Sheet Routine 3D
HCO PL 27 Dec Sec Checks on Staff
HCOB 28 Dec I E-Meter Electrodes, A Dissertation on Soup Cans
HCOB 28 Dec II 3D Rules of Thumb

CLEAN HANDS CONGRESS LECTURES
WASHINGTON, DC

Taking a short break from his heavy schedule of research, lectures and instruction at Saint Hill, Mr. Hubbard flew to Washington where he gave a nine-hour series of lectures on advanced auditing procedures and the technology of Scientology Confessionals. (Available from Golden Era Productions as a series entitled "Expansion of Havingness.")

30 Dec Scientology, Where We Are Going
30 Dec Auditing Perfection and Classes of Auditors
30 Dec Parts of the 3D Package
31 Dec The Goals Problem Mass
31 Dec The E-Meter and Its Use
31 Dec Havingness, Quality of Reach
1 Jan The Valence, How It Works
1 Jan Goals Package Balance of Valences and Identification
1 Jan Effectiveness and Your Effectiveness Now

1962

Mr. Hubbard's most major activity in 1962, in the area of Scientology technology, was overseeing the Saint Hill Special Briefing Course. He delivered more than 150 lectures to Briefing Course students, updating them on each research development and refinement as it was made, and inspecting and correcting their application of what they were learning.

In September, LRH took a short break from his intensive technical and administrative work at Saint Hill and flew to Washington, DC, where he delivered eight lectures in three days to delegates at the Clearing Success Congress.

HUBBARD BRITISH MARK V E-METER

The first British Mark V E-Meter became available in 1962. Its sensitivity range was greatly increased over all previous meters.

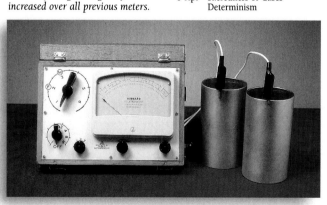

HUBBARD BRITISH MARK V E-METER

A new British Mark V E-Meter became available in 1963 with double the sensitivity of the first Mark V. The Mark IV and Mark V were both in use from 1963 through 1965. The Mark IV was discontinued in December 1965.

1963

While keeping the Saint Hill Special Briefing Course roaring ahead, LRH embarked on what he called "the most intense period of research I've yet done."

In addition to his work in the technical line, Mr. Hubbard made great strides in the field of administration—newly defining the activities of auditors and organizations across the world.

ISSUES

SAINT HILL SPECIAL
BRIEFING COURSE
LECTURES
SUSSEX, ENGLAND

ISSUES

HCO PL	6 Mar	R3M, HCO WW Form G3, Revised, Fast Goals Check
HCOB	8 Mar	Use of the Big Middle Rudiments
HCOB	9 Mar	Routine 2 and 3M, Correction to 3M Steps 13, 14
HCOB	10 Mar	Routine 2-10, 2-12, 2-12A (Also applies to Routine 3M), Vanished R/S or RR
HCO PL	12 Mar	Staff Personnel Allowance, Saint Hill
HCO PL	13 Mar	Amnesty
HCOB	13 Mar II	The End of a GPM
HCOB	14 Mar	Routine 2–Routine 3, ARC Breaks, Handing of
HCO PL	15 Mar II	Checksheet Rating System
HCOB	17 Mar	R2—R3, Corrections, Typographicals and Added Notes
HCOB	18 Mar	R2—R3, Important Data, Don't Force the Pc
HCO PL	20 Mar I	HCO WW Electric Stencil-Cutting Machine
HCO PL	20 Mar II	Self-determinism in Central Organizations
HCOB	23 Mar	Clear and OT
HCO PL	23 Mar I	Clear Test 1963, Issue II
HCO PL	23 Mar II	Policies in Force, Org /Assoc Secs, HCO Secs
HCO PL	23 Mar III	Classification of Auditors, Class II and Goals
HCO PL	29 Mar	Clear Requirement
HCOB	30 Mar	Routine 3M Simplified
HCO PL	2 Apr	Construction Information
HCOB	2 Apr	Diagrams Illustrating Tape of 28 March 1963
HCO PL	4 Apr II	Director of Training Weekly Student Interviews
HCO PL	5 Apr	Organization Students on Saint Hill Course
HCOB	6 Apr	R3M2, What You Are Trying to Do in Clearing
HCOB	8 Apr I	Routine 3M2, Listing and Nulling
HCOB	8 Apr II	Routine 3M2, Corrected Line Plots
HCO PL	11 Apr II	Emergency Library
HCO PL	13 Apr	Policy of HGCs
HCOB	13 Apr	Routine 2G, Original Routine 2, 3GA, 2-10, 2-12, 2-12A and Others Specially Adapted
HCOB	18 Apr	Routine 3M2, Directive Listing

PROFESSIONAL AUDITOR'S CONGRESS
SUSSEX, ENGLAND

On a Saturday afternoon at Saint Hill, LRH gave these two lectures to professional Scientologists and

students currently on course in the Academy of Scientology in London.

20 Apr	What Clearing Is
20 Apr	Basic Purpose

SAINT HILL SPECIAL BRIEFING COURSE LECTURES
SUSSEX, ENGLAND

2 Apr	GPM Items
4 Apr	Anatomy of the GPM
16 Apr	Top of the GPM
18 Apr	Directive Listing
23 Apr	Goals
25 Apr	Finding Goals
30 Apr	Pattern of the GPM
2 May	Running the GPM
14 May	Implant GPMs
15 May	TV Demo: Blocking Out and Dating Incidents
16 May	The Time Track
21 May	The Helatrobus Implants
22 May	TV Demo: Engram Running—Helatrobus Implant Goal
23 May	State of OT
28 May	Handling ARC Breaks
29 May	Programing Cases, Part I
30 May	Programing Cases, Part II
11 Jun	Engram Chain Running
12 Jun	ARC Straightwire
13 Jun	Levels of Case
18 Jun	Beingness
19 Jun	Summary of Modern Auditing
20 Jun	History of Psychotherapy
25 Jun	Modern Processes
26 Jun	TV Demo: Listing Assessment for Engram Running, Part I
27 Jun	TV Demo: Listing Assessment for Engram Running, Part II
9 Jul	The Free Being
10 Jul	Auditing Skills for R3R
10 Jul	Auditing Session: Preliminary Steps of R3R, Part I
10 Jul	Auditing Session: Preliminary Steps of R3R, Part II
11 Jul	ARC Breaks
16 Jul	Tips on Running R3R
17 Jul	Dating
18 Jul	Errors in Time
23 Jul	Between Lives Implants
24 Jul	ARC Breaks and the Comm Cycle
25 Jul	Comm Cycles in Auditing
6 Aug	Auditing Comm Cycles
7 Aug	R2H Fundamentals
8 Aug	R2H Assessment
14 Aug	Auditing Tips
15 Aug	The Tone Arm
20 Aug	The Itsa Line
21 Aug	The Itsa Line (cont.)
22 Aug	Project 80
27 Aug	Rightness and Wrongness
28 Aug	The Tone Arm and the Service Facsimile

29 Aug	The Service Facsimile
3 Sep	R3SC
4 Sep	How to Find a Service Facsimile
5 Sep	Service Fac Assessment
10 Sep	Destimulation of a Case
11 Sep	Service Facs and GPMs
12 Sep	Service Facsimiles
17 Sep	What You Are Auditing
18 Sep	Saint Hill Service Facsimile Handling
19 Sep	Routine 4M TA
24 Sep	Summary I
25 Sep	Summary II: Scientology 0
26 Sep	Summary III: About Level IV Auditing
15 Oct	Essentials of Auditing
16 Oct	The Itsa Maker Line
17 Oct	Level IV Auditing
21 Oct	Attack and GPMs
22 Oct	The Integration of Auditing
23 Oct	Auditing the GPM
29 Oct	Routine 4
30 Oct	R4 Case Assembly
31 Oct	R4M2 Programing
5 Nov	Three Zones of Auditing
7 Nov	Relationship of Training to OT
26 Nov	R4 Auditing
28 Nov	TV Demo: Auditing Demo with Comments by LRH
28 Nov	Seven Classifications
3 Dec	Certifications and Classifications
4 Dec	TV Demo: Basic Auditing—Lecture and Demo
5 Dec	Basic Auditing
10 Dec	Scientology Zero
12 Dec	Summary of OT Processes
31 Dec	Indicators

ISSUES

HCOB	23 Apr	Routine 3M2, Handling the GPM
HCOB	24 Apr	Routine 3M2, Tips, The Rocket Read of a Reliable Item
HCO PL	25 Apr R Rev. 29 Aug 90	Duties of a Staff Member
HCOB	25 Apr	Meter Reading TRs
HCOB	28 Apr	Routine 3, An Actual Line Plot
HCOB	29 Apr	Routine 3, Directive Listing, Listing Liabilities
HCO PL	30 Apr	The Saint Hill Staff Co-audit
HCOB	30 Apr	Routine 3
HCOB	4 May	Routine 3, An Actual Line Plot No. 2
HCOB	5 May	Routine 3, R3 Stable Data
HCOB	8 May	The Nature of Formation of the GPM
HCOB	12 May	Routine 3, RI Form (GPM RI Form Corrected)
HCOB	13 May	Routine 3, Routine 3N Directive Listing with New Routine 3 Model Session
HCO PL	15 May	Instructor Hats

HCOB	15 May	The Time Track and Engram Running by Chains, Bulletin 1
SEC ED	20 May	Scientology Missionary Hat
HCOB	20 May	Routine 3N, Proper Programing, Fast Blowing RIs
HCO PL	24 May	Changes in Basement Student Facilities
HCOB	26 May	Routine 3, Line Plot
HCOB	27 May	Cause of ARC Breaks
HCOB	1 Jun	Routine 2, New Processes
HCOB	4 Jun	Routine 3, Handling GPMs
HCOB Rev. 3 Oct 77	8 Jun R	The Time Track and Engram Running by Chains, Bulletin 2
HCO PL	10 Jun	Scientology Training, Technical Studies
HCO PL	17 Jun	Staff Clearing Program
HCO PL	18 Jun	Tape Release
HCO PL	24 Jun	Review of Departments
HCOB	24 Jun	Routine 3, Engram Running by Chains, Bulletin 3
HCOB	25 Jun	Routine 2H, ARC Breaks by Assessment
HCOB	1 Jul	Routine 3R, Bulletin 4, Preliminary Step
HCOB	5 Jul	ARC Break Assessments
HCOB	9 Jul	A Technical Summary, The Required Skills of Processing and Why
HCOB	14 Jul	Routine 3N, Line Plots
HCOB	21 Jul	Co-audit ARC Break Process
HCOB	22 Jul I	You Can Be Right
HCOB	22 Jul III	Org Technical—HGC Processes and Training
HCO PL	23 Jul	Retreads on Saint Hill Special Briefing Course
HCOB	23 Jul	Auditing Rundown, Missed Withholds, To Be Run in X1 Unit
HCOB	24 Jul	R3N Corrections
HCOB	28 Jul	Time and the Tone Arm
HCOB	29 Jul I	Scientology Review
HCOB	29 Jul II	R3R–R3N–R3T, Cautionary HCOB
HCO PL	30 Jul	Current Planning
HCO PL	2 Aug I	Public Project One
HCO PL	2 Aug II	Saint Hill Course Changes
HCOB	4 Aug	E-Meter Errors, Communication Cycle Error

AZIMUTH ALIGNMENT METER

The Azimuth Alignment Meter became available in 1965. It was a "see-through" meter—the dial being glass both front and back. This enabled an auditor to read a list through the glass dial and see the needle at the same time. It is a Mark V Meter in function.

1964

In May, Mr. Hubbard created *The Auditor*, a new magazine sent out regularly from Saint Hill to swiftly carry information on his latest technical developments as well as news of Saint Hill students and preclears.

Technical progress in 1964 included tremendous achievements in the field of education. Combining his own experiences as a student with observations made in training others, Mr. Hubbard developed Scientology Study Technology and recorded this revolutionary new tech in lectures to students on the Saint Hill Special Briefing Course.

In December of 1964, R6EW Solo auditing materials were made available at Saint Hill Manor.

SAINT HILL SPECIAL BRIEFING COURSE LECTURES

SUSSEX, ENGLAND

THE SCIENTOLOGY PIN (OR MEMBERSHIP PIN)

Worn by members of the Hubbard Association of Scientologists International, a gold lapel-sized pin of the Scientology symbol.

Following the release of the Classification, Gradation and Awareness Chart of Levels and Certificates in 1965, a series of insignia became available that could be worn to show an individual's training level and grade of release.

AUDITOR BLAZER BADGE FOR CLASS IV AUDITOR

This is a shield with two horizontal stripes across the top. The top stripe is yellow with the Roman numerals "0–IV" in red. The second stripe is black with the word "auditor" in gold. The bottom of the shield is green with a gold Scientology symbol. Below the shield is a gold banner with the words "Standard Tech" in red.

HCO PL 11 Dec — Full Table of Courses and Classification, Classification Correction

HCO PL 17 Dec — Tape Prices

HCO PL 18 Dec I — Saint Hill Org Board

HCO PL 18 Dec IV — Re: OIC Data

HCO PL 21 Dec — Address Lists to City Offices

FILMED LECTURES
[Confidential and unpublished]

Two confidential filmed lectures were given by L. Ron Hubbard at Saint Hill Manor, East Grinstead, Sussex, England on December 22, 1964. These films are now part of Grade VI. All materials of Grade VI are confidential and unpublished. TRANSLATIONS: *French, German, Italian and Spanish.*

ISSUE

HCOB 26 Dec — Routine 0A (Expanded)

FILMED LECTURES
[Confidential and unpublished]

Three confidential filmed lectures were given by L. Ron Hubbard at Saint Hill Manor, East Grinstead, Sussex, England on December 30, 1964. Two of these films are now part of Grade VI, and one is part of the Clearing Course. All materials of Grade VI and the Clearing Course are confidential and unpublished. TRANSLATIONS: *French, German, Italian and Spanish.*

Issues

HCO PL 31 Dec I — Certificates

HCO PL 31 Dec III — Use of "Dianetics," "Scientology," "Applied Philosophy"

1965

Great advances were made in Scientology technical and administrative technology in 1965.

Mr. Hubbard codified the organizational technology he had developed in building Saint Hill into a big, rapidly expanding organization and released it in a flood of new HCO Policy Letters. In fact, 1965 was one of the richest years in Scientology history in terms of policy advances and releases.

1965 was also marked by spectacular progress in auditing and training technology. The route to total freedom was fully codified, and the first Classification, Gradation and Awareness Chart of Levels and Certificates was released in May. Power Processing was also begun in May, and in September, the Clearing Course was made available to students who had completed the prerequisite auditing steps.

ARTICLES

	My Philosophy
THE AUDITOR 6 Jan	Healthy Babies

ISSUES

HCO PL 18 Jan — Financial Management, Building Fund Account

HCO PL 21 Jan R I — Vital Data on Promotion, The Fundamentals of Promotion
Rev. 5 Apr 65

HCOB 25 Jan — Definition of "Terminal"

HCO PL 28 Jan — How to Maintain Credit Standing and Solvency

HCO PL 31 Jan — Dev-T

HCO PL 7 Feb — Keeping Scientology Working
KSW Series 1

HCO PL 8 Feb — Dev-T Analysis

HCO PL 10 Feb — Ad and Book Policies

HCO PL 13 Feb I — 1965 Saint Hill Objectives

HCO PL 13 Feb II — Politics

HCO PL 14 Feb — Safeguarding Technology
KSW Series 4

HCO PL 20 Feb — Appointments and Programs

HCO PL 22 Feb I — Inspections

HCO PL 22 Feb II — HCO Area Secretary Saint Hill

HCO PL 22 Feb III — Executive Director Comm Lines

HCO PL 24 Feb — Addendum to HCO PL of 7 Sept. 63, Committees of Evidence, Scientology Jurisprudence, Administration Of

HCO PL 27 Feb — Course Pattern

HCO PL 28 Feb I — Deliver

HCO PL 28 Feb II — Course Checkouts, Twin Checking

THE BOOK OF E-METER DRILLS
by L. Ron Hubbard

First published by the Department of Publications, Worldwide, Saint Hill Manor, East Grinstead, Sussex, England, February 1965. Revised in 1996. Today published by Bridge Publications and New Era Publications.

SAINT HILL SPECIAL BRIEFING COURSE LECTURES
SUSSEX, ENGLAND

2 Mar — Technology and Hidden Standards

9 Mar — The New Organizational Structure

16 Mar — The Progress and Future of Scientology

30 Mar — ARC Breaks and Generalities

6 Apr — Org Board and Livingness

13 Apr — The Lowest Levels

27 Apr — Awareness Levels

ISSUES

HCO PL 1 Mar — General Amnesty

HCO PL 2 Mar — Purchase Order Filing

HCO EXEC LETTER 3 Mar II — What's Coming Next

HCO PL 4 Mar I — Reserved Payment Account

HCO PL 4 Mar RA II — Technical and Policy Distribution
Rev. 7 Jul 83

HCO PL 4 Mar III — HCO Secretary WW

HCO PL 5 Mar I — New Status of Honorary Awards

HCO PL 5 Mar II — Policy: Source Of

HCOB 5 Mar II — *Book of Case Remedies,* Application of Tech

HCO PL 6 Mar — Amnesty Policy

HCO PL 7 Mar RA III — Offenses and Penalties
Rev. 10 Jan 91

HCO PL 7 Mar II — Certificate Cancellation

HCO PL 8 Mar — Board Decisions, Data Evaluation, Raw Data, Judging a Situation, Selection of Key Personnel

HCOB 10 Mar — Words, Misunderstood Goofs
Word Clearing Series 14

HCO PL 13 Mar I — The Comm-Member System

HCO PL 13 Mar II — The Comm-Member System, Routing Policies Section

HCO PL 13 Mar III — The Structure of Organization, What Is Policy?

SEC ED 13 Mar — Registrar Success

HCO PL 15 Mar I — Registrars, CF and Address

HCO PL 17 Mar I — Clearing and Training

HCO PL 17 Mar II — Rights of a Staff Member, Students and Preclears to Justice

HCO PL 17 Mar III — Administering Justice

HCO PL 17 Mar IV — Organizational Suppressive Acts

HCO EXEC LETTER 18 Mar — Justice

HCO EXEC LETTER 21 Mar — PE Comes After They Have Read a Book

HCO PL 21 Mar — Staff Members Auditing Outside Pcs

HCO PL 22 Mar — Current Promotion and Org Program Summary, Membership Rundown

HCO PL 26 Mar RA II — Field Staff Member I/C Hat
Rev. 8 Nov 84 *FSM Series 2*

HCO EXEC LETTER 27 Mar — Confused Presentation Denies Service

HCO PL 27 Mar — The Justice of Scientology, Its Use and Purpose, Being a Scientologist

HCO PL 28 Mar — Emergencies and Accounts Personnel

HCO PL 29 Mar I — Routing Despatches

HCO PL 29 Mar II — Flows and Expansion, The Fast Flow System

HCO PL 29 Mar III — Staff Regulations

POWER PROCESSING MATERIALS
[Confidential and unpublished]

Power materials were made available on 10 May 1965 to the auditors LRH was personally training on this level. They are confidential and unpublished.

ISSUES

SAINT HILL SPECIAL BRIEFING COURSE LECTURES

SUSSEX, ENGLAND

ISSUES

AUDITOR BLAZER BADGE FOR CLASS VI AUDITOR

This is a shield with two horizontal stripes across the top. The top stripe is yellow with the Roman numeral "VI" in red. The second stripe is black with the word "auditor" in gold. The bottom of the shield is blue with a gold Scientology symbol. Below the shield is a gold banner with the words "Standard Tech" in red.

THE POWER RELEASE PIN

For the preclear who has attained Grades V, VA or VI, a release pin with the S and double triangle (Scientology symbol) with the red R encircled by a gold wreath.

THE RELEASE PIN

A small lapel-sized pin. It is the Scientology symbol in gold with a red R (for Release) mounted on it. It signifies a release, Grades 0 through IV.

THE MATERIALS OF THE R6 BANK
[Confidential and unpublished]

A confidential filmed lecture that is now part of the Clearing Course, given by L. Ron Hubbard at Saint Hill Manor, East Grinstead, Sussex, England on September 3, 1965. All materials of the Clearing Course are confidential and unpublished.
TRANSLATIONS: **French, German, Italian and Spanish.**

ISSUE

CLEARING COURSE MATERIALS
[Confidential and unpublished]

The new Clearing Course materials were first presented for study on 5 September, to those eligible to receive them. They are confidential and unpublished.
TRANSLATIONS: **French, German, Italian and Spanish.**

ISSUES

SAINT HILL SPECIAL
BRIEFING COURSE
LECTURES
SUSSEX, ENGLAND

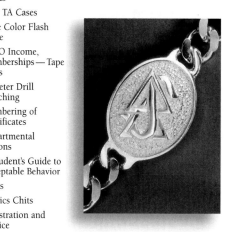

THE CLEAR BRACELET

A Clear is signified by a silver identification bracelet with the S and double triangle on it. The bracelet is sterling silver. The underside bears the word "Clear," L. Ron Hubbard's initials, the engraved name of the person, the date they were declared Clear and their Clear number.

HCO PL 28 Dec RA E-Meters Allowed
Rev. 4 Feb 91

HCO PL 30 Dec   PTS Auditing and
                 Routing

SCIENTOLOGY:
A NEW SLANT
ON LIFE
by L. Ron Hubbard

A collection of the most popular articles and essays by L. Ron Hubbard. First published by Hubbard Communications Office, Worldwide, Saint Hill Manor, East Grinstead, Sussex, England, December 1965. Today published by Bridge Publications and New Era Publications. TRANSLATIONS: Danish, Dutch, French, German, Hebrew, Italian, Portuguese and Swedish.

1966

Early in 1966, Mr. Hubbard turned over his executive duties at Saint Hill and traveled to the Canary Islands to do advanced research. In March he flew on to the southern African country of Rhodesia (since renamed Zimbabwe), where he continued his research and investigated the relationship of the individual to a large group.

Returning to Saint Hill in July, he resumed lecturing to students on the Saint Hill Special Briefing Course, completing this monumental six-year series of lectures and demonstrations in December.

Throughout this time, LRH continued researching new levels. In August, the first Operating Thetan level was released—OT I —followed by OT II in September.

In order to devote his time to lecturing and further research LRH resigned on the 1st of September from all directorships in Scientology organizations. Toward the end of the year, he was awarded his third Explorers Club flag, which he was to carry on a research expedition: the Hubbard Mediterranean Geological Survey Expedition, examining ancient Mediterranean civilizations and amplifying man's knowledge of his history.

WHAT ARE PEOPLE
FOR?
An Introduction to
Scientology

Based on the works of L. Ron Hubbard. Published by the Hubbard College of Scientology, Saint Hill Manor, East Grinstead, Sussex, England, 1966. TRANSLATION: Danish.

ISSUES

HCO PL 4 Jan I   Staff Meeting

HCO PL 4 Jan III Scientology
                   Organizations
                   Communications
                   System: Despatches

HCO PL 4 Jan RA IV Sec EDs and
Rev. 7 May 85   HCO Exec Letters
                     LRH Comm N/W
                     Series 3

HCO PL 4 Jan RA V   Personnel, Staff
Rev. 25 Mar 89   Status

HCO PL 4 Jan VI   LRH Relationships to
                   Orgs

HCO PL 6 Jan   Credit and Discounts

HCO PL 7 Jan I   Leaving Post,
                   Writing Your Hat

HCO PL 7 Jan II   Credit

HCO PL 9 Jan I   OIC Section SH

HCO PL 9 Jan II   International
                   Changes or Area
                   Changes of Address

HCO PL 9 Jan III Accounts,
                   Invalidating

HCO PL 11 Jan   Ad Council and Ad
                   Comms, Orders,
                   Issue Of

HCO PL 12 Jan   Selectees Mailing,
                   Selectee Advice
                   Packets

HCO PL 13 Jan I   Regulations for
                   Auditing of Staff and
                   Students

HCO PL 13 Jan II   Records of Bank
                   Deposits

SEC ED 13 Jan   Intern Training

HCO PL 15 Jan I   Hold the Form of
                   the Org, Don't Bring
                   About Danger
                   Conditions

HCO PL 15 Jan II   Office of the
                   Treasurer

HCO PL 16 Jan R   Danger Condition
Rev. 29 Nov 79

HCO PL 17 Jan I   Unclassed
                   Certificates, HAS,
                   HBA, HQS

HCO PL 17 Jan II   Organization Chart

SEC ED 17 Jan   Distribution Action

HCOB   19 Jan   Danger Conditions,
                   Technical Data for
                   Review Auditors

HCO PL 19 Jan I   Danger Condition,
                   Warning, the Junior
                   Who Accepts Orders
                   from Everyone

HCO PL 19 Jan RA II LRH
Rev. 7 May 84   Communicator
                     Orders
                     LRH Comm N/W
                     Series 4

HCO PL 19 Jan III Danger Condition,
                   Responsibilities of
                   Declaring

HCO PL 20 Jan II   Division 7,
                   International
                   Executive Division,
                   Offices of the HCO
                   Exec Sec and Org
                   Exec Sec Described

HCO PL 21 Jan   Executive Division

SEC ED 21 Jan   To Advisory Council
                   Worldwide

HCOB   21 Jan   S&D Errors

HCO PL 22 Jan   Division Seven

HCO PL 23 Jan   Accounting Policies
                   of Scientology
                   Companies

HCO PL 25 Jan II   Communication
                   Inspector Hat

HCO PL 26 Jan   Int Exec Div
                   Relation to Saint Hill
                   Org

SEC ED 27 Jan   Orders to HCOs

HCOB   28 Jan   Search and
                   Discovery Data, How
                   a Suppressive
                   Becomes One

HCO PL 30 Jan RA I Org LRH
Rev. 7 May 84   Communicator
                    Reports to LRH
                    Comm Int
                    LRH Comm N/W
                    Series 5

HCO PL 30 Jan II   Minimum Personnel
                   of an Org

HCO PL 30 Jan III Accounts Procedures

HCO PL 30 Jan IV   Check Signing
                   Procedure

HCO PL 1 Feb I   Staff Auditor and
                   Supervisor
                   Procurement

HCO PL 1 Feb II   Danger Conditions,
                   Inspections by
                   Executive
                   Secretaries, How to
                   Do Them

HCO PL 1 Feb III HGC Cure, Intern
                   Training and Staff
                   Auditors

HCO PL 1 Feb IV   Statistics, Actions
                   to Take, Statistic
                   Changes

ARTICLE

CERTAINTY 2 Feb Psychotics
VOL. 13, NO. 2

ISSUES

HCO PL 3 Feb I   Legal, Tax,
                   Accountant and
                   Solicitor, Mail and
                   Legal Officer

HCO PL 3 Feb II   Clearing Course,
                   Submission of
                   Folders

HCO PL 3 Feb IV   Sec ED, Change in
                   Issue and Use

HCO PL 3 Feb V   Sec EDs, Definition
                   and Purpose

HCOB   5 Feb I   S and D Warning

HCOB   5 Feb II   "Letting the Pc Itsa,"
                  The Properly Trained
                  Auditor
                  Basic Auditing Series 8

HCOB   9 Feb   Release Grades

HCO PL 10 Feb I   Checksheets, Course

HCO PL 10 Feb R II Tech Recovery
Rev. 22 Feb 79

HCO PL 10 Feb III Bonuses for Service
                   Delivery

HCOB 11 Feb R   Free Needles, How
Rev. 22 Feb 79   to Get Them on a Pc

HCO PL 11 Feb   Shipping Charges

HCOB 12 Feb   The "Dangerous
                  Auditor"

HCO PL 13 Feb I   Personnel Control
                   Officer

HCO PL 13 Feb II   Sec EDs, Sec ED
                   Okay (Continued),
                   Policy Letter
                   Changes and Origins

HCO PL 14 Feb   Doctor Title
                   Abolished

HCO PL 15 Feb I   Attacks on
                   Scientology

HCO PL 16 Feb   Invoice Routing

HCO PL 18 Feb   Attacks on
                   Scientology
                   (Continued)

HCO PL 23 Feb   Appointments and
                   Promotions

HCO PL 24 Feb   Mail Statistic, Dir
                   Comm's Functions

HCO PL 25 Feb I   Communications
                   Functions

HCO PL 28 Feb   Danger Condition
                   Data, Why
                   Organizations Stay
                   Small

ARTICLE

CERTAINTY Mar   What Is Greatness?
VOL. 13, NO. 3

ISSUES

HCO PL 1 Mar R II Executive Division
Rev. 14 Feb 91   Organization and Its
                    Theory and Purpose

HCO PL 3 Mar I   Attacks on
                   Scientology, Sex and
                   Organizations

HCO PL 6 Mar I   Rewards and
                   Penalties, How to
                   Handle Personnel
                   and Ethics Matters

HCO PL 6 Mar II   Statistic Graphs,
                   How to Figure the
                   Scale

HCO PL 7 Mar I   HGC Cure
                   (Continued)

HCO PL 7 Mar II   Star-rates on Tech
                   and Qual Staff

HCO PL 8 Mar   High Crime
                   KSW Series 13

HCO PL 12 Mar   Board Minutes

HCO PL 13 Mar I   Orders, Precedence
                   of Personnel,
                   Titles Of

HCO PL 15 Mar   Corporate Address

SEC ED 17 Mar   Expansion of Your
                   Org

HCO PL 17 Mar   Promotion of Saint
                   Hill *Auditor* Issue
                   Frequency

ARTICLES

ABILITY 179   Times Must
          20 Mar   Change

CERTAINTY Apr   Economics
VOL. 13, NO. 4

AN INTRODUCTION TO
SCIENTOLOGY

A one-hour filmed interview with L. Ron Hubbard answering questions commonly asked about Scientology. Filmed in April 1966. Available in a colorized version on video from Golden Era Productions. TRANSLATIONS: Afrikaans, Arabic, Czechoslovakian, Danish, Dutch, Finnish, French, German, Greek, Hebrew, Hungarian, Italian, Japanese, Korean, Mandarin, Norwegian, Polish, Portuguese, Russian, Serbo-Croatian, Spanish, Swedish, Taiwanese and Urdu.

ISSUES

HCOB   3 Apr   Dianetic Auditing
                  Course

HCO PL 3 Apr   Dianetic Auditor
                  Course

HCO PL 19 Apr   Congress Policies

HCO PL 29 Apr II Policy Checkouts and E-Meter

HCO PL 3 May R Reserve Fund
Rev. 2 Feb 91

HCO PL 7 May LRH Communicator, Issue Authority Of
LRH Comm N/W Series 20

HCO PL 8 May RA LRH
Rev. 7 May 84 Communicator, No Other Hats
LRH Comm N/W Series 6

FILMED LECTURES
[Confidential and unpublished]

L. Ron Hubbard gave four confidential filmed lectures at Saint Hill Manor, East Grinstead, Sussex, England in June 1966, which are now part of the Clearing Course. All materials of the Clearing Course are confidential and unpublished. TRANSLATIONS: French, German, Italian and Spanish.

ISSUES

HCO PL 4 Jun Board of Investigation

HCO PL 7 Jun OIC Publication and Distribution

HCOB 10 Jun I S&D Commands

HCOB 10 Jun II S&D — The Missed Item

SAINT HILL SPECIAL BRIEFING COURSE LECTURES
Sussex, England

19 Jul About Rhodesia

21 Jul Dianetic Auditing

26 Jul The Classification Chart and Auditing

28 Jul Dianetic Auditing and the Mind

2 Aug Suppressives and GAEs

4 Aug Dianetics, Scientology and Society

16 Aug Releases and Clears

18 Aug Study and Intention

23 Aug Organization

25 Aug The Antisocial Personality

1 Sep Gradients and ARC

8 Sep States of Identity

1 Nov Government and Organization

29 Nov Scientology Definitions I: OT and Clear Defined

6 Dec Scientology Definitions II

13 Dec Scientology Definitions III

ISSUES

HCO PL 21 Jun Appointments, LRH Comm and Executive Secretary and Others

HCO PL 29 Jun Keep Academy Checksheets Up-to-Date

HCO PL 1 Jul Information Concerning the WW Time Machine

HCO PL 17 Jul I Despatches, Speed Up; Despatches, Staledate

HCO PL 17 Jul II Evidence, Admissibility of, in Hearings, Boards or Committees

HCO PL 20 Jul RB Staff Status
Rev. 24 Nov 85

HCOB 20 Jul The Type Two PTS

HCO PL 21 Jul I Tech versus Qual

HCO PL 25 Jul Allocation of Quarters, Arrangement of Desks and Equipment

HCO PL 27 Jul Moving

HCO PL 31 Jul R Refund Notice
Rev. 28 Jan 91

HCO PL 1 Aug I Sign-ups and Discounts

HCO PL 1 Aug II Refund Addition

HCO PL 2 Aug I Graph Change, Ad Council Statistic

HCO PL 2 Aug II Dianetic Auditing

HCO PL 4 Aug Clears, Invalidation Of

HCO PL 5 Aug I Registered Mail

HCO PL 5 Aug RA II Chaplain's
Rev. 7 Dec 88 Court, Civil Hearings

SEC ED 5 Aug Successes of Scientology

HCO PL 8 Aug OT Color Flash, Color Flash Addition

HCOB 10 Aug Errors of Students

HCO PL 10 Aug Executive Director Sec EDs

HCO PL 11 Aug Lamps and Security

OT I MATERIALS
[Confidential and unpublished]

On 14 August 1966, the confidential and unpublished materials of OT I, a Solo-audited action, were made available to those who met the requirements to study it.

ISSUES

HCO PL 15 Aug I Information Packets

HCO PL 15 Aug II Ethics Orders

HCO PL 16 Aug II Clearing Course Security

HCO PL 17 Aug Routing and Handling of SHSBC Students

HCO PL 22 Aug I Dead File: Restoration to Good Standing

HCOB 22 Aug Floating Needles, Listing Processes

HCOB 23 Aug Service Facsimile

INTRODUCING THE E-METER
by L. Ron Hubbard

Published by the Hubbard College of Scientology, Saint Hill Manor, East Grinstead, Sussex, England, September 1966. Revised in 1988. TRANSLATIONS: Danish, Dutch, French, German, Italian, Spanish and Swedish.

OT II MATERIALS
[Confidential and unpublished]

In September 1966, the confidential and unpublished materials for OT II were made available for study to Solo auditors who had successfully completed OT I and who met the requirements for beginning the level. TRANSLATIONS: French, German, Italian and Spanish.

ISSUES

HCO PL 1 Sep RA Founder
Rev. 8 May 73

HCO PL 6 Sep The Handling of Purchased or Rented Mailing Lists

HCO PL 9 Sep Security

HCO PL 13 Sep Requirement for Termination on the SHSBC and Enrollment on Solo Course

HCOB 20 Sep Minus Scale Releases: ARC Straightwire, Dianetic

HCOB 21 Sep ARC Break Needle

HCOB 27 Sep The Antisocial Personality, the Anti-Scientologist

HCO PL 30 Sep II OT Regulations

A NEW UNDERSTANDING OF LIFE

Published by the Hubbard College of Scientology, Saint Hill Manor, East Grinstead, Sussex, England, 1966.

ISSUES

HCO PL 5 Oct Students Terminating, Leave of Absence, Blown Students

HCO EXEC 5 Oct A New Pattern of
LETTER Organization

HCO PL 6 Oct RC II Additions to
Rev. 4 Feb 91 HCO Div Account Policy

HCO PL 11 Oct Legal, Tax, Accountant and Solicitor Mail Incoming and Outgoing

HCO PL 12 Oct IV Examinations

HCO PL 12 Oct V Duration of SHSBC and Solo Course Requirements

HCO PL 13 Oct I Invoice Routing

HCO PL 13 Oct IV Advertisements, Continental Magazines and *Auditor*

HCO PL 14 Oct Clearing Course Folders

HCO PL 17 Oct II Bonuses

HCO PL 18 Oct SH Staff Auditor's Purpose

HCO PL 20 Oct I Signatures of Policy Letters

HCO PL 20 Oct II Executives and Governing Body Errors and Answers
AKH Series 1

HCO PL 21 Oct I Six-Department System

HCO PL 21 Oct II City Office System

HCO PL 21 Oct III City Office

HCO PL 21 Oct IV Evening Foundations

HCO PL 31 Oct I Actions, Executive, for Handling Disastrous Occurrences
AKH Series 2

HCO PL 31 Oct R II Job Endangerment
Rev. 5 Mar 68 Chits
AKH Series 3R

HCO PL 31 Oct III Boards of Investigation

ARTICLE

THE AUDITOR 18 What Every Auditor Should Know

ISSUES

HCO PL 1 Nov I Worldwide Organization

HCO PL 3 Nov Leadership
AKH Series 4

HCO PL 6 Nov R I Statistic
Rev. 9 Nov 79 Interpretation, Statistic Analysis
AKH Series 5R

HCO PL 6 Nov II Statistic Interpretation, Estate Statistic

HCO PL 7 Nov Clear Checkouts in Continental Orgs

HCO PL 10 Nov I Good versus Bad Management
AKH Series 6

HCO PL 16 Nov Executive Facilities, Facility Differential
AKH Series 7

HCO PL 17 Nov II Intervention
AKH Series 8

HCOB 18 Nov Rehab on Self Analysis

HCO PL 21 Nov Ideas and Compilations Branch WW

HCOB 30 Nov Assessment for Service Facsimiles

ARTICLE

THE AUDITOR 19 Dianetics,
Dec Scientology and Beyond

ISSUES

HCO PL 4 Dec Expansion, Theory of Policy
AKH Series 9

HCO PL 7 Dec RA Magazines
Rev. 5 Feb 91 Permitted All Orgs

HCO PL 12 Dec New Org Board Design (2)

HCO PL 15 Dec Financial Planning

HCO PL 16 Dec Clearing Course Regulation

LRH ED 20 Dec Tech and Qual Pre-examinations

HCO PL 21 Dec I Advisory Council

HCO PL 21 Dec II Executive Council

HCO PL 21 Dec III Office of LRH Supplies

HCO PL 23 Dec Saint Hill Income Peaks, Reinforcement of *Auditor* Promotion

HCO PL 24 Dec I How to Program an Org, Saint Hill Programs
AKH Series 10

HCO PL 24 Dec II	How to Program an Org, Corrections and Addition, Sequence of Programs Correction *AKH Series 11*	
HCO PL 26 Dec	PTS Sections, Personnel and Execs *AKH Series 12*	
HCO PL 29 Dec	Historical Precedence of Ethics	

1967

In early January, L. Ron Hubbard traveled from Saint Hill to the North African city of Tangier, Morocco to continue his research into the advanced levels of Scientology. Before his departure, he gave instructions for the formation of a special project to ensure the delivery of these and all future advanced levels. Known as the Sea Project, its purpose was to help establish bases where the research of these higher levels could be carried out. The first such base was formed at Tangier.

A short time later he traveled to Las Palmas in the Canary Islands, and the Sea Project was transformed into the Sea Organization religious order, a permanent part of the Scientology network. In November, he returned to England where he accepted delivery of a 3,200-ton vessel, the *Royal Scotman*. Later renamed the *Apollo*, it became the flagship of the Sea Organization.

Amidst all of the tremendous organizational activity of 1967, Mr. Hubbard also made many spectacular technical advances, including the discovery and resolution of one of the most major barriers to man's attainment of full spiritual freedom: OT Section III, the Wall of Fire.

THE OPERATING THETAN SYMBOL

The symbol used for OT activities is an oval O with a horizontal bar and a vertical bar down from its center to the bottom of the O. A person attaining OT VIII may have a wreath completely around the outside of the O. The OT symbol is worn on necklaces and rings.

INFORMATION FOR RELEASES
Taken from the works of L. Ron Hubbard.

Published by the Hubbard College of Scientology, Saint Hill Manor, East Grinstead, Sussex, England, 1967.

ARTICLE

THE AUDITOR 25	Dianetics: Its Relationship to Scientology	

ISSUES

HCOB	2 Jan I	Sub-Zero Releases, Examiner's Safeguard
HCOB	2 Jan II	Dating—Forbidden Words
HCO PL 17 Jan		An Open Letter to All Clears
HCOB	19 Jan	Manifestations of Engrams and Secondaries Further Defined
HCO PL 27 Jan		Clearing and OT Course Reorganization

HCO PL 12 Feb	The Responsibilities of Leaders *AKH Series 13*	
HCO PL 22 Feb I	Office of LRH	
HCO PL 22 Feb II	LRH Property, Building and Plans Branch	
HCO PL 22 Mar I	Personnel Requirement	
HCOB 22 Mar II	Alter-Is and Degraded Beings *AKH Series 14*	
HCO PL 11 Apr	Section III OT Prerequisite	

ARTICLE

ABILITY 15 Jun	Man from Mud	

ISSUES

HCO PL 25 Jun	Scientology Orgs, Tax and Balance Sheets	
HCOB 30 Jun	Evidences of an Aberrated Area	
HCO PL 24 Jul	Fixed Public Consumption of Product	

ARTICLE

THE AUDITOR 27	The Goal of Training	

ISSUES

HCO PL 11 Aug I	Second Dynamic Rules	
HCO PL 11 Aug II	Organization, Definition Of	
HCO PL 11 Aug III	OT Central Committee	
HCO PL 15 Aug I	Discipline, SPs and Admin, How Statistics Crash	
HCO PL 15 Aug II	Important Executive Action	
HCOB 19 Aug	The Supreme Test	
LRH ED 1 Sep	WW Emergency Condition	
HCO PL 6 Sep II	WW Division Reorganization	
HCO PL 8 Sep I	Statistics and Org Board Copies	
HCO PL 8 Sep II	Continental Liaison Officers at WW	
HCO PL 10 Sep	Statistic, GDS Div 6	
HCO PL 12 Sep	Post, Handling Of	
HCOB 13 Sep	Remedy B *Word Clearing Series 27*	
HCO PL 15 Sep I	Release and Clear Checkouts	
HCO PL 15 Sep II	Examiner Bonuses	
HCO PL 15 Sep III	The Supervisor's Code	
LRH ED 15 Sep	ARC Break Registrar	
HCO PL 18 Sep	Complexity and Confronting	
HCOB 18 Sep	Scales	

 RON'S JOURNAL 67

In this recorded message of 20 September, L. Ron Hubbard announced the formation of the Sea Organization and its role in safeguarding the upper end of the Bridge and bringing Scientologists up to and through those advanced levels. He also briefed Scientologists on a

technical breakthrough of extraordinary magnitude: He had successfully mapped the route through the Wall of Fire—OT III—and made it possible for others to follow. TRANSLATIONS: *French, German, Italian and Spanish.*

OT III MATERIALS
[Confidential and unpublished]

In September 1967, the confidential and unpublished materials for OT III were made available for study to those eligible to receive them. Translations: French, German, Italian and Spanish.

 AFFINITY

A twenty-minute film based on the works of L. Ron Hubbard, produced at Saint Hill Manor, East Grinstead, Sussex, England in the autumn of 1967.

ISSUES

LRH ED 20 Sep	"Failure to apply..."	
HCO PL 21 Sep I	WW Income Outgo	
HCO PL 21 Sep II	Worldwide and Saint Hill Functions Redefined	
HCO PL 21 Sep III	International Officers at WW, Alert Council	
HCO PL 23 Sep	New Post Formula, The Conditions Formulas	
HCOB 24 Sep	"The following report..."	
HCO PL 25 Sep	Grades above Clear	
HCO PL 1 Oct	Uses of Orgs *AKH Series 15*	
LRH ED 3 Oct	Special Program, Fast Academies	
HCO PL 4 Oct I	Auditor and Org Individual Stats	
HCO PL 6 Oct I	HCO Exec Sec Condition	
HCO PL 6 Oct R II Rev. 25 Sep 77	Conditions of Liability and Doubt	
HCOB 8 Oct	Clear Checks and Re-Clear Checks	
HCOB 9 Oct RA Rev. 13 Aug 87	Contact Assist	
HCOB 11 Oct	Clay Table Training	
HCO PL 12 Oct I	Operational, Definition Of	
HCO PL 12 Oct II	Sea Org Resignations	
HCO PL 12 Oct III	Charges	
HCO PL 15 Oct	*Auditor* Magazine Success	

ARTICLE

ABILITY 197 15 Oct	Politics	

ISSUES

HCO PL 16 Oct	Suppressives and the Administrator, How to Detect SPs as an Administrator *AKH Series 16*	
HCO PL 18 Oct II	WW—How to Comm to WW, Continental Liaison Officers	

HCO PL 18 Oct III	Policy and HCOB Alterations, High Crime	
HCO PL 18 Oct V	Conditions on Orgs or Divisions or Depts, Clarification	
HCO PL 18 Oct VI	Failure to Follow or Apply Condition	
HCO PL 18 Oct VII	Academy Checksheets, Supervisor Conditions	
HCO PL 19 Oct I	HCO Exec Sec Duties, Org Exec Sec Duties	
HCO PL 19 Oct II	WW Seven Divisions	
HCO PL 20 Oct I	Conditions, How to Assign *AKH Series 17*	
HCO PL 20 Oct R II Rev. 4 Mar 75	Conditions Penalties, New Employees and Persons Newly on Post	
HCO PL 23 Oct	Enemy Formula	
HCO PL 26 Oct	The Public Divisions	
LRH ED 26 Oct	Nine-Division Org	
HCOB 5 Nov	Critics of Scientology	
HCOB 9 Nov	Revision of Remedy A, Remedy B, and S and Ds *Word Clearing Series 28*	
LRH ED 9 Nov	Academy Checksheets	
HCO PL 20 Nov	Out-Tech	
HCO PL 22 Nov RA Rev. 12 Apr 83	Out-Tech *KSW Series 25*	
HCO PL 23 Nov I	Financial Lines and Legal Lines	
HCO PL 23 Nov II	Public Attacks, Legal Point	
HCOB 28 Nov	"The key S&D question..."	
LRH ED 20 Dec	Taxation	
HCO PL 22 Dec	Affluence Attainment	
HCOB 27 Dec	List Handling	
HCO PL 28 Dec	Qual Senior Datum	

1968

Closely following the release of OT III, the next three OT levels—OT IV, V and VI—were released in January of 1968.

In the interest of advancing Scientology's highest levels of spiritual attainment, Mr. Hubbard carried out his research into the upper levels of the Bridge while living aboard the flagship *Apollo*. This setting afforded him a distraction-free research environment and was an altogether logical move, given he had long been a master mariner licensed to captain any vessel in any ocean. At this time, he was also training Sea Org members in their duties as seamen and as highly effective organizational staff and executives.

Further, he was making major strides in nearly every other aspect of Scientology technology, including breakthroughs in handling the effects of drugs, study and effective education, repair of cases slowed or

stalled in auditing, precise metering and fully standardized Grades auditing and case supervision.

In the fall of 1968, Mr. Hubbard called a select group of auditors from around the world to the flagship for a course that would make them true specialists of Standard Tech—the Class VIII Course.

A TEST OF WHOLE TRACK RECALL
by L. Ron Hubbard

Limited first edition published by the Publications Organization, Worldwide, Saint Hill Manor, East Grinstead, Sussex, England, 1968. Later republished as Mission into Time, *1972.*

OT IV, V AND VI MATERIALS
[Confidential and unpublished]

In January 1968, the confidential and unpublished materials for all three levels were made available simultaneously for study to those who met the requirements for beginning one of the levels. Scientologists came to the Advanced Organization aboard the *Apollo* from around the world to obtain the spiritual gains of these OT levels.

ISSUES

HCO PL 3 Jan	Speed of Service	
HCO PL 5 Jan I	Overfilled In-Basket, Bad News	
HCO PL 5 Jan II	Conditions Orders, Executive Ethics	
HCOB 9 Jan	Money Process	
HCOB 13 Jan	S&Ds	
HCOB 16 Jan	Starting of Preclears	
HCOB 19 Jan	S&Ds, S&Ds by Button	
HCO PL 23 Jan	Orders and Responsibility	
HCO PL 28 Jan	OT WW Liaison Unit, OT Central Committee	
HCO PL 6 Feb	Organization— The Flaw	
HCO PL 7 Feb	Fast Flow and Ethics	
HCO PL 8 Feb I	Statistic Rationalization *AKH Series 18*	
HCO PL 8 Feb II	Sea Org Zones of Planning	
HCO PL 22 Feb	Ethics and Admin, Slow Admin	

ARTICLE

THE AUDITOR 34 Mar	Training and Life	

ISSUES

HCO PL 2 Mar I	Advanced Course Security Check	
HCO PL 8 Mar	Checksheets	
HCO PL 11 Mar	False Attestation	
HCOB 12 Mar	Mistakes, Anatomy Of	
HCO PL 13 Mar	Statistics	
LRH ED 13 Mar	New Qual Stat, GDS Qual Div	
HCO PL 14 Mar	Corrected Table of Conditions	
HCO PL 16 Mar	Post Changes	

HCO PL 17 Mar	"Boom Formula" Cancelled	

ARTICLE

ABILITY 207	The Bridge from Chaos to Total Freedom	

ISSUES

HCO PL 15 Apr	"To Ensure Speed and Accuracy..."	
HCOB 18 Apr	Needle Reactions above Grade IV	
LRH ED 28 Apr	"When the Success Story Stat..."	
HCO PL 28 Apr I	Standard Executive Actions	

ARTICLE

THE AUDITOR 36 May	What It Means to Be a Scientologist	

ISSUES

HCO PL 4 May	Handling Situations	
HCOB 4 May	Dianetic Courses, Stuck Pictures	
HCO PL 7 May	The Key Questions, Director of Success Duty	
HCOB 7 May R Rev. 2 Apr 90	Upper Indoc TRs	
HCO PL 9 May	Sea Organization Personnel	
HCO PL 10 May RA Rev. 7 May 84	LRH Comms Functions *LRH Comm N/W Series 7*	
HCOB 20 May	Overt–Motivator Sequence	
HCO PL 21 May	Comm Procedure over Long Distances	
HCO PL 22 May I	Hiring Personnel, Line For	
HCO PL 22 May III	Translations	
HCO PL 22 May IV	OT Section Awards	
HCO PL 23 May I	WW and SH Recombined	
HCOB 24 May	Coaching	
HCO PL 24 May	Immigration Tip	
HCO PL 26 May	Boards of Investigation and Committees of Evidence, Termination Of	
LRH ED 27 May	Minimum Book Stocks	
HCO PL 28 May I	Books	
HCO PL 30 May I	Administration *AKH Series 20*	
HCO PL 30 May II	Communication	
HCO PL 31 May I	Scientology Technology *KSW Series 29*	
HCO PL 31 May II	Auditors	
HCO PL 31 May III	LRH Comm Log	

ARTICLE

CERTAINTY Jun VOL. 15, NO. 6	Scientology and the Group	

ISSUES

HCO PL 5 Jun R III Rev. 8 Nov 84	FSM Commissions *FSM Series 4*	
HCO PL 5 Jun R II Rev. 28 Jan 80	Weekly Book Stock Report Required	
HCO PL 17 Jun	HCO Book Account	
HCO PL 18 Jun	Ethics	

THE SEA ORGANIZATION SYMBOL

The Sea Organization, founded 12 August 1967, is a religious fraternal organization of Scientologists who serve on the staff of advanced churches of Scientology.

The Sea Organization symbol is worn on cloth badges and rings. It is also worn on belt buckles, ties and other items of clothing and accessories.

The laurel wreath represents victory and has been used throughout history to crown poets, artists and champions. It not only represents the physical victory, but the series of inner victories achieved by the individual. It is associated with the head—traditional abode of the spirit.

The star is the symbol of the spirit. The five-pointed star signifies "rising up toward the point of origin."

The laurel wreath and star in combination signify the victory of the spirit. Its proper color is always gold. The star is not trapped in its victory, but is in the open field toward the top of the wreath, allowing free exit beyond its victory. The symbol is in a field of blue, symbolizing truth.

THE CLASS VIII BADGE

The Class VIII Badge is a shield with two horizontal stripes across the top with the word "auditor" and the Roman numeral "VIII." The bottom of the shield contains the Scientology symbol and beneath that the banner with the words "Standard Tech."

The Class VIII Badge is all red with gold lettering and numbering. It is given to permanent Class VIII Auditors only.

PUBLIC DIVISION 6 BADGE

The purpose of Division 6 in Scientology churches—then known as the Distribution Division and today known as the Public Divisions—is to make Scientology grow. Its symbol and the symbol worn by its personnel is the affinity-reality-communication (ARC) triangle interwoven with the symbol for infinity.

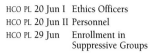

INTRODUCTION TO SCIENTOLOGY ETHICS
by L. Ron Hubbard

First published by the Publications Organization, Worldwide, Saint Hill Manor, East Grinstead, Sussex, England, July 1968. Revised and updated in 1989 and 1998. Today published by Bridge Publications and New Era Publications. TRANSLATIONS: Danish, Dutch, French, German, Hebrew, Hungarian, Italian, Japanese, Norwegian, Portuguese, Russian, Spanish and Swedish.

ARTICLE

ISSUES

THE PHOENIX LECTURES
from lectures by L. Ron Hubbard

Published by the Publications Organization, Worldwide, Saint Hill Manor, East Grinstead, Sussex, England, August 1968. (With the 1985 release of recordings of the original, complete lectures, this book is no longer in print.) TRANSLATIONS: Dutch, French, German and Swedish.

ISSUES

ARTICLE

ISSUES

CLASS VIII COURSE LECTURES
[Confidential and unpublished]
SEA ORGANIZATION FLAGSHIP APOLLO

In September of 1968, a select group of auditors from Scientology organizations around the world were called to the Sea Organization's flagship *Apollo* for what was to be the toughest, most exacting technical course in Scientology history: the Class VIII Course. In a series of nineteen lectures, Mr. Hubbard delineated exactly what *standard* Scientology technology is, the spectacular results it invariably achieves, and precisely how, as Class VIIIs, course graduates would

put it in and keep it in. The lectures are today an integral part of Class VIII Auditor training. (These confidential and unpublished tapes are available for listening only on the Class VIII Auditor Course.)

HUBBARD DIANETICS AUDITOR'S COURSE TEXTBOOK
Compiled from the works of L. Ron Hubbard

Published by the Publications Organization Worldwide, Edinburgh, Scotland, 1968.

ISSUES

ARTICLE

ISSUES

ARTICLE

ISSUES

HCO PL 24 Oct III Supervisor Know-How, R-factor to Students

HCO PL 24 Oct IV Supervisor Know-How, Tips in Handling Students

HCO PL 25 Oct Admin Know-How *AKH Series 21*

HCO PL 26 Oct Executive Council

HCO PL 28 Oct I Press Releases

HCO PL 28 Oct II Classified Materials

HCO PL 29 Oct I Class VIII C/S Qual Stat

HCOB 1 Nov I High TA

HCOB 1 Nov II Overt–Motivator Definitions

HCOB 2 Nov R Case Supervisor, Class VIII, The Basic Processes
Rev. 31 Jan 75

HCO PL 5 Nov R Space Allocation
Rev. 8 Feb 89

HCOB 9 Nov Clearing Commands, All Levels

HCO PL 9 Nov Standard Admin

LRH ED 9 Nov Standard Admin

HCO PL 12 Nov R The Main Weakness
Rev. 11 Jan 89

LRH ED 16 Nov A Fable

HCO PL 17 Nov The Action Affluence Formula

HCO PL 21 Nov I Senior Policy

HCO PL 21 Nov II Photo Policy for Magazines

HCO PL 24 Nov II The Group Officer

HCO PL 26 Nov The Original *Auditor* Journal Policy

LRH ED 29 Nov The War

HCO PL 30 Nov OT Central Committee

HCO PL 2 Dec Gung-ho Groups

HCO PL 3 Dec Gung-ho Groups Policy Letter #2

HCOB 5 Dec Unresolving Cases

HCO PL 6 Dec Qualifications Check 7A

LRH ED 8 Dec Scarcity of Trained Auditors

HCO PL 9 Dec Qual Has No Backlog

HCOB 10 Dec Correction

LRH ED 11 Dec Services, Illegal Offering

LRH ED 13 Dec The Great "Charity" Swindle

HCOB 15 Dec RB L4BRB, For Assessment of All Listing Errors
Rev. 28 Apr 89

HCO PL 16 Dec Security Div 1

HCO PL 23 Dec Good Service

HCOB 26 Dec I The Third Party Law

HCO PL 26 Dec II Gung-ho Group Tech

HCO PL 30 Dec The Public Programs Officer

1969

While continuing to work closely with Sea Org officers and crew to expand Scientology across the world, Mr. Hubbard's work on technical matters remained at its usual rapid pace.

Major advances were made in the area of Dianetics auditing and case supervision, restoring this vital technology to full use and streamlining its application.

Handling the harmful effects of drug use was also an area that received LRH's attention in 1969, with new procedures developed to solve the underlying causes of drug use and relieve its harmful effects.

ARTICLES

THE AUDITOR 44 Jan Start a Scientology Group in Your Area

THE AUDITOR 44 Jan The Value of Scientology

ISSUES

HCOB 5 Jan R Unresolving Cases, Additional Note
Rev. 13 Jan 89

HCOB 8 Jan Drugs and "Insanity" Noncompliance and Alter-Is

HCO PL 12 Jan High Ethics for High Conditions

HCO PL 13 Jan Unusual Favors

HCO PL 14 Jan I OT Orgs
Target Series 1

HCO PL 14 Jan II Spectatorism

HCO PL 16 Jan Targets, Types Of
Target Series 2

HCO PL 18 Jan II Planning and Targets
Target Series 3

LRH ED 20 Jan A Vital Target, Trained Auditor Program

HCO PL 24 Jan I Target Types
Target Series 4

HCO PL 24 Jan II Purpose and Targets
Target Series 5

HCOB/PL 25 Jan Targets and Computers
Computer Series 2
Target Series 6

HCO PL 26 Jan Compliance Reports

HCO PL 27 Jan Dev-T Summary List

HCO PL 30 Jan I Public Divisions Org Board

HCO PL 30 Jan R II Dev-T Summary List Additions
Rev. 21 Oct 80

HCO PL 31 Jan Humanitarian Objective and Gung-ho Groups

HCOB 3 Feb Triple Grades, Flows

HCO PL 3 Feb Public Image

HCO PL 5 Feb R I Code of a Scientologist
Rev. 15 May 73

HCO PL 5 Feb II PRO Actions
PR Series 35

HCO PL 5 Feb III Double Hats

HCOB 9 Feb Research Notes

LRH ED 9 Feb Organizational Intention

HCO PL 12 Feb Religion

HCO PL 13 Feb Ethics Protection, Conditions, Blue Star, Green Star, Gold Star

HCO PL 24 Feb Justice

ARTICLES

FREEDOM 27 Feb A Reason Psychiatric Front Groups Attack Scientology

FREEDOM 27 Feb Druidism and Psychiatry

ISSUE

HCOB 28 Feb Medical Doctors

ARTICLES

FREEDOM 1 Mar Fast Justice

FREEDOM 1 Mar Patriotism

FREEDOM 1 Mar Economics—War and Tax

FREEDOM 1 Mar Today's Terrorism

FREEDOM 3 Mar On Writing to Governments

ISSUES

HCOB 3 Mar Case Gain, Completing Levels
KSW Series 32

HCO PL 7 Mar Organization

ARTICLES

FREEDOM 11 Mar Brainwashing

FREEDOM 11 Mar British "Justice" and Evidence

ISSUES

HCOB 12 Mar II Physically Ill Pcs and Pre-OTs

HCO PL 15 Mar I Third Party, How to Find One

HCOB 17 Mar I Politics

HCOB 17 Mar R II Summary Report Form
Rev. 12 Nov 87
Auditor Admin Series 12RA

ARTICLES

FREEDOM 19 Mar Riots

FREEDOM Mar A Paper on the Difficulties of Researching in the Humanities, A Summary on Scientology for Scientists

ISSUES

HCOB 2 Apr RA Dianetic Assists
Rev. 28 Jul 78

HCO 4 Apr Ron's Journal 1969
INFO LETTER NO. 3, Political Treatment

HCOB 5 Apr New Preclears

HCOB 6 Apr I Fundamental Auditing

HCOB 6 Apr II Dianetics Course Auditing Requirements

HCO PL 6 Apr Dianetics

HCO PL 7 Apr Org Reduction or Eradication

HCOB 17 Apr R I Dianetic Case Supervision
Rev. 25 Jul 78

HCOB 17 Apr II Dianetic Case Failures

HCO PL 20 Apr II Hats, Not Wearing

HCOB 22 Apr I Dianetics versus Scientology

HCOB 22 Apr II Somatics and OTs

HCOB 23 Apr RA I Dianetics, Basic Definitions
Rev. 20 Sep 78

HCOB 23 Apr III Past Lives

HCOB 24 Apr RA I Dianetic Use
Rev. 20 Sep 78

HCOB 24 Apr R II Dianetic Results
Rev. 20 Jul 78

HCOB 26 Apr R Somatics
Rev. 11 Jul 78

HCOB 27 Apr II Dianetic Failures

HCO PL 27 Apr Death Wish

HCOB 28 Apr R High TA in Dianetics
Rev. 20 Sep 78

HCOB 29 Apr R Assessment and Interest
Rev. 23 Apr 96

HCOB 30 Apr Auditor Trust

ARTICLES

FREEDOM 1 May Justice

THE AUDITOR 49 May The Value of Training

FREEDOM May Drug Addiction

ISSUES

HCOB 1 May Grinding Out Engrams

HCOB 7 May IV The Five GAEs

HCOB 7 May R V Floating Needle
Rev. 15 Jul 77

HCOB 7 May VI Summary of How to Write an Auditor's Report, Worksheets and Summary Report, with Some Additional Information

HCOB 8 May I Important Study Data

HCOB 8 May R II Teaching the Dianetics Course
Rev. 31 Mar 77

HCOB 9 May RA Case Supervising New Era Dianetics Folders
Rev. 21 Sep 78

HCOB 11 May R I Meter Trim Check
Rev. 8 Jul 78

HCOB 11 May R II Forcing a Pc
Rev. 12 Oct 69

ARTICLE

FREEDOM 12 May Government and Revolt

ISSUES

HCOB 13 May Peculiarities

HCOB 14 May I Sickness

HCOB 14 May III Cultural Lag

HCOB 15 May Dirty Needle

HCO PL 16 May Course Administration

HCOB 17 May TRs and Dirty Needles

HCOB 18 May R Erasure
Rev. 3 Aug 78

HCOB 19 May RB Drug and Alcohol Cases, Prior Assessing
Rev. 14 Nov 78

HCOB 20 May Keeping Dianetics Working in an Area

HCOB 21 May Assessment

HCOB 22 May Dianetics, Its Background

HCO PL 22 May Orders versus Arbitraries

HCO PL 23 May Dianetic Contract

HCOB 23 May R Auditing Out Sessions, Narrative versus Somatic Chains
Rev. 11 Jul 78

HCOB 24 May I The Difficult Case

HCOB 24 May II Dianetic High Crimes

HCOB 27 May The VIII's Nightmare

HCOB 28 May RA I How Not to
Rev. 21 Sep 78 Erase

HCOB 28 May II Dianetics and
Results, Dianetic
Counseling Groups

HCO PL 29 May Dianetic
Certificates

HCOB 6 Jun Prediction and
Consequences

HCOB 7 Jun R How to Make a
Rev. 13 Aug 87 Person Sober

HCOB 11 Jun Materials, Scarcity Of

HCO PL 12 Jun Dianetic
Registration

ARTICLES

FREEDOM 15 Jun The Bland
Personality

FREEDOM 15 Jun Control "Sciences"

FREEDOM 16 Jun How to Win an
Argument

THE AUDITOR 48 Dianetics
16 Jun

FREEDOM 16 Jun Quackery and
Fakery

ISSUE

HCO PL 17 Jun The Org Image
PR Series 36

ARTICLE

FREEDOM 23 Jun Crime &
Psychiatry

ISSUES

HCOB 28 Jun RA C/S, How to Case
Rev. 21 Sep 78 Supervise Dianetics
Folders

HCOB 16 Jul "I have made a
breakthrough..."

HCOB 17 Jul RB I New Era Dianetics
Rev. 4 Sep 78 Command Training
Drills

HCOB 17 Jul II Flagrant Auditing
Errors

ARTICLE

THE AUDITOR 50 Why Feel Guilty?
Jul

ISSUES

HCOB 19 Jul RA I Dianetics and
Rev. 21 Sep 78 Illness

HCOB 21 Jul II One-Hand
Electrodes

HCOB 22 Jul R I Auditing Speed
Rev. 20 Sep 78

HCOB 22 Jul II High TA Assessment

HCOB 23 Jul Auditor Assignment
Policies

HCOB 24 Jul R Seriously Ill Pcs
Rev. 24 Jul 78

HCOB 27 Jul Antibiotics

HCOB 29 Jul The "Art" of Case
Supervision

HCO PL 29 Jul II Course
Administration, Roll
Book

HCO PL 29 Jul III Completion of
Cycles

HCOB 2 Aug R "LX" Lists
Rev. 4 Sep 78

HCOB 3 Aug R LX2, Emotional
Rev. 22 Aug 78 Assessment List

HCOB 9 Aug R I LX1 (Conditions)
Rev. 21 Aug 78

HCOB 9 Aug RA II Case Folder
Rev. 21 Sep 78 Analysis, New Era
Dianetics

HCOB 15 Aug Flying Ruds

HCOB 16 Aug R Handling Illness in
Rev. 25 Sep 78 Scientology

ARTICLE

THE AUDITOR 23 The New
Aug Dianetics

ISSUE

HCO PL 1 Sep R Counterespionage
Rev. 24 Sep 83

ARTICLE

THE AUDITOR Standard Dianetic
2 Sep Gains

ISSUES

HCO PL 2 Sep I Old ACC Students

HCO PL 2 Sep II Triple Grades

HCO PL 2 Sep IV Failed VIIIs

HCO PL 3 Sep I Former HDAs,
HPAs

HCO PL 3 Sep II Successful Class
VIIIs

HCO PL 8 Sep The Org Exec
Course Introduction

HCO PL 9 Sep R How to Study This
Rev. 17 Jun 85 Course

LRH ED 11 Sep Org Affluences

HCO PL 14 Sep The Key Ingredients
AKH Series 22

HCOB 19 Sep Study Slowness

HCO PL 20 Sep Stability

HCO PL 21 Sep Staff Training Officer

ARTICLES

FREEDOM 24 Sep The Fight for
Freedom

FREEDOM 24 Sep "Cult"

FREEDOM 25 Sep Drug Problems

FREEDOM 25 Sep Tangled Terms

FREEDOM 26 Sep Being Good

FREEDOM 26 Sep The Road Out

FREEDOM 29 Sep Student Victims

ISSUES

HCO PL 4 Oct Organizational
Enturbulence

HCO PL 5 Oct R I Dianetic Courses,
Rev. 10 Dec 69 Wildcat

HCO PL 5 Oct II The Rehabilitation
of Artists

HCOB 5 Oct I Triple Flows

ARTICLE

THE AUDITOR Scientology, The
11 Oct Senior Science

ISSUES

HCO PL 7 Oct Fundamentals of
Administration No. 2

HCO PL 9 Oct Publications Depts
and Orgs, How to
Straighten Out

HCO PL 10 Oct R Downstat Causes
Rev. 13 Feb 91

HCO PL 12 Oct Dianetic Triples
Plural Item

HCO PL 16 Oct Finance Course,
Vital Action

HCOB 17 Oct RB Drugs, Aspirin and
Rev. 8 Apr 88 Tranquilizers

HCO PL 27 Oct I Dev-T
AKH Series 23

ARTICLE

FREEDOM 30 Oct Cultural
Destruction

ISSUES

HCO PL 4 Nov Dev-T Graphed

HCOB 5 Nov R V LX3 (Attitudes)
Rev. 4 Sep 78

HCO PL 8 Nov Tech Services

ARTICLE

FREEDOM 9 Nov Too Many Enemies

ISSUES

HCO PL 10 Nov I FSM Awards

HCO PL 11 Nov I Accounts and PRO
PR Series 37

HCO PL 11 Nov II Promotion and
Motivation

HCO PL 11 Nov III Mission Promotion
Musts

HCO PL 12 Nov Appearance and PRO
PR Series 38

HCO PL 13 Nov I Internships and Case
Supervisors

HCOB 14 Nov Medical Charts

HCOB 15 Nov R I Case Supervision,
Rev. 27 Jul 78 Auditing and Results

HCOB 15 Nov II Case Supervision,
How It Goes
Nonstandard

ARTICLES

FREEDOM 15 Nov Old-Fashioned
Holdovers

FREEDOM 15 Nov A Champion

ISSUES

HCO PL 18 Nov I Central Files, Value
Of — The Gross
Income of the Org
and Why

HCO PL 18 Nov II Dianetics, Right to
Audit

HCO PL 18 Nov III Dianetics, Right to
Teach

HCO PL 23 Nov I Individuals vs.
Groups
PR Series 39

HCO PL 23 Nov II Allowed Technical
Services

LRH ED 23 Nov Reform Mailing
Result

LRH ED 23 Nov Ethics Program No. 1

HCOB 23 Nov RB III Student
Rev. 4 Sep 78 Rescue Intensive

ARTICLES

FREEDOM 25 Nov The Evolution of
Totalitarianism

FREEDOM 25 Nov False Reports

ISSUES

LRH ED 25 Nov Registration

LRH ED 29 Nov Org Services

HCOB 2 Dec Rising TA

HCO PL 2 Dec R Freeloaders
Rev. 17 Jan 91

HCO PL 3 Dec II Issue Authority for
Translations of
Dianetics and
Scientology
Materials

HCO PL 7 Dec I Ethics, the Design Of

HCO PL 7 Dec II The Ethics Officer,
His Character

HCO PL 7 Dec III More on Staff
Member Reports

LRH ED 9 Dec RA Organization
Rev. 8 Jan 91 Program No. 1

HCO PL 9 Dec I How to Prevent an
Ethics Officer from
Doing His Job

HCO PL 9 Dec R II Purchasing from
Rev. 27 Mar 78 Pubs Org

HCO PL 10 Dec Superior Service
Image

HCO PL 11 Dec R I Appearances in
Rev. 16 Sep 88 Public Divs
PR Series 40

HCO PL 11 Dec RB II Training of Clears
Rev. 25 Mar 89

HCO PL 13 Dec Post Transfers

LRH ED 14 Dec Magazines

HCO PL 15 Dec II Orders, Query Of

LRH ED 16 Dec Instant Service
Project

LRH ED 16 Dec Org Image Program
No. 1 US

LRH ED 20 Dec How to Raise Stats

A SUMMARY ON SCIENTOLOGY FOR SCIENTISTS

An article by L. Ron Hubbard

Published by the Church of Scientology of California (Worldwide) Saint Hill Manor, East Grinstead, Sussex, England, 1969.

HOW TO SAVE YOUR MARRIAGE

Taken from the works of L. Ron Hubbard.

Published by Scientology Publications Organization, Copenhagen, Denmark, 1969.

THE BEST OF THE AUDITOR

A collection of articles by L. Ron Hubbard from THE AUDITOR magazine, published by the American Saint Hill Organization, Los Angeles, California, 1969.

DIANETICS CASE HISTORIES BOOK

Staff compiled, published by the Sea Organization, Division 5 Flag, late 1969.

REALITY

A film based on the works of L. Ron Hubbard, produced in Copenhagen, Denmark, in 1969.

1970

Working aboard the Sea Organization flagship *Apollo*, Mr. Hubbard continued to research intensively in the administrative and technical fields.

Having developed a successful and standard system of organization form and function, he turned to streamlining the technology of management. He released the highly workable principles and systems he evolved in series of policy letters covering the handling of logic, personnel, organization and public relations—the first Management Series policy letters.

On the technical front, Mr. Hubbard resolved the mystery of the difficulties sometimes encountered by preclears after exteriorizing and released the technology to handle them—the new Interiorization Rundown. He also began writing series of technical bulletins covering the technologies of case supervision and Word Clearing. And in September 1970, OT VII was released.

FREEDOM

Based on the works of L. Ron Hubbard, this twenty-minute film was produced in Los Angeles, California in 1970. The film includes a demonstration of Dianetics auditing.

ISSUES

HCOB	3 Jan	Triple Errors in Dianetics
LRH ED	14 Jan	Solvency
HCOB	15 Jan I	The Uses of Auditing
HCOB	15 Jan II	Handling with Auditing *KSW Series 17*
LRH ED	17 Jan	The Uses of Auditing, Handling with Auditing, Registrar Advice Form
HCO PL	18 Jan	"The following is a letter..."
HCOB	19 Jan	Registrar's Advice Form
HCO PL	24 Jan	Tech/Admin Ratio
HCOB	29 Jan	Null Lists in Dianetics
HCOB	31 Jan	Withholds, Other People's

ARTICLES

FREEDOM		Failures
THE AUDITOR 51		What Your Donations Buy
THE AUDITOR 51		Dianetics Versus Scientology

ISSUES

HCO PL 4 Feb RA Rev. 28 Jan 91		Pc Application Form for Any Major Auditing Action
HCOB	4 Feb	Pc Application for Major Actions
HCO PL	5 Feb	Statistics, Management By
HCO PL	7 Feb	HCO Makes the Org
HCO PL	9 Feb	Statistical Judgment
HCO PL 10 Feb RA I Rev. 7 Jan 91		Mission, Multiple Ownership
HCO PL 12 Feb RB I Rev. 7 May 84		LRH Comm and HCO ES Responsibility for Lines *LRH Comm N/W Series 8*
HCO PL 12 Feb II		EC WW, Primary Duties Of
HCOB	13 Feb	High TA, *Full Handling Of*
LRH ED	17 Feb	Stat Recovery, an Analysis of Broad Outnesses
HCOB	20 Feb	Floating Needles and End Phenomena

ARTICLE

FREEDOM 20 Feb		Professional Warfare

ISSUES

HCO PL	22 Feb	Celebrity Centre
HCO PL	23 Feb	Quality of Service
HCOB	26 Feb	Standard Tech and Invalidation

ARTICLE

FREEDOM 26 Feb		A Cause of Violence

ISSUES

HCO PL	28 Feb	Field Auditors
LRH ED	1 Mar	Recruit!
HCO PL	3 Mar	How to Write an ED or Order
HCO PL 12 Mar R Rev. 20 Jan 89		Source to Cause
HCOB	15 Mar	Double Folder Danger

ARTICLE

FREEDOM 18 Mar		Civil Rights

ISSUES

HCOB	20 Mar	Ally, Definition Of
HCO PL	24 Mar	A Matter of Orders
HCOB	27 Mar II	Green Form
HCO PL	28 Mar	R6EW and Clear
HCOB	29 Mar	Auditing and Ethics
HCOB	31 Mar	Dianetic TR Notes

ARTICLE

FREEDOM		The Enemies of Scientology
HCOB	1 Apr	Ethics Program No. 1 Case Actions
HCO PL	4 Apr	Power Change Violation Repair Formula

HCO PL 7 Apr RE Rev. 27 Apr 89		Green Form
LRH ED	8 Apr	Flag Executive Briefing Course
HCOB	8 Apr	GF 40 Handling – Clarification

ISSUES

HCO PL	9 Apr	Conference Hats
HCO PL	10 Apr	Conference Planning Officer
HCOB 11 Apr R Rev. 23 Sep 78		Auditing Past Exterior *Int RD Series 6*
HCO PL	11 Apr I	Third Dynamic Tech
HCO PL	11 Apr II	Review Complete?
HCOB/PL	16 Apr	Arbitraries
HCO PL	16 Apr I	Morale
HCO PL	17 Apr I	Department 1
HCO PL	17 Apr II	An Auditor and "The Mind's Protection"
HCO PL	18 Apr I	Ethics and Missions
LRH ED	19 Apr	Mimeo
HCO PL	21 Apr	Field Ethics
HCOB	21 Apr	2-way Comm C/Ses
HCOB 22 Apr R Rev. 2 Aug 89		Clay Table Demo Checkouts
HCO PL 22 Apr Iss. 24 May 98		Power Change Formula Additional Data
HCO PL	23 Apr	SH – UK ANZO – EU Relationships
HCO PL	25 Apr	More on Lines and Hats
HCO PL 26 Apr R Rev. 15 Mar 75		The Anatomy of Thought *Data Series 1R*
HCOB 6 May R Rev. 24 Sep 78		Blows, Auditing Past Exterior *Int RD Series 7*
HCO PL	8 May	Distraction and Noise *AKH Series 24*
HCO PL	10 May	Single Declare *KSW Series 14*
LRH ED	10 May	Lower Grades Upgraded
HCO PL	11 May	Logic *Data Series 2*
HCO PL	11 May-1	Further Illogics *Data Series 2-1*
HCO PL	12 May	Breakthroughs *Data Series 3*

AMERICAN MARK V E-METER

In 1970 the American Mark V E-Meter became available. It and the British Mark V and Azimuth Alignment Meter became the standard meters.

HCO PL 14 May Hat Checkout Sequence

HCO PL 15 May I Data and Situation Analyzing
Data Series 4

HCO PL 15 May II Information Collection
Data Series 5

HCO PL 16 May Institutional and Shock Cases, Petitions From

HCO PL 17 May R Data Systems
Rev. 16 Sep 78 *Data Series 6R*

HCO PL 18 May Familiarity
Data Series 7

HCO PL 19 May Sanity
Data Series 8

LRH ED 20 May The Ideal Org

LRH ED 21 May Fast Flow Grades Cancelled

HCO PL 23 May Errors
Data Series 9

HCOB 27 May R Unreading
Rev. 3 Dec 78 Questions and Items

HCOB 28 May Correction Lists, Use Of

HCOB 30 May R Interiorization
Rev. 23 Sep 78 Intensive, 2-way Comm
Int RD Series 3

HCO PL 30 May Cutatives
KSW Series 7

LRH ED 2 Jun Auditing Sales and Delivery Program #1

LRH ED 3 Jun What Was Wrong

LRH ED 3 Jun Orders to Divisions for Immediate Compliance

HCOB 5 Jun Triple Grades

LRH ED 6 Jun SH Pcs

HCO PL 8 Jun RC II Student Auditing
Rev. 11 Jan 85

HCOB 8 Jun Low TA Handling

HCO PL 10 Jun Public Divisions and Tech/Admin Ratio

LRH ED 11 Jun Auditing Mystery Solved

HCOB 12 Jun Programing of Cases
C/S Series 2

HCOB 13 Jun I Session Priorities, Repair Programs and Their Priority
C/S Series 3

HCOB 13 Jun II Hubbard Consultant, Study Stress Analysis

HCOB 14 Jun The Return Program
C/S Series 4

HCOB 15 Jun Repair Example
C/S Series 5

HCOB 16 Jun What the C/S Is Doing
C/S Series 6
KSW Series 20

HCOB 17 Jun RA Triple/Quad
Rev. 7 Apr 91 Rudiments and Overts

HCO PL 17 Jun RB I Technical
Rev. 25 Oct 83 Degrades
KSW Series 5R

HCO PL 17 Jun II OIC Change, Cable Change

HCOB 19 Jun I C/S Q and A
C/S Series 7

HCOB 19 Jun II Chart of Human Evaluation
C/S Series 8

HCOB 21 Jun Superficial Actions
C/S Series 9
KSW Series 10

LRH ADDRESS
LOS ANGELES, CALIFORNIA

The Grand National Convention of Dianetics and Total Freedom was held in Los Angeles in July 1970. Shortly before the convention, Mr. Hubbard recorded a message to the delegates. He discussed the early days of Dianetics and the tremendous improvements in auditing technology made since then, including the development of Expanded Grades and standardized training.

21 Jun Expanded Grades and Training

ISSUES

HCO PL 23 Jun The Missing Scene
Data Series 10

HCOB 24 Jun Repairing a Repair
C/S Series 10

HCO PL 24 Jun I Management Cycle

HCO PL 24 Jun II Personnel Pools

HCOB 25 Jun I C/S Series 11

HCOB 25 Jun RC II Glossary of
Rev. 16 Aug 89 C/S Terms
C/S Series 12RC
KSW Series 9R

HCOB 30 Jun RA VIII Actions
Rev. 9 Apr 77 *C/S Series 13RA*

HCO PL 30 Jun The Situation
Data Series 11

HCOB 3 Jul C/Sing 2-way Comm
C/S Series 14

HCO PL 5 Jul How to Find and Establish an Ideal Scene
Data Series 12

HCO PL 6 Jul Irrationality
Data Series 13

HCO PL 7 Jul Working and Managing
Data Series 14

HCOB 14 Jul Solo Cans

HCO PL 14 Jul I Registrar Statistic

HCO PL 14 Jul II Hats, Basic and False

HCOB 15 Jul R Unresolved Pains
Rev. 17 Jul 78

HCOB 16 Jul The Psychiatrist at Work

HCO PL 20 Jul Cases and Morale of Staff

HCO PL 8 Aug Wrong Target
Data Series 15

HCO PL 13 Aug I Liabilities of PR
PR Series 1

HCO PL 13 Aug II The Missing Ingredient
PR Series 2

HCO PL 13 Aug III Wrong Publics
PR Series 3

HCOB 16 Aug R Getting the F/N to
Rev. 7 Jul 78 Examiner
C/S Series 15R

HCO PL 16 Aug Statistic Mismanagement

HCOB 20 Aug R Interiorization
Rev. 23 Sep 78 Rundown Musts
Int RD Series 8

HCOB 21 Aug Session Grading
C/S Series 16

HCOB 23 Aug R The Body
Rev. 7 Apr 91 Communication Process

HCOB 26 Aug R Incomplete Cases
Rev. 22 Sep 80 *C/S Series 17R*
KSW Series 15

LRH ED 26 Aug Case and Letter Reg Project #1

LRH ED 27 Aug Auditors Association Project in *Your* Area

LRH ED 27 Aug My Own Objectives

HCOB 28 Aug RB HC Outpoint–
Rev. 27 Jan 81 Pluspoint Lists RB

HCO PL 28 Aug I Control of Statistics

HCO PL 28 Aug R II Auditors
Rev. 16 Jan 75 Association

HCO PL 29 Aug I Personnel Transfers Can Destroy an Org
Personnel Series 1

HCO PL 29 Aug II Personnel Programing
Personnel Series 2

HCO PL 29 Aug III Recruit in Excess
Personnel Series 3

LRH ED 29 Aug Staff Training Pgm No. 2

HCO PL 30 Aug Recruiting Actions
Personnel Series 4

HCO PL 2 Sep II First Policy

LRH ED 4 Sep Gross Divisional Statistics

HCO PL 8 Sep RA Examiner's 24-
Rev. 24 Oct 75 Hour Rule

OT VII MATERIALS
[Confidential and unpublished]

On 9 September 1970, the confidential and unpublished materials for this level were made available for study to those who were eligible to receive them.

ISSUES

HCO PL 10 Sep Transferitis
Personnel Series 5

HCOB 11 Sep RI Chronic Somatic,
Rev. 7 Jul 78 Dianetic Handling Of
C/S Series 18R

HCO PL 12 Sep Training
Personnel Series 6

HCO PL 13 Sep I Hats—Vital Data
Personnel Series 7

HCO PL 13 Sep II Basic Organization
Org Series 1

HCO PL 14 Sep I Cope and Organize
Org Series 2

HCO PL 14 Sep II How to Organize an Org
Org Series 3

HCO PL 15 Sep R Executive
Rev. 25 Apr 79 Responsibility for Training Staff

HCO PL 16 Sep Ethics and Personnel
Personnel Series 8

HCO PL 17 Sep Hats

HCO PL 19 Sep I Investigatory Procedure
Data Series 16

HCO PL 19 Sep II Narrowing the Target
Data Series 17

HCO PL 19 Sep III Summary of Outpoints
Data Series 18

HCOB 21 Sep R Study Definitions
Rev. 19 Mar 91 *Study Series 1R*

HCO PL 21 Sep Cope

HCO PL 22 Sep Hats
Org Series 4
Personnel Series 9

LRH ED 22 Sep Why Orgs Sag

HCO PL 23 Sep Quarters, Policy Regarding, Historical

HCO PL 24 Sep RA Issues — Types Of
Rev. 3 Jul 77

HCO PL 26 Sep III Org Board Cutatives
Org Series 5

HCO PL 27 Sep I Cutative Prices
Org Series 6

HCO PL 30 Sep I Checksheet Format

HCO PL 30 Sep II Credit Collections Defined

HCO PL 1 Oct Hats and Counter-Effort
Org Series 7

HCO PL 3 Oct RA Stat Interpretation
Rev. 27 Aug 82

HCOB 6 Oct Folder Error Summaries
C/S Series 19

HCO PL 6 Oct I Inspection of Low Stats

HCO PL 6 Oct II "Moonlighting"
Personnel Series 10

HCOB 8 Oct Persistent F/N
C/S Series 20
KSW Series 19

HCO PL 8 Oct Organizing and Product
Org Series 8

HCO PL 9 Oct The PR Personality
PR Series 4
Personnel Series 11

HCO PL 10 Oct Utilization

HCOB 13 Oct Course Supervisor Corrections

HCO PL 13 Oct II The Real Why
Data Series 19

HCO PL 14 Oct Division Four Org Board, Ideal Scenes and Stats

HCOB 18 Oct Auditor's Stats on F/N VGI
Auditor Admin Series 17

HCOB 22 Oct II "No Overts" Cases

HCOB 26 Oct III Obnosis and the Tone Scale

HCO PL 28 Oct Organizing and Hats
Org Series 9

HCO PL 29 Oct I The Analysis of Organization by Product
Org Series 10

HCO PL 29 Oct II An Org Board

SCIENTOLOGY 0-8: THE BOOK OF BASICS
by L. Ron Hubbard

First published by the Publications Organization, Copenhagen, Denmark in 1970. Today published by Bridge Publications and New Era Publications. TRANSLATIONS: Danish, Dutch, French, German, Italian, Spanish, Hebrew and Swedish.

ISSUES

HCO PL   1 Nov I   Organization and Morale
Org Series 11

HCO PL   1 Nov II   Use of I&R Form 1

HCO PL   2 Nov II   The Theory of Scientology Organizations
Org Series 12

HCO PL   2 Nov III Responsibility

HCO PL   4 Nov R IV   Estimated Purchase Orders
Rev. 7 Feb 91

HCO PL   7 Nov   "Noise" and Organization

HCOB   10 Nov   C/S Responsibility for Training
C/S Series 21

HCO PL 13 Nov   Planning by Product
Org Series 13

HCO PL 14 Nov   The Product as an Overt Act
Org Series 14

HCO PL 15 Nov R   HCO and Confessionals
Rev. 21 Sep 74

HCO PL 18 Nov II   PR Definition
PR Series 5

HCOB/PL 20 Nov   Organization Misunderstoods
Word Clearing Series 18
Personnel Series 12
Org Series 15

HCO PL 25 Nov   Policy and Orders
Org Series 16

HCO PL 26 Nov   More Outpoints
Data Series 20

HCOB   28 Nov   Psychosis
C/S Series 22

HCO PL   1 Dec   Reality of Products
Org Series 17

HCO PL   6 Dec   Third Dynamic De-aberration
Personnel Series 13
Org Series 18

LRH ED   8 Dec   Life Repair Block

HCOB   10 Dec RA I   Clay Table Work in Training
Rev. 25 Jul 87

HCO PL 14 Dec   Group Sanity
Org Series 19
Personnel Series 14

HCO PL 16 Dec R   SH FSM Bonus Awards
Rev. 17 Apr 75

HCOB   23 Dec   Fast Courses

HCO PL 23 Dec   HCO Traffic

HCO PL 27 Dec   Hats Program Pitfalls
Personnel Series 16

HCO PL 30 Dec   Environmental Control
Org Series 20
Personnel Series 15

THE BACKGROUND AND CEREMONIES OF THE CHURCH OF SCIENTOLOGY WORLDWIDE
based on the works of L. Ron Hubbard

Published by the Church of Scientology, Worldwide, Saint Hill Manor, East Grinstead, Sussex, England, 1970. TRANSLATIONS: Danish and German.

1971

In 1971 Mr. Hubbard carried on along similar lines to the work he had done in 1970, both technically and administratively.

Lecturing to top Scientology executives on the new Flag Executive Briefing Course—the Class VIII of administrative training—he revealed new management technology to be used in administrating churches across the planet.

Continuing to refine auditing and case supervision technology, LRH added nearly 50 new HCO Bulletins to the Case Supervisor Series and polished the technology of the Interiorization Rundown to make it even more precise and effective.

Great advances were also made in the areas of study and education, with many bulletins issued on the technology of Word Clearing. These HCO Bulletins and the study tech LRH had codified in the 1960s gave Course Supervisors and Word Clearers all the tools they needed to get students flying through their training and effectively applying what they learned.

ISSUES

HCOB   2 Jan   Illegal Auditing

HCO PL 4 Jan   Competence

HCOB   4 Jan RA   Exteriorization and High TA, the Interiorization Rundown Revised
Rev. 8 Apr 91
Int RD Series 2R

HCOB   13 Jan R   Exteriorization
Rev. 24 Sep 78   *Int RD Series 9*

HCO PL 13 Jan   Exam 24-Hour Rule (Additional Information)

FLAG EXECUTIVE BRIEFING COURSE LECTURES
SEA ORGANIZATION
FLAGSHIP *APOLLO*

LRH established the Flag Executive Briefing Course in late 1970 to train Scientology executives up to full mastery of the technology of running an organization. These lectures to FEBC students form a vital part of the course, key principles of organizing

any activity and the powerful Product–Organizing Officer system. Together with the course's written materials and practical drills, these lectures make a truly competent executive, capable of expertly running and expanding any organization. (Unpublished work, not available for purchase. Can be heard by those enrolled on the Flag Executive Briefing Course.)

17 Nov   Welcome to the FEBC

18 Jan   PR Becomes a Subject

18 Jan   The Product–Org Officer System, Part I

18 Jan   The Product–Org Officer System, Part II

23 Jan   How to Post an Org

23 Jan   The Org Officer and His Resources, Part I

23 Jan   The Org Officer and His Resources, Part II

ISSUES

HCO PL 19 Jan   Duplicating Functions
Personnel Series 17
Org Series 21

HCO PL 25 Jan   Squirrel Admin
Org Series 22

HCO PL 29 Jan RA   Flag Banking Officers
Rev. 2 Feb 91   *Finance Series 1RA*

HCO PL   5 Feb VI   CF and Address Presorting

HCO PL   6 Feb I   Transferring Funds

HCOB   7 Feb R   Administrative Training Drills, Admin TRs
Rev. 11 Aug 90

LRH ED   9 Feb   Auditors Association

HCO PL   9 Feb   Executive Misbehavior

HCO PL 10 Feb I   Mimeo Files

HCO PL 10 Feb III "An I&R Form 1..."
Personnel Series 18

HCOB   10 Feb   Tech Volume and Two-way Comm

HCO PL 11 Feb RA   Policy Knowledge Function
Rev. 7 May 84   *LRH Comm N/W Series 9*

HCO PL 12 Feb   Hat Knock Off

HCO PL 13 Feb   Financial Planning Tips
Finance Series 2

HCO PL 16 Feb II   Lines and Terminals
Org Series 23

HCO PL 17 Feb RC   Basic FBO Duties
Rev. 2 Feb 91   *Finance Series 3RC*

HCO PL 17 Feb-1 RB   Handling of Bounced Checks and Refunds
Rev. 2 Feb 91   *Finance Series 3-1RB*

HCO PL 21 Feb RA   Supervisor Checkouts
Rev. 25 Jul 87

HCO PL 23 Feb   The Magic Formula

HCO PL 24 Feb   Operating at Risk

HCO PL 26 Feb I   LRH Comm Troubles
LRH Comm N/W Series 10

HCO PL 26 Feb II   Drills

HCO PL 27 Feb I   Books

HCO PL 27 Feb II   First Financial Policy

HCO PL 27 Feb RA III   LRH Comm, New Basic Duties
Rev. 7 May 84   *LRH Comm N/W Series 11*

HCO PL 27 Feb RA IV   LRH Comm Correction Form
Rev. 7 May 84   *LRH Comm N/W Series 12*

HCOB   28 Feb   Metering Reading Items
C/S Series 24

HCO PL   1 Mar RB II   Income Sources
Rev. 2 Feb 91   *Finance Series 4RB*

HCO PL   2 Mar   Mimeo Section

HCO PL   3 Mar   Star-rate Outpoints

HCO PL   4 Mar II   How to Do Theory Checkouts and Examinations

HCOB   5 Mar   The Fantastic New HGC Line
C/S Series 25
Auditor Admin Series 10

HCOB   6 Mar I   New Uses for the Green Form
C/S Series 26

HCOB   6 Mar II   Long C/Ses
C/S Series 27

HCO PL   6 Mar   Line Design, HGC Lines, an Example
Org Series 24

HCOB   7 Mar RB   Use of Quadruple Dianetics
Rev. 3 Feb 89   *C/S Series 28RB*

HCO PL   7 Mar   Handling Overloaded Posts

HCOB   8 Mar R   Case Actions, Off-Line
Rev. 25 Jul 78   *C/S Series 29R*

HCO PL   8 Mar R II   Org Officer
Rev. 22 Apr 82   *Org Series 42*

HCO PL   8 Mar I   Examiner's Form
Auditor Admin Series 11

HCO PL   9 Mar II   Posting an Org Board, How to Put an HCO There, How to Put an Org There

HCO PL 10 Mar RA I   FBO Hat
Rev. 2 Feb 91   *Finance Series 6RA*

HCO PL 10 Mar II   Establishment and the HAS
Org Series 43

HCO PL 11 Mar   Org Board and Production

HCO PL 12 Mar I   Putting an HCO There, How to Establish a Division

HCO PL 12 Mar II   Command Intention and Your Post

HCO PL 12 Mar III CO/ED Inspections

HCOB   14 Mar R   F/N Everything
Rev. 25 Jul 73

HCO PL 14 Mar   On Giving Checkouts

HCO PL 15 Mar RA II   Data Series Auditing
Rev. 21 Sep 81   *Data Series 21RA*

HCOB/PL 16 Mar R I   What Is a Course?
Rev. 29 Jan 75   *KSW Series 27*

HCO PL 16 Mar II   An Operating Standard Rule

HCO PL 16 Mar IV   Lines and Hats
Personnel Series 19
Org Series 25

THE BASIC DIANETICS PICTURE BOOK

based on the works of
L. Ron Hubbard

*Published by Publications Organization,
US. Revised in 1972 and 1991.*

THE BASIC SCIENTOLOGY PICTURE BOOK

based on the works of
L. Ron Hubbard

*First published by Publications
Organization, US. Revised in 1997.
Today published by Bridge Publications
and New Era Publications.
TRANSLATIONS: Danish, Dutch, French,
German, Hebrew, Italian, Japanese,
Norwegian, Portuguese, Spanish and
Swedish.*

1972

Early 1972 found L. Ron Hubbard aboard the flagship *Apollo*, researching, lecturing and overseeing the training of church executives and auditors who had come from around the world for the highest levels of training available.

New achievements in the fields of study and education were made, with several new methods of Word Clearing released. These included the steps needed to bring about a brand–new state: Superliteracy, the ability to comfortably and quickly take data from a page and be able at once to apply it.

BASIC STUDY MANUAL

based on the works of L. Ron Hubbard

Compiled from the works of L. Ron Hubbard by Applied Scholastics, Inc. Revised in 1990. TRANSLATIONS: *French, German, Greek, Hungarian, Italian, Norwegian, Russian and Spanish.*

ISSUES

HCOB	2 Jan	WC1 Comes First *Word Clearing Series 30*
HCOB Rev. 20 Jun 89	3 Jan R	Repairing a Case *C/S Series 69*
HCOB	7 Jan	Training and Interning Staff Auditors
HCO PL Rev. 10 Sep 88	7 Jan R II	Creating Survey Questions *Marketing Series 21 PR Series 14RA*
HCOB Rev. 24 May 98	8 Jan 72 RH II	C/S Checklist on Folders of New Students onto Advanced Courses *Solo C/S Series II RH*
HCO PL Rev. 10 Sep 90	15 Jan RC	Riches or Poverty, the Quality of the Dissem Division, a Dissem Div Checklist for Quality
LRH ED	16 Jan	Your Dissem Division
HCO PL	19 Jan	Specialization
HCOB Rev. 8 Dec 78	20 Jan R	PTS Rundown Addition
HCO PL	21 Jan	Hatting
HCO PL	22 Jan II	Personnel Programing
HCO PL	26 Jan I	Not–Dones, Half–Dones and Backlogs *Exec Series 5 AKH Series 29*
HCOB	27 Jan	Temperatures
HCO PL	31 Jan	The Why Is God *Data Series 22*
HCO PL	1 Feb II	Accounts Policing
HCO PL	3 Feb	Illegal Processing
HCOB	3 Feb	R6EW–OT III, No–Interference Area

HCO PL	6 Feb	Executive Intention *Exec Series 6*
HCOB	7 Feb III	Vitamin and Glandular Deficiency, Important Data All Levels
HCO PL Rev. 21 Oct 80	8 Feb R	Targeting of Divisional Statistics and Quotas *Exec Series 7R*
HCOB Rev. 26 Jan 77	15 Feb R	False TA, Addition 2
HCOB	16 Feb	Talking the TA Down Modified *C/S Series 74*
HCO PL	16 Feb	The Purpose of the Department of Personnel Enhancement
HCO PL	17 Feb	Proper Format and Correct Action *Data Series 23*
HCO PL	18 Feb	The Top Triangle *Exec Series 8*
LRH ED	18 Feb	Survey = Response
HCOB Rev. 25 May 80	18 Feb RA I	False TA Addition 3
HCO PL	21 Feb	Qualities at the Top
HCOB Rev. 8 Jul 74	22 Feb RA	Word Clearing Method 4 *Word Clearing Series 32RA*
HCOB	24 Feb	Word Clearing OCAs *C/S Series 71A*
HCO PL	24 Feb I	Injustice
HCO PL	24 Feb II	Estos *Esto Series 41*
HCOB	26 Feb	Word Clearing Series 15R
HCO PL Rev. 10 Sep 90	26 Feb R I	Order or Chaos, the Quality of the HCO Division, an HCO Div Checklist for Quality
HCO PL Rev. 10 Sep 90	26 Feb R II	Cause or Effect, the Quality of the Qual Division, a Qual Div Checklist for Quality
HCO PL Rev. 10 Sep 90	26 Feb R III	Sanity or Psychosis, the Quality of the Tech Division, a Tech Division Checklist for Quality
HCO PL Rev. 10 Sep 90	26 Feb RA IV	Viability or Liability, the Quality of the Treasury Division, a Treasury Div Checklist for Quality
HCO PL Rev. 10 Sep 90	26 Feb R V	Coordination or Confusion, an Exec Div Checklist for Quality
HCO PL	27 Feb	Routing *Exec Series 9*
HCO PL	29 Feb I	Correct Comm *Exec Series 10*
HCO PL Rev. 3 Nov 90	29 Feb RA II	Handling, Policy, Plans, Programs, Projects and Orders Defined *Data Series 24RA*

ESTABLISHMENT OFFICER LECTURES

SEA ORGANIZATION FLAGSHIP *APOLLO*

Delivered to Flag Executive Briefing Course students aboard the *Apollo*, this series of lectures details the Establishment Officer system, how it relates to the Product–Organizing Officer system and how Establishment Officer technology can be utilized to create rapid and stable expansion in any organization. (Unpublished work, not available for purchase. Can be heard by those enrolled on the Flag Executive Briefing Course and Establishment Officer Course.)

1 Mar	Estos Instant Hat, Part I
1 Mar	Estos Instant Hat, Part II
2 Mar	Evaluation and Handling of Personnel, Part I
2 Mar	Evaluation and Handling of Personnel, Part II
3 Mar	Handling Personnel, Part I
3 Mar	Handling Personnel, Part II
4 Mar	Hold the Form of the Org, Part I
4 Mar	Hold the Form of the Org, Part II
5 Mar	Revision of the Product–Org Officer System, Part I
5 Mar	Revision of the Product–Org Officer System, Part II
6 Mar	F/Ning Staff Members, Part I
6 Mar	F/Ning Staff Members, Part II

ISSUES

HCOB/PL	3 Mar	Exercise
HCO PL Rev. 13 Apr 72	7 Mar R I	The Establishment Officer *Esto Series 1R*
HCO PL	7 Mar II	Course Supervisors
HCO PL Rev. 2 Feb 91	9 Mar RA I	Income Flows and Pools, Principles of Money Management *Finance Series 11RA*
HCO PL	9 Mar II	Hatting the Esto *Esto Series 2*
HCO PL	9 Mar III	Dev–T and Unhattedness *Esto Series 3*
HCO PL	10 Mar	Exec Esto Hatting Duties *Esto Series 4*
HCO PL	13 Mar	Production and Establishment – Orders and Products *Esto Series 5*
HCO PL	14 Mar I	Sequence of Hatting *Esto Series 6*
HCO PL	14 Mar II	Follow Policy and Lines *Esto Series 7*
HCOB	15 Mar	Cramming *Cramming Series 9*
HCO PL	16 Mar I	Look Don't Listen *Esto Series 8*
HCO PL	16 Mar II	Stuck In *Esto Series 9*
HCO PL	16 Mar III	Finance Directives Cancelled
HCO PL	16 Mar V	What Is a Course, High Crime

HCO PL	18 Mar	Files *Esto Series 10*
HCO PL	19 Mar I	C/Sing or Auditing Without Folder Study *Auditor Admin Series 5*
HCO PL	19 Mar II	Learning to Use Data Analysis *Data Series 25*
HCO PL	20 Mar	Auditors
HCOB Rev. 24 Mar 85	22 Mar RA	Disagreement Check
HCO PL	23 Mar	Full Product Clearing Long Form *Esto Series 11*
HCO PL	27 Mar	Study
HCOB Rev. 18 Oct 86	27 Mar RD I	Student Correction List – Revised
HCOB Rev. 12 Jul 88	27 Mar RA II	Course Supervisor Correction List
HCOB Rev. 12 Jul 88	27 Mar RC III	Auditor Correction List, Auditor Recovery
LRH ED	29 Mar	Study and Tech Breakthrough
HCOB Rev. 30 May 72	30 Mar R	The Primary Correction Rundown, Revised *Study Series 5R*

EXPANDED DIANETICS LECTURES

SEA ORGANIZATION FLAGSHIP *APOLLO*

These lectures were given by L. Ron Hubbard to students he was personally training in the specialized data and advanced skills of his latest breakthrough in auditing technology, Expanded Dianetics. In addition to specifics on Expanded Dianetics procedures, he also covered vital data on misunderstood words and their handling and the importance of standard auditor administration. (Unpublished work, not available for purchase. Can be heard by those enrolled on the Expanded Dianetics Auditor Course.)

30 Mar	Expanded Dianetics
7 Apr	Expanded Dianetics and Word Clearing
7 Apr	Auditor Administration
7 Apr	Illness Breakthrough

ISSUES

HCO PL	1 Apr	Making an Executive *Esto Series 12 Exec Series 11*
HCO PL	3 Apr	Doing Work *Esto Series 13*
HCOB	3 Apr	Primary Rundown Note *Study Series 6*
HCOB Rev. 30 May 72	4 Apr R I	Primary Rundown (Revised)
HCO PL	4 Apr I	Ethics *Esto Series 14*
HCO PL	4 Apr II	Org Officers, Product Officers, Estos *Org Series 44 Esto Series 42*

HCO PL   4 Apr R III Ethics and
Rev. 21 Jun 75   Study Tech
*Word Clearing
Series 48*

HCO PL   6 Apr I Product Correction
Esto Series 15

HCO PL   6 Apr R II How to Find a
Rev. 21 Jan 91   Why on a Person
and Handle

HCOB   7 Apr RA Touch Assists,
Rev. 25 Aug 87   Correct Ones

HCO PL   9 Apr R Correct Danger
Rev. 1 Dec 79   Condition Handling

HCOB   10 Apr Pre–OTs Don't C/S
*C/S Series 75
Solo C/S Series 13*

HCOB   11 Apr Further Data on
Correct Danger
Condition Handling
Iss. 12 Aug 96
Esto Series 51

HCO PL 12 Apr Handling Danger
Conditions

HCOB   15 Apr RA Expanded
Rev. 24 Apr 91   Dianetics Series 1RA

HCOB   16 Apr R PTS RD Correction
Rev. 20 Dec 83   List

HCOB   17 Apr R C/Sing a PTS
Rev. 20 Dec 83   Rundown
C/S Series 76R

HCOB   19 Apr "Quickie" Defined
*C/S Series 77
KSW Series 8*

HCOB   20 Apr R I Suppressed Pcs
Rev. 23 Apr 91   and PTS Tech
ExDn Series 4

HCOB   20 Apr II Product Purpose and
Why and W/C Error
Correction
C/S Series 78

HCOB   24 Apr I PTS Interviews
*C/S Series 79
ExDn Series 5*

HCO PL 24 Apr I Hatting the Product
Officer of the
Division
Esto Series 16

HCO PL 24 Apr II Dones

LRH ED 24 Apr Auditor Recovery

HCOB   26 Apr The Glib Student
Study Series 8

HCO PL   2 May RA Numbering of
Rev. 29 Jun 77   Mimeo Issues

HCO PL   3 May R Ethics and
Rev. 18 Dec 77   Executives
Exec Series 12

HCOB   3 May Havingness

HCOB   4 May Six Basic Processes

HCOB   5 May R The Remedy of
Rev. 17 Jan 73   Havingness

HCOB   6 May Remedy of
Havingness – The
Process

HCOB   7 May Expanded GITA

HCOB   8 May The Importance of
Havingness

HCOB   10 May Robotism

HCO PL 12 May R PTS Personnel and
Rev. 27 Oct 82   Finance
*Exec Series 13R
Finance Series 12R
Personnel Series 25R*

HCOB/PL 13 May I Chinese School
*Study Series 4
Esto Series 17*

HCO PL 13 May II Handle

HCO PL 14 May Morale
*Exec Series 22
Esto Series 50*

HCO PL 28 May Boom Data,
Publications Basic
Function

HCO PL   3 Jun R Promotion
Rev. 2 Feb 91   Allocations
Finance Series 13R

HCOB   3 Jun RA PTS Rundown,
Rev. 8 Dec 78   Final Step

HCOB   9 Jun Grammar
*Word Clearing
Series 36*

HCOB   10 Jun I Bypassed Charge

HCOB   10 Jun RA VI The L3RH
Rev. 13 Jun 88   Rundown, Dianetic
Track Repair
NED Series 31

HCO PL 11 Jun Product Officers

HCO PL 12 Jun R Length of Time to
Rev. 24 Jun 88   Evaluate
*Esto Series 18R
Data Series 26R*

HCO PL 13 Jun Program Drill
Esto Series 19

HCO PL 15 Jun R PR Area Control,
Rev. 24 Jan 83   Three Grades of PR
PR Series 11R

HCOB   15 Jun "Dog Pcs"
C/S Series 80

HCOB   16 Jun RA Auditor's Rights
Rev. 7 Dec 76   Modified
C/S Series 81RA

HCOB   19 Jun Dinky Dictionaries
*Word Clearing
Series 37*

HCO PL 20 Jun Registrars and Notes

HCOB   21 Jun R I Method 5
Rev. 20 Feb 89   *Word Clearing
Series 38R*

HCOB   21 Jun II Method 6
*Word Clearing
Series 39*

HCOB   21 Jun III Method 7
*Word Clearing
Series 40*

HCOB   21 Jun R IV Method 8
Rev. 8 Feb 89   *Word Clearing
Series 41R*

HCO PL 24 Jun Posting
Esto Series 43

HCO PL 25 Jun Recovering Students
and Pcs

HCO PL 26 Jun Supervisor Tech
Esto Series 20

HCO PL 28 Jun Files Accuracy
Esto Series 21

HCO PL 14 Jul II Esto Failures
*Esto Series 22
Exec Series 14
Org Series 30*

HCOB   20 Jul I Primary Correction
Rundown Handling

HCOB   20 Jul II Distractive and
Additive Questions
and Orders

HCO PL 23 Jul RB The Vital Necessity
Rev. 11 Jan 91   of Hatting
*Esto Series 23RB
Exec Series 15RB
Org Series 31RB*

HCO PL 25 Jul The Form of the Org
Esto Series 24

HCO PL 27 Jul Form of the Org and
Schedules
Esto Series 25

HCO PL 28 Jul Establishing, Holding
the Form of the Org
*Esto Series 26
Exec Series 16
Org Series 32*

HCO PL   7 Aug R PR and Causation
Rev. 9 Aug 72   *PR Series 17R*

HCO PL   9 Aug Seniority of
Orders

FBDL   10 Aug Magazines

HCOB   10 Aug Dianetic HCOB,
Interest
*C/S Series 82
ExDn Series 6*

HCO PL 11 Aug I Films and Tapes
Not Prohibited

HCO PL 11 Aug II Foundation and
Day Orgs Separate

HCO PL 11 Aug R III Foundation
Rev. 4 Sep 72   Income

HCO PL 11 Aug IV Hatting Officer

HCOB   13 Aug RB Fast Flow Training
Rev. 9 Aug 90

HCOB   16 Aug Flubless C/Sing
C/S Series 84

HCOB   17 Aug RA Method 4 Notes
Rev. 14 Jan 89   *Word Clearing
Series 42RA
Tape Course Series 10R*

HCOB   18 Aug Grammar Definition
*Word Clearing
Series 43*

MISSION
INTO TIME

*Compiled by staff and published by the
Publications Organization, Los Angeles,
California, September 1972.
Re–publication of* A Test of Whole
Track Recall, *1968.*

ISSUES

HCO PL 21 Aug Effective Hatting
Esto Series 27

HCOB   2 Sep Cramming Motto
Cramming Series 10

LRH ED   7 Sep Evaluation

HCO PL   8 Sep Efficiency and Flaps

HCO PL   9 Sep I LRH Income

HCOB   13 Sep Catastrophes From
and Repair of "No
Interest" Items
*C/S Series 85
ExDn Series 7*

HCOB   14 Sep Expanded Dianetics
Case A
ExDn Series 8

HCOB   15 Sep R Expanded Dianetics
Rev. 20 May 77   Case B
ExDn Series 9R

HCOB   18 Sep Expanded Dianetics
Case C
ExDn Series 10

HCOB   19 Oct Expanded Dianetics
Case D
ExDn Series 11

HCOB   20 Oct R Expanded Dianetics
Rev. 25 Jul 77   Case E
ExDn Series 12R

HCOB   21 Oct I Expanded Dianetics
Case F
ExDn Series 13

HCOB   22 Oct R Expanded Dianetics
Rev. 25 May 77   Case G
ExDn Series 14R

HCOB   24 Oct R Expanded Dianetics
Rev. 23 May 77   Case I
ExDn Series 15R

HCOB   25 Oct R Expanded Dianetics
Rev. 11 Jun 77   Case J
ExDn Series 16R

HCOB   29 Oct R Expanded Dianetics
Rev. 23 May 77   Case K
ExDn Series 17R

HCOB   30 Oct R Expanded Dianetics
Rev. 4 Jun 77   Case L
ExDn Series 18R

HCOB   1 Nov Expanded Dianetics
Case M
ExDn Series 19

HCOB   6 Nov Illiteracy and Work
*Word Clearing
Series 44*

HCOB   8 Nov RA The Dianetic Full
Rev. 27 Oct 85   Flow Table
*Auditor Admin
Series 21RA*

HCOB   15 Nov II Students Who
Succeed

HCO PL 21 Nov I How to Handle Black
Propaganda
PR Series 18

1973

Returning to the *Apollo* after several
months in New York City where he
conducted sociological studies,
Mr. Hubbard carried out research in
the areas of vitamins and nutrition.
His discoveries during this time
formed the foundation for major
advances he would make in later
years to fully handle the effects of
drugs and other toxic substances.

ISSUES

HCOB   4 Jan Confront
Study Series 9

HCOB   20 Jan RE The Red Tag Line
Rev. 19 Apr 90   *C/S Series 86RE*

HCOB   30 Jan RE Method 9 Word
Rev. 16 May 84   Clearing the Right
Way
*Word Clearing
Series 46RE*

HCO PL   7 Feb II Mimeo Supply
Conservation

HCO PL   7 Feb III Mimeo File Folders
and Files

HCO PL   7 Feb R IV Mimeo Files
Rev. 22 Mar 73

HCOB   5 Apr Axiom 28 Amended

HCO PL 12 May RC I Post Protection,
Rev. 7 May 84   LRH Communicators
*LRH Comm N/W
Series 15*

HCO PL 25 May Supplementary
Evaluations
Data Series 27

ORGANIZATION EXECUTIVE COURSE VOLUMES 0–7

by L. Ron Hubbard

Compiled by staff between 1969 and 1972 and published for Scientology staff use, these volumes of HCO Policy Letters were first made broadly available in 1973. Published by Scientology Publications Organization, Copenhagen and Publications Organization US, Los Angeles, California. Revised in 1991.

ISSUES

L. RON HUBBARD'S PROFESSIONAL AUDITOR'S BULLETINS
(collections of bulletins issued as books)

(Note: The Professional Auditor's Bulletins written by L. Ron Hubbard are available in the Technical Bulletins *Volumes.)*

1974

The year opened with the announcement of an important technical breakthrough: the Introspection Rundown. Resulting from research and piloting in the closing months of 1973, this powerful series of audited actions locates and corrects the causes of introversion; with these factors handled the person can again extrovert, see his environment and therefore handle and control it.

In February, Mr. Hubbard formed a music and dance troupe aboard the *Apollo* which regularly performed their unique interpretations of local music for residents of the ship's Spanish and Portuguese ports of call. The troupe gained a huge following wherever they appeared and their engagements were anticipated by both fans and the local businesses that benefited from the boost they brought to the island economies. Mr. Hubbard personally instructed the musicians and dancers in artistic presentation, music, composition, sound, arranging and recording. Much of the technology he taught them is now found in the HCO Bulletins of the Art Series, contained in the *Technical Bulletins* Volumes.

THE MANAGEMENT SERIES 1970–1974
by L. Ron Hubbard

Published by Scientology Publications Organization, Copenhagen and Publications Organization US, Los Angeles, California, 1974. Contains the Data Series, Public Relations Series, Personnel Series, Organizing Series, Finance Series, Executive Series and Establishment Officer Series. Revised and expanded into two volumes in 1983 and into three volumes in 1991.

HYMN OF ASIA: AN EASTERN POEM
by L. Ron Hubbard

Published by the Publications Organization, Los Angeles, California, December 1974.

ISSUES

1975

1975 saw Mr. Hubbard move from sea to land, first to Daytona, Florida, and subsequently to Clearwater, Florida, where the Flag Land Base was established. During that period, his work yielded new developments in Dianetics auditing, E–Metering, health, nutrition and dealing with the effects of drugs, as well as further advances in Church administrative technology.

DIANETICS TODAY

Compiled by staff and published by the Publications Organization, Los Angeles, California, March 1975.

DIANETICS AND SCIENTOLOGY TECHNICAL DICTIONARY

Compiled from the works of L. Ron Hubbard, first published by the Publications Organization, Los Angeles, California, June 1975. Revised in 1987. Today published by Bridge Publications and New Era Publications.
TRANSLATION: Italian.

NEW VITALITY RUNDOWN LECTURES

Late 1975, in Daytona, Florida, Mr. Hubbard gave twenty–two lectures to a specially picked team of auditors being trained on a new and confidential auditing rundown. Designed to handle cases that have not progressed well due to suppression or other factors, the New Vitality Rundown is delivered at the Flag Service Organization by auditors trained on the precise technology given in these lectures. (Not available for purchase. Unpublished work, limited to Flag staff enrolled on the New Vitality Rundown Auditor Course.)

1976

At the end of 1975, while living in Dunedin, Florida, Mr. Hubbard engaged in a program to promote ecumenical unity. During this period he recorded and broadcast on radio, congregational choirs of numerous churches of varying faiths. In 1976, he traveled from Florida to Washington, DC, across the United States to Los Angeles, California,

and finally to a ranch at La Quinta in the Southern California desert.

At his new home he continued researching and writing. In addition to numerous technical bulletins, several key HCO Policy Letters on training staff members and how to improve church administration came from his work at this time.

THE POLICY SUBJECT INDEX

Index to the Organization Executive Course and the Management Series volumes, published by Publications Organization US, Los Angeles, California, March 1976. (Also known as the Hubbard Communications Office Policy Letter Subject Index.)

THE TECHNICAL BULLETINS OF DIANETICS AND SCIENTOLOGY

by L. Ron Hubbard

Compilation of L. Ron Hubbard's technical bulletins on Dianetics and Scientology. Published by Scientology Publications Organization, Copenhagen and Publications Organization US, Los Angeles, California, August 1976. Revised in 1991.

HCOB 10 Aug R R/Ses, What They
Rev. 5 Sep 78 Mean

HCO PL 20 Sep The Stat Push
Org Series 35
Exec Series 17

HCO PL 20 Sep – 1 Stat Push Clarified
Add. of 17 Apr 77 *Org Series 35–1*
Exec Series 17–1

HCOB 20 Oct R I PTS Data
Rev. 25 Aug 87

HCOB 20 Oct II PTS Handling

HCOB 24 Oct RA Delivery Repair Lists
Rev. 12 Jul 88 *C/S Series 96RA*

HCO PL 24 Oct RF I Ex-Staff Free
Rev. 2 Aug 90 Service

HCO PL 24 Oct RA II Supervisors Can
Rev. 9 Aug 90 Become Professors

HCO PL 24 Oct R III Senior Case
Rev. 20 Jan 91 Supervisor
Requirements

HCO PL 25 Oct Provisional
Certificate Expiry

HCOB/PL 26 Oct I Auditing Reports,
Falsifying Of
C/S Series 97
Auditor Admin
Series 25

HCOB/PL 28 Oct Auditing Folders,
Omissions in
Completeness
C/S Series 98
Auditor Admin
Series 26

HCO PL 4 Nov RB I Statistic Change,
Rev. 12 Feb 89 Gross Divisional
Statistics, HCOs and
Quals, OIC Cable
Change

HCO PL 4 Nov – 2 HCO Stat Penalty
Add. of 24 Feb 77

HCO PL 10 Nov I Staff Courses
Mandatory in Orgs

HCO PL 11 Nov RB I Statistic Change,
Rev. 20 Nov 84 HCOs and Qual,
Definitions

HCO PL 12 Nov RC Statistic Change,
Rev. 25 Nov 85 Tech Sec Stat

HCO PL 13 Nov RA Professional Rates
Rev. 9 Nov 89

HCO PL 14 Nov Manning Up an Org
Exec Series 18
AKH Series 36
Org Series 36
Personnel Series 28

HCO PL 16 Nov Production Quotas
Exec Series 19
Org Series 37

HCO PL 27 Nov R Restoration of Local
Rev. 30 Jun 89 Control of Personnel
Assignments and
Comm Evs

HCO PL 30 Nov R Only SSO Can TIP
Rev. 25 Apr 79

**MODERN
MANAGEMENT
TECHNOLOGY
DEFINED—HUBBARD
DICTIONARY OF
ADMINISTRATION AND
MANAGEMENT**

*Compiled from the works of L. Ron
Hubbard, first published by Publications
Organization US, Los Angeles,
California, December 1976. Today
published by Bridge Publications and
New Era Publications.*

**THE VOLUNTEER
MINISTER'S HANDBOOK**
by L. Ron Hubbard

*Published by Publications Organization
US, Los Angeles, California, December
1976. TRANSLATION: German.*

ISSUES

HCO PL 6 Dec RB Illegal Pcs,
Rev. 8 Apr 88 Acceptance Of,
High Crime PL

HCO PL 7 Dec Leaving and Leaves

HCOB 10 Dec RB Scientology F/N
Rev. 25 May 80 and TA Position
C/S Series 99RB

RON'S JOURNAL 28

*L. Ron Hubbard recorded a special
message for the staff of Scientology
organizations in December 1976.*

1977

**Living in southern California,
Mr. Hubbard continued his work on
films, writing scripts for eight new
Scientology instruction films.**

**His technical and organizational
research went ahead at full speed,
making significant progress in
such areas as E–Meter use, Word
Clearing, study and training
technology, case repair, handling the
effects of drugs, the technology of
Confessionals, Expanded Dianetics,
marketing, data evaluation and
ethics. Each new advance was
released in HCO Bulletins and HCO
Policy Letters.**

**CAN WE EVER
BE FRIENDS?**

*A recorded lecture delivered by a
minister of Scientology on the truth
about Dianetics and Scientology,
intended for those who have exhibited
coolness or even antagonism toward
the subjects due to misconceptions
about them. Revised and re-recorded
in 1989. Produced by Golden Era
Productions. TRANSLATIONS: Danish,
Dutch, French, German, Italian,
Spanish and Swedish.*

**CAN WE EVER
BE FRIENDS?**

*Booklet published by the Church of
Scientology of California, Worldwide,
Saint Hill, England, 1977. Revised in
1989. TRANSLATIONS: French, German.*

**THE VOLUNTEER
MINISTER BOOKLETS**

*Nine booklets published by Publications
Organization, Los Angeles, California,
1977.*
1. *Communication*
2. *Understanding Others – Affinity,
Reality, Communication*
3. *Do You Make Many Mistakes?*
4. *The Eight Dynamics*
5. *Assists*
6. *The Conditions of Existence*
7. *The Parts of Man*
8. *The Aims of Scientology*
9. *The Third Party Law*

ISSUES

HCO PL 1 Jan RA Marketing Hat
Rev. 29 Aug 79 *Marketing Series 3*

HCOB 10 Jan I How to Win with
Word Clearing
Word Clearing
Series 55

HCOB 10 Jan II Ethics and Word
Clearing
Word Clearing
Series 50

HCOB 13 Jan RB Handling a
Rev. 25 May 80 False TA

HCOB 21 Jan RB False TA Checklist
Rev. 25 May 80

HCOB 22 Jan In–Tech, The Only
Way to Achieve It
Cramming Series 13
KSW Series 21

HCOB 24 Jan Tech Correction
Roundup

HCOB 30 Jan R False TA Data
Rev. 25 May 80

HCOB 5 Feb Jokers and Degraders
C/S Series 100

HCOB 17 Feb R Course Necessities
Rev. 20 Feb 77

HCOB 24 Feb Expanded Dianetics
Cases

HCOB 1 Mar II Confessional Forms

HCOB 1 Mar III Formulating
Confessional
Questions

HCOB 1 Mar IVA Valid Confessional

HCO PL 15 Mar RA Evaluation: The
Rev. 5 Nov 90 Situation
Data Series 41RA

HCOB 16 Mar The Gambler
ExDn Series 22

HCO PL 17 Mar RA Date Coincidence
Rev. 2 Nov 90 *Data Series 42RA*

HCO PL 18 Mar RA Evaluation and
Rev. 6 Nov 90 Programs
Data Series 43RA

HCO PL 18 Mar-1R Evaluation
Rev. 14 Jun 77 Success
Data Series 43–1R

HCO PL 20 Mar R Super Evaluation
Rev. 15 Jun 77 *Data Series 44R*

HCOB 27 Mar R Auditing the Pc
Rev. 23 Apr 91 at Cause
ExDn Series 23

HCOB 5 Apr Expanded Grades

HCO PL 10 Apr Dissemination
Pieces, Stable
Datum, Appearance,
Layout and Design

HCOB 11 Apr List Errors,
Correction Of

HCOB 17 Apr R Recurring Withholds
Rev. 16 Nov 89 and Overts

HCOB 7 May Long Duration Sec
Checking

HCOB 9 May I Foreword of
Expanded Dianetics
Course

HCOB 9 May II Psychosis, More
About
ExDn Series 24

HCOB 31 May LSD, Years After
They Have "Come
Off Of" LSD

HCOB 14 Jun RB Paid Completions
Rev. 11 Apr 91 Simplified

HCO PL 14 Jun RB I All Class IV Orgs,
Rev. 18 Jun 78 OIC Cable Change

HCO PL 14 Jun RA II All Sea Org Orgs,
Rev. 28 Jun 78 OIC Cable Change

HCOB 26 Sep R Art and
Rev. 30 Dec 79 Communication
Art Series 5

HCOB 4 Dec RA Checklist for
Rev. 23 Apr 96 Setting Up Sessions
and an E–Meter

**THE SECRET
OF FLAG RESULTS**

*A film written by L. Ron Hubbard,
produced by Universal Media
Productions and released 9 December
1977. Shows the actions and steps
which lie behind the stellar results of
Flag auditing.*

1978

**This was a landmark year for
technical breakthroughs. In fact, in
Ron's Journal 30, Mr. Hubbard called
it "The Year of Lightning Fast New
Tech." Just a few of these
spectacular new advances are listed
below.**

**New Era Dianetics was released, a
refinement of all previous Dianetics
techniques combined with new
developments to give much faster
results and far higher gain per hour
of auditing.**

**In September, a remarkable new OT
level was released—an audited level
called New Era Dianetics for OTs
(*New OT V*).**

**The Sweat Program, forerunner of
the Purification Program, gave new
hope to those whose spiritual
progress had been hindered by the
effects of drug residues in their
bodies.**

**To give technical training a terrific
boost in speed and accuracy, in 1978
LRH wrote scripts for thirty-three
new technical training films.**

ISSUES

HCOB 6 Feb RD The Purification
Rev. 27 Mar 90 Rundown Replaces
the Sweat Program
Purif RD Series 1R

HCO PL	23 Feb R Rev. 7 May 84	Board of Review *LRH Comm N/W Series 19*
HCOB	26 Feb	Internships Versus Courses
HCOB	19 Mar	Quickie Objectives
HCOB	23 Mar RB Rev. 16 Jan 89	Clearing Words *Word Clearing Series 59RB*
HCOB	27 Mar I	Ethics Penalty for Word Clearers *Word Clearing Series 58*
HCOB	3 Apr R Rev. 23 Dec 89	TR Debug Assessment
HCOB	26 May I	Dianetics: Urgent Command Change
HCOB	2 Jun RC Rev. 18 Jun 88	Cramming Repair Assessment List *Cramming Series 14*
HCOB	2 Jun Add. of 3 Jul 88	RC-1 Cramming Repair Assessment List Word List *Cramming Series 14-1*
HCOB	15 Jun R Rev. 23 Apr 91	"The Key to Expanded Dianetics..." *ExDn Series 25*
HCOB	18 Jun R Rev. 20 Sep 78	Assessment and How to Get the Item *NED Series 4R*
HCOB	19 Jun	Objective ARC *NED Series 3*
HCOB	20 Jun	Identity Rundown *NED Series 15*
HCOB	21 Jun R Rev. 8 Apr 88	New Era Dianetics *NED Series 1R*
HCOB	22 Jun RA Rev. 8 Apr 88	New Era Dianetics Full Pc Program Outline *NED Series 2RA*
HCOB	23 Jun RA Rev. 8 Apr 88	Preclear Checklist *NED Series 16RA*
HCOB	24 Jun RA Rev. 8 Apr 88	Original Assessment Sheet *NED Series 5RA*
HCO PL	25 Jun	Come-on Dissemination *Marketing Series 6*
HCOB	26 Jun RA II Rev. 15 Sep 78	Routine 3RA, Engram Running by Chains *NED Series 6RA*
HCOB	28 Jun RA Rev. 15 Sep 78	R3RA Commands *NED Series 7RA*
HCOB	29 Jun	Disability Rundown *NED Series 14*
HCOB	1 Jul	The Dianetic Prepared Assessment Rundown Action Fifteen *NED Series 13*
HCOB	2 Jul	Dianetic Student Rescue Intensive *NED Series 11*
HCOB	3 Jul R Rev. 22 Sep 78	Relief Rundown *NED Series 10R*
HCOB	4 Jul R Rev. 22 Sep 78	Second Original Assessment *NED Series 12R*
HCOB	9 Jul RA Rev. 8 Apr 88	Dianetic C/S-1 *NED Series 21*
HCOB	11 Jul	The Preassessment List *NED Series 4-1*
HCOB	14 Jul R I Rev. 15 Sep 78	Typical Dianetic Chain *NED Series 22*
HCOB	14 Jul R II Rev. 15 Sep 78	A Typical Narrative Item *NED Series 23*

HCOB	15 Jul RA Rev. 10 Mar 84	Scientology Auditing C/S-1
HCOB	19 Jul	Dianetic Persistent F/Ns *NED Series 17*
HCOB	20 Jul	After the Fact Items *NED Series 18*
HCO PL	20 Jul	Held From Above, Double-Hatting *Org Series 38*
HCOB	21 Jul	What Is a Floating Needle?
HCOB	22 Jul	Assessment TRs
HCOB	23 Jul	List of Perceptics *C/S Series 101*
HCOB	24 Jul	Dianetic Remedies *NED Series 24*
HCO PL	24 Jul	Subproducts, How to Compile a Subproduct List
HCOB	5 Aug	Instant Reads
HCOB	7 Aug	Havingness, Finding and Running the Pc's Havingness Process
HCOB	9 Aug I	New Era Dianetics, A Requisite for Expanded Dianetics
HCOB	9 Aug II	Clearing Commands *Word Clearing Series 52*
HCOB	11 Aug I	Rudiments, Definitions and Patter
HCOB	11 Aug II	Model Session
HCO PL	15 Aug	Chinese Schooling an Org Board
HCOB	21 Aug	Running Flows That Won't Erase
HCOB	26 Aug R Rev. 5 Oct 78	More on Drugs
HCOB	3 Sep	Definition of a Rock Slam
HCOB	5 Sep	Anatomy of a Service Facsimile
HCOB	6 Sep I	Following Up on Dirty Needles
HCOB	6 Sep II	Service Facsimiles and Rock Slams
HCOB	6 Sep III	Routine Three SC-A, Full Service Facsimile Handling Updated with New Era Dianetics
HCOB	7 Sep R Rev. 21 Oct 78	Modern Repetitive Prepchecking
HCOB	8 Sep RB Rev. 16 Nov 87	Mini List of Grade 0–IV Processes
HCOB	10 Sep	NED High Crime *NED Series 25*
HCOB	12 Sep R I Rev. 2 Dec 85	Dianetics Forbidden on Clears and OTs
HCOB	12 Sep II	Overrun by Demanding Earlier Than There Is *NED Series 26*
HCOB	13 Sep I	R3RA Engram Running by Chains and Narrative R3RA —An Additional Difference *NED Series 27*
HCOB	13 Sep II	Clears, OTs and R/Ses
HCO PL	13 Sep	"An old poem..."
HCO PL	15 Sep	Confidentiality of Upper-Level Rundowns

HCOB	16 Sep	Postulate Off Equals Erasure *NED Series 28*
HCOB	19 Sep RI Rev. 31 Jan 79	The End of Endless Drug RDs
HCOB	19 Sep R II Rev. 31 Jan 79	The End of Endless Drug Rundowns Repair List
LRH ED	19 Sep	AD 28, The Year of Technical Breakthroughs

NEW ERA DIANETICS FOR OTs (NEW OT V) MATERIALS
[Confidential and unpublished]

On 15 September 1978, the confidential and unpublished materials of this new, audited OT level were made available for study to members of the Sea Organization enrolled on the Class IX Auditor Course.

ISSUES

HCOB	20 Sep I	An Instant F/N Is a Read
HCOB	20 Sep II	LX List Handling
HCOB	20 Sep R III Rev. 23 Apr 88	NED Auditor Analysis Checklist *NED Series 19R* *C/S Series 103R*
HCOB	24 Sep RB I Rev. 4 Feb 89	The End of Endless Int Repair Rundown *Int RD Series 4RB*
HCOB	24 Sep II	Preassessment, AESPs and Int *Int RD Series 13*
HCOB	24 Sep RC III Rev. 18 Dec 88	Dianetic Clear *CCRD Series 1R*
HCOB	25 Sep RI Rev. 8 Apr 91	Quad Commands for Int Buttons *Int RD Series 5R*
HCOB	25 Sep R II Rev. 4 Feb 89	Star-rate Checkouts for Interiorization Handling *Int RD Series 14R*
HCO PL	27 Sep	Examining Resources *Data Series 45*
LRH ED	28 Sep	The End of Endless Training
HCOB	3 Oct	NED Rule *NED Series 29*
HCOB	4 Oct	Interiorization Handling Simplified *Int RD Series 1*
HCOB	16 Oct I	Repair Correction List
HCOB	16 Oct II	C/S Checklist of Int Errors *Int RD Series 16* *C/S Series 102*
HCO PL	20 Oct	Two-Bit FP *Finance Series 17*
HCO PL	22 Oct	Mistakes *Esto Series 44*

ISSUES

HCOB	30 Oct RI Rev. 3 Aug 83	Courses — Their Ideal Scene
HCOB	30 Oct RII Rev. 26 Jul 86	C/S Series 53, Use Of
HCO PL	8 Nov RB Rev. 5 Nov 79	Senior HCOs, Area and Continental
HCOB	10 Nov RA I Rev. 26 Jul 86	Proclamation, Power to Forgive

HCO PL	10 Nov II	"Power to Forgive" Certificate
HCOB	15 Nov	Dating and Locating
HCOB	19 Nov	L&N Lists — The Item "Me"
HCOB	27 Nov RB Rev. 30 Apr 88	Word Clearing Correction List *Word Clearing Series 35RI*
HCOB	28 Nov	Auditors Who Miss Withholds, Penalty
HCO PL	29 Nov	How You Handle Demands for Personnel *Personnel Series 29* *AKH Series 37*
HCOB	30 Nov RA Rev. 26 Aug 96	Confessional Procedure
HCOB	1 Dec RB Rev. 18 Dec 88	Programing of Clears *C/S Series 113RA*
HCOB	3 Dec	Unreading Flows
HCOB	4 Dec	How to Read Through an F/N
HCOB	5 Dec RB Rev. 18 Dec 88	Clear Data *C/S Series 105RB* *CCRD Series 4R*
HCOB	6 Dec	Revivification
HCO PL	6 Dec	Space Planning
HCOB	8 Dec R II Rev. 27 Jun 88	Green Form and Expanded Green Form 40RF, Use Of
HCO PL	10 Dec RA Rev. 4 Feb 91	Gross Book Sales, Definition
LRH ED	17 Dec	Ron's Journal 30, 1978 The Year of Lightning Fast New Tech
HCO PL	28 Dec	Use of *Big League Sales*
HCOB	29 Dec R Rev. 20 Dec 83	The Suppressed Person Rundown, A Magical New Rundown
HCOB	30 Dec R Rev. 6 Jan 79	Suppressed Person Rundown, Problems Processes
HCOB	31 Dec RA II Rev. 26 Jul 86	Outline of PTS Handling
HCOB	31 Dec RA III Rev. 21 Mar 89	Educating the Potential Trouble Source, The First Step Toward Handling: PTS C/S-1

1979

While supervising the training of a group of auditors selected to deliver a highly precise new auditing rundown, Mr. Hubbard found that many of them had difficulty with their TRs. In 1979 his search for the cause of this one outness and the means to terminatedly handle it led him to a series of discoveries that form the basis for the technology found today in the new Hubbard Professional TR Course, the Hubbard Key to Life Course and the Hubbard Life Orientation Course.

In December, LRH announced a new rundown designed to rid the body of harmful drug residues and toxic substances. The successes from those who had participated in its piloting credited this new action for remarkable increases in their energy level, awareness, alertness, spiritual well-being and ability to think clearly. This new program, the Purification Rundown, is in use today throughout the world.

On the administrative front, 1979 saw the development of a powerful new technology for handling slowed or inadequate production: Debug Tech, consisting of a formidable battery of new technical tools including Crashing Misunderstood Word Finding, False Data Stripping, the Debug Tech Checklist and the Product Debug Repair List.

ISSUES

HCO PL 4 Jan The Ideal Ideal Scene
Data Series 46

LRH ED 6 Jan Correction to Ron's Journal 30 Requirements for Super Power Auditors

HCO PL 6 Jan Financial Planning Regarding Property Renovations and Construction

HCOB 9 Jan BTB Cancellation

HCO PL 13 Jan Orders, Illegal and Cross

HCO PL 17 Jan A New Type of Crime

HCO PL 19 Jan RB I Scholarships, No
Rev. 30 May 89 Discounts

HCO PL 20 Jan Income Cutatives and Salary Sum

HCO PL 23 Jan Unevaluated Orders

HCOB 28 Jan C/S Qualifications

HCO PL 29 Jan Prices, Upper Org

HCO PL 30 Jan Positioning, Philosophic Theory
PR Series 30
Marketing Series 5

HCOB 31 Jan Mood Drills

HCOB 3 Feb R I Change the
Rev. 19 Dec 90 Civilization Eval

HCOB 3 Feb II Confront Tech Has to Be Part of the TR Checksheet

HUBBARD PROFESSIONAL MARK VI E–METER

With the advanced technology of New Era Dianetics for OTs, the Mark V E–Meter proved not to be sensitive enough. A more sensitive meter—the Mark VI—was developed and released as the first OT meter.

HCOB 7 Feb RD E-Meter Drill 5RB,
Rev. 11 Jul 97 Can Squeeze

HCO PL 7 Feb R The Basics of
Rev. 3 Sep 79 Marketing
Marketing Series 7

HCOB/PL 9 Feb R How to Defeat
Rev. 23 Aug 84 Verbal Tech Checklist
KSW Series 23R

HCOB/PL 15 Feb Verbal Tech: Penalties
KSW Series 24

HCO PL 25 Feb R HCO Staff
Rev. 14 May 89 Qualification Requirements

HCOB 4 Mar R Art in Its Basics
Rev. 30 Dec 79 *Art Series 6*

HCOB 5 Mar RB Dianetic Clear
Rev. 2 Dec 85 False Declares

HCO PL 21 Mar R Sliding Scale of
Rev. 6 Dec 89 Pricing

HCO PL 25 Mar A New Hope for Justice

HCOB 26 Mar RB Misunderstood
Rev. 2 Sep 79 Words and Cycles of Action
Esto Series 35RB
Word Clearing Series 60RB
Product Debug Series 7R

HCO PL 5 Apr I FSM Penalty for Refunds, Repayments and Bounced Checks

HCO PL 5 Apr RC II New FSM
Rev. 14 Feb 91 Account
FSM Series 6

HCO PL 10 Apr RA Flag Rep Statistics
Rev. 12 Feb 91

HCOB 15 Apr Fine Arts Versus Illustrations
Art Series 7

HCO PL 25 Apr Estates Production Statistics

HCO PL 1 May RB Clear Certainty
Rev. 18 Dec 88 Rundown: Administration
CCRD Series 3R

HCO PL 27 May Book Sales Commission

HCO PL 7 Jun R I Data Series PLs,
Rev. 14 Jun 79 Use Of
Data Series 47

HCOB/PL 5 Jun Condition
Iss. 13 Aug 96 Formulas – Handling a Withhold

HCOB 10 Jun A Professional
Art Series 8

ARTICLE

FREEDOM Jun AMA... Up to Its Old Tricks

ISSUES

HCOB 17 Jun Crashing Mis-Us: The Key to Completed Cycles of Action and Products
Word Clearing Series 61
Product Debug Series 3

HCOB 18 Jun R The Crashing Mis-U
Rev. 27 Jun 88 Repair List—LC1R
Product Debug Series 4R
Word Clearing Series 62R

HCO PL 24 Jun Crime Additions

HCOB 7 Jul Crashing Mis-U Definition

HCO PL 10 Jul R I Publications
Rev. 26 Nov 79 Organizations Are Sales Organizations

HCO PL 16 Jul I Hubbard Key to Life Course High Crime

HCO PL 16 Jul II Delivering the Hubbard Key to Life Course, the Chicken and Egg Theory

HCOB 16 Jul The "Elusive" Mis-U or Crashing Mis-U
Word Clearing Series 63
Product Debug Series 5

HCOB 17 Jul RB I The Misunderstood
Rev. 26 Feb 89 Word Defined
Word Clearing Series 64RB

HCO PL 21 Jul Magazine Planning

HCO PL 25 Jul Magazine Motifs

THE TECHNICAL BULLETINS OF DIANETICS AND SCIENTOLOGY VOLUME XI, 1976–1978

Compilation of L. Ron Hubbard's technical bulletins on Dianetics and Scientology. Published by Publications Department Advanced Org/Saint Hill Denmark and Publications Organization US, Los Angeles, California, August 1979. Revised and updated in 1991.

ISSUES

HCOB 7 Aug False Data Stripping
Product Debug Series 8
Esto Series 36

HCO PL 9 Aug I Call-in: The Key to Delivery and Future Income

HCO PL 9 Aug R II Service Product
Rev. 19 Nov 79 Officer
Org Series 39
Esto Series 39

HCO PL 9 Aug III Service Call-in Committee

HCOB 19 Aug RA High-Crime
Rev. 27 Aug 84 Checkouts and Word Clearing
Word Clearing Series 47

HCO PL 20 Aug Dianetics and Scientology Are New
Marketing Series 1
PR Series 34

HCOB 21 Aug Twinning

HCOB 23 Aug Definition of TRs
Iss. 9 May 96

HCOB 23 Aug I Crashing Mis–Us, Blocks to Finding Them
Word Clearing Series 65
Product Debug Series 6

HCOB 23 Aug R II Product Debug
Rev. 14 Jun 88 Repair List
Product Debug Series 10R

HCOB 23 Aug R III Debug Tech
Rev. 23 Aug 84 *Product Debug Series 1R*
Esto Series 37R

HCO PL 23 Aug R II Debug Tech
Rev. 24 Jun 88 Checklist
Esto Series 38R
Product Debug Series 2R

SCIENTOLOGY GROUP AUDITOR'S HANDBOOK, VOLUMES I AND II

Compiled by staff and published by Publications Organization US, Los Angeles, California.

1980

Following the release of the Purification Rundown in December of 1979, the new Scientology Drug Rundown was announced, using Scientology auditing techniques to relieve the mental and spiritual ravages of drugs. Another new OT level — the OT Drug Rundown (New OT IV) — was also released in January 1980.

The first of the *Research and Discovery Series* volumes was released in June. Containing transcriptions of Mr. Hubbard's thousands of technical lectures, arranged chronologically and projected to fill approximately 100 encyclopedia-sized books, this monumental set represents the complete running record of his research into the subject of the mind and spirit.

Two brand-new OT levels were released in September: the Hubbard Solo New Era Dianetics for OTs Auditor Course (New OT VI), which gives a person the technology he needs to audit himself on the next level, and New OT VII, Solo New Era Dianetics for OTs.

In addition to these spiritual breakthroughs for mankind, Mr. Hubbard also wrote in 1980 the largest single-volume science fiction novel in the genre's history: *Battlefield Earth: A Saga of the Year 3000*, as well as the first volumes of his 10-volume science fiction opus, *Mission Earth.*

ISSUES

OT DRUG RUNDOWN MATERIALS (NEW OT IV)
[Confidential and unpublished]

On 29 January 1980, the confidential and unpublished materials of this new, audited OT level were made available for study to members of the Sea Organization enrolled on the Class VIII Auditor Course.

ISSUES

THE TECHNICAL BULLETINS OF DIANETICS AND SCIENTOLOGY VOLUME XII, 1978–1979

Compilation of L. Ron Hubbard's technical bulletins on Dianetics and Scientology. Published by Scientology Publications Organization, Copenhagen and Publications Organization US, Los Angeles, California, August 1980. Revised in 1991, and published today by Bridge Publications and New Era Publications.

ISSUE

HUBBARD SOLO NEW ERA
DIANETICS FOR OTS AUDITOR
MATERIALS (NEW OT VI)
[Confidential and unpublished]

& SOLO NEW ERA DIANETICS
FOR OTS MATERIALS
(NEW OT VII)
[Confidential and unpublished]

On 10 September 1980, the
confidential and unpublished
materials of these two new OT
levels were first made available for
study to Scientologists who met the
spiritual and ethical requirements
for these levels.

ISSUES

HCOB 11 Sep L4BRB Word List

HCOB 16 Sep R PTS RD Correction
Rev. 4 Jul 88 List Word List

HCOB 17 Sep R I L3RH Word List
Rev. 8 Apr 88 *NED Series 20–1*

HCOB 17 Sep RA II Green Form
Rev. 28 Jun 90 Word List

HCOB 28 Sep R III Confessional
Rev. 26 Jul 86 Repair List – LCRE
Word List

HCOB 6 Oct I General Staff
Confessional List
Confessional Form 2R

HCOB 6 Oct II Supervisor
Confessional List
Confessional Form 4R

HCO PL 15 Oct R Celebrity Centre
Rev. 4 Feb 91 Magazine, *Celebrity*

HCOB/PL 23 Oct R Chart of Abilities
Rev. 16 Nov 87 Gained for Lower
Levels and Expanded
Lower Grades

HCOB 4 Nov I PRD Confessional
List
*Confessional Form
10RA*

HCOB 5 Nov Returning Tours
Confessional
*Confessional Form
9RA*

HCOB 8 Nov R C/S Series 53RM
Rev. 26 Jul 86 Long Form Word
List

HCOB 12 Nov R I Case Supervisor
Rev. 12 Jul 88 Correction List

HCOB 12 Nov II Registrar and Sales
Personnel
Confessional List
*Confessional Form
6RA*

HCOB 18 Nov R I Auditor Correction
Rev. 12 Jul 88 List, Auditor
Recovery Word List

HCOB 18 Nov R II Case Supervisor
Rev. 12 Jul 88 Correction List Word
List

HCOB 23 Nov Case Supervisor
Confessional
*Confessional
Form 8RA*

HCOB 2 Dec Floating Needle and
TA Position
Modified

HCOB 19 Dec R Rehab Tech
Rev. 16 Nov 87

HCOB 21 Dec RA The Scientology
Rev. 23 Apr 91 Drug Rundown

HCOB 23 Dec R I Executive
Rev. 12 Jul 88 Correction List

HCOB 23 Dec R II Executive
Rev. 12 Jul 88 Correction List
Word List

HCOB 25 Dec I LRH Communicator
Confessional List
Confessional Form 12R

HCOB 25 Dec II Flag Rep
Confessional List
Confessional Form 11R

THE LEARNING BOOK

*Compiled from the works of L. Ron
Hubbard by the faculty of the Delphian
School. Published by Heron Books.
TRANSLATIONS: Chinese, Danish, Dutch,
Finnish, French, German, Italian,
Japanese, Portuguese, Russian,
Spanish and Swedish.*

THE PROBLEM OF LIFE

*A public film written by L. Ron
Hubbard which describes the plight of
those looking for the answer to the
question "What is life?" It opens the
door to Scientology for someone who
has no familiarity with the subject.
Originally released December 1980.
Newly produced by Golden Era
Productions and released in May 1993.*

THE PROBLEM OF LIFE MUSIC

Ten musical compositions from the
music for the film, *The Problem of
Life*, composed by L. Ron Hubbard.

1981

Observing that modern society
lacked a moral code befitting its
pragmatic, fast-paced, high-tech
outlook, in 1981 Mr. Hubbard wrote
The Way to Happiness—a
common–sense nonreligious guide to
help people live happier lives.
Separately, he also announced a new
auditing rundown called the
Happiness Rundown, designed to
alleviate the spiritual trauma of
moral transgressions an individual
had made in life.

1981 was marked by dramatic
changes in the Classification and
Gradation Chart. First, the routes
onto the Bridge were clarified and
opened wide. The lower levels of
auditing and training were also
streamlined, making possible much
smoother and faster progress
upward. The new Hubbard Solo
Auditor Course, Part 1 was released
to all Class V orgs, making it easier
to take the first steps to OT.

A brand-new rundown was released
for those who had just achieved the
state of Clear: the Sunshine

Rundown. And in November, Mr.
Hubbard researched, developed and
released a New OT I, further
streamlining the route to full OT.

ISSUES

HCO PL 5 Jan RA Extension Courses
Rev. 13 Feb 91

HCO PL 8 Jan R Advanced Course
Rev. 3 Oct 88 Regulations and
Security

HCO PL 22 Jan Orders of the Day

HCOB 29 Jan RA I FES Checklists
Rev. 9 Apr 91 and Summary
*Auditor Admin
Series 24RB*

HCOB 29 Jan II HC
Outpoint – Pluspoint
Lists RB Words List

HCOB 13 Feb R Dictionaries
Rev. 25 Jul 87 *Word Clearing
Series 67R*

HCOB 26 Mar R II Expanded Green
Rev. 4 Jul 88 Form 40RF Word
List

HCOB 31 Mar R "Heavy Drug
Rev. 25 Apr 90 History" Defined

HCOB 1 Apr R II Interviews
Rev. 17 Jan 91

HCO PL 5 Apr RA Clear Certificates
Rev. 18 Dec 88 *CCRD Series 16R*

HCOB 10 Apr R Reach and
Rev. 7 Aug 83 Withdraw

HCOB 4 May RA Study Green Form
Rev. 27 Jun 88 *Study Series 10RA*

HCOB 5 May R Study Green Form
Rev. 4 Jul 88 Word List

HCO PL 21 Jul RI What Is a
Rev. 25 Jul 87 Checksheet

HCO PL 23 Jul RI The Use of
Rev. 10 Jan 84 Demonstration
Study Series 12

HCOB 23 Jul Pregnancy and
Auditing

HCOB 29 Jul R Full Assist
Rev. 13 Apr 91 Checklists for
Injuries and Illnesses

HCO PL 4 Aug R Pink Sheets
Rev. 30 Aug 83

HCO PL 9 Sep How to "Sell"
Scientology to Your
Friends
FSM Series 8

HCOB 15 Sep The Criminal Mind

HCO PL 20 Sep Dianetics and
Scientology
Redefined

HCOB 6 Oct Tech Films and
Verbal Tech

HCOB 7 Oct R Method 3 Word
Rev. 30 Aug 83 Clearing
*Word Clearing
Series 31RD*

HCOB 8 Oct R III Word Clearing
Rev. 16 Jan 89 Method 2
*Word Clearing
Series 6RB
Tape Course Series 9RA*

HCO PL 20 Oct R PTS Type A
Rev. 10 Sep 83 Handling

HCO PL 8 Nov RA Who May
Rev. 10 Nov 83 See Technical
Training Films

HCO PL 11 Nov R Policies on Film
Rev. 30 Jan 91 Usage

HCOB 12 Nov RD Grade Chart
Rev. 20 Apr 90 Streamlined for
Lower Grades

HCOB 13 Nov What Tone 40 Is

HCOB 15 Nov R The Sunshine
Rev. 18 Dec 88 Rundown

HCOB 29 Nov Dianetics and
Scientology
Compared to
Nineteenth Century
Practices

HCOB 5 Dec R Setting Up and
Rev. 7 Oct 84 Using a Reel-to-
Reel Tape Player
Tape Course Series 7R

HCOB 12 Dec The Theory of the
New Grade Chart

HCOB 14 Dec The State of Clear

HCOB 15 Dec New Grade Chart
Pc/Pre-OT
Programing

HCOB 17 Dec Post Purpose
Clearing Revived

HCOB 26 Dec Post Purpose
Clearing for
Management Teams
and Executives

Holidays 81/82 Ron's Journal 33

HCO PL 29 Dec Clear Certainty
Iss. 27 Mar 94 Rundown:
Administration
Additional Data
CCRD Series 3R-1

THE WAY TO HAPPINESS

by L. Ron Hubbard

*Paperback booklet; packets of twelve
booklets each. Published by Regent
House Publishers, Los Angeles,
California. New paperback, hardback
and leatherbound editions released in
1984 by Bridge Publications.
TRANSLATIONS: Afrikaans, Arabic,
Bosnian, Chinese, Croatian, Czech,
Danish, Dutch, Finnish, French,
German, Greek, Hebrew, Hungarian,
Italian, Japanese, Norwegian, Polish,
Portuguese, Russian, Serbian,
Spanish, Swedish and Zulu.*

BASIC DICTIONARY OF DIANETICS AND SCIENTOLOGY

based on the works of
L. Ron Hubbard

*Published by Scientology Publications
Organization, Copenhagen, and
Publications US, Los Angeles,
California. A new edition was released
in 1988. TRANSLATIONS: Dutch, French,
German, Italian, Japanese and
Swedish.*

THE CASE HE COULDN'T CRACK

*A film written by L. Ron Hubbard, set at
the Flag Land Base, which describes the
power of standard Flag auditing. Shows
how the application of 100 percent
standard technology cracks any case.*

OT I MATERIALS
[Confidential and unpublished]

In late 1981 the confidential and unpublished written materials of this new OT level were made available for study to those eligible to receive them.

1982

1982 saw the beginning of a new era for Scientology. The Church of Scientology International was formed as the mother church of the Scientology religion and established to provide ethical, effective ecclesiastical management for churches around the world.

That same year saw formation of the Religious Technology Center (RTC), an independent nonprofit religious corporation to which Mr. Hubbard made a free gift of all trademarks of Dianetics and Scientology. With ownership of the marks and control of their licensing and use, RTC assumed responsibility for ensuring the standard application of the technologies of Dianetics and Scientology throughout the world.

In 1982 came the beginning of the computerization of Scientology management, using Mr. Hubbard's phenomenal breakthroughs in the application of computer technology. With new ideas for computer utilization far beyond the scope of the time, computers were being used to the utmost to help forward Scientology's efforts to improve conditions worldwide.

New advances were also made in the areas of Confessionals, E-Metering, study technology, auditing repair and case supervision, marketing, finance, management and ethics technology, with each new development made the subject of an HCO Bulletin or Policy Letter.

ISSUES

HCO PL 17 Jan	What Is an Executive? *Exec Series 22*	
HCOB 19 Jan II	High School Indoctrination	
HCOB 26 Jan Iss. 1 Aug 96	Killing an F/N in Solo Auditing	
HCO PL 1 Feb	Stature	
HCO PL 5 Feb I	Out-Ethics Symptoms	
HCO PL 5 Feb II	Books and Marketing *PR Series 44* *Marketing Series 16*	
HCOB 15 Feb	Freedom of Speech	
HCOB 17 Feb	Prejudice	
HCO PL 18 Feb	Changing Workable Finance Systems *Finance Series 27*	
HCOB 20 Feb	Overts	
HCO PL 24 Feb	Economic Systems	
HCO PL 28 Feb I	News	
HCO PL 28 Feb R III Rev. 4 Feb 91	HCO Book Account Cash–Bills	
HCO PL 3 Mar	The Qual Library	
HCO PL 6 Mar R Rev. 10 Dec 88	Confessional Tech Policies	

HCOB 8 Mar R
Rev. 24 Apr 83 — Confessionals and the Non-Interference Zone

HCO PL 9 Mar RB
Rev. 6 Jan 85 — Eligibility for OT Levels

HCOB 10 Mar — Confessionals—Ethics Reports Required

HCO PL 11 Mar — Proportionate Marketing
Finance Series 30
Marketing Series 17

RJ 34 13 Mar — The Future of Scientology

HCO PL 14 Mar — Financial Irregularities

HCO PL 17 Mar — FBO FP Adjudication
Finance Series 28

HCO PL 19 Mar — Executive Success
Exec Series 23
Finance Series 31
Marketing Series 19

UNDERSTANDING THE E–METER

Compiled from the works of L. Ron Hubbard. Published by Bridge Publications, Los Angeles, California. Revised in 1988.

ISSUES

HCOB 20 Mar R
Rev. 12 Apr 88 — Standards

HCO PL 23 Mar R
Rev. 16 Sep 88 — A Refined Definition of PR
PR Series 28RA

HCOB 25 Mar R
Rev. 16 Apr 90 — Objectives Not Biting

HCO PL 29 Mar — Personnel Policy
Personnel Series 30

HCOB 31 Mar R
Rev. 29 Dec 88 — Basic Study Missed Withhold
Study Series 11R
Word Clearing Series 68R

HCO PL 1 Apr — The Safe Point
PR Series 19R

HCO PL 7 Apr — Out-Ethics Indicators
LRH Comm N/W Series 16

HCOB 11 Apr — Sec Checking Implants

HCOB 13 Apr — Still Needle and Confessionals

HCO PL 15 Apr II — The Counting of Gross Income
Finance Series 29

HCOB 16 Apr — More on PTS Handling

HCOB 26 Apr — The Criminal Mind and the Psychs

HCO PL 28 Apr — The Rights of the Field Auditor

HCO PL 29 Apr II — Field Auditor Fees

LRH ED 4 May — Books Straight Talk

HCOB 6 May — The Cause of Crime

HCO PL 6 May — Books Are Assets
Finance Series 32

LRH ED 9 May — Ron's Journal 35, From Clear to Eternity

HCOB 10 May — OT Levels

HCO PL 10 May — Bookstore Officer Hat

LRH ED 10 May R
Rev. 21 Oct 82 — The Ridge on the Bridge

HCO PL 25 May — Kha-Khan

HCO PL 1 Jul — Management Coordination
AKH Series 41

HCOB 11 Jul I — Questionable Auditing Repair List

HCOB 11 Jul II — Questionable Auditing

HCO PL 16 Jul R
Rev. 30 May 89 — Fully Hatted Org Staff Members, HCO Gross Divisional Statistic

HCO PL 19 Jul — Failed PR
PR Series 45

HCO PL 22 Jul — Knowledge Reports

HCO PL 27 Jul RA
Rev. 2 Feb 91 — Deputy FBOs for Marketing of Org Resources for Exchange (D/FBO for MORE)
Finance Series 33RA

HCOB 10 Aug — OT Maxims

HCO PL 18 Aug RI
Rev. 28 Feb 84 — Targets and Production
Target Series 8
Computer Series 3
AKH Series 42R

HCO PL 18 Aug II — Computers, Danger of Relying On
Computer Series 7

HCO PL 20 Aug — Organizational Basics

HCO PL 22 Aug — Battle Plans
Target Series 9
AKH Series 43

HCOB 25 Aug — The Joy of Creating
Art Series 10

HCOB 26 Aug — Pain and Sex

HCO PL 27 Aug — Vital Data: Power and Affluence Conditions

HCO PL 2 Sep — And That Is Banking
Finance Series 34

HCO PL 3 Sep — Deputy FBO for Marketing of Org Resources for Exchange (D/FBO for MORE) Purpose
Finance Series 35

HCO PL 10 Sep — Exchange, Org Income and Staff Pay
Finance Series 36

HCO PL 12 Sep — PR Functions
PR Series 46

HCO PL 28 Sep — The Basics of Statistics and Management

HCOB 28 Sep — Mixing Rundowns and Repairs
C/S Series 115

HCO PL 29 Sep — Misrepresentation of Dianetics and Scientology
KSW Series 30

HCO PL 12 Oct — Corrupt Activities

HCOB 13 Oct — Ethics and the C/S
C/S Series 116

HCO PL 14 Oct — Why Things Are Evaluated
Data Series 49

HCO PL 27 Oct RA
Rev. 23 Sep 89 — Cash-Bills Defined
Finance Series 38RA

HCO PL 31 Oct — Financial Planning, Responsibility For
Finance Series 39

HCO PL 1 Nov — "Boom Formula" Cancelled

HCO PL 2 Nov — Conditions Handlings

HCO PL 16 Nov — Div 6A Stat Renamed and Redefined: Bodies in the Shop

HCO PL 30 Nov — The Deputy CO or Deputy ED for Delivery and Exchange

HCO PL 18 Dec — Ethics Conditions: Hang-up at Doubt

HCO PL 19 Dec I — "Doing a Quicksilver" Forbidden
Org Series 45
Personnel Series 31

HCO PL 19 Dec RA II
Rev. 26 May 98 — Repairing Past Ethics Conditions

HCO PL 22 Dec RB
Rev. 15 Aug 90 — Service Routes for New Public

HCO PL 24 Dec R
Rev. 19 Feb 91 — Service Routes into SO Orgs

HCOB 27 Dec — Training and OT

HCO PL 29 Dec RI
Rev. 21 Feb 91 — Service Routes into the FSO

HCO PL 29 Dec RA II
Rev. 21 Jan 91 — The Tools of Management
Esto Series 45RA
Org Series 46RA
AKH Series 44RA
Exec Series 24RA

INTRODUCTORY AND DEMONSTRATION PROCESSES AND ASSISTS
based on the works of L. Ron Hubbard

First published by Bridge Publications, revised in December 1992.

RON'S JOURNAL 36: "YOUR NEW YEAR"

In this tape-recorded Ron's Journal, released on New Year's 1982, L. Ron Hubbard urges all Scientologists to move up the Bridge.

1983

Among the new technical releases of 1983 was a vital new auditor training course, the Professional TR Course—featuring Mr. Hubbard's Technical Training Film, *The Professional TR Course* and his latest TR training breakthroughs.

Mr. Hubbard also published new bulletins and policy letters on ethics technology, case supervision, Word Clearing, Confessionals, and several church management breakthroughs. These new technical releases resulted in further expansion of Scientology. Church management was reformed and there were new breakthroughs in public relations.

BRONZE BUST OF L. RON HUBBARD

Large bust of L. Ron Hubbard for display on pedestal.

CAR BADGE

Scientology symbol for use on cars

SOLO WINGS

Gold pin in the form of wings around a Scientology symbol for Solo auditors.

For example, the size of the LRH Comm Network more than doubled. And international dissemination efforts brought Dianetics and Scientology to ever–increasing numbers.

And while continuing his researches into the mind and spirit, he also wrote 50 original stories for new public films on Scientology.

ISSUES

HCO PL	5 Jan	Strategic Planning *AKH Series 46*
HCO PL 9 Jan R I Rev. 2 Feb 91		Viability, the Make–Break Point of an Org *Finance Series 41R*
HCO PL	9 Jan II	Checklist for a Strategic Plan *AKH Series 47*
HCO PL	13 Jan	The Business of Orgs
HCO PL	23 Jan	Auditor Training Prerequisite
HCO PL	30 Jan	Your Post and Life *Esto Series 46* *KSW Series 28*
HCO PL	31 Jan	The Reason for Orgs
HCOB	8 Mar	Handling PTS Situations
HCO PL	7 Apr	Goodwill *Exec Series 25* *PR Series 47*
HCOB	12 Apr	List of Keeping Scientology Working Series
HCOB	3 May	Who or What Is a "C/S"? *C/S Series 117*
HCO PL 13 Jun R Rev. 17 Jan 91		Addition to HCO Gross Divisional Statistic, Fully Hatted Org Staff Members
HCO PL 31 Jul R I Rev. 21 Jan 91		Basic Management Tools *Esto Series 47R* *Org Series 47R* *Exec Series 26R* *AKH Series 48R*
HCO PL	31 Jul II	Management Tools Breakthrough *Esto Series 48* *Org Series 48* *Exec Series 27* *AKH Series 49*
HCO PL 4 Aug R Rev. 2 Feb 91		Financial Planning Program No. 1 *Finance Series 42R*
HCO PL 6 Aug R Rev. 24 Dec 89		What a Professional TR Course Must Consist Of
HCOB	7 Aug	Robotic TRs
HCOB	8 Aug	Cycling Through TRs on a Professional TR Course
HCOB	19 Aug	OT III Course Posh–Up
HCOB	27 Aug	Words and Associations *Word Clearing Series 69*
HCO PL	28 Aug	Spot Checks

THE PROFESSIONAL TR COURSE

Directed and narrated by L. Ron Hubbard, this film shows why TRs are vital in auditing and depicts all aspects of professional TR training. The TRs themselves are covered in detail, portraying exactly how each is done. May be viewed by students in churches of Scientology on courses that include this film. TRANSLATIONS: *Danish, Dutch, French, German, Hebrew, Italian, Japanese, Norwegian, Portuguese, Spanish and Swedish.*

ISSUES

HCOB	10 Sep	PTSness and Disconnection
HCO PL	15 Sep	LRH Comm and PRO *LRH Comm N/W Series 17*
HCO PL	2 Oct	Solo Course Part One, Prerequisites
HCOB	23 Oct	Sec Checking: Note
HCO PL	10 Nov	TR and EM Films, Showing Of

MANAGEMENT SERIES VOLUMES 1 AND 2
by L. Ron Hubbard

Updated edition of the Management Series *Volumes. Compiled and published by Bridge Publications, Los Angeles, California.*

THE ORIGINAL L. RON HUBBARD EXECUTIVE DIRECTIVES
by L. Ron Hubbard

Two–volume reprinting of all the LRH Executive Directives. Published by Bridge Publications, Los Angeles, California.
Series 1–15 September 1966 to 28 April 1968
Series 2–10 May 1968 to 9 March 1969
Series 3–20 January 1969 to 13 March 1983

RON'S JOURNAL 38, TODAY AND TOMORROW: THE PROOF

One-hour recorded journal from L. Ron Hubbard giving news of the unprecedented expansion of Scientology, technical and administrative breakthroughs, and reorganization of the Church. Mr. Hubbard states, "My earnest

---

advice is: Only deal with or associate with those organizations licensed by RTC and auditors in good standing with the Church." Produced in Clearsound by Golden Era Productions.

1984

In addition to the many technical and administrative advances made in 1984, Mr. Hubbard's research in the field of sound culminated in the development of Clearsound technology. This revolutionary technology made it possible to restore early, previously inaudible sound recordings of Mr. Hubbard's lectures so that the advances in spiritual understanding they contained could be made available to all. This began the release of lectures now available today and listed throughout this chronology. This was also the year that the International Association of Scientologists (IAS) was formed and the Pledge to Mankind signed at Saint Hill in England, uniting Scientologists everywhere.

ISSUES

HCOB	3 Jan III	Radiation and Liquids *Purif RD Series 7*
HCOB	10 Jan	The Use of Demonstration *Study Series 12*
HCOB 16 Jan RA I Rev. 27 Jun 89		The Happiness Rundown *HRD Series 1RA*
HCOB	16 Jan II	Repair of Past Cramming *Cramming Series 17*
HCOB	17 Jan	Happiness Rundown Basics *HRD Series 2*
HCOB	18 Jan	How to Audit the HRD *HRD Series 3*
HCOB	19 Jan	Happiness Rundown Command Sheets *HRD Series 4*
HCOB	20 Jan	HRD Precepts Assessment List *HRD Series 4–1*
HCOB 21 Jan R I Rev. 20 Jul 88		Happiness Rundown Repair List (HRL) *HRD Series 5R*
HCOB 21 Jan RA II Rev. 27 Jun 89		C/Sing the Happiness Rundown *HRD Series 6RA*
HCOB 21 Jan R III Rev. 20 Jul 88		Delivery of the Happiness Rundown to Clears and OTs *HRD Series 7R*
HCOB	23 Jan	Drug Rundowns and Radiation
HCOB	27 Jan	FSM Breakthrough, New FSM TRs – Controlling a Conversation
HCOB	1 Feb	How to View Art *Art Series 11*
HCO PL	16 Feb	What Is a Computer? *Computer Series 1*

HCOB	25 Feb		Depth Perspective *Art Series 13*
HCOB	26 Feb I		Color *Art Series 14*
HCOB	26 Feb II		Art and Integration *Art Series 15* *Marketing Series 20*
HCOB/PL	28 Feb		Pretended PTS *C/S Series 118*
HCO PL	29 Feb		Computer Ethics Points *Computer Series 6*
HCOB Rev. 12 Aug 96	2 Mar RA		O/W Write-ups
HCOB Rev. 11 Jun 96	3 Mar R		The Comm Cycle in Solo Auditing *Solo Series 3R*
HCOB	10 Mar I		Message *Art Series 16*
HCOB	10 Mar II		Oils Can Go Rancid *Purif RD Series 8*
HCO PL	20 Mar		Targets, More About *Target Series 7*
HCO PL	27 Mar		Three Classes of People *Esto Series 49*
HCOB	27 Mar		Stalled Dianetic Clear: Solved *C/S Series 119*
HCO PL	28 Mar I		The Stages of Analysis *Data Series 50*
HCO PL	28 Mar II		Executive Posting Qualifications *Personnel Series 32* *Exec Series 28*
HCO PL	2 Apr		"Upside Down" Graphs
HCO PL	6 May		ARC Break Program, Additional Data
HCO PL	7 May		The LRH Comm Network and Its Purpose *LRH Comm N/W Series 1*
HCOB Rev. 11 Jan 90	5 Jun R		False Purpose Rundown *FPRD Series 1R*
HCOB	6 Jun I		Rock Slams, More About
HCOB	6 Jun II		"Murder Routine"
HCOB	6 Jun III		Missed Withhold Handling
HCOB Rev. 12 Jan 90	6 Jun R IV		The "Lost Tech" of Handling Overts and Evil Purposes *FPRD Series 2R*
HCOB	7 Jun		The Prior Confusion: New Tech Breakthrough *FPRD Series 3*
HCOB	8 Jun		Clearing Justifications *FPRD Series 4*
HCOB Rev. 22 Mar 96	9 Jun RA		Auditing the False Purpose Rundown *FPRD Series 5R*
HCOB	10 Jun		False Purpose Rundown Commands *FPRD Series 6*
HCOB	11 Jun		C/Sing the False Purpose Rundown *FPRD Series 7*
HCOB	12 Jun		False Purpose Rundown Auditor Errors *FPRD Series 8*
HCOB Rev. 1 Aug 90	13 Jun R		False Purpose Rundown Correction List *FPRD Series 9R*
HCOB	14 Jun		False Purpose Rundown Basic Form *FPRD Series 10-A*
HCOB	15 Jun II		False Purpose Rundown, Info for Orgs and Missions
HCOB	17 Jun		Evil Purposes and False PR *C/S Series 118-1*
HCO PL	2 Jul		Hatting and the Environment *Esto Series 50* *Exec Series 29*
HCO PL	8 Aug II		Routing Forms, How to Write One
HCO PL Rev. 6 Jul 98	2 Oct RA		Scientology Magistrate

PURIFICATION: AN ILLUSTRATED ANSWER TO DRUGS

A picture book compiled by staff and published by Bridge Publications, Los Angeles, California and New Era Publications, Copenhagen, Denmark. TRANSLATIONS: Danish, Dutch, French, German, Italian, Spanish, Japanese and Swedish.

PURIFICATION RUNDOWN DELIVERY MANUAL

Compiled by staff and published by Bridge Publications, Los Angeles, California. TRANSLATIONS: Danish, Dutch, French, German, Italian, Japanese, Spanish and Swedish.

ISSUES

HCOB Rev. 18 Jun 89	8 Nov R		Security Checker Beingness
HCOB	22 Nov		False Purpose Rundown Correction List Word List *FPRD Series 9-1*

1985

Living at his ranch near San Luis Obispo, California, Mr. Hubbard continued to develop new technology at the lower levels of the Bridge, while also pushing forward his research into the highest levels of OT.

In August he completed and released the Allergy or Asthma Rundown, a new series of auditing steps designed to help relieve mental and spiritual troubles associated with allergies and asthma.

The new Clear Certainty Rundown was completed in December,

providing a complete and streamlined procedure for verifying and validating a person's achievement of the state of Clear. For Clears, a completely new first step toward Operating Thetan was released: New OT I. This level, which replaced OT I, not only gives the Clear terrific case gains, but also builds his certainty and competence as a Solo auditor.

While advancing technical research, Mr. Hubbard also found time to compose and write lyrics for a complete album of Scientology songs. Making musical statements of many of the basic principles of Scientology, the album was recorded and produced in 1986 by Golden Era Productions. The album provided a musical medium for Scientologists to introduce family and friends to the truths of Scientology.

ISSUES

HCO PL	7 Jan		HCO Confessionals
HCO PL	24 Mar		Responsibility, Control and Danger Conditions
HCOB	1 May		Honesty and Case Gain *C/S Series 120*
HCOB/PL	2 May		Responsibility, Definition Of
HCOB	12 May		Exec and Staff Member Form *FPRD Series 10-C*
HCOB	13 May		Second Dynamic Form *FPRD Series 10-D*
HCOB	14 May		Money and Finance Form *FPRD Series 10-E*
HCOB	15 May		Dissemination Form *FPRD Series 10-F*
HCOB	17 May		Auditor Form *FPRD Series 10-H*
HCOB	18 May		Student Form *FPRD Series 10-I*
HCOB/PL	21 May		Two Types of PTSes *C/S Series 121* *FPRD Series 11*
HCO PL	18 Jun		Product Orientation *Org Series 49* *Exec Series 30*
HCOB	2 Jul		Artist Form *FPRD Series 10-G*
HCO PL	3 Aug		Completing Conditions Formulas
HCOB	20 Aug		Sec Checker Form *FPRD Series 10-J*

NEW OT I MATERIALS
[Confidential and unpublished]

On 24 August 1985, the confidential and unpublished materials of this new OT level were made available to those who met the requirements for beginning the level.

ISSUE

HCOB	29 Aug		Allergy or Asthma Rundown

PLAQUE: "PROFESSIONALISM," BY L. RON HUBBARD

Article on professionalism by L. Ron Hubbard, suitable for wall-hanging.

PLAQUE: "CODE OF HONOR," BY L. RON HUBBARD

The Code of Honor, suitable for wall-hanging.

PLAQUE: "JOY OF CREATING," BY L. RON HUBBARD

Calligraphic rendering of "Joy of Creating" in frame, suitable for wall-hanging.

CHURCH OF SCIENTOLOGY INTERNATIONAL RING

A gold ring with the Church of Scientology International symbol.

INTERNATIONAL ASSOCIATION OF SCIENTOLOGISTS PINS

Earned by persons who have contributed to the International Association of Scientologists: Membership Pin, Award Pin and Patron Pin.

THE FUTURE OF SCIENTOLOGY AND WESTERN CIVILIZATION

by L. Ron Hubbard

Transcribed from a recorded lecture. International Association of Scientologists special gift edition. Published by New Era Publications, Copenhagen, Denmark.

ISSUES

HCOB 24 Oct R Rev. 28 Mar 90	Troubleshooting the Purification Rundown Pc *C/S Series 122R Purif RD Series 9R*	
HCOB 25 Oct R Rev. 28 Mar 90	Purification Rundown Correction List *Purif RD Series 10R*	
HCOB 17 Nov R Rev. 18 Dec 88	Clear Certainty Rundown: Purpose *C/S Series 104RB CCRD Series 2R*	
HCOB 18 Nov R Rev. 27 May 94	Clearing, Meter Phenomena and the Clear Certainty Rundown *CCRD Series 11RA*	
HCOB 19 Nov RA Rev. 27 Mar 94	Clear Certainty Rundown: Two-Way Comm Step *CCRD Series 9RA*	
HCOB 20 Nov	Exterior and Clear *CCRD Series 17R*	
HCOB 21 Nov	First Dynamic Form *FPRD Series 10–K*	
HCOB 22 Nov	Field Staff Member Repair and Revitalization List *FSM Series 9*	
HCO PL 23 Nov	INCOMM *Computer Series 4*	
HCOB 23 Nov R Rev. 27 Mar 94	Last Life Clear *CCRD Series 12RA*	
HCOB 24 Nov RA Rev. 27 Mar. 94	Clear Certainty Rundown Assessment List *CCRD Series 10RA*	
HCOB 25 Nov R Rev. 27 Mar 94	Clear Certainty Rundown Word List *CCRD Series 8RA*	
HCOB 26 Nov RA Rev. 27 Mar 94	Clear Certainty Rundown: Procedure *CCRD Series 6RA*	

HCOB 27 Nov R Rev. 27 Mar 94	Clear Certainty Rundown Case Checklist *CCRD Series 14R*	
HCOB 28 Nov R Rev. 27 Mar 94	C/Sing the Clear Certainty Rundown *CCRD Series 15R*	
HCOB 30 Nov R Rev. 27 Mar 94	FES Checklist for Starting the Clear Certainty Rundown *CCRD Series 7R*	
HCOB/PL 2 Dec R Rev. 18 Dec 88	Clear Certainty Rundown, New Service *C/S Series 112RA*	
HCOB 4 Dec	Case Evaluation and Children	
HCOB 5 Dec R Rev. 18 Dec 88	Handling of Past-Life Auditing *C/S Series 123R*	
HCOB 6 Dec R Rev. 18 Dec 88	C/S Study Requirement *C/S Series 106RB*	

NEW OT VIII
[Confidential and unpublished]

By the end of 1985, Mr. Hubbard had completed and codified new OT levels all the way through New OT XV. His New Year's message for 1986 included a very special gift for his friends—the first of these OT Levels, New OT VIII: Truth Revealed. The level was complete, but an ideal space for its delivery was needed—which was accomplished with the purchase of the ship *Freewinds*. New OT VIII was released on the *Freewinds* on 7 June 1988.

RON'S JOURNAL 39: MY NEW YEAR'S GIFT TO YOU

In this special New Year's message for 1986, produced in Clearsound, L. Ron Hubbard announces the levels above New OT VII.

1986

On 24 January 1986, having completed all he set out to do, Mr. Hubbard departed his body. However, he left a wealth of research material yet to be assembled and published, along with instructions as to how this work was to be done. Dedicated staff of the Church of Scientology International took up the task of making this legacy of as-yet-unpublished material available.

In addition to compiling and publishing materials not previously available, a continuing effort has been made to see that the entire legacy of Mr. Hubbard's work is made known—and easily accessible—to all the peoples of Earth. To this end a series of projects have been carried out to assemble and publish new editions of his works: books supplemented with glossaries and indexes to make data more easily located and understood; lectures produced using

Clearsound technology to restore the recordings of Mr. Hubbard's recorded lectures so that every word can be clearly heard, then released with complete transcripts and glossaries; translated editions of books, films and recorded lectures; and new books and films to quickly communicate the truths of Dianetics and Scientology and how they can be used to improve life. This work has been going forward apace since 1986 and will continue for many years to come.

THE ORGANIZATION EXECUTIVE COURSE VOLUME 0

by L. Ron Hubbard

New edition updated by staff with many new LRH policies added. Fully indexed and includes an insert of nine-division org board. Published by Bridge Publications, Los Angeles, California.

ROAD TO FREEDOM

Songs composed by L. Ron Hubbard and performed by the Golden Era Musicians and numerous celebrities. "Thank You for Listening," the last song, is sung by L. Ron Hubbard himself. Released on 13 March, 1986 at L. Ron Hubbard's Birthday Event. Produced in Clearsound on cassette and as a record album. TRANSLATIONS: French, German, Italian, Spanish, Danish, Swedish and Japanese.

ISSUES

HCO PL 10 Jul I	Keeping Admin Working *AKH Series 50*	
HCO PL 10 Jul II	Admin Degrades *AKH Series 51*	
HCO PL 10 Jul III	Admin High Crime *AKH Series 52 Computer Series 5*	

THE HOPE OF MAN

by L. Ron Hubbard

Transcribed from a recorded lecture. International Association of Scientologists special gift edition. Published by Bridge Publications, Los Angeles, California.

MY PHILOSOPHY

A recording in which "My Philosophy," "A Description of Scientology" and "The Aims of Scientology," three of L. Ron Hubbard's powerful writings, are read by Jeff Pomerantz and accompanied by music composed especially for it. Produced by Golden Era Productions. Released in September.

1987

MY PHILOSOPHY

A video presentation of L. Ron Hubbard's 1965 essay, "My Philosophy," with never-before-seen photos of Mr. Hubbard's life. Produced by Golden Era Productions with transcript and glossary.

ISSUES

HCO PL	25 Jul	Knowledge, Definition Of
HCOB	13 Aug	Confessionals — Types of TRs
HCOB Rev. 29 Mar 96	15 Aug R	Unconscious Person Assist
HCOB	25 Aug I	Nerve Assist
HCOB	25 Aug II	Touch Assists, More About

THE GAME CALLED MAN
by L. Ron Hubbard

Transcribed from a recorded lecture. International Association of Scientologists special gift edition. Published by Bridge Publications, Los Angeles, California.

ISSUES

HCOB	28 Oct	The Auditor Admin Series for Use by All Auditors *Auditor Admin Series 1RA*
HCOB	29 Oct	The Folder *Auditor Admin Series 4R*
HCOB	30 Oct	The Yellow Sheet *Auditor Admin Series 6RA*
HCOB	31 Oct	The Folder Summary *Auditor Admin Series 7RA*
HCOB	1 Nov	OCA Graphs *Auditor Admin Series 8R*
HCOB	2 Nov	The Program Sheet *Auditor Admin Series 9RA*
HCOB	5 Nov	The Auditor's Report Form *Auditor Admin Series 13RA*
HCOB	6 Nov	The Worksheets *Auditor Admin Series 14RA*
HCOB	9 Nov	Dianetic Assessment Lists *Auditor Admin Series 19RA*
HCOB	10 Nov	Miscellaneous Reports *Auditor Admin Series 20RA*
HCOB	11 Nov	Folder Error Summary Format *Auditor Admin Series 22RB*
HCOB	12 Nov	Invoice Form and Routing Forms *Auditor Admin Series 23RB*
HCOB	13 Nov	The Pc Folder and Its Contents *Auditor Admin Series 3RA*
HCOB	14 Nov I	Expanded ARC Straightwire Grade Process Checklist
HCOB	14 Nov II	Expanded Grade 0 Process Checklist
HCOB	14 Nov III	Expanded Grade I Process Checklist
HCOB	14 Nov IV	Expanded Grade II Process Checklist
HCOB	14 Nov V	Expanded Grade III Process Checklist
HCOB	14 Nov VI	Expanded Grade IV Process Checklist
HCO PL	27 Nov	Examiner's Form, Additional Data *Auditor Admin Series 11-1*
HCOB	28 Nov	L&N Lists *Auditor Admin Series 18RA*
HCOB	29 Nov	Correction Lists *Auditor Admin Series 16RA*

DIANETICS: EVOLUTION OF A SCIENCE
by L. Ron Hubbard

Beginning with the revolutionary postulate that the human mind should have nearly infinite potential, L. Ron Hubbard followed a trail of research which led to discovery of the reactive mind, man's hidden nemesis. This public film depicts the results of that exploration in the story of a young man who makes his way back, through Dianetics, from a serious injury. Produced by Golden Era Productions. TRANSLATIONS: Danish, Dutch, French, German, Italian, Spanish and Swedish.

1988

THE HISTORY OF THE E-METER

A technical film covering the development of the E-Meter. May be viewed by students in churches of Scientology on courses that include this film. Produced by Golden Era Productions. TRANSLATIONS: Danish, Dutch, French, German, Italian, Spanish and Swedish.

ISSUES

HCOB	8 Apr	The "Bring Back to Life" Assist
HCOB	10 Apr	R3RA Service Facsimile Handling Action Eleven *NED Series 30*
HCOB Rev. 19 Jun 89	4 May R	False Purpose Rundown Executive Posting Qualifications Form *FPRD Series 10-L*

NEW OT VIII MATERIALS
[Confidential and unpublished]

On 7 June 1988, aboard the Freewinds, the confidential and unpublished materials of this Solo-audited OT level were made available for study to those who met the requirements for beginning it.

ISSUES

HCOB	1 Jul	Questionable Auditing Repair List Word List
HCOB	2 Jul	Field Staff Member Repair and Revitalization List Word List *FSM Series 9-1*
HCOB Rev. 28 Mar 90	4 Jul R	Purification Rundown Correction List Word List *Purif RD Series 10-1R*
HCOB	5 Jul	The End of Endless Drug Rundowns Repair List Word List
HCOB	6 Jul	Crashing Mis-U Repair List - LC1R Word List *Product Debug Series 4R-1* *Word Clearing Series 62R-1*
HCOB	7 Jul	Product Debug Repair List Word List *Product Debug Series 10R-1*
HCOB	8 Jul	C/S Series 53RM (Short Form), Short Hi–Lo TA Assessment C/S Word List
HCOB	11 Jul	False Data Stripping Repair List *Product Debug Series 11*
HCOB	12 Jul	False Data Stripping Repair List Word List *Product Debug Series 11-1*
HCOB	20 Jul	Happiness Rundown Repair List Word List *HRD Series 5R-1*
HCO PL	10 Sep	Tabulating Survey Responses *Marketing Series 22*
HCO PL	11 Sep	Ethnic Surveys *PR Series 15* *Marketing Series 23*
HCO PL	12 Sep	Positioning in PR *PR Series 29*
HCO PL	13 Sep	The Positioning Era *Marketing Series 24*
HCO PL	14 Sep	Positioning Surveys *Marketing Series 25*
HCO PL	15 Sep	Naming Services and Products *Marketing Series 26*
HCO PL	16 Sep	Instant Impression *Marketing Series 27*
HCO PL	17 Sep	Survey Network *Marketing Series 28*
HCO PL	18 Sep	PR Texts *PR Series 16*
HCO PL	19 Sep	Clipping Books *PR Series 24*
HCO PL	20 Sep	Documentation and the Dead Agent Caper *PR Series 32*
HCO PL	21 Sep	Press Agentry *PR Series 33*
HCO PL	22 Sep	Creating Overwhelming Popularity *PR Series 41*
HCO PL	23 Sep	Names and the Local Environment *PR Series 42*
HCO PL	24 Sep	PR and Purpose *PR Series 43*
HCO PL	6 Oct	Success Through Communication
HCO PL	18 Dec	The Sunshine Rundown: Administration
HCOB Rev. 30 Jan 90	19 Dec R	Scientology Marriage Counseling

E-METER ESSENTIALS
by L. Ron Hubbard

New edition. Published by Bridge Publications, Los Angeles, California and New Era Publications, Copenhagen, Denmark. TRANSLATIONS: Dutch, French, German, Italian and Spanish.

INTRODUCING THE E-METER
by L. Ron Hubbard

New edition. Published by Bridge Publications, Los Angeles, California and New Era Publications, Copenhagen, Denmark. TRANSLATIONS: Danish, Dutch, French, German, Italian, Spanish and Swedish.

THE BOOK OF E-METER DRILLS
by L. Ron Hubbard

New edition. Published by Bridge Publications, Los Angeles, California and New Era Publications, Copenhagen, Denmark. TRANSLATIONS: Danish, Dutch, French, German, Italian, Spanish and Swedish.

UNDERSTANDING THE E-METER
by L. Ron Hubbard

New edition. Published by Bridge Publications, Los Angeles, California and New Era Publications, Copenhagen, Denmark. TRANSLATIONS: French, German, Italian, Japanese and Spanish.

INDIVIDUAL TRACK MAP
by L. Ron Hubbard

New edition. Published by Bridge Publications, Los Angeles, California for use with New Era Dianetics.

INTERNATIONAL ASSOCIATION OF SCIENTOLOGISTS PIN

Earned by patrons who have contributed to the International Association of Scientologists: Patron with Honors Pin.

RELIGIOUS TECHNOLOGY CENTER RING

A gold ring with the Religious Technology Center symbol.

HUBBARD PROFESSIONAL MARK SUPER VII E-METER

On March 13, 1988, the Mark Super VII E-Meter, designed according to L. Ron Hubbard's specifications, was released. It was the most precise and accurate E-Meter to date, especially suitable for the upper OT levels. Special editions in Gold, Silver and Bronze were issued to commemorate the occasion.

BASIC DICTIONARY OF DIANETICS AND SCIENTOLOGY

by L. Ron Hubbard

New edition. Published by Bridge Publications, Los Angeles, California and New Era Publications, Copenhagen, Denmark. TRANSLATIONS: Dutch, French, German, Italian, Japanese and Swedish.

THE MARRIED COUPLE

A public film that tells the story of a once-happy couple whose relationship deteriorates to the verge of divorce. They receive marriage counseling at a church of Scientology, find the source of their problems and begin to build an honest and lasting relationship. Produced by Golden Era Productions. TRANSLATIONS: Danish, Dutch, French, German, Italian, Spanish and Swedish.

THE TROUBLESHOOTER

This package contains L. Ron Hubbard's bulletins for the analysis and handling of difficulties which may be encountered in an auditing session. TRANSLATIONS: French, German, Italian and Spanish.

PASSPORT UP THE BRIDGE TO FREEDOM

This unique document lists out the training and processing steps on the Bridge to Total Freedom, as well as every book, film and lecture by L. Ron Hubbard. Whenever a step is completed it is officially validated at a Scientology organization with a special passport stamp.

WHAT HAPPENED TO THESE CIVILIZATIONS?

A film that tells why numerous civilizations have failed and the solution to creating a new civilization

that will bring hope to mankind. This public film was released May 9, 1988. Produced by Golden Era Productions. TRANSLATIONS: Brazilian, Danish, Dutch, Finnish, French, German, Greek, Hebrew, Italian, Norwegian, Portuguese, Spanish and Swedish.

1989

ISSUES

HCOB	8 Mar	Word Clearing— Key Datum *Word Clearing Series 45*
HCO PL	21 Mar	PTS People and Leaves

ASSISTS

This film supplements Dianetics and Scientology written materials and lectures about assists, including why they work and how to do them. May be viewed by students in churches of Scientology on courses that include this film. Produced by Golden Era Productions. TRANSLATIONS: Danish, Dutch, French, German, Italian, Portuguese, Spanish and Swedish.

ISSUES

HCOB	2 Jun I	Auditing Repair List for People from EST
HCOB	2 Jun II	EST Confessional Form *Confessional Form 13*
HCOB	3 Jun	Auditing Repair List for People from EST Word List
HCOB	5 Jul	Coaching TRs 0–4
HCOB	24 Sep	Repair List for Treatment from Psychiatrists, Psychologists and Psychoanalysts
HCOB	25 Sep	Repair List for Treatment from Psychiatrists, Psychologists and Psychoanalysts Word List
HCOB	26 Oct	TRs Clay Table Processing: Instructions for the Student Auditor
HCOB	27 Oct	How to Do Clay Table Processing
HCOB	29 Oct	Clay Table Processing Repair List – LCTR
HCOB	30 Oct	Clay Table Processing Repair List Word List
HCOB	16 Nov	Art and Equipment *Art Series 17*
HCOB	23 Dec	TR Debug Assessment Word List

CLAY TABLE PROCESSING PICTURE BOOK

by L. Ron Hubbard

For use by students on the Hubbard Professional TR Course only. Published by Bridge Publications, Los Angeles, California and New Era Publications, Copenhagen, Denmark. TRANSLATIONS: Danish, Dutch, French, German, Hebrew, Italian, Japanese, Portuguese, Norwegian, Spanish and Swedish.

1990

THE SCIENTOLOGY CHARTS PACKAGE

A full package of sixteen Scientology charts and codes that help map the Route to Total Freedom was released at the March 13th event. These can be purchased separately or as a package in a special plastic envelope. The charts and codes in this package include:

Scientology Classification, Gradation and Awareness Chart of Levels and Certificates

The Bridge to Total Freedom

Hubbard Chart of Human Evaluation and Dianetic Processing

Hubbard Chart of Attitudes

The Tone Scale in Full and the Illustrated Tone Scale Chart

The Conditions Formulas

Evaluator's Know-How Chart

The Logics

The Factors

Code of a Scientologist

The Auditor's Code

The Code of Honor

The Creed of the Church of Scientology

ISSUES

HCOB	27 Mar I	The Purification Rundown and Radiation *Purif RD Series 13*
HCOB	27 Mar II	The Purification Rundown: A Long-Range Detoxification Program *Purif RD Series 14*
HCOB	28 Mar	The Role of Oil on the Purification Rundown *Purif RD Series 15*
HCOB	1 Apr	CCHs 8–10
HCOB	2 Apr	Additional Objective Processes for TRs and Objectives Co-audit
HCOB	4 Apr	Model Session for Objectives Co-audits
HCO PL	4 Apr	Course Schedules
HCOB	9 Apr	Objectives Correction List
HCOB	10 Apr	Objectives Correction List Word List
HCOB	12 Apr	Clay Table, Definition of Terms

HUBBARD KEY TO LIFE COURSE BOOKS
by L. Ron Hubbard

The thirteen books of the Hubbard Key to Life Course materials, written and designed by L. Ron Hubbard, utilize 4,000 highly expressive illustrations to define concepts along with words to ensure full comprehension. Released on May 9th, these materials include The New Grammar, How To Use a Dictionary Picture Book and Small Common Words Defined. Published by Bridge Publications, Los Angeles, California.

DIANETICS: THE DYNAMICS OF LIFE

A public film showing the true story of how L. Ron Hubbard embarked on the most daring exploration in all human history—a journey to confront and answer the riddle of life itself. Released in May. Produced by Golden Era Productions. TRANSLATIONS: Danish, Dutch, French, German, Hebrew, Italian, Japanese, Norwegian, Portuguese, Spanish and Swedish.

CLEAR BODY, CLEAR MIND: THE EFFECTIVE PURIFICATION PROGRAM
by L. Ron Hubbard

Released in May, this book makes the full technology of the Purification program available to anyone. Published by Bridge Publications, Los Angeles, California. TRANSLATIONS: French, German and Italian.

ISSUES

HCOB	18 Jun	Pcs Who Refuse Auditing *C/S Series 124*
HCOB	30 Jul	Scientology Auditor Analysis Checklist *C/S Series 125*
HCOB	31 Jul	Confessional Auditor Analysis Checklist *C/S Series 126*
HCOB	1 Aug	The Test of a C/S *C/S Series 127*
HCO PL	2 Aug	Auditing Discounts
HCOB	3 Aug	Auditing and C/Sing Below One's Training Level
HCO PL	29 Aug	Using Orders or Policy to Create Problems
HCO PL	30 Aug	Weekly Staff Meetings
HCO PL	10 Sep I	The Quality of Division 6A, a Division 6A Checklist for Quality
HCO PL	10 Sep II	The Quality of Division 6B, a Division 6B Checklist for Quality
HCO PL	10 Sep III	The Quality of Division 6C, a Division 6C Checklist for Quality
HCO PL	5 Nov R Rev. 20 Sep 96	O/Ws and Evaluation *Data Series 51R*

UPPER INDOC TRS

This film shows exactly how Upper Indoc TRs are done and their result. May be viewed by students in churches of Scientology on courses which include this film. Released by Golden Era Productions in October.

HUBBARD LIFE ORIENTATION COURSE BOOKS
by L. Ron Hubbard

A companion work to the Key to Life Course materials, the Life Orientation Course materials also use full-color illustrations or photographs along with words to bring about full understanding. Published by Bridge Publications, Los Angeles, California and New Era Publications, Copenhagen, Denmark. TRANSLATIONS: French, German, Italian and Spanish.

BASIC STUDY MANUAL
based on the works of L. Ron Hubbard

New edition based on the works of L. Ron Hubbard, and released in December. Published by Applied Scholastics Publications, Los Angeles, California. TRANSLATIONS: German, Italian and Spanish.

DIANETICS: THE DYNAMICS OF LIFE MUSIC

Motion picture soundtrack from the film Dianetics: The Dynamics of Life. In Clearsound.

1991

ISSUES

HCO PL	10 Jan	Confusion Formula, Additional Data
HCO PL	11 Jan	Telex Discipline
HCO PL	21 Jan	Moonripping *Personnel Series 33*
HCO PL	22 Jan	Consequences of Miscramming
HCO PL	23 Jan	Senior Qual Network
HCO PL	28 Jan II	The Tech Estimate Line
HCO PL	28 Jan III	Marketing Posters *Marketing Series 31*
HCO PL	28 Jan IV	Fliers, Definition and Use *Marketing Series 30*
HCO PL	29 Jan I	Repetition of Message *Marketing Series 29*
HCO PL	29 Jan II	Technical Specialist Courses
HCO PL	11 Feb	Upper-Org Central Files and New Names to CF
HCOB	20 Feb R Rev. 13 Jun 96	Solo E-Meter Drills *Solo Series 4R*
HCO PL	21 Feb	Religious Influence in Society

HCO PL	22 Feb	Volunteer Ministers
HCO PL	23 Feb	Body Routing and Its Use
HCO PL	25 Feb	Delivering Public Division Courses
HCO PL	26 Feb	The Organization of the Public Divisions

THE ORGANIZATION EXECUTIVE COURSE VOLUMES
by L. Ron Hubbard

Updated edition containing every issue on administrative technology written by L. Ron Hubbard. Volumes 0–7. Compiled by staff and published by Bridge Publications, Los Angeles, California.

Volume 0: Basic Staff Hat

Volume 1: HCO Division

Volume 2: Dissemination Division

Volume 3: Treasury Division

Volume 4: Technical Division

Volume 5: Qualifications Division

Volume 6: Public Division

Volume 7: Executive Division

THE MANAGEMENT SERIES POLICY VOLUMES 1–3
by L. Ron Hubbard

Updated edition of the Management Series in three volumes, published by Bridge Publications, Los Angeles, California. Contains the Data Series, Public Relations Series, Marketing Series, Personnel Series, Organizing Series, Finance Series, Executive Series, Establishment Officer Series, Computer Series, Target Series, Admin Know-How Series.

THE OEC AND MANAGEMENT SERIES POLICY INDEX

An index to the new Organization Executive Course and Management Series volumes, published by Bridge Publications, Los Angeles, California.

OT VIII BRACELET

A gold bracelet carrying the OT symbol in a wreath may be worn by a Scientologist who has attained the level of New OT VIII.

INTERNATIONAL ASSOCIATION OF SCIENTOLOGISTS PINS

Earned by patrons who have contributed to the International Association of Scientologists: Sponsor, Crusader, Honor Roll, Patron, Patron with Honors, Patron Meritorious, Gold Meritorious, and Senior Honor Roll.

AUDITOR PINS

Class IV Auditor Pin, Class V Auditor Pin and Class V Graduate Auditor Pin.

FIELD STAFF MEMBER PINS

FSM Pin, Senior FSM Pin, Master FSM Pin and Power FSM Pin.

TRAINING PINS

Fast Flow Student Pin, Train for Life Pin, Pro TR Course Pin and Key to Life Pin.

 THE SOLO AUDITOR

In the 1990s, technical advances in film production made it possible to further enhance the standard of the technical training films by greatly improving the visual quality and durability of the films themselves. As a result, some technical training films were newly produced and re-released. One of the first among these was The Solo Auditor, a technical training film written by L. Ron Hubbard to teach basics to new Solo auditors. May be viewed by students in churches of Scientology on the Solo Auditor Course. Produced by Golden Era Productions.

ISSUES

HCOB	19 Apr	A Key Cramming Question *Cramming Series 18*
HCOB	20 Apr	Cramming and Basics *Cramming Series 19*
HCOB	21 Apr	Auditor Coordination Drills *Cramming Series 20*
HCOB	22 Apr	What a Cramming Officer Has to Know *Cramming Series 21*
HCOB	23 Apr	The Tools of a Cramming Officer *Cramming Series 22*
HCOB	24 Apr	Modification of the Primary Rundown
HCOB	25 Apr	Between Session Notes from Pcs
HCOB	26 Apr II	Handling Undeclared States of Release
HCOB	27 Apr I	Discovery on PDH (Pain-Drug-Hypnosis)
HCOB	27 Apr II	PDH Confessional *Confessional Form 14*
HCOB	27 Apr III	Prepared List for Still Needles
HCOB	28 Apr R I Rev. 31 May 95	Barley Formula for Babies
HCOB	29 Apr	Data About Fragrances

HCOB	1 May I	Study of Expanded Dianetics *ExDn Series 0*
HCOB	1 May II	Expanded Dianetics Repair List – L3 EXD *ExDn Series 2*
HCOB	1 May III	Expanded Dianetics Repair List – L3 EXD Word List *ExDn Series 3*
HCOB	1 May IV	Auditing Commands for Running Evil Intentions in Expanded Dianetics *ExDn Series 26*
HCOB	1 May V	Preassessment for Expanded Dianetics *ExDn Series 27*
HCOB	1 May VI	Preassessment List for Left-Side Rundowns *ExDn Series 27-1*
HCOB	1 May VII	Preassessment List for Right-Side Rundowns *ExDn Series 27-2*
HCOB	1 May VIII	Present Time Environment Rundown *ExDn Series 28*
HCOB	1 May IX	Handling Emotional Stresses *ExDn Series 29*
HCOB	1 May X	Past Auditing and Expanded Dianetics *ExDn Series 30*
HCOB	1 May XI	Handling Hidden Standards with Expanded Dianetics *ExDn Series 31*
HCOB	1 May XII	Wants Handled Rundown *ExDn Series 32*
HCOB	1 May XIII	Handling Stuck Points on the Track *ExDn Series 33*
HCOB	1 May XIV	Confessionals and Expanded Dianetics *ExDn Series 34*
HCOB	1 May XV	The Responsibility Rundown *ExDn Series 35*
HCOB	1 May XVI	Expanded Dianetics Service Facsimile Handling *ExDn Series 36*
HCOB	1 May XVII	Metalosis Rundown *ExDn Series 37*
HCOB	1 May XVIII	The OCA Rundown *ExDn Series 38*
HCOB	1 May XIX	C/Sing and Programing Expanded Dianetics *ExDn Series 39*

 UNDERSTANDING: THE UNIVERSAL SOLVENT

A volume of quotations from the works of L. Ron Hubbard. Published by Bridge Publications, Los Angeles, California.

NED FOR OTs AND SOLO NED FOR OTs NEW MATERIALS
[Confidential and unpublished]

At the Flag Land Base on 6 May 1991, confidential and unpublished issues and rundowns not previously available for New OT V, New OT VI and New OT VII were made available for study to those eligible to receive them.

 KNOWINGNESS

The second volume of quotations from the works of L. Ron Hubbard. Published by Bridge Publications, Los Angeles, California.

 THE TECHNICAL BULLETINS OF DIANETICS AND SCIENTOLOGY

by L. Ron Hubbard

Updated edition containing all technical writings of L. Ron Hubbard on Dianetics and Scientology. Eighteen volumes, including thirteen chronological volumes, index and four subject volumes—the Case Supervisor Series, Technical Series, Auditing Rundowns and Grade Processes and Prepared Lists. Published by Bridge Publications, Los Angeles, California.

 THE BOOK OF CASE REMEDIES

by L. Ron Hubbard

New edition including previously unpublished remedies and additional case remedy tools. Published by Bridge Publications, Los Angeles, California and New Era Publications, Copenhagen, Denmark.

 THE BASIC DIANETICS PICTURE BOOK

Based on the works of L. Ron Hubbard

New edition. Published by Bridge Publications, Los Angeles, California and New Era Publications, Copenhagen, Denmark. TRANSLATIONS: Chinese, Danish, Dutch, French, German, Greek, Hebrew, Italian, Japanese, Norwegian, Portuguese, Russian, Spanish and Swedish.

L. RON HUBBARD: CALENDAR

Beautiful wall calendar featuring photographs by L. Ron Hubbard. First in a series to be released each year.

 SCIENTOMETRIC TESTING

Based on the works of L. Ron Hubbard

The manual on the technology of testing based on the works of L. Ron Hubbard. Packaged in a slipcase along with sample testing materials and grading tools. Published by Bridge Publications, Los Angeles, California.

THE STORY OF BOOK ONE

The story of the release of Dianetics: The Modern Science of Mental Health *in May 1950 and the grassroots movement it sparked. This public film was produced by Golden Era Productions and released May 9, 1987 in English. Newly produced and released in 1991 in English, Danish, Dutch, French, German, Hebrew, Italian, Spanish and Swedish.*

1992

HOW TO USE DIANETICS: A VISUAL GUIDEBOOK TO THE HUMAN MIND

A video for Book One auditors which explains exactly what Dianetics is and how to co-audit on it. Released at the May 9th event. Produced by Golden Era Productions. TRANSLATIONS: Danish, Dutch, French, German, Greek, Hungarian, Italian, Japanese, Norwegian, Russian, Spanish and Swedish.

ART
by L. Ron Hubbard

L. Ron Hubbard's writings on art. Published by Bridge Publications, Los Angeles, California.

LEARNING HOW TO LEARN
Based on the works of L. Ron Hubbard

A first study book for children. Fully illustrated. Published in July by Bridge Publications, Los Angeles, California, and New Era Publications, Copenhagen, Denmark. TRANSLATIONS: Hungarian, Russian and Spanish.

STUDY SKILLS FOR LIFE
Based on the works of L. Ron Hubbard

The basic aspects of study technology written and illustrated for teenagers. Published in September by Bridge Publications, Los Angeles, California.

HOW TO USE A DICTIONARY PICTURE BOOK FOR CHILDREN
Based on the works of L. Ron Hubbard

An illustrated book which shows children how to find and understand words using a dictionary. Published in September by Bridge Publications, Los Angeles, California.

GRAMMAR AND COMMUNICATION FOR CHILDREN
Based on the works of L. Ron Hubbard

A simple, illustrated book which teaches the young student the basics of grammar. Published in October by Bridge Publications, Los Angeles, California.

HUBBARD MARK V E-METER

Re-released in September. Made available for Academy co-audits, and although not as advanced as later meters, this less expensive meter is perfectly suited for co-auditing the lower levels.

WHAT IS SCIENTOLOGY?

First edition. A comprehensive encyclopedic reference work on the Scientology religion. English hardback published October 1992 by Bridge Publications, Los Angeles, California. Published by New Era Publications, Copenhagen, Denmark in 1993, in French, German, Italian and Spanish. Also published in paperback. Revised and updated in 1998.

ASSISTS PROCESSING HANDBOOK
by L. Ron Hubbard

The basic Scientology assists which allow anyone to help ease suffering from illness and injuries and greatly speed recovery. Published by Bridge Publications, Los Angeles, California in December 1992.

GROUP AUDITOR'S HANDBOOK
by L. Ron Hubbard

Group Processing is formal auditing delivered to a group of people at the same time. This handbook offers thirty-three processes and full instructions on how a Group Auditor delivers these processes. Published in December 1992 by Bridge Publications, Los Angeles, California.

INTRODUCTORY AND DEMONSTRATION PROCESSES HANDBOOK
by L. Ron Hubbard

Contains over two hundred processes specifically designed to give those new to Scientology a subjective glimpse of how it can improve their lives. Published by Bridge Publications, Los Angeles, California in December 1992.

1993

THE PROBLEM OF LIFE

Written by L. Ron Hubbard, this newly produced public film released in May, opens the door to Scientology for those looking for the answer to the question "What is life?" Produced by Golden Era Productions. TRANSLATIONS: Danish, Dutch, French, German, Hebrew, Italian, Japanese, Norwegian, Spanish and Swedish.

ESTIMATING CASE CONDITIONS BY TESTS AND THE E-METER

Written by L. Ron Hubbard, this training film shows auditors and Scientology staff members how tests are used by different departments in the organization. Released in June. May be viewed by students in churches of Scientology on courses that include this film. Produced by Golden Era Productions.

THE TONE SCALE AND TONE SCALE DRILL FILM

Newly produced and released, The Tone Scale, a Technical Training Film written by L. Ron Hubbard which depicts each and every emotion which can be experienced by an individual and shows how these relate to life. The viewer is then instructed to watch the accompanying drill film to review the tone levels until he knows them fully. May be viewed by students in churches of Scientology on courses that include this film. The Tone Scale was released in September and the Tone Scale Drill Film was released in December. Produced by Golden Era Productions.

LIFE ORIENTATION PIN

Gold-plated "hat in life," symbol for the Hubbard Life Orientation Course.

SAINT HILL SPECIAL BRIEFING COURSE RING

Solid gold signet ring with crest.

AUDITOR PINS

Class VI Auditor Pin, Class VI C/S Pin, Class VIII Auditor Pin and Class VIII C/S Pin.

HOW THE E-METER WORKS

Newly produced and released. All aspects of how an E-Meter works are presented clearly in this Technical Training Film written by L. Ron Hubbard, with answers to any questions regarding the workings of the E-Meter. May be viewed by students in churches of Scientology on courses that include this film. Released in September. Produced by Golden Era Productions.

1994

HOW TO SET UP A SESSION AND AN E-METER

Every aspect of setting up a session is shown in detail in this newly produced technical training film written by L. Ron Hubbard. May be viewed by students in churches of Scientology on courses that include this film. Released in February. Produced by Golden Era Productions.

THE SCIENTOLOGY HANDBOOK
Based on the works of L. Ron Hubbard

This extensive volume details many of the basic principles of Scientology, presenting them in a format which teaches the reader how to apply them in life. An immensely valuable tool, particularly for Volunteer Ministers. Released at the March 13th event, published by Bridge Publications, Los Angeles, California, and New Era Publications, Copenhagen, Denmark. TRANSLATIONS: French, German, Italian and Spanish.

In addition to the complete handbook, each of the chapters is available as a separate booklet. The booklets, and the languages in which each is available, include:
The Technology of Study
(French, German, Greek, Hungarian, Italian and Spanish)
The Dynamics of Existence
(Finnish, French, German, Italian, and Spanish)
The Components of Understanding
(French, German, Italian, Russian and Spanish)
The Emotional Tone Scale
(French, German, Italian, Russian and Spanish)
Communication
(French, German, Italian and Spanish)
Assists for Illnesses and Injuries
(French, German, Italian, Russian and Spanish)

Answers to Drugs
(French, German, Italian and Spanish)
How to Resolve Conflicts
(French, German, Italian and Spanish)
Integrity and Honesty
(French, German, Italian and Spanish)
Ethics and the Conditions
(French, German, Italian and Spanish)
The Cause of Suppression
(Finnish, French, German, Greek, Italian and Spanish)
Solutions for a Dangerous Environment
(French, German, Italian and Spanish)
Marriage
(French, German, Greek, Italian and Spanish)
Children
(French, German, Italian and Spanish)
Tools for the Workplace
(French, German, Italian and Spanish)
Basics of Organizing
(French, German, Italian and Spanish)
Targets and Goals
(French, German, Italian and Spanish)
Investigations
(French, German, Italian and Spanish)
Fundamentals of Public Relations
(French, German, Italian and Spanish)
A Description of the Scientology Religion
(Danish, Dutch, Finnish, French, German, Greek, Italian, Portuguese, Spanish and Swedish)

TONE 40 ASSESSMENT

This Technical Training Film written by L. Ron Hubbard demonstrates the proper way for an auditor to ask an assessment question. The film shows what happens in session and in life when one asks a question correctly. May be viewed by students in churches of Scientology on courses that include this film. Released in May. Produced by Golden Era Productions.

ISSUE

HCOB   4 May   Clear and Release
CCRD Series 5R

RESEARCH AND DISCOVERY SERIES VOLUME 1: BEYOND BOOK ONE – REFINING THE MIRACLE

In light of breakthroughs in sound reproduction allowing indecipherable recordings to be heard and the discovery of early recordings by L. Ron Hubbard, this brand-new volume released May 9 includes full transcripts of the recorded lectures and auditing demonstrations of Mr. Hubbard from 7 June to 17 June 1950. Published by Bridge Publications, Los Angeles, California.

RESEARCH AND DISCOVERY SERIES VOLUME 2: LAWS OF THE MIND – EVOLUTION TO SIMPLICITY

A 763-page volume released in July which includes full transcripts of the taped lectures and auditing demonstrations of L. Ron Hubbard from 19 June to 5 July 1950. Published by Bridge Publications, Los Angeles, California.

USE OF A DOLL IN AUDITING AND TRS

Newly produced Technical Training Film written by L. Ron Hubbard which shows the proper use of dolls in training auditors, released on September 9. May be viewed by students in churches of Scientology on courses that include this film. Produced by Golden Era Productions.

RESEARCH AND DISCOVERY SERIES VOLUME 3: STRAIGHT MEMORY – EXPLORING THE TIME TRACK

A new compilation released on September 9 which includes full transcripts of the taped lectures of L. Ron Hubbard from 6 July to 4 August 1950. Published by Bridge Publications, Los Angeles, California.

RESEARCH AND DISCOVERY SERIES VOLUME 4: THE SIX BRANCHES OF DIANETICS

An extensive new volume first released December 16, which includes full transcripts of the taped lectures and auditing demonstrations of L. Ron Hubbard from 5 August to 29 September 1950. Published by Bridge Publications, Los Angeles, California.

1995

RON SERIES L. RON HUBBARD: A PROFILE

The first of a series of publications known as the RON Series, which include previously unpublished writings, photographs, anecdotes, diary excerpts and more, released at the March 13 Birthday Event. L. Ron Hubbard: A Profile provides an in-depth portrait of Mr. Hubbard's life and accomplishments. Published by Bridge Publications, Los Angeles, California, and New Era Publications, Copenhagen, Denmark. TRANSLATIONS: Danish, Dutch, French, German, Greek, Hungarian, Italian, Japanese, Norwegian, Portuguese, Russian, Spanish and Swedish.

THE ART OF COMMUNICATION

This Technical Training Film, written by L. Ron Hubbard, shows the use of proper communication and TRs in dealing with situations in life. Released in March. May be viewed by students in churches of Scientology on courses that include this film. Produced by Golden Era Productions. TRANSLATIONS: Danish, Dutch, French, German, Hebrew, Japanese, Italian, Portuguese, Spanish and Swedish.

RESEARCH AND DISCOVERY SERIES VOLUME 5: GROUP DIANETICS – BRINGING SANITY TO THE THIRD DYNAMIC

A new and very complete compilation which includes full transcripts of the taped lectures of L. Ron Hubbard from 30 September to 19 December 1950. Released March 24. Published by Bridge Publications, Los Angeles, California.

CONFESSIONAL TRS

Written by L. Ron Hubbard, and released at the May 9 event, this Technical Training Film instructs the auditor in the standard procedure and appropriate beingness used in Confessional auditing and shows the remarkable results which can be obtained. An individual's transgressions against his own and society's mores can condemn one to a living hell. An auditor who administers a standard Confessional can restore anyone to a happy and productive life. May be viewed by students in churches of Scientology on courses that include this film. Produced by Golden Era Productions.

RESEARCH AND DISCOVERY SERIES VOLUME 6: THE DISCOVERY OF THE THETA UNIVERSE

A new volume which includes full transcripts of the taped lectures and auditing demonstrations of L. Ron Hubbard from 20 December 1950 to 6 August 1951. Released at the May 9 event. Published by Bridge Publications, Los Angeles, California.

RON SERIES THE MUSIC MAKER

Focusing on L. Ron Hubbard as director, arranger, performer and composer of music, this issue contains photos, stories and articles that detail his lifelong love of music. Released during the June Freewinds Maiden Voyage Anniversary week. Published by Bridge Publications, Los Angeles, California, and New Era Publications, Copenhagen, Denmark. TRANSLATIONS: Danish, French, German, Italian, Japanese, Spanish and Swedish.

ROAD TO FREEDOM COMPACT DISC

The *Road to Freedom* compact disc featuring Scientology music and lyrics written by L. Ron Hubbard. Produced by Golden Era Productions and released in eight languages in June. TRANSLATIONS: Danish, French, German, Italian, Japanese, Spanish and Swedish.

RON SERIES THE POET/LYRICIST

A collection of sixty-five poems, lyrics and ballads—fifty-three of them never before published—that show Ron's mastery of this art form. Released July 26. Published by Bridge Publications, Los Angeles, California.

RESEARCH AND DISCOVERY SERIES VOLUME 7: EXPLORING THE ENERGY OF LIFE

A new compilation which includes full transcripts of the taped lectures and auditing demonstrations of L. Ron Hubbard from 7 August to 12 October 1951. Released at the Auditors Day event in September. Published by Bridge Publications, Los Angeles, California.

RESEARCH AND DISCOVERY SERIES VOLUME 8: THE VAST TECHNOLOGY OF POSTULATES

A new volume of transcribed early lectures by L. Ron Hubbard which includes full transcripts of the taped lectures and auditing demonstrations from 13 October to 31 December 1951. Released on December 8. Published by Bridge Publications, Los Angeles, California.

RON SERIES THE HUMANITARIAN: THE ROAD TO SELF-RESPECT

This issue of the RON Series provides L. Ron Hubbard's answers to criminality and failing morality. Released in December at the New Years Event. Published by Bridge Publications, Los Angeles, California, and New Era Publications, Copenhagen, Denmark. TRANSLATIONS: Danish, French, German, Italian, Japanese and Spanish.

1996

This year saw the release of the Golden Age of Tech on May 9—a pivotal moment in Scientology history. To launch the Golden Age of Tech, a series of technical programs and breakthroughs were developed to train huge numbers of auditors and enable every one of them to achieve perfection in his auditing skill. Included among these developments were sets of precision drills resulting in gradiently increased abilities; the revolutionary Drills Simulator, which can reproduce session E-Meter phenomena with perfect accuracy so that their handling can be drilled; and the Quantum E-Meter (listed under May 9). In June, this release was followed by further drills for the Advanced levels: the Golden Age of Tech for OTs. Concurrent with the release of the Golden Age of Tech, 750 Supervisors and Word Clearers newly trained to perfection at the Flag Service Org, were returned to their orgs, ready to deliver.

ISSUES

HCOB	7 Mar	Handling a Read
HCOB	21 Apr	Critiquing TRs

ORIENTATION

This film, written by L. Ron Hubbard, and released on March 13, introduces people to the world of Scientology, including its basic books, its organizations and its purposes and orients the viewer to his true nature as a spiritual being. It is required viewing for any person new to Scientology. Produced by Golden Era Productions. TRANSLATIONS: Danish, Dutch, French, German, Hebrew, Italian, Japanese, Portuguese, Spanish and Swedish.

IMAGES OF A LIFETIME

A pictorial biography of L. Ron Hubbard, containing over four hundred photographs of his life, his adventures and his contributions to mankind, released at the March 13 event. Published by Bridge Publications, Los Angeles, California and New Era Publications, Copenhagen, Denmark. TRANSLATIONS: Danish, French, German, Italian, Japanese and Spanish.

THE BOOK OF E-METER DRILLS
by L. Ron Hubbard

New edition. Published by Bridge Publications, Los Angeles, California and New Era Publications, Copenhagen, Denmark. TRANSLATIONS: Danish, Dutch, French, German, Italian, Japanese, Spanish and Swedish.

RON SERIES THE PHILOSOPHER: THE REDISCOVERY OF THE HUMAN SOUL

L. Ron Hubbard presents the truth about life, death and self. Released at the June 6 Freewinds Maiden Voyage Anniversary. Published by Bridge Publications, Los Angeles, California, and New Era Publications, Copenhagen, Denmark. TRANSLATIONS: Danish, French, German, Italian, Japanese and Spanish.

RON SERIES ADVENTURER/EXPLORER: DARING DEEDS AND UNKNOWN REALMS

Tales from L. Ron Hubbard's forty years of adventure and exploration. Released on August 3. Published by Bridge Publications, Los Angeles, California, and New Era Publications, Copenhagen, Denmark. TRANSLATIONS: Danish, French, German, Italian, Japanese and Spanish.

THE CYCLE OF COMMUNICATION

Newly produced and released in September, this film, written by L. Ron Hubbard, covers every aspect of the cycle of communication and demonstrates each one of these in detail. May be viewed by students in churches of Scientology on courses that include this film. Produced by Golden Era Productions. TRANSLATIONS: Danish, Dutch, French, German, Hebrew, Italian, Japanese, Portuguese, Spanish and Swedish.

RON SERIES THE HUMANITARIAN: EDUCATION

L. Ron Hubbard's solutions to the twentieth-century educational crisis. Released in November. Published by Bridge Publications, Los Angeles, California, and New Era Publications, Copenhagen, Denmark. TRANSLATIONS: Danish, French, German, Italian, Japanese and Spanish.

HUBBARD MARK SUPER VII QUANTUM E-METER

Released with the Golden Age of Tech on May 9, the Hubbard Mark Super VII Quantum E-Meter with its variable sensitivity is the greatest advance in metering since the Mark V. It is the OT Meter Mr. Hubbard wanted, but its development was only recently made possible for the first time due to advances in computer technology. On previous meters, when the tone arm went up, the size of the reads got smaller; due to new developments in computerization capabilities, the Quantum's sensitivity stays constant regardless of tone arm position, resulting in reads which are vivid, even at higher TA positions—a tremendous asset in any type of auditing.

RESEARCH AND DISCOVERY SERIES VOLUME 9: THE WHOLE TRACK UNFOLDS

New compilation released in November, including full transcripts of the taped lectures and auditing demonstrations of L. Ron Hubbard from 1 January to 7 March 1952. Published by Bridge Publications, Los Angeles, California.

RON SERIES THE HUMANITARIAN: REHABILITATING A DRUGGED SOCIETY

L. Ron Hubbard's solutions to the plague of drug addiction. Released in December 1996 at the New Year's event. Published by Bridge Publications, Los Angeles, California, and New Era Publications, Copenhagen, Denmark. TRANSLATIONS: Danish, French, German, Italian, Japanese and Spanish.

RESEARCH AND DISCOVERY SERIES VOLUME 10: THE INFINITE POTENTIAL OF THETA

A brand-new compilation which features full transcripts of the taped lectures and auditing demonstrations of L. Ron Hubbard from 8 March to 26 June 1952. Released in December. Published by Bridge Publications, Los Angeles, California.

1997

HUBBARD E-METER DRILLS SIMULATOR

A computerized training aid used in conjunction with an E-Meter to create any type of read, so that real conditions in an auditing session can be simulated in a course room setting and auditors' skills can be polished to perfection. Produced by Golden Era Productions and released at the May 9 event.

RON SERIES LETTERS AND JOURNALS: THE DIANETICS LETTERS

A collection from personal notes, journals and diaries of L. Ron Hubbard during his early years of research into the human mind. Released in May. Published by Bridge Publications, Los Angeles, California.

MAN THE UNFATHOMABLE

Newly produced and released at the May 9 event, a Technical Training Film written by L. Ron Hubbard which explains man's travails in his attempts to help man, and how and why the E-Meter is the breakthrough that solves it. Man is no longer unfathomable. Produced by Golden Era Productions. TRANSLATIONS: Danish, Dutch, French, German, Hebrew, Hungarian, Italian, Japanese, Norwegian, Portuguese, Russian, Spanish and Swedish.

RON SERIES THE WRITER: THE SHAPING OF POPULAR FICTION

First a writer, L. Ron Hubbard continually shared his knowledge of the craft with others. This collection of published and unpublished articles presents his insights into the profession of writing. Released in June. Published by Bridge Publications, Los Angeles, California, and New Era Publications, Copenhagen, Denmark. TRANSLATIONS: Danish, French, German, Italian, Japanese and Spanish.

RESEARCH AND DISCOVERY SERIES VOLUME 11: AESTHETICS AND THE OT

This volume reveals the thetan's aesthetic nature, and includes lectures from 27 June to 31 October 1952. Released in June. Published by Bridge Publications, Los Angeles, California.

E-METER READS AND E-METER READS DRILL FILM

Newly produced and released in June. Written by L. Ron Hubbard, these Technical Training Films demonstrate every different kind of E-Meter read which can be gotten on a pc so an auditor can learn to recognize and identify each of them, and what they mean, instantly. The drill film also enables the audience to drill recognizing the reads many times. May be viewed by students in churches of Scientology on courses that include this film. Produced by Golden Era Productions. TRANSLATIONS: Danish, Dutch, French, German, Hebrew, Italian, Japanese, Norwegian, Portuguese, Spanish and Swedish.

RON SERIES LETTERS AND JOURNALS: LITERARY CORRESPONDENCE

Released in August, L. Ron Hubbard's letters to friends and his personal notes on the craft of writing provide insights into the profession from one of the foremost authors of modern times. Published by Bridge Publications, Los Angeles, California.

RESEARCH AND DISCOVERY SERIES VOLUME 12: THE CREATION OF UNIVERSES

This volume defines the thetan's responsibility for universes and his capabilities for handling these responsibilities—the topic of LRH lectures from 1 November to 30 November 1952. It was released in September. Published by Bridge Publications, Los Angeles, California.

THE AUDITOR'S CODE

A Technical Training Film written by L. Ron Hubbard, released in September, covering the points of the Auditor's Code and its vital part in producing the miraculous wins of auditing. May be viewed by students in churches of Scientology on courses that include this film. Produced by Golden Era Productions. TRANSLATIONS: Danish, Dutch, French, German, Hebrew, Italian, Japanese, Norwegian, Portuguese, Spanish and Swedish.

RON SERIES THE HUMANITARIAN: FREEDOM FIGHTER: ARTICLES AND ESSAYS

Containing forty-six essays and articles by L. Ron Hubbard which champion man's dignity and freedom in a troubled world, this work was released at the IAS event in October. Published by Bridge Publications, Los Angeles, California, and New Era Publications, Copenhagen, Denmark. TRANSLATIONS: French, German, Italian and Spanish.

BODY MOTION READS

A Technical Training Film written by L. Ron Hubbard which offers the most basic audiovisual orientation of the E-Meter, the laws of energy and motion that influence meter phenomena and insights every auditor must have to professionally operate the E-Meter. This film was released in December. May be viewed by students in churches of

Scientology on courses that include this film. Produced by Golden Era Productions. TRANSLATIONS: Danish, Dutch, French, German, Hebrew, Hungarian, Italian, Japanese, Norwegian, Portuguese, Russian, Spanish and Swedish.

1998

PC INDICATORS AND PC INDICATORS DRILL FILM

Written by L. Ron Hubbard, and released in March, these Technical Training Films aid auditors to observe the conditions or circumstances that arise in and out of session which tell him whether the case is running well or badly. The second film enables the audience to drill recognizing them. May be viewed by students in churches of Scientology on courses that include this film. Produced by Golden Era Productions. TRANSLATIONS: Danish, Dutch, French, German, Hebrew, Italian, Japanese, Norwegian, Portuguese, Spanish and Swedish.

TRS IN LIFE

Written and narrated by L. Ron Hubbard, this film shows how—without TRs—life is a struggle instead of a game. It depicts the common denominator of all failures to confront and handle life, why each TR exists and what each is designed to handle. Released May 9. Produced by Golden Era Productions. TRANSLATIONS: Danish, Dutch, French, German, Hebrew, Italian, Japanese, Norwegian, Portuguese, Spanish and Swedish.

THE DIFFERENT TR COURSES AND THEIR CRITICISM

Written by L. Ron Hubbard, this Technical Training Film was released at the May 9 Anniversary event. May be viewed by students in churches of Scientology on courses that include this film. Produced by Golden Era Productions. TRANSLATIONS: Danish, Dutch, French, German, Hebrew, Italian, Japanese, Norwegian, Portuguese, Spanish and Swedish.

RESEARCH AND DISCOVERY SERIES VOLUME 13: OPERATING BY POSTULATES

This volume contains the lectures of the first nine days of the famous Philadelphia Doctorate Course, 1–9 December 1952, covering the mechanics of the mest universe and how a thetan operates in it. Released in May. Published by Bridge Publications, Los Angeles, California.

STATE OF MIND

The eleven songs performed by various artists on this album were inspired by a collection of L. Ron Hubbard's verse, written over a period spanning almost fifty years. Released at the Freewinds Maiden Voyage Anniversary event. Produced by Golden Era Productions.

UPPER INDOC TRS

Written by L. Ron Hubbard, this film shows exactly how Upper Indoc TRs are done and their result. May be viewed by students in churches of Scientology on courses that include this film. Produced by Golden Era Productions. Translated versions released in August. TRANSLATIONS: Danish, Dutch, French, German, Hebrew, Italian, Japanese, Norwegian, Portuguese, Spanish and Swedish.

INTRODUCTION TO SCIENTOLOGY ETHICS
by L. Ron Hubbard

New, greatly expanded and updated edition, released at Auditor's Day event. Published by Bridge Publications, Los Angeles, California and New Era Publications, Copenhagen, Denmark. TRANSLATIONS: Danish, Dutch, French, German, Hebrew, Hungarian, Italian, Japanese, Norwegian, Portuguese, Russian, Spanish and Swedish.

WHAT IS SCIENTOLOGY?

A newly revised and updated edition of the comprehensive reference work covering every aspect of the Scientology religion. Published by Bridge Publications, Los Angeles, California and New Era Publications, Copenhagen, Denmark. TRANSLATIONS: Danish, Dutch, French, German, Hebrew, Hungarian, Italian, Japanese, Norwegian, Portuguese, Russian, Spanish and Swedish.

CHAPTER 49

LIST OF CHURCHES OF SCIENTOLOGY AND OTHER RELATED ORGANIZATIONS

Churches of Scientology and related organizations and groups using the technologies of L. Ron Hubbard exist all over the world.

The address list that follows is as up-to-date as possible, but due to the rapid growth of the religion, the number of churches and related organizations is always increasing.

INTERNATIONAL ASSOCIATION OF SCIENTOLOGISTS

The International Association of Scientologists (IAS) is the official membership association of the Church of Scientology. It unites individuals around the world to achieve the Aims of Scientology. Anyone in agreement with these aims may become a member.

For information concerning the activities of the IAS, to become a member or renew membership in the Association, write to:

INTERNATIONAL ASSOCIATION OF SCIENTOLOGISTS

c/o Saint Hill Manor
East Grinstead, West Sussex
England RH 19 4JY

or

US IAS MEMBERS TRUST

1311 N. New Hampshire Avenue
Los Angeles, California 90027

CHURCH OF SCIENTOLOGY INTERNATIONAL

The Church of Scientology International (CSI) is the mother church of the Scientology religion. It provides ecclesiastical direction, planning and guidance to the network of churches, missions and field auditors which make up the Church of Scientology hierarchy.

Information on churches, missions, field auditors and Volunteer Ministers may be obtained through the organizations listed on pages 978 through 993 of this directory. You can also write to:

CHURCH OF SCIENTOLOGY INTERNATIONAL
6331 Hollywood Boulevard, Suite 1200
Los Angeles, California 90028-6329

or call:
1-800-FOR-LIFE

RELIGIOUS TECHNOLOGY CENTER

Religious Technology Center (RTC) and the Inspector General Network exist to ensure the purity of the Scientology religion. The purpose of RTC is to ensure that the religious technologies of Dianetics and Scientology remain in proper hands and are properly applied.

To report matters of interest to RTC and the Inspector General Network, write to:

**RELIGIOUS
TECHNOLOGY CENTER**
1710 Ivar Avenue, Suite 1100
Los Angeles, California 90028

THE CHURCHES OF SCIENTOLOGY CONTINENTAL LIAISON OFFICES

The ecclesiastical management of Scientology churches within each continental zone is the responsibility of Continental Liaison Offices (CLOs). There are also Operation and Transport Liaison Offices (OTLs) which help manage churches in certain of the larger countries, effectively functioning as a branch of the CLO in their particular country.

Continental Liaison Office Africa
6th Floor, Budget House
130 Main Street
Johannesburg 2001
South Africa

Continental Liaison Office ANZO
201 Castlereagh Street,
3rd Floor
Sydney, New South Wales
2000 Australia
This CLO covers Australia and New Zealand as well as Japan.

Continental Liaison Office Canada
696 Yonge Street
Toronto, Ontario
Canada M4Y 2A7

Continental Liaison Office Eastern United States
349 W. 48th Street
New York, New York 10036

Continental Liaison Office Europe
Store Kongensgade 55
1264 Copenhagen K
Denmark
This CLO covers continental Europe, the Commonwealth of Independent States and Israel.

Continental Liaison Office Latin America
Federación Mexicana de
Dianética A.C.
Pomona, 53
Colonia Roma
C.P. 06700
Mexico, D.F.
This CLO covers Mexico, Central and South America.

Continental Liaison Office United Kingdom
Saint Hill Manor
East Grinstead, West Sussex
England RH19 4JY

Continental Liaison Office Western United States
1308 L. Ron Hubbard Way
Los Angeles, California
90027

Operations & Transport Liaison Office Hungary
Magyarorszag Scientology
1438 Budapest
PO Box 351
Hungary

Operation and Transport Liaison Office Iberia
Asociación Civil de Dianética
C/ Montera 20, 1° dcha.
28013 Madrid
Spain

Operation and Transport Liaison Office Italy
Chiesa Nazionale di
Scientology d'Italia
Via Cadorna, 61
20090 Vimodrone
Milano
Italy

Operation and Transport Liaison Office Russia
c/o Hubbard Humanitarian
    Center
129301 Moscow
Borisa Galushkina Ul. 19A
Russia

THE CHURCHES OF SCIENTOLOGY

For information concerning church services, Volunteer Minister programs and other activities, contact the nearest Church of Scientology.

CHURCH OF SCIENTOLOGY FLAG SHIP SERVICE ORGANIZATION

c/o *Freewinds* Relay Office
118 North Fort Harrison Avenue
Clearwater, Florida 34615

CHURCH OF SCIENTOLOGY FLAG SERVICE ORGANIZATION

210 South Fort Harrison Avenue
Clearwater, Florida 34616

ADVANCED ORGANIZATIONS

AUSTRALIA, NEW ZEALAND & OCEANIA

*Church of Scientology
Advanced Organization
Saint Hill Australia,
New Zealand and Oceania*
19 – 37 Greek Street
Glebe, New South Wales 2037
Australia

EUROPE & AFRICA

*Church of Scientology
Advanced Organization
for Europe and Africa*
Jernbanegade 6
1608 Copenhagen V
Denmark

UNITED KINGDOM

*Advanced Organization
Saint Hill United Kingdom*
Saint Hill Manor
East Grinstead, West Sussex
England RH19 4JY

UNITED STATES

*Church of Scientology
Advanced Organization
of Los Angeles*
1306 L. Ron Hubbard Way
Los Angeles, California 90027

*Church of Scientology
American Saint Hill Organization*
1413 L. Ron Hubbard Way
Los Angeles, California 90027

CELEBRITY CENTRES

CHURCH OF SCIENTOLOGY CELEBRITY CENTRE INTERNATIONAL

5930 Franklin Avenue
Hollywood, California 90028

AUSTRIA

*Church of Scientology
Celebrity Centre Vienna*
Senefeldergasse 11/5
1100 Vienna, Austria

FRANCE

*Church of Scientology
Celebrity Centre Paris*
69, rue Legendre
75017 Paris
France

GERMANY

*Church of Scientology
Celebrity Centre Düsseldorf*
Luisenstraße 23
40215 Düsseldorf
Germany

*Church of Scientology
Celebrity Centre Munich*
Landshuter Allee 42
80637 Munich
Germany

ITALY

*Church of Scientology
Celebrity Centre Florence*
Via Silvestrina 12, 1st Floor
50129 Florence, Italy

UNITED KINGDOM

Church of Scientology
Celebrity Centre London
27 Westbourne Grove
London
England W2 4UA

UNITED STATES

New York
Church of Scientology
Celebrity Centre New York
65 East 82nd Street
New York, New York 10028

Nevada
Church of Scientology
Celebrity Centre Las Vegas
1100 South 10th Street
Las Vegas, Nevada 89104

Oregon
Church of Scientology
Celebrity Centre Portland
708 S.W. Salmon Street
Portland, Oregon 97205

Tennessee
Church of Scientology
Celebrity Centre Nashville
1907 Old Murfreesboro Pike
Nashville, Tennessee 37217

Texas
Church of Scientology
Celebrity Centre Dallas
10500 Steppington Drive,
Suite 100
Dallas, Texas 75230

CLASS V
CHURCHES

ARGENTINA

Dianetics Association of Argentina
1769 Santa Fe Avenue, 2nd Floor
C.P. 1060
Buenos Aires, Argentina

AUSTRALIA

Church of Scientology of Adelaide
24–28 Waymouth Street
Adelaide, South Australia 5000
Australia

Church of Scientology
of Australian Capital Territory
43–45 East Row
Canberra City, ACT 2601
Australia

Church of Scientology of Brisbane
106 Edward Street, 2nd Floor
Brisbane, Queensland 4000
Australia

Church of Scientology of Melbourne
42–44 Russell Street
Melbourne, Victoria 3000
Australia

Church of Scientology of Perth
108 Murray Street, 1st Floor
Perth, Western Australia 6000
Australia

Church of Scientology of Sydney
201 Castlereagh Street
Sydney, New South Wales 2000
Australia

AUSTRIA

Church of Scientology of Austria
Schottenfeldgasse 13–15
1070 Vienna
Austria

BELGIUM

Church of Scientology of Belgium
61, rue du Prince Royal
1050 Brussels
Belgium

CANADA

Church of Scientology of Edmonton
10206 106th Street NW
Edmonton, Alberta
Canada T5J 1H7

Church of Scientology of Kitchener
104 King Street West, 2nd Floor
Kitchener, Ontario
Canada N2G 2K6

Church of Scientology of Montreal
4489 Papineau Street
Montreal, Quebec
Canada H2H 1T7

Church of Scientology of Ottawa
150 Rideau Street, 2nd Floor
Ottawa, Ontario
Canada K1N 5X6

Church of Scientology of Quebec
350 East Charest Boulevard
Quebec, Quebec
Canada G1K 3H5

Church of Scientology of Toronto
696 Yonge Street, 2nd Floor
Toronto, Ontario
Canada M4Y 2A7

Church of Scientology of Vancouver
401 West Hasting Street
Vancouver, British Columbia
Canada V6B 1L5

Church of Scientology of Winnipeg
315 Garry Street, Suite 210
Winnipeg, Manitoba
Canada R3B 2G7

COLOMBIA

Centro Cultural Dianética
Carrera 15 #75035
Santa Fé de Bogotá
Bogotá
Colombia

DENMARK

Church of Scientology of Jylland
Vester Alle 26
8000 Aarhus C
Denmark

Church of Scientology of Copenhagen
Store Kongensgade 55
1264 Copenhagen K
Denmark

Church of Scientology of Denmark
Gammel Kongevej 3–5, 1
1610 Copenhagen V
Denmark

ENGLAND

Church of Scientology
Saint Hill Foundation
Saint Hill Manor
East Grinstead, West Sussex
England RH19 4JY

Church of Scientology of Birmingham
Albert House, 3rd Floor
24 Albert Street
Birmingham
England B4 7UD

Church of Scientology of Brighton
5 St. Georges Place
London Road
Brighton
England BN1 4GA

Church of Scientology of London
68 Tottenham Court Road
London
England W1P 0BB

Church of Scientology of Manchester
258 Deansgate
Manchester
England M3 4BG

Church of Scientology of Plymouth
41 Ebrington Street
Plymouth
Devon
England PL4 9AA

Church of Scientology of Sunderland
51 Fawcett Street
Sunderland
Tyne and Wear
England SR1 1RS

FRANCE

Church of Scientology of Angers
6, avenue Montaigne
49100 Angers
France

Church of Scientology
of Clermont-Ferrand
6, rue Dulaure
63000 Clermont-Ferrand
France

Church of Scientology of Lyon
3, place des Capucins
69001 Lyon
France

Church of Scientology of Paris
7, rue Jules César
75012 Paris
France

Church of Scientology of Saint-Étienne
24, rue Marengo
42000 Saint-Étienne
France

GERMANY

Church of Scientology of Berlin
Sponholzstraße 51–52
12159 Berlin
Germany

Church of Scientology of Düsseldorf
Friedrichstraße 28
40217 Düsseldorf
Germany

Church of Scientology of Eppendorf
Brennerstraße 12
20099 Hamburg
Germany

Church of Scientology of Frankfurt
Kaiserstraße 49
60329 Frankfurt
Germany

Church of Scientology of Hamburg
Steindamm 63
20099 Hamburg
Germany

Church of Scientology of Hanover
Odeonstraße 17
30159 Hanover
Germany

Church of Scientology of Munich
Beichstraße 12
80802 Munich
Germany

Church of Scientology of Stuttgart
Hohenheimerstraße 9
70184 Stuttgart
Germany

ISRAEL

Dianetics and Scientology
College of Israel
12 Shontzion Street
PO Box 57478
61573 Tel Aviv
Israel

ITALY

Church of Scientology of Brescia
Via Fratelli Bronzetti, 20
25122 Brescia
Italy

Church of Scientology of Catania
Via Garibaldi, 9
95121 Catania
Italy

Church of Scientology of Milano
Via Abetone, 10
20137 Milano
Italy

Church of Scientology of Monza
Via Nuova Valassina, 356
20035 Lissone
Italy

Church of Scientology of Novara
Via Passalacqua, 28
28100 Novara
Italy

Church of Scientology of Nuoro
Via Lamarmora, 102
08100 Nuoro
Italy

Church of Scientology of Padova
Via Mameli, 1/5
35131 Padova
Italy

Church of Scientology of Pordenone
Via Montereale, 10/C
33170 Pordenone
Italy

Church of Scientology of Rome
Via del Caravita, 5
00186 Rome
Italy

Church of Scientology of Torino
Via Bersezio, 7
10152 Torino
Italy

Church of Scientology of Verona
Corso Milano, 84
37138 Verona
Italy

JAPAN

Scientology Tokyo
2-11-7, Kita-Otsuka
Toshima-ku
Tokyo, 170-0004
Japan

MEXICO

Asociación Cultural Dianética A.C.
Belisario Domínguez #17-1
Coyoacán, Centro
C.P. 04000
Mexico, D.F.

Centro Cultural Latinoamericano A.C.
Rio Amazonas 11
Colonia Cuahutemoc
C.P. 06500
Mexico, D.F.

Instituto de Filosofia Aplicada A.C.
Isabel La Católica #24
Centro Histórico de la Ciudad
   de Mexico
C.P. 06890
Mexico, D.F.

Instituto Tecnológico de Dianética A.C.
Avenida Chapultepec #40
Colonia Roma
C.P. 11590
Mexico, D.F.

Organización Cultural Dianética A.C.
Avenida de la Paz 2787
Arcos Sur, Sector Juarez
Guadalajara, Jalisco
C.P. 44500
Mexico

Organización Cultural Dianética A.C.
Calle Monterrey #402
Colonia Narvarte
C.P. 03020
Mexico, D.F.

*Organización Desarrollo
Dianética A.C.*
Xola #1113
Esq. Pitágoras
Colonia Narvarte
C.P. 03220
Mexico, D.F.

NETHERLANDS

Church of Scientology of Amsterdam
Nieuwe Zijds Voorburgwal 271
1012 RL Amsterdam
Netherlands

NEW ZEALAND

Church of Scientology of Auckland
159 Queen Street, 3rd Floor
Auckland 1
New Zealand

NORWAY

Church of Scientology of Norway
Lille Grensen 3
0159 Oslo 1
Norway

PORTUGAL

Igreja Portuguesa de Ciéntologia
Rua da Prata 185, 2 Andar
1100 Lisbon
Portugal

SCOTLAND

*Hubbard Academy of Personal
Independence*
20 Southbridge
Edinburgh
Scotland EH1 1LL

SOUTH AFRICA

Church of Scientology of Cape Town
1st Floor, Dorlane House
39 Roeland Street
Cape Town 8001
South Africa

Church of Scientology of Durban
20 Buckingham Terrace
Westville, 3630
Durban
South Africa

Church of Scientology of Johannesburg
4th Floor, Budget House
130 Main Street
Johannesburg 2001
South Africa

*Church of Scientology
of Johannesburg North*
1st Floor, Bordeaux Centre
Gordon Road, Corner Jan Smuts
   Avenue
Blairgowrie, Randburg 2125
South Africa

Church of Scientology of Port Elizabeth
2 St. Christopher's
27 Westbourne Road Central
Port Elizabeth 6001
South Africa

Church of Scientology of Pretoria
307 Ancore Building
Corner Jeppe and Esselen Streets
Sunnyside, Pretoria 0002
South Africa

SPAIN

*Asociación Civil de Dianética de
Barcelona*
Paseo de Domingo, 11
08007 Barcelona
Spain

*Asociación Civil de Dianética de
Madrid*
C/ Montera 20, 1° dcha.
28013 Madrid
Spain

SWEDEN

Church of Scientology of Göteborg
Varmlandsgatan 16, 1 tr.
41328 Göteborg
Sweden

Church of Scientology of Malmö
Porslinsgatan 3
21132 Malmö
Sweden

Church of Scientology of Stockholm
Götgatan 105
11662 Stockholm
Sweden

SWITZERLAND

Church of Scientology of Basel
Herrengrabenweg 56
40054 Basel
Switzerland

Church of Scientology of Bern
Muhlemattstrasse 31
Postfach 384
3000 Bern 14
Switzerland

Church of Scientology of Geneva
4, rue de L'Aubepine
1205 Geneva
Switzerland

Church of Scientology of Lausanne
10, rue de la Madeleine
1003 Lausanne
Switzerland

Church of Scientology of Zurich
Badenerstrasse 141
8004 Zurich
Switzerland

UNITED STATES

Arizona

Church of Scientology of Arizona
2111 W. University Drive
Mesa, Arizona 85201

California

Church of Scientology of Los Angeles
4810 Sunset Boulevard
Los Angeles, California 90027

Church of Scientology of Los Gatos
2155 S. Bascom Avenue, Suite 120
Campbell, California 95008

Church of Scientology of Mountain View
2483 Old Middlefield Way
Mountain View, California 94043

REFERENCES

Church of Scientology of Orange County
1451 Irvine Boulevard
Tustin, California 92680

Church of Scientology of Pasadena
1277 East Colorado Boulevard
Pasadena, California 91106

Church of Scientology of Sacramento
825 15th Street
Sacramento, California 95814-2096

Church of Scientology of San Diego
1330 4th Avenue
San Diego, California 92101

Church of Scientology of San Francisco
83 McAllister Street
San Francisco, California 94102

Church of Scientology of Santa Barbara
524 State Street
Santa Barbara, California 93101

Church of Scientology of Stevens Creek
80 E. Rosemary
San Jose, California 95112

Church of Scientology of the Valley
15643 Sherman Way
Van Nuys, California 91406

Colorado

Church of Scientology of Colorado
3385 S. Bannock Street
Englewood, Colorado 80110

Connecticut

Church of Scientology of New Haven
909 Whalley Avenue
New Haven,
Connecticut 06515-1728

Florida

Church of Scientology of Florida
120 Giralda Avenue
Coral Gables, Florida 33134

Church of Scientology of Orlando
1830 East Colonial Drive
Orlando, Florida 32803-4729

Church of Scientology of Tampa
3617 Henderson Boulevard
Tampa, Florida 33609-4501

Georgia

Church of Scientology of Georgia
1132 W. Peachtree Street
Atlanta, Georgia 30308

Hawaii

Church of Scientology of Hawaii
1148 Bethel Street
Honolulu, Hawaii 96813

Illinois

Church of Scientology of Illinois
3011 N. Lincoln Avenue
Chicago, Illinois 60657-4207

Massachusetts

Church of Scientology of Boston
448 Beacon Street
Boston, Massachusetts 02115

Michigan

Church of Scientology of Ann Arbor
2355 W. Stadium Boulevard
Ann Arbor, Michigan 48103

Church of Scientology of Michigan
321 Williams Street
Royal Oak, Michigan 48067

Minnesota

*Church of Scientology of Minnesota
Twin Cities*
1011 Nicollet Mall
Minneapolis, Minnesota 55403

Missouri

Church of Scientology of Kansas City
3619 Broadway
Kansas City, Missouri 64111

Church of Scientology of Missouri
6901 Delmar Boulevard
University City, Missouri 63130

Nevada

Church of Scientology of Nevada
846 E. Sahara Avenue
Las Vegas, Nevada 89104

New Mexico

Church of Scientology of New Mexico
8106 Menaul Boulevard N.E.
Albuquerque, New Mexico 87110

New York

Church of Scientology of Buffalo
47 W. Huron Street
Buffalo, New York 14202

Church of Scientology of Long Island
99 Railroad Station Plaza
Hicksville, New York 11801-2850

Church of Scientology of New York
227 W. 46th Street
New York, New York 10036-1409

Ohio

Church of Scientology of Cincinnati
215 West 4th Street, 5th Floor
Cincinnati, Ohio 45202-2670

Church of Scientology of Ohio
30 N. High Street
Columbus, Ohio 43215

Oregon

Church of Scientology of Portland
323 S.W. Washington
Portland, Oregon 97204

Pennsylvania

Church of Scientology of Pennsylvania
1315 Race Street
Philadelphia, Pennsylvania 19107

Puerto Rico

Church of Scientology of Puerto Rico
272 JT Piñero Avenue
Hyde Park, Hato Rey
San Juan, Puerto Rico 00918

Texas

Church of Scientology of Texas
2200 Guadalupe
Austin, Texas 78705

Utah

Church of Scientology of Utah
1931 South 1100 East
Salt Lake City, Utah 84106

Washington

*Church of Scientology
of Washington State*
2226 Third Avenue
Seattle, Washington 98121

Washington, DC

*Founding Church of Scientology of
Washington, DC*
1701 20th Street NW
Washington, DC 20009

VENEZUELA

Asociación Cultural Dianética A.C.
Avenida Luis Ernesto Branger EDFF
Urbanización La Alegría
Locales PB 4 Y 5
C.P. 833
Valencia, Venezuela

Asociación Dianética A.C.
Avenida Principal de las Palmas
Cruce Con Calle Carúpano
Quinta Suha, Las Palmas
Caracas, Venezuela

ZIMBABWE

Church of Scientology of Bulawayo
Suite 202, Southampton House
Corner Main and 9th Avenue
Bulawayo, Zimbabwe

Church of Scientology of Harare
1st Floor, Braude Brothers Building
47 Speke Avenue
Harare, Zimbabwe

THE MISSIONS OF SCIENTOLOGY

For information on becoming a missionary or starting a Scientology Mission, write to Scientology Missions International (SMI) or any of the continental SMI offices.

INTERNATIONAL OFFICE

SCIENTOLOGY MISSIONS INTERNATIONAL
6331 Hollywood Boulevard
Los Angeles, California 90028

SMI CONTINENTAL OFFICES

AFRICA

Scientology Missions International African Office
6th Floor, Budget House
130 Main Street
Johannesburg 2001, South Africa

AUSTRALIA, NEW ZEALAND, OCEANIA

Scientology Missions International Australian, New Zealand and Oceanian Office
201 Castlereagh Street
Sydney, New South Wales 2000
Australia

CANADA

Scientology Missions International Canadian Office
696 Yonge Street
Toronto, Ontario
Canada M4Y 2A7

COMMONWEALTH OF INDEPENDENT STATES

Scientology Missions International CIS Office
c/o Hubbard Humanitarian Center
129301 Moscow
Borisa Galushkina Ul. 19A
Russia

EUROPE

Scientology Missions International European Office
Sankt Nikolajvej 4–6
Frederiksberg C
1953 Copenhagen, Denmark

HUNGARY

Scientology Missions International Hungarian Office
1438 Budapest
PO Box 351, Hungary

ITALY

Scientology Missions International Italian Office
Via Cadorna, 61
Vimodrone
20090 Milano, Italy

LATIN AMERICA

Scientology Missions International Latin American Office
Pomona, 53
Colonia Roma
C.P. 06700
Mexico, D.F.

UNITED KINGDOM

Scientology Missions International United Kingdom Office
Saint Hill Manor
East Grinstead, West Sussex
England RH19 4JY

UNITED STATES

Scientology Missions International Eastern United States Office
349 W. 48th Street
New York, New York 10036

Scientology Missions International Flag Land Base Office
118 North Fort Harrison Avenue
Clearwater, Florida 34615

Scientology Missions International Western United States Office
1308 L. Ron Hubbard Way
Los Angeles, California 90027

MISSIONS OF SCIENTOLOGY

Missions and Dianetics Centers

Contact the nearest Scientology mission for information on local services.

ALBANIA

Shoqates Kombetore te Scientologere te shirise
rr "bardhyl" P. 18 shk: 2AP :3
Tirana, Albania

AUSTRALIA

Church of Scientology Mission of Inner West
4 Wangal Place
Five Dock
New South Wales 2046
Australia

Church of Scientology Mission of Melbourne
55 Glenferrie Road
Malvern 3144
Victoria, Australia

AUSTRIA

Scientology Mission Salzburg
Rupertgasse 21
5020 Salzburg, Austria

Scientology Mission Wolfsberg
Wienerstrasse 8
9400 Wolfsberg, Austria

CANADA

Church of Scientology Mission of Beauce
11925 Le Avenue
Ville de St. Georges
Beauce, Quebec
Canada G5Y 2C9

Church of Scientology Mission of Halifax
2589 Windsor Street
Halifax, Nova Scotia
Canada B3K 5C4

Church of Scientology Mission of Vancouver
101-2182 W. 12th Avenue
Vancouver, British Columbia
Canada

Church of Scientology Mission of Victoria
201-610 Johnson Street
Victoria, British Columbia
Canada Z8W 1M4

CHILE

Church of Scientology Mission of Chile
Calle Nuncio Laghi 6558
La Reyna, Chile

COLOMBIA

Asociación Dianética North Bogotá
Avenida 13 #104-91
Bogotá, Colombia

Fundación para el Mejoramiento
Carrera 20 No. 52-27
Santa Fé de Bogotá, D.C.
Colombia

COMMONWEALTH OF INDEPENDENT STATES

Kazakhstan

Dianetics Center of Alma-Ata
AB Box 219
480000 Kazakhstan

Dianetics Center of Karaganda
Ermekova 46
Karaganda
470061 Kazakhstan

Scientology Mission of Pavlodar
637000 Pavlodar
AB Box 2105, Kazakhstan

Moldova

Kishinev Dianetics Center
277028 Kishinev
Dokuchaeva Str. 4-73, Moldova

Russia

Dianetics Center of Barnaul
656014 Barnaul
Vodoprovodnaja Ul. 95
Russia

Dianetics Center of Bryansk
241037 Bryansk
Dokuchaeva Ul. 15-72
Russia

Dianetics Center of Dimitrovgrad
433510 Dimitrovgrad-12
Ulyanovsk Region
AB Box 189, Russia

Dianetics Center of Ekaterinburg
610066 Ekaterinburg
Mira Ul. 8-24
Sverdlovskaya Region
Russia

Glazov Dianetics Center
427600 Glazov
Kirova 71 B, Russia

Dianetics Center of Habarovsk
680021 Habarovsk
Pankova Ul. 13-332
Russia

Dianetics Center of Izhevsk
426006 Izhevsk
Novostroitelnaya Ul. 25-A, 67
Russia

Dianetics Center of Kaliningrad MR
141090 Kaliningrad
Moscow Region
Frunze Ul. 24-13, Russia

Dianetics Humanitarian Center of Kaluga
248016 Kaluga
Engelsa Ul. 9-13, Russia

Dianetics Center of Kazan
420089 Tatarstan
Latyshskih Strelkov Ul. 33-171
Russia

Dianetics Center of Kislovodsk
357746 Kislovodsk
Telmana Ul. 3-6, Russia

Dianetics Center of Kogalym
626481 Kogalym
Mira Ul. 2-12
Tyumen Region, Russia

Dianetics Center of Kostomuksha
186989 Kostomuksha
Geroiev Ul. 2-20
Karelia Region, Russia

Dianetics Center of Krasnoyarsk
663080 Divnogorsk
Naberezhnaya Ul. 41-27
Krasnoyarsk Region, Russia

Dianetics Center of Magnitogorsk
455000 Magnitogorsk
AB Box 3008, Russia

Dianetics Center of Minsk
220017 Minsk
AB Box 4
Belarus, Russia

Dianetics Center of Mitischi
141007 Mitischi
Moscow Region
2 Shelkovsky Proiezd 5/1-62
Russia

Dianetics Center of Moscow
105094 Moscow
Bolshaja Semenovskaja Ul. 42
Russia

Dianetics Center of Murmansk
183766 Murmansk
Perulok Rusanova, 10-514
Russia

Dianetics Center of Nizhnekamsk
423550 Nizhnekamsk
Tatarstan
Urmanche Ul. 3-3, Russia

Dianetics Center of Nizhny Novgorod
603074 Nizhny Novgorod
AB Box 123, Russia

Dianetics Center of Novgorod
173025 Novgorod
AB Box 13, Russia

Dianetics Center of Novgorod II
173001 Novgorod
AB Box 120, Russia

Dianetics Center of Novosibirsk
630104 Novosibirsk
Dostoevskogo 5-31, Russia

Dianetics Center of Novy Urengoy
626718 Novy Urengoy
Youbuleynaya Ul. 1-41
Tyumen Region, Russia

Dianetics Center of Obninsk
249020 Obninsk
Gagarin Ul. 27, Russia

Hubbard Humanitarian Center of Omsk
644043 Omsk
AB Box 3768, Russia

Dianetics Center of Omsk II
644099 Omsk
AB Box 999
Glavpochtamt, Russia

Dianetics Center of Orenburg
460024 Orenburg
Vystavochnaya Ul. 25-213
Russia

Dianetics Center of Oriol
302000 Oriol
Polikarpova Square 32, Russia

Dianetics Center of Penza
440046 Penza
Mira Ul. 55-89, Russia

Dianetics Center of Penza II
440056 Penza
Riabova Ul. 6C, Russia

Dianetics Center of Perm
614000 Perm
AB Box 7026, Russia

Dianetics Center of Petropavlovsk-Kamchatskiy
683006 Petropavlovsk-Kamchatskiy
Kavkazskaja Ul. 30/1-31
Russia

Dianetics Center of Samara
443001 Samara
Leninskaja 22-1-3, Russia

Dianetics Center of Saratov
410601 Saratov
AB Box 1533, Russia

Dianetics Center of St. Petersburg
192007 St. Petersburg
Razezshaja Ul. 44, Russia

*Dianetics Humanitarian Center
of Surgut*
626400 Surgut
Lermontova Ul. 6-1
Tyumen Region, Russia

*Dianetics Humanitarian Center
of Togliatti*
445050 Togliatti
AB Box 14
Samara Region, Russia

Dianetics Center of Troitsk
142092 Troitsk
Sirenevaya 10-87, Russia

Dianetics Center of Tula
300000 Tula
Krasnoarmeysky Prospect 7-127
Russia

Dianetics Center of Ufa
450076 Ufa - 76
AB Box 7527, Russia

Dianetics Center of Vladivostok
690001 Vladivostok
AB Box 1-147, Russia

*Dianetics Humanitarian Center of
Volgograd*
400075 Volgograd
AB Box 6, Russia

Dianetics Center of Voronezh
394000 Voronezh
AB Box 146, Russia

Ukraine

Kharkov Dianetics Center
310052 Ukraine
Kotlova Ul. 83
Dvorets Kulturi Zheleznodorozhnikov
Kharkov 52
A-JA 53
Ukraine

Scientology Mission of Herson
Gastello 4
Herson, Ukraine

Scientology Mission of Kremenchug
315326 Kremenchug
Mira Ul. 3-161, Ukraine

Dianetics Center of Uzgorod
294000 Uzgorod
Dobrianskogo Ul. 10-9, Ukraine

COSTA RICA

Instituto Tecnológico de Dianética
15 Mts. Este de Pali, La Florida
Tibas, San Jose, Costa Rica

CZECH REPUBLIC

*Church of Scientology
Mission of Prague*
Hornokrcska 60
140 00 Prague 4, Czech Republic

DENMARK

*Church of Scientology
Mission of Aalborg*
Boulevarden 39 St.
9000 Aalborg, Denmark

*Church of Scientology
Mission of Copenhagen City*
Bulowsvej 20
1870 Frederiksberg, Denmark

Hubbard Kursus Center
Virklundvej 5
8600 Silkeborg, Denmark

Scientology Kirkens Lyngby Mission
Sorgenfrivej 3
2800 Lyngby, Denmark

Hubbard Dianetik Center of Odense
Absalonsgade 42
5000 Odense C, Denmark

DOMINICAN REPUBLIC

Dianética Santo Domingo
Condominio Ambar Plaza II
Bloque II, Apto. 302
Avenida Núñez de Cáceres Esq.
Sarasota, Santo Domingo
Dominican Republic

ECUADOR

*Church of Scientology
Mission of Guayaquil*
Dom Quisquis 722
Entre Avenida Quito y Machala
Guayaquil, Ecuador

ENGLAND

*Church of Scientology
Mission of Hove Ltd.*
59A Coleridge Street
Hove, East Sussex
England BN3 5AB

*Dianetics and Scientology
Mission of Bournemouth Ltd.*
42 High Street
Poole, Dorset
England BH15 1BT

FINLAND

Scientology Helsinki
Vuorikatu 16 A 5
00100 Helsinki
Finland

FRANCE

*Église de Scientologie
Centre Hubbard de Dianétique*
55, rue des Ayres
33000 Bordeaux, France

Centre de Dianétique de Marseille
58, rue Saint Savournin
13005 Marseille, France

Centre de Dianétique de Nice
28, rue Gioffredo
06000 Nice, France

*Église de Scientologie
Mission de Toulouse*
9, rue Edmond de Planet
31000 Toulouse, France

GERMANY

Scientology Mission Bremen e.V.
Osterdeich 27
28203 Bremen, Germany

Dianetik Lebensberatung
Scientology Dresden e.V.
Bischofsweg 46
01099 Dresden, Germany

Dianetik Göppingen e.V.
Scientology Mission
Geislingerstraße 21
73033 Göppingen, Germany

Scientology Heilbronn
Mission der Scientology Kirche e.V.
Keilstraße 6
74080 Heilbronn, Germany

Mission der Scientology Kirche
Karlstraße 46
76133 Karlsruhe, Germany

Scientology Mission Pasing
Baeckerstraße 31
81241 Munich, Germany

Scientology Kirche Bayern e.V.
Faerberstraße 5
90402 Nuremberg, Germany

Scientology Mission e.V.
Heinestraße 9
72762 Reutlingen, Germany

Scientology Mission Ulm e.V.
Eythstraße 2
89075 Ulm, Germany

Scientology Wiesbaden
Mission der Scientology Kirche e.V.
Mauritiusstraße 14
65183 Wiesbaden, Germany

GREECE

Greek Dianetics and Scientology Centre
Patision 200
11256 Athens, Greece

GUATEMALA

Asociación de Cienciología Aplicada
Dianética de Guatemala
11 Avenida "A" 32-28
Zona 5, Guatemala

HONG KONG

Church of Scientology
Mission of Hong Kong
62–64 Peel Street
Central, Hong Kong

HUNGARY

Magyarorszagi Scientology
Egyhaz Dianetika Kozpont
1067 Budapest
Terez Korut 19. III. em. 33-34
Hungary

Dianetika XVII Misszio
1052 Budapest
Karoly Krt. 4. III/10, Hungary

Church of Scientology Mission of Gyor
Szent Istvan u. 49
9022 Gyor, Hungary

Dianetics Center Kalocsa
Tavasz u. 44
6300 Kalocsa, Hungary

Church of Scientology
M.S.E. Miskolc Mission
3530 Miskolc, Vorosmarty 53 I/2
Hungary

Dianetika Mission Paks
Kodaly Zoltan ut 3. fsz. 0
7032 Paks, Hungary

Scientology Egyhaz Pecsi Misszio
Dianetika Kozpont
7621 Pecs, Jokai ut. 21.
Hungary

Magyarorszagi Scientology Egyhaz
H. Budapest V.
Semmelweis u. 2, Hungary

Church of Scientology
Mission of Szazhalombatta
Beke Str. 8
2440 Szazhalombatta, Hungary

Church of Scientology Mission of Szolnok
Maria ut 19
5000 Szolnok, Hungary

Church of Scientology
Mission of Tatabanya
Dozsakert 49 ep III. em. 1/1
2800 Tatabanya, Hungary

Church of Scientology
Mission of Tiszaujvaros
Szederkenyi ut. 1
3580 Tiszaujvaros, Hungary

Magyarorszagi Szcientologia
Egyhaz Szegedi Misszioja
Szeged PF 1258, Hungary

Church of Scientology
Mission of Dunaujvaros
2400 Dunaujvaros
Romai Krt. 41. I/4, Hungary

Church of Scientology Mission of Eger
Vallon u. 11 IX/27
H. 3300 Eger, Hungary

Church of Scientology
Mission of Erzsebetvaros
1071 Budapest VII Peterdy 39
IV/33, Budapest, Hungary

Church of Scientology
Mission of Kaposvar
7631 Pecs
Nagy Postavolgy 65, Hungary

Church of Scientology
Mission of Nyiregyhaza
4400 Nyiregyhaza
Ungvar Setany 33. IX/34 Hungary

Scientology Egyhaz Pecsi Misszio
Dianetika Kozpont
Postacim: Pecs 2 PF 41
Hungary

Church of Scientology
Mission of Sopron
Balfi u. 56
Sopron 9400, Hungary

Church of Scientology
Mission of Szekesfehervar
Varkor ut 11
8001 Szekesfehervar, Hungary

M.S.E. Dianetika Kozpont Szekszard
7100 Szekszard PF 165, Hungary

INDIA

Dianetics Center of Ambala Cantt
6352 Punjabi Mohalla
Ambala Cantt 133001, India

Patiala Dianetics Center
50, New Lal Bagh
Patiala 147001, India

Scientology Mission of Bombay
433 Adash Magar
New Link Road Oshwara
Jogeshwari West
Mumbai 400102, India

IRELAND

Church of Scientology
Mission of Dublin Ltd.
62/63 Middle Abbey Street
Dublin 1, Ireland

ITALY

Chiesa di Scientology
Missione di Aosta
Corso Battaglione, 13/B
11100 Aosta, Italy

Chiesa di Scientology
Missione di Avellino
Via Derna, 3
83100 Avellino, Italy

Chiesa di Scientology
Missione di Barletta
Via Cialdini, 67/B
70051 Barletta (BA), Italy

Chiesa di Scientology
Missione di Bergamo
Via Roma, 85
24020 Bergamo, Italy

Chiesa di Scientology
Missione di Cagliari
Via Sonnino, 177
09127 Cagliari, Italy

Chiesa di Scientology
Missione di Castelfranco
Via 8/9 Maggio, 59
Cornuda (TV), Italy

Chiesa di Scientology
Missione di Como
Via Torno, 12
22100 Como, Italy

Chiesa di Scientology
Missione di Conegliano
Via E. Cornaro, 12
31025 Santa Lucia di Piave (TV)
Italy

Chiesa di Scientology
Missione di Cosenza
Via Duca degli Abruzzi, 6
87100 Cosenza, Italy

Chiesa di Scientology
Missione di Lecco
Via Mascari, 78
22053 Lecco, Italy

Chiesa di Scientology
Missione di Lucca
Viale G. Puccini, 425/b
S. Anna
55100 Lucca, Italy

Chiesa di Scientology
Missione di Macerata
Via Roma, 13
62100 Macerata, Italy

Chiesa di Scientology
Missione di Mantova
Via Visi, 30
46100 Mantova, Italy

Chiesa di Scientology
Missione di Modena
Via Giardini, 468/C
41100 Modena, Italy

Chiesa di Scientology
Missione di Olbia
Via Gabriele D/Annunzio Centro Martini
07026 Olbia (SS), Italy

Chiesa di Scientology
Missione di Palermo
Via Mariano Stabile, 139
90100 Palermo, Italy

Chiesa di Scientology
Missione di Ragusa
Via Cap. degli Zuavi, 67
96019 Vittoria (RG), Italy

Chiesa di Scientology
Missione di Seregno
Via Magenta, 4
20038 Seregno
Italy

Chiesa di Scientology
Missione di Trieste
Via Mazzini, 44
34122 Trieste
Italy

Chiesa di Scientology
Missione di Vicenza
Viale Milano, 38D
c/o Complesso Polialte
36075 Montecchio Maggiore
Italy

LATVIA

Dianetics Center of Riga
Laspesa Str. 27-4
Riga 1011, Latvia

LITHUANIA

Vilnius Centrinis Dianetika
Lietuva, Vilnius
Centrinis Pastas 2000
A/D 42, Lithuania

MEXICO

Centro de Dianética Hubbard de
Aguascalientes A.C.
Hamburgo No. 127
Fraccionamiento del Valle 1A Sec.
C.P. 20080 Aguascalientes, Ags.
Mexico

Centro Hubbard de Dianética
Fuente de Blanca No. 5
Tecamachalco
Naucalpan Edo. de Mexico
C.P. 53950, Mexico

Dianética y Cienciología
Valle A.C.
Edificio Santos
Avenida Madero 1955 Pte.
Local 712
Zona Centro, Monterrey N.L.
Mexico

Instituto de Dianética Monterrey A.C.
Tulancingo 1262
Col. Mitras
Monterrey N.L., Mexico

Instituto de Filosofía Aplicada de Bajío
Calle Manuel Doblado #111
Zona Centro, Leon Gto.
C.P. 37000, Mexico

Church of Scientology
Mission of Chihuahua
Ortiz del Campo 3309
Colonia San Felipe
Chihuahua, Chihuahua, Mexico

Mission of Satelite
Valle Verde 59
Club de Golf Bellavista
Atizapán, Edo. 52295, Mexico

NEW ZEALAND

Church of Scientology
Mission of Christchurch
PO Box 1843
Christchurch, New Zealand

PAKISTAN

Dianetics Centre
Royal Apts., First Floor
Main University Road
OPP: URDU Science College
Karachi, Pakistan

ROMANIA

Dianetika Kozpont Szekelyudvarhely
1 Decembrie 1918 23/13
Szekelyudvarhely - 4150
Romania

SOUTH AFRICA

Church of Scientology
18 Trilby Street
Oaklands, Johannesburg 2192
South Africa

Church of Scientology
Box 314
Kwaxulma, Soweto 1868
South Africa

SPAIN

Asociación Civil Dianética de Bilbao
C/ Juan de Garay, 3, 1A
48003 Bilbao, Spain

Centro de Eficiencia Personal Dianética
C/ Hermanos Rivas 22-1-1
46018 Valencia, Spain

Centro de Mejoramiento Personal
C/ Viera y Clavijo, 33-2
35002 Las Palmas de Gran Canaria,
Spain

Centro de Mejoramiento Personal
Urbanización Los Mirtos 65
41020 Sevilla, Spain

Centro de Mejoramiento
Personal de Cercedilla
Cambrils 19
28034 Madrid, Spain

SWEDEN

Dianetikhuset
Turegatan 55
11438 Stockholm, Sweden

Scientologi-kyrkan
Hässleholmsmissionen
Stobygatan 16
28100 Hässleholm, Sweden

SWITZERLAND

Chiesa di Scientology
Missione di Ticino
Via Campagna, 30
6982 Serocca D'Agno
Switzerland

Dianetik and Scientology Luzern Mission
Sentimattstrasse 7
6003 Luzern, Switzerland

Mission der Scientology Kirche
Regensbergstrasse 89
8050 Zurich, Switzerland

TAIWAN

Church of Scientology
Mission of Kaohsiung
85 Ton-sing Road
Sin-Sing District
Kaohsiung, Taiwan

Church of Scientology
Mission of Taichung
82-2 Wu-Chuan-5 Street
Taichung, Taiwan

Church of Scientology
Mission of Taipei
8f No. 151 Sect 2
Min-sheng East Rd
Taipei, Taiwan

UNITED STATES

Alaska

Church of Scientology
Mission of Anchorage
1300 E. 68th Avenue, Suite 208A
Anchorage, Alaska 99518

California

Church of Scientology
Mission of Antelope Valley
423 E. Palmdale Boulevard, #3
Palmdale, California 93550

Church of Scientology
Mission of Bay Cities
2975 Treat Boulevard, Suite D
Concord, California 94518

Church of Scientology
Mission of Beverly Hills
109 N. La Cienega Boulevard
Beverly Hills, California 90211

Church of Scientology
Mission of Brand Boulevard
116 S. Louise Street
Glendale, California 91205

Church of Scientology
Mission of Buenaventura
180 N. Ashwood Avenue
Ventura, California 93003

Church of Scientology
Mission of Capitol
9915 Fair Oaks Boulevard, Suite A
Fair Oaks, California 95628

Church of Scientology
Mission of the Diablo Valley
1327 N. Main Street, Suite 103
Walnut Creek, California 94596

Church of Scientology
Mission of Escondido
326 S. Kalmia Street
Escondido, California 92025

Church of Scientology
Mission of the Foothills
2254 Honolulu Avenue
Montrose, California 91020

Church of Scientology
Mission of Marin
1930 4th Street
San Rafael, California 94901

Church of Scientology
Mission of Palo Alto
410 Cambridge Avenue, Suite C
Palo Alto, California 94306

Church of Scientology
Mission of Redwood City
617 Veterans Boulevard, #205
Redwood City, California 94063

Church of Scientology
Mission of River Park
1300 Ethan Way, Suite 100
Sacramento, California 95825

Church of Scientology
Mission of San Bernardino
5 E. Citrus Avenue, Suite 105
Redlands, California 92373

Church of Scientology
Mission of the San Fernando Valley
7457 Densmore
Van Nuys, California 91406

Church of Scientology
Mission of San Francisco
701 Sutter Street
San Francisco, California 94109

Church of Scientology
Mission of San Jose
826 N. Winchester
San Jose, California 95128

Church of Scientology
Mission of Santa Clara Valley
2718 Homestead Road
Santa Clara, California 95051

Church of Scientology
Mission of Santa Rosa
51 "E" Street
Santa Rosa, California 95404

Church of Scientology
Mission of Sherman Oaks
13517 Ventura Boulevard, Suite 7
Sherman Oaks, California 91423

Church of Scientology
Mission of West Valley
9310 Topanga Canyon,
 Prairie Street Entrance
Chatsworth, California 91311

Church of Scientology
Mission of Westwood
3200 Santa Monica Boulevard, Suite 200
Santa Monica, California 90404

Colorado

Church of Scientology
Mission of Alamosa
511 Main Street
Alamosa, Colorado 81101

Church of Scientology
Mission of Boulder
1021 Pearl Street
Boulder, Colorado 80302

Church of Scientology
Mission of Roaring Forks
827 Bennett Avenue
Glenwood Springs, Colorado 81601

Florida

Church of Scientology
Mission of Clearwater
100 N. Belcher Road
Clearwater, Florida 34625

Church of Scientology
Mission of Fort Lauderdale
660 South Federal Highway #200
Pompano Beach, Florida 33062

Church of Scientology
Mission of Palm Beach
PO Box 314
West Palm Beach, Florida 33402

Church of Scientology
Mission of Palm Harbor
565 Hammock Drive
Palm Harbor, Florida 34683

Hawaii

Church of Scientology
Mission of Honolulu
1920 Hoolehua Street
Pearl City, Hawaii 96782

Illinois

Church of Scientology
Mission of Champaign-Urbana
312 W. John Street
Champaign, Illinois 61820

Church of Scientology
Mission of Peoria
2020 N. Wisconsin
Peoria, Illinois 61603

Indiana

Church of Scientology
Mission of Indianapolis
1407 E. 86th Street
Indianapolis, Indiana 46240

Kansas

Church of Scientology
Mission of Wichita
3705 E. Douglas
Wichita, Kansas 67218

Louisiana

Church of Scientology
Mission of Baton Rouge
9432 Common Street
Baton Rouge, Louisiana 70809

Church of Scientology
Mission of Lafayette
104 Westmark Boulevard, Suite 1B
Lafayette, Louisiana 70506

Maine

Church of Scientology
Mission of Brunswick
2 Lincoln Street
Brunswick, Maine 04011

Massachusetts

Church of Scientology
Mission of Merrimack Valley
142 Primrose
Haverhill, Massachusetts 01830

Church of Scientology
Mission of Watertown
313 Common Street #2
Watertown, Massachusetts 02172

Michigan

Church of Scientology
Mission of Genesee County
423 N. Saginaw
Holly, Michigan 48442

Minnesota

Church of Scientology
Mission of Golden Valley
4320 Parklawn Avenue
Edina, Minnesota 55435

Nebraska

Church of Scientology
Mission of Omaha
843 Hidden Hills Drive
Bellevue, Nebraska 68005

Nevada

Church of Scientology
Mission of Las Vegas
3355 Spring Mountain Road, Suite 48
Las Vegas, Nevada 89102

New Hampshire

Church of Scientology
Mission of Greater Concord
PO Box 112
Epsom, New Hampshire 03234

New Jersey

Church of Scientology
Mission of Collingswood
118 W. Merchant Street
Audubon, New Jersey 08106

Church of Scientology
Mission of New Jersey
1029 Teaneck Road
Teaneck, New Jersey 07666

New York

Church of Scientology
Mission of Middletown
21 Mill Street
Liberty, New York 12754

Church of Scientology
Mission of Queens
56-03 214th Street
Bayside, New York 11364

Church of Scientology
Mission of Rockland
7 Panoramic Drive
Valley Cottage, New York 10989

Pennsylvania

Church of Scientology
Mission of Pittsburgh
37 Terrace Drive
Charleroi, Pennsylvania 15022

South Carolina

Church of Scientology
Mission of Charleston
4050 Ashley Phosphate Road
Charleston, South Carolina 29418

Tennessee

Church of Scientology
Mission of Memphis
1440 Central Avenue
Memphis, Tennessee 38104

Texas

Church of Scientology
Mission of Casa Linda
10204 Garland Road
Dallas, Texas 75218

Church of Scientology
Mission of El Paso
6330 North Mesa
El Paso, Texas 79912

Church of Scientology
Mission of Houston
2727 Fondren, Suite 1-A
Houston, Texas 77063

Church of Scientology
Mission of San Antonio
PO Box 29618
San Antonio, Texas 78229

Washington

Church of Scientology
Mission of Bellevue
15424 Bellevue-Redmond Road
Redmond, Washington 98052

Church of Scientology
Mission of Burien
15216 2nd Avenue SW
Seattle, Washington 98166

Church of Scientology
Mission of Seattle
2134 NE 145th Street
Seattle, Washington 98155

Dianetics Center
Mission of Spokane
1432 W. Francis
Spokane, Washington 99205

Wisconsin

Church of Scientology
Mission of Milwaukee
710 E. Silver Spring Drive, Suite E
White Fish Bay, Wisconsin 53217

ZAIRE

Church of Scientology
Mission de Kinshasa
BP 1444 Fele No. 7
Kinshasa/Limete
Zaire

INTERNATIONAL HUBBARD ECCLESIASTICAL LEAGUE OF PASTORS (I HELP)

For information on membership, services and programs for Field Auditors, or Auditors Associations, contact I HELP international headquarters or the nearest I HELP office or call 1-800-HELP-4-YU.

To find out more about the Volunteer Minister Program, or if the assistance of a Volunteer Minister is needed, the number to call is also 1-800-HELP-4-YU.

INTERNATIONAL OFFICE

I HELP INTERNATIONAL
6331 Hollywood Boulevard,
Suite 702
Los Angeles, California 90028

I HELP CONTINENTAL OFFICES

AFRICA

*International Hubbard Ecclesiastical League of Pastors
African Office*
6th Floor, Budget House
130 Main Street
Johannesburg 2001, South Africa

AUSTRALIA

*International Hubbard Ecclesiastical League of Pastors
Australian, New Zealand and Oceanian Office*
201 Castlereagh Street, 3rd Floor
Sydney, New South Wales 2000
Australia

CANADA

*International Hubbard Ecclesiastical League of Pastors
Canadian Office*
696 Yonge Street
Toronto, Ontario, Canada M4Y 2A7

COMMONWEALTH OF INDEPENDENT STATES

*International Hubbard Ecclesiastical League of Pastors
CIS Office*
c/o Hubbard Humanitarian Center
129301 Moscow
Borisa Galushkina Ul. 19A, Russia

EUROPE

*International Hubbard Ecclesiastical League of Pastors
European Office*
Store Kongensgade 55
1264 Copenhagen K, Denmark

HUNGARY

*International Hubbard Ecclesiastical League of Pastors
Hungarian Office*
1438 Budapest
PO Box 351, Hungary

ITALY

*International Hubbard Ecclesiastical League of Pastors
Italian Office*
Via Cadorna, 61
20090 Vimodrone
Milano, Italy

LATIN AMERICA

*International Hubbard Ecclesiastical League of Pastors
Latin American Office*
Pomona, 53
Colonia Roma, C.P. 06700
Mexico, D.F.

UNITED KINGDOM

*International Hubbard Ecclesiastical League of Pastors
United Kingdom Office*
Saint Hill Manor
East Grinstead, West Sussex
England RH19 4JY

UNITED STATES

*International Hubbard Ecclesiastical League of Pastors
Eastern United States Office*
349 W. 48th Street
New York, New York 10036

I HELP Representative Flag Land Base
512 Cleveland Street, Suite 283
Clearwater, Florida 33755

*International Hubbard Ecclesiastical League of Pastors
Western United States Office*
1308 L. Ron Hubbard Way
Los Angeles, California 90027

ASSOCIATION FOR BETTER LIVING AND EDUCATION (ABLE)

For information about ABLE, you can write to ABLE International or any of its continental offices.

INTERNATIONAL OFFICES

ASSOCIATION FOR BETTER LIVING AND EDUCATION INTERNATIONAL
7065 Hollywood Boulevard
Los Angeles, California 90028

ASSOCIATION FOR BETTER LIVING AND EDUCATION EXPANSION OFFICE
118 North Fort Harrison Avenue
Clearwater, Florida 34615

ABLE CONTINENTAL OFFICES

AFRICA

Association for Better Living and Education African Office
6th Floor, Budget House
130 Main Street
Johannesburg 2001, South Africa

AUSTRALIA, NEW ZEALAND, OCEANIA

Association for Better Living and Education Australian, New Zealand and Oceanian Office
201 Castlereagh Street
Sydney, New South Wales 2000
Australia

CANADA

Association for Better Living and Education Canadian Office
696 Yonge Street
Toronto, Ontario, Canada M4Y 2A7

COMMONWEALTH OF INDEPENDENT STATES

Association for Better Living and Education CIS Office
c/o Hubbard Humanitarian Center
129301 Moscow
Borisa Galushkina Ul. 19A, Russia

EUROPE

Association for Better Living and Education European Office
Store Kongensgade 55
1264 Copenhagen K, Denmark

HUNGARY

A Jobb Emberert Alapitvany/ Association for Better Living and Education Hungarian Office
1438 Budapest
PO Box 351, Hungary

ITALY

Association for Better Living and Education Italian Office
Via Cadorna, 61
20090 Vimodrone
Milano, Italy

LATIN AMERICA

Association for Better Living and Education Latin American Office
Pomona, 53
Colonia Roma, C.P. 06700
Mexico, D.F.

UNITED KINGDOM

Association for Better Living and Education United Kingdom Office
Saint Hill Manor
East Grinstead, West Sussex
England RH19 4JY

UNITED STATES

Association for Better Living and Education Eastern United States Office
349 W. 48th Street
New York, New York 10036

Association for Better Living and Education Western United States Office
1308 L. Ron Hubbard Way
Los Angeles, California 90027

NARCONON

For information about the Narconon program or how to start a Narconon drug education or drug rehabilitation center, write to Narconon International or any of the continental Narconon offices.

INTERNATIONAL OFFICE

NARCONON INTERNATIONAL
7065 Hollywood Boulevard
Los Angeles, California 90028

NARCONON CONTINENTAL OFFICES

AFRICA

Narconon Africa
6th Floor, Budget House
130 Main Street
Johannesburg 2001
South Africa

AUSTRALIA, NEW ZEALAND, OCEANIA

Narconon ANZO
PO Box 423, Leichhardt
Sydney, New South Wales 2040
Australia

CANADA

Narconon Canada
696 Yonge Street
Toronto, Ontario
Canada M4Y 2A7

EUROPE

Narconon Europe
Gl. Skovvej 8
2770 Kastrup
Denmark

HUNGARY

Narconon Hungary
1438 Budapest
PO Box 351
Hungary

ITALY

Narconon Italy
c/o Associazione per un
Futuro Migliore
Via Cadamosto, 8
20129 Milano
Italy

LATIN AMERICA

Narconon Latin America
Pomona, 53
Colonia Roma
C.P. 06700
Mexico, D.F.

UNITED KINGDOM

Narconon United Kingdom
47 Kelm Scott Gardens
Shepherds Bush
London
England W12 9DB

UNITED STATES

Narconon Eastern United States
349 W. 48th Street
New York, New York 10036

Narconon Western United States
1308 L. Ron Hubbard Way
Los Angeles, California 90027

NARCONON CENTERS

Narconon drug education and drug rehabilitation services are available at the following Narconon centers.

CANADA

Narconon Montreal Drug Education
4301 Parthenis
Montreal, Quebec
Canada H2H 2G2

Narconon Toronto
156 Mentwood Drive
Toronto, Ontario
Canada M4K 3T6

COLOMBIA

Narconon Colombia
Apartado Aéreo, 251628
Santa Fé de Bogotá
Colombia

COMMONWEALTH OF INDEPENDENT STATES

Kazakhstan

Narconon Alma-Ata
480046 Alma-Ata
Turkiebaeva Ul. 246, Apt. 59
Kazakhstan

Russia

Narconon Dimitrovgrad
433510 Ulianovsk Region
Dimitrovgrad
Lenin Prospect 31a, Apt. 19
Russia

Narconon Ekaterinburg
620027 Ekaterinburg
Mamina Sibirjaka Ul. 51, Apt. 32
Russia

Narconon Moscow
125195 Moscow
Smolnaja Ul. 47
Russia

DENMARK

Narconon Denmark
Amosvej 73
Skellingsted
4440 Morkov
Denmark

FRANCE

Narconon Leman
Le Clos Belle Vue
Le Mont Bene
74420 Saxel
France

GERMANY

Narconon North Germany
An der Bundesstraße 77
25524 Itzehoe
Germany

ITALY

Associazione Narconon La Fenice
Strada Statle, 18
Campora San Giovanni
87032 Amantea (Cosenza)
Italy

Comunita Narconon Alfiere
Via Montefeltro, 16/2
61100 Pesaro
Italy

Comunita Narconon Astore
Via Necropoli, 22
61020 Novilara (Pesaro)
Italy

Comunita Narconon Il Falco
Contrata Monti
87040 Altilia (Cosenza)
Italy

Comunita Narconon Il Gabbiano
c/o Hotel Pegaso
Via Sentinella
73020 Torre Dell'Orso (Lecce)
Italy

Comunita Narconon Grifone
Via Gallinaio, 29
95020 C. da Ficarazzi
Aci Castello (Catania)
Italy

MEXICO

Narconon Mexico
Carr. A Galindo Km. 4.5 FR ACC
Ranch Los Salvadores
S/N Pedro Escobedo, QRO
Mexico

NETHERLANDS

Narconon Holland
c/o Gasthuissingel 16
2012 Dn Haarlem
Netherlands

Narconon Zutphen
Deventerweg 93
7203 AD Zutphen
Netherlands

NEW ZEALAND

Narconon New Zealand (Aotearoa)
c/o Ngati Arohanui Trust
8 Hopetown St.
Ponsoby, Auckland
New Zealand

SPAIN

Asociación Narconon Mediterráneo
Autovía Sevilla-Malaga Km. 14,5
41500 Alcalá de Guadaira
Sevilla
Spain

Asociación Narconon Los Molinos
Villa Mari Solea
C/ San Nicolás S/N
28460 Los Molinos de Guadarrama
Madrid
Spain

Asociación Narconon Retiro
Chalet Herrera
41500 Alcalá de Guadaira
Sevilla
Spain

SWEDEN

Narconon Sweden
National Office
Finnbodavägen 2, 4 tr
13131 Nacka
Sweden

Narconon Göteborg
Kronhusgatan
41105 Göteborg
Sweden

Narconon Huddinge
Vårbackavägen 1
14300 Vårby gård
Stockholm
Sweden

Narconon Knutby
Gränsta
74012 Knutby
Sweden

Narconon Malmö/Eslöv
Södergård-Skarhult
24100 Eslöv
Sweden

SWITZERLAND

Narconon Deutschschweiz
Darl 169
9104 Waldstatt
Switzerland

Narconon Romandie
Les Plans Sur Bex 1888
Vaud
Switzerland

UNITED STATES

Narconon Boston Drug Education
459 Broadway, Suite 102
Everett, Massachusetts 02149

Narconon Chilocco
1000 W. Judo Road
Newkirk, Oklahoma 74647

Narconon Newport Beach
1810 W. Ocean Front
Newport Beach, California 92663

Narconon Northern California
8699 Empire Grade
Santa Cruz, California 95060

Narconon Peer Leader Drug Education
52 Martel Road
Chichester, New Hampshire 03234

CRIMINON

For information about the Criminon program write to:

INTERNATIONAL OFFICE

CRIMINON INTERNATIONAL
7065 Hollywood Boulevard
Los Angeles, California 90028

CRIMINON CONTINENTAL OFFICES

AFRICA

Criminon Africa
6th Floor, Budget House
130 Main Street
Johannesburg 2001, South Africa

AUSTRALIA, NEW ZEALAND, OCEANIA

Criminon ANZO
201 Castlereagh Street
Sydney, New South Wales 2000
Australia

CANADA

Criminon Canada
696 Yonge Street
Toronto, Ontario, Canada M4Y 2A7

COMMONWEALTH OF INDEPENDENT STATES

Criminon CIS
c/o Hubbard Humanitarian Center
129301 Moscow
Borisa Galushkina Ul. 19A, Russia

EUROPE

Criminon Europe
Store Kongensgade 55
1264 Copenhagen K, Denmark

LATIN AMERICA

Criminon Latin America
Pomona, 53, Colonia Roma
C.P. 06700
Mexico, D.F.

UNITED KINGDOM

Criminon United Kingdom
PO Box 128
East Grinstead, West Sussex
England RH19 4GB

UNITED STATES

Criminon Eastern United States
349 W. 48th Street
New York, New York 10036

Criminon Western United States
PO Box 9091
Glendale, California 91226

CRIMINON CENTERS

There are Criminon programs at the following locations.

COLOMBIA

Criminon Colombia
18a Street, 1646 South
Bogotá
Colombia

COMMONWEALTH OF INDEPENDENT STATES

Criminon Moscow
c/o Hubbard Humanitarian Center
129301 Moscow
Borisa Galushkina Ul. 19A
Russia

Criminon Oriol
302030 Oriol
Lenin Ul. 4, Apt. 39
Russia

FRANCE

Criminon France
6, avenue Hoche
Beauchamp 95250
France

HUNGARY

Criminon Tatabanya
Tatabanya 2800
Martirok Ut 108
Hungary

ITALY

Criminon Italy
c/o Associazione per un
Futuro Migliore
Via Cadamosto, 8
20129 Milano
Italy

SPAIN

Criminon Canary Islands
C/ Viera y Clavijo, 33-1
35002 Las Palmas de Gran Canaria
Spain

SWEDEN

Criminon Sweden
Finnbodavägen 2, 4 tr
13131 Nacka
Sweden

SWITZERLAND

Criminon Switzerland
Arbeitsgruppe Zurich
Postfach 8176
8036 Zurich
Switzerland

UNITED STATES

California

Criminon Community Education Center
306 W. Compton Boulevard, Suite 203
Compton, California 90220

Criminon Community Education Center
1043 Glendora Avenue, Suite G
West Covina, California 91790

Connecticut

Criminon Connecticut
PO Box 310202
Newington, Connecticut 06131

Florida

Criminon Florida
PO Box 7727
Clearwater, Florida 34615

Criminon South Florida
PO Box 817211
Hollywood, Florida 33021

Minnesota

Criminon Minnesota
PO Box 82
Newport, Minnesota 55055

New York

Criminon Buffalo
2045 Niagara Street
Buffalo, New York 14207

Ohio

Criminon Ohio
PO Box 09579
Columbus, Ohio 43209

VENEZUELA

Criminon Fundación Auyantepuy
Dandoral Plaza, 122A
Avenida Sucre, Los Dos Caminos
Caracas
Venezuela

APPLIED SCHOLASTICS

For information about Applied Scholastics or how to start a tutoring program or school write to Applied Scholastics International or any of the continental Applied Scholastics offices.

INTERNATIONAL OFFICE

APPLIED SCHOLASTICS INTERNATIONAL
7065 Hollywood Boulevard
Los Angeles, California 90028

APPLIED SCHOLASTICS CONTINENTAL OFFICES

AFRICA

Education Alive Africa
6th Floor, Budget House
130 Main Street
Johannesburg 2001, South Africa

AUSTRALIA

Applied Scholastics
National Office
44 Smith Street
Balmain, New South Wales 2041
Australia

CANADA

Applied Scholastics
National Office
1680 Lakeshore Road West, Unit 5a
Mississauga, Ontario
Canada L5J 1J4

COMMONWEALTH OF INDEPENDENT STATES

Applied Scholastics CIS
c/o Hubbard Humanitarian Center
129301 Moscow
Borisa Galushkina Ul. 19A
Russia

EUROPE

Applied Scholastics Europe
F.F. Ulriks Gade 13
2100 Copenhagen O, Denmark

HUNGARY

Applied Scholastics Hungary
Almassy Ter. 16 1/12
1077 Budapest, Hungary

UNITED KINGDOM

Applied Scholastics
United Kingdom
78 Northwood Road
Thornton Heath
Surrey CR7 8HR
England

UNITED STATES

Applied Scholastics
Eastern United States
349 W. 48th Street
New York, New York 10036

Applied Scholastics
Western United States
17291 Irvine Boulevard, Suite 405
Tustin, California 92780

APPLIED SCHOLASTICS EDUCATIONAL ORGANIZATIONS

L. Ron Hubbard's study technology is used in the following Applied Scholastics schools and other educational organizations.

AUSTRIA

Kreativ College
Rienosslgasse 12
1040 Wien
Austria

BELGIUM

Applied Scholastics
Korte Heistraat 7
2800 Mechelen
Belgium

CZECH REPUBLIC

Applied Scholastics of the Czech Republic
PO Box 192
11121 Prague
Czech Republic

DENMARK

Amager International School
Engvej 141–145
2300 Copenhagen S
Denmark

Applied Scholastics Denmark
F.F. Ulriks Gade 13
2100 Copenhagen O
Denmark

ENGLAND

Greenfields School
Priory Road, Forest Row
East Sussex
England RH18 53D

Greenfields School London
2A The Curve
London
England WC12 0RH

FRANCE

Institut Aubert
62, avenue de Paris
94300 Vincennes
France

HUNGARY

Applied Scholastics Hungary
Almassy Ter. 16 1/12
1077 Budapest
Hungary

JAPAN

Applied Scholastics Japan
8-18 Higashi Hakushima
Naka-ku, Hiroshima
Japan 730

MALAYSIA

Applied Scholastics Institute of Malaysia
No. 42-2a Jalan Tun
Sambanthan 3
50470 Kuala Lumpur
Malaysia

MEXICO

Campaña Mexicana para Mejorar el Estudio
Apartado Postal, 85-061
Admon, Correos 85
Mexico, D.F. 10201

NETHERLANDS

Lafayette School
Fahrenheitstraat 99
1097 Amsterdam
Netherlands

SCOTLAND

Effective Education Edinburgh
14 Efflemont Road
Edinburgh
Scotland EH16 5PX

SOUTH AFRICA

Education Alive Cape Town
51 Station Road, Observatory
Cape Town 7925
South Africa

Education Alive School
6th Floor, Budget House
130 Main Street
Johannesburg 2001
South Africa

Summerhill Preparatory School
PO Box 2465
Halfway House 1685
South Africa

SWEDEN

Applied Scholastics Sweden
Källforsvägen 40
S-124 32 Bandhagen
Sweden

TAIWAN

Applied Scholastics Taiwan
87 No. 6, Lane 71 Sec 4
Nan-King E. Rd
Taipei
Taiwan

UNITED STATES

California

Ability Plus School Orange County
220 El Camino Real
Tustin, California 92780

Applied Scholastics San Francisco
39355 California Street #207
Fremont, California 94538

Delphi Academy Sacramento
5590 Madison Avenue
Sacramento, California 95841

Delphi Academy San Diego
3401 Clarimont Drive
San Diego, California 92117

Delphi Academy San Francisco
890 Palmoroy Avenue #201
Santa Clara, California 95051

Delphi Los Angeles
4490 Cornishon Avenue
La Canada, California 91011

*Hollywood Education
and Literacy Project*
6336 Hollywood Boulevard
Hollywood, California 90028

World Literacy Crusade International
33209 North Alameda
Compton, California 90262

Colorado

Ability Plus School Colorado
3375 S. Bannock, Suite 100A
Englewood, Colorado 80110

Connecticut

Standard Education
168 Prospect Street
Waterbury, Connecticut 06702

Florida

Back to Basics School
253 Grove Circle S.
Dunedin, Florida 34698

Clearwater Academy International
814 Franklin Street
Clearwater, Florida 34616

Creative Learning
5741 SW 45 Terrace
Miami, Florida 33155

Delphi Academy Florida
1831 Drew Street
Clearwater, Florida 34625

Little School
217 Kerry Drive
Clearwater, Florida 33758

Georgia

Lafayette Academy
2417 Canton Road
Marietta, Georgia 30066

Illinois

Chicagoland
9 Walnut Road
Glen Ellyn, Illinois 60137

Massachusetts

Boston Academy
233 Pearl Street
Somerville, Massachusetts 02145

Delphi Academy Boston
564 Blue Hill Avenue
Milton, Massachusetts 02186

Missouri

Ability Plus School St. Louis
10264 Chaucer Avenue
St. Louis, Missouri 63114

Nevada

Mission of the Children
1018 E. Sahara #D
Las Vegas, Nevada 89104

New Hampshire

Bear Hill School, Inc.
PO Box 417
Pittsfield, New Hampshire 03263

Oregon

Columbia Academy
9806 SW Boones Ferry Road
Portland, Oregon 97219

The Delphian School Oregon
20950 S.W. Rock Creek Road
Sheridan, Oregon 97378

Texas

Tanglewood Academy
5714 Dolores Street
Houston, Texas 77057

Utah

Ability Plus School Utah
913 E. Syrena Circle
Sandy, Utah 89094

Virginia

Chesapeake Ability School
5533 Industrial Drive
Springfield, Virginia 22151

Washington

*Washington Academy
of Knowledge*
20853 S.E. 123rd Street
Issaquah, Washington 98027

VENEZUELA

*Centro de Educación Efectiva para
Venezuela*
Avenida Martín Tover cruce
   con Rondon
Edif. Piedra Tranca, Piso 1 Oficina 01
Centro, Valencia
Venezuela

THE WAY TO HAPPINESS

For information about distribution of The Way to Happiness, *the Set a Good Example Contest and other social programs contact The Way to Happiness Foundation or any of its continental offices.*

INTERNATIONAL OFFICE

THE WAY TO HAPPINESS FOUNDATION INTERNATIONAL
PO Box 2930
Los Angeles, California 90028

THE WAY TO HAPPINESS FOUNDATION CONTINENTAL OFFICES

AFRICA

The Way to Happiness Foundation Africa
6th Floor, Budget House
130 Main Street
Johannesburg 2001
South Africa

AUSTRALIA, NEW ZEALAND, OCEANIA

The Way to Happiness Foundation ANZO
201 Castlereagh Street, 3rd Floor
Sydney 2000
Australia

CANADA

The Way to Happiness Foundation Canada
696 Yonge Street
Toronto, Ontario
Canada M4Y 2A7

COMMONWEALTH OF INDEPENDENT STATES

The Way to Happiness Foundation CIS
c/o Hubbard Humanitarian Center
129301 Moscow
Borisa Galushkina Ul. 19A
Russia

EUROPE

The Way to Happiness Foundation Europe
Store Kongensgade 55
1264 Copenhagen K
Denmark

HUNGARY

A Jobb Emberert Alapitvany/ The Way to Happiness Foundation Hungary
1438 Budapest
PO Box 351
Hungary

LATIN AMERICA

The Way to Happiness Foundation Latin America
Pomona, 53
Colonia Roma
C.P. 06700
Mexico, D.F.

UNITED KINGDOM

The Way to Happiness Foundation United Kingdom
Saint Hill Manor
East Grinstead, West Sussex
England RH19 4JY

UNITED STATES

The Way to Happiness Foundation Eastern United States
349 W. 48th Street
New York, New York 10036

The Way to Happiness Foundation Western United States
1308 L. Ron Hubbard Way
Los Angeles, California 90027

WORLD INSTITUTE OF SCIENTOLOGY ENTERPRISES (WISE)

To find out about the publication of L. Ron Hubbard's administrative technology and how to become a member of WISE, contact WISE International or any of its continental offices.

INTERNATIONAL OFFICE

WISE INTERNATIONAL
6331 Hollywood Boulevard,
Suite 701
Los Angeles, California 90028

WISE CONTINENTAL OFFICES

AFRICA

World Institute of Scientology Enterprises
African Office
6th Floor, Budget House
130 Main Street
Johannesburg 2001
South Africa

AUSTRALIA, NEW ZEALAND, OCEANIA

World Institute of Scientology Enterprises
Australian, New Zealand and Oceanian Office
201 Castlereagh Street
Sydney, New South Wales 2000
Australia

CANADA

World Institute of Scientology Enterprises
Canadian Office
696 Yonge Street
Toronto, Ontario
Canada M4Y 2A7

COMMONWEALTH OF INDEPENDENT STATES

World Institute of Scientology Enterprises
CIS Office
c/o Hubbard Humanitarian Center
129301 Moscow
Borisa Galushkina Ul. 19A
Russia

EUROPE

World Institute of Scientology Enterprises
European Office
Store Kongensgade 55
1264 Copenhagen K, Denmark

HUNGARY

World Institute of Scientology Enterprises
Hungarian Office
1438 Budapest
PO Box 351
Hungary

ITALY

World Institute of Scientology Enterprises
Italian Office
Via Cadorna, 61
20090 Vimodrone (Milano)
Italy

LATIN AMERICA

World Institute of Scientology Enterprises
Latin American Office
Pomona, 53
Colonia Roma
C.P. 06700
Mexico, D.F.

UNITED KINGDOM

World Institute of Scientology Enterprises
United Kingdom Office
Saint Hill Manor
East Grinstead, West Sussex
England RH19 4JY

UNITED STATES

World Institute of Scientology Enterprises
Eastern United States Office
349 W. 48th Street
New York, New York 10036

World Institute of Scientology Enterprises
Flag Land Base Office
512 Cleveland Street, #283
Clearwater, Florida 33755

World Institute of Scientology Enterprises
Western United States Office
1308 L. Ron Hubbard Way
Los Angeles, California 90027

WISE CHARTER COMMITTEES

AUSTRALIA

WISE Charter Committee Melbourne
10 Pratt Street
Ringwood
Victoria 3134, Australia

CANADA

WISE Charter Committee Toronto
873 Broadview Avenue,
Lower Level
Toronto, Ontario
Canada M4K 2P9

FRANCE

WISE Charter Committee Paris
3, rue Bernoulli
75008 Paris, France

GERMANY

WISE Charter Committee Frankfurt
Johann-Peter-Bach Straße 10
61130 Nidderau, Germany

WISE Charter Committee Hamburg
Postfach 730404
22124 Hamburg, Germany

WISE Charter Committee Munich
Otto-Gaßner-Straße 1A
D-82319 Starnberg, Germany

WISE Charter Committee Stuttgart
Geislinger Straße 21
D-73033 Göppingen, Germany

ITALY

WISE Charter Committee Milano
Via Paracelso, 12
Palazzo Perseo
20411 Agrate Brianza (Milano)
Italy

MEXICO

WISE Charter Committee Mexico
Alamo 93, Cuarto Piso
Santa Monica, Ttal. Edo. de Mexico
Mexico 54040

NEW ZEALAND

WISE Charter Committee
New Zealand
PO Box 350
Albany, New Zealand

SWITZERLAND

WISE Charter Committee
Deutschschweiz
Postfach 6204
Sempach-Stadt, Switzerland

UNITED KINGDOM

WISE Charter Committee
East Grinstead
Bulrushes Farm, Coombe Hill Road
East Grinstead
England RH19 4LZ

WISE Charter Committee Manchester
59 New Hall Lane
Bolton, England BL1 5LW

UNITED STATES

WISE Charter Committee Clearwater
1227 Turner Street, Suite E
Clearwater, Florida 33756

WISE Charter Committee Los Angeles
440 Western Avenue, Suite 103
Glendale, California 91201

WISE Charter Committee Michigan
6920 Spring Valley, Suite 101
Holland, Ohio 43528

WISE Charter Committee New York
67 Summit Avenue
Hackensack, New Jersey 07601

HUBBARD COLLEGES OF ADMINISTRATION

To find out where to take courses in L. Ron Hubbard's administrative technology, contact the Hubbard College of Administration International or any local Hubbard College.

INTERNATIONAL OFFICE

HUBBARD COLLEGE OF ADMINISTRATION INTERNATIONAL
6565 Sunset Boulevard, #400
Los Angeles, California 90028

HUBBARD COLLEGES

ARGENTINA

Hubbard College of Administration Argentina
Marcos Paz, 2954
1417 Buenos Aires
Argentina

AUSTRALIA

Hubbard College of Administration Brisbane
12B Parkview Street
Milton, Queensland 4064
Australia

Hubbard College of Administration Sydney
15 Parnell Street
2nd Floor, Suite 9
Strathfield, New South Wales 2135
Australia

COMMONWEALTH OF INDEPENDENT STATES

Hubbard College of Administration Irkutsk
665470 Irkutsk
Ussolye-Siberskoye, Kuibysheva Ul. 1a
Irkutsk
Russia

Hubbard College of Administration Kemerovo
650099 Kemerovo
Krasnaya Ul. 8
Russia

Hubbard College of Administration Mariupol
341015 Mariupol
Pr. Metallurgov 88, KV. 41
Ukraine

Hubbard College of Administration Moscow
129226 Moscow
17/2 Selskokhozyaistvennaya Ul.
Russia

Hubbard College of Administration Novgorod
173016 Novgorod
Mendeleeva Ul. 3A
Russia

GERMANY

Hubbard College of Administration Munich
Otto-Gaßner-Straße 1A
D-82319 Starnberg
Germany

HUNGARY

Hubbard College of Administration Budapest
Szombathelyi ter 8.
1119 Budapest
Hungary

ITALY

Hubbard College of Administration Milano
c/o Country Hotel Borromeo
Via Bruno Buozzi
20068 Peschiera Borromeo (Milano)
Italy

MEXICO

Hubbard College of Administration Guadalajara
Lopez Cotilla, 2266
Arcos Vallerta
Guadalajara, Jalisco 44130
Mexico

SOUTH AFRICA

Hubbard College of Administration Johannesburg
PO Box 942 Edenvale
Johannesburg 2094
South Africa

UNITED KINGDOM

Hubbard College of Administration West Sussex
31A High Street
East Grinstead, West Sussex
England RH19 3AF

UNITED STATES

Hubbard College of Administration Santa Clara
901 Campisi Way, Suite 380
Campbell, California 95008

Citizens Commission on Human Rights (CCHR)

To find out what you can do to combat psychiatric abuses against human rights and restore dignity to man, contact the Citizens Commission on Human Rights International or any of its local chapters.

INTERNATIONAL OFFICE

Citizens Commission on Human Rights International
6362 Hollywood Boulevard,
Suite B
Los Angeles, California 90028

CCHR CHAPTERS

AUSTRALIA

Citizens Commission on Human Rights Australian National Office
201 Castlereagh Street, 2nd Floor
Sydney, New South Wales 2000
Australia

Citizens Commission on Human Rights Adelaide
24–28 Waymouth Street, 1st Floor
Adelaide, South Australia 5000
Australia

Citizens Commission on Human Rights Brisbane
106 Edward Street, 2nd Floor
Brisbane, Queensland 4000
Australia

Citizens Commission on Human Rights Canberra
GPO Box 2545
Canberra City, ACT 2601
Australia

Citizens Commission on Human Rights Melbourne
42–44 Russell Street
Melbourne, Victoria 3000
Australia

AUSTRIA

Citizens Commission on Human Rights Austria
Postfach 133
Vienna 1072
Austria

BELGIUM

Citizens Commission on Human Rights Belgium
Boite Postale, 6
B-4650 Herve
Belgium

CANADA

Citizens Commission on Human Rights Canadian National Office
50 Charles Street, Unit 194
Toronto, Ontario
Canada M4Y 2L5

Citizens Commission on Human Rights Quebec
316 St. Joseph East
CP 51069
Quebec, Quebec
Canada 61K 8Z7

Citizens Commission on Human Rights Vancouver
401 West Hasting Street
Vancouver, British Columbia
Canada V6B 1L5

COMMONWEALTH OF INDEPENDENT STATES

Citizens Commission on Human Rights CIS
105275 Moscow
Prospect Budyonogo 31
Russia

DENMARK

Citizens Commission on Human Rights Copenhagen
Store Kongensgade 55
1264 Copenhagen K
Denmark

Citizens Commission on Human Rights Denmark
Lundegaardsvej 19
2900 Hellerup
Denmark

FINLAND

*Citizens Commission
on Human Rights Finland*
PL 76
02771 Espoo
Finland

FRANCE

*Citizens Commission
on Human Rights France*
4, rue Burg
75018 Paris
France

*Citizens Commission
on Human Rights Angers*
21, rue Paul Bert
49000 Angers
France

GERMANY

*Citizens Commission
on Human Rights Berlin*
Postfach 150743
10669 Berlin
Germany

*Citizens Commission
on Human Rights Düsseldorf*
Kruppstr. 49
40227 Düsseldorf
Germany

*Citizens Commission
on Human Rights Hamburg*
Rostocker Straße 20
20099 Hamburg
Germany

*Citizens Commission
on Human Rights Karlsruhe*
Am Wetterbach 100
76228 Karlsruhe
Germany

*Citizens Commission
on Human Rights Württemberg*
Pelargusstraße 1–3
72519 Stuttgart
Germany

GREECE

*Citizens Commission
on Human Rights Greece*
Klissovis 12
Athens 10677
Greece

HUNGARY

*Citizens Commission
on Human Rights Hungary*
Budapest, PF 182
1461, Hungary

ISRAEL

*Citizens Commission
on Human Rights Israel*
Suskin 9
Nahariya 22404
Israel

ITALY

*Citizens Commission on Human Rights
Italian National Office*
Via delle Leghe, 22
20127 Milano
Italy

*Citizens Commission
on Human Rights Garbagnate*
c/o Biblioteca Comunale di Arese
Via dei Platani, 6
20020 Arese (MI)
Italy

*Citizens Commission
on Human Rights Lucca*
Casella Postale
Lucca Centro, 154
55100 Lucca
Italy

*Citizens Commission
on Human Rights Monza*
Casella Postale 1
20048 Carate Brianza (MI)
Italy

*Citizens Commission
on Human Rights Novara 1st*
Via Padri Generoso, 19
28020 Colloro di Presosello (NO)
Italy

*Citizens Commission
on Human Rights Pordenone*
Via Celina, 7
33080 Porchia (PN)
Italy

JAPAN

*Citizens Commission
on Human Rights Hiroshima*
8-18 Higashi Hakushima
Naka-ku
Hiroshima, Japan 730

MEXICO

*Citizens Commission
on Human Rights Mexico*
Tuxpan 68
Colonia Roma
C.P. 06760, Mexico, D.F.

NETHERLANDS

*Citizens Commission
on Human Rights Netherlands*
Postbus 11354
1001 GJ Amsterdam
Netherlands

NEW ZEALAND

*Citizens Commission
on Human Rights New Zealand*
159 Queen Street, 1st Floor
Auckland 1, New Zealand

NORWAY

*Citizens Commission
on Human Rights Norway*
Post Boks 8902
Youngstorvet
0028 Oslo
Norway

PORTUGAL

*Citizens Commission
on Human Rights Portugal*
R. Jorge Barradas 41 3 FTE
1500 Lisbon
Portugal

SOUTH AFRICA

*Citizens Commission
on Human Rights
South African National Office*
PO Box 710
Johannesburg 2000
South Africa

SWEDEN

*Citizens Commission
on Human Rights Sweden*
Johan Enbergs väg 36
171 61 Solna
Sweden

*Citizens Commission
on Human Rights Göteborg*
c/o BETAB
Ångpannegatan 9B 3 tr
417 05 Göteborg
Sweden

SWITZERLAND

*Citizens Commission
on Human Rights Basel*
Feldstrasse 10
4123 Allschwil
Switzerland

*Citizens Commission
on Human Rights Bern*
Postfach 338
3000 Bern 7
Switzerland

*Citizens Commission
on Human Rights Geneva*
Casella Postale 1282
1211 Geneva 1
Switzerland

*Citizens Commission
on Human Rights Lausanne*
Casella Postale 231
1000 Lausanne 17
Switzerland

*Citizens Commission
on Human Rights Ticino*
Casella Postale 613
6512 Giubiasco
Switzerland

*Citizens Commission
on Human Rights Zurich*
Badenerstrasse 141
8004 Zurich
Switzerland

UNITED KINGDOM

*Citizens Commission
on Human Rights United Kingdom
National Office*
PO Box 188
East Grinstead, West Sussex
England RH19 4JF

*Citizens Commission
on Human Rights Manchester*
185 Southfield Road
Waterloo
Huddersfield
England HD5 8RJ

UNITED STATES

Arizona

*Citizens Commission
on Human Rights Phoenix*
PO Box 54463
Phoenix, Arizona 85078

California

*Citizens Commission
on Human Rights Los Angeles*
PO Box 29754
Los Angeles, California 90029

*Citizens Commission on
Human Rights Mountain View*
2483 Old Middlefield Way
Mountain View, California 94043

*Citizens Commission on
Human Rights Orange County*
PO Box 984
Tustin, California 92681

*Citizens Commission
on Human Rights Riverside*
17305 Santa Rosa Mine Road
Perris, California 92570

*Citizens Commission
on Human Rights Sacramento*
825 15th Street
Sacramento, California 95814

*Citizens Commission
on Human Rights San Francisco*
83 McAllister Street
San Francisco, California 94102

*Citizens Commission
on Human Rights South Bay*
80 E. Rosemary
San Jose, California 95112

Colorado

*Citizens Commission
on Human Rights Colorado*
PO Box 9202
Denver, Colorado 80209

Connecticut

*Citizens Commission
on Human Rights Connecticut*
PO Box 17
Higganum, Connecticut 06441

Florida

Citizens Commission
on Human Rights Clearwater
305 North Fort Harrison Avenue
Clearwater, Florida 33755

Massachusetts

Citizens Commission
on Human Rights New England
89 Massachusetts Avenue #213
Boston, Massachusetts 02115

Missouri

Citizens Commission
on Human Rights Kansas City
3619 Broadway
Kansas City, Missouri 64111

Citizens Commission
on Human Rights St. Louis
PO Box 24222
University City, Missouri 63130

Nebraska

Citizens Commission
on Human Rights Nebraska
PO Box 24291
Omaha, Nebraska 68124

New York

Citizens Commission
on Human Rights New York City
244 5th Avenue
New York, New York 10001

Oregon

Citizens Commission
on Human Rights Oregon
PO Box 8842
Portland, Oregon 97207

Citizens Commission
on Human Rights Portland
PO Box 8842
Portland, Oregon 97207

Pennsylvania

Citizens Commission
on Human Rights Philadelphia
PO Box 17313
Philadelphia, Pennsylvania 19105

Texas

Citizens Commission
on Human Rights Texas
711 W. 7th Street #110
Austin, Texas 78701

Citizens Commission
on Human Rights Houston
50 Briar Hollowlane, Suite 300 East
Houston, Texas 77027

Utah

Citizens Commission
on Human Rights Utah
662 South State Street
Salt Lake City, Utah 84111

Washington

Citizens Commission
on Human Rights Seattle
300 Lendra Street B252
Seattle, Washington 98121

Washington, DC

Citizens Commission
on Human Rights DC
1701 20th Street NW
Washington, DC 20009

NATIONAL COMMISSION ON LAW ENFORCEMENT AND SOCIAL JUSTICE

National Commission on Law
Enforcement and Social Justice
9025 Fulbright Avenue
Chatsworth, California 91311

PUBLICATIONS ORGANIZATIONS

Bridge Publications, Inc. publishes the works of L. Ron Hubbard in the United States and Canada. New Era Publications publishes them for the rest of the world.

While all books on Dianetics and Scientology are available in Scientology churches and missions, they can also be purchased directly from the following organizations.

BRIDGE PUBLICATIONS, INC.
4751 Fountain Avenue
Los Angeles, California 90029

NEW ERA PUBLICATIONS INTERNATIONAL ApS
Store Kongensgade 55
1264 Copenhagen K
Denmark

AUSTRALIA

NEW ERA Publications Australia Pty Ltd.
Level 3 Ballarat House
68–72 Wentworth Avenue
Surry Hills, New South Wales
2000 Australia

CANADA

Continental Publications Liaison Office
696 Yonge Street
Toronto, Ontario
Canada M4Y 2A7

COMMONWEALTH OF INDEPENDENT STATES

NEW ERA Publications Group
129301 Moscow
Kasatkina Ul. 16, Building 1
Russia

FRANCE

NEW ERA Publications France E.U.R.L.
105, rue des Moines
75017 Paris
France

GERMANY

NEW ERA Publications Deutschland GmbH
Hittfelder Kirschweg 5a
21220 Seevetal-Maschen
Germany

ITALY

NEW ERA Publications Italia S.r.l.
Via Rucellai, 39
20126 Milano
Italy

JAPAN

NEW ERA Publications Japan, Inc.
3-4-20-503 Mita, Minato-ku
Tokyo, Japan 108

MEXICO

ERA DINÁMICA EDITORES, S.A. de C.V.
Nicolás San Juan, 208
Colonia Narvarte
C.P. 03020
Mexico, D.F.

SOUTH AFRICA

Continental Publications Pty Ltd.
6th Floor, Budget House
130 Main Street
Johannesburg 2001
South Africa

SPAIN

NUEVA ERA DINÁMICA, S.A.
C/ Montera 20, 1° dcha.
28013 Madrid
Spain

UNITED KINGDOM

NEW ERA Publications United Kingdom Ltd.
Saint Hill Manor
East Grinstead, West Sussex
England RH19 4JY

FREEDOM MAGAZINE

To obtain a subscription to Freedom *magazine or to contribute information or news articles for publication, contact* Freedom's *international editorial office or its local offices.*

INTERNATIONAL OFFICE

CHURCH OF SCIENTOLOGY INTERNATIONAL
Freedom *Magazine*
6331 Hollywood Boulevard,
Suite 1200
Los Angeles, California 90028

LOCAL OFFICES

AUSTRALIA

Church of Scientology of Sydney
Freedom *Magazine*
201 Castlereagh Street
Sydney, New South Wales 2000
Australia

AUSTRIA

Church of Scientology of Austria
Freedom *Magazine*
Schottenfeldgasse 13–15
1070 Vienna
Austria

BELGIUM

Church of Scientology of Belgium
Freedom *Magazine*
61, rue du Prince Royal
1050 Brussels
Belgium

DENMARK

Church of Scientology of Denmark
Frihed
Gammel Kongevej 3–5
1610 Copenhagen V
Denmark

FRANCE

Church of Scientology of Paris
Magazine Ethique et Liberté
7, rue Jules César
75012 Paris
France

GERMANY

Church of Scientology of Munich
Freiheit *Magazine*
Beichstraße 12
80802 Munich 80
Germany

GREECE

Dianetics and Scientology Centre
Freedom *Magazine*
Patision 200
11256 Athens
Greece

ITALY

Church of Scientology of Milano
Diritti dell'uomo
Via Abetone, 10
21037 Milano
Italy

JAPAN

Scientology Tokyo
Freedom *Magazine*
2-11-7, Kita-Otsuka
Toshima-ku
Tokyo, 170-0004
Japan

MEXICO

Federación Mexicana de Dianética A.C.
Freedom *Magazine*
Pomona, 53
Colonia Roma
C.P. 06700
Mexico, D.F.

NETHERLANDS

*Church of Scientology
of Amsterdam*
Freedom *Magazine*
Nieuwe Zijds Voorburgwal 271
1012 RL Amsterdam
Netherlands

NEW ZEALAND

*Church of Scientology
of New Zealand*
Freedom *Magazine*
159 Queen Street
Auckland 1
New Zealand

SOUTH AFRICA

*Church of Scientology
of Johannesburg*
Freedom *Magazine*
6th Floor, Budget House
130 Main Street
Johannesburg 2001
South Africa

SPAIN

Church of Scientology of Spain
Ética y Libertad *Magazine*
C/ Montera 20, 1° dcha.
28013 Madrid
Spain

SWEDEN

*Church of Scientology
of Stockholm*
Freedom *Magazine*
Götgatan 105
11662 Stockholm
Sweden

SWITZERLAND

*Church of Scientology
of Lausanne*
Magazine Ethique et Liberté
10, rue de la Madeleine
1003 Lausanne
Switzerland

Church of Scientology of Zurich
Freiheit *Magazine*
Badenerstrasse 141
8004 Zurich
Switzerland

UNITED STATES

*Church of Scientology
Flag Service Organization*
Freedom *Magazine*
503 Cleveland Street
Clearwater, Florida 33755

*Church of Scientology
of Los Angeles*
Freedom *Magazine*
4810 Sunset Boulevard
Los Angeles, California 90027

INTERNET SITES

For more information on subjects in this book, visit any of the following Web sites on the World Wide Web.

www.scientology.org
europe.scientology.org
faq.scientology.org
expansion.scientology.org
www.scientologyhandbook.org
on-line.scientology.org
foundingchurch.scientology.org
www.purification.org
www.studytechnology.org
keytolife.org
drugfreemarshals.org
www.smi.org

www.dianetics.org

www.cchr.org

www.freedommag.org

www.lronhubbard.org
tribute.lronhubbard.org

www.able.org
www.appliedscholastics.org
www.criminon.org
www.narconon.org
www.thewaytohappiness.org

www.wise.org
www.hubbardcollege.org

www.bridgepub.com

www.newerapublications.com

GLOSSARY OF TERMS

Philosophy has always had the liability of gathering to itself a great many new words and labels. The reason for this is that the philosopher finds phenomena in the physical universe or in the mind or humanities which have not hitherto been observed or properly identified. Each one of these tends to require a new word for its description. In actual fact this cycle of new observations requiring new labels is probably the growth of language itself. Language is obviously the product of unsung observers who then popularized a word to describe what had been observed.

The system which has been followed in Dianetics and Scientology in labeling phenomena or observed things was originally to make verbs into nouns or vice versa. The practice of developing new nomenclature was actually held to a minimum. However, it was found that many old words in the field of philosophy, when used, conveyed to people an entirely new idea. The exactness of Dianetics and Scientology required a more precise approach. This approach was achieved by special naming with an eye to minimal confusion with already supposed or known phenomena. The Dianetics and Scientology vocabulary is nevertheless not large.

In the search which brought about Dianetics and Scientology many new phenomena were encountered which resulted, for the first time, in a workable, predictable technology of the spirit. The introduction of a few words of new meaning to make this possible seems to be a small price to pay.

This glossary contains the Dianetics and Scientology terms appearing in *What Is Scientology?*

aberration: a departure from rational thought or behavior. It means basically to err, to make mistakes, or more specifically to have fixed ideas which are not true. The word is also used in its scientific sense. It means departure from a straight line. If a line should go from A to B, then if it is *aberrated* it would go from A to some other point, to some other point, to some other point, to some other point, and finally arrive at B. Taken in this sense, it would also mean the lack of straightness or to see crookedly as, for example, a man sees a horse but thinks he sees an elephant. Aberrated conduct would be wrong conduct, or conduct not supported by reason. When a person has engrams, these tend to deflect what would be his normal ability to perceive truth and bring about an aberrated view of situations which then would cause an aberrated reaction to them. *Aberration* is opposed to sanity, which would be its opposite. From the Latin, *aberrare*, to wander from; Latin, *ab*, away, *errare*, to wander.

ABLE: an acronym for *Association for Better Living and Education International*. See Chapter 31.

action phrases: word phrases contained as part of the content of engrams which dictate some type of "action" in the mind.

affinity: the degree of liking or affection or lack of it. It is the feeling of love or liking for something or someone.

affinity-reality-communication (ARC) triangle: a triangle which is a symbol of the fact that *affinity, reality* and *communication* act together to bring about understanding. No point of the triangle can be raised without also raising the other two points, and no point of it can be lowered without also lowering the other two points. See Chapter 4.

analytical mind: that part of the mind which one consciously uses and is aware of. It is the portion of the mind which thinks, observes data, remembers it and resolves problems. See Chapter 4.

antisocial personality: a person who possesses a distinct set of characteristics and mental attitudes that cause him to suppress other people in his vicinity. This is the person whose behavior is calculated to be disastrous. Also called *suppressive person*. See Chapter 17.

AO: abbreviation for *Advanced Organization*. See Chapter 21.

apparency: something that seems to be, that appears to be a certain way; something that *appears* to be but is different from the way it looks. In Dianetics and Scientology *apparency* is used to mean something that looks one way but is, in actual fact, something else. For example, a person "gives an *apparency* of health," whereas he is actually sick. From the Latin, *apparere*, to appear.

ARC: a word coined from the initial letters of *affinity, reality* and *communication*. See Chapter 4.

ARC break: a sudden drop or cutting of *affinity, reality* or *communication* with someone or something. Upsets with people or things (ARC breaks) come about because of a lessening or sundering of affinity, reality or communication or understanding. Scientologists usually use the term *ARC break* instead of *upset*, because if one discovers which of the three points of understanding have been cut, one can bring about a rapid recovery in the person's state of mind.

assessment: an auditing technique which helps to isolate specific areas or subjects on which a preclear has charge so that they can be addressed in auditing.

auditing: Scientology counseling, taken from the Latin word *audire* which means "to hear or listen." Auditing is a very unique form of personal counseling which helps an individual look at his own existence and improves his ability to confront what he is and where he is. See Chapter 5.

Auditing by List: a technique used in certain auditing procedures.

auditor: a minister or minister-in-training of the Church of Scientology. *Auditor* means one who listens, from the Latin *audire* meaning "to hear or listen." An auditor is a person trained and qualified in applying auditing to individuals for their betterment. An auditor does not do anything *to* a preclear, he works together with the preclear to help the preclear defeat his reactive mind. See Chapter 5.

beingness: the assumption or choosing of a category of identity. Beingness can be assumed by oneself or given to oneself or attained. Examples of beingness would be one's own name, one's profession, one's physical characteristics, one's role in a game—each or all of these could be called one's beingness.

Book One: a colloquial term for the first book published on the subject of Dianetics, *Dianetics: The Modern Science of Mental Health.* A *Book One Auditor* is someone who knows the data in this book and uses it to audit others.

case: a general term for a person being treated or helped. It is also used to mean the entire accumulation of upsets, pain, failures, etc., residing in a preclear's reactive mind.

case gains: the improvements and resurgences a person experiences from auditing; any case betterment according to the preclear.

Case Supervisor: a highly trained auditor who is also trained in the technology of supervising auditing. The Case Supervisor reviews all auditing sessions done by auditors under his charge. His purpose is to see that the technology is standardly applied for the greatest possible benefit for the preclear. See Chapter 14.

CCHR: abbreviation for *Citizens Commission on Human Rights.* See Chapter 29.

charge: harmful energy or force contained in mental image pictures of experiences painful or upsetting to the person, which is handled in auditing. See Chapter 5.

Claims Verification Board: an official group within the Church of Scientology which facilitates refund requests.

Clay Table Processing: a particular process used in certain types of auditing.

Clear: a highly desirable state for the individual, achieved through auditing, which was never attainable before Dianetics. A Clear is a person who no longer has his own reactive mind and therefore suffers none of the ill effects that the reactive mind can cause. The Clear has no engrams which, when restimulated, throw out the correctness of his computations by entering hidden and false data. See Chapter 13.

control: the ability to start, change and stop something. One is successful in his life to the degree that he can start or change or stop the things and people within his environment. For example, a driver who cannot exert control over a car by making it start, move about and stop when he wants it to is quite likely to have accidents. A person who *can* control a car, on the other hand, will be able to arrive where he intends to.

counter-effort: an effort of something or someone in a person's environment against that person.

C/S: abbreviation for *Case Supervisor*. Also used to designate a Case Supervisor direction of what to audit on a preclear (as in "he was given a new C/S"), or the giving of such a direction by the Case Supervisor (as in "the preclear was C/Sed for his next action"). *See also* **Case Supervisor** in this glossary.

CSI: abbreviation for *Church of Scientology International*. See Chapter 22.

Data Series: a series of policy letters written by L. Ron Hubbard which deal with logic, illogic, proper evaluation of data and how to detect and handle the causes of good and bad situations within groups and organizations.

determinism: the ability to direct or determine the actions of someone or something. Thus something done "on one's own determinism" would be caused by the person himself, not by a force exterior to him.

Dianetics: comes from the Greek words *dia*, meaning "through" and *nous*, meaning "soul." Dianetics is a methodology developed by L. Ron Hubbard which can help alleviate unwanted sensations and emotions, irrational fears and psychosomatic illnesses. It is most accurately described as *what the soul is doing to the body through the mind*. See Chapter 4.

dramatization: the acting out of an engram in its entirety or in part by an aberrated person in his current environment. Aberrated conduct is entirely dramatization. For example, a woman receives an engram in which she is kicked in the side and told that she is no good, that

she is always changing her mind. At some time in the future, this engram could be reactivated and the woman might experience a pain in her side, feel that she is no good or get the idea that she is always changing her mind. This would be a dramatization of the engram.

dwindling spiral: a condition characterized by continuous worsening, decreasing or shrinking.

dynamics: the eight urges, drives or impulses of life. See Chapter 4.

E-Meter: short for *Electropsychometer*, a specially designed instrument which helps the auditor and preclear locate areas of spiritual distress or travail. The E-Meter is a religious artifact and can only be used by Scientology ministers or ministers-in-training. It does not diagnose or cure anything. It measures the mental state or change of state of a person and thus is of benefit to the auditor in helping the preclear locate areas to be handled. See Chapter 5.

engram: a recording made by the reactive mind when a person is "unconscious." An engram is not a memory—it is a particular type of mental image picture which is a complete recording, down to the last accurate detail, of every perception present in a moment of partial or full "unconsciousness." See Chapter 4.

enturbulence: turbulence or agitation and disturbance.

Est Repair Rundown: an auditing action designed to repair the damage done to a person mentally and spiritually by the practice of est (Erhard Seminars Training). Est was an offbeat group which used destructive techniques, and some people new to Scientology are found to have been previously involved with est. It is necessary to undo the harmful effects of est before such persons can make adequate progress in Scientology auditing.

exteriorization: the state of the thetan being outside his body with or without full perception, but still able to control and handle the body. When a person goes exterior, he achieves a certainty that he is himself and not his body. See Chapter 4.

floating needle: a rhythmic sweep of the needle on an E-Meter dial at a slow, even pace, back and forth, back and forth. A floating needle means that the charge on a subject being audited has dissipated, and is one of the indications of a process being complete.

FSO: abbreviation for *Flag Service Organization.* See Chapter 21.

FSSO: abbreviation for *Flag Ship Service Organization.* See Chapter 21.

genetic entity: a term coined in early Dianetics research to denote that part of a human being which takes care of the automatic mechanisms of the body, such as heartbeat, respiration, etc.

gradient: a gradual approach to something, taken step by step, so that, finally, quite complicated and difficult activities or concepts can be achieved with relative ease.

grant beingness: to let someone else be what he is. Listening to what someone has to say and taking care to understand them, being courteous, refraining from needless criticism, expressing admiration or affinity are examples of the actions of someone who can grant others beingness.

HASI: an acronym for *Hubbard Association of Scientologists International.* See Chapter 33.

hat: a Scientology slang term for a particular job, taken from the fact that in many professions, such as railroading, the type of hat worn is the badge of the job. The term *hat* is also used to describe the write-ups, checksheets and packs that outline the purposes, know-how and duties of a job in a Scientology organization.

hatting: the training given to a person so that he or she can successfully perform the functions and produce the products of a specific job, duty or activity. *See also* **hat** in this glossary.

havingness: the concept of being able to reach. By *havingness* we mean owning, possessing, being capable of commanding, taking charge of objects, energies and spaces. Specific processes exist in Scientology to help a preclear increase his havingness, and these are appropriately called Havingness Processes.

HCO: abbreviation for *Hubbard Communications Office.* See Chapter 20.

HGC: abbreviation for *Hubbard Guidance Center.* See Chapter 15.

Hubbard Consultant Outpoint-Pluspoint List: a list of illogics (outpoints) and logics (pluspoints) used in an auditing process to help the preclear locate and handle illogical thinking in the area being addressed.

IAS: abbreviation for *International Association of Scientologists.* See Chapter 24.

I HELP: an acronym for *International Hubbard Ecclesiastical League of Pastors.* See Chapter 22.

INCOMM: an acronym for *International Network of Computer Organized Management.* See Chapter 33.

int: short for *interiorization,* the action of going into something too fixedly and becoming part of it too fixedly. *Int* is also used to refer to the auditing procedure which handles the adverse mental and spiritual effects of interiorization.

invalidate: refute, degrade, discredit or deny something someone else considers to be fact.

knowledge-responsibility-control (KRC) triangle: a triangle which is a symbol of the fact that *knowledge*, *responsibility* and *control* act together as a whole entity. In order to handle any area of one's life, it is necessary to *know* something about it, take some *responsibility* for it and *control* it to the degree necessary to achieve the desired result. This triangle interacts best when used with high ARC, thus it interlocks with the ARC triangle. *See also* **affinity-reality-communication (ARC) triangle** and **control** in this glossary.

Listing and Nulling: a specialized technique used in certain auditing processes.

lock: a mental image picture of an experience where one was knowingly or unknowingly reminded of an engram. It does not itself contain a blow or a burn or impact and is not any major cause of upset. It does not contain unconsciousness. It may contain a feeling of pain or illness, etc., but is not itself the source of it. For example, a person sees a cake and feels sick. This is a lock on an engram of being made sick by eating cake. The picture of seeing a cake and feeling sick is a lock on (is locked to) the incident (unseen at the moment) of getting sick eating cake.

mental image pictures: three-dimensional pictures which are continuously made by the mind, moment by moment, containing color, sound and smell, as well as other perceptions. They also include the conclusions or speculations of the individual. Mental image pictures are composed of energy, have mass, exist in space and follow definite routines of behavior, the most interesting of which is the fact that they appear when somebody thinks of something. See Chapter 4.

MEST: a word coined from the initial letters of *matter*, *energy*, *space* and *time*, which are the component parts (elements) of the physical universe.

meter: short for *E-Meter*. *See* **E-Meter** in this glossary.

missed withhold: a withhold which has *almost* been found out by another, that leaves the person who has the withhold in a state of wondering whether or not his hidden deed is known. *See also* **withhold** in this glossary.

NCLE: abbreviation for *National Commission on Law Enforcement and Social Justice.* See Chapter 29.

NED: an acronym for *New Era Dianetics.* See Chapter 13.

New Era Dianetics for OTs (NOTs): a series of auditing actions, delivered as part of the OT levels, developed by L. Ron Hubbard during his research into New Era Dianetics in the late 1970s.

NOTs: an acronym for *New Era Dianetics for OTs. See* **New Era Dianetics for OTs (NOTs)** in this glossary.

Objectives: short for *Objective Processing,* an auditing action which helps a person to look or place his attention outward from himself.

OCA: abbreviation for *Oxford Capacity Analysis.* See Chapter 5.

Operating Thetan: a state of being above Clear, in which the Clear has become refamiliarized with his native capabilities. See Chapter 13.

organizing board: a pattern of organization which expresses every function a Scientology church needs to attend to in order to minister to its congregation. See Chapter 20.

OSA: an acronym for *Office of Special Affairs.* See Chapter 36.

OT: abbreviation for *Operating Thetan. See* **Operating Thetan** in this glossary.

overrun: continue an auditing process or a series of processes past the point of completion.

overt: a harmful act or a transgression against the moral code of a group. When a person does something that is contrary to the moral code he has agreed to, or when he omits to do something that he should have done per that moral code, he has committed an overt. An overt violates what was agreed upon. An overt can be intentional or unintentional.

pan-determined: able to view both sides. Pan-determinism is *across* determinism or determinism of two sides. If a person were playing both sides of a chess game, he would be exercising pan-determinism. *See also* **determinism** in this glossary.

PDH: abbreviation for *pain-drug-hypnosis,* a behavioral modification technique used by military and intelligence services in which pain, drugs or hypnosis, or any combination of these, are administered to drive an individual into a state whereby he can be given suggestions or commands subconsciously. Dianetics auditing can undo the effects of PDH. For more information, see Chapter 35.

perceptic: any sense message such as sight, sound, smell, etc.

postulate: a conclusion, decision or resolution made by the individual himself to resolve a problem or to set a pattern for the future or to nullify a pattern of the past. For example, a person says, "I like Model T Fords. I am never going to drive another car." Years later, no longer consciously aware of this postulate, he will wonder why he is having so much trouble with his Buick; it's because he has made an earlier promise to himself. In order to change he has to change that postulate.

potential trouble source: a person who is in some way connected to and being adversely affected by a suppressive person. Such a person is called a *potential* trouble source because he can be a lot of trouble to himself and to others. *See also* **suppressive person** in this glossary.

preclear: a person who is receiving Scientology or Dianetics auditing on his way to becoming Clear, hence pre-Clear. Through auditing he is finding out more about himself and life. See Chapter 5.

process: an exact set of questions asked or directions given by an auditor to help a person locate areas of spiritual distress, find out things about himself and improve his condition. See Chapter 5.

processing: another word for *auditing. See* **auditing** in this glossary.

PTS: abbreviation for *potential trouble source. See* **potential trouble source** in this glossary.

Qual: short for *Qualifications Division. See* Chapter 20.

RD: abbreviation for *rundown.* See **rundown** in this glossary.

reactive mind: that part of the mind which works on a totally stimulus-response basis, which is not under a person's volitional control, and which exerts force and the power of command over his awareness, purposes, thoughts, body and actions. See Chapter 4.

reality: that which appears to be. Reality is fundamentally agreement—what we agree to be real is real.

rehab: short for *rehabilitation*, an auditing action which is used to help a person regain a former ability, state of being or more optimum condition which has been discredited, denied or suppressed.

restimulation: the "awakening" of an old engram, which occurs when a person's present environment contains enough similarities to the elements found in the engram to cause a reactivation of it. When an engram is restimulated, a person can experience similar pains and emotions to those contained in the original incident.

R6EW: the designation for the auditing process used on Grade VI. See Chapter 46.

RTC: abbreviation for *Religious Technology Center*. See Chapter 23.

rundown: a series of related actions in Scientology which culminate in a specific end result. For example, the Drug Rundown consists of several different auditing processes and actions which, done fully and in sequence, result in the freeing of a person from the mental and spiritual effects of drugs.

Scientology: comes from the Latin *scio,* which means "know" and the Greek word *logos,* meaning "the word or outward form by which the inward thought is expressed and made known." Thus, Scientology means knowing about knowing. Scientology is an applied religious philosophy developed by L. Ron Hubbard. It is the study and handling of the spirit in relationship to itself, universes and other life. See Chapter 4.

Sea Org: short for *Sea Organization.* See Chapter 26.

self-determinism: the condition of determining the actions of self; the ability to direct oneself. *See also* **determinism** in this glossary.

service facsimile: a consideration that one must be consistently in a certain state in order to survive. This consideration will cause the individual to deliberately hold in restimulation selected parts of his reactive mind to explain his failures in life. For example, a person may keep an old injury in restimulation so that his family has to look after him.

SHSBC: abbreviation for *Saint Hill Special Briefing Course.* See Chapter 14.

SMI: an acronym for *Scientology Missions International.* See Chapter 22.

SP: abbreviation for *suppressive person. See* **suppressive person** in this glossary.

stable terminal: someone who is reliable, responsible and who can be depended upon to competently perform the duties of his job.

standard memory banks: recordings in the analytical mind of everything perceived throughout the lifetime up to the present by the individual except painful emotion and physical pain, which are recorded in the reactive mind. See Chapter 4.

suppressive person: a person who possesses a distinct set of characteristics and mental attitudes that cause him to suppress other people in his vicinity. This is the person whose behavior is calculated to be disastrous. Also called *antisocial personality.* See Chapter 17.

theta: energy peculiar to life which acts upon material in the physical universe and animates it, mobilizes it and changes it; natural creative energy of a being which he is free to direct toward survival goals. The term comes from the Greek letter *theta* (θ), which the Greeks used to represent *thought.*

thetan: an immortal spiritual being; the human soul. The term *soul* is not used because it has developed so many other meanings from use in other religions and practices that it doesn't describe precisely what was discovered in Scientology. We use the term *thetan* instead, from the Greek letter *theta (θ),* the traditional symbol for thought or life. One does not *have* a thetan, something one keeps somewhere apart from oneself; one *is* a thetan. The thetan is the person himself, not his body or his name or the physical universe, his mind or anything else. It is that which is aware of being aware; the identity which IS the individual. See Chapter 4.

time track: the consecutive record of mental image pictures which accumulates through a person's life. It is a very accurate record of a person's past. As a rough analogy, the time track could be likened to a motion-picture film—if that film were three-dimensional, had fifty-seven perceptions and could fully react upon the observer. See Chapter 4.

TRs: abbreviation for *training routines,* practical drills which can greatly increase a student's ability in essential auditing skills, such as communication. See Chapter 15.

unmock: become nothing, disappear, cease to exist.

whole track: the whole span of the time track. *See also* **time track** in this glossary.

WISE: an acronym for *World Institute of Scientology Enterprises.* See Chapter 30.

withhold: an overt a person has committed but is not talking about; an unspoken, unannounced transgression against a moral code by which a person was bound. Any withhold comes *after* an overt. *See also* **overt** in this glossary.

WW: abbreviation for Worldwide—the worldwide headquarters of the Church of Scientology at Saint Hill, where management was located until the early 1970s.

INDEX

B

ethnic affairs, efforts of Scientologists on behalf of all minorities, 434

evaluation, for preclear not allowed per Auditor's Code, 165

events, celebrations of Scientology holidays, 387

evil,
definition, 286, 643
difference between good and evil, 285–286, 642–643
logic of Scientology ethics is inarguable and based upon two key concepts: *good* and *evil,* 285
man is basically good, not evil, 3
Zoroaster and beliefs about, 21

Evolution of a Science, film that graphically illustrates the power of LRH's discoveries in field of mind and spirit, 189

Examiner, preclear can tell the Examiner anything he wishes the Case Supervisor to know, 301

"Excalibur,"
manuscript written in 1938 by LRH, 115, 635

Executive Director,
duties of, 373
with his staff, responsible for day-to-day operation of church, 419

Executive Division, description, 373

exhaustion, solution to, covered in *The Problems of Work,* 191

existence, higher states of, attainable through Scientology, 179

Expanded Dianetics,
definition, 248, 259, 837
Hubbard Expanded Dianetics Auditor Course, 849

Expanded Grade 0,
definition, 242
processes address a person's ability to communicate and free him, in his *own* estimation, from any blocks in the area, 242

Expanded Grade I,
definition, 242
helps one gain ability to recognize source of problems, 242

Expanded Grade II,
brings relief from the hostilities and sufferings of life, 242
definition, 242

Expanded Grade III,
definition, 243
freedom to face the future with an enhanced ability to confront, experience and find advantage in the inevitable changes of life, 243

Expanded Grade III, *(cont.)*
processes locate specific incidents where upsetting change occurred in life and address these, 243

Expanded Grade IV,
definition, 243
enables preclear to view himself in relation to all life and free himself from any patterns of thought and action which, while seeming to promote one's survival, in reality do everything but, 243

Expanded Grades, *see also* **Expanded Grade 0; Expanded Grade I; Expanded Grade II; Expanded Grade III; Expanded Grade IV**
description, 836
developed as undercut to Dianetics, 244
each Academy Level corresponds to one of the Expanded Grades, 256
improve the person's abilities, 241
series of auditing processes which restore specific abilities, 241
unburden great deal of reactive mind, 244
use of processes on, 241

Expansion of Havingness, LRH lecture series, description, 888

experts' views on Scientology,
growing authority in humanities and spiritual nature of man, 613
improves spiritual lives of millions, 613
practical religion, 613
vital source of wisdom about spiritual nature of man, 613

Explorers Club,
flag of, awarded to LRH for expedition, 694, 699
LRH elected a member in 1940, 694

expulsion, most extreme penalty that can be leveled at a person by a Scientology justice action, 291

extension courses,
cover L. Ron Hubbard's books, 195
description, 659, 832

exteriorization,
definition, 249, 663
out-of-body experiences and, 709
phenomena of, 150, 152
Scientology belief in, 643

Exteriorization and the Phenomena of Space,
course, description, 862
OT lectures, description, 885

F

Factors, The,
description, 772
use of on Key to Life Course, 228–229

faith,
every Scientologist expected to test knowledge for themselves on purely personal level, 675
Scientology does not depend upon a system of beliefs or, 143

false ideas,
can come from newspapers, radio, TV, textbooks, friends, family, 296
example,
"IQ can't be improved," 601
"Man is a stimulus-response animal," 601
"People can't change," 601
"You're just a piece of meat," 601
may cause difficulty in studying or applying a subject, 296
religion and, 296

false information, *see* **false ideas**

False Purpose Rundown,
description, 842
handles false purposes that can be holding a person back, 248
released in 1984, 596

family,
Chaplain services to help the family, 282
church of Scientology goes to great lengths to reconcile family differences if problem arises, 640
relationships between Scientologists and family members who are not, 639
Scientology views on, 639
second dynamic and, 154

FDA, *see* **Food and Drug Administration**

fear, unevaluated, unknowing and unwanted, caused by reactive mind, 147

FEBC, *see* **Flag Executive Briefing Course**

fetus, perceptions of, 707

field auditor(s), *see also* **field group(s)**
assistance from I HELP, 400
dedicated to helping people in their communities, 382
examples of how they help others, 382
services ministered, 383

field group(s), *see also* **field auditor(s)**
Auditors Association and, 400
International Hubbard Ecclesiastical League of Pastors is mother church for all Scientology volunteer ministers and field groups, 399
relationship to local org, 400

G

N

Q

R

EPILOGUE

The aim of this book was to answer the question, What is Scientology? The objective has been to provide you with information on how Scientology can change your life, and how it is changing the world. With all you have read, you now possess enough information to objectively evaluate the subject.

On a more personal level, however, the time has come to make a decision: You can close this book and walk away, or you can take, not your first step on the road to truth, but your next.